Fundamentals of Advanced Accounting

Seventh Edition

Joe B. Hoyle

Associate Professor of Accounting
Robins School of Business
University of Richmond

Thomas F. Schaefer

KPMG Professor of Accountancy
Mendoza College of Business
University of Notre Dame

Timothy S. Doupnik

Associate Professor of Accounting
School of Business
College of Charleston

FUNDAMENTALS OF ADVANCED ACCOUNTING, SEVENTH EDITION

Published by McGraw-Hill Education, 2 Penn Plaza, New York, NY 10121. Copyright © 2018 by McGraw-Hill Education. All rights reserved. Printed in the United States of America. Previous editions © 2015, 2013, and 2011. No part of this publication may be reproduced or distributed in any form or by any means, or stored in a database or retrieval system, without the prior written consent of McGraw-Hill Education, including, but not limited to, in any network or other electronic storage or transmission, or broadcast for distance learning.

Some ancillaries, including electronic and print components, may not be available to customers outside the United States.

This book is printed on acid-free paper.

1 2 3 4 5 6 7 8 9 LWI 21 20 19 18 17

ISBN   978-1-259-72263-9
MHID   1-259-72263-5

Chief Product Officer, SVP Products & Markets: *G. Scott Virkler*
Vice President, General Manager, Products & Markets: *Marty Lange*
Managing Director: *Tim Vertovec*
Marketing Director: *Natalie King*
Executive Brand Manager: *Becky Olson*
Director, Product Development: *Rose Koos*
Associate Director of Digital Content: *Kevin Moran*
Lead Product Developer: *Kris Tibbetts*
Product Developer: *Kevin Moran*
Marketing Manager: *Zach Rudin*
Market Development Manager: *Cheryl Osgood*
Digital Product Analyst: *Xin Lin*
Director, Content Design & Delivery: *Linda Avenarius*
Program Manager: *Daryl Horrocks*
Content Project Managers: *Dana M. Pauley/Brian Nacik*
Buyer: *Sandy Ludovissy*
Design: *Egzon Shaqiri*
Content Licensing Specialists: *Shawntel Schmitt/DeAnna Dausener*
Cover Image: *© Ilin Sergey/Shutterstock; © Smart Design/Shutterstock*
Compositor: *SPi Global*
Printer: *LSC Communications*

All credits appearing on this page or at the end of the book are considered to be an extension of the copyright page.

Library of Congress Cataloging-in-Publication Data

CIP has been applied for

The Internet addresses listed in the text were accurate at the time of publication. The inclusion of a website does not indicate an endorsement by the authors or McGraw-Hill Education, and McGraw-Hill Education does not guarantee the accuracy of the information presented at these sites.

mheducation.com/highered

To our families

The real purpose of books is to trap the mind into doing its own thinking.

—Christopher Morley

About the Authors

Joe B. Hoyle, *University of Richmond*

Joe B. Hoyle is associate professor of accounting at the Robins School of Business at the University of Richmond, where he teaches intermediate accounting, financial accounting, and advanced accounting. In 2015, he was the first recipient of the J. Michael and Mary Anne Cook Prize for undergraduate teaching. The Cook Prize is awarded by the American Accounting Association and "is the foremost recognition of an individual who consistently demonstrates the attributes of a superior teacher in the discipline of accounting." Professor Hoyle has also been named (in 2007) as the Virginia Professor of the Year by the Carnegie Foundation for the Advancement of Teaching and the Center for Advancement and Support of Education. He has been selected as a Distinguished Educator five times at the University of Richmond and Professor of the Year on two occasions. He has authored a book of essays titled *Tips and Thoughts on Improving the Teaching Process in College,* which is available at http://oncampus.richmond.edu/~ jhoyle/. His blog, *Teaching—Getting the Most from Your Students,* at http://joehoyle-teaching.blogspot.com/ was named the Accounting Education Innovation of the Year for 2013 by the American Accounting Association.

Thomas F. Schaefer, *University of Notre Dame*

Thomas F. Schaefer is the KPMG Professor of Accounting at the University of Notre Dame. He has written a number of articles for scholarly journals such as *The Accounting Review, Journal of Accounting Research, Journal of Accounting & Economics, Accounting Horizons,* and others. His primary teaching and research interests are in financial accounting and reporting. Tom is a past president of the American Accounting Association's Accounting Program Leadership Group. He received the 2007 Joseph A. Silvoso Faculty Merit Award from the Federation of Schools of Accountancy and the 2013 Notre Dame Master of Science in Accountancy Dincolo Outstanding Professor Award.

Timothy S. Doupnik, *College of Charleston*

Timothy S. Doupnik is distinguished professor emeritus of accounting at the University of South Carolina. He is a current member of the accounting faculty at the College of Charleston, where he teaches advanced and international accounting. Tim has published extensively in the area of international accounting in journals such as *The Accounting Review; Accounting, Organizations, and Society; Abacus; International Journal of Accounting;* and *Journal of International Business Studies.* Tim is a past president of the American Accounting Association's International Accounting Section and a recipient of the section's Outstanding International Accounting Educator Award.

Overall—this edition of the text provides relevant and up-to-date accounting standards references to the Financial Accounting Standards Board (FASB) *Accounting Standards Codification*® **(ASC).**

Chapter Changes for *Fundamentals of Advanced Accounting,* 7th Edition:

Chapter 1

- Updated the chapter to reflect *Accounting Standards Update* (ASU) No. 2016-07 to ASC Topic 323, Investments—Equity Method and Joint Ventures, entitled "Simplifying the Transition to the Equity Method of Accounting." The ASU is effective for fiscal years beginning after December 15, 2016.

  The ASU eliminates the requirement to retrospectively apply the equity method to previously held ownership interests in an investee when an increase in ownership results in significant influence and thus qualifies for use of the equity method.

- Updated coverage for *Accounting Standards Update* (ASU) No. 2016-01, Financial Instruments—Overall, which requires equity investments (except those accounted for under the equity method of accounting or those that result in consolidation of the investee) to be measured at fair value with changes in fair value recognized in net income, unless fair values are not readily determinable. Thus, the previously available-for-sale category with fair value changes recorded in other comprehensive income will no longer be available. The ASU is effective for fiscal years beginning after December 15, 2017, with early adoption permitted.

- Eliminated coverage of investee extraordinary items to align the text coverage with *Accounting Standards Update* No. 2015-01 which eliminates the concept of extraordinary items.

- Updated terminology in discussion of intra-entity gross profits to reflect the new revenue recognition standards (ASC 606).

- Updated real-world references.

- Added and revised several end-of-chapter problems.

Chapter 2

- Added new descriptive coverage of three recent real-world business combinations—Facebook and WhatsApp, AT&T and DirecTV, and MeadwestVaco and Rock-Tenn.

- Revised chapter learning objectives to focus on combinations when the acquired firm is dissolved vs. continued existence. The chapter also newly recognizes a learning objective on the related costs that typically accompany business combinations.

- Added an updated appendix on pushdown accounting based on *Accounting Standards Update* (ASU) No. 2014-17, Business Combinations: Pushdown Accounting. The ASU allows companies an option to apply pushdown accounting for newly acquired subsidiaries.

- Updated real-world references.

- In addition to several new and revised end-of-chapter problems, replaced/added new research cases that provide students with real-world applications of financial reporting for business combinations.

Chapter 3

- Added coverage of post-acquisition procedures for excess fair value attributable to subsidiary long-term debt. Moved coverage of pushdown accounting to Chapter 2.

- Added a Discussion Question that addresses worksheet adjustments to the parent's beginning-of-the-year retained earnings.

- Updated real-world references.

- Added an appendix covering *Accounting Standards Update* (ASU 2014-02) to Topic 350, "Intangibles—Goodwill and Other, on Accounting for Goodwill. The ASU provides an external reporting option (i.e., amortization) for private company goodwill accounting. The appendix also covers ASU 2014-18, Accounting for Identifiable Intangible Assets in a Business Combination, an amendment of Business Combinations (Topic 805). The new standards allow private companies an option to simplify their accounting by recognizing fewer intangible assets in future business combinations.

- Added new equity method end-of-chapter problems requiring the preparation of consolidated financial statements subsequent to acquisition. In addition, changed the facts and requirements in several end-of-chapter problems.

- Added a new research and analysis case on Microsoft's 2015 goodwill impairment loss.

Chapter 4

- Updated real-world references.
- Added two new equity method end-of-chapter problems.
- Added new end-of-chapter cases using the financial reports of Starbucks (step-acquisition example) and Costco (various noncontrolling interest figures and interpretations).
- Revised the end-of-chapter comprehensive FASB ASC and IFRS research case. The new case, entitled *Bardeen Electric,* continues to focus on valuation issues accompanying a business combination including alternative goodwill measurement under IFRS. In addition, several other end-of-chapter problems have been revised.

Chapter 5

- Updated terminology in discussion of intra-entity gross profits to reflect the new revenue recognition standards (ASC 606).
- Revised and expanded coverage of the deferral and subsequent recognition of intra-entity gains on long-term assets transfers across affiliates. The revised exposition emphasizes the nature of reallocating intra-entity gains across time increasing consistency with the chapter's coverage of intra-entity gross profits in inventory.
- Updated real-world references.
- Changed the facts and requirements in several end-of-chapter problems.

Chapter 6

- Updated real-world references.
- Expanded coverage of post-control period reporting for primary beneficiaries and variable interest entities including an example of consolidated statement preparation.
- Added and revised several end-of-chapter problems.

Chapter 7

- Reduced the size of Exhibit 7.1 containing exchange rates for selected countries.
- Rewrote the section now titled Forward Contracts that was previously titled Spot and Forward Rates.

- Moved the section on foreign currency borrowing from the end of the chapter to immediately follow the section on foreign currency transactions.
- Moved the portion of the IFRS section at the end of the chapter that deals with foreign currency transactions to immediately follow the section on foreign currency borrowing.
- Expanded the learning objective related to how forward contracts and foreign currency options can be used to hedge foreign exchange risk to include understanding what types of foreign exchange risk can be hedged.
- Added new learning objectives on the accounting guidelines for derivatives and the basics of hedge accounting.
- Updated real-world references including examples of company practices, excerpts from annual reports, and foreign exchange rates.
- Added language to more clearly explain the impact that the accounting for a derivative financial instrument used to hedge a foreign exchange risk has on financial statements within the examples demonstrating the accounting for various types of foreign currency hedges.
- Updated the section at the end of the chapter that summarizes the accounting for derivative financial instruments under IFRS.
- Changed the facts in several end-of-chapter problems.
- Updated the develop your skills assignments based on actual exchange rates.

Chapter 8

- Updated references to actual company practice and related excerpts from annual reports.
- In the section on Exchange Rates Used in Translation, added instruction to first read the related Discussion Question before continuing.
- Removed reference to the theoretical possibility of translating income statement items at the current exchange rate.
- Removed reference to a research study published in 1988 that investigated the weighting of functional currency indicators.
- Moved the section on IFRS from the end of the chapter to immediately after the section describing U.S. authoritative literature.
- Changed facts in several end-of-chapter problems.

Chapter 9

- Revised tables showing the allocation of partnership income/loss across partners to provide additional emphasis on the step-by-step nature of the income distribution across partners.
- Changed the facts and requirements in several end-of-chapter problems.

Chapter 10

- Split an existing end-of-chapter problem with two unrelated parts into two separate problems.
- Added a new end-of-chapter problem related to learning objectives 10-2 and 10-5.
- Changed the facts and requirements in several end-of-chapter problems.

Chapter 11

- Updated numerous references to the financial statements of a wide variety of state and local governments such as the City of Baltimore, the City of Houston, the City of Charlotte, and the City of Dallas.

Chapter 12

- Provided coverage of new pronouncement: *GASB Statement No. 76*, "The Hierarchy of Generally Accepted Accounting Principles for State and Local Governments."
- Provided coverage of new pronouncement: *GASB Statement No. 77*, "Tax Abatement Disclosures."
- Updated references to the financial statements of state and local governments such as the City of Los Angeles, the City of Chicago, the City of Orlando, and the City of Boston.

Students Solve the Accounting Puzzle with 7th Edition Features

The approach used by Hoyle, Schaefer, and Doupnik allows students to think critically about accounting, just as they will in their careers and as they prepare for the CPA exam. Read on to understand how students will succeed as accounting majors and as future CPAs by using *Fundamentals of Advanced Accounting, 7e.*

Thinking Critically

With this text, students gain a well-balanced appreciation of the accounting profession. As *Hoyle 7e* introduces them to the field's many aspects, it often focuses on past controversies and present resolutions. The text shows the development of financial reporting as a product of intense and considered debate that continues today and will in the future.

Readability

The writing style of the previous editions has been highly praised. **Students easily comprehend** chapter concepts because of the conversational tone used throughout the book. The authors have made every effort to ensure that the writing style remains engaging, lively, and consistent.

Real-World Examples

Students are better able to relate what they learn to what they will encounter in the business world after reading these frequent examples. Quotations, articles, and illustrations from *Forbes, The Wall Street Journal, Time,* and *Bloomberg BusinessWeek* are incorporated throughout the text. Data have been pulled from business, not-for-profit, and government financial statements as well as official pronouncements.

EXHIBIT 2.1
Recent Notable Business Combinations

Acquirer	Target	Deal Value
AT&T	DirecTV	$47.4B
Berkshire Hathaway, Inc.	Precision Castparts	$32.0B
Visa, Inc.	Visa Europe Ltd	$23.3B
Facebook, Inc.	WhatsApp	$17.2B
MeadWestvaco	RockTenn	$16.0B
Intel Corporation	Altera Corporation	$15.0B
CVS Health Corporation	Omnicare, Inc.	$12.9B
Marriott	Starwood Hotels Intl	$12.2B
Merck	Cubist	$ 9.5B
Weyerhaeuser	Plum Creek Timber	$ 8.4B
Celgene Corporation	Receptos, Inc.	$ 7.2B
Cox Automotive	Dealertrack Technologies	$ 4.0B
FedEx	TNT Express	$ 4.8B
Expedia	HomeAway	$ 3.9B
Microsemi Corporation	PMC-Sierra, Inc.	$ 2.5B
Constellation Brands	Ballast Point Brewing & Spirits	$ 1.0B

manufacturing, and delivery, substantial savings can result. As an example, Oracle's acquisition of Sun Microsystems creates synergies by enabling Oracle to integrate its software product lines with Sun's hardware specifications. The acquisition further allows Oracle to offer

Discussion Questions

This feature **facilitates student understanding** of the underlying accounting principles at work in particular reporting situations. Similar to minicases, these questions help explain the issues at hand in practical terms. Many times, these cases are designed to demonstrate to students why a topic is problematic and worth considering.

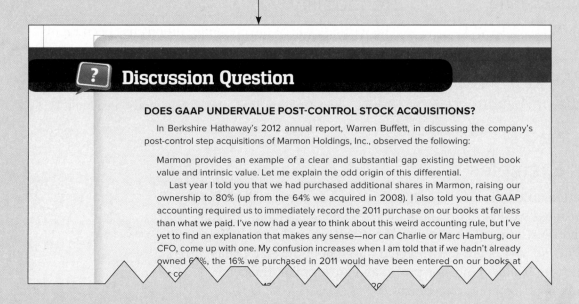

? Discussion Question

DOES GAAP UNDERVALUE POST-CONTROL STOCK ACQUISITIONS?

In Berkshire Hathaway's 2012 annual report, Warren Buffett, in discussing the company's post-control step acquisitions of Marmon Holdings, Inc., observed the following:

Marmon provides an example of a clear and substantial gap existing between book value and intrinsic value. Let me explain the odd origin of this differential.

Last year I told you that we had purchased additional shares in Marmon, raising our ownership to 80% (up from the 64% we acquired in 2008). I also told you that GAAP accounting required us to immediately record the 2011 purchase on our books at far less than what we paid. I've now had a year to think about this weird accounting rule, but I've yet to find an explanation that makes any sense—nor can Charlie or Marc Hamburg, our CFO, come up with one. My confusion increases when I am told that if we hadn't already owned 64%, the 16% we purchased in 2011 would have been entered on our books at

CPA Simulations

Hoyle 7e provides instructors and students access to CPA Simulations that correspond to several key topics and chapters throughout the text. Students can complete these simulations online, allowing them to practice advanced accounting concepts in a web-based interface that mimics the actual CPA exam. There will be no hesitation or confusion when students sit for the real exam; they will know exactly how to maneuver through the computerized test.

End-of-Chapter Materials

As in previous editions, the end-of-chapter material remains a strength of the text. The sheer number of questions, problems, and Internet assignments test and therefore **expand the students' knowledge** of chapter concepts.

Excel Spreadsheet Assignments extend specific problems and are located on the 7th edition Instructor Resources page, with templated versions that can be provided to students for assignments. An Excel icon appears next to those problems that have corresponding spreadsheet assignments.

"Develop Your Skills" asks questions that address the four skills students need to master to pass the CPA exam: Research, Analysis, Spreadsheet, and Communication. An icon indicates when these skills are tested.

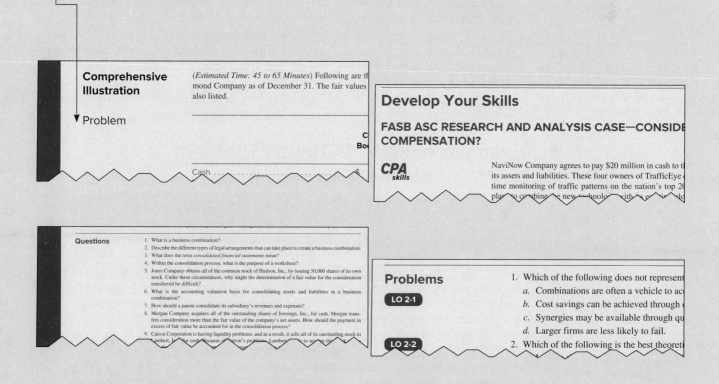

Comprehensive Illustration

▼ Problem

(*Estimated Time: 45 to 65 Minutes*) Following are t̶
mond Company as of December 31. The fair values also listed.

Cash . . . . $

Develop Your Skills

**FASB ASC RESEARCH AND ANALYSIS CASE—CONSIDE
COMPENSATION?**

CPA skills

NaviNow Company agrees to pay $20 million in cash to t̶
its assets and liabilities. These four owners of TrafficEye
time monitoring of traffic patterns on the nation's top 2

Questions

1. What is a business combination?
2. Describe the different types of legal arrangements that can take place to create a business combination.
3. What does the term *consolidated financial statements* mean?
4. Within the consolidation process, what is the purpose of a worksheet?
5. Jones Company obtains all of the common stock of Hudson, Inc., by issuing 50,000 shares of its own stock. Under these circumstances, why might the determination of a fair value for the consideration transferred be difficult?
6. What is the accounting valuation basis for consolidating assets and liabilities in a business combination?
7. How should a parent consolidate its subsidiary's revenues and expenses?
8. Morgan Company acquires all of the outstanding shares of Jennings, Inc., for cash. Morgan transfers consideration more than the fair value of the company's net assets. How should the payment in excess of fair value be accounted for in the consolidation process?
9. Catron Corporation is having liquidity problems, and as a result, it sells all of its outstanding stock to Lambert, Inc., for cash because of Catron's problems, Lamber

---

Problems

LO 2-1

LO 2-2

1. Which of the following does not represent
   a. Combinations are often a vehicle to ac
   b. Cost savings can be achieved through
   c. Synergies may be available through qu
   d. Larger firms are less likely to fail.
2. Which of the following is the best theoreti

The Seventh Edition of Fundamentals of Advanced Accounting has a full Connect package, with the following features available for instructors and students.

- **(New for 7e!) SmartBook** ® is the market-leading adaptive study resource that is proven to strengthen memory recall, increase retention, and boost grades. SmartBook, powered by LearnSmart, is the first and only adaptive reading experience designed to change the way students read and learn. SmartBook delivers a personalized reading experience by highlighting the most impactful concepts a student needs to learn at that moment in time. As a student engages with SmartBook, the reading experience continuously adapts by highlighting content based on what the student has mastered or is ready to learn. This ensures that the student stays focused on the content he or she needs to learn, while simultaneously promoting long-term retention of material. Both students and Instructors can use SmartBook's real-time reports to quickly identify the concepts that require more attention from individual students—or the entire class. The end result? Students are more engaged with course content, can better prioritize their time, and come to class ready to participate.
- The **End-of-Chapter Content** in Connect provides a robust offering of review and question material designed to aid and assess the student's retention of chapter content. The End-of-Chapter content is composed of both static and algorithmic versions of the problems in each chapter, which are designed to challenge students using McGraw-Hill Education's state-of-the-art online homework technology. Connect helps students learn more efficiently by providing feedback and practice material when and where they need it. Connect grades homework automatically, and students benefit from the immediate feedback that they receive, particularly on any questions they may have missed.

Example of End-of-Chapter Problem

Prepare a consolidated balance sheet for Pratt and Spider as of December 31, 2018.

PRATT COMPANY AND SUBSIDIARY Consolidated Balance Sheet December 31, 2018			
Assets		**Liabilities and Owners' Equity**	
Cash			
Total assets		Total liabilities and equities	

- The **Test Bank** for each chapter has been updated for the 7th edition to stay current with new and revised chapter material, with all questions available for assignment through Connect. Instructors can also create tests and quizzes from the Test Bank through our TestGen software, which is available on the Instructor Resources page.
- The **Instructor and Student Resources** have been updated for the 7th edition and are available in the Connect Instructor Resources page. Available resources include Instructor and Solutions Manuals, PowerPoint presentations, Test Bank files, Excel templates, and Chapter Check Figures. All applicable Student Resources will be available in a convenient file that can be distributed to students for classes either directly, through Connect, or via courseware.

McGraw-Hill Connect®
Learn Without Limits

Connect is a teaching and learning platform that is proven to deliver better results for students and instructors.

Connect empowers students by continually adapting to deliver precisely what they need, when they need it, and how they need it, so your class time is more engaging and effective.

73% of instructors who use **Connect** require it; instructor satisfaction **increases** by 28% when **Connect** is required.

Connect's Impact on Retention Rates, Pass Rates, and Average Exam Scores

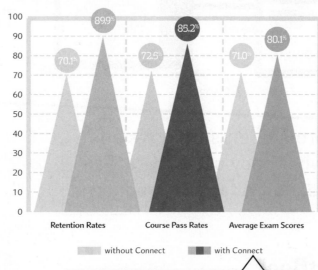

Retention Rates   Course Pass Rates   Average Exam Scores

without Connect   with Connect

Using **Connect** improves retention rates by **19.8%**, passing rates by **12.7%**, and exam scores by **9.1%**.

Analytics

Connect Insight®

Connect Insight is Connect's new one-of-a-kind visual analytics dashboard that provides at-a-glance information regarding student performance, which is immediately actionable. By presenting assignment, assessment, and topical performance results together with a time metric that is easily visible for aggregate or individual results, Connect Insight gives the user the ability to take a just-in-time approach to teaching and learning, which was never before available. Connect Insight presents data that help instructors improve class performance in a way that is efficient and effective.

Impact on Final Course Grade Distribution

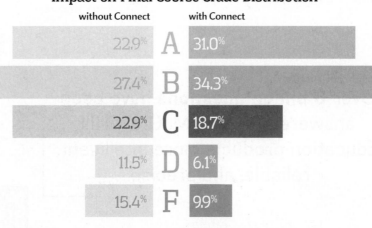

without Connect   with Connect

	without Connect	with Connect
A	22.9%	31.0%
B	27.4%	34.3%
C	22.9%	18.7%
D	11.5%	6.1%
F	15.4%	9.9%

Adaptive

THE **ADAPTIVE** **READING EXPERIENCE**
DESIGNED TO TRANSFORM THE WAY STUDENTS READ

More students earn **A's** and **B's** when they use McGraw-Hill Education **Adaptive** products.

SmartBook®

Proven to help students improve grades and study more efficiently, SmartBook contains the same content within the print book, but actively tailors that content to the needs of the individual. SmartBook's adaptive technology provides precise, personalized instruction on what the student should do next, guiding the student to master and remember key concepts, targeting gaps in knowledge and offering customized feedback, and driving the student toward comprehension and retention of the subject matter. Available on tablets, SmartBook puts learning at the student's fingertips—anywhere, anytime.

Over **8 billion questions** have been answered, making McGraw-Hill Education products more intelligent, reliable, and precise.

STUDENTS WANT

SMARTBOOK®

95% of students reported **SmartBook** to be a more effective way of reading material.

100% of students want to use the Practice Quiz feature available within **SmartBook** to help them study.

100% of students reported having reliable access to off-campus wifi.

90% of students say they would purchase **SmartBook** over print alone.

95% of students reported that **SmartBook** would impact their study skills in a positive way.

*Findings based on 2015 focus group results administered by McGraw-Hill Education

www.mheducation.com

Acknowledgments

We could not produce a textbook of the quality and scope of *Fundamentals of Advanced Accounting* without the help of a great number of people. Special thanks go to the following:

- Gregory Schaefer for his Chapter 2 descriptions of recent business combinations.
- Joyce van der Laan Smith of the University of Richmond and Paul Copley of James Madison University for their work on detailed reviews of the Sixth Edition. Their feedback and direction were instrumental during the revision process.
- Ilene Leopold Persoff of Long Island University (LIU Post) for her work on detailed reviews of the Sixth Edition and for checking the Seventh Edition manuscript, solutions manuals, and test bank files for accuracy. Ilene's subject matter knowledge, detail-oriented nature, and quality of work were instrumental in ensuring that this edition stayed accurate, relevant, and of tremendous quality.

Additionally, we would like to thank Anna Lusher of Slippery Rock University, for updating and revising the PowerPoint presentations; Jack Terry of ComSource Associates for updating the Excel Template Exercises for students to use as they work the select end-of-chapter material; Stacie Hughes of Athens State University, Mark McCarthy of East Carolina University, and Beth Kobylarz of Accuracy Counts for checking the text and Solutions Manual for accuracy; John Abernathy of Kennesaw State University for checking the test bank for accuracy; and Barbara Gershman of Northern Virginia Community College for checking the PowerPoints.

We also want to thank the many people who completed questionnaires and reviewed the book. Our sincerest thanks to them all:

Thomas Collins
University of Wisconsin–Platteville

Charles Lewis
Houston Community College

Waqar Ahmed
University of Illinois

Michael Cohen
Rutgers University

Ling Harris
University of South Carolina

Stacie Hughes
Athens State University

Zane Swanson
University of Central Oklahoma

Amy David
Queens College

John Abernathy
Kennesaw State University

David He
Johns Hopkins University

Suzanne Wright
Penn State University

We also pass along a word of thanks to all the people at McGraw-Hill Education who participated in the creation of this edition. In particular, Dana Pauley, Senior Content Project Manager; Jennifer Pickel, Buyer; Egzon Shaqiri, Designer; Kevin Moran, Associate Director of Digital Content and Product Developer; Becky Olson, Executive Brand Manager; Tim Vertovec, Managing Director; Brian Nacik, Lead Assessment Content Project Manager; and Zach Rudin, Marketing Manager all contributed significantly to the project, and we appreciate their efforts.

Brief Contents

Walkthrough   ix

1. The Equity Method of Accounting for Investments   1

2. Consolidation of Financial Information   39

3. Consolidations—Subsequent to the Date of Acquisition   89

4. Consolidated Financial Statements and Outside Ownership   155

5. Consolidated Financial Statements—Intra-Entity Asset Transactions   211

6. Variable Interest Entities, Intra-Entity Debt, Consolidated Cash Flows, and Other Issues   261

7. Foreign Currency Transactions and Hedging Foreign Exchange Risk   319

8. Translation of Foreign Currency Financial Statements   385

9. Partnerships: Formation and Operation   445

10. Partnerships: Termination and Liquidation   483

11. Accounting for State and Local Governments (Part 1)   517

12. Accounting for State and Local Governments (Part 2)   575

INDEX   631

Contents

Walkthrough   ix

Chapter One
The Equity Method of Accounting for Investments   1

The Reporting of Investments in Corporate Equity Securities   1
   Fair-Value Method   2
   Cost Method (Investments in Equity Securities without Readily Determinable Fair Values)   2
   Consolidation of Financial Statements   3
Discussion Question: Did the Cost Method Invite Earnings Manipulation?   4
   Equity Method   4
International Accounting Standard 28—Investments in Associates   5
Application of the Equity Method   5
   Criteria for Utilizing the Equity Method   5
   Accounting for an Investment—The Equity Method   7
Equity Method Accounting Procedures   9
   Excess of Investment Cost over Book Value Acquired   9
Discussion Question: Does the Equity Method Really Apply Here?   10
   The Amortization Process   12
Equity Method—Additional Issues   14
   Reporting a Change to the Equity Method   14
   Reporting Investee's Other Comprehensive Income and Irregular Items   16
   Reporting Investee Losses   16
   Reporting the Sale of an Equity Investment   17
Deferral of Intra-Entity Gross Profits in Inventory   18
   Downstream Sales of Inventory   19
   Upstream Sales of Inventory   20
Financial Reporting Effects and Equity Method Criticisms   21
   Equity Method Reporting Effects   21
   Criticisms of the Equity Method   22
Fair-Value Reporting for Equity Method Investments   23
Summary   24

Chapter Two
Consolidation of Financial Information   39

Expansion through Corporate Takeovers   40
   Reasons for Firms to Combine   40
   Facebook and WhatsApp   42
   AT&T and DirecTV   42
   MeadwestVaco and Rock-Tenn   43
Business Combinations, Control, and Consolidated Financial Reporting   43
   Business Combinations—Creating a Single Economic Entity   44
   Control—An Elusive Quality   45
   Consolidation of Financial Information   46
Financial Reporting for Business Combinations   47
   The Acquisition Method   47
   Consideration Transferred for the Acquired Business   47
   Contingent Consideration: An Additional Element of Consideration Transferred   47
   Assets Acquired and Liabilities Assumed   48
   Goodwill and Gains on Bargain Purchases   49
Procedures for Consolidating Financial Information   49
   Acquisition Method When Dissolution Takes Place   50
   Related Costs of Business Combinations   54
   The Acquisition Method When Separate Incorporation Is Maintained   55
Acquisition-Date Fair-Value Allocations— Additional Issues   60
   Intangibles   60
   Preexisting Goodwill on Subsidiary's Books   61
   Acquired In-Process Research and Development   62
Convergence between U.S. and International Accounting Standards   63
Summary   63
Appendix A
Legacy Methods of Accounting for Business Combinations   67
Appendix B
Pushdown Accounting   72

Chapter Three
Consolidations—Subsequent to the Date of Acquisition   89

Consolidation—The Effects Created by the Passage of Time   90
   Consolidated Net Income Determination   90
   The Parent's Choice of Investment Accounting   90
Investment Accounting by the Acquiring Company   90
   Internal Investment Accounting Alternatives—The Equity Method, Initial Value Method, and Partial Equity Method   91
Subsequent Consolidation—Investment Recorded by the Equity Method   92
   Acquisition Made during the Current Year   92
   Determination of Consolidated Totals   94
   Consolidation Worksheet   96
   Consolidation Subsequent to Year of Acquisition—Equity Method   98
Subsequent Consolidations—Investment Recorded Using Initial Value or Partial Equity Method   103
   Acquisition Made during the Current Year   103
   Consolidation Subsequent to Year of Acquisition—Initial Value and Partial Equity Methods   107
Discussion Question   111

Discussion Question: How Does a Company Really Decide Which Investment Method to Apply? 112
Excess Fair Value Attributable to Subsidiary Long-Term Debt: Post-Acquisition Procedures 113
Goodwill Impairment 115
  Assigning Goodwill to Reporting Units 116
  Qualitative Assessment Option 116
  Testing Goodwill for Impairment 117
  Illustration—Accounting and Reporting for a Goodwill Impairment Loss 118
  Reporting Units with Zero or Negative Carrying Amounts 119
  Goodwill Impairment Simplified—Proposed Accounting Standards Update (ASU) 119
  Comparisons with International Accounting Standards 120
Amortization and Impairment of Other Intangibles 121
Contingent Consideration 122
  Accounting for Contingent Consideration in Business Combinations 122
Summary 123
Appendix
Private Company Accounting for Business Combinations 127

Chapter Four
Consolidated Financial Statements and Outside Ownership 155

Consolidated Financial Reporting in the Presence of a Noncontrolling Interest 156
  Subsidiary Acquisition-Date Fair Value in the Presence of a Noncontrolling Interest 157
Discussion Question 158
  Allocating Consolidated Net Income to the Parent and Noncontrolling Interest 161
Partial Ownership Consolidations (Acquisition Method) 162
  Illustration—Partial Acquisition with No Control Premium 162
  Illustration—Partial Acquisition with Control Premium 170
  Effects Created by Alternative Investment Methods 174
Revenue and Expense Reporting for Midyear Acquisitions 175
  Consolidating Postacquisition Subsidiary Revenue and Expenses 175
  Acquisition Following an Equity Method Investment 177
Step Acquisitions 177
  Control Achieved in Steps—Acquisition Method 177
  Example: Step Acquisition Resulting in Control—Acquisition Method 177
  Worksheet Consolidation for a Step Acquisition (Acquisition Method) 179
  Example: Step Acquisition Resulting after Control Is Obtained 181
Discussion Question: Does GAAP Undervalue Post-Control Stock Acquisitions? 182

  Parent Company Sales of Subsidiary Stock—Acquisition Method 182
  Cost-Flow Assumptions 184
  Accounting for Shares That Remain 184
Comparisons with International Accounting Standards 184
Summary 185

Chapter Five
Consolidated Financial Statements— Intra-Entity Asset Transactions 211

Intra-Entity Inventory Transfers 212
  The Sales and Purchases Accounts 212
  Intra-Entity Gross Profit—Year of Transfer (Year 1) 213
Discussion Question: Earnings Management 214
  Intra-Entity Gross Profit—Year Following Transfer (Year 2) 215
  Intra-Entity Gross Profit—Effect on Noncontrolling Interest 217
  Intra-Entity Inventory Transfers Summarized 218
  Intra-Entity Inventory Transfers Illustrated: Parent Uses Equity Method 219
  Effects of Alternative Investment Methods on Consolidation 227
Discussion Question: What Price Should We Charge Ourselves? 230
Intra-Entity Land Transfers 232
  Accounting for Land Transactions 232
  Eliminating Intra-Entity Gains—Land Transfers 232
  Recognizing the Effect on Noncontrolling Interest—Land Transfers 234
Intra-Entity Transfer of Depreciable Assets 234
  Deferral and Subsequent Recognition of Intra-Entity Gains 235
  Depreciable Asset Intra-Entity Transfers Illustrated 235
  Years Following Downstream Intra-Entity Depreciable Asset Transfers—Parent Uses Equity Method 238
  Effect on Noncontrolling Interest—Depreciable Asset Transfers 239
Summary 239

Chapter Six
Variable Interest Entities, Intra-Entity Debt, Consolidated Cash Flows, and Other Issues 261

Consolidation of Variable Interest Entities 261
  What Is a VIE? 262
  Consolidation of Variable Interest Entities 263
  Procedures to Consolidate Variable Interest Entities 267
  Consolidation of a Primary Beneficiary and VIE Illustrated 268
Comparisons with International Accounting Standards 271
Intra-Entity Debt Transactions 272

Acquisition of Affiliate's Debt from an Outside Party   273
Accounting for Intra-Entity Debt Transactions—Individual Financial Records   273
Effects on Consolidation Process   275
Assignment of Retirement Gain or Loss   276
Intra-Entity Debt Transactions—Years Subsequent to Effective Retirement   276
Discussion Question: Who Lost This $300,000?   277
Subsidiary Preferred Stock   279
Consolidated Statement of Cash Flows   281
Acquisition Period Statement of Cash Flows   282
Statement of Cash Flows in Periods Subsequent to Acquisition   286
Consolidated Earnings per Share   286
Subsidiary Stock Transactions   288
Changes in Subsidiary Value—Stock Transactions   289
Subsidiary Stock Transactions—Illustrated   292
Summary   296

Chapter Seven
Foreign Currency Transactions and Hedging Foreign Exchange Risk   319

Foreign Exchange Markets   320
Exchange Rate Mechanisms   320
Foreign Exchange Rates   320
Foreign Currency Forward Contracts   321
Foreign Currency Options   322
Foreign Currency Transactions   323
Accounting Issue   324
Balance Sheet Date before Date of Payment   325
International Accounting Standard 21—The Effects of Changes in Foreign Exchange Rates   327
Foreign Currency Borrowing   327
Foreign Currency Loan   328
Hedges of Foreign Exchange Risk   329
Derivatives Accounting   329
Fundamental Requirement of Derivatives Accounting   330
Determination of Fair Value of Derivatives   330
Accounting for Changes in the Fair Value of Derivatives   330
Hedge Accounting   331
Nature of the Hedged Risk   331
Hedge Effectiveness   332
Hedge Documentation   332
Hedging Combinations   332
Hedges of Foreign Currency Denominated Assets and Liabilities   335
Cash Flow Hedge   335
Fair Value Hedge   335
Forward Contract Used to Hedge a Foreign Currency Denominated Asset   335
Forward Contract Designated as Cash Flow Hedge   337
Forward Contract Designated as Fair Value Hedge   340
Discussion Question: Do We Have a Gain or What?   342
Cash Flow Hedge versus Fair Value Hedge   343

Foreign Currency Option Used to Hedge a Foreign Currency Denominated Asset   344
Option Designated as Cash Flow Hedge   345
Option Designated as Fair Value Hedge   347
Hedges of Unrecognized Foreign Currency Firm Commitments   350
Forward Contract Used as Fair Value Hedge of a Firm Commitment   350
Option Used as Fair Value Hedge of Firm Commitment   352
Hedge of Forecasted Foreign Currency Denominated Transaction   355
Forward Contract Cash Flow Hedge of a Forecasted Transaction   355
Option Designated as a Cash Flow Hedge of a Forecasted Transaction   357
Use of Hedging Instruments   358
The Euro   360
International Financial Reporting Standard 9—Financial Instruments   360
Summary   360

Chapter Eight
Translation of Foreign Currency Financial Statements   385

Exchange Rates Used in Translation   386
Discussion Question: How Do We Report This?   387
Translation Adjustments   388
Balance Sheet Exposure   388
Translation Methods   389
Current Rate Method   389
Temporal Method   390
Translation of Retained Earnings   391
Complicating Aspects of the Temporal Method   392
Calculation of Cost of Goods Sold   392
Application of the Lower-of-Cost-or-Net-Realizable-Value Rule   393
Property, Plant, and Equipment, Depreciation, and Accumulated Depreciation   393
Gain or Loss on the Sale of an Asset   393
Treatment of Translation Adjustment   394
Authoritative Guidance   394
Determining the Appropriate Translation Method   395
Highly Inflationary Economies   396
Appropriate Exchange Rate   397
International Accounting Standard 21—The Effects of Changes in Foreign Exchange Rates   398
The Translation Process Illustrated   399
Translation of Financial Statements—Current Rate Method   401
Translation of the Balance Sheet   402
Translation of the Statement of Cash Flows   404
Remeasurement of Financial Statements—Temporal Method   404
Remeasurement of the Income Statement   405
Remeasurement of the Statement of Cash Flows   407

Nonlocal Currency Balances   408
Comparison of the Results from Applying the Two
Different Methods   408
   Underlying Valuation Method   409
   Underlying Relationships   410
Hedging Balance Sheet Exposure   410
*International Financial Reporting Standard 9—Financial
Instruments   411*
Disclosures Related to Translation   411
Consolidation of a Foreign Subsidiary   412
   Translation of Foreign Subsidiary Trial Balance   413
   *Determination of Balance in Investment Account—Equity
   Method   414*
   Consolidation Worksheet   415
Summary   417

Chapter Nine
Partnerships: Formation and Operation   445

Partnerships—Advantages and Disadvantages   446
Alternative Legal Forms   447
   Subchapter S Corporation   447
   Limited Partnerships (LPs)   448
   Limited Liability Partnerships (LLPs)   448
   Limited Liability Companies (LLCs)   448
Partnership Accounting—Capital Accounts   448
   Articles of Partnership   449
Discussion Question: What Kind of Business Is This?   450
   Accounting for Capital Contributions   450
   Additional Capital Contributions and Withdrawals   453
Discussion Question: How Will the Profits Be Split?   454
   Allocation of Income   454
Accounting for Partnership Dissolution   458
   Dissolution—Admission of a New Partner   458
   Dissolution—Withdrawal of a Partner   463
Summary   466

Chapter Ten
Partnerships: Termination and Liquidation   483

Termination and Liquidation—Protecting
the Interests of All Parties   484
   Termination and Liquidation Procedures Illustrated   484
   Statement of Liquidation   487
   Deficit Capital Balance—Contribution by Partner   487
   Deficit Capital Balance—Loss to Remaining Partners   488
Discussion Question: What Happens If a Partner
Becomes Insolvent?   494
Installment Liquidations   495
   Preliminary Distribution of Partnership Assets   495
   Predistribution Plan   497
Summary   500

Chapter Eleven
Accounting for State and Local Governments (Part 1)   517

Introduction to the Financial Reporting for State and Local
Governments   518
   Governmental Accounting—User Needs   519
   Two Sets of Financial Statements   519
   *The Advantage of Reporting Two Sets of Financial
   Statements   521*
   Internal Record-Keeping—Fund Accounting   522
   Fund Accounting Classifications   523
Overview of State and Local Government
Financial Statements   527
   Government-Wide Financial Statements   527
   Fund Financial Statements   529
Accounting for Governmental Funds   533
   *The Importance of Budgets and the Recording of Budgetary
   Entries   533*
   Encumbrances   536
Recognition of Expenditures and Revenues   537
Discussion Question: Is It an Asset or a Liability?   539
   Recognition of Revenues—Overview   541
   *Derived Tax Revenues Such As Income Taxes and Sales
   Taxes   541*
   *Imposed Nonexchange Revenues Such As Property Taxes and
   Fines   542*
   *Government-Mandated Nonexchange Transactions and
   Voluntary Nonexchange Transactions   543*
   Issuance of Bonds   544
   Special Assessments   547
   Interfund Transactions   548
Summary   552

Chapter Twelve
Accounting for State and Local Governments (Part 2)   575

The Hierarchy of U.S. Generally Accepted Accounting
Principles (GAAP) for State and Local Governments   575
   Tax Abatement Disclosure   577
Solid Waste Landfill   578
   Landfills—Government-Wide Financial Statements   579
   Landfills—Fund Financial Statements   580
Defined Benefit Pension Plans   580
Works of Art and Historical Treasures   582
Infrastructure Assets and Depreciation   584
Comprehensive Annual Financial Report   585
The Primary Government and Component Units   586
   Primary Government   586
   Identifying Component Units   587
   Reporting Component Units   588
   Special Purpose Governments   589

Discussion Question: Is It Part of the County?   590
Acquisitions, Mergers, and Transfers of Operations   590
Government-Wide and Fund Financial Statements
Illustrated   591
   *Statement of Net Position—Government-Wide Financial
   Statements   592*
   *Statement of Activities—Government-Wide Financial
   Statements   593*
   *Balance Sheet—Governmental Funds—Fund Financial
   Statements   597*
   *Statement of Revenues, Expenditures, and Other Changes
   in Fund Balances—Governmental Funds—Fund Financial
   Statements   599*

   *Statement of Net Position—Proprietary Funds—Fund
   Financial Statements   599*
   *Statement of Revenues, Expenses, and Other Changes
   in Net Position—Proprietary Funds—Fund Financial
   Statements   603*
   *Statement of Cash Flows—Proprietary Funds—Fund
   Financial Statements   603*
Reporting Public Colleges and Universities   606
Summary   612

Index   631

The Equity Method of Accounting for Investments

The first several chapters of this text present the accounting and reporting for investment activities of businesses. The focus is on investments when one firm possesses either significant influence or control over another through ownership of voting shares. When one firm owns enough voting shares to be able to affect the decisions of another, accounting for the investment can become challenging and complex. The source of such complexities typically stems from the fact that transactions among the firms affiliated through ownership cannot be considered independent, arm's-length transactions. As in many matters relating to financial reporting, we look to transactions with *outside parties* to provide a basis for accounting valuation. When firms are affiliated through a common set of owners, measurements that recognize the relationships among the firms help to provide objectivity in financial reporting.

The Reporting of Investments in Corporate Equity Securities

In its recent annual report, The Coca-Cola Company describes its 28 percent investment in Coca-Cola FEMSA, a Mexican bottling company with operations throughout much of Latin America. The Coca-Cola Company uses the equity method to account for several of its bottling company investments, including Coca-Cola FEMSA. The Coca-Cola Company states,

> We use the equity method to account for investments in companies, if our investment provides us with the ability to exercise significant influence over operating and financial policies of the investee. Our consolidated net income includes our Company's proportionate share of the net income or loss of these companies.
>
> Our judgment regarding the level of influence over each equity method investment includes considering key factors such as our ownership interest, representation on the board of directors, participation in policy-making decisions and material intercompany transactions.

Such information is hardly unusual in the business world; corporate investors frequently acquire ownership shares of both domestic and foreign businesses. These investments can range from the purchase of a few shares to the acquisition of 100 percent control. Although purchases of corporate equity securities (such as the ones made by Coca-Cola) are not uncommon, they pose a considerable number of financial reporting issues because a close relationship has been established without the investor gaining actual control. These issues are currently addressed by the *equity method*. This chapter deals with accounting for stock investments that fall under the application of this method.

Learning Objectives

After studying this chapter, you should be able to:

LO 1-1 Describe in general the various methods of accounting for an investment in equity shares of another company.

LO 1-2 Identify the sole criterion for applying the equity method of accounting and know the guidelines to assess whether the criterion is met.

LO 1-3 Prepare basic equity method journal entries for an investor and describe the financial reporting for equity method investments.

LO 1-4 Allocate the cost of an equity method investment and compute amortization expense to match revenues recognized from the investment to the excess of investor cost over investee book value.

LO 1-5 Understand the financial reporting consequences for:
a. A change to the equity method.
b. Investee's other comprehensive income.
c. Investee losses.
d. Sales of equity method investments.

LO 1-6 Describe the rationale and computations to defer the investor's share of gross profits on intra-entity inventory sales until the goods are either consumed by the owner or sold to outside parties.

LO 1-7 Explain the rationale and reporting implications of fair-value accounting for investments otherwise accounted for by the equity method.

LO 1-1

Describe in general the various methods of accounting for an investment in equity shares of another company.

Generally accepted accounting principles (GAAP) recognize four different approaches to the financial reporting of investments in corporate equity securities:

1. Fair-value method.
2. Cost method for equity securities without readily determinable fair values.
3. Consolidation of financial statements.
4. Equity method.

The financial statement reporting for a particular investment depends primarily on the degree of influence that the investor (stockholder) has over the investee, a factor most often indicated by the relative size of ownership.[1] Because voting power typically accompanies ownership of equity shares, influence increases with the relative size of ownership. The resulting influence can be very little, a significant amount, or, in some cases, complete control.

Fair-Value Method

In many instances, an investor possesses only a small percentage of an investee company's outstanding stock, perhaps only a few shares. Because of the limited level of ownership, the investor cannot expect to significantly affect the investee's operations or decision making. These shares are bought in anticipation of cash dividends or in appreciation of stock market values. Such investments are recorded at cost and periodically adjusted to fair value according to the Financial Accounting Standards Board (FASB) *Accounting Standards Codification* (ASC) Topic 321, "Investments—Equity Securities."

Fair value is defined by the ASC (Master Glossary) as the "price that would be received to sell an asset or paid to transfer a liability in an orderly transaction between market participants at the measurement date." For most investments in equity securities, quoted stock market prices represent fair values.

Because a full coverage of limited ownership investments in equity securities is presented in intermediate accounting textbooks, only the following basic principles are noted here:

- Initial investments in equity securities are recorded at cost and subsequently adjusted to fair value if fair value is readily determinable (typically by reference to market value); otherwise, the investment remains at cost.
- Changes in the fair values of equity securities during a reporting period are recognized as income.[2]
- Dividends declared on the equity securities are recognized as income.

The above procedures are followed for equity security investments (with readily determinable fair values) when the owner possesses neither significant influence nor control.

Cost Method (Investments in Equity Securities without Readily Determinable Fair Values)

When the fair value of an investment in equity securities is not readily determinable, and the investment provides neither significant influence nor control, the investment may be measured at cost. Such investments sometimes can be found in ownership shares of firms that are not publicly traded or experience only infrequent trades.

---

[1] The relative size of ownership is most often the key factor in assessing one company's degree of influence over another. However, as discussed later in this chapter, other factors (e.g., contractual relationships between firms) can also provide influence or control over firms regardless of the percentage of shares owned.

[2] FASB Accounting Standards Update (ASU) No. 2016-01, Financial Instruments—Overall, requires equity investments (except those accounted for under the equity method of accounting or those that result in consolidation of the investee) to be measured at fair value with changes in fair value recognized in net income, unless fair values are not readily determinable. Thus, the previous available-for-sale category with fair value changes recorded in other comprehensive income will no longer be available. The ASU is effective for fiscal years beginning after December 15, 2017, with early adoption permitted.

Investments in equity securities that employ the cost method often continue to be reported at their original cost over time.[3] Income from cost method equity investments usually consists of the investor's share of dividends declared by the investee. However, despite its emphasis on cost measurements, GAAP allows for two fair value assessments that may affect cost method amounts reported on the balance sheet and the income statement.

- First, cost method equity investments periodically must be assessed for impairment to determine if the fair value of the investment is less than its carrying amount. The ASC allows a qualitative assessment to determine if impairment is likely.[4] Because the fair value of a cost method equity investment is not readily available (by definition), if impairment is deemed likely, an entity must estimate a fair value for the investment to measure the amount (if any) of the impairment loss.

- Second, ASC (321-10-35-2) allows for recognition of "observable price changes in orderly transactions for the identical or a similar investment of the same issuer." Any unrealized holding gains (or losses) from these observable price changes are included in earnings with a corresponding adjustment to the investment account. So even if equity shares are only infrequently traded (and thus fair value is not readily determinable), such trades can provide a basis for financial statement recognition under the cost method for equity investments.

Consolidation of Financial Statements

Many corporate investors acquire enough shares to gain actual control over an investee's operations. In financial accounting, such control may be achieved when a stockholder accumulates more than 50 percent of an organization's outstanding voting stock. At that point, rather than simply influencing the investee's decisions, the investor often can direct the entire decision-making process. A review of the financial statements of America's largest organizations indicates that legal control of one or more subsidiary companies is an almost universal practice. PepsiCo, Inc., as just one example, holds a majority interest in the voting stock of literally hundreds of corporations.

Investor control over an investee presents a special accounting challenge. Normally, when a majority of voting stock is held, the investor-investee relationship is so closely connected that the two corporations are viewed as a single entity for reporting purposes.[5] Hence, an entirely different set of accounting procedures is applicable. Control generally requires the consolidation of the accounting information produced by the individual companies. Thus, a single set of financial statements is created for external reporting purposes with all assets, liabilities, revenues, and expenses brought together. The various procedures applied within this consolidation process are examined in subsequent chapters of this textbook.

The FASB ASC Section 810-10-05 on variable interest entities expands the use of consolidated financial statements to include entities that are financially controlled through special contractual arrangements rather than through voting stock interests. Prior to the accounting requirements for variable interest entities, many firms (e.g., Enron) avoided consolidation of entities that they owned little or no voting stock in but otherwise controlled through special contracts. These entities were frequently referred to as "special purpose entities (SPEs)" and provided vehicles for some firms to keep large amounts of assets and liabilities off their consolidated financial statements. Accounting for these entities is discussed in Chapters 2 and 6.

---

[3] Dividends received in excess of earnings subsequent to the date of investment are considered returns of the investment and are recorded as reductions of cost of the investment.

[4] Impairment indicators include assessments of earnings performance, economic environment, going-concern ability, etc. If the qualitative assessment does not indicate impairment, no further testing is required. If an equity security without a readily determinable fair value is impaired, the investor recognizes the difference between the investment's fair value and carrying amount as an impairment loss in net income (ASC 321-10-35-3).

[5] As discussed in Chapter 2, ownership of a majority voting interest in an investee does not always lead to consolidated financial statements.

Discussion Question

DID THE COST METHOD INVITE EARNINGS MANIPULATION?

Prior to GAAP for equity method investments, firms used the cost method to account for their unconsolidated investments in common stock regardless of the presence of significant influence. Under the cost method, when the investee declares a dividend, the investor records "dividend income." The investment account typically remains at its original cost—hence the term *cost method*.

Many firms' compensation plans reward managers based on reported annual income. How might the use of the cost method of accounting for significant influence investments have resulted in unintended wealth transfers from owners to managers? Do the equity or fair-value methods provide similar incentives?

Equity Method

Another investment relationship is appropriately accounted for using the equity method. In many investments, although control is not achieved, the degree of ownership indicates the ability of the investor to exercise *significant influence* over the investee. Recall Coca-Cola's 28 percent investment in Coca-Cola FEMSA's voting stock. Through its ownership, Coca-Cola can undoubtedly influence Coca-Cola FEMSA's decisions and operations.

To provide objective reporting for investments with significant influence, FASB ASC Topic 323, "Investments—Equity Method and Joint Ventures," describes the use of the equity method. The equity method employs the accrual basis for recognizing the investor's share of investee income. Accordingly, the investor recognizes income as it is earned by the investee. As noted in FASB ASC (para. 323-10-05-5), because of its significant influence over the investee, the investor

> has a degree of responsibility for the return on its investment and it is appropriate to include in the results of operations of the investor its share of earnings or losses of the investee.

Furthermore, under the equity method, the investor records its share of investee dividends declared as a decrease in the investment account, not as income.

In today's business world, many corporations hold significant ownership interests in other companies without having actual control. The Coca-Cola Company, for example, owns between 20 and 50 percent of several bottling companies, both domestic and international. Many other investments represent joint ventures in which two or more companies form a new enterprise to carry out a specified operating purpose. For example, Ford Motor Company and Sollers formed FordSollers, a passenger and commercial vehicle manufacturing, import, and distribution company in Russia. Each partner owns 50 percent of the joint venture. For each of these investments, the investors do not possess absolute control because they hold less than a majority of the voting stock. Thus, the preparation of consolidated financial statements is inappropriate. However, the large percentage of ownership indicates that each investor possesses some ability to affect the investee's decision-making process.

Finally, as discussed at the end of this chapter, firms may elect a fair-value option in their financial reporting for certain financial assets and financial liabilities. Among the qualifying financial assets for fair-value reporting are significant influence investments otherwise accounted for by the equity method.

International Accounting Standard 28—Investments in Associates

The International Accounting Standards Board (IASB), similar to the FASB, recognizes the need to take into account the significant influence that can occur when one firm holds a certain amount of voting shares of another. The IASB defines significant influence as the power to participate in the financial and operating policy decisions of the investee, but it is not control or joint control over those policies. The following describes the basics of the equity method in International Accounting Standard (IAS) 28:[6]

> If an investor holds, directly or indirectly (e.g., through subsidiaries), 20 per cent or more of the voting power of the investee, it is presumed that the investor has significant influence, unless it can be clearly demonstrated that this is not the case. Conversely, if the investor holds, directly or indirectly (e.g., through subsidiaries), less than 20 per cent of the voting power of the investee, it is presumed that the investor does not have significant influence, unless such influence can be clearly demonstrated. A substantial or majority ownership by another investor does not necessarily preclude an investor from having significant influence.
>
> Under the equity method, the investment in an associate is initially recognised at cost and the carrying amount is increased or decreased to recognise the investor's share of the profit or loss of the investee after the date of acquisition. The investor's share of the profit or loss of the investee is recognised in the investor's profit or loss. Distributions received from an investee reduce the carrying amount of the investment.

As seen from the above excerpt from *IAS 28,* the equity method concepts and applications described are virtually identical to those prescribed by the FASB ASC.

Application of the Equity Method

An understanding of the equity method is best gained by initially examining the FASB's treatment of two questions:

1. What factors indicate when the equity method should be used for an investment in another entity's ownership securities?
2. How should the investor report this investment and the income generated by it to reflect the relationship between the two entities?

Criteria for Utilizing the Equity Method

LO 1-2

Identify the sole criterion for applying the equity method of accounting and guidance in assessing whether the criterion is met.

The rationale underlying the equity method is that an investor begins to gain the ability to influence the decision-making process of an investee as the level of ownership rises. According to FASB ASC Topic 323 on equity method investments, achieving this "ability to exercise significant influence over operating and financial policies of an investee even though the investor holds 50 percent or less of the common stock" is the sole criterion for requiring application of the equity method [FASB ASC (para. 323-10-15-3)].

Clearly, a term such as *the ability to exercise significant influence* is nebulous and subject to a variety of judgments and interpretations in practice. At what point does the acquisition of one additional share of stock give an owner the ability to exercise significant influence? This decision becomes even more difficult in that only the *ability* to exercise significant influence need be present. There is no requirement that any actual influence must ever be applied.

FASB ASC Topic 323 provides guidance to the accountant by listing several conditions that indicate the presence of this degree of influence:

- Investor representation on the board of directors of the investee.
- Investor participation in the policy-making process of the investee.
- Material intra-entity transactions.

[6] International Accounting Standards Board, IAS 28, "Investments in Associates," Technical Summary (www.iasb.org).

- Interchange of managerial personnel.
- Technological dependency.
- Extent of ownership by the investor in relation to the size and concentration of other ownership interests in the investee.

No single one of these guides should be used exclusively in assessing the applicability of the equity method. Instead, all are evaluated together to determine the presence or absence of the sole criterion: the ability to exercise significant influence over the investee.

These guidelines alone do not eliminate the leeway available to each investor when deciding whether the use of the equity method is appropriate. To provide a degree of consistency in applying this standard, the FASB provides a general ownership test: *If an investor holds between 20 and 50 percent of the voting stock of the investee, significant influence is normally assumed and the equity method is applied.*

> An investment (direct or indirect) of 20 percent or more of the voting stock of an investee shall lead to a presumption that in the absence of predominant evidence to the contrary an investor has the ability to exercise significant influence over an investee. Conversely, an investment of less than 20 percent of the voting stock of an investee shall lead to a presumption that an investor does not have the ability to exercise significant influence unless such ability can be demonstrated.[7]

Limitations of Equity Method Applicability

At first, the 20 to 50 percent rule may appear to be an arbitrarily chosen boundary range established merely to provide a consistent method of reporting for investments. However, the essential criterion is still the ability to significantly influence (but not control) the investee, rather than 20 to 50 percent ownership. If the absence of this ability is proven (or control exists), the equity method should not be applied regardless of the percentage of shares held.

For example, the equity method is not appropriate for investments that demonstrate any of the following characteristics regardless of the investor's degree of ownership:[8]

- An agreement exists between investor and investee by which the investor surrenders significant rights as a shareholder.
- A concentration of ownership operates the investee without regard for the views of the investor.
- The investor attempts but fails to obtain representation on the investee's board of directors.

In each of these situations, because the investor is unable to exercise significant influence over its investee, the equity method is not applied.

Alternatively, if an entity can exercise *control* over its investee, regardless of its ownership level, consolidation (rather than the equity method) is appropriate. FASB ASC (para. 810-10-05-8) limits the use of the equity method by expanding the definition of a controlling financial interest and addresses situations in which financial control exists absent majority ownership interest. In these situations, control is achieved through contractual and other arrangements called *variable interests.*

To illustrate, one firm may create a separate legal entity in which it holds less than 50 percent of the voting interests but nonetheless controls that entity through governance document provisions and/or contracts that specify decision-making power and the distribution of profits and losses. Entities controlled in this fashion are typically designated as *variable interest entities,* and their sponsoring firm may be required to include them in consolidated financial reports despite the fact that ownership is less than 50 percent. For example, the Walt Disney Company reclassified several former equity method investees as variable interest entities and now consolidates these investments.[9]

---

[7] FASB ASC (para. 323-10-15-8).

[8] FASB ASC (para. 323-10-15-10). This paragraph deals specifically with limits to using the equity method for investments in which the owner holds 20 to 50 percent of the outstanding shares.

[9] Chapters 2 and 6 provide further discussions of variable interest entities.

Extensions of Equity Method Applicability

For some investments that either fall short of or exceed 20 to 50 percent ownership, the equity method is nonetheless appropriately used for financial reporting. As an example, The Coca-Cola Company acquired a 16.7 percent investment in Monster Beverage Corporation in 2015. Coca-Cola notes in its annual 2015 financial statements that "Based on our equity ownership percentage, the significance that our expanded distribution and coordination agreements have on Monster's operations, and our representation on Monster's Board of Directors, the Company is accounting for its interest in Monster as an equity method investment."

Conditions can also exist where the equity method is appropriate despite a majority ownership interest. In some instances, rights granted to noncontrolling shareholders restrict the powers of the majority shareholder. Such rights may include approval over compensation, hiring, termination, and other critical operating and capital spending decisions of an entity. If the noncontrolling rights are so restrictive as to call into question whether control rests with the majority owner, the equity method is employed for financial reporting rather than consolidation. For example, prior to its acquisition of BellSouth, AT&T, Inc., stated in its financial reports "we account for our 60 percent economic investment in Cingular under the equity method of accounting because we share control equally with our 40 percent partner BellSouth."

To summarize, the following table indicates the method of accounting that is typically applicable to various stock investments:

Criterion	Normal Ownership Level	Applicable Accounting Method
Inability to significantly influence	Less than 20%	Fair value or cost method
Ability to significantly influence	20%–50%	Equity method or fair value
Control through voting interests	More than 50%	Consolidated financial statements
Control through variable interests (governance documents, contracts)	Primary beneficiary status (no ownership required)	Consolidated financial statements

Accounting for an Investment—The Equity Method

Now that the criteria leading to the application of the equity method have been identified, a review of its reporting procedures is appropriate. Knowledge of this accounting process is especially important to users of the investor's financial statements because the equity method affects both the timing of income recognition as well as the carrying amount of the investment account.

In applying the equity method, the accounting objective is to report the investment and investment income to reflect the close relationship between the investor and investee. After recording the cost of the acquisition, two equity method entries periodically record the investment's impact:

1. The investor's investment account *increases as the investee recognizes and reports income.* Also, the investor recognizes investment income using the accrual method—that is, in the same period as reported by the investee in its financial statements. If an investee reports income of $100,000, a 30 percent owner should immediately increase its own income by $30,000. This earnings accrual reflects the essence of the equity method by emphasizing the connection between the two companies; as the owners' equity of the investee increases through the earnings process, the investment account also increases. Although the investor initially records the acquisition at cost, upward adjustments in the asset balance are recorded as soon as the investee makes a profit. The investor reduces the investment account if the investee reports a loss.

2. The investor decreases its investment account for its share of investee cash dividends. When the investee declares a cash dividend, its owners' equity decreases. The investor mirrors this change by recording a reduction in the carrying amount of the investment rather than recognizing the dividend as revenue. Furthermore, because the investor recognizes income when the investee recognizes it, double counting would occur if the investor also recorded its share of subsequent investee dividends as revenue. Importantly, a cash dividend declaration is not an appropriate point for income recognition. As stated in FASB ASC (para. 323-10-35-4),

> Under the equity method, an investor shall recognize its share of the earnings or losses of an investee in the periods for which they are reported by the investee in its financial statements rather than in the period in which an investee declares a dividend.

Because the investor can influence their timing, investee dividends cannot objectively measure income generated from the investment.

Application of Equity Method	
Investee Event	**Investor Accounting**
Income is recognized.	Proportionate share of income is recognized.
Dividends are declared.	Investor's share of investee dividends reduce the investment account.

Application of the equity method thus causes the investment account on the investor's balance sheet to vary directly with changes in the investee's equity.

In contrast, the fair-value method reports investments at fair value if it is readily determinable. Also, income is recognized both from changes in fair value and upon receipt of dividends. Consequently, financial reports can vary depending on whether the equity method or fair-value method is appropriate.

To illustrate, assume that Big Company owns a 20 percent interest in Little Company purchased on January 1, 2017, for $210,000. Little then reports net income of $200,000, $300,000, and $400,000, respectively, in the next three years while declaring dividends of $50,000, $100,000, and $200,000. The fair values of Big's investment in Little, as determined by market prices, were $245,000, $282,000, and $325,000 at the end of 2017, 2018, and 2019, respectively.

Exhibit 1.1 compares the accounting for Big's investment in Little across the two methods. The fair-value method carries the investment at its market values, presumed to be readily available in this example. Income is recognized both through changes in Little's fair value and as Little declares dividends.

In contrast, under the equity method, Big recognizes income as it is recorded by Little. As shown in Exhibit 1.1, Big recognizes $180,000 in income over the three years, and the

EXHIBIT 1.1 Comparison of Fair-Value Method (ASC 321) and Equity Method (ASC 323)

Year	Income of Little Company	Dividends Declared by Little Company	Accounting by Big Company When Influence Is Not Significant (fair-value method)			Accounting by Big Company When Influence Is Significant (equity method)	
			Dividend Income	Fair-Value Change to Income	Carrying Amount of Investment	Equity in Investee Income*	Carrying Amount of Investment†
2017	$200,000	$ 50,000	$10,000	$ 35,000	$ 245,000	$ 40,000	$240,000
2018	300,000	100,000	20,000	37,000	282,000	60,000	280,000
2019	400,000	200,000	40,000	43,000	325,000	80,000	320,000
Total income recognized			$70,000	$115,000		$180,000	

*Equity in investee income is 20 percent of the current year income reported by Little Company.
†The carrying amount of an investment under the equity method is the original cost plus income recognized less dividends. For 2017, as an example, the $240,000 reported balance is the $210,000 cost plus $40,000 equity income less $10,000 in dividends.

carrying amount of the investment is adjusted upward to $320,000. Dividends from Little are not an appropriate measure of income because of the assumed significant influence over the investee. Big's ability to influence Little's decisions applies to the timing of dividend distributions. Therefore, dividends from Little do not objectively measure Big's income from its investment in Little. As Little records income, however, under the equity method Big recognizes its share (20 percent) of the income and increases the investment account. Thus the equity method reflects the accrual model: The investor recognizes income as it is recognized by the investee, not when the investee declares a cash dividend.

Exhibit 1.1 shows that the carrying amount of the investment fluctuates each year under the equity method. This recording parallels the changes occurring in the net asset figures reported by the investee. If the owners' equity of the investee rises through income, an increase is made in the investment account; decreases such as losses and dividends cause reductions to be recorded. Thus, the equity method conveys information that describes the relationship created by the investor's ability to significantly influence the investee.

LO 1-3

Prepare basic equity method journal entries for an investor and describe the financial reporting for equity method investments.

Equity Method Accounting Procedures

Once guidelines for the application of the equity method have been established, the mechanical process necessary for recording basic transactions is straightforward. The investor accrues its percentage of the earnings reported by the investee each period. Investee dividend declarations reduce the investment balance to reflect the decrease in the investee's book value.[10]

Referring again to the information presented in Exhibit 1.1, Little Company reported a net income of $200,000 during 2017 and declared and paid cash dividends of $50,000. These figures indicate that Little's net assets have increased by $150,000 during the year. Therefore, in its financial records, Big Company records the following journal entries to apply the equity method:

Investment in Little Company	40,000	
Equity in Investee Income		40,000
To accrue earnings of a 20 percent owned investee ($200,000 × 20%).		
Dividend Receivable.	10,000	
Investment in Little Company		10,000
To record a dividend declaration by Little Company ($50,000 × 20%).		
Cash	10,000	
Dividend Receivable.		10,000
To record collection of the cash dividend.		

In the first entry, Big accrues income based on the investee's reported earnings. The second entry reflects the dividend declaration and the related reduction in Little's net assets followed then by the cash collection. The $30,000 net increment recorded here in Big's investment account ($40,000 − $10,000) represents 20 percent of the $150,000 increase in Little's book value that occurred during the year.

LO 1-4

Allocate the cost of an equity method investment and compute amortization expense to match revenues recognized from the investment to the excess of investor cost over investee book value.

Excess of Investment Cost over Book Value Acquired

After the basic concepts and procedures of the equity method are mastered, more complex accounting issues can be introduced. Surely one of the most common problems encountered in applying the equity method occurs when the investment cost exceeds the proportionate book value of the investee company.[11]

---

[10] In this text, the terms *book value* and *carrying amount* are used synonymously. Each refers to either an account balance, an amount appearing in a financial statement, or the amount of net assets (stockholders' equity) of a business entity.

[11] Although encountered less frequently, investments can be purchased at a cost that is less than the underlying book value of the investee. Accounting for this possibility is explored in later chapters.

DOES THE EQUITY METHOD REALLY APPLY HERE?

Abraham, Inc., a New Jersey corporation, operates 57 bakeries throughout the northeastern section of the United States. In the past, its founder, James Abraham, owned all the company's outstanding common stock. However, during the early part of this year, the corporation suffered a severe cash flow problem brought on by rapid expansion. To avoid bankruptcy, Abraham sought additional investment capital from a friend, Dennis Bostitch, who owns Highland Laboratories. Subsequently, Highland paid $700,000 cash to Abraham, Inc., to acquire enough newly issued shares of common stock for a one-third ownership interest.

At the end of this year, the accountants for Highland Laboratories are discussing the proper method of reporting this investment. One argues for maintaining the asset at its original cost: "This purchase is no more than a loan to bail out the bakeries. Mr. Abraham will continue to run the organization with little or no attention paid to us. After all, what does anyone in our company know about baking bread? I would be surprised if Abraham does not reacquire these shares as soon as the bakery business is profitable again."

One of the other accountants disagrees, stating that the equity method is appropriate. "I realize that our company is not capable of running a bakery. However, the official rules state that we must have only the *ability* to exert significant influence. With one-third of the common stock in our possession, we certainly have that ability. Whether we use it or not, this ability means that we are required to apply the equity method."

How should Highland Laboratories account for its investment in Abraham, Inc.?

Unless the investor acquires its ownership at the time of the investee's conception, paying an amount equal to book value is rare. A number of possible reasons exist for a difference between the book value of a company and its fair value as reflected by the price of its stock. A company's fair value at any time is based on a multitude of factors such as company profitability, the introduction of a new product, expected dividend payments, projected operating results, and general economic conditions. Furthermore, stock prices are based, at least partially, on the perceived worth of a company's net assets, amounts that often vary dramatically from underlying book values. Many asset and liability accounts shown on a balance sheet tend to measure historical costs rather than current value. In addition, these reported figures are affected by the specific accounting methods adopted by a company. Inventory costing methods such as LIFO and FIFO, for example, obviously lead to different book values as does each of the acceptable depreciation methods.

If an investment is acquired at a price in excess of the investee's book value, logical reasons should explain the additional cost incurred by the investor. The source of the excess of cost over book value is important. Income recognition requires matching the income generated from the investment with its cost. Excess costs allocated to fixed assets will likely be expensed over longer periods than costs allocated to inventory. In applying the equity method, the cause of such an excess payment can be divided into two general categories:

1. Specifically identifiable investee assets and liabilities can have fair values that differ from their present book values. The excess payment can be identified directly with individual accounts such as inventory, equipment, franchise rights, and so on.

2. The investor may pay an extra amount because it expects future benefits to accrue from the investment. Such benefits could be anticipated as the result of factors such as the estimated profitability of the investee or the expected relationship between the two companies. When

the additional payment cannot be attributed to any specifically identifiable investee asset or liability, the investor recognizes an intangible asset called *goodwill.* For example, eBay Inc. once disclosed in its annual report that goodwill related to its equity method investments was approximately $27.4 million.

As an illustration, assume that Grande Company is negotiating the acquisition of 30 percent of the outstanding shares of Chico Company. Chico's balance sheet reports assets of $500,000 and liabilities of $300,000 for a net book value of $200,000. After investigation, Grande determines that Chico's equipment is undervalued in the company's financial records by $60,000. One of its patents is also undervalued, but only by $40,000. By adding these valuation adjustments to Chico's book value, Grande arrives at an estimated $300,000 worth for the company's net assets. Based on this computation, Grande offers $90,000 for a 30 percent share of the investee's outstanding stock.

Book value of Chico Company [assets minus liabilities (or stockholders' equity)]	$200,000
Undervaluation of equipment	60,000
Undervaluation of patent	40,000
Value of net assets	$300,000
Percentage acquired	30%
Purchase price	$ 90,000

Although Grande's purchase price is in excess of the proportionate share of Chico's book value, this additional amount can be attributed to two specific accounts: Equipment and Patents. No part of the extra payment is traceable to any other projected future benefit. Thus, the cost of Grande's investment is allocated as follows:

Payment by investor		$90,000
Percentage of book value acquired ($200,000 × 30%)		60,000
Payment in excess of book value		30,000
Excess payment identified with specific assets:		
Equipment ($60,000 undervaluation × 30%)	$18,000	
Patent ($40,000 undervaluation × 30%)	12,000	30,000
Excess payment not identified with specific assets—goodwill		$ –0–

Of the $30,000 excess payment made by the investor, $18,000 is assigned to the equipment whereas $12,000 is traced to a patent and its undervaluation. No amount of the purchase price is allocated to goodwill.

To take this example one step further, assume that Chico's owners reject Grande's proposed $90,000 price. They believe that the value of the company as a going concern is higher than the fair value of its net assets. Because the management of Grande believes that valuable synergies will be created through this purchase, the bid price is raised to $125,000 and accepted. This new acquisition price is allocated as follows:

Payment by investor		$125,000
Percentage of book value acquired ($200,000 × 30%)		60,000
Payment in excess of book value		65,000
Excess payment identified with specific assets:		
Equipment ($60,000 undervaluation × 30%)	$18,000	
Patent ($40,000 undervaluation × 30%)	12,000	30,000
Excess payment not identified with specific assets—goodwill		$ 35,000

As this example indicates, *any extra payment that cannot be attributed to a specific asset or liability is assigned to the intangible asset goodwill.* Although the actual purchase price can be computed by a number of different techniques or simply result from negotiations, goodwill is always the excess amount not allocated to identifiable asset or liability accounts.

Under the equity method, the investor enters total cost in a single investment account regardless of the allocation of any excess purchase price. If all parties accept Grande's bid of $125,000, the acquisition is initially recorded at that amount despite the internal assignments made to equipment, patents and goodwill. The entire $125,000 was paid to acquire this investment, and it is recorded as such.

The Amortization Process

In the above transaction, the extra payment over Grande's book value was made for specific identifiable assets (equipment and patents), and goodwill. Even though the actual dollar amounts are recorded within the investment account, a definite historical cost can be attributed to these assets. With a cost to the investor as well as a specified life, the payment relating to each asset (except land, goodwill, and other indefinite life intangibles) should be amortized over an appropriate time period.[12] However, certain intangibles such as goodwill, are considered to have indefinite lives and thus are not subject to amortization.[13]

Goodwill associated with equity method investments, for the most part, is measured in the same manner as goodwill arising from a business combination (see Chapters 2 through 7). One difference is that goodwill arising from a business combination is subject to annual impairment reviews, whereas goodwill implicit in equity method investments is not. Equity method investments are tested in their entirety for permanent declines in value.[14]

To show the amortization process for definite-lived assets, we continue with our Grande and Chico example. Assume, that the equipment has a 10-year remaining life, the patent a 5-year life, and the goodwill an indefinite life. If the straight-line method is used with no salvage value, *the investor's cost* should be amortized initially as follows:[15]

Account	Cost Assigned	Remaining Useful Life	Annual Amortization
Equipment	$18,000	10 years	$1,800
Patent	12,000	5 years	2,400
Goodwill	35,000	Indefinite	–0–
Annual expense (for five years until patent cost is completely amortized)			$4,200

In recording this annual expense, Grande reduces the investment balance in the same way it would amortize the cost of any other asset that had a limited life. Therefore, at the end of the first year of holding the investment, the investor records the following journal entry under the equity method:

Equity in Investee Income	4,200	
Investment in Chico Company		4,200
To record amortization of excess payment allocated to equipment and patent.		

[12] A 2015 FASB *Proposed Accounting Standards Update,* "Simplifying the Equity Method of Accounting," recommended the elimination of the identification and amortization of excess cost over acquired investee book value. However, at a December 2015 meeting, the FASB did not affirm the proposed elimination of current accounting treatment for the excess cost over acquired investee book value and directed its staff to research additional alternatives for improving the equity method.

[13] Other intangibles (such as certain licenses, trademarks, etc.) also can be considered to have indefinite lives and thus are not amortized unless and until their lives are determined to be limited. Further discussion of intangibles with indefinite lives appears in Chapter 3.

[14] Because equity method goodwill is not separable from the related investment, goodwill should not be separately tested for impairment. See also FASB ASC para. 350-20-35-59.

[15] Unless otherwise stated, all amortization computations are based on the straight-line method with no salvage value.

Because this amortization relates to investee assets, the investor does not establish a specific expense account. Instead, as in the previous entry, the expense is recognized by decreasing the the investor's equity income accruing from the investee company.

To illustrate this entire process, assume that Tall Company purchases 20 percent of Short Company for $200,000. Tall can exercise significant influence over the investee; thus, the equity method is appropriately applied. The acquisition is made on January 1, 2017, when Short holds net assets with a book value of $700,000. Tall believes that the investee's building (10-year remaining life) is undervalued within the financial records by $80,000 and equipment with a 5-year remaining life is undervalued by $120,000. Any goodwill established by this purchase is considered to have an indefinite life. During 2017, Short reports a net income of $150,000 and at year-end declares a cash dividend of $60,000.

Tall's three basic journal entries for 2017 pose little problem:

January 1, 2017		
Investment in Short Company	200,000	
Cash		200,000
To record acquisition of 20 percent of the outstanding shares of Short Company.		

December 31, 2017		
Investment in Short Company	30,000	
Equity in Investee Income		30,000
To accrue 20 percent of the 2017 reported earnings of investee ($150,000 × 20%).		
Dividend Receivable	12,000	
Investment in Short Company		12,000
To record a dividend declaration by Short Company ($60,000 × 20%).		

An allocation of Tall's $200,000 purchase price must be made to determine whether an additional adjusting entry is necessary to recognize annual amortization associated with the extra payment:

Payment by investor		$200,000
Percentage of 1/1/17 book value ($700,000 × 20%)		140,000
Payment in excess of book value		60,000
Excess payment identified with specific assets:		
Building ($80,000 × 20%)	$16,000	
Equipment ($120,000 × 20%)	24,000	40,000
Excess payment not identified with specific assets—goodwill		$ 20,000

As can be seen, $16,000 of the purchase price is assigned to a building and $24,000 to equipment, with the remaining $20,000 attributed to goodwill. For each asset with a definite useful life, periodic amortization is required.

Asset	Attributed Cost	Remaining Useful Life	Annual Amortization
Building	$16,000	10 years	$1,600
Equipment	24,000	5 years	4,800
Goodwill	20,000	Indefinite	–0–
Total for 2017			$6,400

At the end of 2017, Tall must also record the following adjustment in connection with these cost allocations:

Equity in Investee Income	6,400	
Investment in Short Company		6,400
To record 2017 amortization of excess payment allocated to building ($1,600) and equipment ($4,800).		

Although these entries are shown separately here for better explanation, Tall would probably net the income accrual for the year ($30,000) and the amortization ($6,400) to create a single entry increasing the investment and recognizing equity income of $23,600. Thus, the first-year return on Tall Company's beginning investment balance (defined as equity earnings/beginning investment balance) is equal to 11.80 percent ($23,600/$200,000).

Equity Method—Additional Issues

The previous sections on equity income accruals and excess cost amortizations provide the basics for applying the equity method. However, several other non-routine issues can arise during the life of an equity method investment. More specifically, special procedures are required in accounting for each of the following:

1. Reporting a change to the equity method.
2. Reporting investee income from sources other than continuing operations.
3. Reporting investee losses.
4. Reporting the sale of an equity investment.

Reporting a Change to the Equity Method

LO 1-5a

Understand the financial reporting consequences for a change to the equity method.

In many instances, an investor's ability to significantly influence an investee is not achieved through a single stock acquisition. The investor could possess only a minor ownership for some years before purchasing enough additional shares to require conversion to the equity method. Before the investor achieves significant influence, any investment should be reported by either the fair-value method, or if the investment fair value is not readily determinable, the cost method. After the investment reaches the point at which the equity method becomes applicable, a technical question arises about the appropriate means of changing from one method to the other.[16]

FASB ASC (para. 323-10-35-33) addresses the issue of how to account for an investment in the common stock of an investee that, through additional stock acquisition or other means (e.g., increased degree of influence, reduction of investee's outstanding stock, etc.) becomes qualified for use of the equity method.

> If an investment qualifies for use of the equity method . . . , the investor shall add the cost of acquiring the additional interest in the investee (if any) to the current basis of the investor's previously held interest and adopt the equity method of accounting as of the date the investment becomes qualified for equity method accounting.

Thus, the FASB requires a prospective approach by requiring that the cost of any new share acquired simply be added to the current investment carrying amount. By mandating prospective treatment, the FASB avoids the complexity of restating prior period amounts.[17]

To illustrate, assume that on January 1, 2017, Alpha Company exchanges $84,000 for a 10 percent ownership in Bailey Company. At the time of the transaction, officials of Alpha do not believe that their company gained the ability to exert significant influence over Bailey. Alpha properly accounts for the investment using the fair-value method and recognizes in net

---

[16] A switch to the equity method also can be required if the investee purchases a portion of its own shares as treasury stock. This transaction can increase the investor's percentage of outstanding stock.

[17] Prior to 2017, the FASB required a retrospective adjustment to an investor's previous ownership shares upon achieving significant influence over an investee.

income its 10 percent ownership share of changes in Bailey's fair value. The fair and book values of Bailey's common stock appear below:

Date	Fair Value	Book Value
January 1, 2017	$840,000	$670,000
December 31, 2017	890,000	715,000

At the end of 2017, Alpha recognizes the increase in its 10 percent share of Bailey's fair value and increases its investment account to $89,000. Because the fair-value method is used to account for the investment, Bailey's $670,000 book value balance at January 1, 2017 does not affect Alpha's accounting.

Then on January 1, 2018, Alpha purchases an additional 30 percent of Bailey's outstanding voting stock for $267,000 and achieves the ability to significantly influence the investee's decision making. Alpha will now apply the equity method to account for its investment in Bailey. To bring about the prospective change to the equity method, Alpha prepares the following journal entry on January 1, 2018:

Investment in Bailey Company.	267,000	
Cash.		267,000
To record an additional 30 percent investment in Bailey Company		

On January 1, 2018, Bailey's carrying amounts for its assets and liabilities equaled their fair values except for a patent, which was undervalued by $175,000 and had a 10-year remaining useful life.

To determine the proper amount of excess fair value amortization required in applying the equity method, Alpha prepares an investment allocation schedule. The fair value of Alpha's total (40 percent) investment serves as the valuation basis for the allocation schedule as of January 1, 2018, the date Alpha achieves the ability to exercise significant influence over Bailey. Below is the January 1, 2018 investment allocation schedule:

Investment Fair Value Allocation Schedule
Investment in Bailey Company
January 1, 2018

Current fair value of initial 10 percent ownership of Bailey	$ 89,000
Payment for additional 30 percent investment in Bailey	267,000
Total fair value of 40 percent investment in Bailey	$356,000
Alpha's share of Bailey's book value (40% × $715,000)	286,000
Investment fair value in excess of Bailey's book value	$ 70,000
Excess fair value attributable to Bailey's patent (40% × $175,000)	$ 70,000
	-0-

We next assume that Bailey reports net income of $130,000 and declares and pays a $50,000 dividend at the end of 2018. Accordingly, Alpha applies the equity method and records the following three journal entries at the end of 2018:

Investment in Bailey Company	45,000	
Equity in Investee Income.		45,000
To accrue 40 percent of the year 2018 income reported by Bailey Company ($130,000 × 40%) – $7,000 excess patent amortization (10-year remaining life).		
Dividend Receivable	20,000	
Investment in Bailey Company		20,000
To record the 2018 dividend declaration by Bailey Company ($50,000 × 40%).		
Cash.	20,000	
Dividend Receivable.		20,000
To record collection of the cash dividend.		

LO 1-5b

Understand the financial reporting consequences for investee's other comprehensive income.

Reporting Investee's Other Comprehensive Income and Irregular Items

In many cases, reported net income and dividends sufficiently capture changes in an investee's owners' equity. By recording its share of investee income and dividends, an investor company typically ensures its investment account reflects its share of the underlying investee equity. However, when an investee company's activities require recognition of other comprehensive income (OCI), its owners' equity (and net assets) will reflect changes not captured in its reported net income.[18]

Equity method accounting requires that the investor record its share of investee OCI which then is included in its balance sheet as Accumulated Other Comprehensive Income (AOCI). As noted by The Coca-Cola Company in its 2014 annual 10-K report,

> AOCI attributable to shareowners of The Coca-Cola Company is separately presented on our consolidated balance sheets as a component of The Coca-Cola Company's shareowners' equity, which also includes our proportionate share of equity method investees' AOCI.

Included in AOCI are items such as accumulated derivative net gains and losses, foreign currency translation adjustments, and certain pension adjustments.

To examine this issue, assume that Charles Company applies the equity method in accounting for its 30 percent investment in the voting stock of Norris Company. No excess amortization resulted from this investment. In 2017, Norris reports net income of $500,000. Norris also reports $80,000 in OCI from pension and other postretirement adjustments. Charles Company accrues earnings of $150,000 based on 30 percent of the $500,000 net figure. However, for proper financial reporting, Charles must recognize an increase in its Investment in Norris account for its 30 percent share of its investee's OCI. This treatment is intended, once again, to mirror the close relationship between the two companies.

The journal entry by Charles Company to record its equity interest in the income and OCI of Norris follows:

Investment in Norris Company	174,000	
Equity in Investee Income		150,000
Other Comprehensive Income of Investee		24,000
To accrue the investee's operating income and other comprehensive income from equity investment.		

OCI thus represents a source of change in investee company net assets that is recognized under the equity method. In the above example, Charles Company includes $24,000 of other comprehensive income in its balance sheet AOCI total.

Other equity method recognition issues arise for irregular items traditionally included within net income. For example, an investee may report income (loss) from discontinued operations as components of its current net income. In such cases, the equity method requires the investor to record and report its share of these items in recognizing equity earnings of the investee.

Reporting Investee Losses

Although most of the previous illustrations are based on the recording of profits, accounting for losses incurred by the investee is handled in a similar manner. The investor recognizes the appropriate percentage of each loss and reduces the carrying amount of the investment account. Even though these procedures are consistent with the concept of the equity method, they fail to take into account all possible loss situations.

Impairments of Equity Method Investments

Investments can suffer permanent losses in fair value that are not evident through equity method accounting. Such declines can be caused by the loss of major customers, changes

[18] OCI is defined as revenues, expenses, gains, and losses that under generally accepted accounting principles are included in comprehensive income but excluded from net income. OCI is accumulated and reported in stockholders" equity.

in economic conditions, loss of a significant patent or other legal right, damage to the company's reputation, and the like. Permanent reductions in fair value resulting from such adverse events might not be reported immediately by the investor through the normal equity entries discussed previously. The FASB ASC (para. 323-10-35-32) provides the following guidance:

> A loss in value of an investment which is other than a temporary decline shall be recognized. Evidence of a loss in value might include, but would not necessarily be limited to, absence of an ability to recover the carrying amount of the investment or inability of the investee to sustain an earnings capacity that would justify the carrying amount of the investment.

Thus, when a permanent decline in an equity method investment's value occurs, the investor must recognize an impairment loss and reduce the asset to fair value.

However, this loss must be permanent before such recognition becomes necessary. Under the equity method, a temporary drop in the fair value of an investment is simply ignored.

Navistar International Corporation, for example, noted the following in its 2015 annual report:

> We assess the potential impairment of our equity method investments and determine fair value based on valuation methodologies, as appropriate, including the present value of estimated future cash flows, estimates of sales proceeds, and market multiples. If an investment is determined to be impaired and the decline in value is other than temporary, we record an appropriate write-down.

Investment Reduced to Zero

Through the recognition of reported losses as well as any permanent drops in fair value, the investment account can eventually be reduced to a zero balance. This condition is most likely to occur if the investee has suffered extreme losses or if the original purchase was made at a low, bargain price. Regardless of the reason, the carrying amount of the investment account is sometimes eliminated in total.

When an investment account is reduced to zero, the investor should discontinue using the equity method rather than establish a negative balance. The investment retains a zero balance until subsequent investee profits eliminate all unrecognized losses. Once the original cost of the investment has been eliminated, no additional losses can accrue to the investor (since the entire cost has been written off).

For example, Sirius XM Holdings Corporation explains in its 2015 financial statements that

> . . . As of December 31, 2015, we had $840 (thousand) in losses related to our investment in Sirius XM Canada that we had not recorded in our consolidated financial statements since our investment balance is zero. Future equity income will be offset by these losses prior to recording equity income in our results.

Reporting the Sale of an Equity Investment

LO 1-5d

Understand the financial reporting consequences for sales of equity method investments.

At any time, the investor can choose to sell part or all of its holdings in the investee company. If a sale occurs, the equity method continues to be applied until the transaction date, thus establishing an appropriate carrying amount for the investment. The investor then reduces this balance by the percentage of shares sold.

As an example, assume that Top Company owns 40 percent of the 100,000 outstanding shares of Bottom Company, an investment accounted for by the equity method. Any excess investment cost over Top's share of Bottom's book value is considered goodwill. Although these 40,000 shares were acquired some years ago for $200,000, application of the equity method has increased the asset balance to $320,000 as of January 1, 2018. On July 1, 2018, Top elects to sell 10,000 of these shares (one-fourth of its investment) for $110,000 in cash, thereby reducing ownership in Bottom from 40 percent to 30 percent. Bottom Company reports net income of $70,000 during the first six months of 2018 and declares and pays cash dividends of $30,000.

Top, as the investor, initially makes the following journal entries on July 1, 2018, to accrue the proper income and establish the correct investment balance:

Investment in Bottom Company	28,000	
Equity in Investee Income		28,000
To accrue equity income for first six months of 2018 ($70,000 × 40%).		
Dividend Receivable	12,000	
Investment in Bottom Company		12,000
To record a cash dividend declaration by Bottom Company ($30,000 × 40%).		
Cash	12,000	
Dividend Receivable		12,000
To record collection of the cash dividend.		

These two entries increase the carrying amount of Top's investment by $16,000, creating a balance of $336,000 as of July 1, 2018. The sale of one-fourth of these shares can then be recorded as follows:

Cash	110,000	
Investment in Bottom Company		84,000
Gain on Sale of Investment		26,000
To record sale of one-fourth of investment in Bottom Company (1/4 × $336,000 = $84,000).		

After the sale is completed, Top continues to apply the equity method to this investment based on 30 percent ownership rather than 40 percent. However, if the sale had been of sufficient magnitude to cause Top to lose its ability to exercise significant influence over Bottom, the equity method would cease to be applicable. For example, if Top Company's holdings were reduced from 40 percent to 15 percent, the equity method might no longer be appropriate after the sale. The remaining shares held by the investor are reported according to the fair-value method with the remaining book value becoming the new *cost* figure for the investment rather than the amount originally paid.

If an investor is required to change from the equity method to the fair-value method, no retrospective adjustment is made. Although, as previously demonstrated, a change to the equity method mandates a restatement of prior periods, the treatment is not the same when the investor's change is to the fair-value method.

Deferral of Intra-Entity Gross Profits in Inventory[19]

LO 1-6

Describe the rationale and computations to defer gross profits on intra-entity inventory sales until the goods are either consumed by the owner or sold to outside parties.

Many equity acquisitions establish ties between companies to facilitate the direct purchase and sale of inventory items. For example, The Coca-Cola Company recently disclosed net sales in excess of $8.9 billion to its equity method investees. The significant influence relationship between an investor and investee in many ways creates its own entity that works to achieve business objectives. Thus, we use the term *intra-entity* to describe sales between an investor and its equity method investee.

Intra-entity sales require special accounting to ensure proper timing for profit recognition. A fundamental accounting concept is that an entity cannot recognize profits through activities with itself. For example, when an investor company sells inventory to its 40 percent-owned investee at a profit, 40 percent of this intra-entity sale effectively is with itself. Consequently, when inventory sales occur between investor and investee, because of their ownership

[19] Intra-entity transfers can involve the sale of items other than inventory. The intra-entity transfer of depreciable fixed assets and land is discussed in a later chapter.

EXHIBIT 1.2
Downstream and Upstream Sales

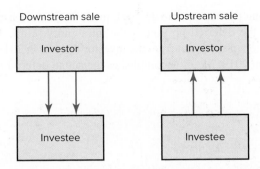

affiliation, the investor delays gross profit recognition until the inventory is sold to an independent party or is consumed.[20]

Importantly, in the presence of significant influence, the amount of profit deferred is limited to the investor's ownership share of the investee. In applying the equity method, the investor therefore defers only its share of the profit from intra-entity sales until the buyer's ultimate disposition of the goods. When the inventory is eventually consumed within operations or resold to an unrelated party, the investor recognizes the remaining gross profit. Accounting for both the profit deferral and subsequent recognition takes place through adjustments to the "Equity in Investee Income" and "Investment" accounts.

Intra-entity inventory sales are identified as either *downstream* or *upstream*. *Downstream sales* refer to the investor's sale of an item to the investee. Conversely, an *upstream sale* describes one that the investee makes to the investor (see Exhibit 1.2). *Although the direction of intra-entity sales does not affect reported equity method balances for investments when significant influence exists, it has definite consequences when financial control requires the consolidation of financial statements, as discussed in Chapter 5.* Therefore, these two types of intra-entity sales are examined separately even at this introductory stage.

Downstream Sales of Inventory

Assume that Major Company owns a 40 percent share of Minor Company and accounts for this investment through the equity method. In 2018, Major sells inventory to Minor at a price of $50,000. This figure includes a gross profit of 30 percent, or $15,000. By the end of 2018, Minor has sold $40,000 of these goods to outside parties while retaining $10,000 in inventory for sale during the subsequent year.

The investor has made downstream sales to the investee. In applying the equity method, recognition of the related profit must be delayed until the buyer disposes of these goods. Although total intra-entity inventory sales amounted to $50,000 in 2018, $40,000 of this merchandise has already been resold to outsiders, thereby justifying the normal reporting of profits. For the $10,000 still in the investee's inventory, the investor delays gross profit recognition. In computing equity income, the investor's portion of the intra-entity profit must be deferred until Minor disposes of the goods.

The gross profit on the original intra-entity sale was 30 percent of the sale price; therefore, Major's profit associated with these remaining items is $3,000 ($10,000 × 30%). *However, because only 40 percent of the investee's stock is held, just $1,200 ($3,000 × 40%) of this profit is deferred.* Major's ownership percentage reflects the intra-entity portion of the profit. The total $3,000 gross profit within the ending inventory balance is not the amount deferred. Rather, 40 percent of that gross profit is viewed as the currently deferred figure.

Remaining Ending Inventory	Gross Profit Percentage	Gross Profit in Ending Inventory	Investor Ownership Percentage	Deferred Intra-Entity Gross Profit
$10,000	30%	$3,000	40%	$1,200

---

[20] When inventory is consumed, for example in a manufacturing process, sales of the resulting production are assumed to generate revenues from outside, unrelated parties.

After calculating the appropriate deferral, the investor decreases current equity income by $1,200 to reflect the deferred portion of the intra-entity profit. This procedure temporarily removes this portion of the profit from the investor's books in 2018 until the investee disposes of the inventory in 2019. Major accomplishes the actual deferral through the following year-end journal entry:

Intra-Entity Gross Profit Deferral

Equity in Investee Income	1,200	
Investment in Minor Company		1,200
To defer gross profit on sale of inventory to Minor Company.		

In the subsequent year, when this inventory is eventually consumed by Minor or sold to unrelated parties, the deferral is no longer needed. Because a sale to an outside party has now occurred, Major should recognize the $1,200. By merely reversing the preceding deferral entry, the accountant succeeds in moving the investor's profit into the appropriate time period. Recognition shifts from the year of inventory transfer to the year in which the sale to customers outside of the affiliated entity takes place.

Subsequent Recognition of Intra-Entity Gross Profit

Investment in Minor Company	1,200	
Equity in Investee Income		1,200
To recognize income on intra-entity sale that now can be recognized after sales to outsiders.		

Upstream Sales of Inventory

Unlike consolidated financial statements (see Chapter 5), the equity method reports upstream sales of inventory in the same manner as downstream sales. Hence, the investor's share of gross profits remaining in ending inventory is deferred until the items are used or sold to unrelated parties. To illustrate, assume that Major Company once again owns 40 percent of Minor Company. During the current year, Minor sells merchandise costing $40,000 to Major for $60,000. At the end of the fiscal period, Major still retains $15,000 of these goods. Minor reports net income of $120,000 for the year.

To reflect the basic accrual of the investee's earnings, Major records the following journal entry at the end of this year:

Income Accrual

Investment in Minor Company	48,000	
Equity in Investee Income		48,000
To accrue income from 40 percent owned investee ($120,000 × 40%).		

The amount of the deferred intra-entity gross profit remaining at year-end is computed using the 33⅓ gross profit percentage of the sales price ($20,000/$60,000):

Remaining Ending Inventory	Gross Profit Percentage	Gross Profit in Ending Inventory	Investor Ownership Percentage	Deferred Intra-Entity Gross Profit
$15,000	33⅓%	$5,000	40%	$2,000

Based on this calculation, a second entry is required of the investor at year-end. Once again, a deferral of the gross profit created by the intra-entity sale is necessary for proper timing of income recognition. *Under the equity method for investments with significant influence, the direction of the sale between the investor and investee (upstream or downstream) has no effect on the final amounts reported in the financial statements.*

Intra-Entity Gross Profit Deferral		
Equity in Investee Income	2,000	
Investment in Minor Company		2,000
To defer recognition of intra-entity gross profit until inventory is used or sold to unrelated parties.		

After the adjustment, Major, the investor, reports earnings from this equity investment of $46,000 ($48,000 − $2,000). The income accrual is reduced because the investor defers its portion of the intra-entity gross profit. When the investor eventually consumes or sells the $15,000 in merchandise, the preceding journal entry is reversed. In this way, the effects of the inventory transfer are reported in the proper accounting period when sales to an outside party allow the recognition of the previously deferred intra-entity gross profit.

In an upstream sale, the investor's own inventory account contains the deferred gross profit. The previous entry, though, defers recognition of this profit by decreasing Major's investment account rather than the inventory balance. An alternative treatment would be the direct reduction of the investor's inventory balance as a means of accounting for this deferred amount. Although this alternative is acceptable, decreasing the investment account remains the traditional approach for deferring gross profits, even for upstream sales.

Whether upstream or downstream, the investor's sales and purchases are still reported as if the transactions were conducted with outside parties. Only the investor's share of the gross profit is deferred, and that amount is adjusted solely through the equity income account. Furthermore, because the companies are not consolidated, the investee's reported balances are not altered at all to reflect the nature of these sales/purchases. Obviously, readers of the financial statements need to be made aware of the inclusion of these amounts in the income statement. Thus, reporting companies must disclose certain information about related-party transactions. These disclosures include the nature of the relationship, a description of the transactions, the dollar amounts of the transactions, and amounts due to or from any related parties at year-end.

Financial Reporting Effects and Equity Method Criticisms

Equity Method Reporting Effects

It is important to realize that business decisions, including equity investments, typically involve the assessment of a wide range of consequences. For example, managers frequently are very interested in how financial statements report the effects of their decisions. This attention to financial reporting effects of business decisions arises because measurements of financial performance often affect the following:

- The firm's ability to raise capital.
- Managerial compensation.
- The ability to meet debt covenants and future interest rates.
- Managers' reputations.

Managers are also keenly aware that measures of earnings per share can strongly affect investors' perceptions of the underlying value of their firms' publicly traded stock. Consequently, prior to making investment decisions, firms will study and assess the prospective effects of applying the equity method on the income reported in financial statements. Additionally, such analyses of prospective reported income effects can influence firms regarding the degree of influence they wish to have, or even on the decision of whether to invest. For example, managers could have a required projected rate of return on an initial investment. In such cases, an analysis of projected income will be made to assist in setting an offer price.

For example, Investmor Co. is examining a potential 25 percent equity investment in Marco, Inc., that will provide a significant level of influence. Marco projects an annual income of $300,000 for the near future. Marco's book value is $450,000, and it has an unrecorded newly developed technology appraised at $200,000 with an estimated useful life of 10 years. In considering offer prices for the 25 percent investment in Marco, Investmor projects equity earnings as follows:

Projected income (25% × $300,000)	$75,000
Excess unpatented technology amortization [(25% × 200,000) ÷10 years]	(5,000)
Annual expected equity in Marco earnings	$70,000

Investmor's required first-year rate of return (before tax) on these types of investments is 20 percent. Therefore, to meet the first-year rate of return requirement involves a maximum price of $350,000 ($70,000 ÷ 20% = $350,000). If the shares are publicly traded (leaving the firm a "price taker"), such income projections can assist the company in making a recommendation to wait for share prices to move to make the investment attractive.

Criticisms of the Equity Method

Over the past several decades, thousands of business firms have accounted for their investments using the equity method. Recently, however, the equity method has come under criticism for the following:

- Emphasizing the 20–50 percent of voting stock in determining significant influence versus control.
- Allowing off-balance-sheet financing.
- Potentially biasing performance ratios.

The guidelines for the equity method suggest that a 20–50 percent ownership of voting shares indicates significant influence that falls short of control. But can one firm exert "control" over another firm absent an interest of more than 50 percent? Clearly, if one firm controls another, consolidation is the appropriate financial reporting technique. However, over the years, firms have learned ways to control other firms despite owning less than 50 percent of voting shares. For example, contracts across companies can limit one firm's ability to act without permission of the other. Such contractual control can be seen in debt arrangements, long-term sales and purchase agreements, and agreements concerning board membership. As a result, control is exerted through a variety of contractual arrangements. For financial reporting purposes, however, if ownership is 50 percent or less, a firm can argue that control technically does not exist.

In contrast to consolidated financial reports, when applying the equity method, the investee's assets and liabilities are not combined with the investor's amounts. Instead, the investor's balance sheet reports a single amount for the investment, and the income statement reports a single amount for its equity in the earnings of the investee. If consolidated, the assets, liabilities, revenues, and expenses of the investee are combined and reported in the body of the investor's financial statements.

Thus, for those companies wishing to actively manage their reported balance sheet numbers, the equity method provides an effective means. By keeping its ownership of voting shares below 50 percent, a company can technically meet the rules for applying the equity method for its investments and at the same time report investee assets and liabilities "off balance sheet." As a result, relative to consolidation, a firm employing the equity method will report smaller values for assets and liabilities. Consequently, higher rates of return for its assets and sales, as well as lower debt-to-equity ratios, could result.

On the surface, it appears that firms can avoid balance sheet disclosure of debts by maintaining investments at less than 50 percent ownership. However, the equity method requires summarized information as to assets, liabilities, and results of operations of the investees to be presented in the notes or in separate statements. Therefore, supplementary information could be available under the equity method that would not be separately identified in consolidation. Nonetheless, some companies have contractual provisions (e.g., debt covenants, managerial compensation agreements) based on ratios in the main body of the financial statements. Meeting the provisions of such contracts could provide managers strong incentives to maintain technical eligibility to use the equity method rather than full consolidation.

LO 1-7

Explain the rationale and reporting implications of fair-value accounting for investments otherwise accounted for by the equity method.

Fair-Value Reporting for Equity Method Investments

Financial reporting standards allow a fair-value option under which an entity may irrevocably elect fair value as the initial and subsequent measurement attribute for certain financial assets and financial liabilities. Under the fair-value option, changes in the fair value of the elected financial items are included in earnings. Among the many financial assets available for the fair-value option were investments otherwise accounted for under the equity method.

For example, Citigroup has reported at fair value certain of its investments that previously were reported using the equity method. In its 2015 annual report, Citigroup noted that "certain investments in non-marketable equity securities and certain investments that would otherwise have been accounted for using the equity method are carried at fair value, since the Company has elected to apply fair-value accounting. Changes in fair value of such investments are recorded in earnings." Many other firms, however, have been reluctant to elect the fair-value option for their equity method investments.

Firms using fair-value accounting simply report the investment's fair value as an asset and changes in fair value as earnings. As such, firms neither compute excess cost amortizations nor adjust earnings for intra-entity profits. Dividends from an investee are included in earnings under the fair-value option. Because dividends typically reduce an investment's fair value, an increase in earnings from investee dividends would be offset by a decrease in earnings from the decline in an investment's fair value.

To illustrate, on January 1, 2017, Westwind Co. pays $722,000 in exchange for 40,000 common shares of Armco, Inc., which has 100,000 common shares outstanding, the majority of which continue to trade on the New York Stock Exchange. During the next two years, Armco reports the following information:

Year	Net Income	Cash Dividends	Common Shares Total Fair Value at December 31
2017	$158,000	$25,000	$1,900,000
2018	125,000	25,000	1,870,000

Westwind elects to use fair-value accounting and accordingly makes the following journal entries for its investment in Armco over the next two years.

Investment in Armco, Inc.	722,000	
Cash		722,000
To record Westwind's initial 40 percent investment in Armco, Inc.		
Cash	10,000	
Dividend Income*		10,000
To recognize 2017 dividends received (40%) as investment income.		
Investment in Armco, Inc.	38,000	
Investment Income		38,000
To recognize Westwind's 40 percent of the 2017 change in Armco's fair value [($1,900,000 × 40%) − $722,000].		
Cash	10,000	
Dividend Income*		10,000
To recognize 2018 dividends received (40%) as investment income.		
Investment Loss	12,000	
Investment in Armco, Inc.		12,000
To recognize Westwind's 40 percent of the 2018 change in Armco's fair value [40% × ($1,870,000 − $1,900,000)].		

*This example assumes dividend declaration and payment occur at the same time.

In its December 31, 2018, balance sheet, Westwind thus reports its Investment in Armco account at $748,000, equal to 40 percent of Armco's total fair value (or $722,000 initial cost adjusted for 2017–2018 fair value changes of $38,000 less $12,000).

In addition to the increasing emphasis on fair values in financial reporting, the fair-value option also was motivated by a perceived need for consistency across various balance sheet items. In particular, the fair-value option is designed to limit volatility in earnings that occurs when some financial items are measured using cost-based attributes and others at fair value.

As FASB ASC (para. 825-10-10-1) observes, the objective of the fair-value option is

to improve financial reporting by providing entities with the opportunity to mitigate volatility in reported earnings caused by measuring related assets and liabilities differently without having to apply complex hedge accounting provisions.

Thus, the fair-value option is designed to match asset valuation with fair-value reporting requirements for many liabilities.

Summary

1. The equity method of accounting for an investment reflects the close relationship that could exist between an investor and an investee. More specifically, this approach is available when the owner achieves the ability to apply significant influence to the investee's operating and financial decisions. Significant influence is presumed to exist at the 20 to 50 percent ownership level. However, the accountant must evaluate each situation, regardless of the percentage of ownership, to determine whether this ability is actually present.

2. To mirror the relationship between the companies, the equity method requires the investor to accrue income when the investee reports it in its financial statements. In recording this profit or loss, the investor separately reports items such as other comprehensive income and discontinued operations, to highlight their special nature. Dividend declarations decrease the owners' equity of the investee company; therefore, the investor reduces the investment account for its share of investee dividends.

3. When acquiring capital stock, an investor often pays an amount that exceeds the investee company's underlying book value. For accounting purposes, such excess payments must be either identified with specific assets and liabilities (such as land or buildings) or allocated to an intangible asset referred to as *goodwill*. The investor then amortizes each assigned cost (except for any amount attributed to land, goodwill, or other indefinite life assets) over the expected useful lives of the assets and liabilities. This amortization affects the amount of equity income recognized by the investor.

4. If the investor sells the entire investment or any portion of it, the equity method is applied until the date of disposal. A gain or loss is computed based on the adjusted book value at that time. Remaining shares are accounted for by means of either the equity method or the fair-value method, depending on the investor's subsequent ability to significantly influence the investee.

5. Inventory (or other assets) can be transferred between investor and investee. Because of the relationship between the two companies, the equity income accrual should be reduced to defer the portion of any gross profit included on these intra-entity sales until the items are either sold to outsiders or consumed. Thus, the amount of intra-entity gross profit in ending inventory decreases the amount of equity income recognized by the investor in the current period although this effect is subsequently reversed.

6. Firms may elect to report significant influence investments at fair value with changes in fair value as earnings. Under the fair-value option, firms simply report the investment's fair value as an asset and changes in fair value as earnings.

Comprehensive Illustration

(*Estimated Time: 30 to 50 Minutes*) Every chapter in this textbook concludes with an illustration designed to assist students in tying together the essential elements of the material presented. After a careful reading of each chapter, attempt to work through the comprehensive problem. Then review the solution that follows the problem, noting the handling of each significant accounting issue.

Problem

Part A

On January 1, 2016, Red Hawk Company pays $70,000 for a 10 percent interest in Wolf Company's common stock. Because market quotes for Wolf's stock are readily available on a continuing basis, the investment account has been appropriately maintained at fair value.

On January 1, 2017, Red Hawk acquires an additional 20 percent of Wolf Company for $176,000. This second purchase provides Red Hawk the ability to exert significant influence over Wolf, and Red Hawk will now apply the equity method. At the time of this transaction, Wolf had a January 1, 2017 book value of $700,000 although Wolf's equipment with a 4-year remaining life was undervalued by $80,000 relative to its fair value.

During these two years, Wolf reported the following operational results (cash dividends are declared and paid in July each year):

Year	Net Income	Cash Dividends	Fair Value at January 1
2016	$210,000	$110,000	$700,000
2017	270,000	110,000	880,000

Required

a. What income did Red Hawk originally report for 2016 in connection with this investment?

b. On comparative financial statements for 2016 and 2017, what figures should Red Hawk report in connection with this investment?

Part B (Continuation of Part A)

In 2018, Wolf Company reports $400,000 in income and $60,000 in other comprehensive income from foreign currency translation adjustments. The company declares and pays a $120,000 cash dividend. During this fiscal year, Red Hawk sells inventory costing $80,000 to Wolf for $100,000. Wolf continues to hold 50 percent of this merchandise at the end of 2018. Red Hawk maintains 30 percent ownership of Wolf throughout the period.

Required

Prepare all necessary journal entries for Red Hawk for the year 2018.

Solution

Part A

a. Red Hawk Company accounts for its investment in Wolf Company at fair value during 2016. Because Red Hawk held only 10 percent of the outstanding shares, significant influence apparently was absent. Because stock quotes were readily available, the investment was periodically updated to fair value. Therefore, the investor recorded both dividends and changes in fair value in its 2016 financial statements as follows:

Dividend income (10% × $110,000)	$11,000
Increase in fair value [10% × ($880,000 − 700,000)]	18,000
Total income recognized from investment in Wolf in 2016	$29,000

b. Changes to the equity method are accounted for prospectively. Therefore, in comparative statements, Red Hawk's 2016 income from its investment in Wolf is $29,000 as reflected in the fair value method shown in part a. above.

Red Hawk's 2017 financial statements will reflect the equity method as a result of the January 1, 2017 share purchase that resulted in significant influence. To determine the 2017 equity method income Red Hawk first evaluates its combined investments in Wolf to determine whether either goodwill or incremental asset values need to be reflected within the equity method procedures.

Fair Value Allocation of 30 Percent Ownership of Wolf Company on January 1, 2017

Fair value of initial 10 percent purchase	$ 88,000
Payment for 20 percent investment at January 1, 2017	176,000
Fair value of 30 percent ownership	264,000
Book value acquired ($700,000 × 30%)	210,000
Fair value in excess of book value	54,000
Excess fair value identified with specific assets:	
Equipment ($80,000 × 30%)	24,000
Excess fair value not identified with specific assets—goodwill	$ 30,000

In allocating Wolf's January 1, 2017 fair value, $24,000 of the payment is attributable to the undervalued equipment with $30,000 assigned to goodwill. Because the equipment now has only a four-year remaining life, annual amortization of $6,000 is appropriate ($24,000/4).

Financial Reporting—2017

Equity in Investee Income (income statement)	
Income reported by Wolf	$270,000
Red Hawk's ownership	30%
Red Hawk's share of Wolf's reported income	$ 81,000
Less: Amortization expense:	
Equipment ($24,000/4 years)	(6,000)
Equity in investee income—2017	$ 75,000
Investment in Wolf (balance sheet)	
Fair value—1/1/17 (above)	$264,000
Equity in investee income (above)	75,000
Less: Investee dividends ($110,000 × 30%)	(33,000)
Investment in Wolf—12/31/17	$306,000

Part B

In July 2018 Wolf declares and pays a $36,000 cash dividend to Red Hawk (30% × $120,000). According to the equity method, this dividend reduces the carrying amount of the investment account:

Dividend Receivable	36,000	
Investment in Wolf Company		36,000
To record the 2018 cash dividend declaration by Wolf Company.		
Cash	36,000	
Dividend Receivable		36,000
To record collection of the cash dividend.		

Red Hawk records no other journal entries in connection with this investment until the end of 2018. At that time, the annual accrual of income as well as the adjustment to record amortization is made (see Part A for computation of expense). The investee's net income is reported separately from its other comprehensive income.

Investment in Wolf Company	138,000	
Equity in Investee Income		120,000
Investee Other Comprehensive Income		18,000
To recognize reported income of investee based on a 30 percent ownership level of $400,000 net income and $60,000 other comprehensive income.		
Equity in Investee Income	6,000	
Investment in Wolf Company		6,000
To record annual amortization on excess payment made in relation to equipment ($24,000/4 years).		

Red Hawk needs to make only one other equity entry during 2018. Intra-entity sales have occurred and Wolf continues to hold a portion of the inventory. Therefore, the investor's share of gross profit must be deferred. The gross profit rate from the sale was 20 percent ($20,000/$100,000). Because the investee still possesses $50,000 of this merchandise, the related gross profit is $10,000 ($50,000 × 20%). However, Red Hawk owns only 30 percent of Wolf's outstanding stock; thus, the intra-entity gross profit in inventory at year-end is $3,000 ($10,000 × 30%). That amount must be deferred until Wolf either consumes the inventory or sells it to unrelated parties.

Equity in Investee Company	3,000	
Investment in Wolf Company		3,000
To defer the investor's share of intra-entity gross profit in ending inventory.		

Questions

1. A company acquires a rather large investment in another corporation. What criteria determine whether the investor should apply the equity method of accounting to this investment?

2. What accounting treatments are appropriate for investments in equity securities without readily determinable fair values?

3. What indicates an investor's ability to significantly influence the decision-making process of an investee?

4. Why does the equity method record dividends from an investee as a reduction in the investment account, not as dividend income?

5. Jones Company owns a 25 percent interest in shares of Sandridge Company common stock. Under what circumstances might Jones decide that the equity method would not be appropriate to account for this investment?

6. Smith, Inc., has maintained an ownership interest in Watts Corporation for a number of years. This investment has been accounted for using the equity method. What transactions or events create changes in the Investment in Watts Corporation account as recorded by Smith?

7. Although the equity method is a generally accepted accounting principle (GAAP), recognition of equity income has been criticized. What theoretical problems can opponents of the equity method identify? What managerial incentives exist that could influence a firm's percentage ownership interest in another firm?

8. Because of the acquisition of additional investee shares, an investor will now change from the fair-value method to the equity method. Which procedures are applied to accomplish this accounting change?

9. Riggins Company accounts for its investment in Bostic Company using the equity method. During the past fiscal year, Bostic reported other comprehensive income from translation adjustments related to its foreign investments. How would this other comprehensive income affect the investor's financial records?

10. During the current year, Davis Company's common stock suffers a permanent drop in market value. In the past, Davis has made a significant portion of its sales to one customer. This buyer recently announced its decision to make no further purchases from Davis Company, an action that led to the loss of market value. Hawkins, Inc., owns 35 percent of the outstanding shares of Davis, an investment that is recorded according to the equity method. How would the loss in value affect this investor's financial reporting?

11. Wilson Company acquired 40 percent of Andrews Company at a bargain price because of losses expected to result from Andrews's failure in marketing several new products. Wilson paid only $100,000, although Andrews's corresponding book value was much higher. In the first year after acquisition, Andrews lost $300,000. In applying the equity method, how should Wilson account for this loss?

12. In a stock acquisition accounted for by the equity method, a portion of the purchase price often is attributed to goodwill or to specific assets or liabilities. How are these amounts determined at acquisition? How are these amounts accounted for in subsequent periods?

13. Princeton Company holds a 40 percent interest in shares of Yale Company common stock. On June 19 of the current year, Princeton sells part of this investment. What accounting should Princeton make on June 19? What accounting will Princeton make for the remainder of the current year?

14. What is the difference between downstream and upstream sales? How does this difference affect application of the equity method?

15. How is the investor's share of gross profit on intra-entity sales calculated? Under the equity method, how does the deferral of gross profit affect the recognition of equity income?

16. How are intra-entity transfers reported in an investee's separate financial statements if the investor is using the equity method?

17. What is the fair-value option for reporting equity method investments? How do the equity method and fair-value accounting differ in recognizing income from an investee?

Problems

LO 1-3

1. When an investor uses the equity method to account for investments in common stock, the investor's share of cash dividends from the investee should be recorded as
   a. A deduction from the investor's share of the investee's profits.
   b. Dividend income.
   c. A deduction from the stockholders' equity account, Dividends to Stockholders.
   d. A deduction from the investment account.
      (AICPA adapted)

LO 1-2

2. Which of the following does not indicate an investor company's ability to significantly influence an investee?
   a. Material intra-entity transactions.
   b. The investor owns 30 percent of the investee but another owner holds the remaining 70 percent.
   c. Interchange of personnel.
   d. Technological dependency.

LO 1-5a

3. Hawkins Company has owned 10 percent of Larker, Inc., for the past several years. This ownership did not allow Hawkins to have significant influence over Larker. Recently, Hawkins acquired an additional 30 percent of Larker and now will use the equity method. How will the investor report change?
   a. A cumulative effect of an accounting change is shown in the current income statement.
   b. A retrospective adjustment is made to restate all prior years presented using the equity method.
   c. No change is recorded; the equity method is used from the date of the new acquisition.
   d. Hawkins will report the change as a component of accumulated other comprehensive income.

LO 1-7

4. Under fair-value accounting for an equity investment, which of the following affects the income the investor recognizes from its ownership of the investee?
   a. The investee's reported income adjusted for excess cost over book value amortizations.
   b. Changes in the fair value of the investor's ownership shares of the investee.
   c. Intra-entity profits from upstream sales.
   d. Other comprehensive income reported by the investee.

LO 1-5c

5. When an equity method investment account is reduced to a zero balance
   a. The investor should establish a negative investment account balance for any future losses reported by the investee.
   b. The investor should discontinue using the equity method until the investee begins paying dividends.
   c. Future losses are reported as unusual items in the investor's income statement.
   d. The investment retains a zero balance until subsequent investee profits eliminate all unrecognized losses.

LO 1-3

6. On January 1, Puckett Company paid $1.6 million for 50,000 shares of Harrison's voting common stock, which represents a 40 percent investment. No allocation to goodwill or other specific account was made. Significant influence over Harrison is achieved by this acquisition and so Puckett applies the equity method. Harrison declared a $2 per share dividend during the year and reported net income of $560,000. What is the balance in the Investment in Harrison account found in Puckett's financial records as of December 31?
   a. $1,724,000
   b. $1,784,000
   c. $1,844,000
   d. $1,884,000

LO 1-3, 1-4

7. In January 2017, Domingo, Inc., acquired 20 percent of the outstanding common stock of Martes, Inc., for $700,000. This investment gave Domingo the ability to exercise significant influence over Martes, whose balance sheet on that date showed total assets of $3,900,000 with liabilities of $900,000. Any excess of cost over book value of the investment was attributed to a patent having a remaining useful life of 10 years.

   In 2017, Martes reported net income of $170,000. In 2018, Martes reported net income of $210,000. Dividends of $70,000 were declared in each of these two years. What is the equity method balance of Domingo's Investment in Martes, Inc., at December 31, 2018?
   a. $728,000
   b. $748,000
   c. $756,000
   d. $776,000

LO 1-3, 1-4

8. Franklin purchases 40 percent of Johnson Company on January 1 for $500,000. Although Franklin did not use it, this acquisition gave Franklin the ability to apply significant influence to Johnson's operating and financing policies. Johnson reports assets on that date of $1,400,000 with liabilities of $500,000. One building with a seven-year remaining life is undervalued on Johnson's books by $140,000. Also, Johnson's book value for its trademark (10-year remaining life) is undervalued by $210,000. During the year, Johnson reports net income of $90,000 while declaring dividends of $30,000. What is the Investment in Johnson Company balance (equity method) in Franklin's financial records as of December 31?

    a. $504,000
    b. $507,600
    c. $513,900
    d. $516,000

LO 1-3, 1-4

9. Evan Company reports net income of $140,000 each year and declares an annual cash dividend of $50,000. The company holds net assets of $1,200,000 on January 1, 2017. On that date, Shalina purchases 40 percent of Evan's outstanding common stock for $600,000, which gives it the ability to significantly influence Evan. At the purchase date, the excess of Shalina's cost over its proportionate share of Evan's book value was assigned to goodwill. On December 31, 2019, what is the Investment in Evan Company balance (equity method) in Shalina's financial records?

    a. $600,000
    b. $660,000
    c. $690,000
    d. $708,000

LO 1-6

10. Perez, Inc., applies the equity method for its 25 percent investment in Senior, Inc. During 2018, Perez sold goods with a 40 percent gross profit to Senior, which sold all of these goods in 2018. How should Perez report the effect of the intra-entity sale on its 2018 income statement?

    a. Sales and cost of goods sold should be reduced by the amount of intra-entity sales.
    b. Sales and cost of goods sold should be reduced by 25 percent of the amount of intra-entity sales.
    c. Investment income should be reduced by 25 percent of the gross profit on the amount of intra-entity sales.
    d. No adjustment is necessary.

LO 1-6

11. Panner, Inc., owns 30 percent of Watkins and applies the equity method. During the current year, Panner buys inventory costing $54,000 and then sells it to Watkins for $90,000. At the end of the year, Watkins still holds only $20,000 of merchandise. What amount of gross profit must Panner defer in reporting this investment using the equity method?

    a. $2,400
    b. $4,800
    c. $8,000
    d. $10,800

LO 1-3, 1-4, 1-6

12. Alex, Inc., buys 40 percent of Steinbart Company on January 1, 2017, for $530,000. The equity method of accounting is to be used. Steinbart's net assets on that date were $1.2 million. Any excess of cost over book value is attributable to a trade name with a 20-year remaining life. Steinbart immediately begins supplying inventory to Alex as follows:

Year	Cost to Steinbart	Transfer Price	Amount Held by Alex at Year-End (at transfer price)
2017	$70,000	$100,000	$25,000
2018	96,000	150,000	45,000

Inventory held at the end of one year by Alex is sold at the beginning of the next.

Steinbart reports net income of $80,000 in 2017 and $110,000 in 2018 and declares $30,000 in dividends each year. What is the equity income in Steinbart to be reported by Alex in 2018?

    a. $34,050
    b. $38,020
    c. $46,230
    d. $51,450

LO 1-3, 1-4

13. On January 3, 2018, Matteson Corporation acquired 40 percent of the outstanding common stock of O'Toole Company for $1,160,000. This acquisition gave Matteson the ability to exercise significant influence over the investee. The book value of the acquired shares was $820,000. Any excess cost over the underlying book value was assigned to a copyright that was undervalued on its balance sheet. This copyright has a remaining useful life of 10 years. For the year ended December 31, 2018, O'Toole reported net income of $260,000 and declared cash dividends of $50,000. At December 31, 2018, what should Matteson report as its investment in O'Toole under the equity method?

LO 1-3

14. On January 1, 2018, Fisher Corporation paid $2,290,000 for 35 percent of the outstanding voting stock of Steel, Inc., and appropriately applies the equity method for its investment. Any excess of cost over Steel's book value was attributed to goodwill. During 2018, Steel reports $720,000 in net income and a $100,000 other comprehensive income loss. Steel also declares and pays $20,000 in dividends.

    a. What amount should Fisher report as its Investment in Steel on its December 31, 2018, balance sheet?

    b. What amount should Fisher report as Equity in Earnings of Steel on its 2018 income statement?

LO 1-3, 1-4

15. On January 1, 2017, Ridge Road Company acquired 20 percent of the voting shares of Sauk Trail, Inc., for $2,700,000 in cash. Both companies provide commercial Internet support services but serve markets in different industries. Ridge Road made the investment to gain access to Sauk Trail's board of directors and thus facilitate future cooperative agreements between the two firms. Ridge Road quickly obtained several seats on Sauk Trail's board which gave it the ability to significantly influence Sauk Trail's operating and investing activities.

    The January 1, 2017, carrying amounts and corresponding fair values for Sauk Trail's assets and liabilities follow:

	Carrying Amount	**Fair Value**
Cash and receivables	$ 110,000	$ 110,000
Computing equipment	5,000,000	5,700,000
Patented technology	100,000	4,000,000
Trademark	150,000	2,000,000
Liabilities	(185,000)	(185,000)

    Also as of January 1, 2017, Sauk Trail's computing equipment had a seven-year remaining estimated useful life. The patented technology was estimated to have a three-year remaining useful life. The trademark's useful life was considered indefinite. Ridge Road attributed to goodwill any unidentified excess cost.

    During the next two years, Sauk Trail reported the following net income and dividends:

	Net Income	**Dividends Declared**
2017	$1,800,000	$150,000
2018	1,985,000	160,000

    a. How much of Ridge Road's $2,700,000 payment for Sauk Trail is attributable to goodwill?

    b. What amount should Ridge Road report for its equity in Sauk Trail's earnings on its income statements for 2017 and 2018?

    c. What amount should Ridge Road report for its investment in Sauk Trail on its balance sheets at the end of 2017 and 2018?

LO 1-3, 1-4, 1-7

16. On January 1, 2017, Alison, Inc., paid $60,000 for a 40 percent interest in Holister Corporation's common stock. This investee had assets with a book value of $200,000 and liabilities of $75,000. A patent held by Holister having a $5,000 book value was actually worth $20,000. This patent had a six-year remaining life. Any further excess cost associated with this acquisition was attributed to goodwill. During 2017, Holister earned income of $30,000 and declared and paid dividends of $10,000. In 2018, it had income of $50,000 and dividends of $15,000. During 2018, the fair value of Allison's investment in Holister had risen from $68,000 to $75,000.

    a. Assuming Alison uses the equity method, what balance should appear in the Investment in Holister account as of December 31, 2018?

    b. Assuming Alison uses fair-value accounting, what income from the investment in Holister should be reported for 2018?

LO 1-3, 1-6

17. On January 1, 2018, Alamar Corporation acquired a 40 percent interest in Burks, Inc., for $210,000. On that date, Burks's balance sheet disclosed net assets with both a fair and book value of $360,000. During 2018, Burks reported net income of $80,000 and declared and paid cash dividends of $25,000. Alamar sold inventory costing $30,000 to Burks during 2018 for $40,000. Burks used all of this merchandise in its operations during 2018. Prepare all of Alamar's 2018 journal entries to apply the equity method to this investment.

LO 1-1, 1-2, 1-3, 1-4, 1-5a

18. Milani, Inc., acquired 10 percent of Seida Corporation on January 1, 2017, for $190,000 and appropriately accounted for the investment using the fair-value method. On January 1, 2018, Milani purchased an additional 30 percent of Seida for $600,000 which resulted in significant influence over Seida. On that date, the fair value of Seida's common stock was $2,000,000 in total. Seida's January 1, 2018, book value equaled $1,850,000, although land was undervalued by $120,000. Any additional excess fair value over Seida's book value was attributable to a trademark with an 8-year remaining life. During 2018, Seida reported income of $300,000 and declared and paid dividends of $110,000. Prepare the 2018 journal entries for Milani related to its investment in Seida.

LO 1-6

19. Tiberend, Inc., sold $150,000 in inventory to Schilling Company during 2017 for $225,000. Schilling resold $105,000 of this merchandise in 2017 with the remainder to be disposed of during 2018. Assuming that Tiberend owns 25 percent of Schilling and applies the equity method, what journal entry is recorded at the end of 2017 to defer the intra-entity gross profit?

LO 1-3, 1-4, 1-6

20. BuyCo, Inc. holds 25 percent of the outstanding shares of Marqueen Company and appropriately applies the equity method of accounting. Excess cost amortization (related to a patent) associated with this investment amounts to $10,000 per year. For 2017, Marqueen reported earnings of $100,000 and declares cash dividends of $30,000. During that year, Marqueen acquired inventory for $50,000, which it then sold to BuyCo for $80,000. At the end of 2017, BuyCo continued to hold merchandise with a transfer price of $32,000.

    a. What Equity in Investee Income should BuyCo report for 2017?

    b. How will the intra-entity transfer affect BuyCo's reporting in 2018?

    c. If BuyCo had sold the inventory to Marqueen, how would the answers to (*a*) and (*b*) have changed?

LO 1-1, 1-2, 1-3, 1-4, 1-5a

21. On January 1, 2016, Halstead, Inc., purchased 75,000 shares of Sedgwick Company common stock for $1,480,000, giving Halstead 25 percent ownership and the ability to apply significant influence over Sedgwick. Any excess of cost over book value acquired was attributed solely to goodwill.

    Sedgwick reports net income and dividends as follows. These amounts are assumed to have occurred evenly throughout these years. Dividends are declared and paid in the same period.

	Net Income	Annual Cash Dividends (paid quarterly)
2016	$340,000	$120,000
2017	480,000	140,000
2018	600,000	160,000

    On July 1, 2018, Halstead sells 12,000 shares of this investment for $25 per share, thus reducing its interest from 25 to 21 percent, but maintaining its significant influence.

    Determine the amounts that would appear on Halstead's 2018 income statement relating to its ownership and partial sale of its investment in Sedgwick's common stock.

LO 1-1, 1-2, 1-3, 1-4, 1-5d

22. Echo, Inc., purchased 10 percent of ProForm Corporation on January 1, 2017, for $345,000 and accounted for the investment using the fair-value method. Echo acquires an additional 15 percent of ProForm on January 1, 2018, for $580,000. The equity method of accounting is now appropriate for this investment. No intra-entity sales have occurred.

    a. How does Echo initially determine the income to be reported in 2017 in connection with its ownership of ProForm?

    b. What factors should have influenced Echo in its decision to apply the equity method in 2018?

    c. What factors could have prevented Echo from adopting the equity method after this second purchase?

    d. What is the objective of the equity method of accounting?

    e. What criticisms have been leveled at the equity method?

f. In comparative statements for 2017 and 2018, how would Echo determine the income to be reported in 2017 in connection with its ownership of ProForm? Why is this accounting appropriate?

g. How is the allocation of Echo's acquisition made?

h. If ProForm declares a cash dividend, what impact does it have on Echo's financial records under the equity method? Why is this accounting appropriate?

i. On financial statements for 2018, what amounts are included in Echo's Investment in ProForm account? What amounts are included in Echo's Equity in Income of ProForm account?

LO 1-3, 1-6

23. Parrot Corporation holds a 42 percent ownership of Sunrise, Inc., and applies the equity method to account for its investment. Parrot assigned the entire original excess purchase price over book value to goodwill. During 2017, the two companies made intra-entity inventory transfers. A portion of this merchandise was not resold until 2018. During 2018, additional transfers were made.

a. What is the difference between upstream transfers and downstream transfers?

b. How does the direction of an intra-entity transfer (upstream versus downstream) affect the application of the equity method?

c. How is the intra-entity gross profit deferral computed in applying the equity method?

d. How should Parrot compute the amount of equity income to be recognized in 2017? What entry is made to record this income?

e. How should Parrot compute the amount of equity income to be recognized in 2018?

f. If none of the transferred inventory had remained at the end of 2017, how would these transfers have affected the application of the equity method?

g. How do these intra-entity transfers affect Sunrise's financial reporting?

LO 1-1, 1-5d

24. Several years ago, Einstein, Inc., bought 40 percent of the outstanding voting stock of Brooks Company. The equity method is appropriately applied. On August 1 of the current year, Einstein sold a portion of these shares.

a. How does Einstein compute the book value of this investment on August 1 to determine its gain or loss on the sale?

b. How should Einstein account for this investment after August 1?

c. If Einstein retains only a 2 percent interest in Brooks so that it holds virtually no influence over Brooks, what figures appear in the investor's income statement for the current year?

d. If Einstein retains only a 2 percent interest in Brooks so that virtually no influence is held, does the investor have to retroactively adjust any previously reported figures?

LO 1-3, 1-4, 1-6

25. Matthew, Inc. owns 30 percent of the outstanding stock of Lindman Company and has the ability to significantly influence the investee's operations and decision making. On January 1, 2018, the balance in the Investment in Lindman account is $335,000. Amortization associated with this acquisition is $9,000 per year. In 2018, Lindman earns an income of $90,000 and declares cash dividends of $30,000. Previously, in 2017, Lindman had sold inventory costing $24,000 to Matthew for $40,000. Matthew consumed all but 25 percent of this merchandise during 2017 and used the rest during 2018. Lindman sold additional inventory costing $28,000 to Matthew for $50,000 in 2018. Matthew did not consume 40 percent of these 2018 purchases from Lindman until 2019.

a. What amount of equity method income would Matthew recognize in 2018 from its ownership interest in Lindman?

b. What is the equity method balance in the Investment in Lindman account at the end of 2018?

LO 1-1, 1-3, 1-4

26. On December 31, 2016, Akron, Inc. purchased 5 Percent of Zip Company's common shares on the open market in exchange for $16,000. On December 31, 2017, Akron, Inc., acquires an additional 25 percent of Zip Company's outstanding common stock for $95,000.

During the next two years, the following information is available for Zip Company:

	Income	Dividends Declared	Common Stock Fair Value (12/31)
2016			$320,000
2017	$ 75,000	$ 7,000	380,000
2018	88,000	15,000	480,000

At December 31, 2017, Zip reports a net book value of $290,000. Akron attributed any excess of its 30 percent share of Zip's fair over book value to its share of Zip's franchise agreements. The franchise agreements had a remaining life of 10 years at December 31, 2017.

a. Assume Akron applies the equity method to its Investment in Zip account:

1. What amount of equity income should Akron report for 2018?
2. On Akron's December 31, 2018, balance sheet, what amount is reported for the Investment in Zip account?

b. Assume Akron uses fair-value accounting for its Investment in Zip account:

1. What amount of income from its investment in Zip should Akron report for 2018?
2. On Akron's December 31, 2018, balance sheet, what amount is reported for the Investment in Zip account?

LO 1-3, 1-4, 1-5d, 1-6

27. Belden, Inc. acquires 30 percent of the outstanding voting shares of Sheffield, Inc. on January 1, 2017, for $312,000, which gives Belden the ability to significantly influence Sheffield. Sheffield has a net book value of $800,000 at January 1, 2017. Sheffield's asset and liability accounts showed carrying amounts considered equal to fair values except for a copyright whose value accounted for Belden's excess cost over book value in its 30 percent purchase. The copyright had a remaining life of 16 years at January 1, 2017. No goodwill resulted from Belden's share purchase.

Sheffield reported net income of $180,000 in 2017 and $230,000 of net income during 2018. Dividends of $70,000 and $80,000 are declared and paid in 2017 and 2018, respectively. Belden uses the equity method.

a. On its 2018 comparative income statements, how much income would Belden report for 2017 and 2018 in connection with the company's investment in Sheffield?

b. If Belden sells its entire investment in Sheffield on January 1, 2019, for $400,000 cash, what is the impact on Belden's income?

c. Assume that Belden sells inventory to Sheffield during 2017 and 2018 as follows:

Year	Cost to Belden	Price to Sheffield	Year-End Balance (at transfer price)
2017	$30,000	$50,000	$20,000 (sold in following year)
2018	33,000	60,000	40,000 (sold in following year)

What amount of equity income should Belden recognize for the year 2018?

LO 1-3, 1-4, 1-5b, 1-6

28. Harper, Inc. acquires 40 percent of the outstanding voting stock of Kinman Company on January 1, 2017, for $210,000 in cash. The book value of Kinman's net assets on that date was $400,000, although one of the company's buildings, with a $60,000 carrying amount, was actually worth $100,000. This building had a 10-year remaining life. Kinman owned a royalty agreement with a 20-year remaining life that was undervalued by $85,000.

Kinman sold inventory with an original cost of $60,000 to Harper during 2017 at a price of $90,000. Harper still held $15,000 (transfer price) of this amount in inventory as of December 31, 2017. These goods are to be sold to outside parties during 2018.

Kinman reported a $40,000 net loss and a $20,000 other comprehensive loss for 2017. The company still manages to declare and pay a $10,000 cash dividend during the year.

During 2018, Kinman reported a $40,000 net income and declared and paid a cash dividend of $12,000. It made additional inventory sales of $80,000 to Harper during the period. The original cost of the merchandise was $50,000. All but 30 percent of this inventory had been resold to outside parties by the end of the 2018 fiscal year.

Prepare all journal entries for Harper for 2017 and 2018 in connection with this investment. Assume that the equity method is applied.

LO 1-3, 1-4, 1-5b, 1-6

29. On January 1, 2018, Pine Company owns 40 percent (40,000 shares) of Seacrest, Inc., which it purchased several years ago for $182,000. Since the date of acquisition, the equity method has been properly applied, and the carrying amount of the investment account as of January 1, 2018, is $293,600. Excess patent cost amortization of $12,000 is still being recognized each year. During 2018, Seacrest reports net income of $342,000 and a $120,000 other comprehensive loss, both incurred uniformly throughout the year. No dividends were declared during the year. Pine sold 8,000 shares of Seacrest on August 1, 2018, for $93,000 in cash. However, Pine retains the ability to significantly influence the investee.

During the last quarter of 2017, Pine sold $50,000 in inventory (which it had originally purchased for only $30,000) to Seacrest. At the end of that fiscal year, Seacrest's inventory retained $10,000 (at sales price) of this merchandise, which was subsequently sold in the first quarter of 2018.

On Pine's financial statements for the year ended December 31, 2018, what income effects would be reported from its ownership in Seacrest?

LO 1-3, 1-4, 1-6

30. On July 1, 2016, Killearn Company acquired 88,000 of the outstanding shares of Shaun Company for $13 per share. This acquisition gave Killearn a 25 percent ownership of Shaun and allowed Killearn to significantly influence the investee's decisions.

    As of July 1, 2016, the investee had assets with a book value of $3 million and liabilities of $74,400. At the time, Shaun held equipment appraised at $364,000 above book value; it was considered to have a seven-year remaining life with no salvage value. Shaun also held a copyright with a five-year remaining life on its books that was undervalued by $972,000. Any remaining excess cost was attributable to goodwill. Depreciation and amortization are computed using the straight-line method. Killearn applies the equity method for its investment in Shaun.

    Shaun's policy is to declare and pay a $1 per share cash dividend every April 1 and October 1. Shaun's income, earned evenly throughout each year, was $598,000 in 2016, $639,600 in 2017, and $692,400 in 2018.

    In addition, Killearn sold inventory costing $91,200 to Shaun for $152,000 during 2017. Shaun resold $92,000 of this inventory during 2017 and the remaining $60,000 during 2018.

    a. Determine the equity income to be recognized by Killearn during each of these years.

    b. Compute Killearn's investment in Shaun Company's balance as of December 31, 2018.

LO 1-1, 1-2, 1-3, 1-4, 1-5d

31. On January 1, 2017, Fisher Corporation purchased 40 percent (80,000 shares) of the common stock of Bowden, Inc., for $982,000 in cash and began to use the equity method for the investment. The price paid represented a $60,000 payment in excess of the book value of Fisher's share of Bowden's underlying net assets. Fisher was willing to make this extra payment because of a recently developed patent held by Bowden with a 15-year remaining life. All other assets were considered appropriately valued on Bowden's books.

    Bowden declares and pays a $100,000 cash dividend to its stockholders each year on September 15. Bowden reported net income of $400,000 in 2017 and $380,000 in 2018. Each income figure was earned evenly throughout its respective years.

    On July 1, 2018, Fisher sold 10 percent (20,000 shares) of Bowden's outstanding shares for $330,000 in cash. Although it sold this interest, Fisher maintained the ability to significantly influence Bowden's decision-making process.

    Prepare the journal entries for Fisher for the years of 2017 and 2018.

LO 1-3, 1-4, 1-6

32. On January 1, 2017, Stream Company acquired 30 percent of the outstanding voting shares of Q-Video, Inc., for $770,000. Q-Video manufactures specialty cables for computer monitors. On that date, Q-Video reported assets and liabilities with book values of $1.9 million and $700,000, respectively. A customer list compiled by Q-Video had an appraised value of $300,000, although it was not recorded on its books. The expected remaining life of the customer list was five years with straight-line amortization deemed appropriate. Any remaining excess cost was not identifiable with any particular asset and thus was considered goodwill.

    Q-Video generated net income of $250,000 in 2017 and a net loss of $100,000 in 2018. In each of these two years, Q-Video declared and paid a cash dividend of $15,000 to its stockholders.

    During 2017, Q-Video sold inventory that had an original cost of $100,000 to Stream for $160,000. Of this balance, $80,000 was resold to outsiders during 2017, and the remainder was sold during 2018. In 2018, Q-Video sold inventory to Stream for $175,000. This inventory had cost only $140,000. Stream resold $100,000 of the inventory during 2018 and the rest during 2019.

    For 2017 and then for 2018, compute the amount that Stream should report as income from its investment in Q-Video in its external financial statements under the equity method.

Develop Your Skills

EXCEL CASE 1

CPA *skills*

On January 1, 2018, Acme Co. is considering purchasing a 40 percent ownership interest in PHC Co., a privately held enterprise, for $700,000. PHC predicts its profit will be $185,000 in 2018, projects a 10 percent annual increase in profits in each of the next four years, and expects to pay a steady annual dividend of $30,000 for the foreseeable future. Because PHC has on its books a patent that is undervalued by $375,000, Acme realizes that it will have an additional amortization expense of $15,000 per year over the next 10 years—the patent's estimated remaining useful life. All of PHC's other assets and liabilities have book values that approximate market values. Acme uses the equity method for its investment in PHC.

Required

1. Using an Excel spreadsheet, set the following values in cells:
   - Acme's cost of investment in PHC.
   - Percentage acquired.
   - First-year PHC reported income.
   - Projected growth rate in income.
   - PHC annual dividends.
   - Annual excess patent amortization.
2. Referring to the values in (1), prepare the following schedules using columns for the years 2018 through 2022.
   - Acme's equity in PHC earnings with rows showing these:
     - Acme's share of PHC reported income.
     - Amortization expense.
     - Acme's equity in PHC earnings.
   - Acme's Investment in PHC balance with rows showing the following:
     - Beginning balance.
     - Equity earnings.
     - Dividends.
     - Ending balance.
   - Return on beginning investment balance = Equity earnings/Beginning investment balance in each year.
3. Given the preceding values, compute the average of the projected returns on beginning investment balances for the first five years of Acme's investment in PHC. What is the maximum Acme can pay for PHC if it wishes to earn at least a 10 percent average return on beginning investment balance? (*Hint:* Under Excel's Data tab, select What-If Analysis, and the Goal Seek capability to produce a 10 percent average return on beginning investment balance by changing the cell that contains Acme's cost of investment in PHC. Excel's Solver should produce an exact answer while Goal Seek should produce a close approximation. You may need to first add in the Solver capability under Excel's Tools menu.)

EXCEL CASE 2

On January 1, Intergen, Inc., invests $200,000 for a 40 percent interest in Ryan, a new joint venture with two other partners, each investing $150,000 for 30 percent interest. Intergen plans to sell all of its production to Ryan, which will resell the inventory to retail outlets. The equity partners agree that Ryan will buy inventory only from Intergen. Also, Intergen plans to use the equity method for financial reporting.

During the year, Intergen expects to incur costs of $850,000 to produce goods with a final retail market value of $1,200,000. Ryan projects that, during this year, it will resell three-fourths of these goods for $900,000. It should sell the remainder in the following year.

The equity partners plan a meeting to set the price Intergen will charge Ryan for its production. One partner suggests a transfer price of $1,025,000 but is unsure whether it will result in an equitable return across the equity holders. Importantly, Intergen agrees that its total rate of return (including its own operations and its investment in Ryan) should be equal to that of the other investors' return on their investments in Ryan. All agree that Intergen's value including its investment in Ryan is $1,000,000.

Required

1. Create an Excel spreadsheet analysis showing the following:
   - Projected income statements for Intergen and Ryan. Formulate the statements to do the following:
     - Link Ryan's cost of goods sold to Intergen's sales (use a starting value of $1,025,000 for Intergen's sales).
     - Link Intergen's equity in Ryan's earnings to Ryan's net income (adjusted for Intergen's gross profit rate × Ryan's ending inventory × 40 percent ownership percentage).
     - Be able to change Intergen's sales and see the effects throughout the income statements of Ryan and Intergen. Note that the cost of goods sold for Intergen is fixed.

- The rate of return for the two 30 percent equity partners on their investment in Ryan.
- The total rate of return for Intergen based on its $1,000,000 value.

2. What transfer price will provide an equal rate of return for each of the investors in the first year of operation? (*Hint:* Under Excel's Data tab, select What-If Analysis and then the Goal Seek capability to produce a zero difference in rates of return across the equity partners by changing the cell that contains Intergen's sales. Excel's Solver add-in will work as well.)

ANALYSIS CASE

Access The Coca-Cola Company's SEC 10-K filing at www.coca-cola.com and address the following:
1. What companies does Coca-Cola describe as significant equity method investments? How do these investments help Coca-Cola?
2. What criteria does Coca-Cola use in choosing to apply the equity method for these investments?
3. How does Coca-Cola describe its application of the equity method?
4. What amount of equity income did Coca-Cola report?
5. Coca-Cola discloses the fair values of its publicly traded bottlers accounted for as equity method investments. List the book values and fair values for these equity method investments that have publically traded data. Discuss the relevance of each of these two values.

RESEARCH AND ANALYSIS CASE—IMPAIRMENT

Wolf Pack Transport Co. has a 25 percent equity investment in Maggie Valley Depot (MVD), Inc., which owns and operates a warehousing facility used for the collection and redistribution of various consumer goods. Wolf Pack paid $1,685,000 for its 25 percent interest in MVD several years ago, including a $300,000 allocation for goodwill as the only excess cost over book value acquired. Wolf Pack Transport has since appropriately applied the equity method to account for the investment. In its most recent balance sheet, because of recognized profits in excess of dividends since the acquisition, Wolf Pack reported a $2,350,000 amount for its Investment in Maggie Valley Depot, Inc., account.

However, competition in the transit warehousing industry has increased in the past 12 months. In the same area as the MVD facility, a competitor company opened two additional warehouses that are much more conveniently located near a major interstate highway. MVD's revenues declined 30 percent as customers shifted their business to the competitor's facilities and the prices for warehouse services declined. The market value of Wolf Pack's stock ownership in MVD fell to $1,700,000 from a high last year of $2,500,000. MVD's management is currently debating ways to respond to these events but has yet to formulate a firm plan.

Required

1. What guidance does the FASB ASC provide for equity method investment losses in value?
2. Should Wolf Pack recognize the decline in the value of its holdings in MVD in its current year financial statements?
3. Should Wolf Pack test for impairment of the value it had initially assigned to goodwill?

RESEARCH CASE—NONCONTROLLING SHAREHOLDER RIGHTS

Consolidated financial reporting is appropriate when one entity has a controlling financial interest in another entity. The usual condition for a controlling financial interest is ownership of a majority voting interest. But in some circumstances, control does not rest with the majority owner—especially when noncontrolling owners are contractually provided with approval or veto rights that can restrict the actions of the majority owner. In these cases, the majority owner employs the equity method rather than consolidation.

Required

Address the following by searching the FASB ASC Topic 810 on consolidation.
1. What are protective noncontrolling rights?
2. What are substantive participating noncontrolling rights?

3. What noncontrolling rights overcome the presumption that all majority-owned investees should be consolidated?

4. Zee Company buys 60 percent of the voting stock of Bee Company with the remaining 40 percent noncontrolling interest held by Bee's former owners, who negotiated the following noncontrolling rights:

    *   Any new debt above $1,000,000 must be approved by the 40 percent noncontrolling shareholders.

    *   Any dividends or other cash distributions to owners in excess of customary historical amounts must be approved by the 40 percent noncontrolling shareholders.

    According to the FASB ASC, what are the issues in determining whether Zee should consolidate Bee or report its investment in Bee under the equity method?

Consolidation of Financial Information

Financial statements published and distributed to owners, creditors, and other interested parties appear to report the operations and financial position of a single company. In reality, these statements frequently represent a number of separate organizations tied together through common control (a *business combination*). When financial statements represent more than one corporation, we refer to them as *consolidated financial statements.*

Consolidated financial statements are typical in today's business world. Most major organizations, and many smaller ones, hold control over an array of organizations. For example, from 2000 through 2016, Cisco Systems, Inc., reported more than 100 business acquisitions that now are consolidated in its financial reports. PepsiCo, Inc., as another example, annually consolidates data from a multitude of companies into a single set of financial statements. By gaining control over these companies (often known as *subsidiaries*)—which include Frito-Lay, Gatorade, Quaker Oats, Sabra, and Tropicana Products—PepsiCo (the *parent*) forms a single business combination and single reporting entity.

The consolidation of financial information as exemplified by Cisco Systems and PepsiCo is one of the most complex procedures in all of accounting. Comprehending this process completely requires understanding the theoretical logic that underlies the creation of a business combination. Furthermore, a variety of procedural steps must be mastered to ensure that proper accounting is achieved for this single reporting entity. The following coverage introduces both of these aspects of the consolidation process.

The FASB *Accounting Standards Codification* (ASC) contains the current accounting standards for business combinations under the following topics:

- "Business Combinations" (Topic 805).
- "Consolidation" (Topic 810).

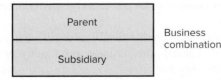

The ASC "Business Combinations" topic provides guidance on the accounting and reporting for business combinations using the *acquisition method*. The acquisition method embraces a *fair-value* measurement attribute. Adoption of this attribute reflects the FASB's increasing emphasis on fair value for measuring and assessing business activity. In the past, financial reporting standards embraced the cost principle to measure and report the

Learning Objectives

After studying this chapter, you should be able to:

LO 2-1   Discuss the motives for business combinations.

LO 2-2   Recognize when consolidation of financial information into a single set of statements is necessary.

LO 2-3   Define the term *business combination* and differentiate across various forms of business combinations.

LO 2-4   Describe the valuation principles of the acquisition method.

LO 2-5   Determine the fair value of the consideration transferred for an acquisition and allocate that fair value to specific assets acquired (including goodwill) and liabilities assumed or to a gain on bargain purchase.

LO 2-6   Prepare an acquiring firm's journal entry to record
   a. a business combination when dissolution takes place.
   b. the various related costs involved in a business combination.
   c. a business combination when the acquired firm retains its separate existence.

LO 2-7   Prepare a worksheet to consolidate the financial statements of two companies that form a business combination in the absence of dissolution.

LO 2-8   Describe the accounting treatment for the various intangible assets often acquired in a business combination.

LO 2-9   Appendix 2A: Identify the general characteristics of the legacy purchase and pooling of interest methods of accounting for past business combinations. Understand the effects that persist today in financial statements from the use of these legacy methods.

LO 2-10   Appendix 2B: Explain the rationale and procedures underlying a subsidiary's election to adopt pushdown accounting.

financial effects of business combinations. This fundamental change from a cost-based to a fair-value model has transformed the way we account for and report business combinations in our society.

The ASC "Consolidation" topic provides guidance on circumstances that require a firm to prepare consolidated financial reports and various other related reporting issues. Basically, consolidated financial reports must be prepared whenever one firm has a controlling financial interest in another. Although ownership of a majority voting interest is the usual condition for a controlling financial interest, the power to control may also exist with a lesser percentage of ownership through governance contracts, leases, or agreement with other stockholders.[1]

In this chapter, we first present expansion through corporate takeovers and present an overview of the consolidation process. Then we present the specifics of the acquisition method of accounting for business combinations where the acquirer obtains complete ownership of another firm. Later, beginning in Chapter 4, we introduce coverage of acquisitions with less than complete ownership.

Financial reporting for business combinations has experienced many changes over the past decade. Prior to the acquisition method requirement, accounting standards allowed either the purchase method or the earlier pooling of interests method of accounting for business combinations. Neither of these methods is now permitted for reporting the formation of new business combinations. However, because of the prospective application of the acquisition method beginning in 2009, legacy effects of these methods remain in many of today's financial statements. Therefore, an appendix to this chapter provides a review of the purchase method and pooling of interests method.

Expansion through Corporate Takeovers

LO 2-1

Discuss the motives for business combinations.

Reasons for Firms to Combine

A frequent economic phenomenon is the combining of two or more businesses into a single entity under common management and control. During recent decades, the United States and the rest of the world have experienced an enormous number of corporate mergers and takeovers, transactions in which one company gains control over another. According to Thomson Reuters, the number of mergers and acquisitions globally in 2015 exceeded 42,300, with a total value of more than $4.7 trillion. Of these deals more than $2.3 trillion involved a U.S. firm. As indicated by Exhibit 2.1, the magnitude of recent combinations continues to be large.

As with any other economic activity, business combinations can be part of an overall managerial strategy to maximize shareholder value. Shareholders—the owners of the firm—hire managers to direct resources so that the firm's value grows over time. In this way, owners receive a return on their investment. Successful firms receive substantial benefits through enhanced share value. Importantly, the managers of successful firms also receive substantial benefits in salaries, especially if their compensation contracts are partly based on stock market performance of the firm's shares.

If the goal of business activity is to maximize the firm's value, in what ways do business combinations help achieve that goal? Clearly, the business community is moving rapidly toward business combinations as a strategy for growth and competitiveness. Size and scale are obviously becoming critical as firms compete in today's markets. Importantly, valuable synergies often accompany business combinations. If large firms can be more efficient in delivering goods and services, they gain a competitive advantage and become more profitable for the owners. Increases in scale can produce larger profits from enhanced sales volume despite smaller (more competitive) profit margins. When two firms integrate successive stages of production and distribution of products, coordinating raw material purchases,

[1] We discuss entities controlled through contractual means (known as variable interest entities) in Chapter 6.

EXHIBIT 2.1
Recent Notable Business Combinations

Acquirer	Target	Deal Value
AT&T	DirecTV	$47.4B
Berkshire Hathaway, Inc.	Precision Castparts	$32.0B
Visa, Inc.	Visa Europe Ltd	$23.3B
Facebook, Inc.	WhatsApp	$17.2B
MeadWestvaco	RockTenn	$16.0B
Intel Corporation	Altera Corporation	$15.0B
CVS Health Corporation	Omnicare, Inc.	$12.9B
Marriott	Starwood Hotels Intl	$12.2B
Merck	Cubist	$ 9.5B
Weyerhaeuser	Plum Creek Timber	$ 8.4B
Celgene Corporation	Receptos, Inc.	$ 7.2B
Cox Automotive	Dealertrack Technologies	$ 4.0B
FedEx	TNT Express	$ 4.8B
Expedia	HomeAway	$ 3.9B
Microsemi Corporation	PMC-Sierra, Inc.	$ 2.5B
Constellation Brands	Ballast Point Brewing & Spirits	$ 1.0B

manufacturing, and delivery, substantial savings can result. As an example, Oracle's acquisition of Sun Microsystems creates synergies by enabling Oracle to integrate its software product lines with Sun's hardware specifications. The acquisition further allows Oracle to offer complete systems made of chips, computers, storage devices, and software with an aim toward increased efficiency and quality.[2] Other cost savings resulting from elimination of duplicate efforts, such as data processing and marketing, can make a single entity more profitable than the separate parent and subsidiary had been in the past. Such synergies often accompany business combinations.

Although no two business combinations are exactly alike, many share one or more of the following characteristics that potentially enhance profitability:

- Vertical integration of one firm's output and another firm's distribution or further processing.
- Cost savings through elimination of duplicate facilities and staff.
- Quick entry for new and existing products into domestic and foreign markets.
- Economies of scale allowing greater efficiency and negotiating power.
- The ability to access financing at more attractive rates. As firm size increases, negotiating power with financial institutions can increase also.
- Diversification of business risk.

Business combinations also occur because many firms seek the continuous expansion of their organizations, often into diversified areas. Acquiring control over a vast network of different businesses has been a strategy utilized by a number of companies (sometimes known as *conglomerates*) for decades. Entry into new industries is immediately available to the parent without having to construct facilities, develop products, train management, or create market recognition. Many corporations have successfully employed this strategy to produce huge, highly profitable organizations. Unfortunately, others discovered that the task of managing a widely diverse group of businesses can be a costly learning experience. Even combinations that are designed to take advantage of operating synergies and cost savings will fail if the integration is not managed carefully.

Overall, the primary motivations for many business combinations can be traced to an increasingly competitive environment. Three recent business combinations provide interesting examples of distinct motivations to combine: Facebook and WhatsApp, AT&T and DirecTV, and Rock-Tenn and MeadwestVaco. Each is discussed briefly in turn.

[2] Ben Worthen, Cari Tuna, and Justin Scheck, "Companies More Prone to Go 'Vertical,'" *The Wall Street Journal,* November 30, 2009.

Facebook and WhatsApp

On October 26, 2014, Facebook completed its acquisition of WhatsApp, the popular internet messaging service with over 600 million users. As stated in its 2014 annual 10-K report, Facebook paid a total of $17.2B in what was one of the largest technology company acquisitions of the year.[3] According to the acquisition agreement, WhatsApp will retain all of its staff and will operate as an independent subsidiary of Facebook, similar to Facebook's 2012 acquisition of Instagram. The steep purchase price was based almost entirely on long-term potential, as in the first six months of 2014, WhatsApp reported just $15M in revenue.[4] Facebook CEO Mark Zuckerberg indicated that his immediate focus was on growing WhatsApp, and that he would not attempt to monetize the service until the number of users reached 1 billion.[5]

Many analysts weighed in on why Facebook would spend over 10% of its net worth for a company with minimal revenue. Aileen Lee, from venture capital firm Kliener Perkins Caufield & Byers, noted that it was important for Facebook to beat out its competition in acquiring a fast growing messaging service like WhatsApp. "These big companies feel like they can't afford to lose mind share and time share to competitors, and they are willing to pay a lot of money for large user bases."[6] Other analysts cited the benefit of an expanded portfolio in protecting against inevitable shifts in online consumer behavior.[7]

Of the total $17.2B purchase consideration, Facebook recognized $15.3B in goodwill. According to Facebook's 2014 10-K, the goodwill value is "primarily attributable to expected synergies from future growth, from potential monetization opportunities, from strategic advantages provided in the mobile ecosystem, and from expansion of our mobile messaging offerings." As is common in high-tech acquisitions, much of the purchase price for WhatsApp was attributed to other intangibles. Facebook reported an additional $2.8B in intangible assets (beyond goodwill) including acquired users, trade name, and acquired technology.

AT&T and DirecTV

On July 24, 2015, AT&T acquired DirecTV for $47.4 billion. According to AT&T's September 30, 2015 10-Q report, $32.7 billion was paid in stock and $14.7 billion in cash. The acquisition made AT&T the nation's leading TV provider, surpassing Comcast for first place.[8] In order to contend with changing consumer demands, many large media companies were turning to mergers as a way to expand offerings. CEO Randall Stephenson commented in a press release that AT&T will now "be able to meet consumers' future entertainment preferences . . .traditional TV service, . . .their favorite content on a mobile device, or video streamed over the Internet to any screen".[9] The acquisition will also provide AT&T access to millions of DirecTV customers in the Latin American market.

The DirecTV acquisition was subject to a series of conditions imposed by the FCC. These conditions included providing discounted broadband service to low-income households, and offering all-fiber access to at least 12.5 million small consumers.[10] Due to antitrust concerns, the FCC and other regulatory agencies had taken an increasingly active role in monitoring mergers in the media industry. Notably, in April of 2015, Comcast withdrew its $45B bid for Time Warner due in large part to resistance from the FCC and Department of Justice.[11]

Intangible assets represented the majority of the value paid for DirecTV. According to its third quarter 2015 10-Q, AT&T reported $35.3 billion in goodwill and $34.7 billion coming

---

[3] Although some news releases cited prices as high as $22 billion, the larger prices evidently included post-acquisition compensation for continuing employees.

[4] *TechCrunch,* Josh Constine, "WhatsApp's First Half of 2014 Revenue Was $15M, Net Loss of $232.5M Was Mostly Issuing Stock," October 28, 2014.

[5] Bloomberg Business, Sarah Frier, "Facebook $22 Billion WhatsApp Deal Buys $10 Million in Sales," October 28, 2014.

[6] *New York Times Dealbook,* David Gelles, "For Facebook, it's Users First and Profits Later," February 20, 2014.

[7] ibid.

[8] *New York Times,* Credit Jonathan Alcorn/Reuters, "F.C.C. Approves AT&T-DirecTV Deal," July 24, 2015.

[9] AT&T press release, "AT&T Completes Acquisition of DIRECTV," Dallas, TX, July 24, 2015.

[10] AT&T 10-Q report for the quarter ending September 30, 2015.

[11] *Los Angeles Times,* Meg James, "AT&T gets FCC approval, immediately completes $49-billion takeover of DirecTV", July 24, 2015.

from other intangible assets such as customer relationships and satellite access rights. As also reflected in the 10-Q, AT&T expects significant synergies as a result of the acquisition, especially in the area of video content cost savings and expanded video service capabilities.

MeadwestVaco and Rock-Tenn

On March 6, 2015, packaging companies MeadwestVaco (MWV) and Rock-Tenn finalized their business combination agreement to become wholly owned subsidiaries of WestRock, a newly formed parent company. WestRock manufactures a variety of consumer and commercial packaging materials, paperboard, and merchandising displays. The company is also one of the largest recyclers of paper.[12]

As part of the business combination, equity of WestRock was divided almost equally, with MWV shareholders owning 50.1% of the new company and Rock-Tenn shareholders getting 49.9%. According to its 2015 annual 10-K report, for financial reporting purposes, Rock-Tenn was treated as the acquiring party. The consideration transferred in the combination was $8.3 billion and was allocated to assets of $16 billion and liabilities of $7.7 billion.[13]

Rock-Tenn had made acquisitions of $7 billion in the 10 years prior to the business combination with MWV and wanted to continue expanding. MWV was attractive to Rock-Tenn because of its diverse and complimentary products as well as its global reach, with plants in Brazil and India. According to Barclay's analyst Scott Gaffner, Rock-Tenn was not in a position to acquire MWV due to its size, and that a "merger of equals" was the best option.[14] From MWV's standpoint, the business combination served as a means to penetrate new end markets and add to its set of global customers.[15]

The prospect of cost synergies was also a large factor for both companies in deciding to combine. In its presentation to investors, Rock-Tenn noted that $550 million in cost savings were achieved related to its 2011 acquisition of Smurfit-Stone. WestRock expects to generate annual cost synergies of $300M resulting from the business combination, to be realized by the third year of operations. Procurement and supply chain integration, production plant optimization, and corporate and overhead reduction are all expected to contribute to the savings.[16]

LO 2-2

Recognize when consolidation of financial information into a single set of statements is necessary.

Business Combinations, Control, and Consolidated Financial Reporting

The consolidation of financial information into a single set of statements becomes necessary when the business combination of two or more companies creates a single economic entity. As stated in FASB ASC (810-10-10-1): "There is a presumption that consolidated financial statements are more meaningful than separate financial statements and that they are usually necessary for a fair presentation when one of the entities in the consolidated group directly or indirectly has a controlling financial interest in the other entities."

Thus, in producing financial statements for external distribution, the reporting entity transcends the boundaries of incorporation to encompass (i.e., consolidate) all companies for which control is present. Even though the various companies may retain their legal identities as separate corporations, the resulting information is more meaningful to outside parties when consolidated into a single set of financial statements.

To explain the process of preparing consolidated financial statements for a business combination, we address three questions:

1. How is a business combination formed?
2. What constitutes a controlling financial interest?
3. How is the consolidation process carried out?

---

[12] www.rocktenn.com/products

[13] Westrock Company 2015 annual 10-K report.

[14] *businessfinancenews.com,* Jason Graul, Rock-Tenn Company, MeadWestvaco Corp. (MWV) Merger: Barclays Views Cost & Operational Synergies, July 15, 2015.

[15] MWV and RockTenn, Investor Presentation, "Creating a Global Packaging Leader," January 26, 2015.

[16] *Ibid,* footnote 11.

LO 2-3

Define the term *business combination* and differentiate across various forms of business combinations.

Business Combinations—Creating a Single Economic Entity

A business combination refers to a transaction or other event in which an acquirer obtains control over one or more businesses.

Business combinations are formed by a wide variety of transactions or events with various formats. For example, each of the following is identified as a business combination although it differs widely in legal form. In every case, two or more enterprises are being united into a single economic entity so that consolidated financial statements are required.

1. One company obtains the assets, and often the liabilities, of another company in exchange for cash, other assets, liabilities, stock, or a combination of these. The second organization normally dissolves itself as a legal corporation. Thus, only the acquiring company remains in existence, having absorbed the acquired net assets directly into its own operations. Any business combination in which only one of the original companies continues to exist is referred to in legal terms as a *statutory merger.*

2. One company obtains all of the capital stock of another in exchange for cash, other assets, liabilities, stock, or a combination of these. After gaining control, the acquiring company can decide to transfer all assets and liabilities to its own financial records with the second company being dissolved as a separate corporation.[17] The business combination is, once again, a statutory merger because only one of the companies maintains legal existence. This statutory merger, however, is achieved by obtaining equity securities rather than by buying the target company's assets. Because stock is obtained, the acquiring company must gain 100 percent control of all shares before legally dissolving the subsidiary.

3. Two or more companies transfer either their assets or their capital stock to a newly formed corporation. Both original companies are dissolved, leaving only the new organization in existence. A business combination effected in this manner is a *statutory consolidation.* The use here of the term *consolidation* should not be confused with the accounting meaning of that same word. In accounting, *consolidation* refers to the mechanical process of bringing together the financial records of two or more organizations to form a single set of statements. A statutory consolidation denotes a specific type of business combination that has united two or more existing companies under the ownership of a newly created company.

4. One company achieves legal control over another by acquiring a majority of voting stock. *Although control is present, no dissolution takes place; each company remains in existence as an incorporated operation.* NBC Universal, as an example, continues to retain its legal status as a corporation after being acquired by Comcast Corporation. Separate incorporation is frequently preferred to take full advantage of any intangible benefits accruing to the acquired company as a going concern. Better utilization of such factors as licenses, trade names, employee loyalty, and the company's reputation can be possible when the subsidiary maintains its own legal identity. Moreover, maintaining an independent information system for a subsidiary often enhances its market value for an eventual sale or initial public offering as a stand-alone entity.

Because the asset and liability account balances are not physically combined as in statutory mergers and consolidations, each company continues to maintain an independent accounting system. To reflect the combination, the acquiring company enters the takeover transaction into its own records by establishing a single investment asset account. However, the newly acquired subsidiary omits any recording of this event; its stock is simply transferred to the parent from the subsidiary's shareholders. Thus, the subsidiary's financial records are not directly affected by a takeover.

5. A final vehicle for control of another business entity does not involve a majority voting stock interest or direct ownership of assets. Control of a variable interest entity (VIE) by design often does not rest with its equity holders. Instead, control is exercised through contractual arrangements with a sponsoring firm that, although it technically may not own the VIE, becomes its "primary beneficiary" with rights to its residual profits. These contracts can take the form of leases, participation rights, guarantees, or other interests. Past use of VIEs

---

[17] Although the acquired company has been legally dissolved, it frequently continues to operate as a separate division within the surviving company's organization.

EXHIBIT 2.2
Business Combinations

Type of Combination	Action of Acquiring Company	Action of Acquired Company
Statutory merger through asset acquisition.	Acquires assets and often liabilities.	Dissolves and goes out of business.
Statutory merger through capital stock acquisition.	Acquires all stock and then transfers assets and liabilities to its own books.	Dissolves as a separate corporation, often remaining as a division of the acquiring company.
Statutory consolidation through capital stock or asset acquisition.	Newly created entity receives assets or capital stock of original companies.	Original companies may dissolve while remaining as separate divisions of newly created company.
Acquisition of more than 50 percent of the voting stock.	Acquires stock that is recorded as an investment; controls decision making of acquired company.	Remains in existence as legal corporation, although now a subsidiary of the acquiring company.
Control through ownership of variable interests (see Chapter 6). Risks and rewards often flow to a sponsoring firm that may or may not hold equity shares.	Establishes contractual control over a variable interest entity to engage in a specific activity.	Remains in existence as a separate legal entity—often a trust or partnership.

was criticized because these structures provided sponsoring firms with off-balance sheet financing and sometimes questionable profits on sales to their VIEs. Prior to 2004, many sponsoring entities of VIEs did not technically meet the definition of a controlling financial interest (i.e., majority voting stock ownership) and thus did not consolidate their VIEs. Current GAAP, however, expands the notion of control and thus requires consolidation of VIEs by their primary beneficiary.

As you can see, business combinations are created in many distinct forms. The specific format is a critical factor in the subsequent consolidation of financial information. Exhibit 2.2 provides an overview of the various combinations.

Control—An Elusive Quality

The definition of control is central to determining when two or more entities become one economic entity and therefore one reporting entity. Control of one firm by another is most often achieved through the acquisition of voting shares. The ASC (810-10-15-8) describes control as follows:

> The usual condition for a controlling financial interest is ownership of a majority voting interest, and, therefore, as a general rule ownership by one reporting entity, directly or indirectly, of more than 50 percent of the outstanding voting shares of another entity is a condition pointing toward consolidation.

By exercising majority voting power, one firm can literally dictate the financing and operating activities of another firm. Accordingly, U.S. GAAP traditionally has pointed to a majority voting share ownership as a controlling financial interest that requires consolidation.

Notably, the power to control may also exist with less than 50 percent of the outstanding shares of another entity. The ASC (810-10-15-8) goes on to observe that:

> The power to control may also exist with a lesser percentage of ownership, for example, by contract, lease, agreement with other stockholders, or by court decree.

Therefore, despite possessing less than 50 percent of the subsidiary's voting stock, one ownership group can enter into contractual arrangement with other ownership groups that provide control.

Alternatively, majority ownership does not always indicate an exclusive ability for one entity to exercise control over another. According to the FASB ASC Glossary, control can also be defined as,

> The direct or indirect ability to determine the direction of management and policies through ownership, contract, or otherwise.

This description recognizes the complex profit-sharing agreements that sometimes accompany economic resource sharing. To reduce their risk, several parties may participate in directing the activities of another entity. For example, a parent with majority ownership may grant certain decision rights to noncontrolling shareholders in exchange for economic support. Such noncontrolling participation rights may be powerful enough to prevent the majority owners from controlling the entity.

As the complexity of ownership arrangements increases, defining when one firm controls another remains a continuing challenge for financial reporting standard setters. Nonetheless, the primary way U.S. firms exercise control remains through the acquisition of a majority of another firm's voting shares. Consequently, in this text, we largely focus on control relationships established through voting interests. In Chapter 6, however, we expand our coverage to include the consolidation of firms where control is exercised through variable interests.

Consolidation of Financial Information

When one company gains control over another, a business combination is established. Financial data gathered from the individual companies are then brought together to form a single set of consolidated statements. Although this process can be complicated, the objectives of a consolidation are straightforward—to report the financial position, results of operations, and cash flows for the combined entity. As a part of this process, reciprocal accounts and intra-entity transactions must be adjusted or eliminated to ensure that all reported balances truly represent the single entity.

Applicable consolidation procedures vary significantly depending on the legal format employed in creating a business combination. *For a statutory merger or a statutory consolidation, when the acquired company (or companies) is (are) legally dissolved, only one accounting consolidation ever occurs.* On the date of the combination, the surviving company simply records the various account balances from each of the dissolving companies. Because the accounts are brought together permanently in this manner, no further consolidation procedures are necessary. After the balances have been transferred to the survivor, the financial records of the acquired companies are closed out as part of the dissolution.

Conversely, in a combination when all companies retain incorporation, a different set of consolidation procedures is appropriate. Because the companies preserve their legal identities, each continues to maintain its own independent accounting records. *Thus, no permanent consolidation of the account balances is ever made. Rather, the consolidation process must be carried out anew each time the reporting entity prepares financial statements for external reporting purposes.*

When separate record-keeping is maintained, the accountant faces a unique problem: The financial information must be brought together periodically without disturbing the accounting systems of the individual companies. Because these consolidations are produced outside the financial records, worksheets traditionally are used to expedite the process. Worksheets are a part of neither company's accounting records nor the resulting financial statements. Instead, they are an efficient structure for organizing and adjusting the information used to prepare externally reported consolidated statements.

Consequently, the legal characteristics of a business combination have a significant impact on the approach taken to the consolidation process:

What is to be consolidated?

- If dissolution takes place, appropriate account balances are physically consolidated in the surviving company's financial records.
- If separate incorporation is maintained, only the financial statement information (not the actual records) is consolidated.

When does the consolidation take place?

- If dissolution takes place, a permanent consolidation occurs at the date of the combination.
- If separate incorporation is maintained, the consolidation process is carried out at regular intervals whenever financial statements are to be prepared.

How are the accounting records affected?

- If dissolution takes place, the surviving company's accounts are adjusted to include appropriate balances of the dissolved company. The dissolved company's records are closed out.
- If separate incorporation is maintained, each company continues to retain its own records. Using worksheets facilitates the periodic consolidation process without disturbing the individual accounting systems.

LO 2-4

Describe the valuation principles of the acquisition method.

Financial Reporting for Business Combinations

The Acquisition Method

Regardless of whether the acquired firm maintains its separate incorporation or dissolution takes place, current standards require the acquisition method to account for business combinations. Applying the acquisition method involves recognizing and measuring

- The consideration transferred for the acquired business and any noncontrolling interest.
- The separately identified assets acquired and liabilities assumed.
- Goodwill, or a gain from a bargain purchase.

Fair value is the measurement attribute used to recognize these and other aspects of a business combination. Therefore, prior to examining specific applications of the acquisition method, we present a brief discussion of the fair-value concept as applied to business combinations.

Consideration Transferred for the Acquired Business

The fair value of the consideration transferred to acquire a business from its former owners is the starting point in valuing and recording a business combination. In describing the acquisition method, the FASB ASC states:

> The consideration transferred in a business combination shall be measured at fair value, which shall be calculated as the sum of the acquisition-date fair values of the assets transferred by the acquirer, the liabilities incurred by the acquirer to former owners of the acquiree, and the equity interests issued by the acquirer. (ASC 805-30-30-7)

The acquisition method thus embraces the fair value of the consideration transferred in measuring the acquirer's interest in the acquired business.[18] Fair value is defined as the price that would be received to sell an asset or paid to transfer a liability in an orderly transaction between market participants at the measurement date. Thus, market values are often the best source of evidence of the fair value of consideration transferred in a business combination. Items of consideration transferred can include cash, securities (either stocks or debt), and other property or obligations.

Contingent Consideration: An Additional Element of Consideration Transferred

Contingent consideration, when present in a business combination, is an additional element of consideration transferred. Contingent consideration can be useful in negotiations when two parties disagree with each other's estimates of future cash flows for the target firm or when

---

[18] An occasional exception occurs in a bargain purchase in which the fair value of the net assets acquired serves as the valuation basis for the acquired firm. Other exceptions include situations in which control is achieved without a transfer of consideration, or determination of the fair value of the consideration transferred is less reliable than other measures of the business fair value.

valuation uncertainty is high.[19] Acquisition agreements often contain provisions to pay former owners (typically cash or additional shares of the acquirer's stock) upon achievement of specified future performance measures. For example, Walt Disney Company disclosed in its 2015 annual report its 2014 acquisition of 100 percent of the outstanding shares of common stock of Maker Studios, Inc. Disney's agreement with the former owners of Maker Studios provided for:

> up to $450 million of additional cash upon final determination of Maker's achievement of certain performance targets for calendar years 2014 and 2015. The [Walt Disney] Company recognized a $198 million liability for the fair value of the contingent consideration (determined by a probability weighting of potential payouts), of which approximately $100 million was paid in fiscal 2015 for calendar year 2014. Subsequent changes in the estimated fair value, if any, will be recognized in earnings.

Disney thus included the fair value of the contingent consideration as a component of the fair value of the consideration transferred for Maker Studios. The acquisition method treats contingent consideration obligations as a negotiated component of the fair value of the consideration transferred. As seen in the above Disney quote, determining the fair value of contingent future payments typically involves probability and risk assessments based on circumstances existing on the acquisition date.

Regardless of the elements that constitute the consideration transferred, the parent's financial statements must now incorporate its newly acquired ownership interest in a controlled entity. In Chapters 2 and 3, we focus exclusively on combinations that result in complete ownership by the acquirer (i.e., no noncontrolling interest in the acquired firm). As described in Chapter 4, in a less-than-100-percent acquisition, the noncontrolling interest also is measured initially at its fair value. Then, the combined fair values of the parent's consideration transferred and the noncontrolling interest comprise the valuation basis for the acquired firm in consolidated financial reports.

Assets Acquired and Liabilities Assumed

A fundamental principle of the acquisition method is that an acquirer must identify the assets acquired and the liabilities assumed in the business combination. Further, once these have been identified, the acquirer measures the assets acquired and the liabilities assumed at their acquisition-date fair values, with only a few exceptions.[20] As demonstrated in subsequent examples, the principle of recognizing and measuring assets acquired and liabilities assumed at fair value applies across all business combinations.

Fair value, as defined by GAAP, is the price that would be received from selling an asset or paid for transferring a liability in an orderly transaction between market participants at the measurement date. However, determining the acquisition-date fair values of the individual assets acquired and liabilities assumed can prove challenging.[21] The ASC (820-10-35-28) points to three sets of valuation techniques typically employed: the market approach, the income approach, and the cost approach.

Market Approach

The market approach estimates fair values using other market transactions involving similar assets or liabilities. In a business combination, assets acquired such as marketable securities and some tangible assets may have established markets that can provide comparable market values for estimating fair values. Similarly, the fair values of many liabilities assumed can be determined by reference to market trades for similar debt instruments.

Income Approach

The income approach relies on multi-period estimates of future cash flows projected to be generated by an asset. These projected cash flows are then discounted at a required rate of

---

[19] Cain, Denis, and Denis, "Earnouts: A Study of Financial Contracting in Acquisition Agreements," *Journal of Accounting and Economics* 51 (2011), 151–170.

[20] Exceptions to the fair-value measurement principle include deferred taxes, certain employee benefits, indemnification assets, reacquired rights, share-based awards, and assets held for sale.

[21] Identifying and measuring the acquired firm's financial statement items can take some time. ASC (805-10-25-14) allows an acquirer to adjust the provisional amounts recognized for a business combination up to a year after the acquisition date.

return that reflects the time value of money and the risk associated with realizing the future estimated cash flows. The multi-period income approach is often useful for obtaining fair-value estimates of intangible assets and acquired in-process research and development.

Cost Approach

The cost approach estimates fair values by reference to the current cost of replacing an asset with another of comparable economic utility. Used assets can present a particular valuation challenge if active markets only exist for newer versions of the asset. Thus, the cost to replace a particular asset reflects both its estimated replacement cost and the effects of obsolescence. In this sense obsolescence is meant to capture economic declines in value including both technological obsolescence and physical deterioration. The cost approach is widely used to estimate fair values for many tangible assets acquired in business combinations such as property, plant, and equipment.

Goodwill, and Gains on Bargain Purchases

In a business combination, the parent must account for both the consideration transferred and the individual amounts of the identified assets acquired and liabilities assumed at their acquisition-date fair values. However, in many cases the respective collective amounts of these two values will differ. Current GAAP accounting for the difference requires one of two outcomes—in one the acquirer recognizes an asset (goodwill), in the other a gain.

When the consideration transferred exceeds the acquisition-date net amount of the identified assets acquired and the liabilities assumed, the acquirer recognizes the asset goodwill for the excess.[22] Goodwill is defined as an asset representing the future economic benefits arising in a business combination that are not individually identified and separately recognized. Goodwill often embodies the expected synergies that the acquirer expects to achieve through control of the acquired firm's assets. Goodwill may also capture non-recognized intangibles of the acquired firm such as employee expertise.

Conversely, if the collective fair value of the net identified assets acquired and liabilities assumed exceeds the consideration transferred, the acquirer recognizes a "gain on bargain purchase." In such cases, the fair value of the net assets acquired replaces the consideration transferred as the valuation basis for the acquired firm. Bargain purchases can result from business divestitures forced by regulatory agencies or other types of distress sales. Before recognizing a gain on bargain purchase, however, the acquirer must reassess whether it has correctly identified and measured all of the acquired assets and liabilities. Illustrations and further discussions of goodwill and of bargain purchase gains follow in the next section.

LO 2-5

Determine the total fair value of the consideration transferred for an acquisition, and allocate that fair value to specific subsidiary assets acquired (including goodwill) and liabilities assumed or to a gain on bargain purchase.

Procedures for Consolidating Financial Information

To demonstrate an application of the acquisition method, assume BigNet Company specializes in communications equipment and business software that provide web-based applications for retail companies. BigNet seeks to expand its operations and plans to acquire Smallport on December 31. Smallport Company owns computers, telecommunications equipment, and software that customize website billing and ordering systems for their customers. BigNet hopes to expand Smallport's customer contracts, utilize its recently developed software, and create other synergies by combining with Smallport.

Exhibit 2.3 lists the December 31 account balances for both BigNet and Smallport. In addition, the estimated fair values of Smallport's assets and liabilities are shown. Although Smallport's computers and equipment have a $400,000 book value, their current fair value is $600,000. Smallport's software has only a $100,000 value on its books; the internal development costs were primarily expensed. The software's observable fair value, however, is $1,200,000. Similarly, although not reflected in its financial records, Smallport has several

---

[22] Assuming a 100% acquisition. For combinations with less than complete ownership, goodwill is computed as the excess of the consideration transferred plus the acquisition-date fair value of the noncontrolling interest over the collective fair values of the net identified assets acquired and liabilities assumed.

EXHIBIT 2.3 Basic Consolidation Information

	BigNet Company Book Values December 31	Smallport Company Book Values December 31	Fair Values December 31
Current assets	$ 1,100,000	$ 300,000	$ 300,000
Computers and equipment (net)	1,300,000	400,000	600,000
Capitalized software (net)	500,000	100,000	1,200,000
Customer contracts	–0–	–0–	700,000
Notes payable	(300,000)	(200,000)	(250,000)
Net assets	**$ 2,600,000**	**$ 600,000**	**$2,550,000**
Common stock—$10 par value	$ (1,600,000)		
Common stock—$5 par value		$ (100,000)	
Additional paid-in capital	(40,000)	(20,000)	
Retained earnings, 1/1	(870,000)	(370,000)	
Dividends declared	110,000	10,000	
Revenues	(1,000,000)	(500,000)	
Expenses	800,000	380,000	
Owners' equity 12/31	**$(2,600,000)**	**$(600,000)**	
Retained earnings, 12/31	(960,000)*	(480,000)*	

*Retained earnings balance after closing out revenues, expenses, and dividends.
Note: Parentheses indicate a credit balance.

large ongoing customer contracts. BigNet estimates the fair value of the customer contracts at $700,000. Smallport also has a $200,000 note payable incurred to help finance the software development. Because interest rates are currently low, this liability (incurred at a higher rate of interest) has a present value of $250,000.

Smallport's net assets (total assets less total liabilities) have a book value of $600,000 but a fair value of $2,550,000. Fair values for only the assets and liabilities are appraised here; the capital stock, retained earnings, dividend, revenue, and expense accounts represent histori-cal measurements rather than any type of future values. Although these equity and income accounts can give some indication of the organization's overall worth, they are not property and thus not transferred in the combination.

Legal as well as accounting distinctions divide business combinations into several separate categories. To facilitate the introduction of consolidation accounting, we present the various procedures utilized in this process according to the following sequence:

1. Acquisition method when dissolution takes place.
2. Acquisition method when separate incorporation is maintained.

Acquisition Method When Dissolution Takes Place

When the acquired firm's legal status is dissolved in a business combination, the continuing firm takes direct ownership of the former firm's assets and assumes its liabilities. Thus, the continuing firm will prepare a journal entry to record

- The fair value of the consideration transferred by the acquiring firm to the former owners of the acquiree, and
- The identified assets acquired and liabilities assumed at their individual fair values.

However, the entry to record the combination further depends on the relation between the consideration transferred and the net amount of the fair values assigned to the identified assets acquired and liabilities assumed. Therefore, we initially provide three illustrations that demon-strate the procedures to record a business combination, each with different amounts of consid-eration transferred relative to the acquired asset and liability fair values. Each example assumes a merger takes place and, therefore, the acquired firm is dissolved. In each situation, the con-sideration transferred is compared to the fair value of the net identifiable assets acquired and liabilities assumed to determine if goodwill or a bargain purchase gain should be recorded.

Consideration Transferred Equals Net Fair Values of Identified Assets Acquired and Liabilities Assumed

Assume that after negotiations with the owners of Smallport, BigNet agrees to pay cash of $550,000 and to issue 20,000 previously unissued shares of its $10 par value common stock (currently selling for $100 per share) for all of Smallport's assets and liabilities. Following the acquisition, Smallport then dissolves itself as a legal entity. The consideration transferred from BigNet to Smallport is computed as follows and in this case, exactly equals the collective fair values of Smallport's assets less liabilities:

Cash payment	$ 550,000
Common stock issued by BigNet ($100 × 20,000 shares)	2,000,000
Total consideration transferred	$2,550,000
Fair value of Smallport's net identifiable assets	$2,550,000

The $2,550,000 fair value of the consideration transferred by BigNet represents the fair value of the acquired Smallport business and serves as the basis for recording the combination in total.

BigNet also must record all of Smallport's identified assets and liabilities at their *individual* fair values. These two valuations present no difficulties because BigNet's consideration transferred exactly equals the $2,550,000 collective net fair values of the individual assets and liabilities acquired as shown in Exhibit 2.3.

Because Smallport Company will be dissolved, BigNet (the surviving company) enters a journal entry in its financial records to record the combination. BigNet has directly acquired the assets and assumed the liabilities of Smallport. Under the acquisition method, BigNet records Smallport's assets and liabilities at fair value ignoring original book values. Revenue, expense, dividend, and equity accounts cannot be transferred to a parent and are not included in recording the business combination.

Acquisition Method: Consideration Transferred Equals Net Identified Asset Fair Values—Subsidiary Dissolved

LO 2-6a

Prepare the journal entry to consolidate the accounts of a subsidiary if dissolution takes place.

BigNet Company's Financial Records—December 31		
Current Assets	300,000	
Computers and Equipment	600,000	
Capitalized Software	1,200,000	
Customer Contracts	700,000	
Notes Payable		250,000
Cash (paid by BigNet)		550,000
Common Stock (20,000 shares issued by BigNet at $10 par value)		200,000
Additional Paid-In Capital		1,800,000
To record acquisition of Smallport Company. Assets acquired and liabilities assumed are recorded at fair value.		

BigNet's financial records now show $1,900,000 in the Computers and Equipment account ($1,300,000 former balance + $600,000 acquired), $1,700,000 in Capitalized Software ($500,000 + $1,200,000), and so forth. Note that the customer contracts, despite being unrecorded on Smallport's books, are nonetheless identified and recognized on BigNet's financial records as part of the assets acquired in the combination. These items have been added into BigNet's balances (see Exhibit 2.3) at their fair values. Conversely, BigNet's revenue balance continues to report the company's own $1,000,000 with expenses remaining at $800,000 and dividends of $110,000. Under the acquisition method, only the subsidiary's revenues, expenses, dividends, and equity transactions that occur subsequent to the takeover affect the business combination.

Consideration Transferred Exceeds Net Amount of Fair Values of Identified Assets Acquired and Liabilities Assumed

In this next illustration, BigNet transfers to the owners of Smallport consideration of $1,000,000 in cash plus 20,000 shares of common stock with a fair value of $100 per share in exchange for ownership of the company. The consideration transferred from BigNet to Smallport is now computed as follows and results in an excess amount exchanged over the fair value of the net assets acquired:

Cash payment	$1,000,000
Common stock issued by BigNet ($100 × 20,000 shares)	2,000,000
Total consideration transferred	$3,000,000
Fair value of Smallport's net identifiable assets	$2,550,000
Goodwill	$ 450,000

As presented in the above calculation, when the consideration transferred in an acquisition exceeds total net fair value of the identified assets and liabilities, the excess ($450,000 in this case) is allocated to an unidentifiable asset known as goodwill. [23] Unlike other assets, we consider goodwill as unidentifiable because we presume it emerges from several other assets acting together to produce an expectation of enhanced profitability. Goodwill essentially captures all sources of profitability beyond what can be expected from simply summing the fair values of the acquired firm's assets and liabilities.

The resulting consideration paid is $450,000 more than the $2,550,000 fair value of Smallport's net identifiable assets and is assigned to the unidentifiable asset Goodwill.

Several factors may have affected BigNet's $3,000,000 acquisition offer. First, BigNet may expect its assets to act in concert with those of Smallport, thus creating synergies that will produce profits beyond the total expected for the separate companies. In our earlier examples, Facebook, WestRock, and AT&T all clearly anticipated substantial synergies from their acquisitions. Other factors such as Smallpot's history of profitability, its reputation, the quality of its personnel, and the current economic condition of the industry in which it operates may also affect the acquisition offer. In general, if a target company is projected to generate unusually high profits relative to its asset base, acquirers frequently are willing to pay a premium price.

Acquisition Method: Consideration Transferred Exceeds Net Identified Asset Fair Values—Subsidiary Dissolved

Returning to BigNet's $3,000,000 consideration, $450,000 is in excess of the fair value of Smallport's net assets. Thus, goodwill of that amount is entered into BigNet's accounting system along with the fair value of each individual asset and liability. BigNet makes the following journal entry at the date of acquisition:

BigNet Company's Financial Records—December 31		
Current Assets	300,000	
Computers and Equipment	600,000	
Capitalized Software	1,200,000	
Customer Contracts	700,000	
Goodwill	450,000	
Notes Payable		250,000
Cash (paid by BigNet)		1,000,000
Common Stock (20,000 shares issued by BigNet at $10 par value)		200,000
Additional Paid-In Capital		1,800,000
To record acquisition of Smallport Company. Assets acquired and liabilities assumed are recorded at individual fair values with excess fair value attributed to goodwill.		

[23] In business combinations, such excess payments are not unusual and can be quite large. When Oracle acquired PeopleSoft, it initially assigned $4.5 billion of its $11 billion purchase price to the fair value of the acquired identified net assets. It assigned the remaining $6.5 billion to goodwill.

Once again, BigNet's financial records now show $1,900,000 in the Computers and Equipment account ($1,300,000 former balance + $600,000 acquired), $1,700,000 in Capitalized Software ($500,000 + $1,200,000), and so forth. As the only change, BigNet records goodwill of $450,000 for the excess consideration paid over the net identified asset fair values.[24]

Bargain Purchase—Consideration Transferred Is Less Than Net Amount of Fair Values of Identified Assets Acquired and Liabilities Assumed

Occasionally, the fair value of the consideration transferred by the acquirer is less than the fair value received in an acquisition. Such bargain purchases typically are considered anomalous. Businesses generally do not sell assets or businesses at prices below their fair values. Nonetheless, bargain purchases do occur—most often in forced or distressed sales.

For example, Westamerica Bank's acquisition of County Bank (California) from the FDIC resulted in a $48.8 million "bargain purchase" gain. The FDIC sold the failed County Bank to Westamerica for $0 and additional guarantees. As a result, Westamerica recorded the combination at the estimated fair value of the net assets acquired and recognized a gain of $48.8 million. This gain treatment is consistent with the view that the acquiring firm is immediately better off by the amount that the fair value acquired in the business combination exceeds the consideration transferred.

To demonstrate accounting for a bargain purchase, our third illustration begins with Big-Net transferring consideration of $2,000,000 to the owners of Smallport in exchange for their business. BigNet conveys no cash and issues 20,000 shares of $10 par common stock that has a $100 per share fair value. The consideration transferred from BigNet to Smallport is now computed as follows and results in a gain on bargain purchase:

Cash payment	$ -0-
Common stock issued by BigNet ($100 × 20,000 shares)	2,000,000
Total consideration transferred	$ 2,000,000
Fair value of Smallport's identifiable net assets	$ 2,550,000
Gain on bargain purchase	$ 550,000

In accounting for this acquisition, at least two competing fair values are present. First, the $2,000,000 consideration transferred for Smallport represents a negotiated transaction value for the business. Second, the net amount of fair values individually assigned to the identified assets acquired and liabilities assumed produces $2,550,000. Additionally, based on expected synergies with Smallport, BigNet's management may believe that the fair value of the business exceeds the net asset fair value. Nonetheless, because the consideration transferred is less than the net asset fair value, a bargain purchase has occurred.

The acquisition method records the identified assets acquired and liabilities assumed at their individual fair values. In a bargain purchase situation, this net asset fair value effectively replaces the consideration transferred as the acquired firm's valuation basis for financial reporting. The consideration transferred serves as the acquired firm's valuation basis only if the consideration equals or exceeds the net amount of fair values for the assets acquired and liabilities assumed (as in the first two examples). In this case, however, the $2,000,000 consideration paid is less than the $2,550,000 net asset fair value, indicating a bargain purchase. Thus, the $2,550,000 net asset fair value serves as the valuation basis for the combination. A $550,000 *gain on bargain purchase* results because the $2,550,000 recorded value is accompanied by a payment of only $2,000,000. The acquirer recognizes this gain on its income statement in the period the acquisition takes place.

---

[24] As discussed in Chapter 3, the assets and liabilities (including goodwill) acquired in a business combination are assigned to reporting units of the combined entity. A reporting unit is simply a line of business (often a segment) in which an acquired asset or liability will be employed. The objective of assigning acquired assets and liabilities to reporting units is to facilitate periodic goodwill impairment testing.

Acquisition Method: Consideration Transferred Is Less Than Net Identified Asset Fair Values—Subsidiary Dissolved

BigNet Company's Financial Records—December 31		
Current Assets..	300,000	
Computers and Equipment	600,000	
Capitalized Software	1,200,000	
Customer Contracts	700,000	
Notes Payable		250,000
Common Stock (20,000 shares issued by BigNet at $10 par value) ...		200,000
Additional Paid-In Capital		1,800,000
Gain on Bargain Purchase		550,000

To record acquisition of Smallport Company. Assets acquired and liabilities assumed are each recorded at fair value. Excess net asset fair value is attributed to a gain on bargain purchase.

LO 2-6a

Prepare the journal entry to consolidate the accounts of a subsidiary if dissolution takes place.

A consequence of implementing a fair-value concept to acquisition accounting is the recognition of an unrealized gain on the bargain purchase. A criticism of the gain recognition is that the acquirer recognizes profit from a buying activity that occurs prior to traditional accrual measures of earned income (i.e., selling activity). Nonetheless, an exception to the general rule of recording business acquisitions at fair value of the consideration transferred occurs in the rare circumstance of a bargain purchase. Thus, in a bargain purchase, the fair values of the assets received and all liabilities assumed in a business combination are considered more relevant for asset valuation than the consideration transferred.

Summary: Acquisition Method When Dissolution Takes Place

When the acquired firm is dissolved in a business combination, the acquiring firm prepares a journal entry to record the combination on its books. The fair value of the consideration transferred by the acquiring firm provides the starting point for recording the acquisition. With few exceptions, the separately identified assets acquired and liabilities assumed are recorded at their individual fair values. Goodwill is recognized if the fair value of the consideration transferred exceeds the net identified asset fair value. If the net identified asset fair value of the business acquired exceeds the consideration transferred, a gain on a bargain purchase is recognized and reported in current income of the combined entity. Exhibit 2.4 summarizes possible allocations using the acquisition method.

Related Costs of Business Combinations

LO 2-6b

Prepare the journal entry to record the various related costs involved in a business combination.

Three additional categories of costs typically accompany business combinations, regardless of whether dissolution takes place. First, firms often engage attorneys, accountants, investment bankers, and other professionals for combination-related services. The acquisition

EXHIBIT 2.4
Consolidation Values—The Acquisition Method

Consolidation Values	Acquisition Accounting
Consideration transferred equals the fair values of net identified assets acquired.	Identified assets acquired and liabilities assumed are recorded at their fair values.
Consideration transferred is greater than the fair values of net identified assets acquired.	Identified assets acquired and liabilities assumed are recorded at their fair values. The excess consideration transferred over the net identified asset fair value is recorded as goodwill.
Bargain purchase—consideration transferred is less than the fair values of net identified assets acquired. The total of the individual fair values of the net identified assets acquired effectively becomes the acquired business fair value.	Identified assets acquired and liabilities assumed are recorded at their fair values. The excess amount of net identified asset fair value over the consideration transferred is recorded as a gain on bargain purchase.

EXHIBIT 2.5
Acquisition Method—Accounting for Costs Frequently Associated with Business Combinations

Types of Combination Costs	Acquisition Accounting
Direct combination costs (e.g., accounting, legal, investment banking, appraisal fees, etc.)	Expense as incurred
Indirect combination costs (e.g., internal costs such as allocated secretarial or managerial time)	Expense as incurred
Amounts incurred to register and issue securities	Reduce the value assigned to the fair value of the securities issued (typically a debit to additional paid-in capital)

method does not consider such expenditures as part of the fair value received by the acquirer. Therefore, professional service fees are expensed in the period incurred. The second category concerns an acquiring firm's internal costs. Examples include secretarial and management time allocated to the acquisition activity. Such indirect costs are reported as current year expenses, too. Finally, amounts incurred to register and issue securities in connection with a business combination simply reduce the otherwise determinable fair value of those securities. Exhibit 2.5 summarizes the three categories of related payments that accompany a business combination and their respective accounting treatments.

To illustrate the accounting treatment of these costs that frequently accompany business combinations, assume the following in connection with BigNet's acquisition of Smallport.

- BigNet pays an additional $100,000 in accounting and attorney fees.
- Internal secretarial and administrative costs of $75,000 are indirectly attributable to BigNet's combination with Smallport.
- Costs to register and issue BigNet's securities issued in the combination total $20,000.

Following the acquisition method, regardless of whether dissolution occurs or separate incorporation is maintained, BigNet would record these transactions as follows:

BigNet Company's Financial Records

Professional Services Expense	100,000	
Cash		100,000
To record as expenses of the current period any direct combination costs.		
Salaries and Administrative Expenses	75,000	
Accounts Payable (or Cash)		75,000
To record as expenses of the current period any indirect combination costs.		
Additional Paid-In Capital	20,000	
Cash		20,000
To record costs to register and issue stock in connection with the Smallport acquisition.		

The Acquisition Method When Separate Incorporation Is Maintained

When each company retains separate incorporation in a business combination, many aspects of the consolidation process are identical to those demonstrated in the previous section. Fair value, for example, remains the basis for initially consolidating the subsidiary's assets and liabilities. Also, the acquiring firm records a journal entry on its books reflecting the investment and the consideration transferred in the combination.

However, several significant differences are evident in combinations in which each company remains a legally incorporated separate entity. Most noticeably, the consolidation of the financial information is only simulated; the acquiring company does not physically record the acquired assets and liabilities. *Because dissolution does not occur, each company maintains independent record-keeping.* To facilitate the preparation of consolidated financial statements, a worksheet and consolidation entries are employed using data gathered from these separate companies.

A worksheet provides the structure for generating financial reports for the single economic entity. An integral part of this process employs consolidation worksheet entries that either adjust or eliminate various account balances of the parent and subsidiary. These adjustments and eliminations are entered on the worksheet to produce consolidated statements as if the financial records had been physically combined. *Because no actual union occurs, neither company ever records consolidation worksheet entries in its journals.* Instead, these adjustments and eliminations appear solely on the worksheet to derive consolidated balances for financial reporting purposes.

Example: (includes stock issue, related combination costs, and contingent consideration)

To illustrate the worksheet mechanics, we again use the Exhibit 2.3 example of BigNet and Smallport. We also include combination costs and contingent consideration. Assume that BigNet acquires Smallport Company on December 31 by issuing 26,000 shares of $10 par value common stock valued at $100 per share (or $2,600,000 in total). BigNet pays fees of $40,000 to a third party for its assistance in arranging the transaction.

Then, to settle a difference of opinion regarding Smallport's fair value, BigNet promises to pay an additional $83,200 to the former owners if Smallport's earnings exceed $300,000 during the next annual period. BigNet estimates a 25 percent probability that the $83,200 contingent payment will be required. A discount rate of 4 percent (to represent the time value of money) yields an expected present value of $20,000 for the contingent liability ($83,200 × 25% × 0.961538). The fair-value approach of the acquisition method views such contingent payments as part of the consideration transferred. According to this view, contingencies have value to those who receive the consideration and represent measurable obligations of the acquirer.[25] Therefore, the fair value of the consideration transferred in this example consists of the following two elements:

Fair value of securities issued by BigNet.	$2,600,000
Fair value of contingent performance liability	20,000
Total fair value of consideration transferred.	$2,620,000

To facilitate a possible future spinoff, BigNet maintains Smallport as a separate corporation with its independent accounting information system intact. Therefore, whenever financial statements for the combined entity are prepared, BigNet utilizes a worksheet in simulating the consolidation of these two companies.

Although the assets and liabilities are not transferred, BigNet must still record the consideration provided to Smallport's owners. When the subsidiary remains separate, the parent establishes an investment account that initially reflects the acquired firm's acquisition-date fair value. Because Smallport maintains its separate identity, BigNet prepares the following journal entries on its books to record the business combination.

LO 2-6c

Prepare the journal entry to record a business combination when the acquired firm retains its separate existence.

LO 2-7

Prepare a worksheet to consolidate the accounts of two companies that form a business combination in the absence of dissolution.

Acquisition Method—Subsidiary Is Not Dissolved

BigNet Company's Financial Records—December 31

Investment in Smallport Company (consideration transferred)	2,620,000	
Contingent Performance Liability.		20,000
Common Stock (26,000 shares issued by BigNet at $10 par value)		260,000
Additional Paid-In Capital (value of shares in excess of par value)		2,340,000
To record acquisition of Smallport Company, which maintains its separate legal identity.		
Professional Services Expense	40,000	
Cash (paid for third-party fees).		40,000
To record combination costs.		

As Exhibit 2.6 demonstrates, a worksheet can be prepared on the date of acquisition to arrive at consolidated totals for this combination. The entire process consists of six steps.

[25] The ASC (805-30-35-1) notes several reasons for contingent consideration including meeting an earnings target, reaching a specified share price, or reaching a milestone on a research and development project.

EXHIBIT 2.6   Acquisition Method—Date of Acquisition

Accounts	BigNet	Smallport	Consolidation Entries Debits	Consolidation Entries Credits	Consolidated Totals
Income Statement					
Revenues	(1,000,000)				(1,000,000)
Expenses	840,000*				840,000
Net income	(160,000)				(160,000)
Statement of Retained Earnings					
Retained earnings, 1/1	(870,000)				(870,000)
Net income (above)	(160,000)*				(160,000)
Dividends declared	110,000				110,000
Retained earnings, 12/31	(920,000)				(920,000)
Balance Sheet					
Current assets	1,060,000*	300,000			1,360,000
Investment in Smallport Company	2,620,000*	–0–		(S) 600,000	–0–
				(A) 2,020,000	
Computers and equipment	1,300,000	400,000	(A) 200,000		1,900,000
Capitalized software	500,000	100,000	(A) 1,100,000		1,700,000
Customer contracts	–0–	–0–	(A) 700,000		700,000
Goodwill	–0–	–0–	(A) 70,000		70,000
Total assets	5,480,000	800,000			5,730,000
Notes payable	(300,000)	(200,000)		(A) 50,000	(550,000)
Contingent performance liability	(20,000)*				(20,000)
Common stock	(1,860,000)*	(100,000)	(S) 100,000		(1,860,000)
Additional paid-in capital	(2,380,000)*	(20,000)	(S) 20,000		(2,380,000)
Retained earnings, 12/31 (above)	(920,000)	(480,000)	(S) 480,000		(920,000)
Total liabilities and equities	(5,480,000)	(800,000)	2,670,000	2,670,000	(5,730,000)

Note: Parentheses indicate a credit balance.
*Balances have been adjusted for consideration transferred and payment of direct acquisition costs. Also note follow-through effects to net income and retained earnings from the expensing of the direct acquisition costs.
(S) Elimination of Smallport's stockholders' equity accounts as of December 31 and book value portion of the investment account.
(A) Allocation of BigNet's consideration fair value in excess of book value.
Note: Parentheses indicate a credit balance.
*Balances have been adjusted for consideration transferred and payment of direct acquisition costs. Also note follow-through effects to net income and retained earnings from the expensing of the direct acquisition costs.
(S) Elimination of Smallport's stockholders' equity accounts as of December 31 and book value portion of the investment account.
(A) Allocation of BigNet's consideration fair value in excess of book value.

Step 1

Prior to constructing a worksheet, the parent prepares a formal allocation of the acquisition-date fair value similar to the equity method procedures presented in Chapter 1.[26] Thus, the following schedule is appropriate for BigNet's acquisition of Smallport:

Acquisition-Date Fair-Value Allocation Schedule		
Fair value of consideration transferred by BigNet		$2,620,000
Book value of Smallport (see Exhibit 2.3).		600,000
Excess of fair value over book value.		$2,020,000
Allocations made to specific accounts based on acquisition-date fair and book value differences (see Exhibit 2.3):		
Computers and equipment ($600,000 – $400,000).	$ 200,000	
Capitalized software ($1,200,000 – $100,000).	1,100,000	
Customer contracts ($700,000 – 0)	700,000	
Notes payable ($250,000 – $200,000).	(50,000)	1,950,000
Excess fair value not identified with specific items—Goodwill		$ 70,000

[26] This allocation procedure is helpful but not critical if dissolution occurs. The asset and liability accounts are simply added directly into the parent's books at their acquisition-date fair value with any excess assigned to goodwill as shown in the previous sections of this chapter.

Note that this schedule initially subtracts Smallport's acquisition-date book value. The resulting $2,020,000 difference represents the total amount needed on the Exhibit 2.6 worksheet to adjust Smallport's individual assets and liabilities from book value to fair value (and to recognize goodwill). Next, the schedule shows how this $2,020,000 total is allocated to adjust each individual item to fair value. The fair-value allocation schedule thus effectively serves as a convenient supporting schedule for the Exhibit 2.6 worksheet and is routinely prepared for every consolidation.

No part of the $2,020,000 excess fair value is attributed to the current assets because their book values equal their fair values. The Notes Payable account shows a negative allocation because the debt's present value exceeds its book value. An increase in debt decreases the fair value of the company's net assets.

Step 2

The consolidation process begins with preparing the first two columns of the worksheet (see Exhibit 2.6) containing the separate companies' acquisition-date book value financial figures (see Exhibit 2.3). BigNet's accounts have been adjusted for the journal entries recorded earlier for the investment and the combination costs. As another preliminary step, Smallport's revenue, expense, and dividend accounts have been closed into its Retained Earnings account. The subsidiary's operations prior to the December 31 takeover have no direct bearing on the operating results of the business combination. These activities occurred before Smallport was acquired; thus, the new owner should not include any precombination subsidiary revenues or expenses in the consolidated statements.

Step 3

Consolidation Entry S eliminates Smallport's stockholders' equity accounts (S is a reference to beginning subsidiary stockholders' equity) as follows:

Consolidation Entry S

Common Stock (Smallport Company)	100,000	
Additional Paid-In Capital (Smallport Company)	20,000	
Retained Earnings (Smallport Company)	480,000	
Investment in Smallport Company		600,000

Consolidation Entry S is a worksheet entry and accordingly does not affect the financial records of either company. The subsidiary balances (Common Stock, Additional Paid-In Capital, and Retained Earnings) represent ownership interests that are now held by the parent—thus they are not represented as equity in the parent's consolidated balance sheet. Moreover, by removing these account balances on the worksheet, only Smallport's assets and liabilities remain to be combined with the parent company figures.

Consolidation Entry S also removes the $600,000 component of the parent's Investment in Smallport Company account balance that equates to the book value of the subsidiary's net assets. For external reporting purposes, BigNet should include each of Smallport's assets and liabilities rather than a single investment balance. In effect, this portion of the parent's Investment in Smallport Company account balance is eliminated and replaced by the specific subsidiary assets and liabilities that are already listed in the second column of the worksheet.

Step 4

Consolidation Entry A removes the $2,020,000 excess payment in the Investment in Smallport Company and assigns it to the specific accounts indicated by the fair-value allocation schedule as follows:

Consolidation Entry A

Computers and Equipment	200,000	
Capitalized Software	1,100,000	
Customer Contracts	700,000	
Goodwill	70,000	
Note Payable		50,000
Investment in Smallport Company		2,020,000

Consequently, Computers and Equipment is increased by $200,000 to agree with Smallport's fair value: $1,100,000 is attributed to Capitalized Software, $700,000 to Customer Contracts, and $50,000 to Notes Payable. The unidentified excess of $70,000 is allocated to Goodwill. This entry for the consolidation worksheet is labeled Entry A to indicate that it represents the allocations made in connection with Smallport's acquisition-date fair value.

Consolidation Entry A also completes the Investment in Smallport Company account balance elimination on the worksheet. The investment remains on BigNet's books, but it does not appear on the consolidated balance sheet. Instead the investment account is replaced on the worksheet with Smallport's actual assets and liabilities as shown in Step 5.

Step 5

All accounts are extended into the Consolidated Totals column. For accounts such as Current Assets, this process simply adds Smallport and BigNet book values. However, when applicable, this extension also includes any allocations to establish the acquisition-date fair values of Smallport's assets and liabilities. Computers and Equipment, for example, is increased by $200,000. By increasing the subsidiary's book value to fair value, the reported balances are the same as in the previous examples when dissolution occurred. The use of a worksheet does not alter the consolidated figures but only the method of deriving those numbers.

Step 6

We subtract consolidated expenses from revenues to arrive at a $160,000 net income. Note that because this is an acquisition-date worksheet, we consolidate no amounts for Smallport's revenues and expenses. Having just been acquired, Smallport has not yet earned any income for BigNet owners. Consolidated revenues, expenses, and net income are identical to BigNet's balances. Subsequent to acquisition, of course, Smallport's revenue and expense accounts will be consolidated with BigNet's (coverage of this topic begins in Chapter 3).

Worksheet Mechanics

In general, totals (such as net income and ending retained earnings) are not directly consolidated across on the worksheet. Rather, the components (such as revenues and expenses) are extended across and then combined vertically to derive the appropriate figure. Net income is then carried down on the worksheet to the statement of retained earnings and used (along with beginning retained earnings and dividends) to compute the December 31 retained earnings balance. In the same manner, ending retained earnings of $920,000 is entered into the balance sheet to arrive at total liabilities and equities of $5,730,000, a number that reconciles with the total of consolidated assets.

Although it remains on BigNet's books, the Investment in Smallport account is eliminated entirely in consolidation. On the worksheet, the investment account is effectively replaced with the acquisition-date fair values of Smallport's assets and liabilities along with goodwill created by the combination.

The balances in the final column of Exhibit 2.6 are used to prepare consolidated financial statements for the business combination of BigNet Company and Smallport Company. The worksheet entries serve as a catalyst to bring together the two independent sets of financial information. The actual accounting records of both BigNet and Smallport remain unaltered by this consolidation process.

Bargain Purchase of a Separately Incorporated Subsidiary

Finally, although not addressed directly by the above example, bargain purchase gains can also occur in acquisitions of separately incorporated subsidiaries. If the consideration transferred is less than the fair value of a newly acquired subsidiary's identifiable net assets, then the parent records a bargain purchase gain on its books as part of the investment journal entry. The bargain purchase gain then appears on the the consolidated income statement for the reporting period that contains the acquisition date.

LO 2-8

Describe the accounting treatment for the various intangible assets often acquired in a business combination.

Acquisition-Date Fair-Value Allocations— Additional Issues

Intangibles

An important element of acquisition accounting is the acquirer's recognition and measurement of the assets acquired and liabilities assumed in the combination. In particular, the advent of the information age brings new measurement challenges for a host of intangible assets that provide value in generating future cash flows. Intangible assets often comprise the largest proportion of an acquired firm. For example, when AT&T acquired AT&T Broadband, it allocated approximately $19 billion of the $52 billion purchase price to franchise costs. These franchise costs form an intangible asset representing the value attributed to agreements with local authorities that allow access to homes.

Intangible assets include both current and noncurrent assets (not including financial instruments) that lack physical substance. In determining whether to recognize an intangible asset in a business combination, two specific criteria are essential.

1. Does the intangible asset arise from contractual or other legal rights?
2. Is the intangible asset capable of being sold or otherwise separated from the acquired enterprise?

Intangibles arising from contractual or legal rights are commonplace in business combinations. Often identified among the assets acquired are trademarks, patents, copyrights, franchise agreements, and a number of other intangibles that derive their value from governmental protection (or other contractual agreements) that allow a firm exclusive use of the asset. Most intangible assets recognized in business combinations meet the contractual-legal criterion.

Also seen in business combinations are intangible assets meeting the separability criterion. An acquired intangible asset is recognized if it is capable of being separated or divided from the acquiree and sold, transferred, licensed, rented, or exchanged individually or together with a related contract, identifiable asset, or liability. The acquirer is not required to have the intention to sell, license, or otherwise exchange the intangible in order to meet the separability criterion. For example, an acquiree may have developed internally a valuable customer list or other noncontractual customer relationships. Although the value of these items may not have arisen from a specific legal right, they nonetheless convey benefits to the acquirer that may be separable through sale, license, or exchange.

Exhibit 2.7 provides an extensive listing of intangible assets with indications of whether they typically meet the legal/contractual or separability criteria.

The FASB (Exposure Draft, *Business Combinations and Intangible Assets,* para. 271) recognized the inherent difficulties in estimating the separate fair values of many intangibles and stated that:

> difficulties may arise in assigning the acquisition cost to individual intangible assets acquired in a basket purchase such as a business combination. Measuring some of those assets is less difficult than measuring other assets, particularly if they are exchangeable and traded regularly in the marketplace. . . . Nonetheless, even those assets that cannot be measured on that basis may have more cash flow streams directly or indirectly associated with them than can be used as the basis for measuring them. While the resulting measures may lack the precision of other measures, they provide information that is more representationally faithful than would be the case if those assets were simply subsumed into goodwill on the grounds of measurement difficulties.

EXHIBIT 2.7   **Illustrative Examples of Intangible Assets That Meet the Criteria for Recognition Separately from Goodwill (FASB ASC paragraphs 805-20-55-11 through 45)**

The following are examples of intangible assets that meet the criteria for recognition as an asset apart from goodwill. The following illustrative list is not intended to be all-inclusive; thus, an acquired intangible asset could meet the recognition criteria of this statement but not be included on that list. Assets designated by the symbol (c) are those that would generally be recognized separately from goodwill because they meet the contractual-legal criterion. Assets designated by the symbol (s) do not arise from contractual or other legal rights but should nonetheless be recognized separately from goodwill because they meet the separability criterion. The determination of whether a specific acquired intangible asset meets the criteria in this statement for recognition apart from goodwill should be based on the facts and circumstances of each individual business combination.*

Marketing-Related Intangible Assets

1. Trademarks, trade names.c
2. Service marks, collective marks, certification marks.c
3. Trade dress (unique color, shape, or package design).c
4. Newspaper mastheads.c
5. Internet domain names.c
6. Noncompetition agreements.c

Customer-Related Intangible Assets

1. Customer lists.s
2. Order or production backlog.c
3. Customer contracts and related customer relationships.c
4. Noncontractual customer relationships.s

Artistic-Related Intangible Assets

1. Plays, operas, and ballets.c
2. Books, magazines, newspapers, and other literary works.c
3. Musical works such as compositions, song lyrics, and advertising jingles.c
4. Pictures and photographs.c
5. Video and audiovisual material, including motion pictures, music videos, and television programs.c

Contract-Based Intangible Assets

1. Licensing, royalty, standstill agreements.c
2. Advertising, construction, management, service, or supply contracts.c
3. Lease agreements.c
4. Construction permits.c
5. Franchise agreements.c
6. Operating and broadcast rights.c
7. Use rights such as landing, drilling, water, air, mineral, timber cutting, and route authorities.c
8. Servicing contracts such as mortgage servicing contracts.c
9. Employment contracts.c

Technology-Based Intangible Assets

1. Patented technology.c
2. Computer software and mask works.c
3. Unpatented technology.s
4. Databases, including title plants.s
5. Trade secrets, including secret formulas, processes, and recipes.c

*The intangible assets designated by the symbol (c) also could meet the separability criterion. However, separability is not a necessary condition for an asset to meet the contractual-legal criterion.

Undoubtedly, as our knowledge economy continues its rapid growth, asset allocations to items such as those identified in Exhibit 2.7 are expected to be frequent.

Preexisting Goodwill on Subsidiary's Books

In our examples of business combinations so far, the assets acquired and liabilities assumed have all been specifically identifiable (e.g., current assets, capitalized software, computers and equipment, customer contracts, and notes payable). However, in many cases, an acquired firm has an unidentifiable asset (i.e., goodwill recorded on its books in connection with a previous business combination of its own). A question arises as to the parent's treatment of this preexisting goodwill on the newly acquired subsidiary's books.

By its very nature, such preexisting goodwill is not considered identifiable by the parent. Therefore, in calculating the new goodwill acquired in the combination, the new owner simply excludes the carrying amount of any preexisting goodwill from the subsidiary's acquisition-date book value. The new owner effectively reallocates any preexisting subsidiary goodwill via a credit in consolidation worksheet Entry A. This worksheet credit to the subsidiary's goodwill balance is then offset by worksheet entries to identifiable assets and liabilities, followed by a debit to the new goodwill from the combination. The logic is that the total business fair value is first allocated to the identified assets and liabilities. Only if an excess amount remains after recognizing the fair values of the net identified assets is any goodwill recognized. Thus, in all business combinations, only goodwill reflected in the current acquisition is brought forward in the consolidated entity's financial reports.

Acquired In-Process Research and Development

The negotiations for a business combination begin with the identification of the tangible and intangible assets acquired and liabilities assumed by the acquirer. The fair values of the acquired individual assets and liabilities then provide the basis for financial statement valuations. Many firms—especially those in pharmaceutical and high-tech industries—have allocated significant portions of acquired businesses to in-process research and development (IPR&D).

Current accounting standards require that acquired IPR&D be measured at acquisition-date fair value and recognized in consolidated financial statements as an asset. However, this was not always the case. Past standards required immediate expense treatment for acquired IPR&D. Nonetheless, arguments about the future economic benefits of IPR&D ultimately persuaded the FASB to require asset recognition. For example, in commenting on the nature of IPR&D as an asset, Pfizer in an October 28, 2005, comment letter to the FASB observed that:

> board members know that companies frame business strategies around IPR&D, negotiate for it, pay for it, fair value it, and nurture it and they view those seemingly rational actions as inconsistent with the notion that IPR&D has no probable future economic benefit.

Asset recognition for acquired IPR&D is now standard even though benefits must be estimated and may be uncertain. To illustrate, when ARCA Biopharma acquired a significant in-process research and development asset through a merger with Nuvelo, Inc., it disclosed the following in its financial statements:

> A valuation firm was engaged to assist ARCA in determining the estimated fair values of these (IPR&D) assets as of the acquisition date. Discounted cash flow models are typically used in these valuations, and the models require the use of significant estimates and assumptions including but not limited to:

- Projecting regulatory approvals.
- Estimating future cash flows from product sales resulting from completed products and in-process projects.
- Developing appropriate discount rates and probability rates by project.

The IPR&D asset is initially considered an indefinite-lived intangible asset and is not subject to amortization. IPR&D is then tested for impairment annually or more frequently if events or changes in circumstances indicate that the asset might be impaired.

Recognizing acquired IPR&D as an asset is clearly consistent with the FASB's fair-value approach to acquisition accounting. Similar to costs that result in goodwill and other internally generated intangibles (e.g., customer lists, trade names, etc.), IPR&D costs are expensed as incurred in ongoing business activities. However, a business combination is considered a significant recognition event for which all fair values transferred in the transaction should be fully accounted for, including any values assigned to IPR&D. Moreover, because the acquirer paid for the IPR&D, an expectation of future economic benefit is assumed and, therefore, the amount is recognized as an asset.

To illustrate further, assume that ClearTone Company pays $2,300,000 in cash for all assets and liabilities of Newave, Inc., in a merger transaction. ClearTone manufactures components for cell phones. The primary motivation for the acquisition is a particularly attractive research and development project under way at Newave that will extend a cell phone's battery life by up to 50 percent. ClearTone hopes to combine the new technology with its manufacturing process and projects a resulting substantial revenue increase. ClearTone is optimistic that Newave will finish the project in the next two years. At the acquisition date, ClearTone prepares the following schedule that recognizes the items of value it expects to receive from the Newave acquisition:

Consideration transferred		$2,300,000
Receivables	$ 55,000	
Patents	220,000	
In-process research and development	1,900,000	
Accounts payable	(175,000)	
Fair value of identified net assets acquired		2,000,000
Goodwill		$ 300,000

ClearTone records the transaction as follows:

Receivables	55,000	
Patents	220,000	
Research and Development Asset	1,900,000	
Goodwill	300,000	
Accounts Payable		175,000
Cash		2,300,000

Research and development expenditures incurred subsequent to the date of acquisition will continue to be expensed. Acquired IPR&D assets initially should be considered indefinite-lived until the project is completed or abandoned. As with other indefinite-lived intangible assets, an acquired IPR&D asset is tested for impairment and is not amortized until its useful life is determined to be no longer indefinite.

Convergence between U.S. and International Accounting Standards

The FASB ASC Topics "Business Combinations" (805) and "Consolidation" (810) represent outcomes of a joint project between the FASB and the International Accounting Standards Board (IASB). The primary objective of the project was stated as follows:

> to develop a single high-quality standard for business combinations that can be used for both domestic and cross-border financial reporting. The goal is to develop a standard that includes a common set of principles and related guidance that produces decision-useful information and minimizes exceptions to those principles. The standard should improve the completeness, relevance, and comparability of financial information about business combinations . . . (FASB Project Updates: *Business Combinations: Applying the Acquisition Method—Joint Project of the IASB and FASB:* October 25, 2007)

The IASB subsequently issued International Financial Reporting Standard 3 (*IFRS 3*) Revised (effective July 2009), which along with FASB ASC Topics 805, "Business Combinations," and 810, "Consolidation," effectively converged the accounting for business combinations internationally. The two standards are identical in most important aspects of accounting for business combinations although differences can result in noncontrolling interest valuation and some other limited applications.[27] The joint project on business combinations represents one of the first successful implementations of the agreement between the two standard-setting groups to coordinate efforts on future work with the goal of developing high-quality comparable standards for both domestic and cross-border financial accounting.

Summary

1. Consolidation of financial information is required for external reporting purposes when one organization gains control of another, thus forming a single economic entity. In many combinations, all but one of the companies is dissolved as a separate legal corporation. Therefore, the consolidation process is carried out fully at the date of acquisition to bring together all accounts into a single set of financial records. In other combinations, the companies retain their identities as separate enterprises and continue to maintain their own separate accounting systems. For these cases, consolidation is a periodic process necessary whenever the parent produces external financial statements. This periodic procedure is frequently accomplished through the use of a worksheet and consolidation entries.

2. Current financial reporting standards require the acquisition method in accounting for business combinations. Under the acquisition method, the fair value of the consideration transferred provides the starting point for valuing the acquired firm. The fair value of the consideration transferred by the acquirer includes the fair value of any contingent consideration. The acquired company assets and liabilities are consolidated at their individual acquisition-date fair values. Direct combination costs are expensed as incurred because they are not part of the acquired business fair value. Also, the fair value of all acquired in-process research and development is recognized as an asset in business combinations and is subject to subsequent impairment reviews.

[27] Chapter 4 of this text provides further discussion of noncontrolling interest accounting differences across U.S. GAAP and IFRS. Other differences are presented in chapters where the applicable topics are covered.

3. If the consideration transferred for an acquired firm exceeds the total fair value of the acquired firm's net assets, the residual amount is recognized in the consolidated financial statements as goodwill, an intangible asset. When a bargain purchase occurs, individual assets and liabilities acquired continue to be recorded at their fair values and a gain on bargain purchase is recognized.

4. Particular attention should be given to the recognition of intangible assets in business combinations. An intangible asset must be recognized in an acquiring firm's financial statements if the asset arises from a legal or contractual right (e.g., trademarks, copyrights, artistic materials, royalty agreements). If the intangible asset does not represent a legal or contractual right, the intangible will still be recognized if it is capable of being separated from the firm (e.g., customer lists, noncontractual customer relationships, unpatented technology).

Comprehensive Illustration

Problem

(*Estimated Time: 45 to 65 Minutes*) Following are the account balances of Miller Company and Richmond Company as of December 31. The fair values of Richmond Company's assets and liabilities are also listed.

	Miller Company Book Values 12/31	Richmond Company Book Values 12/31	Richmond Company Fair Values 12/31
Cash	$ 600,000	$ 200,000	$ 200,000
Receivables	900,000	300,000	290,000
Inventory	1,100,000	600,000	820,000
Buildings and equipment (net)	9,000,000	800,000	900,000
Unpatented technology	–0–	–0–	500,000
In-process research and development	–0–	–0–	100,000
Accounts payable	(400,000)	(200,000)	(200,000)
Notes payable	(3,400,000)	(1,100,000)	(1,100,000)
Totals	$ 7,800,000	$ 600,000	$1,510,000
Common stock—$20 par value	$ (2,000,000)		
Common stock—$5 par value		$ (220,000)	
Additional paid-in capital	(900,000)	(100,000)	
Retained earnings, 1/1	(2,300,000)	(130,000)	
Revenues	(6,000,000)	(900,000)	
Expenses	3,400,000	750,000	
Totals	$ (7,800,000)	$ (600,000)	

Note: Parentheses indicate a credit balance.

Additional Information (not reflected in the preceding figures)

- On December 31, Miller issues 50,000 shares of its $20 par value common stock for all of the outstanding shares of Richmond Company.

- As part of the acquisition agreement, Miller agrees to pay the former owners of Richmond $250,000 if certain profit projections are realized over the next three years. Miller calculates the acquisition-date fair value of this contingency at $100,000.

- In creating this combination, Miller pays $10,000 in stock issue costs and $20,000 in accounting and legal fees.

Required

a. Miller's stock has a fair value of $32 per share. Using the acquisition method:
  1. Prepare the necessary journal entries if Miller dissolves Richmond so it is no longer a separate legal entity.
  2. Assume instead that Richmond will retain separate legal incorporation and maintain its own accounting systems. Prepare a worksheet to consolidate the accounts of the two companies.

b. If Miller's stock has a fair value of $26 per share, describe how the consolidated balances would differ from the results in requirement (a).

Solution

a. 1. In a business combination, the accountant first determines the total fair value of the consideration transferred. Because Miller's stock is valued at $32 per share, the 50,000 issued shares are worth $1,600,000 in total. Included in the consideration transferred is the $100,000 acquisition-date fair value of the contingent performance obligation.

This $1,700,000 total fair value is compared to the $1,510,000 fair value of Richmond's assets and liabilities (including the fair value of IPR&D). Miller recognizes the $190,000 excess fair value ($1,700,000 − $1,510,000) as goodwill. Because dissolution occurs, Miller records on its books the individual fair values of Richmond's identifiable assets and liabilities with the excess recorded as goodwill.

The $10,000 stock issue cost reduces Additional Paid-In Capital. The $20,000 direct combination costs (accounting and legal fees) are expensed when incurred.

Miller Company's Financial Records—December 31

Cash	200,000	
Receivables	290,000	
Inventory	820,000	
Buildings and Equipment	900,000	
Unpatented Technology	500,000	
Research and Development Asset	100,000	
Goodwill	190,000	
Accounts Payable		200,000
Notes Payable		1,100,000
Contingent Performance Obligation		100,000
Common Stock (Miller) (par value)		1,000,000
Additional Paid-In Capital (fair value in excess of par value)		600,000
To record acquisition of Richmond Company		
Professional Services Expense	20,000	
Cash (paid for combination costs)		20,000
To record legal and accounting fees related to the combination.		
Additional Paid-In Capital	10,000	
Cash (stock issuance costs)		10,000
To record payment of stock issuance costs.		

2. Under this scenario, the acquisition fair value is equal to that computed in part (*a*1).

50,000 shares of stock at $32.00 each	$1,600,000
Contingent performance obligation	100,000
Acquisition-date fair value of consideration transferred	$1,700,000

Because the subsidiary is maintaining separate incorporation, Miller establishes an investment account to reflect the $1,700,000 acquisition consideration:

Miller's Financial Records—December 31

Investment in Richmond Company	1,700,000	
Contingent Performance Obligation		100,000
Common Stock (Miller) (par value)		1,000,000
Additional Paid-In Capital (fair value in excess of par value)		600,000
To record investment in Richmond Company.		
Professional Services Expense	20,000	
Cash (paid for combination costs)		20,000
To record legal and accounting fees related to the combination.		
Additional Paid-In Capital	10,000	
Cash (stock issuance costs)		10,000
To record payment of stock issuance costs.		

Because Richmond maintains separate incorporation and its own accounting system, Miller prepares a worksheet for consolidation. To prepare the worksheet, Miller first allocates Richmond's fair value to assets acquired and liabilities assumed based on their individual fair values:

Fair value of consideration transferred by Miller......	$1,700,000
Book value of Richmond	600,000
Excess fair value over book value..................	$1,100,000

Allocations are made to specific accounts based on differences in fair values and book values:

Receivables ($290,000 – $300,000).......................	$(10,000)	
Inventory ($820,000 – $600,000).........................	220,000	
Buildings and equipment ($900,000 – $800,000).............	100,000	
Unpatented technology ($500,000 – 0)	500,000	
In-process research and development	100,000	910,000
Goodwill		$190,000

The following steps produce the consolidated financial statements total in Exhibit 2.8:

Exhibit 2.8   Comprehensive Illustration—Solution—Acquisition Method

MILLER COMPANY AND RICHMOND COMPANY
Consolidation Worksheet
For Period Ending December 31

Accounts	Miller Company	Richmond Company	Consolidation Entries Debit	Consolidation Entries Credit	Consolidated Totals
Income Statement					
Revenues	(6,000,000)				(6,000,000)
Expenses	3,420,000*				3,420,000*
Net income	(2,580,000)				(2,580,000)
Statement of Retained Earnings					
Retained earnings, 1/1	(2,300,000)				(2,300,000)
Net income (above)	(2,580,000)				(2,580,000)
Retained earnings, 12/31	(4,880,000)				(4,880,000)
Balance Sheet					
Cash	570,000*	200,000			770,000
Receivables	900,000	300,000		(A) 10,000	1,190,000
Inventory	1,100,000	600,000	(A) 220,000		1,920,000
Investment in Richmond Company	1,700,000*	–0–		(A) 1,100,000	–0–
				(S) 600,000	
Buildings and equipment (net)	9,000,000	800,000	(A) 100,000		9,900,000
Goodwill	–0–	–0–	(A) 190,000		190,000
Unpatented technology	–0–	–0–	(A) 500,000		500,000
Research and development asset	–0–	–0–	(A) 100,000		100,000
Total assets	13,270,000	1,900,000			14,570,000
Accounts payable	(400,000)	(200,000)			(600,000)
Notes payable	(3,400,000)	(1,100,000)			(4,500,000)
Contingent performance obligation	(100,000)*	–0–			(100,000)
Common stock	(3,000,000)*	(220,000)	(S) 220,000		(3,000,000)
Additional paid-in capital	(1,490,000)*	(100,000)	(S) 100,000		(1,490,000)
Retained earnings, 12/31 (above)	(4,880,000)*	(280,000)†	(S) 280,000		(4,880,000)
Total liabilities and equities	(13,270,000)	(1,900,000)	1,710,000	1,710,000	(14,570,000)

Note: Parentheses indicate a credit balance.
*Balances have been adjusted for issuance of stock, payment of combination expenses, and recognition of contingent performance obligation.
†Beginning retained earnings plus revenues minus expenses.

- Miller's balances have been updated on this worksheet to include the effects of both the newly issued shares of stock, the recognition of the contingent performance liability, and the combination expenses.
- Richmond's revenue and expense accounts have been closed to Retained Earnings. The acquisition method consolidates only postacquisition revenues and expenses.
- Worksheet Entry S eliminates the $600,000 book value component of the Investment in Richmond Company account along with the subsidiary's stockholders' equity accounts.

  Entry A adjusts all of Richmond's assets and liabilities to fair value based on the allocations determined earlier.

b. If the fair value of Miller's stock is $26.00 per share, then the fair value of the consideration transferred in the Richmond acquisition is recomputed as follows:

Fair value of shares issued ($26 × 50,000 shares)	$1,300,000
Fair value of contingent consideration	100,000
Total consideration transferred at fair value	$1,400,000

Because the consideration transferred is $110,000 less than the $1,510,000 fair value of the net assets received in the acquisition, a bargain purchase has occurred. In this situation, Miller continues to recognize each of the separately identified assets acquired and liabilities assumed at their fair values. Resulting differences in the consolidated balances relative to the requirement (*a*) solution are as follows:

- The $110,000 excess fair value recognized over the consideration transferred is recognized as a "gain on bargain purchase."
- Consolidated net income increases by the $110,000 gain to $2,690,000.
- No goodwill is recognized.
- Miller's additional paid-in capital decreases by $300,000 to $1,190,000.
- Consolidated retained earnings increase by the $110,000 gain to $4,990,000.

Also, because of the bargain purchase, the "Investment in Richmond Company" account balance on Miller's separate financial statements shows the $1,510,000 fair value of the net identified assets received. This valuation measure is an exception to the general rule of using the consideration transferred to provide the valuation basis for the acquired firm.

Appendix A

LO 2-9

Identify the general characteristics of the legacy purchase and pooling of interest methods of accounting for past business combinations. Understand the effects that persist today in financial statements from the use of these legacy methods.

Legacy Methods of Accounting For Business Combinations

The acquisition method provides the accounting for business combinations occurring in 2009 and thereafter. However, for decades, business combinations were accounted for using either the **purchase** or **pooling of interests** method. From 2002 through 2008, the purchase method was used exclusively for business combinations. Prior to 2002, financial reporting standards allowed two alternatives: the purchase method and the pooling of interests method. Because the FASB required prospective application of the acquisition method for 2009 and beyond, the purchase and pooling of interests methods continue to provide the basis for financial reporting for pre-2009 business combinations and thus will remain relevant for many years. Literally tens of thousands of past business combinations will continue to be reported in future statements under one of these legacy methods.

The following sections describe the purchase and pooling of interests methods along with comparisons to the acquisition method.

The Purchase Method: An Application of the Cost Principle

A basic principle of the purchase method was to record a business combination at the cost to the new owners. For example, several years ago MGM Grand, Inc., acquired Mirage Resorts, Inc., for approximately $6.4 billion. This purchase price continued to serve as the valuation basis for Mirage Resorts' assets and liabilities in the preparation of MGM Grand's consolidated financial statements.

Several elements of the purchase method reflect a strict application of the cost principle. The following items represent examples of how the cost-based purchase method differs from the fair-value–based acquisition method.

- Acquisition date allocations (including bargain purchases).
- Direct combination costs.
- Contingent consideration.
- In-process research and development.

We next briefly discuss the accounting treatment for these items across the current and previous financial reporting regimes.

Purchase-Date Cost Allocations (Including Bargain Purchases)

In pre-2009 business combinations, the application of the cost principle often was complicated because literally hundreds of separate assets and liabilities were acquired. Accordingly, for asset valuation and future income determination, firms needed a basis to allocate the total cost among the various assets and liabilities received in the bargained exchange. Similar to the acquisition method, the purchase method based its cost allocations on the combination-date fair values of the acquired assets and liabilities. Also closely related to the acquisition method procedures, any excess of cost over the sum of the net identified asset fair values was attributed to goodwill.

But the purchase method stands in marked contrast to the acquisition method in bargain purchase situations. Under the purchase method, a bargain purchase occurred when the sum of the individual fair values of the acquired net assets exceeded the purchase cost. To record a bargain purchase at cost, however, the purchase method required that certain long-term assets be recorded at amounts below their assessed fair values.

For example, assume Adams Co. paid $520,000 for Brook Co. in 2008. Brook has the following assets with appraised fair values:

Accounts receivable	$ 15,000
Land	200,000
Building	400,000
Accounts payable	(5,000)
Total net fair value	$610,000

However, to record the combination at its $520,000 cost, Adams cannot use all of the above fair values. The purchase method solution was to require that Adams reduce the valuation assigned to the acquired long-term assets (land and building) proportionately by $90,000 ($610,000 − $520,000). The total fair value of the long-term assets, in this case $600,000, provided the basis for allocating the reduction. Thus, Adams would reduce the acquired land by (2/6 × $90,000) = $30,000 and the building by (4/6 × $90,000) = $60,000. Adams's journal entry to record the combination using the purchase method would then be as follows:

Accounts Receivable	15,000	
Land ($200,000 − $30,000)	170,000	
Building ($400,000 − $60,000)	340,000	
Accounts Payable		5,000
Cash		520,000

Note that current assets and liabilities did not share in the proportionate reduction to cost. Long-term assets were subject to the reduction because their fair-value estimates were considered less reliable than current items and liabilities. Finally, in rare situations firms recognized an extraordinary gain on a purchase, but only in the very unusual case that the long-term assets were reduced to a zero valuation.

In contrast, the acquisition method embraces the fair-value concept and discards the consideration transferred as a valuation basis for the business acquired in a bargain purchase. Instead, the acquirer measures and recognizes the fair values of each of the assets acquired and liabilities assumed at the date of combination, regardless of the consideration transferred in the transaction. As a result, (1) no assets are recorded at amounts below their assessed fair values, as is the case with bargain purchases accounted for by the purchase method, and (2) a gain on bargain purchase is recognized at the acquisition date.

Direct Combination Costs

Almost all business combinations employ professional services to assist in various phases of the transaction. Examples include target identification, due diligence regarding the value of an acquisition, financing, tax planning, and preparation of formal legal documents. Prior to 2009, under the purchase method, the investment cost basis included direct combination costs. In contrast, the acquisition method considers these costs as payments for services received, not part of the fair value exchanged for the business. Thus, under the acquisition method, direct combination costs are expensed as incurred.

Contingent Consideration

Often business combination negotiations result in agreements to provide additional payments to former owners if they meet specified future performance measures. The purchase method accounted for such contingent consideration obligations as postcombination adjustments to the purchase cost (or stockholders' equity if the contingency involved the parent's equity share value) upon resolution of the contingency. The acquisition method treats contingent consideration obligations as a negotiated component of the fair value of the consideration transferred, consistent with the fair-value measurement attribute.

In-Process Research and Development (IPR&D)

Prior to 2009, financial reporting standards required the immediate expensing of acquired IPR&D if the project had not yet reached technological feasibility and the assets had no future alternative uses. Expensing acquired IPR&D was consistent with the accounting treatment for a firm's ongoing research and development costs.

The acquisition method, however, requires tangible and intangible assets acquired in a business combination to be used in a particular research and development activity, including those that may have no alternative future use, to be recognized and measured at fair value at the acquisition date. These capitalized research and development costs are reported as intangible assets with indefinite lives subject to periodic impairment reviews. Moreover, because the acquirer identified and paid for the IPR&D, the acquisition method assumes an expectation of future economic benefit and therefore recognizes an asset.

The Pooling of Interests Method: Continuity of Previous Ownership

Historically, former owners of separate firms would agree to combine for their mutual benefit and continue as owners of a combined firm. It was asserted that the assets and liabilities of the former firms were never really bought or sold; former owners merely exchanged ownership shares to become joint owners of the combined firm. Combinations characterized by exchange of voting shares and continuation of previous ownership became known as pooling of interests. Rather than an exchange transaction with one ownership group replacing another, a pooling of interests was characterized by a continuity of ownership interests before and after the business combination. Prior to its elimination, this method was applied to a significant number of business combinations.[26] To reflect the continuity of ownership, two important steps characterized the pooling of interests method:

1. The book values of the assets and liabilities of both companies became the book values reported by the combined entity.
2. The revenue and expense accounts were combined retrospectively as well as prospectively. The idea of continuity of ownership gave support for the recognition of income accruing to the owners both before and after the combination.

Therefore, in a pooling, reported income was typically higher than under the contemporaneous purchase accounting. Under pooling, not only did the firms retrospectively combine incomes, but also the smaller asset bases resulted in smaller depreciation and amortization expenses. Because net income reported in financial statements often is used in a variety of contracts, including managerial compensation, managers considered the pooling method an attractive alternative to purchase accounting.

Prior to 2002, accounting and reporting standards allowed both the purchase and pooling of interest methods for business combinations. However, standard setters established strict criteria for use of the pooling method. The criteria were designed to prevent managers from engaging in purchase transactions and then reporting them as poolings of interests. Business combinations that failed to meet the pooling criteria had to be accounted for by the purchase method.

These criteria had two overriding objectives. First, to ensure the complete fusion of the two organizations, one company had to obtain substantially all (90 percent or more) of the voting stock of the other. The second general objective of these criteria was to prevent purchase combinations from being disguised as poolings. Past experience had shown that combination transactions were frequently manipulated so that they would qualify for pooling of interests treatment (usually to increase reported earnings). However, subsequent events, often involving cash being paid or received by the parties, revealed the true nature of the combination: One company was purchasing the other in a bargained exchange. A number of qualifying criteria for pooling of interests treatment were designed to stop this practice.

---

[26] Past prominent business combinations accounted for by the pooling of interests method include Exxon-Mobil, Pfizer-Warner Lambert, Yahoo!-Broadcast.com, and Pepsi-Quaker Oats, among thousands of others.

EXHIBIT 2.9
Precombination
Information for Baker
Company

January 1	Book Values	Fair Values
Current assets	$ 30,000	$ 30,000
Internet domain name	160,000	300,000
Licensing agreements	–0–	500,000
In-process research and development	–0–	200,000
Notes payable	(25,000)	(25,000)
Total net assets	$165,000	$1,005,000

Note: Parentheses indicate a credit balance.

Comparisons across the Pooling of Interests, Purchase, and Acquisition Methods

To illustrate some of the differences across the purchase, pooling of interests, and acquisition methods, assume that on January 1, Archer Inc. acquired Baker Company in exchange for 10,000 shares of its $1.00 par common stock having a fair value of $1,200,000 in a transaction structured as a merger. In connection with the acquisition, Archer paid $25,000 in legal and accounting fees. Also, Archer agreed to pay the former owners additional cash consideration contingent upon the completion of Baker's existing contracts at specified profit margins. The current fair value of the contingent obligation was estimated to be $150,000. Exhibit 2.9 provides Baker's combination-date book values and fair values.

Purchase Method Applied

Archer's valuation basis for its purchase of Baker is computed and allocated as follows:

Fair value of shares issued		$1,200,000
Direct combination costs (legal and accounting fees)		25,000
Cost of the Baker purchase		$1,225,000
Cost allocation:		
Current assets	$ 30,000	
Internet domain name	300,000	
Licensing agreements	500,000	
Research and development expense	200,000	
Notes payable	(25,000)	
Total net fair value of items acquired		1,005,000
Goodwill		$ 220,000

Note the following characteristics of the purchase method from the above schedule.

- The valuation basis is cost and includes direct combination costs but excludes the contingent consideration.
- The cost is allocated to the assets acquired and liabilities assumed based on their individual fair values (unless a bargain purchase occurs and then the long-term items may be recorded as amounts less than their fair values).
- Goodwill is the excess of cost over the fair values of the net assets purchased.
- Acquired in-process research and development is expensed immediately at the purchase date.

Pooling of Interests Method Applied

Because a purchase sale was deemed not to occur, the pooling method relied on previously recorded values reflecting a continuation of previous ownership. Thus, the following asset would be recorded by Archer in a business combination accounted for as a pooling of interests.

	Values Assigned
Current assets	$ 30,000
Internet domain name	160,000
Licensing agreements	–0–
In-process research and development	–0–
Notes payable	(25,000)
Total value assigned within the combination	$165,000

Note the following characteristics of the pooling of interests method from the above schedule.

- Because a pooling of interests was predicated on a continuity of ownership, the accounting incorporated a continuation of previous book values and ignored fair values exchanged in a business combination.
- Previously unrecognized (typically internally developed) intangibles continue to be reported at a zero value postcombination.
- Because the pooling of interests method values an acquired firm at its previously recorded book value, no new amount for goodwill was ever recorded in a pooling.

Acquisition Method Applied

According to the acquisition method, Archer's valuation basis for its acquisition of Baker is computed as follows:

Fair value of shares issued		$1,200,000
Fair value of contingent performance obligation		150,000
Total consideration transferred for the Baker acquisition		$1,350,000
Cost allocation:		
Current assets.	$ 30,000	
Internet domain name	300,000	
Licensing agreements	500,000	
Research and development asset.	200,000	
Notes payable.	(25,000)	
Total net fair value of items acquired		1,005,000
Goodwill		$ 345,000

Note the following characteristics of the acquisition method from the above schedule.

- The valuation basis is fair value of consideration transferred and includes the contingent consideration but excludes direct combination costs.
- The assets acquired and liabilities assumed are recorded at their individual fair values.
- Goodwill is the excess of the consideration transferred over the fair values of the net assets acquired.
- Acquired in-process research and development is recognized as an asset.
- Professional service fees to help accomplish the acquisition are expensed.

The following table compares the amounts from Baker that Archer would include in its combination-date consolidated financial statements under the pooling of interests method, the purchase method, and the acquisition method.

	Values Incorporated in Archer's Consolidated Balance Sheet Resulting from the Baker Transaction		
	Pooling of Interests Method	**Purchase Method**	**Acquisition Method**
Current assets	$ 30,000	$ 30,000	$ 30,000
Internet domain name	160,000	300,000	300,000
Licensing agreements	–0–	500,000	500,000
In-process research and development asset*	–0–	–0–	200,000
Goodwill	–0–	220,000	345,000
Notes payable	(25,000)	(25,000)	(25,000)
Contingent performance obligation	–0–	–0–	(150,000)
Total net assets recognized by Archer	$165,000	$1,025,000	$1,200,000

*Acquired in-process research and development was expensed under the purchase method and not recognized at all under the pooling of interests method.

Several comparisons should be noted across these methods of accounting for business combinations:

- In consolidating Baker's assets and liabilities, the purchase and acquisition methods record fair values. In contrast, the pooling method uses previous book values and ignores fair values. Consequently, although a fair value of $1,350,000 is exchanged, only a net value of $165,000 (assets less liabilities) is reported in the pooling.

- The pooling method, as reflected in the preceding example, typically shows smaller asset values and consequently lowers future depreciation and amortization expenses. Thus, higher future net income was usually reported under the pooling method compared to similar situations that employed the purchase method.

- Under pooling, financial ratios such as Net Income/Total Assets were dramatically inflated. Not only was this ratio's denominator understated through failure to recognize internally developed assets acquired (and fair values in general), but the numerator was overstated through smaller depreciation and amortization expenses.

- Although not shown, the pooling method retrospectively combined the acquired firm's revenues, expenses, dividends, and retained earnings. The purchase and acquisition methods incorporate only postcombination values for these operational items. Also all costs of the combination (direct and indirect acquisition costs and stock issue costs) were expensed in the period of combination under the pooling of interests method.

- Finally, with adoption of the acquisition method, the FASB has moved clearly in the direction of increased management accountability for the fair values of all assets acquired and liabilities assumed in a business combination.

Appendix B

Pushdown Accounting

In the analysis of business combinations to this point, discussion has focused on (1) the recording of the combination by the parent company and (2) required consolidation procedures. An additional reporting issue, however, arises concerning the separate postacquisition financial statements of subsidiary companies than maintain separate incorporation.

This issue has become especially significant in recent years because of business acquisitions by private-equity firms. An organization, for example, might acquire a company, work to improve its business model, and subsequently offer the shares back to the public in hopes of making a large profit. What valuation basis should be used in reporting the subsidiary's financial statements that accompany the initial public offering? In other situations, a subsidiary company may need to provide its own separate financial statements in connection with a new public debt issue. Should the subsidiary's financial statements utilize the new basis of accounting that the parent company established in the acquisition or continue its financial statement carrying amounts established prior to the acquisition?

To illustrate, assume that Strand Company owns one asset: a production machine with a carrying amount of $200,000 but a fair value of $900,000. Parker Corporation pays exactly $900,000 in cash to acquire Strand. Consolidation offers no real problem here: The machine will be reported by the business combination at $900,000.

However, if Strand continues to issue separate financial statements (for example, to its creditors or potential stockholders), should the machine be reported at $200,000 or $900,000? If adjusted, should the $700,000 increase be reported as a gain by the subsidiary or as an addition to contributed capital? Should depreciation be based on $200,000 or $900,000? If the subsidiary is to be viewed as a new entity with a new basis for its assets and liabilities, should Retained Earnings be returned to zero? If the parent acquires only 51 percent of Strand, does that change the answers to the previous questions?

Proponents of pushdown accounting argue that a change in ownership creates a new basis for subsidiary assets and liabilities. An unadjusted balance ($200,000 in the preceding illustration) is a cost figure applicable to previous stockholders. That amount is no longer relevant information. Rather, according to this argument, the fair value at the date control of the company changes is now relevant, a figure best reflected by the consideration transferred to acquire the subsidiary. Balance sheet accounts should be reported at the asset's acquisition-date fair value. ($900,000 in the illustration) rather than the cost incurred by the previous owners of the company. Moreover, the subsidiary can now recognize any previously unrecognized intangible assets as valued by its new owner concurrently with the acquisition.

External Reporting Option for Pushdown Accounting

To address the valuation issues for a subsidiary's separately issued financial statements, the FASB issued Accounting Standards Update (ASU) No. 2014-17, *Business Combinations: Pushdown Accounting* in November 2014. The ASU does not require pushdown accounting, but instead provides an option to apply pushdown accounting following a business combination in which the acquirer obtains control of an acquired entity and the acquired entity maintains separate incorporation. A newly acquired entity (e.g., subsidiary firm) may elect the option to apply pushdown accounting in the reporting period immediately following the acquisition.[27] Alternatively, a newly acquired company may simply choose to continue using its previous accounting valuations in separately issued financial statements.

When an acquired entity elects to apply pushdown accounting, it reflects in its financial statements the valuations for the individual assets and liabilities used by the parent in allocating the consideration transferred in the acquisition. Thus, the parent's acquisition-date valuations for its newly acquired subsidiary are "pushed down" to the subsidiary's financial statements.

As discussed below, the FASB (ASC 805-50-30) provides particular guidance for three accounting issues: goodwill, bargain purchase gains, and acquisition-related liabilities. We then discuss other accounting issues including acquisition-date retained earnings and other owners' equity effects.

Goodwill

When an entity elects pushdown accounting, any goodwill recognized in the combination is reported in the acquired entity's separate financial statements.

Bargain Purchase Gains

An exception to pushdown accounting's general rule of using the parent's valuations for the subsidiary's separate financial statement occurs for bargain purchases. Recall that when the fair values assigned to the subsidiary's collective net assets exceeds the parent's consideration transferred, the parent recognizes a bargain purchase gain on its income statement. In this case, however, pushdown accounting requires that the acquired entity not recognize the gain in its income statement, but instead as an adjustment to its additional paid-in capital. The reflection of the bargain purchase gain in additional paid-in capital prevents income recognition by both the acquirer and the acquiree for the same event.

Acquisition-Related Liabilities

When acquisition-related liabilities arise, pushdown accounting recognizes only the debt that the acquired firm must recognize under other generally accepted accounting principles. Thus if an acquired firm is either jointly or severally liable for repayment of the debt, such debt is pushed down to its separate financial statements, possibly including debt incurred by the acquirer.

Acquisition-Date Subsidiary Retained Earnings

After recognizing the new basis for its assets and liabilities, the acquired firm must then report the effects of the acquisition in its owners' equity section. Because pushdown accounting treats the acquired firm as a new reporting entity, the acquired firm reports zero acquisition-date retained earnings. The elimination of acquisition-date subsidiary retained earnings is consistent with consolidated financial reporting.

Additional Paid-In Capital from Pushdown Accounting

The overall effect of the combined pushdown accounting adjustments to the previous carrying amounts of the subsidiary's assets and liabilities then is reported as an adjustment to the subsidiary's additional paid-in capital attributable to the common shareholders. For example, a subsidiary may report "Additional paid-in capital from pushdown accounting" in its separate balance sheet. The total effect in the additional paid-in capital from pushdown accounting results from both the elimination of acquisition-date retained earnings and the revaluation of the acquired firm's assets and liabilities to the parent's basis.

---

[27] The acquired entity can also elect to apply pushdown accounting in periods subsequent to the acquisition, but must report the election as a retrospective change in accounting principle (ASC Topic 250, Accounting Changes and Error Corrections). Once made, the decision to apply pushdown accounting to a specific change-in-control event is irrevocable.

EXHIBIT 2.10
Pushdown Accounting—
Date of Acquisition

Smallport Company Balance Sheet at January 1	
Current assets	$ 300,000
Computers and equipment	600,000
Capitalized software	1,200,000
Customer contracts	700,000
Goodwill	70,000
Total assets	$ 2,870,000
Liabilities	$ (250,000)
Common stock	(100,000)
Additional paid-in capital excess over par	(20,000)
Additional paid-in capital from pushdown accounting	(2,500,000)
Retained earnings, 1/1	–0–
Total liabilities and equities	$ 2,870,000

Example: Pushdown Accounting

To illustrate an application of pushdown accounting, we use the Exhibit 2.3 BigNet and Smallport Company example presented previously in this chapter. If Smallport Company applies pushdown accounting, its acquisition-date separately reported balance sheet would appear as presented in Exhibit 2.10:

Note that the values for each asset and liability in Smallport's separate balance sheet above are identical to those reported in BigNet's consolidated acquisition-date balance sheet.

Internal Reporting

Pushdown accounting has several advantages for internal reporting. For example, it simplifies the consolidation process. If the subsidiary enters the acquisition-date fair value allocations into its records, worksheet Entry A (to recognize the allocations originating from the fair-value adjustments) is not needed. Amortizations of the excess fair value allocation (see Chapter 3) would be incorporated in subsequent periods as well.

Despite some simplifications to the consolidation process, pushdown accounting does not address the many issues in preparing consolidated financial statements that appear in subsequent chapters of this text. Therefore, it remains to be seen how many acquired companies will choose to elect pushdown accounting. For newly acquired subsidiaries that expect to issue new debt or eventually undergo an initial public offering, fair values may provide investors with a better understanding of the company.

In summary, pushdown accounting provides a newly acquired subsidiary the option to revalue its assets and liabilities to acquisition-date fair values in its separately reported financial statements. This valuation option may be useful when the parent expects to offer the subsidiary shares to the public following a period of planned improvements. Other benefits from pushdown accounting may arise when the subsidiary plans to issue debt and needs its separate financial statements to incorporate acquisition-date fair values and previously unrecognized intangibles in their standalone financial reports.

Questions

1. What is a business combination?
2. Describe the different types of legal arrangements that can take place to create a business combination.
3. What does the term *consolidated financial statements* mean?
4. Within the consolidation process, what is the purpose of a worksheet?
5. Jones Company obtains all of the common stock of Hudson, Inc., by issuing 50,000 shares of its own stock. Under these circumstances, why might the determination of a fair value for the consideration transferred be difficult?
6. What is the accounting valuation basis for consolidating assets and liabilities in a business combination?
7. How should a parent consolidate its subsidiary's revenues and expenses?
8. Morgan Company acquires all of the outstanding shares of Jennings, Inc., for cash. Morgan transfers consideration more than the fair value of the company's net assets. How should the payment in excess of fair value be accounted for in the consolidation process?
9. Catron Corporation is having liquidity problems, and as a result, it sells all of its outstanding stock to Lambert, Inc., for cash. Because of Catron's problems, Lambert is able to acquire this stock at less than the fair value of the company's net assets. How is this reduction in price accounted for within the consolidation process?

10. Sloane, Inc., issues 25,000 shares of its own common stock in exchange for all of the outstanding shares of Benjamin Company. Benjamin will remain a separately incorporated operation. How does Sloane record the issuance of these shares?

11. To obtain all of the stock of Molly, Inc., Harrison Corporation issued its own common stock. Harrison had to pay $98,000 to lawyers, accountants, and a stock brokerage firm in connection with services rendered during the creation of this business combination. In addition, Harrison paid $56,000 in costs associated with the stock issuance. How will these two costs be recorded?

Problems

LO 2-1

1. Which of the following does not represent a primary motivation for business combinations?
   a. Combinations are often a vehicle to accelerate growth and competitiveness.
   b. Cost savings can be achieved through elimination of duplicate facilities and staff.
   c. Synergies may be available through quick entry for new and existing products into markets.
   d. Larger firms are less likely to fail.

LO 2-2

2. Which of the following is the best theoretical justification for consolidated financial statements?
   a. In form the companies are one entity; in substance they are separate.
   b. In form the companies are separate; in substance they are one entity.
   c. In form and substance the companies are one entity.
   d. In form and substance the companies are separate. (AICPA)

LO 2-3

3. What is a statutory merger?
   a. A merger approved by the Securities and Exchange Commission.
   b. An acquisition involving the purchase of both stock and assets.
   c. A takeover completed within one year of the initial tender offer.
   d. A business combination in which only one company continues to exist as a legal entity.

LO 2-4

4. FASB ASC 805, "Business Combinations," provides principles for allocating the fair value of an acquired business. When the collective fair values of the separately identified assets acquired and liabilities assumed exceed the fair value of the consideration transferred, the difference should be:
   a. Recognized as an ordinary gain from a bargain purchase.
   b. Treated as negative goodwill to be amortized over the period benefited, not to exceed 40 years.
   c. Treated as goodwill and tested for impairment on an annual basis.
   d. Applied pro rata to reduce, but not below zero, the amounts initially assigned to specific non-current assets of the acquired firm.

LO 2-8

5. What is the appropriate accounting treatment for the value assigned to in-process research and development acquired in a business combination?
   a. Expense upon acquisition.
   b. Capitalize as an asset.
   c. Expense if there is no alternative use for the assets used in the research and development and technological feasibility has yet to be reached.
   d. Expense until future economic benefits become certain and then capitalize as an asset.

LO 2-8

6. An acquired entity has a long-term operating lease for an office building used for central management. The terms of the lease are very favorable relative to current market rates. However, the lease prohibits subleasing or any other transfer of rights. In its financial statements, the acquiring firm should report the value assigned to the lease contract as
   a. An intangible asset under the contractual-legal criterion.
   b. A part of goodwill.
   c. An intangible asset under the separability criterion.
   d. A building.

LO 2-4

7. When does gain recognition accompany a business combination?
   a. When a bargain purchase occurs.
   b. In a combination created in the middle of a fiscal year.
   c. In an acquisition when the value of all assets and liabilities cannot be determined.
   d. When the amount of a bargain purchase exceeds the value of the applicable noncurrent assets (other than certain exceptions) held by the acquired company.

LO 2-6b

8. According to the acquisition method of accounting for business combinations, costs paid to attorneys and accountants for services in arranging a merger should be
   a. Capitalized as part of the overall fair value acquired in the merger.
   b. Recorded as an expense in the period the merger takes place.

     c. Included in recognized goodwill.

     d. Written off over a five-year maximum useful life.

LO 2-4

9. When negotiating a business acquisition, buyers sometimes agree to pay extra amounts to sellers in the future if performance metrics are achieved over specified time horizons. How should buyers account for such contingent consideration in recording an acquisition?

     a. The amount ultimately paid under the contingent consideration agreement is added to goodwill when and if the performance metrics are met.

     b. The fair value of the contingent consideration is expensed immediately at acquisition date.

     c. The fair value of the contingent consideration is included in the overall fair value of the consideration transferred, and a liability or additional owners' equity is recognized.

     d. The fair value of the contingent consideration is recorded as a reduction of the otherwise determinable fair value of the acquired firm.

LO 2-5

10. An acquired firm's financial records sometimes show goodwill from previous business combinations. How does a parent company account for the preexisting goodwill of its newly acquired subsidiary?

     a. The parent tests the preexisting goodwill for impairment before recording the goodwill as part of the acquisition.

     b. The parent includes the preexisting goodwill as an identified intangible asset acquired.

     c. The parent ignores preexisting subsidiary goodwill and allocates the subsidiary's fair value among the separately identifiable assets acquired and liabilities assumed.

     d. Preexisting goodwill is excluded from the identifiable assets acquired unless the subsidiary can demonstrate its continuing value.

LO 2-5

11. On June 1, Cline Co. paid $800,000 cash for all of the issued and outstanding common stock of Renn Corp. The carrying amounts for Renn's assets and liabilities on June 1 follow:

Cash	$150,000
Accounts receivable	180,000
Capitalized software costs	320,000
Goodwill	100,000
Liabilities	(130,000)
Net assets	$620,000

On June 1, Renn's accounts receivable had a fair value of $140,000. Additionally, Renn's in-process research and development was estimated to have a fair value of $200,000. All other items were stated at their fair values. On Cline's June 1 consolidated balance sheet, how much is reported for goodwill?

     a. $320,000

     b. $120,000

     c. $80,000

     d. $20,000

Problems 12 and 13 relate to the following:

On May 1, Donovan Company reported the following account balances:

Current assets	$ 90,000
Buildings & equipment (net)	220,000
Total assets	$310,000
Liabilities	$ 60,000
Common stock	150,000
Retained earnings	100,000
Total liabilities and equities	$310,000

On May 1, Beasley paid $400,000 in stock (fair value) for all of the assets and liabilities of Donovan, which will cease to exist as a separate entity. In connection with the merger, Beasley incurred $15,000 in accounts payable for legal and accounting fees.

    Beasley also agreed to pay $75,000 to the former owners of Donovan contingent on meeting certain revenue goals during the following year. Beasley estimated the present value of its probability adjusted expected payment for the contingency at $20,000. In determining its offer, Beasley noted the following:

- Donovan holds a building with a fair value $30,000 more than its book value.

- Donovan has developed unpatented technology appraised at $25,000, although is it not recorded in its financial records.
- Donovan has a research and development activity in process with an appraised fair value of $45,000. The project has not yet reached technological feasibility.
- Book values for Donovan's current assets and liabilities approximate fair values.

LO 2-4, 2-5

12. What should Beasley record as total liabilities incurred or assumed in connection with the Donovan merger?
   a. $15,000
   b. $75,000
   c. $95,000
   d. $150,000

LO 2-5, 2-8

13. How much should Beasley record as total assets acquired in the Donovan merger?
   a. $400,000
   b. $420,000
   c. $410,000
   d. $480,000

LO 2-5

14. Prior to being united in a business combination, Atkins, Inc., and Waterson Corporation had the following stockholders' equity figures:

	Atkins	Waterson
Common stock ($1 par value).............	$ 180,000	$ 45,000
Additional paid-in capital.................	90,000	20,000
Retained earnings......................	300,000	110,000

Atkins issues 51,000 new shares of its common stock valued at $3 per share for all of the outstanding stock of Waterson. Immediately afterward, what are consolidated Additional Paid-In Capital and Retained Earnings, respectively?
   a. $104,000 and $300,000
   b. $110,000 and $410,000
   c. $192,000 and $300,000
   d. $212,000 and $410,000

Problems 15 through 18 are based on the following information:

On July 1, TruData Company issues 10,000 shares of its common stock with a $5 par value and a $40 fair value in exchange for all of Webstat Company's outstanding voting shares. Webstat's pre-combination book and fair values are shown below along with book values for TruData's accounts.

	TruData Book Values	Webstat Book Values	Webstat Fair Values
Revenues (1/1 to 7/1).............	$(250,000)	$(130,000)	
Expenses (1/1 to 7/1).............	170,000	80,000	
Retained earnings, 1/1............	(130,000)	(150,000)	
Cash and receivables.............	140,000	60,000	$ 60,000
Inventory.......................	190,000	145,000	175,000
Patented technology (net).........	230,000	180,000	200,000
Land...........................	400,000	200,000	225,000
Buildings and equipment (net)	100,000	75,000	75,000
Liabilities......................	(540,000)	(360,000)	(350,000)
Common stock	(300,000)	(70,000)	
Additional paid-in capital..........	(10,000)	(30,000)	

LO 2-5, 2-9, 2-10

15. On its acquisition-date consolidated balance sheet, what amount should TruData report as goodwill?
   a. –0–
   b. $15,000
   c. $35,000
   d. $100,000

LO 2-5

16. On its acquisition-date consolidated balance sheet, what amount should TruData report as patented technology (net)?
    a. $200,000
    b. $230,000
    c. $410,000
    d. $430,000

LO 2-5, 2-7

17. On its acquisition-date consolidated balance sheet, what amount should TruData report as common stock?
    a. $70,000
    b. $300,000
    c. $350,000
    d. $370,000

LO 2-5, 2-7

18. On its acquisition-date consolidated balance sheet, what amount should TruData report as retained earnings as of July 1?
    a. $130,000
    b. $210,000
    c. $260,000
    d. $510,000

Problems 19 and 20 are based on the following information. The separate condensed balance sheets of Patrick Corporation and its wholly owned subsidiary, Sean Corporation, are as follows:

BALANCE SHEETS
December 31, 2017

	Patrick	Sean
Cash	$ 80,000	$ 60,000
Accounts receivable (net)	140,000	25,000
Inventories	90,000	50,000
Plant and equipment (net)	625,000	280,000
Investment in Sean	460,000	
Total assets	$1,395,000	$415,000
Accounts payable	$ 160,000	$ 95,000
Long-term debt	110,000	30,000
Common stock ($10 par)	340,000	50,000
Additional paid-in capital		10,000
Retained earnings	785,000	230,000
Total liabilities and shareholders' equity	$1,395,000	$415,000

Additional Information:
- On December 31, 2017, Patrick acquired 100 percent of Sean's voting stock in exchange for $460,000.
- At the acquisition date, the fair values of Sean's assets and liabilities equaled their carrying amounts, respectively, except that the fair value of certain items in Sean's inventory were $25,000 more than their carrying amounts.

LO 2-4, 2-5

19. In the December 31, 2017, consolidated balance sheet of Patrick and its subsidiary, what amount of total assets should be reported?
    a. $1,375,000
    b. $1,395,000
    c. $1,520,000
    d. $1,980,000

LO 2-4, 2-5

20. In the December 31, 2017, consolidated balance sheet of Patrick and its subsidiary, what amount of total stockholders' equity should be reported?
    a. $1,100,000
    b. $1,125,000

    c. $1,150,000

    d. $1,355,000

LO 2-8

21. Prycal Co. merges with InterBuy, Inc., and acquires several different categories of intangible assets including trademarks, a customer list, copyrights on artistic materials, agreements to receive royalties on leased intellectual property, and unpatented technology.

    a. Describe the criteria for determining whether an intangible asset acquired in a business combination should be separately recognized apart from goodwill.

    b. For each of the acquired intangibles listed, identify which recognition criteria (separability and legal/contractual) may or may not apply in recognizing the intangible on the acquiring firm's financial statements.

LO 2-6a, 2-6b

22. The following book and fair values were available for Westmont Company as of March 1.

	Book Value	Fair Value
Inventory.	$ 630,000	$ 600,000
Land.	750,000	990,000
Buildings.	1,700,000	2,000,000
Customer relationships	–0–	800,000
Accounts payable.	(80,000)	(80,000)
Common stock	(2,000,000)	
Additional paid-in capital.	(500,000)	
Retained earnings, 1/1.	(360,000)	
Revenues	(420,000)	
Expenses	280,000	

Arturo Company pays $4,000,000 cash and issues 20,000 shares of its $2 par value common stock (fair value of $50 per share) for all of Westmont's common stock in a merger, after which Westmont will cease to exist as a separate entity. Stock issue costs amount to $25,000 and Arturo pays $42,000 for legal fees to complete the transaction. Prepare Arturo's journal entries to record its acquisition of Westmont.

LO 2-6a, 2-6b, 2-8

23. Use the same facts as in problem (22), but assume instead that Arturo pays cash of $4,200,000 to acquire Westmont. No stock is issued. Prepare Arturo's journal entries to record its acquisition of Westmont.

LO 2-4, 2-5, 2-6a, 2-6b, 2-6c

24. Following are preacquisition financial balances for Padre Company and Sol Company as of December 31. Also included are fair values for Sol Company accounts.

	Padre Company Book Values 12/31	Sol Company Book Values 12/31	Sol Company Fair Values 12/31
Cash	$ 400,000	$ 120,000	$ 120,000
Receivables	220,000	300,000	300,000
Inventory.	410,000	210,000	260,000
Land.	600,000	130,000	110,000
Building and equipment (net)	600,000	270,000	330,000
Franchise agreements	220,000	190,000	220,000
Accounts payable.	(300,000)	(120,000)	(120,000)
Accrued expenses	(90,000)	(30,000)	(30,000)
Long-term liabilities.	(900,000)	(510,000)	(510,000)
Common stock—$20 par value	(660,000)		
Common stock—$5 par value		(210,000)	
Additional paid-in capital.	(70,000)	(90,000)	
Retained earnings, 1/1.	(390,000)	(240,000)	
Revenues	(960,000)	(330,000)	
Expenses	920,000	310,000	

Note: Parentheses indicate a credit balance.

On December 31, Padre acquires Sol's outstanding stock by paying $360,000 in cash and issuing 10,000 shares of its own common stock with a fair value of $40 per share. Padre paid legal and accounting fees of $20,000 as well as $5,000 in stock issuance costs.

Determine the value that would be shown in Padre's consolidated financial statements for each of the accounts listed.

Accounts	
Inventory	Revenues
Land	Additional paid-in capital
Buildings and equipment	Expenses
Franchise agreements	Retained earnings, 1/1
Goodwill	Retained earnings, 12/31

LO 2-5, 2-6a, 2-6b, 2-8

25. On May 1, Soriano Co. reported the following account balances along with their estimated fair values:

	Carrying Amount	Fair Value
Receivables	$ 90,000	$ 90,000
Inventory............................	75,000	75,000
Copyrights	125,000	480,000
Patented technology	825,000	700,000
Total assets	$1,115,000	$1,345,000
Current liabilities	$ 160,000	$ 160,000
Long-term liabilities.................	645,000	635,000
Common stock	100,000	
Retained earnings...................	210,000	
Total liabilities and equities...........	$1,115,000	

On that day, Zambrano paid cash to acquire all of the assets and liabilities of Soriano, which will cease to exist as a separate entity. To facilitate the merger, Zambrano also paid $100,000 to an investment banking firm.

The following information was also available:

- Zambrano further agreed to pay an extra $70,000 to the former owners of Soriano only if they meet certain revenue goals during the next two years. Zambrano estimated the present value of its probability adjusted expected payment for this contingency at $35,000.

- Soriano has a research and development project in process with an appraised value of $200,000. However, the project has not yet reached technological feasibility and the project's assets have no alternative future use.

Prepare Zambrano's journal entries to record the Soriano acquisition assuming its initial cash payment to the former owners was

a. $700,000.

b. $800,000.

LO 2-4, 2-5, 2-6b, 2-7

26. On June 30, 2017, Wisconsin, Inc., issued $300,000 in debt and 15,000 new shares of its $10 par value stock to Badger Company owners in exchange for all of the outstanding shares of that company. Wisconsin shares had a fair value of $40 per share. Prior to the combination, the financial statements for Wisconsin and Badger for the six-month period ending June 30, 2017, were as follows:

	Wisconsin	Badger
Revenues	$ (900,000)	$ (300,000)
Expenses	660,000	200,000
Net income.........................	$ (240,000)	$ (100,000)
Retained earnings, 1/1.................	$ (800,000)	$ (200,000)
Net income..........................	(240,000)	(100,000)
Dividends declared...................	90,000	–0–
Retained earnings, 6/30	$ (950,000)	$ (300,000)

(continued)

Cash	$ 80,000	$ 110,000
Receivables and inventory	400,000	170,000
Patented technology (net)	900,000	300,000
Equipment (net)	700,000	600,000
Total assets	$ 2,080,000	$ 1,180,000
Liabilities	$ (500,000)	$ (410,000)
Common stock	(360,000)	(200,000)
Additional paid-in capital	(270,000)	(270,000)
Retained earnings	(950,000)	(300,000)
Total liabilities and equities	$ (2,080,000)	$ (1,180,000)

Wisconsin also paid $30,000 to a broker for arranging the transaction. In addition, Wisconsin paid $40,000 in stock issuance costs. Badger's equipment was actually worth $700,000, but its patented technology was valued at only $280,000.

What are the consolidated balances for the following accounts?

a. Net income.

b. Retained earnings, 1/1/17.

c. Patented technology.

d. Goodwill.

e. Liabilities.

f. Common stock.

g. Additional paid-in capital.

LO 2-4, 2-7

27. On January 1, 2018 Casey Corporation exchanged $3,300,000 cash for 100 percent of the outstanding voting stock of Kennedy Corporation. Casey plans to maintain Kennedy as a wholly owned subsidiary with separate legal status and accounting information systems.

At the acquisition date, Casey prepared the following fair-value allocation schedule:

Fair value of Kennedy (consideration transferred)		$3,300,000
Carrying amount acquired		2,600,000
Excess fair value		$ 700,000
to buildings (undervalued)	$ 382,000	
to licensing agreements (overvalued)	(108,000)	274,000
to goodwill (indefinite life)		$ 426,000

Immediately after closing the transaction, Casey and Kennedy prepared the following postacquisition balance sheets from their separate financial records.

Accounts	Casey	Kennedy
Cash	$ 457,000	$ 172,500
Accounts receivable	1,655,000	347,000
Inventory	1,310,000	263,500
Investment in Kennedy	3,300,000	–0–
Buildings (net)	6,315,000	2,090,000
Licensing agreements	–0–	3,070,000
Goodwill	347,000	–0–
Total assets	$ 13,384,000	$ 5,943,000
Accounts payable	$ (394,000)	$ (393,000)
Long-term debt	(3,990,000)	(2,950,000)
Common stock	(3,000,000)	(1,000,000)
Additional paid-in capital	–0–	(500,000)
Retained earnings	(6,000,000)	(1,100,000)
Total liabilities and equities	$ (13,384,000)	$ (5,943,000)

Prepare an acquisition-date consolidated balance sheet for Casey Corporation and its subsidiary Kennedy Corporation.

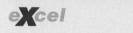

28. On January 1, 2018, Marshall Company acquired 100 percent of the outstanding common stock of Tucker Company. To acquire these shares, Marshall issued $200,000 in long-term liabilities and 20,000 shares of common stock having a par value of $1 per share but a fair value of $10 per share. Marshall paid $30,000 to accountants, lawyers, and brokers for assistance in the acquisition and another $12,000 in connection with stock issuance costs.

Prior to these transactions, the balance sheets for the two companies were as follows:

	Marshall Company Book Value	Tucker Company Book Value
Cash	$ 60,000	$ 20,000
Receivables	270,000	90,000
Inventory	360,000	140,000
Land	200,000	180,000
Buildings (net)	420,000	220,000
Equipment (net)	160,000	50,000
Accounts payable	(150,000)	(40,000)
Long-term liabilities	(430,000)	(200,000)
Common stock—$1 par value	(110,000)	
Common stock—$20 par value		(120,000)
Additional paid-in capital	(360,000)	–0–
Retained earnings, 1/1/18	(420,000)	(340,000)

Note: Parentheses indicate a credit balance.

In Marshall's appraisal of Tucker, it deemed three accounts to be undervalued on the subsidiary's books: Inventory by $5,000, Land by $20,000, and Buildings by $30,000. Marshall plans to maintain Tucker's separate legal identity and to operate Tucker as a wholly owned subsidiary.

a. Determine the amounts that Marshall Company would report in its postacquisition balance sheet. In preparing the postacquisition balance sheet, any required adjustments to income accounts from the acquisition should be closed to Marshall's retained earnings. Other accounts will also need to be added or adjusted to reflect the journal entries Marshall prepared in recording the acquisition.

b. To verify the answers found in part (a), prepare a worksheet to consolidate the balance sheets of these two companies as of January 1, 2018.

29. Pratt Company acquired all of Spider, Inc.'s outstanding shares on December 31, 2018, for $495,000 cash. Pratt will operate Spider as a wholly owned subsidiary with a separate legal and accounting identity. Although many of Spider's book values approximate fair values, several of its accounts have fair values that differ from book values. In addition, Spider has internally developed assets that remain unrecorded on its books. In deriving the acquisition price, Pratt assessed Spider's fair and book value differences as follows:

	Book Values	Fair Values
Computer software	$ 20,000	$ 70,000
Equipment	40,000	30,000
Client contracts	–0–	100,000
In-process research and development	–0–	40,000
Notes payable	(60,000)	(65,000)

At December 31, 2018, the following financial information is available for consolidation:

	Pratt	Spider
Cash	$ 36,000	$ 18,000
Receivables	116,000	52,000
Inventory	140,000	90,000
Investment in Spider	495,000	–0–
Computer software	210,000	20,000

(continued)

Buildings (net)	595,000	130,000
Equipment (net)	308,000	40,000
Client contracts	–0–	–0–
Goodwill	–0–	–0–
Total assets	$ 1,900,000	$ 350,000
Accounts payable	$ (88,000)	$ (25,000)
Notes payable	(510,000)	(60,000)
Common stock	(380,000)	(100,000)
Additional paid-in capital	(170,000)	(25,000)
Retained earnings	(752,000)	(140,000)
Total liabilities and equities	$(1,900,000)	$(350,000)

Prepare a consolidated balance sheet for Pratt and Spider as of December 31, 2018.

LO 2-4, 2-5, 2-6a

30. Allerton Company acquires all of Deluxe Company's assets and liabilities for cash on January 1, 2018, and subsequently formally dissolves Deluxe. At the acquisition date, the following book and fair values were available for the Deluxe Company accounts:

	Book Values	Fair Values
Current assets	$ 60,000	$ 60,000
Building	90,000	50,000
Land	10,000	20,000
Trademark	–0–	30,000
Goodwill	15,000	?
Liabilities	(40,000)	(40,000)
Common stock	(100,000)	
Retained earnings	(35,000)	

Prepare Allerton's entry to record its acquisition of Deluxe in its accounting records assuming the following cash exchange amounts:

1. $145,000.
2. $110,000.

LO 2-4, 2-5, 2-6a, 2-6b

31. On June 30, 2018, Streeter Company reported the following account balances:

Receivables	$ 83,900	Current liabilities	$ (12,900)
Inventory	70,250	Long-term liabilities	(54,250)
Buildings (net)	78,900	Common stock	(90,000)
Equipment (net)	24,100	Retained earnings	(100,000)
Total assets	$257,150	Total liabilities and equities	$ (257,150)

On June 30, 2018, Princeton Company paid $310,800 cash for all assets and liabilities of Streeter, which will cease to exist as a separate entity. In connection with the acquisition, Princeton paid $15,100 in legal fees. Princeton also agreed to pay $55,600 to the former owners of Streeter contingent on meeting certain revenue goals during 2019. Princeton estimated the present value of its probability adjusted expected payment for the contingency at $17,900.

In determining its offer, Princeton noted the following pertaining to Streeter:

- It holds a building with a fair value $43,100 more than its book value.
- It has developed a customer list appraised at $25,200, although it is not recorded in its financial records.
- It has research and development activity in process with an appraised fair value of $36,400. However, the project has not yet reached technological feasibility and the assets used in the activity have no alternative future use.
- Book values for the receivables, inventory, equipment, and liabilities approximate fair values.

Prepare Princeton's accounting entries to record the combination with Streeter.

LO 2-4, 2-5, 2-8, 2-6b

32. SafeData Corporation has the following account balances and respective fair values on June 30:

	Book Values	Fair Values
Receivables	$ 80,000	$ 80,000
Patented technology	100,000	700,000
Customer relationships	–0–	500,000
In-process research and development.	–0–	300,000
Liabilities.	(400,000)	(400,000)
Common stock	(100,000)	
Additional paid-in capital	(300,000)	
Retained earnings deficit, 1/1.	700,000	
Revenues	(300,000)	
Expenses	220,000	

Privacy First, Inc., obtained all of the outstanding shares of SafeData on June 30 by issuing 20,000 shares of common stock having a $1 par value but a $75 fair value. Privacy First incurred $10,000 in stock issuance costs and paid $75,000 to an investment banking firm for its assistance in arranging the combination. In negotiating the final terms of the deal, Privacy First also agrees to pay $100,000 to SafeData's former owners if it achieves certain revenue goals in the next two years. Privacy First estimates the probability adjusted present value of this contingent performance obligation at $30,000.

  a. What is the fair value of the consideration transferred in this combination?

  b. How should the stock issuance costs appear in Privacy First's postcombination financial statements?

  c. How should Privacy First account for the fee paid to the investment bank?

  d. How does the issuance of these shares affect the stockholders' equity accounts of Privacy First, the parent?

  e. How is the fair value of the consideration transferred in the combination allocated among the assets acquired and the liabilities assumed?

  f. What is the effect of SafeData's revenues and expenses on consolidated totals? Why?

  g. What is the effect of SafeData's Common Stock and Additional Paid-In Capital balances on consolidated totals?

  h. If Privacy First's stock had been worth only $50 per share rather than $75, how would the consolidation of SafeData's assets and liabilities have been affected?

LO 2-4, 2-5, 2-6a, 2-6b, 2-6c

LO 2-7, 2-8

33. On January 1, NewTune Company exchanges 15,000 shares of its common stock for all of the outstanding shares of On-the-Go, Inc. Each of NewTune's shares has a $4 par value and a $50 fair value. The fair value of the stock exchanged in the acquisition was considered equal to On-the-Go's fair value. NewTune also paid $25,000 in stock registration and issuance costs in connection with the merger.

Several of On-the-Go's accounts' fair values differ from their book values on this date:

	Book Values	Fair Values
Receivables	$ 65,000	$ 63,000
Trademarks	95,000	225,000
Record music catalog.	60,000	180,000
In-process research and development.	–0–	200,000
Notes payable	(50,000)	(45,000)

Precombination book values for the two companies are as follows:

	NewTune	On-the-Go
Cash	$ 60,000	$ 29,000
Receivables	150,000	65,000
Trademarks	400,000	95,000
Record music catalog.	840,000	60,000
Equipment (net)	320,000	105,000
Totals.	$1,770,000	$354,000

(continued)

Accounts payable...........................	$ (110,000)	$ (34,000)
Notes payable.............................	(370,000)	(50,000)
Common stock	(400,000)	(50,000)
Additional paid-in capital....................	(30,000)	(30,000)
Retained earnings..........................	(860,000)	(190,000)
Totals....................................	$(1,770,000)	$(354,000)

a. Assume that this combination is a statutory merger so that On-the-Go's accounts will be transferred to the records of NewTune. On-the-Go will be dissolved and will no longer exist as a legal entity. Prepare a postcombination balance sheet for NewTune as of the acquisition date.

b. Assume that no dissolution takes place in connection with this combination. Rather, both companies retain their separate legal identities. Prepare a worksheet to consolidate the two companies as of the combination date.

c. How do the balance sheet accounts compare across parts (a) and (b)?

LO 2-4, 2-5, 2-6b, 2-6c, 2-7

34. On December 31, Pacifica, Inc., acquired 100 percent of the voting stock of Seguros Company. Pacifica will maintain Seguros as a wholly owned subsidiary with its own legal and accounting identity. The consideration transferred to the owner of Seguros included 50,000 newly issued Pacifica common shares ($20 market value, $5 par value) and an agreement to pay an additional $130,000 cash if Seguros meets certain project completion goals by December 31 of the following year. Pacifica estimates a 50 percent probability that Seguros will be successful in meeting these goals and uses a 4 percent discount rate to represent the time value of money.

Immediately prior to the acquisition, the following data for both firms were available:

	Pacifica	Seguros Book Values	Seguros Fair Values
Revenues.........................	$(1,200,000)		
Expenses	875,000		
Net income.....................	$ (325,000)		
Retained earnings, 1/1...........	$ (950,000)		
Net income......................	(325,000)		
Dividends declared...............	90,000		
Retained earnings, 12/31	$(1,185,000)		
Cash	$ 110,000	$ 85,000	$ 85,000
Receivables and inventory	750,000	190,000	180,000
Property, plant, and equipment	1,400,000	450,000	600,000
Trademarks	300,000	160,000	200,000
Total assets	$ 2,560,000	$ 885,000	
Liabilities........................	$ (500,000)	$(180,000)	$(180,000)
Common stock	(400,000)	(200,000)	
Additional paid-in capital...........	(475,000)	(70,000)	
Retained earnings.................	(1,185,000)	(435,000)	
Total liabilities and equities.......	$(2,560,000)	$(885,000)	

In addition, Pacifica assessed a research and development project under way at Seguros to have a fair value of $100,000. Although not yet recorded on its books, Pacifica paid legal fees of $15,000 in connection with the acquisition and $9,000 in stock issue costs.

Prepare the following:

a. Pacifica's entries to account for the consideration transferred to the former owners of Seguros, the direct combination costs, and the stock issue and registration costs. (Use a 0.961538 present value factor where applicable.)

b. A postacquisition column of accounts for Pacifica.

c. A worksheet to produce a consolidated balance sheet as of the acquisition date.

Appendix 2A Problems

LO 2-9

35. In a pre-2009 business combination, Acme Company acquired all of Brem Company's assets and liabilities for cash. After the combination Acme formally dissolved Brem. At the acquisition date, the following book and fair values were available for the Brem Company accounts:

	Book Values	Fair Values
Current assets	$ 80,000	$ 80,000
Equipment	120,000	180,000
Trademark	–0–	320,000
Liabilities.	(55,000)	(55,000)
Common stock	(100,000)	
Retained earnings.	(45,000)	

In addition, Acme paid an investment bank $25,000 cash for assistance in arranging the combination.

a. Using the legacy purchase method for pre-2009 business combinations, prepare Acme's entry to record its acquisition of Brem in its accounting records assuming the following cash amounts were paid to the former owners of Brem:

1. $610,000.
2. $425,000.

b. How would these journal entries change if the acquisition occurred post-2009 and therefore Acme applied the acquisition method?

LO 2-9

36. On February 1, Piscina Corporation completed a combination with Swimwear Company. At that date, Swimwear's account balances were as follows:

	Book Values	Fair Values
Inventory.	$ 600,000	$ 650,000
Land.	450,000	750,000
Buildings.	900,000	1,000,000
Unpatented technology.	–0–	1,500,000
Common stock ($10 par value)	(750,000)	
Retained earnings, 1/1.	(1,100,000)	
Revenues	(600,000)	
Expenses	500,000	

Piscina issued 30,000 shares of its common stock with a par value of $25 and a fair value of $150 per share to the owners of Swimwear for all of their Swimwear shares. Upon completion of the combination, Swimwear Company was formally dissolved.

Prior to 2002, business combinations were accounted for using either purchase or pooling of interests accounting. The two methods often produced substantially different financial statement effects. For the scenario above,

a. What are the respective consolidated values for Swimwear's assets under the pooling method and the purchase method?

b. Under each of the following methods, how would Piscina account for Swimwear's current year, but prior to acquisition, revenues and expenses?

• Pooling of interests method.
• Purchase method.

c. Explain the alternative impact of pooling versus purchase accounting on performance ratios such as return on assets and earnings per share in periods subsequent to the combination.

Appendix 2B Problems

LO 2-10

37. What is push-down accounting?

a. A requirement that a subsidiary must use the same accounting principles as a parent company.

b. Inventory transfers made from a parent company to a subsidiary.

c. A subsidiary's recording of the fair-value allocations as well as subsequent amortization.

d. The adjustments required for consolidation when a parent has applied the equity method of accounting for internal reporting purposes.

38. On May 1, Burns Corporation acquired 100 percent of the outstanding ownership shares of Quigley Corporation in exchange for $710,000 cash. At the acquisition date, Quigley's book and fair values were as follows:

	Book Values	Fair Values
Cash	$ 95,000	$ 95,000
Receivables	200,000	200,000
Inventory	210,000	260,000
Land	130,000	110,000
Building and equipment (net)	270,000	330,000
Patented technology	-0-	220,000
Total assets	$905,000	$1,215,000
Accounts payable	$120,000	$ 120,000
Long-term liabilities	510,000	510,000
Common stock ($5 par value)	210,000	
Additional paid-in capital	90,000	
Retained earnings	(25,000)	
Total liabilities and stockholders equity	$905,000	

Burns directs Quigley to seek additional financing for expansion through a new long-term debt issue. Consequently, Quigley will issue a set of financial statements separate from that of its new parent to support its request for debt and accompanying regulatory filings. Quigley elects to apply pushdown accounting in order to show recent fair valuations for its assets.

Prepare a separate acquisition-date balance sheet for Quigley Corporation using pushdown accounting.

Develop Your Skills

FASB ASC RESEARCH AND ANALYSIS CASE—CONSIDERATION OR COMPENSATION?

NaviNow Company agrees to pay $20 million in cash to the four former owners of TrafficEye for all of its assets and liabilities. These four owners of TrafficEye developed and patented a technology for real-time monitoring of traffic patterns on the nation's top 200 frequently congested highways. NaviNow plans to combine the new technology with its existing global positioning systems and projects a resulting substantial revenue increase.

As part of the acquisition contract, NaviNow also agrees to pay additional amounts to the former owners upon achievement of certain financial goals. NaviNow will pay $8 million to the four former owners of TrafficEye if revenues from the combined system exceed $100 million over the next three years. NaviNow estimates this contingent payment to have a probability adjusted present value of $4 million.

The four former owners have also been offered employment contracts with NaviNow to help with system integration and performance enhancement issues. The employment contracts are silent as to service periods, have nominal salaries similar to those of equivalent employees, and specify a profit-sharing component over the next three years (if the employees remain with the company) that NaviNow estimates to have a current fair value of $2 million. The four former owners of TrafficEye say they will stay on as employees of NaviNow for at least three years to help achieve the desired financial goals.

Should NaviNow account for the contingent payments promised to the former owners of TrafficEye as consideration transferred in the acquisition or as compensation expense to employees?

ASC RESEARCH CASE—DEFENSIVE INTANGIBLE ASSET

Ahorita Company manufactures wireless transponders for satellite applications. Ahorita has recently acquired Zelltech Company, which is primarily known for its software communications development but also manufactures a specialty transponder under the trade name "Z-Tech" that competes with one of Ahorita's products. Ahorita will now discontinue Z-Tech and projects that its own product line will see a market share increase. Nonetheless, Ahorita's management will maintain the rights to the Z-Tech trade name as a defensive intangible asset to prevent its use by competitors, despite the fact that its highest and best use would be to sell the trade name. Ahorita estimates that the trade name has an internal value of $1.5 million, but if sold would yield $2 million.

Answer the following with supporting citations from the FASB ASC:

a. How does the FASB ASC Glossary define a defensive intangible asset?

b. According to ASC Topic 805, "Business Combinations," what is the measurement principle that an acquirer should follow in recording identifiable assets acquired in a business combination?

c. According to ASC Topic 820, "Fair Value Measurement," what value premise (in-use or in-exchange) should Ahorita assign to the Z-Tech trade name in its consolidated financial statements?

d. According to ASC Topic 350, "General Intangibles Other Than Goodwill," how should Ahorita determine the estimated useful life of its defensive intangible asset?

RESEARCH CASE—CELGENE'S ACQUISITION OF RECEPTOS, INC.

On August 27, 2015, Celgene Corporation acquired all of the outstanding stock of Receptos, Inc., in exchange for $7.6 billion in cash. Referring to Celgene's 2015 financial statements and its July 14, 2015, press release announcing the acquisition, answer the following questions regarding the Receptos acquisition.

1. Why did Celgene acquire Receptos?

2. What accounting method was used, and for what amount, to record the acquisition?

3. What amount did Celgene include in pre-combination service compensation in the total consideration transferred? What support is provided for this treatment in the Accounting Standards Codification (see ASC 805-30-30, paragraphs 9-13)?

4. What allocations did Celgene make to the assets acquired and liabilities assumed in the acquisition? Provide a calculation showing how Celgene determined the amount allocated to goodwill.

5. Describe the nature of the in-process research and development product rights acquired by Celgene in its acquisition of Receptos.

6. How will Celgene account for the in-process research and development product rights acquired in the Receptos combination?

RESEARCH CASE—ARCTIC CAT'S ACQUISITION OF MOTORFIST, LLC.

In February 2015, Arctic Cat, Inc., acquired the assets and liabilities of MotorFist, LLC, a privately owned company based in Idaho Falls, Idaho, in exchange for $9.118 million in cash and contingent consideration. Referring to Arctic Cat's 2015 annual 10-K report, answer the following questions regarding the MotorFist acquisition.

1. Why did Arctic Cat acquire MotorFist?

2. How was the consideration transferred allocated between cash paid and the contingent consideration?

3. Provide a schedule showing Arctic Cat's allocations of the consideration transferred to the identifiable assets acquired and liabilities assumed with the remainder going to goodwill.

4. What is the maximum potential contingent payout (i.e., earnout) to the former owners of MotorFist? Although not explicitly stated in Arctic Cat's fiscal 2015 10-K report (for the year ended March 31, 2015), what may be some possible factors that entered into the determination of the acquisition-date fair value of the contingent consideration?

EXHIBIT 3.2
Excess Fair-Value
Allocation

PARROT COMPANY		
100 Percent Acquisition of Sun Company		
Allocation of Acquisition-Date Subsidiary Fair Value		
January 1, 2017		
Sun Company fair value (consideration transferred by Parrot Company)..		$800,000
Book value of Sun Company:.................................		
Common stock	$200,000	
Additional paid-in capital...............................	20,000	
Retained earnings, 1/1/17	380,000	(600,000)
Excess of fair value over book value..........................		200,000
Allocation to specific accounts based on fair values:.............		
Trademarks	$ 20,000	
Patented technology	130,000	
Equipment (overvalued).................................	(30,000)	120,000
Excess fair value not identified with specific accounts—goodwill ...		$ 80,000

Parrot considers the economic life of Sun's trademarks as extending beyond the foreseeable future and thus having an indefinite life. Such assets are not amortized but are subject to periodic impairment testing.[4] For the definite lived assets acquired in the combination (patented technology and equipment), we assume that straight-line amortization and depreciation with no salvage value is appropriate.[5]

Parrot paid $800,000 cash to acquire Sun Company, clear evidence of the fair value of the consideration transferred. As shown in Exhibit 3.2, individual allocations are used to adjust Sun's accounts from their book values to their acquisition-date fair values. Because the total value of these assets and liabilities was only $720,000, goodwill of $80,000 must be recognized for consolidation purposes.

Each of these allocated amounts (other than the $20,000 attributed to trademarks and the $80,000 for goodwill) represents a valuation associated with a definite life. As discussed in Chapter 1, Parrot must amortize each allocation over its expected life. The expense recognition necessitated by this fair-value allocation is calculated in Exhibit 3.3.

Two aspects of this amortization schedule warrant further explanation. First, we use the term *amortization* in a generic sense to include both the amortization of definite-lived intangibles and depreciation of tangible assets. Second, the acquisition-date fair value of Sun's equipment is $30,000 *less* than its book value. Therefore, instead of attributing an additional amount to this asset, the $30,000 allocation actually reflects a fair-value reduction. As such, the amortization shown in Exhibit 3.3 relating to Equipment is not an additional expense but instead is an expense reduction.

EXHIBIT 3.3
Annual Excess
Amortization

PARROT COMPANY			
100 Percent Acquisition of Sun Company			
Excess Amortization Schedule—Allocation of Acquisition-Date Fair Values			
Account	**Allocation**	**Remaining Useful Life**	**Annual Excess Amortizations**
Trademarks	$ 20,000	Indefinite	$ –0–
Patented technology	130,000	10 years	13,000
Equipment	(30,000)	5 years	(6,000)
Goodwill	80,000	Indefinite	–0–
			$ 7,000*

*Total excess amortizations will be $7,000 annually for five years until the equipment allocation is fully removed. At the end of each asset's life, future amortizations will change.

[4] In other cases, trademarks can have a definite life and thus would be subject to regular amortization.

[5] Unless otherwise stated, all amortization and depreciation expense computations in this textbook are based on the straight-line method with no salvage value.

Having determined the allocation of the acquisition-date fair value in the previous example as well as the associated amortization, the parent's separate record-keeping for its first year of Sun Company ownership can be constructed. Assume that Sun earns income of $100,000 during the year, declares a $40,000 cash dividend on August 1, and pays the dividend on August 8.

In this first illustration, Parrot has adopted the equity method. Apparently, this company believes that the information derived from using the equity method is useful in its evaluation of Sun.

Application of the Equity Method

	Parrot's Financial Records		
1/1/17	Investment in Sun Company.............................	800,000	
	Cash..		800,000
	To record the acquisition of Sun Company.		
8/1/17	Dividend Receivable.................................	40,000	
	Investment in Sun Company........................		40,000
	To record cash dividend declaration from subsidiary.		
8/8/17	Cash...	40,000	
	Dividend Receivable..............................		40,000
	To record receipt of the subsidiary cash dividend.		
12/31/17	Investment in Sun Company.........................	100,000	
	Equity in Subsidiary Earnings......................		100,000
	To accrue income earned by 100 percent owned subsidiary.		
12/31/17	Equity in Subsidiary Earnings.........................	7,000	
	Investment in Sun Company........................		7,000
	To recognize amortizations on allocations made in acquisition of subsidiary (see Exhibit 3.3).		

Parrot's application of the equity method, as shown in this series of entries, causes the Investment in Sun Company account balance to rise from $800,000 to $853,000 ($800,000 − $40,000 + $100,000 − $7,000). During the same period the parent recognizes a $93,000 equity income figure (the $100,000 earnings accrual less the $7,000 excess amortization expenses).

The consolidation procedures for Parrot and Sun one year after the date of acquisition are illustrated next. For this purpose, Exhibit 3.4 presents the separate 2017 financial statements for these two companies. Parrot recorded both investment-related accounts (the $853,000 asset balance and the $93,000 income accrual) based on applying the equity method.

Determination of Consolidated Totals

Before becoming immersed in the mechanical aspects of a consolidation, the objective of this process should be understood. As indicated in Chapter 2, in the preparation of consolidated financial reports, the subsidiary's revenue, expense, asset, and liability accounts are added to the parent company balances. Within this procedure, several important guidelines must be followed:

- Sun's assets and liabilities are adjusted to reflect the allocations originating from their acquisition-date fair values.
- Because of the passage of time, the income effects (e.g., amortizations) of these allocations must also be recognized within the consolidation process.
- Any reciprocal or intra-entity[6] accounts must be offset. If, for example, one of the companies owes money to the other, the receivable and the payable balances have no connection with an outside party. Thus, when the companies are viewed as a single consolidated entity, the receivable and the payable represent intra-entity balances that should be eliminated for external reporting purposes.

---

[6] The FASB Accounting Standards Codification (ASC) uses the term *intra-entity* to describe transfers of assets across business entities affiliated though common stock ownership or other control mechanisms. The phrase indicates that although such transfers occur across separate legal entities, they are nonetheless made within a commonly controlled entity. Prior to the use of the term intra-entity, such amounts were routinely referred to as intercompany balances.

EXHIBIT 3.4 Separate Records—Equity Method Applied

PARROT COMPANY AND SUN COMPANY
Financial Statements
For Year Ending December 31, 2017

	Parrot Company	Sun Company
Income Statement		
Revenues	$ (1,500,000)	$ (400,000)
Cost of goods sold	700,000	232,000
Amortization expense	120,000	32,000
Depreciation expense	80,000	36,000
Equity in subsidiary earnings	(93,000)	–0–
Net income	$ (693,000)	$ (100,000)
Statement of Retained Earnings		
Retained earnings, 1/1/17	$ (840,000)	$ (380,000)
Net income (above)	(693,000)	(100,000)
Dividends declared*	120,000	40,000
Retained earnings, 12/31/17	$ (1,413,000)	$ (440,000)
Balance Sheet		
Current assets	$ 1,040,000	$ 400,000
Investment in Sun Company (at equity)	853,000	–0–
Trademarks	600,000	200,000
Patented technology	370,000	288,000
Equipment (net)	250,000	220,000
Total assets	$ 3,113,000	$ 1,108,000
Liabilities	$ (980,000)	$ (448,000)
Common stock	(600,000)	(200,000)
Additional paid-in capital	(120,000)	(20,000)
Retained earnings, 12/31/17 (above)	(1,413,000)	(440,000)
Total liabilities and equity	$ (3,113,000)	$(1,108,000)

Note: Parentheses indicate a credit balance.

*Dividends declared, whether currently paid or not, provide the appropriate amount to include in a statement of retained earnings. To help keep the number of worksheet rows (i.e., dividends payable and receivable) at a minimum, throughout this text we assume that dividends are declared and paid in the same period.

The consolidation of the two sets of financial information in Exhibit 3.4 is a relatively uncomplicated task and can even be carried out without the use of a worksheet. Understanding the origin of each reported figure is the first step in gaining a knowledge of this process.

- *Revenues* = $1,900,000. The revenues of the parent and the subsidiary are added together.
- *Cost of goods sold* = $932,000. The cost of goods sold of the parent and subsidiary are added together.
- *Amortization expense* = $165,000. The balances of the parent and of the subsidiary are combined along with the $13,000 additional amortization from the recognition of the excess fair value over book value attributed to the subsidiary's patented technology, as shown in Exhibit 3.3.
- *Depreciation expense* = $110,000. The depreciation expenses of the parent and subsidiary are added together along with the $6,000 reduction in equipment depreciation, as indicated in Exhibit 3.3.
- *Equity in subsidiary earnings* = –0–. The investment income recorded by the parent is eliminated and replaced by adding across the subsidiary's revenues and expenses to the consolidated totals.
- *Net income* = $693,000. Consolidated revenues less consolidated expenses.
- *Retained earnings, 1/1/17* = $840,000. The parent figure only. This acquisition-date parent's balance has yet to be affected by any equity method adjustments.

- *Dividends declared* = $120,000. The parent company balance only because the subsidiary's dividends are attributable intra-entity to the parent, not to an outside party.
- *Retained earnings, 12/31/17* = $1,413,000. Consolidated retained earnings as of the beginning of the year plus consolidated net income less consolidated dividends declared.
- *Current assets* = $1,440,000. The parent's book value plus the subsidiary's book value.
- *Investment in Sun Company* = –0–. The asset recorded by the parent is eliminated and replaced by adding the subsidiary's assets and liabilities across to the consolidated totals.
- *Trademarks* = $820,000. The parent's book value plus the subsidiary's book value plus the $20,000 acquisition-date fair-value allocation. Note that the trademark has an indefinite life and therefore is not amortized.
- *Patented technology* = $775,000. The parent's book value plus the subsidiary's book value plus the $130,000 acquisition-date fair-value allocation less current year amortization of $13,000.
- *Equipment* = $446,000. The parent's book value plus the subsidiary's book value less the $30,000 fair-value reduction allocation plus the current year expense reduction of $6,000.
- *Goodwill* = $80,000. The residual allocation shown in Exhibit 3.2. Note that goodwill is considered to have an indefinite life and thus is not amortized.
- *Total assets* = $3,561,000. A vertical summation of consolidated assets.
- *Liabilities* = $1,428,000. The parent's book value plus the subsidiary's book value.
- *Common stock* = $600,000. The parent's book value. Subsidiary shares owned by the parent are treated·as if they are no longer outstanding.
- *Additional paid-in capital* = $120,000. The parent's book value. Subsidiary shares owned by the parent are treated as if they are no longer outstanding.
- *Retained earnings, 12/31/17* = $1,413,000. Computed previously.
- *Total liabilities and equities* = $3,561,000. A vertical summation of consolidated liabilities and equities.

Consolidation Worksheet

Although the consolidated figures to be reported can be computed as just shown, accountants normally prefer to use a worksheet. A worksheet provides an organized structure for this process, a benefit that becomes especially important in consolidating complex combinations.

For Parrot and Sun, only five consolidation entries are needed to arrive at the same figures previously derived for this business combination. As discussed in Chapter 2, *worksheet entries are the catalyst for developing totals to be reported by the entity but are not physically recorded in the individual account balances of either company.*

Consolidation Entry S

Common Stock (Sun Company)	200,000	
Additional Paid-In Capital (Sun Company)	20,000	
Retained Earnings, 1/1/17 (Sun Company)	380,000	
Investment in Sun Company.		600,000

As shown in Exhibit 3.2, Parrot's $800,000 Investment account balance at January 1, 2017, reflects two components: (1) a $600,000 amount equal to Sun's book value and (2) a $200,000 figure attributed to the acquisition-date difference between the book value and fair value of Sun's assets and liabilities (with a residual allocation made to goodwill). Entry **S** removes the $600,000 component of the Investment in Sun Company account which is then replaced by adding the *book values* of each subsidiary asset and liability across to the consolidated figures. A second worksheet entry (Entry **A**) eliminates the remaining $200,000 portion of the January 1, 2017 Investment in Sun account and replaces it with the specific acquisition-date excess fair over book value allocations along with any goodwill. Importantly, worksheet entries S and A are part of the sequence of worksheet adjustments that bring the investment account to zero.

Entry **S** also removes Sun's stockholders' equity accounts as of the beginning of the year. Because consolidated statements are prepared for the parent company owners, the subsidiary equity accounts are not relevant to the business combination and should be eliminated for consolidation purposes. The elimination is made through this entry because the equity accounts and the $600,000 component of the investment account represent reciprocal balances: Both provide a measure of Sun's book value as of January 1, 2017.

Before moving to the next consolidation entry, a clarification point should be made. In actual practice, worksheet entries are usually identified numerically. However, as in the previous chapter, the label "Entry **S**" used in this example refers to the elimination of Sun's beginning **S**tockholders' Equity. As a reminder of the purpose being served, all worksheet entries are identified in a similar fashion. Thus, throughout this textbook, "Entry **S**" always refers to the removal of the subsidiary's beginning stockholders' equity balances for the year against the book value portion of the investment account.

Consolidation Entry A

Trademarks	20,000	
Patented Technology	130,000	
Goodwill	80,000	
Equipment		30,000
Investment in Sun Company		200,000

Consolidation Entry **A** adjusts the subsidiary balances from their book values to acquisition-date fair values (see Exhibit 3.2) and includes goodwill created by the acquisition. This entry is labeled "Entry **A**" to indicate that it represents the Allocations made in connection with the excess of the subsidiary's fair values over its book values. Sun's accounts are adjusted collectively by the $200,000 excess of Sun's $800,000 acquisition-date fair value over its $600,000 book value.

Consolidation Entry I

Equity in Subsidiary Earnings	93,000	
Investment in Sun Company		93,000

"Entry **I**" (for **I**ncome) removes from the worksheet the subsidiary income recognized by Parrot during the year. For reporting purposes, we must add the subsidiary's individual revenue and expense accounts (and the current excess amortization expenses) to the parent's respective amounts to arrive at consolidated totals. Worksheet entry **I** thus effectively removes the one-line Equity in Subsidiary Earnings which is then replaced with the addition of the subsidiary's separate revenues and expenses (already listed on the worksheet in the subsidiary's balances). The $93,000 figure eliminated here represents the $100,000 income accrual recognized by Parrot, reduced by the $7,000 in excess amortizations. Observe that the entry originally recorded by the parent is simply reversed on the worksheet to remove its impact.

Consolidation Entry D

Investment in Sun Company	40,000	
Dividends Declared		40,000

The dividends declared by the subsidiary during the year also must be eliminated from the consolidated totals. The entire $40,000 dividend goes to the parent, which from the viewpoint of the consolidated entity is simply an intra-entity transfer. The dividend declaration did not affect any outside party. Therefore, "Entry **D**" (for **D**ividends) is designed to offset the impact of this transaction by removing the subsidiary's Dividends Declared account. Because the equity method has been applied, Parrot originally recorded these dividends as a decrease in the Investment in Sun Company account. To eliminate the impact of this reduction, the investment account is increased.

Consolidation Entry E

Amortization Expense	13,000	
Equipment	6,000	
Patented Technology.		13,000
Depreciation Expense		6,000

This final worksheet entry recognizes the current year's excess amortization expenses relating to the adjustments of Sun's assets to acquisition-date fair values. Because the equity method amortization was eliminated within Entry **I**, "Entry **E**" (for **E**xpense) now enters on the worksheet the current year expense attributed to each of the specific account allocations (see Exhibit 3.3). Note that we adjust depreciation expense for the tangible asset *equipment* and we adjust amortization expense for the intangible asset *patented technology*. As mentioned earlier, we refer to the adjustments to all expenses resulting from excess acquisition-date fair-value allocations collectively as *excess amortization expenses*.

Thus, the worksheet entries necessary for consolidation when the parent has applied the equity method are as follows:

Entry S—Eliminates the subsidiary's stockholders' equity accounts as of the beginning of the current year along with the equivalent book value component within the parent's investment account.

Entry A—Recognizes the unamortized allocations as of the beginning of the current year associated with the original adjustments to fair value.

Entry I—Eliminates the impact of intra-entity subsidiary income accrued by the parent.

Entry D—Eliminates the impact of intra-entity subsidiary dividends.

Entry E—Recognizes excess amortization expenses for the current period on the allocations from the original adjustments to fair value.

Exhibit 3.5 provides a complete presentation of the December 31, 2017, consolidation worksheet for Parrot Company and Sun Company. The series of entries just described brings together the separate financial statements of these two organizations. Note that the consolidated totals are the same as those computed previously for this combination.

Observe that Parrot separately reports net income of $693,000 as well as ending retained earnings of $1,413,000, figures that are identical to the totals generated for the consolidated entity. However, subsidiary income earned after the date of acquisition is to be *added* to that of the parent. Thus, a question arises in this example as to why the parent company figures alone equal the consolidated balances of both operations.

In reality, Sun's income for this period is contained in both Parrot's reported balances and the consolidated totals. Through the application of the equity method, the current year earnings of the subsidiary have already been accrued by Parrot along with the appropriate amortization expense. *The parent's Equity in Subsidiary Earnings account is, therefore, an accurate representation of Sun's effect on consolidated net income.* If the equity method is employed properly, the worksheet process simply replaces this single $93,000 balance with the specific revenue and expense accounts that it represents. *Consequently, when the parent employs the equity method, its net income and retained earnings mirror consolidated totals.*

Consolidation Subsequent to Year of Acquisition—Equity Method

In many ways, every consolidation of Parrot and Sun prepared after the date of acquisition incorporates the same basic procedures outlined in the previous section. However, the continual financial evolution undergone by the companies prohibits an exact repetition of the consolidation entries demonstrated in Exhibit 3.5.

As a basis for analyzing the procedural changes necessitated by the passage of time, assume that Parrot Company continues to hold its ownership of Sun Company as of December 31, 2020. This date was selected at random; any date subsequent to 2017 would serve equally well to illustrate this process. As an additional factor, assume that Sun now has a $40,000 liability that is payable to Parrot.

EXHIBIT 3.5   Consolidation Worksheet—Equity Method Applied

PARROT COMPANY AND SUN COMPANY
Consolidation Worksheet
Investment: Equity Method   For Year Ending December 31, 2017

Accounts	Parrot Company	Sun Company	Consolidation Entries Debit	Consolidation Entries Credit	Consolidated Totals
Income Statement					
Revenues	(1,500,000)	(400,000)			(1,900,000)
Cost of goods sold	700,000	232,000			932,000
Amortization expense	120,000	32,000	(E) 13,000		165,000
Depreciation expense	80,000	36,000		(E) 6,000	110,000
Equity in subsidiary earnings	(93,000)	–0–	(I) 93,000		–0–
Net income	(693,000)	(100,000)			(693,000)
Statement of Retained Earnings					
Retained earnings, 1/1/17	(840,000)	(380,000)	(S) 380,000		(840,000)
Net income (above)	(693,000)	(100,000)			(693,000)
Dividends declared	120,000	40,000		(D) 40,000	120,000
Retained earnings, 12/31/17	(1,413,000)	(440,000)			(1,413,000)
Balance Sheet					
Current assets	1,040,000	400,000			1,440,000
Investment in Sun Company	853,000	–0–	(D) 40,000	(S) 600,000 (A) 200,000 (I) 93,000	–0–
Trademarks	600,000	200,000	(A) 20,000		820,000
Patented technology	370,000	288,000	(A) 130,000	(E) 13,000	775,000
Equipment (net)	250,000	220,000	(E) 6,000	(A) 30,000	446,000
Goodwill	–0–	–0–	(A) 80,000		80,000
Total assets	3,113,000	1,108,000			3,561,000
Liabilities	(980,000)	(448,000)			(1,428,000)
Common stock	(600,000)	(200,000)	(S) 200,000		(600,000)
Additional paid-in capital	(120,000)	(20,000)	(S) 20,000		(120,000)
Retained earnings, 12/31/17 (above)	(1,413,000)	(440,000)			(1,413,000)
Total liabilities and equities	(3,113,000)	(1,108,000)	982,000	982,000	(3,561,000)

Note: Parentheses indicate a credit balance.
Consolidation entries:
(S) Elimination of Sun's stockholders' equity January 1 balances and the book value portion of the investment account.
(A) Allocation of Sun's acquisition-date excess fair values over book values.
(I) Elimination of parent's equity in subsidiary earnings accrual.
(D) Elimination of intra-entity dividends.
(E) Recognition of current year excess fair-value amortization and depreciation expenses.

For this consolidation, assume that the January 1, 2020, Sun Company's Retained Earnings balance has risen to $600,000. Because that account had a reported total of only $380,000 on January 1, 2017, Sun's book value apparently has increased by $220,000 during the 2017–2019 period. Although knowledge of individual operating figures in the past is not required, Sun's reported totals help to clarify the consolidation procedures.

Year	Sun Company Net Income	Dividends Declared	Increase in Book Value	Ending Retained Earnings
2017	$100,000	$ 40,000	$ 60,000	$ 440,000
2018	140,000	50,000	90,000	530,000
2019	90,000	20,000	70,000	600,000
	$330,000	$110,000	$220,000	

For 2020, the current year, we assume that Sun reports net income of $160,000 and declares and pays cash dividends of $70,000. Because it applies the equity method, Parrot recognizes earnings of $160,000. Furthermore, as shown in Exhibit 3.3, amortization expense of $7,000 applies to 2020 and must also be recorded by the parent. Consequently, Parrot reports an Equity in Subsidiary Earnings balance for the year of $153,000 ($160,000 − $7,000).

Although this income figure can be reconstructed with little difficulty, the current balance in the Investment in Sun Company account is more complicated. Over the years, the initial $800,000 acquisition price has been subjected to adjustments for

1. The annual accrual of Sun's income.
2. The receipt of dividends from Sun.
3. The recognition of annual excess amortization expenses.

Exhibit 3.6 analyzes these changes and shows the components of the Investment in Sun Company account balance as of December 31, 2020.

Following the construction of the Investment in Sun Company account, the consolidation worksheet developed in Exhibit 3.7 should be easier to understand. Current figures for both companies appear in the first two columns. The parent's investment balance and equity income accrual as well as Sun's income and stockholders' equity accounts correspond to the information given previously. Worksheet entries (lettered to agree with the previous illustration) are then utilized to consolidate all balances.

Several steps are necessary to arrive at these reported totals. The subsidiary's assets, liabilities, revenues, and expenses are added to those same accounts of the parent. The unamortized portion of the original acquisition-date fair-value allocations are included along with current excess amortization expenses. The investment and equity income balances are both eliminated as are the subsidiary's stockholders' equity accounts. Intra-entity dividends are removed as are the existing receivable and payable balances between the two companies.

Consolidation Entry S

Once again, this first consolidation entry offsets reciprocal amounts representing the subsidiary's book value as of the beginning of the current year. Sun's January 1, 2020, stockholders'

EXHIBIT 3.6
Investment Account under Equity Method

PARROT COMPANY Investment in Sun Company Account As of December 31, 2020 Equity Method Applied		
Fair value of consideration transferred at date of acquisition		$ 800,000
Entries recorded in prior years:		
Accrual of Sun Company's income		
2017	$100,000	
2018	140,000	
2019	90,000	330,000
Sun Company—Dividends declared		
2017	$ (40,000)	
2018	(50,000)	
2019	(20,000)	(110,000)
Excess amortization expenses		
2017	$ (7,000)	
2018	(7,000)	
2019	(7,000)	(21,000)
Entries recorded in current year—2020		
Accrual of Sun Company's income	$160,000	
Sun Company—Dividends declared	(70,000)	
Excess amortization expenses	(7,000)	83,000
Investment in Sun Company, 12/31/20		$1,082,000

EXHIBIT 3.7   Consolidation Worksheet Subsequent to Year of Acquisition—Equity Method Applied

	PARROT COMPANY AND SUN COMPANY					
	Consolidation Worksheet					
Investment: Equity Method	For Year Ending December 31, 2020					
Accounts	**Parrot Company**	**Sun Company**	**Consolidation Entries**		**Consolidation Totals**	
			Debit	**Credit**		
Income Statement						
Revenues	(2,100,000)	(600,000)			(2,700,000)	
Cost of goods sold	1,000,000	380,000			1,380,000	
Amortization expense	200,000	20,000	(E) 13,000		233,000	
Depreciation expense	100,000	40,000		(E) 6,000	134,000	
Equity in subsidiary earnings	(153,000)	–0–	(I) 153,000		–0–	
Net income	(953,000)	(160,000)			(953,000)	
Statement of Retained Earnings						
Retained earnings, 1/1/20	(2,044,000)	(600,000)	(S) 600,000		(2,044,000)	
Net income (above)	(953,000)	(160,000)			(953,000)	
Dividends declared	420,000	70,000		(D) 70,000	420,000	
Retained earnings, 12/31/20	(2,577,000)	(690,000)			(2,577,000)	
Balance Sheet						
Current assets	1,705,000	500,000		(P) 40,000	2,165,000	
Investment in Sun Company	1,082,000	–0–	(D) 70,000	(S) 820,000	–0–	
				(A) 179,000		
				(I) 153,000		
Trademarks	600,000	240,000	(A) 20,000		860,000	
Patented technology	540,000	420,000	(A) 91,000	(E) 13,000	1,038,000	
Equipment (net)	420,000	210,000	(E) 6,000	(A) 12,000	624,000	
Goodwill	–0–	–0–	(A) 80,000		80,000	
Total assets	4,347,000	1,370,000			4,767,000	
Liabilities	(1,050,000)	(460,000)	(P) 40,000		(1,470,000)	
Common stock	(600,000)	(200,000)	(S) 200,000		(600,000)	
Additional paid-in capital	(120,000)	(20,000)	(S) 20,000		(120,000)	
Retained earnings, 12/31/20 (above)	(2,577,000)	(690,000)			(2,577,000)	
Total liabilities and equities	(4,347,000)	(1,370,000)	1,293,000	1,293,000	(4,767,000)	

Note: Parentheses indicate a credit balance.
Consolidation entries:
(S)   Elimination of Sun's stockholders' equity January 1 balances and the book value portion of the investment account.
(A)   Allocation of Sun's acquisition-date excess fair values over book values, unamortized balance as of beginning of year.
(I)   Elimination of parent's equity in subsidiary earnings accrual.
(D)   Elimination of intra-entity dividends.
(E)   Recognition of current year excess fair-value amortization and depreciation expenses.
(P)   Elimination of intra-entity receivable/payable.

equity accounts are eliminated against the book value portion of the parent's investment account. Here, though, the amount eliminated is $820,000 rather than the $600,000 shown in Exhibit 3.5 for 2017. Both balances have changed during the 2017–2019 period. Sun's operations caused a $220,000 increase in retained earnings. Parrot's application of the equity method created a parallel effect on its Investment in Sun Company account (the income accrual of $330,000 less dividends collected of $110,000).

Although Sun's Retained Earnings balance is removed in this entry, the income this company earned since the acquisition date is still included in the consolidated figures. Parrot accrues these profits annually through application of the equity method. Thus, elimination of the subsidiary's entire Retained Earnings is necessary; a portion was earned prior to the acquisition and the remainder has already been recorded by the parent.

Entry **S** removes these balances as of the first day of 2020 rather than at the end of the year. The consolidation process is made a bit simpler by segregating the effect of preceding operations from the transactions of the current year. Thus, *all worksheet entries relate specifically to either the previous years (S and A) or the current period (I, D, E, and P).*

Consolidation Entry A

In the initial consolidation (2017), fair-value allocations amounting to $200,000 were entered, but these balances have now undergone three years of amortization. As computed in Exhibit 3.8, expenses for these prior years totaled $21,000, leaving a balance of $179,000. Allocation of this amount to the individual accounts is also determined in Exhibit 3.8 and reflected in worksheet Entry **A.** As with Entry **S,** these balances are calculated as of January 1, 2020, and replaced by current year expenses as shown in Entry **E.**

Consolidation Entry I

As before, this entry eliminates the equity income recorded currently by Parrot ($153,000) in connection with its ownership of Sun. The subsidiary's revenue and expense accounts are left intact so they can be included in the consolidated figures.

Consolidation Entry D

This worksheet entry offsets the $70,000 intra-entity dividends (from Sun to Parrot) during the current period.

Consolidation Entry E

Excess amortization expenses relating to acquisition-date fair-value adjustments are individually recorded for the current period.

Before progressing to the final worksheet entry, note the close similarity of these entries with the five entries incorporated in the 2017 consolidation (Exhibit 3.5). Except for the numerical changes created by the passage of time, the entries are identical.

Consolidation Entry P

This last entry (labeled "Entry **P**" because it eliminates an intra-entity **P**ayable) introduces a new element to the consolidation process. As noted earlier, intra-entity reciprocal accounts do not relate to outside parties. Therefore, Sun's $40,000 payable and Parrot's $40,000 receivable must be removed on the worksheet because the companies are being reported as a single entity.

In reviewing Exhibit 3.7, note several aspects of the consolidation process:

- The stockholders' equity accounts of the subsidiary are removed.
- The Investment in Sun Company and the Equity in Subsidiary Earnings are both removed.
- The parent's Retained Earnings balance is not adjusted. Because the parent applies the equity method this account should be correct.
- The acquisition-date fair-value adjustments to the subsidiary's assets are recognized but only after adjustment for prior periods' annual excess amortization expenses.
- Intra-entity balances such as dividends and receivables/payables are offset.

EXHIBIT 3.8
Excess Amortizations Relating to Individual Accounts as of January 1, 2020

Accounts	Original Allocation	Annual Excess Amortizations			Balance 1/1/20
		2017	2018	2019	
Trademarks	$ 20,000	$ –0–	$ –0–	$ –0–	$ 20,000
Patented technology	130,000	13,000	13,000	13,000	91,000
Equipment	(30,000)	(6,000)	(6,000)	(6,000)	(12,000)
Goodwill	80,000	–0–	–0–	–0–	80,000
	$200,000	$ 7,000	$ 7,000	$ 7,000	$179,000
			$21,000		

LO 3-3b

Prepare consolidated financial statements subsequent to acquisition when the parent has applied **the initial value method** in its internal records.

LO 3-3c

Prepare consolidated financial statements subsequent to acquisition when the parent has applied **the partial equity method** in its internal records.

Subsequent Consolidations—Investment Recorded Using Initial Value or Partial Equity Method

Acquisition Made during the Current Year

As discussed at the beginning of this chapter, the parent company may opt to use the initial value method or the partial equity method for internal record-keeping rather than the equity method. Application of either alternative changes the balances recorded by the parent over time and, thus, the procedures followed in creating consolidations. However, *choosing one of these other approaches does not affect any of the final consolidated figures to be reported.*

When a company utilizes the equity method, it eliminates all reciprocal accounts, assigns unamortized fair-value allocations to specific accounts, and records amortization expense for the current year. Application of either the initial value method or the partial equity method has no effect on this basic process. For this reason, a number of the consolidation entries remain the same regardless of the parent's investment accounting method.

In reality, just three of the parent's accounts actually vary because of the method applied:

- The investment account.
- The income recognized from the subsidiary.
- The parent's retained earnings (in periods after the initial year of the combination).

Only the differences found in these balances affect the consolidation process when another method is applied. Thus, any time after the acquisition date, accounting for these three balances is of special importance.

To illustrate the modifications required by the adoption of an alternative accounting method, the consolidation of Parrot and Sun as of December 31, 2017, is reconstructed. Only one differing factor is introduced: the method by which Parrot accounts for its investment. Exhibit 3.9 presents the 2017 consolidation based on Parrot's use of the initial value method. Exhibit 3.10 demonstrates this same process assuming that the parent applied the partial equity method. Each entry on these worksheets is labeled to correspond with the 2017 consolidation in which the parent used the equity method (Exhibit 3.5). Furthermore, differences with the equity method (both on the parent company records and with the consolidation entries) are highlighted on each of the worksheets.

Initial Value Method Applied—2017 Consolidation

Although the initial value method theoretically stands in marked contrast to the equity method, few reporting differences actually exist. In the year of acquisition, Parrot's income and investment accounts relating to the subsidiary are the only accounts affected.

Under the initial value method, income recognition in 2017 is limited to the $40,000 dividend received by the parent; no equity income accrual is made. At the same time, the investment account retains its $800,000 initial value. Unlike the equity method, no adjustments are recorded in the parent's investment account in connection with the current year operations, subsidiary dividends, or amortization of any fair-value allocations.

After the composition of the dividend income and investment accounts has been established, worksheet entries can be used to produce the consolidated figures found in Exhibit 3.9 as of December 31, 2017.

Consolidation Entry S

As with the previous Entry **S** in Exhibit 3.5, the $600,000 component of the investment account is eliminated against the beginning stockholders' equity account of the subsidiary. Both are equivalent to Sun's net assets at January 1, 2017, and are, therefore, reciprocal balances that must be offset. This entry is not affected by the accounting method in use.

Consolidation Entry A

Sun's $200,000 excess acquisition-date fair value over book value is allocated to Sun's assets and liabilities based on their fair values at the date of acquisition. The $80,000 residual is

EXHIBIT 3.9   Consolidation Worksheet—Initial Value Method Applied

PARROT COMPANY AND SUN COMPANY					
Consolidation Worksheet					
Investment: Initial Value Method		**For Year Ending December 31, 2017**			

Accounts	Parrot Company	Sun Company	Consolidation Entries Debit	Consolidation Entries Credit	Consolidation Totals
Income Statement					
Revenues	(1,500,000)	(400,000)			(1,900,000)
Cost of goods sold	700,000	232,000			932,000
Amortization expense	120,000	32,000	(E) 13,000		165,000
Depreciation expense	80,000	36,000		(E) 6,000	110,000
Dividend income	(40,000)*	–0–	(I) 40,000*		–0–
Net income	(640,000)	(100,000)			(693,000)
Statement of Retained Earnings					
Retained earnings, 1/1/17	(840,000)	(380,000)	(S) 380,000		(840,000)
Net income (above)	(640,000)	(100,000)			(693,000)
Dividends declared	120,000	40,000		(I) 40,000*	120,000
Retained earnings, 12/31/17	(1,360,000)	(440,000)			(1,413,000)
Balance Sheet					
Current assets	1,040,000	400,000			1,440,000
Investment in Sun Company	800,000*	–0–		(S) 600,000	–0–
				(A) 200,000	
Trademarks	600,000	200,000	(A) 20,000		820,000
Patented technology	370,000	288,000	(A) 130,000	(E) 13,000	775,000
Equipment (net)	250,000	220,000	(E) 6,000	(A) 30,000	446,000
Goodwill	–0–	–0–	(A) 80,000		80,000
Total assets	3,060,000	1,108,000			3,561,000
Liabilities	(980,000)	(448,000)			(1,428,000)
Common stock	(600,000)	(200,000)	(S) 200,000		(600,000)
Additional paid-in capital	(120,000)	(20,000)	(S) 20,000		(120,000)
Retained earnings, 12/31/17 (above)	(1,360,000)	(440,000)			(1,413,000)
Total liabilities and equities	(3,060,000)	(1,108,000)	889,000	889,000	(3,561,000)

Note: Parentheses indicate a credit balance.
*Boxed items highlight differences with consolidation in Exhibit 3.5.
Consolidation entries:
- (S)   Elimination of Sun's stockholders' equity January 1 balances and the book value portion of the investment account.
- (A)   Allocation of Sun's acquisition-date excess fair values over book values.
- (I)   Elimination of intra-entity dividend income and dividends declared by Sun.
- (E)   Recognition of current year excess fair-value amortization and depreciation expenses.

Note: Consolidation entry (D) is not needed when the parent applies the initial value method because entry (I) eliminates the intra-entity dividend effects.

attributed to goodwill. This procedure is identical to the corresponding entry in Exhibit 3.5 in which the equity method was applied.

Consolidation Entry I

Under the initial value method, the parent records dividends declared by the subsidiary as income. Entry **I** removes this Dividend Income account along with Sun's Dividends Declared. From a consolidated perspective, these two $40,000 balances represent an intra-entity transfer that had no financial impact outside of the entity. In contrast to the equity method, Parrot has not accrued subsidiary income, nor has amortization been recorded; thus, no further income elimination is needed.

EXHIBIT 3.10 Consolidation Worksheet—Partial Equity Method Applied

PARROT COMPANY AND SUN COMPANY
Consolidation Worksheet
For Year Ending December 31, 2017

Investment: Partial Equity Method

Accounts	Parrot Company	Sun Company	Consolidation Entries Debit	Consolidation Entries Credit	Consolidation Totals
Income Statement					
Revenues	(1,500,000)	(400,000)			(1,900,000)
Cost of goods sold	700,000	232,000			932,000
Amortization expense	120,000	32,000	(E) 13,000		165,000
Depreciation expense	80,000	36,000		(E) 6,000	110,000
Equity in subsidiary earnings	(100,000)*	–0–	(I) 100,000 *		–0–
Net income	(700,000)	(100,000)			(693,000)
Statement of Retained Earnings					
Retained earnings, 1/1/17	(840,000)	(380,000)	(S) 380,000		(840,000)
Net income (above)	(700,000)	(100,000)			(693,000)
Dividends declared	120,000	40,000		(D) 40,000	120,000
Retained earnings, 12/31/17	(1,420,000)	(440,000)			(1,413,000)
Balance Sheet					
Current assets	1,040,000	400,000			1,440,000
Investment in Sun Company	860,000 *	–0–	(D) 40,000	(S) 600,000	–0–
				(A) 200,000	
				(I) 100,000 *	
Trademarks	600,000	200,000	(A) 20,000		820,000
Patented technology	370,000	288,000	(A) 130,000	(E) 13,000	775,000
Equipment (net)	250,000	220,000	(E) 6,000	(A) 30,000	446,000
Goodwill	–0–	–0–	(A) 80,000		80,000
Total assets	3,120,000	1,108,000			3,561,000
Liabilities	(980,000)	(448,000)			(1,428,000)
Common stock	(600,000)	(200,000)	(S) 200,000		(600,000)
Additional paid-in capital	(120,000)	(20,000)	(S) 20,000		(120,000)
Retained earnings, 12/31/17 (above)	(1,420,000)	(440,000)			(1,413,000)
Total liabilities and equities	(3,120,000)	(1,108,000)	989,000	989,000	(3,561,000)

Note: Parentheses indicate a credit balance.
*Boxed items highlight differences with consolidation in Exhibit 3.5.
Consolidation entries:
  (S)   Elimination of Sun's stockholders' equity January 1 balances and the book value portion of the investment account.
  (A)   Allocation of Sun's acquisition-date excess fair values over book values.
  (I)   Elimination of parent's equity in subsidiary earnings accrual.
  (D)   Elimination of intra-entity dividends.
  (E)   Recognition of current year excess fair-value amortization and depreciation expenses.

Dividend Income.	40,000	
Dividends Declared		40,000
To eliminate intra-entity income.		

Consolidation Entry D

When the initial value method is applied, the parent records intra-entity dividends as income. Because these dividends were already removed from the consolidated totals by Entry **I,** no separate Entry **D** is required.

Consolidation Entry E

Regardless of the parent's method of accounting, the reporting entity must recognize excess amortizations for the current year in connection with the original fair-value allocations. Thus, Entry **E** serves to bring the current year expenses into the consolidated financial statements.

Consequently, using the initial value method rather than the equity method changes only Entries **I** and **D** in the year of acquisition. Despite the change in methods, reported figures are still derived by (1) eliminating all reciprocals, (2) allocating the excess portion of the acquisition-date fair values, and (3) recording amortizations on these allocations. As indicated previously, the consolidated totals appearing in Exhibit 3.9 are identical to the figures produced previously in Exhibit 3.5. Although the income and the investment accounts on the parent company's separate statements vary, the consolidated balances are not affected.

One significant difference between the initial value method and equity method does exist: The parent's separate statements do not reflect consolidated income totals when the initial value method is used. Because equity adjustments (such as excess amortizations) are not recorded, neither Parrot's reported net income of $640,000 nor its retained earnings of $1,360,000 provides an accurate portrayal of consolidated figures.

Partial Equity Method Applied—2017 Consolidation

Exhibit 3.10 presents a worksheet to consolidate these two companies for 2017 (the year of acquisition) based on the assumption that Parrot applied the partial equity method. Again, the only changes from previous examples are found in (1) the parent's separate records for this investment and its related income and (2) worksheet Entries **I** and **D.**

As discussed earlier, under the partial equity approach, the parent's record-keeping is limited to two periodic journal entries: the annual accrual of subsidiary income and the recognition of dividends. Hence, within the parent's records, only a few differences exist when the partial equity method is applied rather than the initial value method. The entries recorded by Parrot in connection with Sun's 2017 operations illustrate both of these approaches.

Therefore, by applying the partial equity method, the investment account on the parent's balance sheet rises to $860,000 by the end of 2017. This total is composed of the original $800,000 acquisition-date fair value for Sun adjusted for the $100,000 income recognition and the $40,000 cash dividend. The same $100,000 equity income figure appears within the parent's income statement. These two balances are appropriately found in Parrot's records in Exhibit 3.10.

Because of differences in income recognition and the effects of subsidiary dividends, Entries **I** and **D** again differ on the worksheet. For the partial equity method, the $100,000 equity income is eliminated (Entry **I**) by reversing the parent's entry. Removing this accrual allows the individual revenue and expense accounts of the subsidiary to be reported without double-counting. The $40,000 intra-entity dividend must also be removed (Entry **D**). The Dividends Declared account is simply deleted. However, elimination of the dividend from the

Parrot Company Initial Value Method 2017			Parrot Company Partial Equity Method 2017		
Dividend Receivable	40,000		Dividend Receivable	40,000	
Dividend Income.		40,000	Investment in Sun Company		40,000
Subsidiary dividends declared.			Subsidiary dividends declared.		
Cash	40,000		Cash	40,000	
Dividend Receivable . .		40,000	Dividend Receivable . .		40,000
To record the receipt of the cash dividend.			To record the receipt of the cash dividend.		
			Investment in Sun Company	100,000	
			Equity in Subsidiary Earnings		100,000
			Accrual of subsidiary income.		

Investment in Sun Company actually causes an increase because the dividend was recorded by Parrot as a reduction in that account. All other consolidation entries (Entries **S, A,** and **E**) are the same for all three methods.

LO 3-4

Understand that a parent's internal accounting method for its subsidiary investments has no effect on the resulting consolidated financial statements.

Comparisons across Internal Investment Methods

Consolidated financial worksheets have now been completed when the parent uses the equity, initial value, and partial equity methods. At this point it is instructive to compare the final consolidated balances in Exhibits 3.5, 3.9, and 3.10. Note the identical final consolidated column balances across the three internal methods of investment accounting. Thus, the parent's internal investment method choice has no effect on the resulting consolidated financial statements.

Consolidation Subsequent to Year of Acquisition—Initial Value and Partial Equity Methods

By again incorporating the December 31, 2020, financial data for Parrot and Sun (presented in Exhibit 3.7), consolidation procedures for the initial value method and the partial equity method are examined for years subsequent to the date of acquisition. *In both cases, establishment of an appropriate beginning retained earnings figure becomes a significant goal of the consolidation.*

Conversion of the Parent's Retained Earnings to a Full-Accrual (Equity) Basis

Consolidated financial statements require a *full accrual-based measurement of both income and retained earnings.* The initial value method, however, recognizes income when the subsidiary declares a dividend thus ignoring when the underlying income was earned. The partial equity method only partially accrues subsidiary income. Thus, neither provides a full accrual-based measure of the subsidiary activities on the parent's income. As a result, over time the parent's retained earnings account fails to show a full accrual-based amount. Therefore, new worksheet adjustments are required to convert the parent's beginning of the year retained earnings balance to a full-accrual basis. These adjustments are made to *beginning of the year retained earnings* because current year earnings are readily converted to full-accrual basis by simply combining current year revenue and expenses. The resulting current year combined income figure is then added to the adjusted beginning of the year retained earnings to arrive at a full-accrual ending retained earnings balance.

This concern was not faced previously when the equity method was adopted. Under that approach, the parent's Retained Earnings account balance already reflects a full-accrual basis so that no adjustment is necessary. In the earlier illustration, the $330,000 income accrual for the 2017–2019 period as well as the $21,000 amortization expense was recognized by the parent in applying the equity method (see Exhibit 3.6). Having been recorded in this manner, these two balances form a permanent part of Parrot's retained earnings and are included automatically in the consolidated total. Consequently, if the equity method is applied, the process is simplified; no worksheet entries are needed to adjust the parent's Retained Earnings account to record subsidiary operations or amortization for past years.

Conversely, if a method other than the equity method is used, a worksheet change must be made to the parent's beginning Retained Earnings account (in every subsequent year) to equate this balance with a full-accrual amount. To quantify this adjustment, the parent's recognized income for these past three years under each method is first determined (Exhibit 3.11). For consolidation purposes, the beginning retained earnings account must then be increased or decreased to create the same effect as the equity method.

EXHIBIT 3.11
Retained Earnings
Differences

PARROT COMPANY AND SUN COMPANY Previous Years—2017–2019			
	Equity Method	Initial Value Method	Partial Equity Method
Equity accrual	$330,000	$ –0–	$330,000
Dividend income	–0–	110,000	–0–
Excess amortization expenses	(21,000)	–0–	–0–
Increase in parent's retained earnings	$309,000	$110,000	$330,000

Initial Value Method Applied—Subsequent Consolidation

As shown in Exhibit 3.11, if Parrot applied the initial value method during the 2017–2019 period, it recognizes $199,000 less income than under the equity method ($309,000 − $110,000). Two items cause this difference. First, Parrot has not accrued the $220,000 increase in the subsidiary's book value across the periods prior to the current year. Although the $110,000 in dividends was recorded as income, the parent never recognized the remainder of the $330,000 earned by the subsidiary.[7] Second, no accounting has been made of the $21,000 excess amortization expenses. Thus, the parent's beginning Retained Earnings account is $199,000 ($220,000 − $21,000) below the appropriate consolidated total and must be adjusted.[8]

To simulate the equity method so that the parent's beginning Retained Earnings account reflects a full-accrual basis, this $199,000 increase is recorded through a worksheet entry. The initial value method figures reported by the parent effectively are converted into equity method balances.

Investment in Sun Company...	199,000	
Retained Earnings, 1/1/20 (Parrot Company)		199,000
To convert parent's beginning retained earnings from the initial value method to equity method.		

This adjustment is labeled Entry *C. The C refers to the conversion being made to equity method (full-accrual) totals. The asterisk indicates that this equity simulation relates solely to transactions of prior periods. Thus, *Entry *C should be recorded before the other worksheet entries to align the beginning balances for the year.*

Exhibit 3.12 provides a complete presentation of the consolidation of Parrot and Sun as of December 31, 2020, based on the parent's application of the initial value method. After Entry *C has been recorded on the worksheet, the remainder of this consolidation follows the same pattern as previous examples. Sun's stockholders' equity accounts are eliminated (Entry S) while the allocations stemming from the $800,000 initial fair value are recorded (Entry A) at their unamortized balances as of January 1, 2020 (see Exhibit 3.8). Intra-entity dividend income is removed (Entry I) and current year excess amortization expenses are recognized (Entry E). To complete this process, the intra-entity receivable and payable of $40,000 are offset (Entry P).

In retrospect, the only new element introduced here is the adjustment of the parent's beginning Retained Earnings. For a consolidation produced after the initial year of acquisition, an Entry *C is required if the parent has not applied the equity method.

Partial Equity Method Applied—Subsequent Consolidation

Exhibit 3.13 demonstrates the worksheet consolidation of Parrot and Sun as of December 31, 2020, when the investment accounts have been recorded by the parent using the partial equity method. This approach accrues subsidiary income each year but records no other equity adjustments. Therefore, as of December 31, 2020, Parrot's Investment in Sun Company account has a balance of $1,110,000:

[7] Two different calculations are available for determining the $220,000 in nonrecorded income for prior years: (1) subsidiary income less dividends declared and (2) the change in the subsidiary's book value as of the first day of the current year. The second method works only if the subsidiary has had no other equity transactions such as the issuance of new stock or the purchase of treasury shares. Unless otherwise stated, the assumption is made that no such transactions have occurred.

[8] Because neither the income in excess of dividends nor excess amortization is recorded by the parent under the initial value method, its beginning Retained Earnings account is $199,000 less than the $2,044,000 reported under the equity method (Exhibit 3.7). Thus, a $1,845,000 balance is shown in Exhibit 3.12 ($2,044,000 less $199,000). Conversely, if the partial equity method had been applied, Parrot's absence of amortization would cause the Retained Earnings account to be $21,000 higher than the figure derived by the equity method. For this reason, Exhibit 3.13 shows the parent with a beginning Retained Earnings account of $2,065,000 rather than $2,044,000.

Fair value of consideration transferred for Sun Company 1/1/17		$ 800,000
Sun Company's 2017–2019 increase in book value:		
Accrual of Sun Company's income	$ 330,000	
Sun Company's dividends	(110,000)	220,000
Sun Company's 2020 operations:		
Accrual of Sun Company's income	$ 160,000	
Sun Company's dividends	(70,000)	90,000
Investment in Sun Company, 12/31/20 (Partial equity method)		$1,110,000

EXHIBIT 3.12   **Consolidation Worksheet Subsequent to Year of Acquisition—Initial Value Method Applied**

PARROT COMPANY AND SUN COMPANY
Consolidation Worksheet

Investment: Initial Value Method   **For Year Ending December 31, 2020**

Accounts	Parrot Company	Sun Company	Consolidation Entries Debit	Consolidation Entries Credit	Consolidation Totals
Income Statement					
Revenues	(2,100,000)	(600,000)			(2,700,000)
Cost of goods sold	1,000,000	380,000			1,380,000
Amortization expense	200,000	20,000	(E) 13,000		233,000
Depreciation expense	100,000	40,000		(E) 6,000	134,000
Dividend income	(70,000)*	–0–	(I) 70,000 *		–0–
Net income	(870,000)	(160,000)			(953,000)
Statement of Retained Earnings					
Retained earnings, 1/1/20					
Parrot Company	(1,845,000)†*			(*C) 199,000 *	(2,044,000)
Sun Company		(600,000)	(S) 600,000		–0–
Net income (above)	(870,000)	(160,000)			(953,000)
Dividends declared	420,000	70,000		(I) 70,000 *	420,000
Retained earnings, 12/31/20	(2,295,000)	(690,000)			(2,577,000)
Balance Sheet					
Current assets	1,705,000	500,000		(P) 40,000	2,165,000
Investment in Sun Company	800,000*	–0–	(*C) 199,000	(S) 820,000	–0–
				(A) 179,000	
Trademarks	600,000	240,000	(A) 20,000		860,000
Patented technology	540,000	420,000	(A) 91,000	(E) 13,000	1,038,000
Equipment (net)	420,000	210,000	(E) 6,000	(A) 12,000	624,000
Goodwill	–0–	–0–	(A) 80,000		80,000
Total assets	4,065,000	1,370,000			4,767,000
Liabilities	(1,050,000)	(460,000)	(P) 40,000		(1,470,000)
Common stock	(600,000)	(200,000)	(S) 200,000		(600,000)
Additional paid-in capital	(120,000)	(20,000)	(S) 20,000		(120,000)
Retained earnings, 12/31/20 (above)	(2,295,000)	(690,000)			(2,577,000)
Total liabilities and equities	(4,065,000)	(1,370,000)	1,339,000	1,339,000	(4,767,000)

Note: Parentheses indicate a credit balance.
*Boxed items highlight differences with consolidation in Exhibit 3.7.
†See footnote 8.
Consolidation entries:
   (*C) To convert parent's beginning retained earnings to full accrual basis.
   (S)   Elimination of Sun's stockholders' equity January 1 balances and the book value portion of investment account.
   (A)   Allocation of Sun's excess acquisition-date fair value over book value, unamortized balance as of beginning of year.
   (I)   Elimination of intra-entity dividend income and dividends declared by Sun.
   (E)   Recognition of current year excess fair-value amortization and depreciation expenses.
   (P)   Elimination of intra-entity receivable/payable.
Note: Consolidation entry (D) is not needed when the parent applies the initial value method because entry (I) eliminates the intra-entity dividend effects.

EXHIBIT 3.13 Consolidation Worksheet Subsequent to Year of Acquisition—Partial Equity Method Applied

PARROT COMPANY AND SUN COMPANY
Consolidation Worksheet
Investment: Partial Equity Method — **For Year Ending December 31, 2020**

Accounts	Parrot Company	Sun Company	Consolidation Entries Debit	Consolidation Entries Credit	Consolidation Totals
Income Statement					
Revenues	(2,100,000)	(600,000)			(2,700,000)
Cost of goods sold	1,000,000	380,000			1,380,000
Amortization expense	200,000	20,000	(E) 13,000		233,000
Depreciation expense	100,000	40,000		(E) 6,000	134,000
Equity in subsidiary earnings	(160,000) *	–0–	(I) 160,000 *		–0–
Net income	(960,000)	(160,000)			(953,000)
Statement of Retained Earnings					
Retained earnings, 1/1/20					
Parrot Company	(2,065,000)†*		(*C) 21,000 *		(2,044,000)
Sun Company		(600,000)	(S) 600,000		–0–
Net income (above)	(960,000)	(160,000)			(953,000)
Dividends declared	420,000	70,000		(D) 70,000*	420,000
Retained earnings, 12/31/20	(2,605,000)	(690,000)			(2,577,000)
Balance Sheet					
Current assets	1,705,000	500,000		(P) 40,000	2,165,000
Investment in Sun Company	1,110,000 *	–0–	(D) 70,000	(*C) 21,000 *	–0–
				(S) 820,000	
				(A) 179,000	
				(I) 160,000 *	
Trademarks	600,000	240,000	(A) 20,000		860,000
Patented technology	540,000	420,000	(A) 91,000	(E) 13,000	1,038,000
Equipment (net)	420,000	210,000	(E) 6,000	(A) 12,000	624,000
Goodwill	–0–	–0–	(A) 80,000		80,000
Total assets	4,375,000	1,370,000			4,767,000
Liabilities	(1,050,000)	(460,000)	(P) 40,000		(1,470,000)
Common stock	(600,000)	(200,000)	(S) 200,000		(600,000)
Additional paid-in capital	(120,000)	(20,000)	(S) 20,000		(120,000)
Retained earnings, 12/31/20 (above)	(2,605,000)	(690,000)			(2,577,000)
Total liabilities and equities	(4,375,000)	(1,370,000)	1,321,000	1,321,000	(4,767,000)

Note: Parentheses indicate a credit balance.
*Boxed items highlight differences with consolidation in Exhibit 3.7.
†See footnote 8.
Consolidation entries:
  (*C) To convert parent's beginning retained earnings to full accrual basis.
  (S) Elimination of Sun's stockholders' equity January 1 balances and the book value portion of investment account.
  (A) Allocation of Sun's excess acquisition-date fair over book value, unamortized balance as of beginning of year.
  (I) Elimination of parent's equity in subsidiary earnings accrual.
  (D) Elimination of intra-entity dividends.
  (E) Recognition of current year excess fair-value amortization and depreciation expenses.
  (P) Elimination of intra-entity receivable/payable.

As indicated here and in Exhibit 3.11, Parrot has recognized the yearly equity income accrual but not amortization. When the parent employs the partial equity method, the parent's beginning Retained Earnings account must be adjusted to include this expense. Therefore, Entry *C provides the three-year $21,000 amortization total to simulate the equity method and, hence, consolidated totals.

? Discussion Question

In consolidation worksheet entry *C, we adjust the parent's *beginning of the year* retained earnings to a full accrual basis. Why don't we adjust to the parent's *end of the year* retained earnings balance on the consolidated worksheet?

Clearly, in a consolidated balance sheet, we wish to report the parent's end-of-period consolidated retained earnings at its full accrual GAAP basis. To accomplish this goal, we utilize the following separate individual components of end-of-period retained earnings available on the worksheet.

Beginning of the year balance (after *C adjustment if parent does not employ equity method)
+ Net income (parent's share of consolidated net income adjusted to full accrual by combining revenues and expenses—including excess acquisition-date fair value amortizations)
− Dividends (parent's dividends)
= End of the year balance

The worksheet provides for the computation of current year full accrual consolidated net income via the income statement section. Dividends are already provided in the retained earnings section of the consolidated worksheet. The only component of the ending balance of retained earnings that requires a special adjustment (*C) is the beginning balance.

How does the consolidation worksheet entry *C differ when the parent uses the initial value method versus the partial equity method? Why is no *C adjustment needed when consolidated statements are prepared for the first fiscal year-end after the business combination?

Consolidation Entry *C

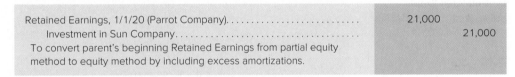

Retained Earnings, 1/1/20 (Parrot Company)................................	21,000	
Investment in Sun Company...		21,000
To convert parent's beginning Retained Earnings from partial equity method to equity method by including excess amortizations.		

By recording Entry ***C** on the worksheet, all of the subsidiary's operational results for the 2017–2019 period are included in the consolidation. As shown in Exhibit 3.13, the remainder of the worksheet entries follow the same basic pattern as that illustrated previously for the year of acquisition (Exhibit 3.10).

Summary of Worksheet Procedures

Having three investment methods available to the parent means that three sets of entries must be understood to arrive at reported figures appropriate for a business combination. The process can initially seem to be a confusing overlap of procedures. However, at this point in the coverage, only three worksheet entries actually are affected by the choice of either the equity method, partial equity method, or initial value method: Entries ***C, I,** and **D.** Furthermore, accountants should never get so involved with a worksheet and its entries that they lose sight of the balances that this process is designed to calculate. Exhibit 3.14 provides a summary of the final consolidated totals and how they are calculated. These figures are never affected by the parent's choice of an accounting method.

After the appropriate balance for each account is understood, worksheet entries assist the accountant in deriving these figures. To help clarify the consolidation process required under each of the three accounting methods, Exhibit 3.14 describes the purpose of each worksheet entry: first during the year of acquisition and second for any period following the year of acquisition.

?

Discussion Question

HOW DOES A COMPANY REALLY DECIDE WHICH INVESTMENT METHOD TO APPLY?

Pilgrim Products, Inc., buys a controlling interest in the common stock of Crestwood Corporation. Shortly after the acquisition, a meeting of Pilgrim's accounting department is convened to discuss the internal reporting procedures required by the ownership of this subsidiary. Each member of the staff has a definite opinion as to whether the equity method, initial value method, or partial equity method should be adopted. To resolve this issue, Pilgrim's chief financial officer outlines several of her concerns about the decision.

> I already understand how each method works. I know the general advantages and disadvantages of all three. I realize, for example, that the equity method provides more detailed information whereas the initial value method is much easier to apply. What I need to know are the factors specific to our situation that should be considered in deciding which method to adopt. I must make a recommendation to the president on this matter, and he will want firm reasons for my favoring a particular approach. I don't want us to select a method and then find out in six months that the information is not adequate for our needs or that the cost of adapting our system to monitor Crestwood outweighs the benefits derived from the data.

What are the factors that Pilgrim's officials should evaluate when making this decision?

EXHIBIT 3.14
Consolidated Totals Subsequent to Acquisition*

Current revenues	Parent revenues are included. Subsidiary revenues are included but only for the period since the acquisition.
Current expenses	Parent expenses are included. Subsidiary expenses are included but only for the period since the acquisition. Amortization expenses of the excess fair-value allocations are included by recognition on the worksheet.
Investment (or dividend) income	Income recognized by parent is eliminated and effectively replaced by the subsidiary's revenues and expenses.
Retained earnings, beginning balance	Parent balance is included. The change in the subsidiary balance since acquisition is included either as a regular accrual by the parent or through a worksheet entry to increase parent balance. Past amortization expenses of the excess fair-value allocations are included either as a part of parent balance or through a worksheet entry.
Assets and liabilities	Parent balances are included. Subsidiary balances are included after adjusting for acquisition-date fair values less amortization to beginning of current period. Intra-entity receivable/payable balances are eliminated.
Goodwill Investment in subsidiary	Original fair-value allocation is included unless reduced by impairment. Asset account recorded by parent is eliminated on the worksheet so that the balance is not included in consolidated figures.
Capital stock and additional paid-in capital	Parent balances only are included although they will have been adjusted at acquisition date if stock was issued.

*The next few chapters discuss the necessity of altering some of these balances for consolidation purposes. Thus, this table is not definitive but is included only to provide a basic overview of the consolidation process as it has been described to this point.

EXHIBIT 3.15 **Consolidation Worksheet Entries**

Equity Method Applied		Initial Value Method Applied	Partial Equity Method Applied
Any Time during Year of Acquisition			
Entry **S**	Beginning stockholders' equity of subsidiary is eliminated against book value portion of investment account.	Same as equity method.	Same as equity method.
Entry **A**	Excess fair value is allocated to assets and liabilities based on difference in book values and fair values; residual is assigned to goodwill.	Same as equity method.	Same as equity method.
Entry **I**	Equity income accrual (including amortization expense) is eliminated.	Dividend income is eliminated.	Equity income accrual is eliminated.
Entry **D**	Intra-entity dividends declared by subsidiary are eliminated.	No entry—intra-entity dividends are eliminated in Entry **I**.	Same as equity method.
Entry **E**	Current year excess amortization expenses of fair-value allocations are recorded.	Same as equity method.	Same as equity method.
Entry **P**	Intra-entity payable/receivable balances are offset.	Same as equity method.	Same as equity method.
Any Time Following Year of Acquisition			
Entry ***C**	No entry—equity income for prior years has already been recognized along with amortization expenses.	Increase in subsidiary's book value during prior years and excess amortization expenses are recognized (conversion is made to equity method).	Excess amortization expenses for prior years are recognized (conversion is made to equity method).
Entry **S**	Same as initial year.	Same as initial year.	Same as initial year.
Entry **A**	Unamortized excess fair value at beginning of year is allocated to specific accounts and to goodwill.	Same as equity method.	Same as equity method.
Entry **I**	Same as initial year.	Same as initial year.	Same as initial year.
Entry **D**	Same as initial year.	Same as initial year.	Same as initial year.
Entry **E**	Same as initial year.	Same as initial year.	Same as initial year.
Entry **P**	Same as initial year.	Same as initial year.	Same as initial year.

Excess Fair Value Attributable to Subsidiary Long-Term Debt: Post-Acquisition Procedures

In the previous consolidation examples for Parrot and Sun Company, the acquisition-date excess fair values were attributed solely to long-term assets. Similarly, however, the acquisition-date fair value of subsidiary long-term debt may also differ from its carrying amount. Although the long-term debt adjustment to fair value is relatively straightforward, the adjustments to interest expense in periods subsequent to acquisition require additional analysis.

In subsequent periods, the acquisition-date fair value adjustment to long-term debt is amortized to interest expense over the remaining life of the debt. When the acquisition-date fair value of subsidiary long-term debt exceeds its carrying amount on the subsidiary's books, the parent increases the value of the debt reported on its consolidated balance sheet (and vice-versa). Consequently, when the parent reflects the increased value of the subsidiary's long-term debt valuation, it must reduce interest expense recognized on the consolidated income statement over the debt's remaining life. When the long-term debt valuation is decreased, interest expense increases.

Exhibit 3.16 summarizes the worksheet effects when acquisition-date long-term debt's carrying amount differs from its fair value.

EXHIBIT 3.16 Long-Term Debt: Consolidation Worksheet Adjustments

Long-Term Debt Valuation at Acquisition Date	Worksheet Adjustment to Long-Term Debt	Worksheet Adjustment to Interest Expense
Fair value > Carrying amount	Increase long-term debt to adjust to fair value (less previous periods interest amortization)	Debit Long-Term Debt and credit Interest Expense
Fair value < Carrying amount	Decrease long-term debt to adjust to fair value (less previous periods interest amortization)	Debit Interest Expense and credit Long-Term Debt

At first glance, it may seem counterintuitive that when long-term debt is ***increased,*** interest expense is ***decreased.*** Certainly for plant assets like equipment, when we increase their carrying amounts to acquisition-date fair values on the worksheet, we increase the related depreciation expense. Why do we seem to do the opposite for long-term liabilities?

The answer can be seen in the fact that even though the acquisition-date value of the subsidiary's long-term debt exceeds its carrying amount, the acquisition does not affect the subsidiary's contractual obligation for repaying the debt. The ultimate amount of debt to be repaid at maturity remains the same. For example, assume Pax Company acquires Sax Company on January 1, 2017. Exhibit 3.17 provides information about Sax Company's long-term debt:

EXHIBIT 3.17
Acquisition-Date Long-Term Debt Valuation

	Long-Term Debt January 1, 2017	Long-Term Debt Maturity Value January 1, 2022
Fair value	$105,000	$100,000
Carrying amount	100,000	100,000

By acquiring Sax, Pax has taken on $105,000 of fair value debt, but will only have to pay back $100,000 at the debt's maturity date. As shown in Exhibit 3.18, the additional $5,000 excess fair over book value (that will not be repaid) is recognized as a reduction in overall interest expense, similar to amortizing a bond premium. Therefore, when consolidated statements are prepared, interest expense is reduced over the life of the long-term debt.

EXHIBIT 3.18
Worksheet Adjustments for Excess Acquisition-Date Fair Value Attributable to Subsidiary Long-Term Debt

December 31, 2017, Consolidation Worksheet		
Consolidation Entry A		
Investment in Sax Company	5,000	
Long-term debt		5,000
To adjust the subsidiary's long-term debt to acquisition-date fair value.		
Consolidation Entry E		
Long-term debt	1,000	
Interest expense		1,000
To recognize the reduction in current year interest expense		
December 31, 2018, Consolidation Worksheet		
Consolidation Entry A		
Investment in Sax Company	4,000	
Long-term debt		4,000
To adjust the subsidiary's long-term debt to unamortized balance as of the beginning of the year ($5,000 − $1,000 from year 2017).		
Consolidation Entry E		
Long-term debt	1,000	
Interest expense		1,000
To recognize the reduction in current year interest expense		

To complete this example, we assume the sole acquistion-date excess fair value adjustment made by Pax Company is to long-term debt, and straight-line amortization is used for the interest adjustments.

Finally, the carrying amount of a subsidiary's long-term debt may exceed its fair value. In that case, a consolidation entry is required to decrease the long-term debt reported in the consolidated balance sheet. Then, in periods subsequent to acquisition, worksheet entries are also needed to increase the amount of interest expense to be recognized in the consolidated income statement.

LO 3-5

Discuss the rationale for the goodwill impairment testing approach.

Goodwill Impairment

FASB ASC Topic 350, "Intangibles—Goodwill and Other," provides accounting standards for determining, measuring, and reporting goodwill impairment losses. Because goodwill is considered to have an indefinite life, an impairment approach is used rather than amortization. The FASB reasoned that although goodwill can decrease over time, it does not do so in the "rational and systematic" manner that periodic amortization suggests. Only upon recognition of an impairment loss (or partial sale of a subsidiary) will goodwill decline from one period to the next. Goodwill impairment losses are reported as operating items in the consolidated income statement.

The notion of an indefinite life allows many firms to report the original amount of goodwill recognized in a business combination. However, goodwill can become impaired, requiring loss recognition and a reduction in the amount reported in the consolidated balance sheet. Evidence shows that goodwill impairment losses can be substantial. Exhibit 3.19 provides examples of some recent goodwill impairment losses. Unlike amortization, which periodically reduces asset values, impairment must first be revealed before a write-down is justified. Accounting standards therefore require periodic tests for goodwill impairment.

Goodwill impairment tests are performed at the reporting unit level within a combined entity. As discussed next, all assets acquired (including goodwill) and liabilities assumed in a business combination must be assigned to *reporting units* within a consolidated enterprise. The goodwill residing in each reporting unit is then separately subjected to periodic impairment reviews. Current financial reporting standards require, at a minimum, an annual assessment for potential goodwill impairment.

Because impairment testing procedures can be costly, the FASB provides firms the option to first conduct a *qualitative* analysis to assess whether further testing procedures are appropriate. If circumstances indicate a potential decline in the fair value of a reporting unit below its carrying amount, then further tests are required to see if goodwill is the source of the decline. Our coverage of goodwill impairment addresses the following:

- The assignment of acquired goodwill to reporting units.
- The option to conduct an annual qualitative test for potential goodwill impairment.
- Goodwill impairment testing procedures.
- A FASB proposal to simplify goodwill impairment testing.
- Comparison with international accounting standards.

EXHIBIT 3.19
Recent Goodwill
Impairments

Microsoft	$5.1 billion
Yahoo!	4.5 billion
Devon Energy	1.9 billion
Rent-a-Center	1.2 billion
Time, Inc.	952 million
J. Crew	676 million
Staples	410 million
The Hershey Company	31 million
Pep Boys	23.9 million

Assigning Goodwill to Reporting Units

Combined companies typically organize themselves into separate *units* along distinct operating lines. Each individual operating unit has responsibility for managing its assets and liabilities to earn profits for the combined entity. These operating units report information about their earnings activities to top management to support decision making. Such operating units are known as *reporting units.*

Following a business combination, the identifiable assets and liabilities acquired are assigned to the firm's reporting units based on where they will be employed. Any amount assigned to goodwill also is assigned to reporting units expected to benefit from the synergies of the combination. Thus, any individual reporting unit where goodwill resides is the appropriate level for goodwill impairment testing.

In practice, firms often assign goodwill to reporting units either at the level of a reporting segment—as described in ASC Topic 280, "Segment Reporting"—or at a lower level within a segment of a combined enterprise. Reporting units may thus include the following:

- A component of an operating segment at a level below that operating segment. Segment management should review and assess performance at this level. Also, the component should be a business in which discrete financial information is available and should differ economically from other components of the operating segment.
- The segments of an enterprise.
- The entire enterprise.

For example, Qorvo, Inc. is a wireless technology firm serving the mobile device, networks infrastructure, and defense and aerospace markets. In its recent annual report Qorvo identified its two business segments, MP and IDP (Mobile Products and Infrastructure and Defense Products), as its reporting units:

> For fiscal 2015, we have determined that our reporting units are MP and IDP for purposes of allocating and testing goodwill. . .Goodwill is allocated to our reporting units based on the expected benefit from the synergies of the business combinations generating the underlying goodwill.

Thus, all goodwill impairment testing is performed at the reporting unit level, rather than collectively at the combined entity level. Separate testing of goodwill within individual reporting units also prevents the masking of goodwill impairment in one reporting unit with contemporaneous increases in the value of goodwill in other reporting units.

LO 3-6

Describe the procedures for conducting a goodwill impairment test.

Qualitative Assessment Option

Because goodwill impairment tests require firms to calculate fair values for their reporting units each year, such a comprehensive measurement exercise can be costly. To help reduce costs, FASB ASC Topic 305 allows an entity the option to first assess qualitative factors to determine whether more rigorous testing for goodwill impairment is needed. The qualitative approach assesses the *likelihood* that a reporting unit's fair value is less than its carrying amount. The more-likely-than-not threshold is defined as having a likelihood of more than 50 percent.

In assessing whether a reporting unit's fair value exceeds its carrying amount, a firm must examine all relevant facts and circumstances, including

- Macroeconomic conditions such as a deterioration in general economic conditions, limitations on accessing capital, fluctuations in foreign exchange rates, or other developments in equity and credit markets.
- Industry and market considerations such as a deterioration in the environment in which an entity operates, an increased competitive environment, a decline (both absolute and relative to its peers) in market-dependent multiples or metrics, a change in the market for an entity's products or services, or a regulatory or political development.
- Cost factors such as increases in raw materials, labor, or other costs that have a negative effect on earnings.
- Overall financial performance such as negative or declining cash flows or a decline in actual or planned revenue or earnings.

- Other relevant entity-specific events such as changes in management, key personnel, strategy, or customers; contemplation of bankruptcy; or litigation.
- Events affecting a reporting unit such as a change in the carrying amount of its net assets, a more-likely-than-not expectation of selling or disposing all, or a portion of, a reporting unit, the testing for recoverability of a significant asset group within a reporting unit, or recognition of a goodwill impairment loss in the financial statements of a subsidiary that is a component of a reporting unit.
- If applicable, a sustained decrease (both absolute and relative to its peers) in share price. (FASB ASC para. 350-20-35-3C)

The underlying rationale for comparing a reporting unit's fair value and carrying amount is as follows. If a reporting unit's fair value is deemed greater than its carrying amount, then its collective net assets are maintaining their value. It then can be argued that a decline in any particular asset (i.e., goodwill) within the reporting unit is also unlikely and no further impairment tests are necessary. On the other hand, if the relevant facts and circumstances listed above suggest that a reporting unit's fair value is likely less than its carrying amount, then more rigorous testing for goodwill impairment is appropriate. Nonetheless, a qualitative assessment of a sufficient fair value for a reporting unit circumvents further goodwill impairment testing.

The FASB ASC (paragraph 350-20-35-28) requires an entity to assess its goodwill for impairment annually for each of its reporting units where goodwill resides. Moreover, more frequent impairment assessment is required if events or circumstances change that make it more likely than not that a reporting unit's fair value has fallen below its carrying amount.

Testing Goodwill for Impairment

Goodwill impairment testing and measurement involves a two-step process.[9] In contrast to the qualitative assessment, Steps 1 and 2 rely on quantitative fair-value measures for reporting units as a whole and for their underlying individual assets and liabilities. If, after performing the qualitative assessment described above, an entity concludes that it is more likely than not that the fair value of a reporting unit is less than its carrying amount, then the entity is required to proceed to the first step of the two-step impairment test.[10]

Step 1: Is the Carrying Amount of a Reporting Unit More Than Its Fair Value?

In the first step of impairment testing, the consolidated entity calculates fair values for each of its reporting units with allocated goodwill. Each reporting unit's fair value is then compared with its carrying amount (*including goodwill*). If an individual reporting unit's fair value exceeds its carrying amount, its goodwill is not considered impaired, and the second step in testing is not performed—goodwill remains at its current carrying amount. However, if the fair value of a reporting unit has fallen below its carrying amount, a potential for goodwill impairment exists. In this case, a second step must be performed to determine whether goodwill has been impaired and to measure the amount of impairment.

Step 2: Is Goodwill's Implied Value Less Than Its Carrying Amount?

If Step 1 indicates potential goodwill impairment, Step 2 then compares the fair value of goodwill to its carrying amount. Because, by definition, goodwill is not separable from other assets, it is not possible to directly observe its fair value. Therefore, an *implied fair value* for goodwill is calculated in a similar manner to the determination of goodwill in a business combination. As stated in the FASB ASC (para. 350-20-35-14):

> The implied fair value of goodwill shall be determined in the same manner as the amount of goodwill recognized in a business combination . . . That is, an entity shall assign the fair value of a reporting unit to all of the assets and liabilities of that unit (including any unrecognized intangible assets) as if the reporting unit had been acquired in a business combination . . .

[9] As discussed later in this chapter, FASB has proposed the elimination of step 2 of the goodwill impairment measurement procedure.

[10] An entity, on the basis of its discretion, may bypass the qualitative assessment for any reporting unit in any period and proceed directly to performing the first step of the impairment test. An entity may resume performing the qualitative assessment in any subsequent period (FASB ASC para. 350-20-35-3B).

The current fair value of the reporting unit is allocated across that unit's identifiable assets and liabilities with any remaining excess considered as the implied value of goodwill.[11] If the implied value of goodwill is less than its carrying amount, impairment has occurred and a loss is recognized. The loss equals the excess of the carrying amount of the reporting unit's goodwill over its implied fair value.[12]

Illustration—Accounting and Reporting for a Goodwill Impairment Loss

To illustrate the testing procedures for goodwill impairment, assume that on January 1, 2017, investors form Newcall Corporation to consolidate the telecommunications operations of DSM, Inc., and VisionTalk Company in a deal valued at $2.2 billion. Newcall organizes each former firm as an operating segment. Additionally, DSM comprises two divisions—DSM Wired and DSM Wireless—that along with VisionTalk are treated as independent reporting units for internal performance evaluation and management reviews. Newcall recognizes $215 million as goodwill at the merger date and allocates this entire amount to its reporting units. That information and each reporting unit's acquisition-date fair values are as follows:

Newcall's Reporting Units	Goodwill	Acquisition-Date Fair Values January 1, 2017
DSM Wired	$22,000,000	$950,000,000
DSM Wireless	155,000,000	748,000,000
VisionTalk	38,000,000	502,000,000

In December 2017, Newcall performs a qualitative analysis for each of its three reporting units to assess potential goodwill impairment. Accordingly, Newcall examines the relevant events and circumstances that may affect the fair values of its reporting units. The analysis reveals that the fair value of each reporting unit likely exceeds its carrying amount except for DSM Wireless. Step 1 of the goodwill impairment test then reveals that DSM Wireless's fair value has fallen to $600 million, well below its current carrying amount. Newcall attributes the decline in value to a failure to realize expected cost-saving synergies with VisionTalk. Then, in Step 2, Newcall compares the implied fair value of the DSM Wireless goodwill to its carrying amount. Newcall derived the implied fair value of goodwill through the following allocation of the December 31, 2017, fair value of DSM Wireless:

DSM Wireless December 31, 2017, fair value		$600,000,000
Fair values of DSM Wireless net assets at December 31, 2017:		
Current assets	$ 50,000,000	
Property	125,000,000	
Equipment	265,000,000	
Subscriber list	140,000,000	
Patented technology	185,000,000	
Current liabilities	(44,000,000)	
Long-term debt	(125,000,000)	
Value assigned to identifiable net assets		$596,000,000
Implied fair value of goodwill		$ 4,000,000
Goodwill carrying amount before impairment		155,000,000
Impairment loss		$151,000,000

Thus, Newcall reports a $151,000,000 goodwill impairment loss as a separate line item in the operating section of its consolidated income statement. Additional disclosures are required describing (1) the facts and circumstances leading to the impairment and (2) the method of determining the fair value of the associated reporting unit (e.g., market prices, comparable business, present value technique, etc.). The reported amounts for the other

[11] This procedure serves only to measure an implied fair value for goodwill. None of the other values allocated to assets and liabilities in the testing comparison are used to adjust their reported amounts.
[12] The loss cannot exceed the carrying amount of goodwill.

assets and liabilities of DSM Wireless remain the same and are not changed based on the goodwill testing procedure.

Reporting Units with Zero or Negative Carrying Amounts

One final issue regarding goodwill impairment testing deserves mentioning. When a reporting unit has a zero or negative carrying amount, the ASC requires a special application of the testing procedure. An exception is needed because a zero or negative carrying amount for a reporting unit accompanied by a positive fair value would always permit an entity to forgo Step 2 of the impairment test even though its underlying goodwill might be impaired. Therefore, in such circumstances, the ASC requires an entity to perform Step 2 of the impairment test when it is more likely than not that a goodwill impairment exists. In judging the likelihood of goodwill impairment, an entity must consider the same factors as in the qualitative assessment for individual reporting units.

Goodwill Impairment Simplified—Proposed Accounting Standards Update (ASU)

In May, 2016, the FASB issued a proposed ASU entitled, "Simplifying the Accounting for Goodwill Impairment."[13] The stated objective of the proposed ASU was "to remove Step 2 from the goodwill impairment test, which includes determining the implied fair value of goodwill and comparing it with the carrying amount of that goodwill." The proposed changes would greatly simplify the accounting procedures previously described above. The changes would also save companies the cost involved in determining fair values for each of the assets and liabilities residing in their reporting units. However, the FASB would continue to require a determination of the fair value of its reporting units, should any fail (or elect to forego) the qualitative goodwill impairment assessment.

The FASB's recommendation partially stems from a post-implementation review of accounting for business combinations. That review concluded that current goodwill accounting produces more complexity and costs than the FASB anticipated. Further, the board concluded that eliminating Step 2 would not significantly reduce the usefulness of the goodwill impairment information provided to users of financial statements.

The proposed ASU changes accounting for goodwill impairment as follows:

> . . .an entity would perform its annual, or any interim, goodwill impairment test by comparing the fair value of a reporting unit with its carrying amount. An entity generally would recognize an impairment charge for the amount by which the carrying amount exceeds the reporting unit's fair value. However, that amount should not exceed the carrying amount of goodwill allocated to that reporting unit. An entity would still have the option to perform the qualitative assessment for a reporting unit to determine if the quantitative impairment test is necessary.[14]

Thus, assuming a reporting unit failed (or elected to forego) the qualitative assessment (a likelihood of more than 50 percent that a reporting unit's fair value is less than its carrying amount), a quantitative comparison would be employed to measure the amount of goodwill impairment. For example, assume the following December 31, 2018 values for Quality Road Company's RNT reporting unit:

December 31, 2018	Fair Value	Carrying Amount
RNT reporting unit as a whole	$1,500,000	$1,625,000*
Goodwill	?	148,000

*Reporting unit's assets (including goodwill) – liabilities.

The December 31, 2018 goodwill impairment loss would be measured simply as follows:

RNT reporting unit fair value	$1,500,000
RNT reporting unit carrying amount	1,625,000
Goodwill impairment loss	$ 125,000

---

[13] Financial Accounting Standards Board, Exposure Draft: Proposed Accounting Standards Update, Intangibles—Goodwill and Other (Topic 350), "Simplifying the Accounting for Goodwill Impairment," May 12, 2016.

[14] *Ibid.*

By eliminating Step 2 of the impairment test, Quality Road Company would benefit by avoiding costs of determining fair values for the RNT reporting unit's identifiable assets and liabilities. Moreover, no fair values would need to be determined for any unrecorded intangibles of the reporting unit.

The only exception to the above impairment measurement occurs when the initially computed goodwill impairment loss exceeds the carrying amount of goodwill. In the above example, the RNT reporting unit's goodwill carrying amount is $148,000, sufficient to absorb the $125,000 impairment. However, if the reporting unit's goodwill carrying amount was less than $125,000, the goodwill impairment loss would be limited to the lower carrying amount. Thus, the impairment loss cannot exceed the carrying amount of any particular reporting unit's goodwill.

Another change to goodwill accounting would be the elimination of the differential impairment analysis required for reporting units with zero or negative carrying amounts. According to the proposed ASU, "the same impairment assessment would apply to all reporting units. An entity would be required to disclose the existence of any reporting units with zero or negative carrying amounts and the amount of goodwill allocated to those reporting units."[15] Therefore, if the proposed ASU is ultimately approved, all reporting units would follow an identical model for assessing goodwill impairment.

Comparisons with International Accounting Standards

International Financial Reporting Standards (IFRS) and U.S. GAAP both require goodwill recognition in a business combination when the fair value of the consideration transferred exceeds the net fair values of the assets acquired and liabilities assumed. Subsequent to acquisition, both IFRS and U.S. GAAP require an assessment for goodwill impairment at least annually and more frequently in the presence of indicators of possible impairment. Also for both sets of standards, goodwill impairments, once recognized, are not recoverable. However, differences exist across the two sets of standards in the way goodwill impairment is tested for and recognized. In particular, goodwill allocation, impairment testing, and determination of the impairment loss differ across the two reporting regimes and are discussed below.

Goodwill Allocation

- *U.S. GAAP.* Goodwill acquired in a business combination is allocated to reporting units expected to benefit from the goodwill. Reporting units are operating segments or a business component one level below an operating segment.
- *IFRS.* International Accounting Standard *(IAS) 36* requires goodwill acquired in a business combination to be allocated to cash-generating units or groups of cash-generating units that are expected to benefit from the synergies of the business combination. Cash-generating groups represent the lowest level within the entity at which the goodwill is monitored for internal management purposes and are not to be larger than an operating segment or determined in accordance with *IFRS 8,* "Operating Segments."

Impairment Testing

- *U.S. GAAP.* Firms have the option to perform a qualitative assessment to evaluate possible goodwill impairment based on a greater than 50 percent likelihood that a reporting unit's fair value is less than its carrying amount. If such a likelihood exists, then a two-step testing procedure is performed. In step one, a reporting unit's total fair value is compared to its carrying amount. If the carrying amount exceeds fair value, then a second step comparing goodwill's implied fair value to its carrying amount is performed.
- *IFRS.* A one-step approach compares the fair and carrying amounts of each cash-generating unit with goodwill. If the carrying amount exceeds the fair value of the cash-generating unit, then goodwill (and possibly other assets of the cash-generating unit) is considered impaired.

Determination of the Impairment Loss

- *U.S. GAAP.* In step two, a reporting unit's implied fair value for goodwill is computed as the excess of the reporting unit's fair value over the fair value of its identifiable net assets.

[15] *Ibid.*

If the carrying amount of goodwill is greater than its implied fair value, an impairment loss is recognized for the difference.

- *IFRS.* Any excess carrying amount over fair value for a cash-generating unit is first assigned to reduce goodwill. If goodwill is reduced to zero, then the other assets of the cash-generating unit are reduced pro-rata based on the carrying amounts of the assets.

Finally, the FASB and IASB have agreed to include impairment recognition and reporting as one of their future convergence projects.

LO 3-7

Describe the rationale and procedures for impairment testing for intangible assets other than goodwill.

Amortization and Impairment of Other Intangibles

As discussed in Chapter 2, the acquisition method governs how we initially consolidate the assets acquired and liabilities assumed in a business combination. Subsequent to acquisition, income determination becomes a regular part of the consolidation process. The fair-value bases (established at the acquisition date) for definite-lived subsidiary assets acquired and liabilities assumed will be amortized over their remaining lives for income recognition. For indefinite-lived assets (e.g., goodwill, certain other intangibles), an impairment model is used to assess whether asset write-downs are appropriate.

Current accounting standards suggest categories of intangible assets for possible recognition when one business acquires another. Examples include noncompetition agreements, customer lists, patents, subscriber lists, databases, trademarks, lease agreements, licenses, and many others. All identified intangible assets should be amortized over their economic useful life unless such life is considered *indefinite*. The term *indefinite life* is defined as a life that extends beyond the foreseeable future. A recognized intangible asset with an indefinite life should not be amortized unless and until its life is determined to be finite. Importantly, *indefinite* does not mean "infinite." Also, the useful life of an intangible asset should not be considered indefinite because a precise finite life is not known.

For intangible assets with finite lives, the amortization method should reflect the pattern of decline in the economic usefulness of the asset. If no such pattern is apparent, the straight-line method of amortization should be used. The amount to be amortized should be the value assigned to the intangible asset less any residual value. In most cases, the residual value is presumed to be zero. However, that presumption can be overcome if the acquiring enterprise has a commitment from a third party to purchase the intangible at the end of its useful life or an observable market exists for the intangible asset.

The length of the amortization period for identifiable intangibles (i.e., those not included in goodwill) depends primarily on the assumed economic life of the asset. Factors that should be considered in determining the useful life of an intangible asset include

- Legal, regulatory, or contractual provisions.
- The effects of obsolescence, demand, competition, industry stability, rate of technological change, and expected changes in distribution channels.
- The enterprise's expected use of the intangible asset.
- The level of maintenance expenditure required to obtain the asset's expected future benefits.

Any recognized intangible assets considered to possess indefinite lives are not amortized but instead are assessed for impairment on an annual basis.[16] Similar to goodwill impairment assessment, an entity has the option to first perform qualitative assessments for its indefinite-lived intangibles to see if further quantitative tests are necessary. According to the FASB ASC (350-30-65-3), if an entity elects to perform a qualitative assessment, it examines events and circumstances to determine whether it is more likely than not (that is, a likelihood of more than 50 percent) that an indefinite-lived intangible asset is impaired. Qualitative factors include costs of using the intangible, legal and regulatory factors, industry and market considerations, and other. If the qualitative assessment indicates impairment is unlikely, no additional tests are needed.

---

[16] An entity has an unconditional option to bypass the qualitative assessment for any indefinite-lived intangible asset in any period and proceed directly to performing the quantitative impairment test.

If the qualitative assessment indicates that impairment is likely, the entity then must perform a quantitative test to determine if a loss has occurred. To test an indefinite-lived intangible asset for impairment, its carrying amount is compared to its fair value. If the fair value is less than the carrying amount, then the intangible asset is considered impaired and an impairment loss is recognized. The asset's carrying amount is reduced accordingly for the excess of its carrying amount over its fair value.

LO 3-8

Understand the accounting and reporting for contingent consideration subsequent to a business acquisition.

Contingent Consideration

Contingency agreements frequently accompany business combinations. In many cases, the target firm asks for consideration based on projections of its future performance. The acquiring firm, however, may not share the projections and, thus, may be unwilling to pay now for uncertain future performance. To close the deal, agreements for the acquirer's future payments to the former owners of the target are common. Alternatively, when the acquirer's stock comprises the consideration transferred, the sellers of the target firm may request a guaranteed minimum market value of the stock for a period of time to ensure a fair price.

Accounting for Contingent Consideration in Business Combinations

As an illustration, assume that Skeptical, Inc., acquires 100 percent of the voting stock of Rosy Pictures Company on January 1, 2017, for the following consideration:

- $550,000 market value of 10,000 shares of its $5-par common stock.
- A contingent payment of $80,000 cash if Rosy Pictures generates cash flows from operations of $20,000 or more in 2017.
- A payment of sufficient shares of Skeptical common stock to ensure a total value of $550,000 if the price per share is less than $55 on January 1, 2018.

Under the acquisition method, each of the three elements of consideration represents a portion of the negotiated fair value of Rosy Pictures and therefore must be included in the recorded value entered on Skeptical's accounting records. For the cash contingency, Skeptical estimates that there is a 30 percent chance that the $80,000 payment will be required. For the stock contingency, Skeptical estimates that there is a 20 percent probability that the 10,000 shares issued will have a market value of $540,000 on January 1, 2018, and an 80 percent probability that the market value of the 10,000 shares will exceed $550,000. Skeptical uses an interest rate of 4 percent to incorporate the time value of money.

To determine the fair values of the contingent consideration, Skeptical computes the present value of the expected payments as follows:

- *Cash contingency* = $80,000 × 30% × [1/(1 + .04)] = $23,077
- *Stock contingency* = $10,000 × 20% × [1/(1 + .04)] = $1,923

Skeptical then records in its accounting records the acquisition of Rosy Pictures as follows:

Investment in Rosy Pictures	575,000	
Common Stock ($5 par)		50,000
Additional Paid-in Capital		500,000
Contingent Performance Obligation		23,077
Additional Paid-in Capital—Contingent Equity Outstanding		1,923
To record acquisition of Rosy Pictures at fair value of consideration transferred including performance and stock contingencies.		

Skeptical will report the contingent cash payment under its liabilities and the contingent stock payment as a component of stockholders' equity. In periods subsequent to acquisition, obligations for contingent consideration that meet the definition of a liability will continue to be measured at fair value with adjustments recognized in income. Those obligations classified as equity are not subsequently remeasured at fair value, consistent with other equity issues (e.g., common stock).

To continue the preceding example, assume that in 2017 Rosy Pictures exceeds the cash flow from operations threshold of $20,000, thus requiring an additional payment of $80,000. Also, Skeptical's stock price had fallen to $54.45 at January 1, 2018. Because the acquisition agreement called for a $550,000 total value at January 1, 2018, Skeptical must issue an additional 101 shares ($5,500 shortfall/$54.45 per share) to the former owners of Rosy Pictures.

Contingent Performance Obligation	23,077	
Loss from Revaluation of Contingent Performance Obligation.	56,923	
Cash		80,000
To record contingent cash payment required by original Rosy Pictures acquisition agreement.		
Additional Paid-in Capital—Contingent Equity Outstanding	1,923	
Common Stock		505
Additional Paid-in Capital		1,418
To record contingent stock issue required by original Rosy Pictures acquisition agreement.		

The loss from revaluation of the contingent performance obligation is reported in Skeptical's consolidated income statement as a component of ordinary income. Regarding the additional required stock issue, note that Skeptical's total paid-in capital remains unchanged from the total $551,923 recorded at the acquisition date.

Summary

1. The procedures used to consolidate financial information generated by the separate companies in a business combination are affected by both the passage of time and the method applied by the parent in accounting for the subsidiary. Thus, no single consolidation process that is applicable to all business combinations can be described.

2. The parent might elect to utilize the equity method to account for a subsidiary. As discussed in Chapter 1, the parent accrues income when earned by the subsidiary. The parent records dividend declarations by the subsidiary as reductions in the investment account. The effects of excess fair-value amortizations or any intra-entity transactions also are reflected within the parent's financial records. The equity method provides the parent with accurate information concerning the subsidiary's impact on consolidated totals; however, it is usually somewhat complicated to apply.

3. The initial value method and the partial equity method are two alternatives to the equity method. The initial value method recognizes only the subsidiary's dividends as income while the asset balance remains at the acquisition-date fair value. This approach is simple and typically reflects cash flows between the two companies. Under the partial equity method, the parent accrues the subsidiary's income as earned but does not record adjustments that might be required by excess fair-value amortizations or intra-entity transfers. The partial equity method is easier to apply than the equity method, and, in many cases, the parent's income is a reasonable approximation of the consolidated total.

4. For a consolidation in any subsequent period, all reciprocal balances must be eliminated. Thus, the subsidiary's equity accounts, the parent's investment balance, intra-entity income, dividends, and liabilities are removed. In addition, the remaining unamortized portions of the fair-value allocations are recognized along with excess amortization expenses for the period. If the equity method has not been applied, the parent's beginning Retained Earnings account also must be adjusted for any previous income or excess amortizations that have not yet been recorded.

5. For each subsidiary acquisition, the parent must assign the acquired assets and liabilities (including goodwill) to individual reporting units of the combined entity. The reporting units should be at operating segment level or lower and serve as the basis for future assessments of fair value. Any value assigned to goodwill is not amortized but instead is tested annually for impairment. Firms have the option to perform a qualitative assessment to evaluate whether a reporting unit's fair value more likely than not exceeds its carrying amount. If the assessment shows excess fair value over carrying amount for the reporting unit, a firm can forgo further testing. Otherwise, a two-step test is performed. First, if the fair value of any reporting unit below its carrying amount, then the implied value of the associated goodwill is recomputed. Second, the recomputed implied value of goodwill is compared to its carrying amount. An impairment loss must then be recognized if the carrying amount of goodwill exceeds its implied value.[17]

6. Subsequent to a business combination, any newly recognized subsidiary identifiable intangible assets (i.e., other than goodwill) considered to possess indefinite lives are not amortized but instead are assessed for impairment on an annual basis. Similar to goodwill impairment assessment, an

[17] A proposed FASB Accounting Standards Update would eliminate the second step of the impairment test. Goodwill would simply be the excess of a reporting unit's carrying amount over its fair value (loss not to exceed goodwill's carrying amount).

entity has the option to first perform qualitative assessments for its indefinite-lived intangibles to see if further quantitative tests are necessary. For intangible assets with finite lives, amortization expense is recognized over the intangible asset's useful life. The amortization method should reflect the pattern of decline in the economic usefulness of the asset. If no such pattern is apparent, the straight-line method of amortization should be used.

7. The acquisition-date fair value assigned to a subsidiary can be based, at least in part, on the fair value of any contingent consideration. For contingent obligations that meet the definition of a liability, the obligation is adjusted for changes in fair value over time with corresponding recognition of gains or losses from the revaluation. For contingent obligations classified as equity, no remeasurement to fair value takes place. In either case the initial value recognized in the combination does not change regardless of whether the contingency is eventually paid or not.

Comprehensive Illustration

Problem

(*Estimated Time: 40 to 65 Minutes*) On January 1, 2016, Top Company acquired all of Bottom Company's outstanding common stock for $842,000 in cash. As of that date, one of Bottom's buildings with a 12-year remaining life was undervalued on its financial records by $72,000. Equipment with a 10-year remaining life was undervalued, but only by $10,000. The book values of all of Bottom's other assets and liabilities were equal to their fair values at that time except for an unrecorded licensing agreement with an assessed value of $40,000 and a 20-year remaining useful life. Bottom's book value at the acquisition date was $720,000.

During 2016, Bottom reported net income of $100,000 and declared $30,000 in dividends. Earnings were $120,000 in 2017 with $20,000 in dividends distributed by the subsidiary. As of December 31, 2018, the companies reported the following selected balances, which include all revenues and expenses for the year:

	Top Company December 31, 2018		Bottom Company December 31, 2018	
	Debit	Credit	Debit	Credit
Buildings..............	$1,540,000		$460,000	
Cash and receivables....	50,000		90,000	
Common stock		$ 900,000		$400,000
Dividends declared......	70,000		10,000	
Equipment	280,000		200,000	
Cost of goods sold	500,000		120,000	
Depreciation expense ...	100,000		60,000	
Inventory..............	280,000		260,000	
Land.................	330,000		250,000	
Liabilities.............		480,000		260,000
Retained earnings, 1/1/18		1,360,000		490,000
Revenues		900,000		300,000

Required

a. If Top applies the equity method, what is its investment account balance as of December 31, 2018?

b. If Top applies the initial value method, what is its investment account balance as of December 31, 2018?

c. Regardless of the accounting method in use by Top, what are the consolidated totals as of December 31, 2018, for each of the following accounts?

Buildings	Revenues
Equipment	Net Income
Land	Investment in Bottom
Depreciation Expense	Dividends Declared
Amortization Expense	Cost of Goods Sold

d. Prepare the worksheet entries required on December 31, 2018, to consolidate the financial records of these two companies. Assume that Top applied the equity method to its investment account.

e. How would the worksheet entries in requirement (d) be altered if Top has used the initial value method?

Solution

a. To determine the investment balances under the equity method, four items must be determined: the initial value assigned, the income accrual, dividends and amortization of excess acquisition-date fair value over book value. Although the first three are indicated in the problem, amortizations must be calculated separately.

An allocation of Bottom's acquisition-date fair values as well as the related amortization expense follows.

Fair value of consideration transferred by Top Company..	$ 842,000
Book value of Bottom Company, 1/1/16	(720,000)
Excess fair value over book value.	$ 122,000

Adjustments to specific accounts based on fair values:

		Remaining Life (years)	Annual Amortization
Buildings.	$ 72,000	12	$6,000
Equipment	10,000	10	1,000
Licensing agreement	40,000	20	2,000
Totals.	$122,000		$9,000

Thus, if Top adopts the equity method to account for this subsidiary, the Investment in Bottom account shows a December 31, 2018, balance of $1,095,000, computed as follows:

Initial value (fair value of consideration transferred by Top)		$ 842,000
Bottom Company's 2016–2017 increase in book value (income less dividends).		170,000
Excess amortizations for 2016–2017 ($9,000 per year for two years).		(18,000)
Current year recognition (2018):		
Equity income accrual (Bottom's revenues less its expenses) . . .	$120,000	
Excess amortization expenses.	(9,000)	
Dividends from Bottom	(10,000)	101,000
Investment in Bottom Company, 12/31/18		$1,095,000

The $120,000 income accrual and the $9,000 excess amortization expenses indicate that an Equity in Subsidiary Earnings balance of $111,000 appears in Top's income statement for the current period.

b. If Top Company applies the initial value method, the Investment in Bottom Company account permanently retains its original $842,000 balance, and the parent recognizes only the intra-entity dividend of $10,000 as income in 2018.

c. • The consolidated Buildings account as of December 31, 2018, has a balance of $2,054,000. Although the two book value figures total only $2 million, a $72,000 allocation was made to this account based on fair value at the date of acquisition. Because this amount is being depreciated at the rate of $6,000 per year, the original allocation will have been reduced by $18,000 by the end of 2018, leaving only a $54,000 increase.

• On December 31, 2018, the consolidated Equipment account amounts to $487,000. The book values found in the financial records of Top and Bottom provide a total of $480,000. Once again, the allocation ($10,000) established by the acquisition-date fair value must be included in the consolidated balance after being adjusted for three years of depreciation ($1,000 × 3 years, or $3,000).

• Land has a consolidated total of $580,000. Because the book value and fair value of Bottom's land were in agreement at the date of acquisition, no additional allocation was made to this account. Thus, the book values are simply added together to derive a consolidated figure.

• *Cost of goods sold* = $620,000. The cost of goods sold of the parent and subsidiary are added together.

• *Depreciation expense* = $167,000. The depreciation expenses of the parent and subsidiary are added together along with the $6,000 additional building depreciation and the $1,000 additional equipment depreciation as presented in the fair-value allocation schedule.

- *Amortization expense* = $2,000. An additional expense of $2,000 is recognized from the amortization of the licensing agreement acquired in the business combination.

- The Revenues account appears as $1.2 million in the consolidated income statement. None of the worksheet entries in this example affects the individual balances of either company. Consolidation results merely from the addition of the two book values.

- Net income for this business combination is $411,000: consolidated expenses of $789,000 subtracted from revenues of $1.2 million.

- The parent's Investment in Bottom account is removed entirely on the worksheet so that no balance is reported. For consolidation purposes, this account is always eliminated so that the individual assets and liabilities of the subsidiary can be included.

- Dividends declared for the consolidated entity should be reported as $70,000, the amount Top distributed. Because Bottom's dividends are entirely intra-entity, they are deleted in arriving at consolidated figures.

d. Consolidation Entries Assuming Equity Method Used by Parent

Entry S

Common Stock (Bottom Company)	400,000	
Retained Earnings, 1/1/18.		
(Bottom Company)	490,000	
Investment in Bottom Company.		890,000

Elimination of subsidiary's beginning stockholders' equity accounts against book value portion of investment account.

Entry A

Buildings.	60,000	
Equipment	8,000	
Licensing Agreement.	36,000	
Investment in Bottom Company.		104,000

To recognize fair-value allocations to the subsidiary's assets in excess of book value. Balances represent original allocations less two years of amortization for the 2016–2017 period.

Entry I

Equity in Subsidiary Earnings	111,000	
Investment in Bottom Company.		111,000

To eliminate parent's equity income accrual, balance is computed in requirement (*a*).

Entry D

Investment in Bottom	10,000	
Dividends Declared		10,000

To eliminate intra-entity dividends from the subsidiary to the parent (and recorded as a reduction in the investment account because the equity method is in use).

Entry E

Depreciation Expense	7,000	
Amortization Expense	2,000	
Equipment		1,000
Buildings.		6,000
Licensing Agreement.		2,000

To recognize excess fair-value depreciation and amortization for 2018.

e. If Top utilizes the initial value method rather than the equity method, three changes are required in the development of consolidation entries:

(1) An Entry *C is required to update the parent's beginning Retained Earnings account as if the equity method had been applied. Both an income accrual as well as excess amortizations for the prior two years must be recognized because these balances were not recorded by the parent.

Entry *C

Investment in Bottom Company............................	152,000	
Retained Earnings, 1/1/18 (Top Company)		152,000

To convert to the equity method by accruing the net effect of the subsidiary's operations (income less dividends) for the prior two years ($170,000) along with excess amortization expenses ($18,000) for this same period.

(2) An alteration is needed in Entry **I** because, under the initial value method, only dividends are recorded by the parent as income.

Entry I

Dividend Income..	10,000	
Dividends Declared		10,000

To eliminate intra-entity dividends recorded by parent as income.

(3) Finally, because the intra-entity dividends have been eliminated in Entry **I,** no separate Entry **D** is needed.

Appendix: Private Company Accounting for Business Combinations

LO 3-9:

Describe the alternative accounting treatments for goodwill and other intangible assets available for business combinations by private companies.

External Reporting Option for Private Company Goodwill Accounting

In January 2014, the Financial Accounting Standards Board (FASB) approved an *Accounting Standards Update* (ASU 2014-02) to Topic 350, "Intangibles—Goodwill and Other, on Accounting for Goodwill." This ASU emerged as a consensus of the FASB's Private Company Council (PCC) and gives private companies an option to apply a simplified alternative to the more complex goodwill accounting model required of public companies. As discussed below, the new standard allows a private company both to amortize goodwill and to apply a simplified impairment test at either the reporting unit or entity level.

The private company standards apply only to businesses that do not meet the definition of a public business entity or a not-for-profit entity. In general, business is a public entity if the Securities and Exchange Commission (or a foreign or other domestic regulatory agency) requires the business to furnish financial statements (ASU 2013-12). In this textbook, our focus is squarely on public business entities. Nonetheless, the goodwill accounting option for private companies provides an interesting alternative that the FASB may someday consider for public entities as well.[18]

The new standard allows a private company to elect to amortize goodwill over a 10-year period.[19] The amortization process effectively treats goodwill as a definite-lived intangible asset. This approach, of course, stands in marked contrast to the goodwill accounting for public companies which treats goodwill as an indefinite-lived asset, prohibits amortization, and requires annual impairment testing for goodwill. In justifying the differential treatment for private companies, the FASB reasoned that, based on research by the PCC, goodwill impairment tests provided

> limited decision-useful information because most users of private company financial statement generally disregard goodwill and goodwill impairment losses in their analysis of a private company's financial condition and operating performance. (ASU 2014-02, Summary)

Equally important, the PCC expressed concerns about the cost and complexity of goodwill impairment tests, especially for private companies. The cost and complexity arise in large part from the efforts required in determining fair values for a company's reporting units and their identifiable assets and liabilities.

In many cases, goodwill amortization will replace the need to periodically assess and, when deemed necessary, write-down goodwill through the recognition of impairment losses. Private companies who elect the alternative goodwill accounting, however, will still be required to test goodwill balances for impairment in some circumstances, although a simplified approach is employed.

---

[18] In November 2014, the FASB directed its staff to extend its research on goodwill amortization to public companies, focusing on the most appropriate useful life if goodwill were amortized and simplifying the goodwill impairment test.

[19] A less-than-10-year amortization period is available if it can be shown to be appropriate (ASC 350-20-35-63).

The goodwill impairment process is simplified in two respects for private companies. First, if a triggering event occurs (i.e., any event or change in circumstances that may have caused the fair value of the acquired entity—or the reporting unit—to fall below its carrying amount), then the unamortized balance of goodwill must be assessed for impairment.[20] However, to save costs and streamline the process, there is no requirement (as exists for public companies) to remeasure each of the entity's (or reporting unit's) separate assets and liabilities at current fair values to compute a residual implied value for goodwill. The measurement of the goodwill impairment loss simply equals the excess (if any) of the fair value of the acquired entity (or reporting unit) over its total carrying amount. The amount of the impairment loss, however, is limited to the remaining unamortized balance in the goodwill account.

Unlike public companies, a private company also has the option to designate and test goodwill for impairment either at the entity level or the reporting unit level—a policy election made at the adoption of the alternative goodwill method. Thus the accounting for goodwill impairment is simplified by both the ability to assess goodwill at the entity level and the use of a single-step test that compares the fair value of the entity to its carrying amount. Similar to public companies, a private company may skip the qualitative assessment. Unlike public companies, a private company can then go directly to a single-step quantitative impairment test.

External Reporting Option for Private Company Accounting for Other Intangible Assets in a Business Combination

In addition to the private company separate guidance for goodwill, the FASB in December 2014 issued ASU 2014-18, "Accounting for Identifiable Intangible Assets in a Business Combination (a consensus of the Private Company Council)," an amendment of Business Combinations (Topic 805). The new standard allows private companies an option to simplify their accounting by recognizing fewer intangible assets in future business combinations. Private companies can now elect to (1) limit the customer-related intangibles it recognizes separately to those capable of being sold or licensed independently from the other assets of the business, and (2) avoid separate recognition of noncompetition agreements.

By limiting the separate recognition of customer-related intangibles (e.g., customer lists, customer relationships, commodity supply contracts, etc.) and noncompetition agreements, the value of these intangible assets is effectively subsumed into goodwill. As with other private company financial reporting options, the FASB cites cost/benefit considerations.

By providing an accounting alternative, this Update reduces the cost and complexity associated with the measurement of certain identifiable intangible assets without significantly diminishing decision-useful information to users of private company financial statements (ASU 2014-18, Summary).

A private company may elect this alternative only if it also elects the private company goodwill accounting alternative which includes goodwill amortization—thus ensuring that any non-recognized intangibles subsumed into goodwill are also subject to amortization. Companies that choose the goodwill accounting alternative, however, are not required to elect the intangible assets accounting alternative.

Questions

1. CCES Corporation acquires a controlling interest in Schmaling, Inc. CCES may utilize any one of three methods to internally account for this investment. Describe each of these methods, and indicate their advantages and disadvantages.

2. Maguire Company obtains 100 percent control over Williams Company. Several years after the takeover, consolidated financial statements are being produced. For each of the following accounts, briefly describe the values that should be included in consolidated totals.
   a. Equipment.
   b. Investment in Williams Company.
   c. Dividends Declared.
   d. Goodwill.
   e. Revenues.
   f. Expenses.
   g. Common Stock.
   h. Net Income.

3. When a parent company uses the equity method to account for an investment in a subsidiary, why do both the parent's Net Income and Retained Earnings account balances agree with the consolidated totals?

[20] Distinct from public company requirements, no annual assessment for goodwill impairment is required for private companies.

4. When a parent company uses the equity method to account for investment in a subsidiary, the amortization expense entry recorded during the year is eliminated on a consolidation worksheet as a component of Entry **I.** What is the necessity of removing this amortization?

5. When a parent company applies the initial value method or the partial equity method to an investment, a worksheet adjustment must be made to the parent's beginning Retained Earnings account (Entry *C) in every period after the year of acquisition. What is the necessity for this entry? Why is no similar entry found when the parent utilizes the equity method?

6. Several years ago, Jenkins Company acquired a controlling interest in Lambert Company. Lambert recently borrowed $100,000 from Jenkins. In consolidating the financial records of these two companies, how will this debt be handled?

7. Benns adopts the equity method for its 100 percent investment in Waters. At the end of six years, Benns reports an investment in Waters of $920,000. What figures constitute this balance?

8. One company acquired another in a transaction in which $100,000 of the acquisition price is assigned to goodwill. Several years later, a worksheet is being produced to consolidate these two companies. How is the reported value of the goodwill determined at this date?

9. When should a parent consider recognizing an impairment loss for goodwill associated with a subsidiary? How should the loss be reported in the financial statements?

10. Reimers Company acquires Rollins Corporation on January 1, 2017. As part of the agreement, the parent states that an additional $100,000 payment to the former owners of Rollins will be made in 2018, if Rollins achieves certain income thresholds during the first two years following the acquisition. How should Reimers account for this contingency in its 2017 consolidated financial statements?

Problems

LO 3-2

1. A company acquires a subsidiary and will prepare consolidated financial statements for external reporting purposes. For internal reporting purposes, the company has decided to apply the initial value method. Why might the company have made this decision?
   a. It is a relatively easy method to apply.
   b. Operating results appearing on the parent's financial records reflect consolidated totals.
   c. GAAP now requires the use of this particular method for internal reporting purposes.
   d. Consolidation is not required when the parent uses the initial value method.

LO 3-2

2. A company acquires a subsidiary and will prepare consolidated financial statements for external reporting purposes. For internal reporting purposes, the company has decided to apply the equity method. Why might the company have made this decision?
   a. It is a relatively easy method to apply.
   b. Operating results appearing on the parent's financial records reflect consolidated totals.
   c. GAAP now requires the use of this particular method for internal reporting purposes.
   d. Consolidation is not required when the parent uses the equity method.

LO 3-4

3. On January 1, 2018, Jay Company acquired all the outstanding ownership shares of Zee Company. In assessing Zee's acquisition-date fair values, Jay concluded that the carrying value of Zee's long-term debt (8-year remaining life) was less than its fair value by $20,000. At December 31, 2018, Zee Company's accounts show interest expense of $12,000 and long-term debt of $250,000. What amounts of interest expense and long-term debt should appear on the December 31, 2018, consolidated financial statements of Jay and its subsidiary Zee?

	Interest expense	Long-term debt
a.	$14,500	$270,000
b.	$14,500	$267,500
c.	$9,500	$270,000
d.	$9,500	$267,500

LO 3-5

4. When should a consolidated entity recognize a goodwill impairment loss?
   a. If both the fair value of a reporting unit and its associated implied goodwill fall below their respective carrying amounts.
   b. Whenever the entity's fair value declines significantly.
   c. If the fair value of a reporting unit with goodwill fall below its carrying amount.
   d. Annually on a systematic and rational basis.

LO 3-1

5. Paar Corporation bought 100 percent of Kimmel, Inc., on January 1, 2015. On that date, Paar's equipment (10-year remaining life) has a book value of $420,000 but a fair value of $520,000. Kimmel has equipment (10-year remaining life) with a book value of $272,000 but a fair value of $400,000. Paar uses the equity method to record its investment in Kimmel. On December 31, 2017, Paar has equipment with a book value of $294,000 but a fair value of $445,200. Kimmel has equipment with a book value of $190,400 but a fair value of $357,000. What is the consolidated balance for the Equipment account as of December 31, 2017?
   a. $574,000
   b. $802,200
   c. $612,600
   d. $484,400

LO 3-4

6. How would the answer to problem (5) have been affected if the parent had applied the initial value method rather than the equity method?
   a. No effect: The method the parent uses is for internal reporting purposes only and has no impact on consolidated totals.
   b. The consolidated Equipment account would have a higher reported balance.
   c. The consolidated Equipment account would have a lower reported balance.
   d. The balance in the consolidated Equipment account cannot be determined for the initial value method using the information given.

LO 3-5

7. Goodwill recognized in a business combination must be allocated among a firm's identified reporting units. If the fair value of a particular reporting unit with recognized goodwill falls below its carrying amount, which of the following is true?
   a. No goodwill impairment loss is recognized unless the implied value for goodwill exceeds its carrying amount.
   b. A goodwill impairment loss is recognized if the carrying amount for goodwill exceeds its implied value.
   c. A goodwill impairment loss is recognized for the excess of a reporting unit's carrying amount over its fair value, not to exceed the carrying amount of goodwill.
   d. The reporting unit reduces the values assigned to its long-term assets (including any unrecognized intangibles) to reflect its fair value.

LO 3-7

8. If no legal, regulatory, contractual, competitive, economic, or other factors limit the life of an intangible asset, the asset's assigned value is allocated to expense over which of the following?
   a. 20 years.
   b. 20 years with an annual impairment review.
   c. Infinitely.
   d. Indefinitely (no amortization) with an annual impairment review until its life becomes finite.

LO 3-7

9. Dosmann, Inc., bought all outstanding shares of Lizzi Corporation on January 1, 2016, for $700,000 in cash. This portion of the consideration transferred results in a fair-value allocation of $35,000 to equipment and goodwill of $88,000. At the acquisition date, Dosmann also agrees to pay Lizzi's previous owners an additional $110,000 on January 1, 2018, if Lizzi earns a 10 percent return on the fair value of its assets in 2016 and 2017. Lizzi's profits exceed this threshold in both years. Which of the following is true?
   a. The additional $110,000 payment is a reduction in consolidated retained earnings.
   b. The fair value of the expected contingent payment increases goodwill at the acquisition date.
   c. Consolidated goodwill as of January 1, 2018, increases by $110,000.
   d. The $110,000 is recorded as an expense in 2018.

Problems 10, 11, and 12 relate to the following:
On January 1, 2016, Phoenix Co. acquired 100 percent of the outstanding voting shares of Sedona Inc., for $600,000 cash. At January 1, 2016, Sedona's net assets had a total carrying amount of $420,000. Equipment (eight-year remaining life) was undervalued on Sedona's financial records by $80,000. Any remaining excess fair over book value was attributed to a customer list developed by Sedona (four-year remaining life), but not recorded on its books. Phoenix applies the equity method to account for its investment in Sedona. Each year since the acquisition, Sedona has declared a $20,000 dividend. Sedona recorded net income of $70,000 in 2016 and $80,000 in 2017.

Selected account balances from the two companies' individual records were as follows:

	Phoenix	Sedona
2018 Revenues	$498,000	$285,000
2018 Expenses	350,000	195,000
2018 Income from Sedona	55,000	
Retained earnings 12/31/18	250,000	175,000

LO 3-3a

10. What is consolidated net income for Phoenix and Sedona for 2018?
    a. $148,000
    b. $203,000
    c. $228,000
    d. $238,000

LO 3-3a

11. What is Phoenix's consolidated retained earnings balance at December 31, 2018?
    a. $250,000
    b. $290,000
    c. $330,000
    d. $360,000

LO 3-3a

12. On its December 31, 2018, consolidated balance sheet, what amount should Phoenix report for Sedona's customer list?
    a. $10,000
    b. $20,000
    c. $25,000
    d. $50,000

LO 3-7

13. Kaplan Corporation acquired Star, Inc., on January 1, 2017, by issuing 13,000 shares of common stock with a $10 per share par value and a $23 market value. This transaction resulted in recognizing $62,000 of goodwill. Kaplan also agreed to compensate Star's former owners for any difference if Kaplan's stock is worth less than $23 on January 1, 2018. On January 1, 2018, Kaplan issues an additional 3,000 shares to Star's former owners to honor the contingent consideration agreement. Which of the following is true?
    a. The fair value of the number of shares issued for the contingency increases the Goodwill account at January 1, 2018.
    b. The parent's additional paid-in capital from the contingent equity recorded at the acquisition date is reclassified as a regular common stock issue on January 1, 2018.
    c. All of the subsidiary's asset and liability accounts must be revalued for consolidation purposes based on their fair values as of January 1, 2018.
    d. The additional shares are assumed to have been issued on January 1, 2017, so that a retrospective adjustment is required.

LO 3-3, 3-4

14. Herbert, Inc., acquired all of Rambis Company's outstanding stock on January 1, 2017, for $574,000 in cash. Annual excess amortization of $12,000 results from this transaction. On the date of the takeover, Herbert reported retained earnings of $400,000, and Rambis reported a $200,000 balance. Herbert reported internal net income of $40,000 in 2017 and $50,000 in 2018 and declared $10,000 in dividends each year. Rambis reported net income of $20,000 in 2017 and $30,000 in 2018 and declared $5,000 in dividends each year.
    a. Assume that Herbert's internal net income figures above do not include any income from the subsidiary.
       • If the parent uses the equity method, what is the amount reported as consolidated retained earnings on December 31, 2017?
       • Would the amount of consolidated retained earnings change if the parent had applied either the initial value or partial equity method for internal accounting purposes?
    b. Under each of the following situations, what is the Investment in Rambis account balance on Herbert's books on January 1, 2018?
       • The parent uses the equity method.
       • The parent uses the partial equity method.
       • The parent uses the initial value method.

c. Under each of the following situations, what is Entry *C on a 2018 consolidation worksheet?
- The parent uses the equity method.
- The parent uses the partial equity method.
- The parent uses the initial value method.

LO 3-3, 3-4

15. Haynes, Inc., obtained 100 percent of Turner Company's common stock on January 1, 2017, by issu-ing 9,000 shares of $10 par value common stock. Haynes's shares had a $15 per share fair value. On that date, Turner reported a net book value of $100,000. However, its equipment (with a five-year remaining life) was undervalued by $5,000 in the company's accounting records. Also, Turner had developed a customer list with an assessed value of $30,000, although no value had been recorded on Turner's books. The customer list had an estimated remaining useful life of 10 years.

The following balances come from the individual accounting records of these two companies as of December 31, 2017:

	Haynes	Turner
Revenues	$(600,000)	$(230,000)
Expenses	440,000	120,000
Investment income	Not given	–0–
Dividends declared	80,000	50,000

The following balances come from the individual accounting records of these two companies as of December 31, 2018:

	Haynes	Turner
Revenues	$(700,000)	$(280,000)
Expenses	460,000	150,000
Investment income	Not given	–0–
Dividends declared	90,000	40,000
Equipment	500,000	300,000

a. What balance does Haynes's Investment in Turner account show on December 31, 2018, when the equity method is applied?

b. What is the consolidated net income for the year ending December 31, 2018?

c. What is the consolidated equipment balance as of December 31, 2018? How would this answer be affected by the investment method applied by the parent?

d. If Haynes has applied the initial value method to account for its investment, what adjustment is needed to the beginning of the Retained Earnings account on a December 31, 2018, consolida-tion worksheet? How would this answer change if the partial equity method had been in use? How would this answer change if the equity method had been in use?

LO 3-6

16. Francisco Inc. acquired 100 percent of the voting shares of Beltran Company on January 1, 2017. In exchange, Francisco paid $450,000 in cash and issued 104,000 shares of its own $1 par value common stock. On this date, Francisco's stock had a fair value of $12 per share. The combination is a statutory merger with Beltran subsequently dissolved as a legal corporation. Beltran's assets and liabilities are assigned to a new reporting unit.

The following reports the fair values for the Beltran reporting unit for January 1, 2017, and December 31, 2018, along with their respective book values on December 31, 2018.

Beltran Reporting Unit	Fair Values 1/1/17	Fair Values 12/31/18	Book Values 12/31/18
Cash	$ 75,000	$ 50,000	$ 50,000
Receivables	193,000	225,000	225,000
Inventory	281,000	305,000	300,000
Patents	525,000	600,000	500,000
Customer relationships	500,000	480,000	450,000
Equipment (net)	295,000	240,000	235,000
Goodwill	?	?	400,000
Accounts payable	(121,000)	(175,000)	(175,000)
Long-term liabilities	(450,000)	(400,000)	(400,000)

a. Prepare Francisco's journal entry to record the assets acquired and the liabilities assumed in the Beltran merger on January 1, 2017.

b. On December 31, 2018, Francisco opts to forgo any goodwill impairment qualitative assessment and estimates that the total fair value of the entire Beltran reporting unit is $1,425,000. What amount of goodwill impairment, if any, should Francisco recognize on its 2018 income statement?

LO 3-6

17. Alomar Co., a consolidated enterprise, conducted an impairment review for each of its reporting units. In its qualitative assessment, one particular reporting unit, Sellers, emerged as a candidate for possible goodwill impairment. Sellers has recognized net assets of $1,094, including goodwill of $755. Seller's fair value is assessed at $1,028 and includes two internally developed unrecognized intangible assets (a patent and a customer list with fair values of $199 and $56, respectively). The following table summarizes current financial information for the Sellers reporting unit:

	Carrying Amounts	Fair Values
Tangible assets, net	$ 84	$ 137
Recognized intangible assets, net	255	326
Goodwill	755	?
Unrecognized intangible assets	0	255
Total	$1,094	$1,028

a. Determine the amount of any goodwill impairment for Alomar's Sellers reporting unit.

b. After recognition of any goodwill impairment loss, what are the reported carrying amounts for the following assets of Alomar's reporting unit Sellers?

- Tangible assets, net.
- Goodwill.
- Patent.
- Customer list.

LO 3-6

18. Destin Company recently acquired several businesses and recognized goodwill in each acquisition. Destin has allocated the resulting goodwill to its three reporting units: Sand Dollar, Salty Dog, and Baytowne. Destin opts to skip the qualitative assessment and therefore performs a quantitative goodwill impairment review annually.

In its current year assessment of goodwill, Destin provides the following individual asset and liability values for each reporting unit:

	Carrying Amounts	Fair Values
Sand Dollar		
Tangible assets	$180,000	$190,000
Trademark	170,000	150,000
Customer list	90,000	100,000
Goodwill	120,000	?
Liabilities	(30,000)	(30,000)
Salty Dog		
Tangible assets	$200,000	$200,000
Unpatented technology	170,000	125,000
Licenses	90,000	100,000
Goodwill	150,000	?
Baytowne		
Tangible assets	$140,000	$150,000
Unpatented technology	–0–	100,000
Copyrights	50,000	80,000
Goodwill	90,000	?

The fair values for each reporting unit (including goodwill) are $510,000 for Sand Dollar, $580,000 for Salty Dog, and $560,000 for Baytowne. To date, Destin has reported no goodwill impairments.

a. How much goodwill impairment should Destin report this year?

b. What changes to the valuations of Destin's tangible assets and identified intangible assets should be reported based on the goodwill impairment tests?

Problems 19 through 21 should be viewed as independent situations. They are based on the following data:

Chapman Company obtains 100 percent of Abernethy Company's stock on January 1, 2017. As of that date, Abernethy has the following trial balance:

	Debit	Credit
Accounts payable		$ 50,000
Accounts receivable	$ 40,000	
Additional paid-in capital		50,000
Buildings (net) (4-year remaining life)	120,000	
Cash and short-term investments	60,000	
Common stock		250,000
Equipment (net) (5-year remaining life)	200,000	
Inventory	90,000	
Land	80,000	
Long-term liabilities (mature 12/31/20)		150,000
Retained earnings, 1/1/17		100,000
Supplies	10,000	
Totals	$600,000	$600,000

During 2017, Abernethy reported net income of $80,000 while declaring and paying dividends of $10,000. During 2018, Abernethy reported net income of $110,000 while declaring and paying dividends of $30,000.

LO 3-3a
19. Assume that Chapman Company acquired Abernethy's common stock for $490,000 in cash. As of January 1, 2017, Abernethy's land had a fair value of $90,000, its buildings were valued at $160,000, and its equipment was appraised at $180,000. Chapman uses the equity method for this investment. Prepare consolidation worksheet entries for December 31, 2017, and December 31, 2018.

LO 3-3b
20. Assume that Chapman Company acquired Abernethy's common stock for $500,000 in cash. Assume that the equipment and long-term liabilities had fair values of $220,000 and $120,000, respectively, on the acquisition date. Chapman uses the initial value method to account for its investment. Prepare consolidation worksheet entries for December 31, 2017, and December 31, 2018.

LO 3-3c
21. Assume that Chapman Company acquired Abernethy's common stock by paying $520,000 in cash. All of Abernethy's accounts are estimated to have a fair value approximately equal to present book values. Chapman uses the partial equity method to account for its investment. Prepare the consolidation worksheet entries for December 31, 2017, and December 31, 2018.

LO 3-3a, 3-3b, 3-4
22. Adams, Inc., acquires Clay Corporation on January 1, 2017, in exchange for $510,000 cash. Immediately after the acquisition, the two companies have the following account balances. Clay's equipment (with a five-year remaining life) is actually worth $440,000. Credit balances are indicated by parentheses.

	Adams	Clay
Current assets	$ 300,000	$ 220,000
Investment in Clay	510,000	–0–
Equipment	600,000	390,000
Liabilities	(200,000)	(160,000)
Common stock	(350,000)	(150,000)
Retained earnings, 1/1/17	(860,000)	(300,000)

In 2017, Clay earns a net income of $55,000 and declares and pays a $5,000 cash dividend. In 2017, Adams reports net income from its own operations (exclusive of any income from Clay) of $125,000 and declares no dividends. At the end of 2018, selected account balances for the two companies are as follows:

	Adams	Clay
Revenues	$(400,000)	$(240,000)
Expenses	290,000	180,000
Investment income	Not given	–0–
Retained earnings, 1/1/18	Not given	(350,000)

(Continued)

(Continued)

	Adams	Clay
Dividends declared.	–0–	8,000
Common stock	(350,000)	(150,000)
Current assets	580,000	262,000
Investment in Clay.	Not given	–0–
Equipment	520,000	420,000
Liabilities.	(152,000)	(130,000)

a. What are the December 31, 2018, Investment Income and Investment in Clay account balances assuming Adams uses the:
- Equity method.
- Initial value method.

b. How does the parent's internal investment accounting method choice affect the amount reported for expenses in its December 31, 2018, consolidated income statement?

c. How does the parent's internal investment accounting method choice affect the amount reported for equipment in its December 31, 2018, consolidated balance sheet?

d. What is Adams's January 1, 2018, Retained Earnings account balance assuming Adams accounts for its investment in Clay using the:
- Equity value method.
- Initial value method.

e. What worksheet adjustment to Adams's January 1, 2018, Retained Earnings account balance is required if Adams accounts for its investment in Clay using the initial value method?

f. Prepare the worksheet entry to eliminate Clay's stockholders' equity.

g. What is consolidated net income for 2018?

LO 3-1, 3-4

23. Following are selected account balances from Penske Company and Stanza Corporation as of December 31, 2018:

	Penske	Stanza
Revenues	$(700,000)	$(400,000)
Cost of goods sold	250,000	100,000
Depreciation expense	150,000	200,000
Investment income	Not given	–0–
Dividends declared.	80,000	60,000
Retained earnings, 1/1/18.	(600,000)	(200,000)
Current assets	400,000	500,000
Copyrights	900,000	400,000
Royalty agreements	600,000	1,000,000
Investment in Stanza	Not given	–0–
Liabilities.	(500,000)	(1,380,000)
Common stock	(600,000) ($20 par)	(200,000) ($10 par)
Additional paid-in capital	(150,000)	(80,000)

On January 1, 2018, Penske acquired all of Stanza's outstanding stock for $680,000 fair value in cash and common stock. Penske also paid $10,000 in stock issuance costs. At the date of acquisition, copyrights (with a six-year remaining life) have a $440,000 book value but a fair value of $560,000.

a. As of December 31, 2018, what is the consolidated copyrights balance?

b. For the year ending December 31, 2018, what is consolidated net income?

c. As of December 31, 2018, what is the consolidated retained earnings balance?

d. As of December 31, 2018, what is the consolidated balance to be reported for goodwill?

LO 3-2, 3-3, 3-4

24. Foxx Corporation acquired all of Greenburg Company's outstanding stock on January 1, 2016, for $600,000 cash. Greenburg's accounting records showed net assets on that date of $470,000, although equipment with a 10-year remaining life was undervalued on the records by $90,000. Any recognized goodwill is considered to have an indefinite life.

Greenburg reports net income in 2016 of $90,000 and $100,000 in 2017. The subsidiary declared dividends of $20,000 in each of these two years.

Account balances for the year ending December 31, 2018, follow. Credit balances are indicated by parentheses.

	Foxx	Greenburg
Revenues	$ (800,000)	$ (600,000)
Cost of goods sold	100,000	150,000
Depreciation expense	300,000	350,000
Investment income	(20,000)	–0–
Net income.	$ (420,000)	$ (100,000)
Retained earnings, 1/1/18.	$(1,100,000)	$ (320,000)
Net income.	(420,000)	(100,000)
Dividends declared.	120,000	20,000
Retained earnings, 12/31/18	$(1,400,000)	$ (400,000)
Current assets	$ 300,000	$ 100,000
Investment in subsidiary	600,000	–0–
Equipment (net)	900,000	600,000
Buildings (net)	800,000	400,000
Land.	600,000	100,000
Total assets	$ 3,200,000	$ 1,200,000
Liabilities.	$ (900,000)	$ (500,000)
Common stock	(900,000)	(300,000)
Retained earnings.	(1,400,000)	(400,000)
Total liabilities and equity	$(3,200,000)	$(1,200,000)

a. Determine the December 31, 2018, consolidated balance for each of the following accounts:

Depreciation Expense	Buildings
Dividends Declared	Goodwill
Revenues	Common Stock
Equipment	

b. How does the parent's choice of an accounting method for its investment affect the balances computed in requirement (a)?

c. Which method of accounting for this subsidiary is the parent actually using for internal reporting purposes?

d. If the parent company had used a different method of accounting for this investment, how could that method have been identified?

e. What would be Foxx's balance for retained earnings as of January 1, 2018, if each of the following methods had been in use?

- Initial value method.
- Partial equity method.
- Equity method.

LO 3-1, 3-3a, 3-4 25. Allison Corporation acquired all of the outstanding voting stock of Mathias, Inc., on January 1, 2017, in exchange for $5,875,000 in cash. Allison intends to maintain Mathias as a wholly owned subsidiary. Both companies have December 31 fiscal year-ends. At the acquisition date, Mathias's stockholders' equity was $2,000,000 including retained earnings of $1,500,000.

At the acquisition date, Allison prepared the following fair value allocation schedule for its newly acquired subsidiary:

Consideration transferred		$5,875,000
Mathias stockholders' equity		2,000,000
Excess fair over book value		$3,875,000
to unpatented technology (8-year remaining life).	$ 800,000	
to patents (10-year remaining life).	2,500,000	
to increase long-term debt (undervalued, 5-year	(100,000)	3,200,000
remaining life)		
Goodwill		$ 675,000

Post-acquisition, Allison employs the equity method to account for its investment in Mathias. During the two years following the business combination, Mathias reports the following income and dividends:

	Income	Dividends
2017	$480,000	$25,000
2018	960,000	50,000

No asset impairments have occurred since the acquisition date.

Individual financial statements for each company as of December 31, 2018, appear below. Parentheses indicate credit balances. Dividends declared were paid in the same period.

Income Statement	Allison	Mathias
Sales	(6,400,000)	(3,900,000)
Cost of goods sold	4,500,000	2,500,000
Depreciation expense	875,000	277,000
Amortization expense	430,000	103,000
Interest expense	55,000	60,000
Equity earnings in Mathias	(630,000)	–0–
Net income	(1,170,000)	(960,000)
Statement of Retained Earnings		
Retained earnings 1/1	(5,340,000)	(1,955,000)
Net income (above)	(1,170,000)	(960,000)
Dividends declared	560,000	50,000
Retained earnings 12/31	(5,950,000)	(2,865,000)
Balance Sheet		
Cash	75,000	143,000
Accounts receivable	950,000	225,000
Inventories	1,700,000	785,000
Investment in Mathias	6,580,000	–0–
Equipment (net)	3,700,000	2,052,000
Patents	95,000	–0–
Unpatented technology	2,125,000	1,450,000
Goodwill	425,000	–0–
Total assets	15,650,000	4,655,000
Accounts payable	(500,000)	(90,000)
Long-term debt	(1,000,000)	(1,200,000)
Common stock	(8,200,000)	(500,000)
Retained earnings 12/31	(5,950,000)	(2,865,000)
Total liabilities and equity	(15,650,000)	(4,655,000)

Required:

a. Show how Allison determined its December 31, 2018, Investment in Mathias balance.

b. Prepare a worksheet to determine the consolidated values to be reported on Allison's financial statements.

LO 3-1, 3-3a

26. On January 3, 2016, Persoff Corporation acquired all of the outstanding voting stock of Sea Cliff, Inc., in exchange for $6,000,000 in cash. Persoff elected to exercise control over Sea Cliff as a wholly owned subsidiary with an independent accounting system. Both companies have December 31 fiscal year-ends. At the acquisition date, Sea Cliff's stockholders' equity was $2,500,000 including retained earnings of $1,700,000.

Persoff pursued the acquisition, in part, to utilize Sea Cliff's technology and computer software. These items had fair values that differed from their values on Sea Cliff's books as follows:

Asset	Book Value	Fair Value	Remaining Useful Life
Patented technology	$140,000	$2,240,000	7 years
Computer software	$ 60,000	$1,260,000	12 years

Sea Cliff's remaining identifiable assets and liabilities had acquisition-date book values that closely approximated fair values. Since acquisition, no assets have been impaired. During the next three years, Sea Cliff reported the following income and dividends:

	Net Income	Dividends
2016	$900,000	$150,000
2017	940,000	150,000
2018	975,000	150,000

December 31, 2018, financial statements for each company appear below. Parentheses indicate credit balances. Dividends declared were paid in the same period.

Income Statement	Persoff	Sea Cliff
Revenues	$ (2,720,000)	$(2,250,000)
Cost of goods sold	1,350,000	870,000
Depreciation expense	275,000	380,000
Amortization expense	370,000	25,000
Equity earnings in Sea Cliff	(575,000)	–0–
Net income	$ (1,300,000)	$ (975,000)
Statement of Retained Earnings		
Retained earnings 1/1	$ (7,470,000)	$(3,240,000)
Net income (above)	(1,300,000)	(975,000)
Dividends declared	600,000	150,000
Retained earnings 12/31	$ (8,170,000)	$(4,065,000)
Balance Sheet		
Current assets	$ 490,000	$ 375,000
Investment in Sea Cliff	7,165,000	–0–
Computer software	300,000	45,000
Patented technology	800,000	80,000
Goodwill	100,000	–0–
Equipment	1,835,000	4,500,000
Total assets	$ 10,690,000	$ 5,000,000
Liabilities	$ (520,000)	$ (135,000)
Common stock	(2,000,000)	(800,000)
Retained earnings 12/31	(8,170,000)	(4,065,000)
Total liabilities and equity	$(10,690,000)	$(5,000,000)

a. Construct Persoff's acquisition-date fair-value allocation schedule for its investment in Sea Cliff.
b. Show how Persoff determined its Equity earnings in Sea Cliff balance for the year ended December 31, 2018.
c. Show how Persoff determined its December 31, 2018, Investment in Sea Cliff balance.
d. Prepare a worksheet to determine the consolidated values to be reported on Persoff's financial statements.

LO 3-1, 3-3a

27. On January 1, 2017, Prestige Corporation acquired 100 percent of the voting stock of Stylene Corporation in exchange for $2,030,000 in cash and securities. On the acquisition date, Stylene had the following balance sheet:

Cash	$ 23,000	Accounts payable	$1,050,000
Accounts receivable	97,000		
Inventory	140,000		
Equipment (net)	1,490,000	Common stock	800,000
Trademarks	850,000	Retained earnings	750,000
	$2,600,000		$2,600,000

At the acquisition date, the book values of Stylene's assets and liabilities were generally equivalent to their fair values except for the following assets:

Asset	Book Value	Fair Value	Remaining Useful Life
Equipment	$1,490,000	$1,610,000	8 years
Customer lists	–0–	160,000	4 years
Trademarks	850,000	900,000	Indefinite

During the next two years, Stylene has the following income and dividends in its own separately prepared financial reports to its parent.

	Net Income	Dividends
2017	$175,000	$25,000
2018	375,000	45,000

Dividends are declared and paid in the same period. The December 31, 2018, separate financial statements for each company appear below. Parentheses indicate credit balances.

Income Statement	Prestige	Stylene
Revenues	$ (4,200,000)	$ (2,200,000)
Cost of goods sold	2,300,000	1,550,000
Depreciation expense	495,000	275,000
Amortization expense	105,000	–0–
Equity earnings in Stylene	(320,000)	–0–
Net income	$ (1,620,000)	$ (375,000)
Statement of Retained Earnings		
Retained earnings 1/1	$ (2,900,000)	$ (900,000)
Net income (above)	(1,620,000)	(375,000)
Dividends declared	150,000	45,000
Retained earnings 12/31	$ (4,370,000)	$ (1,230,000)
Balance Sheet		
Cash	$ 430,000	$ 35,000
Accounts receivable	693,000	75,000
Inventory	890,000	420,000
Investment in Stylene	2,400,000	–0–
Equipment	6,000,000	1,400,000
Customer lists	115,000	–0–
Trademarks	2,500,000	850,000
Goodwill	172,000	–0–
Total assets	$ 13,200,000	$ 2,780,000
Accounts payable	$ (330,000)	$ (750,000)
Common stock	(8,500,000)	(800,000)
Retained earnings 12/31	(4,370,000)	(1,230,000)
Total liabilities and equity	$(13,200,000)	$ (2,780,000)

a. Prepare Prestige's acquisition-date fair-value allocation schedule for its investment in Stylene.

b. Show how Prestige determined its December 31, 2018, Investment in Stylene balance.

c. Prepare a worksheet to determine the balances for Prestige's December 31, 2018, consolidated financial statements.

28. Patrick Corporation acquired 100 percent of O'Brien Company's outstanding common stock on January 1, for $550,000 in cash. O'Brien reported net assets with a carrying amount of $350,000 at that time. Some of O'Brien's assets either were unrecorded (having been internally developed) or had fair values that differed from book values as follows:

	Book Values	Fair Values
Trademarks (indefinite life)	$ 60,000	$160,000
Customer relationships (5-year remaining life)	–0–	75,000
Equipment (10-year remaining life)	342,000	312,000

Any goodwill is considered to have an indefinite life with no impairment charges during the year.

Following are financial statements at the end of the first year for these two companies prepared from their separately maintained accounting systems. O'Brien declared and paid dividends in the same period. Credit balances are indicated by parentheses.

	Patrick	O'Brien
Revenues	$ (1,125,000)	$ (520,000)
Cost of goods sold	300,000	228,000
Depreciation expense	75,000	70,000
Amortization expense	25,000	–0–
Income from O'Brien	(210,000)	–0–
Net Income	$ (935,000)	$ (222,000)
Retained earnings 1/1	$ (700,000)	$ (250,000)
Net Income	(935,000)	(222,000)
Dividends declared	142,000	80,000
Retained earnings 12/31	$ (1,493,000)	$ (392,000)
Cash	$ 185,000	$ 105,000
Receivables	225,000	56,000
Inventory	175,000	135,000
Investment in O'Brien	680,000	–0–
Trademarks	474,000	60,000
Customer relationships	–0–	–0–
Equipment (net)	925,000	272,000
Goodwill	–0–	–0–
Total assets	$ 2,664,000	$ 628,000
Liabilities	$ (771,000)	$ (136,000)
Common stock	(400,000)	(100,000)
Retained earnings 12/31	(1,493,000)	(392,000)
Total liabilities and equity	$ (2,664,000)	$ (628,000)

a. Show how Patrick computed the $210,000 Income of O'Brien balance. Discuss how you determined which accounting method Patrick uses for its investment in O'Brien.

b. Without preparing a worksheet or consolidation entries, determine and explain the totals to be reported for this business combination for the year ending December 31.

c. Verify the totals determined in part (b) by producing a consolidation worksheet for Patrick and O'Brien for the year ending December 31.

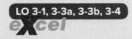

29. Following are separate financial statements of Michael Company and Aaron Company as of December 31, 2018 (credit balances indicated by parentheses). Michael acquired all of Aaron's outstanding voting stock on January 1, 2014, by issuing 20,000 shares of its own $1 par common stock. On the acquisition date, Michael Company's stock actively traded at $23.50 per share.

	Michael Company 12/31/18	Aaron Company 12/31/18
Revenues	$ (610,000)	$ (370,000)
Cost of goods sold	270,000	140,000
Amortization expense	115,000	80,000
Dividend income.	(5,000)	–0–
Net income.	$ (230,000)	$ (150,000)
Retained earnings, 1/1/18.	$ (880,000)	$ (490,000)
Net income (above)	(230,000)	(150,000)
Dividends declared.	90,000	5,000
Retained earnings, 12/31/18	$ (1,020,000)	$ (635,000)
Cash	$ 110,000	$ 15,000
Receivables	380,000	220,000
Inventory.	560,000	280,000
Investment in Aaron Company	470,000	–0–
Copyrights	460,000	340,000
Royalty agreements	920,000	380,000
Total assets	$ 2,900,000	$ 1,235,000
Liabilities.	$ (780,000)	$ (470,000)
Preferred stock	(300,000)	–0–
Common stock	(500,000)	(100,000)
Additional paid-in capital.	(300,000)	(30,000)
Retained earnings, 12/31/18	(1,020,000)	(635,000)
Total liabilities and equity	$ (2,900,000)	$(1,235,000)

On the date of acquisition, Aaron reported retained earnings of $230,000 and a total book value of $360,000. At that time, its royalty agreements were undervalued by $60,000. This intangible was assumed to have a six-year remaining life with no residual value. Additionally, Aaron owned a trademark with a fair value of $50,000 and a 10-year remaining life that was not reflected on its books. Aaron declared and paid dividends in the same period.

a. Using the preceding information, prepare a consolidation worksheet for these two companies as of December 31, 2018.

b. Instead of the initial value method, assume now that Michael applies the equity method to its Investment in Aaron account. What account balances would the parent's individual financial statements then show for the Equity in Subsidiary Earnings, Retained Earnings, and Investment in Aaron accounts?

c. Assuming that Michael applied the equity method to this investment, how would the consolidation entries differ on a December 31, 2018, worksheet?

d. Assuming that Michael applied the equity method to this investment, how would the December 31, 2018, reported consolidated balances differ?

LO 3-1, 3-3, 3-6

30. Giant acquired all of Small's common stock on January 1, 2014, in exchange for cash of $770,000. On that day, Small reported common stock of $170,000 and retained earnings of $400,000. At the acquisition date, $90,000 of the fair-value price was attributed to undervalued land while $50,000 was assigned to undervalued equipment having a 10-year remaining life. The $60,000 unallocated portion of the acquisition-date excess fair value over book value was viewed as goodwill. Over the next few years, Giant applied the equity method to the recording of this investment.

Following are individual financial statements for the year ending December 31, 2018. On that date, Small owes Giant $10,000. Small declared and paid dividends in the same period. Credits are indicated by parentheses.

a. How was the $135,000 Equity in Income of Small balance computed?

b. Without preparing a worksheet or consolidation entries, determine and explain the totals to be reported by this business combination for the year ending December 31, 2018.

c. Verify the amounts determined in part (b) by producing a consolidation worksheet for Giant and Small for the year ending December 31, 2018.

d. If Giant determined that the entire amount of goodwill from its investment in Small was impaired in 2018, how would the parent's accounts reflect the impairment loss? How would the worksheet process change? What impact does an impairment loss have on consolidated financial statements?

	Giant	Small
Revenues	$(1,175,000)	$ (360,000)
Cost of goods sold	550,000	90,000
Depreciation expense	172,000	130,000
Equity in income of Small.	(135,000)	–0–
Net income.	$ (588,000)	$ (140,000)
Retained earnings, 1/1/18.	$(1,417,000)	$ (620,000)
Net income (above)	(588,000)	(140,000)
Dividends declared.	310,000	110,000
Retained earnings, 12/31/18	$(1,695,000)	$ (650,000)
Current assets	$ 398,000	$ 318,000
Investment in Small.	995,000	–0–
Land.	440,000	165,000
Buildings (net)	304,000	419,000
Equipment (net)	648,000	286,000
Goodwill	–0–	–0–
Total assets	$ 2,785,000	$ 1,188,000
Liabilities.	$ (840,000)	$ (368,000)
Common stock	(250,000)	(170,000)
Retained earnings (above).	(1,695,000)	(650,000)
Total liabilities and equity	$(2,785,000)	$(1,188,000)

LO 3-1, 3-3a, 3-3b, 3-4

31. On January 1, 2017, Pinnacle Corporation exchanged $3,200,000 cash for 100 percent of the outstanding voting stock of Strata Corporation. On the acquisition date, Strata had the following balance sheet:

Cash	$ 122,000	Accounts payable	$ 375,000
Accounts receivable.	283,000	Long-term debt	2,655,000
Inventory.	350,000	Common stock	1,500,000
Buildings (net)	1,875,000	Retained earnings.	1,100,000
Licensing agreements	3,000,000		$5,630,000
	$5,630,000		

Pinnacle prepared the following fair-value allocation:

Fair value of Strata (consideration transferred)		$3,200,000
Carrying amount acquired.		2,600,000
Excess fair value		600,000
to buildings (undervalued).	$300,000	
to licensing agreements (overvalued).	(100,000)	200,000
to goodwill (indefinite life)		$ 400,000

At the acquisition date, Strata's buildings had a 10-year remaining life and its licensing agreements were due to expire in 5 years. At December 31, 2018, Strata's accounts payable included an $85,000 current liability owed to Pinnacle. Strata Corporation continues its separate legal existence as a wholly owned subsidiary of Pinnacle with independent accounting records. Pinnacle employs the initial value method in its internal accounting for its investment in Strata.

The separate financial statements for the two companies for the year ending December 31, 2018, follow. Credit balances are indicated by parentheses.

	Pinnacle	Strata
Sales	$ (7,000,000)	$(3,000,000)
Cost of goods sold	4,650,000	1,700,000
Interest expense	255,000	160,000
Depreciation expense	585,000	350,000
Amortization expense		600,000
Dividend income	(50,000)	
Net income	$ (1,560,000)	$ (190,000)
Retained earnings 1/1/18	$ (5,000,000)	$(1,350,000)
Net income	(1,560,000)	(190,000)
Dividends declared	560,000	50,000
Retained earnings 12/31/18	$ (6,000,000)	$(1,490,000)
Cash	$ 433,000	$ 165,000
Accounts receivable	1,210,000	200,000
Inventory	1,235,000	1,500,000
Investment in Strata	3,200,000	
Buildings (net)	5,572,000	2,040,000
Licensing agreements		1,800,000
Goodwill	350,000	
Total assets	$ 12,000,000	$ 5,705,000
Accounts payable	$ (300,000)	$ (715,000)
Long-term debt	(2,700,000)	(2,000,000)
Common stock	(3,000,000)	(1,500,000)
Retained earnings 12/31/18	(6,000,000)	(1,490,000)
Total liabilities and OE	$(12,000,000)	$(5,705,000)

a. Prepare a worksheet to consolidate the financial information for these two companies.

b. Compute the following amounts that would appear on Pinnacle's 2018 separate (nonconsolidated) financial records if Pinnacle's investment accounting was based on the equity method.

- Subsidiary income.
- Retained earnings, 1/1/18.
- Investment in Strata.

c. What effect does the parent's internal investment accounting method have on its consolidated financial statements?

LO 3-1, 3-3, 3-4

32. Following are selected accounts for Mergaronite Company and Hill, Inc., as of December 31, 2018. Several of Mergaronite's accounts have been omitted. Credit balances are indicated by parentheses. Dividends were declared and paid in the same period.

	Mergaronite	Hill
Revenues	$(600,000)	$(250,000)
Cost of goods sold	280,000	100,000
Depreciation expense	120,000	50,000
Investment income	Not given	NA
Retained earnings, 1/1/18	(900,000)	(600,000)
Dividends declared	130,000	40,000
Current assets	200,000	690,000
Land	300,000	90,000
Buildings (net)	500,000	140,000
Equipment (net)	200,000	250,000
Liabilities	(400,000)	(310,000)
Common stock	(300,000)	(40,000)
Additional paid-in capital	(50,000)	(160,000)

Assume that Mergaronite took over Hill on January 1, 2014, by issuing 7,000 shares of common stock having a par value of $10 per share but a fair value of $100 each. On January 1, 2014, Hill's land was undervalued by $20,000, its buildings were overvalued by $30,000, and equipment was undervalued by $60,000. The buildings had a 10-year remaining life; the equipment had a 5-year remaining life. A customer list with an appraised value of $100,000 was developed internally by Hill and was to be written off over a 20-year period.

a. Determine and explain the December 31, 2018, consolidated totals for the following accounts:

Revenues	Amortization Expense	Customer List
Cost of Goods Sold	Buildings	Common Stock
Depreciation Expense	Equipment	Additional Paid-In Capital

b. In requirement (a), why can the consolidated totals be determined without knowing which method the parent used to account for the subsidiary?

c. If the parent uses the equity method, what consolidation entries would be used on a 2018 worksheet?

33. On January 1, 2018, Brooks Corporation exchanged $1,183,000 fair-value consideration for all of the outstanding voting stock of Chandler, Inc. At the acquisition date, Chandler had a book value equal to $1,105,000. Chandler's individual assets and liabilities had fair values equal to their respective book values except for the patented technology account, which was undervalued by $204,000 with an estimated remaining life of six years. The Chandler acquisition was Brooks's only business combination for the year.

In case expected synergies did not materialize, Brooks Corporation wished to prepare for a potential future spin-off of Chandler, Inc. Therefore, Brooks had Chandler maintain its separate incorporation and independent accounting information system as elements of continuing value.

On December 31, 2018, each company submitted the following financial statements for consolidation. Dividends were declared and paid in the same period. Parentheses indicated credit balances.

	Brooks Corp.	Chandler Inc.
Income Statement		
Revenues	$ (640,000)	$ (587,000)
Cost of goods sold	255,000	203,000
Gain on bargain purchase	(126,000)	–0–
Depreciation and amortization	150,000	151,000
Equity earnings from Chandler	(199,000)	–0–
Net income	$ (560,000)	$ (233,000)
Statement of Retained Earnings		
Retained earnings, 1/1	$(1,835,000)	$ (805,000)
Net income (above)	(560,000)	(233,000)
Dividends declared	100,000	40,000
Retained earnings, 12/31	$(2,295,000)	$ (998,000)
Balance Sheet		
Current assets	$ 343,000	$ 432,000
Investment in Chandler	1,468,000	–0–
Trademarks	134,000	221,000
Patented technology	395,000	410,000
Equipment	693,000	341,000
Total assets	$ 3,033,000	$ 1,404,000
Liabilities	$ (203,000)	$ (106,000)
Common stock	(535,000)	(300,000)
Retained earnings, 12/31	(2,295,000)	(998,000)
Total liabilities and equity	$(3,033,000)	$(1,404,000)

a. Show how Brooks determined the following account balances:
- Gain on bargain purchase.
- Earnings from Chandler.
- Investment in Chandler.

b. Prepare a December 31, 2018, consolidated worksheet for Brooks and Chandler.

34. Branson paid $465,000 cash for all of the outstanding common stock of Wolfpack, Inc., on January 1, 2017. On that date, the subsidiary had a book value of $340,000 (common stock of $200,000 and retained earnings of $140,000), although various unrecorded royalty agreements (10-year remaining life) were assessed at a $100,000 fair value. Any remaining excess fair value was considered goodwill.

In negotiating the acquisition price, Branson also promised to pay Wolfpack's former owners an additional $50,000 if Wolfpack's income exceeded $120,000 total over the first two years after the acquisition. At the acquisition date, Branson estimated the probability-adjusted present value of this contingent consideration at $35,000. On December 31, 2017, based on Wolfpack's earnings to date, Branson increased the value of the contingency to $40,000.

During the subsequent two years, Wolfpack reported the following amounts for income and dividends:

	Net Income	Dividends Declared
2017	$65,000	$25,000
2018	75,000	35,000

In keeping with the original acquisition agreement, on December 31, 2018, Branson paid the additional $50,000 performance fee to Wolfpack's previous owners.

Prepare each of the following:

a. Branson's entry to record the acquisition of the shares of its Wolfpack subsidiary.

b. Branson's entries at the end of 2017 and 2018 to adjust its contingent performance obligation for changes in fair value and the December 31, 2018, payment.

c. Consolidation worksheet entries as of December 31, 2018, assuming that Branson has applied the equity method.

d. Consolidation worksheet entries as of December 31, 2018, assuming that Branson has applied the initial value method.

35. Allen Company acquired 100 percent of Bradford Company's voting stock on January 1, 2014, by issuing 10,000 shares of its $10 par value common stock (having a fair value of $14 per share). As of that date, Bradford had stockholders' equity totaling $105,000. Land shown on Bradford's accounting records was undervalued by $10,000. Equipment (with a five-year remaining life) was undervalued by $5,000. A secret formula developed by Bradford was appraised at $20,000 with an estimated life of 20 years.

Following are the separate financial statements for the two companies for the year ending December 31, 2018. There were no intra-entity payables on that date. Credit balances are indicated by parentheses.

	Allen Company	Bradford Company
Revenues	$ (485,000)	$(190,000)
Cost of goods sold	160,000	70,000
Depreciation expense	130,000	52,000
Subsidiary earnings	(66,000)	–0–
Net income	$ (261,000)	$ (68,000)
Retained earnings, 1/1/18	$ (659,000)	$ (98,000)
Net income (above)	(261,000)	(68,000)
Dividends declared	175,500	40,000
Retained earnings, 12/31/18	$ (744,500)	$(126,000)
Current assets	$ 268,000	$ 75,000
Investment in Bradford Company	216,000	–0–
Land	427,500	58,000
Buildings and equipment (net)	713,000	161,000
Total assets	$ 1,624,500	$ 294,000
Current liabilities	$ (190,000)	$(103,000)
Common stock	(600,000)	(60,000)
Additional paid-in capital	(90,000)	(5,000)
Retained earnings, 12/31/18	(744,500)	(126,000)
Total liabilities and equity	$(1,624,500)	$(294,000)

a. Explain how Allen derived the $66,000 balance in the Subsidiary Earnings account.

b. Prepare a worksheet to consolidate the financial information for these two companies.

36. Tyler Company acquired all of Jasmine Company's outstanding stock on January 1, 2016, for $206,000 in cash. Jasmine had a book value of only $140,000 on that date. However, equipment (having an eight-year remaining life) was undervalued by $54,400 on Jasmine's financial records. A building with a 20-year remaining life was overvalued by $10,000. Subsequent to the acquisition, Jasmine reported the following:

	Net Income	Dividends Declared
2016	$50,000	$10,000
2017	60,000	40,000
2018	30,000	20,000

In accounting for this investment, Tyler has used the equity method. Selected accounts taken from the financial records of these two companies as of December 31, 2018, follow:

	Tyler Company	Jasmine Company
Revenues—operating.	$(310,000)	$(104,000)
Expenses	198,000	74,000
Equipment (net)	320,000	50,000
Buildings (net)	220,000	68,000
Common stock	(290,000)	(50,000)
Retained earnings, 12/31/18	(410,000)	(160,000)

Determine and explain the following account balances as of December 31, 2018:

a. Investment in Jasmine Company (on Tyler's individual financial records).

b. Equity in Subsidiary Earnings (on Tyler's individual financial records).

c. Consolidated Net Income.

d. Consolidated Equipment (net).

e. Consolidated Buildings (net).

f. Consolidated Goodwill (net).

g. Consolidated Common Stock.

h. Consolidated Retained Earnings, 12/31/18.

37. On January 1, 2017, Procise Corporation acquired 100 percent of the outstanding voting stock of GaugeRite Corporation for $1,980,000 cash. On the acquisition date, GaugeRite had the following balance sheet:

Cash	$ 14,000	Accounts payable	$ 120,000
Accounts receivable	100,000	Long-term debt	930,000
Land	700,000	Common stock	1,000,000
Equipment (net)	1,886,000	Retained earnings	650,000
	$2,700,000		$2,700,000

At the acquisition date, the following allocation was prepared:

Fair value of consideration transferred		$1,980,000
Book value acquired		1,650,000
Excess fair value over book value		330,000
To in-process research and development	$44,000	
To equipment (8-year remaining life)	56,000	100,000
To goodwill (indefinite life)		$ 230,000

Although at acquisition date Procise had expected $44,000 in future benefits from GaugeRite's in-process research and development project, by the end of 2017 it was apparent that the research project was a failure with no future economic benefits.

On December 31, 2018, Procise and GaugeRite submitted the following trial balances for consolidation. There were no intra-entity payables on that date.

	Procise	GaugeRite
Sales	$ (3,500,000)	$ (1,000,000)
Cost of goods sold	1,600,000	630,000
Depreciation expense	350,000	130,000
Other operating expenses	190,000	30,000
Subsidiary income	(203,000)	–0–
Net income	$ (1,563,000)	$ (210,000)
Retained earnings 1/1/18	$ (3,000,000)	$ (800,000)
Net income	(1,563,000)	(210,000)
Dividends declared	200,000	25,000
Retained earnings 12/31/18	$ (4,363,000)	$ (985,000)
Cash	$ 228,000	$ 50,000
Accounts receivable	840,000	155,000
Inventory	900,000	580,000
Investment in GaugeRite	2,257,000	–0–
Land	3,500,000	700,000
Equipment (net)	4,785,000	1,700,000
Goodwill	290,000	–0–
Total assets	$ 12,800,000	$ 3,185,000
Accounts payable	$ (193,000)	$ (400,000)
Long-term debt	(3,094,000)	(800,000)
Common stock	(5,150,000)	(1,000,000)
Retained earnings 12/31/18	(4,363,000)	(985,000)
Total liabilities and equities	$(12,800,000)	$ (3,185,000)

  a. Show how Procise derived its December 31, 2018, Investment in GaugeRite account balance.

  b. Explain the treatment of the acquired in-process research and development.

  c. Prepare a consolidated worksheet for Procise and GaugeRite as of December 31, 2018.

LO 3-4a, 3-6

38. On January 1, Prine, Inc., acquired 100 percent of Lydia Company's common stock for a fair value of $120,000,000 in cash and stock. Lydia's assets and liabilities equaled their fair values except for its equipment, which was undervalued by $500,000 and had a 10-year remaining life.

    Prine specializes in media distribution and viewed its acquisition of Lydia as a strategic move into content ownership and creation. Prine expected both cost and revenue synergies from controlling Lydia's artistic content (a large library of classic movies) and its sports programming specialty video operation. Accordingly, Prine allocated Lydia's assets and liabilities (including $50,000,000 of goodwill) to a newly formed operating segment appropriately designated as a reporting unit.

    The fair values of the reporting unit's identifiable assets and liabilities through the first year of operations were as follows.

	Fair Values	
Account	**1/1**	**12/31**
Cash	$ 215,000	$ 109,000
Receivables (net)	525,000	897,000
Movie library (25-year remaining life)	40,000,000	60,000,000
Broadcast licenses (indefinite life)	15,000,000	20,000,000
Equipment (10-year remaining life)	20,750,000	19,000,000
Current liabilities	(490,000)	(650,000)
Long-term debt	(6,000,000)	(6,250,000)

However, Lydia's assets have taken longer than anticipated to produce the expected synergies with Prine's operations. Accordingly, Prine reviewed events and circumstances and concluded that Lydia's fair value was likely less than its carrying amount. At year-end, Prine reduced its assessment of the Lydia reporting unit's fair value to $110,000,000.

At December 31, Prine and Lydia submitted the following balances for consolidation. There were no intra-entity payables on that date.

	Prine, Inc.	Lydia Co.
Revenues	$ (18,000,000)	$(12,000,000)
Operating expenses.	10,350,000	11,800,000
Equity in Lydia earnings.	(150,000)	
Dividends declared.	300,000	80,000
Retained earnings, 1/1.	(52,000,000)	(2,000,000)
Cash	260,000	109,000
Receivables (net).	210,000	897,000
Investment in Lydia.	120,070,000	
Broadcast licenses	350,000	14,014,000
Movie library.	365,000	45,000,000
Equipment (net)	136,000,000	17,500,000
Current liabilities	(755,000)	(650,000)
Long-term debt	(22,000,000)	(7,250,000)
Common stock	(175,000,000)	(67,500,000)

a. What is the relevant initial test to determine whether goodwill could be impaired?

b. At what amount should Prine record an impairment loss for its Lydia reporting unit for the year?

c. What is consolidated net income for the year?

d. What is the December 31 consolidated balance for goodwill?

e. What is the December 31 consolidated balance for broadcast licenses?

f. Prepare a consolidated worksheet for Prine and Lydia (Prine's trial balance should first be adjusted for any appropriate impairment loss).

Appendix Problems

LO 3-8

39. Briefly discuss the cost savings that may result from a private company electing to amortize goodwill as opposed to annual impairment testing.

LO 3-8

40. Angela Corporation (a private company) acquired all of the outstanding voting stock of Eddy Tech, Inc., on January 1, 2018, in exchange for $9,000,000 in cash. At the acquisition date, Eddy Tech's stockholders' equity was $7,200,000 including retained earnings of $3,000,000.

At the acquisition date, Angela prepared the following fair value allocation schedule for its newly acquired subsidiary:

Consideration transferred		$9,000,000
Eddy's stockholder's equity		7,200,000
Excess fair over book value		$1,800,000
to patented technology (5-year remaining life).	$ 150,000	
to trade names (indefinite remaining life).	500,000	
to equipment (8-year remaining life)	50,000	700,000
Goodwill		$1,100,000

At the end of 2018, Angela and Eddy Tech report the following amounts from their individually maintained account balances, before consideration of their parent-subsidiary relationship. Parentheses indicate a credit balance.

	Angela	Eddy Tech
Sales	(7,850,000)	(2,400,000)
Cost of goods sold	4,200,000	1,300,000
Depreciation expense	425,000	48,000
Amortization expense	250,000	12,000
Other operating expenses	75,000	53,750
Net income.	(2,900,000)	(986,250)

Required:

Prepare a 2018 consolidated income statement for Angela and its subsidiary Eddy Tech. Assume that Angela, as a private company, elects to amortize goodwill over a 10-year period.

Develop Your Skills

RESEARCH CASE

CPA
skills

Jonas Tech Corporation recently acquired Innovation Plus Company. The combined firm consists of three related businesses that will serve as reporting units. In connection with the acquisition, Jonas requests your help with the following asset valuation and allocation issues. Support your answers with references to FASB ASC as appropriate.

Jonas recognizes several identifiable intangibles from its acquisition of Innovation Plus. It expresses the desire to have these intangible assets written down to zero in the acquisition period.

The price Jonas paid for Innovation Plus indicates that it paid a large amount for goodwill. However, Jonas worries that any future goodwill impairment may send the wrong signal to its investors about the wisdom of the Innovation Plus acquisition. Jonas thus wishes to allocate the combined goodwill of all of its reporting units to one account called *Enterprise Goodwill.* In this way, Jonas hopes to minimize the possibility of goodwill impairment because a decline in goodwill in one business unit could be offset by an increase in the value of goodwill in another business unit.

Required

1. Advise Jonas on the acceptability of its suggested immediate write-off of its identifiable intangibles.
2. Indicate the relevant factors to consider in allocating the value assigned to identifiable intangibles acquired in a business combination to expense over time.
3. Advise Jonas on the acceptability of its suggested treatment of goodwill.
4. Indicate the relevant factors to consider in allocating goodwill across an enterprise's business units.

MICROSOFT IMPAIRMENT ANALYSIS CASE

In 2015 Microsoft Corporation reported a $5.1 billion charge for the impairment of goodwill and a $2.2 billion charge for the impairment of intangible assets in one of its reporting units (segments) in its 10-K annual report. Referring to Microsoft's 2015 financial statements and any other information from the media, address the following:

1. Microsoft's segments serve as its reporting units for assessing goodwill for potential impairments. Which segment suffered a 2015 impairment? Describe the revenue model for this segment.
2. What were the underlying business reasons that required Microsoft to record a goodwill impairment in 2015?
3. How did Microsoft reflect the 2015 goodwill impairment in its income statement and cash flow statement?
4. Describe in your own words the goodwill impairment testing steps performed by Microsoft in 2015 and the consequent loss measurement.

FASB ASC AND IASB RESEARCH CASE

A vice president for operations at Poncho Platforms asks for your help on a financial reporting issue concerning goodwill. Two years ago, the company suffered a goodwill impairment loss for its Chip Integration reporting unit. Since that time, however, the Chip Integration unit has recovered nicely and its current cash flows (and projected cash flows) are at an all-time high. The vice president now asks whether the goodwill loss can be reversed given the reversal of fortunes for the Chip Integration reporting unit.

1. Is impairment of goodwill reversible under U.S. GAAP? How about under IFRS? (Refer to FASB Topic 350, "Intangibles—Goodwill and Other," and *IAS 36,* "Impairment of Assets.")
2. Are goodwill impairment testing procedures the same under IFRS and U.S. GAAP? If not, how is goodwill tested for impairment under IFRS? (Refer to *IAS 36,* "Impairment of Assets.")

EXCEL CASE 1

On January 1, 2017, Innovus, Inc., acquired 100 percent of the common stock of ChipTech Company for $670,000 in cash and other fair-value consideration. ChipTech's fair value was allocated among its net assets as follows:

Fair value of consideration transferred for ChipTech		$670,000
Book value of ChipTech:		
Common stock and Additional Paid-In Capital (APIC)	$130,000	
Retained earnings	370,000	500,000
Excess fair value over book value to		170,000
Trademark (10-year remaining life)	$ 40,000	
Existing technology (5-year remaining life)	80,000	120,000
Goodwill		$ 50,000

The December 31, 2018, trial balances for the parent and subsidiary follow (there were no intra-entity payables on that date):

	Innovus	ChipTech
Revenues	$ (990,000)	$ (210,000)
Cost of goods sold	500,000	90,000
Depreciation expense	100,000	5,000
Amortization expense	55,000	18,000
Dividend income	(40,000)	–0–
Net income	$ (375,000)	$ (97,000)
Retained earnings 1/1/18	$ (1,555,000)	$ (450,000)
Net income	(375,000)	(97,000)
Dividends declared	250,000	40,000
Retained earnings 12/31/18	$ (1,680,000)	$ (507,000)
Current assets	$ 960,000	$ 355,000
Investment in ChipTech	670,000	
Equipment (net)	765,000	225,000
Trademark	235,000	100,000
Existing technology	–0–	45,000
Goodwill	450,000	–0–
Total assets	$ 3,080,000	$ 725,000
Liabilities	$ (780,000)	(88,000)
Common stock	(500,000)	(100,000)
Additional paid-in capital	(120,000)	(30,000)
Retained earnings 12/31/18	(1,680,000)	(507,000)
Total liabilities and equity	$ (3,080,000)	$ (725,000)

Required

a. Using Excel, compute consolidated balances for Innovus and ChipTech. Either use a worksheet approach or compute the balances directly.

b. Prepare a second spreadsheet that shows a 2018 impairment loss for the entire amount of goodwill from the ChipTech acquisition.

EXCEL CASE 2

On January 1, 2017, Hi-Speed.com acquired 100 percent of the common stock of Wi-Free Co. for cash of $730,000. The consideration transferred was allocated among Wi-Free's net assets as follows:

Wi-Free fair value (cash paid by Hi-Speed)		$730,000
Book value of Wi-Free:		
Common stock and additional paid-in capital (APIC)	$130,000	
Retained earnings	370,000	500,000
Excess fair value over book value to		230,000
In-process R&D	$ 75,000	
Computer software (overvalued)	(30,000)	
Internet domain name	120,000	165,000
Goodwill		$ 65,000

At the acquisition date, the computer software had a 4-year remaining life, and the Internet domain name was estimated to have a 10-year remaining life. By the end of 2017, it became clear that the acquired in-process research and development would yield no economic benefits and Hi-Speed.com recognized an impairment loss. At December 31, 2018, Wi-Free's accounts payable included a $30,000 amount owed to Hi-Speed.

The December 31, 2018, trial balances for the parent and subsidiary follow:

	Hi-Speed.com	Wi-Free Co.
Revenues	$ (1,100,000)	$ (325,000)
Cost of goods sold	625,000	122,000
Depreciation expense	140,000	12,000
Amortization expense	50,000	11,000
Equity in subsidiary earnings	(175,500)	–0–
Net income.	$ (460,500)	$ (180,000)
Retained earnings 1/1/18	$ (1,552,500)	$ (450,000)
Net income.	(460,500)	(180,000)
Dividends declared.	250,000	50,000
Retained earnings 12/31/18	$ (1,763,000)	$ (580,000)
Current assets	$ 1,034,000	$ 345,000
Investment in Wi-Free	856,000	–0–
Equipment (net)	713,000	305,000
Computer software.	650,000	130,000
Internet domain name	–0–	100,000
Goodwill	–0–	–0–
Total assets	$ 3,253,000	$ 880,000
Liabilities.	$ (870,000)	$ (170,000)
Common stock	(500,000)	(110,000)
Additional paid-in capital	(120,000)	(20,000)
Retained earnings 12/31/18.	(1,763,000)	(580,000)
Total liabilities and equity	$ (3,253,000)	$ (880,000)

Required

a. Using Excel, prepare calculations showing how Hi-Speed derived the $856,000 amount for its investment in Wi-Free.

b. Using Excel, compute consolidated balances for Hi-Speed and Wi-Free. Either use a worksheet approach or compute the balances directly.

Computer Project

Alternative Investment Methods, Goodwill Impairment, and Consolidated Financial Statements

In this project, you are to provide an analysis of alternative accounting methods for controlling interest investments and subsequent effects on consolidated reporting. The project requires the use of a computer and a spreadsheet software package (e.g., Microsoft Excel, etc.). The use of these tools allows you to assess the sensitivity of alternative accounting methods on consolidated financial reporting without preparing several similar worksheets by hand. Also, by modeling a worksheet process, you can develop a better understanding of accounting for combined reporting entities.

Consolidated Worksheet Preparation

You will be creating and entering formulas to complete four worksheets. The first objective is to demonstrate the effect of different methods of accounting for the investments (equity, initial value, and partial equity) on the parent company's trial balance and on the consolidated worksheet subsequent to acquisition. The second objective is to show the effect on consolidated balances and key financial ratios of recognizing a goodwill impairment loss.

The project requires preparation of the following four separate worksheets:

a. Consolidated information worksheet (follows).
b. Equity method consolidation worksheet.
c. Initial value method consolidation worksheet.
d. Partial equity method consolidation worksheet.

If your spreadsheet package has multiple worksheet capabilities (e.g., Excel), you can use separate worksheets; otherwise, each of the four worksheets can reside in a separate area of a single spreadsheet.

In formulating your solution, each worksheet should link directly to the first worksheet. Also, feel free to create supplemental schedules to enhance the capabilities of your worksheet.

Project Scenario

Pecos Company acquired 100 percent of Suaro's outstanding stock for $1,450,000 cash on January 1, 2017, when Suaro had the following balance sheet:

Assets		Liabilities and Equity	
Cash	$ 37,000	Liabilities	$(422,000)
Receivables	82,000		
Inventory	149,000	Common stock	(350,000)
Land	90,000	Retained earnings	(126,000)
Equipment (net)	225,000		
Software	315,000		
Total assets	$898,000	Total liabilities and equity	$(898,000)

At the acquisition date, the fair values of each identifiable asset and liability that differed from book value were as follows:

Land	$ 80,000	
Brand name	60,000	(indefinite life—unrecognized on Suaro's books)
Software	415,000	(2-year estimated remaining useful life)
In-process R&D	300,000	

Additional Information

- Although at acquisition date Pecos expected future benefits from Suaro's in-process research and development (R&D), by the end of 2017 it became clear that the research project was a failure with no future economic benefits.
- During 2017, Suaro earns $75,000 and pays no dividends.
- Selected amounts from Pecos and Suaro's separate financial statements at December 31, 2018, are presented in the consolidated information worksheet. All consolidated worksheets are to be prepared as of December 31, 2018, two years subsequent to acquisition.
- Pecos's January 1, 2018, Retained Earnings balance—before any effect from Suaro's 2017 income—is $(930,000) (credit balance).
- Pecos has 500,000 common shares outstanding for EPS calculations and reported $2,943,100 for consolidated assets at the beginning of the period.

Following is the consolidated information worksheet.

	A	B	C	D
1	**December 31, 2018, trial balances**			
2				
3		**Pecos**	**Suaro**	
4	Revenues	$ (1,052,000)	$ (427,000)	
5	Operating expenses	821,000	262,000	
6	Goodwill impairment loss	?		
7	Income of Suaro	?		
8	Net income	?	$ (165,000)	
9				
10	Retained earnings—Pecos 1/1/18	?		
11	Retained earnings—Suaro 1/1/18		(201,000)	
12	Net income (above)	?	(165,000)	
13	Dividends declared	200,000	35,000	
14	Retained earnings 12/31/18	?	$ (331,000)	
15				
16	Cash	195,000	95,000	
17	Receivables	247,000	143,000	
18	Inventory	415,000	197,000	
19	Investment in Suaro	?		
20				
21				
22				
23	Land	341,000	85,000	
24	Equipment (net)	240,100	100,000	
25	Software		312,000	
26	Other intangibles	145,000		
27	Goodwill			
28	Total assets	?	$ 932,000	
29				
30	Liabilities	(1,537,100)	(251,000)	
31	Common stock	(500,000)	(350,000)	
32	Retained earnings (above)	?	(331,000)	
33	Total liabilities and equity	?	$ (932,000)	
34				
35	Fair-value allocation schedule			
36	Price paid	1,450,000		
37	Book value	476,000		
38	Excess initial value	974,000	Amortizations	
39	to land	(10,000)	2017	2018
40	to brand name	60,000	?	?

(*continued*)

(*continued*)

	A	B	C	D
41	to software	100,000	?	?
42	to IPR&D	300,000	?	?
43	to goodwill	524,000	?	?
44				
45	Suaro's RE changes	Income	Dividends	
46	2017	75,000	0	
47	2018	165,000	35,000	

Project Requirements

Complete the four worksheets as follows:

1. Input the **consolidated information worksheet** provided and complete the fair-value allocation schedule by computing the excess amortizations for 2017 and 2018.

2. Using separate worksheets, prepare Pecos's trial balances for each of the indicated accounting methods (equity, initial value, and partial equity). **Use only formulas for the Investment in Suaro, the Income of Suaro, and Retained Earnings accounts.**

3. **Using references to other cells only (either from the consolidated information worksheet or from the separate method sheets), prepare for each of the three consolidation worksheets:**
   - Adjustments and eliminations.
   - Consolidated balances.

4. Calculate and present the effects of a 2018 total goodwill impairment loss on the following ratios for the consolidated entity:
   - Earnings per share (EPS).
   - Return on assets.
   - Return on equity.
   - Debt to equity.

   Your worksheets should have the capability to adjust immediately for the possibility that all acquisition goodwill can be considered impaired in 2018.

5. **Prepare a word-processed report that describes and discusses the following worksheet results:**
   a. The effects of alternative investment accounting methods on the parent's trial balances and the final consolidation figures.
   b. The relation between consolidated retained earnings and the parent's retained earnings under each of the three (equity, initial value, partial equity) investment accounting methods.
   c. The effect on EPS, return on assets, return on equity, and debt-to-equity ratios of the recognition that all acquisition-related goodwill is considered impaired in 2018.

Consolidated Financial Statements and Outside Ownership

W al-Mart Stores, Inc. (Walmart), in its 2015 consolidated financial statements, includes the accounts of the company and all of its subsidiaries in which a controlling interest is maintained. For those consolidated subsidiaries where Walmart's ownership is less than 100 percent, the outside stockholders' interests are shown as *noncontrolling interests* in the stockholders' equity section of its consolidated balance sheet. On its consolidated income statement, Walmart also allocates a share of the consolidated net income to the noncontrolling interest.

A number of reasons exist for one company to hold less than 100 percent ownership of a subsidiary. The parent might not have had sufficient resources available to obtain all of the outstanding stock. As a second possibility, a few subsidiary stockholders may elect to retain their ownership, perhaps in hope of getting a better price at a later date.

Lack of total ownership is frequently encountered with foreign subsidiaries. The laws of some countries prohibit outsiders from maintaining complete control of domestic business enterprises. In other areas of the world, a parent can seek to establish better relations with a subsidiary's employees, customers, and local government by maintaining some percentage of native ownership.

LO 4-1

Understand that business combinations can occur with less than complete ownership.

Regardless of the reason for owning less than 100 percent, the parent consolidates the financial data of every subsidiary when control is present. As discussed in Chapter 2, *complete ownership is not a prerequisite for consolidation.* A single economic entity is formed whenever one company is able to control the decision-making process of another.

Although most parent companies own 100 percent of their subsidiaries, a significant number, such as Walmart, establish control with a lesser amount of stock. The remaining outside owners are collectively referred to as *a noncontrolling interest,* which replaces the traditional term *minority interest.*[1] The presence of these other stockholders poses a number of reporting questions for the accountant. Whenever less than 100 percent of

[1] The term *minority interest* had been used almost universally to identify the presence of other outside owners. However, current GAAP refers to these outside owners as the noncontrolling interest. Because this term is more descriptive, it is used throughout this textbook.

Learning Objectives

After studying this chapter, you should be able to:

LO 4-1 Understand that business combinations can occur with less than complete ownership.

LO 4-2 Describe the concepts and valuation principles underlying the acquisition method of accounting for the noncontrolling interest.

LO 4-3 Allocate goodwill acquired in a business combination across the controlling and noncontrolling interests.

LO 4-4 Demonstrate the computation and allocation of consolidated net income in the presence of a noncontrolling interest.

LO 4-5 Identify and calculate the four noncontrolling interest figures that must be included within the consolidation process and prepare a consolidation worksheet in the presence of a noncontrolling interest.

LO 4-6 Identify appropriate placements for the components of the noncontrolling interest in consolidated financial statements.

LO 4-7 Determine the effect on consolidated financial statements of a control premium paid by the parent.

LO 4-8 Understand the impact on consolidated financial statements of a midyear acquisition.

LO 4-9 Understand the impact on consolidated financial statements when a step acquisition has taken place.

LO 4-10 Record the sale of a subsidiary (or a portion of its shares).

a subsidiary's voting stock is held, how should the subsidiary's accounts be valued within consolidated financial statements? How should the presence of these additional owners be acknowledged?

LO 4-2

Describe the concepts and valuation principles underlying the acquisition method of accounting for the noncontrolling interest.

Consolidated Financial Reporting in the Presence of a Noncontrolling Interest

Noncontrolling Interest Defined

The authoritative accounting literature defines a noncontrolling interest as follows:

> The ownership interests in the subsidiary that are held by owners other than the parent is a noncontrolling interest. The noncontrolling interest in a subsidiary is part of the equity of the consolidated group. (FASB ASC 810-10-45-15)

When a parent company acquires a controlling ownership interest with less than 100 percent of a subsidiary's voting shares, it must account for the noncontrolling shareholders' interest in its consolidated financial statements. The noncontrolling interest represents an additional set of owners who have legal claim to the subsidiary's net assets.

Exhibit 4.1 provides a framework for introducing several fundamental challenges in accounting and reporting for a noncontrolling interest. The issues focus on how the parent, in its consolidated financial statements, should

- Recognize the subsidiary's assets and liabilities.
- Assign values to the subsidiary's assets and liabilities.
- Value and disclose the presence of the other owners.

The acquisition method's solution to these challenges involves both the *economic unit concept* and *fair value*. First, the economic unit concept views the parent and subsidiary companies as a single economic unit for financial reporting purposes. Thus, a controlled company must always be consolidated as a whole regardless of the parent's level of ownership. As shown in Exhibit 4.1, when a parent controls a subsidiary through a 70 percent ownership, the parent must consolidate 100 percent of the subsidiary's (and the parent's) assets and liabilities in order to reflect the single economic unit. The consolidated balance sheet then provides an owners' equity amount for the noncontrolling owners' interest—a recognition that the parent does not own 100 percent of the subsidiary's assets and liabilities.

The acquisition method also captures the subsidiary's acquisition-date fair values as the relevant attribute for reporting the financial effects of the business combination—including the noncontrolling interest. Fair values also provide for managerial accountability to investors and creditors for assessing the success or failure of the combination. In contrast, the parent's assets and liabilities remain at their previous carrying amounts.

Control and Accountability

In acquiring a controlling interest, a parent company becomes responsible for managing all the subsidiary's assets and liabilities even though it may own only a partial interest. If a parent can control the business activities of its subsidiary, it directly follows that the parent

EXHIBIT 4.1
Noncontrolling Interest—
Date of Acquisition

PARENT AND 70% OWNED SUBSIDIARY COMPANIES
Consolidated Balance Sheet
Date of Acquisition

Parent's assets (100%)	Parent's liabilities (100%)
Subsidiary's assets (100%)	**Subsidiary's liabilities (100%)**
	Parent company owners' equity
	• 100% of parent's net assets
	• **70% of subsidiary's net assets**
	Noncontrolling owners' interest
	• **30% of subsidiary net assets**

is accountable to its investors and creditors for all of the subsidiary's assets, liabilities, and profits. To provide a complete picture of the acquired subsidiary requires fair-value measurements for both the subsidiary as a whole and its individual assets and liabilities. Thus, for business combinations involving less-than-100 percent ownership, the acquirer recognizes and measures the following at the acquisition date:

- All subsidiary identifiable assets and liabilities at their full fair values.[2]
- Noncontrolling interest at fair value.
- Goodwill or a gain from a bargain purchase.

In concluding that consolidated statements involving a noncontrolling interest should initially show all of the subsidiary's assets and liabilities at their full fair values, the 2005 FASB exposure draft Business Combinations (para. B23.a.) observed:

> The acquirer obtains control of the acquiree at the acquisition date and, therefore, becomes responsible and accountable for all of the acquiree's assets, liabilities, and activities, regardless of the percentage of its ownership in the investee.
> . . . an important purpose of financial statements is to provide users with relevant and reliable information about the performance of the entity and the resources under its control. That applies regardless of the extent of the ownership interest a parent holds in a particular subsidiary. The Boards concluded that measurement at fair value enables users to better assess the cash generating abilities of the identifiable net assets acquired in the business combination and the accountability of management for the resources entrusted to it.

To summarize, even though a company acquires less than 100 percent of another firm, financial reporting standards require the parent to include 100 percent of the assets acquired and liabilities assumed. At the acquisition date, the parent measures at fair value both the subsidiary as a whole and its identifiable assets and liabilities. Also, the parent recognizes the noncontrolling interest at its acquisition-date fair value. However, as discussed below, measuring the fair value of the noncontrolling interest presents some special challenges.

Subsidiary Acquisition-Date Fair Value in the Presence of a Noncontrolling Interest

When a parent company acquires a less-than-100 percent controlling interest in another firm, the acquisition method requires a determination of the acquisition-date fair value of the acquired firm for consolidated financial reporting. The total acquired firm fair value in the presence of a partial acquisition is the sum of the following two components at the acquisition date:

- The fair value of the controlling interest.
- The fair value of the noncontrolling interest.

The sum of these two components serves as the starting point for the parent in valuing and reporting the subsidiary acquisition. If the sum exceeds the collective fair values of the identifiable net assets acquired and liabilities assumed, then goodwill is recognized. Conversely, if the collective fair values of the identifiable net assets acquired and liabilities assumed exceed the total fair value, the acquirer recognizes a gain on bargain purchase.

Measurement of the controlling interest fair value remains straightforward in the vast majority of cases—the consideration transferred by the parent typically provides the best evidence of fair value of the acquirer's interest. However, there is no parallel consideration transferred available to value the noncontrolling interest. Therefore, the parent must employ other valuation techniques to estimate the fair value of the noncontrolling interest at the acquisition date.

Usually, a parent can rely on readily available market trading activity to provide a fair valuation for its subsidiary's noncontrolling interest. Market trading prices for the noncontrolling interest shares in the weeks before and after the acquisition provide an objective measure of their fair value. The fair value of these shares then becomes the initial basis for reporting the noncontrolling interest in consolidated financial statements.

[2] As noted in Chapter 2, exceptions to the fair-value measurement principle include deferred taxes, certain employee benefits, indemnification assets, reacquired rights, share-based awards, and assets held for sale.

? Discussion Question

The FASB received numerous comment letters during its deliberations prior to adopting the current financial accounting standards on business combinations. Many of these letters addressed the FASB's proposed (and ultimately accepted) use of the economic unit concept as a valuation basis for less-than-100-percent acquisitions. A sampling of these letters includes the following observations:

Bob Laux, Microsoft: Microsoft agrees with the Board that the principles underlying standards should strive to reflect the underlying economics of transactions and events. However, we do not believe the Board's conclusion that recognizing the entire economic value of the acquiree, regardless of the ownership interest in the acquiree at the acquisition date, reflects the underlying economics.

Patricia A. Little, Ford Motor Company: We agree that recognizing 100 percent of the fair value of the acquiree is appropriate. We believe that this is crucial in erasing anomalies which were created when only the incremental ownership acquired was fair valued and the minority interest was reflected at its carryover basis.

Sharilyn Gasaway, Alltel Corporation: One of the underlying principles . . . is that the acquirer should measure and recognize the fair value of the acquiree as a whole. If 100 percent of the ownership interests are acquired, measuring and recognizing 100 percent of the fair value is both appropriate and informative. However, if less than 100 percent of the ownership interests are acquired, recognizing the fair value of 100 percent of the business acquired is not representative of the value actually acquired. In the instance in which certain minority owners retain their ownership interest, recognizing the fair value of the minority interest does not provide sufficient benefit to financial statement users to justify the additional cost incurred to calculate that fair value.

PricewaterhouseCoopers: We agree that the noncontrolling interest should be recorded at its fair value when it is initially recorded in the consolidated financial statements. As such, when control is obtained in a single step, the acquirer would record 100 percent of the fair value of the assets acquired (including goodwill) and liabilities assumed.

Loretta Cangialosi, Pfizer: While we understand the motivation of the FASB to account for all elements of the acquisition transaction at fair value, we are deeply concerned about the practice issues that will result. The heavy reliance on expected value techniques, use of the hypothetical market participants, the lack of observable markets, and the obligation to affix values to "possible" and even "remote" scenarios, among other requirements, will all conspire to create a standard that will likely prove to be nonoperational, unauditable, representationally unfaithful, abuse-prone, costly, and of limited (and perhaps negative) shareholder value.

Do you think the FASB made the correct decision in requiring consolidated financial statements to recognize all of the subsidiary's assets and liabilities at fair value regardless of the percentage ownership acquired by the parent?

Acquirers frequently must pay a premium price per share to garner sufficient shares to ensure a controlling interest. A control premium, however, typically is needed only to acquire sufficient shares to obtain a controlling interest. The remaining (noncontrolling interest) shares no longer provide the added benefit of transferring control to the new owner, and, therefore, may sell at a price less than the shares that yielded control. For example, when Expedia, Inc. acquired its 63 percent controlling interest in Trivago, the fair value of the noncontrolling interest excluded any control premium. In discussing the Trivago acquisition, Expedia's 2015 annual report noted

The fair value of the 37% noncontrolling interest was estimated to be $344 million at the time of acquisition based on the fair value per share, excluding the control premium. The control premium was derived directly based on the additional consideration paid to certain shareholders in order to obtain control. The additional consideration was determined to be the best estimate to represent the control premium as it was a premium paid only to the controlling shareholders.

Control premiums are properly included in the fair value of the controlling interest, but as the Expedia-Trivago combination demonstrates, they sometimes do not affect the fair values of the remaining subsidiary shares. Therefore, separate independent valuations for the controlling and noncontrolling interests are often needed for measuring the total fair value of the subsidiary.

In the absence of fair value evidence based on market trades, firms must turn to less objective measures of noncontrolling interest fair value. For example, comparable investments may be available to estimate fair value. Alternatively, valuation models based on subsidiary discounted cash flows or residual income projections can be employed to estimate the acquisition-date fair value of the noncontrolling interest. Finally, if a control premium is unlikely, the consideration paid by the parent can be used to imply a fair value for the entire subsidiary. The noncontrolling interest fair value is then simply measured as its percentage of this implied subsidiary total fair value.

Noncontrolling Interest Fair Value as Evidenced by Market Trades

In the majority of cases, direct evidence based on market activity in the outstanding subsidiary shares (not owned by the parent) will provide the best measure of acquisition-date fair value for the noncontrolling interest. For example, assume that Parker Corporation wished to acquire 9,000 of the 10,000 outstanding equity shares of Strong Company and projected substantial synergies from the proposed acquisition. Parker estimated that a 100 percent acquisition was not needed to extract these synergies. Also, Parker projected that financing more than a 90 percent acquisition would be too costly.

Parker then offered all of Strong's shareholders a premium price for up to 90 percent of the outstanding shares.[3] To induce a sufficient number of shareholders to sell, Parker needed to offer $70 per share, even though the shares had been trading in the $59 to $61 range. During the weeks following the acquisition, the 10 percent noncontrolling interest in Strong Company continues to trade in the $59 to $61 range.

In this case, the $70 per share price paid by Parker does not appear representative of the fair value of all the shares of Strong Company. The fact that the noncontrolling interest shares continue to trade around $60 per share indicates a $60,000 fair value for the 1,000 shares not owned by Parker. Therefore, the valuation of the noncontrolling interest is best evidenced by the traded fair value of Strong's shares, not the price paid by Parker.

The $70 share price paid by Parker nonetheless represents a negotiated value for the 9,000 shares. In the absence of any evidence to the contrary, these shares owned by Parker have a fair value of $630,000 incorporating the additional value Parker expects to extract from synergies with Strong. Thus the fair value of Strong is measured as the sum of the respective fair values of the controlling and noncontrolling interests as follows:

Fair value of controlling interest ($70 × 9,000 shares)	$630,000
Fair value of noncontrolling interest ($60 × 1,000 shares)	60,000
Acquisition-date fair value of Strong Company	$690,000

At the acquisition date, Parker assessed the total fair value of Strong's identifiable net assets at $600,000. Therefore, we compute goodwill as the excess of the acquisition-date fair value of the firm as a whole over the sum of the fair values of the identifiable net assets as follows:

Acquisition-date fair value of Strong Company	$690,000
Fair value of Strong Company's identifiable net assets	600,000
Goodwill	$ 90,000

[3] A more detailed analysis of the effect of a control premium on consolidated financial reporting is presented later in this chapter.

LO 4-3

Allocate goodwill acquired in a business combination across the controlling and noncontrolling interests.

Allocating Acquired Goodwill to the Controlling and Noncontrolling Interests

To properly report ownership equity in consolidated financial statements, acquisition-date goodwill should be apportioned across the controlling and noncontrolling interests. The parent first allocates goodwill to its controlling interest for the excess of the fair value of the parent's equity interest over its share of the fair value of the identifiable net assets. Any remaining goodwill is then attributed to the noncontrolling interest. As a result, the allocated goodwill will not always be proportional to the percentages owned. Continuing the Parker and Strong example, all of the acquisition goodwill is allocated to the controlling interest as follows:

	Controlling Interest	Noncontrolling Interest	Total
Acquisition-date fair value of Strong Company...	$630,000	$60,000	$690,000
Relative fair value of Strong's identifiable net assets (90% and 10% of $600,000)	540,000	60,000	600,000
Goodwill.................................	$ 90,000	$ –0–	$ 90,000

In the unlikely event that the noncontrolling interest's proportionate share of the subsidiary's net asset fair values exceeds its total fair value, such an excess would serve to reduce the goodwill recognized by the parent. For example, if Strong's 10 percent noncontrolling interest had a fair value of $55,000, Strong's total fair value would equal $685,000, and goodwill (all allocated to the controlling interest) would decrease to $85,000. Alternatively, if Strong's 10 percent noncontrolling interest had a fair value of $70,000, Strong's total fair value would equal $700,000. In this case, goodwill would equal $100,000 with $90,000 allocated to the controlling interest and $10,000 allocated to the noncontrolling interest.

Finally, if the total fair value of the acquired firm is less than the collective sum of its identifiable net assets, a *bargain purchase* occurs. In such rare combinations, the parent recognizes the entire gain on bargain purchase in current income. In no case is any amount of the gain allocated to the noncontrolling interest.

Noncontrolling Interest Fair Value Implied by Parent's Consideration Transferred

In other cases, especially when a large percentage of the acquiree's voting stock is purchased, the consideration paid by the parent may be reflective of the acquiree's total fair value. For example, again assume Parker pays $70 per share for 9,000 shares of Strong Company representing a 90 percent equity interest. Also assume that the remaining 1,000 noncontrolling interest shares are not actively traded. If there was no compelling evidence that the $70 acquisition price was not representative of all of Strong's 10,000 shares, then it appears reasonable to estimate the fair value of the 10 percent noncontrolling interest using the price paid by Parker. The total fair value of Strong Company is then estimated at $700,000 and allocated as follows:

Fair value of controlling interest ($70 × 9,000 shares)	$630,000
Fair value of noncontrolling interest ($70 × 1,000 shares).........	70,000
Acquisition-date fair value of Strong Company.................	$700,000

Note that in this case, because the price per share paid by the parent equals the noncontrolling interest per share fair value, goodwill is recognized proportionately across the two ownership groups. Assuming again that the collective fair value of Strong's identifiable net assets equals $600,000, goodwill is recognized and allocated as follows:

	Controlling Interest	Noncontrolling Interest	Total
Acquisition-date fair value of Strong Company	$630,000	$70,000	$700,000
Relative fair value of Strong's identifiable net assets (90% and 10%)	540,000	60,000	600,000
Goodwill	$ 90,000	$10,000	$100,000

LO 4-4

Demonstrate the computation and allocation of consolidated net income in the presence of a noncontrolling interest.

Allocating Consolidated Net Income to the Parent and Noncontrolling Interest

Consolidated net income measures the results of operations for the combined entity. Reflecting the economic unit concept, consolidated net income includes 100 percent of the parent's net income and 100 percent of the subsidiary's net income, adjusted for excess acquisition-date fair value over book value amortizations. Once consolidated net income is determined, it is then allocated to the parent company and the noncontrolling interests. Because the noncontrolling interests' ownership pertains only to the subsidiary, their share of consolidated net income is limited to a share of the subsidiary's net income adjusted for acquisition-date excess fair-value amortizations.[4]

To illustrate, again assume that Parker acquires 90 percent of Strong Company. Further assume that current year consolidated net income equals $108,000 including $10,000 of annual acquisition-date excess fair-value amortization. If Strong reports revenues of $280,000 and expenses of $160,000 based on its internal book values, then the noncontrolling interest share of Strong's income can be computed as follows:

Noncontrolling Interest in Subsidiary Strong Company Net Income	
Strong revenues	$280,000
Strong expenses...	160,000
Strong net income	$120,000
Excess acquisition-date fair-value amortization.......................	10,000
Strong net income adjusted for excess amortization.................	$110,000
Noncontrolling interest percentage....................................	10%
Noncontrolling interest share of adjusted subsidiary net income	$ 11,000

The $11,000 noncontrolling interest share of adjusted subsidiary net income is equivalent to the noncontrolling interest share of consolidated net income. This figure is then simply subtracted from the combined entity's consolidated net income to derive the parent's interest in consolidated net income. Thus, the allocation is presented in Parker's consolidated financial statements as follows:

Consolidated Net Income Allocation	
Consolidated net income	$108,000
Less: Net income attributable to noncontrolling interest...............	11,000
Net income attributable to parent (controlling interest)	$ 97,000

Note that the noncontrolling shareholders' portion of consolidated net income is limited to their 10 percent share of the adjusted *subsidiary* income. These shareholders own a 10 percent interest in the subsidiary company, but no ownership in the parent firm.[5]

---

[4] Adjusting the subsidiary net income for the excess fair-value amortizations recognizes that the noncontrolling interest represents equity in the subsidiary's net assets as remeasured to fair values on the acquisition date.

[5] In this text we assume that the relative ownership percentages of the parent and noncontrolling interest represent an appropriate basis for allocating adjusted subsidiary net income across ownership groups.

LO 4-5

Identify and calculate the four noncontrolling interest figures that must be included within the consolidation process, and prepare a consolidation worksheet in the presence of a noncontrolling interest.

Partial Ownership Consolidations (Acquisition Method)

Having reviewed the basic concepts of accounting for a noncontrolling interest, we now concentrate on the mechanical aspects of the consolidation process when an outside ownership is present. More specifically, we examine consolidations for time periods subsequent to the date of acquisition to analyze the full range of accounting complexities created by a noncontrolling interest. As indicated previously, this discussion centers on the acquisition method as required under generally accepted accounting principles.

The acquisition method focuses on incorporating in the consolidated financial statements 100 percent of the subsidiary's assets and liabilities at their acquisition-date fair values. Note that subsequent to acquisition, changes in current fair values for assets and liabilities are not recognized.[6] Instead, the subsidiary assets acquired and liabilities assumed are reflected in future consolidated financial statements using their acquisition-date fair values net of subsequent excess fair value amortizations (or possibly reduced for impairment).

The presence of a noncontrolling interest does not dramatically alter the consolidation procedures presented in Chapter 3. The unamortized balance of the acquisition-date fair-value allocation must still be computed and included within the consolidated totals. Excess fair-value amortization expenses of these allocations are recognized each year as appropriate. Reciprocal balances are eliminated. Beyond these basic steps, the measurement and recognition of four noncontrolling interest balances add a new dimension to the process of consolidating financial information. The parent company must determine and then enter each of these figures when constructing a worksheet:

- Noncontrolling interest in the subsidiary as of the beginning of the current year.
- Net income attributable to the noncontrolling interest.
- Subsidiary dividends attributable to the noncontrolling interest.
- Noncontrolling interest as of the end of the year (found by combining the three balances above).

Illustration—Partial Acquisition with No Control Premium

To illustrate, assume that King Company acquires 80 percent of Pawn Company's 100,000 outstanding voting shares on January 1, 2017, for $9.75 per share or a total of $780,000 cash consideration. Further assume that the 20 percent noncontrolling interest shares traded both before and after the acquisition date at an average of $9.75 per share. The total fair value of Pawn to be used initially in consolidation is

Consideration transferred by King ($9.75 × 80,000 shares)	$780,000
Noncontrolling interest fair value ($9.75 × 20,000 shares)	195,000
Pawn's acquisition-date fair value	$975,000

Thus King did not pay a control premium to acquire its share of Pawn—both sets of shares have identical per share fair values.

Exhibit 4.2 presents the book value of Pawn's accounts as well as the fair value of each asset and liability on the acquisition date. Pawn's total fair value is attributed to Pawn's assets and liabilities as shown in Exhibit 4.3. Annual amortization relating to these allocations also is included in this schedule. Although expense figures are computed for only the initial years, some amount of amortization is recognized in each of the 20 years following the acquisition (the life assumed for the patented technology).

Exhibit 4.3 shows first that all identifiable assets acquired and liabilities assumed are adjusted to their full individual fair values at the acquisition date. The noncontrolling

[6] Exceptions common to all firms (whether subject to consolidation or not) include recognizing changing fair values for marketable equity securities and other financial instruments.

EXHIBIT 4.2
Subsidiary Accounts—Date of Acquisition

PAWN COMPANY
Account Balances
January 1, 2017

	Book Value	Fair Value	Difference
Current assets	$ 440,000	$440,000	$ –0–
Trademarks (indefinite life)	260,000	320,000	60,000
Patented technology (20-year remaining life) ..	480,000	600,000	120,000
Equipment (10-year remaining life)............	110,000	100,000	(10,000)
Long-term liabilities (8 years to maturity).......	(550,000)	(510,000)	40,000
Net assets...................................	$ 740,000	$950,000	$210,000
Common stock.............................	$(230,000)		
Retained earnings, 1/1/17..................	(510,000)		

Note: Parentheses indicate a credit balance.

EXHIBIT 4.3   Excess Fair-Value Allocations

KING COMPANY AND 80% OWNED SUBSIDIARY PAWN COMPANY
Fair-Value Allocation and Amortization
January 1, 2017

	Allocation	Remaining Life (years)	Annual Excess Amortizations
Pawn's acquisition-date fair value (100%).....................	$975,000		
Pawn's acquisition-date book value (100%)..................	(740,000)		
Fair value in excess of book value...........................	$235,000		
Adjustments (100%) to			
Trademarks.....................................	$ 60,000	indefinite	$ –0–
Patented technology...............................	120,000	20	6,000
Equipment......................................	(10,000)	10	(1,000)
Long-term liabilities (8 years to maturity)...................	40,000	8	5,000
Goodwill..	$ 25,000	indefinite	$ –0–
Annual amortizations of excess fair value over book value (initial years)			$ 10,000

Goodwill Allocation to the Controlling and Noncontrolling Interests

	Controlling Interest	Noncontrolling Interest	Total
Fair value at acquisition date................................	$780,000	$195,000	$975,000
Relative fair value of Pawn's identifiable net assets (80% and 20%)..	760,000	190,000	950,000
Goodwill..	$ 20,000	$ 5,000	$ 25,000

interest will share proportionately in these fair-value adjustments. Exhibit 4.3 also shows that any excess fair value not attributable to Pawn's identifiable net assets is assigned to goodwill. Because the controlling and noncontrolling interests' acquisition-date fair values are identical at $9.75 per share, the resulting goodwill is allocated proportionately across these ownership interests.

Consolidated financial statements will be produced for the year ending December 31, 2018. This date is arbitrary. Any time period subsequent to 2017 could serve to demonstrate the applicable consolidation procedures. Having already calculated the acquisition-date fair-value allocations and related amortization, the accountant can construct a consolidation of these two companies along the lines demonstrated in Chapter 3. Only the presence of the 20 percent noncontrolling interest alters this process.

To complete the information needed for this combination, assume that Pawn Company reports the following changes in retained earnings since King's acquisition:

Current year (2018)

Net income.	$90,000
Less: Dividends declared	(50,000)
Increase in retained earnings.	$40,000

Prior years (only 2017 in this illustration):

Increase in retained earnings.	$70,000

Assuming that King Company applies the equity method, the Investment in Pawn Company account as of December 31, 2018, can be constructed as shown in Exhibit 4.4. Note that the $852,000 balance is computed based on applying King's 80 percent ownership to Pawn's income (less amortization) and dividends. Although 100 percent of the subsidiary's assets, liabilities, revenues, and expenses will be combined in consolidation, the internal accounting for King's investment in Pawn is based on its 80 percent ownership. This technique facilitates worksheet adjustments that allocate various amounts to the noncontrolling interest. Exhibit 4.5 presents the separate financial statements for these two companies as of December 31, 2018, and the year then ended, based on the information provided.

Consolidated Totals

Although the inclusion of a 20 percent outside ownership complicates the consolidation process, the 2018 totals to be reported by this business combination can nonetheless be determined without the use of a worksheet:

- *Revenues* = $1,340,000. The revenues of the parent and the subsidiary are added together. The acquisition method includes the subsidiary's revenues in total although King owns only 80 percent of the stock.
- *Cost of Goods Sold* = $544,000. The parent and subsidiary balances are added together.
- *Depreciation Expense* = $79,000. The parent and subsidiary balances are added together along with the $1,000 reduction in equipment depreciation as indicated in Exhibit 4.3.
- *Amortization Expense* = $181,000. The parent and subsidiary balances are added together along with the $6,000 additional patented technology amortization expense as indicated in Exhibit 4.3.
- *Interest Expense* = $120,000. The parent and subsidiary balances are added along with an additional $5,000. Exhibit 4.3 shows Pawn's long-term debt reduced by $40,000 to fair value. Because the maturity value remains constant, the $40,000 represents a discount amortized to interest expense over the remaining eight-year life of the debt.

EXHIBIT 4.4
Equity Method Investment Balance

KING COMPANY
Investment in Pawn Company
Equity Method
December 31, 2018

Acquisition price for 80% interest.		$780,000
Prior year (2017):		
Increase in retained earnings (80% × $70,000).	$56,000	
Excess amortization expenses (80% × $10,000) (Exhibit 4.3) . .	(8,000)	48,000
Current year (2018):		
Income accrual (80% × $90,000) .	72,000	
Excess amortization expense (80% × $10,000) (Exhibit 4.3) . . .	(8,000)	
Equity in subsidiary earnings.	64,000*	
Dividends from Pawn (80% × $50,000) .	(40,000)	24,000
Balance, 12/31/18 .		$852,000

*This figure appears in King's 2018 income statement. See Exhibit 4.5.

EXHIBIT 4.5
Separate Financial Records

KING COMPANY AND PAWN COMPANY		
Separate Financial Statements		
For December 31, 2018, and the Year Then Ended		
	King	Pawn
Revenues	$ (910,000)	$ (430,000)
Cost of goods sold	344,000	200,000
Depreciation expense..........................	60,000	20,000
Amortization expense..........................	100,000	75,000
Interest expense	70,000	45,000
Equity in subsidiary earnings (see Exhibit 4.4)	(64,000)	–0–
Net income	$ (400,000)	$ (90,000)
Retained earnings, 1/1/18.......................	$ (860,000)	$ (580,000)
Net income (above)............................	(400,000)	(90,000)
Dividends declared	60,000	50,000
Retained earnings, 12/31/18	$(1,200,000)	$ (620,000)
Current assets	$ 726,000	$ 445,000
Trademarks...................................	304,000	295,000
Patented technology...........................	880,000	540,000
Equipment (net)	390,000	160,000
Investment in Pawn Company (see Exhibit 4.4)	852,000	–0–
Total assets................................	$ 3,152,000	$ 1,440,000
Long-term liabilities	$(1,082,000)	$ (590,000)
Common stock................................	(870,000)	(230,000)
Retained earnings, 12/31/18.....................	(1,200,000)	(620,000)
Total liabilities and equities	$(3,152,000)	$(1,440,000)

Note: Parentheses indicate a credit balance.

- *Equity in Subsidiary Earnings* = –0–. The parent's investment income is replaced with the subsidiary's separate revenues and expenses which are then included in the consolidated totals.
- *Consolidated Net Income* = $416,000. The consolidated entity's total earnings before allocation to the controlling and noncontrolling ownership interests.
- *Net Income Attributable to Noncontrolling Interest* = $16,000. The outside owners are assigned 20 percent of Pawn's reported net income of $90,000 less $10,000 total excess fair-value amortization. The acquisition method shows this amount as an allocation of consolidated net income.
- *Net Income Attributable to King Company (Controlling Interest)* = $400,000. The acquisition method shows this amount as an allocation of consolidated net income.
- *Retained Earnings, 1/1* = $860,000. The parent company figure equals the consolidated total because the equity method was applied. If the initial value method or the partial equity method had been used, the parent's balance would require adjustment to include any unrecorded figures.
- *Dividends Declared* = $60,000. Only the parent company balance is reported. Eighty percent of the subsidiary's dividends are distributable to the parent and are thus eliminated. The remaining distribution goes to the outside owners and serves to reduce the noncontrolling interest balance.
- *Retained Earnings, 12/31* = $1,200,000. The balance is found by adding the controlling interest's share of consolidated net income to the beginning consolidated retained earnings balance and then subtracting the parent's dividends. Because the equity method is utilized, the parent company figure reflects the total for the business combination.
- *Current Assets* = $1,171,000. The parent's and subsidiary's book values are added.

- *Trademarks* = $659,000. The parent's book value is added to the subsidiary's book value plus the $60,000 allocation of the acquisition-date fair value (see Exhibit 4.3).
- *Patented Technology* = $1,528,000. The parent's book value is added to the subsidiary's book value plus the $120,000 excess fair-value allocation less two years' excess amortizations of $6,000 per year (see Exhibit 4.3).
- *Equipment* = $542,000. The parent's book value is added to the subsidiary's book value less the $10,000 acquisition-date fair-value reduction plus two years' expense reductions of $1,000 per year (see Exhibit 4.3).
- *Investment in Pawn Company* = –0–. The balance reported by the parent is eliminated so that the subsidiary's assets and liabilities can be included in the consolidated totals.
- *Goodwill* = $25,000. The total goodwill allocation shown in Exhibit 4.3 is reported.
- *Total Assets* = $3,925,000. This balance is a summation of the consolidated assets.
- *Long-Term Liabilities* = $1,642,000. The parent's book value is added to the subsidiary's book value less the $40,000 acquisition-date fair-value allocation net of two years' amortizations of $5,000 per year (see Exhibit 4.3).
- *Noncontrolling Interest in Subsidiary* = $213,000. The outside ownership is 20 percent of the subsidiary's year-end book value adjusted for any unamortized excess fair value attributed to the noncontrolling interest:

Noncontrolling interest in Pawn at 1/1/18	
20% of $810,000 beginning book value—common stock plus 1/1/18 retained earnings	$162,000
20% of unamortized excess fair-value allocations as of 1/1	45,000
Noncontrolling interest in Pawn 1/1/18	$207,000
Net income attributable to noncontrolling interest (see page 165).	16,000
Dividends distributable to noncontrolling interest (20% of $50,000 total).	(10,000)
Noncontrolling interest in Pawn at 12/31/18.	$213,000

- *Common Stock* = $870,000. Only the parent's balance is reported.
- *Retained Earnings, 12/31* = $1,200,000. Computed on page 165.
- *Total Liabilities and Equities* = $3,925,000. This total is a summation of consolidated liabilities, noncontrolling interest, and equities.

Alternative Calculation of Noncontrolling Interest at December 31, 2018

The acquisition method requires that the noncontrolling interest in the subsidiary's net assets be measured at fair value at the date of acquisition. Subsequent to acquisition, however, the noncontrolling interest value is adjusted for its share of subsidiary net income, excess fair-value amortizations, and dividends. The following schedule demonstrates how the noncontrolling interest's acquisition-date fair value is adjusted to show the ending consolidated balance sheet amount.

Fair value of 20% noncontrolling interest in Pawn at acquisition date . . .		$195,000
20% of $70,000 change in Pawn's 2017 retained earnings	14,000	
20% of excess fair-value amortizations.	(2,000)	12,000
2018 net income allocation [20% × ($90,000 − $10,000)]		16,000
2018 dividends (20% × $50,000)		(10,000)
Noncontrolling interest in Pawn at December 31, 2018.		$213,000

As can be seen in the above schedule, the fair-value principle applies only to the initial noncontrolling interest valuation.

Worksheet Process—Acquisition Method

The consolidated totals for King and Pawn also can be determined by means of a worksheet as shown in Exhibit 4.6. Comparing this example with Exhibit 3.7 in Chapter 3 indicates that the presence of a noncontrolling interest does not create a significant number of changes in the consolidation procedures.

EXHIBIT 4.6   Noncontrolling Interest (No Control Premium) Illustrated

			KING COMPANY AND PAWN COMPANY Consolidation Worksheet For Year Ending December 31, 2018			
Investment: Equity Method					**Ownership: 80%**	
Accounts	**King Company***	**Pawn Company***	**Consolidation Entries**		**Noncontrolling Interest**	**Consolidated Totals**
			Debit	**Credit**		
Revenues	(910,000)	(430,000)				(1,340,000)
Cost of goods sold	344,000	200,000				544,000
Depreciation expense	60,000	20,000		(E) 1,000		79,000
Amortization expense	100,000	75,000	(E) 6,000			181,000
Interest expense	70,000	45,000	(E) 5,000			120,000
Equity in Pawn's earnings (see Exhibit 4.4)	(64,000)	–0–	(I) 64,000			–0–
Separate company net income	(400,000)	(90,000)				
Consolidated net income						(416,000)
Net income attributable to noncontrolling interest					(16,000)	16,000
Net income attributable to King Company						(400,000)
Retained earnings, 1/1	(860,000)	(580,000)	(S) 580,000			(860,000)
Net income (above)	(400,000)	(90,000)				(400,000)
Dividends declared	60,000	50,000		(D) 40,000	10,000	60,000
Retained earnings, 12/31	(1,200,000)	(620,000)				(1,200,000)
Current assets	726,000	445,000				1,171,000
Trademarks	304,000	295,000	(A) 60,000			659,000
Patented technology	880,000	540,000	(A) 114,000	(E) 6,000		1,528,000
Equipment (net)	390,000	160,000	(E) 1,000	(A) 9,000		542,000
Investment in Pawn Company (see Exhibit 4.4)	852,000	–0–	(D) 40,000	(S) 648,000 (A) 180,000 (I) 64,000		–0–
Goodwill	–0–	–0–	(A) 25,000			25,000
Total assets	3,152,000	1,440,000				3,925,000
Long-term liabilities	(1,082,000)	(590,000)	(A) 35,000	(E) 5,000		(1,642,000)
Common stock	(870,000)	(230,000)	(S) 230,000			(870,000)
Noncontrolling interest in Pawn, 1/1				(S) 162,000 (A) 45,000	(207,000)	
Noncontrolling interest in Pawn, 12/31					(213,000)	(213,000)
Retained earnings, 12/31	(1,200,000)	(620,000)				(1,200,000)
Total liabilities and equities	(3,152,000)	(1,440,000)	1,160,000	1,160,000		(3,925,000)

*See Exhibit 4.5.
Note: Parentheses indicate a credit balance.
Consolidation entries:
(S) Elimination of subsidiary's stockholders' equity along with recognition of January 1 noncontrolling interest.
(A) Allocation of subsidiary total fair value in excess of book value, unamortized balances as of January 1.
(I)   Elimination of intra-entity income (equity accrual less amortization expenses).
(D) Elimination of intra-entity dividends.
(E) Recognition of amortization expenses of fair-value allocations.

The worksheet still includes elimination of the subsidiary's stockholders' equity accounts (Entry **S**) although, as explained next, this entry is expanded to record the beginning noncontrolling interest for the year. The second worksheet entry (Entry **A**) recognizes the excess acquisition-date fair-value allocations at January 1 after one year of amortization with an additional adjustment to the beginning noncontrolling interest. Intra-entity income and dividends are removed also (Entries **I** and **D**) while current-year excess amortization expenses are recognized (Entry **E**). The differences from the Chapter 3 illustrations relate exclusively to the recognition of the three components of the noncontrolling interest. In addition, *a separate Noncontrolling Interest column is added to the worksheet to accumulate these components to form the year-end figure to be reported on the consolidated balance sheet.*

Noncontrolling Interest—Beginning of Year

Under the acquisition method, the noncontrolling interest shares proportionately in the fair values of the subsidiary's identifiable net assets as adjusted for excess fair-value amortizations. On the consolidated worksheet, this total net fair value is represented by two components:

1. Pawn's stockholders' equity accounts (common stock and beginning retained earnings) indicate a January 1, 2018, book value of $810,000.
2. January 1, 2018, acquisition-date fair-value net of previous year's amortizations (in this case 2017 only).

Therefore, the January 1, 2018, balance of the 20 percent outside ownership is computed as follows:

20% × $810,000 subsidiary book value at 1/1/18.	$162,000
20% × $225,000* unamortized excess fair-value allocation at 1/1/18	45,000
Noncontrolling interest in Pawn at 1/1/18	$207,000
*Acquisition-date excess fair over book value (Exhibit 4.3).	$235,000
Less: 2017 excess fair over book value amortization	(10,000)
Unamortized excess fair over book value amount at 1/1/18	$225,000

The $207,000 noncontrolling interest balance at 1/1/18 is recognized on the worksheet through Entry **S** ($162,000) and Entry **A** ($45,000):

Consolidation Entry S

Common Stock (Pawn)	230,000	
Retained Earnings, 1/1/18 (Pawn)	580,000	
Investment in Pawn Company (80%)		648,000
Noncontrolling Interest in Pawn Company, 1/1/18 (20%)		162,000

To eliminate beginning stockholders' equity accounts of subsidiary along with book value portion of investment (equal to 80 percent ownership). Noncontrolling interest of 20 percent is also recognized.

Consolidation Entry A

Trademarks	60,000	
Patented Technology	114,000	
Liabilities	35,000	
Goodwill	25,000	
Equipment		9,000
Investment in Pawn Company (80%)		180,000
Noncontrolling Interest in Pawn Company, 1/1/18 (20%)		45,000

To recognize unamortized excess fair value as of January 1, 2018, to Pawn's assets acquired and liabilities assumed in the combination. Also to allocate the unamortized fair value to the noncontrolling interest. Goodwill is attributable proportionately to controlling and noncontrolling interests.

The total $207,000 balance assigned here to the outside owners at the beginning of the year is extended to the Noncontrolling Interest worksheet column (see Exhibit 4.6).

To complete the required worksheet adjustments, Entries **I, D,** and **E** are prepared as follows:

Consolidation Entry I

Equity in Pawn's Earnings	64,000	
Investment in Pawn Company		64,000
To eliminate intra-entity income accrual comprising subsidiary income less excess acquisition-date fair-value amortizations.		

Consolidation Entry D

Investment in Pawn Company	40,000	
Dividends Declared		40,000
To eliminate intra-entity dividends.		

Consolidation Entry E

Amortization Expense	6,000	
Interest Expense	5,000	
Equipment (net)	1,000	
Depreciation Expense		1,000
Patented Technology.		6,000
Long-Term Liabilities		5,000
To recognize current year excess fair-value amortizations.		

Noncontrolling Interest—Share of Current Year Consolidated Net Income

Exhibit 4.6 shows the noncontrolling interest's share of current year earnings is $16,000. The amount is based on the subsidiary's $90,000 net income (Pawn Company column) less excess acquisition-date fair-value amortizations. Thus, King assigns $16,000 to the outside owners computed as follows:

Net Income Attributable to Noncontrolling Interest	
Pawn Company net income	$90,000
Excess acquisition-date fair-value amortization.	10,000
Net income adjusted for excess amortizations	$80,000
Noncontrolling interest percentage	20%
Net income attributable to noncontrolling interest in Pawn	$16,000

In effect, 100 percent of each subsidiary revenue and expense account (including excess acquisition-date fair-value amortizations) is consolidated with an accompanying 20 percent allocation to the noncontrolling interest. The 80 percent net effect corresponds to King's ownership.

Because $16,000 of consolidated net income accrues to the noncontrolling interest, this amount is added to the $207,000 beginning balance assigned (in Entries **S** and **A**) to these outside owners. The noncontrolling interest increases because the subsidiary generated a profit during the period.

Although we could record this allocation through an additional worksheet entry, the $16,000 is usually shown, as in Exhibit 4.6, by means of a columnar adjustment. The current year accrual is simultaneously entered in the Income Statement section of the consolidated column as an allocation of consolidated net income and in the Noncontrolling Interest column as an increase. This procedure assigns a portion of the combined earnings to the outside owners rather than to the parent company owners.

Noncontrolling Interest—Dividends

The $40,000 dividend to the parent company is eliminated routinely through Entry **D,** but the remainder of Pawn's dividend went to the noncontrolling interest. The impact of the dividend (20 percent of the subsidiary's total) distributable to the other owners must be acknowledged. As shown in Exhibit 4.6, this remaining $10,000 is extended directly into the Noncontrolling Interest column on the worksheet as a reduction. It represents the decrease in the underlying claim of the outside ownership that resulted from the subsidiary's dividend declaration.

Noncontrolling Interest—End of Year

The ending assignment for these other owners is calculated by a summation of

Noncontrolling interest in Pawn beginning of year—credit balance	$207,000
Net income attributable to noncontrolling interest	16,000
Less: Dividends to the outside owners	(10,000)
Noncontrolling interest in Pawn end of year—credit balance	$213,000

The Noncontrolling Interest column on the worksheet in Exhibit 4.6 accumulates these figures. The $213,000 total is then transferred to the balance sheet, where it appears in the consolidated financial statements.

LO 4-6

Identify appropriate placements for the components of the noncontrolling interest in consolidated financial statements.

Consolidated Financial Statements

Having successfully consolidated the information for King and Pawn, the resulting financial statements for these two companies are produced in Exhibit 4.7. These figures are taken from the consolidation worksheet.

Exhibit 4.7 shows first the consolidated income statement. Consolidated net income is computed at the combined entity level as $416,000 and then allocated to the noncontrolling and controlling interests. The statement of changes in owners' equity provides details of the ownership changes for the year for both the controlling and noncontrolling interest shareholders. Finally, note the placement of the noncontrolling interest in the subsidiary's equity squarely in the consolidated owners' equity section.[7]

LO 4-7

Determine the effect on consolidated financial statements of a control premium paid by the parent.

Illustration—Partial Acquisition with Control Premium

To illustrate the valuation implications for an acquisition involving a control premium, again assume that King Company acquires 80 percent of Pawn Company's 100,000 outstanding voting shares on January 1, 2017. We also again assume that Pawn's shares traded before the acquisition date at an average of $9.75 per share. In this scenario, however, we assume that to acquire sufficient shares to gain control King pays $11 per share or a total of $880,000 cash consideration for its 80 percent interest. King thus pays a control premium of $1.25 ($11 − $9.75) per share to acquire Pawn. King anticipates that synergies with Pawn will create additional value for King's shareholders. Finally, following the acquisition, the remaining 20 percent noncontrolling interest shares continue to trade at $9.75.

The total fair value of Pawn to be used initially in consolidation is thus recomputed as follows:

Consideration transferred by King ($11.00 × 80,000 shares)	$ 880,000
Noncontrolling interest fair value ($9.75 × 20,000 shares)	195,000
Pawn's total fair value at January 1, 2017	$1,075,000

[7] If appropriate, each component of other comprehensive income is allocated to the controlling and noncontrolling interests. The statement of changes in owners' equity would also provide an allocation of accumulated other comprehensive income elements across the controlling and noncontrolling interests.

EXHIBIT 4.7
Consolidated Statements with Noncontrolling Interest—Acquisition Method

KING COMPANY AND PAWN COMPANY
Consolidated Financial Statements
Income Statement
Year Ended December 31, 2018

Revenues	$1,340,000
Cost of goods sold	(544,000)
Depreciation expense	(79,000)
Amortization expense	(181,000)
Interest expense	(120,000)
Consolidated net income	$ 416,000
To noncontrolling interest	16,000
To King Company (controlling interest)	$ 400,000

Statement of Changes in Owners' Equity
Year Ended December 31, 2018

	King Company Owners		Noncontrolling Interest
	Retained Earnings	Common Stock	
Balance, January 1	$ 860,000	$870,000	$207,000
Net income	400,000		16,000
Less: Dividends	(60,000)		(10,000)
Balance, December 31	$1,200,000	$870,000	$213,000

Balance Sheet
At December 31, 2018

Assets

Current assets	$1,171,000
Trademarks	659,000
Patented technology	1,528,000
Equipment (net)	542,000
Goodwill	25,000
Total assets	$3,925,000

Liabilities

Long-term liabilities	$1,642,000

Owners' Equity

Common stock—King Company	870,000
Noncontrolling interest in Pawn	213,000
Retained earnings	1,200,000
Total liabilities and owners' equity	$3,925,000

In keeping with the acquisition method's requirement that identifiable assets acquired and liabilities assumed be adjusted to fair value, King allocates Pawn's total fair value as follows:

Fair value of Pawn at January 1, 2017		$1,075,000
Book value of Pawn at January 1, 2017		(740,000)
Fair value in excess of book value		$ 335,000
Adjustments to		
Trademarks	$ 60,000	
Patented technology	120,000	
Equipment	(10,000)	
Long-term liabilities	40,000	210,000
Goodwill		$ 125,000

Note that the *identifiable* assets acquired and liabilities assumed are again adjusted to their full individual fair values at the acquisition date. Only the amount designated as goodwill is changed to $125,000 from $25,000 in the original fair-value allocation example as shown in Exhibit 4.3. In this case, King allocates $120,000 of the $125,000 total goodwill amount to its own interest as follows:

	Controlling Interest	Noncontrolling Interest	Total
Fair value at acquisition date	$880,000	$195,000	$1,075,000
Relative fair value of Pawn's identifiable net assets (80% and 20%)	760,000	190,000	950,000
Goodwill	$120,000	$ 5,000	$ 125,000

The initial acquisition-date fair value of $195,000 for the noncontrolling interest includes only a $5,000 goodwill allocation from the combination. Because the parent paid an extra $1.25 per share more than the fair value of the noncontrolling interest shares, more goodwill is allocated to the parent.

Next we separate the familiar consolidated worksheet entry **A** into two components labeled **A1** and **A2.** The **A1** worksheet entry allocates the excess acquisition-date fair value to the *identifiable* assets acquired and liabilities assumed (trademarks, patented technology, equipment, and liabilities). Note that the relative ownership percentages of the parent and noncontrolling interest (80 percent and 20 percent) provide the basis for allocating the net $200,000 adjustment to the parent's Investment account ($160,000) and the 1/1/18 balance of the noncontrolling interest ($40,000).

Next, consolidated worksheet entry **A2** provides the recognition and allocation of the goodwill balance taking into account the differing per share prices of the parent's consideration transferred and the noncontrolling interest fair value. Note that the presence of a control premium affects primarily the parents' shares, and thus goodwill is disproportionately (relative to the ownership percentages) allocated to the controlling and noncontrolling interests. Exhibit 4.8 shows the consolidated worksheet for this extension to the King and Pawn example.

Consolidation Entry A1 (see page 171 for excess fair value allocations)

Trademarks	60,000	
Patented Technology	114,000	
Liabilities	35,000	
Equipment		9,000
Investment in Pawn Company (80%)		160,000
Noncontrolling Interest in Pawn 1/1/18 (20%)		40,000

Consolidation Entry A2

Goodwill	125,000	
Investment in Pawn Company		120,000
Noncontrolling Interest in Pawn 1/1/18		5,000

EXHIBIT 4.8   Noncontrolling Interest (Control Premium) Illustrated

KING COMPANY AND PAWN COMPANY
Consolidation Worksheet

Investment: Equity Method		For Year Ending December 31, 2018				*Ownership: 80%*
			Consolidation Entries		**Noncontrolling**	**Consolidated**
Accounts	**King Company**	**Pawn Company**	**Debit**	**Credit**	**Interest**	**Totals**
Revenues	(910,000)	(430,000)				(1,340,000)
Cost of goods sold	344,000	200,000				544,000
Depreciation expense	60,000	20,000		(E) 1,000		79,000
Amortization expense	100,000	75,000	(E) 6,000			181,000
Interest expense	70,000	45,000	(E) 5,000			120,000
Equity in Pawn's earnings	(64,000)	–0–	(I) 64,000			–0–
Separate company net income	(400,000)	(90,000)				
Consolidated net income						(416,000)
Net income attributable to noncontrolling interest					(16,000)	16,000
Net income attributable to King Company						(400,000)
Retained earnings, 1/1	(860,000)	(580,000)	(S) 580,000			(860,000)
Net income (above)	(400,000)	(90,000)				(400,000)
Dividends declared	60,000	50,000		(D) 40,000	10,000	60,000
Retained earnings, 12/31	(1,200,000)	(620,000)				(1,200,000)
Current assets	626,000	445,000				1,071,000
Trademarks	304,000	295,000	(A1) 60,000			659,000
Patented technology	880,000	540,000	(A1) 114,000	(E) 6,000		1,528,000
Equipment (net)	390,000	160,000	(E) 1,000	(A1) 9,000		542,000
Investment in Pawn Company	952,000	–0–	(D) 40,000	(S) 648,000		–0–
				(A1) 160,000		
				(A2) 120,000		
				(I) 64,000		
Goodwill	–0–	–0–	(A2) 125,000			125,000
Total assets	3,152,000	1,440,000				3,925,000
Long-term liabilities	(1,082,000)	(590,000)	(A1) 35,000	(E) 5,000		(1,642,000)
Common stock	(870,000)	(230,000)	(S) 230,000			(870,000)
Noncontrolling interest in Pawn 1/1				(S) 162,000		
				(A1) 40,000		
				(A2) 5,000	(207,000)	
Noncontrolling interest in Pawn 12/31					(213,000)	(213,000)
Retained earnings, 12/31	(1,200,000)	(620,000)				(1,200,000)
Total liabilities and equities	(3,152,000)	(1,440,000)	1,260,000	1,260,000		(3,925,000)

Note: Parentheses indicate a credit balance.
Consolidation entries:
(S) Elimination of subsidiary's stockholders' equity along with recognition of January 1 noncontrolling interest.
(A1) Allocation of subsidiary identifiable net asset fair value in excess of book value, unamortized balances as of January 1.
(A2) Allocation of goodwill to parent and noncontrolling interest.
(I) Elimination of intra-entity income (equity accrual less amortization expenses).
(D) Elimination of intra-entity dividends.
(E) Recognition of amortization expenses of fair-value allocations.

The worksheet calculates the December 31, 2018, noncontrolling balance as follows:

Pawn January 1, 2018: 20% book value	$162,000
January 1, 2018: 20% excess fair-value allocation for Pawn's identifiable net assets ($200,000 × 20%) + $5,000 goodwill allocation	45,000
Noncontrolling interest at January 1, 2018	$207,000
2018 consolidated net income allocation	16,000
Noncontrolling interest share of Pawn dividends	(10,000)
Noncontrolling interest in Pawn, December 31, 2018.	$213,000

Note that the $45,000 January 1 excess fair-value allocation to the noncontrolling interest includes the noncontrolling interest's full share of the *identifiable* assets acquired and liabilities assumed in the combination but only $5,000 for goodwill. Because King Company paid a $100,000 control premium (80,000 shares × $1.25), the additional $100,000 is allocated entirely to the controlling interest.

By comparing Exhibits 4.6 and 4.8 we can assess the effect of the separate acquisition-date valuations for the controlling and noncontrolling interests. As seen in the differences across Exhibits 4.6 and 4.8 calculated next, the presence of King's control premium affects the goodwill component in the consolidated financial statements and little else.

	Exhibit 4.6	Exhibit 4.8	Difference
On King's Separate Financial Statements			
Current assets	$ 726,000	$ 626,000	−$100,000
Investment in Pawn	852,000	952,000	+ 100,000
On the Consolidated Balances			
Current assets	1,171,000	1,071,000	− 100,000
Goodwill	25,000	125,000	+ 100,000

Because King paid an additional $100,000 for its 80 percent interest in Pawn, the initial value assigned to the Investment account increases and current assets (i.e., additional cash paid for the acquisition) decreases by $100,000. The extra $100,000 then simply increases goodwill on the consolidated balance sheet. Note that the noncontrolling interest amount remains unchanged at $213,000 across Exhibits 4.6 and 4.8, consistent with the fact that its acquisition-date fair value was left unchanged at $195,000.

Effects Created by Alternative Investment Methods

In the King and Pawn illustrations, the parent uses the equity method and bases all worksheet entries on that approach. As discussed in Chapter 3, had King incorporated the initial value method or the partial equity method, a few specific changes in the consolidation process would be required although the reported figures would be identical.

Initial Value Method

The initial value method ignores two accrual-based adjustments. First, the parent recognizes dividend income rather than an equity income accrual. Thus, the parent does not accrue the percentage of the subsidiary's net income earned in past years in excess of dividends (the increase in subsidiary retained earnings). Second, the parent does not record amortization expense under the initial value method and therefore must include it in the consolidation process if proper totals are to be achieved. Because neither of these figures is recognized in applying the initial value method, an Entry *C is added to the worksheet to convert the previously recorded balances to the equity method. The parent's beginning Retained Earnings is affected by this adjustment as well as the Investment in Subsidiary account. The exact amount is computed as follows.

Conversion to Equity Method from Initial Value Method (Entry *C)
Combine:

1. The increase (since acquisition) in the subsidiary's retained earnings during past years (net income less dividends) times the parent's ownership percentage, and
2. The parent's percentage of total amortization expense for these same past years.

The parent's use of the initial value method requires an additional procedural change. Under this method, the parent recognizes income when its subsidiary declares a dividend. Entry (**I**) removes both intra-entity dividend income and subsidiary dividends to the parent. Thus, when the initial value method is used, Entry **D** is unnecessary.

Partial Equity Method

Again, an Entry ***C** is needed to convert the parent's retained earnings as of January 1 to the equity method. In this case, however, only the amortization expense for the prior years must be included. Recall that under the partial equity method, although the parent accrues its share of reported subsidiary income, it does not recognize any acquisition-date excess fair value amortization expenses.

LO 4-8

Understand the impact on consolidated financial statements of a midyear acquisition.

Revenue and Expense Reporting for Midyear Acquisitions

In virtually all of our previous examples, the parent gains control of the subsidiary on the first day of the fiscal year. How is the consolidation process affected if an acquisition occurs on a midyear (any other than the first day of the fiscal year) date?

When a company gains control at a midyear date, a few obvious changes are needed. The new parent must compute the subsidiary's book value as of that date to determine excess total fair value over book value allocations (e.g., intangibles). Excess amortization expenses as well as any equity accrual and dividend distributions are recognized for a period of less than a year. Finally, because only net income earned by the subsidiary after the acquisition date accrues to the new owners, it is appropriate to include only postacquisition revenues and expenses in consolidated totals.

Consolidating Postacquisition Subsidiary Revenue and Expenses

Following a midyear acquisition, a parent company excludes current-year subsidiary revenue and expense amounts that have accrued prior to the acquisition date from its consolidated totals. For example, when Comcast acquired AT&T Broadband, its December 31 year-end income statement included AT&T Broadband revenues and expenses only subsequent to the acquisition date. Comcast reported $8.1 billion in revenues that year. However, in a pro forma schedule, Comcast noted that had it included AT&T Broadband's revenues from January 1, total revenue for the year would have been $16.8 billion. However, because the $8.7 billion additional revenue ($16.8 billion − $8.1 billion) was not earned by Comcast owners, Comcast excluded this preacquisition revenue from its consolidated total.

To further illustrate the complexities of accounting for a midyear acquisition, assume that Tyler Company acquires 90 percent of Steven Company on July 1, 2018, for $900,000 and prepares the following fair-value allocation schedule:

Steven Company fair value, 7/1/18...................		$1,000,000
Steven Company book value, 7/1/18.................		
Common stock	$600,000	
Retained earnings, 7/1/18	200,000	800,000
Excess fair value over book value......................		$ 200,000
Adjust trademark to fair value (4-year remaining life)........		200,000
Goodwill...		$ –0–

The affiliates report the following 2018 income statement amounts from their own separate operations:

	Tyler	Steven
Revenues	$450,000	$300,000
Expenses	325,000	150,000
Dividends (declared quarterly)	100,000	20,000

Assuming that all revenues and expenses occurred evenly throughout the year, the December 31, 2018, consolidated income statement appears as follows:

TYLER COMPANY **Consolidated Income Statement** **For the Year Ended December 31, 2018**	
Revenues	$600,000
Expenses	425,000
Consolidated net income	$175,000
To noncontrolling interest	5,000
To Tyler Company (controlling interest)	$170,000

The consolidated income statement components are computed below:

- *Revenues* = $600,000. Combined balances of $750,000 less $150,000 ($\frac{1}{2}$ of Steven's revenues).
- *Expenses* = $425,000. Combined balances of $475,000 less $75,000 ($\frac{1}{2}$ of Steven's expenses) plus $25,000 excess amortization ($200,000 ÷ 4 years × $\frac{1}{2}$ year).
- *Net Income Attributable to Noncontrolling Interest* = $5,000. 10% × ($150,000 Steven's income − $50,000 excess amortization) × $\frac{1}{2}$ year.

In this example, preacquisition subsidiary revenue and expense accounts are eliminated from the consolidated totals. Note also that by excluding 100 percent of the preacquisition income accounts from consolidation, the noncontrolling interest is viewed as coming into being as of the parent's acquisition date.[8]

A midyear acquisition requires additional adjustments when preparing consolidating worksheets. The balances the subsidiary submits for consolidation typically include results for its entire fiscal period. Thus, in the December 31 financial statements, the book value of the firm acquired on a midyear date is reflected by a January 1 retained earnings balance plus revenues, expenses, and dividends from the beginning of the year to the acquisition date. To effectively eliminate subsidiary book value as of the acquisition date, Consolidation Entry **S** includes these items in addition to the other usual elements of book value (i.e., stock accounts). To illustrate, assuming that both affiliates submit fiscal year financial statements for consolidation, Tyler would make the following 2018 consolidation worksheet entry:

Consolidation Worksheet Entry S

Common Stock—Steven	600,000	
Retained Earnings—Steven (1/1/18)*	135,000	
Revenues	150,000	
Dividends Declared—Steven		10,000
Expenses		75,000
Noncontrolling Interest (7/1/18)		80,000
Investment in Steven		720,000

*To arrive at Steven's January 1 retained earning balance, we use the July 1 balance of $200,000 less income from the first six months of $75,000 (1/2 of $150,000 annual Steven income) plus $10,000 dividends declared.

Through Entry **S,** preacquisition subsidiary revenues, expenses, and dividends are effectively

- Included as part of the subsidiary book value elimination in the year of acquisition.
- Included as components of the beginning value of the noncontrolling interest.
- Excluded from the consolidated income statement and statement of retained earnings.

[8] Current practice provides comparability across fiscal years through pro forma disclosures of various categories of revenue and expense as if the combination had occurred at the beginning of the reporting period. With the advent of modern information systems, separate cutoffs for revenues and expenses are readily available.

Acquisition Following an Equity Method Investment

In many cases, a parent company owns a noncontrolling equity interest in a firm prior to obtaining control. In such cases, as the preceding example demonstrates, the parent consolidates the postacquisition revenues and expenses of its new subsidiary. Because the parent owned an equity investment in the subsidiary prior to the control date, however, the parent reports on its income statement the "equity in earnings of the investee" that accrued up to the date control was obtained. In this case, in the year of acquisition, the consolidated income statement reports both combined revenues and expenses (postacquisition) of the subsidiary and equity method income (preacquisition).

In subsequent years, the need to separate pre- and postacquisition amounts is limited to ensuring that excess amortizations correctly reflect the midyear acquisition date. Finally, if the parent employs the initial value method of accounting for the investment in subsidiary on its books, the conversion to the equity method must also reflect only postacquisition amounts.

LO 4-9

Understand the impact on consolidated financial statements when a step acquisition has taken place.

Step Acquisitions

When Ticketmaster Entertainment Corporation increased its percentage ownership in Front Line Company from 39.4 percent to 82.3 percent, it began consolidating its investment in Front Line. Prior to the acquisition of control through majority ownership, the investment in Front Line was accounted for using the equity method of accounting.

In all previous consolidation illustrations, control over a subsidiary was assumed to have been achieved through a single transaction. Obviously, Ticketmaster's takeover of Front Line shows that a combination also can be the result of a series of stock purchases. These step acquisitions further complicate the consolidation process. The financial information of the separate companies must still be brought together, but varying amounts of consideration have been transferred to former owners at several different dates. How do the initial acquisitions affect this process?

Control Achieved in Steps—Acquisition Method

A **step acquisition** occurs when control is achieved in a series of equity acquisitions, as opposed to a single transaction. As with all business combinations, the acquisition method measures the acquired firm (including the noncontrolling interest) at fair value at the date control is obtained. The acquisition of a controlling interest is considered an important economic, and therefore measurement, event. Consequently, the parent utilizes a single uniform valuation basis for all subsidiary assets acquired and liabilities assumed—fair value at the date control is obtained.

If the parent previously held a noncontrolling interest in the acquired firm, the parent remeasures that interest to fair value and recognizes a gain or loss. For example, when eBay increased its equity ownership from 10 percent to 93 percent, it obtained control over GittiGidiyor, a Turkish online marketplace. To measure the subsidiary's acquisition-date fair value, eBay revalued its previously held 10 percent equity interest to fair value and recognized a $17 million gain. As a result, eBay increased its investment account for both the cash paid for the newly acquired shares and the increase in the fair value of its previously owned shares in GittiGidiyor.

If after obtaining control, the parent increases its ownership interest in the subsidiary, no further remeasurement takes place. The parent simply accounts for the additional subsidiary shares acquired as an equity transaction—consistent with any transactions with other owners, as opposed to outsiders. Next we present an example of consolidated reporting when the parent obtains a controlling interest in a series of steps. Then, we present an example of a parent's post-control acquisition of its subsidiary's shares.

Example: Step Acquisition Resulting in Control—Acquisition Method

To illustrate, assume that Arch Company obtains control of Zion Company through two cash acquisitions. The details of each acquisition are provided in Exhibit 4.9. Assuming that Arch has gained the ability to significantly influence Zion's decision-making process, the first investment, for external reporting purposes, is accounted for by means of the equity method as discussed in Chapter 1. Thus, Arch must determine any allocations and amortization associated with its purchase price (see Exhibit 4.10). A customer base with a 22-year estimated remaining life represented the initial excess payment.

Application of the equity method requires the accrual of investee income by the parent while any dividends from the investee are recorded as a decrease in the Investment account. Arch must also reduce both the income and asset balances in recognition of the annual $2,000 amortization indicated in Exhibit 4.10. Following the information provided in Exhibits 4.9 and 4.10, over the next two years, Arch Company's Investment in Zion account grows to $190,000:

Price paid for 30% investment in Zion—1/1/16	$164,000
Accrual of 2016 equity income ($60,000 × 30%)	18,000
Share of dividends 2016 ($20,000 × 30%)	(6,000)
Amortization for 2016	(2,000)
Accrual of 2017 equity income ($80,000 × 30%)	24,000
Share of dividends 2017 ($20,000 × 30%)	(6,000)
Amortization for 2017	(2,000)
Investment in Zion—1/1/18	$190,000

On January 1, 2018, Arch's ownership is increased to 80 percent by the purchase of another 50 percent of Zion Company's outstanding common stock for $350,000. Although the equity method can still be utilized for internal reporting, this second acquisition necessitates the preparation of consolidated financial statements beginning in 2018. Arch now controls Zion; the two companies are viewed as a single economic entity for external reporting purposes.

Once Arch gains control over Zion on January 1, 2018, the acquisition method focuses exclusively on control-date fair values and considers any previous amounts recorded by the acquirer as irrelevant for future valuations. Thus, in a step acquisition all previous values for the investment, prior to the date control is obtained, are remeasured to fair value on the date control is obtained.

We add the assumption that the $350,000 consideration transferred by Arch in its second acquisition of Zion represents the best available evidence for measuring the fair value of Zion Company at January 1, 2018. Therefore, an estimated fair value of $700,000 ($350,000 ÷ 50%) is assigned to Zion Company as of January 1, 2018, and provides the valuation basis for the assets acquired, the liabilities assumed, and the 20 percent noncontrolling interest.

EXHIBIT 4.9
Consolidation Information for a Step Acquisition

ARCH COMPANY'S ACQUISITIONS OF ZION COMPANY SHARES				
	Consideration Transferred	Percentage Acquired	Zion Company (100%)	
			Book Value	Fair Value
January 1, 2016	$164,000	30%	$400,000	$546,667
January 1, 2018	350,000	50	500,000	700,000

Zion Company's Income and Dividends for 2016–2018		
	Income	Dividends
2016	$ 60,000	$ 20,000
2017	80,000	20,000
2018	100,000	20,000

EXHIBIT 4.10
Allocation of First Noncontrolling Acquisition

ARCH COMPANY AND ZION COMPANY	
Fair Value Allocation and Amortization	
January 1, 2016	
Fair value of consideration transferred	$ 164,000
Book value equivalent of Arch's ownership ($400,000 × 30%)	(120,000)
Customer base	$ 44,000
Assumed remaining life	22 years
Annual amortization expense	$ 2,000

Exhibit 4.11 shows Arch's allocation of Zion's $700,000 acquisition-date fair value, first to the ownership interests and then to Zion's assets.

Note that the acquisition method views a multiple-step acquisition as essentially the same as a single-step acquisition. In the Arch Company and Zion Company example, once control is evident, the only relevant values in consolidating the accounts of Zion are fair values at January 1, 2018. A new basis of accountability arises for Zion Company on that single date because obtaining control of another firm is considered a significant remeasurement event. Previously owned noncontrolling blocks of stock are consequently revalued to fair value on the date control is obtained.

In revaluing a previous stock ownership in the acquired firm, the acquirer recognizes any resulting gain or loss in income. Therefore, on January 1, 2018, Arch increases the Investment in Zion account to $210,000 (30% × $700,000 fair value) and records the revaluation gain as follows:

Investment in Zion..	20,000	
Gain on Revaluation of Zion...............................		20,000

Fair value of Arch's 30% investment in Zion at 1/1/18 (30% × $700,000).......................................	$210,000
Book value of Arch's 30% investment in Zion at 1/1/18	190,000
Gain on revaluation of Zion to fair value....................	$ 20,000

Worksheet Consolidation for a Step Acquisition (Acquisition Method)

To continue the example, the amount in Arch Company's 80 percent Investment in Zion account is updated for 2018:

Investment in Zion (after revaluation on 1/1/18)............	$210,000
January 1, 2018—Second acquisition price paid...........	350,000
Equity income accrual—2018 (80% × $100,000)...........	80,000
Amortization of customer base (80% × $10,000)...........	(8,000)
Share of Zion dividends—2018 (80% × $20,000)	(16,000)
Investment in Zion—12/31/18	$616,000

The worksheet for consolidating Arch Company and Zion Company is shown in Exhibit 4.12. Observe that
- The consolidation worksheet entries are essentially the same as if Arch had acquired its entire 80 percent ownership on January 1, 2018.

EXHIBIT 4.11
Allocation of Acquisition-Date Fair Value

ARCH COMPANY AND ZION COMPANY Zion Fair Value at Date Control Is Obtained January 1, 2018	
Fair value of Arch's 50% equity acquisition................	$ 350,000
Fair value of 30% equity already owned by Arch	210,000
Fair value of 20% noncontrolling interest	140,000
Total fair value assigned to Zion Company	$ 700,000

Excess Fair over Book Value Allocation and Amortization January 1, 2018	
Zion Company fair value.....................	$ 700,000
Zion Company book value....................	(500,000)
Customer base...............................	$ 200,000
Assumed remaining life	20 years
Annual amortization expense	$ 10,000

- The noncontrolling interest is allocated 20 percent of the excess fair-value allocation from the customer base.
- The noncontrolling interest is allocated 20 percent of Zion's 2018 income less its share of the excess amortization attributable to the customer base.
- The gain on revaluation of Arch's initial investment in Zion is recognized as income of the current period.

EXHIBIT 4.12   Step Acquisition Illustrated

			Consolidation Entries			
ARCH COMPANY AND ZION COMPANY Consolidation Worksheet						
Investment: Equity Method		For Year Ending December 31, 2018				*Ownership: 80%*
Accounts	**Arch Company**	**Zion Company**	**Debit**	**Credit**	**Noncontrolling Interest**	**Consolidated Totals**
Income Statement						
Revenues	(600,000)	(260,000)				(860,000)
Expenses	425,000	160,000	(E) 10,000			595,000
Equity in subsidiary earnings	(72,000)	–0–	(I) 72,000			–0–
Gain on revaluation of Zion	(20,000)	–0–				(20,000)
Separate company net income	(267,000)	(100,000)				
Consolidated net income						(285,000)
Net income attributable to noncontrolling interest					(18,000)	18,000
Net income attributable to Arch Company						(267,000)
Statement of Retained Earnings						
Retained earnings, 1/1						
Arch Company	(758,000)					(758,000)
Zion Company		(230,000)	(S) 230,000			
Net income (above)	(267,000)	(100,000)				(267,000)
Dividends declared	125,000	20,000		(D) 16,000	4,000	125,000
Retained earnings, 12/31	(900,000)	(310,000)				(900,000)
Balance Sheet						
Current assets	509,000	280,000				789,000
Land	205,000	90,000				295,000
Buildings (net)	646,000	310,000				956,000
Investment in Zion Company	616,000	–0–	(D) 16,000	(A) 160,000 (S) 400,000 (I) 72,000		–0–
Customer base	–0–	–0–	(A) 200,000	(E) 10,000		190,000
Total assets	1,976,000	680,000				2,230,000
Liabilities	(461,000)	(100,000)				(561,000)
Noncontrolling interest in Zion Company, 1/1	–0–	–0–		(S) 100,000 (A) 40,000	(140,000)	
Noncontrolling interest in Zion Company, 12/31	–0–	–0–			(154,000)	(154,000)
Common stock	(355,000)	(200,000)	(S) 200,000			(355,000)
Additional paid-in capital	(260,000)	(70,000)	(S) 70,000			(260,000)
Retained earnings, 12/31 (above)	(900,000)	(310,000)				(900,000)
Total liabilities and equities	(1,976,000)	(680,000)	798,000	798,000		(2,230,000)

Note: Parentheses indicate a credit balance.
 Consolidation entries:
(S) Elimination of subsidiary's stockholders' equity along with recognition of 1/1 noncontrolling interest.
(A) Allocation of subsidiary total fair value in excess of book value, unamortized balances as of 1/1.
(I) Elimination of intra-entity income (equity accrual less amortization expenses).
(D) Elimination of intra-entity dividends.
(E) Recognition of amortization expenses on fair-value allocations.

Example: Step Acquisition Resulting after Control Is Obtained

The previous example demonstrates a step acquisition with control achieved with the most recent purchase. Post-control acquisitions by a parent of a subsidiary's stock, however, often continue as well. Recall that the acquisition method measures an acquired firm at its fair value on the date control is obtained.

A parent's subsequent subsidiary stock acquisitions do not affect these initially recognized fair values. For example, when Walmart increased its ownership in Walmart Chile from 75 percent to 100 percent, it did not change the valuation bases of Walmart Chile's assets. The acquisition of the 25 percent noncontrolling interest was treated as an equity transaction with a corresponding adjustment to additional paid-in capital. As the Walmart example shows, once the subsidiary's valuation basis is established as of the date control is obtained, as long as control is maintained, this valuation basis remains the same. Any further purchases (or sales) of the subsidiary's stock are treated as equity transactions.

To illustrate a post-control step acquisition, assume that on January 1, 2017, Amanda Co. obtains 70 percent of Schallman, Inc., for $350,000 cash. We also assume that the $350,000 consideration paid represents the best available evidence for measuring the fair value of the noncontrolling interest. Therefore, Schallman Company's total fair value is assessed at $500,000 ($350,000 ÷ 70%). Because Schallman's net assets' book values equal their collective fair values of $400,000, Amanda recognizes goodwill of $100,000. Then, on January 1, 2018, when Schallman's book value has increased to $420,000, Amanda buys another 20 percent of Schallman for $95,000, bringing its total ownership to 90 percent. Under the acquisition method, the valuation basis for the subsidiary's net assets was established on January 1, 2017, the date Amanda obtained control. Subsequent transactions in the subsidiary's stock (purchases or sales) are now viewed as transactions in the combined entity's own stock. Therefore, when Amanda acquires additional shares post-control, it recognizes the difference between the fair value of the consideration transferred and the underlying subsidiary valuation as an adjustment to Additional Paid-In Capital.

The difference between the $95,000 price and the underlying consolidated subsidiary value is computed as follows:

1/1/18 price paid for 20% interest		$ 95,000
Noncontrolling interest (NCI) acquired:		
Book value (20% of $420,000)	$84,000	
Goodwill (20% of $100,000)	20,000	
Noncontrolling interest book value (20%) 1/1/18		104,000
Additional paid-in capital from 20% NCI acquisition		$ 9,000

Amanda then prepares the following journal entry to record the acquisition of the 20 percent noncontrolling interest:

Investment in Schallman	104,000	
Cash		95,000
Additional Paid-In Capital		9,000

By purchasing 20 percent of Schallman for $95,000, the consolidated entity's owners have acquired a portion of their own firm at a price $9,000 less than consolidated book value. From a worksheet perspective, the $104,000 increase in the investment account simply replaces the 20 percent allocation to the noncontrolling interest. Note that the $95,000 exchanged for the 20 percent interest in Schallman's net assets does not affect consolidated asset valuation. The basis for the reported values in the consolidated financial statements was established on the date control was obtained.

DOES GAAP UNDERVALUE POST-CONTROL STOCK ACQUISITIONS?

In Berkshire Hathaway's 2012 annual report, Warren Buffett, in discussing the company's post-control step acquisitions of Marmon Holdings, Inc., observed the following:

> Marmon provides an example of a clear and substantial gap existing between book value and intrinsic value. Let me explain the odd origin of this differential.
>
> Last year I told you that we had purchased additional shares in Marmon, raising our ownership to 80% (up from the 64% we acquired in 2008). I also told you that GAAP accounting required us to immediately record the 2011 purchase on our books at far less than what we paid. I've now had a year to think about this weird accounting rule, but I've yet to find an explanation that makes any sense—nor can Charlie or Marc Hamburg, our CFO, come up with one. My confusion increases when I am told that if we hadn't already owned 64%, the 16% we purchased in 2011 would have been entered on our books at our cost.
>
> In 2012 (and in early 2013, retroactive to year end 2012) we acquired an additional 10% of Marmon and the same bizarre accounting treatment was required. The $700 million write-off we immediately incurred had no effect on earnings but did reduce book value and, therefore, 2012's gain in net worth.
>
> The cost of our recent 10% purchase implies a $12.6 billion value for the 90% of Marmon we now own. Our balance-sheet carrying value for the 90%, however, is $8 billion. Charlie and I believe our current purchase represents excellent value. If we are correct, our Marmon holding is worth at least $4.6 billion more than its carrying value.

How would you explain the accounting valuations for the post-control step acquisitions to the Berkshire Hathaway executives? Do you agree or disagree with the GAAP treatment of reporting additional investments in subsidiaries when control has previously been established?

LO 4-10

Record the sale of a subsidiary (or a portion of its shares).

Parent Company Sales of Subsidiary Stock—Acquisition Method

Frequently, a parent company will sell a portion or all of the shares it owns of a subsidiary. For example, when General Electric Company reported the sale of its NBC Universal business, it noted in its financial statements:

> We transferred the assets of the NBCU business and Comcast transferred certain of its assets to a newly formed entity, NBC Universal LLC (NBCU LLC). In connection with the transaction, we received $6,197 million in cash from Comcast and a 49% interest in NBCU LLC. Comcast holds the remaining 51% interest in NBCU LLC. We will account for our investment in NBCU LLC under the equity method. As a result of the transaction, we expect to recognize a small after-tax gain . . .

Importantly, the accounting effect from selling subsidiary shares depends on whether the parent continues to maintain control after the sale. If the sale of the parent's ownership interest results in the loss of control of a subsidiary as in the GE example above, it recognizes any resulting gain or loss in consolidated net income.

If the parent sells some subsidiary shares but retains control, it recognizes no gains or losses on the sale. Under the acquisition method, as long as control remains with the parent, transactions in the stock of the subsidiary are considered to be transactions in the equity of the consolidated entity. Because such transactions are considered to occur with owners, the parent records any difference between proceeds of the sale and carrying amount as additional paid-in capital.

Sale of Subsidiary Shares with Control Maintained

To illustrate, assume Adams Company owns 100 percent of Smith Company's 25,000 voting shares and appropriately carries the investment on its books at January 1, 2018, at $750,000 using the equity method. Assuming Adams sells 5,000 shares to outside interests for $165,000 on January 1, 2018, the transaction is recorded as follows:

Cash	165,000	
Investment in Smith		150,000
Additional Paid-In Capital from Noncontrolling Interest Transaction		15,000
To record sale of 5,000 Smith shares to noncontrolling interest with excess of sale proceeds over carrying amount attributed to additional paid-in capital.		

The $15,000 "gain" on sale of the subsidiary shares is not recognized in income, but is reported as an increase in owners' equity. This equity treatment for the "gain" is consistent with the economic unit notion that as long as control is maintained, payments received from owners of the firm are considered contributions of capital. The ownership group of the consolidated entity specifically includes the noncontrolling interest. Therefore, the above treatment of sales to an ownership group is consistent with accounting for other stock transactions with owners (e.g., treasury stock transactions).

Sale of Subsidiary Shares with Control Lost

The loss of control of a subsidiary is a remeasurement event that can result in gain or loss recognition. The gain or loss is computed as the difference between the sale proceeds and the carrying amount of the shares sold. Using the Adams and Smith example above, assume now that instead of selling 5,000 shares, Adams sells 20,000 of its shares in Smith to outside interests on January 1, 2018, and keeps the remaining 5,000 shares. Assuming sale proceeds of $675,000, we record the transaction as follows:

Cash	675,000	
Investment in Smith		600,000
Gain on Sale of Smith Investment		75,000
To record sale of 20,000 Smith shares, resulting in the loss of control over Smith Company.		

If the former parent retains any of its former subsidiary's shares, the retained investment should be remeasured to fair value on the date control is lost. Any resulting gain or loss from this remeasurement should be recognized in the parent's net income.

In our Adams and Smith example, Adams still retains 5,000 shares of Smith Company (25,000 original investment less 20,000 shares sold). Assuming further that the $675,000 sale price for the 20,000 shares sold represents a reasonable value for the remaining shares of $33.75, Adams's shares now have a fair value of $168,750 ($33.75 × 5,000 shares). Adams would thus record the revaluation of its retained 5,000 shares of Smith as follows:

Investment in Smith...	18,750	
Gain on Revaluation of Retained Smith Shares to Fair Value....		18,750
To record the revaluation of Smith shares to a $33.75 per share fair value from their previous equity method January 1, 2018, carrying amount of $30.00 per share.		

The above revaluation of retained shares reflects the view that the loss of control of a subsidiary is a significant economic event that changes the fundamental relationship between the former parent and subsidiary. Also, the fair value of the retained investment provides the users of the parent's financial statements with more relevant information about the investment.

Cost-Flow Assumptions

If it sells less than an entire investment, the parent must select an appropriate cost-flow assumption when it has made more than one purchase. In the sale of securities, the use of specific identification based on serial numbers is acceptable, although averaging or FIFO assumptions often are applied. Use of the averaging method is especially appealing because all shares are truly identical, creating little justification for identifying different cost figures with individual shares.

Accounting for Shares That Remain

If Adams sells only a portion of the investment, it also must determine the proper method of accounting for the shares that remain. Three possible scenarios are described below:

1. Adams could have so drastically reduced its interest that the parent no longer controls the subsidiary or even has the ability to significantly influence its decision making. For example, assume that Adams's ownership drops from 80 to 5 percent. In the current period prior to the sale, the 80 percent investment is reported by means of the equity method with the market-value method used for the 5 percent that remains thereafter. Consolidated financial statements are no longer applicable.

2. Adams could still apply significant influence over Smith's operations although it no longer maintains control. A drop in the level of ownership from 80 to 30 percent normally meets this condition. In this case, the parent utilizes the equity method for the entire year. Application is based on 80 percent until the time of sale and then on 30 percent for the remainder of the year. Again, consolidated statements cease to be appropriate because control has been lost.

3. The decrease in ownership could be relatively small so that the parent continues to maintain control over the subsidiary even after the sale. Adams's reduction of its ownership in Smith from 80 to 60 percent is an example of this situation. After the disposal, consolidated financial statements are still required, but the process is based on the *end-of-year ownership percentage*. Because only the retained shares (60 percent in this case) are consolidated, the parent must separately recognize any current year income accruing to it from its terminated interest. Thus, Adams shows earnings on this portion of the investment (a 20 percent interest in Smith for the time during the year that it is held) in the consolidated income statement as a single-line item computed by means of the equity method.

Comparisons with International Accounting Standards

As observed in previous chapters of this text, the accounting and reporting standards for business combinations between U.S. and international standards have largely converged with FASB ASC Topic 805 and *IFRS 3R,* each of which carries the title "Business Combinations" and ASC Topic 810: Consolidation. Each set of standards requires the acquisition method and embraces a fair-value model for the assets acquired and liabilities assumed in a business combination. Both sets of standards treat exchanges between the parent and the noncontrolling interest as equity transactions, unless control is lost. However, as seen below, the accounting for the noncontrolling interest can diverge across the two reporting regimes.

- *U.S. GAAP.* In reporting the noncontrolling interest in consolidated financial statements, U.S. GAAP requires a fair-value measurement attribute, consistent with the overall valuation principles for business combinations. Thus, acquisition-date fair value provides a basis for reporting the noncontrolling interest, which is adjusted for its share of subsidiary income and dividends subsequent to acquisition.

- *IFRS.* In contrast, *IFRS 3R* allows an option for reporting the noncontrolling interest for each business combination. Under IFRS, the noncontrolling interest may be measured either at its acquisition-date fair value, which can include goodwill, or at a proportionate share of the acquiree's identifiable net asset fair value, which excludes goodwill. The IFRS proportionate-share option effectively assumes that any goodwill created through the business combination applies solely to the controlling interest.

Summary

1. A parent company need not acquire 100 percent of a subsidiary's stock to form a business combination. Only control over the decision-making process is necessary, a level that has historically been achieved by obtaining a majority of the voting shares. Ownership of any subsidiary stock that is retained by outside unrelated parties is collectively referred to as a noncontrolling interest.

2. A consolidation takes on an added degree of complexity when a noncontrolling interest is present. The noncontrolling interest represents a group of subsidiary owners and their equity is recognized by the parent in its consolidated financial statements.

3. The valuation principle for the noncontrolling interest is acquisition-date fair value. The fair value of the noncontrolling interest is added to the consideration transferred by the parent to determine the acquisition-date fair value of the subsidiary. This fair value is then allocated to the subsidiary's assets acquired and liabilities assumed based on their individual fair values. At the acquisition date, each of the subsidiary's assets and liabilities is included in consolidation at its individual fair value regardless of the degree of parent ownership. Any remaining excess fair value beyond the total assigned to the identifiable net assets is recognized as goodwill.

4. The fair value of the noncontrolling interest is adjusted over time for subsidiary income (less excess fair-value amortization) and subsidiary dividends.

5. Consolidated goodwill is allocated across the controlling and noncontrolling interests based on the excess of their respective acquisition-date fair values less their percentage share of the identifiable subsidiary net asset fair value. The goodwill allocation, therefore, does not necessarily correspond proportionately to the ownership interest of the parent and the noncontrolling interest.

6. Four noncontrolling interest figures appear in the annual consolidation process. First, a beginning-of-the-year balance in the book value of the subsidiary's net assets is recognized on the worksheet (through Entry **S**) followed by the noncontrolling interest's share of the unamortized excess acquisition-date fair values of the subsidiary's assets and liabilities (including a separate amount for goodwill if appropriate). Next, the noncontrolling interest share of the subsidiary's net income for the period (recorded by a columnar entry) is recognized. Subsidiary dividends to these unrelated owners are entered as a reduction of the noncontrolling interest. The final balance for the year is found as a summation of the Noncontrolling Interest column and is presented on the consolidated balance sheet, within the Stockholders' Equity section.

7. When a midyear business acquisition occurs, consolidated revenues and expenses should not include the subsidiary's current year preacquisition revenues and expenses. Only postacquisition subsidiary revenues and expenses are consolidated.

8. A parent can obtain control of a subsidiary by means of several separate purchases occurring over time, a process often referred to as a step acquisition. Once control is achieved, the acquisition method requires that the parent adjust to fair value all prior investments in the acquired firm and recognize any gain or loss. The fair values of these prior investments, along with the consideration transferred in the current investment that gave the parent control, and the noncontrolling interest fair value all constitute the total fair value of the acquired company.

9. When a parent sells some of its ownership shares of a subsidiary, it must establish an appropriate investment account balance to ensure an accurate accounting. If the equity method has not been used, the parent's investment balance is adjusted to recognize any income or amortization previously omitted. The resulting balance is then compared to the amount received for the stock to arrive at either an adjustment to additional paid-in capital (control maintained) or a gain or loss (control lost). Any shares still held will subsequently be reported through either consolidation, the equity method, or the fair-value method, depending on the influence retained by the parent.

Comprehensive Illustration

Problem

(*Estimated Time: 60 to 75 Minutes*) On January 1, 2014, Father Company acquired an 80 percent interest in Sun Company for $425,000. The acquisition-date fair value of the 20 percent noncontrolling interest's ownership shares was $102,500. Also as of that date, Sun reported total stockholders' equity of $400,000: $100,000 in common stock and $300,000 in retained earnings. In setting the acquisition price, Father appraised four accounts at values different from the balances reported within Sun's financial records.

Buildings (8-year remaining life)	Undervalued by $20,000
Land	Undervalued by $50,000
Equipment (5-year remaining life)	Undervalued by $12,500
Royalty agreement (20-year remaining life)	Not recorded, valued at $30,000

As of December 31, 2018, the trial balances of these two companies are as follows:

	Father Company	Sun Company
Debits		
Current assets	$ 605,000	$ 280,000
Investment in Sun Company	425,000	–0–
Land	200,000	300,000
Buildings (net)	640,000	290,000
Equipment (net)	380,000	160,000
Expenses	550,000	190,000
Dividends declared	90,000	20,000
Total debits	$2,890,000	$1,240,000
Credits		
Liabilities	$ 910,000	$ 300,000
Common stock	480,000	100,000
Retained earnings, 1/1/18	704,000	480,000
Revenues	780,000	360,000
Dividend income	16,000	–0–
Total credits	$2,890,000	$1,240,000

Included in these figures is a $20,000 payable that Sun owes to the parent company. No goodwill impairments have occurred since the Sun Company acquisition.

Required

a. Determine consolidated totals for Father Company and Sun Company for the year 2018.

b. Prepare worksheet entries to consolidate the trial balances of Father Company and Sun Company for the year 2018.

c. Assume instead that the acquisition-date fair value of the noncontrolling interest was $104,500. What balances in the December 31, 2018, consolidated statements would change?

Solution

a. The consolidation of Father Company and Sun Company begins with the allocation of the subsidiary's acquisition-date fair value as shown in Exhibit 4.13. Because this consolidation is taking place after several years, the unamortized balances for the various allocations at the beginning of the current year also should be determined (see Exhibit 4.14).

Next, the parent's method of accounting for its subsidiary should be ascertained. The continuing presence of the original $425,000 acquisition price in the investment account indicates that Father is applying the initial value method. This same determination can be made from the Dividend Income account, which equals 80 percent of the subsidiary's dividends. Thus, Father's accounting records have ignored the increase in Sun's book value as well as the excess amortization expenses for the prior periods of ownership. These amounts have to be added to the parent's January 1, 2018, Retained Earnings account to arrive at the proper consolidated balance.

During the 2014–2017 period of ownership, Sun's Retained Earnings account increased by $180,000 ($480,000 − $300,000). Father's 80 percent interest necessitates an accrual of $144,000

EXHIBIT 4.13 Excess Fair-Value Allocations

FATHER COMPANY AND SUN COMPANY
Acquisition-Date Fair-Value Allocation and Amortization
2014–2017

	Allocation	Remaining Life (years)	Annual Excess Amortization
Acquisition-date fair value	$527,500		
Sun book value (100%)	400,000		
Excess fair value	127,500		
Allocation to specific subsidiary accounts based on fair value:			
Buildings	$ 20,000	8	$ 2,500
Land	50,000	indefinite	–0–
Equipment	12,500	5	2,500
Royalty agreement	30,000	20	1,500
Goodwill	$ 15,000		
Annual excess amortization expenses			$ 6,500

Goodwill Allocation to the Controlling and Noncontrolling Interests

	Controlling Interest	Noncontrolling Interest	Total
Acquisition-date fair value	$425,000	$102,500	$527,500
Relative fair value of Sun's net identifiable assets (80% and 20%)	410,000	102,500	512,500
Goodwill	$ 15,000	$ –0–	$ 15,000

EXHIBIT 4.14 Excess Fair-Value Allocation Balances

FATHER COMPANY AND SUN COMPANY
Unamortized Excess Fair- over Book-Value Allocation
January 1, 2018, Balances

Account	Excess Original Allocation	Excess Amortization 2014–2017	Balance 1/1/18
Buildings	$ 20,000	$10,000	$ 10,000
Land	50,000	–0–	50,000
Equipment	12,500	10,000	2,500
Royalty agreement	30,000	6,000	24,000
Goodwill	15,000	–0–	15,000
Total	$127,500	$26,000	$101,500

($180,000 × 80%) for these years. In addition, the acquisition-date fair-value allocations require the recognition of $20,800 in excess amortization expenses for this same period ($6,500 × 80% × 4 years). Thus, a net increase of $123,200 ($144,000 – $20,800) is needed to adjust the parent's beginning retained earnings balance to reflect the equity method.

Once the adjustment from the initial value method to the equity method is determined, the consolidated figures for 2018 can be calculated:

Current Assets = $865,000. The parent's book value is added to the subsidiary's book value. The $20,000 intra-entity balance is eliminated.

Investment in Sun Company = –0–. The intra-entity ownership is eliminated so that the subsidiary's specific assets and liabilities can be consolidated.

Land = $550,000. The parent's book value is added to the subsidiary's book value plus the $50,000 excess fair-value allocation (see Exhibit 4.13).

Buildings (*net*) = $937,500. The parent's book value is added to the subsidiary's book value plus the $20,000 fair-value allocation (see Exhibit 4.14) and less five years of amortization (2014 through 2018).

Equipment (net) = $540,000. The parent's book value is added to the subsidiary's book value. The $12,500 fair-value allocation has been completely amortized after five years.

Royalty Agreement = $22,500. The original residual allocation from the acquisition-date fair value is recognized after taking into account five years of amortization (see Exhibit 4.13).

Goodwill = $15,000. Original acquisition-date value assigned.

Liabilities = $1,190,000. The parent's book value is added to the subsidiary's book value. The $20,000 intra-entity balance is eliminated.

Revenues = $1,140,000. The parent's book value is added to the subsidiary's book value.

Expenses = $746,500. The parent's book value is added to the subsidiary's book value plus current year amortization expenses on the fair-value allocations (see Exhibit 4.13).

Consolidated Net Income = $393,500. The combined total of consolidated revenues and expenses.

Net Income Attributable to Noncontrolling Interest = $32,700. The outside owners are assigned a 20 percent share of the subsidiary's net income less excess fair-value amortizations: 20% × ($170,000 − $6,500).

Net Income Attributable to Father Company = $360,800. Consolidated net income less the amount allocated to the noncontrolling interest.

Common Stock = $480,000. Only the parent company's balance is reported.

Retained Earnings, 1/1/18 = $827,200. Only the parent company's balance after a $123,200 increase to convert from the initial value method to the equity method.

Dividends Declared = $90,000. Only parent company dividends are consolidated. Subsidiary dividends distributable to the parent are eliminated; the remainder reduce the Noncontrolling Interest balance.

Retained Earnings 12/31/18 = $1,098,000. The parent's adjusted beginning balance of $827,200, plus $360,800 net income to the controlling interest, less $90,000 dividends declared by Father Company.

Dividend Income = –0–. The intra-entity dividend declarations are eliminated.
Noncontrolling Interest in Subsidiary, 12/31/18 = $162,000.

NCI in Sun's 1/1/18 book value (20% × $580,000)	$116,000
NCI in unamortized excess fair-value allocations (20% × $86,500)	17,300
January 1, 2018, NCI in Sun's fair value	133,300
NCI in Sun's net income [20% × ($360,000 − 196,500)]	32,700
NCI dividend share (20% × $20,000)	(4,000)
Noncontrolling interest in Sun Company, December 31, 2018	$162,000

b. Six worksheet entries are necessary to produce a consolidation worksheet for Father Company and Sun Company.

Entry *C

Investment in Sun Company	123,200	
Retained Earnings, 1/1/18 (parent)		123,200

This increment is required to adjust the parent's Retained Earnings from the initial value method to the equity method.
The amount is $144,000 (80% of the $180,000 increase in the subsidiary's book value during previous years) less $20,800 in excess amortization over this same 4-year period ($6,500 × 80% × 4 years).

Entry S

Common Stock (subsidiary)	100,000	
Retained Earnings, 1/1/18 (subsidiary)	480,000	
Investment in Sun Company (80%)		464,000
Noncontrolling Interest in Sun Company (20%)		116,000

To eliminate beginning stockholders' equity accounts of the subsidiary and recognize the beginning balance book value attributed to the outside owners (20%).

Entry A1 and A2 Combined

Buildings	10,000	
Land	50,000	
Equipment	2,500	
Royalty Agreement	24,000	
Goodwill	15,000	
Investment in Sun Company		84,200
Noncontrolling Interest in Sun Company		17,300

To recognize unamortized excess fair- over book-value allocations as of the first day of the current year (see Exhibit 4.14). All goodwill is attributable to the controlling interest.

Entry I

Dividend Income	16,000	
Dividends Declared		16,000

To eliminate intra-entity dividend declarations recorded by parent (using the initial value method) as income.

Entry E

Depreciation Expense	5,000	
Amortization Expense	1,500	
Buildings		2,500
Equipment		2,500
Royalty Agreement		1,500

To recognize excess amortization expenses for the current year (see Exhibit 4.13).

Entry P

Liabilities	20,000	
Current Assets		20,000

To eliminate the intra-entity receivable and payable.

c. If the acquisition-date fair value of the noncontrolling interest were $104,500, then Sun's fair value would increase by $2,000 to $529,500 and goodwill would increase by the same $2,000 to $17,000. The entire $2,000 increase in goodwill would be allocated to the noncontrolling interest as follows:

	Controlling Interest	Noncontrolling Interest	Total
Acquisition-date fair value	$425,000	$104,500	$529,500
Relative fair value of Sun's identifiable net assets (80% and 20%)	410,000	102,500	512,500
Goodwill	$ 15,000	$ 2,000	$ 17,000

Therefore, the consolidated balance sheet would show goodwill at $17,000 (instead of $15,000) and the noncontrolling interest in Sun Company balance would show $164,000 (instead of $162,000).

Questions

1. What does the term *noncontrolling interest* mean?
2. Atwater Company acquires 80 percent of the outstanding voting stock of Belwood Company. On that date, Belwood possesses a building with a $160,000 book value but a $220,000 fair value. At what value would this building be consolidated?
3. What is a control premium and how does it affect consolidated financial statements?
4. Where should the noncontrolling interest's claims be reported in a set of consolidated financial statements?
5. How is the noncontrolling interest in a subsidiary company calculated as of the end of a reporting period?

6. December 31 consolidated financial statements are being prepared for Allsports Company and its new subsidiary acquired on July 1 of the current year. Should Allsports adjust its consolidated balances for the preacquisition subsidiary revenues and expenses?

7. Tree, Inc., has held a 10 percent interest in the stock of Limb Company for several years. Because of the level of ownership, this investment has been accounted for using the fair-value method. At the beginning of the current year, Tree acquires an additional 70 percent interest, which provides the company with control over Limb. In preparing consolidated financial statements for this business combination, how does Tree account for the previous 10 percent ownership interest?

8. Duke Corporation owns a 70 percent equity interest in Salem Company, a subsidiary corporation. During the current year, a portion of this stock is sold to an outside party. Before recording this transaction, Duke adjusts the book value of its investment account. What is the purpose of this adjustment?

9. In question (8), how would the parent record the sales transaction?

10. In question (8), how would Duke account for the remainder of its investment subsequent to the sale of this partial interest?

Problems

LO 4-1

1. What is a basic premise of the acquisition method regarding accounting for a noncontrolling interest?

    a. Consolidated financial statements should be primarily for the benefit of the parent company's stockholders.

    b. Consolidated financial statements should be produced only if both the parent and the subsidiary are in the same basic industry.

    c. A subsidiary is an indivisible part of a business combination and should be included in its entirety regardless of the degree of ownership.

    d. Consolidated financial statements should not report a noncontrolling interest balance because these outside owners do not hold stock in the parent company.

LO 4-2

2. Mittelstaedt, Inc., buys 60 percent of the outstanding stock of Sherry, Inc. Sherry owns a piece of land that cost $212,000 but had a fair value of $549,000 at the acquisition date. What value should be attributed to this land in a consolidated balance sheet at the date of takeover?

    a. $549,000

    b. $337,000

    c. $127,200

    d. $421,800

LO 4-2

3. Jordan, Inc., holds 75 percent of the outstanding stock of Paxson Corporation. Paxson currently owes Jordan $400,000 for inventory acquired over the past few months. In preparing consolidated financial statements, what amount of this debt should be eliminated?

    a. –0–

    b. $100,000

    c. $300,000

    d. $400,000

LO 4-2

4. On January 1, 2017, Grand Haven, Inc., reports net assets of $760,000 although equipment (with a four-year remaining life) having a book value of $440,000 is worth $500,000 and an unrecorded patent is valued at $45,000. Van Buren Corporation pays $692,000 on that date to acquire an 80 percent equity ownership in Grand Haven. If the patent has a remaining life of nine years, at what amount should the patent be reported on Van Buren's consolidated balance sheet at December 31, 2018?

    a. $28,000

    b. $35,000

    c. $36,000

    d. $40,000

LO 4-6

5. The noncontrolling interest represents an outside ownership in a subsidiary that is not attributable to the parent company. Where in the consolidated balance sheet is this outside ownership interest recognized?

    a. In the liability section.

    b. In a mezzanine section between liabilities and owners' equity.

    c. In the owners' equity section.

    d. The noncontrolling interest is not recognized in the consolidated balance sheet.

LO 4-4

6. On January 1, 2017, Chamberlain Corporation pays $388,000 for a 60 percent ownership in Neville. Annual excess fair-value amortization of $15,000 results from the acquisition. On December 31, 2018, Neville reports revenues of $400,000 and expenses of $300,000 and Chamberlain reports revenues of $700,000 and expenses of $400,000. The parent figures contain no income from the subsidiary. What is consolidated net income attributable to Chamberlain Corporation?

    a. $385,000

    b. $351,000

    c. $366,000

    d. $400,000

Problems 7 and 8 relate to the following:

On January 1, 2016, Pride Corporation purchased 90 percent of the outstanding voting shares of Star, Inc., for $540,000 cash. The acquisition-date fair value of the noncontrolling interest was $60,000. At January 1, 2016, Star's net assets had a total carrying amount of $420,000. Equipment (eight-year remaining life) was undervalued on Star's financial records by $80,000. Any remaining excess fair value over book value was attributed to a customer list developed by Star (four-year remaining life), but not recorded on its books. Star recorded net income of $70,000 in 2016 and $80,000 in 2017. Each year since the acquisition, Star has declared a $20,000 dividend. At January 1, 2018, Pride's retained earnings show a $250,000 balance.

Selected account balances for the two companies from their separate operations were as follows:

	Pride	Star
2018 Revenues	$498,000	$285,000
2018 Expenses	350,000	195,000

LO 4-4

7. What is consolidated net income for 2018?

    a. $194,000

    b. $197,500

    c. $203,000

    d. $238,000

LO 4-4

8. Assuming that Pride, in its internal records, accounts for its investment in Star using the equity method, what amount of retained earnings would Pride report on its January 1, 2018, consolidated balance sheet?

    a. $250,000

    b. $286,000

    c. $315,000

    d. $360,000

LO 4-8

9. James Company acquired 85 percent of Mark-Right Company on April 1. On its December 31 consolidated income statement, how should James account for Mark-Right's revenues and expenses that occurred before April 1?

    a. Include 100 percent of Mark-Right's revenues and expenses and deduct the preacquisition portion as noncontrolling interest in net income.

    b. Exclude 100 percent of the preacquisition revenues and 100 percent of the preacquisition expenses from their respective consolidated totals.

    c. Exclude 15 percent of the preacquisition revenues and 15 percent of the preacquisition expenses from consolidated expenses.

    d. Deduct 15 percent of the net combined revenues and expenses relating to the preacquisition period from consolidated net income.

LO 4-9

10. Amie, Inc., has 100,000 shares of $2 par value stock outstanding. Prairie Corporation acquired 30,000 of Amie's shares on January 1, 2015, for $120,000 when Amie's net assets had a total fair value of $350,000. On July 1, 2018, Prairie bought an additional 60,000 shares of Amie from a single stockholder for $6 per share. Although Amie's shares were selling in the $5 range around July 1, 2018, Prairie forecasted that obtaining control of Amie would produce significant revenue synergies to justify the premium price paid. If Amie's identifiable net assets had a fair value of $500,000 at July 1, 2018, how much goodwill should Prairie report in its postcombination consolidated balance sheet?

    a. $60,000

    b. $90,000

    c. $100,000

    d. $–0–

LO 4-9

11. A parent buys 32 percent of a subsidiary in one year and then buys an additional 40 percent in the next year. In a step acquisition of this type, the original 32 percent acquisition should be

    a. Maintained at its initial value.

    b. Adjusted to its equity method balance at the date of the second acquisition.

    c. Adjusted to fair value at the date of the second acquisition with a resulting gain or loss recorded.

    d. Adjusted to fair value at the date of the second acquisition with a resulting adjustment to additional paid-in capital.

LO 4-4, 4-8

12. On April 1, Pujols, Inc., exchanges $430,000 fair-value consideration for 70 percent of the outstanding stock of Ramirez Corporation. The remaining 30 percent of the outstanding shares continued to trade at a collective fair value of $165,000. Ramirez's identifiable assets and liabilities each had book values that equaled their fair values on April 1 for a net total of $500,000. During the remainder of the year, Ramirez generates revenues of $600,000 and expenses of $360,000 and declared no dividends. On a December 31 consolidated balance sheet, what amount should be reported as noncontrolling interest?

    a. $219,000

    b. $237,000

    c. $234,000

    d. $250,500

LO 4-10

13. McKinley, Inc., owns 100 percent of Jackson Company's 45,000 voting shares. On June 30, McKinley's internal accounting records show a $192,000 equity method adjusted balance for its investment in Jackson. McKinley sells 15,000 of its Jackson shares on the open market for $80,000 on June 30. How should McKinley record the excess of the sale proceeds over its carrying amount for the shares?

    a. Reduce goodwill by $64,000.

    b. Recognize a gain on sale for $16,000.

    c. Increase its additional paid-in capital by $16,000.

    d. Recognize a revaluation gain on its remaining shares of $48,000.

Use the following information for Problems 14 through 16:

West Company acquired 60 percent of Solar Company for $300,000 when Solar's book value was $400,000. The newly comprised 40 percent noncontrolling interest had an assessed fair value of $200,000. Also at the acquisition date, Solar had a trademark (with a 10-year remaining life) that was undervalued in the financial records by $60,000. Also, patented technology (with a 5-year remaining life) was undervalued by $40,000. Two years later, the following figures are reported by these two companies (stockholders' equity accounts have been omitted):

	West Company Book Value	Solar Company Book Value	Solar Company Fair Value
Current assets	$620,000	$300,000	$320,000
Trademarks	260,000	200,000	280,000
Patented technology	410,000	150,000	150,000
Liabilities	(390,000)	(120,000)	(120,000)
Revenues	(900,000)	(400,000)	
Expenses	500,000	300,000	
Investment income	Not given		

LO 4-2

14. What is the consolidated net income before allocation to the controlling and noncontrolling interests?

    a. $400,000

    b. $486,000

    c. $491,600

    d. $500,000

LO 4-4, 4-5

15. Assuming Solar Company has declared no dividends, what are the noncontrolling interest's share of the subsidiary's income and the ending balance of the noncontrolling interest in the subsidiary?

    a. $26,000 and $230,000

    b. $28,800 and $252,000

    c. $34,400 and $240,800

    d. $40,000 and $252,000

LO 4-2

16. What is the consolidated trademarks balance?
    a. $508,000
    b. $514,000
    c. $520,000
    d. $540,000

Use the following information for Problems 17 through 21:

On January 1, Park Corporation and Strand Corporation had condensed balance sheets as follows:

	Park	Strand
Current assets	$ 70,000	$20,000
Noncurrent assets	90,000	40,000
Total assets.........................	$160,000	$60,000
Current liabilities......................	$ 30,000	$10,000
Long-term debt.......................	50,000	–0–
Stockholders' equity	80,000	50,000
Total liabilities and equities	$160,000	$60,000

On January 2, Park borrowed $60,000 and used the proceeds to obtain 80 percent of the outstanding common shares of Strand. The acquisition price was considered proportionate to Strand's total fair value. The $60,000 debt is payable in 10 equal annual principal payments, plus interest, beginning December 31. The excess fair value of the investment over the underlying book value of the acquired net assets is allocated to inventory (60 percent) and to goodwill (40 percent). On a consolidated balance sheet as of January 2, what should be the amount for each of the following?

LO 4-2

17. Current assets:
    a. $105,000
    b. $102,000
    c. $100,000
    d. $90,000

LO 4-2

18. Noncurrent assets:
    a. $130,000
    b. $134,000
    c. $138,000
    d. $140,000

LO 4-2

19. Current liabilities:
    a. $50,000
    b. $46,000
    c. $40,000
    d. $30,000

LO 4-2

20. Noncurrent liabilities:
    a. $110,000
    b. $104,000
    c. $90,000
    d. $50,000

LO 4-2

21. Stockholders' equity:
    a. $80,000
    b. $90,000
    c. $95,000
    d. $130,000
    (AICPA adapted)

LO 4-4, 4-5

22. On January 1, 2017, Harrison, Inc., acquired 90 percent of Starr Company in exchange for $1,125,000 fair-value consideration. The total fair value of Starr Company was assessed at $1,200,000. Harrison computed annual excess fair-value amortization of $8,000 based on the difference between Starr's total fair value and its underlying book value. The subsidiary reported net

income of $70,000 in 2017 and $90,000 in 2018 with dividend declarations of $30,000 each year. Apart from its investment in Starr, Harrison had net income of $220,000 in 2017 and $260,000 in 2018.

a. What is the consolidated net income in each of these two years?

b. What is the balance of the noncontrolling interest in Starr at December 31, 2018?

LO 4-2, 4-4, 4-5

23. On January 1, 2018, Johnsonville Enterprises, Inc., acquired 80 percent of Stayer Company's outstanding common shares in exchange for $3,000,000 cash. The price paid for the 80 percent ownership interest was proportionately representative of the fair value of all of Stayer's shares.

At acquisition date, Stayer's books showed assets of $4,200,000 and liabilities of $1,600,000. The recorded assets and liabilities had fair values equal to their individual book values except that a building (10-year remaining life) with book value of $195,000 had an appraised fair value of $345,000. Stayer's books showed a $175,500 carrying amount for this building at the end of 2018.

Also, at acquisition date Stayer possessed unrecorded technology processes (zero book value) with an estimated fair value of $1,000,000 and a 20-year remaining life. For 2018 Johnsonville reported net income of $650,000 (before recognition of Stayer's income), and Stayer separately reported earnings of $350,000. During 2018, Johnsonville declared dividends of $85,000 and Stayer declared $50,000 in dividends.

Compute the amounts that Johnsonville Enterprises should report in its December 31, 2018, consolidated financial statements for the following items:

a. Stayer's building (net of accumulated depreciation).

b. Stayer's technology processes (net of accumulated amortization).

c. Net income attributable to the noncontrolling interest.

d. Net income attributable to controlling interest.

e. Noncontrolling interest in Stayer.

LO 4-4, 4-5, 4-7

24. On January 1, Patterson Corporation acquired 80 percent of the 100,000 outstanding voting shares of Soriano, Inc., in exchange for $31.25 per share cash. The remaining 20 percent of Soriano's shares continued to trade for $30 both before and after Patterson's acquisition.

At January 1, Soriano's book and fair values were as follows:

	Book Values	Fair Values	Remaining Life
Current assets	$ 80,000	$ 80,000	
Buildings and equipment	1,250,000	1,000,000	5 years
Trademarks	700,000	900,000	10 years
Patented technology	940,000	2,000,000	4 years
	$2,970,000		
Current liabilities	$ 180,000	$ 180,000	
Long-term notes payable	1,500,000	1,500,000	
Common stock	50,000		
Additional paid-in capital	500,000		
Retained earnings	740,000		
	$2,970,000		

In addition, Patterson assigned a $600,000 value to certain unpatented technologies recently developed by Soriano. These technologies were estimated to have a three-year remaining life.

During the year, Soriano declared a $30,000 dividend for its shareholders. The companies reported the following revenues and expenses from their separate operations for the year ending December 31.

	Patterson	Soriano
Revenues	$3,000,000	$1,400,000
Expenses	1,750,000	600,000

a. What amount should Patterson recognize as the total value of the acquisition in its January 1 consolidated balance sheet?

b. What valuation principle should Patterson use to report each of Soriano's identifiable assets and liabilities in its January 1 consolidated balance sheet?

c. For years subsequent to acquisition, how will Soriano's identifiable assets and liabilities be valued in Patterson's consolidated financial statements?

d. How much goodwill resulted from Patterson's acquisition of Soriano?

e. What is the consolidated net income for the year and what amounts are allocated to the controlling and noncontrolling interests?

f. What is the noncontrolling interest amount reported in the December 31 consolidated balance sheet?

g. Assume instead that, based on its share prices, Soriano's January 1 total fair value was assessed at $2,250,000. How would the reported amounts for Soriano's net assets change on Patterson's acquisition-date consolidated balance sheet?

LO 4-9

25. On January 1, 2017, Palka, Inc., acquired 70 percent of the outstanding shares of Sellinger Company for $1,141,000 in cash. The price paid was proportionate to Sellinger's total fair value, although at the acquisition date, Sellinger had a total book value of $1,380,000. All assets acquired and liabilities assumed had fair values equal to book values except for a patent (six-year remaining life) that was undervalued on Sellinger's accounting records by $240,000. On January 1, 2018, Palka acquired an additional 25 percent common stock equity interest in Sellinger Company for $415,000 in cash. On its internal records, Palka uses the equity method to account for its shares of Sellinger.

During the two years following the acquisition, Sellinger reported the following net income and dividends:

	2017	2018
Net income.....................	$340,000	$440,000
Dividends declared..............	150,000	180,000

a. Show Palka's journal entry to record its January 1, 2018, acquisition of an additional 25 percent ownership of Sellinger Company shares.

b. Prepare a schedule showing Palka's December 31, 2018, equity method balance for its Investment in Sellinger account.

LO 4-2, 4-7, 4-8

26. Parker, Inc., acquires 70 percent of Sawyer Company for $420,000. The remaining 30 percent of Sawyer's outstanding shares continue to trade at a collective value of $174,000. On the acquisition date, Sawyer has the following accounts:

	Book Value	Fair Value
Current assets	$ 210,000	$ 210,000
Land............................	170,000	180,000
Buildings........................	300,000	330,000
Liabilities.......................	(280,000)	(280,000)

The buildings have a 10-year remaining life. In addition, Sawyer holds a patent worth $140,000 that has a five-year remaining life but is not recorded on its financial records. At the end of the year, the two companies report the following balances:

	Parker	Sawyer
Revenues	$(900,000)	$(600,000)
Expenses	600,000	400,000

a. Assume that the acquisition took place on January 1. What figures would appear in a consolidated income statement for this year?

b. Assume that the acquisition took place on April 1. Sawyer's revenues and expenses occurred uniformly throughout the year. What amounts would appear in a consolidated income statement for this year?

LO 4-2, 4-4, 4-5

27. On January 1, Beckman, Inc., acquires 60 percent of the outstanding stock of Calvin for $36,000. Calvin Co. has one recorded asset, a specialized production machine with a book value of $10,000 and no liabilities. The fair value of the machine is $50,000, and the remaining useful life is estimated to be 10 years. Any remaining excess fair value is attributable to an unrecorded process

trade secret with an estimated future life of four years. Calvin's total acquisition-date fair value is $60,000.

At the end of the year, Calvin reports the following in its financial statements:

Revenues	$50,000	Machine	$ 9,000	Common stock	$10,000
Expenses	20,000	Other assets	26,000	Retained earnings	25,000
Net income	$30,000	Total assets	$35,000	Total equity	$35,000
Dividends declared	$ 5,000				

Determine the amounts that Beckman should report in its year-end consolidated financial statements for noncontrolling interest in subsidiary income, noncontrolling interest, Calvin's machine (net of accumulated depreciation), and the process trade secret.

LO 4-1, 4-5, 4-6

28. Plaza, Inc., acquires 80 percent of the outstanding common stock of Stanford Corporation on January 1, 2018, in exchange for $900,000 cash. At the acquisition date, Stanford's total fair value, including the noncontrolling interest, was assessed at $1,125,000. Also at the acquisition date, Stanford's book value was $690,000.

Several individual items on Stanford's financial records had fair values that differed from their book values as follows:

	Book Value	Fair Value
Tradenames (indefinite life).	$ 360,000	$383,000
Property and equipment (net, 8-year remaining life)	290,000	330,000
Patent (14-year remaining life)	132,000	272,000

For internal reporting purposes, Plaza, Inc., employs the equity method to account for this investment. The following account balances are for the year ending December 31, 2018, for both companies.

	Plaza	Stanford
Revenues	$(1,400,000)	$ (825,000)
Cost of goods sold	774,000	395,750
Depreciation expense	328,000	36,250
Amortization expense	–0–	28,000
Equity in income of Stanford.	(280,000)	–0–
Net income.	$ (578,000)	$ (365,000)
Retained earnings, 1/1/18.	$(1,275,000)	$ (530,000)
Net income.	(578,000)	(365,000)
Dividends declared.	300,000	50,000
Retained earnings, 12/31/18	$(1,553,000)	$ (845,000)
Current assets	$ 860,000	$ 432,250
Investment in Stanford.	1,140,000	–0–
Tradenames.	240,000	360,000
Property and equipment (net).	1,030,000	253,750
Patents	–0–	104,000
Total assets	$ 3,270,000	$ 1,150,000
Accounts payable.	$ (142,000)	$ (145,000)
Common stock	(300,000)	(120,000)
Additional paid-in capital.	(1,275,000)	(40,000)
Retained earnings (above).	(1,553,000)	(845,000)
Total liabilities and equities.	$(3,270,000)	$(1,150,000)

At year-end, there were no intra-entity receivables or payables.

Prepare a worksheet to consolidate the financial statements of Plaza, Inc., and its subsidiary Stanford.

LO 4-3, 4-5, 4-7

29. On January 1, 2016, Parflex Corporation exchanged $344,000 cash for 90 percent of Eagle Corporation's outstanding voting stock. Eagle's acquisition date balance sheet follows:

Cash and receivables	$ 15,000	Liabilities	$ 76,000
Inventory	35,000	Common stock	150,000
Property and equipment (net)	350,000	Retained earnings	174,000
	$400,000		$400,000

On January 1, 2016, Parflex prepared the following fair-value allocation schedule:

Consideration transferred by Parflex....................	$344,000
10% noncontrolling interest fair value....................	36,000
Fair value of Eagle	380,000
Book value of Eagle.......................................	324,000
Excess fair over book value	56,000
to equipment (undervalued, remaining life of 9 years)...............	18,000
to goodwill (indefinite life)........................	$ 38,000

The companies' financial statements for the year ending December 31, 2018, follow:

	Parflex	Eagle
Sales	$ (862,000)	$(366,000)
Cost of goods sold.............................	515,000	209,000
Depreciation expense	191,200	67,000
Equity in Eagle's earnings......................	(79,200)	–0–
Separate company net income	$ (235,000)	$ (90,000)
Retained earnings 1/1.........................	$ (500,000)	$(278,000)
Net income...................................	(235,000)	(90,000)
Dividends declared............................	130,000	27,000
Retained earnings 12/31......................	$ (605,000)	$(341,000)
Cash and receivables..........................	$135,000	$ 82,000
Inventory....................................	255,000	136,000
Investment in Eagle	488,900	–0–
Property and equipment (net)..................	964,000	328,000
Total assets	$ 1,842,900	$ 546,000
Liabilities...................................	$ (722,900)	(55,000)
Common stock—Parflex.......................	(515,000)	–0–
Common stock—Eagle.........................	–0–	(150,000)
Retained earnings 12/31.......................	(605,000)	(341,000)
Total liabilities and owners' equity..............	$(1,842,900)	$(546,000)

At year-end, there were no intra-entity receivables or payables.

a. Compute the goodwill allocation to the controlling and noncontrolling interest.
b. Show how Parflex determined its "Investment in Eagle" account balance.
c. Determine the amounts that should appear on Parflex's December 31, 2018, consolidated statement of financial position and its 2018 consolidated income statement.

LO 4-3, 4-5, 4-7

30. On January 1, 2017, Holland Corporation paid $8 per share to a group of Zeeland Corporation shareholders to acquire 60,000 shares of Zeeland's outstanding voting stock, representing a 60 percent ownership interest. The remaining 40,000 shares of Zeeland continued to trade in the market close to its recent average of $6.50 per share both before and after the acquisition by Holland. Zeeland's acquisition date balance sheet follows:

Current assets	$ 14,000	Liabilities	$ 212,000
Property and equipment (net)	268,000	Common stock	100,000
Patents	190,000	Retained earnings	160,000
	$472,000		$472,000

On January 1, 2017, Holland assessed the carrying amount of Zeeland's equipment (5-year remaining life) to be undervalued by $55,000. Holland also determined that Zeeland possessed unrecorded patents (10-year remaining life) worth $285,000. Zeeland's acquisition-date fair values for its current assets and liabilities were equal to their carrying amounts. Any remaining excess of Zeeland's acquisition-date fair value over its book value was attributed to goodwill.

The companies' financial statements for the year ending December 31, 2018, follow:

	Holland	Zeeland
Sales	$ (640,500)	$(428,500)
Cost of goods sold	325,000	200,000
Depreciation expense	80,000	34,000
Amortization expense	14,000	21,000
Other operating expenses	52,000	63,500
Equity in Zeeland earnings	(42,300)	–0–
Separate company net income.	$ (211,800)	$(110,000)
Retained earnings 1/1	$ (820,200)	$(296,500)
Net income.	(211,800)	(110,000)
Dividends declared.	50,000	30,000
Retained earnings 12/31	$ (982,000)	$(376,500)
Current assets	$ 125,000	$ 81,500
Investment in Zeeland	562,500	–0–
Property and equipment (net).	837,000	259,000
Patents	149,000	147,500
Total assets.	$ 1,673,500	$ 488,000
Liabilities.	$ (371,500)	$ (11,500)
Common stock - Holland.	(320,000)	–0–
Common stock - Zeeland	–0–	(100,000)
Retained earnings 12/31.	(982,000)	(376,500)
Total liabilities and owners equity.	$(1,673,500)	$(488,000)

At year-end, there were no intra-entity receivables or payables.

a. Compute the amount of goodwill recognized in Holland's acquisition of Zeeland and the allocation of goodwill to the controlling and noncontrolling interest.

b. Show how Holland determined its December 31, 2018, Investment in Zeeland account balance.

c. Prepare a worksheet to determine the amounts that should appear on Holland's December 31, 2018, consolidated financial statements.

LO 4-8, 4-9

31. On January 1, 2018, Morey, Inc., exchanged $178,000 for 25 percent of Amsterdam Corporation. Morey appropriately applied the equity method to this investment. At January 1, the book values of Amsterdam's assets and liabilities approximated their fair values.

On June 30, 2018, Morey paid $560,000 for an additional 70 percent of Amsterdam, thus increasing its overall ownership to 95 percent. The price paid for the 70 percent acquisition was proportionate to Amsterdam's total fair value. At June 30, the carrying amounts of Amsterdam's assets and liabilities approximated their fair values. Any remaining excess fair value was attributed to goodwill.

Amsterdam reports the following amounts at December 31, 2018 (credit balances shown in parentheses):

Revenues	$(210,000)
Expenses	140,000
Retained earnings, January 1	(200,000)
Dividends declared, October 1	20,000
Common stock	(500,000)

Amsterdam's revenue and expenses were distributed evenly throughout the year and no changes in Amsterdam's stock have occurred.

Using the acquisition method, compute the following:

a. The acquisition-date fair value of Amsterdam to be included in Morey's June 30 consolidated financial statements.

b. The revaluation gain (or loss) reported by Morey for its 25 percent investment in Amsterdam on June 30.

c. The amount of goodwill recognized by Morey on its December 31 balance sheet (assume no impairments have been recognized).

d. The noncontrolling interest amount reported by Morey on its

- June 30 consolidated balance sheet.

- December 31 consolidated balance sheet.

LO 4-10

32. Posada Company acquired 7,000 of the 10,000 outstanding shares of Sabathia Company on January 1, 2016, for $840,000. The subsidiary's total fair value was assessed at $1,200,000 although its book value on that date was $1,130,000. The $70,000 fair value in excess of Sabathia's book value was assigned to a patent with a five-year remaining life.

On January 1, 2018, Posada reported a $1,085,000 equity method balance in the Investment in Sabathia Company account. On October 1, 2018, Posada sells 1,000 shares of the investment for $191,000. During 2018, Sabathia reported net income of $120,000 and declared dividends of $40,000. These amounts are assumed to have occurred evenly throughout the year.

a. How should Posada report the 2018 income that accrued to the 1,000 shares prior to their sale?

b. What is the effect on Posada's financial statements from this sale of 1,000 shares?

c. How should Posada report in its financial statements the 6,000 shares of Sabathia it continues to hold?

LO 4-5

33. On January 1, 2016, Telconnect acquires 70 percent of Bandmor for $490,000 cash. The remaining 30 percent of Bandmor's shares continued to trade at a total value of $210,000. The new subsidiary reported common stock of $300,000 on that date, with retained earnings of $180,000. A patent was undervalued in the company's financial records by $30,000. This patent had a five-year remaining life. Goodwill of $190,000 was recognized and allocated proportionately to the controlling and noncontrolling interests. Bandmor earns net income and declares cash dividends as follows:

Year	Net Income	Dividends
2016	$ 75,000	$39,000
2017	96,000	44,000
2018	110,000	60,000

On December 31, 2018, Telconnect owes $22,000 to Bandmor.

a. If Telconnect has applied the equity method, what consolidation entries are needed as of December 31, 2018?

b. If Telconnect has applied the initial value method, what Entry *C is needed for a 2018 consolidation?

c. If Telconnect has applied the partial equity method, what Entry *C is needed for a 2018 consolidation?

d. What noncontrolling interest balances will appear in consolidated financial statements for 2018?

LO 4-2, 4-3, 4-5

34. Miller Company acquired an 80 percent interest in Taylor Company on January 1, 2016. Miller paid $664,000 in cash to the owners of Taylor to acquire these shares. In addition, the remaining 20 percent of Taylor shares continued to trade at a total value of $166,000 both before and after Miller's acquisition.

On January 1, 2016, Taylor reported a book value of $600,000 (Common Stock = $300,000; Additional Paid-In Capital = $90,000; Retained Earnings = $210,000). Several of Taylor's buildings that had a remaining life of 20 years were undervalued by a total of $80,000.

During the next three years, Taylor reports income and declares dividends as follows:

Year	Net Income	Dividends
2016	$ 70,000	$10,000
2017	90,000	15,000
2018	100,000	20,000

Determine the appropriate answers for each of the following questions:

a. What amount of excess depreciation expense should be recognized in the consolidated financial statements for the initial years following this acquisition?

b. If a consolidated balance sheet is prepared as of January 1, 2016, what amount of goodwill should be recognized?

c. If a consolidation worksheet is prepared as of January 1, 2016, what Entry S and Entry A should be included?

d. On the separate financial records of the parent company, what amount of investment income would be reported for 2016 under each of the following accounting methods?

- The equity method.
- The partial equity method.
- The initial value method.

e. On the parent company's separate financial records, what would be the December 31, 2018, balance for the Investment in Taylor Company account under each of the following accounting methods?

- The equity method.
- The partial equity method.
- The initial value method.

f. As of December 31, 2017, Miller's Buildings account on its separate records has a balance of $800,000 and Taylor has a similar account with a $300,000 balance. What is the consolidated balance for the Buildings account?

g. What is the balance of consolidated goodwill as of December 31, 2018?

h. Assume that the parent company has been applying the equity method to this investment. On December 31, 2018, the separate financial statements for the two companies present the following information:

	Miller Company	Taylor Company
Common stock	$500,000	$300,000
Additional paid-in capital	280,000	90,000
Retained earnings, 12/31/18	620,000	425,000

What will be the consolidated balance of each of these accounts?

LO 4-1, 4-8

35. Following are several account balances taken from the records of Karson and Reilly as of December 31, 2018. A few asset accounts have been omitted here. All revenues, expenses, and dividend declarations occurred evenly throughout the year. Annual tests have indicated no goodwill impairment.

	Karson	Reilly
Sales	$ (800,000)	$(500,000)
Cost of goods sold	400,000	280,000
Operating expenses	200,000	100,000
Investment income	not given	–0–
Retained earnings, 1/1	(1,400,000)	(700,000)
Dividends declared	80,000	20,000
Trademarks	600,000	200,000
Royalty agreements	700,000	300,000
Licensing agreements	400,000	400,000
Liabilities	(500,000)	(200,000)
Common stock ($10 par value)	(400,000)	(100,000)
Additional paid-in capital	(500,000)	(600,000)

On July 1, 2018, Karson acquired 80 percent of Reilly for $1,330,000 cash consideration. In addition, Karson agreed to pay additional cash to the former owners of Reilly if certain performance measures are achieved after three years. Karson assessed a $30,000 fair value for the contingent performance obligation as of the acquisition date and as of December 31, 2018.

On July 1, 2018, Reilly's assets and liabilities had book values equal to their fair value except for some trademarks (with five-year remaining lives) that were undervalued by $150,000. Karson estimated Reilly's total fair value at $1,700,000 on July 1, 2018.

For the following items, what balances would be reported on Karson's December 31, 2018, consolidated financial statements?

Sales   Consolidated Net Income
Expenses   Retained Earnings, 1/1
Noncontrolling Interest in   Trademarks
   Subsidiary's Net Income   Goodwill

36. Nascent, Inc., acquires 60 percent of Sea-Breeze Corporation for $414,000 cash on January 1, 2015. The remaining 40 percent of the Sea-Breeze shares traded near a total value of $276,000 both before and after the acquisition date. On January 1, 2015, Sea-Breeze had the following assets and liabilities:

	Book Value	Fair Value
Current assets	$150,000	$150,000
Land	200,000	200,000
Buildings (net) (6-year remaining life)	300,000	360,000
Equipment (net) (4-year remaining life)	300,000	280,000
Patent (10-year remaining life)	–0–	100,000
Liabilities	(400,000)	(400,000)

The companies' financial statements for the year ending December 31, 2018, follow:

	Nascent	Sea-Breeze
Revenues	$ (600,000)	$ (300,000)
Operating expenses	410,000	210,000
Investment income	(42,000)	–0–
Net income	$ (232,000)	$ (90,000)
Retained earnings, 1/1/18	$ (700,000)	$ (300,000)
Net income	(232,000)	(90,000)
Dividends declared	92,000	70,000
Retained earnings, 12/31/18	$ (840,000)	$ (320,000)
Current assets	$ 330,000	$ 100,000
Land	220,000	200,000
Buildings (net)	700,000	200,000
Equipment (net)	400,000	500,000
Investment in Sea-Breeze	414,000	–0–
Total assets	$ 2,064,000	$ 1,000,000
Liabilities	$ (500,000)	$ (200,000)
Common stock	(724,000)	(480,000)
Retained earnings, 12/31/18	(840,000)	(320,000)
Total liabilities and equities	$(2,064,000)	$(1,000,000)

Answer the following questions:
  a. How can the accountant determine that the parent has applied the initial value method?
  b. What is the annual excess amortization initially recognized in connection with this acquisition?
  c. If the parent had applied the equity method, what investment income would the parent have recorded in 2018?
  d. What amount should the parent report as retained earnings in its January 1, 2018, consolidated balance sheet?
  e. What is consolidated net income for 2018 and what amounts are attributable to the controlling and noncontrolling interests?
  f. Within consolidated statements at January 1, 2018, what balance is included for the subsidiary's Buildings account?
  g. What is the consolidated Buildings reported balance as of December 31, 2018?

LO 4-5

LO 4-1, 4-5, 4-7

37. On January 1, 2017, Paloma Corporation exchanged $1,710,000 cash for 90 percent of the outstanding voting stock of San Marco Company. The consideration transferred by Paloma provided a reasonable basis for assessing the total January 1, 2017, fair value of San Marco Company. At the acquisition date, San Marco reported the following owners' equity amounts in its balance sheet:

Common stock	$400,000
Additional paid-in capital	60,000
Retained earnings.	265,000

In determining its acquisition offer, Paloma noted that the values for San Marco's recorded assets and liabilities approximated their fair values. Paloma also observed that San Marco had developed internally a customer base with an assessed fair value of $800,000 that was not reflected on San Marco's books. Paloma expected both cost and revenue synergies from the combination.

At the acquisition date, Paloma prepared the following fair-value allocation schedule:

Fair value of San Marco Company.	$1,900,000
Book value of San Marco Company	725,000
Excess fair value	1,175,000
to customer base (10-year remaining life)	800,000
to goodwill	$ 375,000

At December 31, 2018, the two companies report the following balances:

	Paloma	San Marco
Revenues	$(1,843,000)	$ (675,000)
Cost of goods sold	1,100,000	322,000
Depreciation expense	125,000	120,000
Amortization expense	275,000	11,000
Interest expense	27,500	7,000
Equity in income of San Marco.	(121,500)	–0–
Net income.	$ (437,000)	$ (215,000)
Retained earnings, 1/1.	$(2,625,000)	$ (395,000)
Net income.	(437,000)	(215,000)
Dividends declared.	350,000	25,000
Retained earnings, 12/31	$(2,712,000)	$ (585,000)
Current assets	$ 1,204,000	$ 430,000
Investment in San Marco	1,854,000	–0–
Buildings and equipment.	931,000	863,000
Copyrights	950,000	107,000
Total assets	$ 4,939,000	$ 1,400,000
Accounts payable	$ (485,000)	$ (200,000)
Notes payable	(542,000)	(155,000)
Common stock	(900,000)	(400,000)
Additional paid-in capital	(300,000)	(60,000)
Retained earnings, 12/31	(2,712,000)	(585,000)
Total liabilities and equities.	$(4,939,000)	$(1,400,000)

At year-end, there were no intra-entity receivables or payables.

a. Determine the consolidated balances for this business combination as of December 31, 2018.

b. If instead the noncontrolling interest's acquisition-date fair value is assessed at $167,500, what changes would be evident in the consolidated statements?

LO 4-5, 4-6, 4-7

38. The Holtz Corporation acquired 80 percent of the 100,000 outstanding voting shares of Devine, Inc., for $7.20 per share on January 1, 2017. The remaining 20 percent of Devine's shares also traded actively at $7.20 per share before and after Holtz's acquisition. An appraisal made on that date determined that all book values appropriately reflected the fair values of Devine's underlying accounts except that a building with a five-year future life was undervalued by $85,500 and a fully amortized

trademark with an estimated 10-year remaining life had a $64,000 fair value. At the acquisition date, Devine reported common stock of $100,000 and a retained earnings balance of $226,500.

Following are the separate financial statements for the year ending December 31, 2018:

	Holtz Corporation	Devine, Inc.
Sales..	$ (641,000)	$(399,000)
Cost of goods sold	198,000	176,000
Operating expenses	273,000	126,000
Dividend income	(16,000)	–0–
Net income	$ (186,000)	$ (97,000)
Retained earnings, 1/1/18	$ (762,000)	$(296,500)
Net income (above)	(186,000)	(97,000)
Dividends declared	70,000	20,000
Retained earnings, 12/31/18.........................	$ (878,000)	$(373,500)
Current assets	$ 121,000	$ 120,500
Investment in Devine, Inc............................	576,000	–0–
Buildings and equipment (net).......................	887,000	335,000
Trademarks...	149,000	236,000
Total assets.......................................	$ 1,733,000	$ 691,500
Liabilities	$ (535,000)	$(218,000)
Common stock	(320,000)	(100,000)
Retained earnings, 12/31/18 (above)	(878,000)	(373,500)
Total liabilities and equities	$(1,733,000)	$(691,500)

At year-end, there were no intra-entity receivables or payables.

a. Prepare a worksheet to consolidate these two companies as of December 31, 2018.

b. Prepare a 2018 consolidated income statement for Holtz and Devine.

c. If instead the noncontrolling interest shares of Devine had traded for $4.76 surrounding Holtz's acquisition date, what is the impact on goodwill?

LO 4-1, 4-5, 4-6

39. Padre, Inc., buys 80 percent of the outstanding common stock of Sierra Corporation on January 1, 2018, for $802,720 cash. At the acquisition date, Sierra's total fair value, including the noncontrolling interest, was assessed at $1,003,400 although Sierra's book value was only $690,000. Also, several individual items on Sierra's financial records had fair values that differed from their book values as follows:

	Book Value	Fair Value
Land	$ 65,000	$ 290,000
Buildings and equipment (10-year remaining life).....................	287,000	263,000
Copyright (20-year remaining life).............	122,000	216,000
Notes payable (due in 8 years)	(176,000)	(157,600)

For internal reporting purposes, Padre, Inc., employs the equity method to account for this investment. The following account balances are for the year ending December 31, 2018, for both companies.

	Padre	Sierra
Revenues	$(1,394,980)	$ (684,900)
Cost of goods sold	774,000	432,000
Depreciation expense..............................	274,000	11,600
Amortization expense..............................	0	6,100
Interest expense	52,100	9,200
Equity in income of Sierra.........................	(177,120)	–0–
Net income	$ (472,000)	$ (226,000)

(*continued*)

(continued)

	Padre	Sierra
Retained earnings, 1/1/18	$(1,275,000)	$ (530,000)
Net income	(472,000)	(226,000)
Dividends declared	260,000	65,000
Retained earnings, 12/31/18	$(1,487,000)	$ (691,000)
Current assets	$ 856,160	$ 764,700
Investment in Sierra................................	927,840	–0–
Land	360,000	65,000
Buildings and equipment (net).......................	909,000	275,400
Copyright..	–0–	115,900
Total assets.......................................	$ 3,053,000	$ 1,221,000
Accounts payable	$ (275,000)	$ (194,000)
Notes payable	(541,000)	(176,000)
Common stock.....................................	(300,000)	(100,000)
Additional paid-in capital	(450,000)	(60,000)
Retained earnings (above)...........................	(1,487,000)	(691,000)
Total liabilities and equities	$(3,053,000)	$(1,221,000)

At year-end, there were no intra-entity receivables or payables.

Prepare a worksheet to consolidate the financial statements of these two companies.

40. Adams Corporation acquired 90 percent of the outstanding voting shares of Barstow, Inc., on December 31, 2016. Adams paid a total of $603,000 in cash for these shares. The 10 percent non-controlling interest shares traded on a daily basis at fair value of $67,000 both before and after Adams's acquisition. On December 31, 2016, Barstow had the following account balances:

	Book Value	Fair Value
Current assets	$160,000	$160,000
Land......................................	120,000	150,000
Buildings (10-year remaining life)...........	220,000	200,000
Equipment (5-year remaining life)	160,000	200,000
Patents (10-year remaining life)	–0–	50,000
Notes payable (due in 5 years)	(200,000)	(180,000)
Common stock	(180,000)	
Retained earnings, 12/31/16	(280,000)	

December 31, 2018, adjusted trial balances for the two companies follow:

	Adams Corporation	Barstow, Inc.
Debits		
Current assets	$ 610,000	$ 250,000
Land..	380,000	150,000
Buildings	490,000	250,000
Equipment...	873,000	150,000
Investment in Barstow, Inc	702,000	–0–
Cost of goods sold	480,000	90,000
Depreciation expense..............................	100,000	55,000
Interest expense	40,000	15,000
Dividends declared	110,000	70,000
Total debits.......................................	$3,785,000	$1,030,000
Credits		
Notes payable	$ 860,000	$ 230,000
Common stock.....................................	510,000	180,000
Retained earnings, 1/1/18..........................	1,367,000	340,000
Revenues	940,000	280,000
Investment income	108,000	–0–
Total credits	$3,785,000	$1,030,000

At year-end, there were no intra-entity receivables or payables.

    a. Prepare schedules for acquisition-date fair-value allocations and amortizations for Adams's investment in Barstow.

    b. Determine Adams's method of accounting for its investment in Barstow. Support your answer with a numerical explanation.

    c. Without using a worksheet or consolidation entries, determine the balances to be reported as of December 31, 2018, for this business combination.

    d. To verify the figures determined in requirement (*c*), prepare a consolidation worksheet for Adams Corporation and Barstow, Inc., as of December 31, 2018.

LO 4-1, 4-4, 4-8

41. Following are the individual financial statements for Gibson and Davis for the year ending December 31, 2018:

	Gibson	Davis
Sales.	$ (600,000)	$ (300,000)
Cost of goods sold	300,000	140,000
Operating expenses	174,000	60,000
Dividend income	(24,000)	–0–
Net income	$ (150,000)	$ (100,000)
Retained earnings, 1/1/18	$ (700,000)	$ (400,000)
Net income	(150,000)	(100,000)
Dividends declared	80,000	40,000
Retained earnings, 12/31/18	$ (770,000)	$ (460,000)
Cash and receivables	$ 248,000	$ 100,000
Inventory	500,000	190,000
Investment in Davis	528,000	–0–
Buildings (net)	524,000	600,000
Equipment (net)	400,000	400,000
Total assets	$ 2,200,000	$ 1,290,000
Liabilities	(800,000)	(490,000)
Common stock	(630,000)	(340,000)
Retained earnings, 12/31/18	(770,000)	(460,000)
Total liabilities and stockholders' equity	$(2,200,000)	$(1,290,000)

    Gibson acquired 60 percent of Davis on April 1, 2018, for $528,000. On that date, equipment owned by Davis (with a five-year remaining life) was overvalued by $30,000. Also on that date, the fair value of the 40 percent noncontrolling interest was $352,000. Davis earned income evenly during the year but declared the $40,000 dividend on November 1, 2018.

    a. Prepare a consolidated income statement for the year ending December 31, 2018.

    b. Determine the consolidated balance for each of the following accounts as of December 31, 2018:

      Goodwill   Buildings (net)
      Equipment (net)   Dividends Declared
      Common Stock

LO 4-2, 4-3, 4-6, 4-7, 4-8

42. On July 1, 2018, Truman Company acquired a 70 percent interest in Atlanta Company in exchange for consideration of $720,000 in cash and equity securities. The remaining 30 percent of Atlanta's shares traded closely near an average price that totaled $290,000 both before and after Truman's acquisition.

    In reviewing its acquisition, Truman assigned a $100,000 fair value to a patent recently developed by Atlanta, even though it was not recorded within the financial records of the subsidiary. This patent is anticipated to have a remaining life of five years.

    The following financial information is available for these two companies for 2018. In addition, the subsidiary's income was earned uniformly throughout the year. The subsidiary declared dividends quarterly.

	Truman	Atlanta
Revenues	$ (670,000)	$ (400,000)
Operating expenses	402,000	280,000
Income of subsidiary	(35,000)	–0–
Net income	$ (303,000)	$ (120,000)
Retained earnings, 1/1/18	$ (823,000)	$ (500,000)
Net income (above)	(303,000)	(120,000)
Dividends declared	145,000	80,000
Retained earnings, 12/31/18	$ (981,000)	$ (540,000)
Current assets	$ 481,000	$ 390,000
Investment in Atlanta	727,000	–0–
Land	388,000	200,000
Buildings	701,000	630,000
Total assets	$ 2,297,000	$ 1,220,000
Liabilities	$ (816,000)	$ (360,000)
Common stock	(95,000)	(300,000)
Additional paid-in capital	(405,000)	(20,000)
Retained earnings, 12/31/18	(981,000)	(540,000)
Total liabilities and stockholders' equity	$(2,297,000)	$(1,220,000)

Answer each of the following:

a. How did Truman allocate Atlanta's acquisition-date fair value to the various assets acquired and liabilities assumed in the combination?

b. How did Truman allocate the goodwill from the acquisition across the controlling and noncontrolling interests?

c. How did Truman derive the Investment in Atlanta account balance at the end of 2018?

d. Prepare a worksheet to consolidate the financial statements of these two companies as of December 31, 2018. At year-end, there were no intra-entity receivables or payables.

LO 4-9

43. On January 1, 2017, Allan Company bought a 15 percent interest in Sysinger Company. The acquisition price of $184,500 reflected an assessment that all of Sysinger's accounts were fairly valued within the company's accounting records. During 2017, Sysinger reported net income of $100,000 and declared cash dividends of $30,000. Allan possessed the ability to influence significantly Sysinger's operations and, therefore, accounted for this investment using the equity method.

On January 1, 2018, Allan acquired an additional 80 percent interest in Sysinger and provided the following fair-value assessments of Sysinger's ownership components:

Consideration transferred by Allan for 80% interest	$1,400,000
Fair value of Allan's 15% previous ownership	262,500
Noncontrolling interest's 5% fair value	87,500
Total acquisition-date fair value for Sysinger Company	$1,750,000

Also, as of January 1, 2018, Allan assessed a $400,000 value to an unrecorded customer contract recently negotiated by Sysinger. The customer contract is anticipated to have a remaining life of four years. Sysinger's other assets and liabilities were judged to have fair values equal to their book values. Allan elects to continue applying the equity method to this investment for internal reporting purposes.

At December 31, 2018, the following financial information is available for consolidation:

	Allan Company	Sysinger Company
Revenues	$ (931,000)	$ (380,000)
Operating expenses	615,000	230,000
Equity earnings of Sysinger	(47,500)	–0–
Gain on revaluation of Investment in Sysinger to fair value	(67,500)	–0–
Net income	$ 431,000	$ 150,000

(continued)

(*continued*)

	Allan Company	Sysinger Company
Retained earnings, January 1	$ (965,000)	$ (600,000)
Net income.	(431,000)	(150,000)
Dividends declared	140,000	40,000
Retained earnings, December 31.	$(1,256,000)	$ (710,000)
Current assets	$ 288,000	$ 540,000
Investment in Sysinger (equity method).	1,672,000	–0–
Property, plant, and equipment.	826,000	590,000
Patented technology.	850,000	370,000
Customer contract	–0–	–0–
Total assets.	$ 3,636,000	$ 1,500,000
Liabilities	$(1,300,000)	$ (90,000)
Common stock	(900,000)	(500,000)
Additional paid-in capital	(180,000)	(200,000)
Retained earnings, December 31.	(1,256,000)	(710,000)
Total liabilities and equities	$(3,636,000)	$(1,500,000)

a. How should Allan allocate Sysinger's total acquisition-date fair value (January 1, 2018) to the assets acquired and liabilities assumed for consolidation purposes?

b. Show how the following amounts on Allan's preconsolidation 2018 statements were derived:

- Equity in earnings of Sysinger.

- Gain on revaluation of Investment in Sysinger to fair value.

- Investment in Sysinger.

c. Prepare a worksheet to consolidate the financial statements of these two companies as of December 31, 2018.

At year-end, there were no intra-entity receivables or payables.

LO 4-9

e**X**cel

44. On January 1, 2017, Bretz, Inc., acquired 60 percent of the outstanding shares of Keane Company for $573,000 in cash. The price paid was proportionate to Keane's total fair value although at the date of acquisition, Keane had a total book value of $810,000. All assets acquired and liabilities assumed had fair values equal to book values except for a copyright (six-year remaining life) that was undervalued in Keane's accounting records by $120,000. During 2017, Keane reported net income of $150,000 and declared cash dividends of $80,000. On January 1, 2018, Bretz bought an additional 30 percent interest in Keane for $300,000.

The following financial information is for these two companies for 2018. Keane issued no additional capital stock during either 2017 or 2018. Also, at year-end, there were no intra-entity receivables or payables.

	Bretz, Inc.	Keane Company
Revenues	$ (402,000)	$ (300,000)
Operating expenses	200,000	120,000
Equity in Keane earnings	(144,000)	–0–
Net income	$ (346,000)	$ (180,000)
Retained earnings, 1/1	$ (797,000)	$ (500,000)
Net income (above)	(346,000)	(180,000)
Dividends declared	143,000	60,000
Retained earnings, 12/31.	$(1,000,000)	$ (620,000)
Current assets	$ 224,000	$ 190,000
Investment in Keane Company	994,500	–0–
Trademarks.	106,000	600,000
Copyrights.	210,000	300,000
Equipment (net)	380,000	110,000
Total assets.	$ 1,914,500	$ 1,200,000

(*continued*)

(continued)

	Bretz, Inc.	Keane Company
Liabilities	$ (453,000)	$ (200,000)
Common stock	(400,000)	(300,000)
Additional paid-in capital	(60,000)	(80,000)
Additional paid-in capital—step acquisition.	(1,500)	–0–
Retained earnings, 12/31.	(1,000,000)	(620,000)
Total liabilities and equities	$(1,914,500)	$(1,200,000)

a. Show the journal entry Bretz made to record its January 1, 2018, acquisition of an additional 30 percent of Keane Company shares.

b. Prepare a schedule showing how Bretz determined the Investment in Keane Company balance as of December 31, 2018.

c. Prepare a consolidated worksheet for Bretz, Inc., and Keane Company for December 31, 2018.

Develop Your Skills

ACCOUNTING THEORY RESEARCH CASE

The FASB ASC paragraph 810-10-45-16 states: "The noncontrolling interest shall be reported in the consolidated statement of financial position within equity, separately from the parent's equity. That amount shall be clearly identified and labeled, for example, as noncontrolling interest in subsidiaries."

However, prior to issuing this current reporting requirement, the FASB considered several alternative display formats for the noncontrolling interest. Access the precodification standard, *SFAS 160,* "Noncontrolling Interest in Consolidated Financial Statements," at www.fasb.org to answer the following:

1. What alternative financial statement display formats did the FASB consider for the noncontrolling interest?

2. What criteria did the FASB use to evaluate the desirability of each alternative?

3. In what specific ways did FASB *Concept Statement 6* affect the FASB's evaluation of these alternatives?

RESEARCH CASE: STARBUCKS' STEP ACQUISITIONS OF STARBUCKS COFFEE JAPAN

Since 1995, Starbucks Corporation had owned a 39.5 percent equity interest in Starbucks Coffee Japan, Ltd. ("Starbucks Japan"). Its joint venture partner, Sazaby League of Japan also owned a 39.5 percent equity interest in Starbucks Japan. The remaining 21 percent equity interest was held by public shareholders and option holders.

On October 31, 2014, Starbucks acquired all of Sazaby League's shares of Starbucks Coffee Japan, bringing Starbucks' total ownership to 79 percent. Starbucks paid Sazaby $508.7 million for the additional 39.5 percent ownership. Later in 2014, Starbucks acquired the remaining 21 percent of Starbucks Coffee Japan. Access Starbucks' 2015 10-K annual report and answer the following:

1. What amount did Starbucks estimate for the October 31, 2014, acquisition-date fair value of Starbucks Japan? (*Hint:* include the acquisition-date estimated fair value of the remaining 21 percent noncontrolling interest in Starbucks Japan total fair value.)

2. How did Starbucks allocate the acquisition-date fair value of Starbucks Japan among the assets acquired and liabilities assumed?

3. How does Starbucks explain the three different valuation bases for the following items?
   - Amount paid to Sazaby for 39.5 percent share purchase
   - The fair value of Starbucks' pre-existing 39.5 equity interest
   - The fair value of the 21 percent noncontrolling interest

4. How did Starbucks account for its 39.5 percent ownership interest in Starbucks Japan prior to the acquisition of its controlling interest?

5. Upon acquisition of its controlling interest on October 31, 2014, how did Starbucks account for the change in fair value of its original 39.5 percent ownership interest?

6. Upon acquisition of the 21 percent noncontrolling interest, how did Starbucks account for the difference between the amount paid and the underlying carrying amount of Starbucks Japan?

RESEARCH CASE: COSTCO'S NONCONTROLLING INTERESTS

Costco Wholesale Corporation owns and operates membership warehouses in the United States, Canada, United Kingdom, Mexico, Japan, Australia, and Spain. Costco also engages in retail operations through majority owned subsidiaries in Korea and Taiwan. The outside equity interests (not owned by Costco) in the Korean and Taiwanese subsidiaries are presented collectively as noncontrolling interests in Costco's consolidated financial statements.

Access Costco's 2015 10-K annual report and answer the following:

1. How does Costco present the noncontrolling interest in the following financial statements?
   - Consolidated Balance Sheet
   - Consolidated Income Statement
   - Consolidated Statement of Other Comprehensive Income
   - Consolidated Statement of Cash Flows

2. Explain how Costco's presentations of the noncontrolling interest reflect the acquisition method for consolidated financial reporting as a single economic entity.

BARDEEN ELECTRIC: FASB ASC AND IFRS RESEARCH CASE

On October 18, 2017, Armstrong Auto Corporation ("Armstrong") announced its plan to acquire 80 percent of the outstanding 500,000 shares of Bardeen Electric Corporation's ("Bardeen") common stock in a business combination following regulatory approval. Armstrong will account for the transaction in accordance with ASC 805, "Business Combinations."

On December 1, 2017, Armstrong purchased an 80 percent controlling interest in Bardeen's outstanding voting shares. On this date, Armstrong paid $40 million in cash and issued one million shares of Armstrong common stock to the selling shareholders of Bardeen. Armstrong's share price was $26 on the announcement date and $24 on the acquisition date.

Bardeen's remaining 100,000 shares of common stock had been purchased for $3,000,000 by a small number of original investors. These shares have never been actively traded. Using other valuation techniques (comparable firms, discounted cash flow analysis, etc.), Armstrong estimated the fair value of Bardeen's noncontrolling shares at $16,500,000.

The parties agreed that Armstrong would issue to the selling shareholders an additional one million shares contingent upon the achievement of certain performance goals during the first 24 months following the acquisition. The acquisition-date fair value of the contingent stock issue was estimated at $8 million.

Bardeen has a research and development (R&D) project underway to develop a superconductive electrical/magnetic application. Total costs incurred to date on the project equal $4,400,000. However, Armstrong estimates that the technology has a fair value of $11 million. Armstrong considers this R&D as in-process because it has not yet reached technological feasibility and additional R&D is needed to bring the project to completion. No assets have been recorded in Bardeen's financial records for the R&D costs to date.

Bardeen's other assets and liabilities (at fair values) include the following:

Cash	$ 425,000
Accounts receivable	788,000
Land	3,487,000
Building	16,300,000
Machinery	39,000,000
Patents	7,000,000
Accounts payable	(1,500,000)

Neither the receivables nor payables involve Armstrong.

Answer the following questions citing relevant support from the ASC and IFRS.

1. What is the total consideration transferred by Armstrong to acquire its 80 percent controlling interest in Bardeen?

2. What values should Armstrong assign to identifiable intangible assets as part of the acquisition accounting?

3. What is the acquisition-date value assigned to the 20 percent noncontrolling interest? What are the potential noncontrolling interest valuation alternatives available under IFRS?

4. Under U.S. GAAP, what amount should Armstrong recognize as goodwill from the Bardeen acquisition? What alternative goodwill valuations are allowed under IFRS?

Consolidated Financial Statements— Intra-Entity Asset Transactions

Learning Objectives

After studying this chapter, you should be able to:

LO 5-1 Understand why intra-entity asset transfers create accounting effects within the financial records of affiliated companies that must be eliminated or adjusted in preparing consolidated financial statements.

LO 5-2 Demonstrate the consolidation procedures to eliminate intra-entity sales and purchases balances.

LO 5-3 Explain why consolidated entities defer intra-entity gross profit in ending inventory and the consolidation procedures required to subsequently recognize profits.

LO 5-4 Understand that the consolidation process for inventory transfers is designed to defer the intra-entity gross profit remaining in ending inventory from the year of transfer into the year of disposal or consumption.

LO 5-5 Explain the difference between upstream and downstream intra-entity transfers and how each affects the computation of noncontrolling interest balances.

LO 5-6 Prepare the consolidation entry to defer any gain created by an intra-entity transfer of land from the accounting records of the year of transfer and subsequent years.

LO 5-7 Prepare the consolidation entries to remove the effects of upstream and downstream intra-entity fixed asset transfers across affiliated entities.

C hapter 1 analyzed the deferral and subsequent recognition of gross profits created by inventory transfers between two affiliated companies in connection with equity method accounting. The central theme of that discussion is that intra-entity[1] profits cannot be recognized until the goods are ultimately sold to an unrelated party or consumed in the production process. This same accounting logic applies to transactions between companies within a business combination. Such sales within a single economic entity create neither profits nor losses. In reference to this issue, FASB ASC 810-10-45-1 states,

> As consolidated financial statements are based on the assumption that they represent the financial position and operating results of a single economic entity, such statements shall not include gain or loss on transactions among the entities in the consolidated group. Accordingly, any intra-entity profit or loss on assets remaining within the consolidated group shall be eliminated; the concept usually applied for this purpose is gross profit or loss.

The elimination of the accounting effects created by intra-entity transfers is one of the most significant problems encountered in the consolidation process. Such transfers are especially common in companies organized as a vertically integrated chain of organizations. For example, after acquiring its bottling companies PepsiCo noted,

> we acquired PBG and PAS to create a more fully integrated supply chain and go-to-market business model, improving the effectiveness and efficiency of the distribution of our brands and enhancing our revenue growth.

[1] The FASB *Accounting Standards Codification* (ASC) uses the term *intra-entity* to describe transfers of assets across entities affiliated through common ownership or other control mechanisms. The term indicates that although such transfers occur across separate legal entities, they are nonetheless made within a consolidated entity. In addition to the term *intra-entity,* such transfers are routinely referred to as *intercompany.*

Entities such as Pepsico reduce their costs by developing affiliations in which one operation furnishes products to another. As *Mergers & Acquisitions* observed,

> Downstream acquisitions . . . are aimed at securing critical sources of materials and components, streamlining manufacturing and materials planning, gaining economies of scale, entering new markets, and enhancing overall competitiveness. Manufacturers that combine with suppliers are often able to assert total control over such critical areas as product quality and resource planning.[2]

Intra-entity asset transactions take several forms. In particular, inventory transfers are especially prevalent. However, the sale of land and depreciable assets also can occur between the parties within a combination. This chapter examines the consolidation procedures for each of these different types of intra-entity asset transfers.[3]

Intra-Entity Inventory Transfers

LO 5-1

Understand why intra-entity asset transfers create accounting effects within the financial records of affiliated companies that must be eliminated or adjusted in preparing consolidated financial statements.

As previous chapters discussed, companies that make up a business combination frequently retain their legal identities as separate operating centers and maintain their own record-keeping. Thus, inventory sales between these companies trigger the independent accounting systems of both parties. The seller duly records revenue, and the buyer simultaneously enters the purchase into its accounts. For internal reporting purposes, recording an inventory transfer as a sale/purchase provides vital data to help measure the operational efficiency of each enterprise.[4]

Despite the internal information benefits of accounting for the transaction in this manner, from a consolidated perspective neither a sale nor a purchase has occurred. *An intra-entity transfer is merely the internal movement of inventory, an event that creates no net change in the financial position of the business combination taken as a whole.* Thus, in producing consolidated financial statements, the recorded effects of these transfers are eliminated so that consolidated statements reflect only transactions (and thus profits) with outside parties. Worksheet entries serve this purpose; they adapt the financial information reported by the separate companies to the perspective of the consolidated enterprise. The entire impact of the intra-entity transfer must be identified and then removed. Deleting the effects of the actual transfer is described here first.

The Sales and Purchases Accounts

LO 5-2

Demonstrate the consolidation procedures to eliminate intra-entity sales and purchases balances.

To account for related companies as a single economic entity requires eliminating all intra-entity sales/purchases balances. For example, if Arlington Company makes an $80,000 inventory sale to Zirkin Company, an affiliated party within a business combination, both parties record the transfer in their internal records as a normal sale/purchase. The following consolidation worksheet entry is then necessary to remove the resulting balances from the externally reported figures. Cost of Goods Sold is reduced here under the assumption that the Purchases account usually is closed out prior to the consolidation process.

Consolidation Entry TI		
Sales	80,000	
Cost of Goods Sold (purchases component)		80,000
To eliminate effects of intra-entity transfer of inventory. (Labeled **"TI"** in reference to the transferred inventory.)		

---

[2] "Acquiring along the Value Chain," *Mergers & Acquisitions,* June-July 1996, p. 8.

[3] In practice, the terms *intra-entity transaction* and *intra-entity transfer* are used interchangeably. Some argue that the use of the term *transaction* should be reserved for activities with entities outside the condolidated group.

[4] For all intra-entity transfers, the two parties involved view the events from different perspectives. Thus, the transfer is both a sale and a purchase, often creating both a receivable and a payable. To indicate the dual nature of such transfers, these accounts are indicated within this text as sales/purchases, receivables/payables, and so on.

In the preparation of consolidated financial statements, the preceding elimination must be made for all intra-entity inventory transfers. The total recorded (intra-entity) sales figure is deleted regardless of whether the transfer was downstream (from parent to subsidiary) or upstream (from subsidiary to parent). Furthermore, any gross profit included in the transfer price does not affect this sales/purchases elimination. Because the entire amount of the transfer occurred between related parties, the total effect must be removed in preparing the consolidated statements.

Intra-Entity Gross Profit—Year of Transfer (Year 1)

Removal of the sale/purchase is often just the first in a series of consolidation entries necessitated by inventory transfers. Despite the previous elimination, gross profits in ending inventory created by such sales can still exist in the accounting records at year-end. These profits initially result when the merchandise is priced at more than historical cost. Actual transfer prices are established in several ways, including the normal sales price of the inventory, sales price less a specified discount, or at a predetermined markup above cost. For example, in past financial statements, Ford Motor Company explained that

> intercompany sales among geographic areas consist primarily of vehicles, parts, and components manufactured by the company and various subsidiaries and sold to different entities within the consolidated group; transfer prices for these transactions are established by agreement between the affected entities.

Regardless of the method used for this pricing decision, gross profits that remain in inventory at year-end as a result of intra-entity sales during the period must be removed in arriving at consolidated figures.

All Inventory Remains at Year-End

LO 5-3

Explain why consolidated entities defer intra-entity gross profit in ending inventory and the consolidation procedures required subsequently to recognize profits.

In the preceding illustration, assume that Arlington acquired or produced this inventory at a cost of $50,000 and then sold it to Zirkin, an affiliated party, at the indicated $80,000 price. From a consolidated perspective, the inventory still has a historical cost of only $50,000. However, Zirkin's records now reflect the inventory at the $80,000 transfer price. In addition, because of the markup, Arlington's records show a $30,000 gross profit from this intra-entity sale. However, because the transaction did not occur with an outside party, recognition of this profit is not appropriate for the combination as a whole.

Thus, although the consolidation entry **TI** shown earlier eliminated the sale/purchase figures, the $30,000 inflation created by the transfer price still exists in two areas of the individual statements:

- Ending inventory remains overstated by $30,000.
- Gross profit is artificially overstated by this same amount.

Correcting the ending inventory requires only reducing the asset. However, correcting gross profit requires a careful analysis of the effect of the intra-entity transfer on the Cost of Goods Sold account. The ending inventory total serves as a negative component within the Cost of Goods Sold computation; it represents the portion of acquired inventory that was not sold. Thus, the $30,000 overstatement of the inventory that is still held incorrectly decreases this expense (the inventory that was sold). *Despite Entry TI, the inflated ending inventory figure causes Cost of Goods Sold to be too low and, thus, profits to be too high by $30,000.* For consolidation purposes, we increase Cost of Goods Sold by this amount through a worksheet adjustment that properly removes the gross profit from consolidated net income.

Consequently, if all of the transferred inventory is retained by the business combination at the end of the year, the following worksheet entry also must be included to eliminate the effects of the seller's gross profit that remains within the buyer's ending inventory:

Consolidation Entry G—Year of Transfer (Year 1)		
All Inventory Remains		
Cost of Goods Sold (ending inventory component)........................	30,000	
Inventory (balance sheet account)		30,000
To remove gross profit in ending inventory created by intra-entity sale.		

Discussion Question

EARNINGS MANAGEMENT

Enron Corporation's 2001 third-quarter 10-Q report disclosed the following activities with LJM2, a nonconsolidated special purpose entity (SPE) that was formed by Enron:

> In June 2000, LJM2 purchased dark fiber optic cable from Enron for a purchase price of $100 million. LJM2 paid Enron $30 million in cash and the balance in an interest-bearing note for $70 million. Enron recognized $67 million in pretax earnings in 2000 related to the asset sale. Pursuant to a marketing agreement with LJM2, Enron was compensated for marketing the fiber to others and providing operation and maintenance services to LJM2 with respect to the fiber. LJM2 sold a portion of the fiber to industry participants for $40 million, which resulted in Enron recognizing agency fee revenue of $20.3 million.

As investigations later discovered, Enron controlled LJM2 in many ways.

The FASB ASC now requires the consolidation of SPEs (as variable interest entities) that are essentially controlled by their primary beneficiary.

By selling goods to SPEs that it controlled but did not consolidate, did Enron overstate its earnings? What effect does consolidation have on the financial reporting for transactions between a firm and its controlled entities?

This entry (labeled **G** for gross profit) reduces the consolidated Inventory account to its original $50,000 historical cost. Furthermore, increasing Cost of Goods Sold by $30,000 effectively removes the intra-entity amount from recognized gross profit. Thus, this worksheet entry resolves both reporting problems created by the transfer price markup.

Only a Portion of Inventory Remains

Obviously, a company does not buy inventory to hold it for an indefinite time. It either uses the acquired items within the company's operations or resells them to unrelated, outside parties. Intra-entity profits ultimately are recognized by subsequently consuming or reselling these goods. Therefore, only the transferred inventory still held at year-end continues to be recorded in the separate statements at a value more than the historical cost. For this reason, *the ending inventory intra-entity gross profit elimination (Entry **G**) is based not on total intra-entity sales but only on the amount of transferred merchandise retained within the business at the end of the year.*

To illustrate, assume that Arlington transferred inventory costing $50,000 to Zirkin, a related company, for $80,000, thus recording a gross profit of $30,000. Assume further that by year-end Zirkin has resold $60,000 of these goods to unrelated parties but retains the other $20,000 (for resale in the following year). From the viewpoint of the consolidated company, it has now completed the revenue recognition process on the $60,000 portion of the intra-entity sale and need not make an adjustment for consolidation purposes.

Nonetheless, any gross profit recorded in connection with the $20,000 in merchandise that remains is still a component within Zirkin's Inventory account. Because the gross profit rate was $37\frac{1}{2}$ percent ($30,000 gross profit/$80,000 transfer price), this retained inventory is stated at a value $7,500 more than its original cost ($20,000 × $37\frac{1}{2}$%). The required reduction (Entry **G**) is not the entire $30,000 shown previously but only the $7,500 intra-entity gross profit that remains in ending inventory.

Consolidation Entry G—Year of Transfer (Year 1)		
25% of Inventory Remains (replaces previous entry)		
Cost of Goods Sold (ending inventory component).........................	7,500	
Inventory		7,500
To defer the intra-entity gross profit in ending inventory in year of transfer.		

LO 5-4

Understand that the consolidation process for inventory transfers is designed to defer the intra-entity gross profit in ending inventory from the year of transfer into the year of disposal or consumption.

Intra-Entity Gross Profit—Year Following Transfer (Year 2)

Whenever intra-entity profit is present in ending inventory, one further consolidation entry is eventually required. Although Entry **G** removes the gross profit from the *consolidated* inventory balances in the year of transfer, the $7,500 overstatement remains within the separate financial records of the buyer and seller. The effects of this deferred gross profit are carried into their beginning balances in the subsequent year. Hence, a worksheet adjustment is necessary in the period following the transfer. For consolidation purposes, the ending inventory portion of intra-entity gross profit must be adjusted in two successive years (from ending inventory in the year of transfer and from beginning inventory of the next period).

Referring again to Arlington's sale of inventory to Zirkin, the $7,500 intra-entity gross profit is still in Zirkin's Inventory account at the start of the subsequent year. Once again, the overstatement is removed within the consolidation process but this time from the beginning inventory balance (which appears in the financial statements only as a positive component of cost of goods sold). This elimination is termed *Entry *G.* The asterisk indicates that a previous year transfer created the intra-entity gross profits.

Consolidation Entry *G—Year Following Transfer (Year 2)		
Retained Earnings (beginning balance of seller)...........................	7,500	
Cost of Goods Sold (beginning inventory component).................		7,500
To remove from retained earnings the gross profit in beginning inventory and to currently recognize the profit through a reduction in cost of goods sold.		

Reducing Cost of Goods Sold (beginning inventory) through this worksheet entry increases the gross profit reported for this second year. For consolidation purposes, the gross profit on the transfer is recognized in the period in which the items are actually sold to outside parties. As shown in the following diagram, Entry **G** initially deferred the $7,500 intra-entity gross profit in the year of transfer. Entry ***G** now increases consolidated net income (by decreasing cost of goods sold) to reflect the sales activity with outside parties in the current year.

In Entry ***G,** removal of the $7,500 from beginning inventory (within Cost of Goods Sold) appropriately increases current net income and should not pose a significant conceptual problem. However, the rationale for decreasing the seller's beginning Retained Earnings deserves further explanation. This reduction removes the intra-entity gross profit in ending inventory

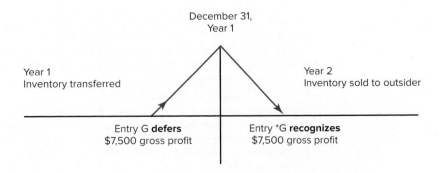

(recognized by the seller in the year of transfer) so that the profit is reported in the period when a sale to an outside party takes place. Despite the consolidation entries in Year 1, the $7,500 gross profit remained on this company's separate books and was closed to Retained Earnings at the end of the period. Recall that consolidation entries are never posted to the individual affiliate's books. Therefore, from a consolidated view, the buyer's Cost of Goods Sold (through the beginning inventory component) and the seller's Retained Earnings accounts as of the beginning of Year 2 contain the intra-entity profit, and must both be reduced in Entry *G.[5]

Intra-Entity Beginning Inventory Profit Adjustment—Downstream Sales When Parent Uses Equity Method

The worksheet eliminations for intra-entity sales/purchases (Entry TI) and intra-entity gross profit in ending inventory (Entry G) are both standard, regardless of the circumstances of the consolidation. In contrast, for one specific situation, the consolidation entry to recognize intra-entity beginning inventory gross profit differs from the Entry *G just presented. If (1) the original transfer is downstream (intra-entity sales made by the parent), and (2) the parent applies the equity method for internal accounting purposes, then the **Investment in Subsidiary** account replaces the parent's beginning Retained Earnings in Consolidation Entry *G as follows:

Consolidation Entry *G—Year Following Transfer (Year 2) (replaces previous Entry *G for downstream transfers when the equity method is used)		
Investment in Subsidiary	7,500	
Cost of Goods Sold (beginning inventory component)		7,500
To recognize previously deferred intra-entity downstream inventory gross profit as part of current year net income when the parent uses the equity method.		

Why debit the Investment in Subsidiary (and not the parent's beginning Retained Earnings) account in this situation? When the parent uses the equity method in its internal records, it recognizes beginning inventory gross profits on its books (and defers intra-entity ending inventory gross profits) as part of its equity income accruals. Therefore, both the parent's net income and retained earnings appropriately reflect consolidated balances.

Consolidation Entry I, however, removes the current year equity income accruals from the Investment in Subsidiary account as part of the investment account elimination sequence. With the equity income removed, the beginning inventory intra-entity profit reappears as a credit to the Investment in Subsidiary account's beginning of the year balance. Following our example, Consolidation Entry *G is thus needed to transfer the original $7,500 Year 1 Investment in Subsidiary account credit to a Year 2 earnings credit (through Cost of Goods Sold). Consolidation Entry *G also ensures that the Investment in Subsidiary account is brought to a zero balance on the worksheet.[6]

---

[5] For upstream intra-entity profit in beginning inventory, the subsidiary's retained earnings remain overstated and must be adjusted through Consolidation Entry *G.

[6] An acceptable alternative to recognizing intra-entity inventory profits in the subsidiary's beginning inventory (downstream sale) when the parent uses the equity method (*G) is as follows:

Equity in Subsidiary Earnings	7,500	
Cost of Goods Sold		7,500

In this case, Consolidation Entry I removes the *remaining* amount of the Equity in Subsidiary Earnings against the Investment in Subsidiary account. In either alternative adjustment for recognizing intra-entity inventory gross profits in beginning inventory, the final consolidated balances are exactly the same: Equity in Subsidiary Earnings =0, Investment in Subsidiary =0, and Cost of Goods Sold is reduced by $7,500.

EXHIBIT 5.1
Relationship between Gross Profit Rate and Markup on Cost

In determining appropriate amounts of intra-entity profits for deferral and subsequent recognition in consolidated financial reports, two alternative—but mathematically related—profit percentages are often seen. Recalling that Gross Profit = Sales − Cost of Goods Sold, then

$$\textbf{Gross profit rate (GPR)} = \frac{\text{Gross profit}}{\text{Sales}} = \frac{MC}{1 + MC}$$

$$\textbf{Markup on cost (MC)} = \frac{\text{Gross profit}}{\text{Cost of goods sold}} = \frac{GPR}{1 - GPR}$$

Example:

Sales (transfer price)	$1,000
Cost of goods sold	800
Gross profit	$ 200

Here the *GPR* = (200/1,000) = 20% and the *MC* = (200/800) = 25%. In most intra-entity purchases and sales, the sales (transfer) price is known and therefore the *GPR* is the simplest percentage to use to determine the amount of intra-entity profit.

$$\text{Intra-entity profit} = \text{Transfer price} \times GPR$$

Instead, if the markup on cost is available, it readily converts to a *GPR* by the preceding formula. In this case (0.25/1.25) =20%.

To summarize, for **intra-entity beginning inventory profits resulting from downstream transfers when the parent applies the equity method:**

- The parent's beginning retained earnings reflect the consolidated balance from application of the equity method and need no adjustment.
- The parent's Investment in Subsidiary account as of the beginning of Year 2 contains a credit from the deferral of Year 1 intra-entity downstream profits.
- Worksheet Entry *G debits the Investment account and credits Cost of Goods Sold, effectively recognizing the profit in the year of sale to outsiders.

Finally, various markup percentages determine the dollar values for intra-entity profit deferrals. Exhibit 5.1 shows formulas for both the gross profit rate and markup on cost and the relationship between the two.

LO 5-5

Explain the difference between upstream and downstream intra-entity transfers and how each affects the computation of noncontrolling interest balances.

Intra-Entity Gross Profit—Effect on Noncontrolling Interest

The worksheet entries just described appropriately account for the effects of intra-entity inventory transfers on business combinations. However, one question remains: What impact do these procedures have on the measurement of a noncontrolling interest? In regard to this issue, paragraph 810-10-45-18 of the FASB ASC states,

> The amount of intra-entity profit or loss to be eliminated in accordance with paragraph 810-10-45-1 is not affected by the existence of a noncontrolling interest. The complete elimination of the intra-entity income or loss is consistent with the underlying assumption that consolidated financial statements represent the financial position and operating results of a single economic entity. The elimination of the intra-entity income or loss may be allocated between the parent and noncontrolling interests.

The last sentence indicates that alternative approaches are available in computing the noncontrolling interest's share of a subsidiary's net income. According to this pronouncement, gross profits in inventory resulting from intra-entity transfers *may or may not* affect recognition of outside ownership. Because the amount attributed to a noncontrolling interest reduces consolidated net income, the handling of this issue can affect the reported profitability of a business combination.

To illustrate, assume that Large Company owns 70 percent of the voting stock of Small Company. To avoid extraneous complications, assume that no amortization expense resulted from this acquisition. Assume further that Large reports current net income (from separate operations) of $500,000 while Small earns $100,000. During the current period, intra-entity transfers of $200,000 occur with a total markup of $90,000. At the end of the year, a $40,000 intra-entity gross profit remains within the inventory accounts.

Clearly, the consolidated net income prior to the reduction for the 30 percent noncontrolling interest is $560,000, the two net income balances less the intra-entity gross profit in ending inventory. The problem facing the accountant is the computation of the noncontrolling interest's share of Small's net income. Because of the flexibility allowed by the FASB ASC, this figure may be reported as either $30,000 (30 percent of the $100,000 earnings of the subsidiary) or $18,000 (30 percent of reported net income after that figure is reduced by the $40,000 intra-entity gross profit in ending inventory).

To appropriately measure this noncontrolling interest allocation, the direction of the intra-entity transfer must be considered. If a transfer is downstream (the parent sells inventory to the subsidiary), a logical view would seem to be that the intra-entity gross profit in inventory is that of the parent company. The parent made the original sale; therefore, the gross profit is included in its financial records. Because the subsidiary's net income is unaffected, little justification exists for adjusting the noncontrolling interest to reflect the deferral of the intra-entity gross profit. Consequently, in the example of Large and Small, if the transfers were downstream, the 30 percent noncontrolling interest would be $30,000 based on Small's reported net income of $100,000.

In contrast, when the subsidiary sells inventory to the parent (an upstream transfer), the subsidiary recognizes the entire gross profit in its financial records even though part of the gross profit is deferred from a consolidation perspective. A reasonable conclusion is that because the subsidiary created the gross profit, owners of the noncontrolling interest are entitled to a portion of that profit.

In this textbook, the noncontrolling interest's share of consolidated net income is computed based on the reported net income of the subsidiary after adjusting for intra-entity gross profit in inventories from *upstream* sales. Returning to Large Company and Small Company, if the $40,000 intra-entity gross profit results from an upstream sale from subsidiary to parent, only $60,000 of Small's $100,000 net income should be recognized currently for consolidation purposes. The allocation to the noncontrolling interest is, therefore, reported as $18,000, or 30% of the $60,000 subsidiary net income after adjusting for the intra-entity profit remaining in ending inventory.

Although the noncontrolling interest figure is based here on the subsidiary's reported net income adjusted for the effects of upstream intra-entity transfers, GAAP, as quoted earlier, does not require this treatment. Giving effect to upstream transfers in this calculation but not to downstream transfers is no more than an attempt to select the most logical approach from among acceptable alternatives.[7]

Intra-Entity Inventory Transfers Summarized

To assist in overcoming the complications created by intra-entity transfers, we demonstrate the consolidation process in three different ways:

1. Before proceeding to a numerical example, review the impact of intra-entity transfers on consolidated figures. Ultimately, the accountant must understand how the balances reported by a business combination are derived when intra-entity gross profit in inventory result from either upstream or downstream sales.

2. Next, two different consolidation worksheets are produced: one for downstream transfers and the other for upstream. The various consolidation procedures used in these worksheets are explained and analyzed.

3. Finally, several of the consolidation worksheet entries are shown side by side to illustrate the differences created by the direction of the transfers.

[7] The 100 percent allocation of downstream profits to the parent affects its application of the equity method. As seen later in this chapter, in applying the equity method, the parent removes 100 percent of intra-entity profits resulting from downstream sales from its investment and equity earnings accounts rather than its percentage ownership in the subsidiary.

The Development of Consolidated Totals

A summary of the effects of intra-entity inventory transfers on consolidated totals follows:

Revenues. Parent and subsidiary balances are combined, but all intra-entity transfers are then removed.

Cost of Goods Sold. Parent and subsidiary balances are combined, but all intra-entity transfers are removed. The resulting total is decreased by any intra-entity gross profit in beginning inventory (thus raising net income) and increased by any intra-entity gross profit in ending inventory (reducing net income).

Net Income Attributable to the Noncontrolling Interest. The subsidiary's reported net income is adjusted for any excess acquisition-date fair-value amortizations and the effects of intra-entity gross profits in inventory from upstream transfers (but not downstream transfers) and then multiplied by the percentage of outside ownership.

Retained Earnings at the Beginning of the Year. As discussed in previous chapters, if the equity method is applied, the parent's balance mirrors the consolidated total. When any other method is used, the parent's beginning Retained Earnings must be converted to the equity method by Entry *C. Accruals for this purpose must recognize (1) the effects on reported subsidiary net income of intra-entity gross profits in beginning inventory that arose from upstream sales in the prior year, and (2) prior years' excess acquisition-date fair-value amortizations.

Inventory. Parent and subsidiary balances are combined. Any intra-entity gross profit remaining at the end of the current year is removed to adjust the reported balance to historical cost.

Noncontrolling Interest in Subsidiary at End of Year. The final total begins with the noncontrolling interest at the beginning of the year. This figure is based on the subsidiary's book value on that date plus its share of any unamortized acquisition-date excess fair value less its share of gross profits in beginning inventory that arose from upstream sales in the prior year. The beginning balance is updated by adding the portion of the subsidiary's net income assigned to these outside owners (as described above) and subtracting the noncontrolling interest's share of subsidiary dividends.

Intra-Entity Inventory Transfers Illustrated: Parent Uses Equity Method

To examine the various consolidation procedures required by intra-entity inventory transfers, assume that Top Company acquires 80 percent of the voting stock of Bottom Company on January 1, 2017. The parent pays $400,000 and the acquisition-date fair value of the noncontrolling interest is $100,000. Top allocates the entire $50,000 excess fair value over book value to adjust a database owned by Bottom to fair value. The database has an estimated remaining life of 20 years. Top Company applies the equity method to its investment in Bottom.[8]

The subsidiary reports net income of $30,000 in 2017 and $70,000 in 2018, the current year. The subsidiary declares dividends of $20,000 in the first year and $50,000 in the second. After the takeover, intra-entity inventory transfers between the two companies occurred as shown in Exhibit 5.2. A $10,000 intra-entity receivable and payable also exists as of December 31, 2018.

EXHIBIT 5.2
Intra-Entity Transfers

	2017	2018
Transfer prices	$80,000	$100,000
Historical cost	60,000	70,000
Gross profit	$20,000	$ 30,000
Inventory remaining at year-end (at transfer price)	$16,000	$ 20,000
Gross profit percentage	25%	30%
Gross profit remaining in year-end inventory	$ 4,000	$ 6,000

[8] Later in this chapter, we extend the example to when the parent applies the initial value method.

EXHIBIT 5.3
Investment Balances—
Equity Method—
Downstream Sales

Investment in Bottom Company Analysis 1/1/17 to 12/31/18		
Consideration paid (fair value) 1/1/17.		$ 400,000
Bottom Company reported net income for 2017.	$30,000	
Database amortization.	(2,500)	
Bottom Company adjusted 2017 net income.	$27,500	
Top's ownership percentage	80%	
Top's share of Bottom Company's net income.	$22,000	
Deferred profit from Top's 2017 downstream sales	(4,000)	
Equity in earnings of Bottom Company, 2017.		$ 18,000
Top's share of Bottom Company dividends, 2017 (80%)		(16,000)
Balance 12/31/17.		$ 402,000
Bottom Company reported net income for 2018.	$70,000	
Database amortization.	(2,500)	
Bottom Company adjusted 2018 net income.	$67,500	
Top's ownership percentage	80%	
Top's share of Bottom Company's net income.	$54,000	
Recognized profit from Top's 2017 downstream sales.	4,000	
Deferred profit from Top's 2018 downstream sales	(6,000)	
Equity in earnings of Bottom Company, 2018.		$ 52,000
Top's share of Bottom Company dividends, 2018 (80%)		(40,000)
Balance 12/31/18.		$ 414,000

The 2018 consolidation of Top and Bottom is presented twice. First, we assume the intra-entity transfers are downstream from parent to subsidiary. Second, consolidated figures are recomputed with the transfers being viewed as upstream. This distinction between upstream and downstream transfer becomes significant when the parent uses the equity method and in the presence of a noncontrolling interest.

Downstream Inventory Transfers: Parent Uses the Equity Method

To understand the consolidation procedures for intra-entity inventory transfers, it's useful first to analyze the parent's internal accounting for the investment. Under the equity method, the parent's investment-related accounts are subjected to (1) income accrual, (2) excess fair over book value amortization, (3) adjustments required by intra-entity gross profit in inventory, and (4) dividends. Exhibit 5.3 shows the changes to the Investment in Bottom Company from the acquisition date until the end of the current year (2018).

Note in particular the computations of Top's equity in earnings of Bottom Company in Exhibit 5.3. First, the calculations for equity method income are identical to those presented in Chapter 4, with the addition of an adjustment for intra-entity profits. Also observe that the $4,000 intra-entity profit deferred in 2017 is subsequently recognized in 2018. Thus, the $4,000 intra-entity profit is not eliminated but simply reallocated across time to the period when it is recognized by the consolidated entity. Next observe that, because the inventory transfers are downstream from parent to subsidiary, 100 percent of the profit deferral and subsequent recognition is allocated to the parent's equity earnings and investment account. As a result, the intra-entity profit reallocation across time affects neither Bottom's net income nor the noncontrolling interest.

Exhibit 5.4 presents the worksheet to consolidate these two companies for the year ending December 31, 2018. Most of the worksheet entries found in Exhibit 5.4 are described and analyzed in previous chapters of this textbook. Thus, we examine only three of these entries in detail along with the computation of the net income attributable to the noncontrolling interest.

First, Consolidation Entry *G adjusts for the intra-entity gross profit carried over in the beginning inventory from the 2017 intra-entity downstream transfers.

EXHIBIT 5.4 Downstream Inventory Transfers

TOP COMPANY AND BOTTOM COMPANY
Consolidation Worksheet
For Year Ending December 31, 2018

Investment: Equity Method   *Ownership: 80%*

Accounts	Top Company	Bottom Company	Consolidation Entries Debit	Consolidation Entries Credit	Noncontrolling Interest	Consolidated Totals
Income Statement						
Sales	(600,000)	(300,000)	(TI) 100,000			(800,000)
Cost of goods sold	320,000	180,000	(G) 6,000	(*G) 4,000		402,000
				(TI) 100,000		
Operating expenses	170,000	50,000	(E) 2,500			222,500
Equity in earnings of Bottom	(52,000)		(I) 52,000			–0–
Separate company net income	(162,000)	(70,000)				
Consolidated net income						(175,500)
Net income attributable to noncontrolling interest					(13,500)	13,500
Net income to Top Company						(162,000)
Statement of Retained Earnings						
Retained earnings, 1/1/18						
Top Company	(652,000)					(652,000)
Bottom Company		(310,000)	(S) 310,000			
Net income (above)	(162,000)	(70,000)				(162,000)
Dividends declared	70,000	50,000		(D) 40,000	10,000	70,000
Retained earnings, 12/31/18	(744,000)	(330,000)				(744,000)
Balance Sheet						
Cash and receivables	280,000	120,000		(P) 10,000		390,000
Inventory	220,000	160,000		(G) 6,000		374,000
Investment in Bottom	414,000		(D) 40,000	(I) 52,000		
			(*G) 4,000	(S) 368,000		–0–
				(A) 38,000		
Land	410,000	200,000				610,000
Plant assets (net)	190,000	170,000				360,000
Database			(A) 47,500	(E) 2,500		45,000
Total assets	1,514,000	650,000				1,779,000
Liabilities	(340,000)	(170,000)	(P) 10,000			(500,000)
Noncontrolling interest in Bottom Company, 1/1/18				(S) 92,000		
				(A) 9,500	(101,500)	
Noncontrolling interest in Bottom Company, 12/31/18					(105,000)	(105,000)
Common stock	(430,000)	(150,000)	(S) 150,000			(430,000)
Retained earnings, 12/31/18 (above)	(744,000)	(330,000)				(744,000)
Total liabilities and equities	(1,514,000)	(650,000)	722,000	722,000		(1,779,000)

Note: Parentheses indicate a credit balance.

†Because intra-entity sales are made downstream (by the parent), the subsidiary's adjusted net income is the $70,000 reported less $2,500 excess amortization figure with a 20% allocation to the noncontrolling interest ($13,500).

‡Boxed items highlight differences with upstream transfers examined in Exhibit 5.6.

Consolidation entries:

(*G) Recognition of intra-entity beginning inventory gross profit in current period consolidated net income. Downstream sales are attributed to parent.

(S) Elimination of subsidiary's stockholders' equity accounts along with recognition of the noncontrolling interest as of January 1.

(A) Allocation of excess fair value over subsidiary's book value, unamortized balance as of January 1.

(I) Elimination of intra-entity income remaining after *G elimination.

(D) Elimination of intra-entity dividend.

(E) Recognition of amortization expense for current year on excess fair value allocated to database.

(P) Elimination of intra-entity receivable/payable balances.

(TI) Elimination of intra-entity sales/purchases balances.

(G) Deferral of intra-entity ending inventory gross profit from current period consolidated net income and removal of intra-entity gross profit from ending inventory.

Consolidation Entry *G

Investment in Bottom	4,000	
Cost of Goods Sold		4,000

To remove 2017 intra-entity gross profit in inventory from seller's beginning balance and recognize the gross profit in 2018 following sales to outsiders. Top uses the equity method and intra-entity sales were downstream.

The gross profit rate (Exhibit 5.2) on these items was 25 percent ($20,000 gross profit/$80,000 transfer price), indicating an intra-entity profit of $4,000 (25 percent of the remaining $16,000 in inventory). To recognize this gross profit in 2018, Entry *G reduces Cost of Goods Sold (or the beginning inventory component of that expense) by that amount. The reduction in Cost of Goods Sold creates an increase in current year net income. From a consolidation perspective, the gross profit is correctly recognized in 2018 when the inventory is sold to an outside party. The debit to the Investment in Bottom account becomes part of the sequence of adjustments to bring that account to a zero balance in consolidation.

Consolidation Entry TI

Sales	100,000	
Cost of Goods Sold		100,000

To eliminate current year intra-entity sales/purchases.

Entry TI eliminates the intra-entity sales/purchases for 2018. The entire $100,000 transfer recorded by the two parties during the current period is removed to arrive at consolidated figures for the business combination.

Consolidation Entry G

Cost of Goods Sold	6,000	
Inventory		6,000

To defer intra-entity gross profit in ending inventory.

Entry G defers the intra-entity gross profit remaining in ending inventory at the end of 2018. The $20,000 in transferred merchandise (Exhibit 5.2) that Bottom has not yet sold has a gross profit rate of 30 percent ($30,000 gross profit/$100,000 transfer price); thus, the intra-entity gross profit amounts to $6,000. On the worksheet, Entry G eliminates this overstatement in the Inventory asset balance as well as the ending inventory (credit) component of Cost of Goods Sold. Because the gross profit must be deferred, the increase in this expense appropriately decreases consolidated net income.

Net Income Attributable to the Noncontrolling Interest

In this first illustration, the intra-entity transfers are downstream. Thus, the deferred intra-entity gross profits are considered to relate solely to the parent company, creating no effect on the subsidiary or the outside ownership. For this reason, the noncontrolling interest's share of consolidated net income is unaffected by the downstream intra-entity profit deferral and subsequent recognition. Therefore, Top allocates $13,500 of Bottom's net income to the noncontrolling interest computed as 20 percent of $67,500 ($70,000 reported net income less $2,500 current year database excess fair-value amortization).

By including these entries along with the other routine worksheet eliminations and adjustments, the accounting information generated by Top and Bottom is brought together into a single set of consolidated financial statements. However, this process does more than simply delete intra-entity transfers; it also affects reported net income. A $4,000 gross profit is removed on the worksheet from 2017 figures and subsequently recognized in 2018 (Entry ***G**). A $6,000 gross profit is deferred in a similar fashion from 2018 (Entry **G**) and subsequently recognized in 2019. However, these changes do not affect the noncontrolling interest because the transfers were downstream.

Special Equity Method Procedures for Deferred Intra-Entity Profits from Downstream Transfers

Exhibit 5.3 presents the parent's equity method investment accounting procedures in the presence of deferred intra-entity gross profits resulting from downstream inventory transfers. This application of the equity method differs from that presented in Chapter 1 for a significant influence (typically 20 to 50 percent ownership) investment. For significant influence investments, an investor company defers intra-entity gross profits in inventory only to the extent of its percentage ownership, regardless of whether the profits resulted from upstream or downstream transfers. In contrast, Exhibit 5.3 shows a 100 percent deferral in 2017, with a subsequent 100 percent recognition in 2018, for intra-entity gross profits resulting from Top's inventory transfers to Bottom, its 80 percent–owned subsidiary.

Why the distinction? When control (rather than just significant influence) exists, 100 percent of all intra-entity gross profits are removed from consolidated net income regardless of the direction of the underlying sale.[9] The 100 percent intra-entity profit deferral on Top's books for downstream sales ensures that none of the deferral will be allocated to the noncontrolling interest. As discussed previously, when the parent is the seller in an intra-entity transfer, little justification exists to allocate a portion of the gross profit deferral to the noncontrolling interest. In contrast, for an upstream sale, the subsidiary recognizes the gross profit on its books. Because the noncontrolling interest owns a portion of the subsidiary (but not of the parent), partial allocation of intra-entity gross profit deferrals and subsequent recognitions to the noncontrolling interest is appropriate when resulting from upstream sales.

Upstream Inventory Transfers: Parent Uses the Equity Method

A different set of consolidation procedures is necessary if the intra-entity transfers are upstream from Bottom to Top. As previously discussed, upstream gross profits are attributed to the subsidiary rather than to the parent company. Therefore, had these transfers been upstream, both the $4,000 beginning inventory gross profit recognition (Entry ***G**) and the $6,000 intra-entity gross profit deferral (Entry **G**) would be considered adjustments to Bottom's reported totals.

In contrast to the downstream example in Exhibit 5.3, Exhibit 5.5 includes the intra-entity profit deferrals and subsequent recognitions in the adjustments to Bottom's net income. Because the inventory transfers are upstream from subsidiary to parent, only 80 percent of the profit deferral and subsequent recognition is allocated to the parent's equity earnings and investment account. As a result, the intra-entity profit reallocation across time affects both the subsidiary's reported net income and the noncontrolling interest. Similar to the previous example, the $4,000 intra-entity profit is not eliminated, but simply reallocated across time to the period when it is recognized by the consolidated entity.

To illustrate the effects of upstream inventory transfers, in Exhibit 5.6, we consolidate the financial statements of Top and Bottom again. *The individual records of the two companies are changed from Exhibit 5.4 to reflect the parent's application of the equity method for upstream sales.* This change creates several important differences between Exhibits 5.4 and 5.6.

---

[9] When only significant influence is present, purchasing-related decisions are typically made in conjunction with the interests of other outside owners of the investee. Profits are partially deferred because sales are considered to be partially made to the other outside owners. When control is present, decision making usually rests exclusively with the majority owner, providing little basis for objective profit measurement in the presence of intra-entity sales.

EXHIBIT 5.5
Investment Balances—
Equity Method—Upstream
Sales

Investment in Bottom Company Analysis 1/1/17 to 12/31/18		
Consideration paid (fair value) 1/1/17		$400,000
Bottom Company reported net income for 2017	$30,000	
Database amortization	(2,500)	
Deferred profit from Bottom's 2017 upstream sales	(4,000)	
Bottom Company adjusted 2017 net income	$23,500	
Top's ownership percentage	80%	
Equity in earnings of Bottom Company, 2017		$ 18,800
Top's share of Bottom Company dividends, 2017 (80%)		(16,000)
Balance 12/31/17		$402,800
Bottom Company reported net income for 2018	$70,000	
Database amortization	(2,500)	
Recognized profit from Bottom's 2017 upstream sales	4,000	
Deferred profit from Bottom's 2018 upstream sales	(6,000)	
Bottom Company's adjusted 2018 net income	$65,500	
Top's ownership percentage	80%	
Equity in earnings of Bottom Company, 2018		$ 52,400
Top's share of Bottom Company dividends, 2018 (80%)		(40,000)
Balance 12/31/18		$415,200

Because the intra-entity sales are upstream, the $4,000 beginning intra-entity gross profit (Entry *G) deferral no longer involves a debit to the parent's Investment in Bottom account. Recall that Top and Bottom, as separate legal entities, maintain independent accounting information systems. Thus, when it transferred inventory to Top in 2017, Bottom recorded the transfer as a regular sale even though the counterparty (Top) is a member of the consolidated group. Because $16,000 of these transfers remain in Top's inventory, $4,000 of gross profit (25 percent) is deferred from a consolidated perspective as of January 1, 2018. Also from a consolidated standpoint, Bottom's January 1, 2018, Retained Earnings are overstated by the $4,000 gross profit from the 2017 intra-entity transfers. Thus, Exhibit 5.6 shows a worksheet adjustment that reduces Bottom's January 1, 2018, Retained Earnings balance. Similar to Exhibit 5.4, the credit to Cost of Goods Sold increases consolidated net income to recognize the profit in 2018 from sales to outsiders as follows:

Consolidation Entry *G

Retained earnings—Bottom	4,000	
Cost of Goods Sold		4,000

To remove 2017 intra-entity gross profit in inventory from seller's beginning balance and recognize the gross profit in 2018 following sales to outsiders. Top uses the equity method and intra-entity sales were upstream.

Following this adjustment, Bottom's beginning Retained Earnings on the worksheet becomes $306,000. Reassigning the $4,000 gross profit from 2017 into 2018 dictates the adjustment of the subsidiary's beginning Retained Earnings balance (as the seller of the goods) to $306,000 from the $310,000 found in the company's separate records on the worksheet.

Consolidation Entry S eliminates a portion of the parent's investment account and provides the initial noncontrolling interest balance. This worksheet entry also removes the stockholders equity accounts of the subsidiary as of the beginning of the current year. Thus, the

EXHIBIT 5.6 **Upstream Inventory Transfers**

TOP COMPANY AND BOTTOM COMPANY
Consolidation Worksheet
For Year Ending December 31, 2018

Investment: Equity Method   *Ownership: 80%*

Accounts	Top Company	Bottom Company	Consolidation Entries Debit	Consolidation Entries Credit	Noncontrolling Interest	Consolidated Totals
Income Statement						
Sales	(600,000)	(300,000)	(TI)100,000			(800,000)
Cost of goods sold	320,000	180,000	(G) 6,000	(*G) 4,000		402,000
				(TI)100,000		
Operating expenses	170,000	50,000	(E) 2,500			222,500
Equity in earnings of Bottom	(52,400)		(I) 52,400‡			
Separate company net income	(162,400)	(70,000)				
Consolidated net income						(175,500)
Net income attributable to noncontrolling interest					(13,100)†	13,100
Net income to Top Company						(162,400)
Statement of Retained Earnings						
Retained earnings, 1/1/18						
Top Company	(652,800)					(652,800)
Bottom Company		(310,000)	(*G) 4,000			
			(S) 306,000			
Net income (above)	(162,400)	(70,000)				(162,400)
Dividends declared	70,000	50,000		(D) 40,000	10,000	70,000
Retained earnings, 12/31/18	(745,200)	(330,000)				(745,200)
Balance Sheet						
Cash and receivables	280,000	120,000		(P) 10,000		390,000
Inventory	220,000	160,000		(G) 6,000		374,000
Investment in Bottom	415,200		(D) 40,000	(I) 52,400		–0–
				(S) 364,800		
				(A) 38,000		
Land	410,000	200,000				610,000
Plant assets (net)	190,000	170,000				360,000
Database			(A) 47,500	(E) 2,500		45,000
Total assets	1,515,200	650,000				1,779,000
Liabilities	(340,000)	(170,000)	(P) 10,000			(500,000)
Noncontrolling interest in Bottom Company, 1/1/18				(S) 91,200		
				(A) 9,500	(100,700)	
Noncontrolling interest in Bottom Company, 12/31/18					(103,800)	(103,800)
Common stock	(430,000)	(150,000)	(S) 150,000			(430,000)
Retained earnings, 12/31/18 (above)	(745,200)	(330,000)				(745,200)
Total liabilities and equities	(1,515,200)	(650,000)	718,400	718,400		(1,779,000)

Note: Parentheses indicate a credit balance.

†Because intra-entity sales were upstream, the subsidiary's $70,000 net income is decreased for the $6,000 gross profit deferred into next year and increased for $4,000 gross profit deferred from the previous year. After further reduction for $2,500 excess amortization, the resulting $65,500 provides the noncontrolling interest with a $13,100 allocation (20%).

‡Boxed items highlight differences with downstream transfers examined in Exhibit 5.4. Consolidation entries:

(*G)   Recognition of intra-entity beginning inventory gross profit in current period consolidated net income. Upstream sales are attributed to the subsidiary.

(S   Elimination of adjusted stockholders' equity accounts along with recognition of the noncontrolling interest as of January 1.

(A)   Allocation of excess fair value over subsidiary's book value, unamortized balance as of January 1.

(I)   Elimination of intra-entity income.

(D)   Elimination of intra-entity dividends.

(E)   Recognition of amortization expense for current year on database.

(P)   Elimination of intra-entity receivable/payable balances.

(TI)   Elimination of intra-entity sales/purchases balances.

(G)   Deferral of intra-entity ending inventory gross profit from current period consolidated net income and removal of intra-entity gross profit from ending inventory.

above $4,000 reduction in Bottom's January 1, 2018, Retained Earnings to defer the intra-entity gross profit affects Entry **S.** After posting Entry ***G,** only $306,000 remains as the subsidiary's January 1, 2018, Retained Earnings, which along with Bottom's common stock is eliminated as follows:

Consolidation Entry S

Common Stock—Bottom	150,000	
Retained earnings—Bottom	306,000	
Investment in Bottom		364,800
Noncontrolling Interest		91,200

This combined equity elimination figure ($456,000) above forms the basis for the 20 percent noncontrolling interest ($91,200) and the elimination of the 80 percent parent company investment ($364,800).

In comparing the consolidated totals across Exhibits 5.4 and 5.6, note that consolidated net income, inventory, total assets, and total liabilities and equities are all identical. The sole effect of the direction of the intra-entity inventory transfers (upstream or downstream) resides in the allocation of the temporary income effects of profit deferral and subsequent recognition to the controlling and noncontrolling interests.

Finally, to complete the consolidation, the noncontrolling interest's share of consolidated net income entered on the worksheet is $13,100, computed as follows:

Bottom reported net income, 2018	$70,000
Excess fair-value database amortization ($50,000/20 years)	(2,500)
2017 intra-entity gross profit recognized	4,000
2018 intra-entity gross profit deferred	(6,000)
Bottom 2018 net income adjusted	$65,500
Noncontrolling interest percentage	20%
Net income attributable to the noncontrolling interest, 2018	$13,100

Upstream transfers affect this computation although the downstream sales in the previous example did not. Thus, the noncontrolling interest balance reported previously in the income statement in Exhibit 5.4 differs from the allocation in Exhibit 5.6.

Consolidations—Downstream versus Upstream Transfers

To help clarify the effect of downstream and upstream transfers when the parent uses the equity method, we compare two of the worksheet entries in more detail:

Downstream Transfers		Upstream Transfers	
(Exhibit 5.4)		(Exhibit 5.6)	
Entry *G		**Entry *G**	
Investment in		Retained Earnings,	
Bottom	4,000	1/1/18—Bottom	4,000
Cost of Goods Sold	4,000	Cost of Goods Sold	4,000
To remove 2017 intra-entity gross profit from seller's beginning balance and recognize the gross profit in 2018.		To remove 2017 intra-entity gross profit from seller's beginning balance and recognize the gross profit in 2018.	

Downstream Transfers			Upstream Transfers		
Entry S			**Entry S**		
Common stock—Bottom	150,000		Common stock—Bottom	150,000	
Retained Earnings, 1/1/18—Bottom	310,000		Retaining Earnings, 1/1/18—Bottom (as adjusted)	306,000	
Investment in Bottom (80%)		368,000	Investment in Bottom (80%)		364,800
Noncontrolling interest—1/1/18..... (20%)		92,000	Noncontrolling interest—1/1/18 (20%)		91,200
To remove subsidiary's stockholders' equity accounts and portion of investment balance. Book value at beginning of year is appropriate.			To remove subsidiary's stockholders' equity accounts (as adjusted in Entry *G) and portion of investment balance. Adjusted book value at beginning of year is appropriate.		
Net Income Attributable to the Noncontrolling Interest = $13,500. 20% of Bottom's reported net income less excess database amortization			**Net Income Attributable to the Noncontrolling Interest** = $13,100. 20% of Bottom's net income (after adjustment for intra-entity gross profit in inventory and excess database amortization).		

Effects of Alternative Investment Methods on Consolidation

In Exhibits 5.3 through 5.6 the parent company utilized the equity method. When the parent uses either the initial value or the partial equity method, consolidation procedures normally continue to follow the same patterns analyzed in the previous chapters of this textbook. However, these alternative methods lack the full accrual properties of the equity method. Therefore, an additional worksheet adjustment (*C) is needed to ensure the consolidated financial statements reflect a full accrual GAAP basis. As was the case previously, the worksheet adjustments depend on whether the intra-entity inventories result from downstream or upstream sales.

Using the same example, we now assume the parent applies the **initial value method.** Given that the subsidiary declares and pays dividends of $20,000 in 2017 and $50,000 in 2018, Top records dividend income of $16,000 ($20,000 × 80%) and $40,000 ($50,000 × 80%) during these two years.

Exhibits 5.7 and 5.8 present the worksheets to consolidate these two companies for the year ending December 31, 2018. As in the previous examples, most of the worksheet entries found in Exhibits 5.7 and 5.8 are described and analyzed in previous chapters of this textbook. Additionally, many of the worksheet entries required by intra-entity sales are identical to those used when the parent applies the equity method. Thus, only Consolidation Entries *C and *G are examined in detail separately for downstream intra-entity sales (Exhibit 5.7) and upstream intra-entity sales (Exhibit 5.8).

*Downstream Transfers—Consolidation Entries *C and *G: Parent Uses Initial Value Method*

Consolidation Entry *C is required in periods subsequent to acquisition whenever the parent does not apply the equity method. This adjustment converts the parent's beginning Retained Earnings to a full-accrual consolidated total. In the current illustration, Top did not accrue its portion of the 2017 increase in Bottom's book value [($30,000 net income less $20,000 in dividends) × 80%, or $8,000] or record the $2,000 amortization expense for this same period.

EXHIBIT 5.7 Downstream Inventory Transfers

			Consolidation Entries			
Accounts	**Top Company**	**Bottom Company**	**Debit**	**Credit**	**Noncontrolling Interest**	**Consolidated Totals**

TOP COMPANY AND BOTTOM COMPANY
Consolidation Worksheet
Investment: Initial Value Method   For Year Ending December 31, 2018   *Ownership: 80%*

Accounts	**Top Company**	**Bottom Company**	Debit	Credit	**Noncontrolling Interest**	**Consolidated Totals**
Income Statement						
Sales	(600,000)	(300,000)	(TI)100,000			(800,000)
Cost of goods sold	320,000	180,000	(G) 6,000	(*G) 4,000		402,000
				(TI)100,000		
Operating expenses	170,000	50,000	(E) 2,500			222,500
Dividend income	(40,000)		(I) 40,000			
Separate company net income	(150,000)	(70,000)				
Consolidated net income						(175,500)
Net income attributable to noncontrolling interest					(13,500)†	13,500
Net income to Top Company						(162,000)
Statement of Retained Earnings						
Retained Earnings, 1/1/18						
Top Company	(650,000)		(*G) 4,000	(*C) 6,000		(652,000)
Bottom Company		(310,000)	(S) 310,000‡			
Net income (above)	(150,000)	(70,000)				(162,000)
Dividends declared	70,000	50,000		(I) 40,000	10,000	70,000
Retained earnings, 12/31/18	(730,000)	(330,000)				(744,000)
Balance Sheet						
Cash and receivables	280,000	120,000		(P) 10,000		390,000
Inventory	220,000	160,000		(G) 6,000		374,000
Investment in Bottom	400,000		(*C) 6,000			–0–
				(S) 368,000		
				(A) 38,000		
Land	410,000	200,000				610,000
Plant assets (net)	190,000	170,000				360,000
Database	–0–	–0–	(A) 47,500	(E) 2,500		45,000
Total assets	1,500,000	650,000				1,779,000
Liabilities	(340,000)	(170,000)	(P) 10,000			(500,000)
Noncontrolling interest in Bottom Company, 1/1/18				(S) 92,000		
				(A) 9,500	(101,500)	
Noncontrolling interest in Bottom Company, 12/31/18					105,000	(105,000)
Common stock	(430,000)	(150,000)	(S) 150,000			(430,000)
Retained earnings, 12/31/18 (above)	(730,000)	(330,000)				(744,000)
Total liabilities and equities	(1,500,000)	(650,000)	676,000	676,000		(1,779,000)

Note: Parentheses indicate a credit balance.

†Because intra-entity sales are made downstream (by the parent), the subsidiary's adjusted net income is the $70,000 reported figure less $2,500 excess amortization with a 20% allocation to the noncontrolling interest ($13,500).

‡Boxed items highlight differences with upstream transfers examined in Exhibit 5.8.

Consolidation entries:

(*G)   Recognition of intra-entity beginning inventory gross profit in current period consolidated net income. Downstream sales are attributed to the parent.

(*C)   Recognition of increase in book value and amortization relating to ownership of subsidiary for year prior to the current year.

(S)   Elimination of subsidiary's stockholders' equity accounts along with recognition of the noncontrolling interest as of January 1.

(A)   Allocation of subsidiary's fair value in excess of book value, unamortized balance as of January 1.

(I)   Elimination of intra-entity dividends recorded by parent as dividend income.

(E)   Recognition of amortization expense for current year on database.

(P)   Elimination of intra-entity receivable/payable balances.

(TI)   Elimination of intra-entity sales/purchases balances.

(G)   Deferral of intra-entity ending inventory gross profit from current period consolidated net income and removal of intra-entity gross profit from ending inventory.

EXHIBIT 5.8 Upstream Inventory Transfers

TOP COMPANY AND BOTTOM COMPANY
Consolidation Worksheet

Investment: *Initial Value Method* | For Year Ending December 31, 2018 | *Ownership: 80%*

Accounts	Top Company	Bottom Company	Consolidation Entries Debit	Consolidation Entries Credit	Noncontrolling Interest	Consolidated Totals
Income Statement						
Sales	(600,000)	(300,000)	(TI)100,000			(800,000)
Cost of goods sold	320,000	180,000	(G) 6,000	(*G) 4,000		402,000
				(TI)100,000		
Operating expenses	170,000	50,000	(E) 2,500			222,500
Dividend income	(40,000)		(I) 40,000			
Separate company net income	(150,000)	(70,000)				
Consolidated net income						(175,500)
Net income attributable to noncontrolling interest					(13,100)†	13,100
Net income to Top Company						(162,400)
Statement of Retained Earnings						
Retained earnings, 1/1/18						
Top Company	(650,000)			(*C) 2,800		(652,800)
Bottom Company		(310,000)	(*G) 4,000			
			(S) 306,000‡			
Net income (above)	(150,000)	(70,000)				(162,400)
Dividends declared	70,000	50,000		(I) 40,000	10,000	70,000
Retained earnings, 12/31/18	(730,000)	(330,000)				(745,200)
Balance Sheet						
Cash and receivables	280,000	120,000		(P) 10,000		390,000
Inventory	220,000	160,000		(G) 6,000		374,000
Investment in Bottom	400,000		(*C) 2,800			–0–
				(S) 364,800		
				(A) 38,000		
Land	410,000	200,000				610,000
Plant assets (net)	190,000	170,000				360,000
Database	–0–	–0–	(A) 47,500	(E) 2,500		45,000
Total assets	1,500,000	650,000				1,779,000
Liabilities	(340,000)	(170,000)	(P) 10,000			(500,000)
Noncontrolling interest in Bottom Company, 1/1/18				(S) 91,200		
				(A) 9,500	(100,700)	
Noncontrolling interest in Bottom Company, 12/31/18					(103,800)	(103,800)
Common stock	(430,000)	(150,000)	(S) 150,000			(430,000)
Retained earnings, 12/31/18 (above)	(730,000)	(330,000)				(745,200)
Total liabilities and equities	(1,500,000)	(650,000)	668,800	668,800		(1,779,000)

Note: Parentheses indicate a credit balance.

†Because intra-entity sales were upstream, the subsidiary's $70,000 net income is decreased for the $6,000 gross profit deferred into next year and increased for $4,000 gross profit deferred from the previous year. After further reduction for $2,500 excess amortization, the resulting $65,500 provides the noncontrolling interest with a $13,100 allocation (20%).

‡Boxed items highlight differences with downstream transfers examined in Exhibit 5.7. Consolidation entries:

(*G)   Recognition of intra-entity beginning inventory gross profit in current period consolidated net income. Upstream sales are attributed to the subsidiary.

(*C)   Recognition of increase in book value and amortization relating to ownership of subsidiary for year prior to the current year.

(S)   Elimination of adjusted stockholders' equity accounts along with recognition of the noncontrolling interest as of January 1.

(A)   Allocation of subsidiary's fair value in excess of book value, unamortized balance as of January 1.

(I)   Elimination of intra-entity dividends recorded by parent as dividend income.

(E)   Recognition of amortization expense for current year on fair value allocated to value of database.

(P)   Elimination of intra-entity receivable/payable balances. (TI) Elimination of intra-entity sales/purchases balances.

(G)   Deferral of intra-entity ending inventory gross profit from current period consolidated net income and removal of intra-entity gross profit from ending inventory.

? Discussion Question

WHAT PRICE SHOULD WE CHARGE OURSELVES?

Slagle Corporation is a large manufacturing organization. Over the past several years, it has obtained an important component used in its production process exclusively from Harrison, Inc., a relatively small company in Topeka, Kansas. Harrison charges $90 per unit for this part:

Variable cost per unit	$40
Fixed cost assigned per unit	30
Markup.	20
Total price	$90

In hope of reducing manufacturing costs, Slagle purchases all of Harrison's outstanding common stock. This new subsidiary continues to sell merchandise to a number of outside customers as well as to Slagle. Thus, for internal reporting purposes, Slagle views Harrison as a separate profit center.

A controversy has now arisen among company officials about the amount that Harrison should charge Slagle for each component. The administrator in charge of the subsidiary wants to continue the $90 price. He believes this figure best reflects the division's profitability: "If we are to be judged by our profits, why should we be punished for selling to our own parent company? If that occurs, my figures will look better if I forget Slagle as a customer and try to market my goods solely to outsiders."

In contrast, the vice president in charge of Slagle's production wants the price set at variable cost, total cost, or some derivative of these numbers. "We bought Harrison to bring our costs down. It only makes sense to reduce the transfer price; otherwise the benefits of acquiring this subsidiary are not apparent. I pushed the company to buy Harrison; if our operating results are not improved, I will get the blame."

Will the decision about the transfer price affect consolidated net income? Which method would be easiest for the company's accountant to administer? As the company's accountant, what advice would you give to these officials?

Because the parent recognized neither number in its financial records, the worksheet process adjusts the parent's beginning retained earnings by $6,000 as follows:

Consolidation Entry *C		
Investment in Bottom	6,000	
Retained Earnings—Top		6,000
To convert Top's retained earnings to the accrual basis. Intra-entity sales were downstream and therefore do not affect the adjustment.		

The intra-entity inventory transfers do not affect this entry because they were downstream; the gross profits had no impact on the net income recognized by the subsidiary.

Under the initial value method, the parent makes no entries in its internal financial records to adjust for the intra-entity sales. Because in this case the sales are downstream, the parent's January 1, 2018, Retained Earnings will be overstated from a consolidated view by the intra-entity $4,000 gross profit in beginning inventory recognized from its 2017 intra-entity sales.

Consolidation entry ***G** corrects this overstatement and appropriately recognizes (through the credit to Cost of Goods Sold) the profit in the current year as follows:

Consolidation Entry *G		
Retained Earnings—Top	4,000	
Cost of Goods Sold		4,000
To remove 2017 intra-entity gross profit in inventory from seller's beginning balance and recognize the gross profit in 2018 following sales to outsiders. Top uses the initial value method and intra-entity sales were downstream.		

Note that the above entry *G simply reassigns the intra-entity beginning inventory gross profit from downstream transfers to 2018 from 2017.

Upstream Transfers—Consolidation Entries *C and *G: Parent Uses Initial Value Method

We now change the example by assuming the intra-entity transfers are upstream from Bottom to Top. In this case, the $4,000 intra-entity gross profit remaining in Top's 2017 ending inventory has been recorded by Bottom as part of its 2017 net income and retained earnings. Because $4,000 of Bottom's 2017 net income is deferred until 2018, the increase in the subsidiary's book value in the previous year is only $6,000 rather than $10,000 ($30,000 net income less $20,000 in dividends) as reported. Consequently, conversion to the equity method (Entry ***C**) requires an increase of just $2,800:

$6,000 net increase (after intra-entity profit deferral) in subsidiary's book value during 2017 × 80%	$4,800
2017 amortization expense (80% × $2,500)	(2,000)
Increase in parent's beginning retained earnings (Entry *C)	$2,800

In applying the initial value method in its financial records, the parent did not recognize the increase in subsidiary book value, excess fair-value amortization, or any effects from intra-entity transfers remaining in inventory. The worksheet process thus adjusts the parent's beginning retained earnings by $2,800 as shown here.

Consolidation Entry *C		
Investment in Bottom	2,800	
Retained Earnings—Top		2,800
To convert Top's retained earnings to the accrual basis. Intra-entity sales were upstream.		

In this case the intra-entity inventory transfers affect Consolidation Entry *C because they were downstream; the gross profits directly affected the net income recognized by the subsidiary.

Using the initial value method, the parent makes no entries in its internal financial records to adjust for the intra-entity sales. Because in this case the sales are upstream, the subsidiary's January 1, 2018, Retained Earnings will be overstated from a consolidated view by the intra-entity gross profit in beginning inventory. Consolidation entry *G corrects this overstatement and appropriately recognizes the profit in the current year as follows:

Consolidation Entry *G		
Retained Earnings—Bottom	4,000	
Cost of Goods Sold		4,000
To remove 2017 intra-entity gross profit in inventory from seller's beginning balance and recognize the gross profit in 2018 following sales to outsiders. Top uses the initial value method and intra-entity sales were upstream.		

Note again how the above entry *G simply reassigns the intra-entity beginning inventory gross profit to 2018 from 2017.

Finally, if the parent had applied the **partial equity method** in its internal records, little would change in the consolidation processes previously described for the equity method. The primary change would involve inclusion of a Consolidation Entry *C. Because the parent would have recorded changes in reported subsidiary book value, the *C adjustment would be computed only for (1) previous years' excess fair over book value amortizations and (2) the immediate past year's intra-entity profit deferral.

LO 5-6

Prepare the consolidation entry to defer any gain created by an intra-entity transfer of land from the accounting records of the year of transfer and subsequent years.

Intra-Entity Land Transfers

Although not as prevalent as inventory transactions, intra-entity sales of other assets occur occasionally. The final two sections of this chapter examine the worksheet procedures that noninventory transfers necessitate. We first analyze land transactions and then discuss the effects created by the intra-entity sale of depreciable assets such as buildings and equipment.

Accounting for Land Transactions

The consolidation procedures necessitated by intra-entity land transfers partially parallel those for intra-entity inventory. As with inventory, the sale of land creates a series of effects on the individual records of the two companies. The worksheet process must then adjust the account balances to reflect the perspective of a single economic entity.

By reviewing the sequence of events occurring in an intra-entity land sale, the similarities to inventory transfers can be ascertained as well as the unique features of this transaction.

1. The original seller of the land reports a gain (losses are rare in intra-entity asset transfers), even though the transaction occurred between related parties. At the same time, the acquiring company capitalizes the inflated transfer price rather than the land's historical cost to the business combination.

2. The gain the seller recorded is closed into Retained Earnings at the end of the year. From a consolidated perspective, this account has been artificially increased by a related party. Thus, both the buyer's Land account and the seller's Retained Earnings account continue to contain the intra-entity gain.

3. The gain on the original transfer is recognized in consolidated net income only when the land is subsequently disposed of to an outside party. Therefore, appropriate consolidation techniques must be designed to eliminate the intra-entity gain each period until the time of resale.

Clearly, two characteristics encountered in inventory transfers also exist in intra-entity land transactions: inflated book values and intra-entity gains subsequently culminated through sales to outside parties. Despite these similarities, significant differences exist. Because of the nature of the transaction, the individual companies do not use sales/purchases accounts when land is transferred. Instead, the seller establishes a separate gain account when it removes the land from its books. And because it's an intra-entity gain, the balance must be eliminated when preparing consolidated statements.

In addition, the subsequent resale of land to an outside party does not always occur in the year immediately following the transfer. Although inventory is normally disposed of within a relatively short time, the buyer often holds land for years if not permanently. Thus, the overvalued Land account can remain on the acquiring company's books indefinitely. As long as the land is retained, the effects of the intra-entity gain (the equivalent of Entry *G in inventory transfers) must be eliminated for each subsequent consolidation. By repeating this worksheet entry every year, the consolidated financial statements properly state both the Land and the Retained Earnings accounts.

Eliminating Intra-Entity Gains—Land Transfers

To illustrate these worksheet procedures, assume that Hastings Company and Patrick Company are related parties. On July 1, 2018, Hastings sold land that originally cost $60,000 to Patrick at a $100,000 transfer price. The seller reports a $40,000 gain; the buyer records the land at the $100,000 acquisition price. At the end of this fiscal period, the intra-entity effect of this transaction must be eliminated for consolidation purposes:

Consolidation Entry TL (year of transfer)		
Gain on Sale of Land	40,000	
Land.		40,000
To eliminate effects of intra-entity transfer of land. (Labeled **"TL"** in reference to the transferred land.)		

This worksheet entry eliminates the intra-entity gain from the 2018 consolidated statements and returns the land to its recorded value at date of transfer, for consolidated purposes. However, as with the transfer of inventory, the effects created by the original transaction remain in the financial records of the individual companies for as long as the property is held. The gain recorded by Hastings carries through to Retained Earnings while Patrick's Land account retains the inflated transfer price. *Therefore, for every subsequent consolidation until the land is eventually sold, the elimination process must be repeated.* Including the following entry on each subsequent worksheet removes the intra-entity gain from the asset and from the earnings reported by the combination:

Consolidation Entry *GL (every year following transfer)		
Retained Earnings (beginning balance of seller).	40,000	
Land.		40,000
To eliminate effects of intra-entity transfer of land made in a previous year. (Labeled "***GL**" in reference to the gain on a land transfer occurring in a prior year.)		

Note that the reduction in Retained Earnings is changed to an increase in the Investment in Subsidiary account when the original sale is downstream and the parent has applied the equity method. In that specific situation, equity method adjustments have already corrected the timing of the parent's intra-entity gain. Removing the gain has created a reduction in the Investment account that is appropriately allocated to the subsidiary's Land account on the worksheet. Conversely, if sales were upstream, the Retained Earnings of the seller (the subsidiary) continue to be overstated even if the parent applies the equity method.

One final consolidation concern exists in accounting for intra-entity transfers of land. If the property is ever sold to an outside party, the company making the sale records a gain or loss based on its recorded book value. However, this cost figure is actually the internal transfer price. The gain or loss being recognized is incorrect for consolidation purposes; it has not been computed by comparison to the land's historical cost. Again, the separate financial records fail to reflect the transaction from the perspective of the single economic entity.

Therefore, if the company eventually sells the land, it must recognize the gain deferred at the time of the original transfer. Gain recognition is appropriate once the property is sold to outsiders. On the worksheet, the gain is removed one last time from beginning Retained Earnings (or the investment account, if applicable). In this instance, though, the worksheet entry reclassifies the amount as a recognized gain. Thus, the gain recognition is reallocated from the year of transfer into the fiscal period in which the land is sold to the unrelated party.

Returning to the previous illustration, Hastings acquired land for $60,000 and sold it to Patrick, a related party, for $100,000. Consequently, the $40,000 intra-entity gain was eliminated on the consolidation worksheet in the year of transfer as well as in each succeeding period. However, if this land is subsequently sold to an outside party for $115,000, Patrick recognizes only a $15,000 gain. From the viewpoint of the business combination, the land (having been bought for $60,000) was actually sold at a $55,000 gain. To correct the reporting, the following consolidation entry must be made in the year that the property is sold to the unrelated party. This adjustment increases the $15,000 gain recorded by Patrick to the consolidated balance of $55,000:

Consolidation Entry *GL (year of sale to outside party)		
Retained Earnings (Hastings)	40,000	
Gain on Sale of Land		40,000
To remove intra-entity gain from year of transfer so that total profit can be recognized in the current period when land is sold to an outside party.		

As in the accounting for inventory transfers, the entire consolidation process demonstrated here accomplishes two major objectives:

1. It reports historical cost for the transferred land for as long as it remains within the business combination.
2. It defers income recognition until the land is sold to outside parties.

Recognizing the Effect on Noncontrolling Interest—Land Transfers

The preceding discussion of intra-entity land transfers ignores the possible presence of a noncontrolling interest. In constructing financial statements for an economic entity that includes outside ownership, the guidelines already established for inventory transfers remain applicable.

If the original sale was a *downstream* transaction, neither the annual deferral nor the eventual recognition of the intra-entity gain has any effect on the noncontrolling interest. The rationale for this treatment, as previously indicated, is that profits from downstream transfers relate solely to the parent company.

Conversely, if the transfer is made *upstream,* deferral and recognition of gains are attributed to the subsidiary and, hence, to the noncontrolling interest. As with inventory, all noncontrolling interest balances are computed on the reported earnings of the subsidiary after adjustment for any upstream transfers.

To reiterate, the accounting consequences stemming from land transfers are these:

1. In the year of transfer, any intra-entity gain is deferred and the Land account is reduced to historical cost. When an upstream sale creates the gain, the amount also is excluded in calculating the noncontrolling interest's share of the subsidiary's net income for that year.
2. Each year thereafter, the intra-entity gain will be removed from the seller's beginning Retained Earnings. If the transfer was upstream, eliminating this earlier gain directly affects the balances recorded within both Entry *C (if conversion to the equity method is required) and Entry S. The additional equity accrual (Entry *C, if needed) as well as the elimination of beginning Stockholders' Equity (Entry S) must be based on the newly adjusted balance in the subsidiary's Retained Earnings. This deferral process also has an impact on the noncontrolling interest's share of the subsidiary's net income, but only in the year of transfer and the eventual year of sale.
3. If the land is ever sold to an outside party, the original gain is recognized and reported in consolidated net income.

LO 5-7

Prepare the consolidation entries to remove the effects of upstream and downstream intra-entity fixed asset transfers across affiliated entities.

Intra-Entity Transfer of Depreciable Assets

Just as related parties can transfer inventory and land, the intra-entity sale of a host of other assets is possible. Equipment, patents, franchises, buildings, and other long-lived assets can be involved. Accounting for such intra-entity transactions resembles that demonstrated for land sales. However, the subsequent calculation of depreciation or amortization provides an added challenge in the development of consolidated financial statements.[10]

[10] To avoid redundancy within this analysis, all further references are made to depreciation expense alone, although this discussion is equally applicable to the amortization of intangible assets and the depletion of wasting assets.

Deferral and Subsequent Recognition of Intra-Entity Gains

When faced with intra-entity sales of depreciable assets, financial reporting objectives remain unchanged: *defer intra-entity gains, re-establish historical cost balances, and recognize appropriate income within the consolidated financial statements.* More specifically, we defer gains created by intra-entity transfers until such time as the subsequent use or resale of the asset consummates the original transaction. For inventory sales, the culminating disposal normally occurs currently or in the year following the transfer. In contrast, transferred land may be kept indefinitely, thus deferring the recognition of the intra-entity profit indefinitely.

When depreciable asset sales occur across firms within a consolidated entity, the accounting effects for both the seller and buyer of the depreciable asset must be analyzed in preparing consolidated financial statements. For example, assume a parent company sells a delivery truck to its subsidiary at a transfer price in excess of the parent's carrying amount for the asset. In recording the sale, the parent recognizes a gain on its books. Clearly, this is an intra-entity gain that must be removed in consolidation.

In the subsidiary's financial records, the purchased truck is recorded at the transfer price and subsequently depreciated. However, because of the parent-subsidiary control relationship, no sale of the truck occurred with an outside entity. Consequently, from a consolidated reporting perspective, the carrying amount of the truck account becomes overstated and further results in overstated depreciation expense and accumulated depreciation. The resulting overstatements of the truck, depreciation expense, and accumulated depreciation must also be removed in consolidation.

However, as the subsidiary uses the truck to generate revenues over time, the decline in the truck's future economic benefit can be viewed as an indirect, gradual sale to outsiders. From a consolidated perspective, as the truck is consumed in producing revenues from outsiders, it becomes gradually "sold" and the intra-entity gain can be gradually recognized. Thus, for depreciable asset transfers, the ultimate recognition of any gain on sale typically occurs over a period of several years.

Because of the long-term nature of depreciable assets, so long as the entity owns the asset, the effects of an intra-entity transfer must be accounted for in preparing the consolidated entity's financial statements. In the year of the intra-entity fixed asset transfer, consolidation procedures to remove the intra-entity gain and its effects on the asset, depreciation expense, and accumulated depreciation are relatively straightforward. First, a worksheet entry eliminates the gain and returns the asset and accumulated depreciation accounts to their pre-transfer amounts. Then, a second worksheet entry accordingly reduces the overstated current year depreciation expense and related accumulated depreciation.

In years subsequent to the intra-entity asset transfer, we observe that the gain on sale recognized by the seller has now been closed to Retained Earnings. The overstated depreciation expense also has been closed to the Retained Earnings of the buyer. Consolidation worksheet entries thus reflect the net effect of the gain on sale and the overstated depreciation on the affiliate's separate accounting records. Below we provide an illustration of the consolidated worksheet entries in the year of the intra-entity transfer followed by the year subsequent to the intra-entity transfer.

Depreciable Asset Intra-Entity Transfers Illustrated

To examine the consolidation procedures required by the intra-entity transfer of a depreciable asset, assume that Able Company sells equipment to Baker Company at the current market value of $90,000. Able originally acquired the equipment for $100,000 several years ago; since that time, it has recorded $40,000 in accumulated depreciation. The transfer is made on January 1, 2017, when the equipment has a 10-year remaining life.[11]

---

[11] Although this example assumes an intra-entity gain on sale, intra-entity losses may occur as well. If the loss cannot be attributed to an asset impairment, then parallel consolidation procedures to those provided in the example, reflecting a loss, would be appropriate.

Year of Intra-Entity Transfer

The 2017 effects on the separate financial accounts of the two companies can be quickly enumerated:

1. Baker, as the buyer, enters the equipment into its records at the $90,000 transfer price. However, from a consolidated view the asset has not been sold, and therefore the $60,000 book value ($100,000 cost less $40,000 accumulated depreciation) remains appropriate.

2. Able, as the seller, reports a $30,000 gain, although the consolidated entity has not yet sold the asset to outsiders. After preparation of the 12/31/17 consolidated financial statements, Able then closes this gain to its Retained Earnings account.

3. Assuming application of the straight-line depreciation method with no salvage value, Baker records expense of $9,000 at the end of 2017 ($90,000 transfer price/10 years). The proper depreciation expense for consolidation, however, is based on the asset's carrying amount to the consolidated entity at the date of the intra-entity transfer. Consolidated depreciation expense for this asset would thus be $6,000 ($60,000 carrying amount/10 remaining years). This requires a $3,000 consolidated worksheet adjustment to depreciation expense.

To report these events as seen by the consolidated entity, we first acknowledge that an asset write-up cannot be recognized based on an intra-entity transfer. A consolidated worksheet entry must therefore return the asset to its pre-transfer carrying amount based on historical cost. Moreover, both the $30,000 intra-entity gain and the $3,000 overstatement in depreciation expense must be eliminated on the worksheet. The two consolidation entries for 2017 are shown below:

Consolidation Entry TA (year of transfer)[12]		
Gain on Sale of Equipment	30,000	
Equipment	10,000	
Accumulated Depreciation		40,000
To remove intra-entity gain and return equipment accounts to balances based on original historical cost. (Labeled **"TA"** in reference to transferred asset.)		

Consolidation Entry ED (year of transfer)		
Accumulated Depreciation	3,000	
Depreciation Expense		3,000
To eliminate overstatement of depreciation expense caused by inflated transfer price. (Labeled **"ED"** in reference to excess depreciation.) *Entry must be repeated for all 10 years of the equipment's remaining life.*		

From the viewpoint of a single consolidated entity, these entries accomplish several objectives:

- Reinstate the asset's historical cost of $100,000.
- Return the January 1, 2017, book value to the appropriate $60,000 figure by recognizing accumulated depreciation of $40,000.
- Eliminate the $30,000 intra-entity gain recorded by Able so the amount does not appear in the consolidated income statement.

---

[12] If the worksheet uses only one account for a net depreciated asset, this entry would have been

Gain on sale	30,000	
Equipment (net)		30,000
To reduce the $90,000 to original $60,000 book value at date of transfer rather than reinstating original balances.		

- Reduce depreciation for the year from $9,000 to $6,000, the appropriate expense based on pre-transfer carrying amount of the asset.
- Although the gain is eliminated, the credit to depreciation expense increases consolidated net income serving as a partial recognition of the gain for 2017.

Over the remaining life of the asset, consolidation entries serve to reallocate the gain from the year of transfer to each of the 10 years following the transfer as the asset is consumed in the production process. Recall that for intra-entity gross profit in ending inventory, the ultimate recognition of the profit deferral was achieved on the consolidated worksheet through a credit to *cost of goods sold.* In a parallel fashion, deferred intra-entity profits on depreciable asset transfers are achieved on the consolidated worksheet through a credit to *depreciation expense.*

In the year of the intra-entity depreciable asset transfer, the preceding consolidation entries **TA** and **ED** are applicable regardless of whether the transfer was upstream or downstream. They are likewise applicable regardless of whether the parent applies the equity method, initial value method, or partial equity method of accounting for its investment. As discussed subsequently, however, in the years following the intra-entity transfer, we make a slight modification to consolidation entry ***TA** for downstream transfers when the equity method is applied.

Years Following the Intra-Entity Transfer

Again, the preceding worksheet entries do not actually remove the effects of the intra-entity transfer from the individual records of these two organizations. Both the intra-entity gain and the excess depreciation expense remain on the separate books and are closed into Retained Earnings of the respective companies at year-end. Similarly, the Equipment account with the related Accumulated Depreciation continues to hold balances based on the transfer price, not historical cost. *Thus, for every subsequent period, the separately reported figures must be adjusted on the worksheet to present the consolidated totals from a single entity's perspective.*

To derive worksheet entries at any future point, the balances in the accounts of the individual companies must be ascertained and compared to the figures appropriate for the consolidated entity. As an illustration, the separate records of Able and Baker two years after the transfer (December 31, 2018) follow. Consolidated totals are calculated based on the original historical cost of $100,000 and accumulated depreciation of $40,000.

Account	Individual Records	Consolidated Perspective	Worksheet Adjustments
Equipment 12/31/18	$90,000	$100,000	$10,000
Accumulated Depreciation 12/31/18	(18,000)	(52,000)*	(34,000)
Depreciation Expense for 2018	9,000	6,000	(3,000)
1/1/18 Retained Earnings effect	(21,000)†	6,000	27,000

Note: Parentheses indicate a credit balance.
*Accumulated depreciation before transfer $(40,000) plus 2 years × $(6,000). †Intra-entity transfer gain ($30,000) less one year's depreciation of $9,000.

Because the intra-entity transfer's effects remain in the separate financial records, the various accounts must be adjusted in each subsequent consolidation. Moreover, the amounts involved must be updated every period because of the continual impact of depreciation recorded by the buyer. Continuing our example, to adjust the individual figures to the consolidated totals derived above, the 2018 worksheet includes the following entries:

Consolidation Entry *TA (year following transfer)		
Equipment	10,000	
Retained Earnings, 1/1/18 (Able)	27,000	
Accumulated Depreciation		37,000
To return the Equipment account to original historical cost and adjust the 1/1/18 balances of Retained Earnings and Accumulated Depreciation.		

Consolidation Entry ED (year following transfer)		
Accumulated Depreciation	3,000	
Depreciation Expense		3,000
To remove excess depreciation expense on the intra-entity transfer price and adjust Accumulated Depreciation to its 12/31/18 consolidated balance.		
Note that the $34,000 increase in 12/31/18 consolidated Accumulated Depreciation results from a $37,000 credit in Entry ***TA** and a $3,000 debit in Entry **ED.**		

We observe that in consolidation entry ***TA,** $27,000 of the original intra-entity gain on sale is removed from Retained Earnings. Then, in consolidation entry **ED,** the $3,000 credit to Depreciation Expense serves to increase consolidated net income by $3,000. Essentially, the remaining intra-entity gain as of the beginning of the year is removed from Retained Earnings and partially recognized as a current year increase in consolidated net income (via the decrease in depreciation expense).[13]

The ***TA** adjustment to the Equipment account remains constant over the life of the asset. However, the ***TA** adjustments to beginning Retained Earnings and Accumulated Depreciation vary with each succeeding consolidation. At December 31, 2017, the individual companies closed out both the intra-entity gain of $30,000 and $9,000 depreciation expense on their books. *Importantly, the $9,000 depreciation expense was overstated by $3,000 from a consolidated perspective.* Therefore, as reflected in Entry ***TA,** the beginning Retained Earnings account for the 2018 consolidation is overstated by a net amount of only $27,000 rather than $30,000. *Over the life of the asset, the intra-entity gain in consolidated retained earnings will be systematically reduced to zero as excess depreciation expense ($3,000) is closed out each year on the books of the company that possesses the asset.* Hence, on subsequent consolidation worksheets, the beginning Retained Earnings account decreases by this amount: $27,000 in 2018, $24,000 in 2019, $21,000 in the following period, and so on. This reduction continues until, at the end of 10 years, the intra-entity gain has been completely recognized in the consolidation process.

Similarly, the change in beginning Accumulated Depreciation varies with each succeeding consolidation. At December 31, 2017, the buyer recorded a $3,000 overstatement of depreciation expense and Accumulated Depreciation. Therefore, as reflected in Entry ***TA,** the Accumulated Depreciation account at the beginning of 2018 is undervalued by a net amount of only $37,000 rather than $40,000.

If this equipment is ever resold to an outside party, the remaining portion of the gain is immediately recognized by the consolidated entity. As in the previous discussion of land, the remaining intra-entity profit existing at the date of resale must be recognized on the consolidated income statement to arrive at the appropriate amount of gain or loss on the sale.

Years Following Downstream Intra-Entity Depreciable Asset Transfers—Parent Uses Equity Method

Consolidation entry ***TA** requires a slight modification when the intra-entity depreciable asset transfer is downstream and the parent uses the equity method. In applying the equity method, the parent adjusts its book income for both the original transfer gain and periodic depreciation expense adjustments. Thus, in downstream intra-entity transfers when the equity method is used, from a consolidated view, the parent's Retained Earnings balance has been already reduced for the gain. Therefore, continuing with the previous example, the following worksheet consolidation entries would be made for a downstream sale assuming that (1) Able is the parent and (2) Able has applied the equity method to account for its investment in Baker.

---

[13] Alternatively, because the straight line method is used, the depreciation expense adjustment can also be computed as the original gain on sale divided by the remaining life of the transferred asset ($30,000/10 years).

Consolidation Entry *TA (year following transfer)

Equipment	10,000	
Investment in Baker	27,000	
Accumulated Depreciation		37,000

Consolidation Entry ED (year following transfer)

Accumulated Depreciation	3,000	
Depreciation Expense		3,000

In Entry ***TA,** note that the Investment in Baker account replaces the parent's Retained Earnings. This temporary increase to the Investment account then effectively allocates the adjustments necessitated by the intra-entity transfer to the appropriate subsidiary Equipment and Accumulated Depreciation accounts.

Effect on Noncontrolling Interest—Depreciable Asset Transfers

Because of the lack of official guidance, no easy answer exists as to the assignment of any income effects created within the consolidation process. Consistent with the previous sections of this chapter, all income is assigned here to the original seller. In Entry ***TA,** for example, the beginning Retained Earnings account of Able (the seller) is reduced. Both the intra-entity gain on the transfer and the excess depreciation expense subsequently recognized are assigned to that party.

Thus, again, downstream sales are assumed to have no effect on any noncontrolling interest values. The parent rather than the subsidiary made the sale. Conversely, the impact on net income created by upstream sales must be considered in computing the balances attributed to these outside owners. Currently, this approach is one of many acceptable alternatives. However, in its future deliberations on consolidation policies and procedures, the FASB could mandate a specific allocation pattern.

Summary

1. The transfer of assets, especially inventory, between the members of a consolidated entity is a common practice. In producing consolidated financial statements, any effects on the separate accounting records created by such transfers must be removed because the transactions did not occur with an outside unrelated party.

2. Inventory transfers are the most prevalent form of intra-entity asset transaction. Despite being only a transfer, one company records a sale while the other reports a purchase. These balances are reciprocals that must be offset on the worksheet in the process of producing consolidated figures.

3. Additional accounting problems result if inventory is transferred at a markup. Any portion of the merchandise still held at year-end is valued at more than historical cost because of the inflation in price. Furthermore, the gross profit that the seller reports on these goods must be deferred from a consolidation perspective. Thus, this gross profit must be removed from the ending Inventory account, a figure that appears as an asset on the balance sheet and as a negative component within cost of goods sold.

4. Intra-entity inventory gross profits in ending inventory also create a consolidation problem in the year following the transfer. Within the separate accounting systems, the seller closes the gross profit to Retained Earnings. The buyer's ending Inventory balance becomes the next period's beginning balance (within Cost of Goods Sold). Therefore, the inflation must be removed again but this time in the subsequent year. The seller's beginning Retained Earnings is decreased to eliminate the intra-entity gross profit while Cost of Goods Sold is reduced to remove the overstatement from the beginning inventory component. However, when the parent applies the equity method and sales are downstream, the parent's Retained Earnings are correctly stated from a consolidated view. Therefore, in this case, the Investment in Subsidiary account is used in the beginning intra-entity inventory profit adjustment, instead of the parent's Retained Earnings. Through this process, the intra-entity profit is deferred from the year of transfer so that recognition can be made at the point of disposal or consumption.

5. The deferral and subsequent recognition of intra-entity gross profits raise a question concerning the measurement of noncontrolling interest balances: Does the change in the period of recognition alter these calculations? Although the issue is currently under debate, no formal answer to this question is yet found in official accounting pronouncements. In this textbook, the deferral of profits from upstream transfers (from subsidiary to parent) is assumed to affect the noncontrolling interest whereas downstream transactions (from parent to subsidiary) do not. When upstream transfers are involved, noncontrolling interest values are based on the gross profit recognized after adjustment for any intra-entity gross profit remaining in inventory.

6. Inventory is not the only asset that can be transferred between the members of a consolidated entity. For example, transfers of land sometimes occur. Again, if the transfer price exceeds original cost, the buyer's records state the asset at an inflated value while the seller recognizes an intra-entity gain. As with inventory, the consolidation process must return the asset's recorded balance to cost while deferring the gain. Repetition of this procedure is necessary in every consolidation for as long as the land remains within the consolidated entity.

7. The consolidation process required by the intra-entity transfer of depreciable assets differs somewhat from that demonstrated for inventory and land. The intra-entity gain created by the transaction must still be deferred along with an adjustment for the asset's overstatement. However, because of subsequent depreciation, these adjustments systematically change from period to period. Additionally, because the excess depreciation is closed annually to Retained Earnings, the overstatement of the equity account resulting from the intra-entity gain is constantly reduced. To produce consolidated figures at any point in time, the remaining overstatement in these figures (as well as in the current depreciation expense) must be determined and removed. Overall, the intra-entity gain is removed from the year of the depreciable asset transfer and subsequently recognized over the remaining life of the asset. Consolidation worksheet entries that serve to reduce depreciation expense become the vehicle for recognizing the annual portion of the intra-entity gain.

Comprehensive Illustration

Problem

(*Estimated Time: 45 to 65 Minutes*) On January 1, 2016, Daisy Company acquired 80 percent of Rose Company for $594,000 in cash. Rose's total book value on that date was $610,000 and the fair value of the noncontrolling interest was $148,500. The newly acquired subsidiary possessed a trademark (10-year remaining life) that, although unrecorded on Rose's accounting records, had a fair value of $75,000. Any remaining excess acquisition-date fair value was attributed to goodwill.

Daisy decided to acquire Rose so that the subsidiary could furnish component parts for the parent's production process. During the ensuing years, Rose sold inventory to Daisy as follows:

Year	Cost to Rose Company	Transfer Price	Gross Profit Rate	Transferred Inventory Still Held at End of Year (at transfer price)
2016	$100,000	$140,000	28.6%	$20,000
2017	100,000	150,000	33.3	30,000
2018	120,000	160,000	25.0	68,000

Any transferred merchandise that Daisy retained at year-end was always put into production during the following period.

On January 1, 2017, Daisy sold Rose several pieces of equipment that had a 10-year remaining life and were being depreciated on the straight-line method with no salvage value. This equipment was transferred at an $80,000 price, although it had an original $100,000 cost to Daisy and a $44,000 book value at the date of exchange.

On January 1, 2018, Daisy sold land to Rose for $50,000, its fair value at that date. The original cost had been only $22,000. By the end of 2018, Rose had made no payment for the land.

The following separate financial statements are for Daisy and Rose as of December 31, 2018. Daisy has applied the equity method to account for this investment.

	Daisy Company	Rose Company
Sales	$ (900,000)	$ (500,000)
Cost of goods sold	598,000	300,000
Operating expenses.	210,000	80,000
Gain on sale of land	(28,000)	–0–
Equity in earnings of Rose Company	(60,000)	–0–
Net income.	$ (180,000)	$ (120,000)
Retained earnings, 1/1/18.	$ (620,000)	$ (430,000)
Net income.	(180,000)	(120,000)
Dividends declared.	55,000	50,000
Retained earnings, 12/31/18	$ (745,000)	$ (500,000)
Cash and accounts receivable	$ 348,000	$ 410,000
Inventory.	430,400	190,000
Investment in Rose Company.	737,600	–0–
Land.	454,000	280,000
Equipment	270,000	190,000
Accumulated depreciation	(180,000)	(50,000)
Total assets	$ 2,060,000	$ 1,020,000
Liabilities.	(715,000)	(120,000)
Common stock	(600,000)	(400,000)
Retained earnings, 12/31/18	(745,000)	(500,000)
Total liabilities and equities.	$ (2,060,000)	$(1,020,000)

Required

Answer the following questions:

a. By how much did Rose's book value increase during the period from January 1, 2016, through December 31, 2017?

b. During the initial years after the takeover, what annual amortization expense was recognized in connection with the acquisition-date excess of fair value over book value?

c. What amount of intra-entity gross profit exists within the parent's inventory figures at the beginning and at the end of 2018?

d. Equipment has been transferred between the companies. What amount of additional depreciation is recognized in 2018 because of this transfer?

e. The parent reports Income of Rose Company of $60,000 for 2018. How was this figure calculated?

f. Without using a worksheet, determine consolidated totals.

g. Prepare the December 31, 2018, worksheet entries required by the transfers of inventory, land, and equipment.

Solution

a. The subsidiary's acquisition-date book value is given as $610,000. At the beginning of 2018, the company's common stock and retained earnings total is $830,000 ($400,000 and $430,000, respectively). In the previous years, Rose's book value has apparently increased by $220,000 ($830,000 − $610,000).

b. To determine amortization, an allocation of Daisy's acquisition-date fair value must first be made. The $75,000 allocation needed to show Daisy's equipment at fair value leads to additional annual expense of $7,500 for the initial years of the combination. The $57,500 assigned to goodwill is not subject to amortization.

Acquisition-Date Fair-Value Allocation and Excess Amortization Schedule

Consideration paid by Daisy for 80% of Rose.	$ 594,000
Noncontrolling interest (20%) fair value	148,500
Rose's fair value at acquisition date	$ 742,500
Book value of Rose Company	(610,000)
Excess fair value over book value.	$ 132,500

		Remaining Life (Years)	Annual Excess Amortizations	Excess Amortizations 2016–2018	Unamortized Balance, 12/31/18
Trademark	$ 75,000	10	$ 7,500	$ 22,500	$52,500
Goodwill	57,500	indefinite	–0–	–0–	57,500
Totals.........	$132,500		$ 7,500	$ 22,500	

c. Of the inventory transferred to Daisy during 2017, $30,000 is still held at the beginning of 2018. This merchandise contains an intra-entity gross profit of $10,000 ($30,000 × 33.3% gross profit rate for that year). At year-end, $17,000 ($68,000 remaining inventory × 25% gross profit rate) remains as intra-entity gross profit in the ending inventory.

d. Additional depreciation for the net addition of 2018 is $3,600. Equipment with a book value of $44,000 was transferred at a price of $80,000. The net of $36,000 to this asset's account balances would be written off over 10 years for an extra $3,600 per year during the consolidation process.

e. According to the separate statements given, the subsidiary reports net income of $120,000. However, in determining the net income allocation between the parent and the noncontrolling interest, this reported figure must be adjusted for the effects of *any upstream transfers*. Because Rose sold the inventory upstream to Daisy, the $10,000 gross profit deferred in requirement (c) from 2017 into the current period is attributed to the subsidiary (as the seller). Likewise, the $17,000 intra-entity gross profit at year-end is viewed as a reduction in Rose's net income.

All other transfers are downstream and not considered to have an effect on the subsidiary. Therefore, the Equity in earnings of Rose Company balance can be verified as follows:

Company's reported net income—2018	$120,000
Recognition of 2017 intra-entity gross profit........................	10,000
Deferral of 2018 intra-entity gross profit	(17,000)
Excess amortization expense—2018 (see requirement [b])	(7,500)
Recognized subsidiary net income from consolidated perspective	105,500
Parent's ownership percentage......................................	80%
Equity income before downstream transfer effects	$ 84,400
Adjustments attributed to parent's ownership......................	
Deferral of intra-entity gain—land	(28,000)
Removal of excess depreciation (see requirement [d])	3,600
Equity in earnings of Rose Company—2018.........................	$ 60,000

f. Each of the 2018 consolidated totals for this business combination can be determined as follows:

Sales = $1,240,000. The parent's balance is added to the subsidiary's balance less the $160,000 in intra-entity transfers for the period.

Cost of Goods Sold = $745,000. The computation begins by adding the parent's balance to the subsidiary's balance less the $160,000 in intra-entity transfers for the period. The $10,000 intra-entity gross profit in inventory from the previous year is deducted to recognize this income currently. Next, the $17,000 ending intra-entity gross profit is added to cost of goods sold to defer the income until a later year when the goods are sold to an outside party.

Operating Expenses =$293,900. The parent's balance is added to the subsidiary's balance. Annual excess fair-value amortization of $7,500 [see requirement (b)] is also included. Excess depreciation of $3,600 resulting from the transfer of equipment [see requirement (e)] is removed.

Gain on Sale of Land = 0. This amount is eliminated for consolidation purposes because the transaction was intra-entity.

Equity in Earnings of Rose Company = 0. The equity earnings figure is removed and replaced with the subsidiary's actual revenues and expenses in the consolidated financial statements.

Net Income Attributable to Noncontrolling Interest = $21,100. Requirement (e) shows the subsidiary's net income from a consolidated perspective as $105,500 after adjustments for intra-entity upstream gains and excess fair-value amortization. Because outsiders hold 20 percent of the subsidiary, a $21,100 allocation ($105,500 × 20%) is made.

Consolidated Net Income = $201,100 computed as Sales less Cost of Goods Sold and Operating Expenses. The consolidated net income is then distributed: $21,100 to the noncontrolling interest and $180,000 to the parent company owners.

Retained Earnings, 1/1/18 = $620,000. The equity method has been applied; therefore, the parent's balance equals the consolidated total.

Dividends Declared = $55,000. Only the parent's dividends are shown in the consolidated statements. Distributions from the subsidiary to the parent are eliminated as intra-entity transfers. Any dividends distributable to the noncontrolling interest reduce the ending balance attributed to these outside owners.

Cash and Accounts Receivable = $708,000. The two balances are added after removal of the $50,000 intra-entity receivable created by the transfer of land.

Inventory = $603,400. The two balances are added after removal of the $17,000 ending intra-entity gross profit [see requirement (c)].

Investment in Rose Company = 0. The investment balance is eliminated and replaced with actual assets and liabilities of the subsidiary.

Land = $706,000. The two balances are added. The $28,000 intra-entity gain created by the transfer is removed.

Equipment = $480,000. The two balances are added. Because of the intra-entity transfer, $20,000 must also be included to adjust the $80,000 transfer price to the original $100,000 cost of the asset.

Accumulated Depreciation = $278,800. The balances are combined and adjusted for $52,400 to reinstate the historical balance for the equipment transferred across affiliates ($56,000 written off at date of transfer less $3,600 for the previous year's depreciation on the intra-entity gain). Then, an additional $3,600 is removed for the current year's depreciation on the intra-entity gain.

Trademark = $52,500. The amount from the original $75,000 acquisition-date excess fair-value allocation less three years' amortization at $7,500 per year.

Goodwill = $57,500. The amount from the original allocation of Rose's acquisition-date fair value.

Total Assets = $2,328,600. This figure is a summation of the preceding consolidated assets.

Liabilities = $785,000. The two balances are added after removal of the $50,000 intra-entity payable created by the transfer of land.

Noncontrolling Interest in Subsidiary, 12/31/18 = $198,600. This figure is composed of several different balances:

Rose 20% book value (adjusted for upstream intra-entity profits) at 1/1/18 . .	$164,000
20% of 1/1/18 unamortized excess fair-value allocation for Rose's net identifiable assets and goodwill ($117,500 × 20%).	23,500
Noncontrolling interest at 1/1/18.	$187,500
2018 Rose net income allocation	21,100
Noncontrolling interest share of Rose dividends	(10,000)
December 31, 2018, balance	$198,600

Common Stock = $600,000. Only the parent company balance is reported within the consolidated statements.

Retained Earnings, 12/31/18 = $745,000. The retained earnings amount is found by adding the parent's (Daisy) share of consolidated net income to the beginning Retained Earnings balance and then subtracting the parent's dividends. All of these figures have been computed previously.

Total Liabilities and Equities = $2,328,600. This figure is the summation of all consolidated liabilities and equities.

g.

**Consolidation Worksheet Entries
to Adjust for Intra-Entity Transfers
December 31, 2018**

Inventory

Entry *G

Retained Earnings, 1/1/18—Subsidiary	10,000	
Cost of Goods Sold		10,000

To remove 2017 intra-entity gross profit from beginning balances of the current year. Because transfers were upstream, retained earnings of the subsidiary (as the original seller) are reduced. Balance is computed in requirement (c).

(continued)

**Consolidation Worksheet Entries
to Adjust for Intra-Entity Transfers
December 31, 2018**

Entry TI

Sales...	160,000	
Cost of Goods Sold...		160,000
To eliminate current year intra-entity transfer of inventory.		

Entry G

Cost of Goods Sold..	17,000	
Inventory...		17,000
To remove 2018 intra-entity gross profit from ending accounts of the current year. Balance is computed in requirement (c).		

Land

Entry TL

Gain on Sale of Land..	28,000	
Land...		28,000
To eliminate gross profit created on first day of current year by an intra-entity transfer of land.		

Equipment

Entry *TA

Equipment..	20,000	
Investment in Rose Company.......................................	32,400	
Accumulated Depreciation.......................................		52,400
To remove remaining gain (as of January 1, 2018) created by intra-entity transfer of equipment and to adjust equipment and accumulated depreciation to historical cost figures.		

Equipment is increased from the $80,000 transfer price to $100,000 cost.

    Accumulated depreciation of $56,000 was eliminated at time of transfer. Excess depreciation of $3,600 per year has been recorded for the prior year ($3,600); thus, the accumulated depreciation is now only $52,400 less than the cost-based figure.

    The intra-entity gain on the transfer was $36,000 ($80,000 less $44,000). That figure has now been reduced by one year of excess depreciation ($3,600). Because the parent used the equity method and this transfer was downstream, the adjustment here is to the investment account rather than the parent's beginning Retained Earnings.

Entry ED

Accumulated Depreciation......................................	3,600	
Operating Expenses (depreciation)...........................		3,600
To eliminate the current year overstatement of depreciation created by inflated transfer price.		

Questions

1. Intra-entity transfers between the component companies of a business combination are quite common. Why do these intra-entity transactions occur so frequently?

2. Barker Company owns 80 percent of the outstanding voting stock of Walden Company. During the current year, intra-entity sales amount to $100,000. These transactions were made with a gross profit rate of 40 percent of the transfer price. In consolidating the two companies, what amount of these sales would be eliminated?

3. Padlock Corp. owns 90 percent of Safeco, Inc. During the year, Padlock sold 3,000 locking mechanisms to Safeco for $900,000. By the end of the year, Safeco had sold all but 500 of the locking mechanisms to outside parties. Padlock marks up the cost of its locking mechanisms by 60 percent in computing its sales price to affiliated and nonaffiliated customers. How much intra-entity profit remains in Safeco's inventory at year-end?

4. How are intra-entity inventory gross profits created, and what consolidation entries does the presence of these gross profits necessitate?

5. James, Inc., sells inventory to Matthews Company, a related party, at James's standard gross profit rate. At the current fiscal year-end, Matthews still holds some portion of this inventory. If consolidated financial statements are prepared, why are worksheet entries required in two different fiscal periods?

6. How do intra-entity profits present in any year affect the noncontrolling interest calculations?

7. A worksheet is being developed to consolidate Allegan, Incorporated, and Stark Company. These two organizations have made considerable intra-entity transactions. How would the consolidation process be affected if these transfers were downstream? How would consolidated financial statements be affected if these transfers were upstream?

8. King Company owns a 90 percent interest in the outstanding voting shares of Pawn Company. No excess fair-value amortization resulted from the acquisition. Pawn reports a net income of $110,000 for the current year. Intra-entity sales occur at regular intervals between the two companies. Intra-entity gross profits of $30,000 were present in the beginning inventory balances, whereas $60,000 in similar gross profits were recorded at year-end. What is the noncontrolling interest's share of consolidated net income?

9. When a subsidiary sells inventory to a parent, the intra-entity profit is removed from the subsidiary's net income for consolidation and reduces the income allocation to the noncontrolling interest. Is the profit permanently eliminated from the noncontrolling interest, or is it merely shifted from one period to the next? Explain.

10. The consolidation process applicable when intra-entity land transfers have occurred differs somewhat from that used for intra-entity inventory sales. What differences should be noted?

11. A subsidiary sells land to the parent company at a significant gain. The parent holds the land for two years and then sells it to an outside party, also for a gain. How does the business combination account for these events?

12. Why does an intra-entity sale of a depreciable asset (such as equipment or a building) require subsequent adjustments to depreciation expense within the consolidation process?

13. If a seller makes an intra-entity sale of a depreciable asset at a price above book value, the seller's beginning Retained Earnings is reduced when preparing each subsequent consolidation. Why does the amount of the adjustment change from year to year?

Problems

LO 5-1

1. What is the primary reason we defer financial statement recognition of gross profits on intra-entity sales for goods that remain within the consolidated entity at year-end?
   a. Revenues and COGS must be recognized for all intra-entity sales regardless of whether the sales are upstream or downstream.
   b. Intra-entity sales result in gross profit overstatements regardless of amounts remaining in ending inventory.
   c. Gross profits must be deferred indefinitely because sales among affiliates always remain in the consolidated group.
   d. When intra-entity sales remain in ending inventory, control of the goods has not changed.

LO 5-3

2. James Corporation owns 80 percent of Carl Corporation's common stock. During October, Carl sold merchandise to James for $250,000. At December 31, 40 percent of this merchandise remains in James's inventory. Gross profit percentages were 20 percent for James and 30 percent for Carl. The amount of intra-entity gross profit in inventory at December 31 that should be eliminated in the consolidation process is
   a. $24,000
   b. $30,000
   c. $20,000
   d. $75,000

LO 5-5

3. In computing the noncontrolling interest's share of consolidated net income, how should the subsidiary's net income be adjusted for intra-entity transfers?
   a. The subsidiary's reported net income is adjusted for the impact of upstream transfers prior to computing the noncontrolling interest's allocation.
   b. The subsidiary's reported net income is adjusted for the impact of all transfers prior to computing the noncontrolling interest's allocation.
   c. The subsidiary's reported net income is not adjusted for the impact of transfers prior to computing the noncontrolling interest's allocation.
   d. The subsidiary's reported net income is adjusted for the impact of downstream transfers prior to computing the noncontrolling interest's allocation.

LO 5-2, 5-3

4. Parkette, Inc., acquired a 60 percent interest in Skybox Company several years ago. During 2017, Skybox sold inventory costing $160,000 to Parkette for $200,000. A total of 18 percent of this inventory was not sold to outsiders until 2018. During 2018, Skybox sold inventory costing $297,500 to Parkette for $350,000. A total of 30 percent of this inventory was not sold to outsiders until 2019. In 2018, Parkette reported cost of goods sold of $607,500 while Skybox reported $450,000. What is the consolidated cost of goods sold in 2018?

   a. $698,950
   b. $720,000
   c. $1,066,050
   d. $716,050

LO 5-2, 5-3

5. Top Company holds 90 percent of Bottom Company's common stock. In the current year, Top reports sales of $800,000 and cost of goods sold of $600,000. For this same period, Bottom has sales of $300,000 and cost of goods sold of $180,000. During the current year, Top sold merchandise to Bottom for $100,000. The subsidiary still possesses 40 percent of this inventory at the current year-end. Top had established the transfer price based on its normal gross profit rate. What are the consolidated sales and cost of goods sold?

   a. $1,000,000 and $690,000
   b. $1,000,000 and $705,000
   c. $1,000,000 and $740,000
   d. $970,000 and $696,000

LO 5-2, 5-3, 5-5

6. Use the same information as in problem (5) except assume that the transfers were from Bottom Company to Top Company. What are the consolidated sales and cost of goods sold?

   a. $1,000,000 and $720,000
   b. $1,000,000 and $755,000
   c. $1,000,000 and $696,000
   d. $970,000 and $712,000

LO 5-3, 5-4, 5-5

7. Angela, Inc., holds a 90 percent interest in Corby Company. During 2017, Corby sold inventory costing $77,000 to Angela for $110,000. Of this inventory, $40,000 worth was not sold to outsiders until 2018. During 2018, Corby sold inventory costing $72,000 to Angela for $120,000. A total of $50,000 of this inventory was not sold to outsiders until 2019. In 2018, Angela reported separate net income of $150,000 while Corby's net income was $90,000 after excess amortizations. What is the noncontrolling interest in the 2018 income of the subsidiary?

   a. $8,000
   b. $8,200
   c. $9,000
   d. $9,800

LO 5-7

8. Dunn Corporation owns 100 percent of Grey Corporation's common stock. On January 2, 2017, Dunn sold to Grey $40,000 of machinery with a carrying amount of $30,000. Grey is depreciating the acquired machinery over a five-year remaining life by the straight-line method. The net adjustments to compute 2017 and 2018 consolidated net income would be an increase (decrease) of

	2017	2018
a.	$(8,000)	$2,000
b.	$(8,000)	–0–
c.	$(10,000)	$2,000
d.	$(10,000)	–0–

(AICPA adapted)

LO 5-7

9. Thomson Corporation owns 70 percent of the outstanding stock of Stayer, Incorporated. On January 1, 2016, Thomson acquired a building with a 10-year life for $460,000. Thomson depreciated the building on the straight-line basis assuming no salvage value. On January 1, 2018, Thomson sold this building to Stayer for $430,400. At that time, the building had a remaining life of eight years but still no expected salvage value. In preparing financial statements for 2018, how does this transfer affect the computation of consolidated net income?

   a. Net income is reduced by $62,400.
   b. Net income is reduced by $59,440.
   c. Net income is reduced by $70,200.
   d. Net income is reduced by $54,600.

Use the following data for Problems 10–15:

On January 1, Jarel acquired 80 percent of the outstanding voting stock of Suarez for $260,000 cash consideration. The remaining 20 percent of Suarez had an acquisition-date fair value of $65,000. On January 1, Suarez possessed equipment (five-year remaining life) that was undervalued on its books by $25,000. Suarez also had developed several secret formulas that Jarel assessed at $50,000. These formulas, although not recorded on Suarez's financial records, were estimated to have a 20-year future life.

As of December 31, the financial statements appeared as follows:

	Jarel	Suarez
Revenues	$ (300,000)	$(200,000)
Cost of goods sold	140,000	80,000
Expenses	20,000	10,000
Net income.	$ (140,000)	$(110,000)
Retained earnings, 1/1.	$ (300,000)	$(150,000)
Net income.	(140,000)	(110,000)
Dividends declared.	–0–	–0–
Retained earnings, 12/31	$ (440,000)	$(260,000)
Cash and receivables.	$ 210,000	$ 90,000
Inventory.	150,000	110,000
Investment in Suarez	260,000	–0–
Equipment (net)	440,000	300,000
Total assets	$ 1,060,000	$ 500,000
Liabilities.	$ (420,000)	$(140,000)
Common stock	(200,000)	(100,000)
Retained earnings, 12/31	(440,000)	(260,000)
Total liabilities and equities.	$(1,060,000)	$(500,000)

Included in the above statements, Jarel sold inventory costing $80,000 to Suarez for $100,000. Of these goods, Suarez still owns 60 percent on December 31.

LO 5-2

10. What is the total of consolidated revenues?
    a. $500,000
    b. $460,000
    c. $420,000
    d. $400,000

LO 5-2, 5-3

11. What is the total of consolidated cost of goods sold?
    a. $140,000
    b. $152,000
    c. $132,000
    d. $145,000

LO 3-1

(Chapter 3)

12. What is the total of consolidated expenses?
    a. $30,000
    b. $36,000
    c. $37,500
    d. $39,000

LO 5-5

13. What is the consolidated total of noncontrolling interest appearing on the balance sheet?
    a. $85,500
    b. $83,100
    c. $87,000
    d. $70,500

LO 5-7

14. What is the consolidated total for equipment (net) at December 31?
    a. $735,000.
    b. $740,000.
    c. $760,000.
    d. $765,000.

LO 5-3

15. What is the consolidated total for inventory at December 31?
    a. $240,000
    b. $248,000
    c. $250,000
    d. $260,000

LO 5-2, 5-3, 5-5

16. Following are several figures reported for Allister and Barone as of December 31, 2018:

	Allister	Barone
Inventory.	$ 500,000	$300,000
Sales .	1,000,000	800,000
Investment income .	not given	
Cost of goods sold .	500,000	400,000
Operating expenses.	230,000	300,000

Allister acquired 90 percent of Barone in January 2017. In allocating the newly acquired subsidiary's fair value at the acquisition date, Allister noted that Barone had developed a customer list worth $78,000 that was unrecorded on its accounting records and had a 4-year remaining life. Any remaining excess fair value over Barone's book value was attributed to goodwill. During 2018, Barone sells inventory costing $130,000 to Allister for $180,000. Of this amount, 10 percent remains unsold in Allister's warehouse at year-end.

Determine balances for the following items that would appear on Allister's consolidated financial statements for 2018:

Inventory
Sales
Cost of Goods Sold
Operating Expenses
Net Income Attributable to Noncontrolling Interest

LO 5-3, 5-4, 5-5

17. On January 1, 2017, Corgan Company acquired 80 percent of the outstanding voting stock of Smashing, Inc., for a total of $980,000 in cash and other consideration. At the acquisition date, Smashing had common stock of $700,000, retained earnings of $250,000, and a noncontrolling interest fair value of $245,000. Corgan attributed the excess of fair value over Smashing's book value to various covenants with a 20-year remaining life. Corgan uses the equity method to account for its investment in Smashing.

During the next two years, Smashing reported the following:

	Net Income	Dividends Declared	Inventory Purchases from Corgan
2017	$150,000	$35,000	$100,000
2018	130,000	45,000	120,000

Corgan sells inventory to Smashing using a 60 percent markup on cost. At the end of 2017 and 2018, 40 percent of the current year purchases remain in Smashing's inventory.

a. Compute the equity method balance in Corgan's Investment in Smashing, Inc., account as of December 31, 2018.

b. Prepare the worksheet adjustments for the December 31, 2018, consolidation of Corgan and Smashing.

LO 5-1, 5-3, 5-4, 5-5, 5-6, 5-7

18. Placid Lake Corporation acquired 80 percent of the outstanding voting stock of Scenic, Inc., on January 1, 2017, when Scenic had a net book value of $400,000. Any excess fair value was assigned to intangible assets and amortized at a rate of $5,000 per year.

Placid Lake's 2018 net income before consideration of its relationship with Scenic (and before adjustments for intra-entity sales) was $300,000. Scenic reported net income of $110,000. Placid Lake declared $100,000 in dividends during this period; Scenic paid $40,000. At the end of 2018, selected figures from the two companies' balance sheets were as follows:

	Placid Lake	Scenic
Inventory.	$140,000	$ 90,000
Land.	600,000	200,000
Equipment (net).	400,000	300,000

During 2017, intra-entity sales of $90,000 (original cost of $54,000) were made. Only 20 percent of this inventory was still held within the consolidated entity at the end of 2017. In 2018, $120,000 in intra-entity sales were made with an original cost of $66,000. Of this merchandise, 30 percent had not been resold to outside parties by the end of the year.

Each of the following questions should be considered as an independent situation for the year 2018.

a. What is consolidated net income for Placid Lake and its subsidiary?

b. If the intra-entity sales were upstream, how would consolidated net income be allocated to the controlling and noncontrolling interest?

c. If the intra-entity sales were downstream, how would consolidated net income be allocated to the controlling and noncontrolling interest?

d. What is the consolidated balance in the ending Inventory account?

e. Assume that no intra-entity inventory sales occurred between Placid Lake and Scenic. Instead, in 2017, Scenic sold land costing $30,000 to Placid Lake for $50,000. On the 2018 consolidated balance sheet, what value should be reported for land?

f. Assume that no intra-entity inventory or land sales occurred between Placid Lake and Scenic. Instead, on January 1, 2017, Scenic sold equipment (that originally cost $100,000 but had a $60,000 book value on that date) to Placid Lake for $80,000. At the time of sale, the equipment had a remaining useful life of five years. What worksheet entries are made for a December 31, 2018, consolidation of these two companies to eliminate the impact of the intra-entity transfer? For 2018, what is the noncontrolling interest's share of Scenic's net income?

19. On January 1, 2017, Doone Corporation acquired 60 percent of the outstanding voting stock of Rockne Company for $300,000 consideration. At the acquisition date, the fair value of the 40 percent noncontrolling interest was $200,000 and Rockne's assets and liabilities had a collective net fair value of $500,000. Doone uses the equity method in its internal records to account for its investment in Rockne. Rockne reports net income of $160,000 in 2018. Since being acquired, Rockne has regularly supplied inventory to Doone at 25 percent more than cost. Sales to Doone amounted to $250,000 in 2017 and $300,000 in 2018. Approximately 30 percent of the inventory purchased during any one year is not used until the following year.

a. What is the noncontrolling interest's share of Rockne's 2018 income?

b. Prepare Doone's 2018 consolidation entries required by the intra-entity inventory transfers.

20. Protrade Corporation acquired 80 percent of the outstanding voting stock of Seacraft Company on January 1, 2017, for $612,000 in cash and other consideration. At the acquisition date, Protrade assessed Seacraft's identifiable assets and liabilities at a collective net fair value of $765,000 and the fair value of the 20 percent noncontrolling interest was $153,000. No excess fair value over book value amortization accompanied the acquisition.

The following selected account balances are from the individual financial records of these two companies as of December 31, 2018:

	Protrade	Seacraft
Sales	$880,000	$600,000
Cost of goods sold	410,000	317,000
Operating expenses	174,000	129,000
Retained earnings, 1/1/18	980,000	420,000
Inventory	370,000	144,000
Buildings (net)	382,000	181,000
Investment income	Not given	–0–

Each of the following problems is an independent situation:

a. Assume that Protrade sells Seacraft inventory at a markup equal to 60 percent of cost. Intra-entity transfers were $114,000 in 2017 and $134,000 in 2018. Of this inventory, Seacraft retained and then sold $52,000 of the 2017 transfers in 2018 and held $66,000 of the 2018 transfers until 2019.

Determine balances for the following items that would appear on consolidated financial statements for 2018:

Cost of Goods Sold
Inventory
Net Income Attributable to Noncontrolling Interest

b. Assume that Seacraft sells inventory to Protrade at a markup equal to 60 percent of cost. Intra-entity transfers were $74,000 in 2017 and $104,000 in 2018. Of this inventory, $45,000 of the 2017 transfers were retained and then sold by Protrade in 2018, whereas $59,000 of the 2018 transfers were held until 2019.

Determine balances for the following items that would appear on consolidated financial statements for 2018:

Cost of Goods Sold
Inventory
Net Income Attributable to Noncontrolling Interest

c. Protrade sells Seacraft a building on January 1, 2017, for $128,000, although its book value was only $74,000 on this date. The building had a five-year remaining life and was to be depreciated using the straight-line method with no salvage value.

Determine balances for the following items that would appear on consolidated financial statements for 2018:

Buildings (net)
Operating Expenses
Net Income Attributable to Noncontrolling Interest

LO 5-3, 5-4, 5-5

21. Akron, Inc., owns all outstanding stock of Toledo Corporation. Amortization expense of $15,000 per year for patented technology resulted from the original acquisition. For 2018, the companies had the following account balances:

	Akron	Toledo
Sales	$1,100,000	$600,000
Cost of goods sold	500,000	400,000
Operating expenses	400,000	220,000
Investment income	Not given	–0–
Dividends declared	80,000	30,000

Intra-entity sales of $320,000 occurred during 2017 and again in 2018. This merchandise cost $240,000 each year. Of the total transfers, $70,000 was still held on December 31, 2017, with $50,000 unsold on December 31, 2018.

a. For consolidation purposes, does the direction of the transfers (upstream or downstream) affect the balances to be reported here?

b. Prepare a consolidated income statement for the year ending December 31, 2018.

LO 5-7

22. On January 1, 2017, QuickPort Company acquired 90 percent of the outstanding voting stock of NetSpeed, Inc., for $810,000 in cash and stock options. At the acquisition date, NetSpeed had common stock of $800,000 and Retained Earnings of $40,000. The acquisition-date fair value of the 10 percent noncontrolling interest was $90,000. QuickPort attributed the $60,000 excess of NetSpeed's fair value over book value to a database with a five-year remaining life.

During the next two years, NetSpeed reported the following:

	Net Income	Dividends Declared
2017	$ 80,000	$8,000
2018	115,000	8,000

On July 1, 2017, QuickPort sold communication equipment to NetSpeed for $42,000. The equipment originally cost $48,000 and had accumulated depreciation of $9,000 and an estimated remaining life of three years at the date of the intra-entity transfer.

a. Compute the equity method balance in QuickPort's Investment in NetSpeed, Inc., account as of December 31, 2018.

b. Prepare the worksheet adjustments for the December 31, 2018, consolidation of QuickPort and NetSpeed.

LO 5-7

23. Padre holds 100 percent of the outstanding shares of Sonora. On January 1, 2016, Padre transferred equipment to Sonora for $95,000. The equipment had cost $130,000 originally but had a $50,000 book value and five-year remaining life at the date of transfer. Depreciation expense is computed according to the straight-line method with no salvage value.

Consolidated financial statements for 2018 currently are being prepared. What worksheet entries are needed in connection with the consolidation of this asset? Assume that the parent applies the partial equity method.

LO 5-7

24. On January 1, 2018, Ackerman sold equipment to Brannigan (a wholly owned subsidiary) for $200,000 in cash. The equipment had originally cost $180,000 but had a book value of only $110,000 when transferred. On that date, the equipment had a five-year remaining life. Depreciation expense is computed using the straight-line method.

    Ackerman reported $300,000 in net income in 2018 (not including any investment income) while Brannigan reported $98,000. Ackerman attributed any excess acquisition-date fair value to Brannigan's unpatented technology, which was amortized at a rate of $4,000 per year.

    a. What is consolidated net income for 2018?

    b. What is the parent's share of consolidated net income for 2018 if Ackerman owns only 90 percent of Brannigan?

    c. What is the parent's share of consolidated net income for 2018 if Ackerman owns only 90 percent of Brannigan and the equipment transfer was upstream?

    d. What is the consolidated net income for 2019 if Ackerman reports $320,000 (does not include investment income) and Brannigan $108,000 in income? Assume that Brannigan is a wholly owned subsidiary and the equipment transfer was downstream.

LO 5-2, 5-3, 5-4, 5-7

25. Allison Corporation acquired 90 percent of Bretton on January 1, 2016. Of Bretton's total acquisition-date fair value, $60,000 was allocated to undervalued equipment (with a 10-year remaining life) and $80,000 was attributed to franchises (to be written off over a 20-year period).

    Since the takeover, Bretton has transferred inventory to its parent as follows:

Year	Cost	Transfer Price	Remaining at Year-End
2016	$45,000	$90,000	$30,000 (at transfer price)
2017	48,000	80,000	35,000 (at transfer price)
2018	69,000	92,000	50,000 (at transfer price)

On January 1, 2017, Allison sold Bretton a building for $50,000 that had originally cost $70,000 but had only a $30,000 book value at the date of transfer. The building is estimated to have a five-year remaining life (straight-line depreciation is used with no salvage value).

Selected figures from the December 31, 2018, trial balances of these two companies are as follows:

	Allison	Bretton
Sales	$700,000	$400,000
Cost of goods sold	440,000	220,000
Operating expenses	120,000	80,000
Investment income	Not given	–0–
Inventory	210,000	90,000
Equipment (net)	140,000	110,000
Buildings (net)	350,000	190,000

Determine consolidated totals for each of these account balances.

LO 5-3, 5-4, 5-5, 5-7

26. On January 1, 2018, Sledge had common stock of $120,000 and retained earnings of $260,000. During that year, Sledge reported sales of $130,000, cost of goods sold of $70,000, and operating expenses of $40,000.

    On January 1, 2016, Percy, Inc., acquired 80 percent of Sledge's outstanding voting stock. At that date, $60,000 of the acquisition-date fair value was assigned to unrecorded contracts (with a 20-year life) and $20,000 to an undervalued building (with a 10-year remaining life).

    In 2017, Sledge sold inventory costing $9,000 to Percy for $15,000. Of this merchandise, Percy continued to hold $5,000 at year-end. During 2018, Sledge transferred inventory costing $11,000 to Percy for $20,000. Percy still held half of these items at year-end.

    On January 1, 2017, Percy sold equipment to Sledge for $12,000. This asset originally cost $16,000 but had a January 1, 2017, book value of $9,000. At the time of transfer, the equipment's remaining life was estimated to be five years.

    Percy has properly applied the equity method to the investment in Sledge.

    a. Prepare worksheet entries to consolidate these two companies as of December 31, 2018.

    b. Compute the net income attributable to the noncontrolling interest for 2018.

27. Pitino acquired 90 percent of Brey's outstanding shares on January 1, 2016, in exchange for $342,000 in cash. The subsidiary's stockholders' equity accounts totaled $326,000 and the non-controlling interest had a fair value of $38,000 on that day. However, a building (with a nine-year remaining life) in Brey's accounting records was undervalued by $18,000. Pitino assigned the rest of the excess fair value over book value to Brey's patented technology (six-year remaining life).

Brey reported net income from its own operations of $64,000 in 2016 and $80,000 in 2017. Brey declared dividends of $19,000 in 2016 and $23,000 in 2017.

Brey sells inventory to Pitino as follows:

Year	Cost to Brey	Transfer Price to Pitino	Inventory Remaining at Year-End (at transfer price)
2016	$69,000	$115,000	$25,000
2017	81,000	135,000	37,500
2018	92,800	160,000	50,000

At December 31, 2018, Pitino owes Brey $16,000 for inventory acquired during the period.

The following separate account balances are for these two companies for December 31, 2018, and the year then ended. Credits are indicated by parentheses.

	Pitino	Brey
Sales revenues	$ (862,000)	$(366,000)
Cost of goods sold	515,000	209,000
Expenses	185,400	67,000
Equity in earnings of Brey	(68,400)	–0–
Net income	$ (230,000)	$ (90,000)
Retained earnings, 1/1/18	$ (488,000)	$(278,000)
Net income (above)	(230,000)	(90,000)
Dividends declared	136,000	27,000
Retained earnings, 12/31/18	$ (582,000)	$(341,000)
Cash and receivables	$ 146,000	$ 98,000
Inventory	255,000	136,000
Investment in Brey	450,000	–0–
Land, buildings, and equipment (net)	964,000	328,000
Total assets	$1,815,000	$562,000
Liabilities	$ (718,000)	$ (71,000)
Common stock	(515,000)	(150,000)
Retained earnings, 12/31/18	(582,000)	(341,000)
Total liabilities and equities	$(1,815,000)	$(562,000)

Answer each of the following questions:

a. What was the annual amortization resulting from the acquisition-date fair-value allocations?

b. Were the intra-entity transfers upstream or downstream?

c. What intra-entity gross profit in inventory existed as of January 1, 2018?

d. What intra-entity gross profit in inventory existed as of December 31, 2018?

e. What amounts make up the $68,400 Equity Earnings of Brey account balance for 2018?

f. What is the net income attributable to the noncontrolling interest for 2018?

g. What amounts make up the $450,000 Investment in Brey account balance as of December 31, 2018?

h. Prepare the 2018 worksheet entry to eliminate the subsidiary's beginning owners' equity balances.

i. Without preparing a worksheet or consolidation entries, determine the consolidation balances for these two companies.

28. ProForm acquired 70 percent of ClipRite on June 30, 2017, for $910,000 in cash. Based on Clip-Rite's acquisition-date fair value, an unrecorded intangible of $400,000 was recognized and is being amortized at the rate of $10,000 per year. No goodwill was recognized in the acquisition.

The noncontrolling interest fair value was assessed at $390,000 at the acquisition date. The 2018 financial statements are as follows:

	ProForm	ClipRite
Sales	$ (800,000)	$ (600,000)
Cost of goods sold	535,000	400,000
Operating expenses	100,000	100,000
Dividend income	(35,000)	–0–
Net income	$ (200,000)	$ (100,000)
Retained earnings, 1/1/18	$ (1,300,000)	$ (850,000)
Net income	(200,000)	(100,000)
Dividends declared	100,000	50,000
Retained earnings, 12/31/18	$ (1,400,000)	$ (900,000)
Cash and receivables	$ 400,000	$ 300,000
Inventory	290,000	700,000
Investment in ClipRite	910,000	–0–
Fixed assets	1,000,000	600,000
Accumulated depreciation	(300,000)	(200,000)
Totals	$ 2,300,000	$ 1,400,000
Liabilities	$ (600,000)	$ (400,000)
Common stock	(300,000)	(100,000)
Retained earnings, 12/31/18	(1,400,000)	(900,000)
Totals	$ (2,300,000)	$(1,400,000)

ProForm sold ClipRite inventory costing $72,000 during the last six months of 2017 for $120,000. At year-end, 30 percent remained. ProForm sells ClipRite inventory costing $200,000 during 2018 for $250,000. At year-end, 10 percent is left. With these facts, determine the consolidated balances for the following:

Sales

Cost of Goods Sold

Operating Expenses

Dividend Income

Net Income Attributable to Noncontrolling Interest

Inventory

Noncontrolling Interest in Subsidiary, 12/31/18

LO 5-2, 5-3, 5-4, 5-5

29. Compute the balances in problem (28) again, assuming that all intra-entity transfers were made from ClipRite to ProForm.

LO 5-1, 5-2, 5-3, 5-4, 5-5, 5-6, 5-7

30. Following are financial statements for Moore Company and Kirby Company for 2018:

	Moore	Kirby
Sales	$ (800,000)	$ (600,000)
Cost of goods sold	500,000	400,000
Operating and interest expenses	100,000	160,000
Net income	$ (200,000)	$ (40,000)
Retained earnings, 1/1/18	$ (990,000)	$ (550,000)
Net income	(200,000)	(40,000)
Dividends declared	130,000	–0–
Retained earnings, 12/31/18	$(1,060,000)	$ (590,000)

(continued)

	Moore	Kirby
Cash and receivables.	$ 217,000	$ 180,000
Inventory.	224,000	160,000
Investment in Kirby	657,000	–0–
Equipment (net).	600,000	420,000
Buildings.	1,000,000	650,000
Accumulated depreciation—buildings	(100,000)	(200,000)
Other assets.	200,000	100,000
Total assets	$ 2,798,000	$ 1,310,000
Liabilities.	$(1,138,000)	$ (570,000)
Common stock	(600,000)	(150,000)
Retained earnings, 12/31/18	(1,060,000)	(590,000)
Total liabilities and equity	$(2,798,000)	$(1,310,000)

- Moore purchased 90 percent of Kirby on January 1, 2017, for $657,000 in cash. On that date, the 10 percent noncontrolling interest was assessed to have a $73,000 fair value. Also at the acquisition date, Kirby held equipment (four-year remaining life) undervalued in its financial records by $20,000 and interest-bearing liabilities (five-year remaining life) overvalued by $40,000. The rest of the excess fair over book value was assigned to previously unrecognized brand names and amortized over a 10-year life.

- During 2017 Kirby reported a net income of $80,000 and declared no dividends.

- Each year Kirby sells Moore inventory at a 20 percent gross profit rate. Intra-entity sales were $145,000 in 2017 and $160,000 in 2018. On January 1, 2018, 30 percent of the 2017 transfers were still on hand, and on December 31, 2018, 40 percent of the 2018 transfers remained.

- Moore sold Kirby a building on January 2, 2017. It had cost Moore $100,000 but had $90,000 in accumulated depreciation at the time of this transfer. The price was $25,000 in cash. At that time, the building had a five-year remaining life.

Determine all consolidated balances either computationally or by using a worksheet.

LO 5-2, 5-3, 5-4, 5-5

e**X**cel

31. On January 1, 2017, McIlroy, Inc., acquired a 60 percent interest in the common stock of Stinson, Inc., for $372,000. Stinson's book value on that date consisted of common stock of $100,000 and retained earnings of $220,000. Also, the acquisition-date fair value of the 40 percent noncontrolling interest was $248,000. The subsidiary held patents (with a 10-year remaining life) that were undervalued within the company's accounting records by $70,000 and an unrecorded customer list (15-year remaining life) assessed at a $45,000 fair value. Any remaining excess acquisition-date fair value was assigned to goodwill. Since acquisition, McIlroy has applied the equity method to its Investment in Stinson account and no goodwill impairment has occurred. At year end, there are no intra-entity payables or receivables.

Intra-entity inventory sales between the two companies have been made as follows:

Year	Cost to McIlroy	Transfer Price to Stinson	Ending Balance (at transfer price)
2017	$120,000	$150,000	$50,000
2018	112,000	160,000	40,000

The individual financial statements for these two companies as of December 31, 2018, and the year then ended follow:

	McIlroy, Inc.	Stinson, Inc.
Sales	$ (700,000)	$(335,000)
Cost of goods sold	460,000	205,000
Operating expenses.	188,000	70,000
Equity in earnings in Stinson.	(28,000)	–0–
Net income.	$ (80,000)	$ (60,000)

	McIlroy, Inc.	Stinson, Inc.
Retained earnings, 1/1/18.	$ (695,000)	$ (280,000)
Net income.	(80,000)	(60,000)
Dividends declared.	45,000	15,000
Retained earnings, 12/31/18	$ (730,000)	$ (325,000)
Cash and receivables.	$ 248,000	$ 148,000
Inventory.	233,000	129,000
Investment in Stinson	411,000	–0–
Buildings (net)	308,000	202,000
Equipment (net)	220,000	86,000
Patents (net)	–0–	20,000
Total assets	$ 1,420,000	$ 585,000
Liabilities.	$ (390,000)	$ (160,000)
Common stock	(300,000)	(100,000)
Retained earnings, 12/31/18	(730,000)	(325,000)
Total liabilities and equities.	$(1,420,000)	$ (585,000)

a. Show how McIlroy determined the $411,000 Investment in Stinson account balance. Assume that McIlroy defers 100 percent of downstream intra-entity profits against its share of Stinson's income.

b. Prepare a consolidated worksheet to determine appropriate balances for external financial reporting as of December 31, 2018.

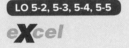

32. On January 1, 2016, Plymouth Corporation acquired 80 percent of the outstanding voting stock of Sander Company in exchange for $1,200,000 cash. At that time, although Sander's book value was $925,000, Plymouth assessed Sander's total business fair value at $1,500,000. Since that time, Sander has neither issued nor reacquired any shares of its own stock.

The book values of Sander's individual assets and liabilities approximated their acquisition-date fair values except for the patent account, which was undervalued by $350,000. The undervalued patents had a five-year remaining life at the acquisition date. Any remaining excess fair value was attributed to goodwill. No goodwill impairments have occurred.

Sander regularly sells inventory to Plymouth. Below are details of the intra-entity inventory sales for the past three years:

Year	Intra-Entity Sales	Intra-Entity Ending Inventory at Transfer Price	Gross Profit Rate on Intra-Entity Inventory Transfers
2016	$125,000	$ 80,000	25%
2017	220,000	125,000	28
2018	300,000	160,000	25

Separate financial statements for these two companies as of December 31, 2018, follow:

	Plymouth	Sander
Revenues	$(1,740,000)	$ (950,000)
Cost of goods sold	820,000	500,000
Depreciation expense	104,000	85,000
Amortization expense	220,000	120,000
Interest expense	20,000	15,000
Equity in earnings of Sander	(124,000)	–0–
Net income	$ (700,000)	$ (230,000)

(continued)

	Plymouth	Sander
Retained earnings 1/1/18	$(2,800,000)	$ (345,000)
Net income	(700,000)	(230,000)
Dividends declared	200,000	25,000
Retained earnings, 12/31/18	$(3,300,000)	$ (550,000)
Cash	$ 535,000	$ 115,000
Accounts receivable	575,000	215,000
Inventory	990,000	800,000
Investment in Sander	1,420,000	–0–
Buildings and equipment	1,025,000	863,000
Patents	950,000	107,000
Total assets	$ 5,495,000	$ 2,100,000
Accounts payable	$ (450,000)	$ (200,000)
Notes payable	(545,000)	(450,000)
Common stock	(900,000)	(800,000)
Additional paid-in capital	(300,000)	(100,000)
Retained earnings, 12/31/18	(3,300,000)	(550,000)
Total liabilities and stockholders' equity	$(5,495,000)	$(2,100,000)

a. Prepare a schedule that calculates the Equity in Earnings of Sander account balance.

b. Prepare a worksheet to arrive at consolidated figures for external reporting purposes. At year-end, there are no intra-entity payables or receivables.

LO 5-2, 5-3, 5-4, 5-5, 5-7 33. On January 1, 2016, Monica Company acquired 70 percent of Young Company's outstanding common stock for $665,000. The fair value of the noncontrolling interest at the acquisition date was $285,000. Young reported stockholders' equity accounts on that date as follows:

Common stock—$10 par value	$300,000
Additional paid-in capital	90,000
Retained earnings.	410,000

In establishing the acquisition value, Monica appraised Young's assets and ascertained that the accounting records undervalued a building (with a five-year remaining life) by $50,000. Any remaining excess acquisition-date fair value was allocated to a franchise agreement to be amortized over 10 years.

During the subsequent years, Young sold Monica inventory at a 30 percent gross profit rate. Monica consistently resold this merchandise in the year of acquisition or in the period immediately following. Transfers for the three years after this business combination was created amounted to the following:

Year	Transfer Price	Inventory Remaining at Year-End (at transfer price)
2016	$60,000	$10,000
2017	80,000	12,000
2018	90,000	18,000

In addition, Monica sold Young several pieces of fully depreciated equipment on January 1, 2017, for $36,000. The equipment had originally cost Monica $50,000. Young plans to depreciate these assets over a six-year period.

In 2018, Young earns a net income of $160,000 and declares and pays $50,000 in cash dividends. These figures increase the subsidiary's Retained Earnings to a $740,000 balance at the end of 2018. During this same year, Monica reported dividend income of $35,000 and an investment account containing the initial value balance of $665,000. No changes in Young's common stock accounts have occurred since Monica's acquisition.

Prepare the 2018 consolidation worksheet entries for Monica and Young. In addition, compute the net income attributable to the noncontrolling interest for 2018.

LO 5-2, 5-3, 5-4, 5-5, 5-7

34. Assume the same basic information as presented in problem (33) except that Monica employs the equity method of accounting. Hence, it reports $102,740 investment income for 2018 with an Investment account balance of $826,220. Under these circumstances, prepare the worksheet entries required for the consolidation of Monica Company and Young Company.

LO 5-1, 5-2, 5-3, 5-4, 5-5, 5-6, 5-7

35. The individual financial statements for Gibson Company and Keller Company for the year ending December 31, 2018, follow. Gibson acquired a 60 percent interest in Keller on January 1, 2017, in exchange for various considerations totaling $570,000. At the acquisition date, the fair value of the noncontrolling interest was $380,000 and Keller's book value was $850,000. Keller had developed internally a customer list that was not recorded on its books but had an acquisition-date fair value of $100,000. This intangible asset is being amortized over 20 years.

    Gibson sold Keller land with a book value of $60,000 on January 2, 2017, for $100,000. Keller still holds this land at the end of the current year.

    Keller regularly transfers inventory to Gibson. In 2017, it shipped inventory costing $100,000 to Gibson at a price of $150,000. During 2018, intra-entity shipments totaled $200,000, although the original cost to Keller was only $140,000. In each of these years, 20 percent of the merchandise was not resold to outside parties until the period following the transfer. Gibson owes Keller $40,000 at the end of 2018.

	Gibson Company	Keller Company
Sales	$ (800,000)	$ (500,000)
Cost of goods sold	500,000	300,000
Operating expenses	100,000	60,000
Equity in earnings of Keller	(84,000)	–0–
Net income	$ (284,000)	$ (140,000)
Retained earnings, 1/1/18	$(1,116,000)	$ (620,000)
Net income (above)	(284,000)	(140,000)
Dividends declared	115,000	60,000
Retained earnings, 12/31/18	$(1,285,000)	$ (700,000)
Cash	$ 177,000	$ 90,000
Accounts receivable	356,000	410,000
Inventory	440,000	320,000
Investment in Keller	726,000	–0–
Land	180,000	390,000
Buildings and equipment (net)	496,000	300,000
Total assets	$ 2,375,000	$ 1,510,000
Liabilities	$ (480,000)	$ (400,000)
Common stock	(610,000)	(320,000)
Additional paid-in capital	–0–	(90,000)
Retained earnings, 12/31/18	(1,285,000)	(700,000)
Total liabilities and equities	$(2,375,000)	$(1,510,000)

    a. Prepare a worksheet to consolidate the separate 2018 financial statements for Gibson and Keller.
    b. How would the consolidation entries in requirement (a) have differed if Gibson had sold a building with a $60,000 book value (cost of $140,000) to Keller for $100,000 instead of land, as the problem reports? Assume that the building had a 10-year remaining life at the date of transfer.

LO 5-2, 5-3, 5-4, 5-6

36. On January 1, 2017, Panther, Inc., issued securities with a total fair value of $577,000 for 100 percent of Stark Corporation's outstanding ownership shares. Stark has long supplied inventory to Panther. The companies expect to achieve synergies with production scheduling and product development with this combination.

    Although Stark's book value at the acquisition date was $300,000, the fair value of its trademarks was assessed to be $45,000 more than their carrying amounts. Additionally, Stark's patented technology was undervalued in its accounting records by $232,000. The trademarks were considered to have indefinite lives, and the estimated remaining life of the patented technology was eight years.

    In 2017, Stark sold Panther inventory costing $75,000 for $125,000. As of December 31, 2017, Panther had resold 74 percent of this inventory. In 2018, Panther bought from Stark $140,000 of inventory that had an original cost of $70,000. At the end of 2018, Panther held $38,000 (transfer price) of inventory acquired from Stark, all from its 2018 purchases.

During 2018, Panther sold Stark a parcel of land for $88,000 and recorded a gain of $16,000 on the sale. Stark still owes Panther $62,000 (current liability) related to the land sale.

At the end of 2018, Panther and Stark prepared the following statements in preparation for consolidation.

	Panther, Inc.	Stark Corporation
Revenues	$ (710,000)	$ (360,000)
Cost of goods sold	305,000	189,000
Other operating expenses	167,000	81,000
Gain on sale of land	(16,000)	–0–
Equity in Stark's earnings	(39,000)	–0–
Net income	$ (293,000)	$ (90,000)
Retained earnings, 1/1/18	$ (367,000)	$ (292,000)
Net income	(293,000)	(90,000)
Dividends declared	80,000	25,000
Retained earnings, 12/31/18	$ (580,000)	$(357,000)
Cash and receivables	$ 102,000	$ 154,000
Inventory	311,000	110,000
Investment in Stark	691,000	–0–
Trademarks	–0–	58,000
Land, buildings, and equip. (net)	638,000	280,000
Patented technology	–0–	125,000
Total assets	$ 1,742,000	$ 727,000
Liabilities	$ (462,000)	$ (220,000)
Common stock	(400,000)	(100,000)
Additional paid-in capital	(300,000)	(50,000)
Retained earnings, 12/31/18	(580,000)	(357,000)
Total liabilities and equity	$(1,742,000)	$ (727,000)

a. Show how Panther computed its $39,000 equity in Stark's earnings balance.

b. Prepare a 2018 consolidated worksheet for Panther and Stark.

Develop Your Skills

EXCEL CASE

On January 1, 2017, James Company purchased 100 percent of the outstanding voting stock of Nolan, Inc., for $1,000,000 in cash and other consideration. At the purchase date, Nolan had common stock of $500,000 and retained earnings of $185,000. James attributed the excess of acquisition-date fair value over Nolan's book value to a trade name with an estimated 25-year remaining useful life. James uses the equity method to account for its investment in Nolan.

During the next two years, Nolan reported the following:

	Income	Dividends Declared	Inventory Transfers to James at Transfer Price
2017	$78,000	$25,000	$190,000
2018	85,000	27,000	210,000

Nolan sells inventory to James after a markup based on a gross profit rate. At the end of 2017 and 2018, 30 percent of the current year purchases remain in James's inventory.

Required

Create an Excel spreadsheet that computes the following:

1. Equity method balance in James' Investment in Nolan, Inc., account as of December 31, 2018.
2. Worksheet adjustments for the December 31, 2018, consolidation of James and Nolan.

Formulate your solution so that Nolan's gross profit rate on sales to James is treated as a variable.

ANALYSIS AND RESEARCH CASE: ACCOUNTING INFORMATION AND SALARY NEGOTIATIONS

Hamilton Hawks Players' Association and Mr. Sideline, the CEO and majority owner of Hamilton Hawks Soccer, Inc, ask your help in resolving a salary dispute. Mr. Sideline presents the following income statement to the players' representatives.

HAMILTON HAWKS SOCCER, INC.
Income Statement

Ticket revenues....................................		$ 3,500,000
Stadium rent expense	$2,500,000	
Ticket expense	30,000	
Promotion expense	80,000	
Player salaries	700,000	
Staff salaries and miscellaneous	265,000	3,575,000
Net income (loss)................................		$ (75,000)

The players contend that their salaries are below market and a raise is warranted. Mr. Sideline argues that the Hamilton Hawks really lose money and, until ticket revenues increase, a salary hike is out of the question.

As a result of your inquiry, you discover that Hamilton Hawks Soccer Company owns 85 percent of the voting stock in Hawks Stadium, Inc. This venue is specifically designed for soccer and is where the Hawks play their entire home game schedule. However, Mr. Sideline does not wish to consider the profits of Hawks Stadium in the negotiations with the players. He claims that "the stadium is really a separate business entity that was purchased separately from the team and therefore does not concern the players. On top of that, we allocate all the ticket revenues to the team's income statement."

The Hawks Stadium income statement appears as follows:

HAWKS STADIUM, INC.
Income Statement

Stadium rent revenue..............................	$2,500,000	
Concession revenue	875,000	
Parking revenue	95,000	$3,470,000
Cost of goods sold................................	270,000	
Depreciation expense	90,000	
Grounds maintenance expense.......................	410,000	
Staff salaries and miscellaneous	200,000	970,000
Net income (loss)................................		$2,500,000

Required

1. What advice would you provide the negotiating parties regarding the issue of considering the Hawks Stadium income statement in their discussions? What authoritative literature could you cite in supporting your advice?
2. What other pertinent information would you need to provide a specific recommendation regarding players' salaries?

Variable Interest Entities, Intra-Entity Debt, Consolidated Cash Flows, and Other Issues

The consolidation of financial information can be a highly complex process often encompassing a number of practical challenges. This chapter examines the procedures required by several additional issues:

- Variable interest entities.
- Intra-entity debt.
- Subsidiary preferred stock.
- The consolidated statement of cash flows.
- Computation of consolidated earnings per share.
- Subsidiary stock transactions.

Variable interest entities emerged over the past two decades as a new type of business structure that provided effective control of one firm by another without overt ownership. In response to the evolving nature of control relationships among firms, the FASB expanded its definition of control beyond the long-standing criterion of a majority voting interest to include control exercised through variable interests. This topic and some of the more traditional advanced business combination subjects listed above provide for further exploration of the complexities faced by the financial reporting community in providing relevant and reliable information to users of consolidated financial reports.

Consolidation of Variable Interest Entities

Several decades ago, many firms began establishing separate business structures to help finance their operations at favorable rates. These structures became commonly known as *special purpose entities* (SPEs), *special purpose vehicles,* or *off-balance-sheet structures.* In this text, we refer to all such entities collectively as *variable interest entities,* or VIEs. Many firms routinely included their VIEs in their consolidated financial reports. However, others sought to avoid consolidation.

VIEs can help accomplish legitimate business purposes. Nonetheless, their use was widely criticized in the aftermath of Enron Corporation's 2001 collapse. Because many firms avoided consolidation and used VIEs for off-balance sheet financing, such entities were often characterized as

LO 6-1

Describe a variable interest entity, a primary beneficiary, and the factors used to decide when a variable interest entity is subject to consolidation.

vehicles to hide debt and mislead investors. Other critics observed that firms with variable interests recorded questionable profits on sales to their VIEs that were not arm's-length transactions.[1] The FASB ASC "Variable Interest Entities" sections within the "Consolidations" Topic were issued in response to such financial reporting abuses.

What Is a VIE?

A VIE can take the form of a trust, partnership, joint venture, or corporation although sometimes it has neither independent management nor employees. Most are established for valid business purposes, and transactions involving VIEs have become widespread. Common examples of VIE activities include transfers of financial assets, leasing, hedging financial instruments, research and development, and other arrangements. An enterprise often creates a VIE to accomplish a well-defined and limited business activity and to provide low-cost financing.

Low-cost financing of asset purchases is frequently a main benefit available through VIEs. Rather than engaging in the transaction directly, a business enterprise may establish a VIE to purchase and finance an asset acquisition. The VIE then leases the asset back to the business enterprise that established the VIE. This strategy saves the business enterprise money because the VIE is often eligible for a lower interest rate. This advantage is achieved for several reasons. First, the VIE typically operates with a very limited set of assets—in many cases just one asset. By isolating an asset in a VIE, the asset's risk is isolated from the business enterprise's overall risk. Thus the VIE creditors remain protected by the specific collateral in the asset. Second, the governing documents can strictly limit the actions of a VIE. These limits further protect lenders by preventing the VIE from engaging in any activities not specified in its agreements. As a major public accounting firm noted,

> The borrower/transferor gains access to a source of funds less expensive than would otherwise be available. This advantage derives from isolating the assets in an entity prohibited from undertaking any other business activity or taking on any additional debt, thereby creating a better security interest in the assets for the lender/investor.[2]

Because governing agreements limit activities and decision making in most VIEs, ownership of a VIE's common stock typically does not provide control of the VIE. In fact, the enterprise that created the VIE may own very little, if any, of the VIE's voting stock. Prior to current consolidation requirements for VIEs, many enterprises left such entities unconsolidated in their financial reports because technically they did not own a majority of the entity's voting stock. In utilizing the VIE as a conduit to provide financing, the related assets and debt were effectively removed from the enterprise's balance sheet.

In general, the party that primarily benefits (or risks losses) from the economic activities of the VIE and has the power to direct the VIE's activities is deemed to have a controlling financial interest in the VIE. We use the term **primary beneficiary** to designate the party with such financial control. The primary beneficiary (most often a business) typically exercises its financial control through governance documents or other contractual agreements that provide it with decision-making authority over the VIE. Once identified, the primary beneficiary must consolidate in its financial statements the VIE's assets, liabilities, revenues, expenses, and noncontrolling interest.

Characteristics of Variable Interest Entities

Similar to most business entities, VIEs generally have assets, liabilities, and investors with equity interests. Unlike most businesses, because a VIE's activities and decision-making can be strictly limited, the role of the equity investors can be fairly minor. The VIE may have been created specifically by the primary beneficiary to provide it with low-cost financing.

---

[1] In its 2001 fourth quarter 10-Q, Enron recorded earnings restatements of more than $400 million related to its failure to properly consolidate several of its SPEs (e.g., Chewco and LJM2). Enron also admitted an improper omission of $700 million of its SPE's debt. Within a month of the restatements, Enron filed for bankruptcy.

[2] KPMG, "Defining Issues: New Accounting for SPEs," March 1, 2002.

Thus, the equity investors may serve simply as a technical requirement to allow the VIE to function as a legal entity. Because they bear relatively low economic risk, equity investors may be provided only a small rate of return.

The small equity investments in a VIE normally are insufficient to induce lenders to provide financing for the VIE. As a result, another party (e.g., the primary beneficiary) must contribute substantial resources—often loans and/or guarantees—to enable the VIE to secure additional financing needed to accomplish its purpose. For example, the primary beneficiary may guarantee the VIE's debt, thus assuming the risk of default. Other contractual arrangements may limit returns to equity holders while participation rights provide increased profit potential and risks to the primary beneficiary. Risks and rewards such as these cause the primary beneficiary's economic interest to vary depending on the created entity's success—hence the term **variable interest entity**. In contrast to a traditional entity, a VIE's risks and rewards frequently are distributed not according to stock ownership but according to other variable interests. Exhibit 6.1 describes variable interests further and provides several examples.

Variable interests increase a firm's risk as the resources it provides (or guarantees) to the VIE increase. With increased risks come incentives to restrict the VIE's decision making. In fact, a firm with variable interests will regularly limit the equity investors' power through the VIE's governance documents. As noted by GAAP literature,

> If the total equity investment at risk is not sufficient to permit the legal entity to finance its activities, the parties providing the necessary additional subordinated financial support most likely will not permit an equity investor to make decisions that may be counter to their interests. (FASB ASC 810-10-05-13)

Although the equity investors are technically the owners of the VIE, in reality they may retain little of the traditional responsibilities, risks, and benefits of ownership. In fact, the equity investors sometimes cede financial control of the VIE to those with variable interests in exchange for a guaranteed rate of return. Alternatively, equity ownership is also a variable interest and a minority equity holder may be the primary beneficiary and end up consolidating the VIE.

Consolidation of Variable Interest Entities

Prior to current financial reporting standards, assets, liabilities, and results of operations for VIEs and other entities frequently were not consolidated with those of the firm that controlled the entity. These firms invoked a reliance on voting interests, as opposed to

EXHIBIT 6.1
Examples of Variable Interests

Variable interests in a variable interest entity are contractual, ownership, or other pecuniary interests in an entity that change with changes in the entity's net asset value. Variable interests absorb portions of a variable interest entity's expected losses if they occur or receive portions of the entity's expected residual returns if they occur.

The following are some examples of variable interests and the related potential losses or returns:

Variable interests	Potential losses or returns
• Participation rights.	• Entitles holder to residual profits.
• Asset purchase options.	• Entitles holder to benefit from increases in asset fair values.
• Guarantees of debt.	• If a VIE cannot repay liabilities, honoring a debt guarantee will produce a loss.
• Subordinated debt instruments.	• If a VIE's cash flow is insufficient to repay all senior debt, subordinated debt may be required to absorb the loss.
• Lease residual value guarantees.	• If leased asset declines below the residual value, honoring the guarantee will produce a loss.
• Common stock	• Entitles holder to residual profits, losses, and dividends.

variable interests, to indicate a lack of a controlling financial interest. As legacy FASB standard *FIN 46R*[3] observed,

> An enterprise's consolidated financial statements include subsidiaries in which the enterprise has a controlling financial interest. That requirement usually has been applied to subsidiaries in which an enterprise has a majority voting interest, but in many circumstances, the enterprise's consolidated financial statements do not include variable interest entities with which it has similar relationships. The voting interest approach is not effective in identifying controlling financial interests in entities that are not controllable through voting interests or in which the equity investors do not bear residual economic risk. (Summary, page 2)

Thus, a business enterprise is required to consolidate the assets and liabilities of a variable interest entity if it can exercise financial control through its role as a primary beneficiary. Variable interests often serve as the vehicle for a controlling financial interest, even in the absence of any equity investment whatsoever.

Business enterprises must first determine if they have a controlling financial interest in any affiliated entity by applying the variable interest model. Each enterprise involved with a VIE must evaluate whether it possesses a controlling financial interest and thus qualifies as the primary beneficiary of the VIE's activities. The VIE's primary beneficiary is then required to include the assets, liabilities, and results of the activities of the VIE in its consolidated financial statements. If the affiliated entity is not a VIE, then a voting interest model is utilized to assess whether financial control exists.

As noted by General Electric Company in its 2015 annual report:

> Our financial statements consolidate all of our affiliates – entities in which we have a controlling financial interest, most often because we hold a majority voting interest. To determine if we hold a controlling financial interest in an entity, we first evaluate if we are required to apply the variable interest entity (VIE) model to the entity, otherwise, the entity is evaluated under the voting interest model.
>
> Where we hold current or potential rights that give us the power to direct the activities of a VIE that most significantly impact the VIE's economic performance, combined with a variable interest that gives us the right to receive potentially significant benefits or the obligation to absorb potentially significant losses, we have a controlling financial interest in that VIE.

Identification of a Variable Interest Entity

An entity qualifies as a VIE if either of the following conditions exists:

- The total equity at risk is not sufficient to permit the entity to finance its activities without additional subordinated financial support provided by any parties, including equity holders. In most cases, if equity at risk is less than 10 percent of total assets, the risk is deemed insufficient.[4]
- The equity investors in the VIE, as a group, lack any one of the following three characteristics of a controlling financial interest:

  1. The power, through voting rights or similar rights, to direct the activities of an entity that most significantly impact the entity's economic performance.
  2. The obligation to absorb the expected losses of the entity (e.g., the primary beneficiary may guarantee a return to the equity investors).
  3. The right to receive the expected residual returns of the entity (e.g., the investors' return may be capped by the entity's governing documents or other arrangements with variable interest holders).

Identification of the Primary Beneficiary of the VIE

Once it is established that a firm has a relationship with a VIE, the firm must determine whether it qualifies as the VIE's primary beneficiary. An enterprise with a variable interest

---

[3] FASB *Interpretation No. 46R (FIN 46R)*, "Consolidation of Variable Interest Entities," December 2003.

[4] Alternatively, a 10 percent or higher equity interest may also be insufficient. According to GAAP, "Some entities may require an equity investment greater than 10 percent of their assets to finance their activities, especially if they engage in high-risk activities, hold high-risk assets, or have exposure to risks that are not reflected in the reported amounts of the entities' assets or liabilities." [FASB ASC (para. 810-10-25-46)]

that provides it with a controlling financial interest in a variable interest entity is the primary beneficiary and will have both of the following characteristics:

- The power to direct the activities of a variable interest entity that most significantly impact the entity's economic performance.
- The obligation to absorb losses of the entity that could potentially be significant to the variable interest entity or the right to receive benefits from the entity that could potentially be significant to the variable interest entity.

Note that these characteristics mirror those that the equity investors often lack in a VIE. Instead, the primary beneficiary will absorb a significant share of the VIE's losses or receive a significant share of the VIE's residual returns or both. The fact that the primary beneficiary may own no voting shares whatsoever becomes inconsequential because such shares do not effectively give the equity investors power to exercise control. Thus, a careful examination of the VIE's governing documents, contractual arrangements among parties involved, and who bears the risk is necessary to determine whether a reporting entity possesses control over a VIE.

The magnitude of the effect of consolidating an enterprise's VIEs can be large. For example, Walt Disney Company consolidates its international theme parks as variable interest entities. In its 2015 annual report, Disney states the following:

> The Company enters into relationships or investments with other entities that may be a variable interest entity (VIE). A VIE is consolidated in the financial statements if the Company has the power to direct activities that most significantly impact the economic performance of the VIE and has the obligation to absorb losses or the right to receive benefits from the VIE that could potentially be significant to the VIE (as defined by ASC 810-10-25-38). Disneyland Paris, HKDL and Shanghai Disney Resort (collectively the International Theme Parks) are VIEs.

As a result of the 2015 consolidation of these VIEs, Disney's total assets increased by $3.98 billion while its total debt increased by $955 million.

Example of a Primary Beneficiary and Consolidated Variable Interest Entity

Assume that Twin Peaks Electric Company seeks to acquire a generating plant for a negotiated price of $400 million from Ace Electric Company. Twin Peaks wishes to expand its market share and expects to be able to sell the electricity generated by the plant acquisition at a profit to its owners.

In reviewing financing alternatives, Twin Peaks observed that its general credit rating allowed for a 4 percent annual interest rate on a debt issue. Twin Peaks also explored the establishment of a separate legal entity whose sole purpose would be to own the electric generating plant and lease it back to Twin Peaks. Because the separate entity would isolate the electric generating plant from Twin Peaks's other risky assets and liabilities and provide specific collateral, an interest rate of 3 percent on the debt is available, producing before-tax savings of $4 million per year. To obtain the lower interest rate, however, Twin Peaks must guarantee the separate entity's debt. Twin Peaks must also maintain certain of its own predefined financial ratios and restrict the amount of additional debt it can assume.

To take advantage of the lower interest rate, on January 1, 2017, Twin Peaks establishes Power Finance Co., an entity designed solely to own, finance, and lease the electric generating plant to Twin Peaks.[5] The documents governing the new entity specify the following:

- The sole purpose of Power Finance is to purchase the Ace electric generating plant, provide equity and debt financing, and lease the plant to Twin Peaks.
- An outside investor will provide $16 million in exchange for a 100 percent nonvoting equity interest in Power Finance.
- Power Finance will issue debt in exchange for $384 million. Because the $16 million equity investment by itself is insufficient to attract low-interest debt financing, Twin Peaks will guarantee the debt.

---

[5] This arrangement is similar to a "synthetic lease" commonly used in utility companies. Synthetic leases also can have tax advantages because the sponsoring firm accounts for them as capital leases for tax purposes.

- Twin Peaks will lease the electric generating plant from Power Finance in exchange for payments of $12 million per year based on a 3 percent fixed interest rate for both the debt and equity investors for an initial lease term of five years.
- At the end of the 5-year lease term (or any extension), Twin Peaks must do one of the following:
  - Renew the lease for five years subject to the approval of the equity investor.
  - Purchase the electric generating plant for $400 million.
  - Sell the electric generating plant to an independent third party. If the proceeds of the sale are insufficient to repay the equity investor, Twin Peaks must make a payment of $16 million to the equity investor.

Once the purchase of the electric generating plant is complete and the equity and debt are issued, Power Finance Company reports the following balance sheet:

POWER FINANCE COMPANY
Balance Sheet
January 1, 2017

Electric Generating Plant	$400M	Long-Term Debt.	$384M
		Owners' Equity	16M
Total Assets	$400M	Total Liabilities and OE	$400M

Exhibit 6.2 shows the relationships between Twin Peaks, Power Finance, the electric generating plant, and the parties financing the asset purchase.

In evaluating whether Twin Peaks Electric Company must consolidate Power Finance Company, two conditions must be met. First, Power Finance must qualify as a VIE by either (1) an inability to secure financing without additional subordinated support or (2) a lack of either the risk of losses or entitlement to residual returns (or both). Second, Twin Peaks must qualify as the primary beneficiary of Power Finance.

In assessing the first condition, several factors point to VIE status for Power Finance. Its owners' equity comprises only 4 percent of total assets, far short of the 10 percent benchmark. Moreover, Twin Peaks guarantees Power Finance's debt, suggesting insufficient equity to finance its operations without additional support. Finally, the equity investor appears to bear

EXHIBIT 6.2
Variable Interest Entity to Facilitate Financing

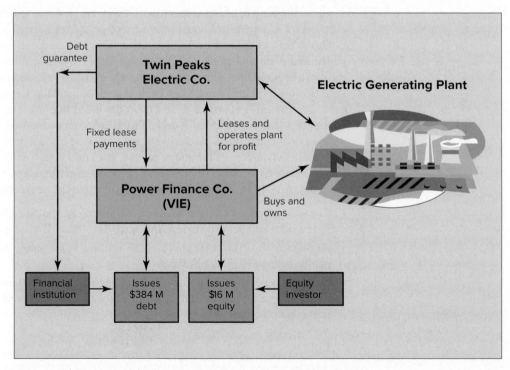

almost no risk with respect to the operations of the Ace electric plant. These characteristics indicate that Power Finance qualifies as a VIE.

In evaluating the second condition for consolidation, an assessment is made to determine whether Twin Peaks qualifies as Power Finance's primary beneficiary. Clearly, Twin Peaks has the power to direct Power Finance's activities. But to qualify for consolidation, Twin Peaks must also have the obligation to absorb losses or the right to receive returns from Power Finance—either of which could potentially be significant to Power Finance. But what possible losses or returns would accrue to Twin Peaks? What are Twin Peaks's variable interests that rise and fall with the fortunes of Power Finance?

As stated in the VIE agreement, Twin Peaks will pay a fixed fee to lease the electric generating plant. It will then operate the plant and sell the electric power in its markets. If the business plan is successful, Twin Peaks will enjoy residual profits from operating while Power Finance's equity investors receive the fixed fee. On the other hand, if prices for electricity fall, Twin Peaks may generate revenues insufficient to cover its lease payments while Power Finance's equity investors are protected from this risk. Moreover, if the plant's fair value increases significantly, Twin Peaks can exercise its option to purchase the plant at a fixed price and either resell it or keep it for its own future use. Alternatively, if Twin Peaks were to sell the plant at a loss, it must pay the equity investors all of their initial investment, furthering the loss to Twin Peaks. Each of these elements points to Twin Peaks as the primary beneficiary of its VIE through variable interests. As the primary beneficiary, Twin Peaks must consolidate the assets, liabilities, and results of operations of Power Finance with its own.

Procedures to Consolidate Variable Interest Entities

As Power Finance's balance sheet exemplifies, VIEs typically possess only a few assets and liabilities. Also, their business activities usually are strictly limited. Thus, the actual procedures to consolidate VIEs are relatively uncomplicated.

Initial Measurement Issues

Just as in business combinations accomplished through voting interests, the financial reporting principles for consolidating variable interest entities require asset, liability, and noncontrolling interest valuations. These valuations initially, and with few exceptions, are based on fair values.

Recall that the acquisition method requires an allocation of the acquired business fair value based on the underlying fair values of its assets and liabilities. The fair-value principle applies to consolidating VIEs in the same manner as business combinations accomplished through voting interests. If the total business fair value of the VIE exceeds the collective fair values of its net assets, goodwill is recognized.[6] Conversely, if the collective fair values of the net assets exceed the total business fair value, then the primary beneficiary recognizes a gain on bargain purchase.

In the previous example, assuming that the debt and noncontrolling interests are stated at fair values, Twin Peaks simply includes in its consolidated balance sheet the Electric Generating Plant at $400 million, the Long-Term Debt at $384 million, and a noncontrolling interest of $16 million.

Consolidation of VIEs Subsequent to Initial Measurement

After the initial measurement, consolidations of VIEs with their primary beneficiaries should follow the same process as if the entity were consolidated based on voting interests. Importantly, all intra-entity transactions between the primary beneficiary and the VIE (including fees, expenses, other sources of income or loss, and intra-entity inventory purchases) must be eliminated in consolidation. Finally, the VIE's income must be allocated among the parties involved (i.e., equity holders and the primary beneficiary). For a VIE, contractual arrangements, as opposed to ownership percentages, typically specify the distribution of its income.

---

[6] The FASB ASC Glossary defines a business as an integrated set of activities and assets that is capable of being conducted and managed for the purpose of providing a return in the form of dividends, lower costs, or other economic benefits directly to investors or other owners, members, or participants. Alternatively, if the activities of the VIE are so restricted that it does not qualify as a business, the excess fair value is recognized as an acquisition loss, as opposed to goodwill.

Therefore, a close examination of these contractual arrangements is needed to determine the appropriate allocation of VIE income to its equity owners and those holding variable interests.

Consolidation of a Primary Beneficiary and VIE Illustrated

LO 6-2

Demonstrate the process to consolidate a primary beneficiary with a variable interest entity.

The next example considers (1) the issues that arise when a primary beneficiary obtains control through variable interests of an existing business, and (2) financial reporting for a VIE in periods subsequent to obtaining control.

Assume that on January 1, 2018, Prescott Corporation provides a $2,200,000 loan to Valente, Inc., a business entity. The loan is due on January 1, 2023. Until receiving the loan from Prescott, Valente had been unable to secure from the debt market the financing needed to continue its operations.

As part of the loan agreement, Valente agrees to provide the following to Prescott during the next five years:

- 5 percent annual interest (market rate) on the loan from Prescott.
- Decision-making power over Valente's operating and financing activities.
- 100 percent participation rights to all of Valente's profits less a $7,000 guaranteed annual dividend to Valente's common shareholders.

At the end of the five-year agreement Prescott has the option of either acquiring ownership of Valente, Inc., for $500,000 or extending the original agreement for an additional five years.

As a result of the agreement, Valente is a variable interest entity and Prescott is its primary beneficiary. Upon consummation of the variable interest agreement, Prescott's and Valente's balance sheets appears below:

January 1, 2018	Prescott	Valente
Cash.	$ 85,000	$ 2,308,000
Accounts receivable	133,000	145,000
Loan receivable from Valente	2,200,000	–0–
Patented technology.	–0–	9,000
Equipment (net)	2,458,000	900,000
Total assets.	$ 4,876,000	$ 3,362,000
Accounts payable	$ (408,000)	$(1,144,000)
Long-term debt.	(954,000)	(2,200,000)
Common stock.	(2,500,000)	(10,000)
Retained earnings, 1/1/18	(1,014,000)	(8,000)
Total liabilities and equity.	$(4,876,000)	$(3,362,000)

At January 1, 2018, Prescott estimated the fair value of Valente's common stock at $143,000. The $125,000 difference between the fair value of the common stock and Valente's book value ($143,000 - $18,000) was attributed entirely to the patented technology with a five-year estimated remaining life.

Exhibit 6.3 shows the consolidation worksheet for Prescott (the primary beneficiary) and Valente (the variable interest entity) at January 1, 2018, the date Prescott obtained financial control over Valente.

Observe that in Exhibit 6.3

- Consolidation Entry **S** eliminates the VIE's owners' equity account balances and recognizes the 100 percent equity ownership as a noncontrolling interest.
- Consolidation Entry **P** eliminates the intra-entity Long-Term Debt and Loan Receivable from Valente.
- Consolidation Entry **A** allocates the excess fair over book value to Patented Technology with a corresponding increase in the noncontrolling interest.
- The noncontrolling interest appears in the consolidated balance sheet at its acquisition-date fair value of $143,000.

EXHIBIT 6.3 Acquisition-Date Consolidation Worksheet—Primary Beneficiary and VIE

PRESCOTT AND VALENTE COMPANY
Consolidation Worksheet
At January 1, 2018

Balance Sheet	Prescott	Valente	Consolidation Entries		Noncontrolling Interest	Consolidated Balance Sheet
Cash	85,000	2,308,000				2,393,000
Accounts receivable	133,000	145,000				278,000
Loan receivable from Valente	2,200,000			(P)2,200,000		–0–
Patented technology		9,000	(A) 125,000			134,000
Equipment (net)	2,458,000	900,000				3,358,000
Total assets	4,876,000	3,362,000				6,613,000
Accounts payable	(408,000)	(1,144,000)				(1,552,000)
Long-term debt	(954,000)	(2,200,000)	(P)2,200,000			(954,000)
Common stock—Prescott	(2,500,000)					(2,500,000)
Common stock—Valente		(10,000)	(S) 10,000			
Retained earnings—Prescott	(1,014,000)					(1,014,000)
Retained earning—Valente		(8,000)	(S) 8,000			
Noncontrolling interest				(S) 18,000		
				(A) 125,000	(143,000)	(143,000)
Total liabilities and equity	(4,876,000)	(3,362,000)	2,343,000	2,343,000		(6,163,000)

Consolidation of VIEs Subsequent to Initial Measurement

Following the first year of operations, Exhibit 6.4 shows the consolidation worksheet for December 31, 2018, at the end of the first year in which Prescott obtained control of the variable interest entity. At the end of the year, Valente paid the guaranteed $7,000 dividend to its equity holders.

The following worksheet entries, as seen in Exhibit 6.4, are used to consolidate the financial statements of Prescott Corporation and its VIE, Valente, as of December 31, 2018:

Consolidation Entry S

Retained earnings—Valente 1/1/18	8,000	
Common stock—Valente	10,000	
Noncontrolling interest		18,000

To eliminate the beginning stockholders' equity of the VIE and recognize the 100 percent equity ownership of the noncontrolling interest.

Consolidation Entry P

Long-term debt	2,200,000	
Loan receivable from Valente		2,200,000

To eliminate the long-term receivable and debt representing Prescott's initial investment in Valente.

Consolidation Entry IE

Interest income	110,000	
Interest expense		110,000

To eliminate the intra-entity interest related to the loan from Prescott to Valente.

Consolidation Entry A

Patented technology	125,000	
Noncontrolling interest		125,000

To allocate the excess fair value to patented technology and credit the noncontrolling interest as part of their fair valuation as of the date Prescott obtained control.

Consolidation Entry E

Other operating expenses	25,000	
Patented technology		25,000

To amortize the excess fair value allocation to unpatented technology over its five-year remaining life.

EXHIBIT 6.4 Consolidation Worksheet for Primary Beneficiary and VIE (Post-Control)

PRESCOTT AND VALENTE COMPANY
Consolidation Worksheet
For the year ended, December 31, 2018

Income Statement	Prescott	Valente	Consolidation Entries		Noncontrolling Interest	Consolidated
Sales	(623,000)	(400,000)				(1,023,000)
Cost of goods sold	230,000	190,000				420,000
Other operating expenses	155,000	55,000	(E)	25,000		235,000
Interest income	(110,000)		(IE)	110,000		–0–
Interest expense		110,000		(IE) 110,000		–0–
Net income	(348,000)	(45,000)				
Consolidated net income						(368,000)
to noncontrolling interest					(7,000)	7,000
to controlling interest						(361,000)
Statement of Retained Earnings						
Retained earnings, 1/1	(1,014,000)	(8,000)	(S)	8,000		(1,014,000)
Net income	(348,000)	(45,000)				(361,000)
Dividends declared	50,000	7,000			7,000	50,000
Retained earnings, 12/31	(1,312,000)	(46,000)				(1,325,000)
Balance Sheet						
Cash	214,000	131,800				345,800
Accounts receivable	258,000	181,000				439,000
Loan receivable from Valente	2,200,000		(P)2,200,000			–0–
Patented technology		7,200	(A) 125,000	(E) 25,000		107,200
Equipment (net)	2,328,000	2,050,000				4,378,000
Total assets	5,000,000	2,370,000				5,270,000
Accounts payable	(434,000)	(114,000)				(548,000)
Long-term debt	(754,000)	(2,200,000)	(P) 2,200,000			(754,000)
Common stock	(2,500,000)	(10,000)	(S) 10,000			(2,500,000)
Retained earnings, 12/31	(1,312,000)	(46,000)				(1,325,000)
			(A) 125,000			
			(S) 18,000		(143,000)	
Noncontrolling interest					(143,000)	(143,000)
Total liabilities and equities	(5,000,000)	(2,370,000)	2,478,000	2,478,000		(5,270,000)

In Exhibit 6.4, we observe that the noncontrolling interest (NCI) column for a VIE differs from a consolidation resulting from voting interest control. For a VIE, contractual arrangements, as opposed to ownership percentages, typically specify the distribution of its income. In Exhibit 6.4, the only income allocation to the NCI is the $7,000 annual dividend guaranteed through the variable interest arrangement. Because of its profit participation rights, Prescott simply receives the remainder of the consolidated net income beyond the $7,000 provided to Valente's equity holders, i.e., the NCI of the consolidated entity.

Also note that the NCI amount recognized after one year did not change from the consolidated balance sheet as of the date control was obtained. The NCI did not change because its entire fixed income share was distributed to the equity holders as a dividend.

Overall, as shown by Exhibit 6.4, consolidation of a VIE with its primary beneficiary follows a similar process as if the entity were consolidated based on voting interests. Importantly, all intra-entity transactions between the primary beneficiary and the VIE (including fees, expenses, other sources of income or loss, and intra-entity transfers) must be eliminated in consolidation. Because VIEs typically have noncontrolling interests, an appropriate allocation of the VIE's net income requires a close examination of the underlying contractual arrangements between the primary beneficiary and other holders of variable interests.

Other Variable Interest Entity Disclosure Requirements

VIE disclosure requirements are designed to provide users of financial statements with more transparent information about an enterprise's involvement in a VIE. The enhanced disclosures are required for any enterprise that holds a variable interest in a VIE.

Included among the enhanced disclosures are requirements to show:

- The VIE's nature, purpose, size, and activities.
- The significant judgments and assumptions made by an enterprise in determining whether it must consolidate a VIE and/or disclose information about its involvement in a VIE.
- The nature of restrictions on a consolidated VIE's assets and on the settlement of its liabilities reported by an enterprise in its statement of financial position, including the carrying amounts of such assets and liabilities.
- The nature of, and changes in, the risks associated with an enterprise's involvement with the VIE.
- How an enterprise's involvement with the VIE affects the enterprise's financial position, financial performance, and cash flows.

Comparisons with International Accounting Standards

Under both U.S. GAAP and IFRS, a controlling financial interest is the critical concept in assessing whether an entity should be consolidated by a reporting enterprise. Nonetheless, the FASB and IASB so far have employed different criteria to determine the existence of control. IFRS employs a single consolidation model for all entities regardless of whether control is evidenced by voting interests or variable interests. In contrast, U.S. GAAP employs separate models for assessing control for variable interest entities and voting interest entities. As a result, current reporting standards differ across jurisdictions for enterprises seeking to determine whether to consolidate another entity. While the FASB continues its deliberations on consolidation policies and procedures, the IASB has issued two updated standards in this area.

The International Accounting Standards Board *IFRS 10,* "Consolidated Financial Statements" and *IFRS 12*, "Disclosure of Interests in Other Entities" cover situations where financial control exists either through a majority voting share or other means. These standards define control to encompass all possible ways (voting power, contractual power, decision-making rights, etc.) in which one entity can exercise power over another. In particular, the criteria for assessing control are

- Power over an investee—does the reporting entity have the current ability to direct activities that significantly affect another entity's returns?

- Exposure to, or rights to, variable returns from involvement with another entity
- Linkage between power and returns—does the investor have the ability to affect its returns through its power?

These criteria recognize one entity can control another through its power to direct its operating and financing activities. For example, even with less than majority ownership, voting interests can provide an enterprise control if the nonowned shares are diffusely held and lack arrangements to act in a coordinated manner. Control can also be achieved through obtaining decision-making rights that relate to the relevant activities of an investee. Importantly, such decision-making rights can extend beyond merely voting rights. By establishing a broad concept of control as opposed to a bright line rule (e.g., consolidate if an entity has majority voting rights or the majority of risks and rewards), the IASB seeks to avoid standards that create structuring opportunities to achieve a particular accounting outcome.[7]

IFRS 12 provides for enhanced disclosures about the relationship between a parent and the entities it controls. These disclosures focus on helping investors understand first why a parent controls (or does not control) another entity and the claims of the noncontrolling interest. Second, the disclosures are designed to help investors evaluate the risks assumed by the parent.[8]

LO 6-3

Demonstrate the consolidation procedures to eliminate all intra-entity debt accounts and recognize any associated gain or loss created whenever one company acquires an affiliate's debt instrument from an outside party.

Intra-Entity Debt Transactions

The previous chapter explored the consolidation procedures required by the intra-entity transfer of inventory, land, and depreciable assets. In preparing consolidated financial statements, all resulting gains were deferred until either the asset was sold to an outside party or consumed through use. Deferral was necessary because these gains, although legitimately recognized by the individual companies, were based on activities of the consolidated entity with itself. The separate financial information of each company was adjusted on the worksheet to be consistent with treating the related companies as a single economic concern.

This same objective applies in consolidating all other intra-entity activities: The financial statements must represent the business combination as one enterprise rather than as a group of independent organizations. Consequently, in designing consolidation procedures for intra-entity transactions, we first isolate the effects recorded by the individual companies. After analyzing the impact of each action, worksheet entries recast these events from the vantage point of the business combination. Although this process involves a number of nuances and complexities, the desire for reporting financial information solely from the perspective of the consolidated entity remains constant.

We introduced the intra-entity sales of inventory, land, and depreciable assets together (in Chapter 5) because these transfers result in similar consolidation procedures. In each case, one of the affiliated companies recognizes a gain prior to the time the consolidated entity is entitled to recognize it. The worksheet entries required by these transactions simply realign the separate financial information to agree with the viewpoint of the business combination. The gain is removed and the inflated asset value is reduced to historical cost.

The next section of this chapter examines the intra-entity acquisition of bonds and notes. Although accounting for the related companies as a single economic entity continues to be the central goal, the consolidation procedures applied to intra-entity debt transactions stand in marked contrast to the process utilized in Chapter 5 for asset transfers.

Before delving into this topic, note that *direct* loans used to transfer funds between affiliated companies create no unique consolidation problems. Regardless of whether bonds or notes generate such amounts, the resulting receivable/payable balances are necessarily identical. Because no money is owed to or from an outside party, these reciprocal accounts must

---

[7] Patrick Finnegan, Board Member of the IASB. "At Long-Last–A Single Model for Consolidation," IFRS Foundation, May 2011 perspectives.

[8] Ibid.

be eliminated in each subsequent consolidation. A worksheet entry simply offsets the two corresponding balances. Furthermore, the interest revenue/expense accounts associated with direct loans also agree and are removed in the same fashion.

Acquisition of Affiliate's Debt from an Outside Party

The difficulties encountered in consolidating intra-entity liabilities relate to a specific type of transaction: the purchase of an affiliate's debt instrument from an outside third party. For example, a subsidiary may have issued bonds in the past that continue to be traded in the open market. If the parent then purchases all or a portion of these outstanding subsidiary bonds in the open market, from a consolidated view, the combined entity (parent and subsidiary) has reacquired its own bonds. Nonetheless, because the companies maintain independent accounting systems, the parent records an Investment in Bonds account as well as periodic interest income. The subsidiary shows the bonds as still outstanding and records periodic interest expense.

Although the individual companies continue to carry both the debt and the investment on their individual financial records, *from a consolidation viewpoint this liability is effectively retired as of the debt reacquisition date.* From that date forward, the debt is no longer owed to a party outside the business combination. Subsequent interest payments are simply intra-entity cash transfers. To create consolidated statements, worksheet entries must be developed to adjust the various balances to report the debt's effective retirement.

Acquiring an affiliate's bond or note from an unrelated party poses no significant consolidation problems if the purchase price equals the corresponding carrying amount of the liability. Reciprocal balances within the individual records would always be identical in value and easily offset in each subsequent consolidation.

Realistically, though, such reciprocity rarely occurs when a debt instrument is purchased from a third party. A variety of economic factors typically produce a difference between the price paid for the investment and the carrying amount of the obligation. The debt is originally sold under market conditions at a particular time. Any premium or discount associated with this issuance is then amortized over the life of the bond, creating a continuous adjustment to its carrying amount. The acquisition of this instrument at a later date is made at a price influenced by current economic conditions, prevailing interest rates, and myriad other financial and market factors.

Therefore, the cost paid to purchase the debt could be either more or less than the carrying amount of the liability currently found within the issuing company's financial records. *To the business combination, this difference is a gain or loss because the acquisition effectively retires the bond; the debt is no longer owed to an outside party.* For external reporting purposes, this gain or loss must be recognized immediately by the consolidated entity.

Accounting for Intra-Entity Debt Transactions—Individual Financial Records

The following accounting problems emerge in consolidating intra-entity debt transactions:

1. Intra-entity investments in debt securities and related debt accounts must be eliminated in consolidation despite their differing balances.
2. Intra-entity interest revenue/expense (as well as any interest receivable/payable accounts) must be removed although these balances also fail to agree in amount.
3. The amortization process for discounts and premiums causes continual changes in each of the preceding accounts.
4. The business combination must recognize the gain or loss on the effective retirement of the debt, even though it is not recognized within the financial records of either company.

To illustrate, assume that Alpha Company possesses an 80 percent interest in the outstanding voting stock of Omega Company. On January 1, 2015, Omega issued $1 million in 10-year bonds paying cash interest of 9 percent annually. Because of market conditions prevailing on that date, Omega sold the debt for $938,555 to yield an effective interest rate of 10 percent per year. Shortly thereafter, the interest rate began to fall, and by January 1, 2017, Omega made the decision to retire this debt prematurely and refinance it at a currently lower rate. To carry out this plan, Alpha purchased all of these bonds in the open market on January 1, 2017, for $1,057,466. This price was based on an effective yield of 8 percent, which is assumed to be in line with the interest rates at the time.

Many reasons could exist for having Alpha, rather than Omega, reacquire this debt. For example, company cash levels at that date could necessitate Alpha's role as the purchasing agent. Also, contractual limitations could prohibit Omega from repurchasing its own bonds.

In accounting for this business combination, Omega Company's bonds have been effectively retired. Thus, the difference between the $1,057,466 payment and the January 1, 2017, carrying amount of the liability must be recognized in the consolidated statements as a gain or loss. The carrying amount for the debt on that date depends on the amortization process. Exhibit 6.5 shows the bond amortization schedule for January 1, 2015, through December 31, 2018.[9]

As seen in Exhibit 6.5, the carrying amount of Omega Company's bonds has increased to $946,651 as of December 31, 2016, the date immediately before the day that Alpha Company acquired the bonds.

Because Alpha paid $110,815 in excess of the recorded liability ($1,057,466 − $946,651), the consolidated entity must recognize a loss of this amount. After the loss has been acknowledged, the bond is considered to be retired and no further reporting is necessary by the *business combination* after January 1, 2017.

Despite the simplicity of this approach for consolidation, neither company separately accounts for the event in this manner. Omega retains the $1 million debt balance within its separate financial records and amortizes the remaining discount each year. Annual cash interest payments of $90,000 (9 percent) continue to be made. At the same time, Alpha records the investment at the historical cost of $1,057,466, an amount that also requires periodic amortization. Furthermore, as the owner of these bonds, Alpha receives the $90,000 interest payments made by Omega.

To organize the accountant's approach to this consolidation, we analyze the subsequent financial records for each company. Omega records only two journal entries during 2017 assuming that interest is paid each December 31:

	Omega Company's Financial Records		
12/31/17	Interest Expense	90,000	
	Cash		90,000
	To record payment of annual cash interest on $1 million, 9 percent bonds payable.		
12/31/17	Interest Expense	4,665	
	Discount on Bonds Payable		4,665
	To adjust interest expense to effective rate based on original yield rate of 10 percent ($946,651 carrying amount for 2017 × 10% = $94,665). Carrying amount increases to $951,316.		

EXHIBIT 6.5
Omega Company Bond Issue Amortization Schedule

Date	Face Value	Unamortized Discount	Carrying Amount	Effective Interest	Cash Interest	Discount Amortized
1/1/15	$1,000,000	$61,445	$938,555			
12/31/15	1,000,000	57,590	942,410	$93,855	$90,000	$3,855
12/31/16	1,000,000	53,349	946,651	94,241	90,000	4,241
12/31/17	1,000,000	48,684	951,316	94,665	90,000	4,665
12/31/18	1,000,000	43,552	956,448	95,132	90,000	5,132

[9] The effective rate method of amortization is demonstrated here because this approach is theoretically preferable. However, the straight-line method can be applied if the resulting balances are not materially different from the figures computed using the effective rate method.

Concurrently, Alpha journalizes entries to record its ownership of this investment:

	Alpha Company's Financial Records		
1/1/17	Investment in Omega Company Bonds	1,057,466	
	Cash		1,057,466
	To record acquisition of $1,000,000 in Omega Company bonds paying 9 percent cash interest, acquired to yield an effective rate of 8 percent.		
12/31/17	Cash	90,000	
	Interest Income		90,000
	To record receipt of cash interest from Omega Company bonds ($1,000,000 × 9%).		
12/31/17	Interest Income	5,403	
	Investment in Omega Company Bonds		5,403
	To reduce $90,000 interest income to effective rate based on original yield rate of 8 percent ($1,057,466 carrying amount for 2017 × 8% = $84,597). Carrying amount decreases to $1,052,063.		

Even a brief review of these entries indicates that the reciprocal accounts to be eliminated within the consolidation process do not agree in amount. You can see the dollar amounts appearing in each set of financial records in Exhibit 6.6. Despite the presence of these recorded balances, none of the four intra-entity accounts (the bond liability, investment, interest expense, and interest revenue) appear in the consolidated financial statements. *The only figure that the business combination reports is the $110,815 loss created by the effective extinguishment of this debt.*

Effects on Consolidation Process

As previous discussions indicated, consolidation procedures convert information generated by the individual accounting systems to the perspective of a single economic entity. A worksheet entry is therefore required on December 31, 2017, to eliminate the intra-entity balances shown in Exhibit 6.6 and to recognize the loss resulting from the effective retirement. Mechanically, the differences in the liability and investment balances as well as the interest expense and interest income accounts stem from the $110,815 difference between the purchase price of the investment and the carrying amount of the liability. Recognition of this loss, in effect, bridges the gap between the divergent figures.

Consolidation Entry B (December 31, 2017)		
Bonds Payable.	1,000,000	
Interest Income	84,597	
Loss on Retirement of Bonds	110,815	
Discount on Bond Payable		48,684
Investment in Omega Company Bonds		1,052,063
Interest Expense		94,665
To eliminate intra-entity bonds and related interest accounts and to recognize loss on effective retirement. (Labeled "**B**" in reference to bonds.)		

The preceding entry successfully transforms the separate financial reporting of Alpha and Omega to that appropriate for the business combination. The objective of the consolidation process has been met: The statements present the bonds as having been retired on January 1, 2017. The debt and the corresponding investment are eliminated along with both interest accounts. Only the loss now appears on the worksheet to be reported within the consolidated financial statements.

EXHIBIT 6.6

	Omega Company Reported Debt	Alpha Company Investment
ALPHA COMPANY AND OMEGA COMPANY Effects of Intra-Entity Debt Transaction 2017		
2017 interest expense*	$ 94,665	$ –0–
2017 interest income†	–0–	(84,597)
Bonds payable	(1,000,000)	–0–
Discount on bonds payable*	48,684	–0–
Investment in bonds, 12/31/17†	–0–	1,052,063
Loss on retirement	–0–	–0–

Note: Parentheses indicate a credit balance.
*Company total is adjusted for 2017 amortization of $4,665 (see journal entry).
†Adjusted for 2017 amortization of $5,403 (see journal entry).

Assignment of Retirement Gain or Loss

An issue in accounting for intra-entity debt repurchases concerns the assignment of any retirement gains or losses. Should the $110,815 loss just reported be attributed to Alpha or to Omega? From a practical perspective, this assignment affects only the consolidated net income allocation to the controlling and noncontrolling interests. In the absence of FASB guidance on the assignment of retirement gain or loss, all income effects in this textbook relating to intra-entity debt transactions are assigned solely to the parent company. Such treatment is consistent with the perspective that the parent company ultimately controls the repurchase decision.

Intra-Entity Debt Transactions—Years Subsequent to Effective Retirement

Even though the preceding Entry **B** correctly eliminates Omega's bonds in the year of retirement for consolidation purposes, the debt remains within the financial accounts of both companies until maturity. Therefore, in each succeeding time period, all balances must again be consolidated so that the liability is always reported as having been extinguished on January 1, 2017. Unfortunately, a simple repetition of Entry **B** is not possible. Developing the appropriate worksheet entry is complicated by the amortization process that produces continual change in the various account balances. Thus, as a preliminary step in each subsequent consolidation, current carrying amounts, as reported by the two parties, must be identified.

To illustrate, the 2018 journal entries for Alpha and Omega follow. Exhibit 6.7 shows the resulting account balances as of the end of that year.

EXHIBIT 6.7

	Omega Company Reported Debt	Alpha Company Investment
ALPHA COMPANY AND OMEGA COMPANY Effects of Intra-Entity Debt Transactions 2018		
2018 interest expense*	$ 95,132	$ –0–
2018 interest income†	–0–	(84,165)
Bonds payable	(1,000,000)	–0–
Discount on bonds payable*	43,552	–0–
Investment in bonds, 12/31/18†	–0–	1,046,228
Income effect within retained earnings, 1/1/18‡	94,665	(84,597)

Note: Parentheses indicate a credit balance.
*Company total is adjusted for 2018 amortization of $5,132 (see journal entry).
†Adjusted for 2018 amortization of $5,835 (see journal entry).
‡The balance shown for the Retained Earnings account of each company represents the 2017 reported interest figures.

? Discussion Question

WHO LOST THIS $300,000?

Several years ago, Penston Company purchased 90 percent of the outstanding shares of Swansan Corporation. Penston made the acquisition because Swansan produced a vital component used in Penston's manufacturing process. Penston wanted to ensure an adequate supply of this item at a reasonable price. The former owner, James Swansan, retained the remaining 10 percent of Swansan's stock and agreed to continue managing this organization. He was given responsibility for the subsidiary's daily manufacturing operations but not for any financial decisions.

Swansan's takeover has proven to be a successful undertaking for Penston. The subsidiary has managed to supply all of the parent's inventory needs and distribute a variety of items to outside customers.

At a recent meeting, Penston's president and the company's chief financial officer began discussing Swansan's debt position. The subsidiary had a debt-to-equity ratio that seemed unreasonably high considering the significant amount of cash flows being generated by both companies. Payment of the interest expense, especially on the subsidiary's outstanding bonds, was a major cost, one that the corporate officials hoped to reduce. However, the bond indenture specified that Swansan could retire this debt prior to maturity only by paying 107 percent of face value.

This premium was considered prohibitive. Thus, to avoid contractual problems, Penston acquired a large portion of Swansan's liability in the open market for 101 percent of face value. Penston's purchase created an effective loss of $300,000 on the debt, the excess of the price over the carrying amount of the debt, as reported on Swansan's books.

Company accountants currently are computing the noncontrolling interest's share of consolidated net income to be reported for the current year. They are unsure about the impact of this $300,000 loss. The subsidiary's debt was retired, but officials of the parent company made the decision. Who lost this $300,000?

Omega Company's Financial Records—December 31, 2018

Interest Expense	90,000	
Cash		90,000
To record payment of annual cash interest on $1 million, 9 percent bonds payable.		
Interest Expense	5,132	
Discount on Bonds Payable		5,132
To adjust interest expense to effective rate based on an original yield rate of 10 percent ($951,316 carrying amount for 2018 × 10% = $95,132). Carrying amount increases to $956,448.		

Alpha Company's Financial Records—December 31, 2018

Cash	90,000	
Interest Income		90,000
To record receipt of cash interest from Omega Company bonds.		
Interest Income	5,835	
Investment in Omega Company Bonds		5,835
To reduce $90,000 interest income to effective rate based on an original yield rate of 8 percent ($1,052,063 carrying amount for 2018 × 8% = $84,165). Carrying amount decreases to $1,046,228.		

After assembling the information in Exhibit 6.7, the necessary December 31, 2018, consolidation entry is prepared. We first assume that the parent applies either the initial value or the partial equity method to its Investment in Omega account. We then show this final consolidation entry assuming the parent applies the equity method.

Parent Applies the Initial Value or Partial Equity Method

To recognize the January 1, 2017, effective retirement on the December 31, 2018, consolidated financial statements, the individual affiliate's balances for the intra-entity bonds and interest income and expense must be removed. Because neither the initial value nor the partial equity method recognizes the retirement loss, the parent's retained earnings will fail to reflect the prior year effective retirement loss. However, retained earnings will reflect past interest income and expense to the extent of any discount or premium amortization.[10] A worksheet adjustment therefore reduces Alpha's January 1, 2018, retained earnings by $110,815 to reflect the original loss net of the prior year's discount and premium amortizations.

Consolidation Entry *B, When Parent Uses the Initial Value or Partial Equity Method (December 31, 2018)		
Bonds Payable.	1,000,000	
Interest Income	84,165	
Retained Earnings—Alpha.	100,747	
Discount on Bond Payable		43,552
Investment in Omega Company Bonds		1,046,228
Interest Expense.		95,132

To eliminate intra-entity bond and related interest accounts and to adjust Alpha's Retained Earnings from $10,068 (currently recorded net debit balance) to $110,815. (Labeled "*B" in reference to prior year bond transaction.)

Analysis of this latest consolidation entry should emphasize several important factors:

1. The individual account balances change during the present fiscal period so that the current consolidation entry differs from Entry **B.** These alterations are a result of the amortization process. To ensure the accuracy of the worksheet entry, the adjusted balances are isolated in Exhibit 6.7.

2. As indicated previously, all income effects arising from intra-entity debt transactions are assigned to the parent company. For this reason, the adjustment to beginning Retained Earnings in Entry ***B** is attributed to Alpha, as is the $10,967 increase in current income ($95,132 interest expense elimination less the $84,165 interest revenue elimination).[11] Consequently, the noncontrolling interest balances are not altered by Entry ***B.**

3. The 2018 reduction to beginning Retained Earnings in Entry ***B** ($100,747) does not agree with the original $110,815 retirement loss. The individual companies have recorded a net deficit balance of $10,068 (the amount by which previous interest expense exceeds interest revenue) at the start of 2018. To achieve the proper consolidated total, an adjustment of only $100,747 is required ($110,815 − $10,068).

Retained earnings balance—consolidation perspective (loss on retirement of debt)		$110,815
Individual retained earnings balances, 1/1/18:		
Omega Company (interest expense—2017)	$94,665	
Alpha Company (interest income—2017).	(84,597)	10,068
Adjustment to consolidated retained earnings, 1/1/18		$100,747

Note: Parentheses indicate a credit balance

[10] If there is no discount or premium amortization, interest revenue will simply offset interest expense, leaving no net effect on retained earnings.

[11] Had the effects of the retirement been attributed solely to the original issuer of the bonds, the $10,967 addition to current income would have been assigned to Omega (the subsidiary), thus creating a change in the noncontrolling interest computations.

The periodic amortization of both the bond payable discount and the premium on the investment impacts the interest expense and revenue recorded by the two companies. As this schedule shows, these two interest accounts do not offset exactly; a $10,068 net residual amount remains in Retained Earnings after the first year. Because this balance continues to increase each year, the subsequent consolidation adjustments to record the loss decrease to $100,747 in 2018 and constantly lesser thereafter. *Over the life of the bond, the amortization process gradually brings the totals in the individual Retained Earnings accounts into agreement with the consolidated balance.*

Parent Applies the Equity Method

Entry ***B** as shown is appropriate for consolidations in which the parent has applied either the initial value or the partial equity method. However, a deviation is required if the parent uses the equity method for internal reporting purposes. Properly applying the equity method ensures that the parent's income and, hence, its retained earnings are correctly stated prior to consolidation. Alpha would have already recognized the loss in accounting for this investment. Consequently, when the parent applies the equity method, no adjustment to Retained Earnings is needed. In this one case, the $100,747 debit in Entry ***B** is made to the Investment in Omega Company (instead of Retained Earnings) because the loss has become a component of that account.

Consolidation Entry *B, When Parent Uses the Equity Method (December 31, 2018)

Bonds Payable.	1,000,000	
Interest Income	84,165	
Investment in Omega	100,747	
Discount on Bond Payable		43,552
Investment in Omega Company Bonds		1,046,228
Interest Expense		95,132

To eliminate intra-entity bond and related interest accounts and to adjust the Investment in Omega from $10,068 (currently recorded net debit balance) to $110,815. (Labeled "***B**" in reference to prior year bond transaction.)

The Entry *B debit to the Investment in Omega account then serves as part of the investment account elimination sequence.

LO 6-4

Understand that subsidiary preferred stock not owned by the parent is a component of the noncontrolling interest and is initially measured at acquisition-date fair value.

Subsidiary Preferred Stock

Although both small and large corporations routinely issue preferred shares, their presence within a subsidiary's equity structure adds a new dimension to the consolidation process. What accounting should be made of a subsidiary's preferred stock and the parent's payments that are made to acquire these shares?

Recall that preferred shares, although typically nonvoting, possess other "preferences" over common shares such as a cumulative dividend preference or participation rights. Some preferred shares even offer limited voting rights. Regardless, preferred shares are part of the subsidiary's stockholders' equity and are treated as such in consolidated financial reports.

The existence of subsidiary preferred shares does little to complicate the consolidation process. The acquisition method measures all business acquisitions (whether 100 percent or less than 100 percent acquired) at their full fair values. In accounting for the acquisition of a subsidiary with preferred stock, the essential process of determining the acquisition-date business fair value of the subsidiary remains intact. Any preferred shares not owned by the parent simply become a component of the noncontrolling interest and are included in the subsidiary business fair-value calculation. The acquisition-date fair value for any subsidiary common and/or preferred shares owned by outsiders becomes the basis for the noncontrolling interest valuation in the parent's consolidated financial reports.

To illustrate, assume that on January 1, 2017, High Company acquires control over Low Company by purchasing 80 percent of its outstanding common stock and 60 percent of its nonvoting, cumulative, preferred stock. Low owns land undervalued in its records by $100,000, but all other assets and liabilities have fair values equal to their book values. High paid $1 million for the common shares and $62,400 for the preferred shares. On the acquisition date, the 20 percent noncontrolling interest in the common shares had a fair value of $250,000 and the 40 percent preferred stock noncontrolling interest had a fair value of $41,600.

Low's capital structure immediately prior to the acquisition is shown below:

Common stock, $20 par value (20,000 shares outstanding).	$ 400,000
Preferred stock, 6% cumulative with a par value of $100	100,000
(1,000 shares outstanding)	
Additional paid-in capital	200,000
Retained earnings	516,000
Total stockholders' equity (book value).	$1,216,000

Exhibit 6.8 shows High's calculation of the acquisition-date fair value of Low and the allocation of the difference between the fair and book values to land and goodwill.

As seen in Exhibit 6.8, the subsidiary's ownership structure (i.e., comprising both preferred and common shares) does not affect the fair-value principle for determining the basis for consolidating the subsidiary. Moreover, the acquisition method follows the same procedure for calculating business fair value regardless of the various preferences the preferred shares may possess. Any cumulative or participating preferences (or other rights) attributed to the preferred shares are assumed to be captured by the acquisition-date fair value of the shares and thus automatically incorporated into the subsidiary's valuation basis for consolidation.

By utilizing the information above, we next construct a basic worksheet entry as of January 1, 2017 (the acquisition date). In the presence of both common and preferred subsidiary shares, combining the customary consolidation entries S and A avoids an unnecessary allocation of the subsidiary's retained earnings across these equity shares. The combined consolidation entry also recognizes the allocations made to the undervalued land and goodwill. No other consolidation entries are needed because no time has passed since the acquisition took place.

Consolidation Entries S and A (combined)		
Common Stock (Low).	400,000	
Preferred Stock (Low).	100,000	
Additional Paid-In Capital (Low)	200,000	
Retained Earnings (Low)	516,000	
Land.	100,000	
Goodwill	38,000	
Investment in Low's Common Stock.		1,000,000
Investment in Low's Preferred Stock.		62,400
Noncontrolling Interest		291,600
To eliminate the subsidiary's common and preferred shares, recognize the fair values of the subsidiary's assets, and recognize the outside ownership.		

The above combined consolidation entry recognizes the noncontrolling interest as the total of acquisition-date fair values of $250,000 for the common stock and $41,600 for the preferred shares. Consistent with previous consolidation illustrations throughout the text, the entire subsidiary's stockholders' equity section is eliminated along with the parent's investment accounts—in this case for both the common and preferred shares.

Allocation of Subsidiary Income

The final factor influencing a consolidation that includes subsidiary preferred shares is the allocation of the company's income between the two types of stock. A division must be made for every period subsequent to the takeover (1) to compute the noncontrolling interest's share and

EXHIBIT 6.8

LOW COMPANY Acquisition-Date Fair Value January 1, 2017	
Consideration transferred for 80% interest in Low's common stock	$1,000,000
Consideration transferred for 60% interest in Low's preferred stock	62,400
Noncontrolling interest in Low's common stock (20%)	250,000
Noncontrolling interest in Low's preferred stock (40%)	41,600
Total fair value of Low on 1/1/17	$1,354,000

HIGH'S ACQUISITION OF LOW Excess Fair Value Over Book Value Allocation January 1, 2017		
Low Company business fair value		$1,354,000
Low Company book value		1,216,000
Excess acquisition-date fair value over book value		$ 138,000
Assigned to land	$100,000	
Assigned to goodwill	38,000	138,000
		$ –0–

(2) for the parent's own recognition purposes. For a cumulative nonparticipating preferred stock such as the one presently being examined, only the specified annual dividend is attributed to the preferred stock with all remaining income assigned to common stock. Consequently, if we assume that Low reports earnings of $100,000 in 2017 while declaring and paying the annual $6,000 dividend on its preferred stock, we allocate income for consolidation purposes as follows:

	Income
Subsidiary total	$100,000
Preferred stock (6% dividend × $100,000 par value of the stock)	$ 6,000
Common stock (residual amount)	94,000

During 2017, High Company, as the parent, is entitled to $3,600 in dividends ($6,000 × 60%) from Low's preferred stock because of its 60 percent ownership. In addition, High holds 80 percent of Low's common stock so that another $75,200 of the income ($94,000 × 80%) is attributed to the parent. The noncontrolling interest in consolidated net income can be calculated in a similar fashion:

		Percentage Outside Ownership	Noncontrolling Interest
Preferred stock dividend	$ 6,000	40%	$ 2,400
Income attributed to common stock	94,000	20	18,800
Noncontrolling interest in consolidated net income			$21,200

LO 6-5

Prepare a consolidated statement of cash flows.

Consolidated Statement of Cash Flows

Current accounting standards require that companies include a statement of cash flows among their consolidated financial reports. The main purpose of the statement of cash flows is to provide information about the entity's cash receipts and cash payments during a period. The statement is also designed to show why an entity's net income is different from its operating cash flows. For a consolidated entity, the cash flows relate to the entire business combination including the parent and all of its subsidiaries.

The statement of cash flows allocates the consolidated entity's overall change in cash during a period to three separate categories:

1. Cash flows from operating activities.
2. Cash flows from investing activities.
3. Cash flows from financing activities.

The cash flows from operating activities can be shown using either the indirect method or the direct method. The indirect method begins with consolidated net income and then adds and subtracts various items to adjust the accrual number to a cash flow amount. The direct method examines cash flows directly from distinct sources that typically include revenues, purchases of inventory, and cash payments of other expenses. However, firms using the direct method must also supplement the statement with the calculation of cash flows from operating activities using the indirect method.

The consolidated statement of cash flows is not prepared from the individual cash flow statements of the separate companies. Instead, the consolidated income statements and balance sheets are first brought together on the worksheet. The cash flows statement is then based on the resulting consolidated figures. Thus, this statement is not actually produced by a consolidation worksheet, but is created from numbers generated by the process. Because special accounting procedures are needed in the period when the parent acquires a subsidiary, we first discuss preparation of the consolidated statement of cash flows for periods in which an acquisition takes place, followed by statement preparation in periods subsequent to acquisition.

Acquisition Period Statement of Cash Flows

If a business combination occurs during a particular reporting period, the consolidated cash flow statement must properly reflect several considerations. For many business combinations, the following issues frequently are present:

Business Acquisitions in Exchange for Cash

Cash purchases of businesses are an investing activity. The *net cash outflow* (cash paid less subsidiary cash acquired) is reported as the amount paid in a business acquisition.[12]

Operating Cash Flow Adjustments

Keeping in mind that the focus is on the consolidated entity's cash flows (not just the parent's), consolidated net income is the starting point for the indirect calculation of consolidated operating cash flows. Recall that consolidated net income includes only postacquisition subsidiary revenues and expenses. Therefore, the adjustment to the accrual-based income number must also reflect only postacquisition amounts for the subsidiary. One important category of adjustments to consolidated net income to arrive at cash flows from operations involves changes in current operating accounts (e.g., accounts receivable, accounts payable, etc.).

For example, an increase in an accounts receivable balance typically indicates that a firm's accrual-based sales exceed the actual cash collections for sales during a period. Therefore, in computing operating cash flows, the increase in accounts receivable are deducted from the sales amount (direct method) or the net income (indirect method). However, when an acquisition takes place, the change in accounts receivable will often include amounts from the newly acquired subsidiary. Because the consolidated entity recognizes only postacquisition subsidiary revenues, such acquired receivables do not reflect sales that have been made by the consolidated entity. Therefore any subsidiary acquisition-date current operating account balances must be removed before calculating the change in accounts receivable.

---

[12] For acquisitions that do not involve cash, or only partially involve cash, the details of the acquisitions should be provided in a supplemental disclosure to the statement of cash flows for "significant noncash investing and financing activities."

In fact, any changes in operating balance sheet accounts (accounts receivable, inventory, accounts payable, etc.) must be computed net of the amounts acquired in the combination. Use of the direct method of presenting operating cash flows also reports the separate computations of cash collected from customers and cash paid for inventory net of acquisition-date balances of newly acquired businesses.

Excess Fair-Value Amortizations

Any adjustments arising from the subsidiary's revenues or expenses (e.g., depreciation, amortization) must reflect only postacquisition amounts. Closing the subsidiary's books at the date of acquisition facilitates the determination of the appropriate current year postacquisition subsidiary effects on the consolidated entity's cash flows.

Subsidiary Dividends Paid

The cash outflow from subsidiary dividends only leaves the consolidated entity when paid to the noncontrolling interest. Thus dividends paid by a subsidiary to its parent do not appear as financing outflows. However, subsidiary dividends paid to the noncontrolling interest are a component of cash outflows from financing activities.

Intra-Entity Transfers

A significant volume of transfers between affiliated companies comprising a business combination often occurs. The resulting effects of intra-entity activities are eliminated in the preparation of consolidated statements. Likewise, the consolidated statement of cash flows does not include the impact of these transfers. Intra-entity sales and purchases do not change the amount of cash held by the business combination when viewed as a whole. Because the statement of cash flows is derived from the consolidated balance sheet and income statement, the impact of all transfers is already removed. Therefore, the proper presentation of cash flows requires no special adjustments for intra-entity transfers. The worksheet entries produce correct balances for the consolidated statement of cash flows.

Consolidated Statement of Cash Flows Illustration

Assume that on July 1, 2017, Pinto Company acquires 90 percent of Salida Company's outstanding stock for $774,000 in cash. At the acquisition date, the 10 percent noncontrolling interest has a fair value of $86,000. Exhibit 6.9 shows book and fair values of Salida's assets and liabilities and Pinto's acquisition-date fair-value allocation schedule.

At the end of 2017, the following comparative balance sheets and consolidated income statement are available:

PINTO COMPANY AND SUBSIDIARY SALIDA COMPANY
Comparative Balance Sheets

	Pinto Co. January 1, 2017	Consolidated December 31, 2017
Cash	$ 170,000	$ 431,000
Accounts receivable (net)	118,000	319,000
Inventory	310,000	395,000
Land	250,000	370,000
Buildings (net)	350,000	426,000
Equipment (net)	1,145,000	1,380,000
Database	–0–	49,000
Total assets	$2,343,000	$3,370,000
Accounts payable	$50,000	$ 45,000
Long-term liabilities	18,000	522,000
Common stock	1,500,000	1,500,000
Noncontrolling interest	–0–	98,250
Retained earnings	775,000	1,204,750
Total liabilities and equities	$2,343,000	$3,370,000

EXHIBIT 6.9

SALIDA COMPANY
Book and Fair Values
July 1, 2017

Account	Book Value	Fair Value
Cash..	$ 35,000	$ 35,000
Accounts receivable......................	145,000	145,000
Inventory................................	90,000	90,000
Land.....................................	100,000	120,000
Buildings................................	136,000	136,000
Equipment................................	259,000	299,000
Database.................................	–0–	50,000
Accounts payable........................	(15,000)	(15,000)
Net book value..........................	$750,000	$860,000

PINTO'S ACQUISITION OF SALIDA
Excess Fair Value over Book Value Allocation
July 1, 2017

Consideration transferred by Pinto....................		$774,000
Noncontrolling interest fair value.....................		86,000
Salida's total fair value..............................		$860,000
Salida's book value..................................		750,000
Excess fair over book value..........................		$110,000
To land.....................................	$ 20,000	
To equipment (5-year remaining life)..............	40,000	
To database (25-year remaining life)..............	50,000	110,000
		$ –0–

PINTO COMPANY AND SUBSIDIARY SALIDA COMPANY
Consolidated Income Statement (partial presentation)
For the Year Ended December 31, 2017

Revenues...		$1,255,000
Cost of goods sold...............................	$600,000	
Depreciation.....................................	124,000	
Database amortization...........................	1,000	
Interest and other expenses......................	35,500	760,500
Consolidated net income.........................		$ 494,500

Additional Information for 2017

- The consolidated income statement totals include Salida's postacquisition revenues and expenses.
- During the year, Pinto paid $50,000 in dividends. On August 1, Salida paid a $25,000 dividend.
- During the year, Pinto issued $504,000 in long-term debt at par value.
- No asset purchases or dispositions occurred during the year other than Pinto's acquisition of Salida.

In preparing the consolidated statement of cash flows, note that each adjustment derives from the consolidated income statement or changes from Pinto's January 1, 2017, balance sheet to the consolidated balance sheet at December 31, 2017.

Depreciation and Amortization

These expenses do not represent current operating cash outflows and thus are added back to convert accrual basis income to cash provided by operating activities.

Increases in Accounts Receivable, Inventory, and Accounts Payable (net of acquisition)

Changes in balance sheet accounts affecting operating cash flows must take into account amounts acquired in business acquisitions. In this case, note that the changes in Accounts Receivable, Inventory, and Accounts Payable are computed as follows:

	Accounts Receivable	Inventory	Accounts Payable
Pinto's balance, 1/1/17..................	$118,000	$310,000	$50,000
Increase from Salida acquisition............	145,000	90,000	15,000
Adjusted beginning balance	263,000	400,000	65,000
Consolidated balance, 12/31/17	319,000	395,000	45,000
Operating cash flow adjustment..........	$ 56,000	$ 5,000	$20,000

Acquisition of Salida Company

The Investing Activities section of the cash flow statement shows increases and decreases in assets purchased or sold involving cash. The cash outflow from the acquisition of Salida Company is determined as follows:

Cash paid for 90% interest in Salida.........	$774,000
Cash acquired	(35,000)
Net cash paid for Salida investment.......	$739,000

Note here that although Pinto acquires only 90 percent of Salida, 100 percent of Salida's cash is offset against the cash consideration paid in the acquisition in determining the investing cash outflow. Ownership divisions between the noncontrolling and controlling interests do not affect reporting for the entity's investing cash flows.

Issue of Long-Term Debt

Pinto Company's issuance of long-term debt represents a cash inflow from financing activities.

Dividends

The dividends paid to Pinto Company owners ($50,000) combined with the dividends paid to the noncontrolling interest ($2,500) represent cash outflows from financing activities.

Based on the consolidated totals from the comparative balance sheets and the consolidated income statement, the following consolidated statement of cash flows is then prepared. Pinto chooses to use the indirect method of reporting cash flows from operating activities.

PINTO COMPANY AND SUBSIDIARY SALIDA COMPANY
Consolidated Statement of Cash Flows (partial presentation)
For the Year Ended December 31, 2017

Consolidated net income.....................		$ 494,500
Depreciation expense.....................	$ 124,000	
Amortization expense.....................	1,000	
Increase in accounts receivable (net of acquisition effects)......	(56,000)	
Decrease in inventory (net of acquisition effects)	5,000	
Decrease in accounts payable (net of acquisition effects).......	(20,000)	54,000
Net cash provided by operating activities		$ 548,500
Purchase of Salida Company (net of cash acquired)...........		
Net cash used in investing activities	$(739,000)	(739,000)
Issue long-term debt.......................................	$ 504,000	
Dividends..	(52,500)	
Net cash provided by financing activities....................		451,500
Increase in Cash, 1/1/17 to 12/31/17....................		**$261,000**

Statement of Cash Flows in Periods Subsequent to Acquisition

Preparing a consolidated statement of cash flows during periods of no acquisition is relatively uncomplicated. As before, consolidated net income is the starting point for the indirect calculation of consolidated operating cash flows. If the operating accounts (e.g., accounts receivable, accounts payable, etc.) do not include amounts acquired in a business combination, then no further special adjustments are required. Because the consolidation process eliminates intra-entity balances, preparation of the operating activity section of the statement of cash flows typically proceeds in a straightforward manner using the already available consolidated income statement and balance sheet amounts. Finally, subsidiary dividends paid to the noncontrolling interest are shown as a component of cash outflows from financing activities.

LO 6-6

Compute basic and diluted earnings per share for a business combination.

Consolidated Earnings per Share

The consolidation process affects one other intermediate accounting topic, the computation of earnings per share (EPS). Publicly held companies must disclose EPS each period.

The following steps calculate such figures:

- Determine basic EPS by dividing the parent's share of consolidated net income (after reduction for preferred stock dividends) by the weighted-average number of common stock shares outstanding for the period. If the reporting entity has no dilutive options, warrants, or other convertible items, only basic EPS is presented on the face of the income statement. However, diluted EPS also must be presented if any dilutive convertibles are present.

- Compute diluted EPS by combining the effects of *any dilutive securities* with basic earnings per share. Stock options, stock warrants, convertible debt, and convertible preferred stock often qualify as dilutive securities.[13]

In most instances, the computation of EPS for a business combination follows the same general pattern. Consolidated net income attributable to the parent company owners along with the number of outstanding parent shares provides the basis for calculating basic EPS. Any convertibles, warrants, or options for the parent's stock that can possibly dilute the reported figure must be included as described earlier in determining diluted EPS.

However, a problem arises if warrants, options, or convertibles that can dilute the subsidiary's earnings are outstanding. Although the parent company is not directly affected, the potential impact of these items on its share of consolidated net income must be given weight in computing diluted EPS for the consolidated income statement. Because of possible conversion, the subsidiary earnings figure included in consolidated net income is not necessarily applicable to the diluted EPS computation. *Thus, the accountant must separately determine the parent's share of subsidiary income that should be used in deriving diluted EPS.*

Finally, the focus is on earnings per share for the parent company stockholders, even in the presence of a noncontrolling interest. As stated in FASB ASC (para. 260-10-45-11A):

> For purposes of computing EPS in consolidated financial statements (both basic and diluted), if one or more less-than-wholly-owned subsidiaries are included in the consolidated group, income from continuing operations and net income shall exclude the income attributable to the noncontrolling interest in subsidiaries.

Thus, consolidated income attributable to the parent's interest forms the basis for the numerator in all EPS calculations for consolidated financial reporting.

---

[13] Complete coverage of the EPS computation can be found in virtually any intermediate accounting textbook. To adequately understand this process, a number of complex procedures must be mastered, including these:

- Calculation of the weighted-average number of common shares outstanding.
- Understanding the method of including stock rights, convertible debt, and convertible preferred stock within the computation of diluted EPS.

Earnings per Share Illustration

Assume Big Corporation has 100,000 shares of its common stock outstanding during the current year. The company also has issued 20,000 shares of nonvoting preferred stock, paying an annual cumulative preferred dividend of $5 per share ($100,000 total). Each of these preferred shares is convertible into two shares of Big's common stock.

Assume also that Big owns 90 percent of Little's common stock and 60 percent of its preferred stock (which pays $12,000 in preferred dividends per year). Annual amortization is $26,000, attributable to various intangibles. Big is preparing its EPS computations for 2017. During the year, Big reported separate income of $600,000 and Little earned $100,000. A simplified consolidation of the figures for the year indicates consolidated net income attributable to Big of $663,000:

Big's separate income for 2017		$600,000
Little's separate income for 2017	$100,000	
Amortization expense resulting from original fair-value allocation	(26,000)	
Little's income after excess fair-value amortization		74,000
Consolidated net income		$674,000
Noncontrolling interest in Little—common stock (10% × $62,000 [$74,000 income less $12,000 preferred stock dividends])	$ (6,200)	
Noncontrolling interest in Little— preferred stock (40% of dividends)	(4,800)	
Net income attributable to the noncontrolling interest		(11,000)
Net income attributable to Big (parent)		$663,000

Little has 20,000 shares of common stock and 4,000 shares of preferred stock outstanding. The preferred shares pay a $3 per year dividend, and each can be converted into two shares of common stock (or 8,000 shares in total). Because Big owns only 60 percent of Little's preferred stock, a $4,800 dividend is distributed each year to the outside owners (40 percent of the $12,000 total payment).

Assume finally that the subsidiary also has $200,000 in convertible bonds outstanding that were originally issued at face value. This debt has both a cash and an effective interest rate of 10 percent ($20,000 per year) and can be converted by the owners into 9,000 shares of Little's common stock. Big owns none of these bonds. Little's tax rate is 30 percent.

To better visualize these factors, the convertible items are scheduled as follows:

Company	Item	Interest or Dividend	Conversion	Big Owns
Big	Preferred stock	$100,000/year	40,000 shares	Not applicable
Little	Preferred stock	12,000/year	8,000 shares	60%
Little	Bonds	14,000/year*	9,000 shares	–0–

*Interest on the bonds is shown net of the 30 percent tax effect ($20,000 interest less $6,000 tax savings). No tax is computed for the preferred shares because distributed dividends do not create a tax impact.

Because the subsidiary has convertible items that can affect the company's outstanding shares and net income, Little's diluted earnings per share must be derived *before* Big's diluted EPS can be determined. As shown in Exhibit 6.10, Little's diluted EPS are $2.38. Two aspects of this schedule should be noted:

- The individual impact of the convertibles ($1.50 for the preferred stock and $1.56 for the bonds) did not raise the EPS figures above the $3.10 basic EPS. Thus, neither the preferred stock nor the bonds are antidilutive, and both are properly included in these computations.

- Absent the presence of the subsidiary's convertible bonds and preferred stock, the parent's share of consolidated net income would form the basis for computing EPS.

EXHIBIT 6.10
Subsidiary's Diluted
Earnings per Share

				LITTLE COMPANY		
				Basic and Diluted Earnings per Common Share		
				For Year Ending December 31, 2017		
	Earnings			Shares		
Little's income after amortization . .	$74,000			20,000		
Preferred stock dividends	(12,000)					
Basic EPS	$62,000			20,000	$3.10	
					($62,000/20,000)	
Effect of possible preferred						
stock conversion:						
Dividends saved	$12,000	New shares		8,000	$1.50 impact	
					(12,000/8,000)	
Effect of possible bond conversion:						
Interest saved (net of taxes).	$14,000			9,000	$ 1.56 impact	
					(14,000/9,000)	
Diluted EPS.	$88,000			37,000	$ 2.38 (rounded)	

As shown in Exhibit 6.10, Little's income is $88,000 for diluted EPS. The issue then becomes how much of this amount should be included in computing the parent's diluted EPS. This allocation is based on the percentage of shares controlled by the parent. Note that if the subsidiary's preferred stock and bonds are converted into common shares, Big's ownership falls from 90 to 62 percent. For diluted EPS, 37,000 shares are appropriate. Big's 62 percent ownership (22,800/37,000) is the basis for allocating the subsidiary's $88,000 income to the parent.

Supporting Calculations for Diluted Earnings per Share

	Little Company Shares	Big's Percentage	Big's Ownership
Common stock	20,000	90%	18,000
Possible new shares—preferred stock	8,000	60	4,800
Possible new shares—bonds	9,000	–0–	–0–
Total	37,000		22,800

Big's ownership (diluted): 22,800/37,000 = 62% (rounded)
Income assigned to Big (diluted earnings per share computation): $88,000 × 62% = $54,560

We can now determine Big Company's EPS. Only $54,560 of subsidiary income is appropriate for computing diluted EPS. Because separate income figures are utilized, Exhibit 6.11 (page 289) shows separate basic and diluted EPS calculations. Consequently, Big Company reports basic EPS of $5.63 and diluted earnings per share of $4.68.

LO 6-7

Demonstrate the accounting effects of subsidiary stock transactions on the parent's financial records and consolidated financial statements.

Subsidiary Stock Transactions

A note to the financial statements of Gerber Products Company disclosed a transaction carried out by one of the organization's subsidiaries: "The Company's wholly owned Mexican subsidiary sold previously unissued shares of common stock to Grupo Coral, S.A., a Mexican food company, at a price in excess of the shares' net book value." The note added that Gerber had increased consolidated Additional Paid-In Capital by $432,000 as a result of this stock sale.

As this illustration shows, subsidiary stock transactions can alter the level of parent ownership. A subsidiary, for example, can decide to sell previously unissued stock to raise needed capital. Although the parent company can acquire a portion or even all of these new shares,

EXHIBIT 6.11

BIG COMPANY AND CONSOLIDATED SUBSIDIARY
Basic Earnings per Common Share
For Year Ending December 31, 2017

	Earnings	Shares	
Consolidated net income (to Big) . .	$663,000		
Big's shares outstanding		100,000	
Preferred stock dividends (Big)	(100,000)		
Basic EPS	$563,000	100,000	$5.63

Diluted Earnings per Common Share
For Year Ending December 31, 2017

	Earnings		Shares	
Computed below	$654,560*			
Big's shares outstanding			100,000	
Preferred stock dividends (Big)	(100,000)			
Effect of possible preferred stock (Big) conversion:				
Dividends saved	100,000	New shares	40,000	$2.50 impact (100,000/40,000)
Diluted EPS	$654,560		140,000	$4.68 (rounded)

*Net income computation:

Big's separate income	$600,000
Portion of Little's income assigned to diluted earnings per share calculation	54,560 (computed in supporting calculations)
Earnings of the business combination applicable to diluted earnings per share	$654,560

such issues frequently are marketed entirely to outsiders. A subsidiary could also be legally forced to sell additional shares of its stock. As an example, companies holding control over foreign subsidiaries occasionally encounter this problem because of laws in the individual localities. Regulations requiring a certain percentage of local ownership as a prerequisite for operating within a country can mandate issuance of new shares. Of course, changes in the level of parent ownership do not result solely from stock sales: A subsidiary also can repurchase its own stock. The acquisition, as well as the possible retirement, of such treasury shares serves as a means of reducing the percentage of outside ownership.

Changes in Subsidiary Value—Stock Transactions

When a subsidiary subsequently buys or sells its own stock, a nonoperational increase or decrease occurs in the company's fair and book value. Because the transaction need not involve the parent, the parent's investment account does not automatically reflect the effect of this change. However, the parent's percentage ownership of the subsidiary may change. *Thus, a separate adjustment must be recorded to maintain reciprocity between the subsidiary's stockholders' equity accounts and the parent's investment balance.* The accountant measures the impact the stock transaction has on the parent to ensure that this effect is appropriately recorded in the parent's investment account and then reflected in the consolidation process.

An overall perspective of accounting for subsidiary stock transactions follows from the fundamental notion that the parent establishes the subsidiary's valuation basis at fair value as of the acquisition date. Over time, the parent adjusts this initial fair value for subsidiary income less excess amortization and subsidiary dividends. If the subsidiary issues (or buys) any of its own stock subsequent to acquisition, the effect on the parent will depend on whether the price received (or paid) is greater or less than the per share subsidiary adjusted fair value at that point in time.

An example demonstrates the mechanics of this issue. Assume that on January 1, 2017, Giant Company acquires in the open market 60,000 of Small Company's outstanding 80,000 shares and prepares the following fair-value allocation schedule:

Consideration transferred by Giant	$480,000	
Noncontrolling interest fair value	160,000	
Small Company acquisition-date fair value		$640,000
Small Company acquisition-date book value		
Common stock (80,000 shares outstanding)	$ 80,000	
Additional paid-in capital	200,000	
Retained earnings, 1/1/17	260,000	540,000
Excess fair value assigned to trademark (10-year remaining life) . . .		$100,000

Assuming Small reports earnings of $50,000 in 2017 and pays no dividends, Giant prepares the following routine consolidation entries for the December 31, 2017, worksheet. Giant uses the equity method to account for its 75 percent interest in Small.

December 31, 2017, Consolidation Worksheet Entries

Consolidation Entry S

Common Stock (Small Company).......................................	80,000	
Additional Paid-In Capital (Small Company).............................	200,000	
Retained Earnings, 1/1/17 (Small Company)	260,000	
Investment in Small Compan'y (75%)		405,000
Noncontrolling Interest in Small Company (25%)		135,000

To eliminate subsidiary's stockholders' equity accounts and recognize noncontrolling interest beginning balance in Small's book value.

Consolidation Entry A

Trademark	100,000	
Investment in Small Company (75%)...............................		75,000
Noncontrolling Interest in Small Company (25%)		25,000

To recognize the excess acquisition-date fair value assigned to Small's trademark with allocations to the controlling and noncontrolling interest.

Consolidation Entry I

Equity in Small's Earnings	30,000	
Investment in Small Company		30,000

To eliminate Giant's equity in Small's earnings (75% × [$50,000 less $10,000 trademark excess amortization]).

Consolidation Entry E

Amortization Expense	10,000	
Trademark		10,000

To recognize the excess trademark amortization ($100,000 ÷ 10 years).

We now introduce a subsidiary stock transaction to demonstrate the effect created on the consolidation process. Assume that on January 1, 2018, Giant announces plans for expansion of Small's operations. To help finance the expansion, Small sells 20,000 previously unissued shares of its common stock to outside parties for $10 per share. After the stock issue, Small's book value is as follows:

Common stock ($1.00 par value with 100,000 shares issued and outstanding).....	$100,000
Additional paid-in capital	380,000
Retained earnings, 1/1/18	310,000
Total stockholders' equity, 1/1/18	$790,000

Note that the common stock and additional paid-in capital balances reflect increases from the new stock issue. Retained earnings have also increased from Small's $50,000 income in 2017 (no dividends). Although Small's book value is now $790,000, its valuation for the consolidated entity is derived from its acquisition-date fair value as adjusted through time as follows:

Consideration transferred	$480,000
Noncontrolling interest acquisition-date fair value	160,000
2017 Small income less excess amortization	40,000
Adjusted subsidiary value, 1/1/18	$680,000
Stock issue proceeds ($10 × 20,000 shares)	200,000
Subsidiary valuation basis, 1/1/18	$880,000

Because of Small's stock issue, Giant no longer possesses a 75 percent interest. Instead, the parent now holds 60 percent (60,000 shares of a total of 100,000 shares) of Small Company. The effect on the parent's ownership can be computed as follows:

Small's valuation basis, 1/1/18 (above)	$880,000
Giant's post-issue ownership (60,000 shares ÷ 100,000 shares)	60%
Giant's post, stock issue ownership balance	$528,000
Giant's equity-adjusted investment account ($480,000 + [75% × $40,000])	510,000
Required adjustment—increase in Giant's additional paid-in capital	$ 18,000

Independent of any action by the parent company, the assigned fair-value equivalency of this investment has risen from $510,000 to $528,000. Small's ability to sell shares of stock at more than the per share consolidated subsidiary value ($680,000 ÷ 80,000 shares = $8.50 per share) created an increased value for the parent. Therefore, Giant records the $18,000 increment as an adjustment to both its investment account (because the underlying value of the subsidiary has increased) and additional paid-in capital:

Giant Company's Financial Records—January 1, 2018		
Investment in Small Company	18,000	
Additional Paid-In Capital (Giant Company)...........................		18,000
To recognize change in equity of business combination created by Small Company issuing 20,000 additional shares of common stock at above the previously assigned fair value.		

Note that the parent reports a change in stockholders' equity (i.e., Additional Paid-In Capital) for effects from subsidiary stock transactions. GAAP literature states that

> [c]hanges in a parent's ownership interest while the parent retains its controlling financial interest in its subsidiary shall be accounted for as equity transactions (investments by owners and distributions to owners acting in their capacity as owners). Therefore, no gain or loss shall be recognized in consolidated net income or comprehensive income. The carrying amount of the noncontrolling interest shall be adjusted to reflect the change in its ownership interest in the subsidiary. Any difference between the fair value of the consideration received or paid and the amount by which the noncontrolling interest is adjusted shall be recognized in equity attributable to the parent. [FASB ASC (para. 810-10-45-23)]

Consistent with this view, this textbook treats the effects from subsidiary stock transactions on the consolidated entity as adjustments to Additional Paid-In Capital.

After the change in the parent's records has been made, the consolidation process can proceed in a normal fashion. Assuming Small reports earnings of $85,000 in 2018 and pays no dividends, Giant prepares the following routine consolidation entries for the December 31, 2018, worksheet. *Although the investment and subsidiary equity accounts are removed here, the change recorded earlier in Giant's Additional Paid-In Capital remains within the consolidated figures.*

December 31, 2018, Consolidation Worksheet Entries

Consolidation Entry S

Common Stock (Small Company)	100,000	
Additional Paid-In Capital (Small Company)	380,000	
Retained Earnings (Small Company)	310,000	
Investment in Small Company (60%)		474,000
Noncontrolling Interest in Small Company (40%)		316,000

To eliminate subsidiary's stockholders' equity accounts and recognize noncontrolling interest book value beginning balance. Small's capital accounts have been updated to reflect the issuance of 20,000 shares of $1 par value common stock at $10 per share.

Consolidation Entry A

Trademark	90,000	
Investment in Small Company (60%)		54,000
Noncontrolling Interest in Small Company (40%)		36,000

To recognize the unamortized excess acquisition-date fair value assigned to Small's trademark as of the beginning of the period with allocations to the controlling and noncontrolling interests' adjusted ownership percentages.

Consolidation Entry I

Equity in Small's Earnings	45,000	
Investment in Small Company		45,000

To eliminate Giant's equity in Small's earnings (60% × [$85,000 − $10,000 trademark excess amortization]).

Consolidation Entry E

Amortization Expense	10,000	
Trademark		10,000

To recognize the excess trademark amortization ($100,000 ÷ 10 years).

The noncontrolling interest now stands at 40 percent ownership. Because these 40 percent owners will share in the profits generated by the subsidiary's trademark, they are allocated a 40 percent share to their overall equity balance in the consolidated financial statements. The noncontrolling interest is also assigned 40 percent of the excess fair-value trademark amortization.

Subsidiary Stock Transactions—Illustrated

No single example can demonstrate the many possible variations that different types of subsidiary stock transactions could create. To provide a working knowledge of this process, we analyze four additional cases briefly, each based on the following scenario:

Assume that Antioch Company acquires 90 percent of the common stock of Westminster Company on January 1, 2017, in exchange for $1,350,000 cash. The acquisition-date fair value of the 10 percent noncontrolling interest is $150,000. At that date, Westminster has the following stockholders' equity accounts:

Common stock—100,000 shares outstanding	$ 200,000
Additional paid-in capital	450,000
Retained earnings, 1/1/17	750,000
Total stockholders' equity	$1,400,000

The $100,000 excess acquisition-date fair over book value was allocated to a customer list with a five-year remaining life. In 2017, Westminster reports $190,000 in earnings and declares a $30,000 dividend. Antioch accrues its share of Westminster's income (less excess fair-value amortization related to the customer list) through application of the equity method. Antioch's equity method balance for its investment in Westminster is computed as follows:

Consideration transferred for 90% of Westminster	$1,350,000
Equity earnings of Westminster (90% × [$190,000 − $20,000 excess amortization])	153,000
Dividends from Westminster (90% × $30,000)	(27,000)
Equity method balance, 12/31/17	$1,476,000

View each of the following cases as an independent situation.

Case 1

Assume that on January 1, 2018, Westminster Company sells 25,000 shares of previously unissued common stock to outside parties for $14.40 per share. This stock issue changes both the parent's percentage interest in the subsidiary and the subsidiary's consolidated valuation basis. The parent's percentage ownership declines to 72 percent (90,000 shares ÷ 125,000 total shares). The subsidiary's valuation basis for consolidation becomes:

Consideration transferred	$1,350,000
Noncontrolling interest acquisition-date fair value	150,000
2017 Westminster income less excess amortization	170,000
Westminster dividends	(30,000)
Stock issue proceeds ($14.40 × 25,000 shares)	360,000
Subsidiary valuation basis, 1/1/18	$2,000,000

Next, the effect on the parent's ownership can be computed as follows:

Westminster's valuation basis, 1/1/18 (above)	$2,000,000
Antioch's post, stock issue ownership (90,000 shares ÷ 125,000 shares)	72%
Antioch's post, stock issue ownership balance	$1,440,000
Antioch's pre, stock issue equity-adjusted investment account (above)	1,476,000
Required adjustment—decrease in Antioch's additional paid-in capital	$ 36,000

To reflect this effect of the stock issue change on its valuation of the subsidiary, the parent makes the following journal entry on its financial records.

Antioch Company's Financial Records		
Additional Paid-In Capital (Antioch Company)	36,000	
Investment in Westminster Company		36,000
To recognize change in equity of business combination created by issuance of 25,000 additional shares of Westminster's common stock.		

Case 2

Assume that on January 1, 2018, Westminster issues 20,000 new shares of common stock for $16 per share. Of this total, Antioch acquires 18,000 shares to maintain its 90 percent level of ownership. Antioch pays a total of $288,000 (18,000 shares × $16) for this additional stock. Outside parties buy the remaining shares.

Under these circumstances, the stock transaction alters the consolidated valuation basis of the subsidiary but not the percentage owned by the parent. Thus, only the subsidiary value must be updated prior to determining the necessity of an equity revaluation:

Consideration transferred	$1,350,000
Noncontrolling interest acquisition-date fair value	150,000
2017 Westminster income less excess amortization	170,000
Westminster dividends	(30,000)
Stock issue proceeds ($16 × 20,000 shares)	320,000
Subsidiary valuation basis 1/1/18	$1,960,000

The effect on the parent's ownership is computed as follows:

Westminster's valuation basis 1/1/18 (above)		$1,960,000
Antioch's post, stock issue ownership (108,000 shares ÷ 120,000 shares)		90%
Antioch's post, stock issue ownership balance		$1,764,000
Antioch's equity-adjusted investment account before stock purchase	$1,476,000	
Additional payment for 18,000 shares of Westminster	288,000	1,764,000
Required adjustment		$ –0–

This case requires no adjustment because Antioch's underlying interest remains aligned with the subsidiary's consolidated valuation basis. Any purchase of new stock by the parent in the same ratio as previous ownership does not affect consolidated Additional Paid-In Capital. The transaction creates no proportionate increase or decrease.

Case 3

Assume that instead of issuing new stock, on January 1, 2018, Westminster reacquires all 10,000 shares owned by the noncontrolling interest. It pays $16 per share for this treasury stock.

This illustration presents another type of subsidiary stock transaction: the acquisition of treasury stock. In this case the effect on the parent can be computed by reference to the amount of noncontrolling interest that must be reduced to zero in the consolidated financial statements.

Noncontrolling interest (NCI) acquisition-date fair value	$150,000
NCI share of 2017 Westminster income less excess amortization ($170,000 × 10%)	17,000
NCI share of Westminster dividends ($30,000 × 10%)	(3,000)
Noncontrolling interest valuation basis at 1/1/18	$164,000
Treasury stock purchase ($16 × 10,000 shares)	(160,000)
Required adjustment—increase in Antioch's additional paid-in capital	$ 4,000

The consolidated entity paid $160,000 to reduce a $164,000 owners' equity interest (the noncontrolling interest) to zero, thus increasing its own equity by $4,000. As usual, the increase in equity is attributed to additional paid-in capital and is recorded on the parent's records.

Antioch Company's Financial Records

Investment in Westminster Company	4,000	
Additional Paid-In Capital (Antioch Company)		4,000
To recognize change in equity of business combination created by acquisition of 10,000 treasury shares by Westminster.		

This third illustration represents a newly introduced subsidiary stock transaction, the purchase of treasury stock. Therefore, display of consolidation Entries **S** and **A** are also presented. These entries demonstrate the worksheet eliminations required when the subsidiary holds treasury shares:

Consolidation Entry S

Common Stock (Westminster Company)	200,000	
Additional Paid-In Capital (Westminster Company)	450,000	
Retained Earnings, 1/1/18 (Westminster Company)	910,000	
Treasury Stock		160,000
Investment in Westminster Company		1,400,000
To eliminate equity accounts of Westminster Company.		

Consolidation Entry A

Customer List	80,000	
Investment in Westminster Company		80,000
To recognize the beginning-of-year unamortized excess acquisition-date fair value allocated to the customer list.		

Note first the absence of a noncontrolling interest entry. Also note that the sum of the credits to the Investment in Westminster account is $1,480,000, which is the pretreasury stock purchase equity method balance of $1,476,000 plus the $4,000 addition from the acquisition of the noncontrolling interest.

Case 4

Assume that on January 1, 2018, Westminster issues a 10 percent stock dividend (10,000 new shares) to its owners when the stock's fair value is $15 per share.

This final case illustrates another example of a subsidiary stock transaction producing no effect on the parent's records. Stock dividends, whether large or small, capitalize a portion of the issuing company's retained earnings without altering total book value. Shareholders recognize the receipt of a stock dividend as a change in the per share value rather than as an adjustment to the investment balance. Because neither party perceives a net effect, the consolidation process proceeds in a routine fashion. Therefore, a subsidiary stock dividend requires no special treatment prior to development of a worksheet.

Consideration transferred	$1,350,000
Noncontrolling interest acquisition-date fair value	150,000
2017 Westminster income less excess amortization	170,000
Westminster dividends	(30,000)
Subsidiary valuation basis, 1/1/18	$1,640,000
Antioch's ownership (adjusted for 10% stock dividend	90%
99,000 ÷ 110,000 shares).	
Antioch's post, stock dividend ownership interest	$1,476,000
Antioch's equity-adjusted investment account.	1,476,000
Adjustment required by stock dividend.	$ –0–

The consolidation Entries **S** and **A** made just after the stock dividend follow. The $1,404,000 component of the investment account is offset against the stockholders' equity of the subsidiary. Although the stock dividend did not affect the parent's investment, the equity accounts of the subsidiary have been realigned in recognition of the $150,000 stock dividend (10,000 shares of $2 par value stock valued at $15 per share):

Consolidation Entry S

Common Stock (Westminster Company)	220,000	
Additional Paid-In Capital (Westminster Company)	580,000	
Retained Earnings, 1/1/18 (Westminster Company)	760,000	
Investment in Westminster Company (90%)		1,404,000
Noncontrolling Interest (10%)		156,000

Consolidation Entry A

Customer List	80,000	
Investment in Westminster Company		72,000
Noncontrolling Interest		8,000
To recognize the beginning-of-year unamortized excess fair value attributable to the customer list.		

Note here that the sum of the credits to the Investment in Westminster account is $1,476,000, which equals the pre–stock dividend equity method balance.

Summary

1. Variable interest entities (VIEs) typically take the form of a trust, partnership, joint venture, or corporation. In most cases, a sponsoring firm creates these entities to engage in a limited and well-defined set of business activities. Control of VIEs, by design, often does not rest with their equity holders. Instead, control is exercised through contractual arrangements with the sponsoring firm that becomes the entity's "primary beneficiary." These contracts can take the form of leases, participation rights, guarantees, or other residual interests. Through contracting, the primary beneficiary bears a significant portion of the risks and receives a significant portion of the rewards of the entity, often without owning any voting shares. Current accounting standards require a business that has a controlling financial interest in a VIE to consolidate the financial statements of the VIE with its own.

2. In periods after the primary beneficiary gains control over a VIE, consolidation procedures follow a similar process as if the entity were controlled by voting interests. All intra-entity transactions between the primary beneficiary and the VIE must be eliminated in consolidation. The consolidated net income distribution to the noncontrolling interest, however, must be based on the contractual agreement with the primary beneficiary, rather than voting interests.

3. If one member of a business combination acquires an affiliate's debt instrument (e.g., a bond or note) from an outside party, the purchase price usually differs from the carrying amount of the liability. Thus, a gain or loss has been incurred from the perspective of the business combination. However, both the debt and investment remain in the individual financial accounts of the two companies, but the gain or loss goes unrecorded. The consolidation process must adjust all balances to reflect the effective retirement of the debt.

4. Following a related party's acquisition of a company's debt, Interest Income and Expense are recognized. Because these accounts result from intra-entity transactions, they also must be removed in every subsequent consolidation along with the debt and investment figures. Retained Earnings also requires adjustment in each year after the purchase to record the impact of the gain or loss.

5. Amortization of intra-entity debt/investment balances often is necessary because of discounts and/or premiums. Consequently, the Interest Income and Interest Expense figures reported by the two parties will not agree. The closing of these two accounts into Retained Earnings each year gradually reduces the consolidation adjustment that must be made to this equity account.

6. When acquired, many subsidiaries have preferred stock outstanding as well as common stock. The existence of subsidiary preferred shares does little to complicate the consolidation process. The acquisition method values all business acquisitions at their full fair values. If a subsidiary has preferred stock, the essential process of determining its acquisition-date business fair value remains

intact. Any preferred shares not owned by the parent simply become a component of the noncontrolling interest and are included in the acquisition-date measure of subsidiary fair value.

7. Every business combination must prepare a statement of cash flows. This statement is not created by consolidating the individual cash flows of the separate companies. Instead, both a consolidated income statement and balance sheet are produced, and the cash flows statement is developed from these figures. Dividends paid to the noncontrolling interest are listed as a financing activity.

8. For most business combinations, the determination of earnings per share (EPS) follows the normal pattern presented in intermediate accounting textbooks. However, if the subsidiary has potentially dilutive items outstanding (stock warrants, convertible preferred stock, convertible bonds, etc.), a different process must be followed. The subsidiary's own diluted EPS is computed as a preliminary procedure. The parent and the outside owners then allocate the earnings used in each of these calculations based on the ownership levels of the subsidiary's shares and the dilutive items. The determination of the EPS figures to be reported for the business combination is based on the portion of consolidated net income assigned to the parent.

9. After the combination is created, a subsidiary may enter into stock transactions such as issuing additional shares or acquiring treasury stock. Such actions normally create a proportional increase or decrease in the subsidiary's equity when compared with the parent's investment. The change is measured and then reflected in the consolidated statements through the Additional Paid-In Capital account. To achieve the appropriate accounting, the parent adjusts the Investment in Subsidiary account as well as its own Additional Paid-In Capital. Because the worksheet does not eliminate this equity balance, the required increase or decrease carries over to the consolidated figures.

Comprehensive Illustration

Problem: Consolidated Statement of Cash Flows and Earnings per Share

(*Estimated Time: 35 to 45 Minutes*) Pop, Inc., acquires 90 percent of the 20,000 shares of Son Company's outstanding common stock on December 31, 2016. Of the acquisition-date fair value, it allocates $80,000 to trademarks, a figure amortized at the rate of $2,000 per year. Comparative consolidated balance sheets for 2018 and 2017 are as follows:

	2018	2017
Cash	$ 210,000	$ 130,000
Accounts receivable	350,000	220,000
Inventory	320,000	278,000
Land, buildings, and equipment (net)	1,090,000	1,120,000
Trademarks	78,000	80,000
Total assets	$2,048,000	$1,828,000
Accounts payable	$ 290,000	$ 296,000
Long-term liabilities	650,000	550,000
Noncontrolling interest	37,800	34,000
Preferred stock (10% cumulative)	100,000	100,000
Common stock (26,000 shares outstanding)	520,000	520,000
Retained earnings, 12/31	450,200	328,000
Total liabilities and stockholders' equity	$2,048,000	$1,828,000

Additional Information for 2018

- Consolidated net income (after adjustments for all intra-entity items) was $178,000.
- Consolidated depreciation and amortization equaled $52,000.

- On April 10, Son sold a building with a $40,000 book value, receiving cash of $50,000. Later that month, Pop borrowed $100,000 from a local bank and purchased equipment for $60,000. These transactions were all with outside parties.

- During the year, Pop declared and paid $40,000 dividends on its common stock and $10,000 on its preferred stock, and Son declared and paid a $20,000 dividend on its common stock.

- Son has long-term convertible debt of $180,000 outstanding included in consolidated liabilities. It recognized interest expense of $16,000 (net of taxes) on this debt during the year. This debt can be exchanged for 10,000 shares of the subsidiary's common stock. Pop owns none of this debt.

- Son recorded $60,000 net income from its own operations. Noncontrolling interest in consolidated net income was $5,800.

- Pop recorded $4,000 in profits on sales of goods to Son. These goods remain in Son's warehouse at December 31.

- Pop applies the equity method to account for its investment in Son. On its own books, Pop recognized $48,200 equity in earnings from Son [90% × ($60,000 less $2,000 amortization) and $4,000 intra-entity gross profit in inventory from its sales to Son].

Required

a. Prepare a consolidated statement of cash flows for Pop, Inc., and Son Company for the year ending December 31, 2018. Use the indirect method for determining the amount of cash provided from operations.[14]

b. Compute basic earnings per share and diluted earnings per share for Pop, Inc.

Solution

a. Consolidated Statement of Cash Flows
The problem specifies that the indirect method should be used in preparing the consolidated statement of cash flows. Therefore, all items that do not represent cash flows from operations must be removed from the $178,000 consolidated net income. For example, both the depreciation and amortization are eliminated (noncash items) as well as the gain on the sale of the building (a nonoperational item). In addition, each of the changes in consolidated Accounts Receivable, Inventory, and Accounts Payable produces a noncash impact on net income. The increase in Accounts Receivable, for example, indicates that the sales figure for the period was larger than the amount of cash collected so that adjustment is required in producing this statement.

From the information given, several nonoperational changes in cash can be determined: the bank loan, the acquisition of equipment, the sale of a building, the dividend paid by Son to the noncontrolling interest, and the dividend paid by the parent. Each of these transactions is included in the consolidated statement of cash flows shown in Exhibit 6.12, which explains the $80,000 increase in cash experienced by the entity during 2018.

b. Earnings per Share
The subsidiary's convertible debt has a potentially dilutive effect on earnings per share. Therefore, diluted EPS cannot be determined for the business combination directly from consolidated net income. First, the diluted EPS figure must be calculated for the subsidiary. This information then is used in the computations made by the consolidated entity.

Diluted EPS of $2.47 for the subsidiary is determined as follows:

Son Company—Diluted Earnings per Share

	Earnings		Shares	
As reported less excess amortization...	$58,000		20,000	$2.90
Effect of possible debt conversion:				
Interest saved (net of taxes).........	16,000	New shares	10,000	$1.60 impact
				(16,000/10,000)
Diluted EPS.........................	$74,000		30,000	$2.47 (rounded)

The parent owns none of the convertible debt included in computing diluted EPS. Pop holds only 18,000 (90 percent of the outstanding common stock) of the 30,000 shares used in this EPS calculation.

[14] Prior to attempting this problem, a review of an intermediate accounting textbook might be useful to obtain a complete overview of the production of a statement of cash flows.

EXHIBIT 6.12

POP, INC., AND SON COMPANY
Consolidated Statement of Cash Flows
Year Ending December 31, 2018

Cash flows from operating activities		
Consolidated net income		$178,000
Adjustments to reconcile consolidated net income to net cash provided by operating activities:		
Depreciation and amortization.	$ 52,000	
Gain on sale of building.	(10,000)	
Increase in accounts receivable	(130,000)	
Increase in inventory	(42,000)	
Decrease in accounts payable.	(6,000)	(136,000)
Net cash provided from operations.		$ 42,000
Cash flows from investing activities		
Purchase of equipment	$ (60,000)	
Sale of building	50,000	
Net cash used in investing activities		(10,000)
Cash flows from financing activities		
Payment of cash dividends—Pop	$ (50,000)	
Payment of cash dividend to noncontrolling owners of Son . .	(2,000)	
Borrowed from bank	100,000	
Net cash provided by financing activities.		48,000
Net increase in cash.		$ 80,000
Cash, January 1, 2018.		130,000
Cash, December 31, 2018		$210,000

Consequently, in determining diluted EPS for the parent company, only $44,400 of the subsidiary's income is applicable:

$$\$74,000 \times 18,000/30,000 = \$44,400$$

Exhibit 6.13 reveals basic EPS of $6.24 and diluted EPS of $5.94. Because the subsidiary's earnings figure is included separately in the computation of diluted EPS, the parent's individual income must be identified in the same manner. Thus, the effect of the equity income and intra-entity (downstream) transactions are taken into account in arriving at the parent's separate earnings.

EXHIBIT 6.13

POP, INC., AND SON COMPANY
Earnings per Share
Year Ending December 31, 2018

	Earnings	Shares	
	Basic Earnings per Share		
Pop's share of consolidated net income	$172,200		
Preferred dividend declared by Pop.	(10,000)		
Basic EPS	162,200	26,000	$6.24 (rounded)
	Diluted Earnings per Share		
Pop's share of consolidated net income	$172,200		
Remove equity income	(48,200)		
Remove intra-entity gross profit.	(4,000)		
Preferred stock dividend.	(10,000)		
Common shares outstanding (Pop, Inc.).		26,000	
Common stock income—Pop (for EPS computations)	$110,000		
Income of Son (for diluted EPS)	44,400		
Diluted EPS.	$154,400	26,000	$5.94 (rounded)

Questions

1. What is a variable interest entity (VIE)?

2. What are variable interests in an entity and how might they provide financial control over an entity?

3. When is a firm required to consolidate the financial statements of a VIE with its own financial statements?

4. A parent company acquires from a third party bonds that had been issued originally by one of its subsidiaries. What accounting problems are created by this purchase?

5. In question (4), why is the consolidation process simpler if the bonds had been acquired directly from the subsidiary than from a third party?

6. When a company acquires an affiliated company's debt instruments from a third party, how is the gain or loss on extinguishment of the debt calculated? When should this balance be recognized?

7. Several years ago, Bennett, Inc., bought a portion of the outstanding bonds of Smith Corporation, a subsidiary organization. The acquisition was made from an outside party. In the current year, how should these intra-entity bonds be accounted for within the consolidation process?

8. One company purchases the outstanding debt instruments of an affiliated company on the open market. This transaction creates a gain that is appropriately recognized in the consolidated financial statements of that year. Thereafter, a worksheet adjustment is required to correct the beginning balance of consolidated Retained Earnings (or the parent's Investment in Subsidiary account when the equity method is employed). Why is the amount of this adjustment reduced from year to year?

9. A parent acquires the outstanding bonds of a subsidiary company directly from an outside third party. For consolidation purposes, this transaction creates a gain of $45,000. Should this gain be allocated to the parent or the subsidiary? Why?

10. Perkins Company acquires 90 percent of the outstanding common stock of the Butterfly Corporation as well as 55 percent of its preferred stock. How should these preferred shares be accounted for within the consolidation process?

11. The income statement and the balance sheet are produced using a worksheet, but a consolidated statement of cash flows is not. What process is followed in preparing a consolidated statement of cash flows?

12. How do noncontrolling interest balances affect the consolidated statement of cash flows?

13. In many cases, EPS is computed based on the parent's portion of consolidated net income and parent company shares and convertibles. However, a different process must be used for some business combinations. When is this alternative approach required?

14. A subsidiary has (1) a convertible preferred stock and (2) a convertible bond. How are these items factored into the computation of earnings per share for the parent company?

15. Why might a subsidiary decide to issue new shares of common stock to parties outside the business combination?

16. Washburn Company owns 75 percent of Metcalf Company's outstanding common stock. During the current year, Metcalf issues additional shares to outside parties at a price more than its per share consolidated value. How does this transaction affect the business combination? How is this impact recorded within the consolidated statements?

17. Assume the same information as in question (16) except that Metcalf issues a 10 percent stock dividend instead of selling new shares of stock. How does this transaction affect the business combination?

Problems

LO 6-1

1. An enterprise that holds a variable interest in a variable interest entity (VIE) is required to consolidate the assets, liabilities, revenues, expenses, and noncontrolling interest of that entity if:
   a. The VIE has issued no voting stock.
   b. The variable interest held by the enterprise involves a lease.
   c. The enterprise has a controlling financial interest in the VIE.
   d. Other equity interests in the VIE have the obligation to absorb the expected losses of the VIE.

LO 6-2

2. Prairie Corporation is a primary beneficiary for Vintage Company, a variable interest entity. When Prairie obtained financial control over Vintage, any excess fair value over Prairie's book value was attributed solely to goodwill. Prairie owns 15 percent of Vintage Company's common stock and participation rights that entitle it to an additional 40 percent of Vintage's net income. In the current year Prairie reports $400,000 of net income before consideration of its investment in Vintage.

Vintage Company reports net income of $100,000. What amount of consolidated net income is attributable to the noncontrolling interest?

  a. $15,000

  b. $45,000

  c. $60,000

  d. $85,000

LO 6-3

3. A parent company buys bonds on the open market that had been previously issued by its subsidiary. The price paid by the parent is less than the carrying amount of the bonds on the subsidiary's records. How should the parent report the difference between the price paid and the carrying amount of the bonds on its consolidated financial statements?

  a. As a loss on retirement of the bonds.

  b. As a gain on retirement of the bonds.

  c. As an increase to interest expense over the remaining life of the bonds.

  d. Because the bonds now represent intra-entity debt, the difference is not reported.

LO 6-3

4. A subsidiary has a debt outstanding that was originally issued at a discount. At the beginning of the current year, the parent company acquired the debt at a slight premium from outside parties. Which of the following statements is true?

  a. Whether the balances agree or not, both the subsequent interest income and interest expense should be reported in a consolidated income statement.

  b. The interest income and interest expense will agree in amount and should be offset for consolidation purposes.

  c. In computing any noncontrolling interest allocation, the interest income should be included but not the interest expense.

  d. Although subsequent interest income and interest expense will not agree in amount, both balances should be eliminated for consolidation purposes.

LO 6-4

5. The parent company acquires all of a subsidiary's common stock but only 70 percent of its preferred shares. This preferred stock pays a 7 percent annual cumulative dividend. No dividends are in arrears at the current time. How is the noncontrolling interest's share of the subsidiary's income computed?

  a. As 30 percent of the subsidiary's preferred dividend.

  b. No allocation is made because the dividends have been paid.

  c. As 30 percent of the subsidiary's income after all dividends have been subtracted.

  d. Income is assigned to the preferred stock based on total par value and 30 percent of that amount is allocated to the noncontrolling interest.

LO 6-5

6. Aceton Corporation owns 80 percent of the outstanding stock of Voctax, Inc. During the current year, Voctax made $140,000 in sales to Aceton. How does this transfer affect the consolidated statement of cash flows?

  a. The transaction should be included if payment has been made.

  b. Only 80 percent of the transfers should be included because the subsidiary made the sales.

  c. Because the transfers were from a subsidiary organization, the cash flows are reported as investing activities.

  d. Because of the intra-entity nature of the transfers, the amount is not reported in the consolidated cash flow statement.

Problems 7 and 8 are based on the following information.

Comparative consolidated balance sheet data for Iverson, Inc., and its 80 percent–owned subsidiary Oakley Co. follow:

	2018	2017
Cash	$ 7,000	$ 20,000
Accounts receivable (net)	55,000	38,000
Merchandise inventory	85,000	45,000
Buildings and equipment (net)	95,000	105,000
Trademark	85,000	100,000
Totals	$327,000	$308,000

(*continued*)

(*continued*)

	2018	2017
Accounts payable	$ 75,000	$ 63,000
Notes payable, long-term	–0–	25,000
Noncontrolling interest.	39,000	35,000
Common stock, $10 par	200,000	200,000
Retained earnings (deficit).	13,000	(15,000)
Totals.	$327,000	$308,000

Additional Information for Fiscal Year 2018

- Iverson and Oakley's consolidated net income was $45,000.
- Oakley paid $5,000 in dividends during the year. Iverson paid $12,000 in dividends.
- Oakley sold $11,000 worth of merchandise to Iverson during the year.
- There were no purchases or sales of long-term assets during the year.

    In the 2018 consolidated statement of cash flows for Iverson Company:

LO 6-5

7. Net cash flows from operating activities were
   a. $12,000
   b. $20,000
   c. $24,000
   d. $25,000

LO 6-5

8. Net cash flows from financing activities were
   a. $(25,000)
   b. $(37,000)
   c. $(38,000)
   d. $(42,000)

LO 6-6

9. Bensman Corporation is computing EPS. One of its subsidiaries has stock warrants outstanding. How do these convertible items affect Bensman's EPS computation?
   a. No effect is created because the stock warrants were for the subsidiary company's shares.
   b. The stock warrants are not included in the computation unless they are antidilutive.
   c. The effect of the stock warrants must be computed in deriving the amount of subsidiary income to be included in making the diluted EPS calculation.
   d. The stock warrants are included only in basic EPS but never in diluted EPS.

LO 6-7

10. Arcola, Inc., acquires all 40,000 shares of Tuscola Company for $725,000. A year later, when Arcola's equity adjusted balance in its investment in Tuscola equals $800,000, Tuscola issues an additional 10,000 shares to outside investors for $25 per share. Which of the following best describes the effect of Tuscola's stock issue on Arcola's investment account?
    a. No effect because the shares were all sold to outside parties.
    b. The investment account is reduced because Arcola now owns a smaller percentage of Tuscola.
    c. The investment account is increased because Arcola's share of Tuscola's value has increased.
    d. No effect because Arcola maintains control over Tuscola despite the new stock issue.

LO 6-3

11. Dane, Inc., owns Carlton Corporation. For the current year, Dane reports net income (without consideration of its investment in Carlton) of $185,000 and the subsidiary reports $105,000. The parent had a bond payable outstanding on January 1, with a carrying amount of $209,000. The subsidiary acquired the bond on that date for $196,000. During the current year, Dane reported interest expense of $18,000 while Carlton reported interest income of $19,000, both related to the intra-entity bond payable. What is consolidated net income?
    a. $289,000
    b. $291,000
    c. $302,000
    d. $304,000

LO 6-6

12. Mattoon, Inc., owns 80 percent of Effingham Company. For the current year, this combined entity reported consolidated net income of $500,000. Of this amount $465,000 was attributable to Mattoon's controlling interest while the remaining $35,000 was attributable to the noncontrolling interest. Mattoon has 100,000 shares of common stock outstanding and Effingham has 25,000 shares outstanding.

Neither company has issued preferred shares or has any convertible securities outstanding. On the face of the consolidated income statement, how much should be reported as Mattoon's earnings per share?

    a. $5.00

    b. $4.65

    c. $4.00

    d. $3.88

LO 6-3

13. Aaron Company's books show current earnings of $430,000 and $46,000 in cash dividends. Zeese Company earns $164,000 in net income and declares $11,500 in dividends. Aaron has held a 70 percent interest in Zeese for several years, an investment with an acquisition-date excess fair over book value attributable solely to goodwill. Aaron uses the initial value method to account for these shares and includes dividend income in its internal earnings reports.

    On January 1 of the current year, Zeese acquired in the open market $64,400 of Aaron's 8 percent bonds. The bonds had originally been issued several years ago at 92, reflecting a 10 percent effective interest rate. On the date of purchase, the carrying amount of the bonds payable was $60,200. Zeese paid $56,000 based on a 12 percent effective interest rate over the remaining life of the bonds.

    What is consolidated net income for this year?

    a. $598,900

    b. $589,450

    c. $438,050

    d. $590,850

LO 6-3

14. Redfield Company reports current earnings of $420,000 while declaring $52,000 in cash dividends. Snedeker Company earns $147,000 in net income and declares $13,000 in dividends. Redfield has held a 70 percent interest in Snedeker for several years, an investment with an acquisition-date excess fair over book value attributable solely to goodwill. Redfield uses the initial value method to account for these shares.

    On January 1 of the current year, Snedeker acquired in the open market $51,600 of Redfield's 8 percent bonds. The bonds had originally been issued several years ago at 92, reflecting a 10 percent effective interest rate. On the date of purchase, the carrying amount of the bonds payable was $50,400. Snedeker paid $49,200 based on a 12 percent effective interest rate over the remaining life of the bonds.

    What is the noncontrolling interest's share of consolidated net income?

    a. $40,200

    b. $44,100

    c. $40,560

    d. $44,460

LO 6-3

15. Pesto Company possesses 80 percent of Salerno Company's outstanding voting stock. Pesto uses the initial value method to account for this investment. On January 1, 2014, Pesto sold 9 percent bonds payable with a $10 million face value (maturing in 20 years) on the open market at a premium of $600,000. On January 1, 2017, Salerno acquired 40 percent of these same bonds from an outside party at 96.6 percent of face value. Both companies use the straight-line method of amortization. For a 2018 consolidation, what adjustment should be made to Pesto's beginning Retained Earnings as a result of this bond acquisition?

    a. $320,000 increase

    b. $326,000 increase

    c. $331,000 increase

    d. $340,000 increase

LO 6-4

16. On January 1, Tesco Company spent a total of $4,384,000 to acquire control over Blondel Company. This price was based on paying $424,000 for 20 percent of Blondel's preferred stock and $3,960,000 for 90 percent of its outstanding common stock. At the acquisition date, the fair value of the 10 percent noncontrolling interest in Blondel's common stock was $440,000. The fair value of the 80 percent of Blondel's preferred shares not owned by Tesco was $1,696,000. Blondel's stockholders' equity accounts at January 1 were as follows:

Preferred stock—9%, $100 par value, cumulative and participating;	
10,000 shares outstanding...	$ 1,000,000
Common stock—$50 par value; 40,000 shares outstanding.................	2,000,000
Retained earnings..	3,000,000
Total stockholders' equity...	$ 6,000,000

Tesco believes that all of Blondel's accounts approximate their fair values within the company's financial statements. What amount of consolidated goodwill should be recognized?

    a. $ 300,000
    b. $ 316,000
    c. $ 364,000
    d. $ 520,000

LO 6-4

17. On January 1, Coldwater Company has a net book value of $2,174,000 as follows:

2,000 shares of preferred stock; par value $100 per share; cumulative, nonparticipating, nonvoting; call value $108 per share	$ 200,000
34,500 shares of common stock; par value $40 per share	1,380,000
Retained earnings	594,000
Total	$2,174,000

Westmont Company acquires all outstanding preferred shares for $214,000 and 60 percent of the common stock for $1,253,280. The acquisition-date fair value of the noncontrolling interest in Coldwater's common stock was $835,520. Westmont believed that one of Coldwater's buildings, with a 12-year remaining life, was undervalued by $63,600 on the company's financial records.
    What amount of consolidated goodwill would be recognized from this acquisition?

    a. $61,600
    b. $65,200
    c. $60,400
    d. $59,200

LO 6-5

18. Premier Company owns 90 percent of the voting shares of Stanton, Inc. Premier reports sales of $480,000 during the current year and Stanton reports $264,000. Stanton sold inventory costing $28,800 to Premier (upstream) during the year for $57,600. Of this amount, 25 percent is still in ending inventory at year-end. Total receivables on the consolidated balance sheet were $81,800 at the first of the year and $119,100 at year-end. No intra-entity debt existed at the beginning or ending of the year. Using the direct method, what is the consolidated amount of cash collected by the business combination from its customers?

    a. $706,700
    b. $649,100
    c. $686,400
    d. $744,000

LO 6-7

19. Aaron owns 100 percent of the 12,000 shares of Veritable, Inc. The Investment in Veritable account has a balance of $588,000, corresponding to the subsidiary's unamortized acquisition-date fair value of $49 per share. Veritable issues 3,000 new shares to the public for $50 per share. How does this transaction affect the Investment in Veritable account?

    a. It is not affected because the shares were sold to outside parties.
    b. It should be increased by $2,400.
    c. It should be increased by $3,000.
    d. It should be decreased by $117,600.

Problems 20 through 22 are based on the following information.
Neill Company purchases 80 percent of the common stock of Stamford Company on January 1, 2017, when Stamford has the following stockholders' equity accounts:

Common stock—40,000 shares outstanding	$100,000
Additional paid-in capital	75,000
Retained earnings, 1/1/17	540,000
Total stockholders' equity	$715,000

To acquire this interest in Stamford, Neill pays a total of $592,000. The acquisition-date fair value of the 20 percent noncontrolling interest was $148,000. Any excess fair value was allocated to goodwill, which has not experienced any impairment.

On January 1, 2018, Stamford reports retained earnings of $620,000. Neill has accrued the increase in Stamford's retained earnings through application of the equity method.

View the following problems as independent situations:

LO 6-7

20. On January 1, 2018, Stamford issues 10,000 additional shares of common stock for $25 per share. Neill acquires 8,000 of these shares. How will this transaction affect the parent company's Additional Paid-In Capital account?

    a. Has no effect on it.

    b. Increases it by $20,500.

    c. Increases it by $36,400.

    d. Increases it by $82,300.

LO 6-7

21. On January 1, 2018, Stamford issues 10,000 additional shares of common stock for $15 per share. Neill does not acquire any of this newly issued stock. How does this transaction affect the parent company's Additional Paid-In Capital account?

    a. Has no effect on it.

    b. Increases it by $44,000.

    c. Decreases it by $35,200.

    d. Decreases it by $55,000.

LO 6-7

22. On January 1, 2018, Stamford reacquires 8,000 of the outstanding shares of its own common stock for $24 per share. None of these shares belonged to Neill. How does this transaction affect the parent company's Additional Paid-In Capital account?

    a. Has no effect on it.

    b. Decreases it by $55,000.

    c. Decreases it by $35,000.

    d. Decreases it by $28,000.

LO 6-2

23. Hillsborough Country Outfitters, Inc., entered into an agreement for HCO Media LLC to exclusively conduct Hillsborough's e-commerce initiatives through a jointly owned (50 percent each) Internet site known as HCO.com. HCO Media receives 2 percent of all sales revenue generated through the site up to a maximum of $500,000 per year. Both Hillsborough and HCO Media pay 50 percent of the costs to maintain the Internet site. However, if HCO Media's fees are insufficient to cover its 50 percent share of the costs, Hillsborough absorbs the loss.

    Assuming that HCO Media qualifies as a VIE, should Hillsborough consolidate HCO Media LLC?

LO 6-2

24. The following describes a set of arrangements between TecPC Company and a variable interest entity (VIE) as of December 31, 2017. TecPC agrees to design and construct a new research and development (R&D) facility. The VIE's sole purpose is to finance and own the R&D facility and lease it to TecPC Company after construction is completed. Payments under the operating lease are expected to begin in the first quarter of 2019.

    The VIE has financing commitments sufficient for the construction project from equity and debt participants (investors) of $4 million and $42 million, respectively. TecPC, in its role as the VIE's construction agent, is responsible for completing construction by December 31, 2018. TecPC has guaranteed a portion of the VIE's obligations during the construction and post-construction periods.

    TecPC agrees to lease the R&D facility for five years with multiple extension options. The lease is a variable rate obligation indexed to a three-month market rate. As market interest rates increase or decrease, the payments under this operating lease also increase or decrease, sufficient to provide a return to the investors. If all extension options are exercised, the total lease term is 35 years.

    At the end of the first five-year lease term or any extension, TecPC may choose one of the following:

    • Renew the lease at fair value subject to investor approval.

    • Purchase the facility at its original construction cost.

    • Sell the facility on the VIE's behalf to an independent third party. If TecPC sells the project and the proceeds from the sale are insufficient to repay the investors their original cost, TecPC may be required to pay the VIE up to 85 percent of the project's cost.

    a. What is the purpose of reporting consolidated statements for a company and the entities that it controls?

    b. When should a VIE's financial statements be consolidated with those of another company?

c. Identify the risks of ownership of the R&D facility that (1) TecPC has effectively shifted to the VIE's owners and (2) remain with TecPC.

d. What characteristics of a primary beneficiary does TecPC possess?

LO 6-2

25. On December 31, 2017, PanTech Company invests $20,000 in SoftPlus, a variable interest entity. In contractual agreements completed on that date, PanTech established itself as the primary beneficiary of SoftPlus. Previously, PanTech had no equity interest in SoftPlus. Immediately after PanTech's investment, SoftPlus presents the following balance sheet:

Cash	$ 20,000	Long-term debt	$120,000
Marketing software	140,000	Noncontrolling interest	60,000
Computer equipment	40,000	PanTech equity interest	20,000
Total assets	$200,000	Total liabilities and equity	$200,000

Each of the above amounts represents an assessed fair value at December 31, 2017, except for the marketing software. Accordingly the December 31 fair value of SoftPlus is assessed at $80,000.

a. If the marketing software was undervalued by $20,000, what amounts for SoftPlus would appear in PanTech's December 31, 2017, consolidated financial statements?

b. If the marketing software was overvalued by $20,000, what amounts for SoftPlus would appear in PanTech's December 31, 2017, consolidated financial statements?

LO 6-2

eXcel

26. On January 1, 2018, Access IT Company exchanged $1,000,000 for 40 percent of the outstanding voting stock of Net Connect. Especially attractive to Access IT was a research project underway at Net Connect that would enhance both the speed and quantity of client-accessible data. Although not recorded in Net Connect's financial records, the fair value of the research project was considered to be $1,960,000.

In contractual agreements with the sole owner of the remaining 60 percent of Net Connect, Access IT was granted (1) various decision-making rights over Net Connect's operating decisions and (2) special service purchase provisions at below-market rates. As a result of these contractual agreements, Access IT established itself as the primary beneficiary of Net Connect. Immediately after the purchase, Access IT and Net Connect presented the following balance sheets:

	Access IT	Net Connect
Cash	$ 61,000	$ 41,000
Investment in Net Connect	1,000,000	
Capitalized software	981,000	156,000
Computer equipment	1,066,000	56,000
Communications equipment	916,000	336,000
Patent		191,000
Total assets	$ 4,024,000	$ 780,000
Long-term debt	(941,000)	(616,000)
Common stock—Access IT	(2,660,000)	
Common stock—Net Connect		(41,000)
Retained earnings	(423,000)	(123,000)
Total liabilities and equity	$(4,024,000)	$(780,000)

Each of the above amounts represents a fair value at January 1, 2018. The fair value of the 60 percent of Net Connect shares not owned by Access IT was $1,500,000.

Prepare an acquisition-date consolidation worksheet for Access IT and its variable interest entity.

LO 6-2

27. On January 1, 2018, Primair Corporation loaned Vista Company $300,000 and agreed to guarantee all of Vista's long-term debt in exchange for (1) decision-making authority over all of Vista's activities and (2) an annual cash payment of 25 percent of Vista's revenues. As a result of the agreement, Primair is the primary beneficiary of Vista (a variable interest entity). Primair's loan to Vista stipulated a 7 percent (market) rate of interest to be paid annually.

On January 1, 2018, Primair estimated that the fair value of Vista's equity shares equaled $150,000 while Vista's book value was $55,000. Any excess fair over book value at that date was attributed to Vista's trademark with an indefinite life.

Because Primair owns no equity in Vista, all of the acquisition-date excess fair over book value is allocated to the non-controlling interest.

Vista paid Primair 25 percent of its 2018 revenues at the end of the year. On December 31, 2018, Primair and Vista submitted the following statements for consolidation. Parentheses indicate credit balances.

	Primair	Vista
Revenues	(839,500)	(188,000)
Cost of good sold	612,000	75,000
Other operating expenses	78,000	25,000
Interest income	(21,000)	–0–
Interest expense	–0–	21,000
Net income	(170,500)	(67,000)
Retained earnings, 1/1	(1,555,000)	(40,000)
Net income	(170,500)	(67,000)
Dividends declared	250,000	–0–
Retained earnings, 12/31	(1,475,500)	(107,000)
Current assets	460,500	50,000
Loan receivable from Vista	300,000	
Equipment (net)	794,000	525,000
Trademark	–0–	45,000
Total assets	1,554,500	620,000
Current liabilities	(29,000)	(18,000)
Long-term debt	–0–	(180,000)
Loan payable to Primair		(300,000)
Common stock	(50,000)	(15,000)
Retained earnings, 12/31	(1,475,500)	(107,000)
Total liabilities and equity	(1,554,500)	(620,000)

In computing the amount of Vista's net income attributable to the non-controlling interest,

- Vista's net income should be reduced by the 25% revenue allocation to Primair.
- Interest expense paid to Primair is not excluded from Vista's net income because it is a contractual distribution of Vista's net income to Primair.

    Prepare the December 31, 2018, consolidation worksheet for Primair and Vista.

LO 6-3

28. Cairns owns 75 percent of the voting stock of Hamilton, Inc. The parent's interest was acquired several years ago on the date that the subsidiary was formed. Consequently, no goodwill or other allocation was recorded in connection with the acquisition. Cairns uses the equity method in its internal records to account for its investment in Hamilton.

    On January 1, 2014, Hamilton sold $1,000,000 in 10-year bonds to the public at 105. The bonds had a cash interest rate of 9 percent payable every December 31. Cairns acquired 40 percent of these bonds at 96 percent of face value on January 1, 2016. Both companies utilize the straight-line method of amortization. Prepare the consolidation worksheet entries to recognize the effects of the intra-entity bonds at each of the following dates.

    a. December 31, 2016

    b. December 31, 2017

    c. December 31, 2018

LO 6-3

29. Highlight, Inc., owns all outstanding stock of Kiort Corporation. The two companies report the following balances for the year ending December 31, 2017:

	Highlight	Kiort
Revenues and interest income	$(670,000)	$(390,000)
Operating and interest expense	540,000	221,000
Other gains and losses	(120,000)	(32,000)
Net income	$(250,000)	$(201,000)

On January 1, 2017, Highlight acquired on the open market bonds for $108,000 originally issued by Kiort. This investment had an effective rate of 8 percent. The bonds had a face value of $100,000 and a cash interest rate of 9 percent. At the date of acquisition, these bonds were shown as liabilities by Kiort with a carrying amount of $84,000 (based on an effective rate of 11 percent). Determine the balances that should appear on a consolidated income statement for 2017.

LO 6-3

30. Several years ago Brant, Inc., sold $900,000 in bonds to the public. Annual cash interest of 9 percent ($81,000) was to be paid on this debt. The bonds were issued at a discount to yield 12 percent. At the beginning of 2016, Zack Corporation (a wholly owned subsidiary of Brant) purchased $180,000 of these bonds on the open market for $201,000, a price based on an effective interest rate of 7 percent. The bond liability had a carrying amount on that date of $760,000. Assume Brant uses the equity method to account internally for its investment in Zack.

    a. What consolidation entry would be required for these bonds on December 31, 2016?

    b. What consolidation entry would be required for these bonds on December 31, 2018?

LO 6-3

31. Opus, Incorporated, owns 90 percent of Bloom Company. On December 31, 2017, Opus acquires half of Bloom's $500,000 outstanding bonds. These bonds had been sold on the open market on January 1, 2015, at a 12 percent effective rate. The bonds pay a cash interest rate of 10 percent every December 31 and are scheduled to come due on December 31, 2025. Bloom issued this debt originally for $435,763. Opus paid $283,550 for this investment, indicating an 8 percent effective yield.

    a. Assuming that both parties use the effective rate method, what gain or loss from the retirement of this debt should be reported on the consolidated income statement for 2017?

    b. Assuming that both parties use the effective rate method, what balances should appear in the Investment in Bloom Bonds account on Opus's records and the Bonds Payable account of Bloom as of December 31, 2018?

    c. Assuming that both parties use the straight-line method, what consolidation entry would be required on December 31, 2018, because of these bonds? Assume that the parent is not applying the equity method.

LO 6-4

32. Hepner Corporation has the following stockholders' equity accounts:

Preferred stock (6% cumulative dividend)	$500,000
Common stock	750,000
Additional paid-in capital	300,000
Retained earnings.	950,000

The preferred stock is participating. Wasatch Corporation buys 80 percent of this common stock for $1,600,000 and 70 percent of the preferred stock for $630,000. The acquisition-date fair value of the noncontrolling interest in the common shares was $400,000 and was $270,000 for the preferred shares. All of the subsidiary's assets and liabilities are viewed as having fair values equal to their book values. What amount is attributed to goodwill on the date of acquisition?

LO 6-4

33. Smith, Inc., has the following stockholders' equity accounts as of January 1, 2018:

Preferred stock—$100 par, nonvoting and nonparticipating, 8% cumulative dividend	$2,000,000
Common stock—$20 par value	4,000,000
Retained earnings.	10,000,000

Haried Company purchases all of Smith's common stock on January 1, 2018, for $14,040,000. The preferred stock remains in the hands of outside parties. Any excess acquisition-date fair value will be assigned to franchise contracts with a 40-year remaining life.

During 2018, Smith reports earning $450,000 in net income and declares $360,000 in cash dividends. Haried applies the equity method to this investment.

    a. What is the noncontrolling interest's share of consolidated net income for this period?

    b. What is the balance in the Investment in Smith account as of December 31, 2018?

    c. What consolidation entries are needed for 2018?

LO 6-4

34. Through the payment of $10,468,000 in cash, Drexel Company acquires voting control over Young Company. This price is paid for 60 percent of the subsidiary's 100,000 outstanding common shares ($40 par value) as well as all 10,000 shares of 8 percent, cumulative, $100 par value preferred stock. Of the total payment, $3.1 million is attributed to the fully participating preferred stock with the remainder paid for the common. This acquisition is carried out on January 1, 2018, when

Young reports retained earnings of $10 million and a total book value of $15 million. The acquisition-date fair value of the noncontrolling interest in Young's common stock was $4,912,000. On this same date, a building owned by Young (with a 5-year remaining life) is undervalued in the financial records by $200,000, while equipment with a 10-year remaining life is overvalued by $100,000. Any further excess acquisition-date fair value is assigned to a brand name with a 20-year remaining life.

During 2018, Young reports net income of $900,000 while declaring $400,000 in cash dividends. Drexel uses the initial value method to account for both of these investments.

Prepare appropriate consolidation entries for 2018.

LO 6-5

35. The following information has been taken from the consolidation worksheet of Peak and its 90 percent–owned subsidiary, Valley:

- Peak reports a $12,000 gain on the sale of a building. The building had a book value of $32,000 but was sold for $44,000 cash.
- Intra-entity inventory transfers of $129,000 occurred during the current period.
- Valley declared and paid a $30,000 dividend during the year with $27,000 of this amount going to Peak.
- Amortization of an intangible asset recognized by Peak's worksheet was $16,000 for the current period.
- Consolidated accounts payable decreased by $11,000 during the year.

Indicate how to reflect each of these events on a consolidated statement of cash flows.

LO 6-5

36. Alford Company and its 80 percent–owned subsidiary, Knight, have the following income statements for 2018:

	Alford	Knight
Revenues	$(500,000)	$(230,000)
Cost of goods sold	300,000	140,000
Depreciation and amortization	40,000	10,000
Other expenses.	20,000	20,000
Gain on sale of equipment	(30,000)	–0–
Equity in earnings of Knight.	(36,200)	–0–
Net income.	$(206,200)	$ (60,000)

Additional Information for 2018

- Intra-entity inventory transfers during the year amounted to $90,000. All intra-entity transfers were downstream from Alford to Knight.
- Intra-entity gross profits in inventory at January 1 were $6,000, but at December 31 they are $9,000.
- Annual excess amortization expense resulting from the acquisition is $11,000.
- Knight paid dividends totaling $20,000.
- The noncontrolling interest's share of the subsidiary's income is $9,800.
- During the year, consolidated inventory rose by $11,000 while accounts receivable and accounts payable declined by $8,000 and $6,000, respectively.

Using either the direct or indirect method, compute net cash flows from operating activities during the period for the business combination.

LO 6-6

37. Porter Corporation owns all 30,000 shares of the common stock of Street, Inc. Porter has 60,000 shares of its own common stock outstanding. During the current year, Porter earns net income (without any consideration of its investment in Street) of $150,000 while Street reports $130,000. Annual amortization of $10,000 is recognized each year on the consolidation worksheet based on acquisition-date fair-value allocations. Both companies have convertible bonds outstanding. During the current year, bond-related interest expense (net of taxes) is $32,000 for Porter and $24,000 for Street. Porter's bonds can be converted into 8,000 shares of common stock; Street's bonds can be converted into 10,000 shares. Porter owns none of these bonds. What are the earnings per share amounts that Porter should report in its current year consolidated income statement?

LO 6-6

38. Primus, Inc., owns all outstanding stock of Sonston, Inc. For the current year, Primus reports net income (exclusive of any investment income) of $600,000. Primus has 100,000 shares of common

stock outstanding. Sonston reports net income of $200,000 for the period with 40,000 shares of common stock outstanding. Sonston also has 10,000 stock warrants outstanding that allow the holder to acquire shares at $10 per share. The value of this stock was $20 per share throughout the year. Primus owns 2,000 of these warrants. What amount should Primus report for diluted earnings per share?

LO 6-6

39. Garfun, Inc., owns all of the stock of Simon, Inc. For 2018, Garfun reports income (exclusive of any investment income) of $480,000. Garfun has 80,000 shares of common stock outstanding. It also has 5,000 shares of preferred stock outstanding that pay a dividend of $15,000 per year. Simon reports net income of $290,000 for the period with 80,000 shares of common stock outstanding. Simon also has a liability for 10,000 of $100 bonds that pay annual interest of $8 per bond. Each of these bonds can be converted into three shares of common stock. Garfun owns none of these bonds. Assume a tax rate of 30 percent. What amount should Garfun report as diluted earnings per share?

LO 6-6

40. The following separate income statements are for Burks Company and its 80 percent–owned subsidiary, Foreman Company:

	Burks	Foreman
Revenues	$(430,000)	$(330,000)
Expenses	280,000	240,000
Gain on sale of equipment	–0–	(30,000)
Equity earnings of subsidiary	(64,000)	–0–
Net income	$(214,000)	$(120,000)
Outstanding common shares	65,000	40,000

Additional Information

- Amortization expense resulting from Foreman's excess acquisition-date fair value is $40,000 per year.
- Burks has convertible preferred stock outstanding. Each of these 8,000 shares is paid a dividend of $4 per year. Each share can be converted into four shares of common stock.
- Stock warrants to buy 20,000 shares of Foreman are also outstanding. For $15, each warrant can be converted into a share of Foreman's common stock. The fair value of this stock is $20 throughout the year. Burks owns none of these warrants.
- Foreman has convertible bonds payable that paid interest of $45,000 (after taxes) during the year. These bonds can be exchanged for 10,000 shares of common stock. Burks holds 10 percent of these bonds, which it bought at book value directly from Foreman.

Compute basic and diluted EPS for Burks Company.

LO 6-7

41. DeMilo, Inc., owns 100 percent of the 40,000 outstanding shares of Ricardo, Inc. DeMilo currently carries the Investment in Ricardo account at $490,000 using the equity method.

Ricardo issues 10,000 new shares to the public for $15.75 per share. How does this transaction affect the Investment in Ricardo account that appears on DeMilo's financial records?

LO 6-7

42. Albuquerque, Inc., acquired 16,000 shares of Marmon Company several years ago for $600,000. At the acquisition date, Marmon reported a book value of $710,000, and Albuquerque assessed the fair value of the noncontrolling interest at $150,000. Any excess of acquisition-date fair value over book value was assigned to broadcast licenses with indefinite lives. Since the acquisition date and until this point, Marmon has issued no additional shares. No impairment has been recognized for the broadcast licenses.

At the present time, Marmon reports $800,000 as total stockholders' equity, which is broken down as follows:

Common stock ($10 par value)	$200,000
Additional paid-in capital	230,000
Retained earnings	370,000
Total	$800,000

View the following as independent situations:

a. Marmon sells 5,000 shares of previously unissued common stock to the public for $47 per share. Albuquerque purchased none of this stock. What journal entry should Albuquerque make to recognize the impact of this stock transaction?

b. Marmon sells 4,000 shares of previously unissued common stock to the public for $33 per share. Albuquerque purchased none of this stock. What journal entry should Albuquerque make to recognize the impact of this stock transaction?

LO 6-7

43. On January 1, 2016, Aronsen Company acquired 90 percent of Siedel Company's outstanding shares. Siedel had a net book value on that date of $480,000: common stock ($10 par value) of $200,000 and retained earnings of $280,000.

Aronsen paid $584,100 for this investment. The acquisition-date fair value of the 10 percent noncontrolling interest was $64,900. The excess fair value over book value associated with the acquisition was used to increase land by $89,000 and to recognize copyrights (16-year remaining life) at $80,000. Subsequent to the acquisition, Aronsen applied the initial value method to its investment account.

In the 2016–2017 period, the subsidiary's retained earnings increased by $100,000. During 2018, Siedel earned income of $80,000 while declaring $20,000 in dividends. Also, at the beginning of 2018, Siedel issued 4,000 new shares of common stock for $38 per share to finance the expansion of its corporate facilities. Aronsen purchased none of these additional shares and therefore recorded no entry. Prepare the appropriate 2018 consolidation entries for these two companies.

LO 6-3

44. Pavin acquires all of Stabler's outstanding shares on January 1, 2015, for $460,000 in cash. Of this amount, $30,000 was attributed to equipment with a 10-year remaining life and $40,000 was assigned to trademarks expensed over a 20-year period. Pavin applies the partial equity method so that income is accrued each period based solely on the earnings reported by the subsidiary.

On January 1, 2018, Pavin reports $300,000 in bonds outstanding with a carrying amount of $282,000. Stabler purchases half of these bonds on the open market for $145,500.

During 2018, Pavin begins to sell merchandise to Stabler. During that year, inventory costing $80,000 was transferred at a price of $100,000. All but $10,000 (at sales price) of these goods were resold to outside parties by year-end. Stabler still owes $33,000 for inventory shipped from Pavin during December.

The following financial figures are for the two companies for the year ending December 31, 2018. Dividends were both declared and paid during the current year. Prepare a worksheet to produce consolidated balances. (Credits are indicated by parentheses.)

	Pavin	Stabler
Revenues	$ (740,000)	$(505,000)
Cost of goods sold	455,000	240,000
Expenses	125,000	158,500
Interest expense—bonds	36,000	–0–
Interest income—bond investment	–0–	(16,500)
Loss on extinguishment of bonds	–0–	–0–
Equity in Stabler's income	(123,000)	–0–
Net income	$ (247,000)	$(123,000)
Retained earnings, 1/1/18	$ (345,000)	$(361,000)
Net income (above)	(247,000)	(123,000)
Dividends declared	155,000	61,000
Retained earnings, 12/31/18	$ (437,000)	$(423,000)
Cash and receivables	$ 217,000	$ 35,000
Inventory	175,000	87,000
Investment in Stabler	613,000	–0–
Investment in Pavin bonds	–0–	147,000
Land, buildings, and equipment (net)	245,000	541,000
Trademarks	–0–	–0–
Total assets	$ 1,250,000	$ 810,000
Accounts payable	$ (225,000)	$(167,000)
Bonds payable	(300,000)	(100,000)
Discount on bonds	12,000	–0–
Common stock	(300,000)	(120,000)
Retained earnings (above)	(437,000)	(423,000)
Total liabilities and stockholders' equity	$(1,250,000)	$(810,000)

45. Fred, Inc., and Herman Corporation formed a business combination on January 1, 2016, when Fred acquired a 60 percent interest in Herman's common stock for $312,000 in cash. The book value of Herman's assets and liabilities on that day totaled $300,000 and the fair value of the noncontrolling interest was $208,000. Patents being held by Herman (with a 12-year remaining life) were undervalued by $90,000 within the company's financial records and a customer list (10-year life) worth $130,000 was also recognized as part of the acquisition-date fair value.

Intra-entity inventory transfers occur regularly between the two companies. Merchandise carried over from one year to the next is always sold in the subsequent period.

Year	Original Cost to Herman	Transfer Price to Fred	Ending Balance at Transfer Price
2016	$80,000	$100,000	$20,000
2017	100,000	125,000	40,000
2018	90,000	120,000	30,000

Fred had not paid for half of the 2018 inventory transfers by year-end.

On January 1, 2017, Fred sold $15,000 in land to Herman for $22,000. Herman is still holding this land.

On January 1, 2018, Herman acquired $20,000 (face value) of Fred's bonds in the open market. These bonds had an 8 percent cash interest rate. On the date of repurchase, the liability was shown within Fred's records at $21,386, indicating an effective yield of 6 percent. Herman's acquisition price was $18,732 based on an effective interest rate of 10 percent.

Herman indicated earning a net income of $25,000 within its 2018 financial statements. The subsidiary also reported a beginning Retained Earnings balance of $300,000, dividends of $4,000, and common stock of $100,000. Herman has not issued any additional common stock since its takeover. The parent company has applied the equity method to record its investment in Herman.

a. Prepare consolidation worksheet adjustments for 2018.

b. Calculate the amount of consolidated net income attributable to the noncontrolling interest for 2018. In addition, determine the ending 2018 balance for noncontrolling interest in the consolidated balance sheet.

c. Determine the consolidation worksheet adjustments needed in 2019 in connection with the intra-entity bonds.

46. On January 1, 2017, Mona, Inc., acquired 80 percent of Lisa Company's common stock as well as 60 percent of its preferred shares. Mona paid $65,000 in cash for the preferred stock, with a call value of 110 percent of the $50 per share par value. The remaining 40 percent of the preferred shares traded at a $34,000 fair value. Mona paid $552,800 for the common stock. At the acquisition date, the noncontrolling interest in the common stock had a fair value of $138,200. The excess fair value over Lisa's book value was attributed to franchise contracts of $40,000. This intangible asset is being amortized over a 40-year period. Lisa pays all preferred stock dividends (a total of $8,000 per year) on an annual basis. During 2017, Lisa's book value increased by $50,000.

On January 2, 2017, Mona acquired one-half of Lisa's outstanding bonds payable to reduce the business combination's debt position. Lisa's bonds had a face value of $100,000 and paid cash interest of 10 percent per year. These bonds had been issued to the public to yield 14 percent. Interest is paid each December 31. On January 2, 2017, these bonds had a total $88,350 carrying amount. Mona paid $53,310, indicating an effective interest rate of 8 percent.

On January 3, 2017, Mona sold Lisa fixed assets that had originally cost $100,000 but had accumulated depreciation of $60,000 when transferred. The transfer was made at a price of $120,000. These assets were estimated to have a remaining useful life of 10 years.

The individual financial statements for these two companies for the year ending December 31, 2018, are as follows:

	Mona, Inc.	Lisa Company
Sales and other revenues..................	$ (500,000)	$ (200,000)
Expenses	220,000	120,000
Dividend income—Lisa common stock.......	(8,000)	–0–
Dividend income—Lisa preferred stock	(4,800)	–0–
Net income.........................	$ (292,800)	$ (80,000)
Retained earnings, 1/1/18.................	$ (700,000)	$ (500,000)
Net income (above)	(292,800)	(80,000)
Dividends declared—common stock.........	92,800	10,000
Dividends declared—preferred stock........	–0–	8,000
Retained earnings, 12/31/18	$ (900,000)	$ (562,000)
Current assets	$ 130,419	$ 500,000
Investment in Lisa—common stock	552,800	–0–
Investment in Lisa—preferred stock	65,000	–0–
Investment in Lisa—bonds..................	51,781	–0–
Fixed assets...............................	1,100,000	800,000
Accumulated depreciation	(300,000)	(200,000)
Total assets	$ 1,600,000	$ 1,100,000
Accounts payable.........................	$ (400,000)	$ (144,580)
Bonds payable.............................	–0–	(100,000)
Discount on bonds payable	–0–	6,580
Common stock	(300,000)	(200,000)
Preferred stock	–0–	(100,000)
Retained earnings, 12/31/18	(900,000)	(562,000)
Total liabilities and equities..............	$(1,600,000)	$(1,100,000)

a. What consolidation worksheet adjustments would have been required as of January 1, 2017, to eliminate the subsidiary's common and preferred stocks?

b. What consolidation worksheet adjustments would have been required as of December 31, 2017, to account for Mona's purchase of Lisa's bonds?

c. What consolidation worksheet adjustments would have been required as of December 31, 2017, to account for the intra-entity sale of fixed assets?

d. Assume that consolidated financial statements are being prepared for the year ending December 31, 2018. Calculate the consolidated balance for each of the following accounts:

Franchises

Fixed Assets

Accumulated Depreciation

Expenses

LO 6-5

47. Bolero Company holds 80 percent of the common stock of Rivera, Inc., and 40 percent of this subsidiary's convertible bonds. The following consolidated financial statements are for 2017 and 2018:

Bolero Company and Consolidated Subsidiary Rivera		
	2017	**2018**
Revenues	$ (900,000)	$(1,030,000)
Cost of goods sold	610,000	650,000
Depreciation and amortization..............	100,000	120,000
Gain on sale of building....................	–0–	(30,000)
Interest expense...........................	40,000	40,000
Consolidated net income	(150,000)	(250,000)
to noncontrolling interest	19,000	21,000
to parent company......................	$ (131,000)	$ (229,000)

(continued)

(continued)

Bolero Company and Consolidated Subsidiary Rivera		
	2017	**2018**
Retained earnings, 1/1.....................	$ (310,000)	$ (381,000)
Net income..............................	(131,000)	(229,000)
Dividends declared........................	60,000	110,000
Retained earnings, 12/31	$ (381,000)	$ (500,000)
Cash	$ 90,000	$ 180,000
Accounts receivable.......................	170,000	150,000
Inventory..................................	210,000	360,000
Buildings and equipment (net)	650,000	710,000
Databases	170,000	155,000
Total assets	$ 1,290,000	$ 1,555,000
Accounts payable.........................	$ (160,000)	$ (110,000)
Bonds payable............................	(410,000)	(520,000)
Noncontrolling interest in Rivera	(42,000)	(61,000)
Common stock	(110,000)	(140,000)
Additional paid-in capital..................	(187,000)	(224,000)
Retained earnings........................	(381,000)	(500,000)
Total liabilities and equities..............	$(1,290,000)	$(1,555,000)

Additional Information for 2018

- The parent issued bonds during the year for cash.
- Amortization of databases amounts to $15,000 per year.
- The parent sold a building with a cost of $80,000 but a $40,000 book value for cash on May 11.
- The subsidiary purchased equipment on July 23 for $205,000 in cash.
- Late in November, the parent issued stock for cash.
- During the year, the subsidiary paid dividends of $10,000. Both parent and subsidiary pay dividends in the same year as declared.

Prepare a consolidated statement of cash flows for this business combination for the year ending December 31, 2018. (Use indirect method.)

48. Following are separate income statements for Austin, Inc., and its 80 percent–owned subsidiary, Rio Grande Corporation as well as a consolidated statement for the business combination as a whole.

	Austin	**Rio Grande**	**Consolidated**
Revenues.............................	$(700,000)	$(500,000)	$(1,200,000)
Cost of goods sold	400,000	300,000	700,000
Operating expenses.....................	100,000	70,000	195,000
Equity in earnings of Rio Grande	(84,000)		
Individual company net income	$(284,000)	$(130,000)	
Consolidated net income			$ (305,000)
Noncontrolling interest in consolidated net income............................			(21,000)
Consolidated net income attributable to Austin			$ (284,000)

Additional Information

- Annual excess fair over book value amortization of $25,000 resulted from the acquisition.
- The parent applies the equity method to this investment.

- Austin has 50,000 shares of common stock and 10,000 shares of preferred stock outstanding. Owners of the preferred stock are paid an annual dividend of $40,000, and each share can be exchanged for two shares of common stock.

- Rio Grande has 30,000 shares of common stock outstanding. The company also has 5,000 stock warrants outstanding. For $10, each warrant can be converted into a share of Rio Grande's common stock. Austin holds half of these warrants. The price of Rio Grande's common stock was $20 per share throughout the year.

- Rio Grande also has convertible bonds, none of which Austin owned. During the current year, total interest expense (net of taxes) was $22,000. These bonds can be exchanged for 10,000 shares of the subsidiary's common stock.

Determine Austin's basic and diluted EPS.

49. On January 1, Paisley, Inc., paid $560,000 for all of Skyler Corporation's outstanding stock. This cash payment was based on a price of $180 per share for Skyler's $100 par value preferred stock and $38 per share for its $20 par value common stock. The preferred shares are voting, cumulative, and fully participating. At the acquisition date, the book values of Skyler's accounts equaled their fair values. Any excess fair value is assigned to an intangible asset and will be amortized over a 10-year period.

During the year, Skyler sold inventory costing $60,000 to Paisley for $90,000. All but $18,000 (measured at transfer price) of this merchandise has been resold to outsiders by the end of the year. At the end of the year, Paisley continues to owe Skyler for the last shipment of inventory priced at $28,000.

Also, on January 2 Paisley sold Skyler equipment for $20,000 although it had a carrying amount of only $12,000 (original cost of $30,000). Both companies depreciate such property according to the straight-line method with no salvage value. The remaining life at this date was four years.

The following financial statements are for each company for the year ending December 31. Determine consolidated financial totals for this business combination.

	Paisley, Inc.	Skyler Corporation
Sales	$ (800,000)	$(400,000)
Cost of goods sold	528,000	260,000
Expenses	180,000	130,000
Gain on sale of equipment	(8,000)	–0–
Net income	$ (100,000)	$ (10,000)
Retained earnings, 1/1	$ (400,000)	$(150,000)
Net income	(100,000)	(10,000)
Dividends declared	60,000	–0–
Retained earnings, 12/31	$ (440,000)	$(160,000)
Cash	$ 30,000	$ 40,000
Accounts receivable	300,000	100,000
Inventory	260,000	180,000
Investment in Skyler Corporation	560,000	–0–
Land, buildings, and equipment	680,000	500,000
Accumulated depreciation	(180,000)	(90,000)
Total assets	$ 1,650,000	$ 730,000
Accounts payable	$ (140,000)	$ (90,000)
Long-term liabilities	(240,000)	(180,000)
Preferred stock	–0–	(100,000)
Common stock	(620,000)	(200,000)
Additional paid-in capital	(210,000)	–0–
Retained earnings, 12/31	(440,000)	(160,000)
Total liabilities and equity	$(1,650,000)	$(730,000)

50. On June 30, 2018, Plaster, Inc., paid $916,000 for 80 percent of Stucco Company's outstanding stock. Plaster assessed the acquisition-date fair value of the 20 percent noncontrolling interest at $229,000. At acquisition date, Stucco reported the following book values for its assets and liabilities:

Cash	$ 60,000
Accounts receivable	127,000
Inventory	203,000
Land	65,000
Buildings	175,000
Equipment	300,000
Accounts payable	(35,000)

On June 30, Plaster allocated the excess acquisition-date fair value over book value to Stucco's assets as follows:

Equipment (3-year remaining life)	$ 75,000
Database (10-year remaining life)	175,000

At the end of 2018, the following comparative (2017 and 2018) balance sheets and consolidated income statement were available:

	Plaster, Inc. December 31, 2017	Consolidated December 31, 2018
Cash	$ 43,000	$ 242,850
Accounts receivable (net)	362,000	485,400
Inventory	415,000	720,000
Land	300,000	365,000
Buildings (net)	245,000	370,000
Equipment (net)	1,800,000	2,037,500
Database	–0–	166,250
Total assets	$3,165,000	$4,387,000
Accounts payable	$ 80,000	$ 107,000
Long-term liabilities	400,000	1,200,000
Common stock	1,800,000	1,800,000
Noncontrolling interest	–0–	255,500
Retained earnings	885,000	1,024,500
Total liabilities and equities	$3,165,000	$4,387,000

PLASTER, INC., AND SUBSIDIARY STUCCO COMPANY
Consolidated Income Statement
For the Year Ended December 31, 2018

Revenues		$1,217,500
Cost of goods sold	$737,500	
Depreciation	187,500	
Database amortization	8,750	
Interest and other expenses	9,750	943,500
Consolidated net income		$ 274,000

Additional Information for 2018

- On December 1, Stucco paid a $40,000 dividend. During the year, Plaster paid $100,000 in dividends.
- During the year, Plaster issued $800,000 in long-term debt at par.
- Plaster reported no asset purchases or dispositions other than the acquisition of Stucco.

  Prepare a 2018 consolidated statement of cash flows for Plaster and Stucco. Use the indirect method of reporting cash flows from operating activities.

Develop Your Skills

EXCEL CASE: INTRA-ENTITY BONDS

CPA *skills*

Place Company owns a majority voting interest in Sassano, Inc. On January 1, 2016, Place issued $1,000,000 of 11 percent 10-year bonds at $943,497.77 to yield 12 percent. On January 1, 2018, Sassano purchased all of these bonds in the open market at a price of $904,024.59 with an effective yield of 13 percent.

Required

Using an Excel spreadsheet, do the following:

1. Prepare amortization schedules for the Place Company bonds payable and the Investment in Place Bonds for Sassano, Inc.
2. Using the values from the amortization schedules, compute the worksheet adjustment for a December 31, 2018, consolidation of Place and Sassano to reflect the effective retirement of the Place bonds. Formulate your solution to be able to accommodate various yield rates (and therefore prices) on the repurchase of the bonds.

Hints

Present value of $1 = 1/(1 + r)n$
Present value of an annuity of $1 = (1 - 1/[1 + r]n)/r$
Where r = effective yield and n = years remaining to maturity

RESEARCH CASE: STATEMENT OF CASH FLOWS

CPA *skills*

Download Pfizer's 2015 annual report (search Pfizer Investor Relations). Locate the firm's consolidated statement of cash flows and answer the following:

- Does the firm employ the direct or indirect method of accounting for operating cash flows?
- Why does the firm account for the changes in balances in operating accounts (e.g., accounts receivable, inventory, accounts payable) in determining operating cash flows as net of acquisitions and divestitures?
- Describe the accounting for cash paid for business acquisitions in the statement of cash flows.
- Describe the accounting for any noncontrolling subsidiary interest and any other business combination–related items in the consolidated statement of cash flows.

FINANCIAL REPORTING RESEARCH AND ANALYSIS CASE

CPA *skills*

The FASB ASC Subtopic "Variable Interest Entities" affects thousands of business enterprises that now, as primary beneficiaries, consolidate entities that qualify as controlled VIEs. Retrieve the annual reports of one or more of the following companies (or any others you may find) that consolidate VIEs:

- The Walt Disney Company.
- General Electric.
- Allegheny Energy.

Required

Write a brief report that describes

1. The reasons for consolidation of the company's VIE(s).
2. The effect of the consolidation of the VIE(s) on the company's financial statements.

Foreign Currency Transactions and Hedging Foreign Exchange Risk

Today, international business transactions are a regular occurrence. In its 2015 annual report, Lockheed Martin Corporation reported export sales of $9.5 billion, representing 21 percent of total sales. Some businesses are very significantly involved in transactions occurring throughout the world as evidenced by this excerpt from Cirrus Logic, Inc.'s fiscal year 2015 annual report: "Export sales, principally to Asia, including sales to U.S.-based customers that manufacture at plants overseas, were approximately $869.9 million in fiscal year 2015, $673.7 million in fiscal year 2014, and $764.9 million in fiscal year 2013. Export sales to customers located in Asia were 92 percent of net sales in fiscal years 2015 and 2014 and 91 percent in fiscal year 2013. All other export sales represented 3 percent of net sales in each of fiscal years 2015, 2014, and 2013."

Collections from export sales or payments for imported items might be made not in U.S. dollars but in pesos, pounds, yen, and the like depending on the negotiated terms of the transaction. As foreign currency exchange rates fluctuate, so does the U.S. dollar value of these export sales and import purchases. Companies often find it necessary to engage in some form of hedging activity to reduce losses arising from fluctuating exchange rates. At the end of fiscal year 2015, in conjunction with its foreign currency hedging activities, Apple, Inc., reported having outstanding foreign exchange contracts with a notional value of $119.2 billion.

This chapter covers accounting issues related to foreign currency transactions and foreign currency hedging activities. To provide background for subsequent discussions of the accounting issues, the chapter begins by describing foreign exchange markets. The chapter then discusses accounting for import and export transactions, followed by coverage of various hedging techniques. Because they are most popular, the discussion concentrates on foreign currency forward contracts and options. Understanding how to account for these items is important for any company engaged in international transactions.

Learning Objectives

After studying this chapter, you should be able to:

LO 7-1 Understand concepts related to foreign currency, exchange rates, and foreign exchange risk.

LO 7-2 Account for foreign currency transactions using the two-transaction perspective, accrual approach.

LO 7-3 Account for foreign currency borrowings.

LO 7-4 Understand the different types of foreign exchange risk that can be hedged and how foreign currency forward contracts and foreign currency options can be used to hedge those risks.

LO 7-5 Understand the accounting guidelines for derivative financial instruments.

LO 7-6 Understand the basic concepts of hedge accounting.

LO 7-7 Account for forward contracts and options used as hedges of foreign currency denominated assets and liabilities.

LO 7-8 Account for forward contracts and options used as hedges of foreign currency firm commitments.

LO 7-9 Account for forward contracts and options used as hedges of forecasted foreign currency transactions.

LO 7-1

Understand concepts related to foreign currency, exchange rates, and foreign exchange risk.

Foreign Exchange Markets

Each country (or group of countries) uses its own currency as the unit of value for the purchase and sale of goods and services. The currency used in the United States is the U.S. dollar, the currency used in Mexico is the Mexican peso, the currency used by a subset of European Union countries is the euro, and so on. If a U.S. citizen travels to Mexico and wishes to purchase local goods, Mexican merchants require payment to be made in Mexican pesos. To make a purchase in Mexico, a U.S. citizen would need to acquire pesos using U.S. dollars. The foreign currency *exchange rate* is the price at which the foreign currency can be acquired (or sold). A variety of factors determine the exchange rate between two currencies; unfortunately for those engaged in international business, the exchange rate can fluctuate over time.[1]

Exchange Rate Mechanisms

Exchange rates have not always fluctuated. During the period 1945–1973, countries fixed the value of their currency in terms of the U.S. dollar, and the value of the U.S. dollar was fixed in terms of gold. In March 1973, most countries allowed their currencies to float in value. Today, several different currency arrangements exist. Some of the more important ones and the countries affected follow:

1. *Independent float:* The value of the currency is allowed to fluctuate freely according to market forces with little or no intervention from the central bank (example countries include Australia, Brazil, Canada, Japan, Sweden, Switzerland, the United Kingdom, and the United States).

2. *Pegged to another currency:* The value of the currency is fixed (pegged) in terms of a particular foreign currency and the central bank intervenes as necessary to maintain the fixed value. For example, Bahrain, Panama, and Saudi Arabia peg their currency to the U.S. dollar. China has pegged its currency, the yuan (or Renminbi), to the U.S. dollar since 1994, while allowing a revaluation in 2005 and again in 2015. By managing the value of its currency (downward) rather than allowing it to float freely, the Chinese government has made it easier for Chinese companies to export their products overseas.

3. *European Monetary System (euro):* In 1998, the countries comprising the European Monetary System adopted a common currency called the *euro* and established a European Central Bank.[2] Until 2002, local currencies such as the German mark and French franc continued to exist but were fixed in value in terms of the euro. On January 1, 2002, local currencies disappeared, and the euro became the currency in 12 European countries. Today, 19 countries are part of the euro zone. The value of the euro floats against other currencies such as the Swiss franc, British pound, and U.S. dollar.

Foreign Exchange Rates

Exchange rates between the U.S. dollar and many foreign currencies are published on a daily basis in *The Wall Street Journal* and major U.S. newspapers. Exchange rates also are available online at websites such as www.oanda.com and www.x-rates.com. To illustrate exchange rates and the foreign currency market, next we examine exchange rates for selected currencies reported for December 1-2, 2015, as shown in Exhibit 7.1.

The exchange rates shown in Exhibit 7.1 are for trades between banks; that is, these are interbank or wholesale prices. Prices charged by banks to retail customers, such as companies engaged in international business, are higher. These are selling rates at which banks will sell currency to one another. The prices that banks are willing to pay to buy foreign currency are

---

[1] Several theories attempt to explain exchange rate fluctuations but with little success, at least in the short term. An understanding of the causes of exchange rate changes is not necessary to comprehend the concepts underlying the accounting for changes in exchange rates.

[2] Most longtime members of the European Union (EU) are "euro zone" countries. The major exception is the United Kingdom, which elected not to participate. Switzerland is another important European country not part of the euro zone because it is not a member of the EU.

EXHIBIT 7.1
Exchange Rates for Selected Currencies (December 1-2, 2015)

Country/Currency	December 1, 2015		December 2, 2015	
	Direct*	Indirect†	Direct*	Indirect†
Euro zone euro................	1.0607	0.9428	1.0685	0.9359
UK pound	1.5078	0.6632	1.5027	0.6655
Canada dollar................	0.7491	1.3349	0.7480	1.3369
Brazil real..................	0.2584	3.8700	0.2595	3.8536
China yuan	0.1560	6.4103	0.1560	6.4103

Source: http://www.oanda.com/currency/historical-rates.
*www.oanda.com/currency/historical-rates.
†Indirect quotes have been calculated by the author.

somewhat less than the selling rates. The difference between the buying and selling rates is the spread through which the banks earn a profit on foreign exchange trades. For example, the December 1, 2015, selling rate for the euro was $1.0607, while the the buying rate was $1.0596. On that date, banks were willing to buy euros for $1.0596 and sell them for $1.0607, earning a profit of $0.0011 per euro.

Two columns of information are shown for each day's exchange rates. The first column reports *direct quotes,* which indicate the number of U.S. dollars needed to purchase one unit of foreign currency. The direct quote for the Brazilian real on December 1 was $0.2584; in other words, 1.0 Brazilian real (BRL) could be purchased for $0.2584. The second column reports *indirect quotes,* which indicate the number of foreign currency units that could be purchased with one U.S. dollar. These rates are simply the inverse of direct quotes (indirect quote = 1 ÷ direct quote). If one BRL can be purchased with $0.2584, then 3.87 BRL can be purchased with $1.00. To avoid confusion, *direct quotes are used exclusively in this chapter.*

The third and fourth columns in Exhibit 7.1 show exchange rates for December 2, 2015. Two of the currencies shown increased in U.S. dollar price (appreciated) from December 1 to December 2, namely the euro and Brazilian real. For example, the euro increased in price by $0.0078 from one day to the next. As a result, the purchase of 100,000 euros on December 2, 2015, would have cost $780 more than on the previous day. In contrast, the U.S. dollar price for two currencies decreased (depreciated) from one day to the next, namely the British pound and Canadian dollar. The Chinese yuan did not change in U.S. dollar value because this currency was effectively pegged to the U.S. dollar.

Foreign Currency Forward Contracts

Foreign currency trades can be executed on a spot or forward basis. The *spot rate* is the price at which a foreign currency can be purchased or sold today. In contrast, the *forward rate* is the price available today at which foreign currency can be purchased or sold sometime in the future. Because many international business transactions take some time to be completed, the ability to lock in a price today at which foreign currency can be purchased or sold at some future date has definite advantages.

A *foreign currency forward contract* can be negotiated by a firm with its bank to exchange foreign currency for U.S. dollars, or vice versa, on a specified future date at a predetermined exchange rate. A forward contract can be written for whatever currency and for whatever future date is required. Entering into a forward contract has no up-front cost; the firm and its bank simply agree today to exchange foreign currency for U.S. dollars at the forward rate on a future date. Similar to how banks make a profit in the spot market, there is a spread between the buying and selling rates in the forward market. For example, on February 1 a bank might agree to buy 500,000 British pounds in three months from one customer at a forward rate of $1.50 and simultaneously agree to sell 500,000 British pounds (GBP) in three months to another customer at a rate of $1.51. In this way, the bank generates a profit of $5,000 (500,000 GBP x $0.01) from entering into these two forward contracts.

The forward rate can exceed the spot rate on a given date, in which case the foreign currency is said to be selling at a *premium* in the forward market, or the forward rate can be less than the spot rate, in which case the currency is selling at a *discount.* Currencies sell at a premium or a discount because of differences in interest rates between two countries. When the interest rate in the foreign country exceeds the domestic interest rate, the foreign currency sells at a discount in the forward market. Conversely, if the foreign interest rate is less than the domestic rate, the foreign currency sells at a premium.[3]

The forward exchange rate for a specific future settlement date will change over time due to changes in the spot exchange rate and/or changes in the differential interest rates between two countries. For example, assume on April 15 the U.S. dollar (USD) per Mexican peso (MXN) spot rate is $0.11 and the forward rate for a forward contract to be settled on June 15 is $0.105. The peso is selling at a discount of $0.005 in the two-month forward market due to a higher interest rate in Mexico than in the United States. If the USD/MXN spot rate decreases to $0.08 on May 15, the forward rate for a June 15 settlement-date forward contract also will decrease, to an amount less than $0.08. The peso will continue to sell at a discount in the one-month forward market because of the higher interest rate in Mexico.

Until December 2014, *The Wall Street Journal* published forward rates offered by New York banks for several major currencies on a daily basis. Since then, it has been difficult for third parties to obtain data on foreign currency forward rates. The spot rate for Swiss francs (CHF) on December 8, 2014, was reported to be $1.0245. On the same day, the one-month forward rate was reported as $1.0250, so the CHF was selling at a premium in the forward market. By entering into a forward contract on December 8, 2014, it would have been possible for a firm to guarantee that CHF could be purchased on January 8, 2015, at a price of $1.0250, regardless of what the spot rate turned out to be on January 8. Entering into the forward contract to purchase CHF would have been beneficial if the spot rate on January 8 was more than $1.0250. On the other hand, such a forward contract would have been detrimental if the spot rate was less than $1.0250. In either case, the firm must execute the forward contract and purchase CHF on January 8 at $1.0250.

As it turned out, the spot rate for CHF on January 8, 2015, was $0.9819, so entering into a one-month forward contract on December 8, 2014, to purchase CHF at $1.0250 on January 8, 2015, would have resulted in a loss because CHF could have been purchased at a lower price using the spot rate on that date.

Foreign Currency Options

To provide companies more flexibility than exists with a forward contract, a market for *foreign currency options* has developed. A foreign currency option gives the holder of the option *the right but not the obligation* to trade foreign currency in the future. A *put* option is for the sale of foreign currency by the holder of the option; a *call* option is for the purchase of foreign currency by the holder of the option. The *strike price* is the exchange rate at which the option will be executed if the option holder decides to exercise the option. The strike price is similar to a forward rate. There are generally several strike prices to choose from at any particular time. Foreign currency options can be purchased on the Philadelphia Stock Exchange or the Chicago Mercantile Exchange, but most foreign currency options are purchased directly from a bank in the so-called over-the-counter (OTC) market. Options purchased in the OTC market usually have a strike price that is equal to the spot rate on that date. These options are said to be "at-the-money."

Unlike a forward contract, for which banks earn their profit through the spread between buying and selling rates, options must actually be purchased by paying an *option premium,* which is a function of two components: intrinsic value and time value. An option's *intrinsic value* is equal to the gain that could be realized by exercising the option immediately. For example, if the spot rate for the euro is $1.00, a *call* option (to purchase euros) with a strike price of $0.97 has an intrinsic value of $0.03 per euro. Euros can be purchased for $0.97 and sold for $1.00, generating a gain of $0.03 per euro. On the other hand, when the spot rate for the euro is $1.00, a *put* option (to sell euros) with a strike price of $0.97 has an intrinsic

---

[3] This relationship is based on the theory of interest rate parity that indicates the difference in national interest rates should be equal to, but opposite in sign to, the forward rate discount or premium. This topic is covered in detail in international finance textbooks.

value of zero. An option with a positive intrinsic value is said to be "in-the-money." The *time value* of an option relates to the fact that the spot rate can change over time and cause the option's intrinsic value to increase. Even though a call option with a strike price of $1.00 has zero intrinsic value when the spot rate is $1.00, it will have a positive time value because there is a chance that the spot rate could increase over the next 90 days and bring the option into the money. As time passes, the time value of an option decreases because there is less time remaining for the option to increase in intrinsic value. The fair value of a foreign currency option on a specific date is the sum of its intrinsic and time values on that date.

The fair value of a foreign currency option can be determined by applying an adaptation of the Black-Scholes option pricing formula. This formula is discussed in detail in international finance books. In very general terms, the value of an option is a function of the difference between the current spot rate and strike price, the difference between domestic and foreign interest rates, the length of time to expiration, and the potential volatility of changes in the spot rate. For purposes of this book, the premium originally paid for a foreign currency option and its subsequent fair value up to the date of expiration derived from applying the pricing formula will be given.

On December 17, 2015, when the USD spot rate for euros was $1.09, the Chicago Mercantile Exchange indicated that a January 2016 call option in euros with a strike price of $1.09 could have been purchased by paying a premium of $0.0068 per euro. Thus, the right to purchase a standard contract of 125,000 euros in December 2016 at a price of $1.09 per euro could have been acquired by paying $850 ($0.0068 × 125,000 euros). Because the spot rate and the strike price were both $1.09, the euro call option had zero intrinsic value and a time value of $850. If the spot rate for euros on January 17, 2016, is more than $1.09, the option will be exercised and euros purchased at the strike price of $1.09. If, on the other hand, the January 17, 2016, spot rate is less than $1.09, the option will not be exercised; instead, euros will be purchased at the lower spot rate. The call option establishes the maximum amount that would have to be paid for euros but does not lock in a disadvantageous price should the spot rate fall below the option strike price. The actual spot rate for euros on January 17, 2016, turned out to be $1.091, so the option would have been exercised and euros purchased for $1.09.

LO 7-2

Account for foreign currency transactions using the two-transaction perspective, accrual approach.

Foreign Currency Transactions

Export sales and import purchases are international transactions; they are components of what is called *trade*. When two parties from different countries enter into a transaction, they must decide which of the two countries' currencies to use to settle the transaction. For example, if a U.S. computer manufacturer sells to a customer in Japan, the parties must decide whether the transaction will be denominated (payment will be made) in U.S. dollars or in Japanese yen.

Assume that a U.S. exporter (Amerco) sells goods to a German importer that will pay in euros (€). In this situation, Amerco has entered into a foreign currency transaction. It must restate the euro amount that it actually will receive into U.S. dollars to account for this transaction. This happens because Amerco keeps its books and prepares financial statements in U.S. dollars. Although the German importer has entered into an international transaction, it does not have a foreign currency transaction (payment will be made in its currency) and no restatement is necessary.

Assume that, as is customary in its industry, Amerco does not require immediate payment and allows its German customer 30 days to pay for its purchases. By doing this, Amerco runs the risk that the euro might depreciate against the U.S. dollar between the sale date and the date of payment. If so, the sale would generate fewer U.S. dollars than it would have had the euro not decreased in value, and the sale is less profitable because it was made on a credit basis. In this situation Amerco is said to have an *exposure to foreign exchange risk.* Specifically, Amerco has a transaction exposure that can be summarized as follows:

- *Export sale:* A transaction exposure exists when the exporter *allows the buyer to pay in a foreign currency* and *allows the buyer to pay sometime after the sale has been made.* The exporter is exposed to the risk that the foreign currency might depreciate (decrease in value) between the date of sale and the date payment is received, thereby decreasing the U.S. dollars ultimately collected.
    - Note that there is no exposure to foreign exchange risk if the exporter requires the foreign customer to make payment on the date of sale. In that case, the exporter would receive foreign currency and immediately convert it into U.S. dollars at the spot rate on the date of sale.
- *Import purchase:* A transaction exposure exists when the importer *is required to pay in foreign currency* and *is allowed to pay sometime after the purchase has been made.* The importer is exposed to the risk that the foreign currency might appreciate (increase in price) between the date of purchase and the date of payment, thereby increasing the U.S. dollars that have to be paid for the imported goods.
    - Note that there is no exposure to foreign exchange risk if the importer makes payment in foreign currency on the date of purchase. In that case, the importer converts U.S. dollars into foreign currency at the spot rate on the date of purchase and immediately makes payment.

Accounting Issue

The major issue in accounting for foreign currency transactions is how to deal with the change in U.S. dollar value of the sales revenue and account receivable resulting from the export when the foreign currency changes in value. (The corollary issue is how to deal with the change in the U.S. dollar value of the account payable and goods being acquired in an import purchase.) For example, assume that Amerco, a U.S. company, sells goods to a German customer at the price of 1 million euros when the spot exchange rate is $1.32 per euro. If payment were received at the sale date, Amerco could have converted 1 million euros into $1,320,000; this amount clearly would be the amount at which the sales revenue would be recognized. Instead, Amerco allows the German customer 30 days to pay for its purchase. At the end of 30 days, the euro has depreciated to $1.30 and Amerco is able to convert the 1 million euros received on that date into only $1,300,000. How should Amerco account for this $20,000 decrease in value?

FASB *ASC* 830-20 Foreign Currency Matters–Foreign Currency Transactions requires companies to use what can be referred to as a *two-transaction perspective* in accounting for foreign currency transactions. This perspective treats the export sale and the subsequent collection of cash as two separate transactions. Because management has made two decisions— (1) to make the export sale and (2) to extend credit in foreign currency to the customer—the company should report the income effect from each of these decisions separately. The U.S. dollar value of the sale is recorded at the date the sale occurs. At that point, the sale has been completed; there are no subsequent adjustments to the Sales account. Any difference between the number of U.S. dollars that could have been received at the date of sale and the number of U.S. dollars actually received at the date of collection due to fluctuations in the exchange rate is a result of the decision to extend foreign currency credit to the customer. This difference is treated as a foreign exchange gain or loss that is reported separately from Sales in the income statement.

Similarly, an import purchase denominated in a foreign currency and the subsequent payment of cash must be accounted for separately. The U.S. dollar value of the goods purchased is recorded at the date of purchase, with no subsequent adjustments to the cost of the goods. Any difference between the number of U.S. dollars that could have been paid on the date of purchase and the actual number of U.S. dollars that is paid on the payment date due to a change in the exchange rate is treated as a foreign exchange gain or loss.

Using the two-transaction perspective to account for its export sale to the German customer, Amerco would make the following journal entries:

Date of Sale:	Accounts Receivable (€)......................	1,320,000	
	Sales		1,320,000
	To record the sale and euro receivable at the spot rate of $1.32.		
Date of Collection:	Foreign Exchange Loss	20,000	
	Accounts Receivable (€)		20,000
	To adjust the value of the euro receivable to the new spot rate of $1.30 and record a foreign exchange loss resulting from the depreciation in the euro.		
	Cash.......................................	1,300,000	
	Accounts Receivable (€)		1,300,000
	To record the receipt of 1 million euros and conversion into U.S. dollars at the spot rate of $1.30.		

Sales are reported in income at the amount that would have been received if the customer had not been given 30 days to pay the 1 million euros—that is, $1,320,000. A separate Foreign Exchange Loss of $20,000 is reported in net income to indicate that because of the decision to extend foreign currency credit to the German customer and because the euro decreased in value, Amerco actually received fewer U.S. dollars.[4]

Note that Amerco keeps its Account Receivable (€) account separate from its U.S. dollar receivables. Companies engaged in international trade need to keep separate receivable and payable accounts in each of the currencies in which they have transactions. Each foreign currency receivable and payable should have a separate account number in the company's chart of accounts.

We can summarize the relationship between fluctuations in exchange rates and foreign exchange gains and losses as follows:

		Foreign Currency (FC)	
Transaction	**Type of Exposure**	**Appreciates**	**Depreciates**
Export sale	Asset (receivable)	Gain	Loss
Import purchase	Liability (payable)	Loss	Gain

A foreign currency receivable arising from an export sale creates an *asset exposure* to foreign exchange risk. If the foreign currency appreciates, the foreign currency asset increases in U.S. dollar value and a foreign exchange gain arises; depreciation of the foreign currency causes a foreign exchange loss. A foreign currency payable arising from an import purchase creates a *liability exposure* to foreign exchange risk. If the foreign currency appreciates, the foreign currency liability increases in U.S. dollar value and a foreign exchange loss results; depreciation of the currency results in a foreign exchange gain.

Balance Sheet Date before Date of Payment

The question arises as to what adjustments should be made if a balance sheet date falls between the date of sale (or purchase) and the date of collection (or payment). For example, assume that Amerco shipped goods to its German customer on December 1, 2017, with payment to be received on March 1, 2018. Assume that at December 1, the spot rate for the euro was $1.32, but by December 31, the euro has appreciated to $1.33. Is any adjustment needed at December 31, 2017, when the books are closed to account for the fact that the foreign currency receivable has changed in U.S. dollar value since December 1?

Authoritative accounting literature requires foreign currency balances such as a foreign currency receivable or a foreign currency payable to be revalued at the balance sheet date to account for the change in exchange rates. Under the two-transaction perspective, this means that a foreign exchange gain or loss arises at the balance sheet date. The next question then is

---

[4] Note that the foreign exchange loss results because the customer is allowed to pay in euros and is given 30 days to pay. If the transaction were denominated in U.S. dollars, no loss would result, nor would there be a loss if the euros had been received at the date the sale was made.

what should be done with these foreign exchange gains and losses that have not yet been realized in cash. Should they be included in net income?

U.S. GAAP requires unrealized foreign exchange gains and losses to be reported in net income in the period in which the exchange rate changes. This is consistent with accrual accounting as it results in reporting the effect of a rate change that will have an impact on cash flow in the period when the event causing the impact takes place. Thus, any change in the exchange rate from the date of sale to the balance sheet date results in a foreign exchange gain or loss to be reported in net income in that period. Any change in the exchange rate from the balance sheet date to the date of collection results in a second foreign exchange gain or loss that is reported in net income in the second accounting period. Amerco makes the following journal entries under this approach:

12/1/17	Accounts Receivable (€)...................	1,320,000	
	Sales		1,320,000
	To record the sale and euro receivable at the spot rate of $1.32.		
12/31/17	Accounts Receivable (€)...................	10,000	
	Foreign Exchange Gain		10,000
	To adjust the value of the euro receivable to the new spot rate of $1.33 and record a foreign exchange gain in 2017 net income resulting from the appreciation in the euro since December 1.		
3/1/18	Foreign Exchange Loss	30,000	
	Accounts Receivable (€)		30,000
	To adjust the value of the euro receivable to the new spot rate of $1.30 and record a foreign exchange loss in 2018 net income resulting from the depreciation in the euro since December 31.		
	Cash..	1,300,000	
	Accounts Receivable (€)		1,300,000
	To record the receipt of 1 million euros and conversion at the spot rate of $1.30.		

The net impact on income in 2017 is a sale of $1,320,000 and a foreign exchange gain of $10,000; in 2018, Amerco records a foreign exchange loss of $30,000. This results in a net increase of $1,300,000 in Retained Earnings that is balanced by an equal increase in Cash over the two-year period. Over the two-year period Amerco recognizes a net foreign exchange loss of $20,000.

One criticism of the accrual approach is that it leads to a violation of conservatism when an unrealized foreign exchange gain arises at the balance sheet date. In fact, this is one of only a few situations in U.S. GAAP in which it is acceptable to recognize an unrealized gain in net income. (This treatment is similar to how changes in the fair value of equity investments are recognized.)

Restatement at the balance sheet date is required for all foreign currency assets and liabilities carried on a company's books. In addition to foreign currency payables and receivables arising from import and export transactions, companies might have dividends receivable from foreign subsidiaries, loans payable to foreign lenders, or lease payments receivable from foreign customers that are denominated in a foreign currency and therefore must be restated at the balance sheet date. Each of these foreign currency denominated assets and liabilities is exposed to foreign exchange risk; therefore, fluctuation in exchange rates result in foreign exchange gains and losses on all foreign currency denominated assets and liabilities.

Many U.S. companies report foreign exchange gains and losses on the income statement in a line item often titled Other income (expense). Companies include other incidental gains and losses such as gains and losses on sales of assets in this line item as well. Companies are required to disclose the magnitude of foreign exchange gains and losses if material. For example, in the Notes to Financial Statements in its 2014 annual report, Merck indicated that the income statement item Other (Income) Expense, Net, included exchange losses of $180 million in 2014, $290 million in 2013, and $185 million in 2012.

International Accounting Standard 21—The Effects of Changes in Foreign Exchange Rates

Similar to U.S. GAAP, *IAS 21,* "The Effects of Changes in Foreign Exchange Rates," also requires the use of a two-transaction perspective in accounting for foreign currency transactions with unrealized foreign exchange gains and losses accrued in net income in the period of exchange rate change. There are no substantive differences between IFRS and U.S. GAAP in the accounting for foreign currency transactions.

LO 7-3

Account for foreign currency borrowings.

Foreign Currency Borrowing

In addition to the receivables and payables that arise from import and export activities, companies often must account for foreign currency borrowings, another type of foreign currency transaction. Companies borrow foreign currency from foreign lenders either to finance foreign operations or perhaps to take advantage of more favorable interest rates. The facts that both the principal and interest are denominated in foreign currency and both create an exposure to foreign exchange risk complicate accounting for a foreign currency borrowing.

To demonstrate the accounting for foreign currency debt, assume that on July 1, 2017, Multicorp International borrowed 1 billion Japanese yen (¥) on a one-year note at a per annum interest rate of 5 percent. Interest is payable and the note comes due on July 1, 2018. The following exchange rates apply:

Date	U.S. Dollars per Japanese Yen Spot Rate
July 1, 2017	$0.00921
December 31, 2017	0.00932
July 1, 2018	0.00937

On July 1, 2017, Multicorp borrows ¥1 billion and converts it into $9,210,000 in the spot market. On December 31, 2017, Multicorp must revalue the Japanese yen note payable with an offsetting foreign exchange gain or loss reported in income and must accrue interest expense and interest payable. Interest is calculated by multiplying the loan principal in yen by the relevant interest rate. The amount of interest payable in yen is then translated to U.S. dollars at the spot rate to record the accrual journal entry. On July 1, 2018, any difference between the amount of interest accrued at year-end and the actual U.S. dollar amount that must be spent to pay the accrued interest is recognized as a foreign exchange gain or loss. These journal entries account for this foreign currency borrowing:

7/1/17	Cash	9,210,000	
	Note Payable (¥)		9,210,000
	To record the ¥ note payable at the spot rate of $0.00921 and the conversion of ¥1 billion into U.S. dollars.		
12/31/17	Interest Expense	233,000	
	Accrued Interest Payable (¥)		233,000
	To accrue interest for the period July 1– December 31, 2017: ¥1 billion × 5% × ½ year = ¥25 million × $0.00932 = $233,000.		

(*continued*)

(continued)

	Foreign Exchange Loss	110,000	
	Note Payable (¥)		110,000
	To revalue the ¥ note payable at the spot rate of $0.00932 and record a foreign exchange loss of $110,000 [¥1 billion × ($0.00932 − $0.00921)].		
7/1/18	Interest Expense	234,250	
	Accrued Interest Payable (¥).		234,250
	To accrue interest for the period January 1–July 1, 2018: ¥1 billion × 5% × ½ year = ¥25 million × $0.00937 = $234,250.		
	Foreign Exchange Loss	1,250	
	Accrued Interest Payable (¥)		1,250
	To revalue the ¥ interest payable that was accrued on December 31, 2017, at the spot rate of $0.00937 and record a foreign exchange loss of $1,250 [¥25 million × ($0.00937 − $0.00932)].		
	Accrued Interest Payable (¥)	468,500	
	Cash.		468,500
	To record the cash interest payment of $468,500 [¥50 million × the spot rate of $0.00937] and remove the ¥ accrued interest payable from the books.		
	Foreign Exchange Loss	50,000	
	Note Payable (¥)		50,000
	To revalue the ¥ note payable at the spot rate of $0.00937 and record a foreign exchange loss of $50,000 [¥1 billion × ($0.00937 − $0.00932)].		
	Note Payable (¥).	9,370,000	
	Cash.		9,370,000
	To record repayment of the ¥1 billion note through purchase of ¥1 billion at the spot rate of $0.00937 and remove the ¥ note payable from the books..		

The total U.S. dollar borrowing cost on the 1 billion Japanese yen note payable is equal to the difference between the U.S. dollar cash outflows and cash inflow: $9,370,000 + $468,500 − $9,210,000 = $628,500. This borrowing cost is reflected in Multicorp's financial statements as a combination of interest expense ($467,250) and foreign exchange loss ($161,250). Taking the exchange rate effect on the cost of borrowing into consideration results in an "effective" interest rate of 6.8% ($628,500/$9,210,000), even though the stated interest rate is only 5%.

Foreign Currency Loan

At times companies lend foreign currency to related parties, creating the opposite situation from a foreign currency borrowing. The accounting involves keeping track of a note receivable and related interest receivable, both of which are denominated in foreign currency. Fluctuations in the U.S. dollar value of the principal and interest generally give rise to foreign exchange gains and losses that would be included in net income. An exception arises when the foreign currency loan is made on a long-term basis to a foreign branch, subsidiary, or equity method affiliate. Foreign exchange gains and losses on "intra-entity foreign currency transactions that are of a long-term investment nature (that is, settlement is not planned or anticipated in the foreseeable future)" are deferred in accumulated other comprehensive income until the loan is repaid.[5] Only the foreign exchange gains and losses related to the interest receivable are recorded currently in net income.

LO 7-4

Understand the different types of foreign exchange risk that can be hedged and how foreign currency forward contracts and foreign currency options can be used to hedge those risks.

Hedges of Foreign Exchange Risk

In the example provided in the earlier section on foreign currency transactions, Amerco has an asset exposure in euros when it sells goods to the German customer and allows the customer three months to pay for its purchase. If the euro depreciates over the next three months, Amerco will incur a net foreign exchange loss. For many companies, the uncertainty of not knowing exactly how many U.S. dollars an export sale will generate is of great concern. To avoid this uncertainty, companies often use derivative financial instruments to hedge against the effect of unfavorable changes in the value of foreign currencies. A derivative financial instrument, or simply derivative, derives its value from some "underlying." In the case of foreign currency derivatives, the underlying is the currency exchange rate. The two most common derivatives used to hedge foreign exchange risk are *foreign currency forward contracts* and *foreign currency options*. In our example, Amerco will receive euros in three months when it collects the receivable and it will need to sell those euros at that time. Through a forward contract, Amerco can lock in the price at which it will sell the euros it receives in three months. An option establishes a price at which Amerco will be able, but is not required, to sell the euros it receives in three months. If Amerco enters into a forward contract or purchases a put option on the date the sale is made, the derivative is being used as a *hedge of a recognized foreign currency denominated asset* (the euro account receivable).

Companies engaged in foreign currency activities often enter into hedging arrangements as soon as they receive a noncancelable sales order or place a noncancelable purchase order. A noncancelable order that specifies the foreign currency price and date of delivery is known as a *foreign currency firm commitment*. Assume that on June 1, Amerco accepts an order to sell parts to a customer in South Korea at a price of 5 million Korean won. The parts will be delivered and payment will be received on August 15. On June 1, before the sale has been made, Amerco enters into a forward contract to sell 5 million Korean won on August 15. In this case, Amerco is using a foreign currency derivative as a *hedge of an unrecognized foreign currency firm commitment*.

Some companies have foreign currency transactions that occur on a regular basis and can be reliably forecasted. For example, Amerco regularly purchases materials from a supplier in Hong Kong for which it pays in Hong Kong dollars. Even if Amerco has no contract to make future purchases, it has an exposure to foreign currency risk if it plans to continue making purchases from the Hong Kong supplier. Assume that on October 1, Amerco forecasts that it will make a purchase from the Hong Kong supplier in one month. To hedge against a possible increase in the price of the Hong Kong dollar, Amerco acquires a call option on October 1 to purchase Hong Kong dollars in one month. The foreign currency option represents a *hedge of a forecasted foreign currency denominated transaction*.

LO 7-5

Understand the accounting guidelines for derivative financial instruments.

Derivatives Accounting

FASB *ASC* Topic 815, "Derivatives and Hedging," governs the accounting for derivatives, including those used to hedge foreign exchange risk. This authoritative literature provides guidance for hedges of the following sources of foreign exchange risk:

1. Recognized foreign currency denominated assets and liabilities.
2. Unrecognized foreign currency firm commitments.
3. Forecasted foreign currency denominated transactions.
4. Net investments in foreign operations.

Different accounting applies to each type of foreign currency hedge. This chapter demonstrates the accounting for the first three types of hedges. The next chapter covers hedges of net investments in foreign operations.

[5] FASB ASC (para. 830-20-35-3b).

Fundamental Requirement of Derivatives Accounting

The fundamental requirement of FASB *ASC* 815 is that companies carry all derivatives on the balance sheet at their fair value. Derivatives are reported on the balance sheet as assets when they have a positive fair value and as liabilities when they have a negative fair value. The first issue in accounting for derivatives is the determination of fair value.

The fair value of derivatives can change over time, causing adjustments to be made to the carrying values of the assets and liabilities. The second issue in accounting for derivatives is the treatment of the gains and losses that arise from these fair value changes.

Determination of Fair Value of Derivatives

The *fair value of a foreign currency forward contract* is determined by reference to changes in the forward rate over the life of the contract, discounted to the present value. Three pieces of information are needed to determine the fair value of a forward contract at any point in time:

1. The forward rate when the forward contract was entered into.
2. The current forward rate for a contract that matures on the same date as the forward contract entered into.
3. A discount rate—typically, the company's incremental borrowing rate.

Assume that Exim Company enters into a forward contract with its bank on December 1 to sell 1 million Mexican pesos on March 1 at a forward rate of $0.085 per peso, or a total of $85,000. Exim incurs no cost to enter into the forward contract, which has no value on December 1. On December 31, when Exim closes its books to prepare financial statements, the forward rate to sell Mexican pesos on March 1 has changed to $0.082. On that date, a forward contract for the delivery of 1 million pesos could be negotiated, resulting in a cash inflow of only $82,000 on March 1. This represents a favorable change in the value of Exim's forward contract of $3,000 ($85,000 − $82,000). The undiscounted fair value of the forward contract on December 31 is $3,000. Assuming that the company's incremental borrowing rate is 12 percent per annum, the undiscounted fair value of the forward contract must be discounted at the rate of 1 percent per month for two months (from the current date of December 31 to the settlement date of March 1). The fair value of the forward contract at December 31 is $2,940.90 ($3,000 × 0.9803).[6]

The manner in which the *fair value of a foreign currency option* is determined depends on whether the option is traded on an exchange or has been acquired in the over-the-counter market. The fair value of an exchange-traded foreign currency option is its current market price quoted on the exchange. For over-the-counter options, fair value can be determined by obtaining a price quote from an option dealer (such as a bank). If dealer price quotes are unavailable, the company can estimate the value of an option using the modified Black-Scholes option pricing model (briefly mentioned earlier). Regardless of who does the calculation, principles similar to those of the Black-Scholes pricing model can be used to determine the fair value of the option.

Accounting for Changes in the Fair Value of Derivatives

Changes in the fair value of derivatives must be included in *comprehensive income,* which consists of two components: *net income* and *other comprehensive income.* Other comprehensive income consists of income items that current authoritative accounting literature require to be deferred in stockholders' equity such as unrealized gains and losses on available-for-sale debt securities. Other comprehensive income is accumulated and reported as a separate line in the stockholders' equity section of the balance sheet. This book uses the account title *Accumulated Other Comprehensive Income* to describe this stockholders' equity line item.

In accordance with U.S. GAAP, gains and losses arising from changes in the fair value of derivatives are recognized initially either (1) in net income or (2) in other comprehensive income (reflected on the balance sheet in accumulated other comprehensive income).

---

[6] The present value factor for two months at 1 percent per month is calculated as $1/1.01^2$, or 0.9803.

Recognition treatment depends partly on whether the company uses derivatives for hedging purposes or for speculation.

Although using derivatives for speculation is not commonly done by nonfinancial institutions, financial entities might acquire derivative financial instruments as investments for speculative purposes. For example, assume that the three-month forward rate for British pounds is $2.00, and a speculator believes the British pound spot rate in three months will be $1.97. In that case, the speculator would enter into a three-month forward contract to sell British pounds. At the future date, the speculator purchases pounds at the spot rate of $1.97 and sells them at the contracted forward rate of $2.00, reaping a gain of $0.03 per British pound. Of course, such an investment might as easily generate a loss if the spot rate does not move as expected. For speculative derivatives, the change in the fair value of the derivative must be recognized immediately as a gain or loss in net income.[7]

The accounting for changes in the fair value of derivatives used for hedging depends on the nature of the foreign exchange risk being hedged and on whether the derivative qualifies for *hedge accounting.*

LO 7-6

Understand the basic concepts of hedge accounting.

Hedge Accounting

Companies enter into hedging relationships to minimize the adverse effect that changes in exchange rates have on cash flows and net income. As such, companies would like to account for hedges in a way that recognizes the gain or loss from the hedge in net income in the same period as the loss or gain on the risk being hedged. This approach is known as *hedge accounting.* U.S. GAAP allows hedge accounting for foreign currency derivatives only if three conditions are satisfied:

1. The derivative is used to hedge either a cash flow exposure or a fair value exposure to foreign exchange risk.
2. The derivative is highly effective in offsetting changes in the cash flows or fair value related to the hedged item.
3. The derivative is properly documented as a hedge.

Each of these conditions is discussed in turn.

Nature of the Hedged Risk

Derivatives for which companies wish to use hedge accounting must be designated as either a *cash flow hedge* or a *fair value hedge.* For hedges of recognized foreign currency assets and liabilities and hedges of foreign currency firm commitments, companies must choose between the two types of designation. Hedges of forecasted foreign currency transactions can qualify only as cash flow hedges. Accounting procedures differ for the two types of hedges. In general, gains and losses on cash flow hedges are included in other comprehensive income (and therefore deferred on the balance sheet in accumulated other comprehensive income), and gains and losses on fair value hedges are recognized immediately in net income.

A *fair value exposure* exists if changes in exchange rates can affect the fair value of an asset or liability reported on the balance sheet. To qualify for hedge accounting, the fair value risk must have the potential to affect net income if it is not hedged. For example, a fair value risk is associated with a foreign currency account receivable. If the foreign currency depreciates, the receivable must be written down with an offsetting loss recognized in net income. The authoritative literature has determined that a fair value exposure also exists for foreign currency firm commitments.

A *cash flow exposure* exists if changes in exchange rates can affect the amount of cash flow to be realized from a foreign currency transaction with changes in cash flow reflected in net income. A foreign currency account receivable, for example, has both a fair value exposure and a cash flow exposure. A cash flow exposure exists for (1) recognized foreign currency

---

[7] In the next section we will see that the change in fair value of a derivative designated as the fair value hedge of a foreign currency denominated asset or liability also is recognized immediately in net income.

assets and liabilities, (2) foreign currency firm commitments, and (3) forecasted foreign currency transactions.

Hedge Effectiveness

For hedge accounting to be used initially, the hedge must be expected to be highly effective in generating gains and losses that offset losses and gains on the item being hedged. The hedge actually must be effective in generating offsetting gains and losses for hedge accounting to continue to be applied over the life of the hedge.

At inception, a foreign currency derivative can be considered an effective hedge if the critical terms of the hedging instrument match those of the hedged item. Critical terms include the currency type, currency amount, and settlement date. For example, a forward contract to purchase 100,000 Canadian dollars in 30 days would be an effective hedge of a 100,000 Canadian dollar liability that is payable in 30 days.

Hedge Documentation

For hedge accounting to be applied, U.S. GAAP requires formal documentation of the hedging relationship at the inception of the hedge (i.e., on the date a foreign currency forward contract is entered into or a foreign currency option is acquired). The hedging company must prepare a document that identifies the hedged item (for example, a 100,000 Canadian dollar liability), the hedging instrument (a forward contract to purchase 100,000 Canadian dollars), the nature of the risk being hedged (a cash flow exposure), how the hedging instrument's effectiveness will be assessed (through reference to changes in the forward rate), and the risk management objective and strategy for undertaking the hedge (to minimize risk associated with a possible Canadian dollar appreciation).

Hedging Combinations

The specific accounting procedures followed and journal entries needed to account for a foreign currency hedging relationship are determined by a combination of the following factors:

1. The type of foreign currency item being hedged:
   a. Foreign currency denominated asset or liability.
   b. Foreign currency firm commitment.
   c. Forecasted foreign currency transaction.
2. The type of hedging instrument used:
   a. Forward contract.
   b. Option.
3. The nature of the hedged risk:
   a. Cash flow exposure.
   b. Fair value exposure.
4. The nature of the foreign currency item being hedged:
   a. Asset (existing or future).
   b. Liability (existing or future).

In the next three sections in this chapter we discuss the accounting for hedges of (1) foreign currency denominated assets/liabilities, (2) foreign currency firm commitments, and (3) forecasted foreign currency transactions. We demonstrate through examples the use of both forward contracts and options to hedge these items, and we selectively demonstrate the accounting for both cash flow and fair value hedges. We focus on hedges entered into by an exporter that has a current or future foreign currency asset that is exposed to foreign exchange risk. The comprehensive example at the end of this chapter demonstrates the accounting for hedges entered into by an importer that has an existing or future foreign currency liability. Exhibit 7.2 provides an overall summary of the procedures followed in accounting for hedges of foreign exchange risk for those combinations presented in this chapter. By examining this exhibit, the similarities and differences in the procedures followed and accounting entries prepared to account for each hedge combination can be discerned.

EXHIBIT 7.2 Summary of Accounting for Hedges of Foreign Exchange Risk

| Date | Hedge of a Foreign Currency Denominated Asset or Liability | | | | Hedge of a Foreign Currency Firm Commitment | | Hedge of a Forecasted Foreign Currency Transaction | |
| | Cash Flow Hedge | | Fair Value Hedge | | Fair Value Hedge | | Cash Flow Hedge | |
	Forward Contract	Option	Forward Contract	Option	Forward Contract	Option	Forward Contract	Option
A. Initiation Date	1. Recognize the transaction (sale or purchase) and foreign currency denominated asset or liability 2. No entry related to forward contract (zero fair value)	1. Recognize the transaction (sale or purchase) and foreign currency denominated asset or liability 2. Recognize option as an asset (purchase price is fair value)	1. Recognize the transaction (sale or purchase) and foreign currency denominated asset or liability 2. No entry related to forward contract (zero fair value)	1. Recognize the transaction (sale or purchase) and foreign currency denominated asset or liability 2. Recognize option as an asset (purchase price is fair value)	1. No entry related to the firm commitment (zero value) 2. No entry related to forward contract (zero fair value)	1. No entry related to the firm commitment 2. Recognize option as an asset (purchase price is fair value)	1. No entry related to the forecasted transaction 2. No entry related to forward contract (zero fair value)	1. No entry related to the forecasted transaction 2. Recognize option as an asset (purchase price is fair value)
B. Balance Sheet Date	1. Adjust hedged asset or liability to fair value, with counterpart (change in fair value) reported as foreign exchange gain or loss in net income 2. Adjust forward contract to fair value (either an asset or a liability), with counterpart (change in fair value) reported in AOCI	1. Adjust hedged asset or liability to fair value, with counterpart (change in fair value) reported as foreign exchange gain or loss in net income 2. Adjust option to fair value (either an asset or zero value), with counterpart (change in fair value) reported in AOCI	1. Adjust hedged asset or liability to fair value, with counterpart (change in fair value) reported as foreign exchange gain or loss in net income 2. Adjust forward contract to fair value (either an asset or a liability), with counterpart (change in fair value) reported as gain or loss in net income	1. Adjust hedged asset or liability to fair value, with counterpart (change in fair value) reported as foreign exchange gain or loss in net income 2. Adjust option to fair value (either an asset or zero value), with counterpart (change in fair value) reported as gain or loss in net income	1. Adjust forward contract to fair value (either an asset or a liability), with counterpart (change in fair value) reported as gain or loss in net income 2. Adjust firm commitment to fair value (based on change in forward rate), with counterpart (change in fair value) reported as gain or loss in net income	1. Adjust option to fair value (either an asset or zero value), with counterpart (change in fair value) reported as gain or loss in net income 2. Adjust firm commitment to fair value (based on change in spot rate), with counterpart (change in fair value) reported as gain or loss in net income	1. N/A 2. Adjust forward contract to fair value (either an asset or a liability), with counterpart (change in fair value) reported in AOCI	1. N/A 2. Adjust option to fair value (either an asset or zero value), with counterpart (change in fair value) reported in AOCI

(continued)

EXHIBIT 7.2 (Continued)

| | Hedge of a Foreign Currency Denominated Asset or Liability | | | | Hedge of a Foreign Currency Firm Commitment | | Hedge of a Forecasted Foreign Currency Transaction | |
| | Cash Flow Hedge | | Fair Value Hedge | | Fair Value Hedge | | Cash Flow Hedge | |
Date	Forward Contract	Option	Forward Contract	Option	Forward Contract	Option	Forward Contract	Option
	3. Transfer an amount from AOCI to net income to offset the foreign exchange gain or loss on the hedged asset or liability recognized in B.1 4. Transfer from AOCI to net income (as discount expense or premium revenue) the current period's amortization of discount or premium	3. Transfer an amount from AOCI to net income to offset the foreign exchange gain or loss on the hedged asset or liability recognized in B.1 4. Transfer from AOCI to net income (as expense) the change in time value on the option	3. N/A 4. N/A	3. N/A 4. N/A	3. N/A 4. N/A	3. N/A 4. N/A	3. N/A 4. Transfer from AOCI to net income (as discount expense or premium revenue) the current period's amortization of discount or premium	3. N/A 4. Transfer from AOCI to net income (as option expense) the change in time value on the option
C. Settlement Date	1.–4. Repeat steps B.1.–B.4 5. Recognize settlement of the foreign currency denominated asset or liability 6. Recognize settlement of the forward contract*	1.–4. Repeat steps B.1.–B.4 5. Recognize settlement of the foreign currency denominated asset or liability 6. Recognize exercise (or expiration) of the option*	1.–2. Repeat steps B.1. and B.2 3. Recognize settlement of the foreign currency denominated asset or liability 4. Recognize settlement of the forward contract&	1.–2. Repeat steps B.1. and B.2 3. Recognize settlement of the foreign currency denominated asset or liability 4. Recognize exercise (or expiration) of the option&	1.–2. Repeat steps B.1. and B.2 3. Recognize the transaction (sale or purchase) 4. Recognize settlement of the forward contract# 5. Close the balance in the firm commitment account as an adjustment to net income	1.–2. Repeat steps B.1. and B.2 3. Recognize the transaction (sale or purchase) 4. Recognize exercise (or expiration) of the option# 5. Close the balance in the firm commitment account as an adjustment to net income	1.–2. Repeat steps B.2. and B.4 3. Recognize the transaction (sale or purchase) 4. Recognize settlement of the forward contract# 5. Close the balance in AOCI related to the forward contract as an adjustment to net income	1.–2. Repeat steps B.2. and B.4 3. Recognize the transaction (sale or purchase) 4. Recognize exercise (or expiration) of the option# 5. Close the balance in AOCI related to the option as an adjustment to net income

*Step 6 precedes step 5 in the case of a foreign currency denominated liability.
&Step 4 precedes step 3 in the case of a foreign currency denominated liability.
#Step 4 precedes step 3 in the case of a foreign currency purchase transaction.

Account for forward contracts and options used as hedges of foreign currency denominated assets and liabilities.

Hedges of Foreign Currency Denominated Assets and Liabilities

Hedges of foreign currency denominated assets and liabilities, such as accounts receivable and accounts payable, can qualify as either *cash flow hedges* or *fair value hedges*. To qualify as a cash flow hedge, the hedging instrument must completely offset the variability in the cash flows associated with the foreign currency receivable or payable. If the hedging instrument does not qualify as a cash flow hedge or if the company elects not to designate the hedging instrument as a cash flow hedge, the hedge is designated as a fair value hedge. The following summarizes the basic accounting for the two types of hedges of foreign currency denominated assets and liabilities.

Cash Flow Hedge

At each balance sheet date, the following procedures are required:

1. The hedged asset (foreign currency account receivable) or liability (foreign currency account payable) is adjusted to fair value based on changes in the spot exchange rate, and a foreign exchange gain or loss is recognized in net income (Cash Flow Hedge Step B.1. in Exhibit 7.2).

2. To comply with the fundamental requirement of derivatives accounting, the derivative hedging instrument (forward contract or option) is adjusted to fair value (resulting in an asset or liability reported on the balance sheet) with the counterpart recognized as a change in Accumulated Other Comprehensive Income (AOCI) (Cash Flow Hedge Step B.2. in Exhibit 7.2).

3. An amount equal to the foreign exchange gain or loss on the hedged asset or liability is then transferred from AOCI to net income; the net effect is to offset any gain or loss on the hedged asset or liability (Cash Flow Hedge Step B.3. in Exhibit 7.2).

4. An additional amount is removed from AOCI and recognized in net income to reflect (a) the current period's amortization of the original discount or premium on the forward contract (if a forward contract is the hedging instrument) or (b) the change in the *time value* of the option (if an option is the hedging instrument) (Cash Flow Hedge Step B.4. in Exhibit 7.2).

Fair Value Hedge

At each balance sheet date, the following procedures are required:

1. Adjust the hedged asset or liability to fair value based on changes in the spot exchange rate and recognize a foreign exchange gain or loss in net income (Fair Value Hedge Step B.1. in Exhibit 7.2).

2. Adjust the derivative hedging instrument to fair value (resulting in an asset or liability reported on the balance sheet) and recognize the counterpart as a gain or loss in net income (Fair Value Hedge Step B.2. in Exhibit 7.2).

Forward Contract Used to Hedge a Foreign Currency Denominated Asset

We now return to the Amerco example in which the company has a foreign currency account receivable to demonstrate the accounting for a hedge of a recognized foreign currency denominated asset.[8] In the preceding example, Amerco has an asset exposure in euros when it sells goods to the German customer and allows the customer three months to pay for its purchase. To hedge its exposure to a possible decline in the U.S. dollar value of the euro, Amerco enters into a forward contract.

---

[8] The comprehensive illustration at the end of this chapter demonstrates the accounting for the hedge of a foreign currency denominated liability.

Assume that on December 1, 2017, the three-month forward rate for euros is $1.305 and Amerco signs a contract with New Manhattan Bank to deliver 1 million euros in three months in exchange for $1,305,000. No cash changes hands on December 1, 2017. Because the spot rate on December 1 is $1.32, the euro (€) is selling at a discount in the three-month forward market (the forward rate is less than the spot rate). Because the euro is selling at a discount of $0.015 ($1.305 - $1.320) per euro, Amerco receives $15,000 less than it would had payment been received at the date the goods are delivered ($1,305,000 versus $1,320,000). This $15,000 reduction in cash flow can be considered as an expense; it is the cost of extending foreign currency credit to the foreign customer.[9] Conceptually, this expense is similar to the transaction loss that arises on the export sale. It exists only because the transaction is denominated in a foreign currency. The major difference is that Amerco knows the exact amount of the discount expense at the date of sale, whereas when it is left unhedged, Amerco does not know the size of the transaction loss until three months pass. (In fact, it is possible that the unhedged receivable could result in a transaction gain rather than a transaction loss.)

Because the future spot rate turns out to be only $1.30, selling euros at a forward rate of $1.305 is obviously better than leaving the euro receivable unhedged: Amerco will receive $5,000 more as a result of the hedge. This can be viewed as a gain resulting from the use of the forward contract. Unlike the discount expense, the exact size of this gain is not known until three months pass. (In fact, it is possible that use of the forward contract could result in an additional loss. This would occur if the spot rate on March 1, 2018, is more than the forward rate of $1.305.)

Amerco must account for its foreign currency transaction and the related forward contract simultaneously but separately. The process can be better understood by referring to the steps involving the three parties—Amerco, the German customer, and New Manhattan Bank—shown in Exhibit 7.3.

Because the settlement date, currency type, and currency amount of the forward contract match the corresponding terms of the account receivable, the hedge is expected to be highly effective. If Amerco properly designates the forward contract as a hedge of its euro account receivable position, it may apply hedge accounting. Because it completely offsets the variability in the cash flows related to the account receivable, Amerco may designate the forward

EXHIBIT 7.3
Hedge of a Foreign Currency Account Receivable with a Forward Contract

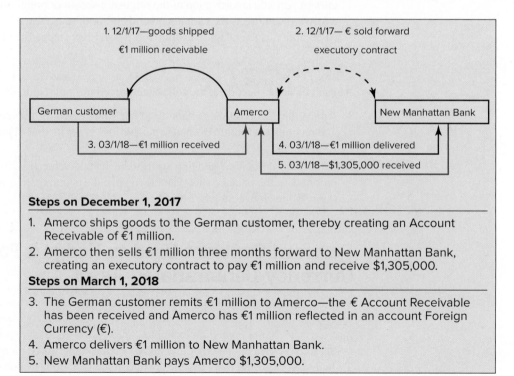

Steps on December 1, 2017

1. Amerco ships goods to the German customer, thereby creating an Account Receivable of €1 million.
2. Amerco then sells €1 million three months forward to New Manhattan Bank, creating an executory contract to pay €1 million and receive $1,305,000.

Steps on March 1, 2018

3. The German customer remits €1 million to Amerco—the € Account Receivable has been received and Amerco has €1 million reflected in an account Foreign Currency (€).
4. Amerco delivers €1 million to New Manhattan Bank.
5. New Manhattan Bank pays Amerco $1,305,000.

[9] This should not be confused with the cost associated with normal credit risk—that is, the risk that the customer will not pay for its purchase. That is a separate issue unrelated to the currency in which the transaction is denominated.

contract as a cash flow hedge. Alternatively, because changes in the spot rate affect not only the cash flows but also the fair value of the foreign currency receivable, Amerco may elect to account for this forward contract as a fair value hedge.

In either case, Amerco determines the fair value of the forward contract by referring to the change in the forward rate for a contract maturing on March 1, 2018. The relevant exchange rates, U.S. dollar value of the euro receivable, and fair value of the forward contract are determined as follows:

		Account Receivable (€)		Forward Rate to 3/1/18	Forward Contract	
Date	Spot Rate	U.S. Dollar Value	Change in U.S. Dollar Value		Fair Value	Change in Fair Value
12/1/17	$1.32	$1,320,000	—	$1.305	$ –0–	—
12/31/17	1.33	1,330,000	+$10,000	1.316	(10,783)*	–$10,783
3/1/18	1.30	1,300,000	– 30,000	1.30	5,000†	+ 15,783

*$1,305,000 − $1,316,000 = $(11,000) × 0.9803 = $(10,783), where 0.9803 is the present value factor for two months at an annual interest rate of 12 percent (1 percent per month) calculated as $1/1.01^2$.

†$1,305,000 − $1,300,000 = $5,000. This is the difference between the dollars that will be received when the forward contract is executed (based on the original forward rate) and the dollars that would have been received if no forward contract had been entered into (based on the spot rate on the date the euros are received).

Amerco pays nothing to enter into the forward contract at December 1, 2017, and the forward contract has a fair value of zero on that date. The original discount on the forward contract is $15,000, determined by the difference in the euro spot rate and three-month forward rate on December 1, 2017 [($1.305 − $1.32) × €1 million]. At December 31, 2017, the forward rate for a contract to deliver euros on March 1, 2018, is $1.316. Amerco could enter into a forward contract on December 31, 2017, to sell 1 million euros for $1,316,000 on March 1, 2018. Because Amerco is committed to sell 1 million euros for $1,305,000, the nominal value of the forward contract is $(11,000). The fair value of the forward contract is the present value of this amount. Assuming that Amerco has an incremental borrowing rate of 12 percent per year (1 percent per month) and discounting for two months (from December 31, 2017, to March 1, 2018), the fair value of the forward contract at December 31, 2017, is $(10,783). Because the fair value is negative, the forward contract is a liability on December 31, 2017. On March 1, 2018, the forward rate to sell euros on that date is, by definition, the spot rate of $1.30. At that rate, Amerco could sell 1 million euros for $1,300,000. Because Amerco has a contract to sell euros for $1,305,000, the fair value of the forward contract on March 1, 2018, is $5,000. At this point, the forward contract is an asset because it has a positive fair value. From December 31, 2017, to March 1, 2018, the fair value of the forward contract has increased by $15,783.

Forward Contract Designated as Cash Flow Hedge

Assume that Amerco designates the forward contract as a *cash flow hedge* of a foreign currency denominated asset. In this case, it allocates the original forward discount or premium to net income over the life of the forward contract using an effective interest method. The company prepares the following journal entries to account for the foreign currency transaction and the related forward contract:

2017 Journal Entries—Forward Contract Designated as a Cash Flow Hedge

12/1/17	Accounts Receivable (€)...............................	1,320,000	
	Sales		1,320,000
	To record the sale and €1 million account receivable at the spot rate of $1.32 (Cash Flow Hedge Step A.1. in Exhibit 7.2).		
	Amerco makes no formal entry for the forward contract because it is an executory contract (no cash changes hands) and has a fair value of zero (Cash Flow Hedge Step A.2. in Exhibit 7.2).		

Amerco prepares a memorandum designating the forward contract as a hedge of the risk of changes in the cash flow to be received on the foreign currency account receivable resulting from changes in the U.S. dollar–euro exchange rate. Following steps B.1.-B.4. in accounting for a cash flow hedge presented in Exhibit 7.2, the company prepares the following journal entries on December 31:

12/31/17	Accounts Receivable (€)...................................	10,000	
	Foreign Exchange Gain		10,000
	To adjust the value of the € receivable to the new spot rate of $1.33 and record a foreign exchange gain resulting from the appreciation of the € since December 1 (Cash Flow Hedge Step B.1. in Exhibit 7.2).		
	Accumulated Other Comprehensive Income (AOCI)............	10,783	
	Forward Contract......................................		10,783
	To record the forward contract as a liability at its fair value of $10,783 with a corresponding debit to AOCI (Cash Flow Hedge Step B.2. in Exhibit 7.2).		
	Loss on Forward Contract	10,000	
	Accumulated Other Comprehensive Income (AOCI)		10,000
	To record a loss on forward contract to offset the foreign exchange gain on account receivable with a corresponding credit to AOCI (Cash Flow Hedge Step B.3. in Exhibit 7.2).		
	Discount Expense	5,019	
	Accumulated Other Comprehensive Income (AOCI)		5,019
	To allocate the forward contract discount to net income over the life of the contract using the effective interest method with a corresponding credit to AOCI (Cash Flow Hedge Step B.4. in Exhibit 7.2).		

The first entry at December 31, 2017, serves to revalue the foreign currency account receivable and recognize a foreign exchange gain of $10,000 in net income. Because the forward contract has a negative fair value of $(10,783), GAAP requires it to be reported on the balance sheet as a liability. Thus, the second entry makes a credit of $10,783 to Forward Contract. Under cash flow hedge accounting, the change in the fair value of the forward contract, which has gone from $0 to $(10,783) is not recognized immediately in income, but is instead deferred in stockholders' equity. Thus, the debit of $10,783 in the second entry is made to AOCI. The third entry achieves the objective of hedge accounting by transferring $10,000 from AOCI to a loss on forward contract. As a result of this entry, the loss on forward contract of $10,000 and the foreign exchange gain on the account receivable of $10,000 exactly offset one another, and the net impact on income is zero. As a result of the second and third entries, the forward contract is reported on the balance sheet as a liability at fair value of $(10,783); a loss on forward contract is recognized in the amount of $10,000 to offset the foreign exchange gain; and AOCI has a negative (debit) balance of $783. The second and third entries could be combined into one entry as follows:

Loss on Forward Contract...	10,000	
Accumulated Other Comprehensive Income (AOCI)......................	783	
Forward Contract		10,783

The negative balance in AOCI of $783 can be viewed as that portion of the loss on the forward contract (decrease in fair value of the forward contract) that is not recognized in net income but instead is deferred in stockholders' equity. Under cash flow hedge accounting, a loss on the hedging instrument (forward contract) is recognized only to the extent that it offsets a gain on the item being hedged (account receivable).

The last entry uses the effective interest method to allocate a portion of the $15,000 forward contract discount as an expense to net income. The company calculates the implicit interest rate associated with the forward contract by considering the fact that the forward contract will generate cash flow of $1,305,000 from a foreign currency asset with an initial value of $1,320,000. Because the discount of $15,000 accrues over a three-month period, the effective interest rate is calculated as $1-\sqrt[3]{[\$1,305,000/\$1,320,000]} = .0038023$ The amount of discount to be allocated to net income for the month of December 2017 is $1,320,000 × .0038023 = $5,019. A debit of $5,019 is made to Discount Expense in the last journal entry on December 31, 2017. By making the credit in this journal entry to AOCI, the theoretically correct amounts are reported in net income and on the balance sheet, and the balance sheet remains in balance.

The impact on net income for the year 2017 follows:

Sales.		$1,320,000
Foreign exchange gain.	$10,000	
Loss on forward contract	(10,000)	
Net gain (loss).		–0–
Discount expense		(5,019)
Impact on net income		$1,314,981

Assets		Liabilities and Stockholders' Equity	
Accounts receivable (€)	$1,330,000	Forward contract	$ 10,783
		Retained earnings	1,314,981
		AOCI.	4,236
			$1,330,000

2018 Journal Entries—Forward Contract Designated as Cash Flow Hedge

From December 31, 2017, to March 1, 2018, the euro account receivable decreases in value by $30,000 and the forward contract increases in value by $15,873. In addition, on March 1, 2018, the remaining discount on forward contract must be amortized to expense. The company prepares the following journal entries on March 1 to reflect these changes:

Date	Account	Debit	Credit
3/1/18	Foreign Exchange Loss	30,000	
	Accounts Receivable (€)		30,000
	To adjust the value of the € receivable to the new spot rate of $1.30 and record a foreign exchange loss resulting from the depreciation of the € since December 31 (Cash Flow Hedge Step C.1. in Exhibit 7.2).		
	Forward Contract	15,783	
	Accumulated Other Comprehensive Income (AOCI)		15,783
	To adjust the carrying value of the forward contract to its current fair value of $5,000 with a corresponding credit to AOCI (Cash Flow Hedge Step C.2. in Exhibit 7.2).		
	Accumulated Other Comprehensive Income (AOCI)	30,000	
	Gain on Forward Contract.		30,000
	To record a gain on forward contract to offset the foreign exchange loss on account receivable with a corresponding debit to AOCI (Cash Flow Hedge Step C.3. in Exhibit 7.2).		
	Discount Expense.	9,981	
	Accumulated Other Comprehensive Income (AOCI)		9,981
	To allocate the remaining forward contract discount to net income ($15,000 – 5,019 = $9,981) with a corresponding credit to AOCI (Cash Flow Hedge Step C.4. in Exhibit 7.2).		

As a result of these entries, the balance in AOCI is zero: $4,236 + $15,783 − $30,000 + $9,981 = $0.

The next two journal entries recognize the receipt of euros from the customer, close out the euro account receivable, and record the settlement of the forward contract.

3/1/18	Foreign Currency (€).	1,300,000	
	Accounts Receivable (€)		1,300,000
	To record receipt of €1 million from the German customer as an asset (Foreign Currency) at the spot rate of $1.30 (Cash Flow Hedge Step C.5. in Exhibit 7.2).		
	Cash.	1,305,000	
	Foreign Currency (€).		1,300,000
	Forward Contract.		5,000
	To record settlement of the forward contract (i.e., record receipt of $1,305,000 in exchange for delivery of €1 million) and remove the forward contract from the accounts (Cash Flow Hedge Step C.6. in Exhibit 7.2).		

The impact on net income for the year 2018 follows:

Foreign exchange loss	$(30,000)	
Gain on forward contract	30,000	
Net gain (loss).		–0–
Discount expense		$(9,981)
Impact on net income		$(9,981)

The net effect on the balance sheet over the two years is a $1,305,000 increase in Cash with a corresponding increase in Retained Earnings of $1,305,000 ($1,314,981 − $9,981). The cumulative amount recognized as Discount Expense of $15,000 reflects the cost of extending credit to the German customer.

The net benefit from entering into the forward contract is $5,000. This "gain" is not directly reflected in net income. However, it can be calculated as the difference between the net gain on the forward contract ($10,000 loss in 2017 plus $30,000 gain in 2018 = $20,000 net gain) and the cumulative amount of discount expense ($15,000) recognized over the two periods: $20,000 − $15,000 = $5,000.

Effective Interest versus Straight-Line Methods

Use of the effective interest method results in allocating the forward contract discount $5,019 at the end of the first month and $9,981 at the end of the next two months. Straight-line allocation of the $15,000 discount on a monthly basis results in a reasonable approximation of these amounts:

$$12/31/17 \qquad \$15,000 \times \tfrac{1}{3} = \$5,000$$

$$3/1/18 \qquad \$15,000 \times \tfrac{2}{3} = \$10,000$$

Determining the effective interest rate is complex and provides no conceptual insights. For the remainder of this chapter, we use straight-line allocation of forward contract discounts and premiums. The important thing to keep in mind in this example is that with a cash flow hedge, an expense equal to the original forward contract discount is recognized in net income over the life of the contract.

What if the forward rate on December 1, 2017, had been $1.326 (i.e., the euro was selling at a premium in the forward market)? In that case, Amerco would receive $6,000 more through the forward sale of euros ($1,326,000) than had it received the euros at the date of sale ($1,320,000). Amerco would allocate the forward contract premium as an increase in net income at the rate of $2,000 per month: $2,000 at December 31, 2017, and $4,000 at March 1, 2018.

Forward Contract Designated as Fair Value Hedge

Assume that Amerco decides to designate the forward contract not as a cash flow hedge but as a fair value hedge. In that case, it takes the gain or loss on the forward contract directly to net income and does not separately amortize the original discount on the forward contract.

2017 Journal Entries—Forward Contract Designated as a Fair Value Hedge

12/1/17	Accounts Receivable (€)................................	1,320,000	
	Sales		1,320,000
	To record the sale and €1 million account receivable at the spot rate of $1.32 (Fair Value Hedge Step A.1. in Exhibit 7.2).		

The forward contract requires no formal entry (Fair Value Hedge Step A.2. in Exhibit 7.2). A memorandum designates the forward contract as a hedge of the risk of changes in the fair value of the foreign currency account receivable resulting from changes in the U.S. dollar–euro exchange rate.

Following the two steps in accounting for a fair value hedge presented in Exhibit 7.2, the company prepares the following entries on December 31:

12/31/17	Accounts Receivable (€).............................	10,000	
	Foreign Exchange Gain		10,000
	To adjust the value of the € receivable to the new spot rate of $1.33 and record a foreign exchange gain resulting from the appreciation of the € since December 1 (Fair Value Hedge Step B.1. in Exhibit 7.2).		
	Loss on Forward Contract	10,783	
	Forward Contract................................		10,783
	To record the forward contract as a liability at its fair value of $10,783 and record a forward contract loss for the change in the fair value of the forward contract since December 1 (Fair Value Hedge Step B.2. in Exhibit 7.2).		

The first entry at December 31, 2017, serves to revalue the foreign currency account receivable and recognize a foreign exchange gain of $10,000. The second entry recognizes the forward contract as a liability of $10,783 on the balance sheet. Because the forward contract has been designated as a fair value hedge, the debit in the second entry recognizes the entire change in fair value of the forward contract as a loss in net income; there is no deferral of loss in stockholders' equity. A net loss of $783 is reported in net income as a result of these two entries.

The impact on net income for the year 2017 is as follows:

Sales................................		$1,320,000
Foreign exchange gain................	$10,000	
Loss on forward contract	(10,783)	
Net gain (loss).......................		(783)
Impact on net income...............		$1,319,217

The effect on the December 31, 2017, balance sheet follows:

Assets		Liabilities and Stockholders' Equity	
Accounts receivable (€)......	$1,330,000	Forward contract	$ 10,783
		Retained earnings	1,319,217
			$1,330,000

[?] Discussion Question

DO WE HAVE A GAIN OR WHAT?

Ahnuld Corporation, a health juice producer, recently expanded its sales through exports to foreign markets. Earlier this year, the company negotiated the sale of several thousand cases of turnip juice to a retailer in the country of Tcheckia. The customer is unwilling to assume the risk of having to pay in U.S. dollars. Desperate to enter the Tcheckian market, the vice president for international sales agrees to denominate the sale in tchecks, the national currency of Tcheckia. The current exchange rate for 1 tcheck is $2.00. In addition, the customer indicates that it cannot pay until it sells all of the juice. Payment of 100,000 tchecks is scheduled for six months from the date of sale.

Fearful that the tcheck might depreciate in value over the next six months, the head of the risk management department at Ahnuld Corporation enters into a forward contract to sell tchecks in six months at a forward rate of $1.80. The forward contract is designated as a fair value hedge of the tcheck receivable. Six months later, when Ahnuld receives payment from the Tcheckian customer, the exchange rate for the tcheck is $1.70. The corporate treasurer calls the head of the risk management department into her office.

> **Treasurer:** I see that your decision to hedge our foreign currency position on that sale to Tcheckia was a bad one.
>
> **Department head:** What do you mean? We have a gain on that forward contract. We're $10,000 better off from having entered into that hedge.
>
> **Treasurer:** That's not what the books say. The accountants have recorded a net loss of $20,000 on that particular deal. I'm afraid I'm not going to be able to pay you a bonus this year. Another bad deal like this one and I'm going to have to demote you back to the interest rate swap department.
>
> **Department head:** Those bean counters have messed up again. I told those guys in international sales that selling to customers in Tcheckia was risky, but at least by hedging our exposure, we managed to receive a reasonable amount of cash on that deal. In fact, we ended up with a gain of $10,000 on the hedge. Tell the accountants to check their debits and credits again. I'm sure they just put a debit in the wrong place or some accounting thing like that.

Have the accountants made a mistake? Does the company have a loss, a gain, or both from this forward contract?

2018 Journal Entries—Forward Contract Designated as a Fair Value Hedge

The company prepares the following entries on March 1:

3/1/18	Foreign Exchange Loss	30,000	
	Accounts Receivable (€)		30,000
	To adjust the value of the € receivable to the new spot rate of $1.30 and record a foreign exchange loss resulting from the depreciation of the € since December 31 (Fair Value Hedge Step C.1. in Exhibit 7.2).		
	Forward Contract.	15,783	
	Gain on Forward Contract		15,783
	To adjust the carrying value of the forward contract to its current fair value of $5,000 and record a forward contract gain for the change in the fair value since December 31 (Fair Value Hedge Step C.2. in Exhibit 7.2).		

(continued)

(*continued*)

3/1/18	Foreign Currency (€)	1,300,000	
	Accounts Receivable (€)		1,300,000
	To record receipt of €1 million from the German customer as an asset at the spot rate of $1.30 (Fair Value Hedge Step C.3. in Exhibit 7.2).		
	Cash	1,305,000	
	Foreign Currency (€)		1,300,000
	Forward Contract		5,000
	To record settlement of the forward contract (i.e., record receipt of $1,305,000 in exchange for delivery of €1 million) and remove the forward contract from the accounts (Fair Value Hedge Step C.4. in Exhibit 7.2).		

The impact on net income for the year 2018 follows:

Foreign exchange loss	$ (30,000)
Gain on forward contract	15,783
Impact on net income	$(14,217)

The net effect on the balance sheet for the two periods is an increase of $1,305,000 in Cash with a corresponding increase in Retained Earnings of $1,305,000 ($1,319,217 − $14,217).

Under fair value hedge accounting, the company does not amortize the original forward contract discount systematically over the life of the contract. Instead, it recognizes the discount in income as the difference between the foreign exchange Gain (Loss) on the account receivable and the Gain (Loss) on the forward contract—that is, $(783) in 2017 and $(14,217) in 2018. The net impact on net income over the two years is $(15,000), which reflects the cost of extending credit to the German customer. The net gain on the forward contract of $5,000 ($10,783 loss in 2017 and $15,783 gain in 2018) reflects the net benefit (i.e., increase in cash inflow) from Amerco's decision to hedge the euro receivable.

Companies often cannot or do not bother to designate as hedges the forward contracts they use to hedge foreign currency denominated assets and liabilities. In those cases, the company accounts for the forward contract as if it were a speculative investment. The company reports an undesignated forward contract on the balance sheet at fair value as an asset or liability and immediately recognizes changes in the fair value of the forward contract in net income. This accounting treatment is exactly the same as if the forward contract had been designated as a fair value hedge. The only difference between a forward contract designated as a fair value hedge of a foreign currency denominated asset or liability and an undesignated (speculative) forward contract is the manner in which the company discloses it in the notes to the financial statements. E.I. du Pont de Nemours and Company provided the following disclosure related to this in its 2014 Form 10-K (page F-43):

Derivatives Not Designated in Hedging Relationships

Foreign Currency Contracts
The company routinely uses forward exchange contracts to reduce its net exposure, by currency, related to foreign currency-denominated monetary assets and liabilities of its operations so that exchange gains and losses resulting from exchange rate changes are minimized. The netting of such exposures precludes the use of hedge accounting; however, the required revaluation of the forward contracts and the associated foreign currency-denominated monetary assets and liabilities intends to achieve a minimal earnings impact, after taxes.

Cash Flow Hedge versus Fair Value Hedge

A forward contract used to hedge a foreign currency denominated asset or liability can be designated as either a cash flow hedge or a fair value hedge when it completely offsets the variability in cash flows associated with the hedged item. The total impact on income is the same regardless of whether the forward contract is designated as a fair value hedge or as a cash flow hedge. In our example, Amerco recognized an expense (or loss) of $15,000 in both cases, and the company knew what the total expense was going to be as soon as the contract was signed.

A benefit to designating a forward contract as a cash flow hedge is that the company knows the forward contract's effect on net income *each year* as soon as the contract is signed. The net impact on income is the periodic amortization of the forward contract discount or premium. In our example, Amerco knew on December 1, 2017, that it would recognize a discount expense of $5,000 in 2017 and $10,000 in 2018. The impact on each year's income is not as systematic when the forward contract is designated as a fair value hedge—loss of $783 in 2017 and $14,217 in 2018. Moreover, the company does not know what the net impact on 2017 income will be until December 31, 2017, when the euro account receivable and the forward contract are revalued. Because of the potential for greater volatility in periodic net income that results from a fair value hedge, companies may prefer to designate forward contracts used to hedge a foreign currency denominated asset or liability as cash flow hedges.

Foreign Currency Option Used to Hedge a Foreign Currency Denominated Asset

As an alternative to a forward contract, Amerco could hedge its exposure to foreign exchange risk arising from the euro account receivable by purchasing a foreign currency put option. A put option would give Amerco the right but not the obligation to sell 1 million euros on March 1, 2018, at a predetermined strike price. Assume that on December 1, 2017, Amerco purchases an over-the-counter option from its bank with a strike price of $1.32 when the spot rate is $1.32 and pays a premium of $0.009 per euro.[10] Thus, the purchase price for the option is $9,000 (€1 million × $0.009).

Because the strike price and spot rate are the same, no intrinsic value is associated with this option. The premium is based solely on time value; that is, it is possible that the euro will depreciate and the spot rate on March 1, 2018, will be less than $1.32, in which case the option will be "in the money." If the spot rate for euros on March 1, 2018, is less than the strike price of $1.32, Amerco will exercise its option and sell its 1 million euros at the strike price of $1.32. If the spot rate for euros in three months is more than the strike price of $1.32, Amerco will not exercise its option but will sell euros at the higher spot rate. By purchasing this option, Amerco is guaranteed a minimum cash flow from the export sale of $1,311,000 ($1,320,000 from exercising the option less the $9,000 cost of the option). There is no limit to the maximum number of U.S. dollars that Amerco could receive.

As is true for other derivative financial instruments, authoritative accounting literature requires foreign currency options to be reported on the balance sheet at fair value. The fair value of a foreign currency option at the balance sheet date is determined by reference to the premium quoted by banks on that date for an option with a similar expiration date. Banks (and other sellers of options) determine the current premium by incorporating relevant variables at the balance sheet date into the modified Black-Scholes option pricing model. Changes in value for the euro account receivable and the foreign currency option are summarized as follows:

| | | Account Receivable (€) | | | Foreign Currency Option | |
Date	Spot Rate	U.S. Dollar Value	Change in U.S. Dollar Value	Option Premium for 3/1/18	Fair Value	Change in Fair Value
12/1/17	$1.32	$1,320,000	$ –0–	$0.009	$9,000	$ –0–
12/31/17	1.33	1,330,000	+ 10,000	0.006	6,000	– 3,000
3/1/18	1.30	1,300,000	– 30,000	0.020	20,000	+ 14,000

The fair value of the foreign currency put option at December 1 is its cost of $9,000. The spot rate for the euro increases during December, which causes a decrease in the fair value of the put

---

[10] The seller of the option determined the price of the option (the premium) by using a variation of the Black-Scholes option pricing formula.

option; the right to sell euros at $1.32 is of even less value when the spot rate is $1.33 (on December 31) than when the spot rate was $1.32 (on December 1). The bank determines the fair value of the option at December 31 to be $6,000. By March 1, the euro spot rate has decreased to $1.30. By exercising its option on March 1 at the strike price of $1.32, Amerco will receive $1,320,000 from its export sale, rather than only $1,300,000 if it were required to sell euros in the spot market on March 1. Thus, the option has a fair value of $20,000 on March 1.

We can decompose the fair value of the foreign currency option into its intrinsic value and time value components as follows:

Date	Fair Value	Intrinsic Value	Time Value	Change in Time Value
12/1/17	$ 9,000	$ –0–	$9,000	$ –0–
12/31/17	6,000	–0–	6,000	–3,000
3/1/18	20,000	20,000	–0–	–6,000

Because the option strike price is less than or equal to the spot rate at both December 1 and December 31, the option has no intrinsic value at those dates. The entire fair value is attributable to time value only. On March 1, the date of expiration, no time value remains, and the entire amount of fair value is attributable to intrinsic value.

Option Designated as Cash Flow Hedge

Assume that Amerco designates the foreign currency option as a *cash flow hedge* of a foreign currency denominated asset. In this case, Amerco recognizes the change in the option's time value immediately in net income. The company prepares the following journal entries to account for the foreign currency transaction and the related foreign currency option:

2017 Journal Entries—Option Designated as a Cash Flow Hedge

12/1/17	Accounts Receivable (€)................................	1,320,000	
	Sales		1,320,000
	To record the sale and €1 million account receivable at the spot rate of $1.32 (Cash Flow Hedge Step A.1. in Exhibit 7.2).		
	Foreign Currency Option	9,000	
	Cash...		9,000
	To record the purchase of the foreign currency option as an asset at its fair value of $9,000 (Cash Flow Hedge Step A.2. in Exhibit 7.2).		

From December 1 to December 31, the euro account receivable increases in value by $10,000 and the option decreases in value by $3,000. The company prepares the following journal entries on December 31 to reflect these changes:

12/31/17	Accounts Receivable (€)	10,000	
	Foreign Exchange Gain...........................		10,000
	To adjust the value of the € receivable to the new spot rate of $1.33 and record a foreign exchange gain resulting from the appreciation of the € since December 1 (Cash Flow Hedge Step B.1. in Exhibit 7.2).		
	Accumulated Other Comprehensive Income (AOCI)	3,000	
	Foreign Currency Option..........................		3,000
	To adjust the fair value of the option from $9,000 to $6,000 with a corresponding debit to AOCI (Cash Flow Hedge Step B.2. in Exhibit 7.2).		
	Loss on Foreign Currency Option	10,000	
	Accumulated Other Comprehensive Income (AOCI) ...		10,000

(*continued*)

(continued)

To record a loss on foreign currency option to offset the foreign exchange gain on the account receivable with a corresponding credit to AOCI (Cash Flow Hedge Step B.3. in Exhibit 7.2).		
Option Expense..................................	3,000	
Accumulated Other Comprehensive Income (AOCI)...		3,000
To recognize the change in the time value of the option as a decrease in net income with a corresponding credit to AOCI (Cash Flow Hedge Step B.4. in Exhibit 7.2).		

The first three journal entries prepared on December 31 result in the euro account receivable and the foreign currency option being reported on the balance sheet at fair value with a net gain (loss) of zero reflected in net income, which is consistent with the concept of hedge accounting. The final entry serves to amortize a portion of the option cost to expense in net income. On March 1, the remaining $6,000 of option cost will be expensed.

The impact on net income for the year 2017 follows:

Sales................................		$1,320,000
Foreign exchange gain................	$ 10,000	
Loss on foreign currency option........	(10,000)	
Net gain (loss).......................		–0–
Option expense......................		(3,000)
Impact on net income................		$1,317,000

The effect on the December 31, 2017, balance sheet is as follows:

Assets		Liabilities and Stockholders' Equity	
Cash......................	$ (9,000)	Retained earnings...........	$1,317,000
Accounts receivable (€)......	1,330,000	AOCI......................	10,000
Foreign currency option......	6,000		$1,327,000
	$1,327,000		

At March 1, 2018, the option has increased in fair value by $14,000—time value decreases by $6,000 and intrinsic value increases by $20,000. The accounting entries made in 2018 are presented next:

2018 Journal Entries—Option Designated as a Cash Flow Hedge

3/1/18	Foreign Exchange Loss................................	30,000	
	Accounts Receivable (€)...........................		30,000
	To adjust the value of the € receivable to the new spot rate of $1.30 and record a foreign exchange loss resulting from the depreciation of the € since December 31 (Cash Flow Hedge Step C.1. in Exhibit 7.2).		
	Foreign Currency Option.............................	14,000	
	Accumulated Other Comprehensive Income (AOCI)...		14,000
	To adjust the fair value of the option from $6,000 to $20,000 with a corresponding credit to AOCI (Cash Flow Hedge Step C.2. in Exhibit 7.2).		
	Accumulated Other Comprehensive Income (AOCI).......	30,000	
	Gain on Foreign Currency Option..................		30,000
	To record a gain on foreign currency option to offset the foreign exchange gain on account receivable with a corresponding debit to AOCI (Cash Flow Hedge Step C.3. in Exhibit 7.2).		
	Option Expense....................................	6,000	
	Accumulated Other Comprehensive Income (AOCI)...		6,000
	To recognize the change in the time value of the option as a decrease in net income with a corresponding credit to AOCI (Cash Flow Hedge Step C.4. in Exhibit 7.2).		

The first three entries on March 1 result in the euro account receivable and the foreign currency option being reported at their fair values, with a net gain (loss) of zero. The fourth entry amortizes the remaining cost of the option to expense. As a result of these entries, the balance in AOCI is zero: $10,000 + $14,000 − $30,000 + $6,000 = $0.

The next two journal entries recognize the receipt of euros from the customer, close out the euro account receivable, and record the exercise of the foreign currency option.

3/1/18	Foreign Currency (€)	1,300,000	
	Accounts Receivable (€)		1,300,000
	To record receipt of €1 million from the German customer as an asset at the spot rate of $1.30 (Cash Flow Hedge Step C.5. in Exhibit 7.2).		
	Cash	1,320,000	
	Foreign Currency (€)		1,300,000
	Foreign Currency Option		20,000
	To record exercise of the option (i.e., record receipt of $1,320,000 in exchange for delivery of €1 million) and remove the foreign currency option from the accounts (Cash Flow Hedge Step C.6. in Exhibit 7.2).		

The impact on net income for the year 2018 follows:

Foreign exchange loss	$(30,000)	
Gain on foreign currency option	30,000	
Net gain (loss)		–0–
Option expense		(6,000)
Impact on net income		$(6,000)

Over the two accounting periods, Amerco reports sales of $1,320,000 and a cumulative option expense of $9,000. The net effect on the balance sheet is an increase in the cash account of $1,311,000 ($1,320,000 − $9,000) with a corresponding increase in the retained earnings account of $1,311,000 ($1,317,000 − $6,000).

The net benefit from having acquired the option is $11,000. This is the difference between the amount Amerco received from executing the option ($1,320,000) and the amount Amerco would have received if it had not acquired the option ($1,300,000), net of the option's cost ($9,000): $1,320,000 − $1,300,000 − $9,000 = $11,000. Amerco indirectly reflects this "gain" in net income as the net gain on foreign currency option ($10,000 loss in 2017 plus $30,000 gain in 2018) less the cumulative option expense ($9,000) recognized over the two accounting periods: $20,000 − $9,000 = $11,000.

Option Designated as Fair Value Hedge

Assume that Amerco decides not to designate the foreign currency option as a cash flow hedge but to treat it as a fair value hedge. In that case, it takes the gain or loss on the option directly to net income. The change in the time value of the option is not recognized, so there is no option expense recorded.

2017 Journal Entries—Option Designated as a Fair Value Hedge

12/1/17	Accounts Receivable (€)	1,320,000	
	Sales		1,320,000
	To record the sale and €1 million account receivable at the spot rate of $1.32 (Fair Value Hedge Step A.1. in Exhibit 7.2).		

(*continued*)

(continued)

	Foreign Currency Option............................	9,000	
	Cash		9,000
	To record the purchase of the foreign currency option as an asset at its fair value of $9,000 (Fair Value Hedge Step A.2. in Exhibit 7.2).		
12/31/17	Accounts Receivable (€)	10,000	
	Foreign Exchange Gain..........................		10,000
	To adjust the value of the € receivable to the new spot rate of $1.33 and record a foreign exchange gain resulting from the appreciation of the € since December 1 (Fair Value Hedge Step B.1. in Exhibit 7.2).		
	Loss on Foreign Currency Option	3,000	
	Foreign Currency Option..........................		3,000
	To adjust the fair value of the option from $9,000 to $6,000 and record a loss on foreign currency option for the change in the fair value of the option since December 1 (Fair Value Hedge Step B.2. in Exhibit 7.2).		

The impact on net income for the year 2017 follows:

Sales.....................................		$1,320,000
Foreign exchange gain....................	$10,000	
Loss on foreign currency option	(3,000)	
Net gain (loss)............................		7,000
Impact on net income...................		$1,327,000

2018 Journal Entries—Option Designated as a Fair Value Hedge

3/1/18	Foreign Exchange Loss	30,000	
	Accounts Receivable (€)		30,000
	To adjust the value of the € receivable to the new spot rate of $1.30 and record a foreign exchange loss resulting from the depreciation of the € since December 31 (Fair Value Hedge Step C.1. in Exhibit 7.2).		
	Foreign Currency Option	14,000	
	Gain on Foreign Currency Option		14,000
	To adjust the fair value of the option from $6,000 to $20,000 and record a gain on foreign currency option for the change in fair value since December 31 (Fair Value Hedge Step C.2. in Exhibit 7.2).		
	Foreign Currency (€)................................	1,300,000	
	Accounts Receivable (€)		1,300,000
	To record receipt of €1 million from the German customer as an asset at the spot rate of $1.30 (Fair Value Hedge Step C.3. in Exhibit 7.2).		
	Cash	1,320,000	
	Foreign Currency (€).............................		1,300,000
	Foreign Currency Option.........................		20,000
	To record exercise of the option (i.e., record receipt of $1,320,000 in exchange for delivery of €1 million) and remove the foreign currency option from the accounts (Fair Value Hedge Step C.4. in Exhibit 7.2).		

The impact on net income for the year 2018 follows:

Foreign exchange loss	$(30,000)
Gain on foreign currency option	14,000
Impact on net income	$(16,000)

Over the two accounting periods, Amerco reports sales of $1,320,000 and a cumulative net loss of $9,000 ($7,000 net gain in 2017 and $16,000 net loss in 2018). The net effect on the balance sheet is an increase in cash of $1,311,000 ($1,320,000 − $9,000) with a corresponding increase in retained earnings of $1,311,000 ($1,327,000 − $16,000). The net benefit from having acquired the option is $11,000. Amerco reflects this in net income through the net gain on foreign currency option ($3,000 loss in 2017 and $14,000 gain in 2018) recognized over the two accounting periods.

The accounting for an option used as a fair value hedge of a foreign currency denominated asset or liability is the same as if the option had been considered a speculative derivative. The only advantage to designating the option as a fair value hedge relates to the disclosures made in the notes to the financial statements.

Spot Rate Exceeds Strike Price

If the spot rate at March 1, 2018, had been more than the strike price of $1.32, Amerco would allow its option to expire unexercised. Instead it would sell its foreign currency (€) at the spot rate. The fair value of the foreign currency option on March 1, 2018, would be zero. The journal entries for 2017 to reflect this scenario would be the same as the preceding ones. The option would be reported as an asset on the December 31, 2017, balance sheet at $6,000 and the € receivable would have a carrying value of $1,330,000. The entries on March 1, 2018, assuming a spot rate on that date of $1.325 (rather than $1.30), would be as follows:

3/1/18	Foreign Exchange Loss	5,000	
	Accounts Receivable (€)		5,000
	To adjust the value of the € receivable to the new spot rate of $1.325 and record a foreign exchange loss resulting from the depreciation of the € since December 31 (Fair Value Hedge Step C.1. in Exhibit 7.2).		
	Loss on Foreign Currency Option.	6,000	
	Foreign Currency Option		6,000
	To adjust the fair value of the option from $6,000 to $0 and record a loss on foreign currency option for the change in fair value since December 31 (Fair Value Hedge Step C.2. in Exhibit 7.2).		
	Foreign Currency (€).	1,325,000	
	Accounts Receivable (€)		1,325,000
	To record receipt of €1 million from the German customer as an asset at the spot rate of $1.325 (Fair Value Hedge Step C.3. in Exhibit 7.2).		
	Cash.	1,325,000	
	Foreign Currency (€).		1,325,000
	To record the sale of €1 million at the spot rate of $1.325 (Fair Value Hedge Step C.4. in Exhibit 7.2).		

The overall impact on net income for the year 2018 is as follows:

Foreign exchange loss	$ (5,000)
Loss on foreign currency option	(6,000)
Impact on net income	$(11,000)

LO 7-8

Account for forward contracts and options used as hedges of foreign currency firm commitments.

Hedges of Unrecognized Foreign Currency Firm Commitments

In the examples thus far, Amerco does not enter into a hedge of its export sale until it actually makes the sale. Assume now that on December 1, 2017, Amerco receives and accepts an order from a German customer to deliver goods on March 1, 2018, at a price of 1 million euros. Assume further that under the terms of the sales agreement, Amerco will ship the goods to the German customer on March 1, 2018, and will receive immediate payment on delivery. In other words, Amerco will not extend credit to the German customer. Although Amerco will not make the sale until March 1, 2018, it has a firm commitment to make the sale and receive 1 million euros in three months. This creates a euro asset exposure to foreign exchange risk as of December 1, 2017. On that date, Amerco wants to hedge against an adverse change in the value of the euro over the next three months. This is known as a *hedge of a foreign currency firm commitment*. U.S. GAAP allows hedges of firm commitments to be designated either as cash flow or fair value hedges. However, because the results of fair value hedge accounting are intuitively more appealing, we do not cover cash flow hedge accounting for firm commitments.

A firm commitment is an executory contract; the company has not delivered goods nor has the customer paid for them. Normally, executory contracts are not recognized in financial statements. However, when a firm commitment is hedged using a derivative financial instrument, hedge accounting requires explicit recognition on the balance sheet at fair value of both the derivative financial instrument (forward contract or option) and the firm commitment. The change in fair value of the firm commitment results in a gain or loss that offsets the loss or gain on the hedging instrument (forward contract or option), thus achieving the goal of hedge accounting. This raises the conceptual question of how to measure the fair value of the firm commitment. When a forward contract is used as the hedging instrument, the fair value of the firm commitment is determined through reference to changes in the forward exchange rate. Changes in the spot exchange rate are used to determine the fair value of the firm commitment when a foreign currency option is the hedging instrument.

Forward Contract Used as Fair Value Hedge of a Firm Commitment

To hedge its firm commitment exposure to a decline in the U.S. dollar value of the euro, Amerco decides to enter into a forward contract on December 1, 2017. Assume that on that date, the three-month forward rate for euros is $1.305 and Amerco signs a contract with New Manhattan Bank to deliver 1 million euros in three months in exchange for $1,305,000. No cash changes hands on December 1, 2017. Amerco measures the fair value of the firm commitment through changes in the forward rate. Because the fair value of the forward contract is also measured using changes in the forward rate, the gains and losses on the firm commitment and forward contract exactly offset. The fair value of the forward contract and firm commitment are determined as follows:

Date	Forward Rate to 3/1/18	Forward Contract		Firm Commitment	
		Fair Value	Change in Fair Value	Fair Value	Change in Fair Value
12/1/17	$ 1.305	$ –0–	$ –0–	$ –0–	$ –0–
12/31/17	1.316	(10,783)*	– 10,783	10,783*	+ 10,783
3/1/18	1.30 (spot)	5,000†	+ 15,783	(5,000)†	– 15,783

*($1,305,000 – $1,316,000) = $(11,000) × 0.9803 = $(10,783), where 0.9803 is the present value factor for two months at an annual interest rate of 12 percent (1 percent per month) calculated as $1/1.01^2$.
†($1,305,000 – $1,300,000) = $5,000.

Amerco pays nothing to enter into the forward contract at December 1, 2017. Both the forward contract and the firm commitment have a fair value of zero on that date. As a result, there are no journal entries needed on December 1, 2017. At December 31,

2017, the forward rate for a contract to deliver euros on March 1, 2018, is $1.316. A forward contract could be entered into on December 31, 2017, to sell 1 million euros for $1,316,000 on March 1, 2018. Because Amerco is committed to sell 1 million euros for $1,305,000, the value of the forward contract is $(11,000); present value is $(10,783), a liability. The fair value of the firm commitment is also measured through reference to changes in the forward rate. As a result, the fair value of the firm commitment is equal in amount but of opposite sign to the fair value of the forward contract. At December 31, 2017, the firm commitment is an asset of $10,783. To apply the two steps in accounting for a fair value hedge of a firm commitment at the balance sheet date, on December 31, 2017, Amerco will:

1. Adjust the forward contract to fair value, which results in the recognition of a liability of $10,783, and recognize the counterpart as a loss in net income (Fair Value Hedge Step B.1. in Exhibit 7.2).
2. Adjust the firm commitment to fair value, which results in the recognition of an asset of $10,783, and recognize the counterpart as a gain on firm commitment in net income (Fair Value Hedge Step B.2. in Exhibit 7.2).

The journal entries in 2017 to account for the forward contract fair value hedge of a foreign currency firm commitment are as follows:

2017 Journal Entries—Forward Contract Fair Value Hedge of Firm Commitment

12/1/17	There is no entry to record either the sales agreement or the forward contract because both are executory contracts. A memorandum designates the forward contract as a hedge of the risk of changes in the fair value of the firm commitment resulting from changes in the U.S. dollar–euro forward exchange rate (Fair Value Hedge Steps A.1. and A.2. in Exhibit 7.2).		
12/31/17	Loss on Forward Contract	10,783	
	Forward Contract.		10,783
	To record the forward contract as a liability at its fair value of $(10,783) and record a forward contract loss for the change in the fair value of the forward contract since December 1 (Fair Value Hedge Step B.1. in Exhibit 7.2).		
	Firm Commitment.	10,783	
	Gain on Firm Commitment.		10,783
	To record the firm commitment as an asset at its fair value of $10,783 and record a firm commitment gain for the change in the fair value of the firm commitment since December 1 (Fair Value Hedge Step B.2. in Exhibit 7.2).		

Consistent with the objective of hedge accounting, the gain on the firm commitment offsets the loss on the forward contract, and the impact on 2017 net income is zero. Amerco reports the forward contract as a liability and reports the firm commitment as an asset on the December 31, 2017, balance sheet. This achieves the objective of making sure that derivatives are reported on the balance sheet and ensures that there is no impact on net income.

On March 1, 2018, the forward rate to sell euros on that date, by definition, is the spot rate, $1.30. At that rate, Amerco could sell 1 million euros for $1,300,000. Because Amerco has a contract to sell euros for $1,305,000, the fair value of the forward contract on March 1, 2018, is $5,000 (an asset). The firm commitment has a value of $(5,000), a liability.

On March 1, 2018, Amerco first recognizes changes in the fair value of the forward contract and firm commitment since December 31. The company then records the sale and the settlement of the forward contract. Finally, the $5,000 balance in the firm commitment account is closed as an adjustment to net income. The required journal entries are as follows:

2018 Journal Entries—Forward Contract Fair Value Hedge of Firm Commitment

3/1/18	Forward Contract.	15,783	
	Gain on Forward Contract		15,783
	To adjust the fair value of the forward contract from $(10,783) to $5,000 and record a forward contract gain for the change in fair value since December 31 (Fair Value Hedge Step C.1. in Exhibit 7.2).		
	Loss on Firm Commitment	15,783	
	Firm Commitment		15,783
	To adjust the fair value of the firm commitment from $10,783 to $(5,000) and record a firm commitment loss for the change in fair value since December 31 (Fair Value Hedge Step C.2. in Exhibit 7.2).		
	Foreign Currency (€).	1,300,000	
	Sales		1,300,000
	To record the sale and the receipt of €1 million as an asset at the spot rate of $1.30 (Fair Value Hedge Step C.3. in Exhibit 7.2).		
	Cash.	1,305,000	
	Foreign Currency (€).		1,300,000
	Forward Contract.		5,000
	To record settlement of the forward contract (receipt of $1,305,000 in exchange for delivery of €1 million) and remove the forward contract from the accounts (Fair Value Hedge Step C.4. in Exhibit 7.2).		
	Firm Commitment.	5,000	
	Adjustment to Net Income—Firm Commitment		5,000
	To close the firm commitment as an adjustment to net income (Fair Value Hedge Step C.5. in Exhibit 7.2).		

Once again, the gain on forward contract and the loss on firm commitment offset. As a result of the last entry, the export sale increases 2018 net income by $1,305,000 ($1,300,000 in sales plus a $5,000 adjustment to net income). This exactly equals the amount of cash received. In practice, companies use a variety of account titles for the adjustment to net income that results from closing the firm commitment account.

The net gain on forward contract of $5,000 ($10,783 loss in 2017 plus $15,783 gain in 2018) measures the net benefit to the company from hedging its firm commitment. Without the forward contract, Amerco would have sold the 1 million euros received on March 1, 2018, at the spot rate of $1.30 generating cash flow of $1,300,000. Through the forward contract, Amerco is able to sell the euros for $1,305,000, a net gain of $5,000.

Option Used as Fair Value Hedge of Firm Commitment

Now assume that to hedge its exposure to a decline in the U.S. dollar value of the euro, Amerco purchases a put option to sell 1 million euros on March 1, 2018, at a strike price of $1.32. The premium for such an option on December 1, 2017, is $0.009 per euro. With this option, Amerco is guaranteed a minimum cash flow from the export sale of $1,311,000 ($1,320,000 from option exercise less $9,000 cost of the option).

Amerco measures the fair value of the firm commitment by referring to changes in the U.S. dollar–euro spot rate. In this case, Amerco must discount the fair value of the firm commitment to its present value. The fair value and changes in fair value for the firm commitment and foreign currency option are summarized here:

| | Option Premium | Foreign Currency Option | | | Firm Commitment | |
Date	for 3/1/18	Fair Value	Change in Fair Value	Spot Rate	Fair Value	Change in Fair Value
12/1/17	$0.009	$ 9,000	$ –0–	$1.32	$ –0–	$ –0–
12/31/17	0.006	6,000	– 3,000	1.33	9,803*	+ 9,803
3/1/18	0.020	20,000	+14,000	1.30	(20,000)†	–29,803

*$1,330,000 − $1,320,000 = $10,000 × 0.9803 = $9,803, where 0.9803 is the present value factor for two months at an annual interest rate of 12 percent (1 percent per month) calculated as $1/1.01^2$.
†$1,300,000 − $1,320,000 = $(20,000).

At December 1, 2017, given the spot rate of $1.32, the firm commitment to receive 1 million euros in three months would generate a cash flow of $1,320,000. At December 31, 2017, the cash flow that the firm commitment could generate increases by $10,000 to $1,330,000. The fair value of the firm commitment at December 31, 2017, is the present value of $10,000 discounted at 1 percent per month for two months. Amerco determines the fair value of the firm commitment on March 1, 2018, by referring to the change in the spot rate from December 1, 2017, to March 1, 2018. Because the spot rate declines by $0.02 over that period, the firm commitment to receive 1 million euros has a fair value of $(20,000) on March 1, 2018. The journal entries to account for the foreign currency option and related foreign currency firm commitment are discussed next:

2017 Journal Entries—Option Fair Value Hedge of Firm Commitment

12/1/17	Foreign Currency Option	9,000	
	Cash.		9,000
	To record the purchase of the foreign currency option as an asset (Fair Value Hedge Step A.2. in Exhibit 7.2).		

There is no entry to record the sales agreement because it is an executory contract (Fair Value Hedge Step A.1. in Exhibit 7.2). Amerco prepares a memorandum to designate the option as a hedge of the risk of changes in the fair value of the firm commitment resulting from changes in the spot exchange rate.

12/31/17	Loss on Foreign Currency Option	3,000	
	Foreign Currency Option.		3,000
	To adjust the fair value of the option from $9,000 to $6,000 and record the change in the value of the option as a loss (Fair Value Hedge Step B.1. in Exhibit 7.2).		
	Firm Commitment	9,803	
	Gain on Firm Commitment		9,803
	To record the firm commitment as an asset at its fair value of $9,803 and record a firm commitment gain for the change in the fair value of the firm commitment since December 1 (Fair Value Hedge Step B.2. in Exhibit 7.2).		

Because the fair value of the firm commitment is based on changes in the spot rate whereas the fair value of the option is based on a variety of factors, the gain on the firm commitment and loss on the option do not exactly offset.

The impact on net income for the year 2017 is as follows:

Gain on firm commitment	$ 9,803
Loss on foreign currency option	(3,000)
Impact on net income	$ 6,803

The effect on the December 31, 2017, balance sheet follows:

Assets		Liabilities and Stockholders' Equity	
Cash.....................	$ (9,000)	Retained earnings	$6,803
Foreign currency option....	6,000		
Firm commitment..........	9,803		
	$ 6,803		

On March 1, 2018, following fair value hedge accounting procedures, Amerco first recognizes changes in the fair value of the option and of the firm commitment since December 31. The company then records the sale and the exercise of the option. Finally, the $20,000 balance in the firm commitment account is closed as an adjustment to net income. The required journal entries are as follows:

2018 Journal Entries—Option Fair Value Hedge of Firm Commitment

3/1/18	Foreign Currency Option	14,000	
	Gain on Foreign Currency Option		14,000
	To adjust the fair value of the foreign currency option from $6,000 to $20,000 and record a gain on foreign currency option for the change in fair value since December 31 (Fair Value Hedge Step C.1. in Exhibit 7.2)		
	Loss on Firm Commitment	29,803	
	Firm Commitment		29,803
	To adjust the fair value of the firm commitment from $9,803 to $(20,000) and record a firm commitment loss for the change in fair value since December 31 (Fair Value Hedge Step C.2. in Exhibit 7.2)		
	Foreign Currency (€)...............................	1,300,000	
	Sales		1,300,000
	To record the sale and the receipt of €1 million as an asset at the spot rate of $1.30 (Fair Value Hedge Step C.3. in Exhibit 7.2).		
	Cash..	1,320,000	
	Foreign Currency (€)............................		1,300,000
	Foreign Currency Option		20,000
	To record exercise of the foreign currency option (receipt of $1,320,000 in exchange for delivery of €1 million) and remove the foreign currency option from the accounts (Fair Value Hedge Step C.4. in Exhibit 7.2).		
	Firm Commitment....................................	20,000	
	Adjustment to Net Income—Firm Commitment		20,000
	To close the firm commitment as an adjustment to net income (Fair Value Hedge Step C.5. in Exhibit 7.2).		

The following is the impact on net income for the year 2018:

Sales...	$1,300,000
Loss on firm commitment	(29,803)
Gain on foreign currency option.......................	14,000
Adjustment to net income—firm commitment	20,000
Impact on net income.............................	$1,304,197

The net increase in net income over the two accounting periods is $1,311,000 ($6,803 in 2017 plus $1,304,197 in 2018), which exactly equals the net cash flow realized on the export sale ($1,320,000 from exercising the option less $9,000 to purchase the option). The net gain on the option of $11,000 (loss of $3,000 in 2017 plus gain of $14,000 in 2018) reflects the net benefit from having entered into the hedge. Without the option, Amerco would have sold the 1 million euros received on March 1, 2018, at the spot rate of $1.30 for $1,300,000.

LO 7-9

Account for forward contracts and options used as hedges of forecasted foreign currency transactions.

Hedge of Forecasted Foreign Currency Denominated Transaction

Cash flow hedge accounting also is used for foreign currency derivatives used to hedge the cash flow risk associated with a forecasted foreign currency transaction. For hedge accounting to apply, the forecasted transaction must be probable (likely to occur), the hedge must be highly effective in offsetting fluctuations in the cash flow associated with the foreign currency risk, and the hedging relationship must be properly documented.

Accounting for a hedge of a forecasted transaction differs from accounting for a hedge of a foreign currency firm commitment in two ways:

1. Unlike the accounting for a firm commitment, there is no recognition of the forecasted transaction or gains and losses on the forecasted transaction. (Because there is no recognition of an asset or liability, there is no fair value exposure to foreign exchange risk. Thus, fair value hedge accounting is not appropriate for hedges of forecasted transactions.)

2. The company reports the hedging instrument (forward contract or option) at fair value, but because no gain or loss occurs on the forecasted transaction to offset against, the company does not report changes in the fair value of the hedging instrument as gains and losses in net income. Instead, it reports them in other comprehensive income. On the projected date of the forecasted transaction, the company transfers the cumulative change in the fair value of the hedging instrument from accumulated other comprehensive income (balance sheet) to net income (income statement).

Forward Contract Cash Flow Hedge of a Forecasted Transaction

To demonstrate the accounting for a hedge of a forecasted foreign currency transaction, assume that Amerco has a long-term relationship with its German customer and can reliably forecast that the customer will require delivery of goods costing 1 million euros in March 2018. Confident that it will receive 1 million euros on March 1, 2018, Amerco enters into a forward contract on December 1, 2017, to sell 1 million euros on March 1, 2018, at a rate of $1.30. The facts are essentially the same as those for the hedge of a firm commitment except that Amerco does not receive a sales order from the German customer until late February 2018. Relevant exchange rates and the fair value of the forward contract are as follows:

Date	Forward Rate to 3/1/18	Forward Contract Fair Value	Forward Contract Change in Fair Value
12/1/17	$1.305	$ –0–	$ –0–
12/31/17	1.316	(10,783)*	– 10,783
3/1/18	1.30 (spot)	5,000	+ 15,783

*($1,305,000 − $1,316,000) = $(11,000) × 0.9803 = $(10,783), where 0.9803 is the present value factor for two months at an annual interest rate of 12 percent (1 percent per month) calculated as $1/1.01^2$. The original discount on the forward contract is determined by the difference in the € spot rate and the three-month forward rate on December 1, 2017: ($1.305 − $1.32) × €1 million = $15,000.

2017 Journal Entries—Forward Contract Hedge of a Forecasted Transaction

12/1/17	There is no entry to record either the forecasted sale or the forward contract. A memorandum designates the forward contract as a hedge of the risk of changes in the cash flows related to the forecasted sale resulting from changes in the spot rate (Cash Flow Hedge Steps A.1. and A.2. in Exhibit 7.2).

On December 31, the forward contract is recognized as a liability at its fair value, with the counterpart reflected in AOCI, and discount expense is recognized due to the passage of time, with the counterpart also reflected in AOCI. The necessary journal entries are:

12/31/17	Accumulated Other Comprehensive Income (AOCI)	10,783	
	Forward Contract		10,783
	To record the forward contract as a liability at its fair value of $10,783 with a corresponding debit to AOCI (Cash Flow Hedge Step B.2. in Exhibit 7.2).		
	Discount Expense.	5,000	
	Accumulated Other Comprehensive Income (AOCI) . .		5,000
	To record straight-line allocation of the forward contract discount: $15,000 × ⅓ = $5,000 (Cash Flow Hedge Step B.4. in Exhibit 7.2).		

Discount expense reduces 2017 net income by $5,000. The impact on the December 31, 2017, balance sheet is as follows:

Assets	Liabilities and Stockholders' Equity	
No effect	Forward contract	$10,783
	Retained earnings	(5,000)
	AOCI.	(5,783)
		$ –0–

On March 1, 2018, the carrying value of the forward contract is adjusted to fair value and the discount is amortized to expense. Then, the sale and the settlement of the forward contract are recorded. Finally, the balance in AOCI related to the hedge of the forecasted transaction is closed as an adjustment to net income. The following entries are required:

2018 Journal Entries—Forward Contract Hedge of a Forecasted Transaction

3/1/18	Forward Contract.	15,783	
	Accumulated Other Comprehensive Income (AOCI). . .		15,783
	To adjust the carrying value of the forward contract to its current fair value of $5,000 with a corresponding credit to AOCI (Cash Flow Hedge Step C.1. in Exhibit 7.2).		
3/1/18	Discount Expense	10,000	
	Accumulated Other Comprehensive Income (AOCI). . .		10,000
	To record straight-line allocation of the forward contract discount: $15,000 × ⅔ = $10,000 (Cash Flow Hedge Step C.2. in Exhibit 7.2).		
	Foreign Currency (€).	1,300,000	
	Sales		1,300,000
	To record the sale and the receipt of €1 million as an asset at the spot rate of $1.30 (Cash Flow Hedge Step C.3. in Exhibit 7.2).		
	Cash.	1,305,000	
	Foreign Currency (€).		1,300,000
	Forward Contract.		5,000
	To record settlement of the forward contract (receipt of $1,305,000 in exchange for delivery of €1 million) and remove the forward contract from the accounts (Cash Flow Hedge Step C.4. in Exhibit 7.2).		
	Accumulated Other Comprehensive Income (AOCI).	20,000	
	Adjustment to Net Income–Forecasted Transaction. . . .		20,000
	To close AOCI as an adjustment to net income (Cash Flow Hedge Step C.5. in Exhibit 7.2).		

As a result of these entries, the forward contract liability reported at December 31, 2017, has been reduced to zero, as has the balance in AOCI related to this forward contract.

The impact on net income for the year 2018 follows:

Sales.	$1,300,000
Discount expense	(10,000)
Adjustment to net income–forecasted transaction	20,000
Impact on net income	$1,310,000

Over the two accounting periods, the net impact on net income is $1,305,000, which equals the amount of net cash inflow realized from the sale.

Option Designated as a Cash Flow Hedge of a Forecasted Transaction

Now assume that Amerco hedges its forecasted foreign currency transaction by purchasing a 1 million euro put option on December 1, 2017. The option, which expires on March 1, 2018, has a strike price of $1.32 and a premium of $0.009 per euro. The fair value of the option at relevant dates is as follows (same as in previous examples):

Date	Option Premium for 3/1/18	Foreign Currency Option				
		Fair Value	Change in Fair Value	Intrinsic Value	Time Value	Change in Time Value
12/1/17	$0.009	$ 9,000	$ –0–	$ –0–	$9,000	$ –0–
12/31/17	0.006	6,000	– 3,000	–0–	6,000	– 3,000
3/1/18	0.020	20,000	+14,000	20,000	–0–	– 6,000

2017 Journal Entries—Option Hedge of a Forecasted Transaction

12/1/17	Foreign Currency Option.	9,000	
	Cash		9,000
	To record the purchase of the foreign currency option as an asset (Cash Flow Hedge Step A.2. in Exhibit 7.2).		
	There is no entry to record the forecasted sale. A memorandum designates the foreign currency option as a hedge of the risk of changes in the cash flows related to the forecasted sale (Cash Flow Hedge Step A.1. in Exhibit 7.2).		

At December 31, the carrying value of the option is decreased for the change in fair value since December 1, and the change in the time value of the option is recognized as option expense. The required journal entries are as follows:

12/31/17	Accumulated Other Comprehensive Income (AOCI).	3,000	
	Foreign Currency Option		3,000
	To adjust the carrying value of the option to its fair value with a corresponding debit to AOCI (Cash Flow Hedge Step B.2. in Exhibit 7.2).		
	Option Expense	3,000	
	Accumulated Other Comprehensive Income (AOCI) . . .		3,000
	To recognize the change in the time value of the option as a decrease in net income with a corresponding credit to AOCI (Cash Flow Hedge Step B.4. in Exhibit 7.2).		

The impact on net income for the year 2017 follows:

Option expense	$(3,000)
Impact on net income	$(3,000)

A foreign currency option of $6,000 is reported as an asset on the December 31, 2017, balance sheet. Cash is decreased by $9,000, and Retained Earnings is decreased by $3,000.

On March 1, 2018, first the carrying value of the option is adjusted to fair value and the change in the time value of the option is recognized as option expense. Then, the sale and the exercise of the foreign currency option are recorded. Finally, the balance in AOCI related to the hedge of the forecasted transaction is closed as an adjustment to net income. The following entries are required:

2018 Journal Entries—Option Hedge of a Forecasted Transaction

3/1/18	Foreign Currency Option.	14,000	
	Accumulated Other Comprehensive Income (AOCI) . . .		14,000
	To adjust the carrying value of the option to its fair value with a corresponding credit to AOCI (Cash Flow Hedge Step C.1. in Exhibit 7.2).		
	Option Expense.	6,000	
	Accumulated Other Comprehensive Income (AOCI) . . .		6,000
	To recognize the change in the time value of the option as a decrease in net income with a corresponding credit to AOCI (Cash Flow Hedge Step C.2. in Exhibit 7.2).		
	Foreign Currency (€)	1,300,000	
	Sales		1,300,000
	To record the sale and the receipt of €1 million as an asset at the spot rate of $1.30 (Cash Flow Hedge Step C.3. in Exhibit 7.2).		
	Cash	1,320,000	
	Foreign Currency (€)		1,300,000
	Foreign Currency Option.		20,000
	To record the exercise of the foreign currency option (receipt of $1,320,000 in exchange for delivery of €1 million) and remove the foreign currency option from the accounts (Cash Flow Hedge Step C.4. in Exhibit 7.2).		
	Accumulated Other Comprehensive Income (AOCI)	20,000	
	Adjustment to Net Income—Forecasted Transaction . . .		20,000
	To close AOCI as an adjustment to net income (Cash Flow Hedge Step C.5. in Exhibit 7.2).		

The following is the impact on net income for the year 2018:

Sales.	$1,300,000
Option expense	(6,000)
Adjustment to net income—forecasted transaction	20,000
Impact on net income	$1,314,000

Over the two periods, a total of $1,311,000 is recognized as net income, which is equal to the net cash inflow realized from the export sale ($1,320,000 from the sale less $9,000 for the option).

Use of Hedging Instruments

There are probably as many different corporate strategies regarding hedging foreign exchange risk as there are companies exposed to that risk. Some companies require hedges of all foreign currency transactions. Others require the use of a forward contract hedge when the forward rate results in a larger cash inflow or smaller cash outflow than with the spot rate. Still other companies have proportional hedging policies that require hedging on some predetermined percentage (e.g., 50 percent, 60 percent, or 70 percent) of transaction exposure. For example, on page 79 of its 2014 annual report, Johnson Controls, Inc., states: "The Company hedges 70% to 90% of the nominal amount of each of its known foreign exchange transactional exposures."

Companies are required to provide information on the use of derivative financial instruments to hedge foreign exchange risk in the notes to financial statements. Exhibit 7.4 presents disclosures made by Abbott Laboratories in its 2014 annual report. Abbott Labs uses forward contracts to hedge foreign exchange risk associated with anticipated foreign currency transactions, foreign currency denominated payables and receivables, and foreign currency borrowings. Much of its hedging activity relates to intra-entity transactions involving foreign subsidiaries. The table in Exhibit 7.4 discloses that (1) Abbott's forward contracts primarily are to sell foreign currencies to receive U.S. dollars, (2) 49 percent of Abbott's $15,562 million in forward contracts at December 31, 2014, was in euros, and (3) the net fair value of all the company's forward contracts was positive and reported on the balance sheet as an asset (receivable).

Abbott Labs uses forward contracts exclusively to manage its foreign exchange risk. Thermo Fischer Scientific uses foreign currency forward contracts as well as options to hedge exposures resulting from changes in currency exchange rates. In contrast, The Coca-Cola Company employs a combination of forward contracts, currency options, and collars[11] in its foreign exchange risk-hedging strategy.

EXHIBIT 7.4   Disclosures Related to Hedging Foreign Exchange Risk in Abbott Laboratories' 2014 Annual Report

Foreign Currency Sensitive Financial Instruments

Certain Abbott foreign subsidiaries enter into foreign currency forward exchange contracts to manage exposures to changes in foreign exchange rates for anticipated intercompany purchases by those subsidiaries whose functional currencies are not the U.S. dollar. These contracts are designated as cash flow hedges of the variability of the cash flows due to changes in foreign exchange rates and are marked-to-market with the resulting gains or losses reflected in Accumulated other comprehensive income (loss). Gains or losses will be included in Cost of products sold at the time the products are sold, generally within the next twelve to eighteen months. At December 31, 2014 and 2013, Abbott held $1.5 billion and $135 million, respectively, of such contracts. Contracts held at December 31, 2014 will mature in 2015 or 2016 depending on the contract. Contacts held at December 31, 2013 matured in 2014.

Abbott enters into foreign currency forward exchange contracts to manage its exposure to foreign currency denominated intercompany loans and trade payables and third-party trade payables and receivables. The contracts are marked-to-market, and resulting gains or losses are reflected in income and are generally offset by losses or gains on the foreign currency exposure being managed. At December 31, 2014 and 2013, Abbott held $14.1 billion and $13.8 billion, respectively, of such contracts, which generally mature in the next twelve months.

The following table reflects the total foreign currency forward contracts outstanding at December 31, 2014.

(dollars in millions)	Contract Amount	Weighted Average Exchange Rate	Fair and Carrying Value Receivable/ (Payable)
Receive primarily U.S. Dollars in exchange for the following currencies:			
Euro	$ 7,574	1.2458	$ 19
British pound	1,295	1.5790	9
Japanese yen	2,258	115.0311	56
Canadian dollar	371	1.1197	13
All other currencies	4,064	N/A	31
Total	$15,562		$128

[11] A foreign currency collar is created by simultaneously purchasing a call option and selling a put option in a foreign currency to fix a range of prices at which the foreign currency can be purchased at a predetermined future date.

The Euro

The introduction of the euro as a common currency throughout much of Europe in 2002 reduced the need for hedging in that region of the world. For example, a German company purchasing goods from a Spanish supplier no longer has an exposure to foreign exchange risk because both countries use a common currency. This is also true for German subsidiaries of U.S. parent companies. However, any euro-denominated transactions between the U.S. parent and its German (or other euro zone) subsidiary continue to be exposed to foreign exchange risk.

One advantage of the euro for U.S. companies is that a euro account receivable from sales to a customer in, say, the Netherlands acts as a natural hedge of a euro account payable on purchases from, say, a supplier in Italy. Assuming that similar amounts and time periods are involved, any foreign exchange loss (gain) arising from the euro payable is offset by a foreign exchange gain (loss) on the euro receivable. A company does not need to hedge the euro account payable with a hedging instrument such as a foreign currency option.

International Financial Reporting Standard 9— Financial Instruments

IFRS 9, "Financial Instruments," provides guidance on the accounting for hedging instruments including those used to hedge foreign exchange risk. Rules and procedures in *IFRS 9* related to foreign currency hedge accounting generally are consistent with U.S. GAAP. Similar to current U.S. standards, *IFRS 9* allows hedge accounting for foreign currency–denominated assets and liabilities, firm commitments, and forecasted transactions when documentation requirements and effectiveness tests are met and requires hedges to be designated as cash flow or fair value hedges. While the hedge accounting models in U.S. GAAP and IFRS are based on similar principles, a number of differences exist in the application guidance provided by the two sets of standards.

One difference between the two sets of standards relates to the type of financial instrument that can be designated as a foreign currency cash flow hedge. Under U.S. GAAP, only derivative financial instruments can be used as a cash flow hedge, whereas *IFRS 9* also allows nonderivative financial instruments, such as foreign currency loans, to be designated as hedging instruments in a foreign currency cash flow hedge.

The standards also differ with regard to the recognition of changes in fair value of forward contracts used as fair value hedges. *IFRS 9* allows companies to choose between recognizing these changes either in net income (as is required under U.S. GAAP) or in other comprehensive income.

Another difference relates to the accounting for the time value of options. Under *IFRS 9,* the initial time value of an option must be amortized to net income on a systematic and rational (e.g., straight-line) basis. To achieve this, changes in time value are reflected initially in AOCI rather than in net income, with an amount equal to the current period's amortization reclassified from AOCI to net income. The total amount recognized as option expense in net income will be the same under both IFRS and U.S. GAAP, but the timing of income statement recognition is likely to differ.

Summary

1. Several exchange rate systems are used around the world. Most national currencies fluctuate in value against other currencies over time. However, some countries have pegged their national currency to the U.S. dollar.

2. Exposure to foreign exchange risk exists when a payment to be made or to be received is denominated (stated) in terms of a foreign currency. Appreciation in a foreign currency results in a foreign exchange gain when the foreign currency is to be received and a foreign exchange loss when the foreign currency is to be paid. Conversely, a decrease in the value of a foreign currency results in a foreign exchange loss when the foreign currency is to be received and a foreign exchange gain when the foreign currency is to be paid.

3. Companies must revalue foreign currency assets and liabilities to their current U.S. dollar value using current exchange rates when financial statements are prepared. The change in U.S. dollar

value of foreign currency balances is recognized as a foreign exchange gain or loss in net income in the period in which the exchange rate change occurs. This is known as the two-transaction perspective, accrual approach.

4. Borrowing foreign currency creates two exposures to foreign exchange risk. Foreign exchange gains and losses both on the foreign currency note payable and on the accrued foreign currency interest payable are recognized in net income over the life of the debt.

5. IFRS rules related to the accounting for foreign currency transactions generally are consistent with U.S. GAAP. *IAS 21* requires a two-transaction, accrual approach in accounting for foreign currency transactions.

6. Exposure to foreign exchange risk can be eliminated through hedging. Hedging involves establishing a price today at which a foreign currency to be received in the future can be sold in the future or at which a foreign currency to be paid in the future can be purchased in the future.

7. The two most popular derivative financial instruments for hedging foreign exchange risk are foreign currency forward contracts and foreign currency options. A *forward contract* is a binding agreement to exchange currencies at a predetermined rate. An *option* gives the buyer the right, but not the obligation, to exchange currencies at a predetermined rate.

8. Hedge accounting is appropriate when three criteria are met: (1) the derivative is used to hedge either a fair value exposure or cash flow exposure to foreign exchange risk, (2) the derivative is highly effective in offsetting changes in the fair value or cash flows related to the hedged item, and (3) the derivative is properly documented as a hedge. Hedge accounting requires reporting gains and losses on the hedging instrument in net income in the same period as gains and losses on the item being hedged.

9. Companies must report all derivatives, including forward contracts and options, on the balance sheet at their fair value. Changes in fair value are included in accumulated other comprehensive income if the derivative is designated as a cash flow hedge and in net income if it is designated as a fair value hedge.

10. Authoritative accounting literature provides guidance for hedges of (a) recognized foreign currency denominated assets and liabilities, (b) unrecognized foreign currency firm commitments, and (c) forecasted foreign currency denominated transactions. Cash flow hedge accounting can be used for all three types of hedges; fair value hedge accounting can be used only for (a) and (b).

11. If a company hedges a foreign currency firm commitment and designates the hedging instrument as a fair value hedge, it should recognize gains and losses on the hedging instrument as well as on the underlying firm commitment in net income. The firm commitment account created to offset the gain or loss on firm commitment is treated as an adjustment to the underlying transaction when it takes place.

12. If a company hedges a forecasted transaction, it must designate the hedging instrument as a cash flow hedge and report changes in the fair value of the hedging instrument in accumulated other comprehensive income. The cumulative change in fair value reported in other comprehensive income is included in net income in the period in which the forecasted transaction was originally anticipated to take place.

13. Similar to U.S. GAAP, *IFRS 9* allows hedge accounting for hedges of foreign currency assets and liabilities, firm commitments, and forecasted transactions, provided that the hedge is properly documented and is effective. Foreign currency hedging instruments are designated either as a cash flow or a fair value hedge; in either case the hedging instrument must be reported at fair value. Unlike U.S. GAAP, when a fair value hedge is designated, *IFRS 9* allows fair value changes to be reported in accumulated other comprehensive income. Similarly, the change in time value of an option is reported in AOCI.

Comprehensive Illustration

Problem

(Estimated Time: 60 to 75 minutes) Zelm Company is a U.S. company that produces electronic switches for the telecommunications industry. Zelm regularly imports component parts from a supplier located in Guadalajara, Mexico, and makes payments in Mexican pesos. The following spot exchange rates, forward exchange rates, and call option premium for Mexican pesos exist during the period August to October.

		U.S. Dollar per Mexican Peso	
Date	Spot Rate	Forward Rate to October 31	Call Option Premium for October 31 (strike price $0.080)
August 1	$0.080	$0.085	$0.0052
September 30	0.086	0.088	0.0095
October 31	0.091	0.091	0.0110

Part A

On August 1, Zelm imports parts from its Mexican supplier at a price of 1 million Mexican pesos. It receives the parts on August 1 but does not pay for them until October 31. In addition, on August 1, Zelm enters into a forward contract to purchase 1 million pesos on October 31. It appropriately designates the forward contract as a *cash flow hedge* of the Mexican peso liability exposure. Zelm's incremental borrowing rate is 12 percent per annum (1 percent per month), and the company uses a straight-line method on a monthly basis for allocating forward discounts and premiums.

Part B

The facts are the same as in Part A with the exception that Zelm designates the forward contract as a *fair value hedge* of the Mexican peso liability exposure.

Part C

On August 1, Zelm imports parts from its Mexican supplier at a price of 1 million Mexican pesos. It receives the parts on August 1 but does not pay for them until October 31. In addition, on August 1 Zelm purchases a three-month call option on 1 million Mexican pesos with a strike price of $0.080. The option is appropriately designated as a *cash flow hedge* of the Mexican peso liability exposure.

Part D

On August 1, Zelm orders parts from its Mexican supplier at a price of 1 million Mexican pesos. It receives the parts and pays for them on October 31. On August 1, Zelm enters into a forward contract to purchase 1 million Mexican pesos on October 31. It designates the forward contract as a *fair value hedge* of the Mexican peso firm commitment. Zelm determines the fair value of the firm commitment by referring to changes in the forward exchange rate.

Part E

On August 1, Zelm orders parts from its Mexican supplier at a price of 1 million Mexican pesos. It receives the parts and pays for them on October 31. On August 1, Zelm purchases a three-month call option on 1 million Mexican pesos with a strike price of $0.080. The option is appropriately designated as a *fair value hedge* of the Mexican peso firm commitment. The fair value of the firm commitment is by reference to changes in the spot exchange rate.

Part F

Zelm anticipates that it will import component parts from its Mexican supplier in the near future. On August 1, Zelm purchases a three-month call option on 1 million Mexican pesos with a strike price of $0.080. It appropriately designates the option as a *cash flow hedge* of a forecasted Mexican peso transaction. Zelm receives and pays for parts costing 1 million Mexican pesos on October 31.

Required

Prepare journal entries for each of these independent situations in accordance with U.S. GAAP and determine the impact each situation has on the September 30 and October 31 trial balances.

Solution

Part A. Forward Contract Cash Flow Hedge of a Recognized Foreign Currency Liability

8/1	Parts Inventory	80,000	
	Accounts Payable (Mexican pesos)		80,000
	To record the purchase of parts and a peso account payable at the spot rate of $0.080.		

The forward contract requires no formal entry. Zelm prepares a memorandum to designate the forward contract as a hedge of the risk of changes in the cash flow to be paid on the foreign currency payable resulting from changes in the U.S. dollar–Mexican peso exchange rate.

9/30	Foreign Exchange Loss	6,000	
	Accounts Payable (Mexican pesos)		6,000
	To adjust the value of the Mexican peso payable to the new spot rate of $0.086 and record a foreign exchange loss resulting from the appreciation of the peso since August 1.		
	Forward Contract.	2,970	
	Accumulated Other Comprehensive Income (AOCI)		2,970
	To record the forward contract as an asset at its fair value of $2,970 with a corresponding credit to AOCI.		

Zelm determines the fair value of the forward contract by referring to the change in the forward rate for a contract that settles on October 31: ($0.088 − $0.085) × 1 million pesos = $3,000. The present value of $3,000 discounted for one month (from October 31 to September 30) at an interest rate of 12 percent per year (1 percent per month) is calculated as follows: $3,000 × 0.9901 = $2,970.

	Accumulated Other Comprehensive Income (AOCI)	6,000	
	Gain on Forward Contract.		6,000
	To record a gain on forward contract to offset the foreign exchange loss on account payable with a corresponding debit to AOCI.		
	Premium Expense.	3,333	
	Accumulated Other Comprehensive Income (AOCI) . . .		3,333
	To allocate the forward contract premium to income over the life of the contract using a straight-line method on a monthly basis ($5,000 × ⅔ = $3,333).		

The original premium on the forward contract is determined by the difference in the peso spot rate and three-month forward rate on August 1: ($0.085 − $0.080) × 1 million pesos = $5,000.

Trial Balance—September 30	Debit	Credit
Parts inventory	$80,000	$ −0−
Accounts Payable (Mexican pesos)		86,000
Forward Contract (asset).	2,970	
AOCI.		303
Foreign exchange loss	6,000	
Gain on forward contract		6,000
Premium expense	3,333	−0−
	$92,303	$92,303

10/31	Foreign Exchange Loss	5,000	
	Accounts Payable (Mexican pesos)		5,000
	To adjust the value of the Mexican peso payable to the new spot rate of $0.091 and record a foreign exchange loss resulting from the appreciation of the peso since September 30.		
	Forward Contract.	3,030	
	Accumulated Other Comprehensive Income (AOCI).		3,030
	To adjust the carrying value of the forward contract to its current fair value of $6,000 with a corresponding credit to AOCI.		

The current fair value of the forward contract is determined by referring to the difference in the spot rate on October 31 and the original forward rate: ($0.091 − $0.085) × 1 million pesos = $6,000. The forward contract adjustment on October 31 is calculated as the difference in the current fair value and the carrying value at September 30: $6,000 − $2,970 = $3,030.

Accumulated Other Comprehensive Income (AOCI).....	5,000	
Gain on Forward Contract........................		5,000
To record a gain on forward contract to offset the foreign exchange loss on account payable with a corresponding debit to AOCI.		
Premium Expense.....................................	1,667	
Accumulated Other Comprehensive Income (AOCI)...		1,667
To allocate the forward contract premium to income over the life of the contract using a straight-line method on a monthly basis ($5,000 × ⅓ = $1,667).		
Foreign Currency (Mexican pesos).....................	91,000	
Cash..		85,000
Forward Contract.................................		6,000
To record settlement of the forward contract: Record payment of $85,000 in exchange for 1 million pesos, record the receipt of 1 million pesos as an asset at the spot rate of $0.091, and remove the forward contract from the accounts.		
Accounts Payable (pesos).............................	91,000	
Foreign Currency (pesos)........................		91,000
To record remittance of 1 million pesos to the Mexican supplier.		

Trial Balance—October 31	Debit	Credit
Cash...		$85,000
Parts inventory.......................................	$80,000	–0–
Retained earnings, 9/30.............................	3,333	–0–
Foreign exchange loss...............................	5,000	–0–
Gain on forward contract............................	–0–	5,000
Premium expense....................................	1,667	–0–
	$90,000	$90,000

Part B. Forward Contract Fair Value Hedge of a Recognized Foreign Currency Liability

8/1	Parts Inventory.....................................	80,000	
	Accounts Payable (Mexican pesos)............		80,000
	To record the purchase of parts and a Mexican peso account payable at the spot rate of $0.080.		

The forward contract requires no formal entry. A memorandum designates the forward contract as a hedge of the risk of changes in the cash flow to be paid on the foreign currency payable resulting from changes in the U.S. dollar–peso exchange rate.

9/30	Foreign Exchange Loss............................	6,000	
	Accounts Payable (Mexican pesos).............		6,000
	To adjust the value of the peso payable to the new spot rate of $0.086 and record a foreign exchange loss resulting from the appreciation of the peso since August 1.		
	Forward Contract..................................	2,970	
	Gain on Forward Contract.....................		2,970
	To record the forward contract as an asset at its fair value of $2,970 and record a forward contract gain for the change in the fair value of the forward contract since August 1.		

Trial Balance—September 30	Debit	Credit
Parts inventory...	$80,000	$ –0–
Accounts payable (Mexican pesos)......................		86,000
Forward contract (asset)................................	2,970	–0–
Foreign exchange loss.................................	6,000	–0–
Gain on forward contract..............................	–0–	2,970
	$88,970	$88,970

		Debit	Credit
10/31	Foreign Exchange Loss	5,000	
	Accounts Payable (Mexican pesos)...............		5,000
	To adjust the value of the peso payable to the new spot rate of $0.091 and record a foreign exchange loss resulting from the appreciation of the peso since September 30.		
	Forward Contract	3,030	
	Gain on Forward Contract......................		3,030
	To adjust the carrying value of the forward contract to its current fair value of $6,000 and record a forward contract gain for the change in fair value since September 30.		
	Foreign Currency (Mexican pesos)	91,000	
	Cash		85,000
	Forward Contract		6,000
	To record settlement of the forward contract: Record payment of $85,000 in exchange for 1 million pesos, record the receipt of 1 million pesos as an asset at the spot rate of $0.091, and remove the forward contract from the accounts.		
	Accounts Payable (pesos)...........................	91,000	
	Foreign Currency (pesos)		91,000
	To record remittance of 1 million pesos to the Mexican supplier.		

Trial Balance—October 31	Debit	Credit
Cash	$ –0–	$85,000
Parts inventory......................................	80,000	–0–
Retained earnings, 9/30	3,030	–0–
Foreign exchange loss................................	5,000	–0–
Gain on forward contract.............................	–0–	3,030
	$88,030	$88,030

Part C. Option Cash Flow Hedge of a Recognized Foreign Currency Liability

The following schedule summarizes the changes in the components of the fair value of the peso call option with a strike price of $0.080:

Date	Spot Rate	Option Premium	Fair Value	Change in Fair Value	Intrinsic Value	Time Value	Change in Time Value
8/1	$0.080	$0.0052	$ 5,200	$ –0–	$ –0–	$5,200*	$ –0–
9/30	0.086	0.0095	9,500	+4,300	6,000[†]	3,500[†]	– 1,700
10/31	0.091	0.0110	11,000	+1,500	11,000	–0–[‡]	– 3,500

*Because the strike price and spot rate are the same, the option has no intrinsic value. Fair value is attributable solely to the time value of the option.

[†]With a spot rate of $0.086 and a strike price of $0.08, the option has an intrinsic value of $6,000. The remaining $3,500 of fair value is attributable to time value.

[‡]The time value of the option at maturity is zero.

8/1	Parts Inventory	80,000	
	Accounts Payable (Mexican pesos)		80,000
	To record the purchase of parts and a peso account payable at the spot rate of $0.080.		
	Foreign Currency Option	5,200	
	Cash.		5,200
	To record the purchase of a foreign currency option as an asset.		
9/30	Foreign Exchange Loss	6,000	
	Accounts Payable (pesos)		6,000
	To adjust the value of the peso payable to the new spot rate of $0.086 and record a foreign exchange loss resulting from the appreciation of the peso since August 1.		
	Foreign Currency Option	4,300	
	Accumulated Other Comprehensive Income (AOCI) . . .		4,300
	To adjust the fair value of the option from $5,200 to $9,500 with a corresponding credit to AOCI.		
	Accumulated Other Comprehensive Income (AOCI).	6,000	
	Gain on Foreign Currency Option		6,000
	To record a gain on forward currency option to offset the foreign exchange loss on account payable with a corresponding debit to AOCI.		
	Option Expense	1,700	
	Accumulated Other Comprehensive Income (AOCI) . . .		1,700
	To recognize the change in the time value of the foreign currency option as an expense with a corresponding credit to AOCI.		

Trial Balance—September 30	Debit	Credit
Cash		$ 5,200
Parts inventory.	$80,000	–0–
Foreign currency option (asset)	9,500	–0–
Accounts payable (Mexican pesos).	–0–	86,000
Foreign exchange loss.	6,000	–0–
Gain on foreign currency option	–0–	6,000
Option expense.	1,700	–0–
	$97,200	$97,200

10/31	Foreign Exchange Loss	5,000	
	Accounts Payable (Mexican pesos).		5,000
	To adjust the value of the peso payable to the new spot rate of $0.091 and record a foreign exchange loss resulting from the appreciation of the peso since September 30.		
	Foreign Currency Option.	1,500	
	Accumulated Other Comprehensive Income (AOCI) . .		1,500
	To adjust the carrying value of the foreign currency option to its current fair value of $11,000 with a corresponding credit to AOCI.		
	Accumulated Other Comprehensive Income (AOCI)	5,000	
	Gain on Foreign Currency Option		5,000
	To record a gain on foreign currency option to offset the foreign exchange loss on account payable with a corresponding debit to AOCI.		
	Option Expense.	3,500	
	Accumulated Other Comprehensive Income (AOCI). . .		3,500
	To recognize the change in the time value of the foreign currency option as an expense with a corresponding credit to AOCI.		

Foreign Currency (Mexican pesos)	91,000	
Cash		80,000
Foreign Currency Option.		11,000

To record exercise of the foreign currency option: Record
payment of $80,000 in exchange for 1 million pesos,
record the receipt of 1 million pesos as an asset at the spot
rate of $0.091, and remove the option from the accounts.

Accounts Payable (pesos)	91,000	
Foreign Currency (pesos)		91,000

To record remittance of 1 million pesos to the Mexican
supplier.

Trial Balance—October 31	Debit	Credit
Cash ($5,200 credit balance + $80,000 credit).	$ –0–	$85,200
Parts inventory	80,000	–0–
Retained earnings, 9/30	1,700	–0–
Foreign exchange loss	5,000	–0–
Gain on foreign currency option	–0–	5,000
Option expense	3,500	–0–
	$90,200	$90,200

Part D. Forward Contract Fair Value Hedge of a Foreign Currency Firm Commitment

8/1	The forward contract or the purchase order requires no formal entry. A memorandum would be prepared designating the forward contract as a fair value hedge of the foreign currency firm commitment.		
9/30	Forward Contract	2,970	
	Gain on Forward Contract.		2,970
	To record the forward contract as an asset at its fair value of $2,970 and record a forward contract gain for the change in the fair value of the forward contract since August 1.		
	Loss on Firm Commitment.	2,970	
	Firm Commitment		2,970
	To record the firm commitment as a liability at its fair value of $2,970 based on changes in the forward rate and record a firm commitment loss for the change in fair value since August 1.		

Trial Balance—September 30	Debit	Credit
Forward contract (asset).	$2,970	$ –0–
Firm commitment (liability)	–0–	2,970
Gain on forward contract.	–0–	2,970
Loss on firm commitment.	2,970	–0–
	$5,940	$5,940

10/31	Forward Contract.	3,030	
	Gain on Forward Contract		3,030
	To adjust the carrying value of the forward contract to its current fair value of $6,000 and record a forward contract gain for the change in fair value since September 30.		
	Loss on Firm Commitment	3,030	
	Firm Commitment		3,030
	To adjust the value of the firm commitment to $6,000 based on changes in the forward rate and record a firm commitment loss for the change in fair value since September 30.		

Foreign Currency (Mexican pesos).....................	91,000	
Cash..		85,000
Forward Contract.................................		6,000
To record settlement of the forward contract: Record payment of $85,000 in exchange for 1 million pesos, record the receipt of 1 million pesos as an asset at the spot rate of $0.091, and remove the forward contract from the accounts.		
Parts Inventory	91,000	
Foreign Currency (Mexican pesos).................		91,000
To record the purchase of parts through the payment of 1 million pesos to the Mexican supplier.		
Firm Commitment....................................	6,000	
Adjustment to Net Income–Firm Commitment........		6,000
To close the firm commitment account as an adjustment to net income.		

(*Note:* The final entry to close the Firm Commitment account to Adjustment to Net Income must be made *only* in the period in which Parts Inventory affects net income through Cost of Goods Sold. The Firm Commitment account remains on the books as a liability until that point in time.)

Trial Balance—October 31	Debit	Credit
Cash...	$ –0–	$85,000
Parts inventory (cost of goods sold)...................	91,000	–0–
Gain on forward contract	–0–	3,030
Loss on firm commitment	3,030	–0–
Adjustment to net income–firm commitment	–0–	6,000
	$94,030	$94,030

Part E. Option Fair Value Hedge of a Foreign Currency Firm Commitment

8/1	Foreign Currency Option..........................	5,200	
	Cash		5,200
	To record the purchase of a foreign currency option as an asset.		
9/30	Foreign Currency Option..........................	4,300	
	Gain on Foreign Currency Option		4,300
	To adjust the fair value of the option from $5,200 to $9,500 and record an option gain for the change in fair value since August 1.		
	Loss on Firm Commitment	5,940	
	Firm Commitment		5,940
	To record the firm commitment as a liability at its fair value of $5,940 based on changes in the spot rate and record a firm commitment loss for the change in fair value since August 1.		

The fair value of the firm commitment is determined by referring to changes in the spot rate from August 1 to September 30: ($0.080 − $0.086) × 1 million pesos = $(6,000). This amount must be discounted for one month at 12 percent per annum (1 percent per month): $(6,000) × 0.9901 = $(5,940).

Trial Balance—September 30	Debit	Credit
Cash...	$ –0–	$ 5,200
Foreign currency option (asset).......................	9,500	–0–
Firm commitment (liability)	–0–	5,940
Gain on foreign currency option	–0–	4,300
Loss on firm commitment	5,940	–0–
	$15,440	$15,440

10/31	Foreign Currency Option.............................	1,500	
	Gain on Foreign Currency Option..................		1,500
	To adjust fair value of the option from $9,500 to $11,000 and record an option gain for the change in fair value since September 30.		
	Loss on Firm Commitment.............................	5,060	
	Firm Commitment....................................		5,060
	To adjust the fair value of the firm commitment from $5,940 to $11,000 and record a firm commitment loss for the change in fair value since September 30.		

The fair value of the firm commitment is determined by referring to changes in the spot rate from August 1 to October 31: ($0.080 − $0.091) × 1 million pesos = $(11,000).

	Foreign Currency (Mexican pesos)......................	91,000	
	Cash..		80,000
	Foreign Currency Option...........................		11,000
	To record exercise of the foreign currency option: Record payment of $80,000 in exchange for 1 million pesos, record the receipt of 1 million pesos as an asset at the spot rate of $0.091, and remove the option from the accounts.		
	Parts Inventory.......................................	91,000	
	Foreign Currency (pesos)..........................		91,000
	To record the purchase of parts through the payment of 1 million pesos to the Mexican supplier.		
	Firm Commitment......................................	11,000	
	Adjustment to Net Income–Firm Commitment........		11,000
	To close Firm Commitment account to Adjustment to Net Income.		

(*Note:* The final entry to close the Firm Commitment to Adjustment to Net Income is made *only* in the period in which Parts Inventory affects net income through Cost of Goods Sold. The Firm Commitment account remains on the books as a liability until that point in time.)

Trial Balance—October 31	Debit	Credit
Cash ($5,200 credit balance + $80,000 credit)...........	$ –0–	$85,200
Parts inventory (cost of goods sold)...................	91,000	–0–
Retained earnings, 9/30..............................	1,640	–0–
Gain on foreign currency option.......................	–0–	1,500
Loss on firm commitment..............................	5,060	–0–
Adjustment to net income–firm commitment............	–0–	11,000
	$97,700	$97,700

Part F. Option Cash Flow Hedge of a Forecasted Foreign Currency Transaction

8/1	Foreign Currency Option.............................	5,200	
	Cash..		5,200
	To record the purchase of a foreign currency option as an asset.		
9/30	Foreign Currency Option.............................	4,300	
	Accumulated Other Comprehensive Income (AOCI)...		4,300
	To adjust the fair value of the option from $5,200 to $9,500 with a corresponding adjustment to AOCI.		
	Option Expense......................................	1,700	
	Accumulated Other Comprehensive Income (AOCI)...		1,700
	To recognize the change in the time value of the foreign currency option as an expense with a corresponding credit to AOCI.		

Trial Balance—September 30	Debit	Credit
Cash	$ –0–	$ 5,200
Foreign currency option (asset)	9,500	–0–
Accumulated other comprehensive income	–0–	6,000
Option expense.....................................	1,700	–0–
	$11,200	$11,200

		Debit	Credit
10/31	Foreign Currency Option.............................	1,500	
	Accumulated Other Comprehensive Income (AOCI)..		1,500
	To adjust the fair value of the option from $9,500 to $11,000 with a corresponding adjustment to AOCI.		
	Option Expense......................................	3,500	
	Accumulated Other Comprehensive Income (AOCI)..		3,500
	To recognize the change in the time value of the foreign currency option as an expense with a corresponding credit to AOCI.		
	Foreign Currency (Mexican pesos)	91,000	
	Cash		80,000
	Foreign Currency Option.........................		11,000
	To record exercise of the foreign currency option: Record payment of $80,000 in exchange for 1 million pesos, record the receipt of 1 million pesos as an asset at the spot rate of $0.091, and remove the option from the accounts.		
	Parts Inventory.....................................	91,000	
	Foreign Currency (Mexican pesos)		91,000
	To record the purchase of parts through the payment of 1 million pesos to the Mexican supplier.		
	Accumulated Other Comprehensive Income (AOCI)	11,000	
	Adjustment to Net Income–Forecasted Transaction..		11,000
	To close AOCI as an adjustment to net income.		

(*Note:* The final entry to close AOCI to Adjustment to Net Income is made at the date that the forecasted transaction was expected to occur, regardless of when the parts inventory affects net income.)

Trial Balance—October 31	Debit	Credit
Cash ($5,200 credit balance + $80,000 credit).........	$ –0–	$85,200
Parts inventory (cost of goods sold)	91,000	–0–
Retained earnings, 9/30.............................	1,700	–0–
Foreign currency option expense.....................	3,500	–0–
Adjustment to net income–forecasted transaction	–0–	11,000
	$96,200	$96,200

Questions

1. What concept underlies the two-transaction perspective in accounting for foreign currency transactions?

2. A company makes an export sale denominated in a foreign currency and allows the customer one month to pay. Under the two-transaction perspective, accrual approach, how does the company account for fluctuations in the exchange rate for the foreign currency?

3. What factors create a foreign exchange gain on a foreign currency transaction? What factors create a foreign exchange loss?

4. In what way is the accounting for a foreign currency borrowing more complicated than the accounting for a foreign currency account payable?

5. What does the term *hedging* mean? Why do companies elect to follow this strategy?

6. How does a foreign currency option differ from a foreign currency forward contract?

7. How does the timing of hedges of (*a*) foreign currency denominated assets and liabilities, (*b*) foreign currency firm commitments, and (*c*) forecasted foreign currency transactions differ?

8. Why would a company prefer a foreign currency option over a forward contract in hedging a foreign currency firm commitment? Why would a company prefer a forward contract over an option in hedging a foreign currency asset or liability?

9. How do companies report foreign currency derivatives, such as forward contracts and options, on the balance sheet?

10. How does a company determine the fair value of a foreign currency forward contract? How does it determine the fair value of an option?

11. What is hedge accounting?

12. Under what conditions can companies use hedge accounting to account for a foreign currency option used to hedge a forecasted foreign currency transaction?

13. What are the differences in accounting for a forward contract used as (*a*) a cash flow hedge and (*b*) a fair value hedge of a foreign currency denominated asset or liability?

14. What are the differences in accounting for a forward contract used as a fair value hedge of (*a*) a foreign currency denominated asset or liability and (*b*) a foreign currency firm commitment?

15. What are the differences in accounting for a forward contract used as a cash flow hedge of (*a*) a foreign currency denominated asset or liability and (*b*) a forecasted foreign currency transaction?

16. How are changes in the fair value of an option accounted for in a cash flow hedge? In a fair value hedge?

Problems

LO 7-1

1. Which of the following combinations correctly describes the relationship between foreign currency transactions, exchange rate changes, and foreign exchange gains and losses?

Type of Transaction	Foreign Currency	Foreign Exchange Gain or Loss
a. Export sale	Appreciates	Loss
b. Import purchase	Appreciates	Gain
c. Import purchase	Depreciates	Gain
d. Export sale	Depreciates	Gain

LO 7-2

2. In accounting for foreign currency transactions, which of the following approaches is used in the United States?

   a. One-transaction perspective; accrue foreign exchange gains and losses.

   b. One-transaction perspective; defer foreign exchange gains and losses.

   c. Two-transaction perspective; defer foreign exchange gains and losses.

   d. Two-transaction perspective; accrue foreign exchange gains and losses.

LO 7-2

3. On October 1, 2017, Tile Co., a U.S. company, purchased products from Azulejo, a Portuguese company, with payment due on December 1, 2017. If Tile's 2017 operating income included no foreign exchange gain or loss, the transaction could have

   a. Been denominated in U.S. dollars.

   b. Resulted in an unusual gain.

   c. Generated a foreign exchange gain to be reported as a deferred charge on the balance sheet.

   d. Generated a foreign exchange loss to be reported as a separate component of stockholders' equity.

LO 7-2

4. Brief, Inc., had a receivable from a foreign customer that is payable in the customer's local currency. On December 31, 2017, Brief correctly included this receivable for 200,000 local currency units (LCU) in its balance sheet at $110,000. When Brief collected the receivable on February 15, 2018, the U.S. dollar equivalent was $120,000. In Brief's 2018 consolidated income statement, how much should it report as a foreign exchange gain?

   a. $–0–

   b. $10,000

   c. $15,000

   d. $25,000

LO 7-2, 7-3

5. On July 1, 2017, Mifflin Company borrowed 200,000 euros from a foreign lender evidenced by an interest-bearing note due on July 1, 2018. The note is denominated in euros. The U.S. dollar equivalent of the note principal is as follows:

Date	Amount
July 1, 2017 (date borrowed)	$225,000
December 31, 2017 (Mifflin's year-end)	220,000
July 1, 2018 (date repaid)	210,000

In its 2018 income statement, what amount should Mifflin include as a foreign exchange gain or loss on the note?

a. $15,000 gain

b. $15,000 loss

c. $10,000 gain

d. $10,000 loss

LO 7-1, 7-2

6. Grace Co. had a Chinese yuan payable resulting from imports from China and a Mexican peso receivable resulting from exports to Mexico. Grace recorded foreign exchange losses related to both its yuan payable and peso receivable. Did the foreign currencies increase or decrease in dollar value from the date of the transaction to the settlement date?

	Yuan	Peso
a.	Increase	Increase
b.	Increase	Decrease
c.	Decrease	Increase
d.	Decrease	Decrease

LO 7-2, 7-3

7. Matthias Corp. had the following foreign currency transactions during 2017:

- Purchased merchandise from a foreign supplier on January 20 for the U.S. dollar equivalent of $60,000 and paid the invoice on April 20 at the U.S. dollar equivalent of $50,000.

- On September 1, borrowed the U.S. dollar equivalent of $300,000 evidenced by a note that is payable in the lender's local currency in one year. On December 31, the U.S. dollar equivalent of the principal amount was $320,000.

In Matthias's 2017 income statement, what amount should be included as a net foreign exchange gain or loss?

a. $10,000 gain

b. $10,000 loss

c. $20,000 gain

d. $30,000 loss

LO 7-7

8. A U.S. exporter has a Thai baht account receivable resulting from an export sale on June 1 to a customer in Thailand. The exporter signed a forward contract on June 1 to sell Thai baht and designated it as a cash flow hedge of a recognized Thai baht receivable. The spot rate was $0.022 on that date, and the forward rate was $0.021. Which of the following did the U.S. exporter report in net income?

a. Discount expense

b. Discount revenue

c. Premium expense

d. Premium revenue

LO 7-8

9. St. Philip Company ordered parts costing €100,000 from a foreign supplier on January 15 when the spot rate was $0.20 per €. A one-month forward contract was signed on that date to purchase €100,000 at a forward rate of $0.23. The forward contract is properly designated as a fair value hedge of the €100,000 firm commitment. On February 15, when the company receives the parts, the spot rate is $0.22. At what amount should St. Philip Company carry the parts inventory on its books?

a. $20,000

b. $21,000

c. $22,000

d. $23,000

LO 7-5

10. On December 1, 2017, Ringling Company (a U.S.-based company) entered into a three-month forward contract to purchase 1,000,000 pesos on March 1, 2018. The following U.S. dollar per peso exchange rates apply:

Date	Spot Rate	Forward Rate (to March 1, 2018)
December 1, 2017	$0.044	$0.047
December 31, 2017	0.046	0.049
March 1, 2018	0.050	N/A

Ringling's incremental borrowing rate is 12 percent. The present value factor for two months at an annual interest rate of 12 percent (1 percent per month) is 0.9803.

Which of the following correctly describes the manner in which Ringling Company will report the forward contract on its December 31, 2017, balance sheet?

a. As an asset in the amount of $1,960.60.

b. As an asset in the amount of $2,940.90.

c. As a liability in the amount of $980.30.

d. As a liability in the amount of $2,940.90.

Use the following information for Problems 11 and 12.

MNC Corp. (a U.S.-based company) sold parts to a South Korean customer on December 1, 2017, with payment of 10 million South Korean won to be received on March 31, 2018. The following exchange rates apply:

Date	Spot Rate	Forward Rate (to March 31, 2018)
December 1, 2017	$0.0035	$0.0034
December 31, 2017	0.0033	0.0032
March 31, 2018	0.0038	N/A

MNC's incremental borrowing rate is 12 percent. The present value factor for three months at an annual interest rate of 12 percent (1 percent per month) is 0.9706.

LO 7-2

11. Assuming that MNC did not enter into a forward contract, how much foreign exchange gain or loss should it report on its 2017 income statement with regard to this transaction?

a. $5,000 gain

b. $3,000 gain

c. $2,000 loss

d. $1,000 loss

LO 7-7

12. Assuming that MNC entered into a forward contract to sell 10 million South Korean won on December 1, 2017, as a fair value hedge of a foreign currency receivable, what is the net impact on its net income in 2017 resulting from a fluctuation in the value of the won?

a. No impact on net income.

b. $58.80 decrease in net income.

c. $2,000 decrease in net income.

d. $1,941.20 increase in net income.

LO 7-9

13. On March 1, Pimlico Corporation (a U.S.-based company) expects to order merchandise from a supplier in Sweden in three months. On March 1, when the spot rate is $0.10 per Swedish krona, Pimlico enters into a forward contract to purchase 500,000 Swedish kroner at a three-month forward rate of $0.12. At the end of three months, when the spot rate is $0.115 per Swedish krona, Pimlico orders and receives the merchandise, paying 500,000 kroner. What amount does Pimlico report in net income as a result of this cash flow hedge of a forecasted transaction?

a. $10,000 premium expense plus a $7,500 positive adjustment to net income when the merchandise is purchased.

b. $10,000 Discount expense plus a $5,000 positive adjustment to net income when the merchandise is purchased.

c. $2,500 premium expense plus a $5,000 negative adjustment to net income when the merchandise is purchased.

d. $2,500 premium expense plus a $2,500 positive adjustment to net income when the merchandise is purchased.

LO 7-9

14. Torres Corporation (a U.S.-based company) expects to order goods from a foreign supplier at a price of 100,000 pounds, with delivery and payment to be made on September 20. On July 20, Torres purchased a two-month call option on 100,000 pounds and designated this option as a cash flow hedge of a forecasted foreign currency transaction. The option has a strike price of $1.25 per pound and costs $600. The spot rate for pounds is $1.25 on June 20 and $1.30 on September 20. What amount will Torres Corporation report as an option expense in net income for the quarter ended September 30?

   a. $300

   b. $600

   c. $2,000

   d. $5,000

Use the following information for Problems 15 through 17.

On September 1, 2017, Jensen Company received an order to sell a machine to a customer in Canada at a price of 100,000 Canadian dollars. Jensen shipped the machine and received payment on March 1, 2018. On September 1, 2017, Jensen purchased a put option giving it the right to sell 100,000 Canadian dollars on March 1, 2018, at a price of $80,000. Jensen properly designated the option as a fair value hedge of the Canadian dollar firm commitment. The option cost $2,000 and had a fair value of $2,300 on December 31, 2017. The fair value of the firm commitment was measured by referring to changes in the spot rate. The following spot exchange rates apply:

Date	U.S. Dollar per Canadian Dollar
September 1, 2017	$0.80
December 31, 2017	0.79
March 1, 2018	0.77

Jensen Company's incremental borrowing rate is 12 percent. The present value factor for two months at an annual interest rate of 12 percent (1 percent per month) is 0.9803.

LO 7-8

15. What was the net impact on Jensen Company's 2017 income as a result of this fair value hedge of a firm commitment?

   a. $–0–.

   b. $680.30 decrease in income.

   c. $300 increase in income.

   d. $980.30 increase in income.

LO 7-8

16. What was the net impact on Jensen Company's 2018 income as a result of this fair value hedge of a firm commitment?

   a. $–0–.

   b. $1,319.70 decrease in income.

   c. $77,980.30 increase in income.

   d. $78,680.30 increase in income.

LO 7-8

17. What was the net increase or decrease in cash flow from having purchased the foreign currency option to hedge this exposure to foreign exchange risk?

   a. $–0–.

   b. $1,000 increase in cash flow.

   c. $1,500 decrease in cash flow.

   d. $3,000 increase in cash flow.

Use the following information for Problems 18 through 20.

On June 1, 2017, Micro Corp. received an order for parts from a Mexican customer at a price of 1,000,000 Mexican pesos with a delivery date of July 31, 2017. On June 1, when the U.S. dollar–Mexican peso spot rate is $0.115, Micro Corp. entered into a two-month forward contract to sell 1,000,000 pesos at a forward rate of $0.12 per peso. Micro designates the forward contract as a fair value hedge of the firm commitment to receive pesos, and the fair value of the firm commitment is measured by referring to changes in the peso forward rate. Micro delivers the parts and receives payment on July 31, 2017, when the peso spot rate is $0.118. On June 30, 2017, the Mexican peso spot rate is $0.123, and the forward contract has a fair value of $2,400.

LO 7-8

18. What is the net impact on Micro's net income for the quarter ended June 30, 2017, as a result of this forward contract hedge of a firm commitment?

    a. $–0–.

    b. $2,400 increase in net income.

    c. $4,000 decrease in net income.

    d. $8,000 increase in net income.

LO 7-8

19. What is the net impact on Micro's net income for the quarter ended September 30, 2017, as a result of this forward contract hedge of a firm commitment?

    a. $–0–.

    b. $115,000 increase in net income.

    c. $118,000 increase in net income.

    d. $120,000 increase in net income.

LO 7-8

20. What is Micro's net increase or decrease in cash flow from having entered into this forward contract hedge?

    a. $–0–.

    b. $1,000 increase in cash flow.

    c. $1,500 decrease in cash flow.

    d. $2,000 increase in cash flow.

Use the following information for Problems 21 and 22.
On November 1, 2017, Dos Santos Company forecasts the purchase of raw materials from a Brazilian supplier on February 1, 2018, at a price of 200,000 Brazilian reals. On November 1, 2017, Dos Santos pays $1,500 for a three-month call option on 200,000 reals with a strike price of $0.40 per real. Dos Santos properly designates the option as a cash flow hedge of a forecasted foreign currency transaction. On December 31, 2017, the option has a fair value of $1,100. The following spot exchange rates apply:

Date	U.S. Dollar per Brazilian Real
November 1, 2017	$0.40
December 31, 2017	0.38
February 1, 2018	0.41

LO 7-9

21. What is the net impact on Dos Santos Company's 2017 net income as a result of this hedge of a forecasted foreign currency transaction?

    a. $–0–.

    b. $400 decrease in net income.

    c. $1,000 decrease in net income.

    d. $1,400 decrease in net income.

LO 7-9

22. What is the net impact on Dos Santos Company's 2018 net income as a result of this hedge of a forecasted foreign currency transaction? Assume that the raw materials are consumed and become a part of the cost of goods sold in 2018.

    a. $80,000 decrease in net income.

    b. $80,600 decrease in net income.

    c. $81,100 decrease in net income.

    d. $83,100 decrease in net income.

LO 7-2

23. Turbo Corporation (a U.S.-based company) acquired merchandise on account from a foreign supplier on November 1, 2017, for 100,000 markkas. It paid the foreign currency account payable on January 17, 2018. The following exchange rates for 1 markka are known:

November 1, 2017	$0.754
December 31, 2017	0.742
January 15, 2018	0.747

  a. How does the fluctuation in exchange rates affect Turbo's 2017 income statement?

  b. How does the fluctuation in exchange rates affect Turbo's 2018 income statement?

LO 7-2

24. On December 20, 2017, Butanta Company (a U.S. company headquartered in Miami, Florida) sold parts to a foreign customer at a price of 50,000 ostras. Payment is received on January 10, 2018. Currency exchange rates for 1 ostra are as follows:

December 20, 2017	$1.05
December 31, 2017	1.02
January 10, 2018	0.98

  a. How does the fluctuation in exchange rates affect Butanta's 2017 income statement?

  b. How does the fluctuation in exchange rates affect Butanta's 2018 income statement?

LO 7-2

25. Peerless Corporation (a U.S. company) made a sale to a foreign customer on September 15, for 100,000 crowns. It received payment on October 15. The following exchange rates for 1 crown apply:

September 15	$0.60
September 30	0.66
October 15	0.62

Prepare all journal entries for Peerless in connection with this sale, assuming that the company closes its books on September 30 to prepare interim financial statements.

LO 7-2

26. On December 15, 2017, Lisbeth Inc. (a U.S. company) purchases merchandise inventory from a foreign supplier for 50,000 schillings. Lisbeth agrees to pay in 45 days after it sells the merchandise. Lisbeth makes sales rather quickly and pays the entire obligation on January 25, 2018. Currency exchange rates for 1 schilling are as follows:

December 15, 2017	$0.28
December 31, 2017	0.30
January 25, 2018	0.33
January 31, 2018	0.34

Prepare all journal entries for Lisbeth Company in connection with this purchase and payment.

LO 7-2

27. Voltac Corporation (a U.S. company located in Charlotte, North Carolina) has the following import/export transactions denominated in Mexican pesos in 2017:

March 1	Bought inventory costing 100,000 pesos on credit.
May 1	Sold 60 percent of the inventory for 80,000 pesos on credit.
August 1	Collected 70,000 pesos from customers.
September 1	Paid 60,000 pesos to suppliers.

Currency exchange rates for 1 peso for 2017 are as follows:

March 1	$0.10
May 1	0.12
August 1	0.13
September 1	0.14
December 31	0.15

For each of the following accounts, how much will Voltac report on its 2017 financial statements?

a. Inventory.

b. Cost of Goods Sold.

c. Sales.

d. Accounts Receivable.

e. Accounts Payable.

f. Cash.

LO 7-3

28. On April 1, 2017, Mendoza Company borrowed 500,000 euros for one year at an interest rate of 5 percent per annum. Mendoza must make its first interest payment on the loan on October 1, 2017, and will make a second interest payment on March 31, 2018, when the loan is repaid. Mendoza prepares U.S.-dollar financial statements and has a December 31 year-end. Prepare all journal entries related to this foreign currency borrowing assuming the following exchange rates for 1 euro:

April 1, 2017	$1.10
October 1, 2017	1.20
December 31, 2017	1.24
March 31, 2018	1.28

LO 7-2

29. Benjamin, Inc., operates an export/import business. The company has considerable dealings with companies in the country of Camerrand. The denomination of all transactions with these companies is alaries (AL), the Camerrand currency. During 2017, Benjamin acquires 20,000 widgets at a price of 8 alaries per widget. It will pay for them when it sells them. Currency exchange rates for 1 AL are as follows:

September 1, 2017	$0.46
December 1, 2017	0.44
December 31, 2017	0.48
March 1, 2018	0.45

a. Assume that Benjamin acquired the widgets on December 1, 2017, and made payment on March 1, 2018. What is the effect of the exchange rate fluctuations on reported income in 2017 and in 2018?

b. Assume that Benjamin acquired the widgets on September 1, 2017, and made payment on December 1, 2017. What is the effect of the exchange rate fluctuations on reported income in 2017?

c. Assume that Benjamin acquired the widgets on September 1, 2017, and made payment on March 1, 2018. What is the effect of the exchange rate fluctuations on reported income in 2017 and in 2018?

LO 7-3

30. On September 30, 2017, Ericson Company negotiated a two-year, 1,000,000 dudek loan from a foreign bank at an interest rate of 2 percent per year. It makes interest payments annually on September 30 and will repay the principal on September 30, 2019. Ericson prepares U.S.-dollar financial statements and has a December 31 year-end.

a. Prepare all journal entries related to this foreign currency borrowing assuming the following exchange rates for 1 dudek:

September 30, 2017	$0.100
December 31, 2017	0.105
September 30, 2018	0.120
December 31, 2018	0.125
September 30, 2019	0.150

b. Taking the exchange rate effect on the cost of borrowing into consideration, determine the effective interest rate in dollars on the loan in each of the three years 2017, 2018, and 2019.

LO 7-7

31. Brandlin Company of Anaheim, California, sells parts to a foreign customer on December 1, 2017, with payment of 16,000 korunas to be received on March 1, 2018. Brandlin enters into a forward

contract on December 1, 2017, to sell 16,000 korunas on March 1, 2018. Relevant exchange rates for the koruna on various dates are as follows:

Date	Spot Rate	Forward Rate (to March 1, 2018)
December 1, 2017	$2.70	$2.775
December 31, 2017	2.80	2.900
March 1, 2018	2.95	N/A

Brandlin's incremental borrowing rate is 12 percent. The present value factor for two months at an annual interest rate of 12 percent (1 percent per month) is 0.9803. Brandlin must close its books and prepare financial statements at December 31.

a. Assuming that Brandlin designates the forward contract as a cash flow hedge of a foreign currency receivable and recognizes any premium or discount using the straight-line method, prepare journal entries for these transactions in U.S. dollars. What is the impact on 2017 net income? What is the impact on 2018 net income? What is the impact on net income over the two accounting periods?

b. Assuming that Brandlin designates the forward contract as a fair value hedge of a foreign currency receivable, prepare journal entries for these transactions in U.S. dollars. What is the impact on 2017 net income? What is the impact on 2018 net income? What is the impact on net income over the two accounting periods?

LO 7-7

32. Use the same facts as in Problem 31 except that Brandlin Company purchases materials from a foreign supplier on December 1, 2017, with payment of 16,000 korunas to be made on March 1, 2018. The materials are consumed immediately and recognized as cost of goods sold at the date of purchase. On December 1, 2017, Brandlin enters into a forward contract to purchase 16,000 korunas on March 1, 2018.

a. Assuming that Brandlin designates the forward contract as a cash flow hedge of a foreign currency payable and recognizes any premium or discount using the straight-line method, prepare journal entries for these transactions in U.S. dollars. What is the impact on 2017 net income? What is the impact on 2018 net income? What is the impact on net income over the two accounting periods?

b. Assuming that Brandlin designates the forward contract as a fair value hedge of a foreign currency payable, prepare journal entries for these transactions in U.S. dollars. What is the impact on net income in 2017 and in 2018? What is the impact on net income over the two accounting periods?

LO 7-7

33. On June 1, Alexander Corporation sold goods to a foreign customer at a price of 1,000,000 pesos and will receive payment in three months on September 1. On June 1, Alexander acquired an option to sell 1,000,000 pesos in three months at a strike price of $0.062. Relevant exchange rates and option premiums for the peso are as follows:

Date	Spot Rate	Put Option Premium for September 1 (strike price $0.062)
June 1	$0.062	$0.0025
June 30	0.066	0.0018
September 1	0.061	N/A

Alexander must close its books and prepare its second-quarter financial statements on June 30.

a. Assuming that Alexander designates the foreign currency option as a cash flow hedge of a foreign currency receivable, prepare journal entries for these transactions in U.S. dollars. What is the impact on net income over the two accounting periods?

b. Assuming that Alexander designates the foreign currency option as a fair value hedge of a foreign currency receivable, prepare journal entries for these transactions in U.S. dollars. What is the impact on net income over the two accounting periods?

LO 7-7

34. On June 1, Cairns Corporation purchased goods from a foreign supplier at a price of 1,000,000 francs and will make payment in three months on September 1. On June 1, Cairns acquired an

option to purchase 1,000,000 francs in three months at a strike price of $0.852. Relevant exchange rates and option premiums for the franc are as follows:

Date	Spot Rate	Call Option Premium for September 1 (strike price $0.852)
June 1	$0.852	$0.002
June 30	0.858	0.007
September 1	0.872	N/A

Cairns must close its books and prepare its second-quarter financial statements on June 30.

a. Assuming that Cairns designates the foreign currency option as a cash flow hedge of a foreign currency payable, prepare journal entries for these transactions in U.S. dollars. What is the impact on net income over the two accounting periods?

b. Assuming that Cairns designates the foreign currency option as a fair value hedge of a foreign currency payable, prepare journal entries for these transactions in U.S. dollars. What is the impact on net income over the two accounting periods?

LO 7-7

35. On November 1, 2017, Bernard Company (a U.S.-based company) sold merchandise to a foreign customer for 100,000 FCUs with payment to be received on April 30, 2018. At the date of sale, Bernard entered into a six-month forward contract to sell 100,000 FCUs. The company properly designates the forward contract as a cash flow hedge of a foreign currency receivable. The following exchange rates apply:

Date	Spot Rate	Forward Rate (to April 30, 2018)
November 1, 2017	$0.21	$0.20
December 31, 2017	0.19	0.17
April 30, 2018	0.18	N/A

Bernard's incremental borrowing rate is 12 percent. The present value factor for four months at an annual interest rate of 12 percent (1 percent per month) is 0.9610.

a. Prepare all journal entries, including December 31 adjusting entries, to record the sale and forward contract.

b. What is the impact on net income in 2017?

c. What is the impact on net income in 2018?

LO 7-7

36. Eximco Corporation (based in Champaign, Illinois) has a number of transactions with companies in the country of Mongagua, where the currency is the mong. On November 30, 2017, Eximco sold equipment at a price of 500,000 mongs to a Mongaguan customer that will make payment on January 31, 2018. In addition, on November 30, 2017, Eximco purchased raw materials from a Mongaguan supplier at a price of 300,000 mongs; it will make payment on January 31, 2018. To hedge its net exposure in mongs, Eximco entered into a two-month forward contract on November 30, 2017, to deliver 200,000 mongs to the foreign currency broker in exchange for $104,000. Eximco properly designates its forward contract as a fair value hedge of a foreign currency receivable. The following rates for the mong apply:

Date	Spot Rate	Forward Rate (to January 31, 2018)
November 30, 2017	$0.53	$0.52
December 31, 2017	0.50	0.48
January 31, 2018	0.49	N/A

Eximco's incremental borrowing rate is 12 percent. The present value factor for one month at an annual interest rate of 12 percent (1 percent per month) is 0.9901.

a. Prepare all journal entries, including December 31 adjusting entries, to record these transactions and the forward contract.

b. What is the impact on net income in 2017?

c. What is the impact on net income in 2018?

LO 7-7, 7-8

37. On October 1, 2017, Sharp Company (based in Denver, Colorado) entered into a forward contract to sell 100,000 rubles in four months (on January 31, 2018) and receive $39,000 in U.S. dollars. Exchange rates for the ruble follow:

Date	Spot Rate	Forward Rate (to January 31, 2018)
October 1, 2017	$0.35	$0.39
December 31, 2017	0.38	0.41
January 31, 2018	0.40	N/A

Sharp's incremental borrowing rate is 12 percent. The present value factor for one month at an annual interest rate of 12 percent (1 percent per month) is 0.9901. Sharp must close its books and prepare financial statements on December 31.

a. Prepare journal entries, assuming that Sharp entered into the forward contract as a fair value hedge of a 100,000 ruble receivable arising from a sale made on October 1, 2017. Include entries for both the sale and the forward contract.

b. Prepare journal entries, assuming that Sharp entered into the forward contract as a fair value hedge of a firm commitment related to a 100,000 ruble sale that will be made on January 31, 2018. Include entries for both the firm commitment and the forward contract. The fair value of the firm commitment is measured by referring to changes in the forward rate.

LO 7-8

38. On August 1, Ling-Harvey Corporation (a U.S.-based importer) placed an order to purchase merchandise from a foreign supplier at a price of 400,000 ringgits. Ling-Harvey will receive and make payment for the merchandise in three months on October 31. On August 1, Ling-Harvey entered into a forward contract to purchase 400,000 ringgits in three months at a forward rate of $0.60. It properly designates the forward contract as a fair value hedge of a foreign currency firm commitment. The fair value of the firm commitment is measured by referring to changes in the forward rate. Relevant exchange rates for the ringgit are as follows:

Date	Spot Rate	Forward Rate (to October 31)
August 1	$0.60	$0.60
September 30	0.63	0.66
October 31	0.68	N/A

Ling-Harvey's incremental borrowing rate is 12 percent. The present value factor for one month at an annual interest rate of 12 percent (1 percent per month) is 0.9901. Ling-Harvey must close its books and prepare its third-quarter financial statements on September 30.

a. Prepare journal entries for the forward contract and firm commitment through October 31.

b. Assuming the inventory is sold in the fourth quarter, what is the impact on net income over the two accounting periods?

c. What net cash outflow results from the purchase of merchandise from the foreign supplier?

LO 7-8

39. On June 1, Vandervelde Corporation (a U.S.-based manufacturing firm) received an order to sell goods to a foreign customer at a price of 100,000 leks. Vandervelde will ship the goods and receive payment in three months on September 1. On June 1, Vandervelde purchased an option to sell 100,000 leks in three months at a strike price of $1.00. It properly designated the option as a fair value hedge of a foreign currency firm commitment. The fair value of the firm commitment is measured by referring to changes in the spot rate. Relevant exchange rates and option premiums for the lek are as follows:

Date	Spot Rate	Put Option Premium for September 1 (strike price $1.00)
June 1	$1.00	$0.020
June 30	0.94	0.028
September 1	0.88	N/A

Vandervelde's incremental borrowing rate is 12 percent. The present value factor for two months at an annual interest rate of 12 percent (1 percent per month) is 0.9803. Vandervelde Corporation must close its books and prepare its second-quarter financial statements on June 30.

a. Prepare journal entries for the foreign currency option and firm commitment.

b. What is the impact on net income over the two accounting periods?

c. What is the net cash inflow resulting from the sale of goods to the foreign customer?

LO 7-8

40. Spitz Company ordered merchandise from a foreign supplier on November 20 at a price of 100,000 forints when the spot rate was $0.50 per forint. Delivery and payment were scheduled for December 20. On November 20, Spitz acquired a call option on 100,000 forints at a strike price of $0.50, paying a premium of $0.01 per forint. It designates the option as a fair value hedge of a foreign currency firm commitment. The fair value of the firm commitment is measured by referring to changes in the spot rate. The merchandise arrives and Spitz makes payment according to schedule. Spitz sells the merchandise by December 31, when it closes its books.

a. Assuming a spot rate of $0.53 per forint on December 20, prepare all journal entries to account for the foreign currency option, foreign currency firm commitment, and purchase of inventory.

b. Assuming a spot rate of $0.48 per forint on December 20, prepare all journal entries to account for the foreign currency option, foreign currency firm commitment, and purchase of inventory.

LO 7-9

41. Based on past experience, Leickner Company expects to purchase raw materials from a foreign supplier at a cost of 1,000,000 marks on March 15, 2018. To hedge this forecasted transaction, the company acquires a three-month call option to purchase 1,000,000 marks on December 15, 2017. Leickner selects a strike price of $0.58 per mark, paying a premium of $0.005 per unit, when the spot rate is $0.58. The spot rate increases to $0.584 at December 31, 2017, causing the fair value of the option to increase to $8,000. By March 15, 2018, when the raw materials are purchased, the spot rate has climbed to $0.59, resulting in a fair value for the option of $10,000.

a. Prepare all journal entries for the option hedge of a forecasted transaction and for the purchase of raw materials, assuming that December 31 is Leickner's year-end and that the raw materials are included in the cost of goods sold in 2018.

b. What is the overall impact on net income over the two accounting periods?

c. What is the net cash outflow to acquire the raw materials?

LO 7-7, 7-8

42. Vino Veritas Company, a U.S.-based importer of wines and spirits, placed an order with a French supplier for 1,000 cases of wine at a price of 200 euros per case. The total purchase price is 200,000 euros. Relevant exchange rates for the euro are as follows:

Date	Spot Rate	Forward Rate to October 31	Call Option Premium for October 31 (strike price $1.00)
September 15	$1.00	$1.06	$0.035
September 30	1.05	1.09	0.070
October 31	1.10	1.10	0.100

Vino Veritas Company has an incremental borrowing rate of 12 percent (1 percent per month) and closes the books and prepares financial statements at September 30.

a. Assume that the wine arrived on September 15, and the company made payment on October 31. There was no attempt to hedge the exposure to foreign exchange risk. Prepare journal entries to account for this import purchase.

b. Assume that the wine arrived on September 15, and the company made payment on October 31. On September 15, Vino Veritas entered into a 45-day forward contract to purchase 200,000 euros. It properly designated the forward contract as a fair value hedge of a foreign currency payable. Prepare journal entries to account for the import purchase and foreign currency forward contract.

c. Vino Veritas ordered the wine on September 15. The wine arrived and the company paid for it on October 31. On September 15, Vino Veritas entered into a 45-day forward contract to purchase 200,000 euros. The company properly designated the forward contract as a fair value hedge of a foreign currency firm commitment. The fair value of the firm commitment is measured by referring to changes in the forward rate. Prepare journal entries to account for the foreign currency forward contract, firm commitment, and import purchase.

d. The wine arrived on September 15, and the company made payment on October 31. On September 15, Vino Veritas purchased a 45-day call option for 200,000 euros. It properly designated the option as a cash flow hedge of a foreign currency payable. Prepare journal entries to account for the import purchase and foreign currency option.

e. The company ordered the wine on September 15. It arrived on October 31, and the company made payment on that date. On September 15, Vino Veritas purchased a 45-day call option for 200,000 euros. It properly designated the option as a fair value hedge of a foreign currency firm commitment. The fair value of the firm commitment is measured by referring to changes in the spot rate. Prepare journal entries to account for the foreign currency option, firm commitment, and import purchase.

Develop Your Skills

RESEARCH CASE—INTERNATIONAL FLAVORS AND FRAGRANCES

Many companies make annual reports available on their corporate web page, often under an Investors tab. Annual reports also can be accessed through the SEC's EDGAR system at www.sec.gov (under Filings, click Company Filings Search, type in Company Name, and under Filing Type, search for 10-K).

Access the most recent annual report for International Flavors and Fragrances (IFF) to complete the following requirements.

Required

1. Identify the location(s) in the annual report where IFF provides disclosures related to its management of foreign exchange risk.
2. Determine the types of hedging instruments the company uses and the types of hedges in which it engages.
3. Determine the manner in which the company discloses the fact that its foreign exchange hedges are effective in offsetting gains and losses on the underlying items being hedged.

ACCOUNTING STANDARDS CASE—FORECASTED TRANSACTIONS

Fergusson Corporation, a U.S. company, manufactures components for the automobile industry. In the past, Fergusson purchased actuators used in its products from a supplier in the United States. The company plans to shift its purchases to a supplier in Portugal. Fergusson's CFO expects to place an order with the Portuguese supplier in the amount of 200,000 euros in three months. In contemplation of this future import, the CFO purchased a euro call option to hedge the cash flow risk that the euro might appreciate against the U.S. dollar over the next three months. The CFO is aware that a foreign currency option used to hedge the cash flow risk associated with a forecasted foreign currency transaction may be designated as a hedge for accounting purposes only if the forecasted transaction is probable. However, he is unsure how he should demonstrate that the anticipated import purchase from Portugal is likely to occur. He wonders whether management's intention to make the purchase is sufficient.

Required

Search current U.S. authoritative accounting literature to determine whether management's intent is sufficient to assess that a forecasted foreign currency transaction is likely to occur. If not, what additional evidence must be considered? Identify the FASB ASC guidance for answering these questions.

EXCEL CASE—DETERMINE FOREIGN EXCHANGE GAINS AND LOSSES

Import/Export Company, a U.S. company, made a number of import purchases and export sales denominated in foreign currency in 2015. Information related to these transactions is summarized in the following table. The company made each purchase or sale on the date in the Transaction Date column and made payment in foreign currency or received payment on the date in the Settlement Date column.

Foreign Currency	Type of Transaction	Amount in Foreign Currency	Transaction Date	Settlement Date
Brazilian real (BRL)	Import purchase	(130,000)	1/10/2015	5/10/2015
Chilean peso (CLP)	Import purchase	(30,000,000)	1/10/2015	5/10/2015
Swiss franc (CHF)	Export sale	50,000	1/10/2015	4/10/2015
Swiss franc (CHF)	Import purchase	(50,000)	4/10/2015	7/10/2015
Euro	Export sale	45,000	1/10/2015	4/10/2015
Euro	Export sale	45,000	4/10/2015	7/10/2015
Chinese yuan (CNY)	Import purchase	(300,000)	1/10/2015	7/10/2015

Required

1. Create an electronic spreadsheet with the information from the preceding table. Label columns as follows:

   Foreign Currency

   Type of Transaction

   Amount in Foreign Currency

   Transaction Date

   Exchange Rate at Transaction Date

   $ Value at Transaction Date

   Settlement Date

   Exchange Rate at Settlement Date

   $ Value at Settlement Date

   Foreign Exchange Gain (Loss)

2. Use historical exchange rate information available on the Internet at www.x-rates.com, Historic Lookup, to find the 2015 exchange rates between the U.S. dollar and each foreign currency on the relevant transaction and settlement dates.

3. Complete the electronic spreadsheet to determine the foreign exchange gain (loss) on each transaction. Determine the total net foreign exchange gain (loss) reported in Import/Export Company's 2015 income statement.

4. Explain why a foreign exchange gain arises for some transactions and a foreign exchange loss occurs for other transactions.

ANALYSIS CASE—CASH FLOW HEDGE

On February 1, 2017, Linber Company forecasted the purchase of component parts on May 1, 2017, at a price of 100,000 euros. On that date, Linber entered into a forward contract to purchase 100,000 euros on May 1, 2017. It designated the forward contract as a cash flow hedge of the forecasted transaction. The spot rate for euros on February 1, 2017, was $1 per euro. On May 1, 2017, the forward contract was settled, and the component parts were received and paid for. The parts were consumed in the second quarter of 2017.

Linber's financial statements reported the following amounts related to this cash flow hedge (credit balances in parentheses):

Income Statement	First Quarter 2017	Second Quarter 2017
Premium expense	$4,000	$ 2,000
Cost of goods sold	–0–	103,000
Adjustment to net income	–0–	3,000

Balance Sheet	3/31/17	5/1/17
Forward contract (liability)	$(1,980)*	$ –0–
AOCI (credit)	(2,020)	–0–
Change in cash	–0–	(106,000)

*$2,000 × 0.9901 = $1,980, where 0.9901 is the present value factor for one month at an annual interest rate of 12 percent calculated as 1/1.01.

Required

1. On February 1, 2017, what was the U.S. dollar per euro forward rate to May 1, 2017?
2. On March 31, 2017, what was the U.S. dollar per euro forward rate to May 1, 2017?
3. Was Linber better off or worse off as a result of having entered into this cash flow hedge of a forecasted transaction? By what amount?
4. What does the total premium expense of $6,000 reflect?

INTERNET CASE—HISTORICAL EXCHANGE RATES

The Pier Ten Company, a U.S. company, made credit sales to four customers in Asia on September 15, 2015, and received payment on October 15, 2015. Information related to these sales is as follows:

Customer	Location	Invoice Price
Rama Properties Ltd.	New Delhi	3,319,000 Indian rupees (INR)
Luzon Island Group	Manila	2,337,000 Philippine pesos (PHP)
Mishima Industries Inc.	Tokyo	6,017,000 Japanese yen (JPY)
Melayu Trading Company	Kuala Lumpur	214,800 Malaysian ringgit (MYR)

The Pier Ten Company's fiscal year ends September 30.

Required

1. Use historical exchange rate information available on the Internet at www.x-rates.com, Historical Lookup, to find exchange rates between the U.S. dollar and each foreign currency for September 15, September 30, and October 15, 2015.
2. Determine the foreign exchange gains and losses that Pier Ten would have recognized in net income in the fiscal years ended September 30, 2015, and September 30, 2016, and the overall foreign exchange gain or loss for each transaction. Determine for which transaction, if any, it would have been important for Pier Ten to hedge its foreign exchange risk.
3. Pier Ten could have acquired a one-month put option on September 15, 2015, to hedge the foreign exchange risk associated with each of the four export sales. In each case, the put option would have cost $100 with the strike price equal to the September 15, 2015, spot rate. Determine for which hedges, if any, Pier Ten would have recognized a net gain on the foreign currency option.

COMMUNICATION CASE—FORWARD CONTRACTS AND OPTIONS

Palmetto Bug Extermination Corporation (PBEC), a U.S. company, regularly purchases chemicals from a supplier in Switzerland with the invoice price denominated in Swiss francs. PBEC has experienced several foreign exchange losses in the past year due to increases in the U.S. dollar price of the Swiss currency. As a result, Dewey Nukem, PBEC's CEO, has asked you to investigate the possibility of using derivative financial instruments, specifically foreign currency forward contracts and foreign currency options, to hedge the company's exposure to foreign exchange risk.

Required

Draft a memo to CEO Nukem comparing the advantages and disadvantages of using forward contracts and options to hedge foreign exchange risk. Recommend the type of hedging instrument you believe the company should employ and justify this recommendation.

Translation of Foreign Currency Financial Statements

- Fluor Corporation said on Monday it would buy Dutch engineering and construction firm Stork from its private equity owner Arle Capital, for $755 million . . . Fluor said the acquisition would combine well with its own operations in the same industry and give it access to Stork's customer base, which spans the globe but is most focused in Europe.[1]

- Omnicom Group Inc., the world's second largest advertising company, has agreed to pay 1 billion reais ($270 million) for Brazil's Grupo ABC, growing Omnicom's publicity, branding services, and content in Latin America's largest economy, a source with direct knowledge of the transaction said on Friday.[2]

- *Kellogg Co is setting up a joint venture with the African arm of Singapore's Tolaram Group to bolster its breakfast and snack food offerings in West Africa.* Kellogg will also pay $450 million for a 50 percent stake in Lagos, Nigeria-based Multipro, a food sales and distribution company owned by Tolaram, with an option to buy a stake in Tolaram's African unit.[3]

Recent announcements such as these are common in today's global economy. Companies establish operations in foreign countries for a variety of reasons including to develop new markets for their products, take advantage of lower production costs, or gain access to raw materials. Some multinational companies have reached a stage in their development in which domestic operations are no longer considered to be of higher priority than international operations. For example, in 2015, U.S.–based International Flavors and Fragrances, Inc., had operations in 38 countries and generated 76 percent of its net sales outside North America; Merck & Co., Inc., generated 56 percent of its sales and had 32 percent of its property, plant, and equipment outside of the United States.

Foreign operations create numerous managerial problems for the parent company that do not exist for domestic operations. Some of these problems arise from cultural differences between the home and foreign countries. Other problems exist because foreign operations generally are

Learning Objectives

After studying this chapter, you should be able to:

LO 8-1 Explain the theoretical underpinnings and the limitations of the current rate and temporal methods.

LO 8-2 Describe guidelines for determining when foreign currency financial statements are to be translated using the current rate method and when they are to be remeasured using the temporal method.

LO 8-3 Translate a foreign subsidiary's financial statements into its parent's reporting currency using the current rate method and calculate the related translation adjustment.

LO 8-4 Remeasure a foreign subsidiary's financial statements using the temporal method and calculate the associated remeasurement gain or loss.

LO 8-5 Understand the rationale for hedging a net investment in a foreign operation and describe the treatment of gains and losses on hedges used for this purpose.

LO 8-6 Prepare a consolidation worksheet for a parent and its foreign subsidiary.

[1] Reuters U.S. Edition Online, "Fluor to buy Stork of the Netherlands for $755 million," December 7, 2015, www.reuters.com.

[2] Reuters U.S. Edition Online, "Omnicom to buy Brazil advertising group ABC, source says," November 20, 2015, www.reuters.com.

[3] Reuters U.S. Edition Online, "Kellogg to spend $450 million to expand in Africa," September 15, 2015,"" www.reuters.com.

required to comply with the laws and regulations of the foreign country. For example, most countries require companies to prepare financial statements in the local currency using local accounting rules.

To prepare worldwide consolidated financial statements, a U.S. parent company must (1) convert the foreign GAAP financial statements of its foreign operations into U.S. GAAP and (2) translate the financial statements from the foreign currency into U.S. dollars. This conversion and translation process must be carried out regardless of whether the foreign operation is a branch, joint venture, majority-owned subsidiary, or affiliate accounted for under the equity method. This chapter deals with the issue of translating foreign currency financial statements into the parent's reporting currency.

Two major theoretical issues are related to the translation process: (1) which *translation method* should be used (the current rate method or the temporal method) and (2) where the resulting *translation adjustment* should be reported in the consolidated financial statements (as a translation gain/loss in net income or as a component of accumulated other comprehensive income in equity). In this chapter, these two issues are examined first from a conceptual perspective and second by the manner in which the FASB in the United States has resolved these issues. The chapter also discusses IFRS on this topic.

Exchange Rates Used in Translation

Two methods currently are used in the United States and most other countries to translate foreign currency financial statements into the parent company's reporting currency, and *two types of exchange rates* are used in applying these methods:

1. *Historical exchange rate:* the exchange rate that existed when a transaction occurred.
2. *Current exchange rate:* the exchange rate that exists at the balance sheet date.

Translation methods differ as to which balance sheet and income statement accounts are translated at historical exchange rates and which are translated at current exchange rates. Before continuing on to the next paragraph, please read the Discussion Question: How Do We Report This?

Assume that the company described in the Discussion Question began operations in Gualos on December 31, 2016, when the exchange rate was $0.20 per vilsek. When Southwestern Corporation prepared its consolidated balance sheet at December 31, 2016, it had no choice about the exchange rate used to translate the Land account into U.S. dollars. It translated the Land account carried on the foreign subsidiary's books at 150,000 vilseks at an exchange rate of $0.20; $0.20 was both the *historical* and *current* exchange rate for the Land account at December 31, 2016.

Consolidated Balance Sheet: 12/31/16	
Land (150,000 vilseks × $0.20)	$30,000

During the first quarter of 2017, the vilsek appreciates relative to the U.S. dollar by 15 percent; the exchange rate at March 31, 2017, is $0.23 per vilsek. In preparing its balance sheet at the end of the first quarter of 2017, Southwestern must decide whether the Land account carried on the subsidiary's balance sheet at 150,000 vilseks should be translated into dollars using the *historical exchange rate* of $0.20 or the *current exchange rate* of $0.23.

If the historical exchange rate is used at March 31, 2017, Land continues to be carried on the consolidated balance sheet at $30,000 with no change from December 31, 2016.

Historical Rate—Consolidated Balance Sheet: 3/31/17	
Land (150,000 vilseks × $0.20)	$30,000

? Discussion Question

HOW DO WE REPORT THIS?

Southwestern Corporation operates throughout Texas buying and selling widgets. To expand into more profitable markets, the company recently decided to open a small subsidiary in the nearby country of Gualos. The currency in Gualos is the vilsek. For some time, the government of that country held the exchange rate constant: 1 vilsek equaled $0.20 (or 5 vilseks equaled $1.00). Initially, Southwestern invested cash in this new operation; its $90,000 was converted into 450,000 vilseks ($90,000 × 5). Southwestern used one-third of this money (150,000 vilseks, or $30,000) to purchase land to hold for the possible construction of a plant, invested one-third in short-term marketable securities, and spent one-third in acquiring inventory for future resale.

Shortly thereafter, the Gualos government officially revalued the currency so that 1 vilsek was worth $0.23. Because of the strength of the local economy, the vilsek gained buying power in relation to the U.S. dollar. The vilsek then was considered more valuable than in the past. Southwestern's accountants realized that a change had occurred; each of the assets (land, inventory, and marketable securities) was now worth more in U.S. dollars than the original $30,000 investment: 150,000 vilseks × $0.23 = $34,500. Two of the company's top officers met to determine the appropriate method for reporting this change in currency values.

Controller: Nothing has changed. Our cost is still $30,000 for each item. That's what we spent. Accounting uses historical cost wherever possible. Thus, we should do nothing.

Finance director: Yes, but the old rates are meaningless now. We would be foolish to report figures based on a rate that no longer exists. The cost is still 150,000 vilseks for each item. You are right, the cost has not changed. However, the vilsek is now worth $0.23, so our reported value must change.

Controller: The new rate affects us only if we take money out of the country. We don't plan to do that for many years. The rate will probably change 20 more times before we remove money from Gualos. We've got to stick to our $30,000 historical cost. That's our cost and that's good, basic accounting.

Finance director: You mean that for the next 20 years we will be translating balances for external reporting purposes using an exchange rate that has not existed for years? That doesn't make sense. I have a real problem using an antiquated rate for the inventory and marketable securities. They will be sold for cash when the new rate is in effect. These balances have no remaining relation to the original exchange rate.

Controller: You misunderstand the impact of an exchange rate fluctuation. Within Gualos, no impact occurs. One vilsek is still one vilsek. The effect is realized only when an actual conversion takes place into U.S. dollars at a new rate. At that point, we will properly measure and report the gain or loss. That is when realization takes place. Until then our cost has not changed.

Finance director: I simply see no value at all in producing financial information based entirely on an exchange rate that does not exist. I don't care when realization takes place.

Controller: You've got to stick with historical cost, believe me. The exchange rate today isn't important unless we actually convert vilseks to dollars.

How should Southwestern report each of these three assets on its current balance sheet? Does the company have a gain because the value of the vilsek has increased relative to the U.S. dollar?

If the current exchange rate is used, Land is carried on the consolidated balance sheet at $34,500, an increase of $4,500 from December 31, 2016.

Current Rate—Consolidated Balance Sheet: 3/31/17	
Land (150,000 vilseks × $0.23)	$34,500

Translation Adjustments

To keep the accounting equation (A = L + OE) in balance, the increase of $4,500 in the Land account on the asset (A) side of the consolidated balance sheet when the current exchange rate is used must be offset by an equal $4,500 *increase* in owners' equity (OE) on the other side of the balance sheet. The increase in owners' equity is called a *positive translation adjustment.* It has a *credit* balance.

The increase in dollar value of the Land due to the vilsek's appreciation creates a positive translation adjustment. This is true for any asset on the Gualos subsidiary's balance sheet that is translated at the *current* exchange rate. *Assets translated at the current exchange rate when the foreign currency has appreciated generate a positive (credit) translation adjustment.*

Liabilities on the Gualos subsidiary's balance sheet that are translated at the current exchange rate also increase in dollar value when the vilsek appreciates. For example, Southwestern would report Notes Payable of 10,000 vilseks at $2,000 on the December 31, 2016, balance sheet and at $2,300 on the March 31, 2017, balance sheet. To keep the accounting equation in balance, the increase in liabilities (L) must be offset by a *decrease* in owners' equity (OE), giving rise to a *negative translation adjustment.* This has a *debit* balance. *Liabilities translated at the current exchange rate when the foreign currency has appreciated generate a negative (debit) translation adjustment.*

Balance Sheet Exposure

Balance sheet items (assets and liabilities) translated at the *current* exchange rate change in dollar value from balance sheet to balance sheet as a result of the change in exchange rate. These items are *exposed* to translation adjustment. Balance sheet items translated at *historical* exchange rates do not change in dollar value from one balance sheet to the next. These items are *not* exposed to translation adjustment. Exposure to translation adjustment is referred to as *balance sheet, translation,* or *accounting exposure. Transaction exposure,* discussed in the previous chapter, arises when a company has foreign currency receivables and payables and can be contrasted with *balance sheet exposure* in the following way: *Transaction exposure gives rise to foreign exchange gains and losses that are ultimately realized in cash; translation adjustments arising from balance sheet exposure do not directly result in cash inflows or outflows.*

Each item translated at the current exchange rate is exposed to translation adjustment. In effect, a separate translation adjustment exists for each of these exposed items. However, negative translation adjustments on liabilities offset positive translation adjustments on assets when the foreign currency appreciates. If total exposed assets equal total exposed liabilities throughout the year, the translation adjustments (although perhaps significant on an individual basis) net to a zero balance. The *net* translation adjustment needed to keep the consolidated balance sheet in balance is based solely on the *net asset* or *net liability* exposure.

A foreign operation has a *net asset balance sheet exposure* when assets translated at the current exchange rate are higher in amount than liabilities translated at the current exchange rate. A *net liability balance sheet exposure* exists when liabilities translated at the current exchange rate are higher than assets translated at the current exchange rate. The following summarizes the relationship between exchange rate fluctuations, balance sheet exposure, and translation adjustments:

Balance Sheet Exposure	Foreign Currency (FC)	
	Appreciates	**Depreciates**
Net asset	Positive translation adjustment	Negative translation adjustment
Net liability	Negative translation adjustment	Positive translation adjustment

Exactly how to handle the translation adjustment in the consolidated financial statements is a matter of some debate. The major issue is whether the translation adjustment should be treated as a *translation gain or loss reported in net income* (and then closed to retained earnings) or whether the translation adjustment should be treated as a *direct adjustment to owners' equity* (in accumulated other comprehensive income) *without affecting net income.* We consider this issue in more detail later after examining methods of translation.

LO 8-1

Explain the theoretical underpinnings and the limitations of the current rate and temporal methods.

Translation Methods

Two major translation methods are currently used: (1) the current rate method and (2) the temporal method. In this section, we discuss the concepts and basic procedures of each method from the perspective of a U.S.–based multinational company translating foreign currency financial statements into U.S. dollars.

Current Rate Method

The basic assumption underlying the *current rate method* is that a company's *net investment* in a foreign operation is *exposed* to foreign exchange risk. In other words, a foreign operation represents a foreign currency net asset and if the foreign currency *decreases* in value against the U.S. dollar, a *decrease in the U.S. dollar value of the foreign currency net asset* occurs. This decrease in U.S. dollar value of the net investment will be reflected by reporting a *negative* (debit balance) translation adjustment in the consolidated financial statements. If the foreign currency *increases* in value, an *increase in the U.S. dollar value of the net asset* occurs and will be reflected through a *positive* (credit balance) translation adjustment.

To measure the net investment's exposure to foreign exchange risk, *all assets and all liabilities* of the foreign operation are translated at the *current* exchange rate. Stockholders' equity items are translated at historical rates. *The balance sheet exposure under the current rate method is equal to the foreign operation's net asset (total assets minus total liabilities) position.*[4]

Total assets > Total liabilities → Net asset exposure

A positive translation adjustment arises when the foreign currency appreciates, and a negative translation adjustment arises when the foreign currency depreciates.

To reiterate, assets and liabilities are translated at the current rate and stockholders' equity is translated at historical rates to reflect the fact that the current rate method assumes that the company's net investment in a foreign operation is exposed to foreign exchange risk; net investment is equal to stockholders' equity.

Another reason to translate equity accounts at historical rates is so that the translated amount for the subsidiary's equity accounts will be equal to the original amount of the investment in subsidiary on the parent's balance sheet. Otherwise, the parent will not be able to exactly eliminate the investment in subsidiary account against the subsidiary's stockholders' equity accounts on the consolidation worksheet.

As mentioned, the major difference between the translation adjustment and a foreign exchange gain or loss is that the translation adjustment is not necessarily realized through inflows and outflows of cash. The translation adjustment that arises when using the current rate method is unrealized. It can become a realized gain or loss only if the foreign operation is sold (for its book value) and the foreign currency proceeds from the sale are converted into U.S. dollars.

The current rate method requires translation of all income statement items at the exchange rate in effect at the date of accounting recognition. For example, January 1 sales revenue should be translated at the January 1 exchange rate, January 2 sales at the January 2 exchange rate, and so on. With so many transactions, this would be overly burdensome. Thus, in many cases, an assumption can be made that the revenue or expense is incurred evenly throughout

---

[4] In rare cases, a foreign subsidiary could have liabilities higher than assets (negative stockholders' equity). In those cases, a net liability exposure exists under the current rate method.

the accounting period and a weighted average-for-the-period exchange rate can be used for translation. However, when an income account, such as a gain or loss, occurs at a specific point in time, the exchange rate at that date should be used for translation.

Temporal Method

The basic objective underlying the *temporal method* of translation is to produce a set of U.S. dollar–translated financial statements as if the foreign subsidiary had actually used U.S. dollars in conducting its operations. Continuing with the Gualos subsidiary example, Southwestern, the U.S. parent, should report the Land account on the consolidated balance sheet at the amount of U.S. dollars that it would have spent if it had sent dollars to the subsidiary to purchase land. Because the land cost 150,000 vilseks at a time when one vilsek could be acquired with $0.20, the parent would have sent $30,000 to the subsidiary to acquire the land; this is the land's historical cost *in U.S. dollar terms*. The following rule is consistent with the temporal method's underlying objective:

1. Assets and liabilities carried on the foreign operation's balance sheet at *historical cost* are translated at *historical* exchange rates to yield an equivalent historical cost in U.S. dollars.
2. Conversely, assets and liabilities carried at a *current or future value* are translated at the *current* exchange rate to yield an equivalent current value in U.S. dollars.

Application of this rule maintains the underlying valuation method (current value or historical cost) that the foreign subsidiary uses in accounting for its assets and liabilities. In addition, stockholders' equity accounts are translated at historical exchange rates. Similar to the current rate method, this ensures that the translated amount of subsidiary's stockholders' equity is equal to the original amount of the investment in subsidiary on the parent's balance sheet.

Cash, marketable securities, receivables, and most liabilities are carried at current or future value and translated at the *current* exchange rate under the temporal method.[5] The temporal method generates either a net asset or a net liability balance sheet exposure, depending on whether cash plus marketable securities plus receivables are more than or less than liabilities.

Cash + Marketable securities + Receivables > Liabilities → Net asset exposure
Cash + Marketable securities + Receivables < Liabilities → Net liability exposure

Because the amount of liabilities (current plus long term) translated at the current exchange rate usually exceeds the amount of assets translated at the current exchange rate, *a net liability exposure generally exists when the temporal method is used.*

One way to understand the concept of exposure underlying the temporal method is to suppose that the parent actually carries on its balance sheet the foreign operation's cash, marketable securities, receivables, and payables. For example, consider the Japanese subsidiary of a U.S. parent company. The Japanese subsidiary's yen receivables that result from sales in Japan may be thought of as Japanese yen receivables of the U.S. parent that result from export sales to Japan. If the U.S. parent had yen receivables on its balance sheet, a decrease in the yen's value would result in a *foreign exchange loss*. A foreign exchange loss also occurs on the Japanese yen held in cash by the U.S. parent and on the Japanese yen–denominated marketable securities. A foreign exchange gain on the parent's Japanese yen payables resulting from foreign purchases would offset these foreign exchange losses. Whether a net gain or a net loss exists depends on the relative amount of yen cash, marketable securities, and receivables versus yen payables. Under the temporal method, the translation adjustment measures the "net foreign exchange gain or loss" on the foreign

---

[5] Under current authoritative literature, all marketable equity securities and marketable debt securities that are classified as "trading" or "available for sale" are carried at fair value. Marketable debt securities classified as "held to maturity" are carried at amortized cost. Throughout the remainder of this chapter, we will assume that all marketable securities are reported at fair value.

operation's cash, marketable securities, receivables, and payables, *as if those items were actually carried on the parent's books.*

Again, the major difference between the translation adjustment resulting from the use of the temporal method and a foreign exchange gain or loss is that the translation adjustment is not necessarily realized through inflows or outflows of cash. The U.S. dollar translation adjustment in this case *is realized* only if (1) the parent sends U.S. dollars to the Japanese subsidiary to pay all of its yen liabilities and (2) the subsidiary converts its yen receivables and marketable securities into yen cash and then sends this amount plus the amount in its yen cash account to the U.S. parent, which converts it into U.S. dollars.

The temporal method translates income statement items at exchange rates that exist when the revenue is generated or the expense is incurred. For most items, an assumption can be made that the revenue or expense is incurred evenly throughout the accounting period and an average-for-the-period exchange rate can be used for translation. However, some expenses are related to assets carried at historical cost—for example, cost of goods sold, depreciation of property, plant, and equipment, and amortization of intangibles. Because the related assets are translated at historical exchange rates, these expenses must be translated at historical rates as well.

The current rate method and temporal method are the two methods currently used in the United States and in all countries that have adopted International Financial Reporting Standards as their local GAAP. A summary of the appropriate exchange rates for selected financial statement items under these two methods is presented in Exhibit 8.1.

Translation of Retained Earnings

Stockholders' equity items are translated at historical exchange rates under both the current rate and temporal methods. This creates somewhat of a problem in translating retained

EXHIBIT 8.1
Exchange Rates for Selected Financial Statement Items

	Temporal Method Exchange Rate	Current Rate Method Exchange Rate
	Balance Sheet	**Balance Sheet**
Assets		
Cash and receivables	Current	Current
Marketable securities	Current*	Current
Inventory at net realizable value	Current	Current
Inventory at cost	Historical	Current
Prepaid expenses	Historical	Current
Property, plant, and equipment	Historical	Current
Intangible assets	Historical	Current
Liabilities		
Current liabilities	Current	Current
Deferred income	Historical	Current
Long-term debt	Current	Current
Stockholders' equity		
Capital stock	Historical	Historical
Additional paid-in capital	Historical	Historical
Retained earnings	Composite	Composite
Dividends	Historical	Historical
	Income Statement	**Income Statement**
Revenues	Average	Average
Most expenses	Average	Average
Cost of goods sold	Historical	Average
Depreciation of property, plant, and equipment	Historical	Average
Amortization of intangibles	Historical	Average

*Marketable debt securities classified as held to maturity are carried at amortized cost and translated at the historical exchange rate under the temporal method.

earnings. Retained earnings is an accumulation of all of the net income less dividends declared by a company since its inception. At the end of the first year of a company's operations, foreign currency (FC) retained earnings (R/E) is translated as follows:

Net income in FC	[translated per method used to translate income statement items]	= Net income in $
− Dividends in FC	× historical exchange rate when declared	= −Dividends in $
Ending R/E in FC		Ending R/E in $

The ending dollar amount of retained earnings in Year 1 becomes the beginning dollar retained earnings for Year 2, and the translated retained earnings in Year 2 (and subsequent years) are then determined as follows:

Beginning R/E in FC	(carried forward from last year's translation)	= Beginning R/E in $
+ Net income in FC	[translated per method used to translate income statement items]	= + Net income in $
− Dividends in FC	× historical exchange rate when declared	= − Dividends in $
Ending R/E in FC		Ending R/E in $

The same approach translates retained earnings under both the current rate and the temporal methods. The only difference is that translation of the current period net income is calculated differently under the two methods.

Complicating Aspects of the Temporal Method

Under the temporal method, keeping a record of the acquisition date exchange rates is necessary when translating inventory, prepaid expenses, property, plant and equipment, and intangible assets because these assets, carried at historical cost, are translated at historical exchange rates. Keeping track of the historical rates for these assets is not necessary under the current rate method. Translating these assets at historical rates makes the application of the temporal method more complicated than the current rate method.

Calculation of Cost of Goods Sold

Under the *current rate method,* the account Cost of Goods Sold (COGS) in foreign currency (FC) is simply translated using the average-for-the-period exchange rate (ER):

$$COGS \text{ in } FC \times Average \text{ } ER = COGS \text{ in } \$$$

Under the *temporal method,* no single exchange rate can be used to directly translate COGS in FC into COGS in dollars. Instead, COGS must be decomposed into beginning inventory, purchases, and ending inventory, and each component of COGS must then be translated at its appropriate historical rate. For example, if a company acquires beginning inventory (FIFO basis) in the year 2017 evenly throughout the fourth quarter of 2016, then it uses the average exchange rate in the fourth quarter of 2016 to translate beginning inventory. Likewise, it uses the fourth quarter (4thQ) 2017 exchange rate to translate ending inventory. When purchases can be assumed to have been made evenly throughout 2017, the average 2017 exchange rate is used to translate purchases:

Beginning inventory in FC	×	Historical ER (4thQ 2016)	=	Beginning inventory in $
+ Purchases in FC	×	Average ER (2017)	=	+ Purchases in $
− Ending inventory in FC	×	Historical ER (4thQ 2017)	=	− Ending inventory in $
COGS in FC				COGS in $

Application of the Lower-of-Cost-or-Net-Realizable-Value Rule

Under the *current rate method,* the ending inventory reported on the foreign currency balance sheet is translated at the current exchange rate regardless of whether it is carried at cost or a lower net realizable value. Application of the *temporal method* requires the inventory's foreign currency cost to be translated into U.S. dollars at the historical exchange rate and foreign currency net realizable value to be translated into U.S. dollars at the current exchange rate. The *lower of the dollar cost and dollar net realizable value* is reported on the consolidated balance sheet. As a result, inventory can be carried at foreign currency cost on the foreign currency balance sheet and at U.S. dollar–translated net realizable value on the U.S. dollar consolidated balance sheet, and vice versa.

Property, Plant, and Equipment, Depreciation, and Accumulated Depreciation

The *temporal method* requires translating property, plant, and equipment acquired at different times at different (historical) exchange rates. The same is true for depreciation of property, plant, and equipment and accumulated depreciation related to property, plant, and equipment.

For example, assume that a company purchases a piece of equipment on January 1, 2015, for FC 1,000 when the exchange rate is $1.00 per FC. It purchases another item of equipment one year later on January 1, 2016, for FC 5,000 when the exchange rate is $1.20 per FC. Both pieces of equipment have a five-year useful life. The temporal method reports the amount of the equipment on the consolidated balance sheet on December 31, 2017, when the exchange rate is $1.50 per FC, as follows:

$$
\begin{array}{llll}
\text{FC } 1{,}000 \times \$1.00 & = \$1{,}000 \\
5{,}000 \times \ \ 1.20 & = \ \ 6{,}000 \\
\hline
\text{FC } 6{,}000 & \ \ \ \ \ \ \ \ \ \ \$7{,}000 \\
\end{array}
$$

Depreciation expense for 2017 under the temporal method is calculated as shown here:

$$
\begin{array}{llll}
\text{FC } \ \ \ 200 \times \$1.00 & = \$ \ \ 200 \\
1{,}000 \times \ \ 1.20 & = \ \ 1{,}200 \\
\hline
\text{FC } 1{,}200 & \ \ \ \ \ \ \ \ \$1{,}400 \\
\end{array}
$$

Accumulated depreciation under the temporal method is calculated as shown:

$$
\begin{array}{llll}
\text{FC } \ \ \ 600 \times \$1.00 & = \$ \ \ 600 \\
2{,}000 \times \ \ 1.20 & = \ \ 2{,}400 \\
\hline
\text{FC } 2{,}600 & \ \ \ \ \ \ \ \ \$3{,}000 \\
\end{array}
$$

Similar procedures apply for intangible assets as well.

The *current rate method* reports equipment on the December 31, 2017, balance sheet at $9,000 (FC 6,000 × $1.50). Depreciation expense is translated at the average exchange rate of $1.40 to be $1,680 (FC 1,200 × $1.40), and accumulated depreciation is $3,900 (FC 2,600 × $1.50 = $3,900).

In this example, the foreign subsidiary has only two pieces of equipment requiring translation. In comparison with the current rate method, the temporal method can require substantial additional work for subsidiaries that own hundreds and thousands of items of property, plant, and equipment.

Gain or Loss on the Sale of an Asset

Assume that a foreign subsidiary sells land that cost FC 1,000 at a selling price of FC 1,200. The subsidiary reports an FC 200 gain on the sale of land on its income statement. It acquired the land when the exchange rate was $1.00 per FC; it made the sale when the exchange rate was $1.20 per FC; and the exchange rate at the balance sheet date is $1.50 per FC. How should the gain on the sale of an asset be translated into U.S. dollars?

The *current rate method* translates the gain on sale of land at the exchange rate in effect at the date of sale:

$$FC\ 200 \times \$1.20 = \$240$$

The *temporal method* cannot translate the gain on the sale of land directly. Instead, it requires translating the cash received and the cost of the land sold into U.S. dollars separately, with the difference being the U.S. dollar value of the gain. In accordance with the rules of the temporal method, the Cash account is translated at the exchange rate on the date of sale, and the Land account is translated at the historical rate:

Cash	FC 1,200	×	$1.20	=	$1,440
Land	1,000	×	1.00	=	1,000
Gain	FC 200				$ 440

Treatment of Translation Adjustment

The *first issue* related to the translation of foreign currency financial statements is selecting the appropriate method. The *second issue* in financial statement translation relates to deciding *where to report the resulting translation adjustment in the consolidated financial statements.* There are two prevailing schools of thought with regard to this second issue:

1. *Translation gain or loss:* This treatment considers the translation adjustment to be a gain or loss analogous to the gains and losses arising from foreign currency transactions and reports it in net income in the period in which the fluctuation in the exchange rate occurs.

The first of two conceptual problems with treating translation adjustments as gains or losses in income is that the gain or loss is unrealized; that is, no cash inflow or outflow accompanies it. The second problem is that the gain or loss could be inconsistent with economic reality. For example, the depreciation of a foreign currency can have a *positive* impact on the foreign operation's export sales and income, but the particular translation method used gives rise to a translation *loss.*

2. *Cumulative translation adjustment in other comprehensive income:* The alternative to reporting the translation adjustment as a gain or loss in net income is to include it in other comprehensive income. In effect, this treatment defers the gain or loss in stockholders' equity (Accumulated Other Comprehensive Income or AOCI) until it is realized in some way. As a balance sheet account, the cumulative translation adjustment is not closed at the end of an accounting period and fluctuates in amount over time.

The two major translation methods and the two possible treatments for the translation adjustment give rise to these four possible combinations:

Combination	Translation Method	Treatment of Translation Adjustment
A	Temporal	Gain or loss in Net Income
B	Temporal	Deferred in Other Comprehensive Income
C	Current rate	Gain or loss in Net Income
D	Current rate	Deferred in Other Comprehensive Income

Authoritative Guidance

Prior to 1975, the United States had no authoritative guidance on which translation method to use or where to report the translation adjustment in the consolidated financial statements. Different companies used different combinations. As an indication of the importance of this particular accounting issue, the first official pronouncement issued by the newly created FASB in 1974 was *SFAS 1,* "Disclosure of Foreign Currency Translation Information." It did not express a preference for any particular combination but simply required disclosure of the method used and the treatment of the translation adjustment.

The use of different combinations by different companies created a lack of comparability across companies. To eliminate this noncomparability, in 1975 the FASB issued *SFAS 8,* "Accounting for the Translation of Foreign Currency Transactions and Foreign Currency Financial Statements." It mandated use of the *temporal method* with all companies reporting *translation gains or losses* in net income for all foreign operations.

U.S. multinational companies (MNCs) strongly opposed *SFAS 8.* Specifically, they considered reporting translation gains and losses in income to be inappropriate because they are unrealized. Moreover, because currency fluctuations often reversed themselves in subsequent quarters, artificial volatility in quarterly earnings resulted.

After releasing two exposure drafts proposing new translation rules, the FASB finally issued *SFAS 52,* "Foreign Currency Translation," in 1981. This resulted in a complete overhaul of U.S. GAAP with regard to foreign currency translation. A narrow four-to-three vote of the board approving *SFAS 52* indicates how contentious the issue of foreign currency translation has been. Despite the narrow vote, *SFAS 52* has stood the test of time and was incorporated into the FASB *Accounting Standards Codification®* (ASC) in 2009 as part of Topic 830, "Foreign Currency Matters."

Determining the Appropriate Translation Method

LO 8-2

Describe guidelines for determining when foreign currency financial statements are to be translated using the current rate method and when they are to be remeasured using the temporal method.

Implicit in the *temporal method* is the assumption that foreign subsidiaries of U.S. MNCs have very close ties to their parent companies and that they would actually carry out their day-to-day operations and keep their books in the U.S. dollar if they could. To reflect the integrated nature of the foreign subsidiary with its U.S. parent, the translation process should create a set of U.S. dollar–translated financial statements as if the foreign subsidiary had actually used the dollar in carrying out its activities. This is the *U.S. dollar perspective* to translation.

In developing the current authoritative guidance, the FASB recognized two types of foreign entities. First, some foreign entities are so closely integrated with their parents that they conduct much of their business in U.S. dollars. *Second, other foreign entities are relatively self-contained and integrated with the local economy; primarily, they use a foreign currency in their daily operations.* For the first type of entity, the FASB determined that the U.S. dollar perspective still applies and, therefore, use of the temporal method with translation gains and losses reported in net income is still relevant.

For the second relatively independent type of entity, a *local currency perspective* to translation is applicable. For this type of entity, the FASB determined that a different translation methodology, namely the *current rate method,* should be used for translation and that translation adjustments should be reported as a *separate component in accumulated other comprehensive income* on the balance sheet.

Functional Currency

To determine whether a specific foreign operation is integrated with its parent or self-contained and integrated with the local economy, the FASB created the concept of the *functional currency.* The functional currency is the primary currency of the foreign entity's operating environment. It can be either the parent's currency (U.S.$ for a U.S.–based company) or a foreign currency (generally the local currency). The functional currency orientation results in the following rule:

Functional Currency	Translation Method	Translation Adjustment
U.S. dollar	Temporal method	Gain (loss) in Net Income
Foreign currency	Current rate method	Separate component of Other Comprehensive Income (Stockholders' Equity)

In addition to introducing the concept of the *functional currency,* the FASB introduced some new terminology. The *reporting currency* is the currency in which the entity prepares its financial statements. For U.S.–based corporations, this is the U.S. dollar. If a foreign operation's functional currency is the U.S. dollar, foreign currency balances must be *remeasured* into U.S. dollars using the temporal method with translation adjustments reported as *remeasurement gains and losses* in net income. When a foreign currency is the functional currency, foreign currency balances are *translated* using the current rate method and a *translation adjustment* is reported in the stockholders' equity section of the balance sheet.

The functional currency is essentially a matter of fact. However, in some cases the facts will not clearly indicate a single functional currency. Management's judgment is essential in assessing the facts to determine a foreign entity's functional currency. Indicators provided by the FASB to guide parent company management in its determination of a foreign entity's functional currency are presented in Exhibit 8.2. Current authoritative literature provides no guidance as to how to weight these indicators in determining the functional currency. Leaving the decision about identifying the functional currency up to management allows some flexibility in this process.

Highly Inflationary Economies

Multinationals do not need to determine the functional currency of those foreign entities located in a *highly inflationary economy*. In those cases, entities must use the *temporal method with remeasurement gains or losses reported in net income*.

A country is defined as having a *highly inflationary economy* when its cumulative three-year inflation exceeds 100 percent. With compounding, this equates to an average of approximately 26 percent per year for three years in a row. Countries that have met this definition at some time include Argentina, Brazil, Israel, Mexico, and Turkey. In any given year, a country may or may not be classified as highly inflationary, depending on its most recent three-year experience with inflation.

One reason for this rule is to avoid a "disappearing plant problem" caused by using the current rate method in a country with high inflation. Remember that under the current rate method, all assets (including fixed assets) are translated at the current exchange rate. To see the problem this creates in a highly inflationary economy, consider the following hypothetical example.

The Brazilian subsidiary of a U.S. parent purchased land at the end of 1984 for 10,000,000 cruzeiros (Cr$) when the exchange rate was $0.001 per Cr$. Under the *current rate method,* Land is reported in the parent's consolidated balance sheet (B.S.) at $10,000:

	Historical Cost		Current ER		Consolidated B.S.
1984	Cr$ 10,000,000	×	$0.001	=	$10,000

In 1985, Brazil experienced roughly 200 percent inflation. Accordingly, with the forces of purchasing power parity at work, the cruzeiro plummeted against the U.S. dollar to a value of

EXHIBIT 8.2
Indicators for Determining the Functional Currency

	Indication That Functional Currency Is the:	
Indicator	**Foreign Currency**	**Parent's Currency**
Cash flow	Primarily in FC and does not affect parent's cash flows.	Directly impacts parent's cash flows on a current basis.
Sales price	Not affected on short-term basis by changes in exchange rate.	Affected on short-term basis by changes in exchange rate.
Sales market	Active local sales market.	Sales market mostly in parent's country or sales denominated in parent's currency.
Expenses	Primarily local costs.	Primarily costs for components obtained from parent's country.
Financing	Primarily denominated in foreign currency and FC cash flows adequate to service obligations.	Primarily from parent or denominated in parent currency or FC cash flows not adequate to service obligations.
Intra-entity transactions	Low volume of intra-entity transactions, not extensive interrelationship with parent's operations.	High volume of intra-entity transactions and extensive interrelationship with parent's operations.

$0.00025 at the end of 1985. Under the current rate method, the parent's consolidated balance sheet reports Land at $2,500, and a negative translation adjustment of $7,500 results:

	Historical Cost		Current ER		Consolidated B.S.
1985	Cr$ 10,000,000	×	$0.00025	=	$2,500

Using the current rate method, 75 percent of the Land's U.S. dollar value "disappeared" in one year—and land is not even a depreciable asset!

In the exposure draft that led to the current authoritative guidance on translation, the FASB proposed requiring companies with operations in highly inflationary countries to first *restate* the foreign financial statements for inflation and then *translate* all financial statement accounts using the current exchange rate. For example, with 200 percent inflation in 1985, the Land account would have been written up to Cr$ 40,000,000 and then translated at the current exchange rate of $0.00025, producing a U.S. dollar–translated amount of $10,000, the same as in 1984.

Companies objected to making inflation adjustments, however, because of a lack of reliable inflation indices in many countries. The FASB backed off from requiring the *restate/ translate* approach; instead it requires using the temporal method in highly inflationary countries. In the previous example, under the *temporal method,* a firm uses the historical rate of $0.001 to translate the land value year after year. The firm carries land on the consolidated balance sheet at $10,000 each year, thereby avoiding the disappearing plant problem.

Once a country is classified as highly inflationary, a decrease in the cumulative three-year inflation rate below 100 percent is not necessarily sufficient to remove it from this classification. FASB ASC 830-10-55-25 and the SEC staff suggest that if there is no evidence to suggest that the drop below 100 percent is "other than temporary," the country should continue to be viewed as highly inflationary. The magnitude of the decrease below 100 percent, the length of time the rate is under 100 percent, and the country's current economic conditions should be taken into account in the "other than temporary" analysis.

In recent years, only a few countries in the world have met the FASB's definition of highly inflationary. One of the most significant countries recently exceeding this threshold is Venezuela, which has been identified as highly inflationary since January 2010.[6] Many U.S. companies, especially those in the energy industry, have subsidiaries in Venezuela. In 2010, those U.S. parent companies that previously designated their Venezuelan operation as having the local currency as functional currency, and therefore used the current rate method for translation, were compelled to change their translation method to the temporal method and begin reporting remeasurement gains and losses in net income.

Appropriate Exchange Rate

In some countries, such as Venezuela, there is more than one rate at which the local currency can be converted into foreign currency. Often there is an "official rate" that is available from the Central Bank, and a "parallel rate" that is available in the open (sometimes illegal) market. Or in some countries there is one rate for certain types of transactions and another rate for other transactions. For example, in January 2010, in conjunction with an official devaluation of the local currency, the Venezuelan government established an exchange rate of 2.6 bolivar fuertes (BsF) per one U.S. dollar for *essential* imports (such as food and medicine), and an exchange rate of BsF 4.3 per U.S.$ for the import of *nonessential* goods. The existence of multiple exchange rates raises the question of which exchange rate to use in the financial statement translation process.

When the temporal method is used, ASC 830-20-30-3 indicates that the appropriate rate to use is the applicable rate at which a transaction could be settled, which is a matter for management judgment. In the case of Venezuela, for example, the Center for Audit Quality's International Practices Task Force (IPTF) determined that while Venezuelan law generally requires

[6] The International Practices Task Force (IPTF) of the Center for Audit Quality (CAQ) SEC Regulations Committee monitors the inflationary status of certain countries and identifies those that meet the FASB's definition of highly inflationary. In May 2015, Malawi, Sudan, and Venezuela were the only countries identified by the IPTF with three-year cumulative inflation rates exceeding 100 percent. http://www.thecaq.org/docs/default-source/iptf-highlights/iptf-may-2015-highlights.pdf?sfvrsn=2.

foreign currency transactions to be settled at the official exchange rate, because some transactions denominated in U.S. dollars may be settled using the parallel rate of exchange, either exchange rate might be appropriate for the translation of U.S.$-denominated assets and liabilities.

In contrast, when the current rate method is used, ASC 830-30-45-6 states that the exchange rate applicable for converting dividend remittances into U.S. dollars should be used to translate financial statements. Generally, this will be the official exchange rate established by the Central Bank or other governmental authority.

International Accounting Standard 21—The Effects of Changes in Foreign Exchange Rates

IAS 21, "The Effects of Changes in Foreign Exchange Rates," provides guidance in IFRS with respect to the translation of foreign currency financial statements. *IAS 21* generally follows the functional currency approach introduced by the FASB. Under *IAS 21,* as is true under U.S. GAAP, a foreign subsidiary's financial statements are translated using the current rate method when a foreign currency is the functional currency and are remeasured using the temporal method when the parent company's currency is the functional currency. Significant differences between IFRS and U.S. GAAP relate to (*a*) the hierarchy of factors used to determine the functional currency and (*b*) the method used to translate the foreign currency statements of a subsidiary located in a hyperinflationary country.

Although stated differently, the factors to be considered in determining the functional currency of a foreign subsidiary in *IAS 21* generally are consistent with U.S. GAAP functional currency indicators. Specifically, *IAS 21* indicates that the *primary* factors to be considered are:

1. The currency that mainly influences sales price.
2. The currency of the country whose competitive forces and regulations mainly determine sales price.
3. The currency that mainly influences labor, material, and other costs of providing goods and services.

Other factors to be considered are:

1. The currency in which funds from financing activities are generated.
2. The currency in which receipts from operating activities are retained.
3. Whether the foreign operation carries out its activities as an extension of the parent or with a significant degree of autonomy.
4. The volume of transactions with the parent.
5. Whether cash flows generated by the foreign operation directly affect the cash flows of the parent.
6. Whether cash flows generated by the foreign operation are sufficient to service its debt.

IAS 21 states that when the above indicators are mixed and the functional currency is not obvious, the parent must give priority to the primary indicators in determining the foreign entity's functional currency.

As noted earlier, U.S. GAAP is silent with respect to weights to be assigned to various indicators to determine the functional currency and there is no hierarchy provided. Because of this difference in the functional currency determination process, it is possible that a foreign subsidiary could be determined to have a functional currency under IFRS that would be different from the functional currency determined under U.S. GAAP.

Under *IAS 21,* the financial statements of a foreign subsidiary located in a hyperinflationary economy are translated into the parent's currency using a two-step process. First, the financial statements are restated for local inflation in accordance with *IAS 29,* "Financial Reporting in Hyperinflationary Economies." Second, each financial statement line item, which has now been restated for local inflation, is translated using the current exchange rate. In effect, neither the temporal method nor the current rate method is used when the subsidiary is located in a country experiencing hyperinflation. Because all balance sheet accounts, including stockholders' equity, are translated at the current exchange rate, a translation adjustment does not exist.

Unlike U.S. GAAP, IFRS does not provide a bright-line threshold to identify a hyperinflationary economy. Instead, *IAS 29* provides a list of characteristics that indicate hyperinflation, including (*a*) the general population prefers to keep its wealth in a relatively stable foreign currency; (*b*) interest rates, wages, and other prices are linked to a price index; and (*c*) the cumulative rate of inflation over three years is approaching, or exceeds, 100 percent. As noted earlier in this chapter, under current U.S. GAAP, the financial statements of a foreign subsidiary located in a highly inflationary economy must be translated using the temporal method, and high inflation is defined as a cumulative three-year inflation of 100 percent or more.

The Translation Process Illustrated

To provide a basis for demonstrating the translation and remeasurement procedures prescribed by current authoritative literature, assume that USCO (a U.S.–based company) forms a wholly owned subsidiary in Switzerland (SWISSCO) on December 31, 2016. On that date, USCO invested $300,000 in exchange for all of the subsidiary's common stock. Given the exchange rate of $0.60 per Swiss franc (CHF), the initial capital investment was CHF 500,000, of which CHF 150,000 was immediately invested in inventory and the remainder held in cash. Thus, SWISSCO began operations on January 1, 2017, with stockholders' equity (net assets) of CHF 500,000 and net monetary assets of CHF 350,000. (Recall that monetary assets consist primarily of cash, receivables, and marketable securities.)

SWISSCO
Opening Balance Sheet
January 1, 2017

Assets	CHF	Liabilities and Equity	CHF
Cash	CHF 350,000	Common stock	CHF 100,000
Inventory.	150,000	Additional paid-in capital	400,000
	CHF 500,000		CHF 500,000

During 2017, SWISSCO purchased property, plant, and equipment, acquired a patent, and purchased additional inventory, primarily on account. It negotiated a five-year loan to help finance the purchase of equipment. It sold goods, primarily on account, and incurred expenses. It generated income after taxes of CHF 470,000 and declared dividends of CHF 150,000 on October 1, 2017.

As a company incorporated in Switzerland, SWISSCO accounts for its activities using IFRS, which differs from U.S. GAAP in many respects. As noted in the introduction to this chapter, to prepare consolidated financial statements, USCO must first convert SWISSCO's financial statements to a U.S. GAAP basis.[7] SWISSCO's U.S. GAAP financial statements for the year 2017 in Swiss francs appear in Exhibit 8.3.

EXHIBIT 8.3
Foreign Currency Financial Statements

SWISSCO
Income Statement
For Year Ending December 31, 2017

	CHF
Sales	4,000,000
Cost of goods sold	(3,000,000)
Gross profit	1,000,000
Depreciation expense	(100,000)
Amortization expense	(10,000)
Other expenses	(220,000)
Income before income taxes	670,000
Income taxes	(200,000)
Net income	470,000

(continued)

[7] Differences in accounting rules across countries are discussed in more detail in Chapter 11.

Statement of Retained Earnings
For Year Ending December 31, 2017

	CHF
Retained earnings, 1/1/17	–0–
Net income, 2017	470,000
Less: Dividends, 10/1/17	(150,000)
Retained earnings, 12/31/17	320,000

Balance Sheet December 31, 2017

Assets	CHF	Liabilities and Equity	CHF
Cash	130,000	Accounts payable	600,000
Accounts receivable	200,000	Total current liabilities	600,000
Inventory*	400,000	Long-term debt	250,000
Total current assets	730,000	Total liabilities	850,000
Property, plant & equipment	1,000,000	Common stock	100,000
Accumulated depreciation	(100,000)	Additional paid-in capital	400,000
Patents, net	40,000	Retained earnings	320,000
Total assets	1,670,000	Total equity	820,000
		Total liabilities and equity	1,670,000

Statement of Cash Flows
For Year Ending December 31, 2017

	CHF
Operating activities:	
Net income	470,000
Add: Depreciation expense	100,000
Amortization expense	10,000
Increase in accounts receivable	(200,000)
Increase in inventory	(250,000)
Increase in accounts payable	600,000
Net cash from operations	730,000
Investing activities:	
Purchase of property, plant & equipment	(1,000,000)
Acquisition of patent	(50,000)
Net cash from investing activities	(1,050,000)
Financing activities:	
Proceeds from long-term debt	250,000
Payment of dividends	(150,000)
Net cash from financing activities	100,000
Decrease in cash	(220,000)
Cash at 12/31/16	350,000
Cash at 12/31/17	130,000

*Inventory is valued at FIFO cost under the lower-of-cost-or-market-value rule; ending inventory was acquired evenly throughout the fourth quarter.

To properly translate the Swiss franc financial statements into U.S. dollars, USCO must gather exchange rates between the Swiss franc and U.S. dollar at various points in time. Relevant exchange rates (in U.S. dollars) are as follows:

January 1, 2017..	$0.60
Rate when property, plant & equipment was acquired and long-term debt was incurred, March 15, 2017...................	0.61
Rate when patent was acquired, April 10, 2017	0.62
Average 2017	0.65
Rate when dividends were declared, October 1, 2017................	0.67
Average fourth quarter 2017......................................	0.68
December 31, 2017	0.70

The Swiss franc steadily appreciated against the dollar during the year, from a value of $0.60 on January 1 to $0.70 on December 31.

LO 8-3

Translate a foreign subsidiary's financial statements into its parent's reporting currency using the current rate method and calculate the related translation adjustment.

Translation of Financial Statements—Current Rate Method

The first step in translating foreign currency financial statements is to determine the functional currency. Assuming that the Swiss franc is the functional currency, the current rate method must be used with the cumulative translation adjustment reported in a separate component of stockholders' equity on the balance sheet. The amount of the cumulative translation adjustment can be determined indirectly as the amount that is needed to keep the translated balance sheet in balance. Translating the income statement first, followed by the statement of retained earnings, and then the balance sheet, facilitates the translation adjustment being reported in the balance sheet. (Conversely, the balance sheet is remeasured first when the temporal method is used.) Translation of the income statement and statement of retained earnings into U.S. dollars using the current rate method is shown in Exhibit 8.4.

EXHIBIT 8.4
Translation of Income Statement and Statement of Retained Earnings— Current Rate Method

SWISSCO
Income Statement
For Year Ending December 31, 2017

	CHF	Translation Rate*	U.S.$
Sales........................	CHF 4,000,000	0.65 A	$2,600,000
Cost of goods sold	(3,000,000)	0.65 A	(1,950,000)
Gross profit..................	1,000,000		650,000
Depreciation expense.........	(100,000)	0.65 A	(65,000)
Amortization expense.........	(10,000)	0.65 A	(6,500)
Other expenses..............	(220,000)	0.65 A	(143,000)
Income before income taxes...	670,000		435,500
Income taxes.................	(200,000)	0.65 A	(130,000)
Net income	CHF 470,000		$ 305,500

Statement of Retained Earnings
For Year Ending December 31, 2017

	CHF	Translation Rate*	U.S.$
Retained earnings, 1/1/17	CHF –0–		$ –0–
Net income, 2017	470,000	From income statement	305,500
Dividends, 10/1/17	(150,000)	0.67 H	(100,500)
Retained earnings, 12/31/17 ..	CHF 320,000		$ 205,000

*Indicates the exchange rate used and whether the rate is the current (C), average (A), or historical (H) rate.

All revenues and expenses are translated at the exchange rate in effect at the date of accounting recognition. We utilize the weighted average exchange rate for 2017 here because each revenue and expense in this illustration would have been recognized evenly throughout the year. However, when an income account, such as a gain or loss, occurs at a specific point in time, the exchange rate as of that date is applied. Depreciation and amortization expenses also are translated at the average rate for the year. These expenses accrue evenly throughout the year even though the journal entry to recognize them might not have been made until year-end for convenience.

The translated amount of net income for 2017 is brought down from the income statement into the statement of retained earnings. Dividends are translated at the exchange rate on the date of declaration.

Translation of the Balance Sheet

Looking at SWISSCO's translated balance sheet in Exhibit 8.5, note that all assets and liabilities are translated at the current exchange rate. Common stock and additional paid-in capital are translated at the exchange rate on the day the common stock was originally acquired by the parent company. Retained earnings at December 31, 2017, is brought down from the statement of retained earnings. Application of these procedures results in total assets of $1,169,000 and total liabilities and equities of $1,100,000. The balance sheet is brought into balance by creating a positive translation adjustment of $69,000 that is treated as an increase in Stockholders Equity.

Note that the translation adjustment for 2017 is a *positive* $69,000 (credit balance). The sign of the translation adjustment (positive or negative) is a function of two factors: (1) the nature of the balance sheet exposure (asset or liability) and (2) the change in the exchange rate

EXHIBIT 8.5
Translation of Balance Sheet—Current Rate Method

SWISSCO
Balance Sheet December 31, 2017

	CHF	Translation Rate	U.S.$
Assets			
Cash	CHF 130,000	0.70 C	$91,000
Accounts receivable	200,000	0.70 C	140,000
Inventory	400,000	0.70 C	280,000
Total current assets	730,000		511,000
Property, plant & equipment	1,000,000	0.70 C	700,000
Less: Accumulated depreciation	(100,000)	0.70 C	(70,000)
Patents, net	40,000	0.70 C	28,000
Total assets	CHF 1,670,000		$1,169,000
Liabilities and Equities			
Accounts payable	CHF 600,000	0.70 C	$ 420,000
Total current liabilities	600,000		420,000
Long-term debt	250,000	0.70 C	175,000
Total liabilities	850,000		595,000
Common stock	100,000	0.60 H	60,000
Additional paid-in capital	400,000	0.60 H	240,000
Retained earnings	320,000	From statement of R/E	205,000
Cumulative translation adjustment		To balance	69,000
Total equity	820,000		574,000
Total liabilities and equity	CHF 1,670,000		$1,169,000

(appreciation or depreciation). In this illustration, SWISSCO has a *net asset exposure* (total assets translated at the current exchange rate are more than total liabilities translated at the current exchange rate), and the Swiss franc has *appreciated,* creating a *positive translation adjustment.*

The translation adjustment can be derived as the amount needed to bring the balance sheet back into balance. The translation adjustment also can be calculated by considering the impact of exchange rate changes on the beginning balance and subsequent changes in the net asset position summarized as follows:

1. Translate the net asset balance of the subsidiary at the beginning of the year at the exchange rate in effect on that date (*a*).

2. Translate individual increases and decreases in the net asset balance during the year at the rates in effect when those increases and decreases occurred (*b*). Only a few events, such as net income, dividends, stock issuance, and the acquisition of treasury stock, actually change net assets. Transactions such as the acquisition of equipment or the payment of a liability have no effect on total net assets.

3. Combine the translated beginning net asset balance (*a*) and the translated value of the individual changes (*b*) to arrive at the relative value of the net assets being held prior to the impact of any exchange rate fluctuations during the year (*c*).

4. Translate the ending net asset balance at the current exchange rate to determine the reported value after all exchange rate changes have occurred (*d*).

5. Compare the translated value of the net assets prior to any rate changes (*c*) with the ending translated value (*d*). The difference is the result of exchange rate changes during the period. If (*c*) is higher than (*d*), a negative (debit) translation adjustment arises. If (*d*) is higher than (*c*), a positive (credit) translation adjustment results.

Computation of Translation Adjustment

Based on the process just described, the translation adjustment for SWISSCO in this example is calculated as follows:

Net asset balance, 1/1/17	CHF 500,000 × 0.60 = $300,000		(*a*)
Change in net assets:			
Net income, 2017	470,000 × 0.65 = 305,500		(*b*)
Dividends declared, 10/1/17	(150,000) × 0.67 = (100,500)		(*b*)
Net asset balance, 12/31/17	CHF 820,000	$505,000	(*c*)
Net asset balance, 12/31/17 at current			
exchange rate	CHF 820,000 × 0.70 = 574,000		(*d*)
Translation adjustment, 2017 (positive).		$(69,000)	

The process just described and demonstrated is used to calculate the current period's translation adjustment. Because SWISSCO began operations at the beginning of the current year, the $69,000 translation adjustment is the only amount that will be needed to keep the U.S. dollar consolidated balance sheet in balance. In subsequent years, a cumulative translation adjustment comprising the current year's translation adjustment plus translation adjustments from prior years will be included in stockholders' equity on the U.S. dollar consolidated balance sheet. Companies report the cumulative translation adjustment in Accumulated Other Comprehensive Income, along with unrealized foreign exchange gains and losses, gains and losses on cash flow hedges, unrealized gains and losses on available-for-sale marketable securities, and adjustments for pension accounting.

The cumulative translation adjustment remains within accumulated other comprehensive income only until the foreign operation is sold or liquidated. In the period in which sale or liquidation occurs, the cumulative translation adjustment related to the particular foreign entity is removed from accumulated other comprehensive income and included as part of the gain or loss on the sale of the investment. In effect, the accumulated unrealized foreign exchange gain or loss that has been deferred in accumulated other comprehensive income becomes realized when the entity is disposed of.

Translation of the Statement of Cash Flows

The current rate method requires translating all operating items in the statement of cash flows at the average-for-the-period exchange rate (see Exhibit 8.6). This is the same rate used for translating income statement items. Although the ending balances in Accounts Receivable, Inventory, and Accounts Payable on the balance sheet are translated at the current exchange rate, the average rate is used for the *changes* in these accounts because those changes are caused by operating activities (such as sales and purchases) that are translated at the average rate.

Investing and financing activities are translated at the exchange rate on the day the activity took place. Although long-term debt is translated in the balance sheet at the current rate, in the statement of cash flows, it is translated at the historical rate when the debt was incurred.

The $(4,500) "effect of exchange rate change on cash" is a part of the overall translation adjustment of $69,000. It represents that part of the translation adjustment attributable to a decrease in Cash and is derived as a balancing amount.

LO 8-4

Remeasure a foreign subsidiary's financial statements using the temporal method and calculate the associated remeasurement gain or loss.

Remeasurement of Financial Statements—Temporal Method

Now assume that a careful examination of the functional currency indicators in Exhibit 8.2 leads USCO's management to conclude that SWISSCO's functional currency is the U.S. dollar. In that case, the Swiss franc financial statements must be remeasured into U.S. dollars using the temporal method and the remeasurement gain or loss must be reported in income. To ensure that the remeasurement gain or loss is reported in income, it is easiest to remeasure the balance sheet first (as shown in Exhibit 8.7).

EXHIBIT 8.6
Translated Statement of Cash Flows—Current Rate Method

SWISSCO
Statement of Cash Flows
For Year Ending December 31, 2017

	CHF	Translation Rate	U.S.$
Operating activities:			
Net income	CHF 470,000	0.65 A	$305,500
Add: Depreciation	100,000	0.65 A	65,000
Amortization	10,000	0.65 A	6,500
Increase in accounts receivable	(200,000)	0.65 A	(130,000)
Increase in inventory	(250,000)	0.65 A	(162,500)
Increase in accounts payable	600,000	0.65 A	390,000
Net cash from operations	730,000		474,500
Investing activities:			
Purchase of property, plant & equipment . .	(1,000,000)	0.61 H	(610,000)
Acquisition of patent	(50,000)	0.62 H	(31,000)
Net cash from investing activities	(1,050,000)		(641,000)
Financing activities:			
Proceeds from long-term debt	250,000	0.61 H	152,500
Payment of dividends	(150,000)	0.67 H	(100,500)
Net cash from financing activities	100,000		52,000
Decrease in cash	(220,000)		(114,500)
Effect of exchange rate change on cash		To balance	(4,500)
Cash at December 31, 2016	CHF 350,000	0.60 H	210,000
Cash at December 31, 2017	CHF 130,000	0.70 C	$ 91,000

EXHIBIT 8.7
Remeasurement of Balance Sheet—Temporal Method

SWISSCO
Balance Sheet
December 31, 2017

	CHF	Remeasurement Rate	U.S.$
Assets			
Cash...........................	CHF 130,000	0.70 C	$91,000
Accounts receivable	200,000	0.70 C	140,000
Inventory	400,000	0.68 H	272,000
Total current assets............	730,000		503,000
Property, plant & equipment	1,000,000	0.61 H	610,000
Less: Accumulated depreciation....	(100,000)	0.61 H	(61,000)
Patents, net.....................	40,000	0.62 H	24,800
Total assets...................	CHF 1,670,000		$1,076,800
Liabilities and Equities			
Accounts payable	CHF 600,000	0.70 C	$ 420,000
Total current liabilities...........	600,000		420,000
Long-term debt...................	250,000	0.70 C	175,000
Total liabilities.................	850,000		595,000
Common stock..................	100,000	0.60 H	60,000
Additional paid-in capital	400,000	0.60 H	240,000
Retained earnings	320,000	To balance	181,800
Total equity...................	820,000		481,800
Total liabilities and equity........	CHF 1,670,000		$1,076,800

According to the procedures outlined in Exhibit 8.1, the temporal method remeasures cash, receivables, and liabilities into U.S. dollars using the current exchange rate of $0.70. Inventory (carried at FIFO cost), property, plant & equipment, patents, and contributed capital (common stock and additional paid-in capital) are remeasured at historical rates. These procedures result in total assets of $1,076,800, liabilities of $595,000, and contributed capital of $300,000. To balance the balance sheet, retained earnings must total $181,800. We verify the accuracy of this amount later.

Remeasurement of the Income Statement

Exhibit 8.8 shows the remeasurement of SWISSCO's income statement and statement of retained earnings. Revenues and expenses incurred evenly throughout the year (sales, other expenses, and income taxes) are remeasured at the average exchange rate of $0.65. Expenses related to assets remeasured at historical exchange rates (depreciation expense and amortization expense) are remeasured at relevant historical rates.

The following procedure remeasures cost of goods sold at historical exchange rates. Beginning inventory acquired on January 1 is remeasured at the exchange rate on that date ($0.60). Purchases made evenly throughout the year are remeasured at the average rate for the year ($0.65). Ending inventory (at FIFO cost) is purchased evenly throughout the fourth quarter of 2017 and the average exchange rate for the quarter ($0.68) is used to remeasure that component of cost of goods sold. These procedures result in cost of goods sold of $1,930,500, calculated as follows:

Beginning inventory, 1/1/17	CHF 150,000 × 0.60 =	$ 90,000
Plus: Purchases, 2017........................	3,250,000 × 0.65 =	2,112,500
Less: Ending inventory, 12/31/17..............	(400,000) × 0.68 =	(272,000)
Cost of goods sold, 2017	CHF3,000,000	$1,930,500

EXHIBIT 8.8
Remeasurement of Income Statement and Statement of Retained Earnings— Temporal Method

SWISSCO
Income Statement For Year Ending December 31, 2017

	CHF	Remeasurement Rate	U.S.$
Sales..............................	CHF 4,000,000	0.65A	$2,600,000
Cost of goods sold	(3,000,000)	Calculation	(1,930,500)
Gross profit.......................	1,000,000		669,500
Depreciation expense..............	(100,000)	0.61H	(61,000)
Amortization expense..............	(10,000)	0.62H	(6,200)
Other expenses	(220,000)	0.65A	(143,000)
Income before income taxes........	670,000		459,300
Income taxes.....................	(200,000)	0.65A	(130,000)
Income before remeasurement loss ..	470,000		329,300
Remeasurement Loss		To balance	(47,000)
Net income.....................	CHF 470,000	Below	$ 282,300

Statement of Retained Earnings
For Year Ending December 31, 2017

	CHF	Remeasurement Rate	U.S.$
Retained earnings, 1/1/17	CHF –0–		$ –0–
Net income, 2017	470,000	To balance	282,300
Dividends........................	(150,000)	0.67 H	(100,500)
Retained earnings, 12/31/17	CHF 320,000	Above	$ 181,800

The ending balances in retained earnings on the balance sheet and on the statement of retained earnings must reconcile with one another. Because dividends are remeasured into a U.S. dollar equivalent of $100,500 and the ending balance in retained earnings on the balance sheet is $181,800, net income must be $282,300.

Reconciling the amount of income reported in the statement of retained earnings and in the income statement requires a remeasurement loss of $47,000 in calculating net income. Without this remeasurement loss, the income statement, statement of retained earnings, and balance sheet are not consistent with one another.

The remeasurement loss can be calculated by considering the impact of exchange rate changes on the subsidiary's balance sheet exposure. Under the temporal method, SWISSCO's balance sheet exposure is defined by its net monetary asset or net monetary liability position. SWISSCO began 2017 with net monetary assets (cash) of CHF 350,000. During the year, however, expenditures of cash and the incurrence of liabilities caused monetary liabilities (accounts payable + long-term debt = CHF 850,000) to exceed monetary assets (cash + accounts receivable = CHF 330,000). A net monetary liability position of CHF 520,000 exists at December 31, 2017. The remeasurement loss is computed by translating the beginning net monetary asset position and subsequent changes in monetary items at appropriate exchange rates and then comparing this with the dollar value of net monetary liabilities at year-end based on the current exchange rate:

Computation of Remeasurement Loss

Net monetary assets, 1/1/17..................	CHF 350,000 × 0.60 =	$ 210,000
Increase in monetary assets:		
Sales, 2017.............................	4,000,000 × 0.65 =	2,600,000
Decreases in monetary assets and increases in monetary liabilities:		
Purchases, 2017	(3,250,000) × 0.65 =	(2,112,500)
Other expenses, 2017	(220,000) × 0.65 =	(143,000)

Income taxes, 2017	(200,000)	× 0.65	=	(130,000)
Purchase of property, plant & equipment, 3/15/17.	(1,000,000)	× 0.61	=	(610,000)
Acquisition of patent, 4/10/17	(50,000)	× 0.62	=	(31,000)
Dividends, 10/1/17	(150,000)	× 0.67	=	(100,500)
Net monetary liabilities, 12/31/17	CHF (520,000)			$ (317,000)
Net monetary liabilities, 12/31/17 at the current exchange rate.	CHF (520,000)	× 0.70	=	(364,000)
Remeasurement loss				$ 47,000

Had SWISSCO maintained its net monetary asset position of CHF 350,000 for the entire year, a $35,000 remeasurement gain would have resulted. The CHF held in cash was worth $210,000 (CHF 350,000 × $0.60) at the beginning of the year and $245,000 (CHF 350,000 × $0.70) at year-end. However, the net monetary asset position is not maintained because of changes during the year in monetary items other than the original cash balance. Indeed, a net monetary liability position arises over the course of the year. The foreign currency *appreciation* coupled with an increase in *net monetary liabilities* generates a *remeasurement loss* for the year.

Remeasurement of the Statement of Cash Flows

In remeasuring the statement of cash flows (shown in Exhibit 8.9), the U.S. dollar value for net income comes directly from the remeasured income statement. Depreciation and amortization are remeasured at the rates used in the income statement, and the remeasurement loss

EXHIBIT 8.9
Remeasurement of Statement of Cash Flows— Temporal Method

SWISSCO Statement of Cash Flows For Year Ending December 31, 2017			
	CHF	Remeasurement Rate	U.S.$
Operating activities:			
Net income	CHF 470,000	From I/S	$ 282,300
Add: Depreciation expense.	100,000	0.61 H	61,000
Amortization expense.	10,000	0.62 H	6,200
Remeasurement loss		From I/S	47,000
Increase in accounts receivable	(200,000)	0.65 A	(130,000)
Increase in inventory.	(250,000)	*	(182,000)
Increase in accounts payable	600,000	0.65 A	390,000
Net cash from operations.	730,000		474,500
Investing activities:			
Purchase of property and equipment	(1,000,000)	0.61 H	(610,000)
Acquisition of patent.	(50,000)	0.62 H	(31,000)
Net cash from investing activities.	(1,050,000)		(641,000)
Financing activities:			
Proceeds from long-term debt	250,000	0.61 H	152,500
Payment of dividends	(150,000)	0.67 H	(100,500)
Net cash from financing activities.	100,000		52,000
Decrease in cash.	(220,000)		(114,500)
Effect of exchange rate changes on cash. . . .		To balance	(4,500)
Cash at December 31, 2016.	CHF 350,000	0.60 H	$ 210,000
Cash at December 31, 2017.	CHF 130,000	0.70 C	$ 91,000

*In remeasuring cost of goods sold earlier, beginning inventory was remeasured as $90,000 and ending inventory was remeasured as $272,000: an increase of $182,000.

is added back to net income because it is a noncash item. The increases in accounts receivable and accounts payable relate to sales and purchases and therefore are remeasured at the average rate. The U.S. dollar value for the increase in inventory is determined by referring to the remeasurement of the cost of goods sold.

The resulting U.S. dollar amount of "net cash from operations" ($474,500) is exactly the same as when the current rate method was used in translation. In addition, the investing and financing activities are translated in the same manner under both methods. This makes sense; the amount of cash inflows and outflows is a matter of fact and is not affected by the particular translation methodology employed.

Nonlocal Currency Balances

One additional issue related to the translation of foreign currency financial statements needs to be considered. How should a company deal with nonlocal currency balances in the foreign currency financial statements of their foreign operations? For example, if any of the accounts of the Swiss subsidiary are denominated in a currency other than the Swiss franc, those balances would first have to be restated into francs in accordance with the rules discussed in the previous chapter. Both the foreign currency balance and any related foreign exchange gain or loss would then be translated (or remeasured) into U.S. dollars.

For example, assume that SWISSCO borrows 100,000 euros on January 1, 2017. Exchange rates in 2017 between the Swiss franc (CHF) and euro (€) and between the CHF and U.S. dollar ($) are as follows:

	CHF per €	$ per CHF
January 1, 2017	CHF 1.20	$0.60
Average, 2017	CHF 1.22	$0.65
December 31, 2017	CHF 1.25	$0.70

On December 31, 2017, SWISSCO remeasures the €100,000 note payable into CHF using the current rate as follows: €100,000 × CHF 1.25 = CHF 125,000. SWISSCO also recognizes a CHF 5,000 [€100,000 × (CHF 1.25 − CHF 1.20)] foreign exchange loss. To consolidate SWISSCO's CHF financial statements with those of its parent, the note payable remeasured in CHF is then translated into $ using the current exchange rate, and the related foreign exchange loss in CHF is translated into $ using the average exchange rate as follows:

Note payable	CHF 125,000 × $0.70 C = $87,500
Foreign exchange loss	CHF 5,000 × $0.65 A = $3,250

A note payable of $87,500 will be reported on the consolidated balance sheet, and a loss of $3,250 will be reflected in the measurement of consolidated net income.

The comprehensive illustration at the end of this chapter further demonstrates how nonlocal currency balances of a foreign entity are treated in the preparation of consolidated financial statements.

Comparison of the Results from Applying the Two Different Methods

The determination of the foreign subsidiary's functional currency (and the use of different translation methods) can have a significant impact on consolidated financial statements. The following chart shows differences for SWISSCO in several key items under the two different translation methods:

Item	Translation Method		Difference
	Current Rate	Temporal	
Net income (NI)	$ 305,500	$ 282,300	+ 8.2%
Total assets (TA)	1,169,000	1,076,800	+ 8.6
Total equity (TE)	574,000	481,800	+ 19.1
Return on equity (NI/TE)	53.2%	58.6%	− 9.2

In this illustration, if the Swiss franc is determined to be SWISSCO's functional currency (and the current rate method is applied), net income reported in the consolidated income statement would be 8.2 percent more than if the U.S. dollar is the functional currency (and the temporal method is applied). In addition, total assets would be 8.6 percent more and total equity would be 19.1 percent more using the current rate method. Because of the larger amount of equity, return on equity (net income/total equity) using the current rate method is 9.2 percent less.

Note that the current rate method does not always result in higher net income and a higher amount of equity than the temporal method. For example, had SWISSCO maintained its net monetary asset position, it would have computed a remeasurement gain under the temporal method leading to higher income than under the current rate method. Moreover, if the Swiss franc had depreciated during 2017, the temporal method would have resulted in higher net income.

The important point is that determining the functional currency and resulting translation method can have a significant impact on the amounts a parent company reports in its consolidated financial statements. The appropriate determination of the functional currency is an important issue.

> "Within rather broad parameters," says Peat, Marwick, Mitchell partner James Weir, "choosing the functional currency is basically a management call. So much so, in fact, that Texaco, Occidental, and Unocal settled on the dollar as the functional currency for most of their foreign operations, whereas competitors Exxon, Mobil, and Amoco chose primarily the local currencies as the functional currencies for their foreign businesses."[8]

Different functional currencies selected by different companies in the same industry could have a significant impact on the comparability of financial statements within that industry. Indeed, one concern that those FASB members dissenting on the current standard raised was that the functional currency rules might not result in similar accounting for similar situations.

In addition to differences in amounts reported in the consolidated financial statements, the results of the SWISSCO illustration demonstrate several conceptual differences between the two translation methods.

Underlying Valuation Method

Using the temporal method, SWISSCO remeasured its property, plant, and equipment as follows:

$$\text{Property, plant, and equipment CHF } 1,000,000 \times \$0.61 \text{ H} = \$610,000$$

By multiplying the historical cost in Swiss francs by the historical exchange rate, $610,000 represents the U.S. dollar–equivalent historical cost of this asset. It is the amount of U.S. dollars that the parent company would have had to pay to acquire assets having a cost of CHF 1,000,000 when the exchange rate was $0.61 per Swiss franc.

Property, plant, and equipment was translated under the current rate method as follows:

$$\text{Property, plant, and equipment CHF } 1,000,000 \times \$0.70 \text{ C} = \$700,000$$

The $700,000 amount is not readily interpretable. It does not represent the U.S. dollar–equivalent historical cost of the asset; that amount is $610,000. Nor does it represent the U.S.

[8] John Heins, "Plenty of Opportunity to Fool Around," *Forbes*, June 2, 1986, p. 139.

dollar–equivalent fair value of the asset because CHF 1,000,000 is not the fair value of the asset in Switzerland. The $700,000 amount is simply the product of multiplying two numbers together!

Underlying Relationships

The following table reports the values for selected financial ratios calculated from the original foreign currency financial statements and from the U.S. dollar–translated statements using the two different translation methods:

Ratio	CHF	U.S.$ Temporal	U.S.$ Current Rate
Current ratio (current assets/current liabilities)	1.22	1.20	1.22
Debt/equity ratio (total liabilities/total equities)	1.04	1.23	1.04
Gross profit ratio (gross profit/sales)	25%	25.8%	25%
Return on equity (net income/total equity)	57.3%	58.6%	53.2%

The temporal method distorts all of the ratios measured in the foreign currency. The subsidiary appears to be less liquid, more highly leveraged, and more profitable than it does in Swiss franc terms.

The current rate method maintains the first three ratios but distorts return on equity. The distortion occurs because income was translated at the average-for-the-period exchange rate whereas total equity was translated at the current exchange rate. In fact, the use of the average rate for income and the current rate for assets and liabilities distorts any ratio combining balance sheet and income statement figures, such as turnover ratios.

LO 8-5

Understand the rationale for hedging a net investment in a foreign operation and describe the treatment of gains and losses on hedges used for this purpose.

Hedging Balance Sheet Exposure

When the U.S. dollar is the functional currency or when a foreign operation is located in a highly inflationary economy, remeasurement gains and losses are reported in the consolidated income statement. Management of U.S. multinational companies could wish to avoid reporting remeasurement losses in net income because of the perceived negative impact this has on the company's stock price. Likewise, when the foreign currency is the functional currency, management could wish to avoid negative translation adjustments because of the adverse impact on the debt-to-equity ratio.

> More and more corporations are hedging their translation exposure—the recorded value of international assets such as plant, equipment and inventory—to prevent gyrations in their quarterly accounts. Though technically only paper gains or losses, translation adjustments can play havoc with balance-sheet ratios and can spook analysts and creditors alike.[9]

Translation adjustments and remeasurement gains or losses are functions of two factors: (1) changes in the exchange rate and (2) balance sheet exposure. Although a company can do little if anything to influence exchange rates, parent companies can use several techniques to hedge the balance sheet exposures of their foreign operations.

Parent companies can hedge balance sheet exposure by using a derivative financial instrument, such as a forward contract or foreign currency option, or a nonderivative hedging instrument, such as a foreign currency borrowing. To illustrate, assume that SWISSCO's functional currency is the Swiss franc; this creates a net asset balance sheet exposure. USCO believes that the Swiss franc will depreciate, thereby generating a negative translation adjustment that will reduce consolidated stockholders' equity. USCO could hedge this balance sheet exposure by borrowing Swiss francs for a period of time, thus creating an offsetting Swiss franc liability exposure. As the Swiss franc depreciates, the U.S. dollar value of the Swiss franc borrowing decreases and USCO will be able to repay the Swiss franc borrowing using fewer U.S. dollars. This generates a foreign exchange gain, which offsets the negative translation

[9] Ida Picker, "Indecent Exposure," *Institutional Investor,* September 1991, p. 82.

adjustment arising from the translation of SWISSCO's financial statements. As an alternative to the Swiss franc borrowing, USCO might have acquired a Swiss franc put option to hedge its balance sheet exposure. A put option gives the company the right to sell Swiss francs at a predetermined strike price. As the Swiss franc depreciates, the fair value of the put option should increase, resulting in a gain. Current standards provide that the gain or loss on a hedging instrument designated and effective as a *hedge of the net investment in a foreign operation* should be reported in the same manner as the translation adjustment being hedged. Thus, the foreign exchange gain on the Swiss franc borrowing or the gain on the foreign currency option would be included in accumulated other comprehensive income along with the negative translation adjustment arising from the translation of SWISSCO's financial statements. In the event that the gain on the hedging instrument is larger than the translation adjustment being hedged, the excess is taken to net income.

The paradox of hedging a balance sheet exposure is that in the process of avoiding an unrealized translation adjustment, realized foreign exchange gains and losses can result. Consider USCO's foreign currency borrowing to hedge a Swiss franc balance sheet exposure. At the initiation of the loan, USCO converts the borrowed Swiss francs into U.S. dollars at the spot exchange rate. When the liability matures, USCO purchases Swiss francs at the spot rate prevailing at that date to repay the loan. The change in exchange rate over the life of the loan generates a *realized* gain or loss. If the Swiss franc depreciates as expected, a realized foreign exchange gain that offsets the negative translation adjustment in accumulated other comprehensive income results. Although the net effect on accumulated other comprehensive income is zero, a net increase in cash occurs as a result of the hedge. If the Swiss franc unexpectedly appreciates, a realized foreign exchange loss occurs. This is offset by a positive translation adjustment in accumulated other comprehensive income, but a net decrease in cash exists. While a hedge of a net investment in a foreign operation eliminates the possibility of reporting a negative translation adjustment in accumulated other comprehensive income, gains and losses realized in cash can result.

International Financial Reporting Standard 9— Financial Instruments

As noted in the previous chapter, there is considerable similarity between IFRS and U.S. GAAP with respect to the accounting for derivative financial instruments used to hedge foreign exchange risk. Similar to U.S. GAAP, *IFRS 9* also allows hedge accounting for hedges of net investments in a foreign operation. The gain or loss on the hedging instrument is recognized in Accumulated Other Comprehensive Income (AOCI) along with the translation adjustment that is being hedged. Under both IFRS and U.S. GAAP, the cumulative translation adjustment and cumulative net gain or loss on the net investment hedge are transferred from AOCI to net income when the foreign subsidiary is sold or otherwise disposed of.

Disclosures Related to Translation

Current standards require firms to present an analysis of the change in the cumulative translation adjustment account in the financial statements or notes thereto. Many companies comply with this requirement directly in their statement of comprehensive income. Other companies provide separate disclosure in the notes; see Exhibit 8.10 for an example of this disclosure for Mondelez International, Inc.

An analysis of the Currency Translation Adjustments column in Exhibit 8.10 indicates a negative translation adjustment of $952 million in 2013 and a negative translation adjustment of $3,995 million in 2014. From the signs of these adjustments, one can infer that, in aggregate, the foreign currencies in which Mondelez International has operations depreciated against the U.S. dollar in both 2013 and 2014, with a much larger depreciation taking place in 2014. The negative translation adjustment of $3,995 million in 2014 is quite large, being equal to 156 percent of 2014 pretax income of $2,554 million.

EXHIBIT 8.10   **Mondelez International, Inc., 2014 Annual Report**

Note 14 Reclassifications from Accumulated Other Comprehensive Earnings / (Losses)

The components of accumulated other comprehensive earnings / (losses) attributable to Mondelez International during 2014 and 2013 were:

(in millions)	Currency Translation Adjustments	Pension and Other Benefits	Derivatives Accounted for as Hedges	Total
Balances at January 1, 2013	$ (399)	$(2,229)	$ (38)	$(2,666)
Other comprehensive earnings / (losses), before reclassifications:				
Currency translation adjustment	(952)	(29)	–	(981)
Pension and other benefits	–	713	–	713
Derivatives accounted for as hedges	(99)	–	169	70
Losses / (gains) reclassified as net earnings	–	197	72	269
Tax (expense) / benefit	36	(244)	(86)	(294)
Total other comprehensive earnings / (losses)				(223)
Balances at December 31, 2013	$(1,414)	$(1,592)	$ 117	$(2,889)
Other comprehensive earnings / (losses), before reclassifications:				
Currency translation adjustment (1)	(3,995)	146	–	(3,849)
Pension and other benefits	–	(1,388)	–	(1,388)
Derivatives accounted for as hedges	595	–	(166)	429
Losses / (gains) reclassified as net earnings	–	174	(45)	129
Tax (expense) / benefit	(228)	386	92	250
Total other comprehensive earnings / (losses)				(4,429)
Balances at December 31, 2014	$(5,042)	$(2,274)	$ (2)	$(7,318)

(1) The consolidated statement of comprehensive earnings for the year ended December 31, 2014, includes $(33) million of currency translation adjustment attributable to noncontrolling interests.

Although not specifically required to do so, many companies describe their translation procedures in their "summary of significant accounting policies" in the notes to the financial statements. The following excerpt from International Business Machines (IBM) Corporation's 2014 annual report illustrates this type of disclosure. Note that IBM uses the terms *translated* and *translation gains and losses* (rather than remeasured and remeasurment gains and losses) in describing its accounting policy with regard to foreign entities that operate in U.S. dollars:

Translation of Non-U.S. Currency Amounts—Assets and liabilities of non-U.S. subsidiaries that have a local functional currency are translated to United States (U.S.) dollars at year-end exchange rates. Translation adjustments are recorded in OCI. Income and expense items are translated at weighted-average rates of exchange prevailing during the year.

Inventories, property, plant and equipment—net, and other non-monetary assets and liabilities of non-U.S. subsidiaries and branches that operate in U.S. dollars are translated at the approximate exchange rates prevailing when the company acquired the assets or liabilities. All other assets and liabilities denominated in a currency other than U.S. dollars are translated at year-end exchange rates with the transaction gain or loss recognized in other (income) and expense. Income and expense items are translated at the weighted-average rates of exchange prevailing during the year. These translation gains and losses are included in net income for the period in which exchange rates change.

LO 8-6

Prepare a consolidation worksheet for a parent and its foreign subsidiary.

Consolidation of a Foreign Subsidiary

This section of the chapter demonstrates the procedures used to consolidate a foreign subsidiary's financial statements with those of its parent. The treatment of the excess of fair value over book value requires special attention. As an item denominated in foreign currency, translation of the excess gives rise to a translation adjustment recorded on the consolidation worksheet.

On January 1, 2016, Altman, Inc., a U.S.-based manufacturing firm, acquired 100 percent of Bradford Ltd. in Great Britain. Altman paid 25 million British pounds (£25,000,000), which was equal to Bradford's fair value. Bradford's balance sheet on January 1, 2016, which reflects a book value of £22,700,000, showed the following totals:

Cash	£ £925,000	Accounts payable	£ 675,000
Accounts receivable	1,400,000	Long-term debt	4,000,000
Inventory	6,050,000	Common stock	20,000,000
Property, plant & equipment (net)	£19,000,000	Retained earnings	2,700,000
Total	£27,375,000	Total	£ 27,375,000

The £2,300,000 excess of fair value over book value resulted from undervalued land (part of Property, plant & equipment) and therefore is not subject to amortization. Altman uses the equity method to account for its investment in Bradford.

On December 31, 2017, two years after the acquisition date, Bradford submitted the following trial balance for consolidation (credit balances are in parentheses):

Cash	£ 600,000
Accounts receivable	2,700,000
Inventory	9,000,000
Property, plant & equipment (net)	17,200,000
Accounts payable	(500,000)
Long-term debt	(2,000,000)
Common stock	(20,000,000)
Retained earnings, 1/1/17	(3,800,000)
Sales	(13,900,000)
Cost of goods sold	8,100,000
Depreciation expense	900,000
Other expenses	950,000
Dividends declared, 6/30/17	750,000
	£ –0–

Although Bradford generated net income of £1,100,000 in 2016, it neither declared nor paid dividends that year. Other than the payment of dividends in 2017, no intra-entity transactions occurred between the two affiliates. Altman has determined the British pound to be Bradford's functional currency.

Relevant exchange rates for the British pound were as follows:

	January 1	June 30	December 31	Average
2016	$1.51	N/A	$1.56	$1.54
2017	1.56	$1.58	1.53	1.55

Translation of Foreign Subsidiary Trial Balance

The initial step in consolidating the foreign subsidiary is to translate its trial balance from British pounds into U.S. dollars. Because the British pound has been determined to be the functional currency, this translation uses the current rate method. The historical exchange rate for translating Bradford's common stock and January 1, 2016, retained earnings is the exchange rate that existed at the acquisition date—$1.51.

	British Pounds	Rate	U.S. Dollars
Cash	£ 600,000	1.53 C	£ 918,000
Accounts receivable	2,700,000	1.53 C	4,131,000
Inventory	9,000,000	1.53 C	13,770,000
Property, plant & equipment (net)	17,200,000	1.53 C	26,316,000
Accounts payable	(500,000)	1.53 C	(765,000)

(continued)

(*continued*)

	British Pounds	Rate	U.S. Dollars
Long-term debt	(2,000,000)	1.53 C	(3,060,000)
Common stock	(20,000,000)	1.51 H	(30,200,000)
Retained earnings, 1/1/17	(3,800,000)	*	(5,771,000)
Sales	(13,900,000)	1.55 A	(21,545,000)
Cost of goods sold	8,100,000	1.55 A	12,555,000
Depreciation expense	900,000	1.55 A	1,395,000
Other expenses	950,000	1.55 A	1,472,500
Dividends declared, 6/30/17	750,000	1.58 H	1,185,000
Cumulative translation adjustment			(401,500)
	£ –0–		$ –0–
*Retained Earnings, 1/1/16	£2,700,000	1.51 H	$4,077,000
Net Income, 2016	1,100,000	1.54 A	1,694,000
Retained Earnings, 12/31/16	£3,800,000		$5,771,000

A positive (credit balance) cumulative translation adjustment of $401,500 is required to make the trial balance actually balance. The cumulative translation adjustment is calculated as follows:

Net assets, 1/1/16..............	£22,700,000	1.51 H	$34,277,000
Change in net assets, 2016.......			
Net income, 2016............	1,100,000	1.54 A	1,694,000
Net assets, 12/31/16	£23,800,000		$35,971,000
Net assets, 12/31/16, at current exchange rate..................	£23,800,000	1.56 C	37,128,000
Translation adjustment, 2016 (positive).....................			$ (1,157,000)
Net assets, 1/1/17..............	£23,800,000	1.56 H	$37,128,000
Change in net assets, 2017.......			
Net income, 2017............	3,950,000	1.55 A	6,122,500
Dividends, 6/30/17	(750,000)	1.58 H	(1,185,000)
Net assets, 12/31/17	£27,000,000		$42,065,500
Net assets, 12/31/17, at current exchange rate	£27,000,000	1.53 C	$41,310,000
Translation adjustment, 2017 (negative)................			755,500
Cumulative translation adjustment, 12/31/17 (positive)............			$ (401,500)

The translation adjustment in 2016 is positive because the British pound appreciated against the U.S. dollar that year; the translation adjustment in 2017 is negative because the British pound depreciated against the U.S. dollar that year.

Determination of Balance in Investment Account—Equity Method

The original value of the investment in Bradford, the net income earned by Bradford, and the dividends paid by Bradford are all denominated in British pounds. Relevant amounts must be translated from pounds into U.S. dollars so Altman can account for its investment in Bradford under the equity method. In addition, the translation adjustment calculated each year is included in the Investment in Bradford account to update the foreign currency investment to its U.S. dollar equivalent. The counterpart is recorded as a translation adjustment on Altman's books:

12/31/16	Investment in Bradford.	$1,157,000	
	Cumulative Translation Adjustment.		$1,157,000
	To record the positive translation adjustment related to the investment in a British subsidiary when the British pound appreciated.		
12/31/17	Cumulative Translation Adjustment.	$ 755,500	
	Investment in Bradford.		$ 755,500
	To record the negative translation adjustment related to the investment in a British subsidiary when the British pound depreciated.		

As a result of these two journal entries, Altman has a cumulative translation adjustment of $401,500 on its separate balance sheet.

The carrying value of the investment account in U.S. dollar terms at December 31, 2017, is determined as follows:

Investment in Bradford	British Pounds	Exchange Rate	U.S. Dollars
Original value	£25,000,000	1.51 H	$37,750,000
Bradford net income, 2016	1,100,000	1.54 A	1,694,000
Translation adjustment, 2016			1,157,000
Balance, 12/31/16.	£26,100,000		$40,601,000
Bradford net income, 2017	3,950,000	1.55 A	6,122,500
Bradford dividends, 6/30/17	(750,000)	1.58 H	(1,185,000)
Translation adjustment, 2017			(755,500)
Balance, 12/31/17.	£29,300,000		$44,783,000

In addition to Altman's $44,783,000 investment in Bradford, it has equity income on its December 31, 2017, trial balance in the amount of $6,122,500.

Consolidation Worksheet

Once the subsidiary's trial balance has been translated into dollars and the carrying value of the investment is known, the consolidation worksheet at December 31, 2017, can be prepared. As is true in the consolidation of domestic subsidiaries, the investment account, the subsidiary's equity accounts, and the effects of intra-entity transactions must be eliminated. The excess of fair value over book value at the date of acquisition also must be allocated to the appropriate accounts (in this example, Property, plant & equipment).

Unique to the consolidation of foreign subsidiaries is the fact that the excess of fair value over book value, denominated in foreign currency, also must be translated into the parent's reporting currency. When the foreign currency is the functional currency, the excess is translated at the current exchange rate with a resulting translation adjustment. The excess is not carried on either the parent's or the subsidiary's books but is recognized only in the consolidation worksheet. *Neither the parent nor the subsidiary has recorded the translation adjustment related to the excess, and it also must be entered in the consolidation worksheet.* Exhibit 8.11 presents the consolidation worksheet of Altman and Bradford at December 31, 2017.

Explanation of Consolidation Entries

S—Eliminates the subsidiary's stockholders' equity accounts as of the beginning of the current year along with the equivalent book value component within the original value of the Investment in Bradford account.

A—Allocates the excess of fair value over book value at the date of acquisition to land (Property, plant & equipment) and eliminates that amount within the original value of the Investment in Bradford account.

I—Eliminates the amount of equity income recognized by the parent in the current year and included in the Investment in Bradford account under the equity method.

EXHIBIT 8.11 Consolidation Worksheet—Parent and Foreign Subsidiary

ALTMAN, INC., AND BRADFORD LTD.
Consolidation Worksheet
For Year Ending December 31, 2017

Accounts	Altman	Bradford	Consolidated Entries Debits	Consolidated Entries Credits	Consolidated Totals
Income Statement					
Sales	$ (32,489,000)	$ (21,545,000)			$ (54,034,000)
Cost of goods sold	16,000,000	12,555,000			28,555,000
Depreciation expense	9,700,000	1,395,000			11,095,000
Other expenses	2,900,000	1,472,500			4,372,500
Equity income	(6,122,500)		(I) 6,122,500		–0–
Net income	$ (10,011,500)	$ (6,122,500)			$ (10,011,500)
Statement of Retained Earnings					
Retained earnings, 1/1/17	$ (25,194,000)	$ (5,771,000)	(S) 5,771,000		$ (25,194,000)
Net income (above)	(10,011,500)	(6,122,500)			(10,011,500)
Dividends	1,500,000	1,185,000		(D) 1,185,000	1,500,000
Retained earnings, 12/31/17	$ (33,705,500)	$ (10,708,500)			$ (33,705,500)
Balance Sheet					
Cash	$ 3,649,800	$ 918,000			$ 4,567,800
Accounts receivable	3,100,000	4,131,000			7,231,000
Inventory	11,410,000	13,770,000			25,180,000
Investment in Bradford	44,783,000			(S) 35,971,000	–0–
				(A) 3,473,000	
			(D) 1,185,000	(I) 6,122,500	
				(T) 401,500	
Property, plant and equipment (net)	39,500,000	26,316,000	(A) 3,473,000		
			(E) 46,000		69,335,000
Total assets	$ 102,442,800	$ 45,135,000			$ 106,313,800
Accounts payable	$ (2,500,000)	$ (765,000)			$ (3,265,000)
Long-term debt	(22,728,800)	(3,060,000)			(25,788,800)
Common stock	(43,107,000)	(30,200,000)	(S) 30,200,000		(43,107,000)
Retained earnings, 12/31/17 (above)	(33,705,500)	(10,708,500)			(33,705,500)
Cumulative translation adjustment	(401,500)	(401,500)	(T) 401,500	(E) 46,000	(447,500)
Total liabilities and equities	$ (102,422,800)	$ (45,135,000)	$47,199,000	$47,199,000	$(106,313,800)

D—Eliminates the subsidiary's dividend payment that was a reduction in the Investment in Bradford account under the equity method.

T—Eliminates the cumulative translation adjustment included in the Investment in Bradford account under the equity method and the cumulative translation adjustment on the subsidiary's translated books.

E—Revalues the excess of fair value over book value for the change in exchange rate since the date of acquisition with the counterpart recognized as an increase in the consolidated cumulative translation adjustment. The revaluation is calculated as follows:

Excess of Fair Value over Book Value			
U.S. dollar equivalent at 12/31/17	$2,300,000 × $1.53	=	$3,519,000
U.S. dollar equivalent at 1/1/16	2,300,000 × $1.51	=	3,473,000
Cumulative translation adjustment related to excess, 12/31/17			$ 46,000

Summary

1. Because many companies have significant financial involvement in foreign countries, the process by which foreign currency financial statements are translated into U.S. dollars has special accounting importance. The two major issues related to the translation process are (1) which method to use and (2) where to report the resulting translation adjustment in the consolidated financial statements.

2. Translation methods differ on the basis of which accounts are translated at the current exchange rate and which are translated at historical rates. Accounts translated at the current exchange rate are exposed to translation adjustment. Different translation methods give rise to different concepts of balance sheet exposure and translation adjustments of differing signs and magnitude.

3. The temporal method translates assets carried at current value (cash, marketable securities, receivables) and liabilities at the current exchange rate. This method translates assets carried at historical cost and stockholders' equity at historical exchange rates. When liabilities are more than the sum of cash, marketable securities, and receivables, a net liability balance sheet exposure exists. Foreign currency appreciation results in a negative translation adjustment (remeasurement loss). Foreign currency depreciation results in a positive translation adjustment (remeasurement gain). By translating assets carried at historical cost at historical exchange rates, the temporal method maintains the underlying valuation method used by the foreign operation but distorts relationships in the foreign currency financial statements.

4. The current rate method translates all assets and liabilities at the current exchange rate, giving rise to a net asset balance sheet exposure. Foreign currency appreciation results in a positive translation adjustment. Foreign currency depreciation results in a negative translation adjustment. By translating assets carried at historical cost at the current exchange rate, the current rate method maintains relationships in the foreign currency financial statements but distorts the underlying valuation method used by the foreign operation.

5. Current U.S. accounting procedures require two separate procedures for translating foreign currency financial statements into the parent's reporting currency. *Translation* through use of the current rate method is appropriate when the foreign operation's functional currency is a foreign currency. In this case, the translation adjustment is reported in the Accumulated Other Comprehensive Income account and reflected on the balance sheet as a separate component of stockholders' equity. *Remeasurement* by using the temporal method is appropriate when the operation's functional currency is the U.S. dollar. Remeasurement also is applied when the operation is in a country with a highly inflationary economy. In these situations, the translation adjustment is treated as a remeasurement gain or loss in net income.

6. IFRS and U.S. GAAP have broadly similar rules with regard to the translation of foreign currency financial statements. Differences exist with respect to the determination of functional currency, with *IAS 21* establishing a hierarchy of functional currency indicators, and in translating financial statements of foreign entities located in high inflation countries. For these entities, *IAS 21* requires financial statements to first be restated for local inflation and then be translated into the parent's currency using the current exchange rate for all financial statement items.

7. Some companies hedge their balance sheet exposures to avoid reporting remeasurement losses in net income and/or negative translation adjustments in accumulated other comprehensive income. Gains and losses on derivative or nonderivative instruments used to hedge net investments in foreign operations are reported in the same manner as the translation adjustment being hedged.

Comprehensive Illustration

Problem

(*Estimated Time: 55 to 65 Minutes*) Arlington Company is a U.S.-based organization with numerous foreign subsidiaries. As a preliminary step in preparing consolidated financial statements for 2017, it must translate the financial information from each foreign operation into its reporting currency, the U.S. dollar.

Arlington owns a Swedish subsidiary that has been in business for several years. On December 31, 2016, this entity's balance sheet was translated from Swedish kroner (SEK) (its functional currency) into U.S. dollars as prescribed by U.S. GAAP. Equity accounts at that date follow (all credit balances):

Common stock	SEK 110,000 =	$21,000
Retained earnings	194,800 =	36,100
Cumulative translation adjustment		3,860

At the end of 2017, the Swedish subsidiary produced the following trial balance. These figures include all of the entity's transactions for the year except for the results of several transactions related to sales made to a Chinese customer. A separate ledger has been maintained for these transactions denominated in Chinese renminbi (RMB). This ledger follows the company's trial balance.

Trial Balance—Swedish Subsidiary
December 31, 2017

	Debit	Credit
Cash...	SEK 41,000	
Accounts receivable	126,000	
Inventory	128,000	
Property, plant & equipment	388,000	
Accumulated depreciation............................		SEK 98,100
Accounts payable		39,000
Notes payable		56,000
Bonds payable......................................		125,000
Common stock......................................		110,000
Retained earnings, 1/1/17		194,800
Sales..		350,000
Cost of goods sold	165,000	
Depreciation expense................................	10,900	
Salary expense......................................	36,000	
Rent expense	12,000	
Interest expense	10,000	
Other expenses.....................................	31,000	
Dividends, 7/1/17	25,000	
Totals	SEK 972,900	SEK 972,900

Ledger—Transactions in Chinese Renminbi
December 31, 2017

	Debit	Credit
Cash...	RMB 10,000	
Accounts receivable	28,000	
Property, plant & equipment	20,000	
Accumulated depreciation............................		RMB 4,000
Notes payable		15,000
Sales..		44,000
Depreciation expense................................	4,000	
Interest expense	1,000	
Totals...	RMB 63,000	RMB 63,000

Additional Information

- The Swedish subsidiary began selling to the Chinese customer at the beginning of the current year. At that time, it borrowed 20,000 RMB to acquire a truck for delivery purposes. It paid one-fourth of that debt before the end of the year. The subsidiary made sales to China evenly during the period.

- The U.S. dollar exchange rates for 1 SEK are as follows:

January 1, 2017	$0.200 = 1.00 SEK
Weighted average rate for 2017	0.192 = 1.00
July 1, 2017	0.190 = 1.00
December 31, 2017	0.182 = 1.00

- The exchange rates applicable for the remeasurement of 1 RMB into Swedish kroner are as follows:

January 1, 2017	1.25 SEK	= 1.00 RMB
Weighted average rate for 2017	1.16	= 1.00
December 1, 2017	1.101	= 1.00
December 31, 2017	1.04	= 1.00

- The Swedish subsidiary expended SEK 10,000 during the year on development activities. In accordance with IFRS, this cost has been capitalized within the Property, plant & equipment account. This expenditure had no effect on the depreciation recognized for the year.

Required

a. Prepare the Swedish kroner trial balance for the Swedish subsidiary for the year ending December 31, 2017. Verify, through separate calculation, the amount of remeasurement gain/loss derived as a plug figure in the trial balance.

b. Translate the Swedish kroner trial balance into U.S. dollars to facilitate Arlington Company's preparation of consolidated financial statements. Verify, through separate calculation, the amount of cumulative translation adjustment derived as a plug figure in the trial balance.

Solution

Part A

Remeasurement of Foreign Currency Balances

A portion of the Swedish subsidiary's operating results is presently stated in Chinese renminbi. These balances must be remeasured into the functional currency, the Swedish krona, before the translation process can begin. In remeasuring these accounts using the temporal method, the krona value of the monetary assets and liabilities is determined by using the current (C) exchange rate (1.04 SEK per RMB) whereas all other accounts are remeasured at historical (H) or average (A) rates.

Remeasurement of Foreign Currency Balances

	Renminbi					Kroner	
	Debit	Credit		Rate		Debit	Credit
Cash	10,000		× 1.04	C	=	10,400	
Accounts receivable...............	28,000		× 1.04	C	=	29,120	
Property, plant & equipment........	20,000		× 1.25	H	=	25,000	
Accumulated depreciation		4,000	× 1.25	H	=		5,000
Notes payable....................		15,000	× 1.04	C	=		15,600
Sales		44,000	× 1.16	A	=		51,040
Depreciation expense	4,000		× 1.25	H	=	5,000	
Interest expense..................	1,000		× 1.16	A	=	1,160	
	63,000	63,000				70,680	71,640
Remeasurement loss						960	
Total...........................						71,640	71,640

Remeasurement Loss for 2017

Net monetary asset balance, 1/1/17................		–0–				–0–
Increases in net monetary items: Operations (sales less interest expense).....................	RMB 43,000	× 1.16	A	=		SEK 49,880
Decreases in net monetary items: Purchased truck, 1/1/17		(20,000)	× 1.25	H	=	(25,000)
Net monetary assets, 12/31/17.....	RMB 23,000					SEK 24,880
Net monetary assets, 12/31/17, at current exchange rate.........	RMB 23,000	× 1.04	C	=		SEK 23,920
Remeasurement loss (gain).......						SEK 960

The net monetary asset exposure (cash and accounts receivable > notes payable) and depreciation of the Chinese renminbi create a remeasurement loss of SEK 960.

The remeasured figures from the Chinese operation must be combined in some manner with the subsidiary's trial balance denominated in Swedish kroner. For example, a year-end adjustment can be recorded in the Swedish subsidiary's accounting system to add the remeasured balances for financial reporting purposes, as follows:

12/31/17 Adjustment	Kroner Debit	Kroner Credit
Cash	10,400	
Accounts receivable	29,120	
Property, plant & equipment	25,000	
Depreciation expense.	5,000	
Interest expense	1,160	
Remeasurement loss.	960	
Accumulated depreciation.		5,000
Notes payable		15,600
Sales		51,040
To record in Swedish kroner the foreign currency transactions originally denominated in renminbi.		

One more adjustment is necessary before translating the subsidiary's Swedish krona financial statements into the parent's reporting currency. The development costs incurred by the Swedish entity should be reclassified as an expense as required by U.S. authoritative literature. After this adjustment, the Swedish subsidiary's statements conform with U.S. GAAP.

Alternatively, the results from remeasuring the Chinese renminbi balances into Swedish kroner and reclassification of development costs can be added to the Swedish subsidiary's unadjusted trial balance as follows:

12/31/17 Adjustment	Kroner Debit	Kroner Credit
Other expenses.	10,000	
Property, plant & equipment.		10,000
To adjust property, plant & equipment and expenses in Swedish kroner to be in compliance with U.S. GAAP.		

Preparation of Adjusted Trial Balance in Swedish Kroner

	Unadjusted Debit	Unadjusted Credit	Adjustments Debit	Adjustments Credit	Adjusted Debit	Adjusted Credit
Cash	41,000		10,400		51,400	
Accounts receivable	126,000		29,120		155,120	
Inventory	128,000				128,000	
Property, plant & equipment	388,000		25,000	10,000	403,000	
Accumulated depreciation		98,100		5,000		103,100
Accounts payable		39,000				39,000
Notes payable		56,000		15,600		71,600
Bonds payable		125,000				125,000
Common stock		110,000				110,000
Retained earnings, 1/1/17		194,800				194,800
Sales		350,000		51,040		401,040
Cost of goods sold	165,000				165,000	
Depreciation expense	10,900		5,000		15,900	
Salary expense	36,000				36,000	
Rent expense	12,000				12,000	
Interest expense	10,000		1,160		11,160	

(*continued*)

(continued)

	Unadjusted		Adjustments		Adjusted	
	Debit	Credit	Debit	Credit	Debit	Credit
Other expenses	31,000		10,000		41,000	
Remeasurement loss			960		960	
Dividends, 7/1/17	25,000				25,000	
Total	972,900	972,900	81,640	81,640	1,044,540	1,044,540

Having established all account balances in the functional currency (Swedish kroner), the subsidiary's trial balance now can be translated into U.S. dollars. Under the current rate method, the dollar values to be reported for income statement items are based on the average exchange rate for the current year. All assets and liabilities are translated at the current exchange rate at the balance sheet date, and equity accounts are translated at historical rates in effect at the date of accounting recognition.

Part B

Translation of Swedish Kroner Trial Balance into U.S. Dollars

	Swedish Kroner		Rate			U.S. Dollars	
	Debit	Credit				Debit	Credit
Cash	51,400		× 0.182	C	=	9,354.80	
Accounts receivable	155,120		× 0.182	C	=	28,231.84	
Inventory	128,000		× 0.182	C	=	23,296.00	
Property, plant & equipment	403,000		× 0.182	C	=	73,346.00	
Accumulated depreciation		103,100	× 0.182	C	=		18,764.20
Accounts payable		39,000	× 0.182	C	=		7,098.00
Notes payable		71,600	× 0.182	C	=		13,031.20
Bonds payable		125,000	× 0.182	C	=		22,750.00
Common stock		110,000	Given				21,000.00
Retained earnings, 1/1/17		194,800	Given				36,100.00
Sales		401,040	× 0.192	A	=		76,999.68
Cost of goods sold	165,000		× 0.192	A	=	31,680.00	
Depreciation expense	15,900		× 0.192	A	=	3,052.80	
Salary expense	36,000		× 0.192	A	=	6,912.00	
Rent expense	12,000		× 0.192	A	=	2,304.00	
Interest expense	11,160		× 0.192	A	=	2,142.72	
Other expenses	41,000		× 0.192	A	=	7,872.00	
Remeasurement loss	960		× 0.192	A	=	184.32	
Dividends, 7/1/17	25,000		× 0.190	H	=	4,750.00	
Total	1,044,540	1,044,540				193,126.48	195,743.08
Cumulative translation adjustment						2,616.60	
Total						195,743.08	195,743.08

The cumulative translation adjustment at 12/31/17 comprises the beginning balance (given) plus the translation adjustment for the current year:

Cumulative Translation Adjustment	
Balance, 1/1/17	$ 3,860.00
Translation adjustment for 2017	(6,476.60)
Balance, 12/31/17	$(2,616.60)

The negative translation adjustment for 2017 of $6,476.60 is calculated by considering the effect of exchange rate changes on net assets:

Translation Adjustment for 2017					
Net assets, 1/1/17	SEK 304,800*	×	0.200 C	=	$ 60,960.00
Increase in net assets:					
Net income, 2017.	119,020	×	0.192 A	=	22,851.84
Decrease in net assets:					
Dividends, 7/1/17	(25,000)	×	0.190 H	=	(4,750.00)
Net assets, 12/31/17	SEK 398,820†				$ 79,061.84
Net assets, 12/31/17, at current exchange rate	SEK 398,820	×	0.182 C	=	72,585.24
Translation adjustment, 2017— negative					$ 6,476.60

*Indicated by January 1, 2017, stockholders' equity balances—Common Stock, SEK 110,000; Retained Earnings, SEK 194,800.
† Indicated by December 31, 2017, stockholders' equity balances—Common Stock, SEK 110,000; Retained Earnings, SEK 288,820.

Questions

1. What are the two major issues related to the translation of foreign currency financial statements?
2. What causes balance sheet (or translation) exposure to foreign exchange risk? How does balance sheet exposure compare with transaction exposure?
3. Why might a company want to hedge its balance sheet exposure? What is the paradox associated with hedging balance sheet exposure?
4. How are gains and losses on financial instruments used to hedge the net investment in a foreign operation reported in the consolidated financial statements?
5. What concept underlies the temporal method of translation? What concept underlies the current rate method of translation? How does balance sheet exposure differ under these two methods?
6. In translating the financial statements of a foreign subsidiary, why is the value assigned to retained earnings especially difficult to determine? How is this problem normally resolved?
7. What are the major procedural differences in applying the current rate and temporal methods of translation?
8. Clarke Company has a subsidiary operating in a foreign country. In relation to this subsidiary, what does the term *functional currency* mean? How is the functional currency determined?
9. A translation adjustment must be calculated and disclosed when financial statements of a foreign subsidiary are translated into the parent's reporting currency. How is this figure computed, and where is the amount reported in the financial statements?
10. In preparing the consolidation worksheet for a parent company and its foreign subsidiary, what consolidation entries are made related to the cumulative translation adjustment?
11. When is remeasurement rather than translation appropriate? How does remeasurement differ from translation?
12. Which translation method does U.S. GAAP require for operations in highly inflationary countries? What is the rationale for mandating use of this method?
13. In what ways does IFRS differ from U.S. GAAP with respect to the translation of foreign currency financial statements?

Problems

LO 8-2

1. What is a subsidiary's functional currency?
   a. The parent's reporting currency.
   b. The currency used by the parent to acquire the subsidiary.
   c. The currency in which the entity primarily generates and expends cash.
   d. Always the currency of the country in which the company has its headquarters.

LO 8-3, 8-4

2. In comparing the current rate and temporal methods of translation, which of the following is true?
   a. The reported balance of accounts receivable is normally the same under both methods.
   b. The reported balance of inventory is normally the same under both methods.

    c. The reported balance of equipment is normally the same under both methods.

    d. The reported balance of depreciation expense is normally the same under both methods.

LO 8-3

3. Which of the following statements is true for the translation process using the current rate method?

    a. A translation adjustment can affect consolidated net income.

    b. Equipment is translated at the historical exchange rate in effect at the date of its purchase.

    c. A translation adjustment is created by the change in the relative value of a subsidiary's monetary assets and monetary liabilities caused by exchange rate fluctuations.

    d. A translation adjustment is created by the change in the relative value of a subsidiary's net assets caused by exchange rate fluctuations.

LO 8-2, 8-3

4. A foreign subsidiary of Thun Corporation has one asset (inventory) and no liabilities. The functional currency for this subsidiary is the yuan. The inventory was acquired for 100,000 yuan when the exchange rate was $0.16 = 1 yuan. Consolidated statements are to be produced, and the current exchange rate is $0.12 = 1 yuan. Which of the following statements is true for the consolidated financial statements?

    a. A remeasurement gain must be reported.

    b. A positive translation adjustment must be reported.

    c. A negative translation adjustment must be reported.

    d. A remeasurement loss must be reported.

LO 8-3

5. At what rates should the following balance sheet accounts in foreign statements be translated (using the current rate method) into U.S. dollars?

	Equipment	Accumulated Depreciation—Equipment
a.	Current	Current
b.	Current	Average for year
c.	Historical	Current
d.	Historical	Historical

Problems 6 and 7 are based on the following information.

Certain balance sheet accounts of a foreign subsidiary of Orchid Company have been stated in U.S. dollars as follows:

	Stated at	
	Current Rates	**Historical Rates**
Accounts receivable, current	$200,000	$220,000
Accounts receivable, long term	100,000	110,000
Land	50,000	55,000
Patents	80,000	85,000
	$430,000	$470,000

LO 8-2, 8-3

6. This subsidiary's functional currency is a foreign currency. What total should Orchid's balance sheet include for the preceding items?

    a. $430,000.

    b. $435,000.

    c. $440,000.

    d. $450,000.

LO 8-2, 8-4

7. This subsidiary's functional currency is the U.S. dollar. What total should Orchid's balance sheet include for the preceding items?

    a. $430,000.

    b. $435,000.

    c. $440,000.

    d. $450,000.

Problems 8 and 9 are based on the following information.

Newberry, Inc., whose reporting currency is the U.S. dollar ($), has a subsidiary in Argentina, whose functional currency also is the $. The subsidiary acquires inventory on credit on November 1, 2017, for 100,000 pesos that is sold on January 17, 2018, for 130,000 pesos. The subsidiary pays for the inventory on January 31, 2018. Currency exchange rates are as follows:

November 1, 2017	$0.16 = 1 peso
December 31, 2017	0.17 = 1
January 17, 2018	0.18 = 1
January 31, 2018	0.19 = 1

LO 8-2, 8-3

8. What amount does Newberry's consolidated balance sheet report for this inventory at December 31, 2017?
   a. $16,000.
   b. $17,000.
   c. $18,000.
   d. $19,000.

LO 8-2, 8-3

9. What amount does Newberry's consolidated income statement report for cost of goods sold for the year ending December 31, 2018?
   a. $16,000.
   b. $17,000.
   c. $18,000.
   d. $19,000.

Problems 10 and 11 are based on the following information.

A Clarke Corporation subsidiary buys marketable equity securities and inventory on April 1, 2017, for 100,000 won each. It pays for both items on June 1, 2017, and they are still on hand at year-end. Inventory is carried at cost under the lower-of-cost-or-net realizable rule. Currency exchange rates for 1 won follow:

January 1, 2017	$0.15 = 1 won
April 1, 2017	0.16 = 1
June 1, 2017	0.17 = 1
December 31, 2017	0.19 = 1

LO 8-2, 8-4

10. Assume that the won is the subsidiary's functional currency. What balances does a consolidated balance sheet report as of December 31, 2017?
    a. Marketable equity securities = $16,000 and Inventory = $16,000.
    b. Marketable equity securities = $17,000 and Inventory = $17,000.
    c. Marketable equity securities = $19,000 and Inventory = $16,000.
    d. Marketable equity securities = $19,000 and Inventory = $19,000.

LO 8-2, 8-4

11. Assume that the U.S. dollar is the subsidiary's functional currency. What balances does a consolidated balance sheet report as of December 31, 2017?
    a. Marketable equity securities = $16,000 and Inventory = $16,000.
    b. Marketable equity securities = $17,000 and Inventory = $17,000.
    c. Marketable equity securities = $19,000 and Inventory = $16,000.
    d. Marketable equity securities = $19,000 and Inventory = $19,000.

LO 8-2, 8-4

12. A U.S. company's foreign subsidiary had these amounts in local currency units (LCU) in 2017:

Cost of goods sold	LCU 5,000,000
Beginning inventory	500,000
Ending inventory	600,000

The average exchange rate during 2017 was $1.00 = LCU 1. The beginning inventory was acquired when the exchange rate was $0.80 = LCU 1. Ending inventory was acquired when the exchange rate was $1.10 = LCU 1. The exchange rate at December 31, 2017, was $1.15 = LCU 1. Assuming that the foreign country is highly inflationary, at what amount should the foreign subsidiary's cost of goods sold be reflected in the U.S. dollar income statement?

a. $4,440,000.

b. $4,840,000.

c. $5,000,000.

d. $5,750,000.

LO 8-3

13. Yang Corporation starts a foreign subsidiary on January 1 by investing 20,000 rand. Yang owns all of the shares of the subsidiary's common stock. The foreign subsidiary generates 40,000 rand of net income throughout the year and pays no dividends. The rand is the foreign subsidiary's functional currency. Currency exchange rates for 1 rand are as follows:

January 1	$0.25 = 1 rand
Average for the year	0.28 = 1
December 31	0.31 = 1

In preparing consolidated financial statements, what translation adjustment will Yang report at the end of the current year?

a. $400 positive (credit).

b. $1,000 positive (credit).

c. $1,400 positive (credit).

d. $2,400 positive (credit).

LO 8-1

14. In the translated financial statements, which method of translation maintains the underlying valuation methods used in preparing the foreign currency financial statements?

a. Current rate method; income statement translated at average exchange rate for the year.

b. Current rate method; income statement translated at exchange rate at the balance sheet date.

c. Temporal method.

d. Monetary/nonmonetary method.

LO 8-4

15. Charleston Corporation operates a branch operation in a foreign country. Although this branch operates in euros, the U.S. dollar is its functional currency. Thus, a remeasurement is necessary to produce financial information for external reporting purposes. The branch began the year with 500,000 euros in cash and no other assets or liabilities. However, the branch immediately used 300,000 euros to acquire a warehouse. On May 1, it purchased inventory costing 100,000 euros for cash that it sold on July 1 for 160,000 euros cash. The branch transferred 10,000 euros to the parent on October 1 and recorded depreciation on the warehouse of 10,000 euros for the year. Currency exchange rates for 1 euro follow:

January 1	$1.14 = 1 euro
May 1	1.18 = 1
July 1	1.20 = 1
October 1	1.18 = 1
December 31	1.08 = 1
Average for the year	1.16 = 1

What is the remeasurement gain or loss to be recognized in the consolidated income statement?

a. $100 gain.

b. $200 gain.

c. $100 loss.

d. $200 loss.

LO 8-4

16. Which of the following items is remeasured using the current exchange rate under the temporal method?

a. Bonds payable.

b. Dividends declared.

c. Additional paid-in capital.

d. Amortization of intangibles.

LO 8-2

17. In accordance with U.S. generally accepted accounting principles, which translation combination is appropriate for a foreign operation whose functional currency is the U.S. dollar?

	Method	Treatment of Translation Adjustment
a.	Current rate	Other comprehensive income
b.	Current rate	Gain or loss in net income
c.	Temporal	Other comprehensive income
d.	Temporal	Gain or loss in net income

LO 8-3

18. A foreign subsidiary's functional currency is its local currency, which has not experienced significant inflation. The current exchange rate at the balance sheet date is the appropriate exchange rate for translating:

	Insurance Expense	Prepaid Insurance
a.	Yes	Yes
b.	Yes	No
c.	No	Yes
d.	No	No

LO 8-5

19. The functional currency of Bertrand, Inc.'s Irish subsidiary is the euro. Bertrand borrowed euros as a partial hedge of its investment in the subsidiary. Since then, the euro has decreased in value. Bertrand's negative translation adjustment on its investment in the subsidiary exceeded its foreign exchange gain on its euro borrowing. How should Bertrand report the effects of the negative translation adjustment and foreign exchange gain in its consolidated financial statements?

  a. Report the translation adjustment in accumulated other comprehensive income on the balance sheet and the foreign exchange gain as a gain on the income statement.

  b. Report the translation adjustment in the income statement and defer the foreign exchange gain in accumulated other comprehensive income on the balance sheet.

  c. Report the translation adjustment less the foreign exchange gain in accumulated other comprehensive income on the balance sheet.

  d. Report the translation adjustment less the foreign exchange gain in the income statement.

Problems 20 and 21 are based on the following information.

McCarthy, Inc.'s Brazilian subsidiary borrowed 100,000 euros on January 1, 2017. Exchange rates between the Brazilian real (BRL) and euro (€) and between the U.S. dollar ($) and BRL are as follows:

	BRL per €	US$ per BRL
January 1, 2017	BRL 4.2	$ 0.28
Average, 2017	BRL 4.3	$ 0.25
December 31, 2017.	BRL 4.6	$ 0.20

LO 8-4

20. At what amount should the Brazilian subsidiary's euro note payable be reported on McCarthy's December 31, 2017, consolidated balance sheet?
  a. $84,000.
  b. $86,000.
  c. $92,000.
  d. $128,800.

LO 8-4

21. What amount of foreign exchange gain or loss should be reflected in McCarthy's 2017 consolidated net income?
  a. $8,000 loss.
  b. $10,000 loss.
  c. $2,000 gain.
  d. $5,000 gain.

LO 8-3

22. On January 1, Narnevik Corporation formed a subsidiary in a foreign country. On April 1, the subsidiary purchased inventory on account at a cost of 250,000 local currency units (LCU). One-fifth of this inventory remained unsold on December 31, while 30 percent of the account payable had not yet been paid. The U.S. $ per LCU exchange rates were as follows:

January 1	$0.60
April 1	0.58
Average for the current year	0.56
December 31	0.54

At what amounts should the December 31 balances in inventory and accounts payable be translated into U.S. dollars using the current rate method?

LO 8-3, 8-4

23. The following accounts are denominated in rubles as of December 31, 2017. For reporting purposes, these accounts need to be stated in U.S. dollars. For each account, indicate the exchange rate that would be used to translate the ruble balance into U.S. dollars under the current rate method. Then, again for each account, indicate the exchange rate that would be used to remeasure the ruble balance to U.S. dollars using the temporal method. The company was started in 2012. The buildings were acquired in 2013 and the patents in 2015.

	Translation	Remeasurement
Accounts payable		
Accounts receivable		
Accumulated depreciation—buildings		
Advertising expense		
Amortization expense (patents)		
Buildings		
Cash		
Common stock		
Depreciation expense		
Dividends (10/1/17)		
Notes payable—due in 2020		
Patents (net)		
Salary expense		
Sales		

Exchange rates for 1 ruble are as follows:

2012	1 ruble = $0.28
2013	1 = 0.26
2015	1 = 0.25
January 1, 2017	1 = 0.24
April 1, 2017	1 = 0.23
July 1, 2017	1 = 0.22
October 1, 2017	1 = 0.20
December 31, 2017	1 = 0.16
Average for 2017	1 = 0.19

LO 8-1, 8-3, 8-4

24. On December 18, 2017, Stephanie Corporation acquired 100 percent of a Swiss company for 4.0 million Swiss francs (CHF), which is indicative of book and fair value. At the acquisition date, the exchange rate was $1.00 = CHF 1. On December 18, 2017, the book and fair values of the subsidiary's assets and liabilities were:

Cash	CHF	800,000
Inventory		1,300,000
Property, plant & equipment		4,000,000
Notes payable		(2,100,000)

Stephanie prepares consolidated financial statements on December 31, 2017. By that date, the Swiss franc has appreciated to $1.10 = CHF 1. Because of the year-end holidays, no transactions took place prior to consolidation.

a. Determine the translation adjustment to be reported on Stephanie's December 31, 2017, consolidated balance sheet, assuming that the Swiss franc is the Swiss subsidiary's functional currency. What is the economic relevance of this translation adjustment?

b. Determine the remeasurement gain or loss to be reported in Stephanie's 2017 consolidated net income, assuming that the U.S. dollar is the functional currency. What is the economic relevance of this remeasurement gain or loss?

LO 8-3, 8-4

25. The Isle of Palms Company (IOP), a U.S.-based entity, has a wholly owned subsidiary in Israel that has been determined as having the Israeli shekel (ILS) as its functional currency. On October 1, 2016, the Israeli subsidiary borrowed 500,000 Swiss francs (CHF) from a bank in Geneva for two years at an interest rate of 5 percent per year. The note payable and accrued interest are payable at the date of maturity. On December 31, 2017, the Israeli subsidiary has the following foreign currency balances on its books:

Interest expense..............	CHF 25,000
Interest payable	CHF 31,250
Note payable.................	CHF 500,000

Relevant exchange rates between the Israeli shekel (ILS) and Swiss franc (CHF), and between the U.S. dollar (USD) and Israeli shekel (ILS) follow:

	ILS per CHF	USD per ILS
October 1, 2016	3.86	0.30
January 1, 2017..	3.91	0.29
Average for 2017	3.95	0.27
December 31, 2017...................................	4.02	0.25

a. Determine the Israeli shekel amounts at which the Swiss franc balances should be reported on the Israel subsidiary's December 31, 2017, trial balance.

b. Determine the U.S. dollar amounts at which the Swiss franc balances should be included in IOP's 2017 consolidated financial statements.

LO 8-3

26. Sullivan's Island Company began operating a subsidiary in a foreign country on January 1, 2017, by investing capital in the amount of 60,000 pounds. The subsidiary immediately borrowed 140,000 pounds on a five-year note with 10 percent interest payable annually beginning on January 1, 2018. The subsidiary then purchased for 200,000 pounds a building that had a 10-year expected life and no salvage value and is to be depreciated using the straight-line method. Also on January 1, 2017, the subsidiary rented the building for three years to a group of local attorneys for 8,000 pounds per month. By year-end, rent payments totaling 80,000 pounds had been received, and 16,000 pounds was in accounts receivable. On October 1, 4,000 pounds was paid for a repair made to the building. The subsidiary transferred a cash dividend of 12,000 pounds back to Sullivan's Island Company on December 31, 2017. The functional currency for the subsidiary is the pound. Currency exchange rates for 1 pound follow:

January 1, 2017	$2.00 = 1 pound
October 1, 2017.................	2.05 = 1
December 31, 2017.............	2.08 = 1
Average for 2017	2.04 = 1

Prepare an income statement, statement of retained earnings, and balance sheet for this subsidiary in pounds and then translate these amounts into U.S. dollars.

LO 8-3

27. Refer to the information in problem 26. Prepare a statement of cash flows in pounds for Sullivan's Island Company's foreign subsidiary and then translate these amounts into U.S. dollars.

LO 8-3, 8-4

28. Rolfe Company (a U.S.-based company) has a subsidiary in Nigeria where the local currency unit is the naira (NGN). On December 31, 2016, the subsidiary had the following balance sheet (amounts are in thousands (000's)):

Cash	NGN 16,000	Note payable........	NGN 20,000
Inventory....................	10,000	Common stock	20,000
Land........................	4,000	Retained earnings....	10,000
Building....................	40,000		
Accumulated depreciation	(20,000)		
	NGN 50,000		NGN 50,000

The subsidiary acquired the inventory on August 1, 2016, and the land and building in 2010. It issued the common stock in 2008. During 2017, the following transactions took place:

2017	
Feb. 1	Paid 8,000,000 NGN on the note payable.
May 1	Sold entire inventory for 16,000,000 NGN on account.
June 1	Sold land for 6,000,000 NGN cash.
Aug. 1	Collected all accounts receivable.
Sept. 1	Signed long-term note to receive 8,000,000 NGN cash.
Oct. 1	Bought inventory for 20,000,000 NGN cash.
Nov. 1	Bought land for 3,000,000 NGN on account.
Dec. 1	Declared and paid 3,000,000 NGN cash dividend to parent.
Dec. 31	Recorded depreciation for the entire year of 2,000,000 NGN.

The U.S dollar ($) exchange rates for 1 NGN are as follows:

2008	NGN 1 = $0.0048
2010	1 = 0.0042
August 1, 2016..................	1 = 0.0062
December 31, 2016..............	1 = 0.0064
February 1, 2017	1 = 0.0066
May 1, 2017....................	1 = 0.0068
June 1, 2017...................	1 = 0.0070
August 1, 2017	1 = 0.0074
September 1, 2017	1 = 0.0076
October 1, 2017................	1 = 0.0078
November 1, 2017...............	1 = 0.0080
December 1, 2017..............	1 = 0.0082
December 31, 2017.............	1 = 0.0084
Average for 2017................	1 = 0.0074

a. Assuming the NGN is the subsidiary's functional currency, what is the translation adjustment determined solely for 2017?

b. Assuming the U.S.$ is the subsidiary's functional currency, what is the remeasurement gain or loss determined solely for 2017?

LO 8-3, 8-4

29. Zugar Company is domiciled in a country whose currency is the dinar. Zugar begins 2017 with three assets: cash of 20,000 dinars, accounts receivable of 80,000 dinars, and land that cost 200,000 dinars when acquired on April 1, 2016. On January 1, 2017, Zugar has a 150,000 dinar note payable, and no other liabilities. On May 1, 2017, Zugar renders services to a customer for 120,000 dinars, which was immediately paid in cash. On June 1, 2017, Zugar incurred a 100,000 dinar operating expense, which was immediately paid in cash. No other transactions occurred during the year. Currency exchange rates for 1 dinar follow:

April 1, 2016	$0.33 = 1 dinar
January 1, 2017	0.36 = 1
May 1, 2017....................	0.37 = 1
June 1, 2017....................	0.39 = 1
December 31, 2017..............	0.41 = 1

a. Assume that Zugar is a foreign subsidiary of a U.S. multinational company that uses the U.S. dollar as its reporting currency. Assume also that the dinar is the subsidiary's functional currency. What is the translation adjustment for this subsidiary for the year 2017?

b. Assume that Zugar is a foreign subsidiary of a U.S. multinational company that uses the U.S. dollar as its reporting currency. Assume also that the U.S. dollar is the subsidiary's functional currency. What is the remeasurement gain or loss for 2017?

c. Assume that Zugar is a foreign subsidiary of a U.S. multinational company. On the December 31, 2017, balance sheet, what is the translated value of the Land account? On the December 31, 2017, balance sheet, what is the remeasured value of the Land account?

30. Lancer, Inc. (a U.S.-based company), establishes a subsidiary in a foreign country on January 1, 2016. The following account balances for the year ending December 31, 2017, are stated in kanquo (KQ), the local currency:

Sales	KQ 200,000
Inventory (bought on 3/1/17)	100,000
Equipment (bought on 1/1/16)	80,000
Rent expense	10,000
Dividends (declared on 10/1/17)	20,000
Notes receivable (to be collected in 2020)	30,000
Accumulated depreciation—equipment	24,000
Salary payable	5,000
Depreciation expense	8,000

The following U.S.$ per KQ exchange rates are applicable:

January 1, 2016	$0.13
Average for 2016	0.14
January 1, 2017	0.18
March 1, 2017	0.19
October 1, 2017	0.21
December 31, 2017	0.22
Average for 2017	0.20

Lancer is preparing account balances to produce consolidated financial statements.

a. Assuming that the kanquo is the functional currency, what exchange rate would be used to report each of these accounts in U.S. dollar consolidated financial statements?

b. Assuming that the U.S. dollar is the functional currency, what exchange rate would be used to report each of these accounts in U.S. dollar consolidated financial statements?

31. Board Company has a foreign subsidiary that began operations at the start of 2017 with assets of 132,000 kites (the local currency unit) and liabilities of 54,000 kites. During this initial year of operation, the subsidiary reported a profit of 26,000 kites. It distributed two dividends, each for 5,000 kites with one dividend declared on March 1 and the other on October 1. Applicable exchange rates for 1 kite follow:

January 1, 2017 (start of business)	$0.80
March 1, 2017	0.78
Weighted average rate for 2017	0.77
October 1, 2017	0.76
December 31, 2017	0.75

a. Assume that the kite is this subsidiary's functional currency. What translation adjustment would Board report for the year 2017?

b. Assume that on October 1, 2017, Board entered into a forward exchange contract to hedge the net investment in this subsidiary. On that date, Board agreed to sell 200,000 kites in three months at a forward exchange rate of $0.76/1 kite. Prepare the journal entries required by this forward contract.

c. Compute the net translation adjustment for Board to report in accumulated other comprehensive income for the year 2017 under this second set of circumstances.

LO 8-3, 8-4

32. Kingsfield establishes a subsidiary operation in a foreign country on January 1, 2017. The country's currency is the kumquat (KQ). To start this business, Kingsfield invests 10,000 kumquats. Of this amount, it spends 3,000 kumquats immediately to acquire equipment. Later, on April 1, 2017, it also purchases land. All subsidiary operational activities occur at an even rate throughout the year. The U.S. dollar ($) exchange rates for the kumquat for 2017 follow:

January 1	$1.71
April 1	1.59
June 1	1.66
Weighted average	1.64
December 31	1.62

As of December 31, 2017, the subsidiary reports the following trial balance:

	Debits	Credits
Cash	KQ 8,000	
Accounts receivable	9,000	
Equipment	3,000	
Accumulated depreciation		KQ 600
Land	5,000	
Accounts payable		3,000
Notes payable (due 2025)		5,000
Common stock		10,000
Dividends declared (6/1/17)	4,000	
Sales		25,000
Salary expense	5,000	
Depreciation expense	600	
Miscellaneous expenses	9,000	
Totals	KQ 43,600	KQ 43,600

A corporation based in East Lansing, Michigan, Kingsfield uses the U.S. dollar as its reporting currency.

  a. Assume that the subsidiary's functional currency is the kumquat. Prepare a trial balance for it in U.S. dollars so that 2017 consolidated financial statements can be prepared.

  b. Assume that the subsidiary's functional currency is the U.S. dollar. Prepare a trial balance for it in U.S. dollars so that 2017 consolidated financial statements can be prepared.

LO 8-3

33. Livingston Company is a wholly owned subsidiary of Rose Corporation. Livingston operates in a foreign country with financial statements recorded in goghs (GH), the company's functional currency. Financial statements for the year 2017 are as follows:

Income Statement
For Year Ending December 31, 2017

Sales	GH 270,000
Cost of goods sold	(155,000)
Gross profit	115,000
Less: Operating expenses	(54,000)
Gain on sale of equipment	10,000
Net income	GH 71,000

Statement of Retained Earnings
For Year Ending December 31, 2017

Retained earnings, 1/1/17	GH 216,000
Net income	71,000
Less: Dividends	(26,000)
Retained earnings, 12/31/17	GH 261,000

Balance Sheet
December 31, 2017

Assets

Cash	GH 44,000
Receivables	116,000
Inventory	58,000
Property, plant and equipment (net)	339,000
Total assets	GH 557,000

Liabilities and Equities

Liabilities	GH 176,000
Common stock	120,000
Retained earnings, 12/31/17	261,000
Total liabilities and equities	GH 557,000

Additional Information

- The common stock was issued in 2010 when the exchange rate was $2.08 per GH; property, plant, and equipment was acquired in 2011 when the rate was $2.00 per GH.
- As of January 1, 2017, the retained earnings balance was translated as $396,520.
- The U.S.$ per GH exchange rates for 2017 follow:

January 1	$1.67
April 1	1.61
September 1	1.72
December 31	1.54
Weighted average	1.59

- Inventory was acquired evenly throughout the year.
- The December 31, 2016, balance sheet reported a translation adjustment with a debit balance of $85,000.
- Dividends were declared on April 1, 2017, and a piece of equipment was sold on September 1, 2017.

    Assume that the gogh is Livingston Company's functional currency. Translate the 2017 foreign currency financial statements into the parent's reporting currency, the U.S. dollar.

LO 8-3, 8-4

34. The following account balances are for the Agee Company as of January 1, 2017, and December 31, 2017. All amounts are denominated in kroner (Kr).

	January 1, 2017	December 31, 2017
Accounts payable	(15,000)	(25,000)
Accounts receivable	54,000	104,000
Accumulated depreciation—buildings	(45,000)	(50,000)
Accumulated depreciation—equipment	–0–	(7,500)
Bonds payable—due 2020	(64,000)	(64,000)
Buildings	134,000	105,000
Cash	60,000	10,500
Common stock	(69,000)	(82,000)
Depreciation expense	–0–	40,000
Dividends (10/1/17)	–0–	57,000
Equipment	–0–	64,000
Gain on sale of building	–0–	(8,500)
Rent expense	–0–	21,500
Retained earnings	(55,000)	(55,000)
Salary expense	–0–	45,000
Sales	–0–	(162,000)
Utilities expense	–0–	7,000

Additional Information

- Agee issued additional shares of common stock during the year on April 1, 2017. Common stock at January 1, 2017, was sold at the start of operations in 2010.
- Agee purchased buildings in 2011 and sold one building with a book value of Kr 1,500 on July 1 of the current year.
- Equipment was acquired on April 1, 2017.

Relevant exchange rates for 1 Kr were as follows:

2010	$2.90
2011	2.70
January 1, 2017	3.00
April 1, 2017	3.10
July 1, 2017	3.30
October 1, 2017	3.40
December 31, 2017	3.50
Average for 2017	3.20

a. Assuming the U.S. dollar is the functional currency, what is the remeasurement gain or loss for 2017? The December 31, 2016, U.S. dollar–translated balance sheet reported retained earnings of $145,200, which included a remeasurement loss of $28,300.

b. Assuming the foreign currency is the functional currency, what is the translation adjustment for 2017? The December 31, 2016, U.S. dollar–translated balance sheet reported retained earnings of $162,250 and a cumulative translation adjustment of $9,650 (credit balance).

35. Sendelbach Corporation is a U.S.-based organization with operations throughout the world. One of its subsidiaries is headquartered in Toronto. Although this wholly owned company operates primarily in Canada, it engages in some transactions through a branch in Mexico. Therefore, the subsidiary maintains a ledger denominated in Mexican pesos (Ps) and a general ledger in Canadian dollars (C$). As of December 31, 2017, the subsidiary is preparing financial statements in anticipation of consolidation with the U.S. parent corporation. Both ledgers for the subsidiary are as follows:

LO 8-3, 8-4

Main Operation—Canada

	Debit	Credit
Accounts payable		C$ 35,000
Accumulated depreciation		27,000
Buildings and equipment	C$ 167,000	
Cash	26,000	
Common stock		50,000
Cost of goods sold	203,000	
Depreciation expense	8,000	
Dividends, 4/1/17	28,000	
Gain on sale of equipment, 6/1/17		5,000
Inventory	98,000	
Notes payable—due in 2020		76,000
Receivables	68,000	
Retained earnings, 1/1/17		135,530
Salary expense	26,000	
Sales		312,000
Utility expense	9,000	
Branch operation	7,530	
Totals	C$640,530	C$640,530

Branch Operation—Mexico

	Debit	Credit
Accounts payable		Ps 49,000
Accumulated depreciation		19,000
Building and equipment	Ps 40,000	
Cash	59,000	
Depreciation expense	2,000	
Inventory (beginning—income statement)	23,000	
Inventory (ending—income statement)		28,000
Inventory (ending—balance sheet)	28,000	
Purchases	68,000	
Receivables	21,000	
Salary expense	9,000	
Sales		124,000
Main office		30,000
Totals	Ps 250,000	Ps 250,000

Additional Information

- The Canadian subsidiary's functional currency is the Canadian dollar, and Sendelbach's reporting currency is the U.S. dollar. The Canadian and Mexican operations are not viewed as separate accounting entities.
- The building and equipment used in the Mexican operation were acquired in 2007 when the currency exchange rate was C$0.25 = Ps 1.
- Purchases of inventory were made evenly throughout the fiscal year.
- Beginning inventory was acquired evenly throughout 2016; ending inventory was acquired evenly throughout 2017.
- The Main Office account on the Mexican records should be considered an equity account. This balance was remeasured into C$7,530 on December 31, 2017.
- Currency exchange rates for 1 Ps applicable to the Mexican operation follow:

Weighted average, 2016	C$0.30
January 1, 2017	0.32
Weighted average rate for 2017	0.34
December 31, 2017	0.35

- The December 31, 2016, consolidated balance sheet reported a cumulative translation adjustment with a $36,950 credit (positive) balance.
- The subsidiary's common stock was issued in 2004 when the exchange rate was $0.45 = C$1.
- The subsidiary's December 31, 2016, retained earnings balance was C$135,530, an amount that has been translated into U.S.$70,421.
- The applicable currency exchange rates for 1 C$ for translation purposes are as follows:

January 1, 2017	U.S.$0.70
April 1, 2017	0.69
June 1, 2017	0.68
Weighted average rate for 2017	0.67
December 31, 2017	0.65

a. Remeasure the Mexican operation's account balances into Canadian dollars. (Note: Back into the beginning net monetary asset or liability position.)

b. Prepare financial statements (income statement, statement of retained earnings, and balance sheet) for the Canadian subsidiary in its functional currency, Canadian dollars.

c. Translate the Canadian dollar functional currency financial statements into U.S. dollars so that Sendelbach can prepare consolidated financial statements.

36. On January 1, 2016, Cayce Corporation acquired 100 percent of Simbel Company for consideration transferred with a fair value of $126,000. Cayce is a U.S.-based company headquartered in Buffalo, New York, and Simbel is in Cairo, Egypt. Cayce accounts for its investment in Simbel under the initial value method. Any excess of fair value of consideration transferred over book value is attributable to undervalued land on Simbel's books. Simbel had no retained earnings at the date of acquisition. Following are the 2017 financial statements for the two operations. Information for Cayce and for Simbel is in U.S. dollars ($) and Egyptian pounds ($E), respectively.

	Cayce Corporation	Simbel Company
Sales	$ 200,000	£E 800,000
Cost of goods sold	(93,800)	(420,000)
Salary expense	(19,000)	(74,000)
Rent expense	(7,000)	(46,000)
Other expenses	(21,000)	(59,000)
Dividend income—from Simbel	13,750	–0–
Gain on sale of building, 10/1/17	–0–	30,000
Net income	$ 72,950	£E 231,000
Retained earnings, 1/1/17	$ 318,000	£E 133,000
Net income	72,950	231,000
Dividends	(24,000)	(50,000)
Retained earnings, 12/31/17	$ 366,950	£E 314,000
Cash and receivables	$ 110,750	£E 146,000
Inventory	98,000	297,000
Prepaid expenses	30,000	–0–
Investment in Simbel (initial value)	126,000	–0–
Property, plant & equipment (net)	398,000	455,000
Total assets	$ 762,750	£E 898,000
Accounts payable	$ 60,800	£E 54,000
Notes payable—due in 2020	132,000	140,000
Common stock	120,000	240,000
Additional paid-in capital	83,000	150,000
Retained earnings, 12/31/17	366,950	314,000
Total liabilities and equities	$ 762,750	£E 898,000

Additional Information

- During 2016, the first year of joint operation, Simbel reported income of $E 163,000 earned evenly throughout the year. Simbel declared a dividend of $E 30,000 to Cayce on June 1 of that year. Simbel also declared the 2017 dividend on June 1.

- On December 9, 2017, Simbel classified a $E 10,000 expenditure as a rent expense, although this payment related to prepayment of rent for the first few months of 2018.

- The exchange rates for 1 $E are as follows:

January 1, 2016	$0.300
June 1, 2016	0.290
Weighted average rate for 2016	0.288
December 31, 2017	0.280
June 1, 2017	0.275
October 1, 2017	0.273
Weighted average rate for 2017	0.274
December 31, 2017	0.270

Translate Simbel's 2017 financial statements into U.S. dollars and prepare a consolidation worksheet for Cayce and its Egyptian subsidiary. Assume that the Egyptian pound is the subsidiary's functional currency.

LO 8-1, 8-3, 8-4

37. Diekmann Company, a U.S.-based company, acquired a 100 percent interest in Rakona A.S. in the Czech Republic on January 1, 2016, when the exchange rate for the Czech koruna (Kčs) was $0.05. Rakona's financial statements as of December 31, 2017, two years later, follow:

Balance Sheet
December 31, 2017

Assets

Cash	Kčs	2,000,000
Accounts receivable (net)		3,300,000
Inventory		8,500,000
Equipment		25,000,000
Less: Accumulated depreciation		(8,500,000)
Building		72,000,000
Less: Accumulated depreciation		(30,300,000)
Land		6,000,000
Total assets	Kčs	78,000,000

Liabilities and Stockholders' Equity

Accounts payable	Kčs	2,500,000
Long-term debt		50,000,000
Common stock		5,000,000
Additional paid-in capital		15,000,000
Retained earnings		5,500,000
Total liabilities and stockholders' equity	Kčs	78,000,000

Income Statement
For Year Ending December 31, 2017

Sales	Kčs	25,000,000
Cost of goods sold		(12,000,000)
Depreciation expense—equipment		(2,500,000)
Depreciation expense—building		(1,800,000)
Research and development expense		(1,200,000)
Other expenses (including taxes)		(1,000,000)
Net income	Kčs	6,500,000
Plus: Retained earnings, 1/1/17		500,000
Less: Dividends, 2017		(1,500,000)
Retained earnings, 12/31/17	Kčs	5,500,000

Additional Information

- The January 1, 2017, beginning inventory of Kčs 6,000,000 was acquired on December 18, 2016, when the exchange rate was $0.043. Purchases of inventory were acquired uniformly during 2017. The December 31, 2017, ending inventory of Kčs 8,500,000 was acquired in the latter part of 2017 when the exchange rate was $0.032. All depreciable assets (equipment and buildings) were on the books when the subsidiary was acquired except for Kčs 5,000,000 of equipment acquired on January 3, 2017, when the exchange rate was $0.036, and Kčs 12,000,000 in buildings acquired on March 5, 2017, when the exchange rate was $0.034. Straight-line depreciation is 10 years for equipment and 40 years for buildings. A full year's depreciation is taken in the year of acquisition.

- Dividends were declared and paid on December 15, 2017, when the exchange rate was $0.031.

- Other exchange rates for 1 Kčs follow:

January 1, 2017	$0.040
Average 2017	0.035
December 31, 2017	0.030

Part I. Translate the Czech koruna financial statements at December 31, 2017, in the following three situations:

   a. The Czech koruna is the functional currency. The December 31, 2016, U.S. dollar–translated balance sheet reported retained earnings of $22,500. The December 31, 2016, cumulative translation adjustment was negative $202,500 (debit balance).

   b. The U.S. dollar is the functional currency. The December 31, 2016, U.S. dollar–remeasured balance sheet reported retained earnings (including a 2016 remeasurement gain) of $353,000.

   c. The U.S. dollar is the functional currency. Rakona has no long-term debt. Instead, it has common stock of Kčs 20,000,000 and additional paid-in capital of Kčs 50,000,000. The December 31, 2016, U.S. dollar–remeasured balance sheet reported a negative balance in retained earnings of $147,000 (including a 2016 remeasurement loss).

Part II. Explain the positive or negative sign of the translation adjustment in Part I(*a*) and explain why a remeasurement gain or loss exists in Parts I(*b*) and I(*c*).

38. Millager Company is a U.S.-based multinational corporation with the U.S. dollar (USD) as its reporting currency. To prepare consolidated financial statements for 2017, the company must translate the accounts of its subsidiary in Mexico, Cadengo S.A. On December 31, 2016, Cadengo's balance sheet was translated from Mexican pesos (MXN) (its functional currency) into U.S. dollars as prescribed by U.S. GAAP. Equity accounts at that date follow:

December 31, 2016	MXN	USD
Common stock	12,000,000	1,000,000
Retained earnings.	2,500,000	200,000
Cumulative translation adjustment (debit balance).		(40,000)

Early in 2017, Cadengo negotiated a 5,000 Brazilian real (BRL) loan from a bank in Rio de Janeiro and established a sales office in Brazil.

At the end of 2017, Cadengo provided Millager a trial balance that includes all of Cadengo's Mexican peso-denominated transactions for the year. A separate ledger has been maintained for transactions carried out by the Brazilian sales office that are denominated in BRL. A trial balance for the Brazilian real-denominated transactions follows Cadengo's MXN trial balance.

CADENGO S.A.
Trial Balance
December 31, 2017

	Debit	Credit
Cash.	MXN 1,000,000	
Accounts receivable	3,000,000	
Inventory	5,000,000	
Land	2,000,000	
Machinery and equipment	15,000,000	
Accumulated depreciation.		MXN 6,000,000
Accounts payable		1,500,000
Notes payable		4,000,000
Common stock.		12,000,000
Retained earnings, 1/1/17		2,500,000
Sales.		34,000,000
Cost of goods sold	28,000,000	
Depreciation expense.	600,000	
Rent expense	3,000,000	
Interest expense	400,000	
Dividends, 7/1/17	2,000,000	
Total	MXN60,000,000	MXN60,000,000

BRAZILIAN SALES OFFICE
Trial Balance
December 31, 2017

	Debit	Credit
Cash..	BRL 5,500	
Accounts receivable	28,000	
Notes payable		BRL 5,000
Sales..		35,000
Rent expense	6,000	
Interest expense	500	
Total.......................................	BRL 40,000	BRL 40,000

Additional Information

The Mexican peso exchange rate for 1 Brazilian real (MXN/BRL) and the U.S. dollar exchange rate for 1 Mexican peso (USD/MXN) during 2017 follow:

Date	MXN/BRL	USD/MXN
January 1, 2017..........................	6.00	0.080
Average 2017	6.20	0.075
July 1, 2017	6.28	0.073
December 31, 2017......................	6.30	0.072

a. Using an electronic spreadsheet, prepare the Mexican peso trial balance for Cadengo S.A. for the year ending December 31, 2017. Verify the amount of remeasurement gain/loss derived as a plug figure in the spreadsheet through separate calculation.

b. Using a second electronic worksheet, translate Cadengo S.A.'s Mexican peso trial balance into U.S. dollars to facilitate Millager Company's preparation of consolidated financial statements. Verify the amount of cumulative translation adjustment derived as a plug figure in the spreadsheet through separate calculation. Note: An additional row must be inserted in the trial balance for the remeasurement gain/loss calculated in part a.

Develop Your Skills

RESEARCH CASE 1—FOREIGN CURRENCY TRANSLATION AND HEDGING ACTIVITIES

Many companies make annual reports available on their corporate website, often under an Investors tab. Annual reports also can be accessed through the SEC's EDGAR system at www.sec.gov (under Filings, click Company Filings Search, type in Company Name, and under Filing Type, search for 10-K).

Access the most recent annual report for a U.S.-based multinational company with which you are familiar to complete the following requirements.

Required

a. Identify the location(s) in the annual report that provides disclosures related to the translation of foreign currency financial statements and foreign currency hedging.

b. Determine whether the company's foreign operations have a predominant functional currency.

c. Determine the amount of remeasurement gain or loss, if any, reported in net income in each of the three most recent years.

d. Determine the amount of translation adjustment, if any, reported in other comprehensive income in each of the three most recent years. Explain the sign (positive or negative) of the translation adjustment in each of the three most recent years.

e. Determine whether the company hedges net investments in foreign operations. If so, determine the type(s) of hedging instrument used.

RESEARCH CASE 2—FOREIGN CURRENCY TRANSLATION DISCLOSURES IN THE COMPUTER INDUSTRY

Many companies make annual reports available on their corporate website, often under an Investors tab. Annual reports also can be accessed through the SEC's EDGAR system at www.sec.gov (under Filings, click Company Filings Search, type in Company Name, and under Filing Type, search for 10-K).

Access the most recent annual report for the following U.S.-based multinational corporations to complete the requirements:
International Business Machines Corporation.
Intel Corporation.

Required

a. Identify the location(s) in the annual report that provides disclosures related to foreign currency translation and foreign currency hedging.
b. Determine whether the company's foreign operations have a predominant functional currency.
c. Determine the amount of translation adjustment, if any, reported in other comprehensive income in each of the three most recent years. Explain the sign (positive or negative) of the translation adjustment in each of the three most recent years. Compare the relative magnitude of these translation adjustments for the two companies.
d. Determine whether each company hedges net investments in foreign operations. If so, determine the type(s) of hedging instrument used.

ACCOUNTING STANDARDS CASE 1—MORE THAN ONE FUNCTIONAL CURRENCY

Lynch Corporation has a wholly owned subsidiary in Mexico (Lynmex) with two distinct and unrelated lines of business. Lynmex's Small Appliance Division manufactures small household appliances such as toasters and coffeemakers at a factory in Monterrey, Nuevo Leon, and sells them directly to retailers such as Gigantes throughout Mexico. Lynmex's Electronics Division imports finished products produced by Lynch Corporation in the United States and sells them to a network of distributors operating throughout Mexico.
Lynch's CFO believes that the two divisions have different functional currencies. The functional currency of the Small Appliance Division is the Mexican peso, whereas the functional currency of the Electronics Division is the U.S. dollar. The CFO is unsure whether to designate the Mexican peso or the U.S. dollar as Lynmex's functional currency, or whether the subsidiary can be treated as two separate foreign operations with different functional currencies.

Required

Search current U.S. authoritative accounting literature to determine how the functional currency should be determined for a foreign entity that has more than one distinct and separable operation. Identify the source of guidance for answering this question.

ACCOUNTING STANDARDS CASE 2—CHANGE IN FUNCTIONAL CURRENCY

Hughes Inc. has a wholly owned subsidiary in Canada that previously had been determined as having the Canadian dollar as its functional currency. Due to a recent restructuring, Hughes Inc.'s CFO believes that the functional currency of the Canadian company has changed to the U.S. dollar. A large cumulative translation adjustment related to the Canadian subsidiary is included in accumulated other comprehensive income on Hughes Inc.'s balance sheet. The CFO is unsure whether the cumulative translation adjustment should be removed from equity, and if so, to what other account it should be transferred. He also questions whether the change in functional currency qualifies as a change in accounting principle, which would require retrospective application of the temporal method in translating the Canadian subsidiary's financial statements. He wonders, for example, whether the Canadian subsidiary's nonmonetary assets need to be restated as if the temporal method had been applied in previous years.

Required

Search current U.S. authoritative accounting literature for guidance on how to handle a change in functional currency from a foreign currency to the U.S. dollar. Summarize that guidance to answer the CFO's questions. Identify the source of guidance for answering these questions.

EXCEL CASE—TRANSLATING FOREIGN CURRENCY FINANCIAL STATEMENTS

CPA skills

Charles Edward Company established a subsidiary in a foreign country on January 1, 2017, by investing FC 3,200,000 when the exchange rate was $0.50/FC. Charles Edward negotiated a bank loan of FC 3,000,000 on January 5, 2017, and purchased plant and equipment in the amount of FC 6,000,000 on January 8, 2017. It depreciated plant and equipment on a straight-line basis over a 10-year useful life. It purchased its beginning inventory of FC 1,000,000 on January 10, 2017, and acquired additional inventory of FC 4,000,000 at three points in time during the year at an average exchange rate of $0.43/FC. It uses the first-in, first-out (FIFO) method to determine cost of goods sold. Additional exchange rates per FC 1 during the year 2017 follow:

January 1–31, 2017	$0.50
Average 2017	0.45
December 31, 2017	0.38

The foreign subsidiary's income statement for 2017 and balance sheet at December 31, 2017, follow:

INCOME STATEMENT
For the Year Ended December 31, 2017
FC (in thousands)

Sales	FC 5,000
Cost of goods sold	3,000
Gross profit	2,000
Selling expense	400
Depreciation expense	600
Income before tax	1,000
Income taxes	300
Net income	700
Retained earnings, 1/1/17	–0–
Retained earnings, 12/31/17	FC 700

BALANCE SHEET
At December 31, 2017
FC (in thousands)

Cash	FC 1,000
Inventory	2,000
Property, plant & equipment	6,000
Less: Accumulated depreciation	(600)
Total assets	FC 8,400
Current liabilities	FC 1,500
Long-term debt	3,000
Contributed capital	3,200
Retained earnings	700
Total liabilities and stockholders' equity	FC 8,400

As the controller for Charles Edward Company, you have evaluated the characteristics of the foreign subsidiary to determine that the FC is the subsidiary's functional currency.

Required

a. Use an electronic spreadsheet to translate the foreign subsidiary's FC financial statements into U.S. dollars at December 31, 2017, in accordance with U.S. GAAP. Insert a row in the spreadsheet after retained earnings and before total liabilities and stockholders' equity for the cumulative translation adjustment. Calculate the translation adjustment separately to verify the amount obtained as a balancing figure in the translation worksheet.

b. Use an electronic spreadsheet to remeasure the foreign subsidiary's FC financial statements in U.S. dollars at December 31, 2017, assuming that the U.S. dollar is the subsidiary's functional currency. Insert a row in the spreadsheet after depreciation expense and before income before taxes for the remeasurement gain (loss).

c. Prepare a report for James Benjamin, CEO of Charles Edward, summarizing the differences that will be reported in the company's 2017 consolidated financial statements because the FC, rather than the U.S. dollar, is the foreign subsidiary's functional currency. In your report, discuss the relationship between the current ratio, the debt-to-equity ratio, and profit margin calculated from the FC financial statements and from the translated U.S. dollar financial statements. Also discuss the meaning of the translated U.S. dollar amounts for inventory and for fixed assets.

EXCEL AND ANALYSIS CASE—PARKER, INC., AND SUFFOLK PLC

On January 1, 2016, Parker, Inc., a U.S.-based firm, acquired 100 percent of Suffolk PLC located in Great Britain for consideration paid of 52,000,000 British pounds ($), which was equal to fair value. The excess of fair value over book value is attributable to land (part of property, plant, and equipment) and is not subject to depreciation. Parker accounts for its investment in Suffolk at cost. On January 1, 2016, Suffolk reported the following balance sheet:

Cash	$ 2,000,000	Accounts payable	$ 1,000,000
Accounts receivable	3,000,000	Long-term debt	8,000,000
Inventory	14,000,000	Common stock	44,000,000
Property, plant, and equipment (net)	40,000,000	Retained earnings	6,000,000
	$59,000,000		$59,000,000

Suffolk's 2016 income was recorded at $2,000,000. It declared and paid no dividends in 2016.

On December 31, 2017, two years after the date of acquisition, Suffolk submitted the following trial balance to Parker for consolidation:

Cash	$ 1,500,000
Accounts Receivable	5,200,000
Inventory	18,000,000
Property, Plant, and Equipment (net)	36,000,000
Accounts Payable	(1,450,000)
Long-Term Debt	(5,000,000)
Common Stock	(44,000,000)
Retained Earnings, 1/1/17	(8,000,000)
Sales	(28,000,000)
Cost of Goods Sold	16,000,000
Depreciation	2,000,000
Other Expenses	6,000,000
Dividends (1/30/17)	1,750,000
	–0–

Other than paying dividends, no intra-entity transactions occurred between the two companies. Relevant exchange rates for the British pound follow:

	January 1	January 30	Average	December 31
2016	$1.60	$1.61	$1.62	$1.64
2017	1.64	1.65	1.66	1.68

The December 31, 2017, financial statements (before consolidation with Suffolk) follow. Dividend income is the U.S. dollar amount of dividends received from Suffolk translated at the $1.65/$ exchange rate at January 30, 2017. The amounts listed for dividend income and all affected accounts (i.e., net income, December 31 retained earnings, and cash) reflect the $1.65/$ exchange rate at January 30, 2017. Credit balances are in parentheses.

Parker	
Sales.	$ (70,000,000)
Cost of goods sold	34,000,000
Depreciation.	20,000,000
Other expenses	6,000,000
Dividend income	(2,887,500)
Net income	$ (12,887,500)
Retained earnings, 1/1/17.	$ (48,000,000)
Net income, 2017	(12,887,500)
Dividends, 1/30/17	4,500,000
Retained earnings, 12/31/17	$ (56,387,500)
Cash.	$ 3,687,500
Accounts receivable	10,000,000
Inventory	30,000,000
Investment in Suffolk.	83,200,000
Plant and equipment (net).	105,000,000
Accounts payable	(25,500,000)
Long-term debt.	(50,000,000)
Common stock.	(100,000,000)
Retained earnings, 12/31/17	(56,387,500)
	–0–

Parker's chief financial officer (CFO) wishes to determine the effect that a change in the value of the British pound would have on consolidated net income and consolidated stockholders' equity. To help assess the foreign currency exposure associated with the investment in Suffolk, the CFO requests assistance in comparing consolidated results under actual exchange rate fluctuations with results that would have occurred had the dollar value of the pound remained constant or declined during the first two years of Parker's ownership.

Required

Use an electronic spreadsheet to complete the following four parts:

Part I. Given the relevant exchange rates presented,

a. Translate Suffolk's December 31, 2017, trial balance from British pounds to U.S. dollars. The British pound is Suffolk's functional currency.

b. Prepare a schedule that details the change in Suffolk's cumulative translation adjustment (beginning net assets, income, dividends, etc.) for 2016 and 2017.

c. Prepare the December 31, 2017, consolidation worksheet for Parker and Suffolk.

d. Prepare the 2017 consolidated income statement and the December 31, 2017, consolidated balance sheet.

*Note:*Worksheets should possess the following qualities:

- Each spreadsheet should be programmed so that all relevant amounts adjust appropriately when different values of exchange rates (subsequent to January 1, 2016) are entered into it.
- Be sure to program Parker's dividend income, cash, and retained earnings to reflect the dollar value of alternative January 30, 2017, exchange rates.

Part II. Repeat tasks (*a*), (*b*), (*c*), and (*d*) from Part I to determine consolidated net income and consolidated stockholders' equity if the exchange rate had remained at $1.60/$ over the period 2016 to 2017.

Part III. Repeat tasks (*a*), (*b*), (*c*), and (*d*) from Part I to determine consolidated net income and consolidated stockholders' equity if the following exchange rates had existed:

	January 1	January 30	Average	December 31
2016	$1.60	$1.59	$1.58	$1.56
2017	1.56	1.55	1.54	1.52

Part IV. Prepare a report that provides Parker's CFO the risk assessments requested. Focus on profitability, cash flow, and the debt-to-equity ratio.

Partnerships: Formation and Operation

A reader of college accounting textbooks might well conclude that business activity is carried out exclusively by corporations. Because most large companies are legally incorporated, a vast majority of textbook references and illustrations concern corporate organizations. Contrary to the perception being relayed, partnerships (as well as sole proprietorships) make up a vital element of the business community. The Internal Revenue Service projects that by 2016, nearly 4.7 million partnership income tax returns will be filed (as compared to nearly 8.1 million corporation income tax returns).[1]

The partnership form serves a wide range of business activities, from small local operations to worldwide enterprises. The following examples exist in the U.S. economy:

- Individual proprietors often join together to form a partnership as a way to reduce expenses, expand services, and add increased expertise. As will be discussed, partnerships also provide important tax benefits.

- A partnership is a common means by which friends and relatives can easily create and organize a business endeavor.

- Historically, doctors, lawyers, and other professionals have formed partnerships because of legal prohibitions against the incorporation of their practices. Although most states now permit alternative forms for such organizations, operating as a partnership or sole proprietorship is still necessary in many areas.

Over the years, some partnerships have grown to enormous sizes. Buckeye Partners, for example, primarily operates pipeline systems in the United States; in 2015 Buckeye had revenues of more than $3.4 billion. The international accounting firm of PricewaterhouseCoopers recently reported revenues of more than $35 billion.[2] In 2015, Deloitte indicated operations in more than 150 countries,[3] and Ernst & Young reported having more than 212,000 employees.[4]

[1] www.irs.gov/taxstats.
[2] "Global Annual Review 2015," pwc.com.
[3] "Deloitte 2015 Global Report," deloitte.com.
[4] "EY at a glance," ey.com.

Learning Objectives

After studying this chapter, you should be able to:

LO 9-1 Explain the advantages and disadvantages of the partnership versus the corporate form of business.

LO 9-2 Describe the purpose of the articles of partnership and list specific items that should be included in this agreement.

LO 9-3 Prepare the journal entry to record the initial capital investment made by a partner.

LO 9-4 Use both the bonus method and the goodwill method to record a partner's capital investment.

LO 9-5 Demonstrate the impact that the allocation of partnership income has on the partners' individual capital balances.

LO 9-6 Allocate income to partners when interest and/or salary factors are included.

LO 9-7 Explain the meaning of partnership dissolution and understand that a dissolution will often have little or no effect on the operations of the partnership business.

LO 9-8 Prepare journal entries to record the acquisition by a new partner of either all or a portion of a current partner's interest.

LO 9-9 Prepare journal entries to record a new partner's admission by a contribution made directly to the partnership.

LO 9-10 Prepare journal entries to record the withdrawal of a current partner.

LO 9-1

Explain the advantages and disadvantages of the partnership versus the corporate form of business.

Partnerships—Advantages and Disadvantages

The popularity of partnerships derives from several advantages inherent to this type of organization. An analysis of these attributes explains why millions of enterprises in the United States are partnerships rather than corporations.

One of the most common motives is the ease of formation. Only an oral agreement is necessary to create a legally binding partnership. In contrast, depending on specific state laws, incorporation requires filing a formal application and completing various other forms and documents. Operators of small businesses may find the convenience and reduced cost involved in creating a partnership to be an especially appealing characteristic. As the American Bar Association notes:

> The principal advantage of partnerships is the ability to make virtually any arrangements defining their relationship to each other that the partners desire. There is no necessity, as there is in a corporation, to have the ownership interest in capital and profits proportionate to the investment made; and losses can be allocated on a different basis from profits. It is also generally much easier to achieve a desirable format for control of the business in a partnership than in a corporation, since the control of a corporation, which is based on ownership of voting stock, is much more difficult to alter.
>
> Partnerships are taxed on a conduit or flow-through basis under subchapter K of the Internal Revenue Code. This means that the partnership itself does not pay any taxes. Instead the net income and various deductions and tax credits from the partnership are passed through to the partners based on their respective percentage interest in the profits and losses of the partnership, and the partners include the income and deductions in their individual tax returns.[5]

Thus, partnership revenue and expense items (as defined by the tax laws) must be assigned directly each year to the individual partners who pay the income taxes. Passing income balances through to the partners in this manner avoids double taxation of the profits that are earned by a business and then distributed to its owners. A corporation's income is taxed twice: when earned and again when conveyed as a dividend. A partnership's income is taxed only at the time that the business initially earns it.

For example, assume that a business earns $100. After paying any income taxes, the remainder is immediately conveyed to its owners. An income tax rate of 30 percent is assumed for both individuals and corporations. Corporate dividends paid to owners, however, are taxed either 0 percent, 15 percent, or 20 percent depending on their overall earnings level.[6] As the following table shows, if this business is a partnership rather than a corporation, the owners have $10.50 more expendable income, which is 10.5 percent of the business income. Although significant in amount, this difference narrows as tax rates are lowered.

	Partnership	Corporation
Income before income taxes	$ 100.00	$ 100.00
Income taxes paid by business (30%)	–0–	(30.00)
Income distributed to owners	$ 100.00	$ 70.00
Income taxes paid by owners*	(30.00)	(10.50)
Expendable income	$ 70.00	$ 59.50

*30 percent assumed rate on ordinary income.
15 percent assumed rate on dividend income.

Historically, a second tax advantage has long been associated with partnerships. Because income is taxable to the partners as the business earns it, any operating losses can be used to reduce their personal taxable income directly. In contrast, a corporation is viewed as legally

[5] American Bar Association, *Family Legal Guide,* 3rd ed. (New York: Random House Reference, 2004).

[6] The American Taxpayer Relief Act of 2012 increased capital gains and dividend tax rates from 15 percent to 20 percent for single taxpayers and married taxpayers with incomes in the top tax bracket. Capital gains will continue to be taxed at 15 percent for individuals in the middle tax brackets. Earners in the lowest two income tax brackets will pay 0 percent on investment income. An additional 3.8 percent Medicare tax on net investment income applies to capital gains and dividends for those with modified adjusted gross incomes over various upper income thresholds.

separate from its owners, so losses cannot be passed through to them. A corporation has the ability to carry back any net operating losses and reduce previously taxed income (usually for the two prior years) and carry forward remaining losses to decrease future taxable income (for up to 20 years). However, if a corporation is newly formed or has not been profitable, operating losses provide no immediate benefit to a corporation or its owners as losses do for a partnership.

The tax advantage of deducting partnership losses is limited, however. For tax purposes, ownership of a partnership is labeled as a passive activity unless the partner materially participates in the actual business activities. Passive activity losses thus serve only to offset other passive activity profits. In most cases, these partnership losses cannot be used to reduce earned income such as salaries. Thus, unless a taxpayer has significant passive activity income (from rents, for example), losses reported by a partnership create little or no tax advantage unless the partner materially participates in the actual business activity.

The partnership form of business also has certain significant disadvantages. Perhaps the most severe problem is the unlimited liability that each partner automatically incurs. Partnership law specifies that any partner can be held personally liable for *all* debts of the business. The potential risk is especially significant when coupled with the concept of *mutual agency*. This legal term refers to the right that each partner has to incur liabilities in the name of the partnership. Consequently, partners acting within the normal scope of the business have the power to obligate the company for any amount. If the partnership fails to pay these debts, creditors can seek satisfactory remuneration from any partner that they choose.

Such legal concepts as unlimited liability and mutual agency describe partnership characteristics that have been defined and interpreted over a number of years. To provide consistent application across state lines in regard to these terms as well as many other legal aspects of a partnership, the Uniform Partnership Act (UPA) was created. This act, which was first proposed in 1914 (and revised in 1997), now has been adopted by all states in some form. It establishes uniform standards in such areas as the nature of a partnership, the relationship of the partners to outside parties, and the dissolution of the partnership. For example, Section 6 of the act provides the most common legal definition of a partnership: "an association of two or more persons to carry on a business as co-owners for profit."

Alternative Legal Forms

Because of the possible owner liability, partnerships often experience difficulty in attracting large amounts of capital. Potential partners frequently prefer to avoid the risk that is a basic characteristic of a partnership. However, the tax benefits of avoiding double taxation still provide a strong pull toward the partnership form. Hence, in recent years, a number of alternative types of organizations have been developed. The availability of these legal forms depends on state laws as well as applicable tax laws. In each case, however, the purpose is to limit the owners' personal liability while providing the tax benefits of a partnership.[7]

Subchapter S Corporation

A Subchapter S corporation (often referred to as an *S corporation*) is created as a corporation and, therefore, has all of the legal characteristics of that form.[8] According to the U.S. tax laws, if the corporation meets certain regulations, it will be taxed in virtually the same way as a partnership. Thus, the Subchapter S corporation pays no income taxes although any income (and losses) pass directly through to the taxable income of the individual owners. This form avoids double taxation, and the owners do not face unlimited liability. To qualify, the business can have only one class of stock and is limited to 100 stockholders. All owners must be individuals, estates, certain tax-exempt entities, or certain types of trusts. The most significant problem associated with this business form is that its growth potential is limited because of the restriction on the number and type of owners.

[7] Many factors should be considered in choosing a specific legal form for an organization. The information shown here is merely an overview. For more information, consult a tax guide or a business law textbook. Also see Hopson and Hopson, "Making the Right Choice of Business Entity," *CPA Journal*, October 2014.

[8] Unless a corporation qualifies as a Subchapter S corporation or some other legal variation, it is referred to as a *Subchapter C corporation*. Therefore, a vast majority of all businesses are C corporations.

Limited Partnerships (LPs)

A *limited partnership* is a type of investment designed primarily for individuals who want the tax benefits of a partnership but who do not wish to work in a partnership or have unlimited liability. In such organizations, a number of limited partners invest money as owners but are not allowed to participate in the company's management. These partners can still incur a loss on their investment, but the amount is restricted to what has been contributed. To protect the creditors of a limited partnership, one or more general partners must be designated to assume responsibility for all obligations created in the name of the business.

Buckeye Partners, L.P. is an example of a limited partnership that trades on the New York Stock Exchange. Buckeye's December 31, 2015, balance sheet reported capital of $3.7 billion for its limited partners.

Many limited partnerships were originally formed as tax shelters to create immediate losses (to reduce the taxable income of the partners) with profits spread out into the future. As mentioned earlier, tax laws limit the deduction of passive activity losses, and this significantly reduced the formation of limited partnerships.

Limited Liability Partnerships (LLPs)

The *limited liability partnership* has most of the characteristics of a general partnership except that it significantly reduces the partners' liability. Partners may lose their investment in the business and are responsible for the contractual debts of the business. The advantage here is created in connection with any liability resulting from damages. In such cases, the partners are responsible for only their own acts or omissions plus the acts and omissions of individuals under their supervision.

As Section 306(c) of the Uniform Partnership Act notes,

> An obligation of a partnership incurred while the partnership is a limited liability partnership, whether arising in contract, tort, or otherwise, is solely the obligation of the partnership. A partner is not personally liable, directly or indirectly, by way of contribution or otherwise, for such an obligation solely by reason of being or so acting as a partner.

Thus, a partner in the Houston office of a public accounting firm would probably not be held liable for a poor audit performed by that firm's San Francisco office. Not surprisingly, limited liability partnerships have become very popular with professional service organizations that have multiple offices. For example, all of the four largest accounting firms are LLPs.

Limited Liability Companies (LLCs)

The limited liability company is a relatively new type of organization in the United States although it has long been used in Europe and other areas of the world. It is classified as a partnership for tax purposes and court purposes. However, depending on state laws, the owners risk only their own investments. Thus, similar to a Subchapter S entity, the LLC provides liability protection for its owners and managers. In contrast to a Subchapter S corporation, the number of owners is not usually restricted so that growth may be easier to accomplish.

Partnership Accounting—Capital Accounts

Despite legal distinctions, questions should be raised as to the need for an entirely separate study of partnership accounting:

- Does an association of two or more persons require accounting procedures significantly different from those of a corporation?
- Does proper accounting depend on the legal form of an organization?

The answers to these questions are both yes and no. Accounting procedures are normally standardized for assets, liabilities, revenues, and expenses regardless of the legal form of a business. *Partnership accounting, though, does exhibit unique aspects that warrant study, but they lie primarily in the handling of the partners' capital accounts.*

The stockholders' equity accounts of a corporation do not correspond directly with the capital balances found in a partnership's financial records. The various equity accounts reported by an incorporated enterprise display a greater range of information. This characteristic reflects the wide variety of equity transactions that can occur in a corporation as well as the influence of state and federal laws. Government regulation has had an enormous effect on the accounting for corporate equity transactions in that extensive disclosure is required to protect stockholders and other outside parties such as potential investors.

To provide adequate information and to meet legal requirements, corporate accounting must provide details about numerous equity transactions and account balances. For example, the amount of a corporation's paid-in capital is shown separately from earned capital and other comprehensive income; the par value of each class of stock is disclosed; treasury stock, stock options, stock dividends, and other capital transactions are reported based on prescribed accounting principles.

In contrast, partnerships provide only a limited amount of equity disclosure primarily in the form of individual capital accounts that are accumulated for every partner or every class of partners. These balances measure each partner's or group's interest in the book value of the net assets of the business. Thus, the equity section of a partnership balance sheet is composed solely of capital accounts that can be affected by many different events: contributions from partners as well as distributions to them, earnings, and any other equity transactions.

However, partnership accounting does not differentiate between the various sources of ownership capital. Disclosing the composition of the partners' capital balances has not been judged necessary because partnerships have historically tended to be small with equity transactions that were rarely complex. Additionally, absentee ownership is not common, a factor that minimizes both the need for government regulation and outside interest in detailed information about the capital balances.

Articles of Partnership

LO 9-2

Describe the purpose of the articles of partnership and list specific items that should be included in this agreement.

Because the demand for information about capital balances is limited, accounting principles specific to partnerships are based primarily on traditional approaches that have evolved over the years rather than on official pronouncements. These procedures attempt to mirror the relationship between the partners and their business especially as defined by the partnership agreement. This legal covenant, which may be either oral or written, is often referred to as the *articles of partnership* and forms the central governance for a partnership's operation. The financial arrangements spelled out in this contract establish guidelines for the various capital transactions. Therefore, the articles of partnership, rather than either laws or official rules, provide much of the underlying basis for partnership accounting.

Because the articles of partnership are a negotiated agreement that the partners create, an unlimited number of variations can be encountered in practice. Partners' rights and responsibilities frequently differ from business to business. Consequently, firms often hire accountants in an advisory capacity to participate in creating this document to ensure the equitable treatment of all parties. Although the articles of partnership may contain a number of provisions, an explicit understanding should always be reached in regard to the following:

- Name and address of each partner.
- Business location.
- Description of the nature of the business.
- Rights and responsibilities of each partner.
- Initial contribution to be made by each partner and the method to be used for valuation.
- Specific method by which profits and losses are to be allocated.
- Periodic withdrawal of assets by each partner.
- Procedure for admitting new partners.
- Method for arbitrating partnership disputes.
- Life insurance provisions enabling remaining partners to acquire the interest of any deceased partner.
- Method for settling a partner's share in the business upon withdrawal, retirement, or death.

Discussion Question

WHAT KIND OF BUSINESS IS THIS?

After graduating from college, Shelley Williams held several different jobs but found that she did not enjoy working for other people. Finally, she and Yvonne Hargrove, her college roommate, decided to start a business of their own. They rented a small building and opened a florist shop selling cut flowers such as roses and chrysanthemums that they bought from a local greenhouse.

Williams and Hargrove agreed orally to share profits and losses equally, although they also decided to take no money from the operation for at least four months. No other arrangements were made, but the business did reasonably well and, after the first four months had passed, each began to draw out $500 in cash every week.

At year-end, they took their financial records to a local accountant so that they could get their income tax returns completed. He informed them that they had been operating as a partnership and that they should draw up a formal articles of partnership agreement or consider incorporation or some other legal form of organization. They confessed that they had never really considered the issue and asked for his advice on the matter.

What advice should the accountant give to these clients?

LO 9-3

Prepare the journal entry to record the initial capital investment made by a partner.

Accounting for Capital Contributions

Several types of capital transactions occur in a partnership: allocation of profits and losses, retirement of a current partner, admission of a new partner, and so on. The initial transaction, however, is the contribution the original partners make to begin the business. In the simplest situation, the partners invest only cash amounts. For example, assume that Carter and Green form a business to be operated as a partnership. Carter contributes $50,000 in cash and Green invests $20,000. The initial journal entry to record the creation of this partnership follows:

Cash	70,000	
Carter, Capital		50,000
Green, Capital		20,000
To record cash contributed to start new partnership.		

The assumption that only cash was invested avoids complications in this first illustration. Often, though, one or more of the partners transfers noncash assets such as inventory, land, equipment, or a building to the business. Although fair value is used to record these assets, a case could be developed for initially valuing any contributed asset at the partner's current book value. According to the concept of unlimited liability (as well as present tax laws), a partnership does not exist as an entity apart from its owners. A logical extension of the idea is that the investment of an asset is not a transaction occurring between two independent parties such as would warrant revaluation. This contention holds that the semblance of an arm's-length transaction is necessary to justify a change in the book value of any account.

Although retaining the recorded value for assets contributed to a partnership may seem reasonable, this method of valuation proves to be inequitable to any partner investing appreciated property. A $50,000 capital balance always results from a cash investment of that amount, but recording other assets depends entirely on the original book value.

For example, should a partner who contributes a building having a recorded value of $18,000 but a fair value of $50,000 be credited with only an $18,000 interest in the partnership? Because $50,000 in cash and $50,000 in appreciated property are equivalent contributions, a $32,000 difference in the partners' capital balances cannot be justified. To prevent such inequities, each item transferred to a partnership is initially recorded for external reporting purposes at current value.[9]

Requiring revaluation of contributed assets can, however, be advocated for reasons other than just the fair treatment of all partners. Despite some evidence to the contrary, a partnership can be viewed legitimately as an entity standing apart from its owners. As an example, a partnership maintains legal ownership of its assets and (depending on state law) can initiate lawsuits. For this reason, accounting practice traditionally has held that the contribution of assets (and liabilities) to a partnership is an exchange between two separately identifiable parties that should be recorded based on fair values.

Determining an appropriate valuation for each capital balance is more than just an accounting exercise. Over the life of a partnership, these figures serve in a number of important capacities:

1. The totals in the individual capital accounts often influence the assignment of profits and losses to the partners.
2. The capital account balance is usually one factor in determining the final distribution that will be received by a partner at the time of withdrawal or retirement.
3. Ending capital balances indicate the allocation to be made of any assets that remain following the liquidation of a partnership.

To demonstrate, assume that Carter invests $50,000 in cash to begin the previously discussed partnership and Green contributes the following assets:

	Book Value to Green	Fair Value
Inventory	$ 9,000	$10,000
Land	14,000	11,000
Building	32,000	46,000
Totals	$55,000	$67,000

As an added factor, Green's building is encumbered by a $23,600 mortgage that the partnership has agreed to assume.

Green's net investment is equal to $43,400 ($67,000 less $23,600). The following journal entry records the formation of the partnership created by these contributions:

Cash	50,000	
Inventory	10,000	
Land	11,000	
Building	46,000	
Mortgage Payable		23,600
Carter, Capital		50,000
Green, Capital		43,400
To record properties contributed to start partnership. Assets and liabilities are recorded at fair value.		

We should make one additional point before leaving this illustration. Although having contributed inventory, land, and a building, Green holds no further right to these individual assets; they now belong to the partnership. The $43,400 capital balance represents an ownership interest in the business as a whole but does not constitute a specific claim to any asset. Having transferred title to the partnership, Green has no more right to these assets than does Carter.

[9] For federal income tax purposes, the $18,000 book value is retained as the basis for this building, even after transfer to the partnership. Within the tax laws, no difference is seen between partners and their partnership so that no adjustment to fair value is warranted.

Intangible Contributions

In forming a partnership, the contributions made by one or more of the partners may go beyond assets and liabilities. A doctor, for example, can bring a particular line of expertise to a partnership, and a practicing dentist might have already developed an established patient list. These attributes, as well as many others, are frequently as valuable to a partnership as cash and fixed assets. *Hence, formal accounting recognition of such special contributions may be appropriately included as a provision of any partnership agreement.*

To illustrate, assume that James and Joyce plan to open an advertising agency and decide to organize the endeavor as a partnership. James contributes cash of $70,000, and Joyce invests only $10,000. Joyce, however, is an accomplished graphic artist, a skill that is considered especially valuable to this business. Therefore, in producing the articles of partnership, the partners agree to start the business with equal capital balances. Often such decisions result only after long, and sometimes heated, negotiations. Because the value assigned to an intangible contribution such as artistic talent is arbitrary at best, proper reporting depends on the partners' ability to arrive at an equitable arrangement.

In recording this agreement, James and Joyce have two options: (1) the bonus method and (2) the goodwill method. Each of these approaches achieves the desired result of establishing equal capital account balances. Recorded figures can vary significantly, however, depending on the procedure selected. Thus, the partners should reach an understanding prior to beginning business operations as to the method to be used. The accountant can help avoid conflicts by assisting the partners in evaluating the impact created by each of these alternatives.

The Bonus Method The bonus method assumes that a specialization such as Joyce's artistic abilities does *not* constitute a recordable partnership asset with a measurable cost. Hence, this approach recognizes only the assets that are physically transferred to the business (such as cash, patents, inventory). Although these contributions determine total partnership capital, the establishment of specific capital balances is viewed as an independent process based solely on the partners' agreement. Because the initial equity figures result from negotiation, they do not need to correspond directly with the individual investments.

James and Joyce have contributed a total of $80,000 in identifiable assets to their partnership and have decided on equal capital balances. According to the bonus method, this agreement is fulfilled simply by splitting the $80,000 capital evenly between the two partners. The following entry records the formation of this partnership under this assumption:

Cash	80,000	
James, Capital		40,000
Joyce, Capital		40,000
To record cash contributions with bonus to Joyce because of artistic abilities.		

Joyce received a *capital bonus* here of $30,000 (the $40,000 recorded capital balance in excess of the $10,000 cash contribution) from James in recognition of the artistic abilities she brought into the business.

The Goodwill Method The goodwill method is based on the assumption that an implied value can be calculated mathematically and recorded for any intangible contribution made by a partner. In the present illustration, Joyce invested $60,000 less cash than James but receives an equal amount of capital according to the partnership agreement. Proponents of the goodwill method argue that Joyce's artistic talent has an apparent value of $60,000, a figure that should be included as part of this partner's capital investment. If not recorded, Joyce's primary contribution to the business is ignored completely within the accounting records.

Cash	80,000	
Goodwill	60,000	
James, Capital		70,000
Joyce, Capital		70,000
To record cash contributions with goodwill attributed to Joyce in recognition of artistic abilities.		

Comparison of Methods   Both approaches achieve the intent of the partnership agreement: to record equal capital balances despite a difference in the partners' cash contributions. The bonus method allocates the $80,000 invested capital according to the percentages designated by the partners, whereas the goodwill method capitalizes the implied value of Joyce's intangible contribution.

Although nothing prohibits the use of either technique, the recognition of goodwill poses definite theoretical problems. In previous discussions of both the equity method (Chapter 1) and business combinations (Chapter 2), goodwill was recognized but only as a result of an acquisition made by the reporting entity. Consequently, this asset had a historical cost in the traditional accounting sense. Partnership goodwill has no such cost; the business recognizes an asset even though no funds have been spent.

The partnership of James and Joyce, for example, is able to record $60,000 in goodwill without any expenditure. Furthermore, the value attributed to this asset is based solely on a negotiated agreement between the partners; the $60,000 balance has no objectively verifiable basis. Thus, although partnership goodwill is sometimes encountered in actual practice, this "asset" should be viewed with a strong degree of professional skepticism.

Additional Capital Contributions and Withdrawals

Subsequent to forming a partnership, the owners may choose to contribute additional capital amounts during the life of the business. These investments can be made to stimulate expansion or to assist the business in overcoming working capital shortages or other problems. Regardless of the reason, the contribution is again recorded as an increment in the partner's capital account based on fair value. For example, in the previous illustration, assume that James decides to invest another $5,000 cash in the partnership to help finance the purchase of new office furnishings. The partner's capital account balance is immediately increased by this amount to reflect the transfer to the partnership.[10]

In many instances, the articles of partnership allow withdrawals on a regular periodic basis as a reward for ownership or as compensation for work performed for the business. Often such distributions are recorded initially in a separate drawing account that is closed into the individual partner's capital account at year-end. Assume, for illustration purposes, that James and Joyce take out $1,200 and $1,500, respectively, from their business. The journal entry to record these payments is as follows:

James, Drawing	1,200	
Joyce, Drawing	1,500	
Cash		2,700
To record withdrawal of cash by partners.		

Larger amounts might also be withdrawn from a partnership on occasion. A partner may have a special need for money or just desire to reduce the basic investment that has been made in the business. Such transactions are usually sporadic occurrences and entail amounts significantly higher than the partner's periodic drawing. The articles of partnership may require prior approval by the other partners.

[10] The partners also may reverse this process by withdrawing assets from the business for their own personal use. To protect the interests of the other partners, the articles of partnership should clearly specify the amount and timing of such withdrawals.

Discussion Question

HOW WILL THE PROFITS BE SPLIT?

James J. Dewars has been the sole owner of a small CPA firm for the past 20 years. Now 52 years old, Dewars is concerned about the continuation of his practice after he retires. He would like to begin taking more time off now although he wants to remain active in the firm for at least another 8 to 10 years. He has worked hard over the decades to build up the practice so that he presently makes a profit of $180,000 annually.

Lewis Huffman has been working for Dewars for the past four years. He now earns a salary of $68,000 per year. He is a very dedicated employee who generally works 44 to 60 hours per week. In the past, Dewars has been in charge of the larger, more profitable audit clients whereas Huffman, with less experience, worked with the smaller clients. Both Dewars and Huffman do some tax work although that segment of the business has never been emphasized.

Sally Scriba has been employed for the past seven years with another CPA firm as a tax specialist. She has no auditing experience but has a great reputation in tax planning and preparation. She currently earns an annual salary of $80,000.

Dewars, Huffman, and Scriba are negotiating the creation of a new CPA firm as a partnership. Dewars plans to reduce his time in this firm although he will continue to work with many of the clients that he has served for the past two decades. Huffman will begin to take over some of the major audit jobs. Scriba will start to develop an extensive tax practice for the firm.

Because of the changes in the firm, the three potential partners anticipate earning a total net income in the first year of operations of between $130,000 and $260,000. Thereafter, they hope that profits will increase at the rate of 10 to 20 percent annually for the next five years or so.

How should this new partnership allocate its future net income among these partners?

LO 9-5

Demonstrate the impact that the allocation of partnership income has on the partners' individual capital balances.

Allocation of Income

At the end of each fiscal period, partnership revenues and expenses are closed out, accompanied by an allocation of the resulting net income or loss to the partners' capital accounts. Because a separate capital balance is maintained for each partner, a method must be devised for this assignment of annual income. Because of the importance of the process, the articles of partnership should always stipulate the procedure the partners established. If no arrangement has been specified, state partnership law normally holds that all partners receive an equal allocation of any income or loss earned by the business. If the partnership agreement specifies only the division of profits, then losses must be divided in the same manner as directed for profit allocation.

The profit allocation pattern can be important to the success of any organization because it can help emphasize and reward outstanding performance. Therefore, many partner compensation plans recognize contributions to revenue, growth, time spent with the firm, management skill development, or any other attribute the partnership deems important. Profit allocations plans can thus become complex in attempting to recognize and reward the various elements of each partner's contributions to the firm's success. Alternatively, partnerships can avoid all complications by assigning net income on an equal basis among all partners.

As an initial illustration, assume that Tinker, Evers, and Chance form a partnership by investing cash of $120,000, $90,000, and $75,000, respectively. The articles of partnership agreement specifies that Evers will be allotted 40 percent of all profits and losses because of previous business experience. Tinker and Chance are to divide the remaining 60 percent equally. This agreement also stipulates that each partner is allowed to withdraw $10,000 in cash annually from the business. The amount of this withdrawal does not directly depend on the method utilized for income allocation. *From an accounting perspective, the assignment of income and the setting of withdrawal limits are two separate decisions.*

At the end of the first year of operations, the partnership reports net income of $60,000. To reflect the changes made in the partners' capital balances, the closing process consists of the following two journal entries. The assumption is made here that each partner has taken the allowed amount of drawing during the year. In addition, for convenience, all revenues and expenses already have been closed into the Income Summary account.

Tinker, Capital	10,000	
Evers, Capital...	10,000	
Chance, Capital...	10,000	
Tinker, Drawing..		10,000
Evers, Drawing		10,000
Chance, Drawing		10,000
To close out drawing accounts recording payments made to the three partners.		

Income Summary	60,000	
Tinker, Capital (30%)...		18,000
Evers, Capital (40%)		24,000
Chance, Capital (30%)		18,000
To allocate net income based on provisions of partnership agreement.		

Statement of Partners' Capital

Because a partnership does not separately disclose a retained earnings balance, the statement of retained earnings usually reported by a corporation is replaced by a statement of partners' capital. The following financial statement is based on the data presented for the partnership of Tinker, Evers, and Chance. The changes made during the year in the individual capital accounts are outlined along with totals representing the partnership as a whole:

TINKER, EVERS, AND CHANCE
Statement of Partners' Capital
For Year Ending December 31, Year 1

	Tinker, Capital	Evers, Capital	Chance, Capital	Totals
Capital balances beginning of year	$120,000	$ 90,000	$75,000	$ 285,000
Allocation of net income	18,000	24,000	18,000	60,000
Drawings	(10,000)	(10,000)	(10,000)	(30,000)
Capital balances end of year.............	$128,000	$104,000	$83,000	$ 315,000

LO 9-6

Allocate income to partners when interest and/or salary factors are included.

Alternative Allocation Techniques—Example 1

Assigning net income based on a ratio may be simple, but this approach is not necessarily equitable to all partners. For example, assume that Tinker does not participate in the partnership's operations but is the contributor of the highest amount of capital. Evers and Chance both work full-time in the business, but Evers has considerably more experience in this line of work.

Under these circumstances, no single ratio is likely to reflect properly the various contributions made by each partner. Indeed, an unlimited number of alternative allocation plans could be devised in hopes of achieving fair treatment for all parties. For example, because of the different levels of capital investments, consideration should be given to including interest within the allocation process to reward the contributions. A compensation allowance is also a possibility, usually in an amount corresponding to the number of hours worked or the level of a partner's business expertise.

To demonstrate one possible option, assume that Tinker, Evers, and Chance begin their partnership based on the original facts except that they arrive at a more detailed method of allocating profits and losses. After considerable negotiation, an articles of partnership agreement credits each partner annually for interest in an amount equal to 10 percent of that partner's beginning capital balance for the year. Evers and Chance also will be allotted $15,000 each as a compensation allowance in recognition of their participation in daily operations. Any remaining profit or loss will be split 3:4:3, with the largest share going to Evers because of the work experience that this partner brings to the business. As with any appropriate allocation, this pattern attempts to provide fair treatment for all three partners.

Under this arrangement, the $60,000 net income earned by the partnership in the first year of operation would be allocated as follows. The sequential alignment of the various provisions is irrelevant except that the ratio, which is used to assign the remaining profit or loss, must be calculated last.

Allocation of Partnership Net Income	Tinker	Evers	Chance	Total
Net Income				$ 60,000
Interest (10% of beginning capital)	$12,000	$9,000	$7,500	(28,500)
Net income remaining after interest				$ 31,500
Compensation allowance	0	15,000	15,000	(30,000)
Net income remaining after interest and compensation				$ 1,500
Remaining income distribution . . .	450 (30%)	600 (40%)	450 (30%)	(1,500)
Net income allocation totals	$12,450	$24,600	$22,950	$ 0

Importantly, the schedule computing the division of income must be completed prior to determining the final capital balances for the partners. For the Tinker, Evers, and Chance partnership, the allocations just calculated lead to the following year-end closing entry:

Income Summary	60,000	
Tinker, Capital		12,450
Evers, Capital		24,600
Chance, Capital		22,950
To allocate income for the year to the individual partners' capital accounts based on partnership agreement.		

Alternative Allocation Techniques—Example 2

As the preceding illustration indicates, the assignment process is no more than a series of mechanical steps reflecting the change in each partner's capital balance resulting from the provisions of the partnership agreement. The number of different allocation procedures that could be employed is limited solely by the partners' imagination. Although interest, compensation allowances, and various ratios are the predominant factors encountered in practice, other possibilities exist. Therefore, another approach to the allocation process is presented to further illustrate some of the variations that can be utilized. A two-person partnership is used here to simplify the computations.

Assume that Webber and Rice formed a partnership several years ago to operate a coffee shop. Webber contributed the initial capital, and Rice manages the business. With the assistance of their accountant, they wrote an articles of partnership agreement that contains the following provisions:

1. Each partner is allowed to draw $1,000 in cash from the business every month. Any withdrawal in excess of that figure will be accounted for as a direct reduction to the partner's capital balance.

2. Partnership profits and losses will be allocated each year according to the following plan:

   a. Each partner will earn 15 percent interest based on the monthly average capital balance for the year (calculated without regard for normal drawings or current income).

b. As a reward for operating the business, Rice is to receive credit for a bonus equal to 20 percent of the year's net income. However, no bonus is earned if the partnership reports a net loss.

c. The two partners will divide any remaining profit or loss equally.

Assume that Webber and Rice subsequently begin the current year with capital balances of $150,000 and $30,000, respectively. On April 1 of that year, Webber invests an additional $8,000 cash in the business, and on July 1, Rice withdraws $6,000 in excess of the specified drawing allowance. Assume further that the partnership reports income of $30,000 for the current year.

Because the interest factor established in this allocation plan is based on a monthly average figure, the specific amount to be credited to each partner is determined by means of a preliminary calculation:

Webber—Interest Allocation

Beginning balance . . .	$150,000 × 3 months =	$ 450,000
Balance, April 1	$158,000 × 9 months =	1,422,000
		1,872,000
		× $\frac{1}{12}$
Monthly average capital balance		156,000
Interest rate		× 15%
Interest credited to Webber		$ 23,400

Rice—Interest Allocation

Beginning balance . . .	$30,000 × 6 months =	$180,000
Balance, July 1	$24,000 × 6 months =	144,000
		324,000
		× $\frac{1}{12}$
Monthly average capital balance		27,000
Interest rate		× 15%
Interest credited to Rice		$ 4,050

Following this initial computation, the actual income assignment can proceed according to the provisions specified in the articles of partnership. The stipulations drawn by Webber and Rice must be followed exactly, even though the business's $30,000 profit for the current year is not sufficient to cover both the interest and the bonus. Income allocation is a mechanical process that should always be carried out as stated in the articles of partnership without regard to the specific level of income or loss.

Based on the plan that was created, Webber's capital increases by $21,675 during the current year but Rice's account increases by only $8,325:

Allocation of Partnership Net Income	Weber	Rice	Total
Net Income			$ 30,000
Interest (above).	$23,400	$4,050	(27,450)
Net income remaining after interest.			$ 2,550
Bonus to Rice (20% × $30,000)	0	6,000	(6,000)
Net income remaining after interest and bonus. . . .			(3,450)
Remaining income (loss) distribution	(1,725) (50%)	(1,725) (50%)	$ 3,450
Net income allocation totals	$21,675	$8,325	$ 0

As discussed above, the interest and bonus allocations sum to $33,450 and thus exceed the available net income of $30,000. The remaining overallocation of $3,450 is then treated as a loss in allocating the partnership's income to the individual partners.

LO 9-7

Explain the meaning of partnership dissolution and understand that a dissolution will often have little or no effect on the operations of the partnership business.

Accounting for Partnership Dissolution

Many partnerships limit capital transactions almost exclusively to contributions, drawings, and profit and loss allocations. Normally, though, over any extended period, changes in the members who make up a partnership occur. Employees may be promoted into the partnership or new owners brought in from outside the organization to add capital or expertise to the business. Current partners eventually retire, die, or simply elect to leave the partnership. Large operations may even experience such changes on a routine basis.

Regardless of the nature or the frequency of the event, any alteration in the specific individuals composing a partnership automatically leads to legal dissolution. In many instances, the breakup is merely a prerequisite to the formation of a new partnership. For example, if Abernethy and Chapman decide to allow Miller to become a partner in their business, the legally recognized partnership of Abernethy and Chapman has to be dissolved first. The business property as well as the right to future profits can then be conveyed to the newly formed partnership of Abernethy, Chapman, and Miller. The change is a legal one. Actual operations of the business would probably continue unimpeded by this alteration in ownership.

Conversely, should the partners so choose, dissolution can be a preliminary step in the termination and liquidation of the business. The death of a partner, lack of sufficient profits, or internal management differences can lead the partners to break up the partnership business. Under this circumstance, the partnership sells properties, pays debts, and distributes any remaining assets to the individual partners. Thus, in liquidations (which are analyzed in detail in the next chapter), both the partnership and the business cease to exist.

Dissolution—Admission of a New Partner

One of the most prevalent changes in the makeup of a partnership is the addition of a new partner. An employee may have worked for years to gain this opportunity, or a prospective partner might offer the new investment capital or business experience necessary for future business success. An individual can gain admittance to a partnership in one of two ways: (1) by purchasing an ownership interest from a current partner or (2) by contributing assets directly to the business.

In recording either type of transaction, the accountant has the option, once again, to retain the book value of all partnership assets and liabilities (as exemplified by the bonus method) or revalue these accounts to their present fair values (the goodwill method). The decision as to a theoretical preference between the bonus and goodwill methods hinges on one single question: *Should the dissolved partnership and the newly formed partnership be viewed as two separate reporting entities?*

If the new partnership is merely an extension of the old, no basis exists for restatement. The transfer of ownership is a change only in a legal sense and has no direct impact on business assets and liabilities. However, if the continuation of the business represents a legitimate transfer of property from one partnership to another, revaluation of all accounts and recognition of goodwill can be justified.

Because both approaches are encountered in practice, this textbook presents each. However, the concerns previously discussed in connection with partnership goodwill still exist: Recognition is not based on historical cost, and no objective verification of the capitalized amount can be made. One alternative revaluation approach that attempts to circumvent the problems involved with partnership goodwill has been devised. This hybrid method revalues all partnership assets and liabilities to fair value without making any corresponding recognition of goodwill.

LO 9-8

Prepare journal entries to record the acquisition by a new partner of either all or a portion of a current partner's interest.

Admission through Purchase of a Current Interest

As mentioned, one method of gaining admittance to a partnership is by the purchase of a current interest. One or more partners can choose to sell their portion of the business to an outside party. This type of transaction is most common in operations that rely primarily on monetary capital rather than on the business expertise of the partners.

In making a transfer of ownership, a partner can actually convey only three rights:

1. *The right of co-ownership in the business property.* This right justifies the partner's periodic drawings from the business as well as the distribution settlement paid at liquidation or at the time of a partner's withdrawal.

2. *The right to share in profits and losses as specified in the articles of partnership.*
3. *The right to participate in the management of the business.*

Unless restricted by the articles of partnership, every partner has the power to sell or assign the first two of these rights at any time. Their transfer poses no threat of financial harm to the remaining partners. In contrast, partnership law states that the right to participate in the management of the business can be conveyed only with the consent of all partners. This particular right is considered essential to the future earning power of the enterprise as well as the maintenance of business assets. Therefore, current partners are protected from the intrusion of parties who might be considered detrimental to the management of the company.

As an illustration, assume that Scott, Thompson, and York formed a partnership several years ago. Subsequently, York decides to leave the partnership and offers to sell his interest to Morgan. Although York may transfer the right of property ownership as well as the specified share of future profits and losses, the partnership does not automatically admit Morgan. York legally remains a partner until such time as both Scott and Thompson agree to allow Morgan to participate in the management of the business.

To demonstrate the accounting procedures applicable to the transfer of a partnership interest, assume that the following information is available relating to the partnership of Scott, Thompson, and York:

Partner	Capital Balance	Profit and Loss Ratio
Scott	$ 50,000	20%
Thompson	30,000	50
York	20,000	30
Total capital	$100,000	

As often happens, the relationship of the capital accounts to one another does not correspond with the partners' profit and loss ratio. Capital balances are historical cost figures. They result from contributions and withdrawals made throughout the life of the business as well as from the allocation of partnership income. Therefore, any correlation between a partner's recorded capital at a particular point in time and the profit and loss percentage would probably be coincidental. Scott, for example, has 50 percent of the current partnership capital ($50,000/$100,000) but is entitled to only a 20 percent allocation of income.

Instead of York selling his interest to Morgan, assume that each of these three partners elects to transfer a 20 percent interest to Morgan for a total payment of $30,000. According to the sales contract, *the money is to be paid directly to the owners.*

One approach to recording this transaction is that, because Morgan's purchase is carried out between the individual parties, the acquisition has no impact on partnership assets and liabilities. Because the business is not involved directly, the transfer of ownership requires a simple capital reclassification without any accompanying revaluation. This approach is similar to the bonus method; only a legal change in ownership is occurring so that revaluation of neither assets or liabilities nor goodwill is appropriate.

Book Value Method		
Scott, Capital (20% of capital balance)	10,000	
Thompson, Capital (20%)	6,000	
York, Capital (20%)	4,000	
Morgan, Capital (20% of total)		20,000
To reclassify capital to reflect Morgan's acquisition. Money is paid directly to partners.		

An alternative for recording Morgan's acquisition relies on a different perspective of the new partner's admission. Legally, the partnership of Scott, Thompson, and York is transferring all assets and liabilities to the partnership of Scott, Thompson, York, and Morgan.

Therefore, according to the logic underlying the goodwill method, a transaction is occurring between two separate reporting entities, an event that necessitates the complete revaluation of all assets and liabilities.

Because Morgan is paying $30,000 for a 20 percent interest in the partnership, the implied value of the business as a whole is $150,000 ($30,000/20%). However, the book value is only $100,000; thus, a $50,000 upward revaluation is indicated. This adjustment is reflected by restating specific partnership asset and liability accounts to fair value with any remaining balance recorded as goodwill.

Goodwill (Revaluation) Method		
Goodwill (or specific accounts)...	50,000	
Scott, Capital (20% of goodwill).......................................		10,000
Thompson, Capital (50%)...		25,000
York, Capital (30%)...		15,000
To recognize goodwill and revaluation of assets and liabilities based on value of business implied by Morgan's purchase price.		

Note that this entry credits the $50,000 revaluation to the original partners based on the profit and loss ratio rather than on capital percentages. Recognition of goodwill (or an increase in the book value of specific accounts) indicates that unrecorded gains have accrued to the business during previous years of operation. Therefore, the equitable treatment is to allocate this increment among the partners according to their profit and loss percentages. After the implied value of the partnership is established, the reclassification of ownership can be recorded based on the new capital balances as follows:

Scott, Capital (20% × new $60,000 capital balance)......................	12,000	
Thompson, Capital (20% × $55,000)	11,000	
York, Capital (20% × $35,000)...	7,000	
Morgan, Capital (20% × $150,000 new total).......................		30,000
To reclassify capital to reflect Morgan's acquisition. Money is paid directly to partners.		

LO 9-9

Prepare journal entries to record a new partner's admission by a contribution made directly to the partnership.

Admission by a Contribution Made to the Partnership

Entrance into a partnership is not limited solely to the purchase of a current partner's interest. An outsider may be admitted to the ownership by contributing cash or other assets directly to the business rather than to the partners. For example, assume that King and Wilson maintain a partnership and presently report capital balances of $80,000 and $20,000, respectively. According to the articles of partnership, King is entitled to 60 percent of all profits and losses with the remaining 40 percent credited each year to Wilson. By agreement of the partners, Goldman is allowed to enter the partnership for a payment of $20,000 *with this money going into the business.* Based on negotiations that preceded the acquisition, all parties have agreed that Goldman receives an initial 10 percent interest in the net assets of the partnership.

Bonus Credited to Original Partners The bonus (or no revaluation) method maintains the same recorded value for all partnership assets and liabilities despite Goldman's admittance. The capital balance for this new partner is simply set at the appropriate 10 percent level based on the total net assets of the partnership after the payment is recorded. Because $20,000 is invested, total reported capital increases to $120,000. Thus, Goldman's 10 percent interest is computed as $12,000. *The $8,000 difference between the amount contributed and this allotted capital balance is viewed as a bonus.* Because Goldman is willing to accept a capital balance that is less than his investment, this bonus is attributed to the original partners (again based on their profit and loss ratio). As a result of the nature of the transaction, no need exists to recognize goodwill or revalue any of the assets or liabilities.

Cash	20,000	
Goldman, Capital (10% of total capital)		12,000
King, Capital (60% of bonus)		4,800
Wilson, Capital (40% of bonus)		3,200
To record Goldman's entrance into partnership with $8,000 extra payment recorded as a bonus to the original partners.		

Goodwill Credited to Original Partners   The goodwill method views Goldman's payment as evidence that the partnership as a whole possesses an actual value of $200,000 ($20,000/10%). Because, even with the new partner's investment, only $120,000 in net assets is reported, a valuation adjustment of $80,000 is implied.[11] Over the previous years, unrecorded gains have apparently accrued to the business. This $80,000 figure might reflect the need to revalue specific accounts such as inventory or equipment, although the entire amount, or some portion of it, may simply be recorded as goodwill.

Goodwill (or specific accounts)	80,000	
King, Capital (60% of goodwill)		48,000
Wilson, Capital (40%)		32,000
To recognize goodwill based on Goldman's purchase price.		
Cash	20,000	
Goldman, Capital		20,000
To record Goldman's admission into partnership.		

Comparison of Bonus Method and Goodwill Method   Completely different capital balances as well as asset and liability figures result from these two approaches. In both cases, however, the new partner is credited with the appropriate 10 percent of total partnership capital.

	Bonus Method	Goodwill Method
Assets less liabilities (as reported)	$100,000	$100,000
Goldman's contribution	20,000	20,000
Goodwill	–0–	80,000
Total	$120,000	$200,000
Goldman's capital	$ 12,000	$ 20,000

Because Goldman contributed an amount more than 10 percent of the partnership's resulting book value, this business is perceived as being worth more than the recorded accounts indicate. Therefore, the bonus in the first instance and the goodwill in the second were both assumed as accruing to the two original partners. Such a presumption is not unusual in an established business, especially if profitable operations have developed over a number of years.

Hybrid Method of Recording Admission of New Partner   One other approach to Goldman's admission can be devised. Assume that the assets and liabilities of the King and Wilson partnership have a book value of $100,000 as stated earlier. Also assume that a piece of land held by the business is actually worth $30,000 more than its currently recorded book value. Thus, the identifiable assets of the partnership are worth $130,000. Goldman pays $20,000 for a 10 percent interest.

[11] In this example, because $20,000 is invested in the business, total capital to be used in the goodwill computation has increased to $120,000. If, as in the previous illustration, payment had been made directly to the partners, the original capital of $100,000 is retained in determining goodwill.

In this approach, the identifiable assets (such as land) are revalued but no goodwill is recognized.

Land.	30,000	
King, Capital (60% of revaluation)		18,000
Wilson, Capital (40%)		12,000
To record current fair value of land in preparation for admission of new partner.		

The admission of Goldman and the payment of $20,000 bring the total capital balance to $150,000. Because Goldman is acquiring a 10 percent interest, a capital balance of $15,000 is recorded. The extra $5,000 payment ($20,000 − $15,000) is attributed as a bonus to the original partners. In this way, asset revaluation and a capital bonus are both used to align the accounts.

Cash	20,000	
Goldman, Capital (10% of total capital)		15,000
King, Capital (60% of bonus)		3,000
Wilson, Capital (40% of bonus)		2,000
To record entrance of Goldman into partnership and bonus assigned to original partners.		

Bonus or Goodwill Credited to New Partner   As previously discussed, Goldman also may be contributing some attribute other than tangible assets to this partnership. Therefore, the articles of partnership may be written to credit the new partner, rather than the original partners, with either a bonus or goodwill. Because of an excellent professional reputation, valuable business contacts, or myriad other possible factors, Goldman might be able to negotiate a beginning capital balance in excess of the $20,000 cash contribution. This same circumstance may also result if the business is desperate for new capital and is willing to offer favorable terms as an enticement to the potential partner.

To illustrate, assume that Goldman receives a 20 percent interest in the partnership (rather than the originally stated 10 percent) in exchange for the $20,000 cash investment. The specific rationale for the higher ownership percentage need not be identified.

The bonus method sets Goldman's initial capital at $24,000 (20 percent of the $120,000 book value). To achieve this balance, a capital bonus of $4,000 must be credited to Goldman and taken from the present partners:

Cash	20,000	
King, Capital (60% of bonus)	2,400	
Wilson, Capital (40% of bonus)	1,600	
Goldman, Capital		24,000
To record Goldman's entrance into partnership with reduced payment reported as a bonus from original partners.		

If goodwill rather than a bonus is attributed to the *entering partner,* a mathematical problem arises in determining the implicit value of the business as a whole. In the current illustration, Goldman paid $20,000 for a 20 percent interest. Therefore, the value of the company is calculated as only $100,000 ($20,000/20%), a figure that is less than the $120,000 in net assets reported after the new contribution. Negative goodwill appears to exist. One possibility is that individual partnership assets are overvalued and require reduction. As an alternative, the cash contribution might not be an accurate representation of the new partner's investment. Goldman could be bringing an intangible contribution (goodwill) to the business along with the $20,000. This additional amount must be determined algebraically:

$$\text{Goldman's capital} = 20\% \text{ of partnership capital}$$

Therefore:

$$\$20,000 + \text{Goodwill} = 0.20\,(\$100,000 + \$20,000 + \text{Goodwill})$$

$$\$20,000 + \text{Goodwill} = \$20,000 + \$4,000 + 0.20\,\text{Goodwill}$$

$$0.80\,\text{Goodwill} = \$4,000$$

$$\text{Goodwill} = \$5,000$$

If the partners determine that Goldman is, indeed, making an intangible contribution (a particular skill, for example, or a loyal clientele), Goldman should be credited with a $25,000 capital investment: $20,000 cash and $5,000 goodwill. When added to the original $100,000 in net assets reported by the partnership, this contribution raises the total capital for the business to $125,000. As the articles of partnership specified, Goldman's interest now represents a 20 percent share of the partnership ($25,000/$125,000).

Recognizing $5,000 in goodwill has established the proper relationship between the new partner and the partnership. Therefore, the following journal entry reflects this transaction:

Cash	20,000	
Goodwill	5,000	
Goldman, Capital		25,000
To record Goldman's entrance into partnership with goodwill attributed to this new partner.		

Dissolution—Withdrawal of a Partner

LO 9-10

Prepare journal entries to record the withdrawal of a current partner.

Admission of a new partner is not the only method by which a partnership can undergo a change in composition. Over the life of the business, partners might leave the organization. Death or retirement can occur, or a partner may simply elect to withdraw from the partnership. The articles of partnership also can allow for the expulsion of a partner under certain conditions. Again, any change in membership legally dissolves the partnership, although its operations usually continue uninterrupted under the remaining partners' ownership.

Regardless of the reason for dissolution, some method of establishing an equitable settlement of the withdrawing partner's interest in the business is necessary. Often, the partner (or the partner's estate) may simply sell the interest to an outside party, with approval, or to one or more of the remaining partners. As an alternative, the business can distribute cash or other assets as a means of settling a partner's right of co-ownership. Consequently, many partnerships hold life insurance policies solely to provide adequate cash to liquidate a partner's interest upon death.

Whether death or some other reason caused the withdrawal, a final distribution will not necessarily equal the book value of the partner's capital account. A capital balance is only a recording of historical transactions and rarely represents the true value inherent in a business. Instead, payment is frequently based on the value of the partner's interest as ascertained by either negotiation or appraisal. Because a settlement determination can be derived in many ways, the articles of partnership should contain exact provisions regulating this procedure.

The withdrawal of an individual partner and the resulting distribution of partnership property can, as before, be accounted for by either the bonus (no revaluation) method or the goodwill (revaluation) method. Again, a hybrid option is also available.

As in earlier illustrations, if a bonus is recorded, the amount can be attributed to either of the parties involved: the withdrawing partner or the remaining partners. Conversely, any revaluation of partnership property (as well as the establishment of a goodwill balance) is allocated among all partners to recognize possible unrecorded gains. The hybrid approach restates assets and liabilities to fair value but does not record goodwill. This last alternative reflects the legal change in ownership but avoids the theoretical problems associated with partnership goodwill.

Accounting for the Withdrawal of a Partner

To demonstrate the various approaches that can be taken to account for a partner's withdrawal, assume that the partnership of Duncan, Smith, and Windsor has existed for a number of years. At the present time, the partners have the following capital balances as well as the indicated profit and loss percentages:

Partner	Capital Balance	Profit and Loss Ratio
Duncan.............................	$ 70,000	50%
Smith.................................	20,000	30
Windsor	10,000	20
Total capital.........................	$ 100,000	

Windsor decides to withdraw from the partnership, but Duncan and Smith plan to continue operating the business. As per the original partnership agreement, a final settlement distribution for any withdrawing partner is computed based on the following specified provisions:

- An independent expert will appraise the business to determine its estimated fair value.
- Any individual who leaves the partnership will receive cash or other assets equal to that partner's current capital balance after including an appropriate share of any adjustment indicated by the previous valuation. The allocation of unrecorded gains and losses is based on the normal profit and loss ratio.

Following Windsor's decision to withdraw from the partnership, its property is immediately appraised. Total fair value is estimated at $180,000, a figure $80,000 in excess of book value. According to this valuation, land held by the partnership is currently worth $50,000 more than its original cost. In addition, $30,000 in goodwill is attributed to the partnership based on its value as a going concern. *Therefore, Windsor receives $26,000 on leaving the partnership: the original $10,000 capital balance plus a 20 percent share of this $80,000 increment.* The amount of payment is not in dispute, but the method of recording the withdrawal is.

Bonus Method Applied   If the partnership used the bonus method to record this transaction, the extra $16,000 paid to Windsor is simply assigned as a decrease in the remaining partners' capital accounts. Historically, Duncan and Smith have been credited with 50 percent and 30 percent of all profits and losses, respectively. This same relative ratio is used now to allocate the reduction between these two remaining partners on a ⅝ and ⅜ basis:

Bonus Method		
Windsor, Capital (to remove account balance)	10,000	
Duncan, Capital (⅝ of excess distribution).................................	10,000	
Smith, Capital (⅜ of excess distribution)...................................	6,000	
Cash		26,000
To record Windsor's withdrawal with $16,000 excess distribution taken from remaining partners.		

Goodwill Method Applied   This same transaction can also be accounted for by means of the goodwill (or revaluation) approach. The appraisal indicates that land is undervalued on the partnership's records by $50,000 and that goodwill of $30,000 has apparently accrued to the business over the years. The first two of the following entries recognize these valuations. The adjustments properly equate Windsor's capital balance with the $26,000 cash amount to be distributed. Windsor's equity balance is merely removed in the final entry at the time of payment.

Land Revaluation

Land.	50,000	
Duncan, Capital (50%)		25,000
Smith, Capital (30%)		15,000
Windsor, Capital (20%)		10,000

To recognize land value as a preliminary step to Windsor's withdrawal.

Goodwill Recognition

Goodwill	30,000	
Duncan, Capital (50%)		15,000
Smith, Capital (30%)		9,000
Windsor, Capital (20%)		6,000

To recognize goodwill at the time of ownership change.

Windsor, Capital (to remove account balance)	26,000	
Cash		26,000

To distribute cash to Windsor in settlement of partnership interest.

After the land revaluation, Windsor's recorded capital balance increases to $20,000. The remaining unrecorded increase in partnership value is then assigned to the intangible asset goodwill. Goodwill represents an asset that captures the intangible increase in partnership value attributable to the past efforts of the individual partners.[12] Upon withdrawal, a partner is entitled to share in any unrecorded increase in partnership value based on his or her profit and loss ratio. The extra $6,000 paid to Windsor (beyond the $20,000 adjusted capital balance) thus is consistent with the $30,000 overall recognition of partnership goodwill: ($6,000 ÷ 20%) = $30,000.

The implied value of a partnership as a whole, however, cannot be determined directly from the amount distributed to a withdrawing partner. For example, paying Windsor $26,000 did not indicate that total capital should be $130,000 ($26,000 ÷ 20%). This computation is appropriate only when (1) a new partner is admitted or (2) the percentage of capital is the same as the profit and loss ratio. Here, an outside valuation of the business indicated that it was worth $80,000 more than book value. As a 20 percent owner, Windsor was entitled to $16,000 of that amount, raising the partner's capital account from $10,000 to $26,000, the amount of the final payment.

Hybrid Method Applied   As indicated previously, a hybrid approach also can be adopted to record a partner's withdrawal. It also recognizes asset and liability revaluations but ignores goodwill. A bonus must then be recorded to reconcile the partner's adjusted capital balance with the final distribution.

The following journal entry, for example, does not record goodwill. However, the book value of the land is increased by $50,000 in recognition of present worth. This adjustment increases Windsor's capital balance to $20,000, a figure that is still less than the $26,000 distribution. The $6,000 difference is recorded as a bonus taken from the remaining two partners according to their relative profit and loss ratio.

Hybrid Method

Land.	50,000	
Duncan, Capital (50%)		25,000
Smith, Capital (30%)		15,000
Windsor, Capital (20%)		10,000

To adjust Land account to fair value as a preliminary step in Windsor's withdrawal.

[12] The value of many partnerships derives overwhelmingly from intangibles such as professional reputation and expertise. Because increases in intangible partnership value are difficult to quantify on an ongoing basis, they typically go unrecorded until a change in partnership ownership forces a reckoning.

Windsor, Capital (to remove account balance)	20,000	
Duncan, Capital (⅝ of bonus)	3,750	
Smith, Capital (⅜ of bonus)	2,250	
Cash		26,000
To record final distribution to Windsor with $6,000 bonus taken from remaining partners.		

Summary

1. A partnership is defined as "an association of two or more persons to carry on a business as co-owners for profit." This form of business organization exists throughout the U.S. economy ranging in size from small, part-time operations to international enterprises. The partnership format is popular for many reasons, including the ease of creation and the avoidance of the double taxation that is inherent in corporate ownership. However, the unlimited liability incurred by each general partner normally restricts the growth potential of most partnerships. Thus, although the number of partnerships in the United States is large, the size of each tends to be small.

2. Over the years, a number of different types of organizations have been developed to take advantage of both the single taxation of partnerships and the limited liability afforded to corporate stockholders. Such legal forms include S corporations, limited partnerships, limited liability partnerships, and limited liability companies.

3. The unique elements of partnership accounting are found primarily in the capital accounts accumulated for each partner. The basis for recording these balances is the articles of partnership, a document that should be established as a prerequisite to the formation of any partnership. One of the principal provisions of this agreement is each partner's initial investment. Noncash contributions such as inventory or land are entered into the partnership's accounting records at fair value.

4. In forming a partnership, the partners' contributions need not be limited to tangible assets. A particular line of expertise possessed by a partner and an established clientele are attributes that can have a significant value to a partnership. Two methods of recording this type of investment are found in practice. The bonus method recognizes only identifiable assets. The capital accounts are then aligned to indicate the balances negotiated by the partners. According to the goodwill approach, all contributions (even those of a nebulous nature such as expertise) are valued and recorded, often as goodwill.

5. Another accounting issue to be resolved in forming a partnership is the allocation of annual net income. In closing out the revenue and expense accounts at the end of each period, some assignment must be made to the individual capital balances. Although an equal division can be used to allocate any profit or loss, partners frequently devise unique plans in an attempt to be equitable. Such factors as time worked, expertise, and invested capital should be considered in creating an allocation procedure.

6. Over time, changes occur in the makeup of a partnership because of death or retirement or because of the admission of new partners. Such changes dissolve the existing partnership, although the business frequently continues uninterrupted through a newly formed partnership. If, for example, a new partner is admitted by the acquisition of a present interest, the capital balances can simply be reclassified to reflect the change in ownership. As an alternative, the purchase price may be viewed as evidence of the underlying value of the organization as a whole. Based on this calculation, asset and liability balances are adjusted to fair value, and any residual goodwill is recognized.

7. Admission into an existing partnership also can be achieved by a direct capital contribution from the new partner. Because of the parties' negotiations, the amount invested will not always agree with the beginning capital balance attributed to the new partner. The bonus method resolves this conflict by simply reclassifying the various capital accounts to align the balances with specified totals and percentages. No revaluation is carried out under this approach. Conversely, according to the goodwill method, all asset and liability accounts are adjusted first to fair value. The price the new partner paid is used to compute an implied value for the partnership, and any excess over fair value is recorded as goodwill.

8. The composition of a partnership also can undergo changes because of the death or retirement of a partner. Individuals may decide to withdraw. Such changes legally dissolve the partnership, although business operations frequently continue under the remaining partners' ownership. In compensating the departing partner, the final asset distribution may differ from the ending capital balance. This disparity can, again, be accounted for by means of the bonus method, which adjusts the remaining capital accounts to absorb the bonus. The goodwill approach by which all assets and liabilities are restated to fair value with any goodwill being recognized also can be applied. Finally, a hybrid method revalues the assets and liabilities but ignores goodwill. Under this last approach, any amount paid to the departing partner in excess of the newly adjusted capital balance is accounted for by means of the bonus method.

Comprehensive Illustration

Problem

(*Estimated Time: 30 to 55 Minutes*) Heyman and Mullins begin a partnership on January 1, 2017. Heyman invests $40,000 cash and inventory costing $15,000 but with a current appraised value of only $12,000. Mullins contributes a building with a $40,000 book value and a $48,000 fair value. The partnership also accepts responsibility for a $10,000 note payable owed in connection with this building.

The partners agree to begin operations with equal capital balances. The articles of partnership also provide that at each year-end profits and losses are allocated as follows:

1. For managing the business, Heyman is credited with a bonus of 10 percent of partnership income after subtracting the bonus. No bonus is accrued if the partnership records a loss.
2. Both partners are entitled to interest equal to 10 percent of the average monthly capital balance for the year without regard for the income or drawings of that year.
3. Any remaining profit or loss is divided 60 percent to Heyman and 40 percent to Mullins.
4. Each partner is allowed to withdraw $800 per month in cash from the business.

On October 1, 2017, Heyman invested an additional $12,000 cash in the business. For 2017, the partnership reported income of $33,000.

Lewis, an employee, is allowed to join the partnership on January 1, 2018. The new partner invests $66,000 directly into the business for a one-third interest in the partnership property. The revised partnership agreement still allows for both the bonus to Heyman and the 10 percent interest, but all remaining profits and losses are now split 40 percent each to Heyman and Lewis with the remaining 20 percent to Mullins. Lewis is also entitled to $800 per month in drawings.

Mullins chooses to withdraw from the partnership a few years later. After negotiations, all parties agree that Mullins should be paid a $90,000 settlement. The capital balances on that date were as follows:

Heyman, capital.	$88,000
Mullins, capital	78,000
Lewis, capital	72,000

Required:

a. Assuming that this partnership uses the bonus method exclusively, make all necessary journal entries. Entries for the monthly drawings of the partners are not required.

b. Assuming that this partnership uses the goodwill method exclusively, make all necessary journal entries. Again, entries for the monthly drawings are not required.

Solution

a. **Bonus Method**
2017

Jan. 1   All contributed property is recorded at fair value. Under the bonus method, total capital is then divided as specified between the partners.

Cash	40,000	
Inventory.	12,000	
Building.	48,000	
Note Payable.		10,000
Heyman, Capital (50%).		45,000
Mullins, Capital (50%)		45,000
To record initial contributions to partnership along with equal capital balances.		

Oct. 1

Cash	12,000	
Heyman, Capital		12,000
To record additional investment by partner.		

Dec. 31 Both the bonus assigned to Heyman and the interest accrual must be computed as preliminary steps in the income allocation process. Because the bonus is based on income after subtracting the bonus, the amount must be calculated algebraically:

$$
\begin{aligned}
\text{Bonus} &= 0.10\,(\$33{,}000 - \text{Bonus}) \\
\text{Bonus} &= \$3{,}300 - 0.10\,\text{Bonus} \\
1.10\,\text{Bonus} &= \$3{,}300 \\
\text{Bonus} &= \$3{,}000
\end{aligned}
$$

According to the articles of partnership, the interest allocation is based on a monthly average figure. Mullins's capital balance of $45,000 did not change during the year; therefore $4,500 (10 percent) is the appropriate interest accrual for that partner. However, because of the October 1, 2017, contribution, Heyman's interest must be determined as follows:

Beginning balance	$45,000 × 9 months = $405,000
New balance	$57,000 × 3 months = 171,000
	576,000
	× ¹⁄₁₂
Monthly average—capital balance	48,000
Interest rate	× 10%
Interest credited to Heyman.	$ 4,800

Following the bonus and interest computations, the $33,000 income earned by the business is allocated according to the previously specified arrangement:

	Heyman	Mullins	Totals
Net Income			$ 33,000
Bonus to Heyman	3,000		(3,000)
Income remaining after bonus.			$ 30,000
Interest on monthly average capital balance	4,800	4,500	(9,300)
Income remaining after bonus and interest			$ 20,700
Remaining income allocation.	12,420 (60%)	8,280 (40%)	(20,700)
Net income allocation total	$ 20,220	$ 12,780	$ 0

The partnership's closing entries for the year would be recorded as follows:

Heyman, Capital	9,600	
Mullins, Capital.	9,600	
Heyman, Drawing.		9,600
Mullins, Drawing		9,600
To close out $800 per month drawing accounts for the year.		
Income Summary	33,000	
Heyman, Capital		20,220
Mullins, Capital		12,780
To close out profit for year to capital accounts as computed above.		

At the end of this initial year of operation, the partners' capital accounts hold these balances:

	Heyman	Mullins	Totals
Beginning balance.	$45,000	$45,000	$ 90,000
Additional investment	12,000	–0–	12,000
Drawing	(9,600)	(9,600)	(19,200)
Net income (above)	20,220	12,780	33,000
Total capital.	$67,620	$48,180	$115,800

2018

Jan. 1   Lewis contributed $66,000 to the business for a one-third interest in the partnership property. Combined with the $115,800 balance previously computed, the partnership now has total capital of $181,800. Because no revaluation is recorded under the bonus approach, a one-third interest in the partnership equals $60,600 ($181,800 × ⅓). Lewis has invested $5,400 in excess of this amount, a balance viewed as a bonus accruing to the original partners:

Cash	66,000	
Lewis, Capital.		60,600
Heyman, Capital (60% of bonus)		3,240
Mullins, Capital (40% of bonus).		2,160
To record Lewis's entrance into partnership with bonus to original partners.		

Several years later   The final event in this illustration is Mullins's withdrawal from the partnership. Although this partner's capital balance reports only $78,000, the final distribution is set at $90,000. The extra $12,000 payment represents a bonus assigned to Mullins, an amount that decreases the capital of the remaining two partners. Because Heyman and Lewis have previously accrued equal 40 percent shares of all profits and losses, the reduction is split evenly between the two.

Mullins, Capital.	78,000	
Heyman, Capital (½ of bonus payment)	6,000	
Lewis, Capital (½ of bonus payment).	6,000	
Cash		90,000
To record withdrawal of Mullins with a bonus from remaining partners.		

b. **Goodwill Method**

2017

Jan. 1   The fair value of Heyman's contribution is $52,000, whereas Mullins is investing only a net $38,000 (the value of the building less the accompanying debt). Because the capital accounts are initially to be equal, Mullins is presumed to be contributing goodwill of $14,000.

Cash	40,000	
Inventory.	12,000	
Building.	48,000	
Goodwill	14,000	
Note payable.		10,000
Heyman, Capital		52,000
Mullins, Capital		52,000
Creation of partnership with goodwill attributed to Mullins.		

Oct. 1

Cash	12,000	
Heyman, Capital.		12,000
To record additional contribution by partner.		

Dec. 31   Although Heyman's bonus is still $3,000 as derived in requirement (*a*), the interest accruals must be recalculated because the capital balances are different. Mullins's capital for the entire year was $52,000; thus, interest of $5,200 (10 percent) is appropriate. However, Heyman's balance changed during the year so that a monthly average must be determined as a basis for computing interest:

Beginning balance	$52,000 × 9 months =	$468,000
New balance	$64,000 × 3 months =	192,000
		660,000
		× 1/12
Monthly average—capital balance		55,000
Interest rate		× 10%
Interest credited to Heyman.		$ 5,500

The $33,000 partnership income is allocated as follows:

	Heyman	Mullins	Totals
Net Income			$ 33,000
Bonus to Heyman	$ 3,000		(3,000)
Income remaining after bonus			$ 30,000
Interest on monthly average capital balance	5,500	5,200	(10,700)
Income remaining after bonus and interest			$ 19,300
Remaining income allocation	11,580 (60%)	7,720 (40%)	(19,300)
Net income allocation total	$ 20,080	$ 12,920	$ 0

The closing entries made under the goodwill approach would be as follows:

Heyman, Capital	9,600	
Mullins, Capital.	9,600	
Heyman, Drawing..		9,600
Mullins, Drawing		9,600
To close out drawing accounts for the year................		
Income Summary	33,000	
Heyman, Capital		20,080
Mullins, Capital		12,920
To assign profits per allocation schedule.		

After the closing process, the capital balances are composed of the following items:

	Heyman	Mullins	Totals
Beginning balance	$ 52,000	$52,000	$104,000
Additional investment..............	12,000	–0–	12,000
Drawing..........................	(9,600)	(9,600)	(19,200)
Net income......................	20,080	12,920	33,000
Total capital	$ 74,480	$55,320	$129,800

2018

Jan. 1   Lewis's investment of $66,000 for a one-third interest in the partnership property implies that the business as a whole is worth $198,000 ($66,000 divided by ⅓). After adding Lewis's contribution to the present capital balance of $129,800, the business reports total net assets of only $195,800. Thus, a $2,200 increase in value ($198,000 − $195,800) is indicated and will be recognized at this time. Under the assumption that all partnership assets and liabilities are valued appropriately, this entire balance is attributed to goodwill.

Goodwill	2,200	
Heyman, Capital (60%).................................		1,320
Mullins, Capital (40%).................................		880
To recognize goodwill based on Lewis's acquisition price.		
Cash	66,000	
Lewis, Capital.		66,000
To admit Lewis to the partnership.		

Several years later   To conclude this illustration, Mullins's withdrawal must be recorded. This partner is to receive a distribution that is $12,000 more than the corresponding capital balance of $78,000. Because Mullins is entitled to a 20 percent share of profits and losses, the additional $12,000 payment indicates that the partnership as a whole is undervalued by $60,000 ($12,000/20%). Only in that circumstance would the extra payment to Mullins be justified. Therefore, once again, goodwill is recognized and is followed by the final distribution.

Goodwill	60,000	
Heyman, Capital (40%).		24,000
Mullins, Capital (20%)		12,000
Lewis, Capital (40%)		24,000
Recognition of goodwill based on withdrawal amount paid to		
Mullins.		
Mullins, Capital.	90,000	
Cash		90,000
To distribute money to partner.		

Questions

1. What are the advantages of operating a business as a partnership rather than as a corporation? What are the disadvantages?
2. How does partnership accounting differ from corporate accounting?
3. What information do the capital accounts found in partnership accounting convey?
4. Describe the differences between a Subchapter S corporation and a Subchapter C corporation.
5. A company is being created and the owners are trying to decide whether to form a general partnership, a limited liability partnership, or a limited liability company. What are the advantages and disadvantages of each of these legal forms?
6. What is an articles of partnership agreement, and what information should this document contain?
7. What valuation should be recorded for noncash assets transferred to a partnership by one of the partners?
8. If a partner is contributing attributes to a partnership such as an established clientele or a particular expertise, what two methods can be used to record the contribution? Describe each method.
9. What is the purpose of a drawing account in a partnership's financial records?
10. At what point in the accounting process does the allocation of partnership income become significant?
11. What provisions in a partnership agreement can be used to establish an equitable allocation of income among all partners?
12. If no agreement exists in a partnership as to the allocation of income, what method is appropriate?
13. What is a partnership dissolution? Does dissolution automatically necessitate the cessation of business and the liquidation of partnership assets?
14. By what methods can a new partner gain admittance into a partnership?
15. When a partner sells an ownership interest in a partnership, what rights are conveyed to the new owner?
16. A new partner enters a partnership and goodwill is calculated and credited to the original partners. How is the specific amount of goodwill assigned to these partners?
17. Under what circumstance might goodwill be allocated to a new partner entering a partnership?
18. When a partner withdraws from a partnership, why is the final distribution often based on the appraised value of the business rather than on the book value of the capital account balance?

Problems

LO 9-1

1. Which of the following is *not* a reason for the popularity of partnerships as a legal form for businesses?
   a. Partnerships may be formed merely by an oral agreement.
   b. Partnerships can more easily generate significant amounts of capital.
   c. Partnerships avoid the double taxation of income that is found in corporations.
   d. In some cases, losses may be used to offset gains for tax purposes.

LO 9-1

2. How does partnership accounting differ from corporate accounting?
   a. The matching principle is not considered appropriate for partnership accounting.
   b. Revenues are recognized at a different time by a partnership than is appropriate for a corporation.
   c. Individual capital accounts replace the contributed capital and retained earnings balances found in corporate accounting.
   d. Partnerships report all assets at fair value as of the latest balance sheet date.

LO 9-2

3. Which of the following best describes the articles of partnership agreement?

    a. The purpose of the partnership and partners' rights and responsibilities are required elements of the articles of partnership.

    b. The articles of partnership are a legal covenant and must be expressed in writing to be valid.

    c. The articles of partnership are an agreement that limits partners' liability to partnership assets.

    d. The articles of partnership are a legal covenant that may be expressed orally or in writing, and forms the central governance for a partnership's operations.

LO 9-9

4. Pat, Jean Lou, and Diane are partners with capital balances of $50,000, $30,000, and $20,000, respectively. These three partners share profits and losses equally. For an investment of $50,000 cash (paid to the business), MaryAnn will be admitted as a partner with a one-fourth interest in capital and profits. Based on this information, which of the following best justifies the amount of MaryAnn's investment?

    a. MaryAnn will receive a bonus from the other partners upon her admission to the partnership.

    b. Assets of the partnership were overvalued immediately prior to MaryAnn's investment.

    c. The book value of the partnership's net assets was less than the fair value immediately prior to MaryAnn's investment.

    d. MaryAnn is apparently bringing goodwill into the partnership, and her capital account will be credited for the appropriate amount.

LO 9-10

5. A partnership has the following capital balances:

Henry (50% of gains and losses)	$ 135,000
Thomas (30%)	85,000
Catherine (20%).	80,000

    Anne is going to invest $125,000 into the business to acquire a 40 percent ownership interest. Goodwill is to be recorded. What will be Anne's beginning capital balance?

    a. $125,000

    b. $170,000

    c. $200,000

    d. $245,000

LO 9-8

6. A partnership has the following capital balances:

Comprix (35% of gains and losses)	$150,000
Heflin (40%)	300,000
Kaplan (25%)	320,000

    Mahar is going to pay a total of $200,000 directly to these three partners to acquire a 25 percent ownership interest from each. Goodwill is to be recorded. What is Heflin's capital balance after the transaction?

    a. $225,000

    b. $234,000

    c. $312,000

    d. $360,000

LO 9-9

7. The capital balance for Maxwell is $110,000 and for Russell is $40,000. These two partners share profits and losses 70 percent (Maxwell) and 30 percent (Russell). Evan invests $50,000 in cash into the partnership for a 30 percent ownership. The bonus method will be used. What is Russell's capital balance after Evan's investment?

    a. $35,000

    b. $37,000

    c. $40,000

    d. $43,000

LO 9-9

8. Bishop has a capital balance of $120,000 in a local partnership, and Cotton has a $90,000 balance. These two partners share profits and losses by a ratio of 60 percent to Bishop and 40 percent to Cotton. Lovett invests $60,000 in cash in the partnership for a 20 percent ownership. The goodwill method will be used. What is Cotton's capital balance after this new investment?

    a. $99,600

    b. $102,000

    c. $112,000

    d. $126,000

LO 9-9

9. The capital balance for Messalina is $210,000 and for Romulus is $140,000. These two partners share profits and losses 60 percent (Messalina) and 40 percent (Romulus). Claudius invests $100,000 in cash in the partnership for a 20 percent ownership. The bonus method will be used. What are the capital balances for Messalina, Romulus, and Claudius after this investment is recorded?

   a. $216,000, $144,000, $90,000

   b. $218,000, $142,000, $88,000

   c. $222,000, $148,000, $80,000

   d. $240,000, $160,000, $100,000

LO 9-6

10. A partnership begins its first year with the following capital balances:

Alfred, Capital	$ 50,000
Bernard, Capital.	60,000
Collins, Capital.	70,000

The articles of partnership stipulate that profits and losses be assigned in the following manner:

- Each partner is allocated interest equal to 5 percent of the beginning capital balance.
- Bernard is allocated compensation of $18,000 per year.
- Any remaining profits and losses are allocated on a 3:3:4 basis, respectively.
- Each partner is allowed to withdraw up to $5,000 cash per year.

Assuming that the net income is $60,000 and that each partner withdraws the maximum amount allowed, what is the balance in Collins capital account at the end of that year?

   a. $70,800

   b. $86,700

   c. $73,500

   d. $81,700

LO 9-4, 9-5, 9-6

11. A partnership begins its first year of operations with the following capital balances:

Winston, Capital.	$110,000
Durham, Capital.	80,000
Salem, Capital	110,000

According to the articles of partnership, all profits will be assigned as follows:

- Winston will be awarded an annual salary of $20,000 with $10,000 assigned to Salem.
- The partners will be attributed interest equal to 10 percent of the capital balance as of the first day of the year.
- The remainder will be assigned on a 5:2:3 basis, respectively.
- Each partner is allowed to withdraw up to $10,000 per year.

The net loss for the first year of operations is $20,000 and net income for the subsequent year is $40,000. Each partner withdraws the maximum amount from the business each period. What is the balance in Winston's capital account at the end of the second year?

   a. $102,600

   b. $104,400

   c. $108,600

   d. $109,200

LO 9-10

12. A partnership has the following capital balances:

Allen, Capital	$60,000
Burns, Capital.	30,000
Costello, Capital	90,000

Profits and losses are split as follows: Allen (20 percent), Burns (30 percent), and Costello (50 percent). Costello wants to leave the partnership and is paid $100,000 from the business based on provisions in the articles of partnership. If the partnership uses the bonus method, what is the balance of Burns's capital account after Costello withdraws?

   a. $24,000

   b. $27,000

   c. $33,000

   d. $36,000

Problems 13 and 14 are *independent* problems based on the following scenario:

At year-end, the Circle City partnership has the following capital balances:

Manning, Capital	$130,000
Gonzalez, Capital	110,000
Clark, Capital	80,000
Freeney, Capital	70,000

Profits and losses are split on a 3:3:2:2 basis, respectively. Clark decides to leave the partnership and is paid $90,000 from the business based on the original contractual agreement.

LO 9-10

13. The payment made to Clark beyond his capital account was for Clark's share of previously unrecognized goodwill. After recognizing partnership goodwill, what is Manning's capital balance after Clark withdraws?
    a. $133,000
    b. $137,500
    c. $140,000
    d. $145,000

LO 9-10

14. If instead the partnership uses the bonus method, what is the balance of Manning's capital account after Clark withdraws?
    a. $100,000
    b. $126,250
    c. $130,000
    d. $133,750

Problems 15 and 16 are *independent* problems based on the following capital account balances:

William (40% of gains and losses)	$ 220,000
Jennings (40%)	160,000
Bryan (20%)	110,000

LO 9-8

15. Darrow invests $270,000 in cash for a 30 percent ownership interest. The money goes to the original partners. Goodwill is to be recorded. How much goodwill should be recognized, and what is Darrow's beginning capital balance?
    a. $410,000 and $270,000
    b. $140,000 and $270,000
    c. $140,000 and $189,000
    d. $410,000 and $189,000

LO 9-9

16. Darrow invests $250,000 in cash for a 30 percent ownership interest. The money goes to the business. No goodwill or other revaluation is to be recorded. After the transaction, what is Jennings's capital balance?
    a. $160,000
    b. $168,000
    c. $170,200
    d. $171,200

LO 9-9

17. Lear is to become a partner in the WS partnership by paying $80,000 in cash to the business. At present, the capital balance for Hamlet is $70,000 and for MacBeth is $40,000. Hamlet and MacBeth share profits on a 7:3 basis. Lear is acquiring 40 percent of the new partnership.
    a. If the goodwill method is applied, what will the three capital balances be following the payment by Lear?
    b. If the bonus method is applied, what will the three capital balances be following the payment by Lear?

LO 9-9

18. The Distance Plus partnership has the following capital balances at the beginning of the current year:

Tiger (50% of profits and losses)	$85,000
Phil (30%)	60,000
Ernie (20%)	55,000

Each of the following questions should be viewed independently.

  a. If Sergio invests $100,000 in cash in the business for a 25 percent interest, what journal entry is recorded? Assume that the bonus method is used.

  b. If Sergio invests $60,000 in cash in the business for a 25 percent interest, what journal entry is recorded? Assume that the bonus method is used.

  c. If Sergio invests $72,000 in cash in the business for a 25 percent interest, what journal entry is recorded? Assume that the goodwill method is used.

LO 9-9

19. A partnership has the following account balances: Cash $50,000; Other Assets $600,000; Liabilities $240,000; Nixon, Capital (50 percent of profits and losses) $200,000; Hoover, Capital (20 percent) $120,000; and Polk, Capital (30 percent) $90,000. Each of the following questions should be viewed as an independent situation:

  a. Grant invests $80,000 in the partnership for an 18 percent capital interest. Goodwill is to be recognized. What are the capital accounts thereafter?

  b. Grant invests $100,000 in the partnership to get a 20 percent capital balance. Goodwill is not to be recorded. What are the capital accounts thereafter?

LO 9-9

20. The Prince-Robbins partnership has the following capital account balances on January 1, 2018:

Prince, Capital	$70,000
Robbins, Capital	60,000

  Prince is allocated 80 percent of all profits and losses with the remaining 20 percent assigned to Robbins after interest of 10 percent is given to each partner based on beginning capital balances.

  On January 2, 2018, Jeffrey invests $37,000 cash for a 20 percent interest in the partnership. This transaction is recorded by the goodwill method. After this transaction, 10 percent interest is still to go to each partner. Profits and losses will then be split as follows: Prince (50 percent), Robbins (30 percent), and Jeffrey (20 percent). In 2018, the partnership reports a net income of $15,000.

  a. Prepare the journal entry to record Jeffrey's entrance into the partnership on January 2, 2018.

  b. Determine the allocation of income at the end of 2018.

LO 9-6

21. The partnership agreement of Jones, King, and Lane provides for the annual allocation of the business's profit or loss in the following sequence:

  • Jones, the managing partner, receives a bonus equal to 20 percent of the business's profit.
  • Each partner receives 15 percent interest on average capital investment.
  • Any residual profit or loss is divided equally.

  The average capital investments for 2018 were as follows:

Jones.	$100,000
King	200,000
Lane.	300,000

  How much of the $90,000 partnership profit for 2018 should be assigned to each partner?

LO 9-4, 9-5, 9-6

22. Purkerson, Smith, and Traynor have operated a bookstore for a number of years as a partnership. At the beginning of 2018, capital balances were as follows:

Purkerson.	$60,000
Smith	40,000
Traynor	20,000

  Due to a cash shortage, Purkerson invests an additional $8,000 in the business on April 1, 2018.
  Each partner is allowed to withdraw $1,000 cash each month.

  The partners have used the same method of allocating profits and losses since the business's inception:

  • Each partner is given the following compensation allowance for work done in the business: Purkerson, $18,000; Smith, $25,000; and Traynor, $8,000.
  • Each partner is credited with interest equal to 10 percent of the average monthly capital balance for the year without regard for normal drawings.
  • Any remaining profit or loss is allocated 4:2:4 to Purkerson, Smith, and Traynor, respectively. The net income for 2018 is $23,600. Each partner withdraws the allotted amount each month.

  What are the ending capital balances for 2018?

LO 9-4, 9-5, 9-6

23. On January 1, 2017, the dental partnership of Angela, Diaz, and Krause was formed when the partners contributed $30,000, $58,000, and $60,000, respectively. Over the next three years, the business reported net income and (loss) as follows:

2017	$70,000
2018	42,000
2019	(25,000)

During this period, each partner withdrew cash of $15,000 per year. Krause invested an additional $5,000 in cash on February 9, 2018.

At the time that the partnership was created, the three partners agreed to allocate all profits and losses according to a specified plan written as follows:

- Each partner is entitled to interest computed at the rate of 10 percent per year based on the individual capital balances at the beginning of that year.
- Because of prior work experience, Angela is entitled to an annual salary allowance of $12,000 per year and Diaz is entitled to an annual salary allowance of $9,000 per year.
- Any remaining profit will be split as follows: Angela, 20 percent; Diaz, 40 percent; and Krause, 40 percent. If a net loss remains after the initial allocations to the partners, the balance will be allocated: Angela, 30 percent; Diaz, 50 percent; and Krause, 20 percent.

Determine the ending capital balance for each partner as of the end of each of these three years.

LO 9-10

24. The E.N.D. partnership has the following capital balances as of the end of the current year:

Pineda.	$230,000
Adams.	190,000
Fergie	160,000
Gomez.	140,000
Total capital	$720,000

Answer each of the following *independent* questions:

a. Assume that the partners share profits and losses 3:3:2:2, respectively. Fergie retires and is paid $190,000 based on the terms of the original partnership agreement. If the goodwill method is used, what is the capital balance of the remaining three partners?

b. Assume that the partners share profits and losses 4:3:2:1, respectively. Pineda retires and is paid $280,000 based on the terms of the original partnership agreement. If the bonus method is used, what is the capital balance of the remaining three partners?

LO 9-10

25. The partnership of Matteson, Richton, and O'Toole has existed for a number of years. At the present time the partners have the following capital balances and profit and loss sharing percentages:

Partner	Capital Balance	Profit and Loss Percentage
Matteson	$ 90,000	30%
Richton	150,000	50
O'Toole	100,000	20

O'Toole elects to withdraw from the partnership, leaving Matteson and Richton to operate the business. Following the original partnership agreement, when a partner withdraws, the partnership and all of its individual assets are to be reassessed to current fair values by an independent appraiser. The withdrawing partner will receive cash or other assets equal to that partner's current capital balance after including an appropriate share of any adjustment indicated by the appraisal. Gains and losses indicated by the appraisal are allocated using the regular profit and loss percentages.

An independent appraiser is hired and estimates that the partnership as a whole is worth $600,000. Regarding the individual assets, the appraiser finds that a building with a book value of $180,000 has a fair value of $220,000. The book values for all other identifiable assets and liabilities are the same as their appraised fair values.

Accordingly, the partnership agrees to pay O'Toole $120,000 upon withdrawal. Matteson and Richton, however, do not wish to record any goodwill in connection with the change in ownership. Prepare the journal entry to record O'Toole's withdrawal from the partnership.

LO 9-2, 9-4, 9-6, 9-9

26. In the early part of 2018, the partners of Hugh, Jacobs, and Thomas sought assistance from a local accountant. They had begun a new business in 2017 but had never used an accountant's services.

Hugh and Jacobs began the partnership by contributing $150,000 and $100,000 in cash, respectively. Hugh was to work occasionally at the business, and Jacobs was to be employed full-time. They decided that year-end profits and losses should be assigned as follows:

- Each partner was to be allocated 10 percent interest computed on the beginning capital balances for the period.
- A compensation allowance of $5,000 was to go to Hugh with a $25,000 amount assigned to Jacobs.
- Any remaining income would be split on a 4:6 basis to Hugh and Jacobs, respectively.

In 2017, revenues totaled $175,000, and expenses were $146,000 (not including the partners' compensation allowance). Hugh withdrew cash of $9,000 during the year, and Jacobs took out $14,000. In addition, the business paid $7,500 for repairs made to Hugh's home and charged it to repair expense.

On January 1, 2018, the partnership sold a 15 percent interest to Thomas for $64,000 cash. This money was contributed to the business with the bonus method used for accounting purposes.

Answer the following questions:

a. Why was the original profit and loss allocation, as just outlined, designed by the partners?

b. Why did the drawings for 2017 not agree with the compensation allowances provided for in the partnership agreement?

c. What journal entries should the partnership have recorded on December 31, 2017?

d. What journal entry should the partnership have recorded on January 1, 2018?

LO 9-3, 9-9, 9-10

27. Following is the current balance sheet for a local partnership of doctors:

Cash and current		Liabilities..................	$ 40,000
assets	$ 30,000	A, capital..................	20,000
Land......................	180,000	B, capital..................	40,000
Building and equipment		C, capital..................	90,000
(net)	100,000	D, capital.................	120,000
Totals.................	$310,000	Totals..................	$310,000

The following questions represent *independent* situations:

a. E is going to invest enough money in this partnership to receive a 25 percent interest. No goodwill or bonus is to be recorded. How much should E invest?

b. E contributes $36,000 in cash to the business to receive a 10 percent interest in the partnership. Goodwill is to be recorded. Profits and losses have previously been split according to the following percentages: A, 30 percent; B, 10 percent; C, 40 percent; and D, 20 percent. After E makes this investment, what are the individual capital balances?

c. E contributes $42,000 in cash to the business to receive a 20 percent interest in the partnership. Goodwill is to be recorded. The four original partners share all profits and losses equally. After E makes this investment, what are the individual capital balances?

d. E contributes $55,000 in cash to the business to receive a 20 percent interest in the partnership. No goodwill or other asset revaluation is to be recorded. Profits and losses have previously been split according to the following percentages: A, 10 percent; B, 30 percent; C, 20 percent; and D, 40 percent. After E makes this investment, what are the individual capital balances?

e. C retires from the partnership and, as per the original partnership agreement, is to receive cash equal to 125 percent of her final capital balance. No goodwill or other asset revaluation is to be recognized. All partners share profits and losses equally. After the withdrawal, what are the individual capital balances of the remaining partners?

LO 9-5, 9-6, 9-9

28. Boswell and Johnson form a partnership on May 1, 2016. Boswell contributes cash of $50,000; Johnson conveys title to the following properties to the partnership:

	Book Value	Fair Value
Land........................	$15,000	$28,000
Building and equipment......	35,000	36,000

The partners agree to start their partnership with equal capital balances. No goodwill is to be recognized.

According to the articles of partnership written by the partners, profits and losses are allocated based on the following formula:

- Boswell receives a compensation allowance of $1,000 per month.
- All remaining profits and losses are split 60:40 to Johnson and Boswell, respectively.
- Each partner can make annual cash drawings of $5,000 beginning in 2017.

Net income of $11,000 is earned by the business during 2016.

Walpole is invited to join the partnership on January 1, 2017. Because of her business reputation and financial expertise, she is given a 40 percent interest for $54,000 cash. The bonus approach is used to record this investment, made directly to the business. The articles of partnership are amended to give Walpole a $2,000 compensation allowance per month and an annual cash drawing of $10,000. Remaining profits are now allocated:

Johnson	48%
Boswell	12
Walpole	40

All drawings are taken by the partners during 2017. At year-end, the partnership reports an earned net income of $28,000.

On January 1, 2018, Pope (previously a partnership employee) is admitted into the partnership. Each partner transfers 10 percent to Pope, who makes the following payments directly to the partners:

Johnson	$ 5,672
Boswell	7,880
Walpole	8,688

Once again, the articles of partnership must be amended to allow for the entrance of the new partner. This change entitles Pope to a compensation allowance of $800 per month and an annual drawing of $4,000. Profits and losses are now assigned as follows:

Johnson	40.5%
Boswell	13.5
Walpole	36.0
Pope	10.0

For the year of 2018, the partnership earned a profit of $46,000, and each partner withdrew the allowed amount of cash.

Determine the capital balances for the individual partners as of the end of each year: 2016 through 2018.

LO 9-4, 9-5, 9-6, 9-9

29. Gray, Stone, and Lawson open an accounting practice on January 1, 2016, in San Diego, California, to be operated as a partnership. Gray and Stone will serve as the senior partners because of their years of experience. To establish the business, Gray, Stone, and Lawson contribute cash and other properties valued at $210,000, $180,000, and $90,000, respectively. An articles of partnership agreement is drawn up. It has the following stipulations:

- Personal drawings are allowed annually up to an amount equal to 10 percent of the beginning capital balance for the year.
- Profits and losses are allocated according to the following plan:
  1. A salary allowance is credited to each partner in an amount equal to $8 per billable hour worked by that individual during the year.
  2. Interest is credited to the partners' capital accounts at the rate of 12 percent of the average monthly balance for the year (computed without regard for current income or drawings).
  3. An annual bonus is to be credited to Gray and Stone. Each bonus is to be 10 percent of net income after subtracting the bonus, the salary allowance, and the interest. Also included in the agreement is the provision that there will be no bonus if there is a net loss or if salary and interest result in a negative remainder of net income to be distributed.
  4. Any remaining partnership profit or loss is to be divided evenly among all partners.

Because of financial shortfalls encountered in getting the business started, Gray invests an additional $9,100 on May 1, 2016. On January 1, 2017, the partners allow Monet to buy into the partnership. Monet contributes cash directly to the business in an amount equal to a 25 percent interest in the book value of the partnership property subsequent to this contribution. The partnership agreement as to splitting profits and losses is not altered upon Monet's entrance into the firm; the general provisions continue to be applicable.

The billable hours for the partners during the first three years of operation follow:

	2016	2017	2018
Gray...............	1,710	1,800	1,880
Stone..............	1,440	1,500	1,620
Lawson	1,300	1,380	1,310
Monet	–0–	1,190	1,580

The partnership reports net income for 2016 through 2018 as follows:

2016...............	$ 65,000
2017...............	(20,400)
2018...............	152,800

Each partner withdraws the maximum allowable amount each year.

a. Determine the allocation of income for each of these three years (to the nearest dollar).

b. Prepare in appropriate form a statement of partners' capital for the year ending December 31, 2018.

LO 9-8, 9-9, 9-10

30. A partnership of attorneys in the St. Louis, Missouri, area has the following balance sheet accounts as of January 1, 2018:

Assets	$320,000	Liabilities.............	$120,000
		Athos, capital.........	80,000
		Porthos, capital	70,000
		Aramis, capital........	50,000

According to the articles of partnership, Athos is to receive an allocation of 50 percent of all partnership profits and losses while Porthos receives 30 percent and Aramis, 20 percent. The book value of each asset and liability should be considered an accurate representation of fair value.

For each of the following *independent* situations, prepare the journal entry or entries to be recorded by the partnership. (Round to nearest dollar.)

a. Porthos, with permission of the other partners, decides to sell half of his partnership interest to D'Artagnan for $50,000 in cash. No asset revaluation or goodwill is to be recorded by the partnership.

b. All three of the present partners agree to sell 10 percent of each partnership interest to D'Artagnan for a total cash payment of $25,000. Each partner receives a negotiated portion of this amount. Goodwill is recorded as a result of the transaction.

c. D'Artagnan is allowed to become a partner with a 10 percent ownership interest by contributing $30,000 in cash directly into the business. The bonus method is used to record this admission.

d. Use the same facts as in requirement (c) except that the entrance into the partnership is recorded by the goodwill method.

e. D'Artagnan is allowed to become a partner with a 10 percent ownership interest by contributing $12,222 in cash directly to the business. The goodwill method is used to record this transaction.

f. Aramis decides to retire and leave the partnership. An independent appraisal of the business and its assets indicates a current fair value of $280,000. Goodwill is to be recorded. Aramis will then be given the exact amount of cash that will close out his capital account.

LO 9-2, 9-3, 9-5, 9-6, 9-8, 9-10

31. Steve Reese is a well-known interior designer in Fort Worth, Texas. He wants to start his own business and convinces Rob O'Donnell, a local merchant, to contribute the capital to form a partnership. On January 1, 2016, O'Donnell invests a building worth $52,000 and equipment valued at $16,000 as well as $12,000 in cash. Although Reese makes no tangible contribution to the partnership, he will operate the business and be an equal partner in the beginning capital balances.

To entice O'Donnell to join this partnership, Reese draws up the following profit and loss agreement:

- O'Donnell will be credited annually with interest equal to 20 percent of the beginning capital balance for the year.
- O'Donnell will also have added to his capital account 15 percent of partnership income each year (without regard for the preceding interest figure) or $4,000, whichever is larger. All remaining income is credited to Reese.
- Neither partner is allowed to withdraw funds from the partnership during 2016. Thereafter, each can draw $5,000 annually or 20 percent of the beginning capital balance for the year, whichever is larger.

The partnership reported a net loss of $10,000 during the first year of its operation. On January 1, 2017, Terri Dunn becomes a third partner in this business by contributing $15,000 cash to the partnership. Dunn receives a 20 percent share of the business's capital. The profit and loss agreement is altered as follows:

- O'Donnell is still entitled to (1) interest on his beginning capital balance as well as (2) the share of partnership income just specified.
- Any remaining profit or loss will be split on a 6:4 basis between Reese and Dunn, respectively.

Partnership income for 2017 is reported as $44,000. Each partner withdraws the full amount that is allowed.

On January 1, 2018, Dunn becomes ill and sells her interest in the partnership (with the consent of the other two partners) to Judy Postner. Postner pays $46,000 directly to Dunn. Net income for 2018 is $61,000 with the partners again taking their full drawing allowance.

On January 1, 2019, Postner withdraws from the business for personal reasons. The articles of partnership state that any partner may leave the partnership at any time and is entitled to receive cash in an amount equal to the recorded capital balance at that time plus 10 percent.

a. Prepare journal entries to record the preceding transactions on the assumption that the bonus (or no revaluation) method is used. Drawings need not be recorded, although the balances should be included in the closing entries.

b. Prepare journal entries to record the previous transactions on the assumption that the goodwill (or revaluation) method is used. Drawings need not be recorded, although the balances should be included in the closing entries.

(Round all amounts to the nearest dollar.)

Develop Your Skills

RESEARCH CASE

Go to the Buckeye Partners, L.P. website where forms filed with the SEC are available through the Investor Center. Find Buckeye's recent annual financial statements in their 10–K report for the partnership.

Required

Review Buckeye's financial statements as well as the accompanying notes. List and briefly discuss information included for this partnership that would typically not appear in financial statements produced for a corporation.

ANALYSIS CASE

Erin Carson, Megyn Delaney, and Caitlin Erikson form a partnership as a first step in creating a business. Carson invests most of the capital but does not plan to be actively involved in the day-to-day operations. Delaney has had some experience and is expected to do a majority of the daily work. Erikson has been in this line of business for some time and has many connections. Therefore, she will devote a majority of her time to getting new clients.

Required

Write a memo to these three partners suggesting at least two different ways in which the profits of the partnership can be allocated each year in order to be fair to all parties.

COMMUNICATION CASE 1

Kelly Fernandez and Michael Webster have decided to create a business. They have financing available and have a well-developed business plan. However, they have not yet decided which type of legal business structure would be best for them.

Required

Write a report for these two individuals outlining the types of situations in which the corporate form of legal structure would be the best choice.

COMMUNICATION CASE 2

Use the information in Communication Case 1.

Required

Write a report for these two individuals outlining the types of situations in which the partnership form of legal structure would be the best choice.

EXCEL CASE

The Ace and Deuce partnership has been created to operate a law firm. The partners are attempting to devise a fair system to allocate profits and losses. Ace plans to work more billable hours each year than Deuce. However, Deuce has more experience and can charge a higher hourly rate. Ace expects to invest more money in the business than Deuce.

Required

Build a spreadsheet that can be used to allocate profits and losses to these two partners each year. The spreadsheet should be constructed so that the following variables can be entered:

>   Net income for the year.
>   Number of billable hours for each partner.
>   Hourly rate for each partner.
>   Capital investment by each partner.
>   Interest rate on capital investment.
>   Profit and loss ratio.

Use this spreadsheet to determine the allocation if partnership net income for the current year is $200,000, the number of billable hours is 2,000 for Ace and 1,500 for Deuce, the hourly rate for Ace is $20 and for Deuce is $30, and investment by Ace is $80,000 and by Deuce is $50,000. Interest on capital will be accrued each year at 10 percent of the beginning balance. Any remaining income amount will be split 50–50.

Use the spreadsheet a second time but make these changes: Deuce reports 1,700 billable hours, Ace invests $100,000, and interest will be recognized at a 12 percent annual rate. How do these three changes impact the allocation of the $200,000?

Partnerships: Termination and Liquidation

P artnerships can be rather frail organizations. Termination of business activities followed by the liquidation of partnership property can take place for a variety of reasons, both legal and personal.

In any firm, unless there is continuous open and candid communication among equity partners, and acceptance and buy-in for the business plan chosen by the firm, sooner or later there will be a dissolution of the firm.

The form of the dissolution is irrelevant, whether by withdrawal of individual partners or wholesale departure and formal liquidation. The end result will be the same: The original dream of harmonious and collegial growth of the firm will come to an end.[1]

Although a business organized as a partnership can exist indefinitely through periodic changes within the ownership, the actual cessation of operations is not an uncommon occurrence. "Sooner or later, all partnerships end, whether a partner dies, moves to Hawaii, or gets into a different line of business."[2] The partners simply might become incompatible and choose to cease operations. The same decision could be made if profits fail to reach projected levels.[3]

The liquidation of a partnership generally involves three important steps:

1. Noncash partnership assets are sold for cash, and gains and losses on the sales are allocated to the capital accounts of individual partners on the basis of their profit and loss ratios.

2. Partnership liabilities and expenses incurred during the liquidation are paid from the partnership's available cash. Liquidation expenses are allocated to partners' capital accounts on the basis of profit and loss ratios.

3. Any partnership cash remaining after paying liabilities and liquidation expenses is distributed to the individual partners on the basis of their respective capital balances.

The accountant can summarize and keep track of these steps in a *statement of partnership liquidation*.

Learning Objectives

After studying this chapter, you should be able to:

LO 10-1 Determine amounts to be paid to partners in a liquidation.

LO 10-2 Prepare journal entries to record the transactions incurred in the liquidation of a partnership.

LO 10-3 Determine the distribution of available cash when one or more partners has a deficit capital balance or becomes personally insolvent.

LO 10-4 Prepare a proposed schedule of liquidation based on safe capital balances to determine an equitable preliminary distribution of available partnership assets.

LO 10-5 Develop a predistribution plan to guide the distribution of assets in a partnership liquidation.

[1] Edward Poll, "Commentary: Coach's Corner: Reuniting a Firm Divided," *Massachusetts Lawyers Weekly*, pNA. Retrieved July 11, 2007, from *InfoTrac OneFile* via Thomson Gale.
[2] Camilla Cornell, "Breaking Up (with a Business Partner) Is Hard to Do," *Profit*, November 2004, p. 69.
[3] Sue Shellenbarger, "Cutting Losses When Partners Face a Breakup," *The Wall Street Journal*, May 21, 1991, p. B1.

The liquidation of a partnership becomes more complicated when:

- One or more partners have a negative (deficit) capital balance. A deficit (debit) capital balance can exist either at the beginning of the liquidation process or can arise during the liquidation as partners' capital balances absorb losses from noncash asset sales and liquidation expenses. In some cases, a partner with a deficit capital balance will have sufficient personal assets to be able to make a contribution to the partnership to eliminate the deficit. In other cases, a partner will be personally insolvent and the other partners will have to absorb the deficit through reductions in their capital accounts.

- The liquidation takes place over an extended period of time. In this case, the partners are likely to request that cash be distributed to them as it becomes available through the liquidation of partnership assets. The accountant can facilitate the distribution of cash in installments by calculating the *safe payments* that can be made without running the risk that an individual partner will incur a deficit capital balance. The accountant might choose to prepare a cash *predistribution plan* in advance of any sales of noncash assets to guide the distribution of installment payments during the course of the partnership liquidation.

Termination and Liquidation—Protecting the Interests of All Parties

As the chapter on bankruptcy discussed, accounting for the termination and liquidation of a business can prove to be a delicate task.

Beyond the goal of merely reporting transactions, the accountant must work to ensure the equitable treatment of all parties involved in the liquidation. The accounting records are the basis for allocating available assets to creditors and to the individual partners. If assets are limited, the accountant also might have to make recommendations as to the appropriate method for distributing any remaining funds. Protecting the interests of partnership creditors is an especially significant duty because the Uniform Partnership Act specifies that they have first priority to the assets held by the business at dissolution. The accountant's desire for an equitable settlement is enhanced, no doubt, in that any party to a liquidation who is not treated fairly can seek legal recovery from the responsible party.

Not only the creditors but also the partners themselves have a great interest in the financial data produced during the period of liquidation. They must be concerned with the possibility of incurring substantial monetary losses. The potential for loss is especially significant because of the unlimited liability to which the partners are exposed.

As long as a partnership can meet all of its obligations, the risk of partners is normally no more than that of corporate stockholders; the most they can lose is their capital investment. However, should the partnership become insolvent, each partner faces the possibility of having to satisfy *all* remaining partnership obligations personally. Although any partner suffering more than a proportionate share of these losses can seek legal retribution from the other partners, this process is not always an effective remedy. The other partners may themselves be personally insolvent, or anticipated legal costs might discourage the damaged party from seeking recovery. Therefore, each partner usually has a keen interest in monitoring the progress of a liquidation as it transpires.

Termination and Liquidation Procedures Illustrated

LO 10-1

Determine amounts to be paid to partners in a liquidation.

The procedures involved in terminating and liquidating a partnership are basically mechanical. Partnership assets are converted into cash that is then used to pay business obligations as well as liquidation expenses. *Any remaining assets are distributed to the individual partners based on their final capital balances.* Once assets have been distributed, the partnership's books are permanently closed. If each partner has a capital balance large enough to absorb all liquidation losses, the accountant should experience little difficulty in recording this series of transactions.

To illustrate the typical process, assume that Morgan and Houseman have been operating an art gallery as a partnership for a number of years. Morgan and Houseman allocate all profits and losses on a 6:4 basis, respectively. On May 1, 2017, the partners decide to terminate business activities, liquidate all noncash assets, and dissolve their partnership. Although they give no specific explanation for this action, any number of reasons could exist. The partners, for example, could have come to a disagreement so that they no longer believe they can work together. Another possibility is that business profits have become inadequate to warrant the continuing investment of their time and capital.

Following is a balance sheet for the partnership of Morgan and Houseman as of the termination date. The partnership has $75,000 of noncash assets to be liquidated. The revenue, expense, and drawing accounts have been closed as a preliminary step in terminating the business. A separate reporting of the gains and losses that occur during the final winding-down process will subsequently be made.

MORGAN AND HOUSEMAN
Balance Sheet
May 1, 2017

Assets		Liabilities and Capital	
Cash	$ 45,000	Liabilities	$ 32,000
Accounts receivable	12,000	Morgan, capital	50,000
Inventory	22,000	Houseman, capital	38,000
Land, building, and equipment (net)	41,000		
Total assets	$120,000	Total liabilities and capital	$120,000

We assume that the liquidation of Morgan and Houseman proceeds in an orderly fashion through the following events:

2017

June 1	The inventory is sold at auction for $15,000.
July 15	Of the total accounts receivable, the partnership collected $9,000 and wrote off the remainder as bad debts.
Aug. 20	The fixed assets are sold for a total of $29,000.
Aug. 25	All partnership liabilities are paid.
Sept. 10	A total of $3,000 in liquidation expenses is paid to cover costs such as accounting and legal fees as well as the commissions incurred in disposing of partnership property.
Oct. 15	All remaining cash is distributed to the owners based on their final capital account balances.

The partnership of Morgan and Houseman incurred a number of losses in liquidating its property. Losses often are expected because the need for immediate sale usually holds a high priority in a liquidation. Furthermore, a portion of the assets used by any business, such as its equipment and buildings, could have value that is strictly limited to a particular type of operation. If the assets are not easily adaptable, disposal at any reasonable price often proves to be a problem.

To record the liquidation of Morgan and Houseman, the following journal entries would be made. Rather than report specific income and expense balances, gains and losses are traditionally recorded directly to the partners' capital accounts. Because operations have ceased, determination of a separate net income figure for this period would provide little informational value. *Instead, a primary concern of the parties involved in any liquidation is keeping track of the continuing changes in each partner's capital balance.*

LO 10-2

Prepare journal entries to record the transactions incurred in the liquidation of a partnership.

6/1/17	Cash	15,000	
	Morgan, Capital (60% of loss)	4,200	
	Houseman, Capital (40% of loss)	2,800	
	Inventory		22,000
	To record sale of partnership inventory at a $7,000 loss.		
7/15/17	Cash	9,000	
	Morgan, Capital	1,800	
	Houseman, Capital	1,200	
	Accounts Receivable		12,000
	To record collection of accounts receivable with write-off of remaining $3,000 in accounts as bad debts.		
8/20/17	Cash	29,000	
	Morgan, Capital	7,200	
	Houseman, Capital	4,800	
	Land, Building, and Equipment (net)		41,000
	To record sale of fixed assets and allocation of $12,000 loss.		
8/25/17	Liabilities	32,000	
	Cash		32,000
	To record payment made to settle the liabilities of the partnership.		
9/10/17	Morgan, Capital	1,800	
	Houseman, Capital	1,200	
	Cash		3,000
	To record payment of liquidation expenses with the amounts recorded as direct reductions to the partners' capital accounts.		

After liquidating the partnership assets and paying off all obligations, the $63,000 cash that remains can be distributed to Morgan and Houseman on the basis of their capital balances. The following schedule determines the partners' ending capital account balances and, thus, the appropriate distribution of the final cash balance.

Cash and Capital Account Balances

	Cash	Morgan, Capital	Houseman, Capital
Beginning balances*	$ 45,000	$50,000	$38,000
Sold inventory	15,000	(4,200)	(2,800)
Collected accounts receivable	9,000	(1,800)	(1,200)
Sold fixed assets	29,000	(7,200)	(4,800)
Paid liabilities	(32,000)	–0–	–0–
Paid liquidation expenses	(3,000)	(1,800)	(1,200)
Final totals	$ 63,000	$35,000	$28,000

*Because of the presence of other assets as well as liabilities, the beginning balances in Cash and in the capital accounts are not equal.

After the ending capital balances have been calculated, the remaining cash can be distributed to the partners to close out the financial records of the partnership:

10/15/17	Morgan, Capital	35,000	
	Houseman, Capital	28,000	
	Cash		63,000
	To record distribution of cash to partners in accordance with final capital balances.		

Statement of Liquidation

Liquidation can take a considerable length of time to complete. Because the various parties involved seek continually updated financial information, the accountant should produce frequent reports summarizing transactions as they occur. Consequently, a statement (often referred to as the *statement of liquidation*) can be prepared at periodic intervals to disclose

- Transactions to date.
- Assets still held by the partnership.
- Liabilities remaining to be paid.
- Current cash and capital balances.

Although the preceding Morgan and Houseman example has been condensed into a few events occurring during a relatively brief period of time, partnership liquidations usually require numerous transactions that transpire over months and, perhaps, even years. By receiving frequent statements of liquidation, both the creditors and the partners are able to stay apprised of the results of this lengthy process.

See Exhibit 10.1 for the final statement of liquidation for the partnership of Morgan and Houseman. The accountant should have distributed previous statements at each important juncture of this liquidation to meet the informational needs of the parties involved. The example here demonstrates the stair-step approach incorporated in preparing a statement of liquidation. The effects of each transaction (or group of transactions) are outlined in a horizontal fashion so that current account balances and all prior transactions are evident. This structuring also facilitates the preparation of future statements: A new layer summarizing recent events can simply be added at the bottom each time a new statement is to be produced.

LO 10-3

Determine the distribution of available cash when one or more partners has a deficit capital balance or becomes personally insolvent.

Deficit Capital Balance—Contribution by Partner

In Exhibit 10.1, the liquidation process ended with both partners having positive capital balances. Thus, each partner was able to share in the remaining $63,000 cash. Unfortunately, such an outcome is not always the case. At the end of a liquidation, one or more partners could have a negative capital account, or the partnership could be unable to generate even enough cash to satisfy all of its creditors' claims. Such deficits are most likely to occur when

EXHIBIT 10.1

	Cash	Noncash Assets	Liabilities	Morgan, Capital (60%)	Houseman, Capital (40%)
MORGAN AND HOUSEMAN Statement of Partnership Liquidation Final Balances					
Beginning balances, 5/1/17	$ 45,000	$ 75,000	$ 32,000	$ 50,000	$ 38,000
Sold inventory, 6/1/17	15,000	(22,000)	–0–	(4,200)	(2,800)
Updated balances	60,000	53,000	32,000	45,800	35,200
Collected receivables, 7/15/17	9,000	(12,000)	–0–	(1,800)	(1,200)
Updated balances	69,000	41,000	32,000	44,000	34,000
Sold fixed assets, 8/20/17	29,000	(41,000)	–0–	(7,200)	(4,800)
Updated balances	98,000	–0–	32,000	36,800	29,200
Paid liabilities, 8/25/17	(32,000)		(32,000)	–0–	–0–
Updated balances	66,000	–0–	–0–	36,800	29,200
Paid liquidation expenses, 9/10/17	(3,000)			(1,800)	(1,200)
Updated balances	63,000	–0–	–0–	35,000	28,000
Distributed remaining cash, 10/15/17	(63,000)			(35,000)	(28,000)
Closing balances	$ –0–	$ –0–	$ –0–	$ –0–	$ –0–

the partnership is already insolvent at the start of the liquidation or when the disposal of non-cash assets results in material losses. Under these circumstances, the accounting procedures to be applied depend on legal regulations as well as the individual actions of the partners.

To illustrate, assume that the partnership of Holland, Dozier, and Ross was terminated at the beginning of the current year. Business activities ceased and all noncash assets were subsequently converted into cash. During the liquidation process, the partnership incurred a number of large losses that have been allocated to the partners' capital accounts on a 4:4:2 basis, respectively. A portion of the resulting cash is then used to pay all partnership liabilities and liquidation expenses.

Following these transactions, assume that only the following four account balances remain open within the partnership's records:

Cash	$20,000	Holland, Capital	$ (6,000)
		Dozier, Capital	15,000
		Ross, Capital	11,000
		Total	$20,000

Holland has a negative capital balance of $6,000; the assigned share of partnership losses has exceeded this partner's capital balance at the date the partnership terminated. In such cases, the Uniform Partnership Act (Section 807[b]) stipulates that the partner "shall contribute to the partnership an amount equal to any excess charges over the credits in the partner's account . . ." Therefore, Holland legally is required to convey an additional $6,000 to the partnership to eliminate the deficit balance. This contribution raises the cash balance to $26,000, which allows a complete distribution to be made to Dozier ($15,000) and Ross ($11,000) based on their capital account balances. The journal entry for this final payment closes out the partnership records:

Cash	6,000	
Holland, Capital		6,000
To record contribution made by Holland to extinguish negative capital balance.		
Dozier, Capital	15,000	
Ross, Capital	11,000	
Cash		26,000
To record distribution of remaining cash to partners in accordance with their ending capital balances.		

Deficit Capital Balance—Loss to Remaining Partners

Unfortunately, an alternative scenario could easily arise for the previous partnership liquidation. Although Holland's capital account shows a $6,000 deficit balance, this partner could resist any attempt to force an additional investment, especially because the business is in the process of being terminated. The possibility of such recalcitrance is enhanced if the individual is having personal financial difficulties. Thus, the remaining partners may eventually have to resort to formal litigation to gain Holland's contribution. Until that legal action is concluded, the partnership records remain open although inactive.

Distribution of Safe Payments

While awaiting the final resolution of this matter, no compelling reason exists for the partnership to continue holding $20,000 in cash. These funds will eventually be paid to Dozier and Ross regardless of any action that Holland takes. An immediate transfer should be made to these two partners to allow them the use of their money. However, because Dozier has a $15,000 capital account balance and Ross currently reports $11,000, a complete distribution is not possible. A method must be devised, therefore, to allow for a fair allocation of the available $20,000.

To ensure the equitable treatment of all parties, this initial distribution is based on the assumption that the $6,000 capital deficit will prove to be a total loss to the partnership. Holland may, for example, be completely insolvent so that no additional payment will ever be forthcoming. By making this conservative presumption, the accountant is able to calculate the lowest possible amounts (or *safe balances)* that Dozier and Ross must retain in their capital accounts to be able to absorb all future losses. Based upon these safe capital balances, the accountant can determine the amount of *safe payments* that can be made to Dozier and Ross without running the risk that future losses will cause either of these partners to have a deficit capital balance.

Should Holland's $6,000 deficit (or any portion of it) prove uncollectible, the loss will be written off against the capital accounts of Dozier and Ross. Allocation of this potential loss is based on the relative profit and loss ratio specified in the articles of partnership. According to the information provided, Dozier and Ross are credited with 40 percent and 20 percent of all partnership income, respectively. This 40:20 ratio equates to a 2:1 relationship (or $\frac{2}{3}$:$\frac{1}{3}$) between the two. Thus, if no part of the $6,000 deficit balance is ever recovered from Holland, $4,000 (two-thirds) of the loss will be assigned to Dozier and $2,000 (one-third) to Ross:

Allocation of Potential $6,000 Loss

Dozier................	$\frac{2}{3}$ of $(6,000) = $(4,000)
Ross	$\frac{1}{3}$ of $(6,000) = $(2,000)

These amounts represent the maximum potential reductions that the two remaining partners could still incur. Depending on Holland's actions, Dozier could be forced to absorb an additional $4,000 loss, and Ross's capital account could decrease by as much as $2,000. These balances must therefore remain in the respective capital accounts until the issue is resolved. Hence, a safe payment of $11,000 may be made to Dozier at the present time; this distribution reduces that partner's capital account from $15,000 to the minimum $4,000 level. Likewise, a $9,000 payment to Ross decreases the $11,000 capital balance to the $2,000 limit. Thus, $11,000 and $9,000 are the safe payments that can be distributed to the partners without fear of creating new deficits in the future.

Dozier, Capital..	11,000	
Ross, Capital	9,000	
Cash		20,000
To record distribution of safe payments of cash to Dozier and Ross based on the assumption that Holland will not contribute further to the partnership.		

After this $20,000 cash distribution, only a few other events can occur during the remaining life of the partnership. Holland, either voluntarily or through legal persuasion, could contribute the entire $6,000 needed to eradicate the capital deficit. If so, the money should be immediately turned over to Dozier ($4,000) and Ross ($2,000) based on their remaining capital balances. This final distribution effectively closes the partnership records.

A second possibility is that Dozier and Ross could be unable to recover any part of the deficit from Holland. These two remaining partners must then absorb the $6,000 loss themselves. Because adequate safe capital balances have been maintained, recording a complete default by Holland serves to close out the partnership books.

Dozier, Capital ($\frac{2}{3}$ of loss)	4,000	
Ross, Capital ($\frac{1}{3}$ of loss)..	2,000	
Holland, Capital...		6,000
To record allocation of deficit capital balance of insolvent partner.		

Deficit Is Partly Collectible

One other ending to this partnership liquidation is possible. The partnership could recover a portion of the $6,000 from Holland, but the remainder could prove to be uncollectible. Holland could become bankrupt, or the other partners could simply give up trying to collect from him. The partners could also negotiate this settlement to avoid protracted legal actions.

To illustrate, assume that Holland manages to contribute $3,600 to the partnership but subsequently files for relief under the provisions of the bankruptcy laws. In a later legal arrangement, $1,000 additional cash goes to the partnership, but the final $1,400 will never be collected. This series of events creates the following effects within the liquidation process:

1. The $3,600 contribution made by Holland is distributed to Dozier and Ross based on a new computation of their safe capital balances.
2. The $1,400 default is charged against the two positive capital balances in accordance with the relative profit and loss ratio.
3. The final $1,000 contribution made by Holland is then paid to Dozier and Ross in amounts equal to their ending capital balances, a transaction that closes the partnership's financial records.

The distribution of the first $3,600 depends on a recalculation of the minimum capital balances that Dozier and Ross must maintain to absorb all potential losses. Each of these computations is necessary because of a basic fact: Holland's remaining deficit balance ($2,400 at this time) could prove to be a total loss. This approach guarantees that the other two partners will continue to report sufficient capital until the liquidation is ultimately resolved.

	Current Capital		Allocation of Potential Loss		Safe Payments
Dozier	$4,000	–	⅔ of $(2,400) = $(1,600)	=	$2,400
Ross	$2,000	–	⅓ of $(2,400) = $ (800)	=	$1,200

Thus, the $3,600 in cash that is now available is distributed immediately to Dozier and Ross as safe payments:

Cash	3,600	
Holland, Capital		3,600
Dozier, Capital	2,400	
Ross, Capital	1,200	
Cash		3,600
To record capital contribution by Holland and subsequent distribution of funds to Dozier and Ross as safe payments.		

After recording this $3,600 contribution from Holland and the subsequent disbursement, the partnership's capital accounts stay open, registering the following balances:

Holland, Capital (deficit)	$(2,400)
Dozier, Capital	1,600
Ross, Capital	800

These accounts continue to remain on the partnership books until the final resolution of Holland's obligation.

LO 10-5

10. Carney, Pierce, Menton, and Hoehn are partners who share profits and losses on a 4:3:2:1 basis, respectively. They are beginning to liquidate the business. At the start of this process, capital balances are

Carney, capital	$60,000
Pierce, capital	27,000
Menton, capital	43,000
Hoehn, capital	20,000

Which of the following statements is true?
   a. The first available $2,000 will go to Hoehn.
   b. Carney will be the last partner to receive any available cash.
   c. The first available $3,000 will go to Menton.
   d. Carney will collect a portion of any available cash before Hoehn receives money.

LO 10-3, 10-4

11. A partnership has gone through liquidation and now reports the following account balances:

Cash	$ 16,000
Loan from Jones	3,000
Wayman, capital	(2,000) (deficit)
Jones, capital	(5,000) (deficit)
Fuller, capital	13,000
Rogers, capital	7,000

Profits and losses are allocated on the following basis: Wayman, 30 percent; Jones, 20 percent; Fuller, 30 percent; and Rogers, 20 percent. Which of the following events should occur now?
   a. Jones should receive $3,000 cash because of the loan balance.
   b. Fuller should receive $11,800 and Rogers $4,200.
   c. Fuller should receive $10,600 and Rogers $5,400.
   d. Jones should receive $3,000, Fuller $8,800, and Rogers $4,200.

LO 10-1, 10-3, 10-4

12. A partnership has the following account balances: Cash, $70,000; Other Assets, $540,000; Liabilities, $260,000; Nixon (50 percent of profits and losses), $170,000; Cleveland (30 percent), $110,000; Pierce (20 percent), $70,000. The company liquidates, and $8,000 becomes available to the partners. Who gets the $8,000?

LO 10-1, 10-3

13. A local partnership is liquidating and has only two assets (cash of $10,000 and land with a cost of $35,000). All partnership liabilities have been paid. All partners are personally insolvent. The partners have capital balances and share profits and losses as follows.

Brown, capital (40%)	$ 25,000
Fish, capital (30%)	15,000
Stone, capital (30%)	5,000

   a. If the land is sold for $25,000, how much cash does each partner receive in a final settlement?
   b. If the land is sold for $15,000, how much cash does each partner receive in a final settlement?
   c. If the land is sold for $5,000, how much cash does each partner receive in a final settlement?

LO 10-3

14. A local dental partnership has been liquidated and the final capital balances are

Atkinson, capital (40% of all profits and losses)	$ 70,000
Kaporale, capital (30%)	30,000
Dennsmore, capital (20%)	(42,000)
Rasputin, capital (10%)	(58,000)

If Rasputin contributes additional cash of $20,000 to the partnership, what should happen to it?

LO 10-4

15. A partnership currently holds three assets: cash, $10,000; land, $35,000; and a building, $50,000. The partnership has no liabilities. The partners anticipate that expenses required to liquidate their partnership will amount to $5,000. Capital balances are

Ace, capital	$ 25,000
Ball, capital	28,000
Eaton, capital	20,000
Lake, capital	22,000

The partners share profits and losses as follows: Ace (30 percent), Ball (30 percent), Eaton (20 percent), and Lake (20 percent). If a preliminary distribution of cash is to be made, what is the amount of safe payment that can be made to each partner?

LO 10-4

16. The following condensed balance sheet is for the partnership of Hardwick, Saunders, and Ferris, who share profits and losses in the ratio of 4:3:3, respectively:

Cash	$ 90,000	Accounts payable	$ 210,000
Other assets	820,000	Ferris, loan	40,000
Hardwick, loan	30,000	Hardwick, capital	300,000
		Saunders, capital	200,000
		Ferris, capital	190,000
Total assets	$940,000	Total liabilities and capital	$ 940,000

The partners decide to liquidate the partnership. Forty percent of the other assets are sold for $200,000. Prepare a proposed schedule of liquidation at this point in time.

LO 10-5

17. The following condensed balance sheet is for the partnership of Miller, Tyson, and Watson, who share profits and losses in the ratio of 6:2:2, respectively:

Cash	$ 50,000	Liabilities	$ 42,000
Other assets	150,000	Miller, capital	69,000
		Tyson, capital	69,000
		Watson, capital	20,000
Total assets	$200,000	Total liabilities and capital	$200,000

For how much money must the other assets be sold so that each partner receives some amount of cash in a liquidation?

LO 10-4

18. The balance sheet for the Delphine, Xavier, and Olivier partnership follows:

Cash	$ 60,000	Liabilities	$ 40,000
Noncash assets	100,000	Delphine, capital	60,000
		Xavier, capital	40,000
		Olivier, capital	20,000
Total assets	$160,000	Total liabilities and capital	$160,000

Delphine, Xavier, and Olivier share profits and losses in the ratio of 4:4:2, respectively. The partners have agreed to terminate the business and estimate that $12,000 in liquidation expenses will be incurred.

a. What is the amount of cash that safely can be paid to partners prior to liquidation of noncash assets?

b. How should the safe amount of cash determined in (a) be distributed to the partners?

LO 10-3

19. A partnership has liquidated all assets but still reports the following account balances:
The partners split profits and losses as follows: Cisneros, 40 percent; Beck, 20 percent; Sadak, 10 percent; Emerson, 20 percent; and Page 10 percent.

Beck, loan	$ 8,000
Cisneros, capital (40%)	5,000
Beck, capital (20%)	(12,000) (deficit)
Sadak, capital (10%)	(8,000) (deficit)
Emerson, capital (20%)	13,000
Page, capital (10%)	(6,000) (deficit)

Assuming that all partners are personally insolvent except for Sadak and Emerson, how much cash must Sadak now contribute to this partnership?

LO 10-4, 10-5

20. The following balance sheet is for a local partnership in which the partners have become very unhappy with each other.

Cash	$ 40,000	Liabilities	$ 30,000
Land	130,000	Adams, capital	80,000
Building	120,000	Baker, capital	30,000
		Carvil, capital	60,000
		Dobbs, capital	90,000
Total assets	$290,000	Total liabilities and capital	$290,000

To avoid more conflict, the partners have decided to cease operations and sell all assets. Using this information, answer the following questions. Each question should be viewed as an *independent* situation related to the partnership's liquidation.

    a. The $10,000 cash that exceeds the partnership liabilities is to be disbursed immediately. If profits and losses are allocated to Adams, Baker, Carvil, and Dobbs on a 2:3:3:2 basis, respectively, how will the $10,000 be divided?

    b. The $10,000 cash that exceeds the partnership liabilities is to be disbursed immediately. If profits and losses are allocated on a 2:2:3:3 basis, respectively, how will the $10,000 be divided?

    c. The building is immediately sold for $70,000 to give total cash of $110,000. The liabilities are then paid, leaving a cash balance of $80,000. This cash is to be distributed to the partners. How much of this money will each partner receive if profits and losses are allocated to Adams, Baker, Carvil, and Dobbs on a 1:3:3:3 basis, respectively?

    d. Assume that profits and losses are allocated to Adams, Baker, Carvil, and Dobbs on a 1:3:4:2 basis, respectively. How much money must the firm receive from selling the land and building to ensure that Carvil receives a portion?

LO 10-2, 10-4

21. Alex and Bess have been in partnership for many years. The partners, who share profits and losses on a 60:40 basis, respectively, wish to retire and have agreed to liquidate the business. Liquidation expenses are estimated to be $5,000. At the date the partnership ceases operations, the balance sheet is as follows:

Cash	$ 50,000	Liabilities	$ 40,000
Noncash assets	150,000	Alex, capital	90,000
		Bess, capital	70,000
Total assets	$200,000	Total liabilities and capital	$200,000

Part A

Prepare journal entries for the following transactions:

    a. Distributed safe cash payments to the partners.

    b. Paid $30,000 of the partnership's liabilities.

    c. Sold noncash assets for $160,000.

    d. Distributed safe cash payments to the partners.

    e. Paid remaining partnership liabilities of $10,000.

    f. Paid $4,000 in liquidation expenses; no further expenses will be incurred.

    g. Distributed remaining cash held by the business to the partners.

Part B

Prepare a final statement of partnership liquidation.

LO 10-5

22. The partnership of Larson, Norris, Spencer, and Harrison has decided to terminate operations and liquidate all business property. During this process, the partners expect to incur $8,000 in liquidation expenses. All partners are currently solvent.

The balance sheet reported by this partnership at the time that the liquidation commenced follows. The percentages indicate the allocation of profits and losses to each of the four partners.

Cash	$ 28,250	Liabilities	$ 47,000
Accounts receivable	44,000	Larson, capital (20%)	15,000
Inventory	39,000	Norris, capital (30%)	60,000
Land and buildings	23,000	Spencer, capital (20%)	75,000
Equipment	104,000	Harrison, capital (30%)	41,250
Total assets	$238,250	Total liabilities and capital	$238,250

Based on the information provided, prepare a predistribution plan for liquidating this partnership.

LO 10-5

23. The Drysdale, Koufax, and Marichal partnership has the following balance sheet immediately prior to liquidation:

Cash	$ 36,000	Liabilities	$50,000
Noncash assets	204,000	Drysdale, loan	10,000
		Drysdale, capital (50%)	70,000
		Koufax, capital (30%)	60,000
		Marichal, capital (20%)	50,000

a. Liquidation expenses are estimated to be $15,000. Prepare a predistribution schedule to guide the distribution of cash.

b. Assume that assets costing $74,000 are sold for $60,000. How is the available cash to be divided?

LO 10-5

24. A local partnership is to be liquidated. Commissions and other liquidation expenses are expected to total $19,000. The business's balance sheet prior to the commencement of liquidation is as follows:

Cash	$ 27,000	Liabilities	$ 40,000
Noncash assets	254,000	Simpson, capital (20%)	18,000
		Hart, capital (40%)	40,000
		Bobb, capital (20%)	48,000
		Reidl, capital (20%)	135,000
Total assets	$281,000	Total liabilities and capital . . .	$281,000

Prepare a predistribution plan for this partnership.

LO 10-3

25. The partnership of Hendrick, Mitchum, and Redding has the following account balances:

Cash	$ 50,000	Liabilities	$ 30,000
Noncash assets	135,000	Hendrick, capital	100,000
		Mitchum, capital	70,000
		Redding, capital	(15,000)

This partnership is being liquidated. Hendrick and Mitchum are each entitled to 40 percent of all profits and losses with the remaining 20 percent going to Redding.

a. What is the maximum amount that Redding might have to contribute to this partnership because of the deficit capital balance?

b. How should the $20,000 cash that is presently available in excess of liabilities be distributed?

c. If the noncash assets are sold for a total of $50,000, what is the minimum amount of cash that Hendrick could receive?

LO 10-3

26. The partnership of Anderson, Berry, Hammond, and Winwood is being liquidated. It currently holds cash of $20,000 but no other assets. Liabilities amount to $30,000. The capital balances are

Anderson (40% of profits and losses)	$ 20,000
Berry (30%)	12,000
Hammond (20%)	(17,000) (deficit)
Winwood (10%)	(25,000) (deficit)

a. If both Hammond and Winwood are personally insolvent, how much money must Berry contribute to this partnership?

b. If only Winwood is personally insolvent, how much money must Hammond contribute to the partnership? How will these funds be disbursed?

c. If only Hammond is personally insolvent, how much money should Anderson receive from the liquidation?

LO 10-2

27. March, April, and May have been in partnership for a number of years. The partners allocate all profits and losses on a 2:3:1 basis, respectively. Recently, each partner has become personally insolvent and, thus, the partners have decided to liquidate the business in hopes of remedying their personal financial problems. As of September 1, the partnership's balance sheet is as follows:

Cash	$ 11,000	Liabilities	$ 61,000
Accounts receivable	84,000	March, capital	25,000
Inventory	74,000	April, capital	75,000
Land, building, and equipment (net)	38,000	May, capital	46,000
Total assets	$207,000	Total liabilities and capital	$207,000

Prepare journal entries for the following transactions:

a. Sold all inventory for $56,000 cash.

b. Paid $7,500 in liquidation expenses.

c. Paid $40,000 of the partnership's liabilities.

d. Collected $45,000 of the accounts receivable.

e. Distributed safe cash balances; the partners anticipate no further liquidation expenses.

f. Sold remaining accounts receivable for 30 percent of face value.

g. Sold land, building, and equipment for $17,000.

h. Paid all remaining liabilities of the partnership.

i. Distributed cash held by the business to the partners.

LO 10-5

28. The partnership of Winn, Xie, Yang, and Zed has the following balance sheet:

Cash	$ 40,000	Liabilities	$ 66,000
		Winn, capital (50% of profits and losses)	100,000
Other assets	300,000	Xie, capital (30%)	84,000
		Yang, capital (10%)	50,000
		Zed, capital (10%)	40,000

Zed is personally insolvent, and one of his creditors is considering suing the partnership for the $10,000 that is currently owed. The creditor realizes that this litigation could result in partnership liquidation and does not wish to force such an extreme action unless Zed is reasonably sure of obtaining at least $10,000 from the liquidation.

Determine the amount for which the partnership must sell the other assets to ensure that Zed receives $10,000 from the liquidation. Liquidation expenses are expected to be $30,000.

LO 10-4

29. On January 1, the partners of Van, Bakel, and Cox (who share profits and losses in the ratio of 5:3:2, respectively) decide to liquidate their partnership. The trial balance at this date follows:

	Debit	Credit
Cash	$ 28,000	
Accounts receivable	86,000	
Inventory	72,000	
Machinery and equipment, net	209,000	
Van, loan	50,000	
Accounts payable		$ 93,000
Bakel, loan		40,000
Van, capital		128,000
Bakel, capital		100,000
Cox, capital		84,000
Totals	$445,000	$445,000

The partners plan a program of piecemeal conversion of the partnership's assets to minimize liquidation losses. All available cash, less an amount retained to provide for future expenses, is to be distributed to the partners at the end of each month. A summary of the liquidation transactions follows:

January   Collected $51,000 of the accounts receivable; the balance is deemed uncollectible.
Received $48,000 for the entire inventory.
Paid $4,000 in liquidation expenses.

(continued)

(*continued*)

Paid $88,000 to the outside creditors after offsetting a $5,000 credit memorandum received by the partnership on January 11.

Retained $20,000 cash in the business at the end of January to cover any unrecorded liabilities and anticipated expenses. The remainder is distributed to the partners.

February Paid $5,000 in liquidation expenses.

Retained $8,000 cash in the business at the end of the month to cover unrecorded liabilities and anticipated expenses.

March Received $156,000 on the sale of all machinery and equipment.

Paid $7,000 in final liquidation expenses.

Retained no cash in the business.

Prepare a schedule to compute the safe installment payments made to the partners at the end of each of these three months.

LO 10-1, 10-3

30. Following is a series of *independent cases*. In each situation, indicate the cash distribution to be made to partners at the end of the liquidation process. *Unless otherwise stated, assume that all solvent partners will reimburse the partnership for their deficit capital balances.*

Part A

The Buarque, Monte, and Vinicius partnership reports the following accounts. Vinicius is personally insolvent and can contribute only an additional $9,000 to the partnership.

Cash	$ 130,000
Liabilities.	35,000
Monte, loan	20,000
Buarque, capital (50% of profits and losses)	50,000
Monte, capital (25%)	40,000
Vinicius, capital (25%).	(15,000) (deficit)

Part B

Drawdy, Langston, and Pearl operate a local accounting firm as a partnership. After working together for several years, they have decided to liquidate the partnership's property. The partners have prepared the following balance sheet:

Cash	$ 20,000	Liabilities.	$ 40,000
Drawdy, loan	5,000	Langston, loan.	8,000
Noncash assets.	150,000	Drawdy, capital (40%).	65,000
		Langston, capital (30%)	50,000
		Pearl, capital (30%)	12,000
Total assets	$175,000	Total liabilities and capital . .	$175,000

The firm sells the noncash assets for $120,000; it will use $15,000 of this amount to pay liquidation expenses. All three of these partners are personally insolvent.

Part C

Use the same information as in Part B, but assume that the profits and losses are split 2:4:4 to Drawdy, Langston, and Pearl, respectively, and that liquidation expenses are only $6,000.

Part D

Following the liquidation of all noncash assets, the partnership of Krups, Lindau, Riedel, and Schnee has the following account balances. Krups is personally insolvent.

Liabilities.	$ 9,000
Krups, loan	6,000
Krups, capital (30% of profits and losses)	(20,000) deficit
Lindau, capital (30%).	(30,000) deficit
Riedel, capital (20%)	15,000
Schnee, capital (20%).	20,000

LO 10-1, 10-2, 10-5

31. The partnership of Frick, Wilson, and Clarke has elected to cease all operations and liquidate its business property. A balance sheet drawn up at this time shows the following account balances:

Cash	$ 60,000		Liabilities	$ 40,000
Noncash assets	219,000		Frick, capital (60%)	129,000
			Wilson, capital (20%)	35,000
			Clarke, capital (20%)	75,000
Total assets	$279,000		Total liabilities and capital	$279,000

Part A

Prepare a predistribution plan for this partnership

Part B

The following transactions occur in liquidating this business:

1. Distributed cash based on safe capital balances immediately to the partners. Liquidation expenses of $8,000 are estimated as a basis for this computation.
2. Sold noncash assets with a book value of $94,000 for $60,000.
3. Paid all liabilities.
4. Distributed cash based on safe capital balances again.
5. Sold remaining noncash assets for $51,000.
6. Paid actual liquidation expenses of $6,000 only.
7. Distributed remaining cash to the partners and closed the financial records of the business permanently.

Produce a final statement of liquidation for this partnership using the predistribution plan to determine payments of cash to partners based on safe capital balances.

Part C

Prepare journal entries to record the liquidation transactions reflected in the final statement of liquidation.

LO 10-2, 10-5

32. **Part A**

The partnership of Wingler, Norris, Rodgers, and Guthrie was formed several years ago as a local architectural firm. Several partners have recently undergone personal financial problems and have decided to terminate operations and liquidate the business. The following balance sheet is drawn up as a guideline for this process:

Cash	$ 15,000		Liabilities	$ 74,000
Accounts receivable	82,000		Rodgers, loan	35,000
Inventory	101,000		Wingler, capital (30%)	120,000
Land	85,000		Norris, capital (10%)	88,000
Building and equipment (net)	168,000		Rodgers, capital (20%)	74,000
			Guthrie, capital (40%)	60,000
Total assets	$451,000		Total liabilities and capital	$451,000

When the liquidation commenced, liquidation expenses of $16,000 were anticipated as being necessary to dispose of all property.

Prepare a predistribution plan for this partnership.

Part B

The following transactions transpire during the liquidation of the Wingler, Norris, Rodgers, and Guthrie partnership:

1. Collected 80 percent of the total accounts receivable with the rest judged to be uncollectible.
2. Sold the land, building, and equipment for $150,000.
3. Made safe capital distributions.
4. Learned that Guthrie, who has become personally insolvent, will make no further contributions.
5. Paid all liabilities.

6. Sold all inventory for $71,000.
7. Made safe capital distributions again.
8. Paid actual liquidation expenses of $11,000 only.
9. Made final cash disbursements to the partners based on the assumption that all partners other than Guthrie are personally solvent.

Prepare journal entries to record these liquidation transactions.

LO 10-2, 10-5

33. **Part A**

The partnership of Butler, Osman, and Ward was formed several years as a local tax preparation firm. Two partners have reached retirement age and the partners have decided to terminate operations and liquidate the business. Liquidation expenses of $34,000 are expected. The partnership balance sheet at the start of liquidation is as follows:

Cash	$ 30,000	Liabilities	$170,000
Accounts receivable	60,000	Butler, loan	30,000
Office equipment (net)	50,000	Butler, capital (25%)	50,000
Building (net)	110,000	Osman, capital (25%)	30,000
Land	100,000	Ward, capital (50%)	70,000
Total assets	$350,000	Total liabilities and capital	$350,000

Prepare a predistribution plan for this partnership.

Part B

The following transactions transpire in chronological order during the liquidation of the partnership:

1. Collected 90 percent of the accounts receivable and wrote the remainder off as uncollectible.
2. Sold the office equipment for $20,000, the building for $80,000, and the land for $120,000.
3. Made safe capital distributions.
4. Paid all liabilities in full.
5. Paid actual liquidation expenses of $30,000 only.
6. Made final cash distributions to the partners.

Prepare journal entries to record these liquidation transactions.

Develop Your Skills

RESEARCH CASE

CPA *skills*

A client of the CPA firm of Harston and Mendez is a medical practice of seven local doctors. One doctor has been sued for several million dollars as the result of a recent operation. Because of what appears to be this doctor's very poor judgment, a patient died. Although that doctor was solely involved with the patient in question, the lawsuit names the entire practice as a defendant. Originally, four of these doctors formed this business as a general partnership. However, five years ago, the partners converted the business to a limited liability partnership based on the laws of the state in which they operate.

Read the following articles as well as any other published information that is available on partner and partnership liability:

"Partners Forever? Within Andersen, Personal Liability May Bring Ruin," *The Wall Street Journal*, April 2, 2002, p. C1.

"Collapse: Speed of Andersen's Demise Amazing," *Milwaukee Journal Sentinel*, June 16, 2002, p. D1.

Required

Based on the facts presented in this case, answer these questions:

1. What liability do the other six partners in this medical practice have in connection with this lawsuit?
2. What factors will be important in determining the exact liability (if any) of these six doctors?

ANALYSIS CASE

Go to the website www.napico.com and click on "Partnership Financial Information—Click Here." Then click on "2015 Annual Reports" to access the Form 10-K annual report for Real Estate Associates Limited II (Real II).

Read the financial statements contained in the 2015 annual report and the accompanying notes, especially any that discuss the partnership form of organization.

Assume that an investor is considering investing in this partnership and has downloaded this report for study and analysis.

Required

1. What differences exist between Real II's financial statements and those of a corporation?
2. Assume that this investor is not aware of the potential implications of investing in a partnership rather than a corporation. What information is available in these statements to advise this individual of the unique characteristics of this legal business form?

COMMUNICATION CASE

Read the following as well as any other published articles on the bankruptcy of the partnership of Laventhol & Horwath:

> "Laventhol Says It Plans to File for Chapter 11," *The Wall Street Journal,* November 20, 1990, p. A3.
>
> "Laventhol Partners Face Long Process That Could End in Personal Bankruptcy," *The Wall Street Journal,* November 20, 1990, p. B5.
>
> "Laventhol Bankruptcy Filing Indicates Liabilities May Be as Much as $2 Billion," *The Wall Street Journal,* November 23, 1990, p. A4.

Required

Write a report describing the potential liabilities that the members of a partnership could incur.

EXCEL CASE

The partnership of Wilson, Cho, and Arrington has the following account information:

Partner	Capital Balance	Share of Profits and Losses
Wilson	$200,000	40%
Cho	180,000	20
Arrington	110,000	40

This partnership will be liquidated, and the partners are scheduled to receive cash equal to any ending positive capital balance. If a negative capital balance results, the partner is expected to contribute that amount.

Assume that losses of $50,000 occur during the liquidation followed later by additional and final losses of $100,000.

Required

1. Create a spreadsheet to determine the capital balances that remain for each of the three partners after these two losses are incurred.
2. Modify this spreadsheet so that it can be used for different capital balances, different allocation patterns, and different liquidation gains and losses.

Accounting for State and Local Governments (Part 1)

"Financial statements prepared by state and local governments in conformity with generally accepted accounting principles provide citizens and taxpayers, legislative and oversight bodies, municipal bond analysts, and others with information they need to evaluate the financial health of governments, make decisions, and assess accountability. This information is intended, among other things, to assist these users of financial statements in assessing (1) whether a government's current-year revenues were sufficient to pay for current-year services (known as interperiod equity), (2) whether a government complied with finance-related legal and contractual obligations, (3) where a government's financial resources come from and how it uses them, and (4) a government's financial position and economic condition and how they have changed over time."[1]

To even a seasoned veteran of accounting, the financial statements produced by a state or local government can appear to be written in a complex foreign language.

- The 2014 financial statements for Bismarck, North Dakota, report several other financing sources and uses for the city's governmental funds that include $26.9 million from transfers-in and $28.7 million for transfers-out.

- The June 30, 2014, balance sheet for the governmental funds of Portland, Maine, reports total fund balances of $97.2 million.

- The 2015 comprehensive annual financial report (CAFR) for Phoenix, Arizona, contains more than 300 pages of data including the dollar amounts of expenditures made in connection with public safety ($826.5 million), community enrichment ($194.4 million), and environmental services ($16.9 million).

- For 2015, Greensboro, North Carolina, reports two complete and distinct sets of financial statements. The first discloses that the city's governmental activities owed $559.8 million in liabilities as of June 30, 2015, whereas the second indicates that, at the same point in time, the city's governmental funds owed only $15.9 million in liabilities.

- The June 30, 2015, balance sheet for Nashville and Davidson County, Tennessee, reports total deferred outflows of resources of $247.9 million along with total deferred inflows of resources of $1.08 billion.

Even a quick perusal of such information points to fundamental differences between state and local government accounting and the reporting associated with the financial statements created for a for-profit entity. These differences are not accidental. The financial statements produced by state and

Learning Objectives

After studying this chapter, you should be able to:

LO 11-1	Explain the history of and the reasons for the unique characteristics of the financial statements produced by state and local governments.
LO 11-2	Differentiate between the two sets of financial statements produced by state and local governments.
LO 11-3	Understand the reason that fund accounting has traditionally been a prominent factor in the internal recording of state and local governments.
LO 11-4	Identify the three fund types and the individual fund categories within each.
LO 11-5	Understand the basic structure of government-wide financial statements and fund financial statements (as produced for the governmental funds).
LO 11-6	Record the passage of a budget as well as subsequent encumbrances and expenditures.
LO 11-7	Understand the reporting of capital assets, supplies, and prepaid expenses by a state or local government.
LO 11-8	Determine the proper timing for the recognition of revenues from various types of nonexchange transactions.
LO 11-9	Account for the issuance of long-term bonds.
LO 11-10	Account for special assessment projects.
LO 11-11	Record the various types of monetary transfers that occur within the funds maintained by a state or local government.

[1] From GASB Statement 77, *Tax Abatement Disclosures*, August 2015.

local governments are unique for many specific reasons. This chapter and the next present the principles and practices that underlie state and local government accounting and explain the logic behind their application.

These chapters are designed to demonstrate a wide variety of reporting procedures. They also explain the evolution that has led state and local governments to produce financial statements that are markedly different from those of for-profit entities.

LO 11-1

Explain the history of and the reasons for the unique characteristics of the financial statements produced by state and local governments.

Introduction to the Financial Reporting for State and Local Governments

In the United States, thousands of state and local governments touch the lives of the citizenry on a daily basis. In addition to the federal and 50 state governments, 90,056 local governments existed as of the most recent census of governments in 2012. Of these, 38,910 were general purpose local governments—3,031 county governments and 35,879 subcounty governments (19,519 municipal governments and 16,360 township governments). The remainder, which comprised more than half of the total, were special purpose local governments that performed only one function or a very limited number of functions: 12,880 school districts and school system governments and 38,266 special district governments.[2]

Actions of one or more governments affect virtually every citizen each day. Nearly 14.4 million people are employed by state and local governments. Income and sales taxes are collected, property taxes are assessed, schools provide education, police and fire departments maintain public safety, garbage is collected, and roads are paved.[3]

When seeking to understand the financial reporting for state and local governments, the first question that should be addressed is whether a complete set of specialized accounting principles is necessary. Could the financial information of a state or local government be presented fairly by applying the same rules and procedures as a for-profit entity such as Microsoft or Google? In response to that basic question, several major differences were identified in a study by the Governmental Accounting Standards Board (GASB).

> "The primary purpose of governments is to enhance or maintain the well-being of citizens by providing services in accordance with public policy goals. In contrast, business enterprises focus primarily on wealth creation, interacting principally with those segments of society that fulfill their mission of generating a financial return on investment for shareholders."
>
> "The white paper cites several other crucial differences that generate user demand for unique information:
>
> - Governments serve a broader group of stakeholders, including taxpayers, citizens, elected representatives, oversight groups, bondholders, and others in the financial community.
> - Monitoring actual compliance with budgeted public policy priorities is central to government public accountability reporting.
> - Governments exist longer than for-profit businesses and are not typically subject to bankruptcy and dissolution."[4]

Accounting for state and local governments is not merely a matching of expenses with recognized revenues so that net income can be determined. The setting of tax rates and allocation of limited financial resources among such worthy causes as education, police protection, welfare, and the environment create heated debates throughout the nation. Without a profit motive, what should be reported by a government and who are the potential users of that financial information? To keep the public informed, government reporting has focused

---

[2] Government Organization Summary Report: 2012 by Carma Hogue, released September 26, 2013. http://www2.census.gov/govs/cog/g12_org.pdf

[3] http://www.census.gov/govs/apes/

[4] "Users of Governmental Financial Reports Require Substantially Different Information than Users of Business Financial Reports," News Release, March 16, 2006, http://www.gasb.org/cs/ContentServer?pagename=GASB%2FGASBContent_C%2FGASBNewsPage&cid=1176156736250.

historically on identifying the sources of current financial resources and the uses made of those resources.

Indeed, this approach is appropriate for the short-term decisions necessitated by the gathering and utilizing of current financial resources by government officials to carry out public policy. For the longer term, information to reflect the overall financial stability of the government is also needed, especially by creditors who provide funding often through the acquisition of government-issued bonds.

Hence, state and local government officials face a number of unique financial reporting challenges. Those issues are addressed by GASB, which was created in 1984 to serve as the public sector counterpart of the Financial Accounting Standards Board (FASB). GASB holds the primary responsibility in the United States for setting authoritative accounting standards for state and local government units.[5] In the same manner as FASB, GASB is an independent body functioning under the oversight of the Financial Accounting Foundation. Much of this chapter and the next reflect the efforts by GASB to provide relevant information to a wide array of individuals and groups interested in assessing both resource allocation decisions and the financial health of a particular government.[6]

Governmental Accounting—User Needs

The unique aspects of any accounting system should be a direct result of the needs of the people who use the financial statements. Identifying those informational requirements is a logical first step in the study of state and local government accounting. Financial reporting procedures are, thus, best understood as an outgrowth of user needs.

In *Concepts Statement No. 1,* "Objectives of Financial Reporting," GASB recognized this challenge by identifying several distinct groups of primary users of external state and local governmental financial reports:

Citizenry—Want to evaluate the likelihood of tax or service fee increases, to determine the sources and uses of resources, and to forecast revenues in order to influence spending decisions.
Legislative and oversight bodies—Want to assess the overall financial condition when developing budgets and program recommendations, to monitor operating results to assure compliance with mandates, to determine the reasonableness of fees and the need for tax changes, and to ascertain the ability to finance new programs and capital needs.
Investors and creditors—Want to know the amount of available and likely future financial resources, to measure the debt position and the ability to service that debt.[7]

Thus, the quest for useful government reporting encounters a significant obstacle: User needs are so broad that no one set of financial statements or accounting principles can satisfy all expectations. How can voters, bondholders, city officials, and all of the other users of the financial statements produced by state and local governments receive the information they need for decision-making purposes? How can statements that are prepared for citizens also be sufficient for the needs of creditors and investors?

Two Sets of Financial Statements

Eventually, the desire to provide information that could satisfy such broad demands led GASB to require the production of two separate sets of financial statements by state and local

LO 11-2

Differentiate between the two sets of financial statements produced by state and local governments.

---

[5] The National Committee on Municipal Accounting held the authority for state and local government accounting from 1934 until 1941. The National Committee on Governmental Accounting, a quasi-independent agency of the Government Finance Officers Association, established government accounting principles from 1949 through 1954 and again from 1967 until 1983 when GASB was formed. During several time periods, no group held primary responsibility for the development of governmental accounting. For an overview of the work of GASB, see Terry K. Patton and Robert J. Freeman, "The GASB Turns 25: A Retrospective," *Government Finance Review,* April 2009.

[6] In 1990, the Director of the Office of Management and Budget, the Secretary of the Treasury, and the Comptroller General created the Federal Accounting Standards Advisory Board (FASAB). FASAB recommends accounting principles and standards for the U.S. federal government and its agencies to use. Information about FASAB can be found at *Journal of Government Finance Management.*

[7] Government Accounting Standards Board, *Codification of Governmental Accounting and Financial Reporting Standards as of June 30, 2012* (Norwalk, CT, 2012), Appendix B, *Concepts Statement No. 1,* par. 35–37.

governments, each with its own unique principles and objectives. For a complete understanding of state and local government accounting, nothing is more essential than recognizing the need for reporting two sets of statements:

1. **Fund financial statements** provide a picture of the current activities of the government. They report current period revenues and expenditures in connection with individual government functions. These statements also focus on disclosing restrictions that have been placed on the use of any of the financial resources held by these functions. Citizens interested in the operation of the government are likely to study the fund financial statements.
2. **Government-wide financial statements** have a longer-term focus. They report all revenues and all costs as well as all assets and liabilities. Creditors, especially bondholders, are likely to be most interested in government-wide financial statements as they assess the likelihood of being paid when obligations come due.

Fund Financial Statements

Fund financial statements have long been reported by state and local governments. They present individual government activities and the amount of financial resources allocated to them as well as the use made of those resources. By analyzing such statements, citizens can assess the government's fiscal accountability in raising and utilizing money. For example, fund financial statements report the amount spent during the current year on such services as public safety, education, health and sanitation, and the construction of new roads. The primary measurement focus, at least for public service activities, is the amount and changes in *current financial resources* such as cash and receivables. Those are assets that can be spent. In most cases, the timing of recognition is based on *modified accrual accounting.* Modified accrual accounting recognizes (1) revenues when the resulting current financial resources are both measurable and available to be used and (2) expenditures when they reduce current financial resources.

In applying modified accrual accounting, identifying when financial resources are available to be used for current-period expenditures is an important decision. The term "available to be used" means that current financial resources will be received soon enough in the future so that they can be used to pay for current period expenditures. The determination of what is meant by "soon enough" is up to the reporting government.

For example, in 2015, the City of Norfolk, Virginia, disclosed that "the City generally considers revenues, except for grant revenues, to be available if they are collected within 45 days of the end of the fiscal year." Therefore, using modified accrual accounting, a 2015 revenue collected by the City of Norfolk within the first 45 days of 2016 is recognized in 2015 because the money was available to pay for 2015 expenditures. In contrast, the City of Richmond, Virginia, applies a policy of two months and the City of Raleigh, North Carolina, uses 90 days. As shown by these cities, the definition of available to be used can vary from one government to the next. The one exception under modified accrual accounting is the recognition of property taxes where a 60-day maximum period is mandated.

Government-Wide Financial Statements

Government-wide financial statements have only been in existence for a little over 15 years. They were created to present information about a government's financial affairs as a whole. These statements provide a method of assessing operational accountability, the government's ability to meet its operating objectives. This information helps users make evaluations of the financial decisions and long-term stability of the government by allowing them to:

• Determine whether the government's overall financial position improved or deteriorated during the reporting period.
• Understand the cost of providing services to the citizenry.
• See how the government finances its programs.
• Understand the extent to which the government has invested in capital assets, such as roads, bridges, and other infrastructure assets.

This information has become especially relevant in recent years as a number of governments have declared bankruptcy (such as San Bernardino, CA; Stockton, CA; Jefferson County, AL; and Detroit, MI) while others face daunting financial difficulties.[8] The need to assess the risk of financial instability becomes an ever more important aspect of state and local government accounting.

To achieve these reporting goals, the government-wide financial statements' measurement focus is on all *economic resources* (not just current financial resources), and these statements utilize *accrual accounting* for timing purposes much like a for-profit entity. Consequently, these statements report all assets and liabilities (and deferred inflows and outflows of resources) and recognize revenues and expenses in a way that is comparable to business-type accounting.

The Advantage of Reporting Two Sets of Financial Statements

One aspect of governmental reporting has remained constant over the years: the goal of making the government and its officials accountable to the public. Because of the essential role of democracy within U.S. society, the creators of accounting principles have attempted to provide a vehicle for evaluating governmental actions. Citizens should be aware of the methods officials use to raise money and then the allocation made of those scarce financial resources.

Most citizens are both voters and taxpayers. They are especially interested in the results obtained from their involuntary contributions to the government in the form of taxes and tolls. Because elected and appointed officials hold authority over the public's money, governmental reporting has traditionally stressed this stewardship responsibility.

> Accountability is the cornerstone of all financial reporting in government. . . . Accountability requires governments to answer to the citizenry—to justify the raising of public resources and the purposes for which they are used. Governmental accountability is based on the belief that the citizenry has a "right to know," a right to receive openly declared facts that may lead to public debate by the citizens and their elected representatives.[9]

To promote transparency, governmental reporting has historically been directed toward measuring and identifying the current financial resources generated and expended by the various government functions. Fund financial statements allow readers to focus on individual activities. At least in connection with public services, such as the police department and public library, the fund statements answer three relevant questions:

- How did a particular part of the government generate current financial resources?
- Where did those current financial resources go?
- What amount of those current financial resources is presently held?

The term *current financial resources* normally encompasses the monetary assets available for officials to spend to meet the government's needs during the present budget period. Thus, when reporting current financial resources, a government is primarily monitoring cash, investments, and receivables as well as any current claims to those resources. Historically, virtually no emphasis has been placed on accounts such as Buildings, Equipment, and Long-Term Debts that have no direct impact on current financial resources.

Stressing accountability by monitoring the inflows and outflows of current financial resources is an approach that cannot meet all user needs. Prior to the creation of government-wide financial statements, many conventional reporting objectives were ignored. For example, does the government have too much debt to service? As a result, investors and creditors were frequently sharp critics of governmental accounting. "When cities get into financial trouble, few citizens know about it until the day the interest can't be met or the

[8] A fascinating picture of a government in financial crisis can be found at http://www.npr.org/blogs/money/2012/03/23/149057880/how-a-city-goes-broke , which details the difficulties of governing Harrisburg, PA, as it fights through a series of bad financial decisions.
[9] GASB, *Codification*, Appendix B, *Concepts Statement No. 1*, par 56.

teachers paid. . . . Had the books been kept like any decent corporation's that could never have happened."[10]

Consequently, in 1998, GASB created an entirely new dimension for government reporting. A new standard was created to mandate that separate government-wide financial statements be included in the general purpose financial reporting for a state or local government. This second set of statements reports all assets and other resources at the disposal of government officials as well as all liabilities that must eventually be paid. Revenues and expenses are recognized according to accrual accounting to provide a completely different perspective from fund financial statements.

With two sets of financial statements, each user (whether citizen, creditor, or other interested party) can select the information considered to be the most relevant. Of course, not everyone believes that this additional data will always be helpful. "One of the tougher challenges of the current information age is sorting out the information most relevant for decision making from the vast amounts of data generated by today's state-of-the-art information systems. Financial reports cannot simply keep growing in size indefinitely to encompass every new type of information that becomes available."[11]

	Fund Financial Statements[*]	**Government-Wide Financial Statements**
Emphasis	Individual activities (during current period).	Government as a whole.
Measurement focus	Current financial resources (cash, investments, and receivables and claims to those assets).	All economic resources (all assets, liabilities, and other resources).
General information	Inflows and outflows of current financial resources.	Overall financial health.
Timing of recognition	Modified accrual accounting.	Accrual accounting.

[*]The information provided here for fund financial statements only applies to public service activities such as public safety and education. As will be discussed shortly, other activities in fund financial statements are reported more in keeping with government-wide financial statements.

LO 11-3

Understand the reason that fund accounting has traditionally been a prominent factor in the internal recording of state and local governments.

Internal Record-Keeping—Fund Accounting

In gathering financial information, state and local governments have always faced the challenge of reporting a diverse array of activities financed from numerous sources. Accountability and control become special concerns for governments that operate through a multitude of relatively independent departments and functions. Consequently, for internal monitoring purposes, the accounting for many government activities is maintained in a separate quasi-independent bookkeeping system referred to as a *fund* with its own complete set of accounts and balances. In this way, information can be accumulated and organized for every activity (the school system, debt payment, road construction, and the like).

For decades, internal information gathered in this manner has served as the foundation for fund financial statements. An underlying assumption of government reporting has long been that most statement users prefer to see information segregated by function in order to assess each activity individually. How much money did the fire department receive and what was done with that money? The internal accounting records provided that information and the figures were transcribed directly into fund financial statements for external distribution.

Because no common profit motive exists to tie various functions and services together, consolidated activity balances were historically not presented. Combining financial results from the city zoo, fire department, water system, print shop, and a wide variety of other operations would provide figures of questionable utility especially if accountability and control over the usage of current financial resources are primary goals. Financial reporting was designed to provide information about individual activities, not the government as a whole.

[10] Richard Greene, "You Can't Fight City Hall—If You Can't Understand It," *Forbes,* March 3, 1980, p. 92.

[11] Jeffrey L. Esser, "Standard Setting—How Much Is Enough?" *Government Finance Review,* April 2005, p. 3.

The addition of government-wide statements does not affect the use of fund accounting. Consequently, the separate funds monitored by a state or local government still serve as the basic foundation for internal reporting. Although a single list of identifiable functions is not possible, the following are performed by many governments. As will be shown below, most of these are departments or agencies reported within the government's general fund. Some, though, are monitored within separate funds for control purposes or because the nature is different from a typical government activity.

Public safety	Judicial system
Highway maintenance	Debt repayment
Sanitation	Bridge construction
Health	Water and sewer system
Welfare	Municipal swimming pool
Culture and recreation	Data processing center
Education	Endowment funds
Parks	Employee pensions

The number of funds in use depends on the extent of services that the government provides and the grouping of related activities. For example, separate funds might be set up to account for a high school and its athletic programs, or these activities may be combined into a single fund.

> Only the minimum number of funds consistent with legal and operating requirements should be established, however, because unnecessary funds result in inflexibility, undue complexity, and inefficient financial administration.[12]

The requirement that government-wide financial statements must be reported along with fund financial statements was a radical advancement designed to communicate the overall financial health of the government to a broader array of decision makers. One significant outcome was that governments had to start reporting information (the total cost of roads, for example) that had never been accumulated previously because fund accounting monitors changes in current financial resources. As will be seen, a considerable amount of additional information is required to create financial statements that report all of the economic resources of the government as a whole.

Fund Accounting Classifications

LO 11-4

Identify the three fund types and the individual fund categories within each.

For internal record-keeping, all funds (whether accounting for the police department, the municipal golf course, or some other activity) are identified within one of three distinct categories. This classification system provides clearer reporting of the government's various activities. Furthermore, dividing funds into separate groups allows for unique accounting principles to be applied to each.

- *Governmental funds*—include all funds that account for activities a government carries out to provide citizens with services that are financed primarily through taxes and other general revenue sources. For that reason, the fire department and the schools systems are reported within the governmental funds.
- *Proprietary funds*—account for a government's ongoing activities that are similar to those conducted by a for-profit entity. This fund type encompasses operations that assess a user charge so that determining profitability or cost recovery is important. For example, both a municipal golf course and a toll road are typically reported within the proprietary funds.
- *Fiduciary funds*—account for monies held by the government in a trustee or agency capacity. Such assets must be maintained for others and cannot be used by officials for government programs. One common example is the monitoring of assets held in a pension plan for government employees such as teachers or sanitation workers.

---

[12] GASB, *Codification*, Sec. 1100.104.

Governmental Funds

In many state and municipal accounting systems, governmental funds tend to dominate because a service orientation usually prevails. The internal accounting system maintains individual funds for every distinct service function: public safety, libraries, construction of a town hall, and so on.

Each governmental fund accumulates and expends current financial resources to achieve one or more desired public goals. To provide better reported information and control, governmental funds are subdivided into five fund types: the general fund, special revenue funds, capital projects funds, debt service funds, and permanent funds. This classification system forms an overall structure for financial reporting purposes.

The General Fund GASB's definition of the general fund appears to be somewhat understated: "to account for and report all financial resources not accounted for and reported in another fund."[13] This description seems to imply that the general fund records only miscellaneous revenues and expenditures when, in actuality, it reports many of a government's most important ongoing functions. For example, the 2013 fund financial statements for the City of Baltimore, Maryland, disclosed 11 major areas of current expenditures within its general fund:

General government	Recreation and culture
Public safety and regulations	Highways and streets
Conservation of health	Sanitation and waste removal
Social services	Public service
Education	Economic development
Public library	

Expenditures reported for these categories were in excess of $1.49 billion and made up more than 73 percent of the total for all of the city's governmental funds for the year ended June 30, 2013.

Special Revenue Funds Special revenue funds account for resources that are restricted or committed for a specific purpose other than debt payments or capital projects. Because of donor stipulations or legislative mandates, these financial resources must be spent in a designated fashion. Saint Paul, Minnesota, for example, reported 16 individual special revenue funds during the 2014 fiscal year. Sources were as diverse as a city sales tax, administration fees for charitable gambling, and money received from solid waste and recycling programs.

The special revenue funds category is used to record these monies because legal or donor restrictions were attached to the revenue to require that expenditure be limited to specific operating purposes. As an example, according to Saint Paul's comprehensive annual financial report, a special revenue fund designated for "Street Lighting Districts" serves "to account for levied assessments used to operate above standard (ornamental) street lighting systems in various areas of the city, installed at the request of adjacent property owners." In this same manner, the City of Charlotte, North Carolina, uses a special revenue fund to account for money from a room occupancy tax that must go to support the NASCAR Hall of Fame.

Capital Projects Funds As the title implies, this fund type accounts for financial resources restricted, committed, or assigned for capital outlays such as acquiring or constructing bridges, high schools, roads, or municipal office complexes. Funding for these projects can come from a number of sources such as grants, the sale of bonds, or transfers from general revenue. The actual capital asset being purchased or constructed is not reported here. Only the money to finance the acquisition is monitored in a capital projects fund. For example, the Lexington-Fayette Urban County Government in Kentucky reported, as of June 30, 2014, that it held a total of more than $20.1 million of current financial resources in 11 different capital projects funds to be used in a variety of projects such as the acquisition or construction of a cultural center, road projects, public library projects, and computer equipment.

Debt Service Funds These funds record financial resources accumulated to pay long-term liabilities and interest as they come due. However, this fund type does not monitor

---

[13] GASB, *Codification*, Sec. 1300.104.

a government's long-term debt. Debt service funds are created to account for any monetary balances that are restricted, committed, or assigned to make the eventual payments needed to satisfy long-term liabilities. For example, on June 30, 2014, the city of Birmingham, Alabama, reported holding approximately $1.6 million of cash and investments in its debt service funds to pay long-term debt and interest. For the year then ended, more than $20.2 million in principal payments were made from this fund along with $10.7 million in interest payments.

Permanent Funds The permanent funds category accounts for financial resources restricted by external donor, contract, or legislation with the stipulation that the principal can never be spent but any resulting income can be used by the government, often for a specified public program. The City of Dallas, Texas, reported holding $9.7 million as of September 30, 2014, from private donations whose income was designated to maintain four different local parks and to help finance other municipal projects. Such gifts are frequently referred to as *endowments.*

Proprietary Funds

The proprietary funds category accounts for government activities, such as a bus system, toll road, or subway line, that assess a user charge. Such services resemble those found in the business world. Because the user charge helps the government make a profit or, at least, recover part of its cost, proprietary funds are reported in much the same way on both the fund financial statements and the government-wide financial statements. The accounting resembles that of a for-profit activity in that accrual accounting is used to recognize all assets and liabilities.

To facilitate financial reporting, proprietary funds are broken down into two fund types: enterprise funds and internal service funds.

Enterprise Funds Any government operation that is open to the public and financed, at least in part, by user charges is likely to be classified as an enterprise fund. A municipality, for example, might generate revenues from the use of a public swimming pool, golf course, airport, water and sewage service, and the like. The City of Houston generated $1.4 billion in revenue during the year ending June 30, 2015, from three enterprise funds: the city's aviation system, combined utility system, and the convention and entertainment facilities.

The number of enterprise funds has increased rather dramatically over recent years as government officials attempt to expand services without raising taxes. Thus, citizens utilizing a particular service might have to shoulder a higher percentage of its costs. "Enterprise funds have become an attractive alternative revenue source for local governments to recover all or part of the cost of goods or services from those directly benefiting from them."[14]

Enterprise fund activities that collect direct fees from customers resemble business activities. Not surprisingly, even in fund financial statements, the accounting parallels that found in for-profit reporting. Accrual basis accounting is used with a focus on all economic resources and not just on current financial resources.

A question arises, though, as to how much revenue an activity must generate before it is viewed as an enterprise fund. For example, if a city wants to promote mass transit and charges only a nickel to ride on its bus line, should that service be viewed as part of an enterprise fund (a business-type activity) or within the general fund (a governmental activity)?

Any activity that charges the public a user fee may be classified as an enterprise fund. However, this designation is *required* if the activity meets any one of the following criteria. At that point, the amount of revenue is viewed as significant to the operation:

- The activity generates revenues that provide the sole security for the debts of the activity.
- Laws or regulations require recovering the activity's costs (including depreciation and debt service) through fees or charges.
- Fees and charges are set at prices intended to recover costs including depreciation and debt service.

---

[14] Jeffrey Molinari and Charlie Tyer, "Local Government Enterprise Fund Activity: Trends and Implications," *Public Administration Quarterly,* Fall 2003, p. 369.

Internal Service Funds This second proprietary fund type accounts for any operation that provides services to another department or agency within the government for a fee. As with enterprise funds, internal service funds charge for their services. Here the work is for the primary benefit of parties within the government rather than for outside users. As with enterprise funds, internal service funds are accounted for much like for-profit operations found in the private sector.

The City of Lincoln, Nebraska, lists eight operations in its 2014 financial statements that are accounted for as individual internal service funds:

Information services fund—to account for the cost of operating a central data processing facility.

Engineering revolving fund—to account for the cost of operating a central engineering pool.

Insurance revolving fund—to account for the cost of providing several types of self-insurance programs.

Fleet services fund—to account for the operations of a centralized maintenance facility for city equipment.

Police garage fund—to account for the operation of a maintenance facility for police and other government vehicles.

Communication services fund—to account for the costs of providing graphic arts and telecommunications services.

Copy services fund—to account for the cost of providing copy services.

Municipal services center fund—to account for the purchase and operation of a facility to provide a location for various government functions.

Fiduciary Funds

The final classification, fiduciary funds, accounts for assets held in a trustee or agency capacity for external parties so that the money cannot be used to support the reporting government's programs. Like proprietary funds, fiduciary funds use the economic resources measurement focus and accrual accounting for the timing of revenues and expenses. Because these assets are not available for the benefit of the reporting government, fiduciary funds are omitted entirely from government-wide financial statements although separate statements are included within the fund financial statements.

Four different fund types are identified within the fiduciary funds category.

Investment Trust Funds The first fiduciary fund type accounts for the outside portion of investment pools when the reporting government has accumulated financial resources from other governments in order to have more money to invest so that a higher rate of return can be earned. For example, the Commonwealth of Virginia held almost $2.7 billion at June 30, 2015, in a local government investment pool that "helps local governmental entities maximize their rate of return by commingling their resources for investment purposes."

Private-Purpose Trust Funds The second fiduciary fund type accounts for monies held in a trustee capacity for the benefit of specifically designated external parties such as individuals, private organizations, or other governments. The Commonwealth of Virginia has seven private-purpose trust funds including unclaimed property and Virginia529 inVEST (the Virginia College Savings Plan). Notes to the government's 2015 financial statements describe this latter fund as "a defined contribution college savings program in which participants can save for qualified higher education expenses by making contributions and investments into portfolios of their choice." At the end of the 2015 fiscal year, the Commonwealth of Virginia reported $506 million in unclaimed property and $3.1 billion in Virginia529 inVEST.

Pension Trust Funds The third fiduciary fund type accounts for assets held to pay employee retirement benefits. Because of the need to provide adequate money for retired government workers (for a period of time that might last for many years), this fund type can become quite large. The City of Philadelphia, for example, reported assets of more than $6.2 billion in its pension trust fund as of June 30, 2014. This fund reports all assets being held but only the liability amounts that are currently owed. Thus, concern has often been expressed that long-term pension responsibilities are not properly reported in a state or local government's financial statements. Consequently, GASB has now mandated that the size of any unfunded pension obligation must be reported.

Agency Funds   The fourth type of fiduciary fund records any resources a government holds as an agent for individuals, private organizations, or other government units. For example, one government could collect taxes and tolls on behalf of another. Money often passes through the agency fund very quickly. To ensure safety and control, the agency fund maintains this money separately until physically transferred to the proper authority.

LO 11-5

Understand the basic structure of government-wide financial statements and fund financial statements (as produced for the governmental funds).

Overview of State and Local Government Financial Statements

Although a complete analysis of the financial statements of a state or local government is presented in the subsequent chapter, an overview of four basic financial statements will be presented at this point to help illustrate the reporting of certain events. These examples are not complete but can be used to demonstrate the presentation of various transactions and accounts.

Government-Wide Financial Statements

Only two financial statements make up the government-wide financial statements: *the statement of net position* and *the statement of activities.* The reporting is separated into governmental activities (all governmental funds and most internal service funds) and business-type activities (all enterprise funds and any remaining internal service funds).[15] As mentioned earlier, government-wide financial statements do not include the transactions and balances of fiduciary funds because those resources are not available for the benefit of the reporting government. Fiduciary funds are only shown in separate fund financial statements.

Exhibit 11.1 outlines the basic structure of a statement of net position. Because the economic resources measurement focus is used in the government-wide financial statements, all assets and liabilities are reported. In addition, as will be discussed later, GASB has identified several balances that relate to future periods of time but do not qualify as either assets or liabilities. As can be seen in this example, these amounts are shown as deferred outflows or deferred inflows of resources.

The final section of this statement, the net position category, indicates (1) the amount of capital assets being reported less related debt, (2) legal or external restrictions on the use of any of the reported assets or resources, and (3) the total unrestricted amount available for use by government officials. For example, in Exhibit 11.1, the Governmental Activities holds $80 that is unrestricted, whereas the Business-Type Activities has only $30.

The statement of activities in Exhibit 11.2 provides details about revenues and expenses, once again separated into governmental activities and business-type activities. This statement is usually read horizontally first and then vertically. Direct expenses and program revenues are shown for each government function. Program revenues include fines, fees, grants, and the like that the specific activity generates. Thus, a single net revenue or net expense figure is determined for each function as a way of indicating the financial burden or financial benefit to the government and its citizens.

For example, at Point A, a reader can see that maintaining public safety (probably through a police department, a fire department, and, maybe, an ambulance service) has a net cost to the government of $8,820. Direct expenses of $9,700 are partially offset by program revenues of $880 (possibly generated by fines, fees, or other charges). A taxpayer can judge the wisdom of incurring that cost to help ensure public safety, a figure that is more than the $8,100 cost of education as shown two lines below.

[15] Government-wide financial statements report internal service funds as governmental activities if their primary purpose is to serve the governmental funds. Conversely, internal service funds are included with business-type activities if they mainly exist to help one or more enterprise funds. For example, a print shop (an internal service fund) should be reported within the governmental activities if its work is primarily for the benefit of a governmental fund such as the public library. However, if its work is to service a bus line (or some other enterprise fund), the print shop is classified within the business-type activities.

EXHIBIT 11.1
Statement of Net Position
Government-Wide
Financial Statements

	Governmental Activities	Business-Type Activities	Total
Assets			
Cash	$ 100	$ 130	$ 230
Investments	900	40	940
Receivables	600	400	1,000
Internal amounts due	50	(50)	–0–
Supplies and materials	30	40	70
Capital assets (net of depreciation)	2,950	2,750	5,700
Total assets	$4,630	$3,310	$7,940
Deferred Outflows of Resources			
Unamortized cost of debt refunding	$ 200	$ 40	$ 240
Liabilities			
Accounts payable	$ 750	$ 230	$ 980
Noncurrent liabilities	2,300	920	3,220
Total liabilities	$3,050	$ 1,150	$4,200
Deferred Inflows of Resources			
Unavailable property tax collections	$ 100	$ –0–	$ 100
Net Position			
Net investment in capital assets	$1,410	$2,110	$3,520
Restricted for:			
Capital projects	50	–0–	50
Debt service	140	60	200
Unrestricted	80	30	110
Total net position	$1,680	$2,200	$3,880

EXHIBIT 11.2 **Statement of Activities—Government-Wide Financial Statements**

			Net (Expense) Revenue		
Function	Expenses	Program Revenues	Governmental Activities	Business-Type Activities	Total
Governmental activities					
General government	$ 3,200	$ 1,400	$ (1,800)	n/a	$ (1,800)
Public safety	9,700	880	(8,820) Ⓐ	n/a	(8,820)
Public works	2,600	600	(2,000)	n/a	(2,000)
Education	8,400	300	(8,100)	n/a	(8,100)
Total governmental activities	$23,900	$ 3,180	$(20,720)	n/a	$(20,720)
Business-type activities					
Water	$ 3,600	$ 4,030	n/a	$ 430	$ 430
Sewer	4,920	5,610	n/a	690	690
Airport	2,300	3,120	n/a	820	820
Total business-type activities	$10,820	$12,760	n/a	$1,940	$ 1,940
Total government	$34,720	$15,940	$(20,720) Ⓑ	$1,940 Ⓒ	$(18,780)
General revenues:					
Property taxes			$ 20,400 Ⓓ	$ –0–	$ 20,400
Investment earnings			420	70	490
Transfers			600	(600)	–0–
Total general revenues and transfers			$ 21,420	$ (530)	$ 20,890
Change in net position			$ 700 Ⓔ	$1,410 Ⓕ	$ 2,110
Beginning net position			980	790	1,770
Ending net position			$ 1,680	$2,200	$ 3,880

The net expense and net revenue for all governmental activities are then summed vertically to arrive at the total cost of operating the government, an amount that is offset by general revenues such as property taxes and sales taxes. As can be seen, governmental activities had a net cost of $20,720 (Point B), whereas the business-type activities generated a net financial benefit of $1,940 (Point C). At Point D, the statement shows that the government generated property tax revenues of $20,400 to cover virtually all of the cost of providing governmental activities. Investment earnings and transfers more than made up the difference so that the net position of the governmental activities increased by $700 this year (Point E). The net position of the business-type activities increased by $1,410 (Point F).

Fund Financial Statements

Most state or local governments produce quite a number of fund financial statements because of all the diverse functions. However, at this introductory stage, only the two fundamental statements that most parallel the two government-wide statements will be examined. Exhibit 11.3 shows *a balance sheet* for the governmental funds, and Exhibit 11.4 presents *a statement of revenues, expenditures, and changes in fund balances* for those same governmental funds. The balance sheet reports the current financial resources (assets) held by the various funds and the claims to those resources (liabilities).

As can be seen in Exhibit 11.4, three separate categories are present in this fund financial statement. They will each be discussed in detail throughout the remainder of this chapter and the next:

Revenues

Expenditures

Other Financing Sources (Uses)

Note that the figures found in these fund financial statements will not be the same as those presented for the governmental activities in the government-wide statement of net position (Exhibit 11.1) and statement of activities (Exhibit 11.2). For example, the asset total reported

EXHIBIT 11.3   Balance Sheet—Governmental Funds—Fund Financial Statements

	General Fund	Library Program	Other Governmental Funds	Total Governmental Funds
Assets				
Cash	$ 40	$ 10	$ 50	$ 100
Investments	580	120	200	900
Receivables	120	200	210	530
Supplies and materials	10	10	10	30
Total assets	$750	$340	$470	$1,560
Liabilities				
Accounts payable	$230	$170	$110	$ 510
Notes payable—current	200	–0–	100	300
Total liabilities	$430	$170	$210	$ 810
Deferred Inflows of Resources				
Unavailable property tax collections	$100	$–0–	$–0–	$ 100
Fund Balances				
Nonspendable	$ 10	$ 10	$ 10	$ 30
Restricted	100	90	60	250
Committed	30	50	100	180
Assigned	20	20	90	130
Unassigned	60	–0–	–0–	60
Total fund balances	$220	$170	$260	$ 650
Total liabilities, deferred inflows, and fund balances	$750	$340	$470	$1,560

EXHIBIT 11.4   **Statement of Revenues, Expenditures, and Other Changes in Fund Balances—Governmental Funds—Fund Financial Statements**

	General Fund	Library Program	Other Governmental Funds	Total Governmental Funds
Revenues				
Property taxes	$17,200	$ 900	$ 2,300	$20,400
Investment earnings	100	200	180	480
Program revenues	500	100	2,500	3,100
Total revenues	$17,800	$1,200	$ 4,980	$23,980
Expenditures				
Current:				
General government	$ 3,400	$ –0–	$ 100	$ 3,500
Public safety	5,100	–0–	400	5,500
Education	6,700	800	–0–	7,500
Debt service:				
Principal	–0–	–0–	1,000	1,000
Interest	–0–	–0–	600	600
Capital outlay	1,100	300	3,300	4,700
Total expenditures	$16,300	$1,100	$ 5,400	$22,800
Excess (deficiency) of revenues over expenditures	$ 1,500	$ 100	$ (420)	$ 1,180
Other Financing Sources (Uses)				
Bond proceeds	$ –0–	$ –0–	$ 1,000	$ 1,000
Transfers in	–0–	20	580	600
Transfers out	(1,300)	–0–	(1,000)	(2,300)
Total other financing sources and uses	$ (1,300)	$ 20	$ 580	$ (700)
Change in fund balances	$ 200	$ 120	$ 160	$ 480
Fund balances—beginning	20	50	100	170
Fund balances—ending	$ 220	$ 170	$ 260	$ 650

for the governmental activities in Exhibit 11.1 is $4,630, whereas the asset total for all governmental funds in Exhibit 11.3 is only $1,560. These differences result primarily for three reasons:

1. In government-wide statements, internal service funds are grouped with the funds that they primarily benefit. Thus, they are reported with the governmental activities if they assist governmental funds and with business-type activities if they assist enterprise funds. However, fund financial statements show all internal service funds as proprietary funds, not as governmental funds. *Totals will vary between the statements because both governmental funds and some proprietary funds are classified as governmental activities.*

2. Governmental activities apply the economic resources measurement focus. The governmental funds, in the fund statements, use the current financial resources measurement focus. *Different assets and liabilities are being reported by the two sets of statements.*

3. Governmental activities use accrual accounting in government-wide statements, while modified accrual accounting is used in creating fund financial statements for the governmental funds. *The timing of recognition is different.*

Because of these differences, reconciliations are reported between totals presented in Exhibits 11.1 and 11.3 and between Exhibits 11.2 and 11.4. Those reconciliations are discussed in detail in the following chapter.

Major Funds

In both of the fund financial statements presented in Exhibits 11.3 and 11.4, the general fund and every other individual fund that qualifies as major is shown in a separate column. The assumption here is that the Library Program (probably one of this government's special revenue funds if it is financed by a designated tax levy) is the only individual fund outside the general fund that is considered major. Information for all other governmental funds is then grouped into a single column. Consequently, identification of a major fund is quite important for disclosure purposes. A major fund is identified as follows:

> The reporting government's main operating fund (the general fund or its equivalent) should always be reported as a major fund. Other individual governmental and enterprise funds should be reported in separate columns as major funds based on these criteria:
>
> a. Total assets, liabilities, revenues, or expenditures/expenses of that individual governmental or enterprise fund are at least 10 percent of the corresponding total (assets, liabilities, and so forth) for all funds of that category or type (that is, total governmental or total enterprise funds), *and*
>
> b. The same element that met the 10 percent criterion in (a) is at least 5 percent of the corresponding total for all governmental and enterprise funds combined.
>
> In addition to funds that meet the major fund criteria, any other governmental or enterprise fund that the government's officials believe is particularly important to financial statement users (for example, because of public interest or consistency) may be reported as a major fund.[16]

Fund Balances

One other unique aspect of the structure of fund financial statements created for the governmental funds should be noted. A stockholders' equity section is not needed in order to report contributed capital, retained earnings, and the like. There are no stockholders for a state or local government. Instead, "fund balance" accounts, as shown in Exhibit 11.3, are used to indicate the amount of net current financial resources reported by each separate fund.

Fund balance accounts have long been used in governmental accounting in a rather generic fashion. Rules have now been established to standardize the reporting within five categories. These designations should help financial statement readers understand the use that can be made of each fund's net current financial resources. Often, because of legal or external restrictions, some amount of the current financial resources cannot be used by government officials as they please. "The fund balance classifications are GASB's response to credit market participants who sought general information about the availability of reported fund balances."[17]

For example, in Exhibit 11.3, the general fund reports assets of $750, and liabilities and deferred inflows of $430 and $100, indicating a net position of $220. From a reporting perspective, the most significant question to be addressed is: What use can be made of this $220? The purpose of the fund balance classifications, therefore, is to indicate restrictions that limit the ability of government officials to use these resources.

Fund Balance—Nonspendable   As implied by the name, this amount of a fund's current financial resources cannot be spent. This restricted classification is normally necessary for one of two reasons. First, some assets such as supplies and prepaid expenses are simply not in a spendable form. Second, financial resources are occasionally received that cannot be spent because of externally imposed limitations. A cash gift, for example, might be donated by a citizen with the stipulation that only the future income generated from this balance can be used by the government. The fund balance designation indicates that assets are held but not available for government spending. As of June 30, 2015, the City of Asheville, North Carolina, reported that the fund balance—nonspendable for its governmental funds totaled $12.0 million.

---

[16] GASB, *Codification*, Sec. 2200.159.

[17] Paul A. Copley, *Essentials of Accounting for Governmental and Not-for-Profit Organizations,* 12th edition, published by McGraw-Hill Education, 2015, p. 58.

Fund Balance—Restricted This figure indicates the amount of assets held by the government that must be spent in a manner that has been designated by an external party. For example, a grant from another government for a specified purpose such as classroom teachers or playground equipment creates an increase in this category as does a bond covenant that requires the proceeds to be used in a particular manner. The City of Asheville reported a $13.3 million fund balance—restricted as of June 30, 2015.

Fund Balance—Committed Here, assets have been designated for a particular purpose, not by an outside party but rather by the highest level of decision-making authority within the government. A state legislature might vote to set aside $400 million for road construction. On the government's balance sheet, that decision is disclosed by an increase in the reported amount of the "fund balance—committed." Of course, the legislature holds the power to reverse its decision so the commitment is not necessarily binding. The City of Asheville reports its fund balance—committed as $842,052 at June 30, 2015. The amount has been committed for community and economic development. This reporting is explained in a note to the city's financial statements as representing "amounts that can only be spent for specific purposes imposed by majority vote by quorum of City of Asheville's governing body, the City Council (highest level of decision-making authority)."

Fund Balance—Assigned Frequently, in the regular operations of a government, money is designated for a specific purpose without formal action by the highest level of decision-making authority. Usually, these are larger amounts held for a particular purpose. The head of the government's finance committee might designate cash of $1 million to be used in a few months to pay the current installment of a bond. However, if necessary, that money could be switched to some other purpose in the interim. At June 30, 2015, the City of Asheville reports a "fund balance—assigned" of $8.7 million. Of that total, $6.2 million is for capital improvements and $2.5 million for various projects.

Fund Balance—Unassigned This category is normally found in the general fund and reflects any amount of financial resources where no use has yet been designated either externally or internally. This amount is available to government officials for any purpose viewed as appropriate. On the June 30, 2015, balance sheet for the City of Asheville, the "fund balance—unassigned" was listed as $13,111,129.

To illustrate the reporting, note how each of the following transactions affects a city government's balance sheet when it is created as part of the fund financial statements for the governmental funds.

- Supplies costing $30,000 that will be used in the future to beautify the local parks are bought on the last day of the fiscal year. The supplies are shown as an asset with an equal amount reported within the "fund balance—nonspendable" balance.

- A citizen dies and leaves cash and investments valued at a total of $3 million to the city with the requirement that this money must be used for park beautification. At the date of the conveyance, a "fund balance—restricted" balance is established for this amount.

- The highest level of decision makers for this city votes to set aside $110,000 in cash to be used to beautify the local parks. No asset account is affected. The "fund balance—unassigned" drops by $110,000, and the "fund balance—committed" increases to reflect this decision.

- The director of finance for the city sets aside $12,000 in previously unassigned cash to be used to buy new benches for the city's parks. Because the decision was not made at the highest level of decision making, the "fund balance—unassigned" goes down while the "fund balance—assigned" rises. The decision, as well as the authority level of the decision, is being shown in this way.

- The city government receives property tax revenues of $1.4 million. City officials might eventually decide to use some of this money to complete the beautification of the local parks, but no decision has yet been made. In the general fund, assets increase by this amount as does the "fund balance—unassigned." The money is available for use by government officials.

Accounting for Governmental Funds

The remainder of this chapter examines many of the important accounting procedures used within the governmental funds: the general fund, special revenue funds, capital projects funds, debt service funds, and permanent funds. The distinct approach of governmental accounting can be seen best in these five funds. Because of the dual nature of the reporting process, most of accounting procedures will be demonstrated twice, once for governmental fund financial statements and a second time for the government-wide financial statements. The reporting applied to the proprietary funds and the fiduciary funds (as well as the government-wide financial statements as a whole) is more likely to resemble the accounting used by for-profit businesses. It is less unique. Thus, the emphasis here is on the accounting of the individual governmental funds.

One preliminary question to address is whether governments should establish two separate sets of financial records (one for fund statements and another for government-wide statements)? Or, should governments maintain only one set for fund accounting that then must be adjusted rather significantly at the end of each year to create government-wide financial statements?

"Most governments have not changed their day-to-day accounting at all from basic fund accounting. They continue to record their routine transactions, like tax collections and grant reimbursements, on a cash basis. Then at year end when government-wide statements are to be produced, the government records the full accrual amounts as required by GASB. Given the nature of control environments in most governments, they find it easier to record full accrual only at year end."[18]

From an educational perspective, this textbook could follow the lead established in practice of reporting each event initially based on the fund financial statement model. Then, a one-time conversion is made at the end of the year to move from fund financial statements to government-wide statements. Or, the textbook could examine each event and transaction from both a fund financial statement and a government-wide perspective.

The second approach has been adopted here. Therefore, this textbook analyzes individual transactions from both a fund and a government-wide perspective. Comparing the two ways of reporting side-by-side seems a more understandable process than learning fund financial reporting and later converting the resulting balances into a completely different set of figures based on the government-wide approach. However, students need to understand that most state and local governments make fund financial statement journal entries that are only adjusted to government-wide figures at a later time when financial statements are to be prepared.

The Importance of Budgets and the Recording of Budgetary Entries

Budgeting is an essential element of the financial planning, control, and performance evaluation processes of many governments. In contrast to commercial organizations' planning-oriented budgetary practices, governments usually adopt budgets that have the force of law, are subject to sanctions for overspending budgetary authorizations, and have extensive controls to ensure budgetary compliance.[19]

A budget is a legally approved plan for operations. In a chronological sense, the first significant accounting procedure carried out by a state or locality is the recording of budgetary entries. To enhance accountability, government officials are usually required to adopt an annual budget for each separate activity to anticipate the inflow of financial resources and establish approved expenditure levels.

The budget serves several important purposes:

1. *Expresses public policy.* If, for example, more money is budgeted for child care and less for the environment, both positive and negative consequences are likely to occur. Through the budget, citizens are made aware of decisions made by government officials as to the allocation of limited financial resources.

[18] From Jack Reagan, Partner with Grant Thornton. February 27, 2016.
[19] American Institute of Certified Public Accountants, *Audit & Accounting Guide, State and Local Governments,* with conforming changes as of March 1, 2015, para. 11.01.

2. *Serves as an expression of financial intent for the upcoming fiscal year.* The budget presents the financial plan for the government for the current period.

3. *Provides control because it establishes spending limitations for each activity.* Officials typically cannot spend more for a particular activity than has been budgeted unless a special authorization has been passed allowing them to do so.

4. *Offers a means of evaluating performance.* The budget allows a comparison to be made between the actual financial results for the period and the authorized level that has been set and approved.

5. *Indicates whether the government anticipates having sufficient revenues to pay for all of the expenditures that have been approved.* In the current economic climate when many governments face declining revenue totals, the amount and handling of proposed deficits should be of interest to every citizen.

GASB even states that "many believe the budget is the most significant financial document produced by a governmental entity."[20]

After a budget has been enacted into law, formal accounting recognition is frequently required as a means of enhancing the informational benefits. The public has the opportunity to review the amounts of current financial resources expected to be received and expended. By entering budget figures into the accounting records at the start of each fiscal year, comparisons can be made between actual and budgeted figures at any point in time. Then, at the end of the year, the budget entries have served their purpose and are reversed to remove the balances from the accounting records.

In the formal reporting process, budget information must be disclosed for the general fund and each major fund that exists within the special revenue funds. For these funds, governments must report comparisons between (a) the original budget, (b) the final budget, and (c) the actual figures for the period. This information appears as required supplementary information located after the notes to the financial statements. As an allowed alternative, a separate statement can be included within the fund financial statements to show the budget and actual figures.

To illustrate, assume that city officials enact a motel excise tax with the revenue to be used to promote tourism and conventions. Because these receipts are legally restricted for a specified purpose, the city must utilize a special revenue fund. Assume that for the 2017 fiscal year, the tax is expected to generate $490,000 in revenues. Based on this projection, the city council authorizes expenditure of $420,000 (referred to as an *appropriation*) for promotional programs during the current year. Of this amount, $200,000 is designated for salaries, $30,000 for utilities, $80,000 for advertising, and $110,000 for supplies. The $70,000 difference between the anticipated revenue and the appropriation total is a budget surplus to be accumulated by the government for future use or in case actual revenue proves to be too small to support budget plans.

To acknowledge the council's action, the accounting records of this fund include the following journal entry. No similar entry is made within the government-wide financial statements.

Fund Financial Statements—Budgetary Entry

Special Revenue Fund—Tourism and Convention Promotions		
Estimated Revenues—Tax Levy	490,000	
Appropriations—Salaries		200,000
Appropriations—Utilities		30,000
Appropriations—Advertising		80,000
Appropriations—Supplies		110,000
Budgetary Fund Balance		70,000
To record annual budget for tourism and convention promotions to be funded by motel excise tax.		

This entry reveals both the expected level of funding (the tax levy) and the approved amount of expenditures. Each of these figures remains in the records of the special revenue

[20] GASB, *Codification*, Appendix B, *Concepts Statement No. 1*, para. 19.

fund for the entire year to allow for planning, disclosure, and control. The Budgetary Fund Balance account indicates an anticipated surplus (or, in some cases, a shortfall) projected for the period. Here, the current financial resources held by this fund are expected to increase by $70,000 during the year.

In this way, budgetary entries reflect a government's *interperiod equity*. This term refers to the alignment of revenues and spending during a period and the possible shift of payments to future generations. If a government projects revenues as $10 million but approves expenditures of $11 million, the extra million must be financed in some manner, often by the issuance of debt to be repaid in the future. The benefits of the additional expenditures are enjoyed today, but citizens of a later time must bear the cost.

The original budget is not always identical to the final appropriations figure because of later amendments formally made during the year. Government officials can vote to change appropriation levels if more or less money than anticipated becomes available or needs to be changed. For the year ending June 30, 2015, the City of Greensboro, North Carolina, reported that $27,191,555 had originally been appropriated for culture and recreation. That amount was increased during the year to a final budget of $27,831,146, but only $26,197,997 was actually spent.

To continue with this illustration, assume that city officials in charge of tourism appeal to the council for an additional $50,000 to create a special advertising campaign. If approved, the original budgetary entry is adjusted:

Fund Financial Statements—Budget Amendment

Special Revenue Fund—Tourism and Convention Promotions		
Budgetary Fund Balance...	50,000	
Appropriations—Advertising.....................................		50,000
To record an additional appropriation for advertising................		

Now assume that the city actually receives $488,000 in tax revenues during the year and spends $457,000 as follows:

Salaries.....................................	$196,000
Utilities......................................	29,000
Advertising..................................	125,000
Supplies	107,000

This information should be disclosed as follows. The Variance column is recommended but not required:

TOURISM AND CONVENTION PROMOTIONS
Year Ended December 31, 2017
Budget Comparison Schedule

	Budgeted Amounts		Actual Amounts	Variance from Final Budget to Actual Amounts— Positive Impact on Fund Balance (negative)
	Original	Final		
Resources (inflows):				
Tax levy.............................	$490,000	$490,000	$488,000	$ (2,000)
Charges to appropriations (outflows):				
Salaries..............................	$200,000	$200,000	$196,000	$ 4,000
Utilities	30,000	30,000	29,000	1,000
Advertising..........................	80,000	130,000	125,000	5,000
Supplies	110,000	110,000	107,000	3,000
Total charges............................	$420,000	$470,000	$457,000	$13,000
Change in fund balance	$ 70,000	$ 20,000	$ 31,000	$11,000

Encumbrances

One additional budgetary procedure that has historically played a central role in government accounting is the recording of financial commitments referred to as *encumbrances*. In contrast to for-profit accounting, purchase commitments and contracts are often recorded within governmental funds prior to any recognition of an actual liability. This recording of encumbrances provides an efficient method for monitoring financial commitments so that officials do not accidentally overspend a fund's approved appropriations. GASB states that "encumbrances should be recorded for budgetary control purposes, especially in general and special revenue funds." Information on both expended and committed amounts is then available to aid officials as they manage the government's financial resources.

To illustrate, assume that a city's police department orders $18,000 in equipment from an approved vendor. As an ongoing service activity, the police department is accounted for within the general fund.

Fund Financial Statements—Commitment Created by Governmental Fund Activity

General Fund—Police Department

Encumbrances—Equipment	18,000	
Encumbrances Outstanding		18,000
To record a purchase order for equipment.		

When the equipment is eventually received, a legal liability for payment replaces the commitment. The encumbrance is removed from the accounting records and an Expenditures account is recognized to reflect the reduction in current financial resources. Often, because of transportation, discounts, or other price adjustments, the actual cost will differ from the original estimate. The recorded expenditure will not necessarily agree with the corresponding encumbrance.

Because of the current financial resource focus found in the fund financial statements (for the governmental funds), no equipment account entry is recorded for this long-lived asset. Instead, the Expenditures account balance identifies the reason for the reduction in current financial resources.

Assume that the equipment has a total cost of $18,160 once it has been received.

Fund Financial Statements—Equipment Order Received by Governmental Fund Activity

General Fund

Encumbrances Outstanding	18,000	
Encumbrances—Equipment		18,000
To remove encumbrance for equipment that has now been received.		
Expenditures—Equipment	18,160	
Vouchers (or Accounts) Payable		18,160
To record the receipt of equipment and the accompanying liability for its cost.		

In producing government-wide financial statements, the only entry created by this ordering and receiving of equipment is an increase in the asset and related liability when the order is filled. As in for-profit accounting, the commitment is not recorded.

At the end of the fiscal period, any commitments that remain outstanding are removed from the accounting records by reversing the original entry because no transaction has yet occurred. The recording of encumbrances is to help prevent spending more money than the amount authorized for the period.

Assuming that the commitment will still be honored in the subsequent year, is additional reporting needed on the current balance sheet? If the fund balance has already been reclassified as restricted, committed, or assigned in recognition of this eventual expenditure, then no further change is needed. The labeling of the fund balance reflects the decision to use that part of the fund's financial resources to meet this commitment. However, if no fund balance has yet been reported as restricted, committed, or assigned, then a portion of the fund balance should be reclassified as either committed (designated by the highest level of decision-making authority) or assigned (designated by a party other than the highest level of decision-making authority) for the purchase order amount to denote the anticipated use of the fund's assets.[21]

To illustrate, assume that the general fund of the city that ordered the $18,000 in equipment reports assets and deferred outflows of $600,000 and liabilities and deferred inflows of $500,000. On the balance sheet, the fund balance accounts are shown as $40,000 assigned and $60,000 unassigned. At the end of the fiscal year, the $18,000 encumbrance is unfulfilled and removed from the records for that period. However, the decision has been made that the government will pay for the equipment when it arrives in the following year. The reporting of the fund balance figures on the balance sheet can be affected in one of two ways.

1. If the $40,000 fund balance—assigned already includes an $18,000 amount reflecting the commitment for this equipment, no change is necessary. The appropriate amount of the fund's resources is shown as assigned.

2. If the $40,000 fund balance—assigned does not include $18,000 to be spent on this equipment, then the fund balance—unassigned is reduced by that amount, and fund balance—assigned (or possibly committed depending on the level of the decision-making to acquire the equipment) is increased. The reported assets and liabilities are not affected since the equipment has not been received, but the fund balance is shown as assigned (or committed) to indicate that $18,000 of the fund's resources are not freely available to government officials. "Encumbered amounts for specific purposes for which amounts have not been previously restricted, committed, or assigned should not be classified as unassigned but, rather, should be included within committed or assigned fund balance, as appropriate."[22]

Recognition of Expenditures and Revenues

LO 11-6

Record the passage of a budget as well as subsequent encumbrances and expenditures.

Although budgetary and encumbrance entries are unique, their impact on the accounting process is somewhat limited because they do not directly affect a fund's financial results for the period. Conversely, the method by which states and localities record the receipt and disbursement of assets can alter reported data significantly. Because a primary emphasis is on measuring changes in current financial resources, *neither expenses nor capital assets are recorded in the fund financial statements of the governmental funds.* Probably no more significant distinction exists between the fund statements and the government-wide statements.

As shown in the previous purchase of equipment, governmental funds report an Expenditures account in the fund statements. This balance reflects decreases in current financial resources caused by the acquisition of a good or service. The reduction of resources is recorded as an expenditure whether it is for rent, a fire truck, salaries, a computer, or the like. In each case, a good or service is acquired. The statement of revenues, expenditures, and other changes in fund balances (Exhibit 11.4) allows the reader to see the use that has been made of an activity's current financial resources. Spending $1,000 for electricity for the past three months is an expenditure of a governmental fund's current financial resources in exactly the same way that buying a $70,000 ambulance is.

[21] If not already reported as restricted, a fund balance cannot be internally restricted. The restricted designation is used to indicate that external parties or applicable laws created the restriction.
[22] GASB, *Codification*, Sec. 1800.184.

Fund Financial Statements—Expenditures for Expense and Capital Asset by Governmental Fund Activity

Expenditures—Electricity...	1,000	
Vouchers (or Accounts) Payable		1,000
To record charges covering the past three months.		
Expenditures—Ambulance	70,000	
Vouchers (or Accounts) Payable		70,000
To record acquisition of ambulance.		

Within the fund financial statements for the governmental funds, the timing of the recognition of expenditures and revenues follows the *modified accrual basis of accounting.* Under modified accrual accounting, expenditures are recognized at the time that the government incurs a current liability, creating a claim against current financial resources. If the claim is established in one period to be settled in the subsequent period using year-end financial resources, the expenditure and liability are recorded in the initial year. However, as discussed earlier, the maximum length of time for the change in current financial resources to occur—often 60 days into the subsequent period—should be disclosed. Thus, if equipment is received on the last day of one year but payment will not be made until 120 days later, no recording of the expenditure is likely to be made in the first year, depending on the recognition period utilized by the government.

In fund statements, a governmental fund records both operating costs such as salaries and rent and the entire cost of all buildings, machines, and other capital assets as expenditures. No net income figure is calculated for these funds. Thus, computing and recording subsequent depreciation is not relevant to the reporting process and is omitted entirely. Depreciation has no effect on current financial resources.

For the government-wide financial statements, all economic resources are measured. Consequently, the previous two transactions are recorded in this second set of statements when the liability is created, with depreciation subsequently recorded for the ambulance as time passes.

Government-Wide Financial Statements—Recording Expense and Acquisition of Capital Asset

Utilities Expense	1,000	
Vouchers (or Accounts) Payable		1,000
To record electricity charges for the past three months.		
Ambulance..	70,000	
Vouchers (or Accounts) Payable		70,000
To record acquisition of new ambulance.		

Reporting Capital Assets and Infrastructure

LO 11-7

Understand the reporting of capital assets, supplies, and prepaid expenses by a state or local government.

One result of recording only expenditures within the fund statements for the governmental funds is that virtually no assets are reported other than current financial resources such as cash, receivables, and investments. All capital assets are recorded as expenditures at the time of acquisition with that balance closed out at the end of each fiscal period. Note that the balance sheet in Exhibit 11.3 shows no buildings, school facilities, computers, trucks, or other equipment as assets.

Prior to the development of government-wide financial statements, only a minimum amount of information was available about capital assets. A listing was included in the financial statements for informational purposes. Even then, the inclusion of infrastructure items was optional. Infrastructure includes roads, sidewalks, bridges, and the like that are normally stationary and can be preserved for a significant period of time. A bridge, for example, with proper care might last for more than 100 years. To save time and energy, many governments simply did not maintain records of such infrastructure items after the original expenditure.

? Discussion Question

IS IT AN ASSET OR A LIABILITY?

During the long evolution of government accounting, many scholars have discussed its unique features. In the August 1989 issue of the *Journal of Accountancy,* R. K. Mautz described the reporting needs of governments and not-for-profit organizations (such as charities) in "Not-For-Profit Financial Reporting: Another View."

To illustrate the governmental accounting challenges, Mautz examined the method by which a city should record a newly constructed high school building. Conventional business wisdom would say that such a property is an asset owned by the government. Thus, the cost should be capitalized and then depreciated over an estimated useful life. However, in paragraph 26 of FASB *Concepts Statement No. 6,* an essential characteristic of an asset is "a probable future benefit . . . to contribute directly or indirectly to future net cash inflows."

Mautz reasoned that the school building cannot be considered an asset because it provides no net contribution to cash inflows. In truth, a high school requires the government to make significant cash outflows for maintenance, repairs, utilities, salaries, and the like. Public educational facilities (as well as many of the other properties of a government such as a fire station or municipal building) are acquired with the understanding that net cash outflows will result for years to come.

Consequently, Mautz then considered whether the construction of a high school is not actually the establishment of a liability because the government is taking on an obligation that will necessitate future cash payments. He also rejects this idea, once again based on the guidance of *Concepts Statement No. 6* (para. 36), because a probable future transfer or use of assets is not required at a "specified or determinable date, on occurrence of a specified event, or on demand."

Is a high school building an asset or is it a liability? If it is neither, how should the cost be recorded? How is the high school reported in fund financial statements? How is the high school reported in government-wide financial statements? Which of these two approaches best portrays the decision to acquire or construct this building? Can a government possibly be accounted for in the same manner as a for-profit enterprise?

The eventual requirement that government-wide financial statements include all economic resources meant that capital assets (including infrastructure items) had to be recorded and, where applicable, depreciation had to be included. As will be discussed in the following chapter, depreciation of infrastructure can still be avoided under certain circumstances.

Thus, today, the fund financial statements report the amount expended each period by the governmental funds for capital assets, while the government-wide financial statements report those capital assets as well as all infrastructure items.

Supplies and Prepaid Items

In gathering information for government-wide financial statements, the acquisition of supplies and prepaid costs such as rent or insurance is not particularly complicated. An asset is recorded at the time of acquisition and subsequently reclassified to expense as the asset's utility is consumed by use or time. The City and County of Denver, Colorado, reported $2.7 million for prepaid items and other assets in its government-wide statements as of December 31, 2014.

However, reporting prepaid costs and supplies by the governmental funds within the fund financial statements is not so straightforward. These assets have a relatively short life but they are not current financial resources that can be spent. Should the cost incurred be reported as an asset until consumed or recorded directly as an expenditure at the time of acquisition?

Traditionally, governmental funds have used the *purchases method,* which simply records such costs as expenditures at the point that a claim to current financial resources is created. No asset is recorded. Thus, in 2014, the City of Philadelphia discloses that the "supplies of governmental funds are recorded as expenditures when purchased rather than capitalized as inventory." For disclosure purposes, though, any remaining supplies or prepaid items (such as insurance or rent) are entered into the accounting records as assets just prior to production of financial statements. At that time, the asset is recorded along with an offsetting amount in fund balance—nonspendable to inform the reader that assets are included that are not current financial resources available for spending.

The *purchases method* reflects modified accrual accounting because the entire cost is recognized as an expenditure when current financial resources are reduced. However, some governments have chosen to have their governmental funds report supplies and prepaid items using an accepted alternative known as the *consumption method.*

The consumption method parallels the process utilized in creating government-wide financial statements. Supplies or prepayments are recorded as assets when acquired. As the utility is consumed by usage or time, the cost is reclassified into an expenditures account. As explained in 2014 by the City of Birmingham, Alabama, "Inventory consists of expendable supplies held in the General Fund for consumption. The cost is recorded as an expenditure at the time individual inventory items are used (consumption method)." Under this approach, the expenditure is recognized in the period of specific usage. Because these assets cannot be spent for government programs or other needs, an equal portion of the Fund Balance account should be reclassified as nonspendable as shown in the balance sheet in Exhibit 11.3.

To illustrate, assume that a municipality purchases $20,000 in supplies for various general fund activities. During the remainder of the fiscal period, $18,000 of these items are consumed so that only supplies costing $2,000 remain at year-end. These events could be recorded through either of the following sets of entries. Notice that, depending on the approach, the expenditures will increase by either $20,000 or $18,000 in the year of purchase. Because of budgeting limitations, that can be an important difference.

Fund Financial Statements—Supplies and Prepaid Expenses—Governmental Funds

Purchases Method

Expenditures—Supplies...	20,000	
Vouchers (or Accounts) Payable...............................		20,000
To record purchase of supplies for various ongoing activities.		
Inventory of Supplies...	2,000	
Fund Balance—Nonspendable.................................		2,000
To establish balance for supplies remaining at year's end.		

Consumption Method

Inventory of Supplies...	20,000	
Vouchers (or Accounts) Payable...............................		20,000
To record purchase of supplies for various ongoing activities.		
Expenditures—Control..	18,000	
Inventory of Supplies...		18,000
To record consumption of supplies during period. Because an asset that cannot be spent remains on the balance sheet, a $2,000 portion of the Fund Balance is also reclassified from unassigned to nonspendable. This reclassification is normally done in creating the statements and not through a journal entry.		

LO 11-8

Determine the proper timing for the recognition of revenues from various types of nonexchange transactions.

Recognition of Revenues—Overview

The reporting of certain revenues has always posed theoretical issues in governmental accounting. Revenues such as property taxes, income taxes, and many grants do not have the same type of exchange process as is found in for-profit entities. Taxes, fines, and the like are imposed on the citizens to support the government's operations rather than providing a specific good or service in return for payments. Consequently, these revenues are referred to as nonexchange transactions.

To assist in the timing of such revenue recognition, GASB has provided a comprehensive set of guidelines. These rules do not apply to revenues such as interest or rents for which a true exchange process does exist. Instead, they focus on nonexchange transactions, including most taxes, fines, grants, gifts, and the like for which the government does not provide a direct and equal benefit for the amount received.

In a nonexchange transaction, a government (including the federal government, as a provider) either gives value (benefit) to another party without directly receiving equal value in exchange or receives value (benefit) from another party without directly giving equal value in exchange.[23]

For organizational purposes, nonexchange transactions are separated into four distinct classifications, each with its own rules as to proper recognition:

1. *Derived tax revenues.* Some tax assessments occur when an underlying exchange takes place. Income taxes and sales taxes are common examples of derived tax revenues. A sale occurs, for example, and an additional sales tax is charged, or income is earned and an income tax is assessed. The tax is tied to an event.

2. *Imposed nonexchange revenues.* Property taxes, fines, and penalties are viewed as imposed nonexchange revenues. The government makes an assessment, but no underlying exchange occurs. With a property tax, for example, the government is taxing ownership and not a specific event or transaction.

3. *Government-mandated nonexchange transactions.* This category includes monies, such as grants conveyed from one government to another, to help cover the cost of a required program. For example, assume a state specifies that a city must create a homeless shelter and then provides a grant of $900,000 to help defray that cost. The city records this inflow of money as a government-mandated nonexchange transaction. City officials did not make the decision. The state government required the shelter to be constructed and provided a portion of the funding.

4. *Voluntary nonexchange transactions.* In this classification, money has been conveyed willingly to the state or local government by an individual, another government, or an organization, usually for a particular purpose. For example, a state might grant a city $1.3 million to help improve reading programs in local schools. Unless the state had mandated an enhancement in these reading programs, this grant is accounted for as a voluntary nonexchange transaction. The money will provide an important benefit, but no separate government requirement led the state to make the conveyance.

Derived Tax Revenues Such As Income Taxes and Sales Taxes

Accounting for derived tax revenues is relatively straightforward. These revenues are normally recognized in government-wide financial statements when the underlying transaction occurs. When an individual taxpayer earns income, the government should record the resulting income tax revenue. Likewise, when a business makes a sale, the government should recognize the related sales tax revenue.

Assume, for example, that sales by businesses operating within a locality amount to $100 million for the current year and a sales tax of 4 percent is assessed. In the period in which the sales are made, the following entry is required for the $4 million to be collected. The amount should be reported net of any estimated refunds or balances that cannot be collected.

[23] GASB, *Codification*, Sec., N50,104.

Government-Wide Financial Statements—Derived Tax Revenues

Receivable—Sales Taxes	4,000,000	
Revenue—Sales Taxes		4,000,000
To recognize sales tax that will be collected in connection with sales for the current period. Same entry is appropriate for the fund financial statements of the governmental fund if the money qualifies as available to be used.		

For fund financial statements, the preceding rules also apply except for one additional requirement. In connection with governmental funds, as mentioned previously, the financial resources must be "available" before the revenue can be recognized. That is, the amounts must be received during the present year or soon enough thereafter so that the money can be used to satisfy current claims. In that way, the essence of modified accrual accounting is utilized at the fund level of reporting.

Imposed Nonexchange Revenues Such As Property Taxes and Fines

Accounting for imposed nonexchange revenues is more complicated because no underlying transaction exists to guide the timing of the revenue recognition. Interestingly, GASB set up separate rules for recognizing the asset and the related revenue. The receivable is recorded as soon as the government has an enforceable legal claim as defined in that particular jurisdiction. Cash is recorded rather than a receivable if a prepayment is made. For the revenue side of the transaction, recognition is made in the time period when the resulting resources are required to be used or in the first period in which use is permitted.

To illustrate, assume that on October 1, Year 1, property tax assessments totaling $530,000 are mailed by the City of Alban to its citizens to finance the government during Year 2. Assume that according to applicable state law, the city has no enforceable claim until January 1, Year 2 (often referred to as the *lien date*). To encourage early payment, the city allows a 5 percent discount on any amount received by December 31, Year 1.

No entry is recorded on October 1, Year 1. Although the assessments have been delivered, no enforceable legal claim yet exists, and the proceeds from the tax cannot be used until Year 2. However, assume that $30,000 of these assessments are collected from citizens during the final three months of Year 1. After reduction for the 5 percent discount, the collection is $28,500.

Government-Wide Financial Statements and Fund Financial Statements—Property Taxes Prepaid in Year 1 for Year 2

Year 1		
Cash	28,500	
Unavailable Property Tax Collections...........................		28,500
To record collection of property tax prior to the start of the levy year after reduction for 5 percent discount.		

The collection of prepaid taxes does not create a liability; no type of payment or service is required. Because the money cannot be spent until Year 2, it is not yet a revenue. As shown in Exhibit 11.1, this balance represents a deferred inflow of resources on the statement of net position.

Assume that city officials expect to collect 96 percent of the remaining $500,000 in assessments, or $480,000. At the beginning of Year 2, both this receivable and the related revenue are recognized.

- The receivable is reported at that time because an enforceable claim comes into existence.
- For government-wide statements, the revenue is reported in Year 2 because that is the period in which the money can first be used.

Note here in the journal entry that the revenue is reduced directly by the estimate of taxes that are expected to be uncollectible. In addition, the previously collected $28,500 is now recognized in Year 2 as revenue because, once again, this is the period for which use is allowed.

Government-Wide Financial Statement—Property Taxes for Year 2

January 1, Year 2

Property Tax Receivable	500,000	
Allowance for Uncollectible Taxes		20,000
Revenues—Property Taxes		480,000
To recognize property tax assessment for Year 2.		
Unavailable Property Tax Collections	28,500	
Revenues—Property Taxes		28,500
To recognize property tax proceeds for Year 2 collected during Year 1.		

The above recording is the same for the fund financial statements unless some portion of the future cash collection is viewed as not being available to be used this period. Because property taxes are such a significant source of revenue for many governments, a specific 60-day maximum period for recognition has been standardized rather than allowing a government to choose a longer period as a way of increasing the amount of revenue recognized.

To illustrate, assume that records for the past several years indicate that $400,000 of this anticipated $480,000 will be collected during Year 2, another $50,000 in the first 60 days of Year 3, and the final $30,000 beyond 60 days into Year 3. This last $30,000 is not viewed as available to pay for Year 2 expenditures. For that amount, recognition is not appropriate until Year 3. Only $450,000 of the financial resources are expected to be available for Year 2 expenditures. Once again, the unavailable property tax collections amount ($30,000 in this case) is shown as a deferred inflow of resources for the governmental fund. The receivable is recognized but no amount of this $30,000 will be available until Year 3.

Fund Financial Statements—Property Taxes for Year 2—Governmental Funds

January 1, Year 2

Property Tax Receivable	500,000	
Allowance for Uncollectible Taxes		20,000
Revenues—Property Taxes		450,000
Unavailable Property Tax Collections		30,000
To record amount of property taxes measurable and available to be used for Year 2 expenditures. Final $30,000 is not expected until after 60 days into Year 3.		
Unavailable Property Tax Collections	28,500	
Revenues—Property Taxes		28,500
To recognize property tax proceeds for Year 2 collected during Year 1.		

Government-Mandated Nonexchange Transactions and Voluntary Nonexchange Transactions

Although these two sources of revenues are identified separately by GASB, the timing of accounting recognition is the same so they are logically discussed here together. Governments recognize these types of revenue (often coming in the form of a grant) when all eligibility requirements have been met. Until eligibility is established, the existence of some degree of uncertainty precludes recognition. Thus, revenue is reported at the time of eligibility even if the money was actually received earlier.

Eligibility requirements are divided into four general classifications. Applicable requirements must all be met before revenues can be recorded for either government-mandated nonexchange transactions or voluntary nonexchange transactions.

1. *Required characteristics of the recipients.* Governments are often given standards that must be met in advance of receiving funding. To illustrate, assume that a not-for-profit foundation awards a grant to a city to finance improved reading education for all kindergarten children in the school system. Assume also that state law has been changed to mandate that all kindergarten teachers must hold proper certification. Consequently, the not-for-profit foundation has stated that it will only convey the grant to the city when all kindergarten teachers have met the state standard. The city must conform to this law first. Because of this eligibility requirement, recognition of the revenue from this grant is delayed until all teachers have become certified.

2. *Time requirements.* The parties providing the funding can specify when the money is to be used. The time becomes an eligibility requirement. To illustrate, assume that in April, a state government provides a grant to a city to buy milk for each child during the subsequent school year starting in September. The grant should be recognized as revenue in the period of use or in the period when the use of the funds is first permitted. Here, the money cannot be used in April so it is not yet revenue.

3. *Reimbursement.* Many grants and other forms of similar support are designed to reimburse a government for amounts spent according to specified guidelines. These arrangements are often called *expenditure-driven programs.* Assume that a state informs a locality that it will reimburse the city government for money paid to provide books to schoolchildren who could not otherwise afford them. In such cases, proper spending is the eligibility requirement. The city recognizes no revenue until its own money has been spent for these books.

4. *Contingencies.* In voluntary nonexchange transactions (but not in government-mandated nonexchange transactions), funding may be withheld until a specified procurement action has been taken. A grant might be given to buy park equipment, for example, but is only available after an appropriate piece of land has been acquired on which to build the park. Until land is obtained (or other required action is taken) a contingency exists, and the revenue should not be recognized.

For most of these events, a liability is recognized in the government-wide statements if money is received before the eligibility requirements are met. The liability is necessary because the government is obligated to act in some manner. However, if only a time restriction exists, then a deferred inflow of resources is reported (rather than a revenue) because no further action is required. In fund financial statements, if the cash is received but the eligibility requirements have not yet been met, a deferred inflow of resources is reported.

LO 11-9

Account for the issuance of long-term bonds.

Issuance of Bonds

The issuance of bonds serves as a major source of financing for many, if not most, state and local governments. At the end of the fourth quarter of 2014, the total long-term debt outstanding for all state and local governments amounted to the almost unbelievable balance of $2.9 trillion.[24] Money received from the issuance of these debts is used for many purposes, including general financing and a wide variety of construction projects such as roads, bridges, and airports. As of June 30, 2014, the City and County of San Francisco, California, had approximately $12.5 billion of noncurrent bonds, loans, and similar liabilities outstanding. Of that amount, $2.7 billion had been incurred by governmental activities and nearly $9.8 billion by business-type activities.

Because the proceeds of a long-term bond must be repaid, the government recognizes no revenues under either method of financial reporting. The reporting process for the government-wide financial statements is straightforward. Both the cash and the debt are increased to reflect

---

[24] U.S. Federal Reserve, *Federal Reserve Statistical Release,* "Financial Accounts of the United States - Flow of Funds, Balance Sheets, and Integrated Macroeconomic Accounts," Third Quarter 2015 (Washington, D.C.: Federal Reserve, December 10, 2015), Table D.3, p. 5.

the issuance. Conversely, in the fund financial statements, recording is more complicated. Cash is received, but the debt is not a claim on current financial resources. Thus, from that perspective, the inflow of current financial resources creates neither a revenue nor a liability.

Assume, for example, that the Town of Ruark issues $15 million in general obligation bonds at face value to finance the construction of a new school building. Because of the intended use of the proceeds, the town establishes a capital projects fund to monitor the receipt and spending of this cash. To emphasize that the money is not derived from a revenue, Ruark utilizes a special designation, *Other Financing Sources.* Note in Exhibit 11.4 the placement of Other Financing Sources (Uses) at the bottom of the statement of revenues, expenditures, and other changes in fund balance to identify changes in the amount of current financial resources created by transactions other than revenues and expenditures.

The following journal entry reflects the issuance of these bonds as recorded in the fund financial statements.

Fund Financial Statements—Issuance of Bonds—Governmental Funds

Capital Projects Fund—School Building		
Cash	15,000,000	
Other Financing Sources—Bond Proceeds		15,000,000
To record issuance of bonds to finance school construction project.		

The reporting of the governmental funds stresses accountability for the inflows and outflows of current financial resources. Although an inflow of cash has taken place, no revenue was generated. The money came from a loan. This increase in current financial resources is reflected by the Other Financing Sources balance, a measurement account that is closed out at each year-end. The $15 million bond liability is not reported by the capital projects fund because it is not yet a claim to current financial resources. Recognition of long-term debts has traditionally been ignored in the reporting of governmental funds. For example, the balance sheet in Exhibit 11.3 shows no noncurrent liabilities for the governmental funds, only claims to current financial resources. A reader of the financial statements who wants to see the complete record of the government's debts must examine the statement of net position in the government-wide financial statements (see Exhibit 11.1).

Because state and local governments often issue significant amounts of debts, related costs can be quite large. To standardize reporting, GASB has ruled that any debt issuance cost should be recognized as an expense/expenditure when incurred rather than being capitalized.

In addition, if available interest rates are subsequently reduced, bonds are sometimes reacquired by a government so that new financing can be arranged at a lower cost. The difference between the amount paid to retire the original debt and its net carrying amount at that time is not recorded immediately as an expense. Instead, the difference is reported on the statement of net position as a deferred outflow of resources (if more than the net carrying amount is paid) or a deferred inflow of resources (if less than the net carrying amount is paid). This deferred amount is amortized over time against interest expense. The refunding arrangement was set up in hopes of reducing the cost of interest. That justification is reflected in the subsequent handling of the difference.

Thus, the State of Florida reported at June 30, 2014, an "amount deferred on refunding of debt" as a deferred outflow of resources of $120.2 million while showing the same account title as a deferred inflow of resources of $4.0 million. Apparently, several debts had been refunded in recent years.

Payment of Noncurrent Liabilities

The payment of noncurrent liabilities by one of the governmental funds again demonstrates the fundamental differences between the two sets of financial statements.

- For the government-wide statements, the payment of principal and interest is recorded in the same manner as that used by a for-profit organization.

- On fund financial statements, an expenditure is recognized for settlement of the debt and also for the related interest. Both payments reduce current financial resources and are often made from a debt service fund.

Assume as an illustration that a government has a $500,000 bond payment to be made along with three months of interest amounting to $10,000. Government officials have previously set aside sufficient cash in a debt service fund to satisfy this obligation.

Government-Wide Financial Statements—Bond and Interest Payments

Bond Payable.	500,000	
Interest Expense	10,000	
Cash		510,000
To record payment of bond and related interest.		

Fund Financial Statements—Bond and Interest Payments—Governmental Funds

Debt Service Funds		
Expenditure—Bond Principal	500,000	
Expenditure—Interest.	10,000	
Cash		510,000
To record payment of bond and related interest.		

Tax Anticipation Notes

One type of debt is recorded in the same manner for government-wide and fund financial statements. State and local governments often issue short-term debts to provide financing until revenue sources such as property taxes have been collected. For example, if tax receipts are expected at a particular point in time, the government might need to borrow money to finance operations until that date. These short-term liabilities are often referred to as *tax anticipation notes* because they are outstanding only until a sufficient amount of taxes is collected.

As short-term liabilities, these debts are a claim on current financial resources. For fund financial statements, the issuance is not recorded as an other financing source but as a liability in the same manner as in the government-wide financial statements. Amounts paid for interest, though, are still recorded as an expenditure in producing fund statements but as an expense on the government-wide financial statements.

Assume a city borrows $300,000 on a 60-day note on January 1 and agrees to pay back $305,000 on March 1. The city expects to repay the debt with receipts from property tax assessments. In creating both sets of financial statements, cash and the related liability are both increased at the time of issuance.

At repayment, however, different entries are required.

Fund Financial Statements—Payment of Tax Anticipation Notes by Governmental Funds

General Fund		
Tax Anticipation Note Payable	300,000	
Expenditure—Interest.	5,000	
Cash		305,000
To record payment of short-term debt and interest for two months.		

Government-Wide Financial Statements—Payment of Tax Anticipation Notes

Tax Anticipation Note Payable	300,000	
Interest Expense	5,000	
Cash		305,000
To record payment of short-term debt and interest for two months.		

LO 11-10

Account for special assessment projects.

Special Assessments

Governments can provide improvements or services that directly benefit a particular property and then assess the costs (in whole or in part) to the owner. In some cases, owners actually petition the government to initiate such projects to enhance property values. Paving streets, installing water and sewage lines, and constructing curbs and sidewalks are typical examples. To finance the work, the government usually issues debt and places a lien on the property being improved to ensure reimbursement. These are not necessarily small amounts. The City of Fargo, North Dakota, reported special assessment receivables of over $280 million as of December 31, 2014. That balance represents the second biggest asset reported by Fargo with only its infrastructure assets being a larger amount.

Government-wide financial statements handle the debt and subsequent construction project in the same manner as for-profit enterprises. The asset is recorded at cost, and assessments are made and collected. Receipts are then used to settle the debt. To illustrate, assume that a sidewalk is to be added to a neighborhood at a cost of $600,000. The city will issue bonds to finance construction with repayment to be made using funds collected from the owners of the property benefited. Total interest to be paid is $30,000. The assessment to the owners is set at $630,000 to cover all costs.

Government-Wide Financial Statements—Special Assessment Project

Cash	600,000	
Bond Payable—Special Assessment.		600,000
To record debt issued to finance sidewalk construction.		
Infrastructure Asset—Sidewalk.	600,000	
Cash		600,000
To record payment to contractor for the cost of building new sidewalk.		
Taxes Receivable—Special Assessment	630,000	
Revenue—Special Assessment		630,000
To record citizens' charges for special assessment project.		
Cash	630,000	
Taxes Receivable—Special Assessment		630,000
To record collection of money from assessment of citizens for sidewalk construction.		
Bond Payable—Special Assessment.	600,000	
Interest Expense	30,000	
Cash		630,000
To record payment of debt on special assessment bonds.		

In the fund financial statements, this same series of transactions has a completely different appearance. Neither the infrastructure asset nor the long-term debt is recorded because the current financial resources measurement basis is used.

Fund Financial Statements—Special Assessment Project—Governmental Funds

Capital Projects Fund—Special Assessment Project

Cash	600,000	
Other Financing Sources—Bond Proceeds		600,000
To record issuance of bonds to finance sidewalk construction with payment to be made from a special assessment levy.		
Expenditures—Sidewalk	600,000	
Cash		600,000
To record payment to contractor for the cost of constructing sidewalk.		

Debt Service Fund—Special Assessment Project

Taxes Receivable—Special Assessment	630,000	
Revenue—Special Assessment		630,000
To record assessment that will be used to pay bond principal and related interest incurred after construction.		
Cash	630,000	
Taxes Receivable—Special Assessment		630,000
To record collection of assessment paid by citizens to extinguish bond and interest incurred in construction of sidewalk.		
Expenditure—Special Assessment Bond	600,000	
Expenditure—Interest	30,000	
Cash		630,000
To record payment of bonds payable and interest incurred in construction of sidewalk.		

One alternative for the reporting of special assessment projects should be mentioned. In some cases, the government may facilitate a project but accept no legal obligation. The government assumes no liability (either primary or secondary) for the debt. The money goes from the citizens to the government and then directly to the contractors. The government serves merely as a conduit.

If the government has no liability for defaults, overruns, or other related problems, the recording of special assessment assets, liabilities, revenues, expenses, other financing sources, and expenditures is not really relevant to the government and its resources. In that situation, all transactions are recorded in an agency fund as increases and decreases in cash, amounts due from citizens, and amounts due to contractors. No other balances are needed. As a fiduciary fund, no impact appears within the government-wide statements.

LO 11-11

Record the various types of monetary transfers that occur within the funds maintained by a state or local government.

Interfund Transactions

Interfund transactions are commonly used within government units as a way to direct sufficient resources to all activities and functions. Monetary transfers made from the general fund are especially prevalent because general tax revenues are initially accumulated in this fund. For example, in fund financial statements for the year ended June 30, 2014, the City of Houston, Texas, indicated that $335.1 million was transferred out of its general fund to other funds while $72.6 million was transferred in from other funds. Transfers into a fund and out of that same fund are not offset in reporting fund financial statements. There is no netting to arrive at reported amounts.

In contrast, the government-wide financial statements do not report most transfers because they frequently occur solely within the governmental activities. For example, a transfer from the general fund to a debt service fund is reported in both funds on fund financial statements. However, it creates no net impact in the government-wide financial statements because both funds are classified within the governmental activities.

Thus, for government-wide financial reporting, the following distinctions are drawn for transfers:

- *Intra-activity transactions* occur between two governmental funds (so that the net totals reported for governmental activities are not affected) or between two enterprise funds (so that the net totals reported for business-type activities are not affected). Transfers between governmental funds and many of the internal service funds are also included here because, as discussed previously, internal service funds are usually reported as governmental activities. Intra-activity transactions are not reported in government-wide financial statements because no overall change is created in either the governmental activities or the business-type activities.

- *Interactivity transactions* occur between governmental funds and enterprise funds. They impact the total amount of resources reported for both governmental activities and business-type activities; one increases as the other decreases. Thus, interactivity transactions are reported in government-wide financial statements. For example, in Exhibit 11.1, internal amounts due ($50) at year-end are reported as both a positive and a negative within the asset section of the statement of net position and then offset to arrive at overall totals. Likewise, in Exhibit 11.2, transfers ($600) occurring between the two classifications during the year appear at the bottom of the general revenues section. These individual totals are shown and then eliminated so that no amount is reported for the government as a whole. Although most transfers are intra-activity, interactivity transactions are not uncommon. In its June 30, 2014, government-wide financial statements, the City of St. Louis reported (and then eliminated) internal balances of $12.6 million within the asset section of its statement of net position and transfers of $9.4 million in its statement of activities.

Consequently, in discussing interfund transactions, the reporting for government-wide statements is impacted only when an interactivity transaction is involved.

Monetary Transfers

The most common interfund transactions are transfers within the governmental funds to ensure adequate financing of budgeted expenditures. For example, a city council could vote to transfer $800,000 from the general fund to a capital projects fund to cover a portion of the cost of a new school building.

Fund Financial Statements—Intra-Activity Transaction

General Fund		
Other Financing Uses—Transfers Out—Capital Projects Fund.	800,000	
Due to Capital Projects Fund (a payable).		800,000
To record authorization of transfer for school construction.		

Capital Projects Fund—School Building		
Due from General Fund (a receivable)	800,000	
Other Financing Sources—Transfers In—General Fund		800,000
To record authorization of transfer for school construction.		

The *Other Financing Uses/Sources* designations are appropriate here for the fund financial statements. Financial resources are being moved into and out of these funds although neither a revenue nor an expenditure has been recognized. As Exhibit 11.4 shows, these balances are reported by each fund in the statement of revenues, expenditures, and other changes in fund balances. The figures are shown but not offset in any way. Both accounts are then closed out at the end of the current year. In contrast, the *Due to/Due from* accounts in the above entries are the equivalent of interfund payable and receivable balances. Again, no elimination is made in arriving at total figures for the governmental funds.

Because this transfer is an intra-activity transaction, no reporting is made in the government-wide financial statements. Financial resources are simply being shifted within the governmental activities as a whole.

Not all monetary transfers are for normal operating purposes. Nonrecurring or nonroutine transfers can also take place. For example, money might be transferred from the general fund to create or expand an enterprise fund such as a bus or subway system. To illustrate, assume that a city sets aside $20 million of unassigned money to help permanently finance a new subway system that will be open to the public. For convenience, this transaction is recorded as if cash is transferred immediately so that no receivable or payable is necessary:

Fund Financial Statements—Interactivity Transaction

General Fund

Other Financing Uses—Transfers Out—Subway System...............	20,000,000	
Cash		20,000,000
To record transfer to help finance subway system.		

Enterprise Fund—Subway System

Cash	20,000,000	
Capital Contributions		20,000,000
To record receipt of transfer from unrestricted funds.		

Because this transfer is an interactivity transaction (between governmental activities and business-type activities), entries must also be made for the government-wide financial statements. The transfer reduces the assets of the governmental activities but increases the assets in the business-type activities. These two transfer balances will be offset in arriving at totals for the government as a whole.

Government-Wide Financial Statements—Interactivity Transaction

Governmental Activities

Transfers Out—Subway System....................................	20,000,000	
Cash		20,000,000
To record transfer to help finance subway system.		

Business-Type Activities

Cash	20,000,000	
Transfers In—General Fund		20,000,000
To record receipt of transfer from unrestricted funds.		

Internal Exchange Transactions

Some payments made within a government are actually the same as transactions with an outside party. For example, a city will likely compensate its own print shop (or any other internal service fund or enterprise fund) for services or materials acquired just as if the work had been performed by an outside vendor. To avoid confusion in reporting, such transfers are recorded as revenues and as expenditures or expenses. These transactions are not really viewed as transfers. The payments are made for work done or materials acquired and are not designed to shift financial resources from one fund to another.

Fund financial statements record all such internal exchange transactions. However, as previously discussed, most internal service funds are reported within governmental activities on the government-wide statements. Exchanges between a governmental fund and one of these internal service funds will have no net impact on the government-wide figures being reported. The increases and decreases offset. Therefore, those balances are omitted.

To illustrate, assume that a city government pays its print shop (an internal service fund) $15,000 for work done for the police department. In addition, the government pays another $6,000 to a toll road operated as an enterprise fund to allow fire department vehicles to ride on the highway without having to make individual payments.

Fund Financial Statements—Internal Exchange Transaction

General Fund

Expenditures—Printing	15,000	
Expenditures—Toll Road Privileges	6,000	
Cash		21,000
To record payment for printing supplies for use by police department and for use of a toll road by fire department.		

Internal Service Fund—Print Shop

Cash	15,000	
Revenues		15,000
To record collection of money paid by the police department for printed materials.		

Enterprise Fund—Toll Road

Cash	6,000	
Revenues		6,000
To record collection of money from government for fire department vehicular use of toll roads.		

The $15,000 transaction with the print shop is not reflected in the government-wide financial statements if this internal service fund is classified within the governmental activities. In that case, the transfer is the equivalent of an intra-activity transaction. However, the $6,000 payment made by the police department (a governmental activity) to the enterprise fund (a business-type activity) is the same as an interactivity transfer and is reported through the following entries.

Government-Wide Financial Statements—Internal Exchange Transaction

Governmental Activities

Expenses—Toll Road Privileges	6,000	
Cash		6,000
To record payment for use of toll road by fire department's vehicles.		

Business-Type Activities

Cash	6,000	
Revenues		6,000
To record collection of money from government for fire department vehicular use of toll roads.		

Summary

1. Readers of state and local government financial statements have a wide variety of informational needs. No single set of financial statements is capable of meeting all user needs, a factor that has led to the requirement that two sets of statements be reported. Accountability of government officials and control over public spending have always been essential elements of traditional government accounting. GASB has attempted to keep those priorities in place while also broadening the scope of the financial statements being produced.

2. A state or local government unit prepares fund financial statements utilizing fund accounting. In this system, activities are classified into three broad categories (governmental, proprietary, and fiduciary). Governmental funds account for service activities. Proprietary funds account for activities for which a user charge is assessed. Fiduciary funds account for resources that the government holds as a trustee or agent for an external party.

3. Governmental funds have five fund types: the general fund, special revenue funds, capital projects funds, debt service funds, and permanent funds. Proprietary funds comprise enterprise funds and internal service funds whereas fiduciary funds comprise pension trust funds, investment trust funds, private-purpose trust funds, and agency funds.

4. Government-wide financial statements are made up of a statement of net position and a statement of activities that report both governmental activities (the governmental funds and most of the internal service funds) and business-type activities (enterprise funds and occasionally an internal service fund). These statements measure all economic resources. The timing of recognition is guided by accrual accounting.

5. Fund financial statements include a number of financial statements. This chapter focuses on the balance sheet and the statement of revenues, expenditures, and other changes in fund balances for the governmental funds. These statements must show separately the general fund and any other individual fund that qualifies as major. For the governmental funds, these statements report current financial resources (mostly cash, receivables, and investments and claims on those current financial resources). The timing of recognition is guided by modified accrual accounting.

6. "Fund balance" figures reflect the size of the net amount of resources held by a particular fund within the governmental funds. To indicate the government's level of control over these resources, the fund financial statements classify the fund balance as nonspendable (the resource cannot be spent), restricted (use has been designated by a party outside the government), committed (use has been approved by the highest level of authority within the government), assigned (use has been set within the government but not by the highest level of authority), and unassigned (use has not been designated) so that the resources can be freely used by government officials.

7. To aid in control over financial resources and disclose allocation decisions, the approved budgets for many of the governmental funds are recorded each year. The initial budget, a final amended budget, and actual figures for the period are then reported as required supplementary information along with the financial statements (or as a separate statement within the fund financial statements).

8. Monetary commitments for purchase orders and contracts are recorded in the individual governmental funds by recognizing encumbrances. These balances are recorded when the commitment is made and removed when an actual claim to current financial resources first comes into existence. This recording helps government officials avoid spending more than the amounts properly appropriated.

9. The fund financial statements recognize expenditures for capital outlay, long-term debt payment, and expense-type costs when a claim to current financial resources is created. In contrast, government-wide financial statements capitalize capital outlay, reduce liabilities for debt payments, and record expenses.

10. Revenue recognition for nonexchange transactions such as sales taxes and property taxes is based on a classification system. The timing and method of recognition depend on whether the revenue is a derived tax revenue, imposed nonexchange revenue, government-mandated nonexchange transaction, or voluntary nonexchange transaction.

11. The issuance of long-term bonds is recorded as an "other financing source" by the governmental funds because the financial resource inflow is not a revenue. However, the same event is reported as an increase in a long-term liability both in the proprietary funds and in the government-wide financial statements as a whole.

12. Transfers between funds are normally reported as an "other financing source" and "other financing use" within the fund financial statements. To show the impact on each fund type, these balances are not eliminated or offset. The government-wide statements do not report such transactions unless they have an effect on overall governmental activities and business-type activities. If reported, the amounts are offset in arriving at figures for the government as a whole. For internal exchange transactions in which payment is made for a good or service, the fund statements recognize a revenue and an expenditure or expense. The government-wide financial statements normally do not reflect internal exchange transfers unless they occur between an enterprise fund and a governmental fund.

Comprehensive Illustration

Problem

(*Estimated Time: 50 Minutes*). The Town of Drexel has the following financial transactions.

1. The town council adopts an annual budget for the general fund estimating general revenues of $1.7 million, approved expenditures of $1.5 million, and approved transfers out of $120,000.
2. The town levies property taxes of $1.3 million. It expects to collect all but 3 percent of these taxes during the year. Of the levied amount, $40,000 will be collected next year but after more than 60 days.
3. The town orders two new police cars at an approximate cost of $110,000.
4. A transfer of $50,000 is made from the general fund to the debt service fund.
5. The town makes a payment on a bond payable of $40,000 along with $10,000 of interest using the money previously set aside.
6. The Town of Drexel issues a $2 million bond at face value in hopes of acquiring a building to convert into a high school.
7. The two police cars are received with an invoice price of $112,000. The voucher has been approved but will not be paid for three weeks.
8. The town purchases the building for the high school for $2 million in cash and immediately begins renovating it.
9. Depreciation on the new police cars is computed as $30,000 for the period.
10. The town borrows $100,000 on a 30-day tax anticipation note.
11. The Town of Drexel begins a special assessment curbing project. The government issues $800,000 in notes at face value to finance this project. The town has guaranteed the debt if the assessments collected do not cover the entire balance.
12. A contractor completes the curbing project and is paid $800,000 as agreed.
13. The town assesses citizens $850,000 for the completed curbing project.
14. The town collects the special assessments of $850,000 in full and repays the debt plus $50,000 in interest.
15. The town receives a $10,000 cash grant from a regional charity to beautify a local park. The grant must be used to cover the specific costs that the town incurs.
16. The town spends the first $4,000 to beautify the park.

Required

a. Prepare journal entries for the town based on the production of fund financial statements.

b. Prepare journal entries in anticipation of preparing government-wide financial statements.

Solution

a. Fund Financial Statements

1. **General Fund**

Estimated Revenues	1,700,000	
Appropriations		1,500,000
Estimated Other Financing Uses		120,000
Budgetary Fund Balance		80,000

2. **General Fund**

Property Tax Receivable	1,300,000	
Allowance for Uncollectible Taxes		39,000
Unavailable Property Tax Revenues		40,000
Revenues—Property Taxes		1,221,000

3. **General Fund**

Encumbrances—Police Cars	110,000	
Encumbrances Outstanding		110,000

4. **General Fund**

Other Financing Uses—Transfers Out.	50,000	
Cash		50,000

Debt Service Funds

Cash	50,000	
Other Financing Sources—Transfers In		50,000

5. **Debt Service Funds**

Expenditures—Principal	40,000	
Expenditures—Interest	10,000	
Cash		50,000

6. **Capital Projects Funds**

Cash	2,000,000	
Other Financing Sources—Bond Proceeds		2,000,000

7. **General Fund**

Encumbrances Outstanding	110,000	
Encumbrances—Police Cars		110,000
Expenditures—Police Cars	112,000	
Vouchers Payable		112,000

8. **Capital Projects Funds**

Expenditures—Building	2,000,000	
Cash		2,000,000

9. No entry is recorded. Expenditures rather than expenses are recorded by the governmental funds.

10. **General Fund**

Cash	100,000	
Tax Anticipation Note Payable		100,000

11. **Capital Projects Funds**

Cash	800,000	
Other Financing Sources—Special Assessments Note		800,000

12. **Capital Projects Funds**

Expenditures—Curbing	800,000	
Cash		800,000

13. **Debt Service Funds**

Taxes Receivable—Special Assessment	850,000	
Revenues—Special Assessment		850,000

14. **Debt Service Funds**

Cash	850,000	
Taxes Receivable—Special Assessment		850,000
Expenditures—Principal	800,000	
Expenditures—Interest	50,000	
Cash		850,000

15.   **Special Revenue Funds**

Cash	10,000	
Grant Collected in Advance		10,000

16.   **Special Revenue Funds**

Expenditures—Park Beautification	4,000	
Cash		4,000
Grant Collected in Advance	4,000	
Revenues—Grants		4,000

b. *Government-Wide Financial Statements*

1. Budgetary entries are not reported within the government-wide financial statements. Budgets are recorded in the individual funds and are then shown as required supplementary information or in a separate fund financial statement.

2.   **Governmental Activities**

Property Tax Receivable	1,300,000	
Allowance for Uncollectible Taxes		39,000
Revenues—Property Taxes		1,261,000

3. Commitments are not reported in government-wide financial statements.

4. This transfer was entirely within the governmental funds and, therefore, had no net effect on the governmental activities. It is an intra-activity transaction. No journal entry is needed.

5.   **Governmental Activities**

Bonds Payable	40,000	
Interest Expense	10,000	
Cash		50,000

6.   **Governmental Activities**

Cash	2,000,000	
Bonds Payable		2,000,000

7.   **Governmental Activities**

Police Cars (or Vehicles)	112,000	
Vouchers (or Accounts) Payable		112,000

8.   **Governmental Activities**

Building	2,000,000	
Cash		2,000,000

9.   **Governmental Activities**

Depreciation Expense	30,000	
Accumulated Depreciation		30,000

10.   **Governmental Activities**

Cash	100,000	
Tax Anticipation Note Payable		100,000

11.   **Governmental Activities**

Cash	800,000	
Special Assessment Notes Payable		800,000

12. | | | **Governmental Activities** | | |
| --- | --- | --- |
| Infrastructure Assets—Curbing | 800,000 | |
| Cash | | 800,000 |

13. | | | **Governmental Activities** | | |
| --- | --- | --- |
| Taxes Receivable—Special Assessment | 850,000 | |
| Revenues—Special Assessment | | 850,000 |

14. | | | **Governmental Activities** | | |
| --- | --- | --- |
| Cash | 850,000 | |
| Taxes Receivable—Special Assessment | | 850,000 |
| Special Assessment Notes Payable | 800,000 | |
| Interest Expense | 50,000 | |
| Cash | | 850,000 |

15. | | | **Governmental Activities** | | |
| --- | --- | --- |
| Cash | 10,000 | |
| Grant Collected in Advance | | 10,000 |

16. | | | **Governmental Activities** | | |
| --- | --- | --- |
| Expenses—Park Beautification | 4,000 | |
| Cash | | 4,000 |
| Grant Collected in Advance | 4,000 | |
| Revenues—Grants | | 4,000 |

Questions

1. How have users' needs impacted the development of accounting principles for state and local government units?

2. Why have accountability and control been so important in the traditional accounting for state and local government units?

3. How has the dual system of financial statements impacted the financial reporting of state and local governments?

4. What are the basic financial statements that a state or local government now produces?

5. What measurement focus is used in fund financial statements for governmental funds, and what system is applied to determine the timing of revenue and expenditure recognition?

6. What measurement focus is used in government-wide financial statements, and what system is applied to determine the timing of revenue and expense recognition?

7. What assets are viewed as current financial resources?

8. In applying the current financial resources measurement focus, when are liabilities recognized in fund financial statements?

9. What are the three categories of funds? What funds are included in each of these three?

10. What are the five fund types within the governmental funds? What types of events does each of these report?

11. What are the two fund types within the proprietary funds? What types of events does each report?

12. What are the four fund types within the fiduciary funds? What types of events does each report?

13. What are the two major divisions reported in government-wide financial statements? What funds are *not* reported in these financial statements?

14. Fund financial statements have separate columns for each activity. Which activities are reported in this manner?

15. The general fund of a city reports assets of $300,000 and liabilities of $200,000 in the fund financial statements. Explain what is meant by each of the following balances: fund balance—nonspendable of $40,000, fund balance—restricted of $28,000, fund balance—committed of $17,000, fund balance—assigned of $4,000, and fund balance—unassigned of $11,000.

16. Why are budgetary entries recorded in the individual funds of a state or local government?

17. How are budget results shown in the financial reporting of a state or local government?
18. When is an encumbrance recorded? What happens to this balance? How are encumbrances reported in government-wide financial statements?
19. What costs necessitate the reporting of an expenditure by a governmental fund?
20. At what point in time does a governmental fund report an expenditure?
21. How do governmental funds report capital outlay in fund financial statements? How do government-wide financial statements report capital expenditures?
22. What are the two different ways that supplies and prepaid items can be recorded on fund financial statements?
23. What are the four classifications of nonexchange revenues that a state or local government can recognize? In each case, when are revenues normally recognized?
24. When is a receivable recognized for property tax assessments? When is the revenue recognized?
25. How is the issuance of a long-term bond reported on fund financial statements? How is the issuance of a long-term bond reported on government-wide financial statements?
26. What is a special assessment project? How are special assessment projects reported?
27. How are interfund transfers reported in fund financial statements?
28. In government-wide financial statements, how do intra-activity and interactivity transactions differ? How is each type of transaction reported?
29. What is an internal exchange transaction, and how is it reported?

Problems

LO 11-4

1. Which of the following is *not* a governmental fund?
   a. Special revenue fund
   b. Internal service fund
   c. Capital projects fund
   d. Debt service fund

LO 11-4

2. What is the purpose of a special revenue fund?
   a. To account for revenues legally or externally restricted as an operating expenditure.
   b. To account for ongoing activities.
   c. To account for gifts when only subsequently earned income can be expended.
   d. To account for the cost of long-lived assets bought with designated funds.

LO 11-4

3. What is the purpose of enterprise funds?
   a. To account for operations that provide services to other departments within a government.
   b. To account for asset transfers.
   c. To account for ongoing activities such as the police and fire departments.
   d. To account for operations financed in whole or in part by outside user charges.

LO 11-4

4. Which of the following statements is true?
   a. There are three different types of proprietary funds.
   b. There are three different types of fiduciary funds.
   c. There are five different types of fiduciary funds.
   d. There are five different types of governmental funds.

LO 11-1, 11-6

5. A government expects to receive revenues of $400,000 but has approved expenditures of $430,000. The anticipated shortage will have an impact on which of the following terms?
   a. Interperiod equity
   b. Modified accrual accounting
   c. Consumption accounting
   d. Account groups

LO 11-4

6. A citizen of the City of Townsend makes a donation of $22,000 in investments. The citizen has stipulated that the investments be held. Any resulting income must be used to help maintain the city's cemetery. In which fund should this asset be reported?
   a. Special revenue funds
   b. Capital projects funds
   c. Permanent funds
   d. General fund

LO 11-2
7. Which of the following statements is correct about the reporting of governmental funds?
   a. Fund financial statements measure economic resources.
   b. Government-wide financial statements measure only current financial resources.
   c. Fund financial statements measure both economic resources and current financial resources.
   d. Government-wide financial statements measure economic resources.

LO 11-2
8. Which of the following statements is correct about the reporting of governmental funds?
   a. Fund financial statements measure revenues and expenditures based on modified accrual accounting.
   b. Government-wide financial statements measure revenues and expenses based on modified accrual accounting.
   c. Fund financial statements measure revenues and expenses based on accrual accounting.
   d. Government-wide financial statements measure revenues and expenditures based on accrual accounting.

LO 11-2, 11-7
9. During the current year, a government buys land for $80,000. Which of the following is *not* true?
   a. The land could be reported as an asset by the business-type activities in the government-wide financial statements.
   b. The land could be reported as an asset by the governmental activities in the government-wide financial statements.
   c. The land could be reported as an asset by the proprietary funds in the fund financial statements.
   d. The land could be reported as an asset by the governmental funds in the fund financial statements.

LO 11-5
10. The City of Bagranoff holds $90,000 in cash that will be used to make a bond payment when the debt comes due early next year. The assistant treasurer had made that decision. However, just before the end of the current year, the city council formally approved using this money in this way. The city council has been designated as the highest level of decision-making authority for this government. What impact does the council's action have on the reporting of fund financial statements?
    a. Fund balance—unassigned goes down and fund balance—restricted goes up.
    b. Fund balance—assigned goes down and fund balance—committed goes up.
    c. Fund balance—unassigned goes down and fund balance—assigned goes up.
    d. Fund balance—assigned goes down and fund balance—restricted goes up.

LO 11-6
11. Which of the following statements is true concerning the recording of a budget?
    a. At the beginning of the year, debit Appropriations.
    b. A debit to the Budgetary Fund Balance account indicates an expected surplus.
    c. At the beginning of the year, debit Estimated Revenues.
    d. At the end of the year, credit Appropriations.

LO 11-1, 11-2, 11-7
12. The general fund pays rent for two months. Which of the following is *not* correct?
    a. Rent expense should be reported in the government-wide financial statements.
    b. Rent expense should be reported in the general fund.
    c. An expenditure should be reported in the fund financial statements.
    d. If one month of rent is in the first year with the other month in the next year, either the purchases method or the consumption method can be used in fund statements.

LO 11-6, 11-7
13. A purchase order for $3,000 is recorded in the general fund for the purchase of a new computer. The computer is received at an actual cost of $3,020. Which of the following statements is correct?
    a. Machinery is increased in the general fund by $3,020.
    b. An encumbrance account is reduced by $3,020.
    c. An expenditure is increased by $3,020.
    d. An expenditure is recorded for the additional $20.

LO 11-5
14. At the end of the current year, a government reports a fund balance—assigned balance of $9,000 in connection with an encumbrance. What information is being conveyed?
    a. A donor has given the government $9,000 that must be used in a specified fashion.
    b. The government has made $9,000 in commitments in one year that will be honored in the subsequent year.

    c. Encumbrances exceeded expenditures by $9,000 during the current year.

    d. The government spent $9,000 less than was appropriated.

LO 11-2, 11-3, 11-7

15. A government buys equipment for its police department at a cost of $54,000. Which of the following is *not* true?

    a. Equipment will increase by $54,000 in the government-wide financial statements.

    b. Depreciation in connection with this equipment will be reported in the fund financial statements.

    c. The equipment will not appear within the reported assets in the fund financial statements.

    d. An expenditure for $54,000 will be reported in the fund financial statements.

LO 11-3, 11-7

16. A city acquires supplies for its fire department and uses the consumption method of accounting. Which of the following statements is true for the fund statements?

    a. An expenditures account was debited at the time of receipt.

    b. An expense is recorded as the supplies are consumed.

    c. An inventory account is debited at the time of the acquisition.

    d. The supplies are recorded within the General Fixed Assets Account Group.

LO 11-8

17. An income tax is an example of which of the following?

    a. Derived tax revenue.

    b. Imposed nonexchange revenue.

    c. Government-mandated nonexchange revenue.

    d. Voluntary nonexchange transaction.

LO 11-8

18. The state government passes a law requiring localities to upgrade their water treatment facilities. The state then awards a grant of $500,000 to the Town of Midlothian to help pay for this cost. What type of revenue is this grant?

    a. Derived tax revenue.

    b. Imposed nonexchange revenue.

    c. Government-mandated nonexchange revenue.

    d. Voluntary nonexchange transaction.

LO 11-8

19. The state awards a grant of $50,000 to the Town of Glenville. The state will pay the grant money to the town as a reimbursement for money spent on road repair. At the time of the grant, the state pays $8,000 in advance. During the first year of this program, the town spent $14,000 and applied for reimbursement. What amount of revenue should be recognized?

    a. $–0–

    b. $8,000

    c. $14,000

    d. $50,000

LO 11-5, 11-9

20. A city issues a 60-day tax anticipation note to fund operations until taxes have been collected. What recording should it make?

    a. The liability should be reported in the government-wide financial statements; an other financing source should be shown in the fund financial statements.

    b. A liability should be reported in the government-wide financial statements and in the fund financial statements.

    c. An other financing source should be shown in the government-wide financial statements and in the fund financial statements.

    d. An other financing source should be shown in the government-wide financial statements; a liability is reported in the fund financial statements.

LO 11-5, 11-9

21. A city issues five-year bonds payable to finance construction of a new school. What recording should be made?

    a. Report the liability in the government-wide financial statements; show an other financing source in the fund financial statements.

    b. Report a liability in the government-wide financial statements and in the fund financial statements.

    c. Show an other financing source in the government-wide financial statements and in the fund financial statements.

    d. Show an other financing source in the government-wide financial statements; report a liability in the fund financial statements.

LO 11-9

22. The City of Dylan issues a 10-year bond payable of $1 million at face value on the first day of Year 1. Debt issuance costs of $10,000 are paid on that day. For government-wide financial statements, how is this debt issuance cost reported?

    a. $1,000 is recorded as an expense and $9,000 is recorded as an asset.

    b. $1,000 is recorded as an expense and $9,000 is recorded as a deferred outflow of resources.

    c. $10,000 is recorded as an expense.

    d. $10,000 is recorded as an asset.

LO 11-9

23. The City of Frost has a 20-year debt outstanding. On the last day of the current year, this debt has an outstanding balance of $4.8 million and five years remaining until it is due. On that date, the debt is paid off early for $5 million. A new debt is issued (with a lower interest rate) for $5.4 million. How is the $200,000 between the amount paid and the outstanding balance of $4.8 million recognized on government-wide financial statements?

    a. As an expense.

    b. As a reduction in liabilities.

    c. As a deferred outflow of resources on the statement of net position.

    d. As an asset on the statement of net position.

LO 11-2, 11-9

24. A $110,000 payment is made on a long-term liability. Of this amount, $10,000 represents interest. Which of the following is *not* true for the recording of this transaction?

    a. Reduce liabilities by $100,000 in the government-wide financial statements.

    b. Record a $110,000 expenditure in the fund financial statements.

    c. Reduce liabilities by $100,000 in the fund financial statements.

    d. Recognize $10,000 interest expense in the government-wide financial statements.

LO 11-1, 11-10

25. A city constructs a special assessment project (a sidewalk) for which it is secondarily liable. The city issues bonds of $90,000. It authorizes another $10,000 that is transferred out of the general fund. The sidewalk is built for $100,000. The citizens are billed for $90,000. They pay this amount and the debt is paid off. Where is the $100,000 expenditure for construction recorded?

    a. It is not recorded by the city.

    b. It is recorded in the agency fund.

    c. It is recorded in the general fund.

    d. It is recorded in the capital projects fund.

LO 11-4, 11-10

26. A city constructs curbing in a new neighborhood and finances it as a special assessment. Under what condition should these transactions be recorded in an agency fund?

    a. Never; the work is reported in the capital projects funds.

    b. Only if the city is secondarily liable for any debt incurred to finance construction costs.

    c. Only if the city is in no way liable for the costs of the construction.

    d. In all cases.

LO 11-11

27. Which of the following is an example of an interactivity transaction?

    a. Money is transferred from the general fund to the debt service fund.

    b. Money is transferred from the capital projects fund to the general fund.

    c. Money is transferred from the special revenue fund to the debt service fund.

    d. Money is transferred from the general fund to the enterprise fund.

LO 11-5, 11-11

28. Cash of $60,000 is transferred from the general fund to the debt service fund. What is reported on the government-wide financial statements?

    a. No reporting is made.

    b. Other Financing Sources increase by $60,000; Other Financing Uses increase by $60,000.

    c. Revenues increase by $60,000; Expenditures increase by $60,000.

    d. Revenues increase by $60,000; Expenses increase by $60,000.

LO 11-5, 11-11

29. Cash of $60,000 is transferred from the general fund to the debt service fund. What is reported on the fund financial statements?

    a. No reporting is made.

    b. Other Financing Sources increase by $60,000; Other Financing Uses increase by $60,000.

    c. Revenues increase by $60,000; Expenditures increase by $60,000.

    d. Revenues increase by $60,000; Expenses increase by $60,000.

LO 11-5, 11-11

30. Cash of $20,000 is transferred from the general fund to the enterprise fund to pay for work that was done. What is reported on the government-wide financial statements?

    a. No reporting is made.

    b. Other Financing Sources increase by $20,000; Other Financing Uses increase by $20,000.

    c. Revenues increase by $20,000; Expenditures increase by $20,000.

    d. Revenues increase by $20,000; Expenses increase by $20,000.

LO 11-5, 11-11

31. Cash of $20,000 is transferred from the general fund to the enterprise fund to pay for work that was done. What is reported on the fund financial statements?

    a. No reporting is made.

    b. Other Financing Sources increase by $20,000; Other Financing Uses increase by $20,000.

    c. Revenues increase by $20,000; Expenditures increase by $20,000.

    d. Revenues increase by $20,000; Expenses increase by $20,000.

LO 11-3, 11-6

32. The board of commissioners of the City of Hartmoore adopted a general fund budget for the year ending June 30, 2017, that included revenues of $1,000,000, bond proceeds of $400,000, appropriations of $900,000, and operating transfers out of $300,000. If this budget is formally integrated into the accounting records, what journal entry is required at the beginning of the year? What later entry is required?

LO 11-2, 11-6, 11-7

33. A city orders a new computer for its general fund at an anticipated cost of $88,000. Its actual cost when received is $89,400. Payment is subsequently made. Prepare all required journal entries for both fund and government-wide financial statements. What information do the government-wide financial statements present? What information do the fund financial statements present?

LO 11-1, 11-2, 11-7

34. Cash of $90,000 is transferred from a city's general fund to start construction on a police station. The city issues a bond at its $1.8 million face value. The police station is built for $1.89 million. Prepare all necessary journal entries for these transactions for both fund and government-wide financial statements. Assume that the city does not record the commitment. What information do the government-wide financial statements present? What information do the fund financial statements present?

LO 11-5

35. The governmental funds of the City of Westchester report $445,000 in assets and $140,000 in liabilities. The following are some of the assets reported by this government.

    - Prepaid items—$7,000.
    - Cash from a bond issuance that must be spent within the school system according to the bond indenture—$80,000.
    - Supplies—$5,000.
    - Investments given by a citizen that will be sold with the proceeds used to beautify a public park—$33,000.
    - Cash that the assistant director of finance has designated for use in upgrading the local roads—$40,000.
    - Cash from a state grant that must be spent to supplement the pay of local kindergarten teachers—$53,000.
    - Cash that the city council (the highest level of authority in the government) has voted to use to renovate a school gymnasium—$62,000.

    On a balance sheet for the governmental funds, what fund balance amounts will be reported by the City of Westchester?

LO 11-5

36. Government officials of Hampstead County ordered a computer near the end of the current fiscal year for $6,400 for the police department. It did not arrive prior to the end of the year. At its final meeting of the year, the city council (the highest decision-making authority for the government) agreed to pay for the computer when it arrived in the subsequent year. In producing a set of government-wide financial statements and a set of fund financial statements for the current year, how will this purchase order be reported?

LO 11-2, 11-5, 11-11

37. A local government has the following transactions during the current fiscal period. Prepare journal entries without dollar amounts, first for fund financial statements and then for government-wide financial statements.

    a. The budget for the police department, ambulance service, and other ongoing activities is passed. Funding is from property taxes, transfers, and bond proceeds. All monetary outflows will be for expenses and fixed assets. A deficit is projected.

    b. A bond is issued at face value to fund the construction of a new municipal building.

c. A computer is ordered for the tax department.

d. The computer is received.

e. The invoice for the computer is paid.

f. The city council agrees to transfer money from the general fund as partial payment for a special assessments project but has not yet done so. The city will be secondarily liable for any money borrowed for this work.

g. The city council creates a motor pool to service all government vehicles. Money is transferred from the general fund to permanently finance this facility.

h. Property taxes are levied. Although officials believe that most of these taxes should be collected during the current period, a small percentage is estimated to be uncollectible.

i. The city collects grant money from the state that must be spent as a supplement to the salaries of the police force. No entry has been recorded. Appropriate payment of the supplement is viewed as an eligibility requirement.

j. A portion of the grant money in (i) is properly spent.

LO 11-2, 11-4, 11-7, 11-8, 11-11

38. Prepare journal entries for the City of Pudding's governmental funds to record the following transactions, first for fund financial statements and then for government-wide financial statements.

a. A new truck for the sanitation department was ordered at a cost of $94,000.

b. The city print shop did $1,200 worth of work for the school system (but has not yet been paid).

c. An $11 million bond was issued to build a new road.

d. Cash of $140,000 is transferred from the general fund to provide permanent financing for a municipal swimming pool that will be viewed as an enterprise fund.

e. The truck ordered in (a) is received at an actual cost of $96,000. Payment is not made at this time.

f. Cash of $32,000 is transferred from the general fund to the capital projects fund.

g. A state grant of $30,000 is received that must be spent to promote recycling.

h. The first $5,000 of the state grant received in (g) is appropriately expended.

LO 11-2, 11-5, 11-7, 11-8, 11-9, 11-11

39. Prepare journal entries for a local government to record the following transactions, first for fund financial statements and then for government-wide financial statements.

a. The government sells $900,000 in bonds at face value to finance construction of a warehouse.

b. A $1.1 million contract is signed for construction of the warehouse. The commitment is required, if allowed.

c. A $130,000 transfer of unrestricted funds was made for the eventual payment of the debt in (a).

d. Equipment for the fire department is received with a cost of $12,000. When it was ordered, an anticipated cost of $11,800 had been recorded.

e. Supplies to be used in the schools are bought for $2,000 cash. The consumption method is used.

f. A state grant of $90,000 is awarded to supplement police salaries. The money will be paid to reimburse the government after the supplement payments have been made to the police officers.

g. Property tax assessments are mailed to citizens of the government. The total assessment is $600,000, although officials anticipate that 4 percent will never be collected. There is an enforceable legal claim for this money and the government can use it immediately.

LO 11-4, 11-5, 11-6, 11-7, 11-8, 11-9, 11-10, 11-11

40. The following unadjusted trial balances are for the governmental funds of the City of Copeland prepared from the current accounting records:

General Fund

	Debit	Credit
Cash	$ 19,000	
Taxes Receivable	202,000	
Allowance for Uncollectible Taxes		$ 2,000
Vouchers Payable		24,000
Due to Debt Service Fund		10,000
Unavailable Revenues		16,000
Encumbrances Outstanding		9,000
Fund Balance—Unassigned		103,000
Revenues		176,000

(*continued*)

(continued)

General Fund

	Debit	Credit
Expenditures	110,000	
Encumbrances	9,000	
Estimated Revenues	190,000	
Appropriations		171,000
Budgetary Fund Balance		19,000
Totals	$530,000	$530,000

Debt Service Fund

	Debit	Credit
Cash	$ 8,000	
Investments	51,000	
Taxes Receivable	11,000	
Due from General Fund	10,000	
Fund Balance—Committed		$ 45,000
Revenues		20,000
Other Financing Sources—Operating Transfers In		90,000
Expenditures	75,000	
Totals	$155,000	$155,000

Capital Projects Fund

	Debit	Credit
Cash	$ 70,000	
Special Assessments Receivable	90,000	
Contracts Payable		$ 50,000
Unavailable Revenues		90,000
Encumbrances Outstanding		16,000
Fund Balance—Unassigned		–0–
Other Financing Sources		150,000
Expenditures	130,000	
Encumbrances	16,000	
Estimated Other Financing Sources	150,000	
Appropriations		150,000
Totals	$456,000	$456,000

Special Revenue Fund

	Debit	Credit
Cash	$ 14,000	
Taxes Receivable	41,000	
Inventory of Supplies	4,000	
Vouchers Payable		$ 25,000
Grant Revenues Collected in Advance		3,000
Fund Balance—Nonspendable		4,000
Encumbrances Outstanding		3,000
Fund Balance—Unassigned		19,000
Revenues		56,000
Expenditures	48,000	
Encumbrances	3,000	
Estimated Revenues	75,000	
Appropriations		60,000
Budgetary Fund Balance		15,000
Totals	$185,000	$185,000

Based on the information presented for each of these governmental funds, answer the following questions:

  a. How much more money can city officials expend or commit from the general fund during the remainder of the current year without amending the budget?

  b. Why does the capital projects fund have no construction or capital asset accounts?

  c. What does the $150,000 Appropriations balance found in the capital projects fund represent?

  d. Several funds have balances for Encumbrances and Encumbrances Outstanding. How will these amounts be accounted for at the end of the fiscal year?

  e. Why does the Fund Balance—Unassigned account in the capital projects fund have a zero balance?

  f. What are possible explanations for the $150,000 Other Financing Sources balance found in the capital projects fund?

  g. What does the $75,000 balance in the Expenditures account of the debt service fund represent?

  h. What is the purpose of the Special Assessments Receivable found in the capital projects fund?

  i. In the special revenue fund, what is the purpose of the Fund Balance—Nonspendable account?

  j. Why does the debt service fund not have budgetary account balances?

LO 11-2, 11-3, 11-4, 11-5, 11-6, 11-7, 11-8, 11-9, 11-11

41. Following are descriptions of transactions and other financial events for the City of Tetris for the year ending December 2017. Not all transactions have been included here. Only the general fund formally records a budget. No encumbrances were carried over from 2016.

Paid salary for police officers	$ 21,000
Received government grant to pay ambulance drivers.	40,000
Estimated revenues	232,000
Received invoices for rent on equipment used by fire department during last four months of the year	3,000
Paid for newly constructed city hall.	1,044,000
Made commitment to acquire ambulance	111,000
Received cash from bonds sold for construction purposes	300,000
Placed order for new sanitation truck.	154,000
Paid salary to ambulance drivers—money derived from state government grant given for that purpose	24,000
Paid for supplies for school system.	16,000
Made transfer from General Fund to eventually pay off a long-term debt.	33,000
Received but did not pay for new ambulance.	120,000
Levied property tax receivables for 2017. City anticipates that 95% ($190,000) will be collected during the year and 5% will be uncollectible.	200,000
Acquired and paid for new school bus.	40,000
Received cash from business licenses and parking meters (not previously accrued)	14,000
Approved appropriations.	225,000

The following questions are *independent* although each is based on the preceding information. Assume that the government is preparing information for its fund financial statements.

  a. What is the balance in the Budgetary Fund Balance account for the budget for the year? Is it a debit or credit?

  b. Assume that 60 percent of the school supplies are used during the year so that 40 percent remain. If the consumption method is being applied, how is this recorded?

  c. The sanitation truck that was ordered was not received before the end of the year. The commitment will be honored in the subsequent year when the truck arrives. What reporting is made at the end of 2015?

  d. Assume that new ambulance was received on December 31, 2017. Provide all necessary journal entries on that date.

  e. Prepare all journal entries that should have been made when the $33,000 transfer was made for the eventual payment of a long-term debt.

  f. What amount of revenue would be recognized for the period? Explain the composition of this total.

  g. What are the total expenditures? Explain the makeup of this total. Include response to (*b*) here.

  h. What journal entry or entries were prepared when the bonds were issued?

LO 11-2, 11-3, 11-4, 11-5, 11-6, 11-7, 11-8, 11-9, 11-11

42. Chesterfield County had the following transactions. Prepare the entries first for fund financial statements and then for government-wide financial statements.

   a. A budget is passed for all ongoing activities. Revenue is anticipated to be $834,000 with approved spending of $540,000 and operating transfers out of $242,000.

   b. A contract is signed with a construction company to build a new central office building for the government at a cost of $8 million. A budget for this project has previously been recorded.

   c. Bonds are sold for $8 million (face value) to finance construction of the new office building.

   d. The new building is completed. An invoice for $8 million is received and paid.

   e. Previously unrestricted cash of $1 million is set aside to begin paying the bonds issued in (*c*).

   f. A portion of the bonds comes due and $1 million is paid. Of this total, $100,000 represents interest. The interest had not been previously accrued.

   g. Citizens' property tax levies are assessed. Total billing for this tax is $800,000. On this date, the assessment is a legally enforceable claim according to the laws of this state. The money to be received is designated for the current period, and 90 percent is assumed to be collectible in this period with receipt of an additional 6 percent during subsequent periods but in time to be available to pay current period claims. The remainder is expected to be uncollectible.

   h. Cash of $120,000 is received from a toll road. This money is restricted for highway maintenance.

   i. The county received investments valued at $300,000 as a donation from a grateful citizen. Income from these investments must be used to beautify local parks.

LO 11-5

43. The following trial balance is taken from the General Fund of the City of Jennings for the year ending December 31, 2017. Prepare a condensed statement of revenues, expenditures, and other changes in fund balance and also prepare a condensed balance sheet.

	Debit	Credit
Accounts Payable		$ 90,000
Cash	$ 30,000	
Contracts Payable.		90,000
Unavailable Revenues		40,000
Due from Capital Projects Funds	60,000	
Due to Debt Service Funds.		40,000
Expenditures	530,000	
Fund Balance—Unassigned		170,000
Investments	410,000	
Revenues		760,000
Other Financing Sources—Bond Proceeds		300,000
Other Financing Sources—Transfers In		50,000
Other Financing Uses—Transfers Out.	470,000	
Taxes Receivable	220,000	
Vouchers Payable.		180,000
Totals.	$1,720,000	$1,720,000

LO 11-2, 11-5, 11-6, 11-7, 11-8, 11-9

44. A city has only one activity, its school system. The school system is accounted for within the general fund. For convenience, assume that, at the start of 2017, the school system and the city have no assets. During the year, the city assessed $400,000 in property taxes. Of this amount, it collected $320,000 during the year, received $50,000 within a few weeks after the end of the year, and expected the remainder to be collected about six months later. The city makes the following payments during 2017: salary expense, $100,000; rent expense, $70,000; equipment (received on January 1 with a five-year life and no salvage value), $50,000; land, $30,000; and maintenance expense, $20,000.

   In addition, on the last day of the year, the city purchased a $200,000 building by signing a long-term liability. The building has a 20-year life and no salvage value, and the liability accrues interest at a 10 percent annual rate. The city also buys two computers on the last day of the year for $4,000 each. One will be paid for in 30 days and the other in 90 days. The computers should last for four years and have no salvage value. During the year, the school system charged students $3,000 for school fees and collected the entire amount. Any depreciation is recorded using the straight-line method.

   a. Produce a statement of net position and a statement of activities for this city's government-wide financial statements.

b. Produce a balance sheet and a statement of revenues, expenditures, and changes in fund balance for the fund financial statements. Assume that *available* is defined by the city as anything to be received within 60 days.

LO 11-2, 11-4, 11-6, 11-7, 11-8, 11-10

45. The City of Havisham has a fiscal year ending December 31, Year 5. If the city were to produce financial statements right now, the following figures would be included:

   – Governmental activities: Assets = $800,000, Liabilities = $300,000, and Change in Net Position for the period = increase of $100,000

   – Business-type activities: Assets = $500,000, Liabilities = $200,000, and Change in Net Position for the period = increase of $60,000

   – Governmental funds: Assets = $300,000, Liabilities = $100,000, and Change in Fund Balances = increase of $40,000

   – Proprietary funds: Assets = $700,000, Liabilities = $300,000, and Change in Net Assets for the period = increase of $70,000

   Other information: The city council is considered the highest level of decision-making authority for the government. Where applicable, current financial resources are viewed by the government as available if collected within 75 days of the end of a fiscal year.

   For each of the following, indicate whether the overall statement is true or false. Assume that each situation is independent of all others.

   a. In the information provided about the city, an error has apparently been made because the amount of proprietary fund assets ($700,000) cannot be greater than the amount of business-type activity assets ($500,000).

   b. A separate governmental fund (such as money designated for the construction of Highway 61) is reporting assets totaling $32,000. Based on that information alone, this fund must be reported separately as a major fund.

   c. The city starts a bus system to help eliminate traffic congestion. Passengers are charged a nickel for each trip although that fee will not come close to covering the cost of the bus system or pay for its debts. The bus system must be reported as a part of the general fund rather than as a separate enterprise fund.

   d. The city council passes an annual budget for all general fund activities. Revenues are expected to be $1 million and approved expenditures are $900,000. These budgetary amounts are recorded through a journal entry at the beginning of the year (an entry that is removed at the end of the year). In recording this budget, an estimated revenue account is debited for $1 million.

   e. The city council passes an annual budget for all general fund activities. Revenues are expected to be $1 million and approved expenditures are $900,000. These budgetary amounts are recorded through a journal entry at the beginning of the year (that entry is removed at the end of the year). In recording this budget, an expenditures account is debited for $900,000.

   f. The government paid for a 3-year insurance policy on January 1, Year 5, for its school system. If the purchases method had been used, the amount of expenditures reported by the city would be larger for that year than if the consumption method had been used.

   g. Money received from an income tax is classified as derived tax revenue.

   h. After the provided figures were determined, officials learned that the city was entitled to an additional $100,000 in taxes on income earned during Year 5. Starting on January 1, Year 6, the city will collect $1,000 per day of this amount for the next 98 days (the final $2,000 is expected to be uncollectible). As a result of this discovery, the reported change in net position for the governmental activities in government-wide statements for Year 5 will go up by $98,000.

   i. The police department ordered equipment on October 17, Year 5, for $43,000. The equipment was received on December 29, Year 5, but at a cost of $44,000. In the general fund, the encumbrance account was credited for $44,000 and the expenditure account was debited for $44,000 to indicate the switch from monetary commitment to liability.

   j. The police department ordered equipment on October 17, Year 5, for $43,000. The equipment was not received prior to the end of Year 5. The police chief authorized the department to accept and pay for the equipment when it arrived in Year 6. In reporting fund financial statements at the end of Year 5, a fund balance—committed of $43,000 should be reported on the balance sheet for the governmental funds.

   k. A cash amount of $32,000 is transferred from the general fund to a capital projects fund. On the statement of activities, for the government-wide financial statements, this transaction is shown as both a transfer in and a transfer out.

LO 11-5, 11-8, 11-10, 11-11

46. The City of Gargery has a fiscal year ending December 31, Year 5. If the city were to produce financial statements right now, the following figures would be included:

- Governmental activities: Assets = $800,000, Liabilities = $300,000, and Change in Net Position for the period = increase of $100,000.
- Business-type activities: Assets = $500,000, Liabilities = $200,000, and Change in Net Position for the period = increase of $60,000.
- Governmental funds: Assets = $300,000, Liabilities = $100,000, and Change in Fund Balances = increase of $40,000.
- Proprietary funds: Assets = $700,000, Liabilities = $300,000, and Change in Net Assets for the period = increase of $70,000.

Other information: The city council is viewed as the highest level of decision-making authority for the government. Where applicable, current financial resources are viewed by the government as available if collected within 75 days of the end of a fiscal year.

For each of the following, indicate whether the overall statement is true or false. Assume that each situation is independent of all others.

a. A cash amount of $19,000 is transferred from the general fund to an internal service fund to pay for work that was done by the print shop for the school system. On the statement of revenues, expenditures, and other changes in fund balances for the Governmental Funds (in the fund financial statements), this resource outflow is reported as an other financing use.

b. Assume that after the provided figures were determined, city officials learned that $100,000 in property taxes had been assessed but not recorded on December 29, Year 5. Per legal requirements, these taxes were solely to finance government operations in Year 6. Starting on January 1, Year 6, the city will collect $1,000 per day for the next 98 days (the final $2,000 is expected to be uncollectible). The change in net position for the governmental activities in the government-wide statements reported for Year 5 should be increased by $98,000.

c. Assume that after the provided figures were determined, city officials learned that $100,000 in property taxes had been assessed but not recorded on December 29, Year 5. Per legal requirements, these taxes were solely to finance government operations in Year 6. Starting on January 1, Year 6, the city will collect $1,000 per day for the next 98 days (the final $2,000 is expected to be uncollectible). The change in fund balances for the Governmental Funds reported for Year 5 should be increased by $60,000.

d. Assume that after the provided figures were determined, city officials learned that $100,000 in property taxes had been assessed but not recorded on December 29, Year 5. As per legal requirements, these taxes were solely to finance government operations in Year 6. The government collected $5,000 on December 30, Year 5, but the rest will not be collected until June of Year 6. On fund financial statements for the Governmental Funds as of December 31, Year 5, the total liability balance will be increased by $5,000.

e. Investments with a value of $5 million are given to the city by a donor. All income earned from these investments must be used to construct a small library in one of the local neighborhoods but the investments must be held forever. In Year 5, income of $480,000 was received from these investments. However, none of this money has yet been spent. On fund financial statements, the year-end balance sheet for the Governmental Funds must show a "fund balance—restricted" of $5 million and a "fund balance—committed" of $480,000.

f. The State of Virginia requires the City of Gargery to buy equipment to monitor local air quality. The state awards the city $100,000 to help pay for the equipment. This grant is known as a voluntary nonexchange transaction so that this revenue is not recognized until all eligibility requirements are met.

g. The city constructs curbing for a neighborhood in a special assessment project in which the individuals whose property is benefiting from the curbs will pay for the work. The city has no legal responsibility for this work so it is recorded in an agency fund. The money collected should be reported as program revenues on the statement of activities in the government-wide financial statements.

h. On January 1, Year 5, the city is awarded a grant for $130,000 with this money to be used to supplement the salaries of the police and fire department workers. No money will be received by the city until after the salaries have been paid. On December 30, Year 5, all $130,000 is distributed to the appropriate workers and the city applies for reimbursement to receive the grant money. The money will be received within the next month. The $130,000 revenue is recognized in the government-wide financial statements in Year 5 but not in the fund financial statements for Year 5.

LO 11-5, 11-7, 11-8, 11-9, 11-11

47. The following transactions relate to the General Fund of the city of Lost Angels for the year ending December 31, 2017. Prepare a statement of revenues, expenditures, and other changes in fund balance for the general fund for the period to be included in the fund financial statements. Assume that the fund balance at the beginning of the year was $180,000. Assume also that the purchases method is applied to the supplies and that receipt within 60 days is used as the definition of available resources.

    a. Collected property tax revenue of $700,000. A remaining assessment of $100,000 will be collected in the subsequent period. Half of that amount should be collected within 30 days, and the remainder will be received in about five months after the end of the year.

    b. Spent $200,000 on four new police cars with 10-year lives. A price of $207,000 had been anticipated when the cars were ordered. The city calculates all depreciation using the straight-line method with no salvage value. The half-year convention is used.

    c. Transferred $90,000 to a debt service fund.

    d. Issued a long-term bond for $200,000 on July 1. Interest at a 10 percent annual rate will be paid each year starting on June 30, 2018.

    e. Ordered a new computer with a five-year life for $40,000.

    f. Paid salaries of $30,000. Another $10,000 is owed at the end of the year but will not be paid for 30 days.

    g. Received the new computer but at a cost of $41,000; payment is to be made in 45 days.

    h. Bought supplies for $10,000 in cash.

    i. Used $8,000 of the supplies in (h).

LO 11-7, 11-8, 11-9, 11-11

48. Use the transactions in problem (47) but prepare a statement of net position for the government-wide financial statements. Assume that the general fund had $180,000 in cash on the first day of the year and no other assets or liabilities. No amount was restricted, committed, or assigned.

LO 11-1, 11-6

49. Government officials of the City of Jones expect to receive general fund revenues of $400,000 in 2017 but approve spending only $380,000. Later in the year, as they receive more information, they increase the revenue projection to $420,000. Officials also approve the spending of an additional $15,000. For each of the following, indicate whether the statement is true or false and, if false, explain why.

    a. In recording this budget, appropriations should be credited initially for $380,000.

    b. The city must disclose this budgetary data within the required supplemental information section reported after the notes to the financial statements.

    c. When reporting budgetary information for the year, three figures should be reported: amended budget, initial budget, and actual figures.

    d. In making the budgetary entry, a debit must be made to some type of Fund Balance account to indicate the projected surplus and its effect on the size of the fund.

    e. The reporting of the budget is reflected in the government-wide financial statements.

LO 11-8

50. On December 1, 2017, a state government awards a city government a grant of $1 million to be used specifically to provide hot lunches for all schoolchildren. No money is received until June 1, 2018. For each of the following, indicate whether the statement is true or false and, if false, explain why.

    a. Because the government received no money until June 1, 2018, no amount of revenue can be recognized in 2017 on the government-wide financial statements.

    b. If this grant has no eligibility requirements and the money is properly spent in September 2018 for the hot lunches, the revenue should be recognized during that September.

    c. Because this money came from the state government and because that government specified its use, this is a government-mandated nonexchange transaction.

    d. If the government had received the money on December 1, 2017, but eligibility reimbursement requirements had not been met yet, unearned revenue of $1 million would have been recognized on the government-wide financial statements.

LO 11-7, 11-8, 11-9, 11-11

51. Indicate (i) how each of the following transactions impacts the fund balance of the general fund, and its classifications, for fund financial statements and (ii) what impact each transaction has on the net position balance of the Government Activities on the government-wide financial statements.

    a. Issue a five-year bond for $6 million to finance general operations.

    b. Pay cash of $149,000 for a truck to be used by the police department.

    c. The fire department pays $17,000 to a government motor pool that services the vehicles of only the police and fire departments. Work was done on several department vehicles.

d. Levy property taxes of $75,000 for the current year that will not be collected until four months into the subsequent year.

e. Receive a grant for $7,000 that must be returned unless the money is spent according to the stipulations of the conveyance. That is expected to happen in the future.

f. Businesses make sales of $20 million during the current year. The government charges a 5 percent sales tax. Half of this amount is to be collected 10 days after the end of the current year with the remainder to be collected 14 weeks later. "Available" has been defined by this government as 75 days.

g. Order a computer for the school system at an anticipated cost of $23,000.

h. A cash transfer of $18,000 is approved from the general fund to a capital projects fund.

LO 11-4, 11-5, 11-11

52. Fund A transfers $20,000 to Fund B. For each of the following, indicate whether the statement is true or false and, if false, explain why.

a. If Fund A is the general fund and Fund B is an enterprise fund, nothing will be shown for this transfer on the statement of activities within the government-wide financial statements.

b. If Fund A is the general fund and Fund B is a debt service fund, nothing will be shown for this transfer on the statement of activities within the government-wide financial statements.

c. If Fund A is the general fund and Fund B is an enterprise fund, a $20,000 reduction will be reported on the statement of revenues, expenditures, and other changes in fund balance for the governmental funds within the fund financial statements.

d. If Fund A is the general fund and Fund B is a special revenue fund (which is not considered a major fund), no changes will be shown on the statement of revenues, expenditures, and other changes in fund balance within the fund financial statements.

e. If Fund A is the general fund and Fund B is an internal service fund and this is for work done, the general fund will report an expense of $20,000 within the fund financial statements.

Use the following information for Problems 53–59:

Assume that the City of Coyote has already produced its financial statements for December 31, 2017, and the year then ended. The city's general fund was only for education and parks. Its capital projects funds worked with each of these functions at times during the current year. The city also had established an enterprise fund to account for its art museum.

The government-wide financial statements indicated the following figures:

- Education reported net expenses of $600,000.
- Parks reported net expenses of $100,000.
- Art museum reported net revenues of $50,000.
- General government revenues for the year were $800,000 with an overall increase in the city's net position of $150,000.

The fund financial statements indicated the following for the entire year:

- The general fund reported a $30,000 increase in its fund balance.
- The capital projects fund reported a $40,000 increase in its fund balance.
- The enterprise fund reported a $60,000 increase in its net position.

The CPA firm of Abernethy and Chapman has been asked to review several transactions that occurred during 2017 and indicate how to correct any erroneous reporting and the impact of each error. View each of the following situations as independent.

LO 11-2, 11-5, 11-10

53. During 2017, the City of Coyote contracted to build a bus stop for schoolchildren costing $10,000 as a special assessments project for which it collected $10,000 from affected citizens. The government had no obligation in connection with this project. Both a $10,000 revenue and a $10,000 expenditure were recorded in the capital projects fund. In preparing government-wide financial statements, an asset and a general revenue were recorded for $10,000.

a. In the general information above, the capital projects fund reported a $40,000 increase in its fund balance for this year. What was the correct change in the capital projects fund's balance during 2017?

b. In the general information, a $150,000 overall increase in the city's net position was found on the government-wide financial statements. What was the correct overall change in the city's net position on the government-wide financial statements?

LO 11-9

54. On December 30, 2017, the City of Coyote borrowed $20,000 for the general fund on a 60-day note. In that fund, both Cash and Other Financing Sources were recorded. In the general information above for this city, a $30,000 overall increase was reported in the general fund balance. What was the correct change in the general fund's balance for 2017?

LO 11-2, 11-4, 11-5

55. An art display set up for the City of Coyote was recorded within the general fund and generated revenues of $9,000 but had expenditures of $45,000 ($15,000 in expenses and $30,000 to buy land for the display). The CPA firm has determined that this program should have been recorded as an enterprise fund activity because it was offered in association with the art museum.

    a. Based on the information provided, what was the correct change in the fund balance for the general fund for 2017?

    b. What was the correct overall change in the city's net position on the government-wide financial statements?

    c. What was the correct change in the net position of the enterprise fund on the fund financial statements?

LO 11-2, 11-5, 11-8

56. The City of Coyote mailed property tax bills for 2018 to its citizens during August 2017. Payments could be made early to receive a discount. The levy becomes legally enforceable on February 15, 2018. All money received must be spent during 2018 or later. The total assessment is $300,000; 40 percent of that amount, less a 10 percent discount, is collected in 2017. The city expects to receive all of the remaining money during 2018 with no discount. During 2017, the government increased cash as well as a revenue for the amount received. No change was made in creating the government-wide financial statements.

    a. What was the correct overall change in the city's net position as shown on the government-wide financial statements?

    b. What was the correct change for 2017 in the fund balance reported in the general fund?

LO 11-2, 11-5, 11-8

57. The City of Coyote mailed property tax bills for 2018 to its citizens during August 2017. Payments could be made early to receive a discount. The levy becomes legally enforceable on February 15, 2018. All money received must be spent during 2018 or later. The total assessment is $300,000, and 40 percent of that amount is collected in 2017 less a 10 percent discount. The city expects to receive all remaining money during 2018 with no discount. During 2017, the government increased cash and a revenue for the amount received. In addition, a receivable account and an unavailable revenue account for $180,000 were recognized.

    a. In the general information above, an overall increase in the city's net position of $150,000 was found on the government-wide financial statements. What was the correct overall change in the city's net position as reported on the government-wide financial statements?

    b. In the general information above, an overall increase of $30,000 was reported in the general fund balance. What was the correct change during 2017 in the general fund's balance?

LO 11-2, 11-5, 11-7, 11-8

58. In 2017, the City of Coyote received a $320,000 cash grant from the state to reduce air pollution. Assume that although a special revenue fund could have been set up, the money remained in the general fund. Cash was received immediately but had to be returned if the city had not lowered air pollution by 25 percent by 2020. On December 31, 2017, Coyote spent $210,000 of this money for a large machine to help begin the process of reducing air pollution. The machine is expected to last for five years and was recorded as an expenditure in the general fund and as an asset on the government-wide financial statements where it was depreciated based on the straight-line method and the half-year convention. Because the money had been received, all $320,000 was recorded as a revenue on both the fund and the government-wide financial statements.

    a. What was the correct change for 2017 in the total fund balance reported by the general fund?

    b. What was the correct overall change in the net position reported on the government-wide financial statements?

LO 11-2

59. During 2017, the City of Coyote's General Fund received $10,000, which was recorded as a general revenue when it was actually a program revenue earned by its park program.

    a. What was the correct overall change for 2017 in the net position reported on the government-wide financial statements?

    b. In the general information above, the parks reported net expenses for the period of $100,000. What was the correct amount of net expenses reported by the parks?

Develop Your Skills

RESEARCH CASE 1

The City of Hampshore is currently preparing financial statements for the past fiscal year. The city manager is concerned because the city encountered some unusual transactions during the current fiscal period and is unsure as to their handling.

Required

Locate a copy (either in hard copy or online) of GASB's *Codification of Governmental Accounting and Reporting Standards.* Either through an online search or a review of the index, answer each of the following questions.

1. For government accounting, what is the definition of an *extraordinary item?*
2. For government accounting, what is the definition of a *special item?*
3. On government-wide financial statements, how should extraordinary items and special items be reported?

RESEARCH CASE 2

The City of Danmark is preparing financial statements. Officials are currently working on the statement of activities within the government-wide financial statements. A question has arisen as to whether a particular revenue should be identified on government-wide statements as a program revenue or a general revenue.

Required

Locate a copy (either in hard copy or online) of GASB's *Codification of Governmental Accounting and Reporting Standards.* Either through an online search or a review of the index, answer each of the following questions.

1. How is a program revenue defined?
2. What are common examples of program revenues?
3. How is a general revenue defined?
4. What are common examples of general revenues?

ANALYSIS CASE

Search the Internet for the official website of one or more state or local governments. After reviewing this website, determine whether the latest comprehensive annual financial report (CAFR) is available on the site. For example, the most recent comprehensive annual financial report for the City of Des Moines can be found at https://www.dmgov.org/Departments/Finance/Pages/CAFR.aspx. Use the financial statements that you locate to answer the following questions.

Required

1. How does the audit opinion given to this city by its independent auditors differ from the audit opinion rendered on the financial statements for a for-profit business?
2. A reconciliation should be presented to explain the difference between the net changes in fund balances for the governmental funds (fund financial statements) and the change in net position for the governmental activities (government-wide financial statements). What were several of the largest reasons for the difference?
3. What were the city's largest sources of general revenues?
4. What was the total amount of expenditures recorded by the general fund during the period? How were those expenditures classified?
5. What assets are reported for the general fund?

6. Review the notes to the financial statements and then determine the number of days the government uses to define the end-of-year financial resources that are viewed as currently available.

7. Did the size of the general fund balance increase or decrease during the most recent year and by how much?

COMMUNICATION CASE 1

Go to the website www.gasb.org and click on "Projects" included in the list that runs across the top of the page. Then click on "Current Projects & Pre-Agenda Research." Click on one of the current projects that is listed. Read the sections that are titled "Project Plan" and "Recent Minutes."

Required

Write a memo to explain the reason that this issue has been chosen for study by GASB. Describe the progress that has been made to date as well as the potential impact on state and local government accounting.

COMMUNICATION CASE 2

Go to the website www.gasb.org and click on "About Us" included in the list that runs across the top of the page. Then click on "Mission, Vision, and Core Values." Read the information provided by GASB.

Required

Assume that a financial analyst with whom you are working is interested in knowing more about the purpose of GASB. Write a short memo explaining the work of GASB based on its vision, mission, core values, and goals.

COMMUNICATION CASE 3

Obtain a copy of the original version of GASB *Statement 34*. Read paragraphs 239 through 277.

Required

Write a report describing alternatives that the GASB considered when it created *Statement 34*. Indicate the alternative that you would have viewed as most appropriate, and describe why the GASB did not choose it.

COMMUNICATION CASE 4

Search the Internet for the official website of one or more state or local governments. On this website, determine whether the latest comprehensive annual financial report (CAFR) is available. For example, a recent comprehensive annual financial report for the City of Minneapolis can be found at https:// www.talgov.com/traffic/accounting-annualrprts.aspx. Read the Management's Discussion and Analysis (MD&A) that should be located near the beginning of the annual report.

Required

Write a memo to explain four or five of the most interesting pieces of information that the Management's Discussion and Analysis provides.

EXCEL CASE

The City of Bainland has been undergoing financial difficulties because of a decrease in its tax base caused by corporations leaving the area. On January 1, 2017, the city has a fund balance of only $400,000 in its governmental funds. In 2016, the city had revenues of $1.4 million and expenditures of $1.48 million. The city's treasurer has forecast that, unless something is done, revenues will decrease at 2 percent per year while expenditures will increase at 3 percent per year.

Required

1. Create a spreadsheet to predict in what year the government will have a zero fund balance.
2. One proposal is that the city slash its expenditures by laying off government workers. That will lead to a 3 percent decrease in expenditures each year rather than a 3 percent increase. However, because of the unemployment, the city will receive less tax revenue. Thus, instead of a 2 percent decrease in revenues, the city expects a 5 percent decrease per year. Adapt the spreadsheet created in requirement (1) to predict what year the government will have a zero fund balance if this option is taken.
3. Another proposal is to increase spending to draw new businesses to the area. This action will lead to a 7 percent increase in expenditures every year, but revenues are expected to rise by 4 percent per year. Adapt the spreadsheet created in requirement (1) to predict what year the government will have a zero fund balance under this option.

Accounting for State and Local Governments (Part 2)

The previous chapter introduced many of the unique aspects of financial reporting applicable to state and local governments. Fund accounting, budgets, encumbrances, expenditures, revenue recognition, transfers, the issuance of bonds, and the like were all presented in connection with both traditional fund financial statements and the newer government-wide financial statements. This coverage was designed to explain the rationale underlying the accounting required of these government entities, especially the differences caused by the dual nature of the financial reporting process.

The current chapter carries this analysis further, first by delving into more complex financial situations. Many state and local government units are quite large and face numerous transactions as complicated as any encountered by a for-profit business. Tax abatements, solid waste landfills, defined benefit pension plans, donated artworks, and the depreciation of infrastructure assets are all examined to broaden the understanding of state and local government accounting.

Second, the chapter discusses the overall financial reporting model for state and local governments. Within this coverage, the actual composition of a government is examined. Because of the wide variety of agencies, departments, and other activities often connected to a government, determining inclusion within the financial statements is not as easy as in a for-profit business where ownership of more than 50 percent of the voting stock is the primary criterion.

The Hierarchy of U.S. Generally Accepted Accounting Principles (GAAP) for State and Local Governments

State and local governments often face complicated reporting issues. Governmental financial events can be just as unusual and complex as those encountered in large for-profit entities. Officials in cities like Chicago and Boston must manage billion-dollar budgets that include a wide array of monetary resources and costs. Those accounting issues rival anything that companies like Coca-Cola and Proctor & Gamble have to solve.

For a vast majority of transactions, appropriate application of U.S. GAAP is not a serious question. Most events such as tax collections and bond issuances occur with regularity so that the reporting has become

Learning Objectives

After studying this chapter, you should be able to:

LO 12-1 Understand how the hierarchy of U.S. generally accepted accounting principles for state and local government accounting can be used to resolve financial reporting issues.

LO 12-2 Explain the informational benefit from required disclosure of tax abatements provided by state and local governments.

LO 12-3 Recognize the liability caused by the eventual closure and postclosure costs of operating a solid waste landfill.

LO 12-4 Explain the reporting of a net pension liability resulting from a defined benefit pension plan provided to employees by a state or local government.

LO 12-5 Record the donation and acquisition of works of art and historical treasures.

LO 12-6 Explain the reporting and possible depreciation of infrastructure assets.

LO 12-7 Understand the composition of a state or local government's comprehensive annual financial report (CAFR).

LO 12-8 Explain the makeup of a primary government and its relationship to component units and related organizations as well as the combination of governments.

LO 12-9 Describe the physical structure of a complete set of government-wide financial statements and a complete set of fund financial statements.

LO 12-10 Understand the presentation of financial statements for a public college or university.

LO 12-1

Understand how the hierarchy of U.S. generally accepted accounting principles for state and local government accounting can be used to resolve financial reporting issues.

widely accepted. For example, the accounting procedures discussed in the previous chapter are all well established through official pronouncements or long-term practical use.

However, periodically, events can arise or be created that do not lend themselves to easy reporting solutions. Perhaps a new type of transaction is undertaken with an unusual nature or a particular twist that seems unique. To further complicate the reporting, different rules can sometimes provide guidance that seems to be contradictory. For financial statements to be in conformity with U.S. GAAP, state and local government accountants must be able to establish the validity of the suggested reporting. The same challenge holds true for independent auditors (CPAs) who are hired to certify that the information is presented fairly, in all material respects, in accordance with the accounting principles generally accepted in the United States.

When faced with a new or unusual transaction, how do accountants and auditors determine what accounting is consistent with U.S. GAAP? Or, when a variety of sources indicate different possible reporting resolutions, which guidance should be followed?

In 2015, the Governmental Accounting Standards Board (GASB) issued its Statement No. 76, *The Hierarchy of Generally Accepted Accounting Principles for State and Local Governments*. This pronouncement was designed to provide reporting guidance whenever the question of establishing conformity with U.S. GAAP arises. According to this standard, all sources of authoritative U.S. GAAP for state and local governments can be divided into two categories, with Category A having more authority than Category B.

Category A: This first level of authoritative rules is made up of the official statements of the GASB. Those statements are available on the Board's website (www.gasb.org). In addition, prior to the release of Statement No. 76, GASB occasionally issued interpretations to help clarify, explain, or provide more detailed information about various GASB statements. Over the years, the Board issued only a few interpretations and has decided to discontinue any further usage. Going forward, the Board will use other methods (see Category B) to provide this type of guidance about U.S. GAAP. However, previously released interpretations that still remain in effect are included in this highest level of authority.

Category B: The second level is made up of GASB Technical Bulletins, GASB Implementation Guides, and any literature of the American Institute of Certified Public Accountants (AICPA) that has been cleared by GASB. Again, specific listings of these resources can be found on GASB's website.

- Technical bulletins are created when needed to serve much the same function as the interpretations described previously. Technical bulletins outline practical guidance concerning GASB statements. They can be issued by GASB in a shorter period of time to provide solutions for pressing reporting problems. In the past, technical bulletins have not been frequently developed but can still be released whenever a majority of the Board does not object to a proposed method of reporting. In this manner, GASB has an official procedure by which reporting problems can be addressed quickly.

- Implementation guides clarify, explain, or elaborate on existing U.S. GAAP for state and local governments. In contrast to technical bulletins, they do not go beyond that function. Therefore, they do not establish the acceptability of new approaches to reporting issues. Because implementation guides tend to have a broader impact and less urgency, a period of public exposure provides a chance for feedback that can highlight potential problems before the guide is issued. Like technical bulletins, they are released only when a majority of the Board does not object to the guidance being given.

Thus, to establish the validity of a proposed reporting treatment, accountants and auditors first look to Category A and, then, only to Category B if no answer is found at the first level.

What happens if no satisfactory answer can be found in either Category A or Category B? No set of generally accepted accounting principles can ever anticipate all of the wide variety of reporting issues that might be faced by a government. At that point, reasoned judgment becomes essential. "If specific guidance cannot be found in either category, financial statement preparers and auditors are to consider guidance for similar transactions or events."[1]. Is official guidance available that is similar enough to be considered applicable? For example, if a rule on the

---

[1] Stephen J. Gauthier, "New Guidance on the GAAP Hierarchy," *Government Finance* Review, December 2015, pages 47–48.

costing of a highway is provided in a GASB statement, can the same logic be used in accounting for a parking lot? Ultimately, the reporting of complex transactions in governmental accounting (as well as that used with for-profit entities) requires accountants and auditors to have a strong understanding of the purpose of the reporting process and the principles on which it is founded.

For further help, GASB also provides a list of nonauthoritative sources that can be considered in determining the reporting that is most consistent with generally accepted accounting principles: GASB Concepts Statements, pronouncements of other accounting bodies such as FASB and the IASB, practices that are prevalent in state and local governments, published literature of professional associations and regulatory agencies, and accounting textbooks and articles.

No function carried out by an accountant or auditor is more significant than the determination of how a unique transaction or event should be reported to be in conformity with U.S. GAAP. That decision requires both deep knowledge and sound judgment. The nature of the event must be understood completely and then compared to the rules that have been established over the decades. With Statement 76, GASB has specified which of these rules (and other sources of guidance) should be analyzed and which has the most authority.

LO 12-2

Explain the informational benefit from required disclosure of tax abatements provided by state and local governments.

Tax Abatement Disclosure

> For years, taxpayers have questioned whether the estimated $70 billion in subsidies governments shower on the free enterprise system each year are savvy investments or corporate welfare run amok. Soon, they will have more information to make that call. This month, the Governmental Accounting Standards Board – the Norwalk, Connecticut, body that oversees government accounting rules – said it will require governments to disclose how much tax revenue they are foregoing because of incentives provided to businesses. State and local governments, as well as school districts, also will have to disclose the jobs promises and other commitments businesses make in order to avoid paying taxes.[2]

Accounting rules do not always come down to specifying the correct debits and credits that must be entered to reflect a transaction. Disclosure issues can be just as challenging as the reporting of an actual event. One question stands at the center of any disclosure discussion: What information should be provided to create a representative financial picture for interested parties without requiring so much data that (a) readers become overwhelmed and (b) unnecessary costs are incurred? Financial statements should enlighten outside parties and not confuse them with excessive information. In any accounting debate, the reporting entities usually argue for less disclosure whereas the decision makers typically call for more.

Governments often make agreements with outside organizations to forego tax revenues for some period of time in exchange for a specific action. GASB recently ruled (in GASB Statement No. 77, *Tax Abatement Disclosures*) that information about such tax abatement programs is beneficial and worth the associated cost of disclosure. This disclosure is necessary when agreement is reached.

For example, in 2014, the city of Fort Worth, Texas, listed 18 ongoing tax abatement programs provided to individual companies in exchange for commitments that were believed to benefit the city and its citizens.[3] This is a common practice. Fort Worth officials had agreed to approximately one new tax abatement program per year for the previous decade. The benefiting companies were allowed to avoid either a portion or all of their real and personal property taxes for periods of up to ten years by promising to carry out specified projects such as a hotel construction, construction of a new production facility, construction of a data center, and the like. The various investments made by these companies in Fort Worth ranged from $1.5 million to $173 million and were estimated to create or retain area jobs, as few as 7 in one case and as many as 1,940 in another.

These abatement programs represent exchanged promises. The city reduces or eliminates an organization's taxes (for example, sales, income, or property taxes) for a period of time. In return, the organization agrees to a defined action such as keeping operations in the city or the construction of a new facility. These tax abatements were received by companies such as Coca-Cola Enterprises, Blue Cross Blue Shield of Texas, and Omni Fort Worth.

---

[2] Len Boselovic, "Pittsburgh Post—Gazette Len Boselovic's Heard Off the Street Column," *McClatchy Tribune Business News,* August 30, 2015.

[3] http://fortworthtexas.gov/uploadedfiles/hed/business/tax-abatement-agreements-2014.pdf.

In a traditional sense, there is no transaction to report. The choice to forego the collection of taxes is not easy to reflect in a journal entry that would be meaningful. However, the financial impact of such agreements can be quite significant. Is a company's promise to create 20 jobs and invest $1.5 million worth giving up real estate tax collections for ten years? If government officials make such a decision, citizens need to be aware of the financial ramifications.

GASB has now decided that information about tax abatements must be disclosed in a government's financial statements. "Tax abatement has been a common carrot that communities use to attract development. To date, however, cities and other tax-abating governments haven't shared much information about the accumulated financial consequences of those tax breaks. Now, because of an edict from the board that oversees government accounting, they will. That means that the counties, cities and public authorities in seven counties in Northeast Ohio will have to provide details about the roughly $1.4 billion in taxes that are passed up annually. . . . 'I'm going to be the happy recipient of more information,' said Tim Offtermatt, an investment banker with the Cleveland office of Stifel Financial Corp. who specializes in public finance. 'It helps us put together a comprehensive credit package for credit analysts.'"[4]

Based on the GASB statement, a state or local government must disclose significant information about abatement agreements including:

- The purpose of the tax abatement program.
- The type of tax being abated.
- Dollar amount of taxes abated.
- The type of commitments made by the tax abatement recipients.
- Any commitments made by the government (or other parties), for example, agreeing to construct infrastructure assets such as roads.

Interestingly, GASB has been criticized for not also requiring the governments to identify the companies receiving the abatements. Additional criticism came from parties who wanted to know about the long-term financial impact of these abatement decisions. Because of the importance of reported information, few accounting rules manage to escape some level of criticism. "Critics disagree, arguing that governments should at least be required to disclose the names of the largest recipients. One reason for this is that many believe subsidies don't generally help small, homegrown businesses flourish."[5] "Policy Matters Ohio's Schiller questioned the lack of long-term cost projections—a key element in the pension fund crisis. 'It's hard to figure why (GASB) didn't approve any kind of forward-looking cost of this,' Schiller said. 'From (a municipal bond) investor's standpoint, isn't your biggest concern not what they paid last year, but what they have to pay in the future?'"[6]

LO 12-3

Recognize the liability caused by the eventual closure and post-closure costs of operating a solid waste landfill.

Solid Waste Landfill

As of June 30, 2015, the City of Greensboro, North Carolina, reported a $500,000 current liability in its statement of net position as an accrued landfill liability. Then, within its noncurrent liabilities, the city reported an additional obligation of nearly $25 million with the same account title. Both balances were listed under business-type activities.

Many communities operate landfills and they often lead to large liabilities. The notes to the financial statements of the City of Greensboro, North Carolina, as of June 30, 2015, help explain the reporting of the government's landfill debt.

> The City owns and operates a regional landfill site located in the northeast portion of the City. State and federal laws require the City to place a final cover on its White Street landfill site and

---

[4] Jay Miller, "GASB Ruling Will Make Tax Breaks More Transparent," *Crain's Cleveland Business,* September 7, 2015, page 3.

[5] Liz Farmer, "3 Things the New Tax Incentive Disclosures Rules Won't Reveal," *McClatchy Business News,* November 24, 2015.

[6] Jay Miller, "GASB ruling will make tax breaks more transparent," *Crain's Cleveland Business,* September 7, 2015, page 3.

to perform certain maintenance and monitoring functions at the site for thirty years after closure. The City reports a portion of these closure and postclosure care costs as an operating expense in each period based on landfill capacity used as of each June 30. The $25,179,925 reported as landfill closure and postclosure care liability at June 30, 2015, is based on 100% use of the estimated capacity of Phase II and Phase III, Cells 1 and 2. Phase III, Cell 3, is estimated at 49.3% of capacity. . . .

The estimated liability amounts are based on what it would cost to perform all closure and postclosure care in the current year. Actual cost may be higher due to inflation, changes in technology, or changes in regulations. At June 30, 2015, the City had expended $3,876,035 to complete closure for the White Street facility, Phase II and $2,666,334 to begin closure activities at the construction and demolition site located on top of the municipal waste filled space. The balance of closure costs, estimated at $12,853,068, and an estimated $12,326,857 for postclosure care will be funded over the remaining life of the landfill estimated to be 20 to 35 years.

Thousands of state and local governments operate solid waste landfills to provide a place for citizens and local companies to dispose of trash and other forms of garbage and refuse. Governments frequently report landfill operations within their enterprise funds if these facilities require a user fee. However, other landfills are open to the public without fee so that reporting within the general fund is appropriate.

Regardless of the type of fund utilized, solid waste landfills can create huge liabilities for these governments. The U.S. Environmental Protection Agency has strict rules on closure requirements as well as groundwater monitoring and other postclosure activities. Satisfying such requirements can be costly. The operation of a landfill can ultimately necessitate large payments to ensure that the facility is closed properly and then monitored and maintained for an extended period. The relevant accounting question has always been how to report these eventual costs while the landfill is still in operation.

To illustrate, assume that a city opens a landfill in Year 1 that is expected to take 10 years to fill. To determine the annual amount to be reported, the city must estimate the current costs required to close the landfill. Such costs include the amount to be paid to cover the area and for all postclosure maintenance. As mentioned above by the City of Greensboro, the government uses current—rather than an estimate of future—closure and postclosure costs as a better measure of the present obligation. However, such amounts must then be adjusted each period for inflation, technology, and regulation changes.

Assume here that the current cost for closure is set at $10 million and for postclosure maintenance at $4 million for a total obligation of $14 million. Assume that during Year 1 the city makes an initial payment of $300,000 toward these closure costs. At the end of this first year, city engineers determine that 16 percent of the available space has been filled.

Landfills—Government-Wide Financial Statements

Regardless of whether the city reports this solid waste landfill as a governmental activity (within the general fund) or as a business-type activity (within an enterprise fund), the closure and postclosure costs in the government-wide statements must be based on accrual accounting and the economic resources measurement basis. The government anticipates that the total current cost of closure and cleanup is $14 million. Because the landfill is 16 percent filled, $2,240,000 should be accrued at the end of this first year ($14 million × 16%). The initial $300,000 payment made this year reduces the liability being reported:

Government-Wide Financial Statements—Estimated Landfill Closure Costs

Year 1		
Expense—Landfill Closure.	2,240,000	
Landfill Closure Liability.		2,240,000
To recognize the Year 1 portion of total costs		
(16 percent) for eventual closure of landfill.		
Landfill Closure Liability.	300,000	
Cash		300,000
To record first payment of costs necessitated by		
eventual closure of landfill.		

To complete this example, assume that the landfill is judged to be 27 percent filled at the end of Year 2 and the city makes another $300,000 payment toward future closure costs. However, because of inflation and recent changes in technology, the city now believes that current closure costs are $11 million with postclosure costs amounting to $5 million. The current cost of the total landfill obligation has thus jumped from $14 million to $16 million.

Based on this new and revised information, the city should recognize an estimated total cost of $4,320,000 at the end of Year 2 ($16 million × 27%). Because $2,240,000 was recognized in Year 1, the city should accrue an additional $2,080,000 in Year 2 ($4,320,000 − $2,240,000):

Government-Wide Financial Statements—Estimated Landfill Closure Costs

Year 2		
Expense—Landfill Closure......................................	2,080,000	
Landfill Closure Liability....................................		2,080,000
To recognize Year 2 portion of costs for eventual closure of landfill.		
Landfill Closure Liability..	300,000	
Cash..		300,000
To record second payment necessitated by eventual closure of the landfill.		

Consequently, in the city's Year 2 government-wide financial statements, the following is reported regardless of whether the landfill is viewed as part of the general fund (a governmental activity) or as an enterprise fund (a business-type activity):

Expense—Landfill closure	$2,080,000
Landfill closure liability ($2,240,000 + 2,080,000 − 300,000 − 300,000).........	$3,720,000

Landfills—Fund Financial Statements

If a solid waste landfill is maintained as an enterprise fund, reporting is the same in the fund financial statements as shown for the government-wide statements. All economic resources are again measured based on accrual accounting.

However, if the landfill is recorded in the general fund because there is little or no user fee charged, the city reports only the actual change in current financial resources. Despite the huge eventual liability, the reduction in current financial resources is limited to the annual payments of $300,000. The remaining liability is too far into the future to necessitate reporting. When fund financial statements are prepared, the only entry required each year is as follows:

Fund Financial Statements—Payment toward Landfill Closure Costs—Governmental Funds

Year 1 and Year 2 **General Fund**		
Expenditures—Closure Costs.............................	300,000	
Cash...		300,000
To record annual payment toward the eventual closure costs of the city's solid waste landfill.		

LO 12-4

Explain the reporting of a net pension liability resulting from a defined benefit pension plan provided to employees by a state or local government.

Defined Benefit Pension Plans

Many state and local governments provide pension plans for employees such as school teachers, police officers, firefighters, and sanitation workers. An educator in the public schools, for example, might be eligible to retire with full benefits after a specified length of employment (such as 30 years). These plans represent a huge financial obligation for many governments across the United States. In for-profit businesses, defined contribution plans are now much more prevalent than defined benefit plans. However, defined benefit plans (with their potentially huge obligations) continue to be common for government employees. Retirees are usually entitled to future benefits based on a contractually set formula. "Future pension obligations of both companies and state governments collectively amount to trillions of dollars; obligations of numerous pension plans can be measured individually in billions of dollars. Public sector pension obligations generally dwarf those in the private sector."[7]

State and local governments often establish pension trust funds to accumulate and invest monetary resources and eventually pay out pension benefits. Because that money is held for retirees, these pension trusts are classified as fiduciary funds and, thus, are not included in the reporting of government-wide financial statements. A question has long been raised as to what amount of a government's pension obligation should be included in the overall financial reporting. Historically, as long as all funding requirements were met in a timely manner, governments reported no pension liability. Because funding requirements did not always cover the maximum amount of the eventual pension payments, financial analysts have argued that the financial position of many state and local governments was much more precarious than reported.

GASB in its *Statement No. 68,* "Accounting and Financial Reporting for Pensions," now requires a more complete reporting of pension liabilities by state and local governments. Because virtually all of these payments will take place well beyond the current period, this reporting applies almost exclusively to government-wide financial statements (and also to the fund financial statements for proprietary funds). Similar requirements have now been created for postemployment benefit plans other than pension plans to better reflect each government's total obligation.

For pensions, this authoritative guidance establishes several steps to be followed in reporting a government's liability.

- First, the pension benefit payments that will ultimately be required are estimated by an actuary.
- Second, the portion of those payments that are attributable to past periods of employee service is calculated.
- Third, the present value of the payments relating to those past amounts is determined in order to arrive at the government's obligation at the present time.
- Fourth, if that liability balance is larger than the net asset position held in the pension trust fund, the excess is shown in the government-wide financial statements as a net pension liability. Conversely, if the net position of the pension trust is larger than the present value of the pension benefits earned to date, a net pension asset is reported. This net liability or asset is placed on the statement of net position as either a governmental activity or a business-type activity depending on the nature of the party responsible for the payments.

To illustrate, assume that a city government has had a pension plan for several decades to cover all of the teachers in its school system who remain employed for at least three years. A pension trust fund was created years ago that now holds $1 billion in cash and investments. No payments are currently due to retirees. Assume that the total amount of expected pension payments has been determined by an actuary as $10 billion. To date, current and retired employees have only earned $8 billion of that amount. These future cash payments have a present value of $3 billion. On the government-wide financial statements, the city reports $2 billion as the net pension liability. The $1 billion held by government's pension trust fund is subtracted from the $3 billion present value of the future payments to indicate the unfunded portion of the obligation. Because the school system is responsible, the debt is reported within the governmental activities.

---

[7] Kathryn E. Easterday and Tim V. Eaton, "Defined Benefit Pension Plans," *The CPA Journal,* September 1, 2012, p. 22.

A number of complex challenges must be dealt with in applying this reporting rule. Although many of these problems are beyond the scope of this textbook, a brief discussion of several key issues is warranted:

- In any present value computation, the question of an appropriate discount rate is essential. The size of the rate is inversely related to the size of the liability that must be reported. The higher the rate, the more interest is assigned to the future cash flows, leaving a smaller liability balance to report. GASB requires that, in most cases, the present value of the future obligation is determined using the estimated long-term investment yield for the plan's assets.

That decision has proven controversial. Because the expected rate of return on investments is normally higher than other possible discount rates, the remaining pension liability to be reported is smaller. That decrease appears to reduce the apparent future cost of these pension plans to the taxpayers.[8]

> Financial economists have recommended for decades that governments calculate pension liabilities using so-called 'risk-free' rates pegged to high-grade municipal bonds or long-term Treasurys. . . . However, GASB let governments stick with their desired, er, expected rate of return, which is typically about 8 percent. Public pension funds have returned 5.7 percent on average since 2000. Achieving much higher returns over the long run would require markets to perform as well as they did in the 1980s and '90s. Would that be true. Governments have resisted climbing down from Fantasyland because using lower discount rates would explode their liabilities.[9]

- The components to be recognized immediately as pension expense must be identified. GASB lists those as the service cost for the current period, interest expense on the total pension liability, and projected earnings on plan investments. Any increases or decreases in the liability caused by changes in benefit terms are included in pension expense immediately rather than being amortized over time.

- Numerous assumptions (such as the life expectancy of retirees) are necessary to arrive at a total pension liability figure. The impact of changes in those assumptions and differences between those assumptions and actual experience are not included immediately by the government as pension expense. Instead, those amounts are recorded as either deferred outflows of resources or deferred inflows of resources and amortized to pension expense over the average expected remaining service lives of all employees in the pension plan. For example, at June 30, 2015, the state of Tennessee explains its reported deferred inflows of resources as "the primary government has one item that qualifies for reporting in this category. This item is the result of two pension-related factors. The first factor is investment returns were better than projected and the other is the difference between the actual and expected economic and demographic factors that were more favorable than anticipated. In the governmental activities column of the government-wide statement of net position, the state reported $701 million for these factors."

Throughout any analysis of these rules, some elements of the reporting used by for-profit organizations for defined benefit pension plans can be seen. However, several unique aspects have also been introduced by GASB for state and local government entities.

LO 12-5

Record the donation and acquisition of works of art and historical treasures.

Works of Art and Historical Treasures

As will be discussed in the following chapter, private not-for-profit entities have long debated the proper reporting of artworks and other museum pieces whether bought or received by gift. State and local governments can face the same issue. How should works of art, historical artifacts, and other such treasures be reported in governmental financial statements? These properties have value but are they really assets in an accounting sense?

---

[8] "The not-so-Great GASB," *The Economist,* Buttonwood's notebook, May 2, 2013, http://www.economist.com/blogs/buttonwood/2013/05/pensions.

[9] "Pension Accounting for Dummies; New government reporting rules are no better than the old ones," *The Wall Street Journal* (online), July 11, 2012.

Assume, for example, that a city maintains a museum in a building formerly used as a high school. The museum was created to display documents, maps, paintings, and other works that depict the history of the city. Admission is free. No revenue is generated.

The government bought a number of the items on display. Local citizens donated the remaining pieces. Several are quite valuable.

Although optional reporting is allowed, the basic rule in accounting for such items is clear. Other than a few specific exceptions, "governments should capitalize works of art, historical treasures, and similar assets at their historical cost or fair value at date of donation (estimated if necessary) whether they are held as individual items or in a collection."[10]

Thus, the government-wide statement of net position will report an antique map bought for $5,000 as an asset at that cost. A similar map received as a gift is also recorded as a $5,000 asset. Such donations qualify as voluntary nonexchange transactions. In recording the gift, revenue is also recognized for the map's value but only when all eligibility requirements are met. Until that time, a liability is recorded.[11]

For fund financial statements, the museum might be viewed as an enterprise fund if an entrance fee is charged. In that case, the reporting of these assets asset simply replicated. However, if the museum is listed within the governmental funds, any such acquisition is reported as an expenditure (rather than an asset) to reflect the decrease in current financial resources. For gifts of this type property, no entry is made because no change took place in the amount of current financial resources. No money was spent to acquire the map.

In government-wide financial statements, a theoretical problem arises in the recognition of such properties regardless of whether they were purchased or obtained by gift. Do such items qualify as assets to be reported by the government? Historical maps, artistic paintings, and the like are often displayed for the public to see but do not generate any direct cash inflows or other economic benefit. Does that satisfy the characteristics of an asset?

GASB encourages the capitalization of all artworks, historical treasures, and the like as assets. However, if all three of the following criteria are met, the recording of such properties as an asset is optional:

1. It is held for public exhibition, education, or research in furtherance of public service rather than for financial gain.
2. It is protected, kept unencumbered, cared for, and preserved.
3. It is subject to an organizational policy that requires the proceeds from sales of collection items to be used to acquire other items for collections.[12] This last requirement ensures that the work is not being held for investment purposes.

If these guidelines are met, the artwork or historical treasure will not provide direct economic benefit to the government. Although the transaction must be recorded, recognition of an asset is not required. For the government-wide statements, an expense rather than an asset can be recorded whether the item is obtained by purchase or by gift.

In the asset section of its 2014 government-wide financial statements, the City of Chicago reported works of art and historical collections with a reported value of $45.2 million although other items of this type are not capitalized. A footnote explains the reporting of these properties.

> The City has a collection of artwork and historical treasures presented for public exhibition and education that are being preserved for future generations. The proceeds from sales of any pieces of the collection are used to purchase other acquisitions. A portion of this collection is not capitalized or depreciated as part of capital assets.

GASB's handling of artwork and historical treasures closely parallels rules established by FASB for private not-for-profit entities. However, as the next chapter explains, differences do remain.

---

[10] Governmental Accounting Standards Board, *Codification of Governmental Accounting and Financial Reporting Standards as of December 31, 2014,* Sec. 1400.109.

[11] A deferred inflow of resources is recorded rather than a liability if all eligibility requirements have been met except for a time requirement.

[12] GASB, *Codification,* Sec. 1400.109.

One related issue needs to be addressed: depreciation. Does the map on display in the museum actually depreciate in value over time? Does the *Mona Lisa* have a finite life? For such works of art or museum artifacts, depreciation is required but only if the asset is deemed as "exhaustible"—that is, if its utility will be consumed by display, education, or research. Depreciation is not necessary if the item is judged to be inexhaustible. As long as properly maintained, many such properties can be considered as inexhaustible assets so that depreciation is allowed but not required.

LO 12-6

Explain the reporting and possible depreciation of infrastructure assets.

Infrastructure Assets and Depreciation

Many governments hold a significant number of infrastructure assets. As mentioned in the previous chapter, infrastructure is a general term for long-lived capital assets that normally are stationary in nature and can be preserved for a significantly greater number of years than most capital assets. Common examples include roads, bridges, tunnels, lighting systems, curbing, and sidewalks.

At one time in government accounting, the recording of infrastructure items was an optional practice. Now, though, infrastructure costs are recorded as assets in the government-wide statements. As of June 30, 2014, the City of Cincinnati, Ohio, listed infrastructure assets, net of accumulated depreciation, of $584.0 million on its government-wide statements. For governmental funds, these costs continue to be recorded as expenditures in the fund statements because acquisition or construction creates a reduction in current financial resources.

As discussed previously, depreciation is required for all capital assets (such as buildings) that have a finite life as well as capitalized artworks and historical treasures that are deemed to be exhaustible. In creating government-wide financial statements, the need for depreciating infrastructure assets was debated by GASB: Is depreciation appropriate for this type of asset? "The responses to the Statement's exposure draft included arguments that infrastructure assets should not be depreciated because they are intended to be preserved in perpetuity."[13]

For example, construction of the Brooklyn Bridge was finished in 1883 at a cost of about $15 million. That particular piece of infrastructure has operated now for more than 130 years and, with proper maintenance, might well continue to carry traffic for another 130 years. Much the same can be said of many roads, sidewalks, and the like. With appropriate repair and maintenance, such assets could have lives that are almost indefinite. What expected life should New York City use to depreciate the cost incurred in constructing a street such as Fifth Avenue?

Depreciation of infrastructure items is recorded in government-wide financial statements. Not surprisingly, governments tend to depreciate some of their infrastructure over extended periods. The City of Portland, Oregon, with approximately $5.0 billion in infrastructure uses lives that range from 20 to 100 years. The City of Portland, Maine, with $250 million in infrastructure depreciates this cost over periods from 30 to 67 years.

However, a unique alternative to depreciating the cost of eligible infrastructure assets such as the Brooklyn Bridge or Fifth Avenue was created by GASB. This method, known as the *modified approach,* eliminates the need for depreciating infrastructure assets. If specified guidelines are met, a government can choose to expense all maintenance costs each year in lieu of recording depreciation. Additions and improvements must be capitalized, but the cost of maintaining the infrastructure in proper working condition is expensed. Thus, if applied, New York City would expense the amount spent on the repair and other maintenance of Fifth Avenue so that no depreciation of the street's capitalized cost need be recorded. Effectively, proper maintenance of infrastructure assets can extend their lives indefinitely.

Use of the modified approach requires the government to accumulate information about all infrastructure assets within either a network or a subsystem of a network. For example, all roads could be deemed a network while state roads, rural roads, and interstate highways might make up three subsystems of that network.

---

[13] Charlotte A. Pryor, "Local Governments and the Modified Approach to Reporting the Cost of Infrastructure," *Government Accountants Journal,* April 1, 2013.

- For eligible assets, the government must establish a minimum acceptable condition level and then document that this minimum level is being met.
- The government must have an asset management system in place to monitor the eligible assets. This system assesses the ongoing condition to ensure that the eligible assets are, indeed, operating at the predetermined level.

The City of Los Angeles has adopted the modified approach in reporting all of its bridges. In its comprehensive annual financial report, the system used by that government is explained as follows. This description does indicate that the city has properly followed the rules above.

> The modified approach is used in reporting the City's bridges infrastructure system. A comprehensive bridge database system, the Bridges and Tunnel System, enables the City to track the entire bridge inventory, the structural condition of various bridge elements, and bridge sufficiency ratings. Condition assessments of these structures are completed in a three-year cycle. The latest assessment report was as of July 1, 2013. A system of letter grades identifies the condition of each structure. Letter grades "A" through "D" represent the condition of the structure as Very Good, Good to Fair, Fair to Poor, and Very Poor. "F" rating symbolizes a failed condition where replacement of the structure is necessary. These letter grades are based on sufficiency ratings, or the overall condition of the structure based on the last inspection. It is the City's policy that at least 70% of the bridges are rated "B" or better and that no bridge shall be rated less than "D". It is also the intent of the City that at least 80% of bridges be rated "B" or better by 2017. The City performs regular inspection and maintenance of the various structural elements for any defects. Funds for annual estimated inspection, maintenance and repair costs are provided in the City's budget. Bridges infrastructure system is excluded in the determination of depreciation provisions for capital assets, while preservation and maintenance costs are charged to expense.

The modified approach provides a method by which governments can avoid depreciating infrastructure assets such as the Brooklyn Bridge that have virtually an unlimited life. The issue is: How many governments will be like the City of Los Angeles and go to the trouble of creating the standards and documentation required by this approach simply to avoid recording depreciation expense? According to one expert in the field, "There are relatively few governmental entities that have adopted the modified approach. Airports, transportation authorities and large transportation departments are really the only ones that I've seen that follow the modified approach."[14]

LO 12-7

Understand the composition of a state or local government's comprehensive annual financial report (CAFR).

Comprehensive Annual Financial Report

Government-wide financial statements and fund financial statements are most often presented to the public as part of a comprehensive annual financial report (CAFR). The CAFR is not limited to the financial statements and includes an extensive amount of other information about the reporting government. For example, the 2015 CAFR for the City of Orlando, Florida, with total assets of $3.2 billion, was approximately 250 pages long. In comparison, the 2015 financial statements for Walmart, with more than $203 billion in assets, was only about 50 pages.

The CAFR of a state or local government is composed of three broad sections:

1. *Introductory section*—includes a letter of transmittal from appropriate government officials, an organization chart, and a list of principal officers.
2. *Financial section*—presents the general purpose external financial statements (both the government-wide and fund financial statements) and reproduces the auditor's report. The government also presents the management's discussion and analysis (MD&A) and other required supplementary information.
3. *Statistical section*—discloses a wide range of data about the government encompassing both financial and nonfinancial information. This statistical information can be fascinating. In its 2015 CAFR, the City of Buffalo, New York, reports the following for that year

[14] From Jack Reagan, partner, Grant Thornton LLP, Washington, DC, March 27, 2016.

(along with considerable other information): number of police officers (699), number of firefighters (654), traffic violations (40,021), fire stations (20), fire hydrants (7,962), street-lights (31,879), traffic lights (665), acreage for parks (1,842), street resurfacing (472,056 square yards), and materials used to fill potholes (1,452 tons).

The financial section of the CAFR is composed of three distinct sections:

1. Management's discussion and analysis. The MD&A is required supplemental information that "should provide an objective and easily readable analysis of the government's financial activities based on currently known facts, decisions, or conditions."[15]

2. Financial statements:

    a. Government-wide financial statements.
    b. Fund financial statements.
    c. Notes to the financial statements.

3. Required supplementary information (other than the MD&A). This section includes information required by U.S. GAAP but not within the financial statements or accompanying notes. For example, the City of Orlando, Florida, compares budgetary figures here for the city with actual results for each major fund although a separate statement within the fund financial statements could also have been used for this purpose. Orlando also includes required supplementary information about the pensions and postemployment benefits that it provides to former employees including a schedule of employer contributions, a schedule of investment returns, and a schedule of net pension liability.

For many readers, one of the most interesting aspects of the financial section is the MD&A because it provides a plain English description of the past, future, and present of the government's financial situation and operations. As an illustration, the 2015 CAFR for the City of Raleigh, North Carolina, includes a management's discussion and analysis 15 pages in length that presents information such as the following:

- "The parking facilities operations generated $13.2 million of revenues in 2014–15, an increase of 9.1% compared to 2013–14. This was driven by an increase in reserved parking rates and an increase in downtown parking demand."

- "Convention Center operations including the Performing Arts venue delivered $13.3 million of operating revenues in 2014–15, an increase of 3.1% compared to 2013-14. This increase was a result of positive increases in event revenue as compared to the prior year. Operating expenses remained relatively flat as compared to the prior year."

- The City issued $66.7 million in limited obligation bonds to finance the construction of the new communications center and a fire station

The Primary Government and Component Units

LO 12-8

Explain the makeup of a primary government and its relationship to component units and related organizations as well as the combination of governments.

Primary Government

It always should be possible in the public sector to trace financial accountability to elected officials. Consistent with this presumption of the ultimate financial accountability of elected officials, a typical state or local government financial report is built around the core of a single government with an elected governing body, known as the primary government.[16]

Each state and local government will prepare and distribute a CAFR if it qualifies as a reporting entity. However, the composition of a reporting entity must be identified. Normally, the reporting process begins with a primary government such as a town, city, county, or state. A primary government has separate legal status, a separately elected governing board, and is

---

[15] GASB, *Codification, as of December 31, 2014,* Sec. 2200.106.

[16] Stephen J. Gauthier, *Governmental Accounting, Auditing, and Financial Reporting* (Chicago: Government Finance Officers Association, 2012), p. 73.

fiscally independent. Beyond that, each reporting entity also includes all of the organizations, agencies, offices, and departments that are not legally separate from the primary government.

However, many of the activities that interact closely with a primary government are legally separate. Should they also be included as part of the reporting entity and its financial statements? That question is not as complicated in for-profit accounting. Except in rare cases, a business enterprise such as IBM or PepsiCo consolidates all businesses over which it holds control through majority ownership. Control is not so clearly delineated in governmental accounting. Should legally separated organizations be included within a government's CAFR and, if so, what reporting is appropriate?

The almost unlimited number of activities that can be connected to a primary government raises problems for officials who are attempting to outline the parameters of the entity being reported. Organizations such as turnpike commissions, port authorities, public housing boards, and downtown development commissions have become commonplace for many cities and counties. The primary government may have created many of these, but they are structured as legally separate organizations. Such operations are usually designed to focus attention on specific issues or problems.

As an example, notes to the financial statements in the 2015 CAFR for the City of Boston, Massachusetts, identifies four discretely presented component units (Boston Redevelopment Authority, Economic Development Industrial Corporation, Boston Public Health Commission, and Trustees of the Boston Public Library) and one blended component unit (State-Boston Retirement System). The city also recognizes three related organizations (Boston Housing Authority, Boston Industrial Development Finance Authority, and Boston Water and Sewer Commission). Discretely presented component units? Blended component units? Related organizations? How do all of these entities relate to the primary government (the City of Boston) and what impact do they have on the financial reporting for that city?

Identifying Component Units

In its CAFR as of June 30, 2015, the City of Atlanta, Georgia, describes the reporting entity: "The government-wide financial statements include not only the City itself (known as the primary government), but also the legally separate Atlanta Fulton County Recreation Authority and the Atlanta Development Authority (doing business as Invest Atlanta) for which the City is financially accountable. Financial information for these component units is reported separately from the financial information presented for the primary government. The Atlanta Housing Opportunity, Inc. and Atlanta CoRA, Inc., are also component units but their financial statements are blended with the primary government. Other blended component units of the City include Urban Design Commission, Atlanta Public Safety and Judicial Facilities Authority and Solid Waste Management Authority."

When producing a CAFR, the major requirement for inclusion as a component unit is the financial accountability of the primary government. "Financial reporting based on accountability should enable the financial statement reader to focus on the body of organizations that are related by a common thread of accountability to the constituent citizenry."[17] When elected officials of the primary government are financially accountable for an outside organization, it is labeled a component unit. Such legally separate activities are so closely connected to the primary government that omission from the financial statements cannot be justified.

That is the reason the City of Atlanta included the Atlanta Fulton County Recreation Authority and the other activities mentioned above in its CAFR. They qualified as component units. They are not part of the government but are reported to reflect the City of Atlanta's financial accountability.

Because of the potential impact on the financial statements of a primary government, the determination of component units is often of significant importance. Two sets of criteria have been established to indicate financial accountability. If either is met, the activity qualifies as a component unit to be reported within the CAFR of the primary government. A legally separate entity can also be included in this way even if it does not meet either of these criteria if exclusion is believed to be misleading.

[17] GASB, *Codification, as of December 31, 2014,* Sec. 2100.102.

Criterion 1 for Financial Accountability

The separate entity (such as the Atlanta Fulton County Recreation Authority) is viewed as a component unit if it fiscally depends on the primary government (the City of Atlanta). *Fiscal dependency* means that the organization cannot do one or more of the following without approval of the primary government: adopt its own budget, levy taxes or set rates, or issue bonded debt. This criterion also requires that the primary government and the component unit must be financially interdependent (there is a relationship of potential financial benefit or burden between the two).

Criterion 2 for Financial Accountability

First, officials of the primary government must appoint a voting majority of the governing board of the separate organization. Second, either the primary government must be able to impose its will on that board or the separate organization provides a financial benefit or imposes a financial burden on the primary government.

Because of the importance of this identification process, three aspects of these criteria will be explained further to ensure proper application.

Voting Majority of the Governing Board

The authority to elect a voting majority must be substantive. If, for example, the primary government simply confirms the choices made by other parties, then financial accountability is not present. In the same way, financial accountability does not result when the primary government merely selects the governing board from a limited slate of candidates (such as picking three individuals from an approved list of five). The primary government must have the actual responsibility of appointing a voting majority of the board to meet this provision of the second criterion.

Imposition of the Primary Government's Will on the Governing Board

Such power is indicated if the primary government can significantly influence programs, projects, activities, or level of services the separate organization provides. This degree of influence is present if the primary government is able to remove an appointed board member at will, modify or approve budgets, override decisions of the board, modify or approve rate or fee changes, or hire or dismiss the individuals responsible for day-to-day operations. Such possible actions indicate the level of authority held by the primary government.

Financial Benefit or Financial Burden on the Primary Government

A financial connection exists between the separate organization and the primary government if the government is entitled to the organization's resources, the government is legally obligated to finance any deficits or provide support, or the government is responsible for the organization's debts.

Reporting Component Units

After being identified, component units are reported by a primary government in one of two ways: discretely presented or blended. If discretely presented, component units are presented on the far right side of the government-wide statements. For example, as of June 30, 2014, the government-wide statements for the City of Detroit, Michigan, show that the primary government holds total assets and deferred outflows of resources of more than $9.9 billion, whereas its discretely presented component units shown just to the right of the primary government reports similar accounts totaling $473.5 million.

According to notes to the city's financial statements, these component unit figures were gathered from 12 separate organizations:

- Detroit Brownfield Redevelopment Authority.
- Detroit Public Library.
- Detroit Transportation Corporation.
- Downtown Development Authority.
- Eastern Market Corporation.

- Economic Development Corporation.
- Greater Detroit Resource Recovery Authority.
- Local Development Finance Authority.
- Museum of African American History.
- Detroit Land Bank Authority.
- Eight Mile/Woodward Corridor Improvement Authority.
- Detroit Employment Solutions Corporation.

As an alternative placement within the CAFR, a primary government can include a component unit as an actual part of the reporting government as if it were another fund (a process referred to as *blending*). The City of Detroit blends four of its component units: Detroit Building Authority, Detroit General Retirement System Service Corporation, Detroit Police and Fire Retirement System Service Corporation, and the Public Lighting Authority. Although legally separate, each of these components is so intertwined with the primary government that inclusion is necessary to present the financial information in an appropriate fashion. The blending of a component unit is usually up to the judgment of government officials. Blending is required if the separate entity's debt will be repaid entirely, or almost entirely, from resources of the primary government.

The City of Detroit also lists several related organizations. They are not closely tied to the primary government so that less reporting is necessary. The primary government is accountable only because it appoints a voting majority of the outside organization's governing board. Fiscal dependency as defined previously is not present, and the primary government cannot impose its will on the board or gather financial benefits or burdens from the relationship. Consequently, the separate organization does not qualify as a component unit. For a related organization, the primary government must still disclose the nature of the relationship. The City of Detroit discloses related organizations that include the Detroit Historical Society, Detroit Institute of Arts, and Detroit Zoological Society.

Special Purpose Governments

Most individuals think of primary governments in terms of general purpose governments such as states, cities, counties, towns, and the like. However, numerous special purpose governments also exist around the country. As noted at the start of the previous chapter, over 50,000 school systems and other special purpose districts were in existence across the United States. Their qualifications as primary governments can be seen in a note to the 2014 CAFR for the Atlanta Independent School System:

> The Atlanta Independent School System (School System of the District) was established by the Georgia State Legislature and is composed of nine publicly elected members serving four-year terms. The School System has the authority to approve its own budget and to provide for the levy of taxes to cover the cost of operations and maintenance and to cover debt service payments. Additionally, the School System has decision-making authority, the power to approve selection of management personnel, the ability to significantly influence operations, and primary accountability for fiscal matters. Accordingly, the School System is a primary government and consists of all the organizations that compose its legal entity.

Special purpose governments carry out only a single function or a limited number of functions. Common examples include public school districts, colleges and universities, water utilities, hospitals, transit authorities, and library services. For the accountant, one question must be addressed: Is such an operation truly a special purpose government or merely a part of a larger government such as a city or county so that it should be reported as a fund or a component unit. Or, perhaps, it is not a government entity at all but rather a nongovernmental not-for-profit organization.

As shown by the note in the CAFR for the Atlanta Independent School System, an activity or function is deemed a special purpose government if it meets the following criteria:

1. Has a separately elected governing body.
2. Is legally independent, which can be demonstrated by having corporate powers such as the right to sue and be sued as well as the right to buy, sell, and lease property in its own name.

Discussion Question

IS IT PART OF THE COUNTY?

Harland County is in a financially distressed area of Missouri. In hopes of enticing business to this county, the state legislature appropriated $3 million to start an industrial development commission. The federal government provided an additional $1 million. The state appointed 15 individuals to a board to oversee the operations of this commission, and Harland County officials named five additional members. The commission began operations by raising funds from local citizens and businesses. Over the past 12 months, it received $700,000 in donations and pledges. The county provided clerical assistance and allowed the commission to use one wing of a county office building for its headquarters. The Harland County government must approve the commission's annual operating budget. The county will also cover any deficits that might occur.

During the current period, the commission spent $2.4 million and achieved notable success. Several large manufacturing companies recently began to explore the possibility of opening plants in the county.

Harland County is currently preparing its comprehensive annual financial report. Should the county's CAFR include the revenues, expenditures, assets, expenses, and liabilities of the industrial development commission? Is it a fund within the county's primary government, a component unit, or a related organization?

Is the industrial development commission a component unit of the State of Missouri? How should its activities be presented in the state's comprehensive annual financial report?

3. Is fiscally independent of other state and local governments. As mentioned previously, an activity is normally considered to be fiscally independent if its leadership can determine the activity's budget without having to seek the approval of an outside party, levy taxes or set rates without having to seek outside approval, or issue bonded debt without outside approval.

A school system or other government activity that satisfies all three of these requirements is reported as a special purpose government that produces its own CAFR. If that same activity fails to meet any one of these criteria, its financial transactions are likely to be maintained within the general fund or special revenue funds of a city or county government.

LO 12-8

Explain the makeup of a primary government and its relationship to component units and related organizations as well as the combination of governments.

Acquisitions, Mergers, and Transfers of Operations

With so many general purpose governments, special purpose governments, component units, and related organizations, combinations and realignment transactions are common. A city government might take over operations of a homeless shelter from a not-for-profit entity. A toll road operated as a special purpose government might be acquired by a local county. Two independent school systems might be brought together to create more efficient operations. "After voters approved a ballot question last month approving the consolidation of the Atwood-Hammond and Arthur school districts, school officials, teachers and students have begun the process of merging the two districts into a single entity. Atwood-Hammond Superintendent Kenny Schwengel said the two school districts will spend the 2013–14 school year getting ready for the merger, which takes effect on July 1, 2014."[18]

[18] Tim Mitchell, "School Districts Prepare for Merger," *The News-Gazette,* May 20, 2013, http://www.news-gazette.com/news/local/2013-05-20/school-districts-prepare-merger.html.

GASB views a combination as a *merger* if two legally separate entities are brought together to form a new entity and no significant consideration is exchanged. The combination is still a merger even if one of those entities ceases to exist while the other continues to function. The combination of two agencies or two school systems might well meet this criteria. In a merger, because of the lack of paid consideration, the net carrying values for all assets, deferred outflows of resources, liabilities, and deferred inflows of resources are simply combined. Balances are not changed. Additional accounts are neither created nor recognized as a result of this type of combination.

The reporting of an *acquisition* is quite different. In an acquisition, a significant amount of consideration is exchanged. For example, the cash purchase of a special purpose government toll road by a county government is reported as an acquisition if the toll road ceases to exist as a separate entity and becomes part of the county government. In government-wide financial statements, the acquiring government records all acquired assets, deferred outflows of resources, liabilities, and deferred inflows of resources at acquisition value (other than a few specific exceptions such as landfills). Acquisition value is defined by GASB as the market-based entry price—the amount that the government would have to pay to acquire or discharge each separate item. Most of the additional costs incurred to create this type of combination are recorded as expenses (government-wide financial statements) or as expenditures (fund financial statements).

As with for-profit transactions, an acquiring entity might have to pay more than the total acquisition values assigned to the various assets, liabilities, and deferrals. In for-profit accounting—as seen in earlier chapters of this textbook—any excess payment is reported as the asset "goodwill." This balance is then tested periodically for possible impairment. On government-wide financial statements, any excess consideration is reported as a deferred outflow of resources on the statement of net position. The balance is written off to expense over a period of time that is determined based on factors such as the service life of capital assets, technology available, and contracts acquired.

When an acquisition takes place, fund financial statements for the governmental funds record any acquired current financial resources and the claims against those resources. That approach is in line with the usual reporting of those funds. Once again, acquisition value is applied to each balance. Any reduction in current financial resources caused by payment is also recorded. The fund balance reported for that fund is adjusted to reflect the net change. To illustrate, assume cash of $4 million is paid to acquire an outside agency which holds current financial resources having a total acquisition fair value of $1 million and capital assets with a total acquisition fair value of $2 million. In fund financial statements, cash is reduced by $4 million with the acquired current financial resources recorded at $1 million. The capital assets are not reported on fund statements. The fund balance for the acquiring fund must be reduced to reflect the $3 million difference.

Occasionally, an entity will convey one of its activities to another entity. A government might transfer the operations of a soup kitchen to a local charity. A not-for-profit entity might transfer a homeless shelter to the local city. If a government receives an operation purely by transfer, all assets, deferred outflows of resources, liabilities, and deferred inflows of resources are recorded at the previous net carrying amounts. Conversely, if a state or local government is turning over an activity to another party, a gain or loss on disposal is reported depending on whether any resources are received in return.

LO 12-9

Describe the physical structure of a complete set of government-wide financial statements and a complete set of fund financial statements.

Government-Wide and Fund Financial Statements Illustrated

At the core of a governmental reporting entity's CAFR are the general purpose financial statements. These statements are made up of government-wide financial statements and fund financial statements. Government-wide statements present financial information for both governmental activities and business-type activities (and often component units). They measure economic resources and utilize accrual accounting.

Separate fund financial statements are created for the governmental funds, the proprietary funds, and the fiduciary funds. The measurement focus and timing of recognition depend on the fund in question. For governmental funds, the current financial resources measurement focus is used with modified accrual accounting. In contrast, both proprietary funds and fiduciary funds use accrual accounting to report all economic resources.

Four of these statements were outlined briefly in the previous chapter to introduce their basic structure. Now that a deeper understanding of government accounting has been established, government-wide and fund financial statements can be examined in more detail.[19]

Statement of Net Position—Government-Wide Financial Statements

Exhibit 12.1 presents a hypothetical version of the June 30, 2017, statement of net position for the City of Eastern South. As a government-wide financial statement, it reports the economic resources of the government as a whole (except for the fiduciary funds, which are not included because those resources must be used for a purpose outside the government).

Several aspects of this statement of net position should be noted:

- The measurement focus is on the economic resources controlled by the government. Thus, all assets including capital assets are reported. Noncurrent liabilities are presented for the same reason.

- Capital assets other than land, inexhaustible works of art, and construction in progress (and infrastructure assets if the modified approach is applied) are reported net of accumulated depreciation. Other than these exceptions, depreciation of capital assets is required on the government-wide statements. (See Point A.)

- As discussed in the previous chapter, categories titled Deferred Outflows of Resources and Deferred Inflows of Resources are included on this statement. These sections provide a location for balances that do not qualify as either assets or liabilities in government accounting.

- The primary government is divided into governmental activities and business-type activities. Governmental funds are reported as governmental activities, whereas enterprise funds comprise most, if not all, of the business-type activities. Even though recorded within the proprietary funds, most internal service funds are classified as governmental activities. That is appropriate when those services are rendered primarily for the benefit of activities within the governmental funds (for example, a print shop works mainly for the local schools).

- The internal balances shown in the asset section (Point B) reflect receivables and payables between the governmental activities and the business-type activities. These internal balances have no impact outside of the government and are offset so that no effect is created on the totals reported for the primary government.

- Discretely presented component units are grouped and shown to the far right side of the statement (Point C) so that reported amounts do not affect the primary government figures. In contrast, blended component units are included, as appropriate, within either the governmental activities or the business-type activities as if they were individual funds. As seen in the final column of Exhibit 12.1, this city has only one discretely presented component unit: the Eastern South Regional Art Space. The government could also have blended component units but their presence can be ascertained only by a review of the disclosure notes.

- As the Net Position section shows, several amounts have been restricted for capital projects, debt service, and the like. Restrictions are reported in this manner only if usage of those resources has been designated (a) by external parties such as creditors, grantors, or other external party, or (b) as a result of laws that have been passed through constitutional provisions or enabling legislation.

---

[19] The examples presented here illustrate the government-wide financial statements and the fund financial statements for both governmental funds and proprietary funds. Because they are more specialized, the fund financial statements for the fiduciary funds have been omitted.

EXHIBIT 12.1   Government-Wide Financial Statements—Statement of Net Position

CITY OF EASTERN SOUTH
Statement of Net Position
June 30, 2017
(in thousands)

	Primary Government			Component Unit—Eastern South Regional Art Space ©
	Governmental Activities	Business-Type Activities	Total	
Assets				
Cash and investments	$ 232,450	$ 149,333	$ 381,783	$ 25,735
Receviables, net	219,435	59,812	279,247	–0–
Internal balances Ⓑ	23,876	(23,876)	–0–	–0–
Inventories and supplies	11,654	12,922	24,576	2,159
Prepaid items	5,075	2,117	7,192	822
Land and other capital assets not depreciated	250,883	165,873	416,756	1,451
Other capital assets, net of depreciation Ⓐ	821,490	688,523	1,510,013	11,434
Total assets	$1,564,863	$1,054,704	$2,619,567	$41,601
Deferred outflows of resources				
Unamortized excess cost of acquisition	$ 59,447	$ –0–	$ 59,447	$ –0–
Liabilities				
Accounts payable	$ 23,775	$ 14,315	$ 38,090	$ 5,076
Other liabilities and unearned revenue	30,766	5,225	35,991	432
Bonds payable—current	87,922	12,885	100,807	3,124
Landfill closure obligation	–0–	9,078	9,078	–0–
Bonds payable—noncurrent	289,217	221,441	510,658	6,780
Net pension liability	111,000	–0–	111,000	–0–
Lease payable—noncurrent	24,548	21,669	46,217	2,277
Total liabilities	$ 567,228	$ 284,613	$ 851,841	$17,689
Deferred inflows of resources				
Unavailable property tax collections	$ 26,500	$ –0–	$ 26,500	$ –0–
Net Position				
Invested in capital assets, net of related debt	$ 811,487	$ 723,656	$1,535,143	$ 872
Restricted for:				
Capital projects	125,769	19,774	145,543	5,045
Debt service	2,355	1,056	3,411	84
Other	29,267	–0–	29,267	–0–
Unrestricted	61,704	25,605	87,309	17,911
Total net position	$1,030,582	$ 770,091	$1,800,673	$23,912

The notes to the financial statements are an integral part of this statement.

Statement of Activities—Government-Wide Financial Statements

The statement of activities presents a wide array of information about the various functions of a state or local government. As shown in the statement for the City of Eastern South in Exhibit 12.2, the same general classification system of governmental activities, business-type activities, and component units used in Exhibit 12.1 forms the structural basis for reporting. However, the format here is more complex and requires close analysis.

EXHIBIT 12.2 Government-Wide Financial Statements—Statement of Activities

CITY OF EASTERN SOUTH
Statement of Activities
For the Fiscal Year Ended June 30, 2017
(in thousands)

Functions/Programs	Operating Expenses ⑥	Program Revenues ⑤			Net (Expenses) Revenues and Changes in Net Position			Component Unit-Eastern South Regional Art Space
		Charge for Services	Operating Grants and Contributions	Capital Grants and Contributions	Primary Government			
					Governmental Activities	Business-type Activities	Total	
Primary government:								
Governmental activities								
General government	$ (28,055)	$ 6,554	$ 5,472	$ 2,384	$ (13,645)		$ (13,645)	
Police	(103,465)	17,980	13,256	6,747	(65,482) ⓗ		(65,482)	
Fire	(97,687)	5,306	19,821	23,063	(49,497)		(49,497)	
Transportation	(96,088)	31,365	355	16,984 ⓖ	(47,384)		(47,384)	
Economic development	(5,563)	898	143	1,875	(2,647)		(2,647)	
Parks and recreation	(64,725)	17,168	16,778	4,221	(26,558)		(26,558)	
Neighborhood services	(3,965)	649	132	2,993	(191)		(191)	
Library	(17,744)	5,365	2,784	2,257	(7,338)		(7,338)	
Interest on noncurrent debt	(23,550) ⓔ	–0–	–0–	–0–	(23,550)		(23,550)	
Total governmental activities	$ (440,842)	$ 85,285	$58,741	$60,524	$ (236,292) ①		$(236,292)	
Business-type activities								
Water	$ (39,273)	$ 50,877	$ 121	$ 6,339		$ 18,064 ①	$ 18,064	
Sewer	(12,868)	11,836	488	2,451		1,907	1,907	
Parking	(11,776)	25,990	1,342	844		16,400	16,400	
Others	(8,074)	795	5,434	6,009		4,164	4,164	
Total business-type activities	(71,991)	89,498	7,385	15,643		40,535 ⓚ	40,535	
Total primary government	$(512,833)	$174,783	$66,126	$76,167	$(236,292)	$40,535	$(195,757)	
Component unit:								
Eastern South Regional Art Space	$ (8,128)	$ 2,896	$ 1,676	$ –0–				$(3,556) ①

(continued)

EXHIBIT 12.2 (Continued)

General revenues		
Property taxes	$ 111,762 Ⓜ	$ –0–	$ 111,762
Income taxes	49,079	–0–	49,079
Sales Taxes	43,809	–0–	43,809
Unrestricted grants	17,227		17,227
Gain on sale of capital asset	–0–	556	556
Investment earnings	13,244	3,101	16,345
Transfers	18,633	(18,633)	–0– Ⓝ
Total general revenues, transfers and others	$ 253,754	$ (14,976)	$ 238,778
Change in net position	$ 17,462 Ⓣ	$ 25,559	$ 43,021
Net position, beginning of year	$1,013,120	$744,532	$1,757,652
Net position, end of year	$1,030,582	$770,091	$1,800,673

		279
		$ 279
		$ (3,277)
		$27,189
		$23,912

The notes to the financial statements are an integral part of this statement.

- Operating expenses are presented in the first column (Point D). They are not classified according to individual causes such as salaries, rent, depreciation, or insurance. Instead, expenses are shown by function: general government, police, fire, general services, and the like. This approach is viewed as more relevant to the needs of the people reading the statements. "As a minimum, governments should report direct expenses for each function. Direct expenses are those that are specifically associated with a service, program, or department and, thus, are clearly identifiable to a particular function."[20] Expenses are shown in this statement for governmental activities, business-type activities, and discretely presented component units.

- Interest expense on general long-term debt is normally considered an indirect expense because borrowed money can benefit many government activities. However, it is usually a large amount with significant informational value. It can be difficult to allocate among different activities. For those reasons, interest expense can be reported as shown in this example (Point E) as a separate "function."

- After operating expenses have been reported for each function, related program revenues are listed in the next three columns (Point F). Program revenues are derived by the function itself or from outsiders seeking to reduce the government's cost for providing that function. Program revenues are different from general government revenues (such as sales taxes) that are reported toward the bottom of the statement. As Exhibit 12.2 shows, program revenues are usually classified as

  1. *Charges for services.* For example, a monthly charge is normally assessed for water service. Therefore, this first business-type activity shows nearly $50.9 million in program revenues. In contrast, most government functions generate only small amounts of revenue from sources such as parking meter revenues, fines for speeding tickets, concessions at parks, and the like.

  2. *Operating grants and contributions.* This column reports resources received from outside grants and similar sources that were designated for some type of operating purpose. For example, the police department is shown here as having earned approximately $13.3 million in operating grants and contributions during the year.

  3. *Capital grants and contributions.* This column presents outside grants and similar sources that were designated for capital asset additions (rather than operations). For the City of Eastern South, over $16.9 million in capital grants and contributions went to transportation (Point G).

- After operating expenses have been assigned along with related program revenues, a net (expense) or revenue is determined for each function. This figure is an important measure of the financial cost (or benefit) of each of the various government functions. For example, in Exhibit 12.2, the police had $103.5 million in operating expenses but generated enough charges, grants, and contributions so that (at Point H) taxpayers can see that they had to bear a financial burden of roughly $65.5 million for police protection. That cost is significant information to the citizens studying these statements. Are they satisfied with that level of protection? Or, do they wish that some of that money had been spent in other ways? In contrast, the water system reported operating expenses of $39.3 million. Because of its charges, grants, and contributions, this business-type activity still managed to generate net revenues of approximately $18.1 million (see Point I) as a financial benefit for the government.

- All of the governmental activities are combined to report net expenses of $236.3 million (see Point J) while the business-type activities generated total net revenues of approximately $40.5 million (see Point K). The component units reported net expenses of $3.6 million (see Point L). The financial cost or benefit from each government function is evident. Such information leads to informed citizens.

- General revenues are reported next as additions to either the governmental activities, business-type activities, or component units. All taxes are general revenues because they do

---

[20] GASB, *Codification*, Sec. 2200.129.

not reflect a charge for services. They are obtained from the population as a whole. At Point M, property taxes of nearly $112 million are shown as the largest revenue source. That money is taken from the citizens in order to meet the cost of the various governmental activities provided by the City of Eastern South. Significant amounts were also collected as income taxes and sales taxes.

- Transfers of $18.6 million between governmental activities and business-type activities are also shown under general revenues. The inflow and the outflow are offset for reporting purposes to indicate that no impact is created on the total figures for the primary government (Point N).

Balance Sheet—Governmental Funds—Fund Financial Statements

Switching now to fund financial statements, Exhibit 12.3 presents the balance sheet for the governmental funds reported by the City of Eastern South. This statement reports only current financial resources (along with some supplies and prepaid items) as well as all claims to those current financial resources. It was produced using modified accrual accounting for timing purposes. No proprietary funds, discretely presented component units, or fiduciary funds are included. This fund-based statement reflects just the governmental funds. Several parts of this statement should be noted:

- Separate columns are shown for the general fund and any other major fund within the governmental funds. The city has identified two other funds as major. The Highway 61 Construction Fund is a major capital projects fund. The Educational Services Fund is a major special revenue fund. All funds that are not considered major are combined and reported as "Other Governmental Funds."
- The balance sheet reports no capital assets or long-term debts simply because they are neither current financial resources nor claims to current financial resources.
- The Fund Balances figures (Point O) indicate the nonspendable, restricted, committed, assigned, and unassigned categories discussed in the previous chapter.
- The total Fund Balances figure for the governmental funds of $319.2 million (Point P) is significantly different from the $1.0 billion total net position reported for governmental activities in the statement of net position (Exhibit 12.1). To explain that large disparity, a reconciliation is presented along with the balance sheet. This reconciliation starts with the total fund balance figure and shows the differences with the total net position amount. For example, this reconciliation might look something like the following for the City of Eastern South.

Reconciliation of the Balance Sheet
Governmental Funds to the Governmental
Activities in the Statement of Net Position
June 30, 2017
(in thousands)

Total fund balance for governmental funds, June 30, 2017, as reported on balance sheet	$ 319,200
Capital assets reported by governmental activities but not reported in governmental funds	1,021,800
Bonds payable reported by governmental activities but not reported in governmental funds	(422,650)
Other assets and liabilities reported by governmental activities but not reported in governmental funds	(43,866)
Revenues reported by governmental activities but not reported in governmental funds because they are not available	32,845
Internal service funds reported by governmental activities but not reported in governmental funds	123,253
Total net position, governmental activities, June 30, 2017, as reported in statement of net position	$1,030,582

EXHIBIT 12.3 Fund Financial Statements—Balance Sheet for the Governmental Funds

CITY OF EASTERN SOUTH
Governmental Funds
Balance Sheet June 30, 2017
(in thousands)

	General Fund	Highway 61 Construction	Educational Services	Other Governmental Funds	Total Governmental Funds
Assets:					
Cash and investments	$111,673	$87,056	$11,908	$10,905	$221,542
Receivables, net					
Taxes	53,875	–0–	17,854	–0–	71,729
Accounts	108,654	–0–	–0–	–0–	108,654
Inventory of supplies	3,222	2,076	3,112	2,175	10,585
Prepaid Items	887	1,015	1,322	556	3,780
Total assets	$278,311	$90,147	$34,196	$13,636	$416,290
Liabilities:					
Accounts payable	$ 21,659	$ 776	$ 452	$ 298	$ 23,185
Accrued liabilities	7,174	323	2,572	1,963	12,032
Other claims to financial resources	1,128	1,733	–0–	312	3,173
Bonds currently due	25,000	–0–	7,200	–0–	32,200
Total liabilities	$ 54,961	$ 2,832	$10,224	$ 2,573	$ 70,590
Deferred inflows of resources:					
Unavailable property tax collections	$ 26,500	$ –0–	$ –0–	$ –0–	$ 26,500
Total liabilities and deferred inflows of resources	$ 81,461	$ 2,832	$10,224	$ 2,573	$ 97,090
Fund balances: ⓞ					
Nonspendable	$ 11,465	$ 3,091	$ 4,434	$ 2,989	$ 21,979
Restricted	46,717	–0–	19,538	875	67,130
Committed	2,044	1,159	–0–	993	4,196
Assigned	35,009	83,065	–0–	6,206	124,280
Unassigned	101,615	–0–	–0–	–0–	101,615
Total fund balances	$196,850	$87,315	$23,972	$11,063	$319,200 ⓟ
Total liabilities, deferred inflows of resources, and fund balances	$278,311	$90,147	$34,196	$13,636	$416,290

The notes to the financial statements are an integral part of this statement.

Statement of Revenues, Expenditures, and Other Changes in Fund Balances—Governmental Funds—Fund Financial Statements

Exhibit 12.4 presents the statement of revenues, expenditures, and other changes in fund balances for the governmental funds of the City of Eastern South. Once again, the general fund is detailed in a separate column along with each of the other major funds previously identified. Figures for all remaining nonmajor funds are accumulated and shown together.

In examining Exhibit 12.4, note the following:

- Because the current financial resources measurement focus is being utilized, expenditures (Point Q) rather than expenses are reported. For example, Capital Outlay is presented here as a reduction in resources rather than as the acquisition of an asset. In the same way, Debt Service—Principal is reported as an expenditure instead of a decrease in long-term liabilities.
- Because the modified accrual method of accounting is used for timing purposes, reported amounts will be different than those previously shown under accrual accounting. For example, property taxes are reported here as $107.2 million but as $111.8 million in Exhibit 12.2.
- At Point R, Exhibit 12.4 presents other financing sources and uses to reflect the financial impact of the issuance of long-term debt and transfers made between the funds. Current financial resources are changed but no revenues or expenditures take place. Because the fund statements focus on individual activities rather than government-wide figures, no elimination of the transfers is made.

Another reconciliation is needed because of the significant difference that exists between the amounts reported in the statement of revenues, expenditures, and other changes in fund balances and the statement of activities. At Point S, Exhibit 12.4 indicates that the fund balances for the governmental funds increased during the period by over $24.8 million. However, in Exhibit 12.2, Point T reports an increase in the net position of the governmental activities by only $17.5 million. A $7.3 million variation exists between two figures that sound alike. That is a difference that might well be confusing to readers of those two statements.

This reconciliation begins with the change in the total fund balances and makes all necessary adjustments to arrive at the reported change in net position. Those changes often include

- The acquisition of capital assets during the period that decreases the fund balance but not the government's net position.
- The recording of depreciation that decreases the city's net position but not its fund balance.
- The recording of revenues and expenses that do not impact current financial resources but do change the net position of the government.
- The issuance of long-term debt that increases the city's fund balance but not its net position.

Statement of Net Position—Proprietary Funds—Fund Financial Statements

The assets and liabilities of the City of Eastern South's proprietary funds, as reported in the fund financial statements, are presented in Exhibit 12.5. This statement shows individual information about three major enterprise funds, with a single column for the summation of all other enterprise funds. The statement then provides a combined total for all of the enterprise funds. Because of their size, specific information is available for the water fund, sewer fund, and parking fund.

In examining Exhibit 12.5, several features should be noted:

- This fund statement combines and exhibits all internal service funds (Point U) because they are identified as proprietary funds. However, in the government-wide financial statements, these same internal service funds are usually reported as part of governmental activities. Those are the activities that are typically served by these internal operations.

EXHIBIT 12.4 Fund Financial Statements—Statement of Revenues, Expenditures, and Other Changes in Fund Balances

CITY OF EASTERN SOUTH
Governmental Funds
Statement of Revenues, Expenditures, and Other Changes in Fund Balance
For the Fiscal Year Ended June 30, 2017 (in thousands)

	General Fund	Highway 61 Construction	Educational Services	Other Governmental Funds	Total Governmental Funds
Revenues:					
Property taxes	$ 99,737	$ –0–	$ 7,500	$ –0–	$ 107,237
Income taxes	43,556	–0–	–0–	–0–	43,556
Sales taxes	38,760	5,000	–0–	–0–	43,760
Charges for services	61,223	–0–	3,327	1,196	65,746
Fines and penalties	2,657	–0–	–0–	312	2,969
Grants and contributions	87,332	17,901	9,448	1,323	116,004
Investment earnings and miscellaneous	20,775	3,989	2,887	624	28,275
Total revenues	$354,040	$ 26,890	$ 23,162	$ 3,455	$ 407,547
Expenditures: ⓖ					
Current:					
General government	$ 23,909	$ –0–	$ –0–	$ –0–	$ 23,909
Police	79,565	–0–	–0–	–0–	79,565
Fire	81,100	–0–	–0–	–0–	81,100
Transportation	76,826	8,554	–0–	–0–	85,380
Economic development	5,129	–0–	–0–	656	5,785
Parks and recreation	53,119	–0–	547	134	53,800
Neighborhood services	1,445	–0–	1,389	–0–	2,834
Library	6,022	–0–	10,083	–0–	16,105
Capital outlay	42,459	17,809	8,220	2,500	70,988
Debt service:					
Principal	5,334	–0–	2,108	–0–	7,442
Interest	3,989	–0–	434	–0–	4,423
Total expenditures	$378,897	$ 26,363	$ 22,781	$ 3,290	$ 431,331
Excess (deficiency) of revenues over (under) expenditures	$ (24,857)	$ 527	$ 381	$ 165	$ (23,784)
Other financing sources (uses): ⓡ					
Transfers in	$ 16,157	$ 442	$ 2,331	$ 11,090	$ 30,020
Transfers out	(30,050)	–0–	–0–	(6,552)	(36,602)
Issuance of long-term debt	45,000	8,112	2,090	–0–	55,202
Total other financing sources (uses)	$ 31,107	$ 8,554	$ 4,421	$ 4,538	$ 48,620
Net change in fund balances	$ 6,250	$ 9,081	$ 4,802	$ 4,703	$ 24,836 ⓢ
Fund balance, beginning of year	$190,600	$78,234	$19,170	$ 6,360	$294,364
Fund balance, end of year	$196,850	$87,315	$23,972	$11,063	$319,200

The notes to the financial statements are an integral part of this statement.

EXHIBIT 12.5   Fund Financial Statements—Statement of Net Position for Proprietary Funds

CITY OF EASTERN SOUTH
Proprietary Funds
Statement of Net Position
June 30, 2017
(in thousands)

	Water	Sewer	Parking	Other Enterprise Funds	Total Enterprise Funds	Internal Service Funds ⓤ
Assets						
Current assets						
Cash and equivalents	$ 18,400	$ 16,150	$ 17,100	$ 9,225	$ 60,875	$ 5,000
Investments	35,045	12,285	25,803	15,325	88,458	8,882
Receivables, net						
Accounts	22,943	9,076	7,577	3,782	43,378	2,178
Other	8,435	3,081	2,290	2,628	16,434	3,006
Due from other funds	–0–	–0–	366	43	409	9,092
Inventories and supplies	3,642	1,810	1,708	5,762	12,922	722
Prepaid items	461	226	824	606	2,117	658
Total current assets	$ 88,926	$ 42,628	$ 55,668	$ 37,371	$ 224,593	$ 29,538
Noncurrent assets						
Capital assets						
Land	$ 62,981	$ 55,773	$ 29,100	$ 18,019	$ 165,873	$ 9,817
Buildings	388,278	206,149	72,925	45,785	713,137	12,713
Leased property	3,672	8,179	10,433	7,734	30,018	2,058
Vehicles	33,012	26,567	37,007	18,633	115,219	3,118
Equipment	34,227	15,995	4,303	7,883	62,408	5,004
Less: Accumulated depreciation	(83,445)	(77,881)	(41,642)	(29,291)	(232,259)	(11,886)
Total noncurrent assets	$438,725	$234,782	$112,126	$ 68,763	$ 854,396	$ 20,824
Total assets	$527,651	$277,410	$167,794	$106,134	$1,078,989	$ 50,362

(continued)

Liabilities

Current liabilities

Accounts payable and other accrued expenses	$ 9,260	$ 3,065	$ 2,084	$ 1,696	$ 983
Due to other funds	11,522	8,044	4,088	631	375
Unearned revenue	1,418	883	316	154	310
Lease payable, current	327	125	98	114	55
Bonds and notes payable, current	5,837	3,992	1,760	1,296	100
Total current liabilities	$ 28,364	$ 16,109	$ 8,346	$ 3,891	$ 1,823

Noncurrent liabilities

Liability for landfill closure	$ –0–	$ –0–	$ –0–	$ 9,078	$ –0–
Capital lease payable, long-term	3,607	7,503	8,291	2,268	1,323
Bonds and notes payable, long-term	96,048	47,155	26,121	52,117	19,880
Total noncurrent liabilities	99,655	54,658	34,412	63,463	21,203
Total liabilities	$128,019	$ 70,767	$ 42,758	$ 67,354	$ 23,026

Net Position

Invested in capital assets, net of related debt	$389,145	$215,103	$ 92,771	$ 26,637	$ 10,831

Restricted for:

Capital projects	4,083	11,092	415	4,184	–0–
Debt service	227	284	432	113	–0–
Unrestricted	6,177	(19,836)	31,418	7,846	16,505
Total Net Position	$399,632	$206,643	$125,036	$ 38,780	$ 27,336

The notes to the financial statements are an integral part of this statement.

- Because the proprietary funds utilize accrual accounting to measure economic resources, the totals for the enterprise funds in Exhibit 12.5 agree in most ways with the total figures in Exhibit 12.1. The amount of detail, however, is more extensive in the fund financial statements. For example, the statement in Exhibit 12.1 uses only two accounts to describe capital assets, whereas Exhibit 12.5 uses five.

Statement of Revenues, Expenses, and Other Changes in Net Position—Proprietary Funds—Fund Financial Statements

Just as the statement of net position in Exhibit 12.5 provides individual information about specific enterprise funds (and totals for the internal service funds), the statement of revenues, expenses, and changes in net position in Exhibit 12.6 gives the revenues, expenses, nonoperating items, and transfers for those same funds in detail.

As an example, in Exhibit 12.2 operating expenses are listed for each of the business-type activities (water, sewer, parking, and community center). Here, in Exhibit 12.6 (Point V), operating expenses are separately listed by the type of expense for each of the proprietary funds: employee services, services and supplies, depreciation and amortization, utilities, maintenance and repairs, and others. In addition, several nonoperating items are identified including investment earnings and a gain on disposal of a capital asset. Finally, because this statement reflects all changes in the net position of each proprietary activity, transfers are included at the bottom. Thus, extensive information is available about the operation of each of these major enterprise funds, which is the objective of fund financial statements.

Statement of Cash Flows—Proprietary Funds—Fund Financial Statements

One of the most unique aspects of the fund financial statements is the statement of cash flows for the proprietary funds (Exhibit 12.7). Because a proprietary fund operates in a manner similar to a for-profit business, information about cash flows is considered as vital as it is in analyzing Intel or Coca-Cola. However, the physical structure is not entirely the same.

One of the main differences is that the statement of cash flows shown for the proprietary funds has four sections rather than just the three required of for-profit entities:

1. Cash flows from operating activities.
2. Cash flows from noncapital financing activities.
3. Cash flows from capital and related financing activities.
4. Cash flows from investing activities.

- The presentation of cash flows from operating activities (Point W) is similar to that prepared by a for-profit business. However, the direct method of reporting is required rather than being an allowed option as in for-profit accounting. The indirect method that is almost universally used by businesses is not allowed for state and local governments.
- Cash flows from noncapital financing activities includes (1) proceeds and payments on debt *not* attributable to the acquisition or construction of capital assets and (2) grants and subsidies *not* restricted for either capital purposes or operating activities.
- As the title implies, cash flows from capital and related financing activities focus on the amounts spent on capital assets and the source of that funding. Exhibit 12.7 shows typical examples (Point X): proceeds from issuance of debt, acquisition of capital assets, and proceeds from disposition of capital assets.
- Cash flows from investing activities disclose amounts paid and received from investments.
- The government should also provide a reconciliation of operating income to operating cash flows. That information has been omitted here because of space considerations.

EXHIBIT 12.6 Fund Financial Statements—Statement of Changes in Revenues, Expenses, and Other Changes in Net Position for the Proprietary Funds

CITY OF EASTERN SOUTH
Proprietary Funds
Statement of Revenues, Expenses, and Other Changes in Net Position
For the Fiscal Year Ended June 30, 2017
(in thousands)

	Water	Sewer	Parking	Other Enterprise Funds	Total Enterprise Funds	Internal Service Funds ①
Operating revenues:						
Charges for services	$ 50,877	$ 11,836	$ 25,990	$ 795	$ 89,498	$ 9,044
Miscellaneous	3,776	2,189	772	290	7,027	112
Total operating revenues	$ 54,653	$ 14,025	$ 26,762	$ 1,085	$ 96,525	$ 9,156
Operating expenses: ②						
Employee services	$ 16,118	$ 5,017	$ 3,982	$ 1,298	$ 26,415	$ 3,372
Services and supplies	3,109	812	971	618	5,510	611
Depreciation and amortization	6,271	1,219	1,311	294	9,095	476
Utilities	7,216	1,315	2,045	416	10,992	1,342
Maintenance and repairs	3,894	2,119	3,183	1,220	10,416	682
Others	2,665	2,386	284	4,228	9,563	525
Total operating expenses	$ 39,273	$ 12,868	$ 11,776	$ 8,074	$ 71,991	$ 7,008
Total operating income (loss)	$ 15,380	$ 1,157	$ 14,986	$ (6,989)	$ 24,534	$ 2,148
Nonoperating revenues and expenses:						
Grant revenue	$ 2,684	$ 750	$ 1,414	$ 11,153	$ 16,001	$ 447
Investment earnings	704	525	1,561	311	3,101	29
Gain on disposal of capital asset	400	–0–	156	–0–	556	–0–
Total nonoperating revenues and expenses	$ 3,788	$ 1,275	$ 3,131	$ 11,464	$ 19,658	$ 476
Income (loss) before transfers	$ 19,168	$ 2,432	$ 18,117	$ 4,475	$ 44,192	$ 2,624
Transfers to governmental and fiduciary funds	(8,703)	(454)	(9,000)	(476)	(18,633)	–0–
Change in net position	$ 10,465	$ 1,978	$ 9,117	$ 3,999	$ 25,559	$ 2,624
Net position, beginning of year	389,167	204,665	115,919	34,781	744,532	24,712
Net position, end of year	$399,632	$206,643	$125,036	$38,780	$770,091	$27,336

The notes to the financial statements are an integral part of this statement.

EXHIBIT 12.7 Fund Financial Statements—Statement of Cash Flows for Proprietary Funds

CITY OF EASTERN SOUTH
Proprietary Funds
Statement of Cash Flows
For the Fiscal Year Ended June 30, 2017
(in thousands)

	Water	Sewer	Parking	Other Enterprise Funds	Total Enterprise Funds	Internal Service Funds
Cash flows from operating activities: Ⓦ						
Receipts from customers	$ 49,772	$ 12,816	$ 25,045	$ 996	$ 88,629	$ 8,961
Payments to employees	(16,553)	(4,849)	(3,717)	(1,011)	(26,130)	(3,402)
Payments to suppliers	(2,816)	(785)	(963)	(580)	(5,144)	(529)
Payments on operating expenses	(13,287)	(6,612)	(5,030)	(6,016)	(30,945)	(1,873)
Receipts from operating grants	3,178	2,985	1,040	8,211	15,414	–0–
Net cash provided by operating activities	$ 20,294	$ 3,555	$ 16,375	$ 1,600	$ 41,824	$ 3,157
Cash flows from noncapital financing activities:						
Issuance of revenue anticipation notes	$ 5,000	$ –0–	$ 800	$ –0–	$ 5,800	$ –0–
Transfers	(8,703)	(454)	(9,000)	(476)	(18,633)	–0–
Net cash provided by (used for) noncapital financing activities	$ (3,703)	$ (454)	$ (8,200)	$ (476)	$ (12,833)	$ –0–
Cash flows from capital and related financing activities: ⊗						
Proceeds from bonds issued for construction	$ 27,500	$ 8,100	$ 10,500	$ –0–	$ 46,100	$ 2,316
Receipt of capital grants	2,375	–0–	1,100	–0–	3,475	–0–
Received from sale of capital assets	1,980	–0–	753	–0–	2,733	–0–
Paid to acquire capital assets	(28,900)	(17,446)	(2,545)	(5,667)	(54,558)	(1,895)
Paid on bonds issued for construction	(2,300)	(540)	(1,508)	(944)	(5,292)	(135)
Paid interest on bonds issued for construction	(1,122)	(665)	(513)	(1,029)	(3,329)	(271)
Net cash provided by (used for) capital and related financing activities	$ (467)	$ (10,551)	$ 7,787	$ (7,640)	$ (10,871)	$ 15
Cash flows from investing activities:						
Purchase of investments	$ (41,200)	$ (19,884)	$(19,936)	$ (2,415)	$(83,435)	$(6,552)
Received from sale and maturity of investments	35,375	20,900	16,650	7,000	79,925	7,255
Received from investment earnings	704	500	1,510	300	3,014	29
Net cash provided by (used for) investing activities:	$ (5,121)	$ 1,516	$ (1,776)	$ 4,885	$ (496)	$ 732
Net increase (decrease) in cash and cash equivalents	$ 11,003	$ (5,934)	$ 14,186	$ (1,631)	$ 17,624	$ 3,904
Cash and cash equivalents, beginning of year	7,397	22,084	2,914	10,856	43,251	1,096
Cash and cash equivalents, end of year	$ 18,400	$ 16,150	$ 17,100	$ 9,225	$ 60,875	$ 5,000

The notes to the financial statements are an integral part of this statement.

LO 12-10

Understand the presentation of financial statements for a public college or university.

Reporting Public Colleges and Universities

Private schools such as Harvard, Duke, and Stanford follow the FASB *Accounting Standards Codification®*. Authoritative accounting literature on contributions and the proper form of financial statements provides a significant amount of official reporting guidance for these private institutions. As will be discussed in the following chapter, generally accepted accounting principles developed for private not-for-profit organizations have progressed greatly over the years.

In contrast, GASB has retained primary authority over the reporting of public colleges and universities. For decades the question of whether the financial statements prepared for public colleges and universities (such as The Ohio State University and the University of Kansas) should resemble those of private schools has been the subject of much theoretical discussion. Generally, the operations of public colleges and universities differ in at least two important ways from private schools.

- First, state and other governments directly provide a significant amount of funding, lessening the reliance on tuition and fees. For example, the 2014 financial statements for the Oregon University System disclosed federal grants and contracts of $309.8 million, state and local grants and contracts of $17.9 million, and governmental appropriations of $341.9 million.

- Second, because of the ongoing support from the government, public schools often accumulate a smaller amount of endowment funds than private colleges and universities. Private schools usually try to build a large endowment to help ensure financial security. This is a less urgent need for public schools that are backed by the state or another government. For example, at June 30, 2015, Princeton University, a private school, held investments with a fair value of approximately $22.5 billion, an amount (roughly equal to $2.83 million per student) that is nearly beyond the comprehension of officials at most public colleges. On that same date, the University of Georgia reported $201.4 million in investments (about $7,500 per student).

Do these and other differences warrant unique financial statements for public colleges and universities? In many ways, public and private schools are much alike. They both educate students, charge tuition and other fees, conduct scholarly research, maintain libraries and sports teams, operate cafeterias and museums, and the like. What should be the measurement basis and form of the financial statements to reflect the financial activity and position of a public college or university?

Over the years, four alternatives have been suggested for constructing the financial statements that public colleges and universities prepare and distribute:

1. Adopt FASB's requirements so that all colleges and universities (public and private) prepare comparable financial statements. As the next chapter discusses, the private school reporting model is relatively well developed. Some worry that this suggestion presents potential problems. FASB has not had to deal with the intricacies of governmental entities and might fail to comprehend the unique aspects of public schools. The specific reporting needs associated with such institutions might go unnoticed.

2. Apply a more traditional model focusing on fund financial statements and the wide variety of funds that such schools often have to maintain. However, both private not-for-profit organizations and governments (at least in part) have abandoned the reporting of individual funds. For public schools to continue relying on this approach seems somewhat outdated.

3. Create an entirely new set of financial statements designed specifically to meet the unique needs of public colleges and universities. If FASB's *Accounting Standards*

Codification® is not to be followed, the fundamental differences between private and public schools must be significant. Identify those differences and new statements could be developed to reflect the events and transactions of public institutions and satisfy the informational needs of users. Unfortunately, the creation of a new set of financial statements would require an enormous amount of work by GASB. Does the benefit gained from tailor-made financial statements outweigh the cost of producing new standards for the reporting of public schools?

4. Adopt the same reporting model for public schools that has been created for state and local governments. Because a large amount of funding for public schools comes directly from governments, the financial statement format utilized by a city or county could be applied.

GASB has officially selected the fourth option by specifying that public colleges and universities are special purpose governments. "'Public universities, hospitals, utilities, and other business-type activities may operate similar to businesses but they are nonetheless governments—and therefore are accountable to the citizenry.' said GASB Chairman Robert H. Attmore."[21] This decision creates a standard reporting model for schools such as the University of Tennessee and Michigan State University.

Nevertheless, a review of public college and university financial statements shows that many do not prepare both government-wide and fund financial statements. Such schools can logically be viewed as large enterprise funds. They have a user charge (tuition and fees), and they are open to the public. As has been discussed, accounting for enterprise funds in government-wide statements and fund financial statements is very similar. For such proprietary funds, both statements report all economic resources and use accrual accounting.

Thus, having two sets of almost identical statements was viewed by GASB as redundant. For this reason, public schools usually only prepare a single set of statements equivalent to those of an enterprise fund (similar to the previous examples shown in this chapter for the proprietary funds of the City of Eastern South). Consequently, Note 1 to the 2015 financial statements for Middle Tennessee State University provides a common rationale for the method by which the statements are structured.

> For financial statement purposes, Middle Tennessee University is considered a special-purpose government engaged *only in business-type activities.* Accordingly, the financial statements have been prepared using the economic resources measurement focus and the accrual basis of accounting. Revenues are recorded when earned and expenses are recorded when a liability is incurred, regardless of the timing of related cash flows. Grants and similar items are recognized as revenue as soon as all eligibility requirements imposed by the provider have been met. [Emphasis added.]

Exhibit 12.8 presents the financial statements for June 30, 2014, and the year then ended for James Madison University (a public school) for illustration purposes, although the accompanying notes have been omitted. The component unit that is reported here is identified as follows:

> The James Madison University Foundation, Inc. meets the criteria which qualify it as a component unit of the University. The Foundation is a legally separate, tax-exempt organization formed to promote the achievements and further the aims and purposes of the University.

Note, as expected, that these statements are quite similar to the fund financial statements presented in this chapter for the proprietary funds of the City of Eastern South (Exhibits 12.5, 12.6, and 12.7).

---

[21] Business Wire, "GASB Publishes New User Guide on Business-Type Activities," March 12, 2013.

EXHIBIT 12.8

JAMES MADISON UNIVERSITY
Statement of Net Position
As of June 30, 2014

	2014	
	James Madison University	Component Unit
ASSETS		
Current assets:		
Cash and cash equivalents (Note 2)............	$ 134,394,162	$ 3,996,832
Securities lending—Cash and cash equivalents (Note 2)	8,040,739	–
Short-term investments (Note 2)................	260,332	–
Accounts receivable (Net of allowance for doubtful accounts of $598,752) (Note 3)	5,983,689	56,475
Contributions receivable (Net of allowance for doubtful contributions of $37,983) (Note 3)...	–	1,126,150
Due from the Commonwealth (Note 4)	6,364,503	–
Prepaid expenses	10,735,912	90,497
Inventory	955,854	–
Notes receivable (Net of allowance for doubtful accounts of $46,598)	388,080	–
Total current assets........................	167,123,271	5,269,954
Noncurrent assets:		
Restricted cash and cash equivalents (Note 2) ...	41,430,267	–
Endowment investments (Note 2)..............	–	51,529,317
Other long-term investments (Note 2)	2,111,959	42,035,137
Land held for future use	–	4,860,348
Contributions receivable (Net of allowance for doubtful contributions of $33,458) (Note 3)..	–	1,639,479
Prepaid expenses	273,646	–
Notes receivable (Net of allowance for doubtful accounts of $227,508)......................	1,895,267	–
Capital assets, net: (Note 5)		
Nondepreciable...........................	116,972,861	1,250,552
Depreciable	777,424,233	3,859,658
Other assets	–	19,655
Total noncurrent assets	940,108,233	105,194,146
DEFERRED OUTFLOW OF RESOURCES		
Deferred outflow of resources (Note 9)	1,831,849	–
Total assets and deferred outflow of resources	1,109,063,353	110,464,100
LIABILITIES		
Current liabilities:		
Accounts payable and accrued expenses (Note 6)...........................	45,361,541	208,100
Unearned revenue	12,825,654	326,363
Obligations under securities lending............	8,301,071	–

(*continued*)

EXHIBIT 12.8
(Continued)

	2014	
	James Madison University	**Component Unit**
Deposits held in custody for others	7,288,631	–
Long-term liabilities—current portion (Note 7)	16,961,338	234,176
Advance from the Treasurer of Virginia.	50,000	–
Total current liabilities.	90,788,235	768,639
Noncurrent liabilities:		
Long-term liabilities (Note 7)	256,293,156	2,709,394
DEFERRED INFLOW OF RESOURCES		
Related to debt refundings (Note 9)	273,166	–
NET POSITION		
Net investment in capital assets	669,184,291	2,812,432
Restricted for:		
Nonexpendable:		
Scholarships and fellowships	–	36,181,726
Research and public service.	–	2,130,282
Other	–	14,111,315
Expendable:		
Scholarships and fellowships	–	14,718,426
Research and public service.	1,925,310	1,852,860
Debt service	368,013	–
Capital projects	5,885,386	2,230,789
Loans	317,366	–
Other	–	20,053,582
Unrestricted	84,028,430	12,894,655
Total net position.	$ 761,708,796	$106,986,067

The accompanying Notes to Financial Statements are an integral part of this statement.

JAMES MADISON UNIVERSITY
Statement of Revenues, Expenses, and Changes in Net Position
For the Year Ended June 30, 2014

	2014	
	James Madison University	**Component Unit**
Operating revenues:		
Student tuition and fees (Net of scholarship allowances of $13,099,419)	$ 177,989,678	$ –
Gifts and contributions	–	6,465,956
Federal grants and contracts.	13,266,312	–
State grants and contracts	7,895,698	–
Non-governmental grants and contracts.	6,026,609	–
Auxiliary enterprises (Net of scholarship allowances of $9,676,813) (Note 11)	162,183,276	–
Sales and Services of Education and General Activities.	1,816,718	–
Other operating revenues	1,453,033	574,088
Total operating revenues.	370,631,324	7,040,044
Operating expenses (Note 12):		
Instruction	140,358,805	639,174

(continued)

EXHIBIT 12.8
(Continued)

	2014	
	James Madison University	Component Unit
Research	4,842,870	9,881
Public service	13,074,273	90,016
Academic support	39,656,736	736,996
Student services	15,873,848	91,543
Institutional support	25,682,435	5,094,382
Operation and maintenance—plant	39,290,677	57,550
Depreciation	35,036,678	78,567
Student aid	9,759,658	3,073,024
Auxiliary activities (Note 11)	123,981,584	661,907
Total operating expenses	447,557,564	10,533,040
Operating loss	(76,926,240)	(3,492,996)
Nonoperating revenues/(expenses):		
State appropriations (Note 13)	82,188,926	–
Grants and contracts (Note 1 L.)	11,117,769	–
Gifts	847,606	–
Investment income (Net of investment expense of $11,762 for the University and $444,729 for the Foundation)	785,908	11,416,060
In-kind support from James Madison University	–	3,463,148
Interest on capital asset - related debt	(8,365,194)	(45,438)
Gain(Loss) on disposal of plant assets	(1,300,783)	–
Payment to the Commonwealth	(2,890,082)	–
Net nonoperating revenues/(expenses)	82,384,150	14,833,770
Income before other revenues, expenses, gains. or losses	5,457,910	11,340,774
Capital appropriations and contributions (Note 14)	42,411,324	–
Capital gifts	104,435	–
Additions to permanent endowments	–	3,169,548
Net other revenues	42,515,759	3,169,548
Increase in net position	47,973,669	14,510,322
Net position—beginning of year	713,735,127	92,475,745
Net position—end of year	$761,708,796	$106,986,067

The accompanying Notes to Financial Statements are an integral part of this statement.

JAMES MADISON UNIVERSITY
Statement of Cash Flows
For the Year Ended June 30, 2014

	2014
Cash flows from operating activities:	
Student tuition and fees	$ 177,185,743
Grants and contracts	28,222,240
Auxiliary enterprises	161,501,322
Other receipts	3,392,715
Payments for compensation and benefits	(235,225,167)

(*continued*)

EXHIBIT 12.8
(Continued)

	2014
Payments for services, supplies and utilities	(138,986,177)
Payments for scholarships and fellowships	(9,759,658)
Payments for noncapitalized plant improvements and equipment	(24,999,068)
Loans issued to students	(502,121)
Collections of loans from students	482,102
Net cash used by operating activities	(38,688,069)
Cash flows from noncapital financing activities:	
State appropriations	82,190,555
Nonoperating grants and contracts	10,697,170
Payment to the Commonwealth	(2,890,082)
Loans issued to students and employees.	(3,625)
Collections of loans from students and employees	3,520
Gifts and grants for other than capital purposes	847,606
Agency receipts.	104,997,405
Agency payments	(103,188,980)
Net cash provided by noncapital financing activities	92,653,569
Cash flows from capital and related financing activities:	
Capital appropriations and contributions	51,138,411
Proceeds from capital debt	49,979,361
Proceeds from sale of capital assets	53,430
Purchase of capital assets	(83,850,792)
Principal paid on capital debt, leases, and installments	(11,574,326)
Interest paid on capital debt, leases, and installments	(9,202,141)
Net cash used by capital financing activities	(3,456,057)
Cash flows from investing activities:	
Interest on investments	98,060
Interest on cash management pools	1,134,477
Net cash provided by investing activities	1,232,537
Net increase in cash	51,741,980
Cash and cash equivalents—beginning of the year	124,082,449
Cash and cash equivalents—end of the year.	$175,824,429

RECONCILIATION OF NET OPERATING LOSS TO NET CASH USED BY OPERATING ACTIVITIES:

Operating loss	$ (76,926,240)
Adjustments to reconcile net loss to net cash used by operating activities:	
Depreciation expense	35,036,678
Changes in assets and liabilities:	
Receivables, net	619,831
Due from the Commonwealth.	177,302
Prepaid expenses	1,773,297
Inventory	60,151
Notes receivable, net	(8,113)
Accounts payable and accrued expenses	1,323,289
Unearned revenue	(1,092,650)
Accrued compensated absences.	602,752
Accrued retirement plan.	(247,929)
Federal loan programs contributions refundable	(6,437)
Net cash used by operating activities	$ (38,688,069)

(continued)

EXHIBIT 12.8
(Continued)

NONCASH INVESTING, NONCAPITAL FINANCING, AND CAPITAL AND RELATED FINANCING TRANSACTIONS:	
Gift of capital assets	$ 104,435
Amortization of bond premium/discount and gain/loss on debt refinancing	(767,451)
Capitalization of interest revenue and expense, net.	(413,863)
Change in fair value of investments recognized as a component of interest income	68,623
Loss on disposal of capital assets	(1,354,212)

The accompanying Notes to Financial Statements are an integral part of this statement

Summary

1. GASB has established a hierarchy for the generally accepted accounting principles for state and local governments. Two categories of authoritative GAAP are listed. Category A is most important and includes GASB's official statements. Category B is composed of GASB Technical Bulletins, GASB Implementation Guides, and literature of the AICPA cleared by GASB. Sources of nonauthoritative accounting literature include GASB Concepts Statements and pronouncements and other literature of the Financial Accounting Standards Board, Federal Accounting Standards Advisory Board, and International Accounting Standards Board.

2. Governments can give tax breaks to entice desired actions by businesses and other taxpayers. These abatements limit the government's ability to collect tax money. To provide citizens and other interested parties with pertinent information about the actions of government officials, disclosure is required for tax abatements. These disclosures indicate the type of commitment that was made and the benefit expected in return.

3. Solid waste landfills create large potential debts for a government because of eventual closure and postclosure costs. Government-wide statements accrue a liability each period based on the latest current cost estimations and the portion of the property that has been filled to date. Fund financial statements report no expenditures until a claim to current financial resources is made.

4. State and local governments determine amounts to be reported for defined benefit pension plans. Future benefits that have been earned to date are estimated and the present value calculated. If the resulting obligation is greater than the net position held by the related pension trust fund, the excess is shown in government-wide statements as the net pension liability.

5. A state or local government that obtains a work of art or historical treasure normally records it as a capital asset on government-wide financial statements. However, if specified guidelines are met, an expense can replace recognition of the asset. Whether recorded as expense or asset, a state or local government that receives such a work of art or historical treasure through donation must still recognize revenue according to the rules established for voluntary nonexchange transactions. Fund financial statements for the governmental funds report no capital assets and, therefore, do not recognize these items except as expenditures if acquired.

6. Depreciation must be recorded each period for works of art and historical treasures that are capitalized unless they are judged to be inexhaustible.

7. Infrastructure assets are capitalized on government-wide financial statements. Depreciation is recorded over time unless the modified approach is applied. Under this method, a monitoring system is created to ensure that each network of infrastructure is maintained yearly at a predetermined condition. When applied, the cost of this upkeep is expensed by the government in lieu of recording depreciation.

8. A state or local government must include a management's discussion and analysis (MD&A) as part of its general purpose external financial reporting. As with for-profit businesses, this MD&A provides a verbal explanation of the government's operations and financial position.

9. A primary government produces a comprehensive annual financial report (CAFR). Both general purpose governments (such as states, cities, towns, counties, and the like) as well as any special purpose governments (such as some school systems and transit systems) that meet certain provisions are viewed as primary governments. A component unit is any function that is legally separate from a primary government but where financial accountability still exists. In government-wide statements, component units are either discretely presented to the right of the primary government or blended within the actual funds of the primary government.

10. A statement of net position and a statement of activities are prepared as government-wide financial statements based on the economic resources measurement focus and accrual accounting. These statements separate governmental activities from business-type activities. Internal service funds are usually included within the governmental activities. The statement of activities reports expenses by function along with related program revenues to determine the net expense or revenue resulting from each function. The government then lists the various general revenues to show its way of covering the net expenses of the various functions.

11. In fund financial statements reported for the governmental funds, the general fund and any other major fund are reported in separate columns. These statements are based on measuring current financial resources using modified accrual accounting. Additional statements are presented for proprietary funds and fiduciary funds.

12. Financial statements prepared by public colleges and universities must follow the same reporting guidelines as those created for state and local government units. As discussed in the following chapter, those statements will differ in several ways from the statements produced by private schools that follow FASB guidelines. Public schools are normally viewed as special purpose governments. They often assume that they are engaged only in business-type activities like an enterprise fund. Thus, such schools present only the fund financial statements of a proprietary fund.

Comprehensive Illustration

Problem

(*Estimated Time: 40 minutes*) The following is a series of transactions for a city. Indicate how the city reports each transaction within the government-wide financial statements and then on the fund financial statements. Assume that the city follows a policy of considering resources as available if they will be received within 60 days. Incurred liabilities are assumed to be claims to current resources if they will be paid within 60 days.

1. Borrowed money by issuing a 20-year bond for $3 million, its face value. This money is to be used to construct a highway around the city.

2. Transferred cash of $100,000 from the general fund to the debt service funds to make the first payment of principal and interest on the bond in (1).

3. Paid the cash in (2) on the bond. Of this total, $70,000 represents interest; the remainder reduces the principal of the bond payable.

4. Completed construction of the highway and paid the entire $3 million.

5. The highway (in 4) is expected to last 30 years. However, the government qualifies to use the modified approach, which it has adopted for this system. A $350,000 cost is incurred during the year to maintain the highway at an appropriate, predetermined condition. Of this amount, $290,000 was paid immediately, but the other $60,000 will not be paid until the sixth month of the subsequent year.

6. Received lights for the new highway donated from a local business. The lights are valued at $200,000 and should last 20 years. The modified approach is not used for this network of infrastructure. Straight-line depreciation is applied using the half-year convention.

7. Agreed to stop collecting property taxes from the Acme Company for eight years in exchange for the promise that a small manufacturing plant will be built within the city to generate capital investment and new job opportunities for the residents.

8. Recorded cash revenues of $2 million from the local subway system and made salary expense payments of $300,000 to its employees.

9. Opened a solid waste landfill at the beginning of the year that will be used for 20 years. This year an estimated 4 percent of the capacity was filled. The city anticipates closure, and postclosure requirements will be $2 million based on current cost figures although no costs have been incurred to date.

Solution

1. *Government-wide financial statements.* On the statement of net position under the governmental activities column, both cash and noncurrent liabilities increase by $3 million.

   Fund financial statements. The cash balance increases on the balance sheet by $3 million, whereas other financing sources increases by the same amount on the statement of revenues, expenditures, and changes in fund balances. These amounts will be shown in the other governmental funds column unless this particular capital projects fund is judged to be major so that a separate column is required.

2. *Government-wide financial statements.* No recording of this transfer is shown because the amount is an intra-activity transaction entirely carried out within the governmental activities.

Fund financial statements. The cash balance of the general fund on the balance sheet decreases while the cash listed for other governmental funds (or debt service fund) increases. On the statement of revenues, expenditures, and other changes in fund balances, the general fund shows an other financing use of $100,000, whereas the other governmental funds report an other financing source. These balances will not be offset in arriving at total figures.

3. *Government-wide financial statements.* On the statement of net position, cash for the governmental activities decreases by $100,000 and the total reported for noncurrent liabilities drops by $30,000 because of the principal payment. The statement of activities then recognizes $70,000 in interest expense as a governmental activity.

    Fund financial statements. First, cash decreases by $100,000 on the balance sheet under the other governmental funds (or debt service fund) column. Second, on the statement of revenues, expenditures, and changes in fund balances, a $30,000 principal expenditure is reported with a $70,000 interest expenditure. These amounts are shown within other governmental funds (or debt service fund).

4. *Government-wide financial statements.* Under the governmental activities listed on the statement of net position, cash decreases by $3 million and capital assets increases by the same amount. All new infrastructure costs are capitalized.

    Fund financial statements. On the balance sheet, cash reported for other governmental funds decreases. Again, if this particular capital projects fund qualifies as major, the effects are shown in a separate column rather than in the other governmental funds column. The statement of revenues, expenditures, and changes in fund balances reports a $3 million expenditure as a capital outlay.

5. *Government-wide financial statements.* The statement of net position reports a $290,000 decrease in cash under governmental activities and a $60,000 increase in a current liability. The statement of activities includes the $350,000 expense within an appropriate function such as public works. Because the modified approach is being applied, maintenance expense is recognized instead of depreciation expense.

    Fund financial statements. Because the $60,000 liability will not require the use of current financial resources (it will not be paid within 60 days), it is not recorded at this time at the fund level. Thus, the balance sheet reports only a $290,000 drop in cash, probably under the general fund. A $290,000 expenditure is recorded on the statement of revenues, expenditures, and changes in fund balances for public works.

6. *Government-wide financial statements.* The lights do not qualify as works of art or historical treasures and must therefore be reported as capital assets on the statement of net position at the $200,000 value. Based on a 20-year life and the half-year convention, $5,000 in accumulated depreciation must be recognized to reduce the reported net position balance to $195,000. For the statement of activities, a $200,000 revenue is appropriate unless eligibility requirements for the donation have not yet been fulfilled. This revenue should be shown as a program revenue (capital grants and contributions) to offset the expenses reported for public works. Depreciation of $5,000 should also be included as an expense for public works ($200,000/20 years × 0.5 year).

    Fund financial statements. No reporting is required because current financial resources were not affected.

7. *Government-wide financial statements and fund financial statements.* Tax abatement information should be disclosed and include the purpose of the tax abatement program, the tax being abated, dollar amount of taxes abated, the type of commitments made by the tax abatement recipients, and other commitments made by the government such as agreeing to build infrastructure assets like roads or sewer systems.

8. *Government-wide financial statements.* Cash reported on the statement of net position increases under the business-type activities by $1.7 million. The statement of activities reports expenses for the subway system as $300,000 while the related program revenues for charges for services rendered increase by $2 million so that the net revenue resulting from this business-type activity is $1.7 million.

    Fund financial statements. The statement of net position for the proprietary funds (see Exhibit 12.5) should include a separate column for the subway system, assuming that it qualifies as a major fund. Cash in this column increases by $1.7 million. Likewise, the statement of revenues, expenses, and changes in net position for the proprietary funds (see Exhibit 12.6) reports operating revenues of $2 million for the subway system. The list of operating expenses will include personnel services of $300,000. The statement of cash flows (see Exhibit 12.7) also reports both the inflow and outflow of cash under cash flows from operating activities.

9. *Government-wide financial statements.* Because the landfill is 4 percent filled and this is its first year of operations, that portion of the overall $2 million cost ($80,000) must be recognized. The statement of net position shows this amount as a noncurrent liability. The balance is presented as either a governmental activity or a business-type activity, depending on the landfill's fund classification. Likewise, the statement of activities reports the same $80,000 figure as an expense.

   Fund financial statements. This liability does not require the use of current financial resources and is not reported if the landfill is considered a governmental fund. However, if the landfill is viewed as an enterprise fund, the separate statements prepared for the proprietary funds include both the $80,000 expense and liability (see Exhibits 12.5 and 12.6).

Questions

1. Authoritative GAAP for state and local governments is divided into two categories with the first category having more authority than the second. What sources of GAAP are found in both of these categories?

2. The accountants for a city government are attempting to determine the appropriate method of reporting a series of unique financial transactions. They have reviewed all of the authoritative sources of GAAP and have not located an answer. What action should they take next?

3. Officials for the city of Winfield have agreed to forgo real estate taxes normally charged to Jamieson Corporation for the subsequent 10 years. In exchange, Jamieson has agreed to build a distribution facility that is expected to hire 500 new employees. What information must the city provide in its financial statements to inform taxpayers and other interested parties about the nature of this tax abatement?

4. Why does the operation of a solid waste landfill create reporting concerns for a local government?

5. A landfill is scheduled to be filled to capacity gradually over a 10-year period. However, at the end of the first year of operations, the landfill is only 7 percent filled. How much liability for closure and postclosure costs should be recognized on government-wide financial statements? How much liability should be recognized on fund financial statements assuming that the landfill is recorded in an enterprise fund? How much liability should be recognized on fund financial statements assuming that the landfill is recorded in the general fund?

6. The City of VanStone operates a solid waste landfill. This facility is 11 percent full after the first year of operation and 24 percent after the second year. How much expense should be recognized on the government-wide financial statements in the second year for closure costs? Assuming that the landfill is reported in the general fund, what expenditure should be recognized in the second year on the fund financial statements?

7. A teacher working for the City of Lights will be provided with a defined benefit pension plan. The city sets up a pension trust fund to monitor the resources held for these future payments. How is the amount of net pension liability to be reported in the government-wide financial statements determined?

8. The City of Ronchester has a defined benefit pension plan for its firefighters. How is the amount of pension expense determined that should be recognized in the current year?

9. A local citizen gives the City of Salem a painting by Picasso to display in city hall. Under what condition will the city *not* report this painting as a capital asset on its government-wide financial statements? If it does report the painting as a capital asset, must the city report depreciation?

10. Assume in question (9) that the city does not choose to report the painting on the government-wide financial statements as a capital asset. Must the city report a revenue for the gift?

11. Under what condition is the modified approach applied by a state or local government?

12. What impact does the use of the modified approach have on reporting within the government-wide financial statements?

13. What does the management's discussion and analysis (MD&A) normally include? Where does a state or local government present this information?

14. What does a comprehensive annual financial report (known as the CAFR) include?

15. A primary government can be either a general purpose government or a special purpose government. What is the difference in these two? How does an activity qualify as a special purpose government?

16. The Willingham Museum qualifies as a component unit of the City of Willingham. How does an activity or function meet the requirements to be deemed a component unit of a primary government?

17. What is the difference between a blended component unit and a discretely presented component unit?

18. What are the two government-wide financial statements? What does each normally present?

19. What are the two fund financial statements for governmental funds? What information does each normally present?

20. What is the difference in program revenues and general revenues? Why is that distinction important?

21. Why does a government determine the net expenses or revenues for each of the functions within its statement of activities?

22. How are internal service funds reported on government-wide financial statements?

23. In governmental accounting, what is the difference between an acquisition and a merger? What differences exist between the accounting for an acquisition and for a merger?

24. A general purpose government takes over a special purpose government in an acquisition. The consideration is larger than the acquisition value of all assets and liabilities. How is the excess reported?

25. What are some of the major differences that exist between private colleges and universities and public colleges and universities that affect financial reporting?

26. What is the most common form for the financial statements prepared by public colleges and universities?

Problems

LO 12-1

1. Which of the following has the least amount of official authority for the financial reporting of state and local governments?
   a. GASB Technical Bulletins.
   b. GASB Statements of Governmental Accounting Standards.
   c. GASB Concepts Statements.
   d. GASB Implementation Guides.

LO 12-1

2. City government officials are analyzing a complicated financial transaction. A GASB Implementation Guide seems to provide one reporting answer and a GASB Concepts Statement seems to provide a different answer. What reporting is most appropriate?
   a. The government can use either method and still be in conformity with GAAP.
   b. Government officials should follow the guidance provided by the GASB Implementation Guide.
   c. The city's financial statements must be in conformity with the GASB Concepts Statement.
   d. The city's accountants should seek some type of compromise that takes both of these pronouncements into consideration.

LO 12-1

3. The accountants for a city are attempting to determine the proper reporting for a new transaction so that the financial statements are in conformity with generally accepted accounting principles. No authoritative answer can be found. What should happen next?
   a. The city will receive a qualified audit report on its financial statements.
   b. The accountants can report the transaction in the way that they believe is best.
   c. The accountants should study other nonauthoritative sources such as GASB Concepts Statements and the official standards produced by FASB.
   d. The city will separate the transaction and report it separately in such a way as to draw attention to the method of reporting that was followed.

LO 12-3

4. A city agrees to allow the Jones Company to operate within its geographical boundaries without having to pay real estate taxes for the following 10 years. In exchange, Jones agrees to continue employing at least 120 people at all times. For this tax abatement, which of the following does the city not have to disclose?
   a. The party receiving the tax abatement.
   b. The purpose of the tax abatement program.
   c. Dollar amount of taxes abated.
   d. The tax being abated.

LO 12-3

5. A city provides a local business with a tax abatement so that real estate taxes will be avoided for the next five years. In exchange, the business agrees to construct a new facility to hire 50 or more individuals. How is this reported?
   a. Only on the government-wide financial statements.
   b. Only on the fund financial statements.
   c. On both the government-wide and fund financial statements.
   d. Only as a footnote disclosure.

LO 12-3

6. A city creates a solid waste landfill. It assesses a charge to every person or company that uses the landfill based on the amount of materials contributed. In which of the following will the landfill probably be recorded?
   a. General fund.
   b. Special revenues funds.
   c. Internal service funds.
   d. Enterprise funds.

Use the following information for problems 7, 8, and 9

A city starts a solid waste landfill that it expects to fill to capacity gradually over a 10-year period. At the end of the first year, it is 8 percent filled. At the end of the second year, it is 19 percent filled. Currently, the cost of closure and postclosure is estimated at $1 million. None of this amount will be paid until the landfill has reached its capacity.

LO 12-3

7. Which of the following is true for the Year 2 government-wide financial statements?
   a. Both expense and liability will be zero.
   b. Both expense and liability will be $110,000.
   c. Expense will be $110,000 and liability will be $190,000.
   d. Expense will be $100,000 and liability will be $200,000.

LO 12-3

8. If this landfill is judged to be a proprietary fund, what liability will be reported at the end of the second year on fund financial statements?
   a. $–0–
   b. $110,000
   c. $190,000
   d. $200,000

LO 12-3

9. If this landfill is judged to be a governmental fund, what liability will be reported at the end of the second year on fund financial statements?
   a. $–0–
   b. $110,000
   c. $190,000
   d. $200,000

LO 12-4

10. The City of Nomanchester has a defined benefit pension plan for a number of its employees. A pension trust fund has been set up that currently has a net position of $32.7 million because quite a number of investments are being held. An actuary estimates that employees will eventually receive $99.7 million as a result of this pension. However, only $72.4 million of that amount is for past work that has been provided. The present value of the $72.4 million in payments is $49.8 million. On its government-wide financial statements, what amount of net pension liability should be reported?
    a. Zero
    b. $17.1 million
    c. $39.7 million
    d. $67.0 million

LO 12-4

11. The City of Huble has a defined benefit pension plan for a number of its employees. Which of the following is not included immediately in the determination of pension expense that this government should recognize in its government-wide financial statements?
    a. Service cost.
    b. Interest on total pension liability.
    c. Changes in pension liability as a result of a change in benefit terms.
    d. Changes in pension liability as a result of a change in economic or demographic assumptions.

LO 12-5

12. The City of Wilson receives a large sculpture valued at $240,000 as a gift to be placed in front of the municipal building. Which of the following is true for reporting the gift within the government-wide financial statements?
    a. A capital asset of $240,000 must be reported.
    b. No capital asset will be reported.
    c. If conditions are met, recording the sculpture as a capital asset is optional.
    d. The sculpture will be recorded but only for the amount paid by the city.

LO 12-5

13. In Problem 12, which of the following statements is true about reporting a revenue in connection with this gift?
    a. A revenue will be reported.
    b. Revenue is reported but only if the asset is reported.
    c. If the asset is not capitalized, no revenue should be recognized.
    d. As a gift, no revenue would ever be reported.

LO 12-5

14. Assume in Problem 12 that the city reports the work as a capital asset. Which of the following is true?
    a. Depreciation is not recorded because the city has no cost.
    b. Depreciation is not required if the asset is viewed as being inexhaustible.
    c. Depreciation must be recognized because the asset is capitalized.
    d. Because the property was received as a gift, recognition of depreciation is optional.

LO 12-6

15. A city builds sidewalks throughout its various neighborhoods at a cost of $2.1 million. Which of the following is *not* true?
    a. Because the sidewalks qualify as infrastructure, the asset is viewed in the same way as land so that no depreciation is recorded.
    b. Depreciation is required unless the modified approach is utilized.
    c. The modified approach recognizes maintenance expense in lieu of depreciation expense for qualifying infrastructure assets.
    d. The modified approach is allowed only if the city maintains the network of sidewalks at least at a predetermined condition.

LO 12-6

16. Which of the following is true about use of the modified approach?
    a. It can be applied to all capital assets of a state or local government.
    b. It is used to adjust depreciation expense either up or down based on conditions for the period.
    c. It is required for infrastructure assets.
    d. For qualified assets, it eliminates the recording of depreciation.

LO 12-7

17. Which of the following is true about the management's discussion and analysis (MD&A)?
    a. It is an optional addition to the comprehensive annual financial report, but the GASB encourages its inclusion.
    b. It adds a verbal explanation for the numbers and trends presented in the financial statements.
    c. It appears at the very end of a government's comprehensive annual financial report.
    d. It replaces a portion of the fund financial statements traditionally presented by a state or local government.

LO 12-8

18. Which of the following is *not* necessary for a special purpose local government to be viewed as a primary government for reporting purposes?
    a. It must have a separately elected governing body.
    b. It must have specifically defined geographic boundaries.
    c. It must be fiscally independent.
    d. It must have corporate powers to prove that it is legally independent.

LO 12-8

19. An accountant is trying to determine whether the school system of the City of Abraham is fiscally independent. Which of the following is *not* a requirement for being deemed fiscally independent?
    a. Holding property in its own name.
    b. Issuing bonded debt without outside approval.
    c. Passing its own budget without outside approval.
    d. Setting taxes or rates without outside approval.

LO 12-8

20. An employment agency for individuals with disabilities works closely with the City of Hanover. The employment agency is legally separate from the city but still depends on it for financial support, which leads to a potential financial burden for the city. How should Hanover report the employment agency in its comprehensive annual financial report?
    a. Not at all because the agency is legally separate.
    b. As a part of the general fund.
    c. As a component unit.
    d. As a related organization.

LO 12-8

21. The City of Bacon is located in the County of Pork. The city has a school system and reports buildings at a net $3.6 million although they are actually worth $4.2 million. The county has another school system and reports buildings at a net $5.2 million although they are actually worth $5.6 million. Both school systems are viewed as special purpose governments. If the school systems are combined in a merger, what should be reported for the buildings?
    a. $8.6 million
    b. $8.8 million
    c. $9.4 million
    d. $9.8 million

LO 12-8

22. For component units, what is the difference in *discrete presentation* and *blending?*
    a. A blended component unit is shown to the left of the statements; a discretely presented component unit is shown to the right.
    b. A blended component unit is shown at the bottom of the statements; a discretely presented component unit is shown within the statements like a fund.
    c. A blended component unit is shown within the statements like a fund; a discretely presented component unit is shown to the right.
    d. A blended component unit is shown to the right of the statements; a discretely presented component unit is shown in completely separate statements.

LO 12-9

23. A government reports that its public safety function had expenses of $900,000 last year and program revenues of $200,000 so that its net expenses were $700,000. On which financial statement is this information presented?
    a. Statement of activities.
    b. Statement of cash flows.
    c. Statement of revenues and expenditures.
    d. Statement of net position.

LO 12-9

24. Government-wide financial statements make a distinction between program revenues and general revenues. How is that difference shown?
    a. Program revenues are offset against the expenses of a specific function; general revenues are assigned to governmental activities and business-type activities in general.
    b. General revenues are shown at the top of the statement of revenues and expenditures; program revenues are shown at the bottom.
    c. General revenues are labeled as operating revenues; program revenues are shown as miscellaneous income.
    d. General revenues are broken down by type; program revenues are reported as a single figure for the government.

LO 12-9

25. Which of the following is true about the statement of cash flows for the proprietary funds of a state or local government?
    a. The indirect method of reporting cash flows from operating activities is allowed although the direct method is recommended.
    b. The structure of the statement is virtually identical to that of a for-profit business.
    c. The statement is divided into four separate sections of cash flows.
    d. Amounts spent on capital assets are reported in a separate section from amounts raised to finance those capital assets.

LO 12-10

26. Which of the following is most likely to be true about the financial reporting of a public college or university?
    a. It resembles the financial reporting of private colleges and universities.
    b. It will continue to use its own unique style of financial reporting.
    c. It resembles the financial reporting made by a proprietary fund within the fund financial statements for a state or local government.
    d. It will soon be reported using a financial statement format unique to the needs of public colleges and universities that GASB is scheduled to create.

LO 12-3

27. On January 1, 2017, the City of Hastings created a solid waste landfill that it expects to reach capacity gradually over the next 20 years. If the landfill were to be closed at the current time, closure costs would be approximately $1.2 million plus an additional $700,000 for postclosure work. Of these totals, the city must pay $50,000 on December 31 of each year for preliminary closure work.

At the end of 2017, the landfill reached 3 percent of capacity. At the end of 2018, the landfill reached 9 percent of capacity. Also at the end of 2018, a reassessment is made; total closure costs are determined to be $1.4 million rather than $1.2 million.

a. Assuming that the landfill is viewed as an enterprise fund, what journal entries are made in 2017 and 2018 on the government-wide financial statements?

b. Assuming that the landfill is reported within the general fund, what journal entries are made in 2017 and 2018 on the government-wide financial statements?

c. Assuming that the landfill is viewed as an enterprise fund, what journal entries are made in 2017 and 2018 on fund financial statements?

d. Assuming that the landfill is reported within the general fund, what journal entries are made in 2017 and 2018 on fund financial statements?

LO 12-3

28. The City of Lawrence opens a solid waste landfill in 2017 that is at 54 percent of capacity on December 31, 2017. The city had initially anticipated closure costs of $2 million but later that year decided that closure costs would actually be $2.4 million. None of these costs will be incurred until 2021 when the landfill is scheduled to be closed.

a. What will appear on the government-wide financial statements for this landfill for the year ended December 31, 2017?

b. Assuming that the landfill is recorded within the general fund, what will appear on the fund financial statements for this landfill for the year ended December 31, 2017?

LO 12-4

29. The City of Columbus has approximately 2,000 employees. For the past three decades, the city has provided its employees with a defined benefit pension plan. The plan contract calls for specific payment amounts to be made to each retiree based on a set formula. Money is transferred periodically to a pension trust fund where it is accumulated and invested so that eventual payments can be made.

a. Describe how the city determines the amount (if any) of a net pension liability that should be reported within its government-wide financial statements.

b. Describe how the city determines the amount (if any) of pension expense that should be reported within its government-wide financial statements.

c. How is the pension reported in the fund financial statements for the governmental funds?

LO 12-5

30. On January 1, 2017, a rich citizen of the Town of Ristoni donates a painting valued at $300,000 to be displayed to the public in a government building. Although this painting meets the three criteria to qualify as an artwork, town officials choose to record it as an asset. There are no eligibility requirements for the gift. The asset is judged to be inexhaustible so that depreciation will not be reported.

a. For the year ended December 31, 2017, what will be reported on government-wide financial statements in connection with this gift?

b. How does the answer to requirement (a) change if the government decides to depreciate this asset over a 10-year period using straight-line depreciation?

c. How does the answer to requirement (a) change if the government decides not to capitalize the asset?

LO 12-5

31. On January 1, 2017, the City of Graf pays $60,000 for a work of art to display in the local library. The city will take appropriate measures to protect and preserve the piece. However, if the work is ever sold, the money received will go into unrestricted funds. The work is viewed as inexhaustible, but the city has opted to depreciate this cost over 20 years (using the straight-line method).

a. How is this work to be reported on the government-wide financial statements for the year ended December 31, 2017?

b. How is this work to be reported in the fund financial statements for the year ended December 31, 2017?

LO 12-6

32. A city government adds street lights within its boundaries at a total cost of $300,000. The lights should burn for at least 10 years but can last significantly longer if maintained properly. The city sets up a system to monitor these lights with the goal that 97 percent will be working at any one time. During the year, the city spends $48,000 to clean and repair the lights so that they are working according to the specified conditions. However, it spends another $78,000 to construct lights for several new streets in the city.

Describe the various ways these costs could be reported on government-wide statements.

LO 12-7

33. The City of Francois, Texas, has begun the process of producing its current comprehensive annual financial report (CAFR). Several organizations that operate within the city are related in some way

to the primary government. The city's accountant is attempting to determine how these organizations should be included in the reporting process.

a. What is the major criterion for inclusion in a government's CAFR?

b. How does an activity or function qualify as a special purpose government?

c. How is the legal separation of a special purpose government evaluated?

d. How is the fiscal independence of a special purpose government evaluated?

e. What is a component unit, and how is it normally reported on government-wide financial statements?

f. How does a primary government prove that it can impose its will on a component unit?

g. What is meant by the blending of a component unit?

LO 12-4

34. The County of Maxnell decides to create a sanitation department and offer its services to the public for a fee. As a result, county officials plan to account for this activity within the enterprise funds. Prepare journal entries for this operation for the following 2017 transactions as well as necessary adjusting entries at the end of the year. Assume the information is being gathered to prepare fund financial statements. Only entries for the sanitation department are required here:

January 1—Received unrestricted funds of $160,000 from the general fund as permanent financing.

February 1—Borrowed an additional $130,000 from a local bank at a 12 percent annual interest rate.

March 1—Ordered a truck at an expected cost of $108,000.

April 1—Received the truck and made full payment. The actual cost amounted to $110,000. The truck has a 10-year life and no salvage value. Straight-line depreciation is to be used.

May 1—Received a $20,000 cash grant from the state to help supplement the pay of the sanitation workers. The money must be used for that purpose.

June 1—Rented a garage for the truck at a cost of $1,000 per month and paid 12 months of rent in advance.

July 1—Charged citizens $13,000 for services. Of this amount, $11,000 has been collected.

August 1—Made a $10,000 cash payment on the 12 percent note of February 1. This payment covers both interest and principal.

September 1—Paid salaries of $18,000 using the grant received on May 1.

October 1—Paid truck maintenance costs of $1,000.

November 1—Paid additional salaries of $10,000, first using the rest of the grant money received May 1.

December 31—Sent invoices totaling $19,000 to customers for services over the past six months. Collected $3,000 cash immediately.

December 31—A new landfill was opened this year. It is 12 percent filled as of the end of the year. The estimated current cost for the eventual closure of this facility is $4 million although no payments will be made for approximately 9 years.

LO 12-5, 12-7, 12-9

35. The following information pertains to the City of Williamson for 2017, its first year of legal existence. For convenience, assume that all transactions are for the general fund, which has three separate functions: general government, public safety, and health and sanitation.

Receipts:
Property taxes $320,000
Franchise taxes 42,000
Charges for general government services 5,000
Charges for public safety services 3,000
Charges for health and sanitation services 42,000
Issued long-term note payable 200,000
Receivables at end of year:
Property taxes (90% estimated to be collectible) 90,000
Payments:
Salary:
General government 66,000
Public safety 39,000
Health and sanitation 22,000

(*continued*)

Rent:

General government	11,000
Public safety	18,000
Health and sanitation	3,000

Maintenance:

General government	21,000
Public safety	5,000
Health and sanitation	9,000

Insurance:

General government	8,000
Public safety ($2,000 still prepaid at end of year)	11,000
Health and sanitation	12,000
Interest on debt	16,000
Principal payment on debt	4,000
Storage shed	120,000
Equipment	80,000
Supplies (20% still held) (public safety)	15,000
Investments	90,000

Ordered but not received:

Equipment	12,000

Due in one month at end of year:

Salaries:

General government	4,000
Public safety	7,000
Health and sanitation	8,000

Compensated absences (such as vacations and sick days) legally owed to general government workers at year-end total $13,000. These amounts will not be taken by the employees until so late in 2018 that the payment is not viewed as requiring 2017 current financial resources.

The city received a piece of art this year as a donation. It is valued at $14,000. It will be used for general government purposes. There are no eligibility requirements. The city chose not to capitalize this property.

The general government uses the storage shed that was acquired this year. It is being depreciated over 10 years using the straight-line method with no salvage value. The city uses the equipment for health and sanitation and depreciates it using the straight-line method over five years with no salvage value.

The investments are valued at $103,000 at the end of the year.

For the equipment that has been ordered but not yet received, the City Council (the highest decision-making body in the government) has voted to honor the commitment when the equipment is received.

  a. Prepare a statement of activities and a statement of net position for governmental activities for December 31, 2017, and the year then ended.

  b. Prepare a statement of revenues, expenditures, and other changes in fund balances and a balance sheet for the general fund as of December 31, 2017, and the year then ended. Assume that the city applies the consumption method.

LO 12-2, 12-4, 12-8, 12-10

36. The City of Bernard starts the year of 2017 with the following unrestricted amounts in its general fund: cash of $20,000 and investments of $70,000. In addition, it holds a small building bought on January 1, 2016, for general government purposes for $300,000 and related long-term debt of $240,000. The building is being depreciated on the straight-line method over 10 years. The interest rate is 10 percent. The general fund has four separate functions: general government, public safety, public works, and health and sanitation. Other information includes the following:

Receipts:

Property taxes	$510,000
Sales taxes	99,000
Dividend income	20,000
Charges for general government services	15,000
Charges for public safety services	8,000
Charges for public works	4,000

(continued)

Charges for health and sanitation services.	31,000
Charges for landfill.	8,000
Grant to be used for salaries for health workers	
(no eligibility requirements)	25,000
Issued long-term note payable	200,000
Sold above investments	84,000

Receivables at year-end:

Property taxes ($10,000 is expected to be uncollectible).	130,000

Payments:

Salary:

General government.	90,000
Public safety	94,000
Public works	69,000
Health and sanitation (all from grant)	22,000

Utilities:

General government.	9,000
Public safety	16,000
Public works	13,000
Health and sanitation	4,000

Insurance:

General government.	25,000
Public safety	12,000
Public works (all prepaid as of the end of the year)	6,000
Health and sanitation	4,000

Miscellaneous:

General government.	12,000
Public safety	10,000
Public works	9,000
Health and sanitation	7,000
Interest on previous debt.	24,000
Principal payment on previous debt.	10,000
Interest on new debt.	18,000
Building (public works)	210,000
Equipment (public safety).	90,000
Public works supplies (30% still held).	20,000
Investments.	111,000

Ordered but not received:

Equipment.	24,000
Supplies.	7,000

Due at end of year:

Salaries:

General government.	14,000
Public safety	17,000
Public works	5,000

On the last day of the year, the city borrowed $64,000 from a local bank and used that money to buy a truck. The first payment on the loan (plus interest) will be made at the end of the next year.

The city started a landfill this year that it is recording within its general fund. It is included as a public works function. Closure costs today would be $260,000 although the landfill is not expected to be filled for nine more years. The city has incurred no costs to date although the landfill is now 15 percent filled.

For the equipment and supplies that have been ordered but not yet received, the City Council (the highest decision-making body in the government) has voted to honor the commitment when the items are received.

The new building is being depreciated over 20 years using the straight-line method and no salvage value, whereas depreciation of the equipment is similar except that its life is only 10 years. Assume the city records a full year's depreciation in the year of acquisition.

The investments are valued at $116,000 at year-end.

- a. Prepare a statement of activities and a statement of net position for governmental activities for December 31, 2017, and the year then ended.
- b. Prepare a statement of revenues, expenditures, and other changes in fund balances and a balance sheet for the general fund as of December 31, 2017, and the year then ended. Assume that the purchases method is being applied.

LO 12-6, 12-7, 12-8, 12-10
37. The City of Pfeiffer starts the year of 2017 with the general fund and an enterprise fund. The general fund has two activities: education and parks/recreation. For convenience, assume that the general fund holds $123,000 cash and a new school building costing $1 million. The city utilizes straight-line depreciation. The building has a 20-year life and no salvage value. The enterprise fund has $62,000 cash and a new $600,000 civic auditorium with a 30-year life and no salvage value. The enterprise fund monitors just one activity, the rental of the civic auditorium for entertainment and other cultural affairs.

The following transactions for the city take place during 2017. Assume that the city's fiscal year ends on December 31.

- a. Decides to build a municipal park and transfers $70,000 into a capital projects fund and immediately expends $20,000 for a piece of land. The creation of this fund and this transfer were made by the highest level of government authority.
- b. Borrows $110,000 cash on a long-term bond for use in creating the new municipal park.
- c. Assesses property taxes on the first day of the year. The assessment, which is immediately enforceable, totals $600,000. Of this amount, $510,000 will be collected during 2017 and another $50,000 is expected in the first month of 2018. The remainder is expected about half-way through 2018.
- d. Constructs a building in the park in (b) for $80,000 cash so that local citizens can play basketball and other sports. It is put into service on July 1 and should last 10 years with no salvage value.
- e. Builds a sidewalk around the new park for $10,000 cash and puts it into service on July 1. It should last for 10 years, but the city plans to keep it up to a predetermined quality level so that it will last almost indefinitely.
- f. Opens the park and charges an entrance fee of only a token amount so that it records the park, therefore, in the general fund. Collections during this first year total $8,000.
- g. Buys a new parking deck for $200,000, paying $20,000 cash and signing a long-term note for the rest. The parking deck, which is to go into operation on July 1, is across the street from the civic auditorium and is considered part of that activity. It has a 20-year life and no salvage value.
- h. Receives a $100,000 cash grant for the city school system that must be spent for school lunches for the poor. Appropriate spending of these funds is viewed as an eligibility requirement of this grant. During the current year, $37,000 of the amount received was properly spent.
- i. Charges students in the school system a total fee of $6,000 for books and the like. Of this amount, 90 percent is collected during 2017 with the remainder expected to be collected in the first few weeks of 2018.
- j. Buys school supplies for $22,000 cash and uses $17,000 of them. The general fund uses the purchases method.
- k. Receives a painting by a local artist to be displayed in the local school. It qualifies as a work of art, and officials have chosen not to capitalize it. The painting has a value of $80,000. It is viewed as inexhaustible.
- l. Transfers $20,000 cash from the general fund to the enterprise fund as a capital contribution.
- m. Orders a school bus for $99,000.
- n. Receives the school bus and pays an actual cost of $102,000. The bus is put into operation on October 1 and should last for five years with no salvage value.
- o. Pays salaries of $240,000 to school teachers. In addition, owes and will pay $30,000 during the first two weeks of 2018. Vacations worth $23,000 have also been earned but will not be taken until July 2018.
- p. Pays salaries of $42,000 to city auditorium workers. In addition, owes and will pay $3,000 in the first two weeks of 2018. Vacations worth $5,000 have also been earned but will not be taken until July 2018.
- q. Charges customers $130,000 for the rental of the civic auditorium. Of this balance, collected $110,000 in cash and will collect the remainder in April 2018.

r. Pays $9,000 maintenance charges for the building and sidewalk in (*d*) and (*e*).

s. Pays $14,000 on the bond in (*b*) on the last day of 2017: $5,000 principal and $9,000 interest.

t. Accrues interest of $13,000 on the note in (*g*) as of the end of 2017, an amount that it will pay in June 2018.

u. Assumes that a museum that operates within the city is a component unit that will be discretely presented. The museum reports to city officials that it had $42,000 of direct expenses this past year and $50,000 in revenues from admission charges. The only assets that it had at year-end were cash of $24,000, building (net of depreciation) of $300,000, and a long-term liability of $210,000.

Prepare the 2017 government-wide financial statements for this city. Assume the use of the modified approach.

LO 12-6, 12-7, 12-8, 12-10

38. Use the information in problem 37 to prepare the 2017 fund financial statements for the governmental funds and the proprietary funds. A statement of cash flows is not required. Assume that "available" is defined as within 60 days and that all funds are major. The general fund is used for debt repayment. Assume that major funds are labeled as "Special Revenue Fund" and "Capital Projects Fund."

LO 12-4, 12-5, 12-8, 12-10

39. For each of the following, indicate whether the statement is true or false and include a brief explanation for your answer.

a. A pension trust fund appears in the government-wide financial statements but not in the fund financial statements.

b. Permanent funds are included as one of the governmental funds.

c. A fire department placed orders of $20,000 for equipment. The equipment is received but at a cost of $20,800. In compliance with requirements for fund financial statements, an encumbrance of $20,000 was recorded when the order was placed, and an expenditure of $20,800 was recorded when the order was received.

d. The government reported a landfill as an enterprise fund. At the end of Year 1, the government estimated that the landfill will cost $800,000 to clean up when it is eventually full. Currently, it is 12 percent filled. At the end of Year 2, the estimation was changed to $860,000 when it was 20 percent filled. No payments are due for several years. Fund financial statements for Year 2 should report a $76,000 expense.

e. A city reports a landfill in the general fund. At the end of Year 1, the government anticipated the landfill would cost $900,000 to clean up when it is full and reported that it was 11 percent filled. At the end of Year 2, the estimates were changed to $850,000 and 20 percent filled. No payments are due for several years. Government-wide financial statements for Year 2 should report a $71,000 expense.

f. An agency fund has neither revenues nor expenditures but reports expenses.

For problems 40 through 43, use the following introductory information:

The City of Wolfe has issued its financial statements for Year 4 (assume that the city uses a calendar year). The city's general fund is made up of two functions: (1) education and (2) parks. The city also utilizes capital projects funds for ongoing construction and an enterprise fund to account for an art museum. It also has one discretely presented component unit.

The government-wide financial statements indicated the following Year 4 totals:

Education had net expenses of $710,000.

Parks had net expenses of $130,000.

Art museum had net revenues of $80,000.

General revenues were $900,000; the overall increase in net position was $140,000.

The fund financial statements issued for Year 4 indicated the following:

The general fund had an increase of $30,000 in its fund balance.

The capital projects fund had an increase of $40,000 in its fund balance.

The enterprise fund had an increase of $60,000 in its net position.

Officials for Wolfe define "available" as current financial resources to be paid or collected within 60 days.

LO 12-5

40. On the first day of Year 4, the city receives a painting as a gift that qualifies as a work of art. It has a 30-year life, is worth $15,000, and is being displayed at one of the local parks. The accountant accidentally capitalized and depreciated it although officials had wanted to use the allowed alternative.

Respond to the following questions:

a. According to the information provided above, the general fund reported a $30,000 increase in its fund balance. If city officials had used proper alternatives in this reporting, what would have been the correct change in the fund balance for the general fund for the year?

b. According to the information provided above, the parks reported net expenses of $130,000. If city officials had used proper alternatives in this reporting, what was the correct net expense for parks for the year?

c. Assume the same information except that the art was given to the art museum but not recorded at all. What should have been the overall change in net position for Year 4 on government-wide financial statements, assuming that officials still preferred the allowed alternative?

LO 12-8

41. Assume that the one component unit had program revenues of $30,000 and expenses of $42,000 and spent $10,000 for land during Year 4. However, it should have been handled as a blended component unit, not as a discretely presented component unit. According to the information provided above, the overall increase in net position reported was $140,000. What was the correct overall change in the net position in the government-wide financial statements?

LO 12-3

42. The city maintains a landfill that has been recorded during the current year within its parks. The landfill generated program revenues of $4,000 in Year 4 and cash expenses of $15,000. It also paid $3,000 cash for a piece of land. These transactions were recorded as would have been anticipated, but no other recording was made this year. The city assumes that it will have to pay $200,000 to clean up the landfill when it is closed in several years. The landfill was 18 percent filled at the end of Year 3 and is 26 percent filled at the end of Year 4. No payments will be necessary for several more years. For convenience, assume that the entries in all previous years were correctly handled regardless of the situation.

a. The city believes that the landfill was included correctly in all previous years as one of its enterprise funds. According to the information provided, the overall increase in net position reported was $140,000. What is the correct overall change in the net position in the government-wide financial statements?

b. The city believes that the landfill was included correctly in all previous years in one of the enterprise funds. According to the information provided, the enterprise fund reported an increase in its net position of $60,000. What is the correct change in the net position of the enterprise fund in the fund financial statements?

c. The city believes that the landfill was included correctly in all previous years within the general fund. What is the correct change in the fund balance of the general fund?

LO 12-7, 12-9

43. On the first day of the year, the City of Wolfe bought $20,000 of equipment with a 5-year life and no salvage value for its school system. It was capitalized but no other entries were ever made. The machine was monitored using the modified approach.

a. Based on the information provided above, what was the correct overall change in the net position in the government-wide financial statements?

b. What was the correct amount of net expenses for education in the government-wide statements?

LO 12-3

44. A city has a solid waste landfill that was filled 12 percent in Year 1 and 26 percent in Year 2. During those periods, the government expected that total closure costs would be $2 million. As a result, it paid $50,000 to an environmental company on July 1 of each of these two years. Such payments will continue for several years to come. Indicate whether each of the following *independent* statements is true or false and briefly explain each answer. The city has a December 31 year-end.

a. The government-wide financial statements will show a $230,000 expense in Year 2 but only if reported in an enterprise fund.

b. The fund financial statements will show a $50,000 liability in Year 2 if this landfill is reported in the general fund.

c. The fund financial statements will show a $50,000 liability at the end of Year 2 if this landfill is reported in an enterprise fund.

d. If this landfill is reported in an enterprise fund, the government-wide financial statements and the fund financial statements will basically have the same reporting.

e. The government-wide financial statements will show a $420,000 liability at the end of Year 2.

f. Over the landfill's entire life, the amount of expense recognized in the government-wide financial statements will be the same as the amount of expenditures recognized in the fund financial statements. Assume the landfill is reported in the general fund.

LO 12-3

45. Use the same information as in problem 44 except that, by the end of Year 3, the landfill is 40 percent filled. The city now realizes that the total closure costs will be $3 million. Indicate

whether each of the following *independent* statements is true or false and briefly explain each answer.

a. If the city had known the costs were going to be $3 million from the beginning, the reporting on the fund financial statements would have been different in the past years if the landfill had been reported in an enterprise fund.

b. If the landfill is monitored in the general fund, a liability will be reported for the governmental activities in the government-wide financial statements at the end of Year 3.

c. A $680,000 expense should be recognized in Year 3 in the government-wide financial statements.

d. Because the closure costs reflect a future flow of cash, any liability reported in the government-wide financial statements must be reported at present value.

LO 12-5

46. A city receives a copy of its original charter from the year 1799 as a gift from a citizen. The document will be put under glass and displayed in the city hall for all to see. The fair value is estimated at $10,000. Indicate whether each of the following *independent* statements is true or false and briefly explain each answer.

a. If the city government does not have a policy for handling any proceeds if it ever sells the document, the city must report a $10,000 asset within its government-wide financial statements.

b. Assume that this gift qualifies for optional handling and that the city chooses to report it as an asset. For the government-wide financial statements, depreciation is required.

c. Assume this gift qualifies for optional handling and the document is deemed to be exhaustible. The city must report an immediate expense of $10,000 in the government-wide financial statements.

d. Assume that this gift qualifies for optional handling. The city must make a decision as to whether to recognize a revenue of $10,000 in the government-wide financial statements.

e. Assume that this gift qualifies for optional handling. The city can choose to report the gift in the statement of net activities for the government-wide financial statements in a way so that there is no overall net effect.

LO 12-8

47. A city starts a public library that has separate incorporation and gets some of its money for operations from the state and some from private donations. Indicate whether each of the following *independent* statements is true or false and briefly explain each answer.

a. If the city appoints 9 of the 10 directors, it must report the library as a component unit.

b. If the library is a component unit and its financial results are shown as part of the governmental activities of the city, it is known as a *blended component unit*.

c. If the library appoints its own board but the city must approve its budget, the library must be reported as a blended component unit.

LO 12-5, 12-6, 12-8, 12-9

48. The City of Dickens has a fiscal year ending December 31, Year 5. The city council is viewed as the highest level of decision-making authority for the government. For each of the following, indicate whether the overall statement is true or false. Assume that each situation is independent of all others.

a. On December 30, Year 5, the city spends $900,000 on a sidewalk project that is not a special assessment. On the Year 5 financial statements, a reconciliation is presented that starts with the total change in fund balances for the governmental funds and works down to end with the total change in net position for the governmental activities. As a result of this acquisition, this $900,000 must be subtracted as part of this reconciliation.

b. All members of the board of directors for a nature museum are appointed by the city. This fact alone makes this nature museum a component unit of the city.

c. The city appoints none of the governing board of a parks commission. This fact alone prohibits this parks commission from being a component unit of the city.

d. The city has a school system with a separately elected governing board (elected by the public). This fact alone makes the school system a special purpose government with its own financial reporting to be made.

e. The modified approach applies only to infrastructure assets.

f. The modified approach has become widely used in state and local government accounting over the last few years.

g. The city's school system charges students a $10 per person fee each year. In the statement of activities, this fee should be shown as miscellaneous revenue directly under the general revenues.

h. The city receives a work of art worth $100,000 as a gift and also spends $70,000 in cash to buy a second art work. Both art works will be exhibited publicly and properly protected and preserved. The city council passes a resolution that if either item is ever sold the proceeds will be used to buy replacement art works. Both of the art works are viewed as inexhaustible. The city has the option to report both of these pieces of art as expenses rather than as assets in the government-wide financial statements.

i. Assume that the city issues 30-day revenue anticipation notes on December 30, Year 5, to finance the government until new taxes are collected. These notes are issued at their face value of $500,000. On the Year 5 financial statements, there is a reconciliation that starts with the total change in fund balances for the governmental funds and works down to end with the total change in the net position for the governmental activities. As a result of the bond issuance, this $500,000 must be subtracted as part of this reconciliation.

Develop Your Skills

RESEARCH CASE 1

The City of Abernethy has three large bridges built in the later part of the 1980s that were not capitalized at the time. In creating government-wide financial statements, the city's accountant is interested in receiving suggestions as to how to determine a valid amount to report currently for these bridges.

Required

Use a copy of the GASB *Codification of Governmental Accounting and Financial Reporting Standards* as the basis for writing a report to this accountant to indicate various ways to make this calculation. Use the Topical Index or skim Section 1400 which covers "Reporting Capital Assets." Use examples that will help illustrate the process.

RESEARCH CASE 2

Officials for the City of Artichoke, West Virginia, have recently formed a transit authority to create a public transportation system for the community. These same officials are now preparing the city's CAFR for the most recent year. The transit authority has already lost a considerable amount of money and the officials have become interested in its reporting and whether it qualifies as a component unit of the city.

Following are several articles written about the reporting of component units by a state or local government:

"Changes in Component Units," *Government Finance Review,* February 2011.

"GASB Issues Guidance on Financial Reporting Entity, Component Units," *Accounting Policy & Practice Report,* January 7, 2011.

"Financial Reporting for Affiliated Organizations," *The Journal of Government Financial Management,* Winter 2003.

"How to Implement GASB *Statement No. 34,*" *The Journal of Accountancy,* November 2001.

"GASB Issues Guidance on Blending Certain Component Units into Financial Statements," *Investment Weekly News,* February 27, 2016.

"Accounting for Affiliated Organizations," *Government Finance Review,* December 2002.

"Component Unit Reporting in the New Reporting Model," *The CPA Journal,* October 2001.

Required

Read one or more of the above articles and any others that you may discover about component units. Write a memo to these city officials providing as much detailed information about component units and their reporting as you can to help these individuals understand the challenges and difficulties of this reporting.

ANALYSIS CASE 1

Read the following journal article: "25 Years of State and Local Governmental Financial Reporting— An Accounting Standards Perspective," *The Government Accountants Journal*, Fall 1992.

Or, as an alternative possibility, do a search of books in the college library for advanced accounting textbooks or government accounting textbooks that were published prior to 2000.

Required

Accounting for state and local governments has changed considerably in the last 10–20 years. Write a report to highlight some of the differences you noted between the process described before 2000 and the process that has been presented in this chapter and the preceding one in this textbook.

ANALYSIS CASE 2

Go to www.phoenix.gov and do a search for the term "CAFR." Those results should lead to the latest CAFR for the City of Phoenix, Arizona. The financial statements for a state and local government must include a Management's Discussion and Analysis of the information being reported. Read this section of the Phoenix CAFR.

Required

Write a report indicating the types of information found in this government's MD&A.

COMMUNICATION CASE 1

Read the following articles and any other papers that are available on setting governmental accounting standards:

> "The Governmental Accounting Standards Board: Factors Influencing Its Operation and Initial Technical Agenda," *Government Accountants Journal*, Spring 2000.
>
> "Governmental Accounting Standards Come of Age: Highlights from the First 20 Years," *Government Finance Review*, April 2005.
>
> "Forward-Looking Information: What It Is and Why It Matters," *Government Accountants Journal*, December 1, 2010.
>
> "GASB Simplifies GAAP Hierarchy for State and Local Governments," *Business Wire*, June 29, 2015.
>
> "A Century of Governmental Accounting and Financial Reporting Leadership," *Government Finance Review*, April 2006.
>
> "The GASB Turns 25: A Retrospective," *Government Finance Review*, April 2009.
>
> "Proposed Changes to the Process Used to Set the GASB's Technical Agenda," *Government Finance Review*, April 1, 2013.

Required

Write a short paper discussing the evolution of governmental accounting.

COMMUNICATION CASE 2

The City of Larissa recently opened a solid waste landfill to serve the area's citizens and businesses. The city's accountant has gone to city officials for guidance as to whether to record the landfill within the general fund or as a separate enterprise fund. Officials have asked for guidance on how to make that decision and how the answer will impact the government's financial reporting.

Required

Write a memo to the government officials describing the factors that should influence the decision as to the fund in which to report the landfill. Describe the impact that this decision will have on the city's future comprehensive annual financial reports.

EXCEL CASE

Prior to the creation of government-wide financial statements, the City of Loveland did not report the cost of its infrastructure assets. Now city officials are attempting to determine reported values for major infrastructure assets that were obtained prior to the preparation of these statements. The chief concern is determining a value for the city's hundreds of miles of roads that were built at various times over the past several decades. Each road is assumed to last for 50 years (depreciation is 2 percent per year).

As of December 31, 2017, city engineers believed that one mile of new road would cost $2.3 million. For convenience, each road is assumed to have been acquired as of January 1 of the year in which it was put into operation. Officials have done some investigation and believe that the cost of constructing a mile of road has increased by 8 percent each year over the past 30 years.

Required

Build a spreadsheet to determine the value that should now be reported for each mile of road depending on the year it was put into operation. For example, what reported value should be disclosed in the government-wide financial statements for 10 miles of roads put into operation on January 1, 1999?

Index

A

Abbot Laboratories, Inc., 359
Accounting Standards Codification (ASC), of FASB
  Topic 205, "Accounting Changes and Error Corrections," 73n
  Topic 260, "EPS computation," 286
  Topic 280, "Segment Reporting," 116
  Topic 305, on qualitative assessments, 116–117
  Topic 321, "Investments—Equity Securities," 2
  Topic 323, "Investments—Equity Method and Joint Ventures," 4–5, 8, 14, 17
  Topic 350, "Intangibles—Goodwill and Other," 115, 117, 121–122, 127
  Topic 805, on acquisition method, 47
  Topic 805, on business combinations, 63, 75, 184
  Topic 810, on consolidation, 36, 39–40, 43, 45, 63, 184, 208, 211, 217
  Topic 815, on derivatives and hedging, 329–330
  Topic 820, on valuation methods, 48
  Topic 825, on fair value, 24
  Topic 830, on foreign currency transactions, 324, 395
Accounting Standards Update (ASU), of FASB
  No. 2014-17, "Business Combinations: Pushdown Accounting," 73
  No. 2016, "Financial Instruments," 3n
  "Simplifying the Equity Method of Accounting," 12n
Accumulated other comprehensive income (AOCI)
  in derivatives accounting, 335
  in forward contracts, 338–339
  overview, 16
Acquisition date. *See* Consolidations subsequent to acquisition date
Acquisition-date fair value for subsidiaries, 157–161
Acquisition method
  application example, 71–72
  with dissolution, 50–55
  overview, 47, 49–50
  for partial ownership consolidations, 162–175
    alternative investment method effects, 174–175
    with control premium, 170–174
    with no control premium, 162–170
  pooling of interests and purchase method *vs.,* 70
  with separate incorporation, 55–60
  for step acquisitions, 177–179
Acquisitions, mergers, and transfers of operations in state and local government accounting, 590–591
Additional paid-in capital (APIC), 73–74
Affiliate debt acquisition from outside party, 273
Agency funds, of governments, 527
Allegheny Energy Company, 317
Alltel Corporation, 158
Alternative investment method effects, 174–175
Amortization, 12–14, 121
Antitrust concerns, in AT&T acquisition of DirectTV, 42
ARCA Biopharma, 62
Arie Capital, 385
Armco, Inc., 23–24
Articles of partnership, 449–450
Artistic-related intangible assets, 61
Artwork and historical treasures
  state and local government accounting for, 582–584
Assets
  acquired in business combinations, 48–49, 51–54
  capital, by government fund activity, 538
  gains or losses on sales of, 393–394

Assets—*Cont.*
  hedges of foreign currency denominated, 335
  infrastructure, 584–585
  VIEs for low-financing of purchase of, 262
AT&T, Inc., 7, 41–43, 52, 60
AT&T Broadband, 60, 175

B

Balance sheet
  exposure to translation adjustment, 388–389
  at partnership termination, 485–486
Barclay's, 43
Bargain purchases
  in business combinations, 49
  pushdown accounting exception, 73
  of separately incorporated subsidiaries, 60
  valuation basis in, 47n
BellSouth, Inc., 7
Berkshire Hathaway, Inc., 89, 182
Black-Scholes option pricing formula, 323
Blue Cross Blue Shield of Texas, 577
Bond issues, in state and local government
    accounting, 544–547
Bonus method of recording partnership capital
    contributions, 452–453, 460–464
Book value, excess of investment cost over,
    9–12
Borrowing, as foreign currency transaction,
    327–329
Buckeye Partners, 445, 480
Budgets, state and local government, 533–535
Buffett, Warren, 182
Business combinations
  consolidation of financial information
    acquisition method for, 47
    assets acquired and liabilities assumed,
        48–49
    consideration transferred, 47
    contingent consideration transferred, 47–48
    control in, 45–46
    financial information consolidated in, 46–47
    goodwill and gains on bargain purchases, 49
    single economic entity creation, 44–45
  private company accounting for, 127–128

*Business Combinations: Applying the
    Acquisition Method-Joint Project of
    the IASB and Business Combinations
    and Intangible Assets* (Exposure Draft,
    FASB), 60
FASB (FASB Project Update, October 25,
    2007), 63
Business Wire, 629

C

CAFR (comprehensive annual financial report),
    538, 571–572, 585–586
Call options, 322
Cangialosi, Loretta, 158
Capital, 21, 73–74
Capital accounts for partnerships
  accounting for capital contributions, 450–453
  additional capital contributions and
      withdrawals, 453–454
  articles of partnership, 449–450
  income allocation, 454–457
  overview, 448–449
Capital assets, by government fund activity, 538
Capital projects funds, of governments, 524
Carrying amount. *See* Book value
Cash flows
  consolidated statement of, 281–286
  forward contracts on foreign currency as
      hedge for, 337–340, 344
  in fund financial statement in state and local
      government accounting, 603–605
Center for Audit Quality's International
    Practices Task Force (IPTF), 397
Chicago Mercantile Exchange, 322–323
Cingular, Inc., 7
Cirrus Logic, Inc., 319
Cisco Systems, Inc., 39
Citigroup, Inc., 23
Coca-Cola Company, 1, 4, 7, 16, 18, 36, 359,
    575, 577
Coca-Cola FEMSA (Mexico), 1, 4
College and university reporting, public,
    606–612
Comcast Corporation, 42, 44, 175

Compensation, managerial, 21

Comprehensive annual financial report (CAFR), 538, 571–572, 585–586

Conglomerates, 41

Consideration transferred, in business combinations, 47

Consolidated earnings per share, 286–288

Consolidated net income distribution, 161

Consolidated variable interest entities, 265–268

Consolidation Entry A, 58–59, 97–98, 102–104

Consolidation Entry *C, 111

Consolidation Entry D (dividends), 97–98, 103, 105–106

Consolidation Entry E (expenses), 98, 103, 106

Consolidation Entry I (income), 97–98, 102, 104–105

Consolidation Entry P (payables), 103

Consolidation Entry S, 58, 96–98, 100–103

Consolidation of financial information
  business combinations
    acquisition method for, 47
    assets acquired and liabilities assumed, 48–49
    consideration transferred, 47
    contingent consideration transferred, 47–48
    control in, 45–46
    financial information consolidated in, 46–47
    goodwill and gains on bargain purchases, 49
    single economic entity creation, 44–45
  corporate takeovers, 40–43
  criterion for, 7
  FASB ASC Topic 810, 39–40
  for foreign subsidiaries, 412–416
  intangible assets, 60–61
  overview, 3–4
  preexisting goodwill, 61
  procedures for
    acquisition method with dissolution, 50–55
    acquisition method with separate incorporation, 55–60
    overview, 47–50
  research and development in-process, 62–63
  U.S. and international standard convergence, 63

Consolidations subsequent to acquisition date, 89–154
  amortization and impairment of other intangibles, 121
  contingent consideration, 122–123
  equity method for investment recording
    application of, 94
    consolidated totals, 94–96
    consolidation worksheets, 96–98
    overview, 92–94
    subsequent to year of acquisition, 98–102
  excess fair value attributable to subsidiary long-term debt, 113–115
  goodwill impairment
    assigning to reporting units, 116
    example of, 119
    international accounting standards for, 120
    overview, 115
    qualitative assessment option, 116–117
    testing, 117–118
    zero or negative carrying amounts, 119–120
  initial value or partial equity method for investment recording
    current year acquisition, 103–107
    subsequent to year acquisition, 107–113
  investment accounting by acquiring company, 90–92
  passage of time effects, 90

Consumption method of cost recognition, 540

Contingent considerations, 47–48, 69, 122–123

Contract-based intangible assets, 61

Control, in business combinations, 45–46

Control premiums
  partial ownership consolidations with, 170–174
  partial ownership consolidations without, 158, 162–170

Corporate equity securities reporting, 1–4

Corporate takeovers, 40–43

Cost approach to valuation, 49

Costco Wholesale Corporation, 209

Cost-flow, in step acquisitions, 184

Cost method, 2–4, 7

Cost of goods sold, 392

Costs, 54–55

County Bank (California), 53

Current financial resources, of state and local governments, 521

Current rate translation method, 389–390, 401–404

Customer-related intangible assets, 61

D

Debt. *See also* Variable interest entities (VIEs) and intra-entity debt
covenants on, 21
government funds to service, 524–525
long-term, of subsidiaries, 113–115

Deficit capital balance
contribution by partner, 487–488
loss to remaining partners, 488–494
negative, 484

Defined benefit pension plan, state and local government accounting for, 580–582

Deloitte, 445

Depreciable assets, in intra-entity asset transactions, 234–239

Depreciation, of infrastructure assets, 584–585

Derivatives accounting, 329–331

Derived tax revenues, in state and local government accounting, 541–542

Diluted earnings per share, 288

Direct combination costs, 54–55, 68–69

DirectTV, 41–43

"Disappearing plant problem," 396

Dissolution
acquisition method with, 50–55
consolidation requirements with, 45–46

Distribution, of consolidated net income, 161

Diversification of risk, 41

Dividends
Consolidation Entry D for, 97–98, 103, 105–106
investment fair value reduced by, 23
in noncontrolling interest presence, 170

Downstream inventory transfers, 220–223, 226–227

Downstream sales, 19–20

E

Earnings manipulation, 4

Earnings per share, consolidated, 286–288

eBay, Inc., 177

Economic unit concept, 156, 158

Effective interest method, 340

Encumbrances, in state and local government accounting, 536–537

End-of-year ownership percentage, 184

Enron Corporation, 214, 261–262

Enterprise funds, of governments, 525

Equity basis, retained earnings conversion to, 106

Equity method for investment recording
acquisition following, 177
application of, 94
consolidated totals, 94–96
consolidation worksheets, 96–98
conversion from initial value method, 174
inventory in intra-entity asset transactions, 219–227
overview, 91–94
partial, 175
subsequent to year of acquisition, 98–102

Equity method of accounting, 1–38
application of, 5–9
corporate equity securities reporting, 1–4
criticisms of, 22
effects of, 21–22
equity investment sales, 17–18
fair value reporting for, 23–24
International Accounting Standard 28, 5
inventory intra-entity gross profit deferral, 18–21
other comprehensive income and irregular items, 16–17
procedures in, 9–14
reporting changes to, 14–15

Ernst & Young, 445

Estates and trusts, 631–632

European Monetary System, 320, 360

Excess fair value attributable to subsidiary long-term debt, 113–115

Excess of investment cost over book value, 9–12

Exchange rates. *See* Foreign currency transactions and hedging foreign exchange risk

Expected value techniques, 158

Expedia, Inc., 158–159

Expenditure and revenue recognition in state and local government accounting
for bond issues, 544–547
for derived tax revenues, 541–542
for expenses and capital asset by government fund activity, 538
for government-mandated and voluntary nonexchange transactions, 543–544
for imposed nonexchange revenues, 542–543
for interfund transactions, 548–551
overview, 537, 541
for special assessments, 547–548
for supplies and prepaid items, 539–540

Expenses, Consolidation Entry E for, 98, 103, 106

Exxon-Mobil, 69n

F

Facebook, Inc., 41–42, 52

Fair value
of consideration transferred, 51–54
in consolidating variable interest entities, 267
criterion for, 7
of derivatives, 330–331
of equity method investments, 2, 23–24
of excess amortizations, 283
of excess attributable to subsidiary long-term debt, 113–115
forward contracts as hedge for, 340–344, 350–352
income recognition under, 8–9
of intangible assets, 60–61
in noncontrolling interest presence, 156–157
option as hedge for, 352–355
subsidiary acquisition-date, 157–161

FASB (Financial Accounting Standards Board). *See* Financial Accounting Standards Board (FASB)

FDIC (Federal Deposit Insurance Corporation), 53

Fiduciary funds, of governments, 523

Financial Accounting Standards Board (FASB)
ASC Topic 205, "Accounting Changes and Error Corrections," 73n
ASC Topic 260, "EPS computation," 286
ASC Topic 280, "Segment Reporting," 116
ASC Topic 305, on qualitative assessments, 116–117
ASC Topic 321, "Investments—Equity Securities," 2
ASC Topic 323, "Investments—Equity Method and Joint Ventures," 4–5, 8, 14, 17
ASC Topic 350, "Intangibles—Goodwill and Other," 115, 117, 121, 127
ASC Topic 805, on acquisition method, 47
ASC Topic 805, on business combinations, 63, 75, 184
ASC Topic 810, on consolidation, 36, 39–40, 43, 45, 63, 184, 208, 211, 217
ASC Topic 815, on derivatives and hedging, 329–330
ASC Topic 820, on valuation methods, 48
ASC Topic 825, on fair value, 24
ASC Topic 830, on foreign currency transactions, 324, 395
ASU, "Simplifying the Equity Method of Accounting," 12n
ASU No. 2014-17, "Business Combinations: Pushdown Accounting," 3n, 73
ASU No. 2016, "Financial Instruments," 3n
Business Combinations and Intangible Assets (Exposure Draft), 60
Business Combinations draft of 2005, 157–158
Concepts Statement No. 6 on assets, 539
FASB Interpretation No. 46R (FIN 46R) standard, 264
functional currency concept of, 395
Private Company Council (PCC) of, 127–128
Project Updates: *Business Combinations: Applying the Acquisition Method-Joint Project of the IASB and FASB:* October 25, 2007, 63
reporting currency concept of, 395–396

Financial statements, outside ownership and, 155–210
  acquisition method for partial ownership consolidations, 162–175
    alternative investment method effects, 174–175
    with control premium, 170–174
    with no control premium, 162–170
  international accounting standards *vs.*, 184–185
  noncontrolling interest presence and, 156–161
    consolidated net income distribution, 161
    definition of, 156
    subsidiary acquisition-date fair value, 157–161
  revenue and expense reporting for midyear acquisitions, 175–177
  step acquisitions, 177–184
    accounting for remaining shares, 184
    acquisition method, 177–179
    after control obtained, 181–182
    cost-flow assumptions, 184
    parent company sale of subsidiary stock, 182–184
    worksheet consolidation for, 179–180
Financial statements—foreign currency, 385–444. *See also* Foreign currency transactions and hedging foreign exchange risk
  current rate translation method, 389–390, 401–404
  exchange rates in translation of, 386–389
  foreign subsidiary consolidation, 412–416
  guidance on, 394–398
  hedging balance sheet exposure, 410–411
  International Financial Reporting Standards (IFRS) on, 398–399
  remeasurement of, 404–408
  retained earnings translation, 391–392
  temporal rate translation method, 390–394
  translation adjustment treatment, 394
  translation disclosures, 411–412
  translation method effects, 408–410
  translation process illustrated, 399–401

Financial statements—intra-entity asset transactions in, 211–260
  depreciable asset transfers, 234–239
  intra-entity land transfers, 232–234
  inventory transfers
    alternative investment method effects, 227–232
    equity methods to illustrate, 219–227
    gross profit effect on noncontrolling interest, 217–218
    gross profit in year following transfer, 215–217
    gross profit in year of transfer, 213–215
    sales and purchase accounts, 212–213
    summary of, 218–219
Financial statements of state and local governments
  by fund, 529–533
  government-wide, 527–529
  two sets of, 519–522
Fluor Corporation, 385
Ford Motor Company, 4, 158, 213
FordSollers (Russia), 4
Forecasted foreign currency denominated transactions, 355–358
Foreign currency transactions and hedging foreign exchange risk, 319–384. *See also* Financial statements—foreign currency
  accounting for, 323–327
  borrowing as, 327–329
  derivatives accounting, 329–331
  exchange rate mechanisms, 320
  exchange rates, publication of, 320–321
  forward contracts on
    as cash flow hedge, 337–340, 344
    as fair value hedge, 340–344
    overview, 321–322, 335–337
  hedges
    accounting for, 331–334
    of forecasted foreign currency denominated transactions, 355–358
    of foreign currency denominated assets and liabilities, 335
    hedging instruments, 358–360
    of unrecognized foreign currency firm commitments, 350–355

International Financial Reporting Standards
(IFRS) on, 327, 360
options on, 322–323, 344–349
Forward contracts on foreign currency
as cash flow hedge, 337–340, 344,
355–357
as fair value hedge, 340–344
as fair value hedge of firm commitments,
350–352
overview, 321–322
Forward rate, on foreign currency, 321
Frito-Lay North America, 39
Front Line Company, 177
Full-accrual basis, retained earnings conversion
to, 106, 111
Functional currency, FASB concept
of, 395–396
Fund accounting, in state and local government,
522–527
Fund financial statements in state and local
government accounting, 597–605
balance sheet, 597–598
overview, 520, 529–533
statement of cash flows of proprietary funds,
603–605
statement of net position of proprietary funds,
599–603
statement of revenues, expenditures, and other
changes, 599, 603

G

GAAP (generally accepted accounting
principles). *See* Generally accepted
accounting principles (GAAP)
Gaffner, Scott, 43
Gains on bargain purchases, in business
combinations, 49
Gasaway, Sharilyn, 158
GASB (Governmental Accounting Standards
Board). *See* Governmental Accounting
Standards Board (GASB)
Geico, Inc., 89
General Electric Company, 182, 264, 317
General fund, of governments, 524

Generally accepted accounting principles
(GAAP)
on control through voting shares, 45
on corporate equity investment reporting, 2
on fair value assessments, 3
on fair value of derivatives, 330–331, 338
on goodwill assets, 49, 120
on hedge documentation, 332
noncontrolling interest reported in,
184–185
post-control stock acquisitions undervalued
by, 182
for state and local government accounting,
575–578
on unrealized foreign exchange gains and
losses, 326
on variable interest entities, 45, 263,
271–272
Gerber Products Company, 288
GittiGidiyar online marketplace, 177
Goodwill
in business combinations, 49
controlling and noncontrolling interest
allocation of, 160
description of, 11–12
in Facebook acquisition of WhatsApp, 42
generally accepted accounting principles
(GAAP) on, 49
impairment of
assigning to reporting units, 116
example of, 119
international accounting standards for,
120–121
overview, 115
proposed accounting standards update
(ASU), 119–120
qualitative assessment option, 116–117
testing, 117–118
zero or negative carrying amounts, 119
preexisting, 61
private company accounting for, 127–128
Goodwill method of recording partnership
capital contributions, 452–453, 461–465
Government, accounting for. *See* State and local
government, accounting for
Government Accountants Journal, The, 629

Governmental Accounting Standards Board (GASB)
  on artwork and historical treasures capitalization, 583
  on bond issues, 545
  on budgets, 534
  description of, 518–519
  on encumbrances, 536
  general fund definition of, 524
  Hierarchy of Generally Accepted Accounting Principles for State and Local Governments, The (Statement No. 76), 576
  on objectives of financial reporting, 519
  on pension plan accounting (Statement No. 68), 581–582
  on public college and university reporting, 606–607
  on tax abatement disclosures (Statement No. 77), 577
  two sets of financial statements required by, 519–522
Governmental funds, 523
Government Finance Review, 629
Government-wide financial statements
  example of, 591–597
  overview, 520–521
  statement of net position and statement of activities, 527–529
Grupo ABC (Brazil), 385

H

Hamburg, Charlie, 182
Hamburg, Marc, 182
Hedging foreign exchange risk. *See* Foreign currency transactions and hedging foreign exchange risk
Hierarchy of Generally Accepted Accounting Principles for State and Local Governments, The (Statement No. 76 by Governmental Accounting Standards Board), 576
Highly inflationary economies, 396–397
Historical treasures
  state and local government accounting for, 582–584

I

IBM, Inc., 587
Impairment
  of equity method investments, 16–17
  of goodwill, 12
  of intangibles in consolidations subsequent to acquisition date, 121
  international standards for, 120
Imposed nonexchange revenues, in state and local government accounting, 541–543
Income
  allocation of, for partnerships, 454–457
  Consolidation Entry I for, 97–98, 102, 104–105
Income approach to valuation, 48–49
Independent float, as currency arrangement, 320
Inflation, 396–397
Infrastructure assets and depreciation, 584–585
Initial value method for investment recording
  current year acquisition, 103–107
  for deferred intra-entity profits, 227–232
  equity method converted from, 174
  in intra-entity debt transactions, 278–279
  overview, 91–92
  subsequent to year of acquisition, 107–113
Installment partnership liquidation, 495–500
Intangible assets
  acquisition-date fair-value allocations of, 60–61
  in AT&T acquisition of DirectTV, 42–43
  in consolidations, 60–61
  in Facebook acquisition of WhatsApp, 42
  goodwill, 11–12
  impairment of, in consolidations subsequent to acquisition date, 121
  private company accounting for, 127–128
Interest rates, financial reporting effects on, 21
Interfund transactions, in state and local government accounting, 548–551
Internal Revenue Service (IRS), 445
Internal service funds, of governments, 526
International accounting standards (IASs), 5

International Financial Reporting
    Standards (IFRS)
  on business combinations (#3R), 184–185
  on equity method (#28), 5
  on financial instruments (#9), 360
  for financial statements with outside
      ownership, 184–185
  on foreign currency rate changes,
      398–399
  on foreign exchange rates (#21), 327
  on goodwill recognition, 120
  on variable interest entities and intra-entity
      debt, 271–272
International Flavors and Fragrances (IFF),
    Inc., 382, 385
Intra-entity assets. *See* Inventory
Intra-entity asset transactions. *See* Financial
    statements—intra-entity asset transactions in
Intra-entity debt. *See* Variable interest entities
    (VIEs) and intra-entity debt
Intra-entity sales, 18–19. *See also* Inventory
Inventory
  book values affected by costing methods
      for, 10
  intra-entity, 19–21
  in intra-entity asset transactions
    alternative investment method effects,
        227–232
    equity methods to illustrate,
        219–227
    gross profit effect on noncontrolling interest,
        217–218
    gross profit in year following transfer,
        215–217
    gross profit in year of transfer, 213–215
    sales and purchase accounts, 212–213
    summary of, 218–219
  intra-entity gross profit deferral, 18–21
Investment accounting by acquiring company,
    90–92
Investments. *See also* Equity method of
    accounting
  alternative methods in, 174–175
  costs reduced to zero, 17
  excess of cost over book value, 9–12
Investment trust funds, of governments, 526

J

James Madison University, 607–612
Johnson Controls, Inc., 359
Joint ventures, in *Accounting Standards
    Codification* (ASC) Topic 323,
    "Investments—Equity Method and Joint
    Ventures" (FASB), 4
Journal of Accountancy, 539

K

Kellogg Co., 385
Kliener Perkins Caufield & Byers, 42

L

Land transfers, in intra-entity asset transactions,
    232–234
Laux, Bob, 158
Laventhol Partners, 515
Lee, Aileen, 42
Legacy methods of business combination
    accounting, 67–71
Liabilities
  assumed in business combinations, 48–49,
      51–53
  hedges of foreign currency denominated,
      335
  in pushdown accounting, 73
  unlimited, in partnerships, 447
Limited liability companies (LLCs), 448
Limited liability partnerships (LLPs), 448
Limited partnerships (LPs), 448
Little, Patricia A., 158
LJM2 special purpose entity (SPEs), 214
Loans, foreign currency, 328–329
Local government, accounting for. *See* State and
    local government, accounting for
Lockheed Martin Corporation, 319
Long-term debt, excess fair value attributable to
    subsidiary, 113–115
Lower-of-cost-or-net realizable value, for
    inventory, 393

M

Maker Studios, Inc., 48

Managerial compensation, 21

Market approach to valuation, 48

Marketing-related intangible assets, 61

Market trades, noncontrolling interest fair value from, 159

Marmon Holdings, Inc., 182

Mautz, R. K., 539

MeadwestVaco, 41, 43

Merck & Co., Inc., 385

Mergers & Acquisitions, 212

Mergers and acquisitions. *See also* Consolidation of financial information in state and local government accounting, 590–591

MGM Grand, Inc., 67

Michigan State University, 607

Microsoft Corporation, 149, 158

Midyear acquisitions, 175–177

Mirage Resorts, Inc., 67

Monster Beverage Corporation, 7

Multipro (Nigeria), 385

Mutual agency concept, 447

N

NASCAR Hall of Fame, 524

Navistar International Corporation, 17

NBC Universal, 44, 182

NCI (noncontrolling interest). *See* Noncontrolling interest (NCI) presence

Negative carrying amounts of goodwill, 119–120

Net income, 90, 161

New York Stock Exchange (NYSE), 23

Noncontrolling interest (NCI) presence, 155–161

consolidated net income distribution, 161

definition of, 155–156

depreciable asset transfer effect on, 239

inventory in intra-entity asset transactions and, 217–218

subsidiary acquisition-date fair value, 157–161

for variable interest entities (VIEs), 271

Nonexchange transactions, government-mandated and voluntary, 541, 543–544

Not-for-profit entities. *See* Private not-for-profit entities

Nuvelo, Inc., 62

O

OCI (other comprehensive income) and irregular items, 16–17

Off-balance sheet structures, 261

Offtermatt, Tim, 578

Ohio State University, The, 606

Omnicom Group, Inc., 385

Omni Fort Worth (TX), 577

Options
    as cash flow hedge of forecasted transaction, 357–358
    as fair value hedge of firm commitment, 352–355
    foreign currency, 322–323, 344–349

Oracle, Inc., 41

Oregon University System, 606

Other comprehensive income (OCI) and irregular items, 16–17

Outside ownership. *See* Financial statements, outside ownership and

Over-the-counter (OTC) market, 322

P

Parent companies
    investment accounting choice of, 90
    retained earnings converted to full-accrual basis, 106, 111
    sale of stock in subsidiaries by, 182–184

Partial equity method for investment recording
    current year acquisition, 103–107
    in intra-entity debt transactions, 278–279
    in noncontrolling interest presence, 175
    overview, 91–92
    subsequent to year of acquisition, 107–113

Partial ownership consolidations
  with control premiums, 170–174
  without control premiums, 162–170
Partnership formation and operation, 445–482
  advantages and disadvantages of, 446–447
  alternatives to, 447–448
  capital accounts for
    accounting for capital contributions,
      450–453
    additional capital contributions and
      withdrawals, 453–454
    articles of partnership, 449–450
    income allocation, 454–457
    overview, 448–449
  dissolution of
    new partner admission, 458–463
    overview, 458
    partner withdrawal, 463–466
Partnership termination and liquidation,
  483–516
  deficit capital balance—contribution by
    partner, 487–488
  deficit capital balance—loss to remaining
    partners, 488–494
  installment, 495–500
  overview, 484
  procedures illustrated, 484–486
  statement of liquidation, 483, 487
Passage of time effects in consolidations, 90
Payables, 103
PCC (Private Company Council), of FASB,
  127–128
Pegged to other currency, as currency
  arrangement, 320
Pension plans, state and local government
  accounting for, 580–582
Pension trust funds, of governments, 526–527
PepsiCo, Inc., 3, 39, 211–212, 587
Pepsi-Quaker Oats, 69n
Permanent funds, of governments, 525
Pfizer Corporation, 158, 317
Pfizer-Warner Lambert, 69n
Philadelphia Stock Exchange, 322
Pooling of interests method, of business
  combination accounting, 67
Preexisting goodwill, 61

Preferred stock of subsidiaries, 279–281
Prepaid items, state and local government
  accounting for, 539–540
PricewaterhouseCoopers, 158, 445
Primary beneficiary, of VIE, 262, 264–268
Primary government and component units,
  586–590
Princeton University, 606
Private company accounting for business
  combinations, 127–128
Private Company Council (PCC), of FASB,
  127–128
Private-purpose trust funds, of
  governments, 526
Procter & Gamble, Inc., 575
Property, plant, and equipment, depreciation, in
  foreign currency financial statements, 393
Proprietary funds, 523, 599–605
Public college and university reporting,
  606–612
Purchase method, of business combination
  accounting, 67–70
Purchases method of cost recognition, 540
Pushdown accounting, 72–74
Put options, 322

Q

Qorvo, Inc., 116
Qualitative assessment option of goodwill
  impairment, 116–118

R

Readily determinable fair values, 2
Reporting currency, FASB concept of, 395–396
Reputation, financial reporting impact on, 21
Research and development in-process, in
  consolidations, 62–63, 69
Retained earnings
  acquisition-date subsidiary, 73
  of parent company converted to full-accrual
    basis, 106, 111
  in translation of financial statements, 391–392

Revenue and expense reporting for midyear acquisitions, 175–177
Risk, diversification of, 41
Rock-Tenn, Inc., 41, 43

S

Sales and purchase accounts, 212–213
Sales of equity investments, 17–18
Salvage values, 12n
Sazaby League of Japan, 208
Scale, competition and, 40–41
Schwengel, Kenny, 590
Securities, registration and issue costs of, 55
Securities and Exchange Commission (SEC), public entity definition, 127
Separate incorporation
  in acquisitions, 55–60
  consolidation requirements with, 45–46
Shares in step acquisitions, accounting for, 184
Significant influence, ownership level to exercise, 4
Single economic entity creation, business combinations, 44–45
Sirius XM Holdings Corporation, 17
Smurfit-Stone, Inc., 43
Solid waste landfill, state and local government accounting for, 578–580
Sollers (Russia), 4
Special assessments, in state and local government accounting, 547–548
Special purpose entities (SPEs), 3, 214, 261
Special purpose governments, 589–590
Special purpose vehicles, 261
Special revenue funds, of governments, 524
Spot rate, on foreign currency, 321, 349
Starbucks Coffee Japan, Ltd., 208
Starbucks Corporation, 208–209
State and local government, accounting for, 517–630
  acquisitions, mergers, and transfers of operations, 590–591
  art and historical treasures example, 582–584
  budgets and recording budgetary entries, 533–535

comprehensive annual financial report of, 585–586
defined benefit pension plan example, 580–582
encumbrances, 536–537
expenditure and revenue recognition
  bond issues, 544–547
  derived tax revenues, 541–542
  for expenses and capital asset by government fund activity, 538–539
  government-mandated and voluntary nonexchange transactions, 543–544
  imposed nonexchange revenues, 542–543
  interfund transactions, 548–551
  overview, 537, 541
  special assessments, 547–548
  for supplies and prepaid items, 539–540
fund accounting, 522–527
fund financial statements, 597–605
  balance sheet, 597–598
  overview, 529–533
  statement of cash flows of proprietary funds, 603–605
  statement of net position of proprietary funds, 599–603
  statement of revenues, expenditures, and other changes, 599, 603
GAAP for, 575–578
government-wide financial statements, 527–529, 591–597
infrastructure assets and depreciation example, 584–585
overview, 517–519
primary government and component units, 586–590
public college and university reporting, 606–612
solid waste landfill example, 578–580
two sets of financial statements, 519–522
user needs, 519
Statement of liquidation, of partnerships, 487
Statement of partners' capital, 455
Step acquisitions, 177–184
  accounting for remaining shares, 184
  acquisition method for, 177–179
  after control obtained, 181–182

cost-flow assumptions, 184
    parent company sale of subsidiary stock in,
        182–184
    worksheet consolidation for, 179–180
Stifel Financial Corp., 578
Stocks
    GAAP undervaluation of acquisitions of, 182
    of subsidiaries
        illustrations of, 292–296
        overview, 288–289
        preferred, 279–281
        value changes in, 289–292
Straight-line methods, 12n, 340
Strike price, for exchange rates, 322, 349
Subchapter S Corporation, 447
Subsidiaries
    acquisition-date fair value for, 157–161
    acquisition-date retained earnings of, 73
    bargain purchases of separately incorporated, 60
    consolidating postacquisition revenue and
        expenses of, 175–176
    consolidation of foreign, 412–416
    definition, 39
    example of, 43
    excess fair value attributable to long-term debt
        of, 113–115
    parent company sale of stock in, 182–184
    preferred stock of, 279–281
    stock transactions of, 288–296
        illustrations of, 292–296
        overview, 288–289
        value changes in, 289–292
Sun Microsystems, 41
Supplies and prepaid items, state and local
    government accounting for, 539–540
Synergies, 41, 43

T

Tax abatements, 577
Tax anticipation notes, 546
Taxes
    derived revenues from, in state and local
        government accounting, 541–542
    for partnerships, 446

Technology-based intangible assets, 61
Temporal rate translation method, 390–394
Thermo Fischer Scientific, Inc., 359
Thomson Reuters, 40
Ticketmaster Entertainment Corporation, 177
TimeWarner, 42
Tolarom Group (Singapore), 385
Transfers of operations in state and local
    government accounting, 590–591
Translation of foreign currency in financial
    statements. *See* Financial statements—
    foreign currency
Trivago, Inc., 158–159
Trusts. *See* Estates and trusts

U

Uniform Partnership Act, 484, 488,
    495–496
Uniform Partnership Act (UPA), 447–448
University of Georgia, 606
University of Kansas, 606
University of Tennessee, 607
University reporting, public, 606–612
Unrecognized foreign currency firm
    commitments, 350–355
UPA (Uniform Partnership Act), 447–448
Upstream inventory transfers, 223–227
Upstream sales, 19–21

V

Value, maximizing firm, 40
Variable interest entities (VIEs) and intra-entity
    debt, 261–318
    accounting for, 273–275
    affiliate debt acquisition from outside
        party, 273
    cash flows consolidated statement, 281–286
    consolidated earnings per share, 286–288
    consolidation affected by, 275–276
    consolidation of, 261–271
        illustration of, 268–271
        overview, 263–267

Variable interest entities (VIEs) and
　　intra-entity debt—*Cont.*
　　　procedures to, 267–268
　　　VIE definition, 262–263
　　description of, 44–45
　　international accounting standards *vs.*,
　　　271–272
　　overview, 6, 272–273
　　retirement gain or loss assignment, 276
　　subsidiary preferred stock, 279–281
　　subsidiary stock transactions,
　　　288–296
　　　illustrations of, 292–296
　　　overview, 288–289
　　　value changes in, 289–292
　　in years subsequent to effective retirement,
　　　276–279
Vertical integration, in mergers and
　　acquisitions, 41
VIEs (variable interest entities). *See* Variable
　　interest entities (VIEs) and intra-entity debt
Voting shares, control from, 45–46

W

Wall Street Journal, 320, 322, 515
Wal-Mart Stores, Inc., 155, 181
Walt Disney Company, 6, 48, 265, 317
Westamerica Bank, 53
WestRock, Inc., 43, 52
Westwind Co., 23–24
WhatsApp, 41–42
Wills. *See* Estates and trusts

Y

Yahoo!-Broadcast.com, 69n

Z

Zero, investments reduced to, 17
Zero or negative carrying amounts of goodwill,
　　119–120
Zuckerberg, Mark, 42